COUNTRIES AND THEIR CULTURES

Editorial Board

Editors in Chief

MELVIN EMBER, *President, Human Relations Area Files*

CAROL R. EMBER, *Executive Director, Human Relations Area Files*

Advisory Board

H. RUSSELL BERNARD, *University of Florida*

E. PAUL DURRENBERGER, *Pennsylvania State University*

STEVAN HARRELL, *University of Washington*

PAUL HOCKINGS, *University of Illinois, Chicago*

CONRAD P. KOTTAK, *University of Michigan*

LOUISE D. LENNIHAN, *City University of New York*

SUSAN M. PARMAN, *California State University, Fullerton*

PAULA L. W. SABLOFF, *University of Pennsylvania*

NORMAN E. WHITTEN, JR., *University of Illinois, Urbana-Champaign*

Countries and Their Cultures was prepared under the auspices and with the support of the Human Relations Area Files, Inc. (HRAF) at Yale University. The foremost international research organization in the field of cultural anthropology, HRAF is a not-for-profit consortium of 19 Sponsoring Member institutions and more than 400 active and inactive Associate Member institutions in nearly 40 countries. The mission of HRAF is to provide information that facilitates the cross-cultural study of human behavior, society, and culture. The HRAF Collection of Ethnography, which has been building since 1949, contains nearly one million pages of information, indexed according to more than 700 subject categories, on the cultures of the world. An increasing portion of the Collection of Ethnography, which now covers more than 365 cultures, is accessible via the World Wide Web to member institutions. The HRAF Collection of Archaeology, the first installment of which appeared in 1999, is also accessible on the Web to those member institutions opting to receive it.

COUNTRIES AND THEIR CULTURES

VOLUME 2

DENMARK
TO
KYRGYZSTAN

Melvin Ember and Carol R. Ember, Editors

Macmillan Reference USA
an imprint of the Gale Group
New York • Detroit • San Francisco • London • Boston • Woodbridge, CT

Countries and Their Cultures

Macmillan Reference USA
1633 Broadway
New York, NY 10019

Macmillan Reference USA
27500 Drake Rd.
Farmington Hills, MI 48331-3535

Library of Congress Cataloging-in-Publication Data
Countries and their cultures / Melvin Ember and Carol R. Ember, editors.
p.cm.
Includes bibliographical references and index.
ISBN 0-02-864950-8 (set : hc.)
1. Ethnology-Encyclopedias. I. Ember, Melvin. II. Ember, Carol R.
GN307 .C68 2001
306'.03-dc21

2001030188

Volume 1: 0-02-864947-8
Volume 2: 0-02-864948-6
Volume 3: 0-02-864949-4
Volume 4: 0-02-864946-X

Printed in the United States of America

Printing number
1 2 3 4 5 6 7 8 9 10

Front cover photos (clockwise from top): Aymara man with llamas © Gian Berto Vanni/Corbis; Japanese kindergarten students © Don Stevenson/Mira; Hooded men at Oaxaca Festival © Liba Taylor/Corbis; Kava Ceremony, Fiji © Charles & Josette Lenars/Corbis; Wedding service in a Russian Orthodox church © Dean Conger/Corbis; Egyptian ranger battalion demonstration © Corbis; Boy eating lobster at Friendship Regatta festivities © Dean Conger/Corbis; Akha villagers perform a Chi Ji Tsi ritual © Michael Freeman/Corbis. Background: Desert Rose block print by Arlinka Blair © Jonathan Blair/Corbis.

DENMARK

CULTURE NAME

Danish

ORIENTATION

Identification. The name of the country means "Borderlands of the Danes" in reference to a political unit created during the sixth through ninth centuries. This period was marked by a slow progression of sovereignty among the Danes, a people who originated in Skaane (today the southern part of Sweden) but eventually were based in Jutland. By the ninth century the Danes had gained mastery of the area known today as Denmark and maintained control until the late medieval period, including parts of modern Sweden and Norway. In the late medieval period, Denmark was reduced in size to approximately the area of contemporary Denmark.

Denmark is a small nation whose cultural unity is mitigated by regional traditions of rural, urban, and island communities with distinctions based on local language, food, and history. This situation has sometimes created friction between local history and national history.

Denmark historically includes the former colonies Greenland and the Faroe Islands. Greenland gained home rule in 1979. In 1948, the Faroe Islands became a self-governing territory within the Danish state.

Location and Geography. The kingdom of Denmark, which is situated in Scandinavia and northern Europe, is surrounded by the North Sea, Skagerrak, Kattegat, and the Baltic Sea. The country covers approximately 16,634 square miles (43,095 square kilometers). Roughly eighty of its more than four hundred islands are inhabited. Jutland, Zealand, and Funen (Fyn) are the largest and most densely populated regions. There is a relative homogeneity in topography, with few areas at a high elevation. Since the sixteenth century, the capital has been Copenhagen, which is also the largest city.

Demography. The first census in 1769 counted a total of 797,584 people; by 1998, the total population was 5,294,860. Infant mortality, epidemics, war and emigration, better hygiene, food, and housing influenced population changes. The population increased from 2.5 to 5.3 million during the twentieth century, showing an interdependency between decline in population growth and industrialization, with the average number of children per woman decreasing from 4 to 1.5. Free abortion and sterilization rights since 1973 caused slower population growth, which in certain years was negative (1981 through 1984).

Immigration increased from 35,051 in 1988 to 50,105 in 1997. Immigrants from other Scandinavian and northern European countries account for most of the increases, but immigrants from southern Europe and the Middle East are the most noticed in public debate.

Linguistic Affiliation. Danish belongs to the Germanic family language within the Indo-European languages. Linguistic relatives are English, German, Swedish, Norwegian, and Icelandic, all of which descend from the ancient Teutonic language.

Danish is differentiated in individual, geographic, and social dialects. Language varies in terms of pitch, tonality, intonation, and pronunciation. Some dialects are mutually unintelligible. "Standard Danish" is one dialect among many.

There is no secondary language, but several languages, including English, German, French, Spanish, and Russian, are taught in schools. Most Danes can speak some English and German.

Many foreigners complain that Danish is difficult to learn because the same wording can have differing and even opposing meanings, depending on the intonation and context. Also, pronunciation does not necessarily follow spelling.

Symbolism. Markers of the national culture include the national flag (the Dannebrog), the na-

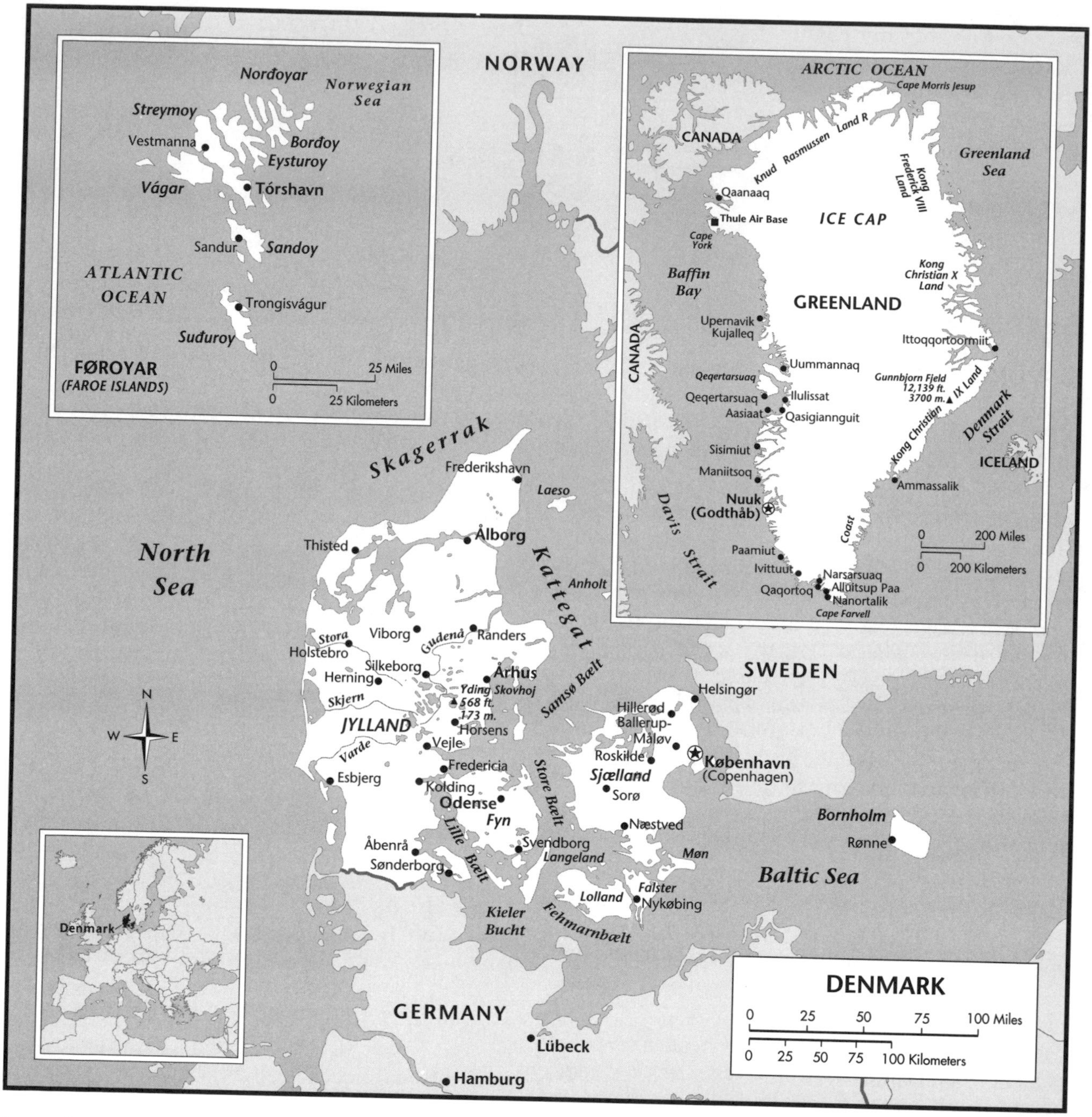

Denmark

tional anthem, public holidays, and hymns, songs, and ballads. According to myth, the national flag descended from the sky to the Danish army during a battle in Estonia in 1219 and was institutionalized as a national symbol in the seventeenth century. The flag—a horizontal white cross on a red field—symbolizes a membership community and a sense of belonging, marking an extensive number of social events. Danes use the flag at festive occasions, including birthdays, weddings, sports events, political meetings, and public holidays. Hymns, songs, and ballads provide metaphors associated with Danish nationality, the mother tongue, school, history, and homeland. The national anthem, *"Der er et Yndigt Land"* ("There Is a Lovely Land"), was written around 1820.

History and Ethnic Relations

Emergence of the Nation. Denmark is a constitutional monarchy and the oldest kingdom in Europe. According to historical sources it dates back to the ninth century, but myth dates it as far back as the sixth century. The recent history of the nation features an outward-looking people focused on trade, welfare, equality, and democracy, which in Danish means "people's government" (*folkestyre*). Fundamental values include a striving for freedom and equality, accomplished after battling for years with neighboring countries in the eighteenth and nineteenth centuries. After centuries of sovereign rule by the king, the first common constitution was completed and signed in 1849, initiating a government with an assembly consisting of a lower house (*Folketing*) and upper house (*Landsting*). The making of a common constitution was an important element in the nineteenth century's political emphasis on the formation of nationhood.

National Identity. Beer, allotment gardens, the flag, the national anthem, democracy, Christmas, folk high schools, personal well-being, and coziness are some of the elements of the national culture, but questions of how the cultural heritage can survive and what it is emphasize the fact that Denmark is a nation of cultural borrowers. Danes constantly negotiate and change their culture in response to contact with people and items from other countries. However, for many people, the national identity lies in the Danish language.

Danes rarely refer to Danishness, a term used for the first time in 1836, but that term has been a hotly debated topic since the increase of immigration in the 1960s and Denmark's affiliation with the European Union (EU) in 1972. Much political and public debate on elements of nationality, sympathies, feeling, and patriotism occurred in the late twentieth century. Many Danes seem to have a strong national identification, although differences exist and a "Danish community" may be more imagined than real in regard to culture and traditions.

Ethnic Relations. Denmark once was considered an open and welcoming country to foreigners, but tensions between native residents and immigrants arose during the last decades of the twentieth century, culminating in the establishment of political parties whose platforms called for the exclusion of inhabitants of foreign ethnicity from social services and other forms of public support. Immigrants of the second and third generations tend to be doubly socialized, displaying competence in Danish values in public and in the native language at home.

Urbanism, Architecture, and the Use of Space

Within a span of one-hundred fifty years, Denmark changed from an agricultural to an industrialized society. In the late nineteenth century, two-thirds of the population lived in rural areas and engaged in agriculture; today, only 15 percent live in rural areas, and many of those people have city jobs.

After the "green wave" of the 1980s, many city dwellers moved to the countryside, hoping to return to nature. However, many returned to urban areas after years of unfulfilled dreams. The long winters; long commutes to work, shopping, and entertainment; and the prevalence of gossip in local rural cultures were unpleasant for people who were accustomed to city life.

In cities, people hope to escape the restraints of social control in rural communities and seek conveniences such as better shopping, entertainment, and job opportunities. Migration to urban areas is common in the pursuit of education, and many young people from the provinces remain in the cities after graduation.

Architecture is marked by a division between the ideals of Denmark as a "fairy-tale country" and as a modern, industrialized one. The first image is characterized by traditional small houses with small windows, low ceilings, straw roofs, and gardens with flowers and vegetables. Even the castles are small and more "cute" than "grandiose." The modern ideal is marked by houses with slender lines and large glass windows or walls, very little outside decoration, and the use of bricks, tile, and ferroconcrete. Common to both architectural traditions is the fact that there are very few tall buildings. Apart from a few buildings from the 1960s in the largest cities, it is unusual to see buildings with more than five floors. Family houses often have one floor, usually with a garden.

Towns and cities are characterized by a center area with older houses (some several centuries old) and a periphery with newer houses, divided into business and residential areas. Village size is from five to one thousand houses, and many villages have been enlarged by new residential areas.

The government is situated in a royal castle built by Christian IV in the seventeenth century in central Copenhagen, symbolizing a harmonious relationship between the government and the royal family. The royal castle and the many statues of kings and politicians in the city support this symbolic harmony.

Even large cities such as Odense, shown here, retain traditional architecture and streetscapes.

Anthropologists have noted a sharp distinction between public and private space and a pronounced preference for the private and domestic sphere in Danish culture. In urban public space, people stand close to one another in buses, subways, parks, and streets, but pretend that they do not see each other. The symbolic demarcation of closed groups such as friends and spectators is clear, with a tendency to form closed circles. An intrusion by strangers often causes offense and creates an even stricter demarcation. In rural areas, people are more likely to connect across public space, greeting and talking about the weather.

Private houses commonly are divided into areas for cooking, dining, and television-viewing and preferably have a private room for each family member. Private homes are considered spaces to "relax" and "be yourself"; many foreigners find it difficult to be invited to the home of a Dane. Usually only family members and close friends have this privilege, experiencing the coziness of a social event celebrated by sitting down, lighting candles, and eating and drinking. Colleagues, sympathetic foreigners, and more distant friends preferably are met only in public (workplace, bar, café, museum).

Food and Economy

Food in Daily Life. Danes eat most of their meals at home and in private settings, although public dining places ranging from small hot dog stands to fancy restaurants are available and are used.

A breakfast of coffee, bread, or cereal is eaten at home. Sunday breakfast commonly includes fresh bakery bread, boiled eggs, juice, tea or coffee, and the Sunday newspaper.

Lunch at a work place, school, or institution is either homemade or available in kitchens or canteens, offering open sandwiches, hot meals, or a buffet table. It also may be bought at butcher shops, cafes, and sandwich bars. Open sandwiches are traditional, consisting of rye bread with salami, liver pâté, herring, roast pork, fried plaice, cod roe, cheese, chocolate, or fruit. Dinner at home traditionally consisted of an appetizer, a main course, and dessert. Soup, porridge and fish dishes were served but today are rarely eaten on a daily basis. A main course is traditionally composed of boiled potatoes, boiled vegetables such as green beans and cauliflower, and fried meat such as meat balls, cutlets, or roast pork served with brown gravy. Pizza, pasta, rice, chicken, and turkey have become common food items among young people. Imported fruit, vegetables, and spices are also common.

Inns often dating back several centuries throughout the country offer traditional Danish food. Pizzerias are found in small towns and cities. In larger cities, there are Chinese, Italian, and Greek restaurants, along with fast-food establishments from America, the Middle East, and South America and restaurants that serve Danish open sandwiches (*smørrebrød*) and pastry. Food taboos include pet animals such as cats, dogs, and horses. The ecological movement and informed consumers have been mutually dependent since the 1970s. The demand for and production of organically grown foods have grown, and most supermarkets offer a range of organically grown vegetables, meat, and dairy products.

Food Customs at Ceremonial Occasions. Danes eat or drink at every social occasion, preferably traditional dishes, cakes, and drinks. However, the act of drinking and eating together is considered more important than what is actually consumed. Formal social occasions include birthdays, weddings, anniversaries, baptisms, confirmations, graduations, and funerals. Private parties held in community centers or restaurants are common. Hosts spend from one to six months' salary on a formal party for rent, food, drinks, and musicians.

Holidays with special meals include New Year's Eve, Easter, Martin Mass, and Christmas. New Year's Eve traditionally is celebrated with boiled cod, Easter with elaborate lunches and roast lamb for dinner, and Martin Mass with roast goose. The traditional Christmas Eve dinner includes roast pork, roast duck, or goose stuffed with prunes, served with pickled red cabbage, white boiled potatoes, fried brown sugared potatoes, and thick brown gravy. Desserts include rice porridge and *ris a la mande* (rice porridge mixed with whipped cream, almonds, and vanilla and served with hot cherry sauce). At Christmas and Easter, special seasoned beers are sold. Christmas is celebrated by eating a traditional extravagant lunch and dinner that bring the family together.

Basic Economy. Natural resources are limited to agricultural land, clay, stone, chalk, lime, peat, and lignite. The economy is therefore heavily dependent on international trade. Farming accounts for two-thirds of the total land area, and agriculture produces enough edible products for three times the population. Industrial exports account for about 75 percent of total exports, while the share of agricultural exports is about 15 percent.

Land Tenure and Property. Most farmers are freeholders, 91 percent of them on individually owned family-run farms, 7 percent on company-run farms, and the rest on farms owned by the state, local authorities, or foundations. Private family houses typically are fenced off to delineate private property, or an invisible line between the garden and the pavement may indicate the border between private and public property. Neighbors discuss which parts outside their homes should be cleared for snow and which parts should be taken care of by municipal services.

Commercial Activities. The major goods produced include foods and beverages, textiles, paper, chemicals, pharmaceuticals, glass, ceramics, bricks, cement, concrete, marine engines, compressors, agriculture and forestry machinery, computers, electric motors, radio and communication equipment, ships, boats, furniture, and toys. Agricultural products include beef, pork, poultry, milk, and eggs.

Major Industries. The main industries are food processing, furniture, diesel engines, and electrical products. Major agricultural products include dairy products, pork, beef, and barley. Commercial fishing includes salmon, herring, cod, plaice, crustaceans and mollusks, mackerel, sprat, eel, lobster, shrimp, and prawns.

Trade. Major commodity groups sold on the international market include animal products (cattle, beef and veal, pigs and pork, poultry, butter, cheese, and eggs), vegetable products (grains, seeds, fruit, flowers, plants, and vegetables), ships, fish, fur, fuel, lubricating goods, and electricity. The major industrial exports are machines and instruments, medicinal and pharmaceutical products, chemical items, industrially prepared agricultural products, fish, crayfish and mollusks, furniture, textiles, and clothing. Imports, which lag slightly behind exports, include automobiles, fuel, consumer goods (food, clothing, electronics, and others), and goods to be further processed at local industries. The major trading partners are Germany, Sweden, Great Britain, France, the Netherlands, the United States, Japan, and Italy.

Division of Labor. The division of labor is determined by gender, industry and socioeconomic status. Although agricultural products constitute a major proportion of exports, only 4 percent of the population is employed in agriculture, which has become highly industrialized and machine-driven. Close to 25 percent of the population is employed in

Two-thirds of Denmark's land and nearly 25 percent of its population is devoted to agriculture.

trade, a similar number in industry, and more than 40 percent in other service.

SOCIAL STRATIFICATION

Classes and Castes. Most national surveys dealing with social strata do not divide the population into different income groups. Instead, the population is categorized into five social layers, according to level of education and occupation.

Those social categories are academics, owners of large farms, and persons with more than fifty employees (4 percent); farmers with at least four employees, owners of companies with more than six employees, and college-educated business owners (7 percent); farmers with a maximum of three employees, owners of small companies, and persons with jobs requiring expertise (21 percent); skilled workers, small landowners, and workers with a professional education (37 percent); and workers without skills training (32 percent).

In the adult population, there has been an increase in unemployed people who receive public support from 6 percent in 1960 to 25 percent today. Increasing demands for skills in reading, writing, mathematics, computers, and stress management are among the factors that have caused this development. Unemployment rates are somewhat higher among ethnic minorities, with persons of Turkish descent having the highest rate.

Figures from 1996 show inequality in income distribution: Twenty percent of the lowest-income families accounted for 6 percent of total income, while 20 percent of the highest-income families accounted for 40 percent of the income.

Symbols of Social Stratification. According to a code of morality (the "Jante Law") which was formulated by the author Aksel Sandemose in his 1933 novel *A Refugee Crosses His Tracks*, a person should not display superiority materially or otherwise. Wealth and high social position are downplayed in public in regard to dress, jewelry, and housing. The point is to be discreet about individual distinction and avoid public boasting while allowing one's wealth to be recognized by persons in a similar economic position.

POLITICAL LIFE

Government. Denmark is a constitutional monarchy in which succession to the throne is hereditary and the ruling monarch must be a member of the national church. The parliament has 179 members, including two from Greenland and two from the Faroe Islands. Members of parliament are elected for four-year terms, but the state minister has the right to dissolve the parliament and force an election. The voting age has been eighteen since 1978. Since 1989, immigrants without Danish nationality have been allowed to vote and be elected in local elections. The minimum percentage of votes required for representation in the parliament is 2 percent.

Leadership and Political Officials. The first political groupings appeared in 1848, shortly before the first constitution was promulgated, and consisted of liberals (farmers), the center (intellectuals), and the right (landowners and higher officials).

Party policy is based on political principles and working programs; the former include fundamental political ideas, while the programs are action-oriented. Currently, ten political parties are represented in the parliament, ranging from socialist to conservative to liberal. Representatives to parliament are elected in local areas and thus represent their home localities as well as a political party.

Liberal parties traditionally strive for individual freedom, including freedom of thought, belief, speech, expression, individual choice, and ownership, and attempt to strengthen the rights of the individual citizen in relation to the state. Conservatives stress individual freedom, choice, and responsibility and attempt to protect the national culture and tradition. Modern conservatism includes confidence in the individual, an open and critical outlook, tolerance, and a free market economy, combined with a commitment to social security. Social Democrats favor a welfare society based on freedom, equal opportunity, equality, dignity, solidarity, cultural freedom and diversity, ecology, and democracy. Socialist parties seek a society based on political, social, and cultural diversity; ecological sustainability; social security; equal opportunity; responsibility for the weak; individual freedom; self-realization; active work for peace and disarmament; and a commitment to end global inequality. The Christian People's Party favors a democracy based on Christian ethical values, focused on individual freedom, social responsibility and security, the family, and medical ethics. For this party, a Christian view of human nature forms the basis for equal human value regardless of race, sex, age, abilities, culture, and religion.

Social Problems and Control. Executive power lies with the monarch, while legislative power is based in the parliament. In executive matters, the monarch exercises authority through government ministers. Judicial power lies with the courts of justice. The most common crimes are offenses against property, offenses against special laws in some municipalities, crimes of violence, and sexual offenses.

The police force consists of approximately 10,000 officers, who work at police stations located in local communities. Traditionally, Danish police have been known for their easy-going manner and "gentle" approach to difficult situations, relying more on dialogue and communication than on brute force. After years of becoming more centralized and distanced from the Danish people, there is now a trend in policing that involves forming new, smaller police stations in more towns and cities. In this new environment, officers are moving out of their cars and walking the streets, gaining closer contact with the people.

In criminal cases, those over the age of 15 may be punished by the courts. Those between 15 and 18 are held in special youth prisons that provide social training. Those above the age of 18 are imprisoned in one of the country's 14 state prisons. Due to a lack of prison space, convicted criminals sometimes wait for up to two years before they are actually imprisoned.

Military Activity. Since World War II, Denmark has been a member of the North Atlantic Treaty Organization (NATO), and it participated in NATO's actions in the Balkan crisis in the 1990s, particularly in Bosnia and Kosovo. Denmark also contributes to the United Nations peace forces in the Middle East and other areas. In 1993, the population voted not to join in the development of a common EU military force.

The military is staffed through a system of compulsory enrollment. The term of service, depending on one's duties, ranges from four to twelve months. Full mobilization in the defense forces involves fifty-eight thousand soldiers, while in the absence of war the number is only fifteen thousand. The defense forces include the navy, air force, home guard, and national rescue corps. The defense budget in 1997 was under 2 percent of the gross national product.

Social Welfare and Change Programs

All residents receive social support when they are unemployed, either through union insurance or locally run programs. Idled workers receive compensation that is equal to slightly less than the lowest

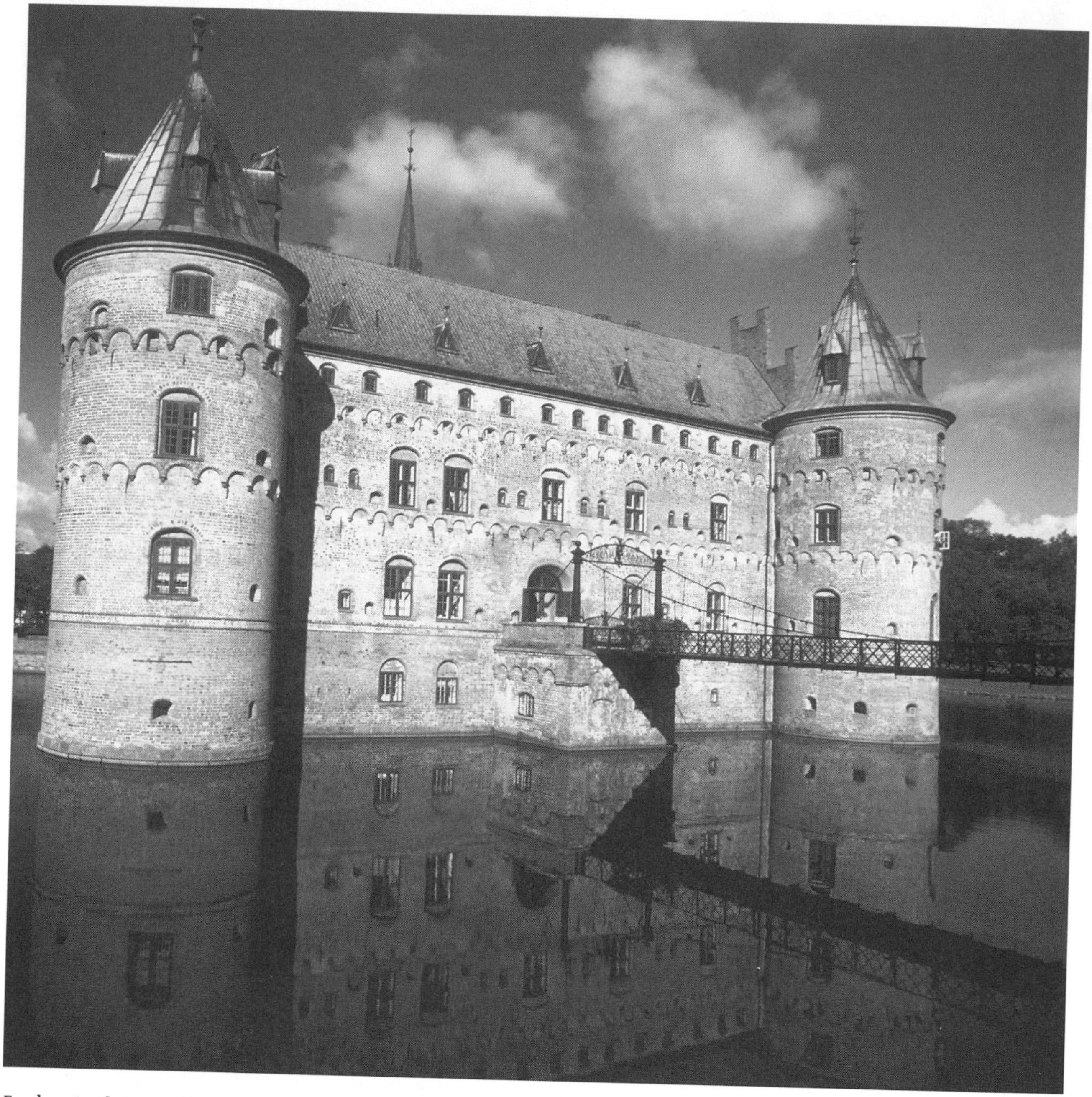

Egeskov Castle is a well-preserved example of Renaissance architecture in Denmark.

wages paid for regular, full-time employment, and they are also guaranteed housing, food, and other basic necessities. After six months of unemployment, an individual meets with an officer from the local unemployment office to formulate a specific strategy for getting a new job. That strategy can include training, further education, or a government job that is supported by the local community in which the person lives.

Public and private programs to aid disabled individuals are found in every major town and city. Food and shelter are always provided, and sometimes disabled persons are placed with a type of foster family.

Nongovernmental Organizations and Other Associations

Danes pursue common interests in leisure, sports, and politics. Associations are essentially nongovernmental, originating in the late nineteenth century, when farmers and workers formed interest groups. Today Denmark has one of the highest proportions of association membership in the world.

More than 90 percent of the population belongs to an organization, and more than 73 percent of the people have multiple memberships in more than three hundred thousand organizations.

Organizations and associations play three important roles. First, they have been able to develop common interests and identities among different groups of people. Second, practical improvements in the form of production, increases in salary, and membership discounts have been achieved. Third, organizations participate in the political struggle for the distribution of values and goods in society.

Gender Roles and Statuses

Division of Labor by Gender. Denmark has the highest percentage of women in the labor market in Europe, with close to 80 percent of women being employed. Since the 1980s, the country has had a public policy of equality of men and women in regard to wages and working conditions, yet men are more likely to get top positions and in general earn higher wages than women. Persistent beliefs associate women with the family and men with work. These practices are enforced by employers who encourage single women and married men to pursue careers.

The Relative Status of Women and Men. Since 1924 there have been women in the government, and the representation of women in politics has grown significantly. Today nine of twenty ministers are women. However, state ministers have always been men. The Equal Status Council was founded in 1974 and closed in 2000, when a new equal status law was issued.

Marriage, Family, and Kinship

Marriage. Individuals are free to choose their marriage partners. Many people cohabit at a young age. Polygyny and polyandry are not allowed, and it is forbidden to marry close family and kin members. Since the late 1980s, homosexuals have had the right to register their partnerships with the local city council. People marry for love, but convenience and economic gains may be equally important. Parents who are not married may wed to give legal security to their children in case of sudden or accidental death.

Forty percent of the adult population is married, 45 percent is unmarried, 7 percent is divorced, and 7 percent is widowed. Divorce typically involves separation followed by a legal procedure.

Domestic Unit. The ideal household unit consists of a married couple and their children who are below age twenty. However, more than 50 percent of households have only one adult (single, divorced with children, or widowed). Extended families living together are rare. Young people usually leave the parental home in their late teens. Previously children stayed in the same town or municipality as their parents, but today families are dispersed across the country. Some people choose to live in shared houses on the basis of similarities in age or ideology or for practical purposes such as ecological farming. A number of collective forms of housing for the elderly have emerged.

Inheritance. For many centuries, men and women have had equal inheritance rights. If one member of a couple dies, the other partner inherits all the possessions of the deceased. If both partners die, their children inherit equal shares of their possessions. There are also special circumstances such as wills, separate estates, joint property, and divided or undivided possession of an estate.

Traditionally, the oldest son inherited the farm or the position as head of the family company after the death of the father. However, the son in this case has to compensate his mother and siblings economically. This tradition extends to the royal family, where the title of king traditionally has been passed from father to oldest son. Because King Frederik IX had no sons, the constitution was changed in 1953 to make it legal for his oldest daughter to inherit the throne.

Kin Groups. Family relations are traced back equally both matrilineally and patrilineally, and active kin groups often extend to the great-grandparents. Rural residents often hold "cousin-parties" (*fætter-kusine-fester*) that are attended by up to 90 people.

Socialization

Infant Care. Three to six months of maternal leave is a legal right, but the mother may share the last three months of that leave with the father. Infants generally are breast-fed until the end of the period of maternal leave. Traditionally, the mother was the primary caregiver, but recently the father and other family members have been recognized as equally important in raising infants. Because Denmark has one of the highest rates of women in the labor market, most infants above six months of age spend the mother's working hours in public nurseries or private child care.

Some Danes, such as these hunters near Alborg, enjoy outdoor leisure activities.

Infant care has been much debated, resulting in great variations in regard to ideas about how much an infant should be carried around, whether it should sleep alone or with the parents, whether parents should attend to a baby every time it cries, and how to manage infants who cry during the night. The overall tendency is that younger parents recognize the individual rights and needs of an infant more than older people do.

Child Rearing and Education. Most children enter kindergarten at age three, and many continue school attendance until their early teens. In 1997, more than 80 percent of three- to six-year-olds attended some kind of day care institution. The pedagogy practiced in nursery schools, kindergartens, and after-school centers is not research-based but is informed by changing ideologies of what children are like and what they need. An ideology of ''self-management'' is practiced in many institutions, leaving it up to the children to decide what they want to do and how, where, and when to do it.

In the ideal family, the mother and father share authority, including their children in decision making. In pedagogical circles, the term ''negotiation-families'' is used to illustrate this situation. Most children are materially well taken care of, with nourishing food, regular supplies of new clothes and toys, and a private room in the family house. Some people argue that working parents compensate for their absence by giving their children toys, videos, and computers.

Higher Education. There are five universities: the University of Copenhagen, the University of Southern Denmark, the University of Aarhus, Aalborg University, and Roskilde University Center. In 1996, 167,764 students were enrolled in those institutions: 93,544 women and 74,220 men. All children in Denmark are obligated to complete nine years of school, either at private or public institutions. After they have fulfilled that requirement, 50 percent of the students choose a trade by entering vocational training, which includes an apprenticeship and formal schooling. Thirty percent select a one- to three-year college training program, which prepares them for teaching, nursing, or other professional occupations. The remaining 20 percent enter university. Nearly two-thirds of graduating students apply for university, but the majority are not admitted; those who are turned down either reapply the next year or select one of the vocational or college options. Admission has become increasingly competitive, based on grade point averages. All higher education is free of charge.

Crowds of tourists and Copenhagen residents mingle along the Stroget, a mile-long pedestrian street along the harbor.

Etiquette

Privacy is a primary value in Danish etiquette. One is not supposed to invite oneself into another person's house or look into other people's land, property, and salary. Danes show few emotions publicly, as the open expression of feelings is considered a sign of weakness. Unless provoked, Danes avoid getting into an argument, and they dislike being interrupted during a conversation.

Informality is considered a virtue. However, informality in social interaction makes it difficult to enter new social circles. At dinner parties, meetings, and conferences, there are no formal introductions, leaving it up to people to initiate interaction.

Religion

Religious Beliefs. Religious freedom is consonant with international standards on the right to freedom of religion. Eighty-six percent of the population belongs to the Evangelical Lutheran Church, which has for centuries been supported by the state and is considered the national church. Numerous other Christian communities exist, including the Catholic Church, the Danish Baptist Church, and the Pentecostal Movement. Other world religions represented in the country are Islam, Judaism, Hinduism, Buddhism, the Baha'i faith, and Sikhism. Recently, religious groups celebrating old Viking gods have emerged.

Religious Practitioners. The majority religion is Christianity, and at birth all Danes are considered to belong to the national church, with an obligation to pay church taxes as part of the income tax.

Since the fifteenth century priests have been educated in a university, and ministers in the national church are officials under the Minister of Ecclesiastical Affairs. The official duties of religious leaders include performing church ceremonies for local members of the national church and keeping a register of births, marriages, and deaths. Many religious practitioners participate in worldly affairs as social workers or advocate for the underprivileged in public debates.

Rituals and Holy Places. Churches are situated within and outside villages, towns, and cities and are surrounded by churchyards with cemeteries. In a Lutheran service, there is a minister, a cantor, a servant, and an organist. Members attend ritual events such as baptisms, confirmations, wedding ceremonies, and funerals and major religious events such as Christmas and Easter. Only a minority of people attend services regularly, and on weekdays churches are virtually empty.

Death and the Afterlife. Danes are not great believers in God; therefore, practices concerning death, the deceased, funerals, and the afterlife are handled in a rational and practical manner.

Dead persons are buried in coffins on the grounds of a church or are cremated and have their ashes buried in the graveyard. Graves are decorated with a gravestone with the deceased's name, dates, and greetings and are surrounded by greenery and flowers. After twenty years the grave is neglected unless family members pay for its care. Generally, religious practitioners are available to support the surviving relatives and talk about life, death, and the afterlife. Neoreligious communities have emerged in which people are guided to the other side to communicate with deceased family members and kin.

Medicine and Health Care

Since 1973, a tax-financed health care system has provided free access to health care throughout the life span within a national system. Treatment for inclusion in this system must adhere to theories and practices based on the sciences of medicine and psychology utilized by organized practitioners trained at accredited colleges and universities.

Most children are born in hospitals. Health visitors give families support for infant care and development. All children are offered an extensive vaccination program and medical examinations on a regular basis (at least once a year) until they leave school.

Fee-for-service health care is available from alternative practitioners and private hospitals. Alternative medicines such as homeopathy, reflexology, acupuncture, massage, diet therapy, and healing have been popular since the 1960s. Alternative explanatory models adhere to notions of holism and energy as important factors in disease and healing, aiming at indirect disease elimination. Alternative medicines have been well received by the population, with 20 percent of the population seeking alternative treatments in the 1980s and more than 30 percent in the 1990s.

In the 1990s, a number of private hospitals offering orthodox medical services and staffed with medical doctors, nurses, and other biomedical professions were established. Limited resources for national health care that caused long waiting lists led to the establishment of private hospitals offering treatments such as hip surgery and bypass operations.

Medical professionals increasingly stress the individual's responsibility for health through changes in lifestyle and personal habits. Smoking, alcohol abuse, poor dietary patterns, and lack of physical exercise are considered the main causes of disease. In surveys of lay perceptions of health and disease, the focus has been on notions of the importance of varied eating patterns, fresh air, regular exercise, a positive mood, and good social relations.

Secular Celebrations

Among the traditional secular celebrations is "Shrovetide" (*fastelavn*), which is held in February and features children dressed in fancy costumes going from house to house singing songs and begging for money, candy, or even buns. The "1st of May Celebrations" were originally intended to celebrate the formation of workers' unions, but they have evolved into public parties with demonstrations, speeches, music, and drinking. "Saint Hans" is a midsummer celebration held on June 23 that features singing, speeches, and a traditional bonfire at which a doll symbolizing a witch is burned. Besides these national celebrations, farmers and other rural residents regularly hold harvest parties in August and September to celebrate crops that have been brought in from the fields.

The Arts and Humanities

Support for the Arts. Artists may join a union from which they receive insurance against unemployment. In this system of employment security, artists must produce input in the form of work, and many artists take menial jobs to maintain their union status. During their training, artists may receive subsidies through the State Education Grant and Loan scheme. A few artists are awarded a civil list pension on the basis of merit and talent. A few excellent artists are fully self-supporting.

Literature. Danish literature was initiated by the historian Saxo Grammaticus, who wrote about Danish history up to the end of the twelfth century, including Scandinavian mythology, with its traditional stories of gods and legendary heroes. Since that time, Denmark has had a long history of poetry and literature, with Hans Christian Andersen and Karen Blixen (Isak Dinesen) being among the most famous writers.

Graphic Arts. There is an extended culture of painting, sculpture, textiles, and pottery. Those subjects are part of the school curriculum and are taught in leisure time courses. Many of the islands are known for their artifacts. Bornholm produces pottery, sculpture, and glass. Artifacts are exhibited at museums and art exhibitions attended by school children, university students, and tourists. Professional artists known outside Denmark include the sculptor Bertel Thorvaldsen (1770–1844) and the contemporary painter Per Kirkeby.

Performance Arts. Music and dance from Europe have been dominant, but genres from Africa and South America have become popular. The Royal Danish Music Conservatory was founded in 1867, and the Rhythmic Music Conservatory was founded in 1986. Conservatories are for those with special talents and ambitions, while many other schools are open to a wider range of people. Danish cinema has been awarded many international prizes.

The State of the Physical and Social Sciences

University life dates back to the fifteenth century, with theology, medicine, and law as the first areas of study. The terminal degree was for centuries the *magistergraden*, which was between a master's and a doctoral degree. Recently this degree has been replaced by the *kandidatgraden*, which is equivalent to a master's degree. Theology was the first social science degree awarded. Major social sciences today are economics, political science, anthropology, and sociology.

The physical sciences are well established. The Technical University of Denmark was founded in 1829 and today is a leading international institution, training construction, chemical, computer, and mechanical engineers. However, young Danes tend to choose humanistic or social science studies over the natural sciences.

Universities are public and are run by the state, as are the Ministry of Research and a number of research councils that fund basic and applied research. Much technical research is applied, supported by public and private authorities, and much natural science research is funded by private companies and foundations. The Danish Technological Institute and the Academy for Technical Sciences are important in technology and information services.

Bibliography

Andersen, Johannes. *Politiske Partier og Politisk Magt i Danmark*, 1982.

Anderson, Benedict. *Imagined Communities: Reflections on the Origin and Spread of Nationalism*, 1983.

Anderson, Robert T. *Denmark: Success of a Developing Nation*, 1975.

Arenas, Julio G., and Rashmi Singla. *Etnisk Minoritetsungdom i Danmark: Om deres Psykosociale Situation*, 1995.

Arendt, Niels Henrik. "Den Danske Folkekirke." In *Kristne Kirkesamfund i Danmark*, Birgitte Larsen and Peter Lodberg, eds., 1998.

Billing, Yvonne Due. "Organisational Cultures, Families, and Careers in Scandinavia." In *Organizational Change and Gender Equity: International Perspectives on Fathers and Mothers at the Workplace*, Linda L. Haas, Philip Hwang, and Graeme Russell, eds., 2000.

Buckser, Andrew S. *Communities of Faith: Sectarianism, Identity, and Social Change on a Danish Island*, 1996.

Coleman, David, and Eskil Wadensjö. *Indvandringen til Danmark: Internationale og Nationale Perspektiver*, 1999.

DIKE. *Danskernes Sundhed mod år 2000*, 1997.

Ejskjær, Inger. *Danish Dialect Research*, 1993.

Faber, Tobias. *A History of Danish Architecture*, 1978.

Fledelius, Hanne, and Birgitte Juul. eds. *Freedom of Religion in Denmark*, 1992.

Gamrath, Helge, and Bjørn Westerbeek. "Historie, Litteratur og Registre." *København før og Nu—og Aldrig*, vol. 11, 1990.

Gupta, Nabatina Datta, and Nina Smith. *Children and Career Interruptions: The Family Gap in Denmark*, 2000.

Hastrup, Bjarne. *Vores Danmark—Dansk Demokrati og Velfærd*, 1994.

Hauge, Hans. *Den Danske Kirke Nationalt Betragtet*, 1998.

Hemmingsen, Knud, and Heino Larsen. *Danmark i Tema og Tabeller*, 1992.

Henriksen, Ingrid. *Indvandrernes levevilkår i Danmark*, 1985.

Herndon, Jeanne H. "Relationships of Some Indo-European Languages with Detail of English Dialects." In Virginia P. Clark, Paul A. Eschholz, and Alfred F. Rosa, *Language: Introductory Readings*, 1985.

Jenkins, Richard. "Fœllesspisning midt i Jylland." *Tidsskriftet Antropologi*, vol. 39, 1999.

Jensen, Sussi, et al. *Hvad er Meningen med Krœft: En Antropologisk Undersøgelse Blandt Danske Patienter og Behandlere*, 1987.

Jensen, Sussi Skov. *Den Syge, den Raske . . . og den Virkelig Sunde*, 1991.

Jensen, Tim. *Religionsguiden—en Vejviser til Flygtninges og Indvandreres Religioner og Trossamfund i Danmark*, 1994.

Kjersgaard, Erik. *A History of Denmark*, 1974.

Kjœrgaard, Thorkild. *The Danish Revolution, 1500–1800: An Ecohistorical Interpretation*, 1994.

Kjøller, Mette, Niels Chr, Rasmussen, et al. *Sundhed og Sygelighed i Danmark—og Udviklingen Siden 1987*, 1995.

Klindt-Jensen, Ole. *Denmark: Before the Vikings*, 1962.

Knudsen, Anne. *Her Går det Godt, Send Flere Penge*, 1996.

———. *Fanden på Væggen*, 1997.

Larsen, Birgitte, and Peter Lodberg, eds. *Kristne Kirkesamfund i Danmark*, 1998.

Lassen, Moses. *Hvem Forsvarer det Flerkulturelle Danmark? Danske Myndigheders Manglende Beskyttelse af Etniske Minoriteter mod Diskrimination*, 1999.

Lauring, Palle. *A History of Denmark*, 1995.

Maruyama, Magoroh. "The Multilateral Mutual Causal Relationships among the Modes of Communication, Sociometric Pattern and the Intellectual Orientation in the Danish Culture." *Phylon*, vol. 22, 1961.

Pedersen, Søren. "Vandringen til og fra Danmark i Perioden 1960–1997." In *Indvandringen til Danmark: Internationale og Nationale Perspektiver*, David Coleman and Eskil Wadensjö, eds., 1999.

Petri, Christian. *Arv og Gave*, 1998.

Ravnkilde, Knud. *From Fettered to Free: The Farmer in Denmark's History*, 1989.

Reddy, Prakash G. *"Danes Are Like That!". Perspectives of an Indian Anthropologist on the Danish Society*, 1993.

Riis, Povl, ed. *Kan vor Nationale Kulturarv Overleve? De Ikke-Materielle Værdiers Art og Veje*, 1999.

Salamon, Karen Lisa Goldschmidt. "I Grunden er vi Enige. En Ekskursion i Skandinavisk Foreningsliv." *Tidsskriftet Antropologi*, vol. 25, 1992.

Sampson, Steven. "Please: No More Danskhed." In Uffe Østergård, ed., *Dansk Identitet?* 1992.

———. " . . . Hvor er mit Fœdreland Dog Hyggeligt." *Tidsskriftet Antropologi*, vol 27, 1993.

Sandemose, Aksel. *A Refugee Crosses His Tracks*, 1936.

Sawyer, Peter. "Da Danmark blev Danmark: Fra ca. år 700 til ca. 1050." In *Danmarkshistorie*, Olaf Olsen, ed., vol. 3, 1988.

Schwartz, Jonathan Matthew. *Reluctant Hosts: Denmark's Reception of Guest Workers*, 1985.

Sehested, Thomas, Carsten Wulff, et al., eds. *Denmark: Based on Text from the Danish National Encyclopedia and Compiled by its Editors*, 1998.

Ssenoga, Geoffrey Bakiraasa. *The Silent Tribe: A Film about the Danes and Denmark*, 1994.

Statistics Denmark. *Statistisk Årbog*, 1998.

———. *Befolkningens Bevœgelser 1997*, 1999.

Thieme, Paul. "The Indo-European Language." In Virginia P. Clark, Paul A. Eschholz, and Alfred F. Rosa, eds., *Language: Introductory Readings* 1985.

Turner, Barry. *The Statesman's Yearbook 1998–99*, 1998.

Web Sites

Danish National Encyclopedia, Danmarks Nationalleksikon: http://www.dnl.dk

Denmark, a publication by The Royal Danish Ministry of Foreign Affairs: http://www.um.dk/english/danmark/danmarksbog

Ministry of Culture, Kulturministeriet: http://www.kulturministeriet.dk

Ministry of the Interior, Indenrigsministeriet: http://www.im.dk

Ministry of Social Affairs, Socialministeriet: http://www.socialministeriet.dk

Ministry of Trade and Industry, Erhvervsministeriet: http://www.em.dk/english/frame.htm

Women in Government: http://hjem.get2net.dk/Womeningovernments/Denmark.htm

—Erling Høg
and Helle Johannessen

Djibouti

Culture Name

Djiboutian

Orientation

Identification. Djibouti is in northeast Africa, on the Red Sea coast, bordered by Eritrea, Ethiopia, and Somalia. The country was created by France in the late nineteenth century during the colonial scramble for Africa. In 1977, it became independent after having been a protectorate and colony for more than a century. Djibouti had no identity as a state or national unit before 1859, when the French concluded a treaty with the local Afar sultan of Obock.

The two dominant ethnic groups—the Issa-Somali and the Afar—have opposed each other on critical occasions, but a minimal shared identity and national consciousness have emerged, buttressed by social and cultural similarities between originally nomadic-pastoral populations that speak related languages, adhere to Islam, and share a way of life. The wealth brought by Djibouti's seaports unite the inhabitants, who share the idea of being an island of relative stability in a volatile region. While the nation has experienced political turbulence and active armed rebellion, there has never been a prolonged civil war. Compromise has shaped its political life. In international and regional affairs, Djibouti tries to avoid being a pawn of the neighboring countries and maintains an independent position.

Location and Geography. Djibouti lies in a hot, arid area of the Horn of Africa. Its area is 8,960 square miles (23,200 square kilometers). The soil is rocky and sandy and lies on volcanic layers. In the hot and humid climate, rainfall is very low. Most of the soil is not suitable for agriculture, and only about 10 percent is used as pasture. The vegetation consists mainly of desert shrubs and acacia trees. There are only a few patches of perennial forest. The traditional mode of life was nomadic pastoralism, in which state borders were not recognized. Fishing in the Red Sea provides a limited source of income; horticulture is possible only on a small scale.

The Bay of Tadjoura cuts into the country from the Gulf of Aden. The terrain is mainly a desertlike plain with some intermediate mountain ranges near Arta and the eastern border. There is one active volcano. There are seasonal streams that flow toward the sea or into the two salt lakes. Apart from Djibouti City, the capital and large urban center, there are a few small towns: Tadjoura, Obock, Dikhil, Ali Sabieh, and Yoboki.

Demography. The population in 1999 was estimated at about 640,000. It is ethnically diverse, and there are significant numbers of expatriates, including Europeans (mainly French) and Arabs (mainly Yemenis). There is a sizable community of Ethiopians and refugees from Eritrea and Somalia. More than half the population lives in Djibouti City.

Linguistic Affiliation. The main indigenous languages are Afar and Issa-Somali, both of which belong to the Cushitic language group. The official national languages are French, which is used in education and administration, and Arabic, which is spoken by Yemeni and other Arab immigrants.

Symbolism. The coat of arms shows two bent olive branches within which a traditional round shield is pictured over a vertical Somali spear topped with a red star and flanked by two Afar daggers to the left and right. It symbolizes the ideal of coexistence of the two dominant communities. The flag is a tricolor with blue, white, and green fields and a red star on the triangular white field on the left.

History and Ethnic Relations

Emergence of the Nation. Politics has been dominated by the complex relations between the Issa-Somali and the Afar. Before the colonial era, they were nomadic pastoralists and traders and were politically highly organized but had no state-forming

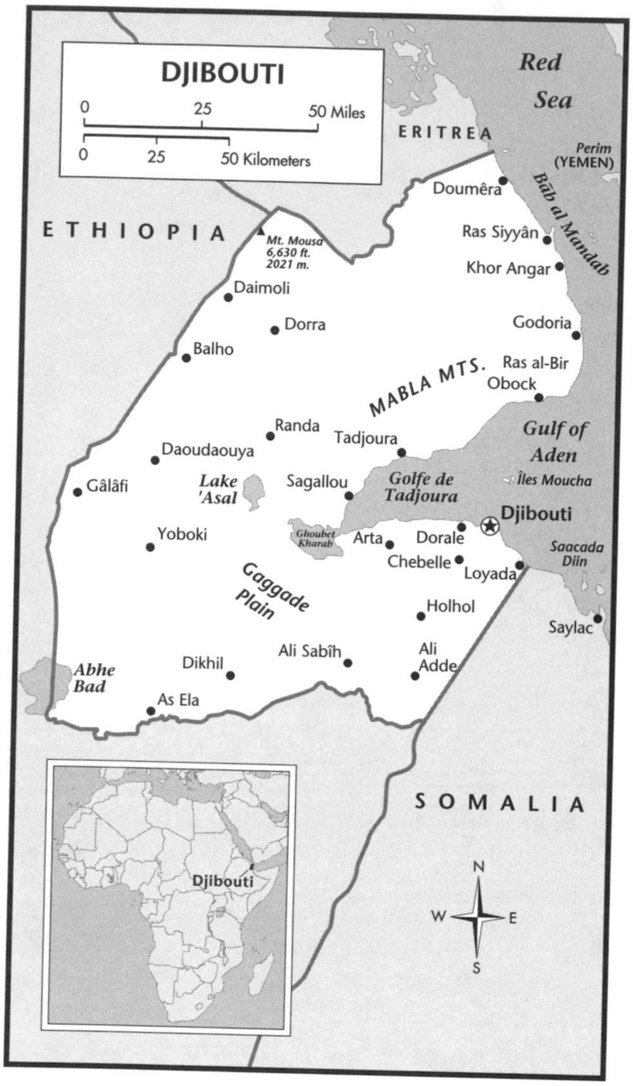

Djibouti

tradition. The Afar had chiefdoms and four sultanates. When the French arrived, about 75 percent of the territory was inhabited by Afar nomads. The Issa had a decentralized political organization based on clan loyalty, although the ruler of Zeila, a trading center on the Somali coast, had great influence over them. The number of Issa and Gadabursi (the third largest group, also Somali) grew steadily in the twentieth century because of immigration from Somalia. The Isaak Somali (about 13 percent of the population) also originated in Somalia.

Before independence, the French alternatively promoted the Issa and the Afar; that divisive policy contributed to postcolonial conflicts.

France created Djibouti as a colony and superimposed a centralist state structure on local pastoral societies. More than two-thirds of the territory traditionally belonged to Afar sultanates, and the remaining southern slice was controlled by Issa nomadic herders. Djibouti as a nation derives its identity from its strategic location and the economic importance of the port. A political crisis occurred with the 1991 armed rebellion of the Front for the Restoration of Unity and Democracy (FRUD), a largely Afar movement that conquered a major part of the country. This crisis pressured the government into opening the political system and holding multiparty elections in 1992. After the elections, a military crackdown was followed by an accommodative policy in which the FRUD was persuaded to join mainstream politics and abandon violence.

National Identity. Djibouti's identity as a nation is a compromise between the political and social aspirations of two communities that have created a social contract within the context of the state that allows them to maintain their independence.

The new President, Ismail Omar Guelleh, who has been in office since 1999, supports economic integration with Ethiopia and has hinted at favoring economic federation with that country.

Ethnic Relations. Though closely related culturally and linguistically, the Afar and the Somali-speaking groups (especially the Issa) have been rivals for power and access to resources. This tension exploded into open armed conflict in the 1990s. After a military campaign to quell the Afar revolt, the government opted for a policy of compromise without endangering Issa dominance, and a full-scale "ethnicization" of politics was averted. There is also tension between the settled population and newcomers (Gadabursi, Isaak, and refugees), which occasionally turns into open conflict.

Urbanism, Architecture, and the Use of Space

Djibouti has no tradition of urban architecture. The indigenous architecture of earlier centuries is found in the capitals of the sultanates of Raheita and Tadjoura, with their old mosques and town centers. Djibouti City was designed by French town planners with a grid street plan and government institutions placed close to each other in the center. The town grew fast, with new neighborhoods added in a less planned fashion. There is a camel market on the outskirts.

In the urban culture, traditional social and cultural features of the indigenous populations tend to fuse and create new forms. In the countryside, the herders' seasonal migrations and transborder crossings of Afar, Issa, and Gadabursi pastoralists show the mobility and free use of space necessary for the survival of humans and herds. These people have huts and furniture that can be easily packed and moved.

FOOD AND ECONOMY

Food in Daily Life. Dairy products and meat from the herds are the traditional foods, along with grain dishes. In the cities, the diet is influenced by Italian and other European foods. A notable feature of the diet is the consumption of the light narcotic leaf *qat,* which is imported from Ethiopia. Qat is consumed recreationally by virtually all men, preferably after lunch, when government offices and work come to a standstill in the midday heat.

Food Customs at Ceremonial Occasions. Qat is used in religious services, allegedly because it enhances concentration, delays sleep, and mutes the appetite.

Basic Economy. Djibouti is a poor but developing country that is dependent on the expanding port and services sector. The economy is unbalanced, with only rudimentary agriculture and a declining livestock economy, but most people still maintain herds and work in agriculture. Infrastructure and communications, except around the port and in the capital, are underdeveloped. Unemployment, poverty, and social insecurity are rampant, especially in the countryside and the working-class neighborhoods in Djibouti City. The government receives subsidies from Arab oil countries and France for balance of payments support and development projects. There is a growing banking and insurance sector, and the telecommunications sector is the best in the region. The currency used is the Djibouti franc.

Land Tenure and Property. Although the government holds most of the land, urban land can be owned privately. Nomadic pastoralists control their traditional pasture areas through customary rights.

Commercial Activities. Djibouti is a free-trade zone. Port activity and related services dwarf other commercial activities, but there is also a small tourist industry. The expenditures of the French army are substantial. Prostitution in Djibouti City is a big business.

Major Industries. The industrial sector employs thirty-five thousand people in a large mineral water bottling plant, leather tanning, construction, a pharmaceuticals factory, abattoirs, salt mining, and a petroleum refinery.

Trade. The transshipment trade through the port is the mainstay of the economy and creates at least 75 percent of the gross domestic product. It has greatly expanded since 1998, when Ethiopia decided to shift all of its import-export activities to Djibouti. Djibouti produces only 5 percent of its own food needs, making it a huge food importer from Ethiopia (grain and other staples) and Somalia (meat and dairy products). The costs of imports are covered by the profitable service sector (the port) and proceeds from contraband trade.

SOCIAL STRATIFICATION

Classes and Castes. Issa and Gadabursi social organization was fairly egalitarian, although it has a patriarchal bias. There are positions of wider authority, such as that of the *ugaz,* a ritual-political clan leader. In the countryside, egalitarianism is still the norm, but there are many impoverished pastoralists as a result of drought, cattle disease, and conflict.

Among the Afar, traditional social stratification was much more hierarchical. The Afar were organized in sultanates and had "tribal" and clan rankings. The Afar distinguish between the more prestigious "red" clans (the Asahimara) and the "white" clans (the Asdohimara), although this division did not coincide with political authority in all regions. In the country as a whole, urbanization, modern state formation and political institutions, and trade have created an urban social stratification based on political power and wealth.

Among the Afar and Somali groups there traditionally are castelike artisan groups that traditionally were held in low esteem. The modern economy gave rise to an incipient class society, including in it the working class. Most workers are state civil servants and port laborers. A relatively large stratum of the population engages in prostitution, works in bars, and trades in contraband. Yemenis traditionally form the trader class.

Symbols of Social Stratification. In line with the socio-economic differentiation into a developing urban society and a largely stagnant agro-pastoral rural society, differences in appearance and life style between social groups are increasingly visible. The urban elites speak French, are well-dressed, have good housing, drive their own cars, and travel abroad frequently for business, education, or leisure. The rural and urban poor have substandard

Tourists may purchase leopard skins and rugs at a market in Djibouti City.

housing, no means of transport, and live under precarious conditions. Most of the rural populations speak Afar or Issa-Somali, not the more prestigious French.

Political Life

Government. Since independence in 1977, there has been a presidential-republican system of government. There is a Chamber of Deputies with sixty-five members that is elected by universal suffrage. Real power lies with the president and his inner circle. The president is also commander in chief of the armed forces. The prime minister, who is always an Afar, is relatively powerless. The country effectively remained an authoritarian one-party state until 1992, when the Afar struggle for more power became a quest for inclusive democracy.

Leadership and Political Officials. Political life since independence has been dominated by a restricted elite of Issa and Afar politicians. In recent years younger politicians have emerged, but they are linked to the same elite. The 1992 constitution limits the number of political parties to four.

There are complex formal and informal rules for the division of power across the various ethnic communities: The president is an Issa; the prime minister is an Afar; and in the Cabinet of Ministers, one seat each is reserved for the Arabs, Isaak, and Gadabursi, while the Afar have one seat more than the Issa. The head of the supreme court is always an Issa.

Social Problems and Control. Unemployment, the decline of pastoral society, a lack of education, and poverty are the major social problems. Prostitution has caused major health problems, including the spread of AIDS. The refugee population strains the national budget and service facilities. In rural areas, communities deal with local political issues and disputes through the use of customary law.

Military Activity. Djibouti has an army of ninety-four hundred men, along with a small navy and air force. Men serve on the basis of conscription. There is a police force of twelve hundred and a national security force of three thousand. In the mid-1990s, the national army grew to a force of twenty thousand to contain the armed revolt led by FRUD. The national security force keeps a tight grip on domestic security. One faction of the FRUD is still active in the Afar part of the country. Djibouti is the base of a large French overseas military force consisting of three thousand men, with one Foreign Legion battalion that helps control the strategic Red Sea en-

French planners laid out the original street grid of Djibouti City.

trance and the port, mediates in domestic conflicts, and protects the republic against its neighbors.

Social Welfare and Change Programs

The Djibouti government is not in a financial position to support extended social and welfare programs. There are state pensions for retired civil servants, but no unemployment benefits or social security provisions, except on a private basis via insurance. There are some vocational training institutes, orphanages and food aid institutions run by Islamic and Christian charities, but they do not cover the needs of the population. Several local nongovernmental organizations are active in addressing problems of urban and rural development. Refugees from Ethiopia and Somalia are cared for partly by the government and by United Nations programs.

Nongovernmental Organizations and Other Associations

With the economy being dominated by the state, the role of nongovernmental organizations and associations is limited. The most important organizations are the trade unions, which have some autonomy.

Gender Roles and Statuses

Division of Labor by Gender. If they are not livestock herders or fishermen, men work largely in the civil service, horticulture, corporate business, the military, and the port services. Women are active as lower civil servants and petty traders, mostly in the informal sector.

The Relative Status of Women and Men. By custom and law men have more rights and higher status than women. Traditional Afar and Issa culture as well as Islam tend to support a pattern of gender roles that give men predominance in public life, business, and politics. Economic necessity, conflict, and migration have made many women the sole household head.

Marriage, Family, and Kinship

Marriage. Descent and family and ethnic group membership remain important in the conclusion of marriages and in family life, especially in the countryside, where rituals around marriage and kinship are still widely observed. Afar have a traditional preference for patrilateral cross-cousin marriage; the Issa and other Somalis are less strict. There is some Afar-Issa intermarriage.

Domestic Unit. The domestic unit in the city is the nuclear family, although members of extended families often live together and provide mutual support. Pastoralists among the Issa, Afar, and Gadabursi live and move together in extended kin groups, accompanied by allies and adopted members. Men make decisions involving the movement of herds and families.

Inheritance. Inheritance follows the tenets of Islamic law, modified by state law inspired by French civil codes.

Kin Groups. In the indigenous Issa and Afar communities, and among the Gadabursi and Isaak Somali, the clan and the lower-level lineage remain important. Membership in these units is identified for marriage purposes, economic networking and mutual assistance, and recourse to customary law for dispute settlement and decisions about inheritance.

SOCIALIZATION

Child Rearing and Education. The family and local community play a crucial role in education and the transmission of culture and morals. Only a minority of children in the countryside, especially in the Afar area, attend schools; often these are Koranic schools with low academic standards. Most children remain in the extended family to assist in economic activities (herding). More than half the population is illiterate. The rural and poor urban populations speak only their indigenous languages. Children are socialized within the family and lineage group and are reared to feel an attachment to kin and community. Among the Somali, children are given more freedom than they are among the Afar, among whom the *fima*, a disciplinary institution, is strong. Exposure to formal schooling is limited to roughly one-third of school-age children, chiefly in Djibouti City.

Higher Education. There are no universities. Many high school graduates go to France to pursue higher education.

ETIQUETTE

The Issa and Afar value the expression of personal independence and courage, but not recklessness. They feel attached to their cultural tradition, or at least to their idea of it. Older people are treated respectfully.

RELIGION

Religious Beliefs. The dominant religion of Djiboutians and Arabs is Islam (95 percent of the population). The ten thousand Europeans are nominally Christians (Catholic). Ethiopians are mostly Ethiopian Orthodox Christian, and Greeks and Armenians are Eastern Orthodox Christian. Islamic beliefs are deeply rooted in Afar and Somali society. Indigenous Issa, Gadabursi, and Afar beliefs combine folk religion and custom with normative Islamic practices. Sufi orders are also prominent. Islam is not used for political purposes by any major party.

Religious Practitioners. Among the Islamic Issa, Gadabursi, and Afar, sheikhs and marabouts occupy a prominent position and play a role in many lifecycle events. There is one diocese for the nine thousand Catholics.

Rituals and Holy Places. There are no Islamic holy places except the tombs of saints and marabouts. Daily life is oriented to the Islamic cycle of religious rituals and holidays.

Death and the Afterlife. Islamic and Christian religious precepts include the belief in the immortality of the soul, ascending to heaven, or descending to hell, according to the merits of an individual's life. All deceased are buried—there is no cremation. In traditional Afar and Issa beliefs, shaped by the continuity of patrilineal ideology, the soul of a deceased rejoins the ancestors, who are occasionally appealed to by the living descendants.

MEDICINE AND HEALTH CARE

Health care is precarious. In Djibouti City, it is available, although not easily accessible to the poor. In rural areas, there are clinics in the major villages, but the nomadic peoples are dependent on traditional remedies.

SECULAR CELEBRATIONS

Independence Day on 27 June is the most important national holiday and unites all Djiboutians in celebration of their national identity. New Year's Day is celebrated on 1 January and Labor Day on 1 May; 11 November, 25 December (Christmas Day), and 31 December (New Year's Eve) are other public holidays.

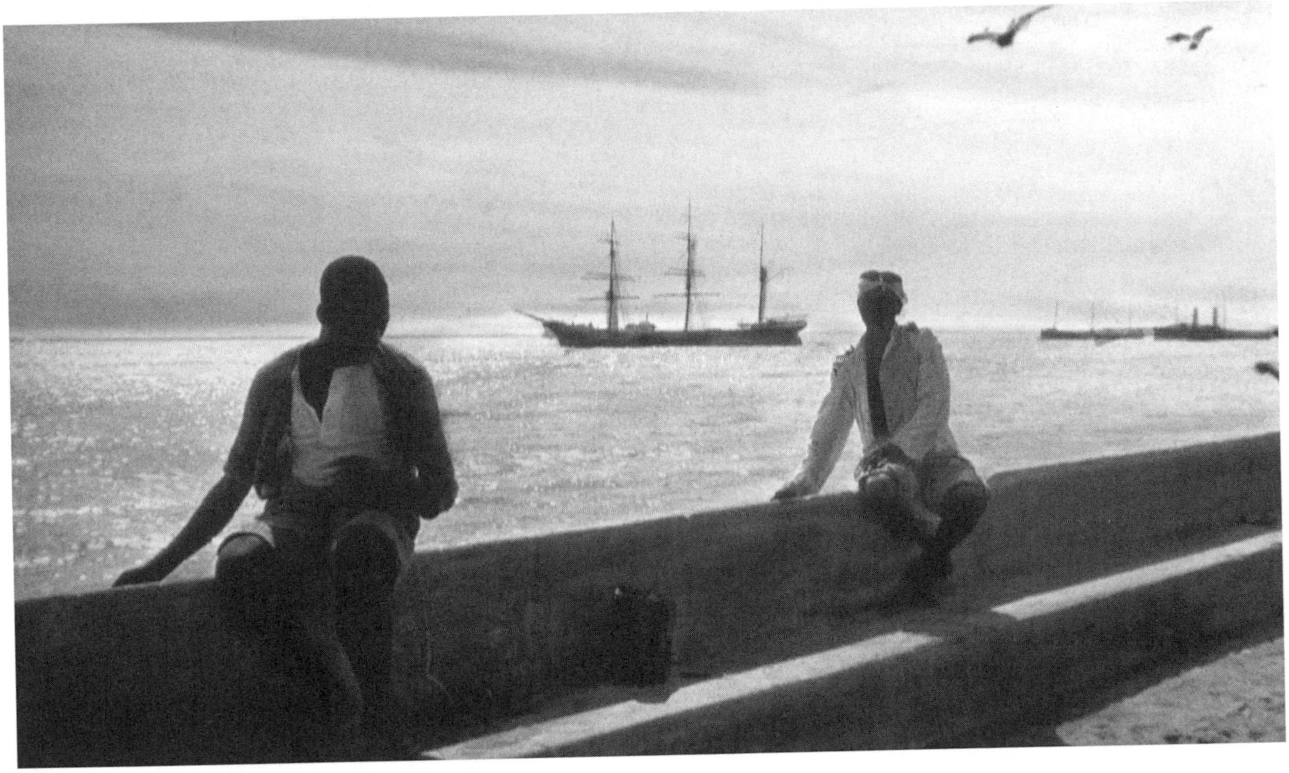

Djibouti's ports are the mainstay of its economy.

The Arts and Humanities

Academic life is lacking, because there are not any universities or a significant intellectual scene. Artists (painters, sculptors, designers) cater to foreign demand. The few literary authors publish in French.

Support for the Arts. The government has few financial or institutional resources to support the arts, but in the capital there is a "people's palace," a national museum, and a national center for the promotion of culture and the arts, where performances and festivals are held. The National Tourism Office has a section to promote interest in the traditional crafts of the country. Connaissance de Djibouti is a study association whose members are interested in retrieving knowledge of the cultures and customs of Djibouti's peoples. Djibouti maintains a cultural exchange and education agreement with France.

Literature. While there is little creative written literature (poetry, novels, drama) to speak of, oral poetry and rhetoric are well developed in Afar and Somali pastoral societies. The Afar are familiar with the *ginnili*, a kind of warrior-poet and diviner, and have a rich oral tradition of folk stories. Among the Somali, poetic talent and verbal skills expressed in songs and epic stories are also highly developed. In recent years there has been a growing number of politicians and intellectuals who write memoirs or reflections on Djibouti society and its problems, but virtually all of them publish in France.

Graphic Arts. Some painters and sculptors in Djibouti town galleries cater largely to French and other foreign visitors.

Performance Arts. There are no major theaters or playwrights in Djibouti, although there are drama performances in the capital's center for culture and art.

The State of the Physical and Social Sciences

Research is done by foreign institutions and individuals, often in partnership with Djibouti scientists educated abroad. There is a French-supported research institute, the Institut Supérieur des Etudes et des Recherches Scientifiques et Techniques. Research on Djibouti society is not well developed.

Bibliography

Ali Coubba. *Le Mal Djiboutien. Rivalités Ethniques et Enjeux Politiques*, 1996.

Ali Moussa Iye. *Le Verdict de l'Arbre*, 1994.

Chire, Anne S. "Djibouti: Migrations de Populations et Insertion Urbaine des Femmes." *L'Afrique Politique,* 120–146. 1998.

Laudouze, André. *Djibouti: Nation Carrefour,* 2nd ed., 1989.

Leclercq, Claude. "La Constitution de la Republique de Djibouti du 15 Septembre 1992." *Revue Juridique et Politique,* 47 (1):71–77, 1993.

Oberlé, Philippe, and Pierre Hugot. *Histoire de Djibouti, des Origines à la République,* 1985.

Rouaud, Alain. "Pour une Histoire des Arabes de Djibouti, 1896–1977." *Cahiers d'Etudes Africaines,* 37 (146):319–348, 1997.

Schraeder, Peter J. "Crystal Anniversary Reflections on the Nascent field of Djiboutian Studies." *A Current Bibliography on African Affairs,* 23 (3):227–247, 1991–1992.

———. "Ethnic Politics in Djibouti: From Eye of the Hurricane to Boiling Cauldron." *African Affairs,* 92 (367):203–221, 1993.

Weber, Olivier, ed. *Corne de l'Afrique. Royaumes Disparus: Ethiopie, Somalie, Djibouti, Yemen,* (special issue of *Autrement,* no. 21), 1987.

—JON G. ABBINK

Dominica

Culture Name

Dominican

Alternative Names

Commonwealth of Dominica; Dominique

Orientation

Identification. Sighted on 3 November 1493 during Christopher Columbus's second voyage to the "New World," Dominica was named for the day: *dies Dominica,* "the Lord's Day" or "Sunday" in Latin. Carib Indians from South America had inhabited the island for almost six hundred years and other Amerindians had been there for as long as three thousand years, but their name for the island, *Waitukubuli,* meaning "Tall is her body," was not recorded for another two centuries. Spain soon lost interest in the island, but France and England fought each other and the Caribs for control throughout the seventeenth and eighteenth centuries. After changing hands several times and two centuries of continuous British rule, Dominica became an independent republic on 3 November 1978.

Location and Geography. Not to be confused with the nearby Dominican Republic, Dominica is located between French-controlled Martinique and Guadeloupe in the eastern Caribbean. The capital, Roseau, is located on the calm Caribbean Sea on the western coast; the rougher Atlantic Ocean forms the island's eastern shore. Though only 29 miles (47 kilometers) long and 16 miles (26 kilometers) wide, those who have tried to settle and develop the island through the centuries have been frustrated with the difficulties of accessing its 290 square miles (751 square kilometers) of land area. With peaks over 4,500 feet (1,370 meters) high, it is the most mountainous island in the Lesser Antilles and one of the last islands in the Caribbean to be colonized. It provided refuge for indigenous Caribs and later for maroons (escaped slaves), and never developed the large-scale sugar plantations that characterized other colonies. Lush tropical rainforests cover two-thirds of the island, and annual rainfall ranges from 50 inches (127 centimeters) on the coast to 300 inches (762 centimeters) in the mountains. Its volcanic origin is evident in bubbling sulphur springs and the Boiling Lake, located in the 17,000-acre (6,885 hectare) Trois Pitons National Park (a UNESCO World Heritage Site since 1998). The island has few white sand beaches, but numerous waterfalls and rivers (Dominicans say there is one for each day of the year).

Demography. The 1991 population census counted 71,183 persons and provided an estimate for 1998 of 74,300 people. About twenty thousand reside in Roseau and its environs, reflecting the "drift" to the urban center during the last several decades of the twentieth century. A majority of the population, 89 percent, is of African descent, 7 percent are of mixed race, and 2 percent are Carib. The remaining 2 percent identify as white, Syrian Lebanese, East Indian, Chinese, and Portuguese.

Linguistic Affiliation. The country's complex colonial past is reflected in its languages. English has been the official language since the British took control in 1763, but it ranges from the standard varieties spoken in Roseau to creolized varieties in rural villages. A distinct English-based creole called Kokoy is spoken in Wesley and Marigot, two villages on the Atlantic coast that were settled by Methodist missionaries, estate owners, and their slave laborers from Antigua and other Leeward Islands in the late eighteenth century. The last fluent speaker of the Carib language reportedly died in the 1920s, although efforts are now being made to revive that language. A French-based creole, known officially as Kwéyòl but also commonly called Patois or Patwa, arose in the early eighteenth century through contact between French colonizers and enslaved West Africans. Once the primary oral lan-

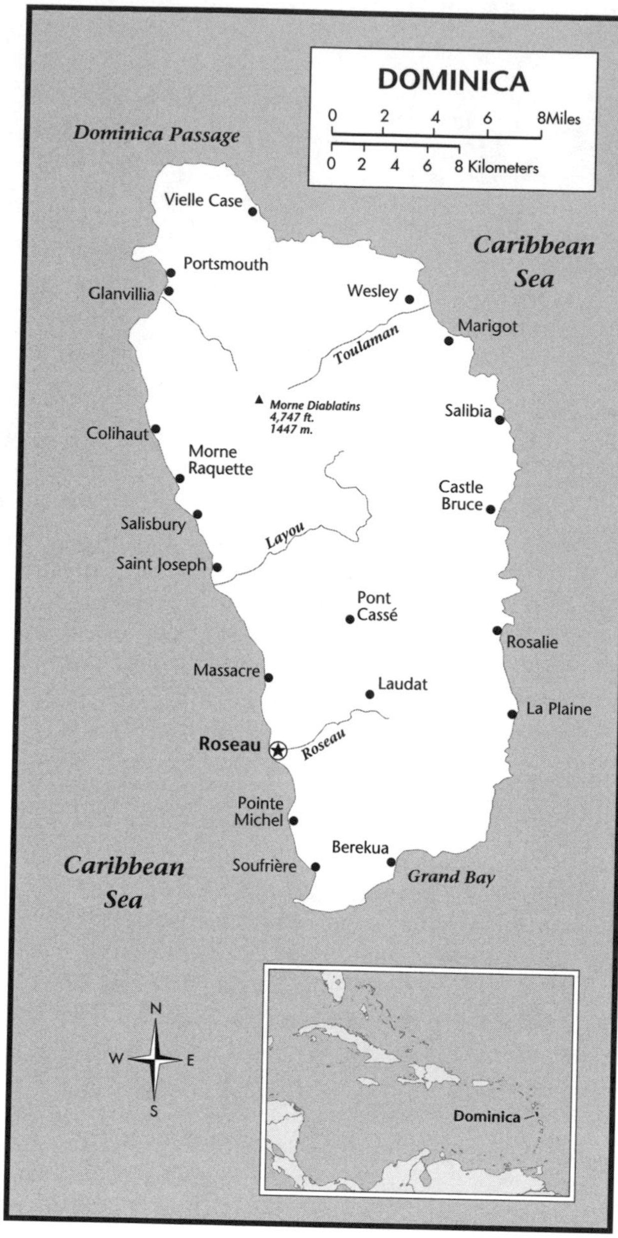

Dominica

guage of the rural population, its use is now declining among the younger generations. The Konmité Pou Etid Kwéyòl (Committee for Creole Studies) was created in 1981 as part of the government's Cultural Division to document, promote, and preserve the language.

Symbolism. Dominica's national motto is *Apres Bondie C'est La Ter,* "After God, it is the land," emphasizing the country's French-creole heritage, strong religious orientation, and dependence on the soil. The national flag depicts a Sisserou parrot, found only in Dominica, within a red circle surrounded by ten green stars representing the parishes of the country; this is centered on a cross in yellow, black, and white stripes on a green background representing the lushness of its rainforests. The three-colored cross symbolizes the Trinity of God; yellow represents the main agricultural products (bananas and citrus); white, the clarity of its rivers and waterfalls; and black, the rich volcanic soil and its African heritage. The national flower, the indigenous Bois Caribe ("Carib wood"), was chosen because of its hardiness and for having persisted throughout human habitation of the island. It is said to represent the nation's history and continuity, and the ruggedness and resourcefulness of its people.

History and Ethnic Relations

Emergence of the Nation. Geography has played a guiding role in the island's history. Due to the mountainous terrain and the resistant Caribs who inhabited it, Dominica was unclaimed by European powers until settled by French planters and missionaries in 1635. England, France's rival, soon vied for control. In 1686 both nations agreed to relinquish the island to the Caribs, yet repeatedly returned. By 1750, the Caribs had retreated to the rugged windward coast (they now reside in an area called the Carib Reserve). In 1763, France ceded Dominica to England in the Treaty of Paris. The French captured the island in 1778, but the English regained control in 1783.

The British concentrated in Roseau, and overseers ran estates for their absentee owners. The French, however, lived on small estates and remained well after the British took official control. A peasant-based agricultural economy and creole culture emerged. Maroons, often supplied with weapons by the French, terrorized the British from 1785 to 1814. Emancipation for all slaves was granted in 1834. Freed slaves from Dominica, Martinique, and Guadeloupe eventually took over the small estates. Dominica became the first and only British Caribbean colony to have a black-controlled legislature following the abolition of slavery. Called the "Mulatto Ascendency," they played a powerful role in politics, government, and cultural affairs into the twentieth century.

Dominica became part of the Leeward Islands in 1833, but changed affiliation to the Windward Islands in 1940. The country became an associated state within the British Commonwealth in 1967 before claiming independence in 1978.

National Identity. Social and political unrest (including attempted coups in 1980 and 1981), economic instability, and the devastating Hurricane David in 1979 complicated the transition to independence. Further divisions included language and historical settlement patterns, as rural villages were relatively isolated from each other and from Roseau and Portsmouth, the second largest town, since colonization. Despite internal differences, the national identity embraced by urban intellectuals and the government was the cultural heritage highlighting French, African, and Carib influence, more than British. A discourse of development unites the country.

Ethnic Relations. The population is predominantly of African descent. The Carib reside primarily on the Carib Reserve, but aside from maintaining some ancestral practices (such as basket weaving and boat making), they live like rural peoples around the island. People who identify as Syrian, Lebanese, and Chinese own some of the largest businesses in Roseau. Although there is some ethnic stereotyping, more salient social divisions fall along class, language, education, and rural and urban lines.

Urbanism, Architecture, and the Use of Space

Roseau is the island's center of government, commerce, health services, education, and communications. The largest French settlement, it was named after the reeds that grow along the nearby Roseau River. French houses grew up haphazardly around a central market square; when the British came to power, they planned the remaining streets and house lots on an orderly grid system. Most buildings are small-scale, ranging from Victorian wood and stone townhouses with large verandas and fretwork to newer, more hurricane-resistant concrete structures. The city is dwarfed by the multi-story cruise ships that call at its newly rebuilt port. A large black and white crucifix and shrine on Morne Bruce overlooks the city. Old stone forts built by the British and expanded by the French include Fort Young in Roseau (now a hotel) and Fort Shirley in Portsmouth (in Cabrits National Park).

Rural villages vary by population and size. Many have a school, health center, post office, one or more churches, and rum shops. Larger villages have a community center and playing field for cricket. Rural homes are traditionally made of wood with galvanized metal roofing, and are perched on stilts. They usually have two or three rooms and a separate outdoor kitchen with a coal pot, fire, or more modern gas stove. Most are sparsely furnished, though those who can afford it fill their homes with store-bought knicknacks, dishes, and appliances. Some larger Western-style concrete houses with recently-available amenities like electricity and indoor plumbing are being built. Yards are kept neat and clean in both rural and urban areas. People socialize at shops, community centers, churches, or on the street.

Food and Economy

Food in Daily Life. Dominica's rich volcanic soil and abundant rainfall are ideal for growing a variety of fruits, vegetables, and root crops. These are sold at market or by street vendors, but people typically grow enough for their own consumption. Bananas and plantains are central to rural diets, and are prepared in a variety of ways. The growing and processing of manioc into cassava bread and farina was once a major subsistence activity, but now wheat bread is widely available from local bakeries. Land crabs, river crayfish, opossum, agouti, and fish are caught where available. Locally raised livestock include goats, pigs, and some cows. Crapaud or "mountain chicken," a type of frog, is the national dish, but a more popular creole dish is roasted breadfruit with salted codfish, onions, and peppers cooked in oil. Imported frozen chicken and turkey parts, tinned milk and sausages, and packaged snacks are increasingly popular. Staple foods like flour, sugar, salt, and rice are purchased in town or from village shops. Individuals often sell homemade cakes, coconut milk ice pops, and sweets from their homes.

Urban residents obtain produce from relatives outside the city or purchase it at market. There are several large American-style supermarkets in Roseau, offering expensive imported goods. Most restaurants are located in Roseau and Portsmouth; in rural areas, shops may sell sandwiches or fried chicken. Kentucky Fried Chicken, an American fast food restaurant, opened in Roseau in 1997. When guests visit a home in both rural and urban areas, it is expected that some food or drink will be offered. Lunch is the largest meal of the day.

Food Customs at Ceremonial Occasions. Holidays and important religious ceremonies are celebrated with the slaughtering of livestock and the preparation of large meals. Guests visit homes throughout the day and are given food, desserts, and alcoholic beverages or other drinks. Catholics make offerings of fruits and vegetables during church services or special masses.

Dominicans socialize on the street and in other public areas.

Basic Economy. Agriculture is the mainstay of the economy, with bananas the chief export crop. Citrus and coconut products are also exported. The economy has historically relied on a successive monocrop strategy, but shifting markets, fluctuating prices, and natural disasters have recently increased calls to diversify.

Land Tenure and Property. In 1763, British surveyors divided the island into lots for sale; only 232 acres went to the Caribs. For the next two centuries, most large estates belonged to British or long-established French families. These were bought up during the "banana boom" of the 1950s by foreign investors and Dominican merchants and professionals moving into agriculture. Small-scale farmers remained scattered between the larger estates. In the 1970s, many estates were sold off in smaller plots. Today, land ownership with deed is highly valued by peasant farmers; land is also rented or worked by squatters. The Carib Reserve was expanded to 3,700 acres by British administrator Hesketh Bell in 1903, but by law it is communally owned by all its residents.

Commercial Activities. Agricultural products and manufactured goods including coconut soaps, bay leaf oils, juice concentrates, rum, cigarettes, paint, and plastic sandals are produced for sale.

Major Industries. The major industries include food processing, coconut product manufacturing, paint production, rum distilling, and handicrafts. There is a small commercial fishing industry and some commerce in timber and pumice. Tourism is developing, but is hindered by a lack of accommodations and an international airport. Billed as "The Nature Island of the Caribbean," recent efforts promote cultural ecotourism. Day cruise ship visits increased dramatically in the 1990s.

Trade. Imports total twice as much as exports. Manufactured goods, food, machinery, and chemicals are imported, chiefly from the United States. Agricultural produce is exported to CARICOM countries and the United Kingdom. CARICOM (Caribbean Community and Common Market), a treaty established and signed by most Caribbean nations in 1973, coordinates foreign policies and economic integration. Bananas are sold to Geest, a British multinational corporation. Merchants travel to neighboring islands to sell agricultural produce and handicrafts.

Division of Labor. Professional positions, including highly desirable government jobs, generally require secondary and usually some post-secondary education. Rural villagers are predominantly peasant farmers, and sometimes run small businesses.

Larger businesses are owned by upper-class Dominicans and Syrian and Lebanese merchants.

Social Stratification

Classes and Castes. Prime determiners of social class are wealth, level of education, occupation, and family history including family name, and class may change through educational advancement or pursuit of a prestigious occupation. The wealthier upper classes are concentrated in Roseau, but there are also marked differences in social class and status in rural villages.

Symbols of Social Stratification. Styles of dress, food, and language were traditionally major symbols of class differentiation, and strongly reflected rural/urban differences. Today, however, rural folk desire the same goods and modern conveniences as urbanites. English still tends to be associated with the educated upper classes and Kwéyòl with lower-class peasants, but this is changing as rural areas become more accessible and education more widespread.

Political Life

Government. Dominica has a British parliamentarian system of government, headed by a president and prime minister. The thirty-member unicameral House of Assembly has twenty-one elected and nine appointed senators, plus the Speaker of the House. A local government system allocates each village a council headed by a chairman (called a chief in the Carib Reserve).

Leadership and Political Officials. There are three principal political parties: the Dominica Freedom Party (DFP), the Dominica Labour Party (DLP), and the United Workers Party (UWP). The DFP, headed by Dame Eugenia Charles, governed from 1980 until 1995. Charles, known as the "Iron Lady of the Caribbean," was the first female Caribbean prime minister. She supported former United States president Ronald Reagan in the 1983 invasion of Grenada. The UWP, under the leadership of Prime Minister Edison James, won the 1995 elections. In 2000, it lost to the DLP and Prime Minister Rosie Douglas, who died after eight months in office. He was replaced by Prime Minister Pierre Charles in October 2000.

Elections are held every five years and are generally peaceful. Supporters travel the island in caravans by political party, and candidates often sprinkle campaign speeches with Kwéyòl during rallies in rural villages. Political officials are generally respected and often invited to attend important meetings and events in villages; they may be severely criticized, however, if popular opinion turns against them.

Social Problems and Control. Since the early 1980s, crime has been very low. The police force is based in Roseau and maintains departments in larger villages. The court system is used to resolve land disputes and slander cases, but problems are usually settled within the family or village.

Military Activity. The police force includes a Special Service Unit and Coast Guard.

Social Welfare and Change Programs

The Social Welfare Department was established in 1945. Since then, it has gradually expanded to include a national system of Social Security and various divisions such as Community Development, Local Government, Youth, Sports, Culture, and the Women's Desk.

Nongovernmental Organizations and Other Associations

Several nongovernmental organizations (NGOs) have been established since independence. They often work together and with the government to utilize limited funds for projects in rural development, agriculture, health, women, and culture. Funding and assistance come from churches (especially the Roman Catholic Church) and several international agencies including UNESCO, UNICEF, and the United States Peace Corps.

Gender Roles and Statuses

Division of Labor by Gender. Women and girls are primarily responsible for childcare, cooking, and household chores. In rural areas, they often grow vegetables and raise small livestock. The majority of vendors at the open-air markets are women, and many women supplement household income by selling homemade sweets and baked goods, weaving baskets, or by working as house cleaners or childcare providers. Men harvest and sell bananas (the main export) and other crops, tend large livestock, fish, hunt, and work in construction. Both men and women are employed as professionals. Men hold more positions of authority in the churches, but both men and women are active in politics and village affairs.

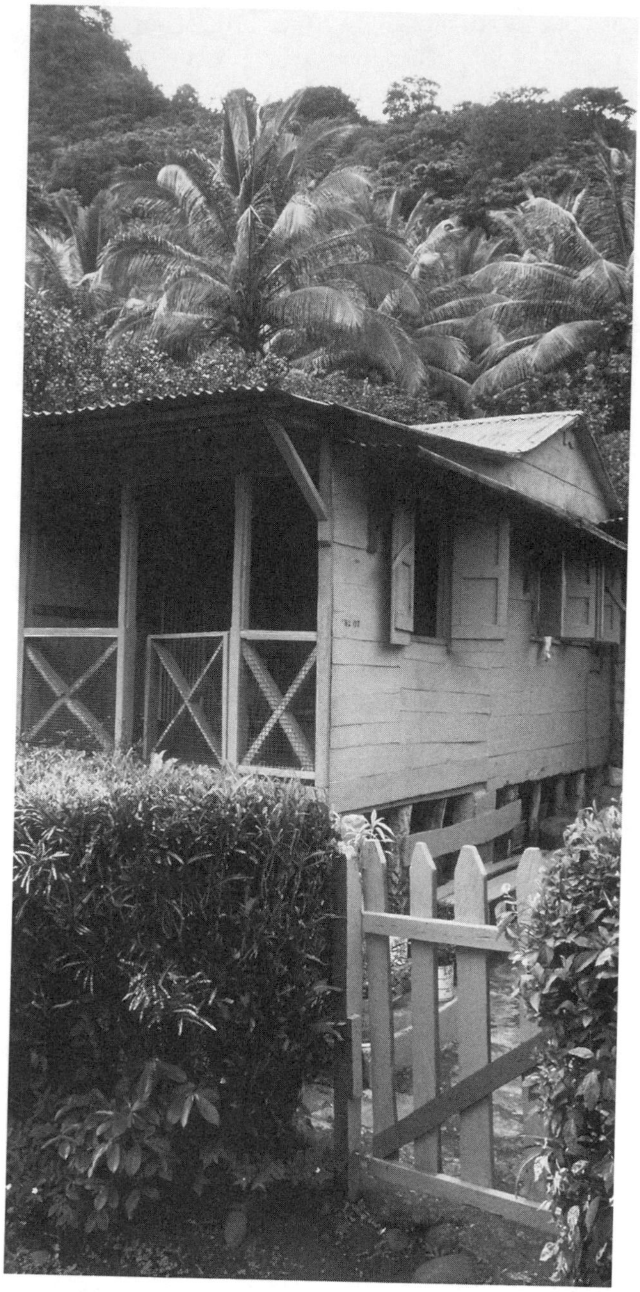

A foundation on stilts, wood construction, and a metal roof typify rural homes.

The Relative Status of Women and Men. Women's work is often valued less than men's work, although women's contributions are equally or more important to household maintenance. Women are criticized if they spend too much time out of the home, while men are allowed more freedom. Women, particularly as mothers, are very involved in community life and are often the center of extensive kin networks.

Marriage, Family, and Kinship

Marriage. Only monogamous marriages are permitted by law. Marriage is based on individual choice, though generally limited by social class and religion. Many young people have children, often with multiple partners, and may cohabit for years before legally marrying, despite church disapproval. Men are expected to contribute financially to their children's upbringing, regardless of their relationship with the mother. Except among the upper classes, marriage usually comes later in life, after age thirty. Divorce is legal, but is rare and is frowned upon.

Domestic Unit. The household may be headed by a man or a woman. Households may consist of one person, a woman and her children (perhaps visited by her boyfriend), a nuclear family with the parents either married or cohabiting, or an extended household that includes several generations. Several families, often related through one matriarch, may have separate homes but share a common piece of land or yard with an outdoor kitchen or other resources.

Inheritance. The predominant inheritance practice is ''family land,'' in which a parcel of land is owned jointly by descendants of the original owner, either male or female. Use of the land is determined by consensus or family tradition. Oral agreements frequently lead to disputes, but no part may be sold unless all co-owners agree.

Kin Groups. Kin groups extend beyond the household to include those related through blood lines, marriage, and friendship both within and outside the village; Dominicans frequently say that everyone on the island is related. Financial and material resources are often shared, and child fostering is common. Many households depend on money sent from relatives who have migrated overseas.

Socialization

Infant Care. Children are cared for primarily by their mothers, but also by other relatives, friends, and neighbors. In rural areas, families rarely have separate cribs or rooms for infants, and they stay with the rest of the family. Small babies are kept at home, but are soon brought along to the fields, river, and elsewhere. When they begin to walk and talk, children are given small household chores. Once they start primary school, they are expected to run errands and look after smaller children.

Child Rearing and Education. Children are expected to be obedient, and corporal punishment is

Uniformed schoolboys wait for the bus in Roseau. Opportunities for education after age fifteen are limited.

used when a child is troublesome or rude. Yet both boys and girls are taught to stand up for themselves and to engage in verbal play and teasing. Education is increasingly valued and is seen as a way out of the rural farming life. Preschool is available to those who can afford it. All children can attend primary school from ages five to fifteen, but must get a high enough score on the Common Entrance Examination by age thirteen to secure one of the limited spaces in a secondary school. As Kwéyòl is widely thought to interfere with children's learning of English, many rural parents now try to speak only English with their children.

Higher Education. Post-secondary education is limited to the Teacher's Training College, the Clifton Dupigny Community College, and a small branch of the University of the West Indies for continuing education. Adult education classes are offered in Roseau, Portsmouth, and occasionally in villages. Further education or training must be obtained on other islands or elsewhere overseas. According to the 1991 census, only 2 percent of the population receives a university education.

Etiquette

Greetings such as "good morning" or "good afternoon" are the most basic form of social interaction. People are expected to greet when they telephone, visit someone's home, or simply pass one another on the street. Strangers are eyed with suspicion, but are treated warmly once introduced. Close friends, especially girls, stand close to one another and often walk with arms around each other's shoulders or waists. Privacy is difficult to maintain but is highly valued; items are concealed when carried in public, and domestic problems are dealt with in the home.

Religion

Religious Beliefs. Roman Catholicism is the religion of over 70 percent of the population. None of the Protestant religions (Methodist, Pentecostal, Seventh Day Adventist, Baptist, Anglican, Jehovah's Witnesses, Church of God) exceed more than 5 percent. Carib and West African beliefs in spirits and obeah (witchcraft) persist despite church disapproval. Rastafarianism is followed by some.

Religious Practitioners. Native Dominicans are now being trained as clergy, but practitioners of the formal religions, particularly Catholic priests and nuns, have generally been foreigners. Obeah practitioners or seers (*gadè*) are native or are from nearby islands.

Rituals and Holy Places. The religions hold services in their respective churches. Residents of smaller villages often must travel to larger villages to attend church. Some villages have stone Roman Catholic churches dating to the seventeenth and eighteenth centuries, although new ones continue to be built in other villages. Many Protestant churches, especially Pentecostal and Seventh Day Adventist, have been built in the latter decades of the twentieth century. The frequency and days of worship depend on the religion.

Death and the Afterlife. Many traditional practices and beliefs, such as the Carib custom of burying the dead in a fetal position, have been abandoned in favor of Christian traditions. All Saints Day is observed by visiting cemeteries and lighting candles on the graves of deceased loved ones.

Medicine and Health Care

Common health problems include parasitic, intestinal, nutritional, venereal, and respiratory diseases, and illnesses like diabetes and hypertension. Dengue fever (but not malaria), teenage pregnancy, and sanitation are major health concerns. Life expectancy is seventy-five years for men and eighty-one years for women. The healthcare system includes a main hospital in Roseau; smaller hospitals in Portsmouth, Grand Bay, and Marigot; and clinics staffed with trained nurses around the island. Doctors, both Dominicans trained abroad and foreigners from technical aid programs and staff hospitals, periodically visit village clinics. There is an off-shore American medical school, Ross University, in Portsmouth. Traditional medical knowledge includes the use of herbs, plants, and tree barks to cure illnesses, induce labor, and so on. A combination of prescription and natural remedies is often used, despite being discouraged by healthcare professionals.

Secular Celebrations

The state's major holiday is Independence Day, 3 November. It is preceded by festivals, competitions, and events starting in August, including Heritage Day, Creole Day (Jounen Kwéyòl), and the three-day World Creole Music Festival, which was begun in 1997. Other secular holidays include Carnival, celebrated the Monday and Tuesday before Ash Wednesday, and New Year's Day. Villages celebrate their patron saints' feasts at various times during the year. Most fishing villages celebrate the Feast of Saint Peter and Saint Paul in June and July.

The Arts and Humanities

Support for the Arts. The arts are largely self-supporting, although major events receive government, international, and private funding. Village cultural groups receive some government assistance, and organizations such as the Cultural Division, Dominica Festivals Commission, and Movement for Cultural Awareness support the arts locally.

Literature. Largely due to the high illiteracy rate prior to the mid-twentieth century, most literature about Dominica has been written by visitors or foreign-born residents. Since the 1970s, there has been a surge of indigenous poetry, short stories, and plays, though much is unpublished or of limited availability. Local historian and anthropologist Lennox Honychurch has published detailed histories and academic scholarship about Dominica.

Graphic Arts. There is a growing local interest in painting, wood carving, pottery, and sculpture. Baskets and handicrafts are sold to tourists.

Performance Arts. African and European-influenced forms of traditional dance, song, music, and storytelling are performed at various cultural shows. The Karifuna Cultural Group was formed in 1978 to revive and promote ancestral Carib cultural expressions. There is a growing interest in modern creative dance.

The State of the Physical and Social Sciences

Lack of funding, resources, and facilities has constrained the development of the physical and social sciences in Dominica. Studies of the environment and people, particularly the Carib, have been carried out by foreign researchers and some Dominicans attending universities abroad. With limited funding, the government's Cultural Division researches and documents cultural and oral traditions.

Bibliography

Andre, Irving W., and Gabriel J. Christian. *In Search of Eden: Dominica, the Travails of a Caribbean Mini-State,* 1992.

Baker, Patrick L. *Centring the Periphery: Chaos, Order, and the Ethnohistory of Dominica,* 1994.

Christie, Pauline. "Language Preference in Two Communities in Dominica, West Indies." *La Linguistique,* 30:7–16, 1994.

Commonwealth of Dominica. *Population and Housing Census,* 1991.

Cultural Division, Government of Dominica. *A Directory of Cultural Activities, Artists and Major Cultural Groups and Institutions in Dominica,* 1993.

Higbie, Janet. *Eugenia: The Caribbean's Iron Lady,* 1993.

Honychurch, Lennox. *Dominica: Isle of Adventure,* 1991.

———. *The Dominica Story: A History of the Island,* 1995.

———. "Carib to Creole: Contact and Culture Exchange in Dominica." Ph.D. Diss., University of Oxford, Trinity, 1997.

Krumeich, Anja. *The Blessings of Motherhood: Health, Pregnancy and Child Care in Dominica,* 1994.

Myers, Robert. *A Resource Guide to Dominica, 1493–1986,* 3 vols., 1987.

Pezeron, Simone Maguy. *The Carib Indians of Dominica Island in the West Indies: Five Hundred Years after Columbus,* 1993.

Stuart, Stephanie. "Dominican Patwa—Mother Tongue or Cultural Relic?" *International Journal of the Sociology of Language,* 102:57–72, 1993.

Taylor, Douglas. *Languages of the West Indies,* 1977.

Trouillot, Michel-Rolph. *Peasants and Capital: Dominica in the World Economy,* 1988.

—Amy L. Paugh

Dominican Republic

Culture Name

Dominican

Orientation

Identification. The Dominican Republic became a nation on 27 February 1844 when a group of revolutionaries seized power from the Haitian rulers of the island of Hispaniola. When Christopher Columbus first discovered the island in 1492, he named it La Isla Española, which became Hispaniola. A few years later the city of Santo Domingo became the Spanish capital of the New World, and because of its location in the trade winds, it was the gateway to the Caribbean. France gained a foothold on the western end of the island, which became prosperous, and by 1795 Spain ceded the entire island to France. By 1804 the black African slaves in the western portion of the island (now Haiti) rebelled against the French and ruled the entire island. French troops eventually reclaimed the island, but were able to occupy only the western end. In 1838 a small group of Spanish-speaking Dominican intellectuals from Santo Domingo organized a secret society called La Trinitaria to overthrow the Haitian rule. The society was established by Juan Pablo Duarte, the son of a wealthy Dominican family. After the overthrow, Pedro Santana, one of the leaders in the revolution, became the first president of the Dominican Republic.

The complex heritage of Arawak, Spanish, African, and French traditions, plus an early independence, set the Dominican Republic apart from other Caribbean islands. Independence was won before slavery was abolished in the Spanish Caribbean and a century before the decolonization of the other islands. The Dominicans consider themselves more Latin American than Caribbean. In addition, they retain close ties with the United States, which occupied the island in the early twentieth century. The national community is struggling to build a democracy against a corrupt and authoritarian political elite.

Location and Geography. The Dominican Republic is located on the eastern two-thirds of the island of Hispaniola and is 18,816 square miles (48,734 square kilometers), about twice the size of New Hampshire. The western portion of the island is occupied by the republic of Haiti. Hispaniola is near the center of the West Indies, a group of islands that extend from Florida to Venezuela. To the north of Hispaniola is the Atlantic Ocean, to the south the Caribbean Sea, to the east Puerto Rico, and to the west Cuba. Hispaniola, Puerto Rico, Cuba, and Jamaica are referred to as the Greater Antilles.

The mountains of the Dominican Republic divide the country into northern, central, and southwestern regions. The northern region includes the Cordillera Septentrional (northern mountain range), the Cibao Valley, which is the country's major agricultural area; and the tropical Samaná Peninsula with its coconut plantations and bay, where humpback whales breed.

The central region is dominated by the Cordillera Central (central range) which ends at the Caribbean Sea. The highest point in the Caribbean is Pico Duarte, which reaches an elevation of over 10,414 feet (3,175 meters) and has alpine forests near the summit. The Caribbean coastal plain includes a series of limestone terraces that gradually rise to a height of about 328 feet (100 meters) and has sugarcane plantations.

The southwestern region lies south of the Valle de San Juan and encompasses the Sierra de Neiba. Much of the region is a desert and it includes Lake Enriquillo, the island's largest lake. Lake Enriquillo is a saltwater lake that lies 150 feet (46 meters) below sea level and is inhabited by unique fauna, including crocodiles, huge iguanas, and flamingos.

The diverse geography of the country includes 800 miles (1,288 kilometers) of coastline with beautiful white-sand beaches and rocky cliffs and

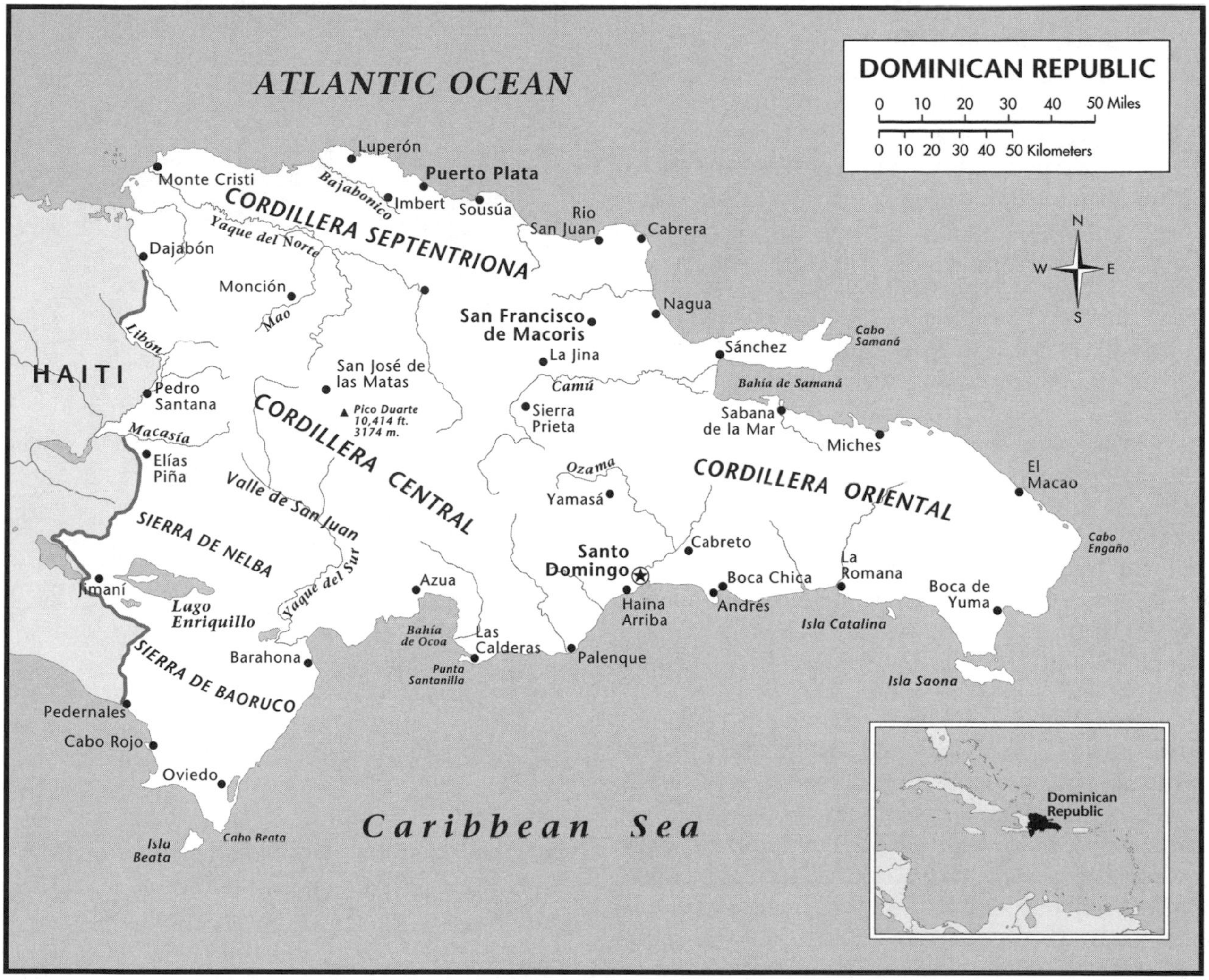

Dominican Republic

warm water, all of which are attractive to tourists. The most significant river in the country, with a drainage basin of 2,720 square miles (7,044 square kilometers), is Yaque del Norte, which starts at Pico Duarte and empties into the Bahia de Monte Cristi on the northwest coast.

The weather is mostly tropical, especially along the southern and eastern coasts. The time and magnitude of the rainy season varies in different parts of the country, but generally occurs in late spring and early fall. In the west and southwestern regions the climate is dry and desertlike because of low rainfall and/or deforestation.

The capital, Santo Domingo, was the first permanent European settlement in the New World and was established by Spain in 1496. The Colonial Zone of Santo Domingo is one of the great treasures of Spanish America today, with many original buildings intact and restored.

Demography. The population of the Dominican Republic is about 8.4 million (2000 estimate) and is increasing at a rate of 1.6 percent per year. More than 1 million Dominicans live full or part time in New York City and are called Dominican Yorks. Seventy-three percent of the population is mixed race—combinations of descendants of Spaniards and other Europeans, West African slaves, and natives. Sixteen percent is Caucasian and 11 percent is black, which includes a Haitian minority.

Dominicans have migrated from rural areas to the cities. The capital, Santo Domingo, has over 2.14 million people, while the population of other large cities, including Santiago de los Caballeros, La Romana, and San Pedro de Macorís, ranges from 124,000 to 364,000. Estimates of the birth rate range from seventeen per thousand (1994) to twenty-five per thousand (2000 estimated). The death rate estimate varies from one per thousand in

1994 to five per thousand (2000 estimated). The infant mortality rate is quite high at thirty-six deaths per thousand live births (2000 estimated). Nevertheless, the total fertility rate is three children born per woman (2000 estimated). The net migration rate is minus four migrants per thousand (2000 estimated).

Linguistic Affiliation. Spanish is the official language and is universally spoken. Dominicans pride themselves on the purity of their Spanish and it is considered by some to be the most classical Castilian spoken in Latin America. Nevertheless, Dominican Spanish has a distinctive accent and incorporates numerous African and Taino (native) expressions. For example, small rural houses are now called *bohios,* after the rectangular houses of the Tainos. A large number of place-names as well as social and cultural terms are inherited from the Tainos. Some English is spoken in Santo Domingo, particularly within the tourist industry. Some Creole is spoken near the Haitian border and in the sugarcane villages, where many Haitian workers live.

Symbolism. The colors and shapes used in the national flag symbolize patriotism and national pride. The flag has a large white cross, a symbol of salvation, that divides it into four quarters. Two quarters are red and two are blue. The blue sections represent liberty, while the red sections symbolize the blood of the heroes who died to preserve it. In the center of the cross is the Dominican coat of arms.

A recent national symbol, constructed in 1992, is the Columbus Lighthouse. It was a work project conceived of by President Joaquín Balaguer when he was 85 years old and blind. It is an enormous cross, flat on the ground, facing the sky and bursting with lights, and was built as a tourist attraction. The physical remains of Columbus have been moved to the lighthouse (although Spain and Cuba also claim to have them). The lighthouse burns so brightly it can be seen from Puerto Rico, but, ironically, it is situated in the midst of a poor neighborhood where the people live without water or electricity and with unpaved, dusty streets and uncollected garbage. A wall was built around the lighthouse to protect the visitors from the neighborhood. Some Dominicans call it the Wall of Shame and argue that the country needs basic services, such as dependable electricity and transportation, not expensive monuments to Columbus. In addition, Dominicans have mixed feelings about Columbus and superstitiously refer to him only as the Great Admiral, believing that to say his name will bring about bad luck.

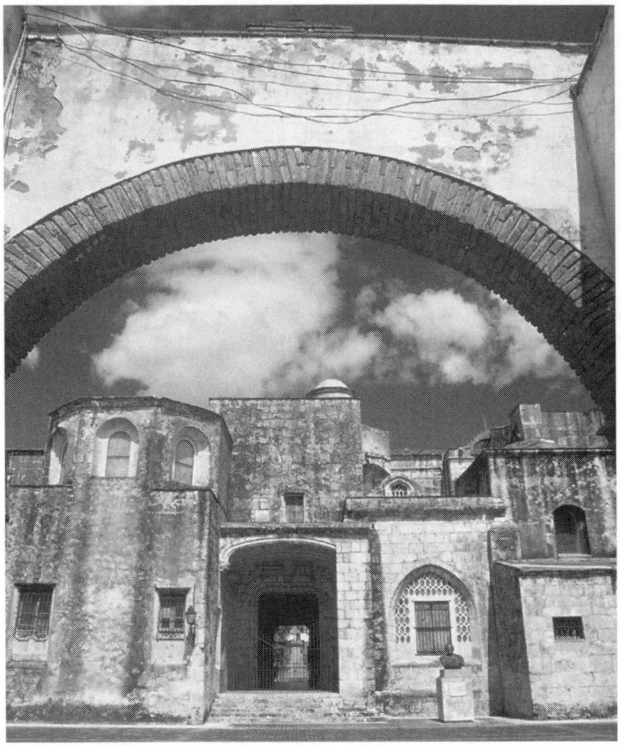

An architectural view of the Cathedral de Santa Maria La Menor.

History and Ethnic Relations

Emergence of the Nation. The Taino were the native people of the Dominican Republic who greeted Columbus. They were a peaceful subgroup of Arawaks who had their origins in the tropical forests of South America. Columbus encountered an island populated by at least 500,000 Tainos living in permanent villages and subsisting on agriculture. The houses were made of wood with thatch roofs, and several families lived together in the same house. Most people used hammocks to sleep in, and goods were stored in baskets hung from the roof and walls. The houses were irregularly arranged around a central plaza, where the larger home of the chief was situated. Villages were arranged into districts, each ruled by one chief, and in turn the districts were grouped into regional chiefdoms headed by the most prominent district chief. There were only two classes of villagers, which chroniclers equated with nobility and commoners. There were no slaves. Instead of simply slashing and burning the forest to make a clearing for agriculture as is common in the Amazon, the Tainos made permanent fields to cultivate root crops. They retarded erosion and improved the drainage, which permitted more lengthy storage of mature tubers. The Tainos mined gold and beat the nuggets into small plates. Then the gold was either inlayed in wooden objects or overlaid on clothing or ornaments. Columbus took special notice of the Tainos' gold work, believing it offered him a chance to repay his debt to the king and queen of Spain. Because nearly all the Tainos died within about three decades of Columbus's arrival, the culture and traditions of these gentle people are not as clearly present in everyday life as, for example, the Maya culture in Mexico today. A more nomadic and warlike group of Arawaks called the Caribs was present on a small portion of the island and are said to have shot arrows at Columbus upon his arrival.

In 1492, when Columbus first landed, he named the island La Isla Española, which later changed to Hispaniola. Although Columbus was a superb navigator, neither he nor his brother Bartholomé could rule the new colony. Both alienated the Spanish by demanding that they work, and they also disrupted the native agriculture by forcing each Indian to dig up a set amount of gold instead of allowing farming. By 1496 many natives had died, and those that rebelled were harshly punished. Food was in short supply and the population of natives was greatly diminished. It was then that Bartholomé transferred the capital from Isabella to the new city of Santo Domingo, located in a more productive region with a good harbor. It was a natural destination for ships following the easterly trade winds from Europe and the Lesser Antilles and remained the Spanish capital of the New World for the next fifty years, when a change in sailing routes made Havana the preferred port. When Columbus returned to Santo Domingo for the third time, he was faced with a revolt by the colonists. To placate the rebels, he distributed not only land but also native communities. Spanish settlers could legally force their Indians to work without wages in a kind of semislavery called *encomienda*, a system that rapidly caused the demise of the Taino Indians because of the harsh forced-labor practices and the diseases the Spanish brought with them. The Spanish imported African slaves to work in the mines and established a strict two-class social system based on race and state domination.

The Spanish abandoned Hispaniola for more economically promising areas such as Cuba and Mexico, but the Spanish institutions of government, economy, and society have persisted in the Dominican Republic. The island became the hiding place for many pirates and was captured for ransom by British admiral Sir Francis Drake. For nearly two hundred years Hispaniola remained in a state of disorganization and depression. In 1697 Spain handed over the western third of Hispaniola to the French, and that portion began to prosper by producing sugar and cotton in an economy based on slavery. By 1795 Spain gave the rest of the island, where most people were barely surviving on subsistence farming, to the French. By 1809 the eastern part of Hispaniola reverted back to Spanish rule. In 1822 the black armies of Haiti invaded and gained control of the entire island, which they maintained until 1844.

On 27 February 1844, Juan Pablo Duarte, the leader of the Dominican independence movement, entered Santo Domingo and declared the eastern two-thirds of Hispaniola an independent nation. He named it the Dominican Republic. The first of the strong-armed leaders called *caudillos*, Pedro Santana, became president. The emerging nation struggled, going in and out of political and economic chaos. Using the Monroe Doctrine to counter what the United States considered potential European intervention, the United States invaded the Dominican Republic in 1916 and occupied it until 1924.

During the period of U.S. occupation, a new class of large landowners resulted from changes made in land-tenure. A new military security force, the Guardia Nacional, was trained by the U.S. Marines to be a counterinsurgency force. In 1930, Rafael Trujillo, who had risen to a position of leadership in the Guardia, used it to acquire and consolidate power. From 1930 to 1961, Trujillo ran the Dominican Republic as his own personal possession, in what has been called the first truly totalitarian state in the hemisphere. He and his friends held nearly 60 percent of the country's assets and controlled its labor force while they abolished personal and political freedoms. He typified the *caudillismo* that has shaped Dominican society.

After Trujillo was assassinated in 1961, his son fled the country and a democratic election was held. Ultimately, the Dominican military with the help of twenty-three thousand U.S. troops defeated the constitutionalists in 1965. The Dominican economic elite, having been reinstalled by the U.S. military, achieved the election of Joaquín Balaguer, one of Trujillo's puppet presidents. Until the early 1970s the Dominican Republic went through a period of economic growth and development arising mainly from public-works projects, foreign investments, increased tourism, and skyrocketing sugar prices. Most of the benefits went to the already wealthy while the unemployment rate, illiteracy, malnutrition, and infant mortality rates were dangerously high. With the mid-1970s surge in oil prices, a crash in the price of sugar, and increases in unemployment and inflation, the Balaguer government was destabilized, and human rights and political freedom were better observed. The country, however, incurred enormous foreign debt, and the International Monetary Fund required drastic austerity measures, such as a government wage freeze, a decrease of funding, an increase in prices of staple goods, and restricted credit. These policies resulted in social unrest and Balaguer, nearly eighty years old and legally blind, regained control of the country. He once again turned to massive public-works projects in an attempt to revitalize the economy, but this time was unsuccessful. Balaguer was forced to step down in 1996 and Leonel Fernández Reyna was elected.

National Identity. A large factor that influences Dominican national identity is its Spanish heritage and early independence. The native population was decimated or assimilated within decades of the arrival of Columbus, and the island was repopulated with Spanish colonists and their African slaves. Spanish is the national language, universally spoken today. Light skin color, which is considered to reflect European ancestry, is valued, while dark skin tones reflect the West African slave ancestry. The Roman Catholic cathedrals still stand and the majority of the population is Roman Catholic. A proud aggressive attitude is admired in sports, business, and politics. Machismo permeates society, especially among rural and low income groups, with males enjoying privileges not accorded to females.

The common expression, *Si Dios quiere* (If God wishes), expresses the belief that personal power is intertwined with one's place in the family, the community, and the grand design of the Deity. People have been forced to accept the strong class system begun by the Spanish and maintained by the strongman leaders where only a few historically prominent families hold a great deal of the wealth and power. Some of the few surviving traits of the gentle Tainos may account for acceptance of the system with relatively few revolts.

The family unit is of primary importance. Relationships among people are more important than schedules and being late for appointments, and people often spend time socializing rather than working. Dominicans are warm, friendly, outgoing, and gregarious. They are very curious about others and forthright in asking personal questions. Children are rarely shy. *Confianze* (trust) is highly valued and not quickly or easily gained by outsiders, perhaps as a result of the human rights and economic abuses the people have suffered at the hands of the powerful.

Ethnic Relations. Dominican society is the cradle of blackness in the Americas. It was the port of entry for the first African slaves, only nine years after Columbus arrived. Blacks and mulattoes make up almost 90 percent of the population. There has been a longstanding tension with Haiti, particularly over the Haitian desire to migrate there. In the early fall of 1937 Trujillo's soldiers used machetes, knives, picks, and shovels to slaughter somewhere between ten thousand and thirty-five thousand Haitian civilians, claiming it was a Dominican peasant uprising. Even loyal personal servants and Haitian spouses of Dominicans were killed by the soldiers. Today there is still great disdain for Haitian and other blacks.

Urbanism, Architecture, and the Use of Space

A massive migration from rural to urban areas characterized the twentieth century. About 60 percent of Dominicans live in urban areas. The capital, Santo Domingo, is the largest city by far and has a population of 2.14 million. Its population approximately doubled every ten years between 1920 and 1970. The second and third largest cities, Santiago and La Romana, also experienced rapid growth, especially in the 1960s and 1970s.

Santo Domingo was a walled city, modeled after those of medieval Spain, and for three decades was the seat of Spanish power and culture in the New World. Today the area known as the *Zona Colonial* stands as a monument to Spain's time as a superpower, with some buildings dating back to the early sixteenth century. The layout of the city followed the classic European grid pattern, with several plazas. Plazas are popular meeting places for area residents, tourists, vendors, taxi drivers, guides, and shoeshine boys. The plazas usually contain shade trees, park benches, and monuments.

Food and Economy

Food in Daily Life. The main meal is served at midday and can last up to two hours. *La bandera* (the flag) is a popular national dish; the white rice and red beans remind people of the flag colors, hence the name. The third ingredient is stewed meat, and it is usually served with fried plantain and a salad. Another favorite dish is *sancocho,* a meat, plantain, and vegetable stew. On the coast, fish and conch are enjoyed, and coconut is used to sweeten many sea-

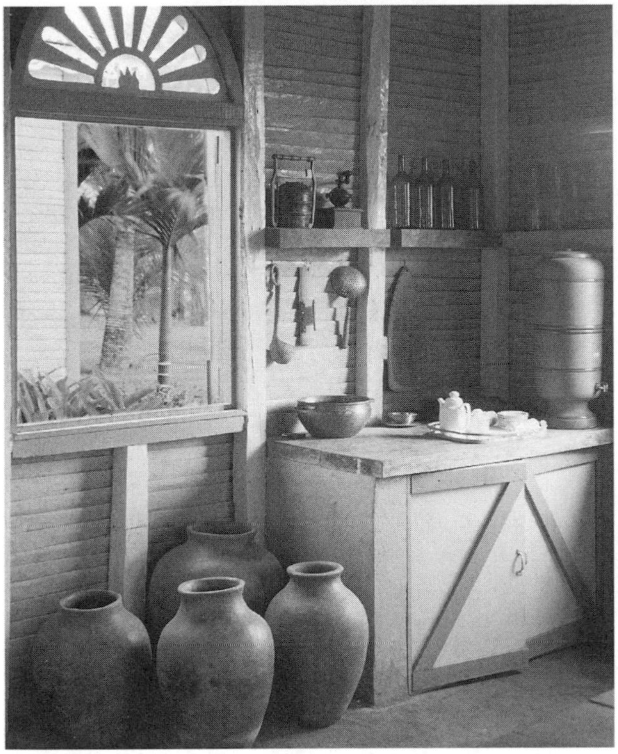

Clay jars provide storage in this kitchen in Santo Domingo.

food dishes. Root vegetables include sweet potatoes, yams, cassava, and potatoes. Small quantities of chicken, beef, pork, or goat are eaten with a meal. Food is generally not spicy.

Dining out is popular and restaurants in Santo Domingo are superior and reasonably priced. The Hotel Lina has been voted one of the ten best restaurants in the world. Even the food sold by street vendors, such as grilled meat or *tostones* (fried plantain patties), is delicious.

Food Customs at Ceremonial Occasions. On special occasions, such as Christmas or Easter, extended families sit down together for large feasts. Roasted pig, pigeon peas (small yellow beans), and boiled chestnuts are served at Christmas. Fish is the traditional dish at Easter.

Basic Economy. The Dominican Republic is among the fastest-growing economies in Latin America. Even though the gross domestic product (GDP) tripled in the last generation, 70 percent of the people are affected by poverty and unemployment is high. Throughout history, the economy has been based on the production and export of sugar. Sugarcane is still a big cash crop, along with rice, plantains (starchy green bananas), and bananas. Fluctuating world prices make the market volatile.

Land Tenure and Property. Land-tenure patterns reflect both Dominican and international politics. Sugar and cattle production require large tracts of land and ownership has changed over time. In 1916 when the United States invaded, the military enacted legislation to facilitate the takeover of Dominican land by U.S. sugar growers. Communal lands were broken up and transferred to private ownership. By 1925 eleven of the twenty-one sugar mills belonged to U.S. corporations and most of the sugar was exported to the United States.

Cattle raising, an important source and symbol of wealth in the countryside, was feasible for many because the animals were branded and left to graze freely on open land. Much of the land was expropriated by Trujillo, and later he established a law requiring livestock to be enclosed, ending the free grazing. By the 1970s the government created state-subsidized credits for cattle production, enabling people to buy land for grazing in an attempt to increase production.

Major Industries. Agriculture, including forestry and fishing, contributed about 13 percent of the GDP in 1996. Industry, including mining, manufacturing, construction, and power, provided about 32 percent of the GDP in 1996. The services sector contributes 55 percent of the GDP. With the relative stability of the Dominican democracy and tax incentives, tourism is the most rapidly growing sector of the economy. With more hotel rooms than any other Caribbean country and beautiful beaches, tourism in the country is now the largest source of foreign exchange, along with manufacturing in the free trade zones. The government is working to increase electric generating capacity, a key to continued economic growth, and the state-owned electric company was ultimately privatized by 2000.

Trade. Mining of ferro-nickel, gold, and silver has recently surpassed sugar as the biggest source of export earnings. Manufacturing of food, petroleum products, beverages, and chemicals contributes about 17 percent of the GDP. A rapidly growing part of the manufacturing sector is occurring in the free trade zones, established for multinational corporations. Products such as textiles, garments, and light electronic goods intended for export are assembled. Industries locate in these zones because they are permitted to pay low wages for labor intensive activities; also, the Dominican government grants exemptions from duties and taxes on exports.

Division of Labor. The Dominican Republic is the world's fourth-largest location of free trade zones, and much of the nation's industrial work occurs there. Two-thirds of these zones are owned by U.S. corporations. The majority of the workers are women; in 1990 the average monthly salary was $59 (U.S.) with no benefits. Most are assembly and factory workers who produce electronics, jewelry, furniture, clothing, and shoes for export. Nevertheless, free trade zones have created much-needed jobs and have brought more advanced technology to the island. Companies pay rent and purchase utilities and supplies.

On most sugarcane farms, working conditions are dreadful, and Dominicans are too proud to work for such low wages. Companies hire Haitians to work the fields for twelve to fifteen hours a day. Workers are as young as eight years old. There are no cooking or sanitary facilities. Children born to Haitian sugarcane workers effectively have no country and no medical or educational benefits.

Social Stratification

Classes and Castes. Dominican social stratification is influenced by racial and economic issues. The upper class is historically descended from European ancestry and is light skinned. The lower class is most often black, descendants of the African slave population or Haitians. The mulattoes are people of mixed African and European ancestry and make up the majority of the population; they have created a growing middle class. This middle class is divided into *indio claro,* who have lighter skin, and *indio obscuro,* who are darker skinned. The term *indio* (Indian) is used because many Dominicans do not yet acknowledge their African roots.

Symbols of Social Stratification. The symbols of social stratification are similar to those in Western cultures. Many of the growing middle-class population own homes and cars, and enjoy updating them with the latest electronic appliances. Their children graduate from high school, and may go on to college. People take pride in their personal appearance and prefer New York fashions and jewelry. However, there is still a large segment of the population which lives in urban slums and poor rural areas without electricity or running water.

Political Life

Government. The Dominican Republic is divided into twenty-nine provinces, each run by a governor who is appointed by the president. The president and vice president and a bicameral Congress of thirty senators and 120 deputies are elected by popular vote every four years. The voting age is eighteen. A nine-member Supreme Court is formally appointed every four years by the Senate, but is greatly influenced by the president.

Leadership and Political Officials. One of the most influential political parties is the Dominican Revolutionary Party (PRD) and it has a liberal philosophy. A spin-off is the Dominican Liberation Party (PLD) and it is considered even more liberal. A conservative group is the Revolutionary Social Christian Party (PRSC).

Unfortunately, many people aspire to be elected to government positions so that they can obtain bribes. Each time government salaries are cut, the corruption in government grows. Also, government contracts are awarded to business in return for money paid directly to the official who makes the decision.

Social Problems and Control. During much of its history the Dominican Republic has been governed by strongarm dictators who have denied human rights to their citizens, particularly darker-skinned people. The most recent constitution was adopted in 1966 after the civil war following Trujillo's rule. Although it puts few limitations on the powers of the president, it stresses civil rights and gives Dominicans liberties they had never before been granted. In 1978 reforms were made to reduce the military's political involvement in order to prevent a coup. The military were given civic duties such as building roads, medical and educational facilities, and houses, and replanting forests. The judicial branch is subject to the political mood since they are appointed every four years. Since the 1960s the court has become more independent, even if it is not an equal branch of government.

Military Activity. Military service is voluntary and lasts for four years. In 1998 the armed forces totaled 24,500 people, with most in the army, followed by the air force and the navy. There are about fifteen thousand members of the paramilitary. The defense budget in 1998 was slightly less than the amount spent on welfare.

Social Welfare and Change Programs

A voluntary national contributory scheme exists to provide insurance coverage for sickness, unemployment, dental injury, maternity, old age, and death. Only about 42 percent of the population benefits from it.

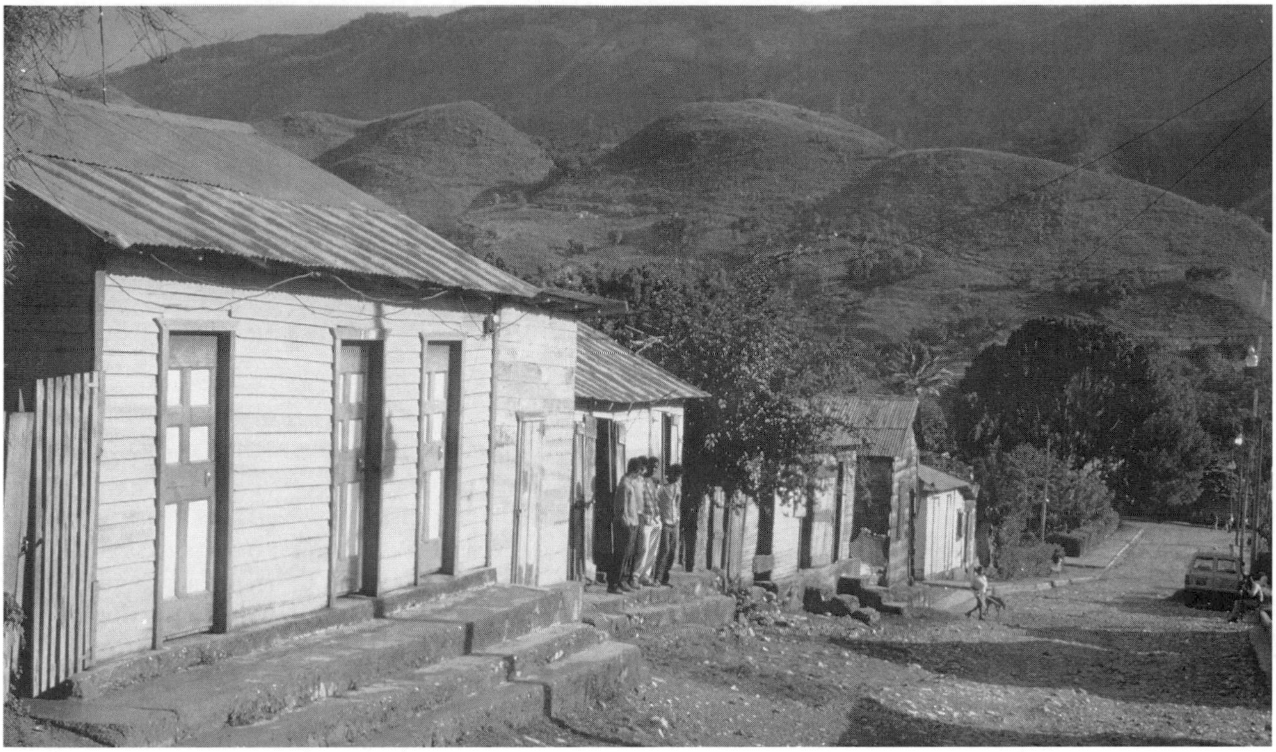

About 40 percent of Dominicans live in rural areas such as the village of Honda Valle.

Nongovernmental Organizations and Other Associations

Many nongovernmental organizations exist. Some collaborate with international organizations such as the United Nations, the World Trade Organization, the International Monetary Fund, the Organization of American States, and private voluntary organizations such as Amnesty International and the International Committee of the Red Cross, CARE, and Catholic Relief Services. They implement a wide variety of projects in agriculture, microenterprise, water and sanitation, and health.

In the 1970s and 1980s, after the end of the Trujillo regime, there was an increase in Dominican interest groups. For example, the Central Electoral Junta is an independent board that monitors elections. The Collective of Popular Organizations is a political pressure group. Many organizations exist to promote business, including the Dominican Center of Promotion of Exportation and the Dominican Sugar Institute.

Gender Roles and Statuses

Division of Labor by Gender. About one-quarter of the lower-class people are unemployed. Among this group, women tend to find jobs more easily than men, especially in rural areas, and are paid less. Women often support their households, but do not make enough to bring them out of poverty.

The Relative Status of Women and Men. In middle-class and upper-class families the structure is patriarchal, and the dominant father-figure is the norm. As women gain control over the number of children they bear, they have been able to gain greater educational and employment opportunities. Among the lower-class families, the structure is often matriarchal because the father does not live in the house.

Marriage, Family, and Kinship

Marriage. Three different types of marital union include church marriages, civil marriages, and consensual or common-law unions. Church and civil marriages are most prevalent among the upper classes and the ceremonies can be costly, whereas consensual unions predominate among the poor. These patterns can be traced back to the Spanish colonial and slave periods. The Spanish settlers brought with them a strong ethic of family solidarity, and the father was the dominant figure. Slave families were broken up and marriages were often not allowed. Informal unions between the Spanish settlers and African slave women were encouraged, and the present-day range of skin tones and mar-

Agriculture represented about 13 percent of the gross domestic product in 1996.

riage practices are reflections of the colonial heritage.

Domestic Unit. The extended family, composed of three or more generations, is prevalent among the Dominican elite. The oldest man holds authority, makes public decisions, and is responsible for the welfare of the family. The oldest married woman commands her household, delivers the more private decisions, and nurtures the family. Married brothers and their wives and children are part of the extended family, and have a strong allegiance to their father. Married daughters become part of their husbands' families.

Consensual unions create a more loosely structured family, and responsibilities fall to the mother. The result is a lower-class household which often becomes an extended matriarchy with the oldest woman at the head and her unmarried children, married daughters, and grandchildren constituting the household. Some men have more than one wife and family and are often absent from a particular household.

Inheritance. Among the two-parent families, land, money, and personal possessions are usually left to the surviving spouse and children. When the household is headed by a woman or when there is a consensual union, inheritance policies are more loosely structured.

Kin Groups. Family loyalty is a virtue ingrained from early childhood when individuals learn that relatives can be trusted and relied on. At every level of society a person looks to family and kin for both social identity and succor. A needy relative might receive the loan of a piece of land, some wage labor, or gifts of food. More affluent relatives may adopt a child from needy relatives and help out the parents of that child as well.

Formal organizations succeed best when they are able to mesh with pre-existing ties of kinship. Until the 1960s and 1970s, most community activities were kin-based and consisted of a few related extended families joined together for endeavors. Families with relatively equal resources shared and cooperated.

When kinship is lacking and where families wish to establish a trusting relationship with other families, they can become *compadres.* Strong emotional bonds link *compadres* or co-parents, and they use the formal "usted" instead of "tu" when addressing one another. Compadres are chosen at baptism and marriage, and the relationship extends to the two couples and their offspring.

SOCIALIZATION

Child Rearing and Education. Public education is provided through the high-school level at no cost except for the school uniform and books. Attendance is mandatory to sixth grade, although many children, particularly girls, drop out before then. Over one thousand schools were destroyed by Hurricane George in 1998. Scarce funding before and after the hurricane has resulted in limited resources and understaffed facilities. Many urban families send their children to private schools. Considering the lack of enforcement of education laws, the adult literacy rate of 83 percent is quite high, nearly double that of neighboring Haiti.

Higher Education. The oldest public university in the New World was built by the Spanish in 1588, and the University of Santo Domingo is its descendant. Most of the twenty-eight Dominican universities are privately owned and offer student loans. Total enrollment for all colleges and universities in 1998 topped 100,000. Some students go abroad to attend schools and universities.

ETIQUETTE

Politeness is a very important aspect of social interaction. When you enter a room or begin a conversation, it is polite to make a general greeting such as *buenos días,* which means "good day." Handshakes are another friendly gesture.

Personal appearance is important to Dominicans and they do their best to look neat and clean. They like the latest in New York fashions. Men wear long pants and stylish shirts except when at the beach or doing manual labor. Professional men wear business suits or the traditional *chacabana,* a white shirt worn over dark trousers. Rural women wear skirts or dresses, but in urban areas jeans and short skirts are acceptable. Bright colors and shiny fabrics are favored. Children are often dressed up, especially for church or visiting. Short pants are not allowed in government buildings and shorts and tank tops are not worn in church.

Formal introductions are rare, but professional titles are used to address respected persons. Older and more prominent people may be addressed as *Don* (for men) or *Doña* (for women), with or without their first names. Most women ride sidesaddle while on the backs of motorcycles, because sitting with the legs apart is considered unladylike. Personal space is limited, touching is normal, and crowding, particularly on public transportation, is common.

Dominicans are animated and often make gestures and use body language. "Come here" is indicated with the palm down and fingers together waving inward. To hail a taxi or bus, one wags a finger or fingers depending on the number of passengers in need of a ride. Dominicans point with puckered lips instead of a finger. Men shake hands firmly when they greet and close friends embrace. Most women kiss each other on both cheeks, and a man who trusts a woman will also kiss her.

RELIGION

Religious Beliefs. About 95 percent of the population is Roman Catholic, even if not all of these people attend church regularly. Catholicism was introduced by Columbus and the Spanish missionaries and even today is an important force in shaping society. Although many Dominicans are fairly secular, children are often taught to ask for a blessing from their parents and other relatives when greeting them. For example, a child might say "Bless me, aunt," and the response is "May God bless you." The dominance of the Catholic Church was diminishing at the end of the twentieth century, due to a decrease in funding, a shortage of priests, and a lack of social programs for the people. Although some Protestants are descendants of non-Spanish immigrants who came to the island in the early 1800s, the Protestant evangelical movement has been gaining more support. The style of worship is much less formal than that of the Catholic Church and emphasizes family rejuvenation, biblical teachings, and economic independence. Despite differences in belief and opinion, there is little conflict between religious groups.

During World War II (1939–1945) the small town of Sosúsa was built by a group of European Jews who escaped persecution, and is still the center for the tiny Jewish population of the island.

Voodoo is practiced secretly, primarily along the border with Haiti, and originated with the African slaves, particularly those from the Dahomey region. Practitioners believe in one God and many lesser spirits. They believe that each individual has a protector spirit who rewards that person with wealth and punishes him or her with illness. Nature spirits oversee the external world. Ancestral spirits are the souls of dead ancestors and will protect the living if properly remembered with funerals and memorials. Because the early colonists forbade the practice of voodoo, people learned to disguise the spirits as Roman Catholic saints. For example, the Madonna who represents motherhood, beauty,

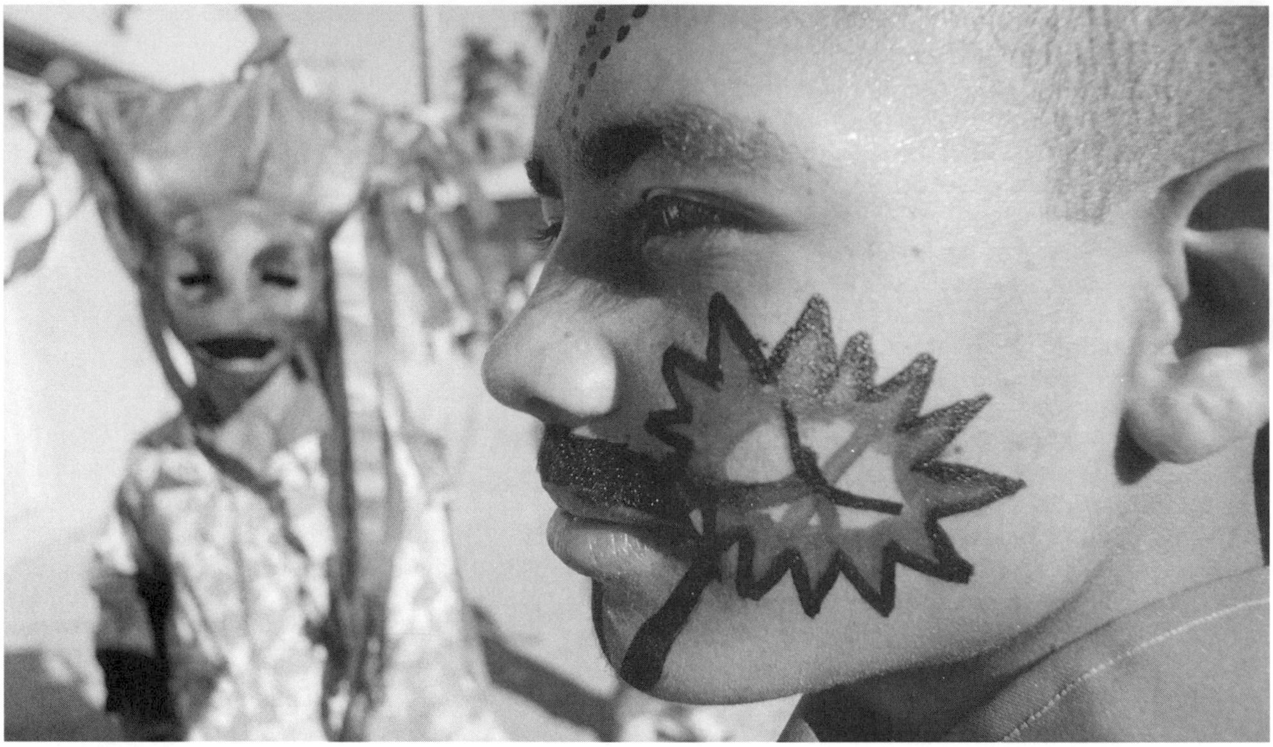

Children with painted faces and costumes participate in the Festival of Cabral, which takes place on Good Friday.

love, and sex is Erzulie. Although many voodoo products are for sale in markets, voodoo is unpopular with most Dominicans.

Religious Practitioners. Roman Catholicism has been combined with traditional folk religion, particularly in rural areas. It is quite common for devout Catholics to consult a folk practitioner for spiritual advice or to prevent some calamity. The *ensalmo* is a healing chant that is usually performed by an elderly woman, and is among the most respected folk practices. Folk healers work through the saints and ask for special help for those in need. A few people are skilled in the use of herbs and other natural objects for healing, and are called witch doctors. They are also believed to have the power to banish evil spirits.

Medicine and Health Care

Public clinics and hospitals provide free care, but people who can afford to prefer to go to private doctors. Public institutions tend to be poorly equipped and understaffed, and the focus is on curative rather than preventive care. There are about one thousand people to each doctor, with over eight hundred people per each hospital bed. There is a separate system for members of the armed forces. Private health care is also available, primarily in urban centers. Many people still consult native healers, including witch doctors, voodoo practitioners, and herbalists. Parasites and infectious diseases are common. Contaminated water must be boiled in rural areas. Malaria and rabies are still a problem. In spite of this, the life expectancy is sixty-eight for men and seventy-two for women.

Secular Celebrations

Secular holidays include New Year's Day on 1 January; Juan Pablo Duarte's Birthday on 26 January; Independence Day from Haiti, celebrated with a carnival featuring parades, costumes and parties on 27 February; Pan-American Day on 14 April; Labor Day on 1 May; the Foundation of Sociedad la Trinitaria on 16 July; the Santo Domingo Merengue Festival, in late July; the founding of Santo Domingo on 5 August; Restoration Day on 16 August; Columbus Day on 12 October; and United Nations Day on 24 October.

The Arts and Humanities

Support for the Arts. There are a variety of organizations and schools which support all forms of art, from fine arts to traditional crafts. The Fine Arts Council controls the Academies of Music, the National Conservatory of Music and Elocution, the School of Scenic Art, the Fine Arts School (in three different cities), and the School of Plastic Arts. The Institute of Dominican Culture promotes cultural tradition and encourages artistic creation and expression of the spirit of the Dominican people. Recently, Dominican artists have gained international recognition.

In the capital city of Santo Domingo there is a neighborhood of Haitian immigrants, which includes many people who try to make a living by selling their paintings to tourists. The paintings are usually oil on canvas and are colorful, stylized, and inexpensive. These people have a history of being mistreated by the police.

Literature. The Dominican literary heritage has historically come from the elite, particularly the Henríque-Ureña family, who had the advantage of formal education. The literary works and style have a European influence, particularly Spanish and French. Gaston Fernando Deligne led the movement into modernism. Don Pedro Mir is known as the National Poet. More recent Dominican authors, such as Julia Alvarez, are leaving the Spanish influences behind and creating a unique Dominican style.

Graphic Arts. Folk arts provide a cottage industry for many. Both glazed and unglazed terra-cotta pottery pieces are sold in markets. Particularly popular are terra-cotta figures for Christmas nativity scenes. Carved calabash or gourds are made into masks or filled with seeds to rattle as maracas. Women in rural areas are well known for their macramé hammocks and bags. Other crafts include basket making, palm weaving, and jewelry made from native coral and seashells. More elaborate jewelry is made from the high-quality native amber and *larimar*, a semiprecious ocean-blue gemstone found only in the Dominican Republic.

Performance Arts. Dominicans love music and dancing. Merengue, with its African tom-tom beat and Spanish salsa spirit, is the most popular. Other influences are the sound of reggae from Jamaica and the Spanish guitar. Music can be heard on every street corner and there are large outdoor festivals. There is also the National Conservatory for Music and Speech.

The State of the Physical and Social Sciences

The University of Santo Domingo, founded in 1538, is autonomous, although state-supported. After the fall of Trujillo, the Madre y Maestra Catholic University and Pedro Henríquez-Ureña National University and others were also formed in Santo Domingo. Likewise, there are universities in most of the largest cities.

Among the oldest of the technical colleges is the Higher Institute of Agriculture, which was founded in 1962. The Institute of Technology of Santo Domingo offers undergraduate and postgraduate teaching and research. The Technological University in Santiago has faculties of social and economic sciences, architecture and engineering, health sciences, and science and humanities. There are also a variety of joint programs such as Indiana University's Underwater Science program, which is supported by the Catholic University of Santo Domingo and grants from local groups for the study of underwater archaeology of the Columbus shipwreck and Taino sites.

Two research institutes are the Dominican Sugar Institute and the Military Cartographic Institute. There is a natural history museum and a museum of Dominican man in the capital. Technology is also being brought into the country by multinational corporations in the free trade zones for light manufacture. United States AID also provides grants for research.

Bibliography

Alvarez-Lopez, Luis, Sherrie Baver, Jean Weisman, Ramona Hernández, and Nancy López. *Dominican Studies: Resources and Research Questions*, 1997.

de Cordoba, Jose. "If We Told You Who This Story Is About, We Might Be Jinxed—Christopher C Is a Curse, say Dominicans, Who Knock When They Hear the Name. *Wall Street Journal*, 22 April 1992.

Doggett, Scott, and Leah Gordon. *Dominican Republic and Haiti*, 1999.

Foley, Erin. *Dominican Republic*, 1995.

Grasmuck, Sherri, and Patricia Pessar. *Between Two Islands: Dominican International Migration*, 1991.

Haggerty, Richard. *Dominican Republic and Haiti: Country Studies*, 1991.

Kryzanek, Michael, and Howard Wiarda. *The Politics of External Influence upon the Dominican Republic*, 1988.

Logan, Rayford. *Haiti and the Dominican Republic*, 1968.

Moya Pons, Frank. *The Dominican Republic: A National History*, 1995.

Novas, Himilce. *Everything You Need to Know about Latino History*, 1994.

Pacini-Hernández, Deborah. *Bachata: A Social History of Dominican Popular Music*, 1995.

Parker, Lonnae. "Soulsa, a Simmering Blend of Cultures. Latino Music Connects with an African Beat." *Washington Post*, 13 January 2000.

Pessar, Patricia. *A Visa for a Dream: Dominicans in the United States*, 1995.

Rogers, Lura, and Barbara Radcliffe Rogers. *The Dominican Republic*, 1999.

Rogozinske, Jan. *A Brief History of the Caribbean from the Arawak and Carib to the Present*, 1999.

Rouse, Irving. *The Tainos: Rise and Decline of the People Who Greeted Columbus*, 1992.

Ruck, Rob. *The Tropic of Baseball: Baseball in the Dominican Republic*, 1991.

Safa, Helen. *The Myth of the Male Breadwinner: Women and Industrialization in the Caribbean*, 1995.

Tores-Saillant, Silvio. "The Tribulations of Blackness: Stages in Dominican Racial Identity." *Latin American Perspectives*, 25 (3): 126–146. 1998.

Walton, Chelle. *Caribbean Ways: A Cultural Guide*, 1993.

Welles, Sumner. *Naboth's Vineyard: The Dominican Republic, 1844–1924*, 2 vols., 1928.

Whiteford, Linda. "Child and Maternal Health and International Economic Policies." *Social Science and Medicine* 7 (11): 1391–1400, 1993.

———. "Contemporary Health Care and the Colonial and Neo-Colonial Experience: The Case of the Dominican Republic." *Social Science and Medicine* 35 (10): 1215–1223, 1992.

Wiarda, Howard. *The Dominican Republic: Nation in Transition*, 1969.

———, and Michael Kryzanek. *The Dominican Republic: A Caribbean Crucible*, 2nd ed., 1992.

World Health Organization. Division of Epidemiological Surveillance. *Demographic Data for Health Situation Assessment and Projections*, 1993.

Wucker, Michele. *Why the Cocks Fight: Dominicans, Haitians, and the Struggle for Hispaniola*, 1999.

Zakrzewski Brown, Isabel. *Culture and Customs of the Dominican Republic*, 1999.

Web Sites

United Nations Development Program. *Human Development Report*, 1999. http://www.undp.org/hdro

U.S. Department of State. Bureau of Western Hemisphere Affairs. http://www.state.gov/www/background_notes/domrep_0010_bgn.html. Background Notes: Dominican Republic, 2000

—Elizabeth Van Eps Garlo

ECUADOR

CULTURE NAME

Ecuadorian; ecuatoriano (masc.), ecuatoriana (fem.)

ALTERNATIVE NAMES

Republic of Ecuador, República del Ecuador (official name, in Spanish), El Ecuador

ORIENTATION

Identification. In 1830, Ecuador took its name from the Spanish word for the equator, which crosses the entire northern sector. The three mainland regions are referred to as the Coast, the Sierra, and Amazonia, or the Oriente (''east''). A constitutional democracy, Ecuador is a multicultural, multiethnic nation–state that many consider multinational. It has one of the highest representations of indigenous cultures in South America and two distinct Afro–Ecuadorian cultures. The dominant populace is descended primarily from Spanish colonists and settlers and to a lesser extent from German, Italian, Lebanese, and Asian immigrants. Spanish is the national language; thirteen indigenous languages are spoken, of which the principal ones are Quichua in the Sierra and the Oriente and Jivaroan in the Oriente.

The citizens take great pride in being Ecuadorian and refer to themselves as *ecuatorianos(-as)* and *gente* (people). Despite continuing discrimination, indigenous and black citizens identify themselves as Ecuadorians as well as native people or black people.

The elites and those in the upper–middle classes are oriented toward education, personal achievement, and the modern consumerism of Euro–North America. People in these classes regard themselves as *muy culto* (''very cultured''), and while they may learn English, French, or German as part of their formal education, most disavow knowledge of any indigenous language.

People in the upper and upper–middle classes generally identify by skin color as *blanco* (''white''), to distinguish themselves from those whom they regard as ''below'' them. The prevalent concept of *mestizaje* is an elitist ideology of racial miscegenation, implying ''whitening.'' Those who self–identify as ''white'' may use the term ''mestizo'' for themselves, as in *blanco–mestizo,* to show how much lighter they are than other ''mestizos.''

Black people, represented by their leaders as Afro–Ecuadorians, *(afroecuatorianos)*, speak Spanish and range through the middle to lower classes. They are concentrated in the northwest coastal province of Esmeraldas, the Chota–Mira River Valley of the northern Andes, and the city of Guayaquil. A sizable black population lives in sectors of the Quito metropolitan area, and there is a concentration in the oil-rich Amazonian region.

The cultures of the indigenous people are rich and varied, but there are commonalities across languages and societies. The Quichua (pronounced Kéechua) speakers of the Andes and Amazonia are differentiated from one another, but come together when common causes arise. Quichua includes the northern dialects of Quechua, the language of the imperial Inca. In Quichua and Quechua people identify as Runa (''fully human''), and their language as *runa shimi* (''human speech'').

All of the nationalities identify in their own languages as both fully human beings and as Ecuadorians. There is no word resembling *indio* (''indian'') in indigenous languages, and the use of that term is deeply resented. In Spanish, the term for indigenous person (*indígena*) is preferred, though *gente* (person, human being) is the most appropriate designation for any Ecuadorian. People throughout Ecuador make it very clear that identification as Ecuadorian is for all people, and is not only for the elite and upper–middle classes.

Location and Geography. Ecuador, which is 109,493 square miles (283,600 square kilometers;

Ecuador

about the size of Oregon), is located in western South America, the second smallest South American nation. Its topography is dramatic. Two cordilleras split the nation into coastal, Andean, and Amazonian regions. The Galápagos Islands lie 600 miles (965 kilometers) off the Pacific coast. The nation is flanked on the north by Colombia and on the east and south by Peru. The coastal region ranges from a tropical rain forest in the north to a mixed wet–dry monsoon region for the rest of the region. A third fairly low cordillera runs intermittently along the coastal strip. The Andes region has a number of snow–capped volcanic mountains, dominated by Chimborazo (20,596 feet; 6,278 meters) and Cotopaxi (19,613 feet; 5,978 meters). Rich, fertile valleys, or basins, lie in the inter–Andean region known as the Corridor of the Volcanoes. The Amazonian topography is highly varied, ranging from mountainous regions that tower well over 6,000 feet (1,829 meters) to Amazonian biotopes.

Demography. The population of Ecuador is estimated as approaching fourteen million and is under–enumerated. It is divided almost evenly between the Coast and the Sierra. The Amazonian region consists of only about 6 percent of the nation's population. Guayaquil, the major coastal city with nearly four million people, and the Andean capital, Quito, with its two million people, constitute the powerful polarities of a political–economic coastal–sierran divide. Both metropolitan areas vie for control of the nation's wealth and power. Indigenous people may comprise as much as 25 percent to 35 percent of the republic, and black people about 7 percent. When those descended from indigenous or Afro–Ecuadorian parents or ancestors are added to these statistics, people who from an elite and upper–middle–class perspective carry the "taint" of ethnicity become the majority. The Quichua–speaking people constitute the largest indigenous population of about two million, followed by the Jivaroans who number between 50,000 and 70,000. The smallest group, the Zaparoans, number only a handful of actual speakers. The other indigenous groups range between 500 and 1300.

Linguistic Affiliation. Spanish, called *castellano*, is the official Ecuadorian language. According to the 1998 constitution, the state guarantees the system of bilingual, intercultural education that uses the principal language of a particular culture and Spanish as the idiom of intercultural relations.

The indigenous nationalities speak various languages that belong to different linguistic families. Quichua is spoken by most indigenous people in the Sierra and by the largest indigenous group in Amazonia. Well–known cultural clusters in the Sierra include the Otavalo of Imbabura–Carchi, the Tigua–Zumbagua of Cotopaxi, the Colta of Chimborazo, the Cañari of Cañar and Azuay, and the Saraguro of Loja. The Awa, Chachi, and Tscháchila of the northern coastal region speak mutually intelligible dialects of Barbacoan. In the Amazonian region, Shuar, Achuar, and Shiwiar are Jivaroan languages, though those identifying with the latter may speak Achuar, Shuar, Quichua, or Záparo. The Waorani, Záparo, and Cofán (A'i) speak languages unrelated to other language families of South America, and the Siona and Secoya speak Western Tukanoan.

Quechua, subsuming Quichua, has twelve million speakers ranging from southern Colombia to Argentina in the Andes, and Colombia, Ecuador, and Peru in Amazonia. It is the largest Native American language. The Jivaroan languages (Shuar, Huambisa, Achuar, and Aguaruna) are spoken in northeastern Peru; Cofán is spoken in Colombia; Siona and Secoya are spoken in Colombia and Peru.

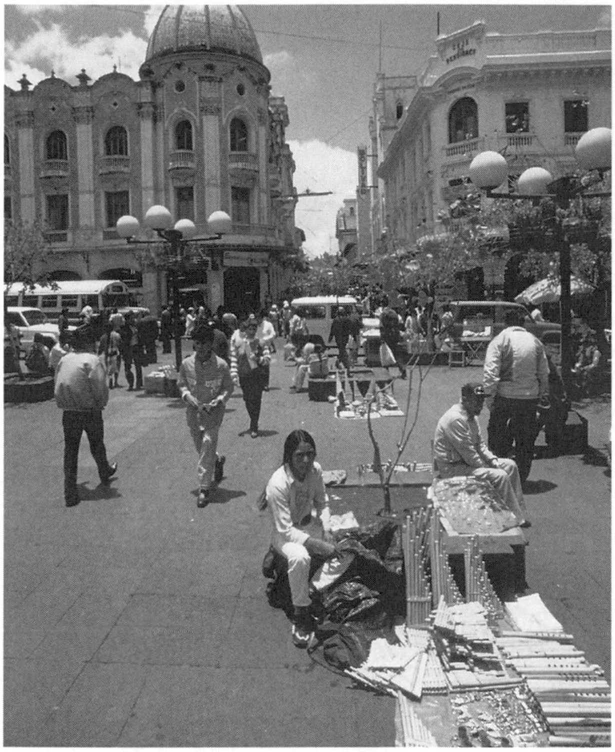

A public square in Quito, the capital of Ecuador.

All indigenous languages are native to South America; they are not derived from pidgin or creole. Black people speak their own dialects of Spanish and generally do not learn indigenous languages. Bilingualism and multilingualism are common in Amazonia, where the Achuar and Canelos Quichua intermarry, and there is increasing intermarriage among people in diverse language families. Spanish is common as a second or third language among indigenous people, and English, French, and German are used by those who have been educated abroad or who have traveled extensively in Europe or the United States.

Symbolism. Identity as Ecuadorian has many key symbols. *La patria* (''the motherland'') is complemented by *el país,* ''the fatherland'' (country). The former is the more powerful evocative referent of collective identity. While *el país* may be in chaos, *la patria* endures. The government, *el gobierno,* is closely related to the fatherland. It expresses itself through *el estado* (''the state''). The people look to the government for sustenance and protection, but also expect corruption. When the government cannot serve the people, they rise up as one. The common collective chant during such uprisings is *el pueblo, unido, jamás será vencido* (''the united people will never be defeated''). The feminine concept of *la nación* (''nation'') is weaker than the other two, as is the collective idea of an *estado–nación* (''nation–state''). While scholars debate whether Ecuador is a true nation or nation–state, the people identify with *la patria* and look to *el gobierno* for salvation of individual and collective self, as citizens of *el país.* ''Governability'' is another key symbol in Ecuador, and every leader has stated that Ecuador is very difficult to govern, or that governability is impossible.

The national flag (the ''tricolor'') emerged in the union of Gran Colombia in 1820s. A broad horizontal yellow stripe represents the sun, fount of all natural abundance; a red stripe is for the blood of the heroes who fell in the making of a nation, specifically those who died in Quito; and the central blue strip is for the sky. The national coat of arms, which is also part of the national flag, features the union of Coast and Sierra. The condor, the national bird, is on top of the coat of arms. In the 1960s the Central Bank of Ecuador took as its emblem a golden sun mask from the La Tolita archaeological culture of Esmeraldas Province. In the 1990s the indigenous organization CONAIE appropriated this same mask as its own emblem of multinationality of *el pueblo.* One of Ecuador's most powerful collective symbols, which appears on some official stationery and in other places, is *¡el Ecuador es, ha sido, y será, país amazónico!* (Ecuador has been, is, and will be, an Amazonian country!). This slogan arose after Peru attacked Ecuador in the war of 1941. After brief but costly wars in 1981 and 1995, the boundary dispute was resolved in October 1998. With the acceptance of the treaty, Ecuadorians everywhere reported feeling as though a limb had been amputated from the collective body of *el país* long after the Peruvian violation of *la patria.* On 12 May 1999, presidents Jamil Mahuad and Alberto Fujimori presented a new symbol of unity—the *Spondylus* shell—evidence of ancient long-distance trade between the native peoples of Ecuador and Peru—renewing their nations' cooperation in development and prosperity.

The national anthem reflects these themes. It is played and sung, often with all of its verses, at all public gatherings in every setting, including those involving nationalities that may be at odds with the government, the nation, and the nation–state. Every television station signs on with the national anthem, often accompanied by pictures of the national flag flying and the golden sun mask radiating. Also included are ethnic and geographic scapes that remind everyone of the topographical and cultural diversity of the country.

Two key symbols represent both cultural–biological centralization and homogenization and diversification, human integrity, and dignity. The first is that of *mestizaje*, which is promulgated by the elite, who descend from Europeans. It refers to a body of blended Ecuadorians who occupy the middle to lower classes. It is confronted constantly by the second symbol of *nacionalidad* ("nationality") which refers to being culturally distinct in an oppressive nationalist state. The most prominent nationality in Ecuador is that of the Quichua-speaking people. In the 1970s their slogan was a common greeting in the Inca Empire: *ama shua, ama llulla, ama quilla* ("don't steal, don't lie, don't be lazy"). The indigenous-based social-political movement *pachakutik* ("return to the land"), formed in 1996, chose as its flag a rainbow spectrum, representing the anaconda, which emerges from the Amazonian lowlands to unite people from the Andes and Amazonia. This rainbow flag was combined with the golden sun and Inca greeting to build a master set of symbols of a diverse yet unified body. These symbols are now nationally recognized, defining an indigenous space of dynamic nationalities within the republic.

History and Ethnic Relations

Emergence of the Nation. Pre-Inca indigenous existence—which is important to the concept of national culture in Ecuador—is difficult to unravel, but it was rich in its diversity, complex in its multiplicity of polities, and left an archaeological record that differentiates its cultures from others in South America. The Incaic period, to which most Ecuadorians refer when discussing the indigenous past, began about 1480 and ended fifty years later with the Spanish conquest led by Francisco Pizarro and Diego Almagro. The Inca, whose northern leader in the 1530s was Atahualpa, probably introduced Quechua, as Quichua, into Andean Ecuador, and they certainly promoted its usage as a political lingua franca. The Spaniards introduced their language as they imposed colonial rule, but Quichua continued to spread.

As the Spanish took over Quito, began the exploration of Amazonia, and sought to establish a viable Pacific port, African-American people began their own conquest of the northwest rain-forest region of what is now Esmeraldas. By the mid-sixteenth century, self-liberated Africans and their offspring controlled what was known as the Zambo Republic (*zambo* refers to intermixture of African and Native peoples). As Quito became a royal court system of the Spanish crown in 1563, it extended bureaucratic control westward to the northwest coast and eastward to the Upper Amazon. In both areas full-scale revolts occurred, with the "Zambos" of the northwest coast and the Quijos and Jivaroans of the Amazonian region resisting all attempts of Spanish incursion. The Spanish were forced to make alliances with the representatives of the Zambo Republic to the west; they managed to subdue the Quijos in the north Amazonian territory, but not the Jivaroans in the center and south Amazonian regions.

The colonial era lasted for three hundred years and caused large-scale depopulation due to disease and the emergence of a system of "racial hybridity" that denied nationality to all those classed as *indio* and *negro*. Through it all there were uprisings, revolts, revolutions, movements of self-assertion, and relationships that promoted subsistence, trade, commerce, and cultural coherence beyond colonial bureaucratic control.

National holidays that proclaim the sequence of events leading to the one hundred fifty years of republican history are 10 August (1809), "shout for Independence," and 24 May (1822), "Battle of Pichincha." After that battle Ecuador broke from Spain, which also governed Peru, and joined the Confederation of Gran Colombia, which also included present-day Colombia and Venezuela. In 1830 Ecuador became an independent republic, gained its name, and began a tumultuous history racked with ethnic clashes and dominated by a white, European-oriented oligarchy.

A unifying force between about 1860 and 1875 was a conservative-Catholic alliance aimed at infrastructural development and consolidation of the *blanco* elite's position against that of the army, which was filled with blacks and mestizos. As conservatism reigned in the Sierra, liberalism grew on the Coast. Political conflicts between liberal and conservative, Coast and Sierra played heavily in national governing throughout the late 1800s and early 1900s led to a series of civil wars, including the assassinations of conservative President Gabriel García Moreno and liberal President Eloy Alfaro Delgado.

The decline of dependency on the world market that accompanied World War I calmed the violence and civil disorder and ushered in an era of internal development. As dependency on world trade returned, violence again became common until the army of the Sierra rebelled against coastal dominance and initiated a new era of Quito-dominated bureaucratic controls that included a central bank (inaugurated 10 August 1927). Between 1925 and 1979, Ecuador's political history, which has a powerful hold on its cultural history, was characterized

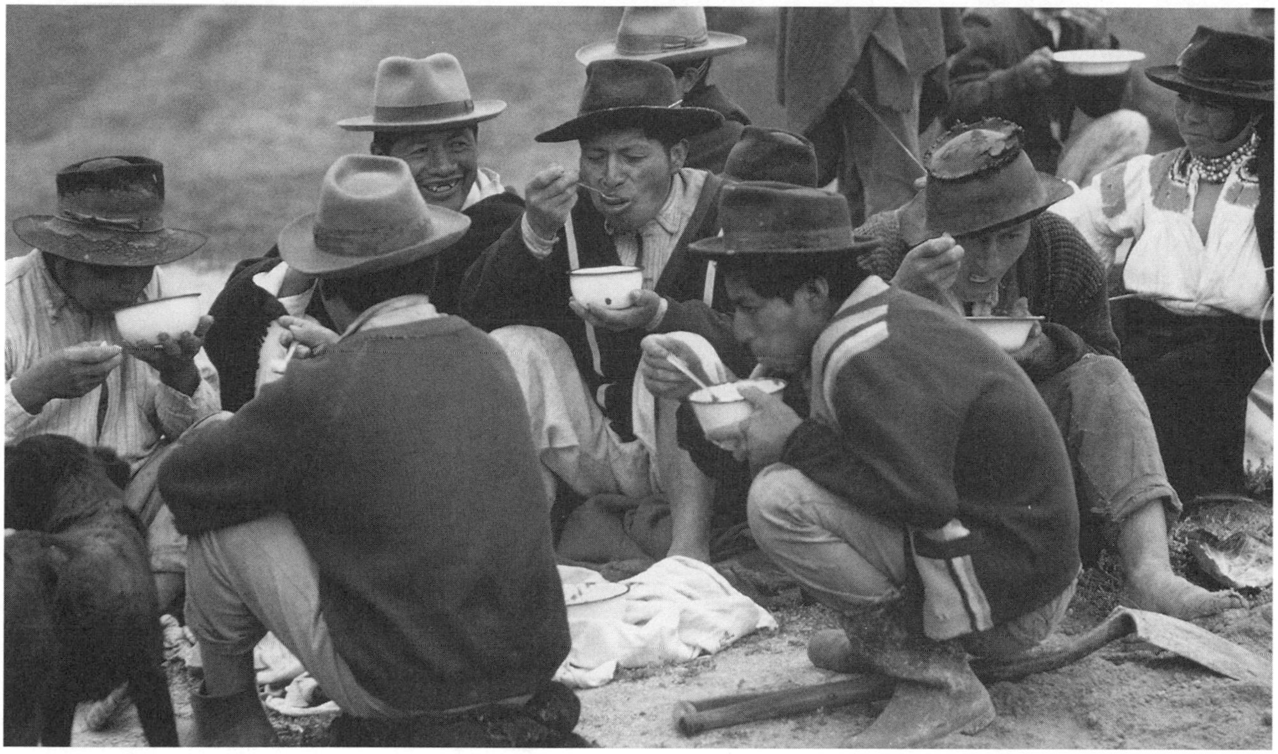

Community workers take a lunch break in Mariano Acosta. In Ecuador, national identity is a state system that owes the poor a livelihood.

by democratic–military dictatorship oscillations, with the democratic regimes being run by great *caudillos* (people who arise in a crisis and rally people of opposing parties to their cause).

Since 1979, after nine years of military dictatorship, Ecuador has had a series of democratic governments, each one strengthening the role of the white elite and increasing the poverty of the rest of the nation. Three elected presidents have failed to fill their terms. In 1981, Jaime Roldós Aguilera perished in a plane crash; in 1997, Abdalá Bucaram Ortiz was ousted by an act of congress and by grass–roots movements for "mental incapacity"; and in 2000, Jamil Mahuad Witt was ousted by a conjuncture of an indigenous and grass–roots uprising and a military coup. Although a growing middle class has been increasingly apparent in the last quarter century, poverty has grown exponentially as an economy of capital dependence has overridden subsistence pursuits. The most recent manifestation of these processes is that of "dollarization" of the national currency in 2000.

National Identity. In all walks of life, people identify as *ecuatorianos(-as)*. National identity emerged historically in several sectors. The elites and the upper–class, along with ideologues in the military and the press, use the concept of "*blanco–mestizo*" to both identify with the masses (through the concept *mestizo*), and to affirm their distance from the masses (through the concept *blanco*). The elites have a concept of *gente de bién*, or *gente bién* ("good people"; "people of good or proper background"). They are complemented by a new elite that sometimes is known as *gente de bienes* ("rich people"). The concept of *sociedad* ("society") refers to the old elite, both internally and among the new rich.

Among the elite and the newer wealthy, identity as Ecuadorian is paralleled by identity as good, righteous, Catholic, civilized, white people, who share a European and United States orientation. Colonial wealth is important, as is the maintenance of high status with great power and substantial wealth. Among the middle classes, the elite focus on whiteness is conjoined with the elitist ambivalent stigma of *mestizaje*. Middle–class commercial people tend to identify with their families, their jobs, and a general sense of the republic without worrying about their ethnicity.

Over half the nation is poor, and poverty is a self–identity referent. Here national identity is with a state system that owes the poor a livelihood. Those who self identify as "fully human" in one of seven or eight language families also identify as being Ecuadorian, but look to themselves and to their own social movements for critical livelihood, and for the political capital by which to construct a nation of indigenous people. Where the elites and middle classes are dominated by capitalist thought and activity, the indigenous people, who are at the forefront of movements of self-affirmation, favor socialist reforms. Black people are caught between the dominant elite, the prejudices of the middle classes, and a tenuous and tentative rapproachment with indigenous people.

Ethnic Relations. Black and indigenous people identify with cultural counterparts in other nations. For example, Quichua-speaking people identify with other such speakers in Colombia, Peru, Bolivia, and Argentina. Jivaroan speakers do the same with Peruvians. Cofán, Secoya, and Siona make little differentiation between themselves and those speaking the same languages who live in adjacent countries. At another level, the very fact of being indigenous, of being "original people," serves as a binding reference not only in South America, but across the Americas and beyond. Black people identify more tenuously with those who would seem to be phenotypically similar, and the processes of identity are stronger within their own regions than they are internationally. In the last decade, movements for black ethnic unity have taken place. Black leaders suffer from a lack of funding while indigenous leaders have considerable resources for international ethnic nationalist movements of self–affirmation.

URBANISM, ARCHITECTURE, AND THE USE OF SPACE

Urbanism permeates the world view of the white–mestizo sectors of Ecuador and is denied by other Ecuadorians. To be urbane in the Sierra is to be a social part of a major city—Quito, Ambato, Riobamba, Cuenca—where whiteness, Catholic Christianity, economic wealth, and ties to political power define the *dignidad* ("dignity") and *gentileza* ("gentility") of those who set themselves off from the majority. In the large coastal cities—Guayaquil and Manta—similar concepts prevail, but the phenomena of being *listo* ("ready to respond") and *vivo* ("ready to seize an opportunity") are more salient than they are in the Sierra. The cultural and political differences between the Coast and the Sierra are great, and each region may constitute a political–economic bloc that severely impedes a national consensus on matters of critical collective concern.

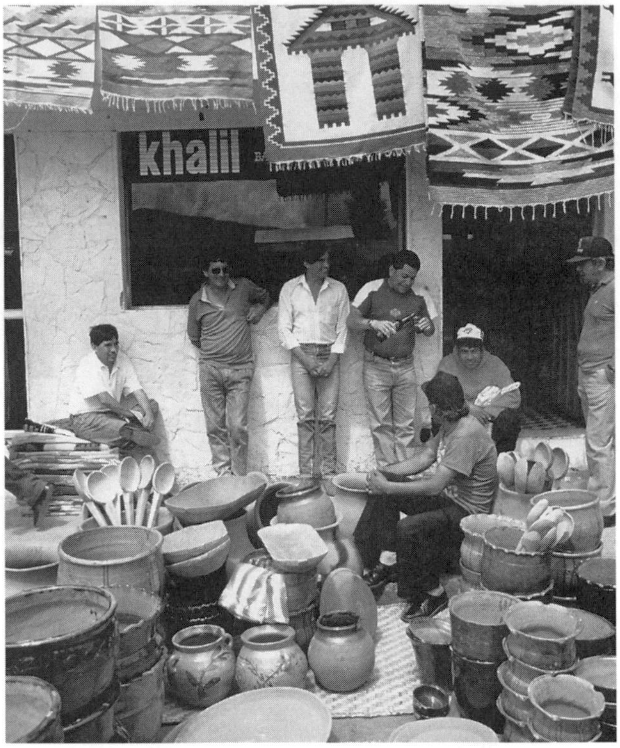

A market in Otavalo.

Both urban–oriented *serranos*, as the highlanders are called, and *costeños*, the people from the Coast, draw a primary contrast between that which is urban and that which is wilderness. The wilderness includes rain forest and dry–forest areas, high mountainous regions ("páramos"), and riverine systems. These are the systems which, in other contexts, define the beauty and romance of the country, that which the tourism industry seeks to "develop" for the benefit of the rich, mobile, and powerful.

Those with wealth and power long ago established what they regard as civilized spaces through the haciendas, which are extensive land holdings surrounding large rural homes. Those in control of their haciendas, called *hacendados*, treated people on their lands by a system known in the Sierra as the *huasipungo* (described by western scholars as "landed slavery"). On the Coast the concept of *concertaje* was very similar, and carried the same meaning. Agrarian reform, which began in the early 1960s and continued through the 1970s, has rectified this system to a large extent, but many large hacendados retain their landed power bases.

For indigenous and Afro–Ecuadorian people, together with their various cultural "mixtures," urban areas and rural areas blend; each depends on the other, and the ability to move between the sites of the "government" and the "home" and the "land" is critically important. Many such people are familiar with one or more of the urban centers of Ecuador, having spent time there in one or another capacity. Most such rural people have relatives and friends in the cities. People in the poor sector are able to move in and out of urban centers because of kinship ties, ties of ritual kinship (*compadrazgo*), and ties of patronage. Social movements usually originate in a rural sector and move toward the governing center.

Architecture can be thought of as a cultural complement to the nation's beautiful, varied scenery. It runs the gamut from humble wattle-and-daub houses with thatched roofs in the northern countryside to the magnificent La Companía Church in Quito with its gold-leaf interior; from thick-walled colonial monasteries to glass-walled, angular skyscrapers. The pace of urbanism has steadily increased since the beginning of petroleum production in the early 1970s, but it has not erased regional architectural styles that rely on natural materials such as palm, mangrove, bamboo, and thatch on the Coast; eucalyptus, maguey stems, earth, pampas grass, and thatch in the Sierra; and palm, bamboo, and thatch in the Oriente. Increasingly, these natural materials are being supplemented or replaced by cut planks, cinder-block, cement, brick, ceramic and asbestos tile, and corrugated metal.

Urban sprawl is visible around the major cities and towns and along the Panamerican highway that runs north-south through the center of the country, but there are vast open spaces in the more rural areas. In the less populous coastal and Amazonian sectors, open spaces abound despite colonization and urbanization. Population density in urban areas, particularly in poorer neighborhoods, is greatly underreported.

The use of personal household space is extremely varied. In general terms, there tends to be a female portion and a male portion of a domicile. Visitors enter through the male side and are received in a *sala* ("living room"). To be polite as a guest is to be seated; hosts move to serve guests. Within this framework there are innumerable variations. For example, among the indigenous Canelos Quichua native peoples of the Bobonaza River region, and radiating out of urban Puyo, the head of the house sits on a round carved wood stool, the seat of power of the water spirit-master Sungui. Guests sit on a long bench that symbolizes the anaconda. The Achuar native people carry this further, insisting that male and female guests be separated: women enter through the female door and sit with the women on small stools, while the men enter through the male side and sit on the anaconda-bench.

Food and Economy

Food in Daily Life. The most basic, ubiquitous prepared food is soup, with many variations according to region and ingredients. Coastal fish and coconut milk chowders, sierran potato-based soups, and Amazonian pepper-pot dishes are joined by chicken consommé, cream of avocado, and cow's foot and tripe soup. The mildly fermented *chicha* made from manioc by indigenous people of Amazonia could be regarded as a soup in its daily, nonceremonial consumption. Other common nonfermented food drinks are made with barley and oatmeal.

The middle and upper classes follow a European model of diet and dining: the primary meal, dinner, features several courses, is served at 2:00 P.M., and may last for two hours. First comes the soup, and then the *segundo* ("second") or *seco* ("dry") courses. It is a time to gather with family at home, or to meet friends or business acquaintances at a restaurant. Workers who travel far from home may take along lunch in a vertically compartmentalized lunch bucket, or buy inexpensive hot food from kiosks or street vendors. These foods include potato and meat soups or stews, *choclos* (corn on the cob), small sausages fried with onions and potatoes, and eggs. Other national favorites from the street to restaurants include *empanadas*, small meat, vegetable, or corn pies; shrimp, bivalves, fish, pork, or beef specialties; and "typical" dishes such as *locro*, a potato and cheese soup, and *llapingachos*, potato-cheese fritters. In urban Quito and Guayaquil one may choose food from Arby's, Domino's Pizza, Kentucky Fried Chicken, McDonald's, or TGI Friday's. A small number of caterers specialize in home-delivered prepared meals to accommodate employed women. Abundant fresh fruits and fruit juices are extremely popular.

Food Customs at Ceremonial Occasions. A variety of special dishes are prepared from fresh ingredients for ceremonial occasions by the woman of the house and her female maids. In the Sierra and parts of the Coast *fanesca*, a hearty soup that combines numerous beans, grains, and other vegetables cooked in fish broth, is served during Holy Week. Native people of Amazonia and the Sierra prepare *chicha*, a brew made from manioc and maize, respectively. This drink is served on all ceremonial occasions, but in Amazonia it also provides daily caloric intake. For the elite, alcoholic drinks, partic-

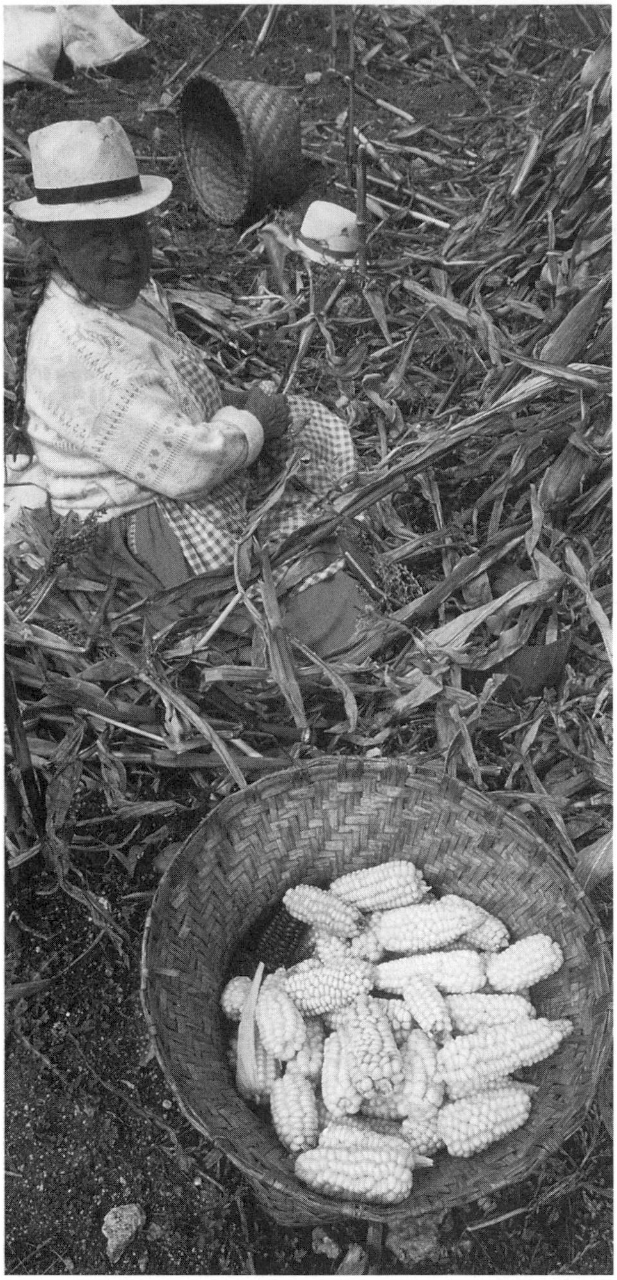

A woman harvesting corn near Cuenca. Probably 50 percent or more Ecuadorans produce their own food.

ularly imported scotch whisky (called *wisky*), and imported beer and wine are served on special occasions. As one descends the class hierarchy, whisky is replaced by bonded rums and raw cane alcohol (*trago*), and domestic beer. In some places, inexpensive Chilean wines supplemented or replaced *chicha* and domestic beer.

Basic Economy. The lush Andean valleys and coastal farms produce vegetables and fruits in great variety and abundance, and there is active interregional marketing. Stable starches are rice, bananas, plantains, and taro, grown on the coast; potatoes, corn, barley, quinoa, and wheat from the Sierra; and, in Amazonia, plantains, bananas, and particularly the root crops manioc and taro. Coffee, sugar, cacao, and coconuts from the coast are widely distributed. Chickens are raised everywhere for meat and for eggs, which are a major source of protein. Other meats are provided by hogs, cattle, and sheep; fish and some game are important in the Oriente. A wide variety of sausages, processed meats, and canned tuna and sardines is available in markets. The dairy industry is strong in the Sierra and the Coast, providing milk and numerous types of cheeses. Supermarkets carry an increasingly wide variety of imported canned and dehydrated soups, as well as nationally produced canned cow's foot and tripe soups.

Until recently, Ecuadorians depended entirely on domestic produce. Probably 50 percent or more of Ecuador's people produced their own food. Such production took place on coastal and sierran haciendas, where the elite controlled the land. Peasants (often indigenous) eked out an existence bordering on abject poverty, often in systems of sharecropping or landed slavery. Since the petroleum boom and the land reforms of the 1970s, more people depend on meager cash incomes to purchase food grown by fewer people. Commercial agriculture and floriculture have increased dramatically with the use of plastic greenhouses—the plastic sheeting is a product of the petrochemical industries. Fish farming (primarily trout and tilapia) and shrimp farming are important sources of food and income.

Land Tenure and Property. Black people of the northwest coast and indigenous people in the Amazonian region have long been excluded from any land tenureship of the property on which they have dwelled, since the mid–16th century in the former, and from time immemorial in the latter. The lands of indigenous and black people in these lowland regions are declared *tierras baldías* ("uninhabited lands") even though they are teeming with Afro–Ecuadorian or indigenous people. During the time of sierran land reforms, they were opened for colonization by poor Andean people. The resulting clashes and conflicts continue.

Commercial Activities. Petroleum, bananas, shrimp and other seafood, timber and wood products, fruits, and flowers constitute Ecuador's primary legal exports. Its major industry is petroleum processing, which takes place in Balao, just outside of the city of Esmeraldas. Most of the oil comes from the Amazonian region, where companies such as Texaco have caused one of the worst oil disasters in the world. Indigenous organizations have tried to sue Texaco in the United States, but the white-mestizo judges and lawyers of Ecuador support Texaco as a major source of national and institutional wealth.

Division of Labor. In the upper and middle classes, family connections and higher education are extremely important for significant participation in many professional and commercial ventures, as are payments to powerful political figures. Manual labor opportunities are often controlled by labor bosses who recruit among poor people and illegally take a portion of the workers' wages. This system, known as *enganche*, exploits especially black and indigenous people by setting them against low-class and usually unionized mestizo workers. People have multiple means of labor mobilization including the community-based *minga*, in which everyone pitches in to accomplish a task.

Social Stratification

Classes and Castes. Ecuador is a highly stratified society with strong symbolic as well as socioeconomic and political ordering. The social structure constitutes a class pyramid. The all-white oligarchies represent the pinnacle of political power, economic control, and social esteem. There is a significant middle class of professional, commercial, and service workers who generally self identify ethnically as *blancos*. Their representations of other people depend on many political and socioeconomic situations and contexts. Power and control are associated with being *blanco*, and upward mobility often involves a process known as *blanqueamiento* (whitening). In vulgar discourse *blanqueamiento* means moving away from any *mancha* (taint, or stain) of the hybrid categories, as well as denying the sources of *indio* and *negro*. Despite quasi-racial categorization and vast differences of wealth, there is a great deal of mobility and fluidity in all social and cultural sectors.

Well over half the nation is composed of those stigmatized as black or "Indian" people and those with ancestry falling into such categories; they are excluded from access to wealth, power, or social esteem. These are the people who must be mobilized in a national election or for collective action, and to whom a *caudillo* must appeal, usually through the assertion of the commonality of all Ecuadorians as *el pueblo*. Ecuadorians whose forefathers came from other lands, especially Lebanon, have been particularly successful in such mobilization and some of them have also been quickly deposed by those mobilized. Recent ex-presidents Bucaram Ortiz and Witt Mahuad illustrate these dual processes of *caudillismo*.

People throughout Ecuador are thoroughly familiar with the economic machinations at the pinnacle of power and argue against aggressive self-serving capitalism and corporate privatization while at the same time looking to patrons in the government for relief from poverty and opportunities to advance socially and economically. The symbolic structure of stratification permeates all dimensions of the republic. Even Amazonian shamans, when in trance, travel to spirit governments to gain the power to cure. In their festivals, black people in Esmeraldas may dramatize diverse relationships with distant central governments.

Political Life

Government. Ecuador is a constitutional democracy. Political life is focused on *caudillos* within a contemporary system of coalitions that features from seven to twenty political parties. Parties constantly coalesce and fragment, but a few, such as the Social Christians, the Leftist Democrats, and various populist parties, endure. The judicial system is based on the Napoleonic code, wherein a person is treated as guilty until proven innocent. The military is the most powerful force within the country, and the police force is substantial. Poor people have little recourse to police help, and the idea and practice of *justicia por propia mano* ("justice by one's own hand") is increasingly prevalent. The military system of socioeconomic mobility stresses the doctrine of *mestizaje*. During social movements, including uprisings, the military takes control but more often than not serves as a forceful mediator rather than as an oppressor.

Social Welfare and Change Programs

National welfare programs, including a social security system with extensive health-care components, exist. It is common for a program to be established with inadequate funding. The concept of a "program without money" is a ubiquitous cultural image that reflects economic reality. The failure of the social security system has provoked numerous protests for reform. Successful efforts for social change usually come from the poor sectors, of which the most powerful are the many indigenous organizations and the national unions representing labor, transportation, and education.

Rugs for sale at a market in Otavalo are an example of indigenous craftsmanship.

Nongovernmental Organizations and Other Associations

Ecuadorians have created some very important nongovernmental organizations (NGOs). Fundación Natura is well known internationally for its efforts at ecological preservation. Since the 1970s, indigenous people have developed, with substantial help from European sources, many organizations, most notably the Confederation of Indigenous People of Ecuador (CONAIE), Ecuador's Indigenous Awakening (ECUARUNANI), the Shuar Federation, and the Confederation of Indigenous People of Amazonian Ecuador (CONFENIAE). The Association of Ecuadorian Blacks (ASONE) is growing in strength. In recent years there has been an explosion of NGOs serving the interests of numerous groups, mainly grass–roots ethnic–, gender–, and labor–based. Active NGOs number over two hundred and are largely sponsored by foreign capital. While many NGOs are real forces in the transformation of institutional dysfunctions, it is often claimed that they contribute to corruption within institutions.

Families with pictures of loved ones at a demonstration in Quito, circa 1989. The Ecuadoran people look to the government for protection, but also expect corruption.

Gender Roles and Statuses

Division of Labor by Gender. Women make up a considerable portion of the workforce and are particularly visible in banking and finance, university teaching and research, and NGOs. They play a prominent role in indigenous and Afro–Ecuadorian mobilizations and movements. They hold high government positions in the national and regional judicial system, the national congress, and the executive branch.

The Relative Status of Women and Men. Gender roles vary greatly across classes and ethnicities, ranging from equal to male–dominated. Context specificity alters gender roles and statuses so that women may control sectors of activity even when ideological maleness is said to prevail. The ideology of *machismo* refers to masculine dominance and sexual conquest. It is said by people in some sectors to be complemented by *marianismo*, which, in reference to the Virgin Mary, designates an ideal of female purity and fidelity. How this somewhat vague ideology, which is not universal in Ecuador and varies enormously by gender, class, and ethnic perspectives, articulates to actual gender roles is not clear, and deserves serious research attention.

Women have gained legal rights over their children and their own property. A woman, even with a stable and enduring marriage, may elect to omit her husband's name from her child's birth certificate to protect that child from possible future bad fatherhood or separation or divorce, in which the father could claim the child.

Marriage, Family, and Kinship

Marriage. Marriage varies greatly, with its expressions ranging from those characteristic of middle–class United States or Europe to a variety of systems that include "trial marriage" and "serial polygyny."

Domestic Unit. The family is a key feature in the social structural and mobility systems of Ecuador. The basic domestic unit focuses on the mother and children with the father as provider. The mother nurtures the children and manages the household; the father legally provides for the family and the home. This system operates at all class levels and across different cultural systems. Overall, strong men try to keep their nuclear and expanded families around them, while bringing in–laws in. Where this succeeds, a kindred political–economic base develops; where it does not, people become attached to relatively more successful kin. Children are cherished, and socialization focuses on the granting of respect to parents, siblings, other relatives, the community, the nation, God, and those who lend a helping hand.

Etiquette

Respeto (respect) is the key to etiquette across all of the class and ethnic divisions and between the genders. To be granted respect is to have *dignidad* (dignity) which is a social cognate of the legal status of *derechos* ("rights"). The granting and receiving—or withholding and denying—of respect governs much of interpersonal relationships. The opposite of respect is *desprecio* (disrespect). One counters disrespect to one's dignity by claiming "rights," and such rights come to one as an *ecuatoriano*, Ecuadorian. All Ecuadorians demand respect in their interactions, and conflict on interpersonal, aggregate, or group bases occurs when disrespect is repeatedly observed or inferred. One of the fundamental features of the black social movement is found in the phrase *el rescate de la dignidad national* ("the rescue of national dignity"). Black leaders say that Ecuador will lack dignity until the ideology of *mestizaje*, with its built-in premise of *blanqueamiento* and subtext of *mejorar la raza* ("improve the race" of indigenous and Afro-Ecuadorian people) is abandoned. The indigenous and black social movements, and movements by women and poor people, are oriented toward achieving the status of dignity through the allocation and/or appropriation of respect.

Religion

Religious Beliefs. White-mestizo religiosity is predominantly Roman Catholic and varies considerably according to social class. Conservative Catholicism is infused with patriotism. Protestantism with many dimensions and sects is common and growing, though with smaller congregations. Overall, a fatalistic world view prevails wherein, ultimately, God's will is seen to dominate events. Phrases such as "if God permits," "if God helps me," and "thanks to God," are ubiquitous. Natural disasters, which are common in Ecuador, are said to be God's punishment for collective sin. The government, though secular, is thought of as a powerful but unconcerned father who cares little for his "children" (citizens), thereby provoking God's wrath.

Rituals and Holy Places. A root metaphor for many Catholics is that of the Passion of Christ. His life symbolizes the value of suffering. Virgins and saints are second to Christ's imagery in widespread Ecuadorian Catholicism. People make pilgrimages to the virgins and saints from great distances, primarily to become healed of physical or mental afflictions. It is believed some saints can heal and inflict harm and that at least one, San Gonzalo, can kill. Syncretisms between Catholic Christianity and local-level beliefs and practices are ubiquitous and permeate every sector of Ecuadorian culture. Indigenous people have a rich spiritual universe, which shamans tap for curing and for sending harm.

Death and the Afterlife. Death occurs, it is said everywhere, "when one's time comes," and this is accompanied by the assertion that "no one knows when my time is to come; when my time is up I die." This knowledge is restricted, according to some, to God ("when God calls me"), but others say even he doesn't know when one's time will be up on this earth. On or near death, saints from heaven and demons from hell come to claim the soul. Conceptions of the afterlife also vary greatly, from pious assertions that the good go to heaven and the bad go to hell, to the Afro-Ecuadorian coastal idea that most souls go to purgatory. Souls are thought to return to earth to seek their households where the living still exist, and this is something that is not wanted. Indigenous people have many concepts of soul movement after death, and the heaven-hell dichotomy, mediated by purgatory, is usually a superficial overlay on indigenous cosmologies and cosmogonies. In the Sierra and the Coast during the Day of the Dead—All Souls Day—which occurs at the end of October or early November, people congregate in cemeteries, socialize with souls of the deceased, and honor death itself through the imagery embodied in special bread-dough figurines and *colada morada*, a drink made with blue-black corn meal, blueberries, blackberries, other fruits, and spices.

Medicine and Health Care

Religion, shamanism, and home remedies are important resources. Traditional and alternative medicines were recognized in the constitutional reform of 1998. Amazonian Quichua shamans and coastal Tsháchila healers are considered to be the most powerful healers and minister to people speaking other languages, including those who come from many classes and backgrounds from the Sierra and the Coast. The use of *Banisteriopsis caapi*, called *ayahuasca* ("soul vine") in Quichua, is widespread and has attracted attention from medical-care personnel, international pharmaceutical companies, and foreign tourists.

Western health-care delivery exists mainly in the large cities, with outlying clinics rarely functioning in anything resembling western designs. While there are exceptions, hospitals are places where people in dire straits go, after trying many possible cures for illness. Pharmacists do a big business in diagnosis and prescription, and almost any drug or medication can be purchased over the counter.

Secular Celebrations

Soccer (*futbol*) is the national passion for the majority of men in every walk of life. As one encounters poverty and ethnic marginality, one finds women playing with men. *Futbol* reflects regional and economic differences. When the national team plays in international matches, a united Ecuadorian presence emerges throughout the country. When not united, Ecuadorians become divided in terms of the racial features of its national team. Some argue that powerful sports figures seek to "lighten" the phenotype of the teams. Attempts at such *blanqueamiento* are vigorously protested by the most prominent black organization, ASONE. The celebrity soccer players can achieve quasi-sainthood, particularly when they die under unforeseen and tragic circumstances. Heroes of other individual sports (e.g. track and field) are also idolized and may become quite prosperous.

The most prominent national secular celebrations are 24 May and 10 August, the two dates of national liberation. The assumption of presidential office always takes place on the latter. Other celebrations are 12 October, Columbus Day, known as the *dia de la raza* ("day of the race"). The elite take this to mean the day of the European (white), Spanish race from which they descend. Other Ecuadorians take this day as a symbol of racial blending, of *mestizaje*. It is a day of infamy for indigenous and black leaders, who are excluded by its symbolism, as they are excluded in everyday life. New Year's Eve features a huge secular festival where prominent figures, called *muñecos* or *años viejos*—effigies or "old years"—are created on platforms on public streets, lampooned, and burned at midnight. Epiphany (6-11 January) is the Three Kings' Day, which is celebrated by indigenous people of the Sierra as a secular festival. Pre-Lenten Carnival is celebrated throughout the country as a big water fight. In June and July, Sierran festivals of Saint Peter, Saint Paul, and Saint John fuse with those of Corpus Christi and the Incaic Inti Raymi solstice celebration, attracting national and international tourists. The founding days of cities and towns are celebrated throughout the nation, while the alleged European–Andean "discovery" of the Amazon on 12 February is acknowledged primarily in the Oriente.

The Arts and Humanities

Support for the Arts. Quito proclaims itself to be the Patrimonio de Humanidad, "the Heritage of Humanity," and in 1999, Cuenca was designated by UNESCO as an international Heritage of Humanity. Two major organizations that support the arts and the humanities are the Casa de la Cultura Ecuatoriana (the House of Ecuadorian Culture), and the Banco Central del Ecuador. These organizations are funded by the federal government. Archaeological and colonial arts are considered national treasures.The Instituto Nacional de Patrimonio Cultural (the National Institute of Ecuadorian Heritage) is involved in the restoration of colonial edifices and some archaeological sites and in preventing national treasures from leaving the country. Excellent newspapers, television documentaries, and ethnographic and historic video productions all feature a wide spectrum of writers, analysts, and commentators, including intellectuals in various sectors of cultural life, as well as in the academies.

Literature. Literature is rich in Ecuador, and includes writings not only by those highly educated and by journalists, but also by self-taught people who have produced works of value. Best known authors include Juan Montalvo, Juan León Mera, Luis A. Martínez, Jorge Icaza, Jorge Enrique Adoum, and Alfredo Pareja Diezcanseco. Artists such as Benjamín Carrión, Oswaldo Guayasamín, Edwardo Kingman, Camilo Egas, and Oswaldo Viteri are internationally known. Julio Jaramillo is the best known national composer.

An internationally significant corpus of literature is produced by black scholars such as Nelson Estupiñán Bass, Argentina Chiriboga, Aldalberto Ortiz, and Preciado Bedoya, among others. Indigenous authors write in Spanish and in Quichua.

Performance Arts. There is a national symphony and national folkloristic ballet in Quito, but Ecuador is probably best known internationally for indigenous bands that combine and recombine various genres of Andean "folk" music. Many come from Otavalo and Salasaca, but groups exist throughout the Andes and the Amazonian region. Black marimba groups from Esmeraldas are becoming internationally known.

THE STATE OF THE PHYSICAL AND SOCIAL SCIENCES

Major universities in Quito and Guayaquil, and smaller ones in other cities, all have curricula in physical and social sciences. Private and public universities vary greatly in their emphases, but offer a respectable array of liberal arts and sciences, medical, legal, and engineering training. Funding comes from the government, from tuition, from foreign aid, and from gifts and private donations. Many Ecuadorians, from all classes and walks of life, earn master's and doctoral degrees in Latin America, the United States, and Europe.

BIBLIOGRAPHY

Acosta-Solis, Misael, et al. *Ecuador: In the Shadow of the Volcano*, 1981.

Adoum, Rosangela. "L'Art Equatorien Préhispanique: Une Autre Monumentalíté," in *Tresors du Nouveau Monde*, 1992

Albán Gómez, Ernestso. *Los Indios y el Estado-País: Pluriculturalidad y Multietnicidad en el Ecuador: Contribuciones al Debate*, 1993.

Almeida, Ileana, et al. *Indios: Realidad Nacional*, 1992.

Ayala Mora, Enrique. *Los Partidos Políticos en el Ecuador: Síntesis Histórica*, 1989.

———, ed. *Nueva Historia del Ecuador*, 12 volumes, 1988–1992.

——— et al. *Pueblos Indios, Estado y Derecho*, 1992.

Cervone, Emma, and Fredy Rivera, eds. *Ecuador Racista: Imágenes e Identidades*, 1999.

Cuvi, Pablo. *Crafts of Ecuador*, 1994.

Donoso Pareja, Miguel. *Ecuador: Identitidad o Esquizofrenia*, 1998.

Espinoza Apolo, Manuel. *Los Mestizos Ecuatorianos: y Las Señas de Identitidad Cultural*, 1977.

Hurtado, Osvaldo, Nick D. Mills, Jr., trans. *Political Power in Ecuador*, 1977.

———. *El Poder Político en el Ecuador*, 10th ed., 1997.

Ibarra, Alicia. *Los Indígenas y el Estado en el Ecuador: La Práctica Neoindigenista*, 1992.

Lane, Kris. *Quito 1599: City and Colony in Transition*, 2001.

Lathrap, Donald W., Donald Collier, and Helen Chandra. *Ancient Ecuador: Culture, Clay and Creativity, 3000–300 B.C.*, 1975.

Lucas, Kintto. *La Rebelión de los Indios*, 2000.

Marcos, Jorge. *Arqueología de la Costa Ecuatoriana: Nuevos Enfoques*, 1986.

Newson, Linda A. *Life and Death in Early Colonial Ecuador*, 1995.

Phelan, John Leddy. *The Kingdom of Quito in Early Colonial Ecuador*, 1967.

Rangles Lara, Rodrigo. *Venturas y Desventuras del Poder*, 1995.

Rowe, Ann Pollard, ed. *Costume and Identity in Highland Ecuador*, 1998.

Salamone, Frank. *Native Lords of Quito in the Age of the Incas*, 1986.

Salvat, Juan, and Eduardo Crespo, eds. *Historia del Arte Ecuatoriano*, 1985.

Weismantel, Mary. *Food, Gender, and Poverty in the Ecuadorian Andes*, 1988.

Whitten, Dorothea S. and Norman E. Whitten, Jr. *From Myth to Creation: Art from Amazonian Ecuador*, 1988.

Whitten, Norman E., Jr. *Sicuanga Runa: The Other Side of Development in Amazonian Ecuador*, 1985.

———. *Black Frontiersmen: Afro-Hispanic Culture of Ecuador and Colombia*, fourth ed., 1994.

———, ed. *Cultural Transformations and Ethnicity in Modern Ecuador*, 1981.

—NORMAN E. WHITTEN, JR.,
DOROTHEA SCOTT WHITTEN,
AND DIEGO QUIROGA

EGYPT

CULTURE NAME

Egyptian; Arab Egyptian; Arab

ALTERNATIVE NAMES

Official name: Arab Republic of Egypt

Previously: The United Arab Republic. Before 1952: The Egyptian Kingdom

ORIENTATION

Identification. Egypt is the internationally used name but not the name used by the people of the country. It derives from the Greek *Aegyptos*, which in turn probably comes from ancient Egyptian words referring to the land (*Hut-ka-ptah*, or "house of the essence [ka] of Ptah," a local god). Western names derive from this, as does the word "Copt" (in Arabic, *qibt*). "Copt" can be taken to mean "Egyptian" in general, but now commonly means an Egyptian Christian, technically one belonging to the majority Coptic Church.

In Arabic, the name is *Misr.* This name is older than the Muslim conquest, but is attested to in the Koran. It can refer to either the whole country or the capital city. The name itself is an icon, spoken, written, or sung.

The population of Egypt is relatively homogeneous. The overwhelming majority (over 90 percent) are Arabic-speaking Sunni Muslims. About 6 percent are Christians, who are indistinguishable in other respects from the Muslims. Most of the Christians belong to the Coptic Orthodox Church, the historic church of Egypt, but minorities within the minority are Catholic or Protestant, or derive from the churches of the Levant (Maronite, Greek Orthodox, Greek Catholic). There are a few small linguistic minorities, of which the largest is the Nubians, who speak two Nubian languages (Kenuz and Mahas) related to the Nilo-Saharan languages of the Sudan. They represent less than 1 percent of Egypt's population, and are concentrated around Aswan. Other linguistic minorities include a few thousand Berber speakers in Siwa oasis, the easternmost outpost of Berber speech, and the small population of Beja (Ababda and Bisharin) in the eastern desert east of Aswan. All these groups are Muslim. There are also urban linguistic enclaves of Armenians, Greeks, Italians, and others. Another urban enclave was the Jews, now largely emigrated, who spoke either Arabic or various European languages. The urban minorities were much larger before the middle of the twentieth century.

Location and Geography. Egypt has an area of 385,229 square miles (1,001,000 square kilometers). The country is separated from its neighbors by either ocean or sparsely populated desert. To the north is the Mediterranean Sea, and to the east the Red Sea. Egypt is separated from Libya and North Africa by the western desert, from Palestine and Israel by the desert of the Sinai Peninsula, and from the centers of population in the Sudan by desert except along the narrow Nile River. Among the major geographical features of Egypt are the Nile River and the Suez Canal, which joins the Red Sea and the Mediterranean Sea, and also separates Egypt proper from Sinai. The highest point is Mount Catherine in the Sinai, at 8,743 feet (2,665 meters).

Egypt is the gift of the Nile. Rainfall is not adequate to sustain agriculture or a settled population, and water instead comes from the Nile. The Nile rises far to the south of Egypt, in Ethiopia and in the drainage basin of Lake Victoria. It reaches Egypt in Lake Nasser, behind the Aswān High Dam. After the dam, the Nile continues to flow north in a single channel paralleled by irrigation canals until it reaches Cairo, 550 miles (860 kilometers) away. North of Cairo, the Nile Delta begins. The Nile breaks into two main channels, the western Rosetta branch and the eastern Damietta branch, for the final 120 miles (200 kilometers) before the water reaches the Mediterranean. The two main regions of

Egypt

Egypt are thus the Valley, or Sa'id, in the south, and the Delta in the north, separated by Cairo at the apex of the Delta.

The Nile receives about 85 percent of its water from the Ethiopian highlands. Before the construction of dams and barrages, floodwaters would spill out of the river's banks and, channeled by sluices and dikes, cover most of the agricultural land. Egyptians then practiced a form of recession agriculture, planting winter crops in the mud left behind by the receding river.

In the twentieth century, people have increased their control of the river. This culminated in the construction of the Aswān High Dam, completed in 1971 but which first held back the floodwaters in 1964. Control of the Nile has made it possible to cultivate year round. On average, there are two crops a year.

About 96 percent of Egypt's population lives in the Nile Valley, which comprises about 4 percent of the area of the country; most of the economic and social activity occurs there. The rest of the country is desert. This includes the scrub desert along the Mediterranean coast between the Nile Delta and Libya, and along the north coast of the Sinai Peninsula; the mountainous desert between the Nile Valley and the Red Sea; and the western desert west of the Nile Valley. Rainfall in these areas is rare to nonexistent. Only the Mediterranean coast has rain that is reliable enough to support marginal human activity, with some agriculture and animal husbandry. The Western Desert has five oases that support a settled population and serve as communication centers (Khārga, Dakhla, Farafra, Baharīya, and Siwa). There are smaller oases in the Sinai peninsula (Firan), and even in the arid Eastern desert there are occasional springs, two of which provide water to Christian monasteries.

It is an article of faith in contemporary Egypt that agriculture and settled life should spread beyond the confines of the Nile Valley. Major efforts have been made to "reclaim" land on the fringes of the Nile Valley, particularly east and west of the Delta. Over a million acres have been reclaimed since the middle of the twentieth century. Recent discovery of fossil underground water in the extreme southwest corner of Egypt is leading to the development of irrigated agriculture in that area.

Demography. At the end of 1996, the total population of Egypt was 65,200,000, of whom about 1,900,000 were considered to be living abroad temporarily, presumably mostly in the oil countries of the Arab Gulf but also including some in the West. The 1996 population represented a 21.7 percent increase over the 1986 population. The annual growth rate was calculated at 2.1 percent, down from 2.8 percent in the period of 1976–1986. The lower growth rate was also reflected in the figure for those under 15 years of age, which was 35 percent of the overall population in 1996 as against 38.8 percent in 1986. Egypt's population is predicted to double between 1996 and 2029. According to the *Egyptian Human Development Report 1997-98*, life expectancy at birth in Egypt was 66.7 years, up from 55 in 1976. Infant mortality was 29 per 1,000 live births in 1996. The total fertility rate was 3.3 in 1997, with urban areas quite a bit lower than rural areas. Just over one-third of the population was below a poverty line based on consumption needs, calculated by the Egyptian government.

Males were 51.2 percent of the total population, contrary to the demographic norm that postulates more women than men. Egypt is part of a broad band of countries, extending east to Korea, where there are "missing women."

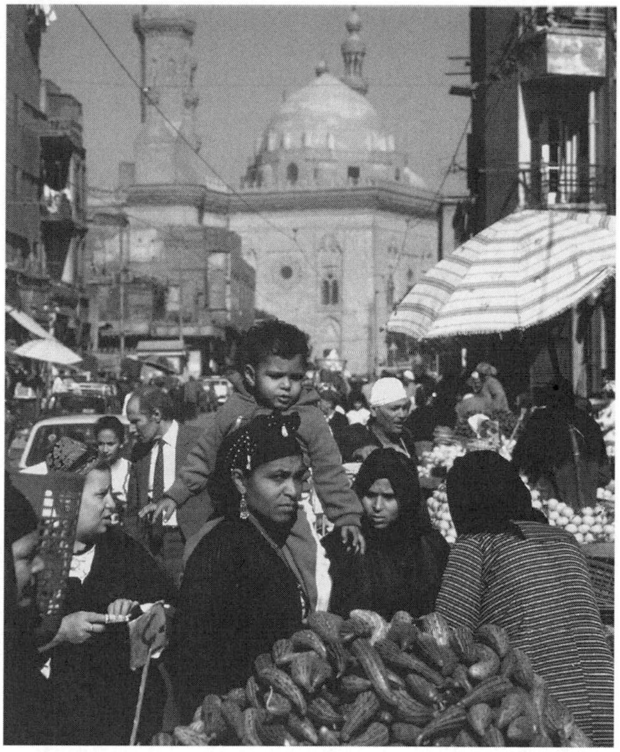

People fill the street in a Cairo market.

The level of education is increasing; those over the age of ten who were literate increased from 50.4 percent in 1986 to 61.4 percent in 1996. Figures for graduates from different levels of education also grew—those holding a higher education degree increased from 4.3 percent in 1986 to 7.3 percent in 1996. The rural population was 57 percent in 1996, compared to 56 percent in 1986, but this includes some people living in settlements of 20,000 or more. A settlement is defined as urban according to its administrative function.

Linguistic Affiliation. Egypt is part of the Arabic speech community of about 250 million people, spread from Morocco to Oman. Arabic is a branch of the Semitic languages, which in turn belongs to the Afro-Asiatic language family together with Berber, Ancient Egyptian, Chadic, and Cushitic. Egypt became Arabic-speaking as a result of the Muslim conquest in the seventh century, though the full replacement of the earlier languages took several centuries. In Egypt, as elsewhere in the Arab world, the Arabic language is characterized by diglossia. That is, there is a substantial difference between the written language, influenced by the Koran, and the spoken language. There are some regional dialects in Egypt, notably the speech of Upper Egypt, but nothing that prevents understanding.

Radio and television impose the Cairo-spoken language as the standard dialect of Egypt. Egyptian cultural influence is transmitted to the rest of the Arabic-speaking world in the Cairo dialect. English is the most common foreign language spoken in Egypt, followed by French.

Symbolism. The dominant symbols in the formal and semiformal sphere derive mainly from aspects of Egypt's history, especially the Pharaonic and Islamic periods.

The three Giza pyramids (sometimes together with the Great Sphinx) represent the most important and obvious visual symbol of the Egyptian nation. It is the most widespread "postcard" image, and also the title of the major daily newspaper *Al-Ahram* (with the three pyramids on the top of the front page). The symbol of Egypt Air, the national airline, is Horus, a figure from ancient Egyptian religion represented as a falcon.

Other symbols derive from the country's Islamic heritage. The nineteenth-century Mohammed Ali mosque built on top of a medieval citadel is visible from different parts of Cairo. Of more architectural significance are the Ibn Tulun and Sultan Hassan mosques in Cairo and the Qaitbey mausoleum and school in the northern cemetery.

One important symbol is derived from the country's geography: the Nile River. The Nile is invoked in different contexts, each representing a facet of the country's identity or prevalent themes of the culture. It is associated with immortality, romance, or glory (the construction of the high dam). In recent years, Nile cruises have become a favored tourist attraction, and "cleaning up the Nile" has become an environmental slogan.

The flag is an abstract tricolor, with black standing for the past of oppression, red for sacrifice, and white for the future. A centerpiece of a falcon completes the design. Reflecting a sense of Arab unity, the flags of several other Arab countries have the same colors. The current national anthem is the music of the song "Biladi" (meaning "My Country"), a patriotic song that was popular during the 1919 uprising against the British occupation.

History and Ethnic Relations

Emergence of the Nation. The land of Egypt has a distinctiveness within the region because of the development of major civilizations in the Nile Valley, sometimes phrased as seven thousand years of civilization. After the Pharaonic and Greco-Roman periods, Christianity came to Egypt. For several centuries Egypt was essentially a Christian country. The Muslim conquest in the seventh century C.E. brought a new force, but it was some time before there was a Muslim majority in Egypt. In the sixteenth century, Egypt became part of the Ottoman Empire, ruled from Constantinople (now Istanbul). On the eve of modernization, Napoleon and the French army conquered Egypt in 1798, and remained through 1801. Many writers identify this period of three years as a major turning point in Egyptian cultural history, while others argue that the process began earlier and lasted longer.

Shortly after the British expelled the French from Egypt in 1801, the Ottoman military leader Muhammad 'Alī Pasha and his troops took over in 1805. Muhammad 'Alī Pasha remained the ruler of Egypt until his death in 1849, and his descendants continued as the rulers until the overthrow of the monarchy in 1952.

The British occupied Egypt in 1882, working under the nominal authority of the descendants of Muhammad 'Alī Pasha. In 1919, in the aftermath of World War I, unrest aiming at Egyptian independence began. The main nationalist political party, the Wafd, was created that year. The agitation resulted in the recognition of Egypt's independence in 1922 and the establishment of a constitution in 1923. This amounted to internal self-government under King Fu'ād, with an elected parliament and a prime minister. In 1936 and 1937 further treaties with the United Kingdom led to international recognition of Egypt's independence, and it joined the League of Nations in 1937. Egypt was the scene of major battles in World War II, and the country formally joined the war in its last year, 1945. At this time, Egypt also joined the United Nations and helped found the Arab League.

In 1952 the "Free Officers" from the Egyptian army forced King Farouk, son of King Fu'ād, to abdicate. A year later the monarchy was abolished and a republic established. Colonel Gamal Abdel Nasser emerged as the strongman of the new regime, and he became president in 1954. The new regime initiated many new social policies in Egypt. This was a genuine revolution that shared power and wealth more equally with all elements of the population and encouraged education for the masses. From a cultural point of view, the new regime released Egyptians from the feeling of oppression due to foreign rule, and allowed for the flowering of an unencumbered Egyptian identity, making it possible to be both modern and Egyptian. This was also the period of maximum Egyptian involvement in warfare. The most devastating moment came with the defeat of

Egyptians standing with a pile of pottery water jugs in Luxor Village along the Nile River. Irrigation is central to Egyptian agriculture and water is supplied by the government.

Egypt by Israel in the Six-Day War in 1967; the Israeli army overran the remainder of Palestine and occupied the Sinai Peninsula.

Anwar el-Sadat became president after Nasser died in 1970. After the fourth war against Israel in 1973, Sadat moved to make peace and to recover the Sinai. Under Sadat, too, many of the social reforms of the Nasser period were frozen or reversed. Sadat was assassinated in 1981 and was succeeded by his vice president, Hosni Mubarak, who was elected for a fourth six-year term in September 1999. To date, all four of Egypt's presidents have been military men.

National Identity. Unlike many third-world countries, Egypt does not have a clear moment when it became "independent." Instead there was a process beginning with the anti-British movement of 1919 and the constitution of 1923, and continuing through international recognition in 1937 and the departure of the last British soldier in 1956. Arguably the process continues still, as Egypt deals with the meaning of an Egyptian identity and national independence in a globalizing world dominated economically and culturally by the United States.

Ethnic Relations. The main issue in ethnic identity arises not within the nation, but in terms of the nation being part of the wider Arab world. People debate whether being Egyptian or being Arab is more important. The Arab world is tied together by shared language and culture, including shared Islamic values and practices, and by a sense of shared political problems—even when countries and people take different positions, they focus on the same problems. Arab unity is concretized in the Arab League, whose headquarters is in Cairo.

Urbanism, Architecture, and the Use of Space

Villages and cities are the two major settlement types. There has been, however, an increasing overlap in social and economic functions which, in turn, manifests itself in an increasing blurring of distinctions regarding architectural features of both city and village.

Villages consist of a core residential area surrounded by fields, and agricultural land. The core consists of contiguous one-story mud-brick houses built along narrow dirt roads. The houses incorporate a stable for the farm animals. Owning a cow or a water buffalo represents a high investment, and since animal theft is feared, farmers are keen to keep their animals closely supervised. Rooftops are used for storage of dung cakes or straw, for ovens and mud granaries, or to keep chickens or rabbits.

Since the mid-1970s the mud-brick houses have progressively been replaced by houses made of fired bricks, and growing population and prosperity have led to an expansion of the built-up surface of the village. Red-brick houses are healthier, provide more amenities, and are more practical for modern life, though they are more expensive and less adapted to the climate. People can build them several stories high, which uses less of the scarce agricultural land.

The money earned by migrants to oil-rich countries was mainly used to build new houses based on urban models. Urban Egyptians generally decried this transformation of the village-scape as a blind emulation of urban lifestyles, and a change for the worse in the peasant character. This alarmed reaction from urban middle-class voices underscores an important aspect of rural-urban relations and perceptions where the "traditional village" is seen as the locus of authenticity and reservoir of tradition of the Egyptian nation.

Each village has at least one mosque. The mosque is communal and public for men. Many of the mosques are collectively built by the villagers themselves. Another public space is the guest house, which is usually a large hall built and used collectively by an extended family. Here mourners receive condolences, and well-wishers extend congratulations for returning pilgrims. Again, guest houses represent mainly male space. Churches often include a space for social gatherings of a family or religious nature. Both women and men actively participate in the marketplace. Weekly markets in big villages or district towns are both a place where commodities are traded and an important social arena where people exchange news and maintain social relationships.

The urban character of the national culture is most apparent in the two major cities: Cairo and Alexandria. One aspect of the political culture is a centralized bureaucracy. This feature manifests itself in a huge government building that dominates Cairo's main square. This building houses various government departments that handle bureaucratic dealings with the public from all over the country. Government buildings are more functional than beautiful.

The architecture and layout of Cairo reflect the various epochs of its history. Very roughly, old Cairo is the medieval part, the heart of popular Cairo, and also where the Islamic and Coptic monuments are. The modern city center was built in the nineteenth century and was modeled after Paris.

Cairo is a continuously expanding city, and numerous squatter settlements are built on the outskirts. These squatter areas have poor water and sewage connections, and lack services such as schools, clinics, and police.

Urban Egyptians usually live in rented apartments. Individual houses are rare. One of the reforms of socialism was to establish a form of rent control that kept rentals low. Newer apartments, however, are not under rent control, and rents are much higher. Some people own apartments in a condominium-like arrangement. Occasionally an extended family may own an entire building and make the apartments available to its members. In the 1980s and 1990s living conditions in urban areas improved, albeit unequally, and such amenities as telephones, television, and air conditioning became more common. Nationwide 73.5 percent of households are connected to the potable water system, and 95.7 percent to the electrical system.

Egypt is crowded. The built-up areas of villages have very high population densities. People have largely accommodated to this forced proximity. In older parts of Cairo the streets are sinuous with many dead ends, while in newer parts, where the building pattern follows the lines of long narrow fields, the streets are themselves long and narrow. Despite or because of the crowding, there is segregation by gender. For example, there are often two different queues for men and for women, and often separate cars for women on trains.

Residential and urban areas, as well as agricultural zones, are spreading into the desert. There has been considerable increase in the use of the coastline, initially by foreign tourists and now increasingly as a vacation area for the Egyptian elite. The tradition of going to the Mediterranean towns in the summer is older, but now some people are exploring areas further afield, particularly along the Sinai coast and on the western shore of the Red Sea.

Food and Economy

Food in Daily Life. Eating is an important social activity, and is central to marking special events and ceremonial occasions.

The most important food item in daily life is the bread loaf. In rural areas, bread is usually baked by women in mud ovens at home. In cities, bread is sold in bakeries. The standard loaf is strictly regulated by the government in terms of weight and

People taking the local ferry in Aswān, Egypt.

price, and is one of the very few items that still receives a state subsidy.

The indigenous cuisine relies heavily on legumes. The main national dish is *foul*. This is a dish of fava beans cooked slowly over low heat and seasoned with salt, lemon, cumin, and oil. It is usually eaten for breakfast. Another common dish is *tamiyya* or falafel which is made from crushed fava beans mixed with onions and leeks and fried in oil. Also popular is *koshari*, a mixture of rice, black lentils, and macaroni covered with tomato sauce and garnished with fried onions. These dishes are prepared at home, but are also sold in stalls all over Cairo.

The level of consumption of animal protein depends almost entirely on wealth (and is itself a sign of wealth). Well-to-do households eat animal protein (beef, lamb, poultry, or fish) every day. Muslims do not eat pork. Less-affluent families eat animal protein once a week or even once a month.

Restaurants are widespread all over the country. They vary from stalls selling traditional street food to posh restaurants serving international cuisine.

One main distinction between traditional, usually rural, and urban middle-class eating habits concerns the seating and service of food. In villages, people sit on a carpet, and food is placed on a very low round wooden table. Each person has a spoon, and everyone eats directly from the service dish. In cities, people sit on chairs around Western-style dining tables. Each person has his or her own plate, spoon, fork, and knife. In rural areas, the main meal is after dark; in the urban areas it is often in late afternoon after office workers return home.

Food Customs at Ceremonial Occasions. Several Muslim feasts are marked by special meals. The 'Id al-Adha, which celebrates Abraham's willingness to sacrifice his son (who is then miraculously turned into a ram), requires those who can afford it to sacrifice a ram. Part of the animal is distributed to the poor and part consumed by members of the household.

The 'Id al-Fitr after the fast of Ramadan is celebrated by baking special cookies (*kahk*) which are later sprinkled with powdered sugar. These cookies are usually offered to guests who bring the greetings of the feast.

The Prophet's Birthday, which marks the birth of the prophet Muhammad, is celebrated by the consumption of *halawet al-mulid,* which is a variety of sweets cooked with different types of nuts.

Children are given dolls (girls) or horses (boys) made entirely of sugar and decorated with colored paper.

On the eve of both Christmas day and Easter day, Orthodox Copts break their fast with a variety of dishes made of beef and poultry. One of the main food items that marks the feast are cookies similar to those prepared for the 'Id al-Fitr. Sham al-Nassim (Easter Monday) is mainly marked by a breakfast of salted fish, spring onion, lettuce, and colored eggs, which is consumed outdoors in gardens and open areas. This festival is celebrated nationwide in practically all regions and by all social classes. It is the ancient Egyptian spring and harvest festival.

Fasting is seen as a spiritual exercise by both Muslims and Christians. The Muslim fast entails abstaining from food and drink from sunrise to sundown, notably during the lunar month of Ramadan (either twenty-nine or thirty days). Some particularly devout Muslims also fast on other days in the Islamic calendar, such as the days celebrating the birth of the prophet Muhammad or his miraculous "Night Journey," the days representing the middle of the lunar month (days thirteen, fourteen, and fifteen), or each Monday and Thursday. The result is that nearly half the days in the year can be considered fasting days by some. Virtually all Egyptian Muslims fast during Ramadan, while the voluntary fasts are followed by a smaller number.

The number of days that Egyptian Christians can theoretically fast is even larger. The number is variable, but it includes over 200 days a year, mostly in the periods leading up to Christmas and Easter, plus the Wednesdays and Fridays of each week outside the fasting periods. Christian fasting means avoiding meat, fish, eggs, milk, butter, and cheese. In the Christian tradition, one theme of fasting is the domination of the body and of emotions by the mind in order to reach a greater purity.

Basic Economy. About 25 percent of the gross domestic product comes from industry and about 18 percent from agriculture. The remaining 57 percent includes all other activities, primarily services, including tourism, and the "informal sector" (small-scale enterprises that often escape government supervision). There is also an extensive network of banks and a major construction industry. A stock market on which about thirty stocks are traded emerged in the 1990s.

Egypt is a rich agricultural country, with some of the highest yields per unit of land in the world. The main crops are cotton, sugarcane, wheat, maize, and fava beans with substantial areas given over to fruit orchards (primarily citrus) and to vegetables. Livestock (cattle, water buffalo, sheep, and goats) is also important and some land is used to grow fodder crops for these animals. There are two crops a year on average. Individual farmers try to be self-sufficient in certain crops such as wheat, but on the whole they market what they grow and procure their own food also from the market.

Elaborate market networks composed of small-scale traders purchase food crops and trade them into the urban areas, or sometimes between rural areas. On the whole, the marketing sector is characterized by a plethora of small units, although a few large-scale trading companies operate. Being too small to bargain on price, farmers have to accept the trader's offer.

The main inputs to agriculture are land, water, and labor. Land is generally owned by private individuals in small holdings, with an average of about 2.5 acres (1 hectare). From 1952 to 1997 tenancies were guaranteed (those renting farmland could not be expelled except under rare conditions), but this guarantee was repealed in 1997. By that year, rented land covered about one-sixth of the farmland, and tenants tended to be poorer than farmers who were also owners. Nevertheless, tenants had learned to treat farmland as if they owned it, and after 1997 had to adjust to higher rents or the loss of the land.

Irrigation is central to Egyptian agriculture, and water is supplied by the government to the farmer through a network of canals. Payment for water is indirect, through the land tax paid by the larger farmers. Water is perceived to be free, and the government continues to support the policy that water should be provided free to farmers. Since farmers must lift the water from the canals to their fields they do incur a cost.

Farm labor is primarily family labor, based on the rural family household. The head of this household mobilizes labor from his family, but may also hire outside labor from time to time, particularly for tasks that require a large group working together. Egyptian agriculture tends to be labor-intensive and indeed could better be described as gardening.

Many members of these rural households work as agricultural laborers or outside agriculture, and it is probable that many of these households would not survive without the income from this work. The most common off-farm sources of income are government work (as teachers, clerks, or guards), private business (trucking agricultural goods or trading), and factory work.

A man collecting water from the Dakhla Oasis. Payment for water use is indirect, with fees generated as a land tax by larger farmers.

In Egyptian agriculture, the tasks that can be done by a tractor (e.g., plowing, hauling) or a water pump are mechanized. Other tasks (e.g., planting, weeding, harvesting) are still done by hand. Since most farmers cannot afford to own machinery, they rent it as they need it. On the whole, tractors and pumps are owned by the richer farmers who rent out their excess capacity.

Major Industries. Egypt is a relatively industrialized country, especially in textiles and garment manufacture, cement, metal works of various kinds, and armaments. Various makes of automobile are assembled in Egypt. In the second half of the twentieth century, many of these industries were government-owned. At the end of the twentieth century, they were in the process of being privatized. There are also many small private workshops producing shoes, door frames, furniture, clothing, aluminum pots, and similar items for local consumption.

Trade. Egypt tends to import more than it exports. Imports include consumer goods, including food, and raw material for industry; exports are largely agricultural products and services. A major Egyptian export consists of workers who labor outside the country but who send money back home.

Social Stratification

Classes and Castes. In Egypt there is an enormous gap between the very wealthy and the very poor. The culture also encourages deference of the weak, poor, or subaltern to the rich and powerful, in terms of speech, posture, and acquiescence. The differences among individuals and families in Egypt can be represented by income level or source of income. They can also be represented in choices of consumption style—housing, transport, dress, language, education, music, and the like. Marriage negotiations bring all these differences of taste and income to the forefront. What is less evident in Egypt is a strong class consciousness that might turn potential classes into real ones. One finds only broad and loose categories that are the subject of much public discussion.

The increasing prosperity of Egypt means that the middle class is increasing in relative size, while the gap between the top and the bottom is increasing. One-third of the population is below a poverty line established by the Egyptian government. The growing middle class aspires to a home, a car, and marriage and family life, and increasingly is able to achieve this.

Political Life

Government. Egypt has had a republican form of government since the overthrow of the monarchy in 1952. The government is headed by a president elected for six years. The president designates a prime minister and a council of ministers. The Parliament is elected for five years from 222 constituencies, each of which elects one person to represent workers and peasants and one other. In addition, the president nominates up to ten others to provide representation to groups that might not otherwise be represented in Parliament. In recent years this has allowed the president to nominate leaders of parties that did not win any seats; Christians, who are rarely elected; and women. In addition, there is a kind of upper house, the Consultative Council, which is two-thirds elected and one-third appointed, and which is supposed to provide for more reflective debate on fundamental issues. Through the minister of interior, the president also names governors for the twenty-six governorates of Egypt. Elected councils function at the local level.

Egypt is a "dominant party" system in which one party regularly controls an enormous majority in Parliament. This dominant party is the National Democratic Party (NDP), which represents the political establishment. There are fourteen other parties, only a few of which have ever been represented in Parliament. These include the Wafd party, heir to the tradition of the struggle for national independence in the 1920s and 1930s, and with a pro-capitalist orientation; the Socialist Labor Party, heavily dominated by Islamic-oriented leaders; the Progressive Party, heir to the Egyptian leftist tradition; and the Liberal Party.

Relatively few women are elected to Parliament, though there are always some. In the late 1970s seats were set aside for women, and this increased their number, but this provision was later ruled unconstitutional. Usually there are a few women ministers. One of the key roles for women in the current political system is the role of the wife of the president. The current "first lady" has taken on a role of organizing campaigns for literacy and health in support of the government's policies.

The extraparliamentary opposition is the Islamic movement, which is not a single movement. Since specifically religious parties, Muslim or Christian, are prohibited, politically active Muslim militants must either join another party, which many do, or remain outside the formal process, which others do. There is a sense in which the main political struggle in Egypt is between the secularists of the NDP, linked to the world of business and the high administration, and the values represented by one or another version of the Islamic trend, representing the "opposition."

In villages and urban neighborhoods there are elected councils that manage zoning, garbage collection, and some public-interest construction, such as a new water system. These local councils work in tandem with local representatives of the different ministries (such as interior, health, or agriculture) to carry out their tasks.

Social Problems and Control. Street crime is relatively rare in Egypt. Most crimes reported in the press are either family dramas or con games of one kind or another. Drugs are illegal, though present, in Egypt, and the users tend to be discreet.

Despite the visible presence of traffic police and police guards in areas where there are foreigners, there are also large areas of Cairo, and many villages, with no police presence at all. People are thus thrown back on their own resources to settle disputes, and there are well-known techniques of intervention (to break up fistfights) and of mediation for more complicated disputes. Even the police often act as mediators rather than prosecutors. In rural Upper Egypt in particular, disputes between extended families over property and power can develop into feuds.

Social control appears to be maintained by a combination of strong values, expressed as Islamic, and by the constant presence of witnesses due to crowded streets and apartments. Anonymity in large Egyptian cities, let alone in villages, is nearly impossible. Perhaps another way to express the same point is to say that Cairo is a village of fifteen million people.

Military Activity. Egypt fought many wars in the second half of the twentieth century, mostly with Israel: around the creation of Israel in 1947–1949; over the nationalization of the Suez Canal Company and the "tripartite aggression" of Israel, France, and the United Kingdom in 1956; the Six-Day War in 1967; the war of attrition in the early 1970s; and the October War of 1973. In addition, Egypt was involved in the Yemeni civil war in the 1960s, when Saudi Arabia was involved on the other side, and contributed troops to the allies who confronted Iraq over the invasion of Kuwait in 1990–1991. Egypt suffered considerable loss of life in the wars with Israel between 1947 and 1973, so the situation since then seems more peaceful.

Social Welfare and Change Programs

Egyptian citizens are entitled to free education and health care, in addition to employment guarantees for graduates. Services are poor, however, and there are many hidden costs, such as time spent waiting. The transition from socialism to the market system has left the majority of the population without a real safety net. Part of the social policy includes efforts to restructure welfare, and to help unemployed youth set up their own businesses. Attempts are underway to establish national health insurance and social security systems.

Nongovernment efforts in the area of welfare are sporadic. There is an increasing return to philanthropy in a traditional sense of charity and patronage, in addition to some community-based foundations and associations that provide services.

Islamist groups have been active in providing services in poor areas, particularly in health care and educational services. This was the main source for their popularity in the past decade. With government restrictions on Islamist groups, however, such activity has been considerably curtailed.

People wait outside a spice shop in Khan el-Khalili. Business queues are often separated by gender.

Nongovernmental Organizations and Other Associations

Egypt has a long tradition of voluntary associations. Currently there are over fourteen thousand associations, most of which are devoted to charitable purposes. They are mostly small and local, and none has a mass membership. After 1964, the associations were governed by a law that stipulated fairly close governmental control. A new law allowing somewhat more flexibility was passed in 1999 but was declared unconstitutional a year later, so the older law continues to apply. This law was contested by many environmental and human rights associations, because it appeared to prevent them from taking political positions.

The main national associations are the professional syndicates for doctors, lawyers, teachers, agricultural officials, and others. They lobby for their members, and also sometimes play a role on the political scene. Their internal politics tends to be a reflection of national politics, with the main competition between the NDP and the Islamists. The professional syndicates are also governed by restrictive laws, and are periodically suspended by the government for infringing these restrictions.

Gender Roles and Statuses

Division of Labor by Gender. Household work and child rearing are almost exclusively women's responsibility. Women also contribute significantly to productive work outside the home, especially in cities. But since the majority of women work in the informal sector, the size of their contribution is often underestimated. In rural areas, women work in the fields in most regions. In addition, women's household responsibilities in villages involve many productive and profitable activities, although they are not generally recognized as "work." These activities include caring for animals and processing dairy products. Women may also take part in some stages of preparing crops for market.

The Relative Status of Women and Men. In general, men and women have equal legal rights. But equality is not determined only by law. For example, the principle of equal pay applies only in the formal sector. Women working in the informal sector are often paid less than men. Women do not have the same legal rights as men in the domain of personal status (marriage, divorce, child custody). Only Egyptian men have the right to pass on Egyptian nationality to their children. Various feminist and human rights groups, however, are active in promoting legal change in areas of discrimination against women.

At home men have more power than women, and are supposed to make the major decisions. Nevertheless, women have much influence and informal power.

Marriage, Family, and Kinship

Marriage. One of the critical decisions a woman can make is the choice of marriage partner. The pattern here is one of negotiation among the members of her family about whom she will marry. She is a participant, and must in some sense agree, but many others are involved, including matchmakers. Similarly a young man may find constraints on his choice of marriage partner.

The trend is for marriage partners to be increasingly more like one another in age and level of education. The old hierarchical marriage is giving way to a companionate marriage, especially in the urban middle classes. Marriage to cousins, however, remains frequent, accounting for 39 percent of marriages in a 1995 sample. Since premarital sex is rare, the pressure to marry is high, and almost everyone marries.

The actual marriage ceremony is distinct from the legal contract of marriage. It is a major event in the lives of all involved. The young couple must prepare a place to live, while at the same time seeing that the often considerable costs of the ceremony are covered. People spend as much as they can, if not more, on a marriage, and in the upper classes, the sky is the limit.

Polygyny (having more than one wife) among Muslims is rare, and declining. Around 5 percent of Muslim men have more than one wife, and most of them only two. A polygynous man usually maintains two households. Divorce is formally easy though families try to reconcile the partners. The rate of divorce is declining, while the absolute number is increasing. When a divorced couple has children, the mother retains custody only while they are young. The father may then claim them. Copts recognize neither polygyny nor divorce.

An important signal of family identity is the personal name. Egyptians frequently do not have "family" names in the current Western sense of a last name that is shared by all members of an extended family. Instead, each person has a given name, followed by the given names of his or her father, grandfather, and so on. For legal purposes one's name is usually "given name, father's name, grandfather's name," resulting in three given names (e.g., Hassan Ali Abdallah). Thus one carries one's paternal lineage and one's status in one's name. In certain parts of rural Egypt, where genealogy is important, people learn to recite a long list of paternal ancestors. Muslim men are likely to have religious names but some have secular names. Christians may carry the names of saints, or may be given names that are Arabic rather than religious. Women also have religious names but sometimes have more fanciful ones, including names of foreign origin. Women often do not change their names upon marriage.

Domestic Unit. Although most households now are organized around a nuclear family, there are some extended family households. Marriage was historically patrilocal (brides moved to the household of the husband), though in cities the young couple often establishes a new residence, at least after a couple of years. Even when residence is not shared, extensive kin ties are maintained through frequent family gatherings. Authority tends to be patriarchal, with the senior male in the household generally given the last word and otherwise expecting deference. Wives, for instance, often are reluctant to assert that they have any serious independent power to make decisions.

Inheritance. Islamic law requires partible inheritance. The property of a dead person must be divided among the heirs, usually children and surviving spouse. Male heirs are favored over female heirs by receiving a share that is twice as large. Moreover, any group of heirs should include a male, even if that means tracking down a distant cousin. A person may not dispose of more than one-third of his or her estate by will, and may not even use this provision to favor one legal heir over another. In other words, a person cannot will this one-third to one son at the expense of another, but could will it to a charity or a nonrelative. Use of this provision is rare, as people accept the Islamic rules and prefer to keep property in the family. Arrangements among heirs, particularly brothers and sisters, however, may result in a different outcome. For instance, a father may set up his daughter in marriage in lieu of an eventual inheritance.

Kin Groups. Egyptian kinship is patrilineal, with individuals tracing their descent through their fathers.

Socialization

Child Rearing and Education. In all parts of Egypt and among all social classes, having children is considered the greatest blessing of all. Caring for children is primarily the women's responsibility. Many Egyptian women (both Copt and Muslim) abide by the Koranic directive to breast-feed children for two years. Grandparents and other members of the extended family play an active role in bringing up children.

There is a general preference for boys over girls, although in infancy and early childhood children of both sexes are treated with equal love and care. The preference to have at least one son is related to the desire to have an heir, and so provide continuity from father to son.

Education is highly valued in Egypt, and families invest a lot in that area. Even low-income families try to educate their children as much as possible. Education, especially having a university degree, is considered an important avenue for social mobility. But many families cannot afford to educate their children beyond the elementary level. In addition, many children have to work at an early age to help support their families.

Etiquette

Public modesty in dress and deportment is highly valued in Egypt. There is a form of dress code that affects women more than men, and that requires clothing that covers all the body but the hands and face. For women, this most visibly means wearing a head scarf that covers the hair and ears and is pinned under the chin, though there are many other styles ranging from simply covering the hair to covering the entire face. This is the sense in which veiling exists in Egypt, but the situation is volatile, with a good deal of variety. Many women do not veil at all. What is proper, or required, or necessary, is hotly debated in contemporary Egypt. The motivations for veiling are numerous, and range from those who accept that this is a requirement of Islam to those who cover themselves essentially to satisfy their relatives, male and female. Men are also enjoined to dress modestly, but the changes are not as striking, involving for instance loose trousers and long sleeves. For both men and women, the principle is that clothes should disguise the shape of the body.

Another rule of etiquette is that greetings must precede all forms of social interaction. A person joining any kind of group, even of strangers, is expected to greet those already present. In less anonymous situations handshakes are due. Embracing is also common as a form of greeting, usually among members of the same sex.

People are generally addressed by their given name, often preceded by a title of some kind (*'am*, or uncle, is the all-purpose title for men; others include *hajj* for a pilgrim returned from Mecca or simply for an older man, *duktor* for a person with a doctorate, and *muhandis* for an engineer). To address someone by name alone is impolite.

One important rule of etiquette is to treat guests cordially and hospitably. An offering, usually tea or a soft drink, is the least a visitor expects. The first drink is sometimes called a "greeting." Cigarettes are often also offered as hospitality. In rural areas, some people avoid visiting those they consider to be of lower status than themselves. From this point of view, visits are always "up," and hospitality is always "down," i.e., the higher-status host provides hospitality for the lower-status guest.

In general, young defer to old and women to men. Members of the younger generation are expected to show signs of respect and not to challenge their seniors and must use the special terms of address for aunts, uncles, and grandparents, as well as for older nonrelatives. Juniors should not raise their voices to elders, nor should they remain seated while an older person is standing up. With increasing disparities between classes and the spread of patronage ties, there is an inflation in deferential terms of address. This includes the resurgence in the use of terms that were previously official titles but were abolished after 1952, such as Pasha and Bey.

Religion

Religious Beliefs. Egypt is a country of "everyday piety." The central belief in Islam is in the oneness of God, whose truths were revealed through the prophet Muhammad. The statement of this basic profession of faith is one of the five pillars of the religion. The other four are the Ramadan fast, the pilgrimage to Mecca, the five daily prayers, and the giving of alms. For many Muslims these five pillars sum up the belief system and indicate the practices. Egyptians frequently invoke the notion of God and his power. Any statement about the future, for instance, is likely to contain the injunction, "God willing," showing that the ultimate determination of the intention is up to God.

In Egypt, there are other possible elaborations. For some, who focus on God as all-powerful, religious practice involves seeking God's help in overcoming problems and seeking favorable outcomes, for instance, with regard to recovery from disease or misfortune. Around this notion has grown up a series of practices involving visits to shrines, often

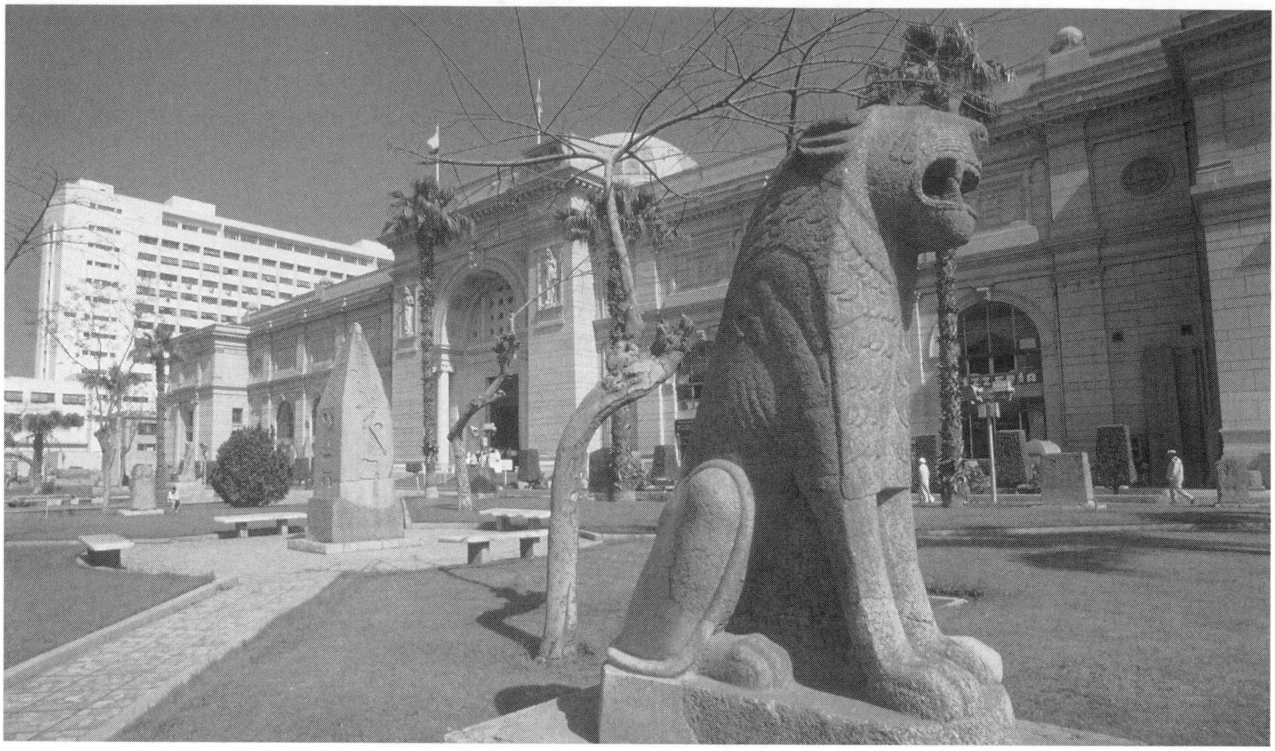

The Egyptian Museum in Cairo features artifacts from the tombs of pharaohs.

where individuals believed to be beloved of God are buried, to seek their intercession with God. Foremost among these shrines are those in Cairo associated with the family of the prophet Muhammad. But every village and town has such shrines, whose importance varies. This form of religion is often attacked by religious purists who argue that to give such importance to these "saints" undercuts the oneness of God.

Also very common in Egypt are associations of mystics (Sufi brotherhoods). These male-dominated groups are under the leadership of a *shaykh*, or a hierarchy of shaykhs, devoted to helping their members attain a mystical experience of union with God. This mystical experience is often attained through collective rituals, proper to each order, called *zikr*. There are nearly one hundred officially recognized associations, plus numerous unrecognized ones, and they claim around six million members (about one third of the adult male population).

Current mainstream practice in Egypt is to focus on the core beliefs of Islam, and to be concerned with learning the "law" of Islam, the particular details of everyday life that believing Muslims must follow to be in accord with God's will as interpreted by specialists. The authority here is the word of God as found in the Koran. The prayer leader (imam) can be anyone in religious good standing, although established mosques usually have a regular imam. The Friday sermon is said by a *khatib*, many of whom are trained in religious institutes. There have been debates over whether women can play these roles, especially that of a teacher of religion to women and girls.

The two top religious leaders in Egyptian Islam are the Shaykh al-Azhar, who heads the religious bureaucracy, and the Grand Mufti, who offers authoritative interpretations of the Koran. The individuals in these posts have been known to take different positions on some issues.

The two main Muslim religious holidays are the feast following Ramadan, the fasting month, and 'Id al-Adha, which corresponds to the Muslim pilgrimage to Mecca. The Ramadan holiday comes after a month of fasting and family visits and people usually just rest. The 'Id al-Adha celebrates Abraham's willingness to sacrifice his son, who then miraculously turned into a ram, so that most families try to sacrifice a ram on this day. Other religious holidays include Moulid an-Nabi, commemorating the birth of the prophet Muhammad, which is especially important for sufis; and Islamic New Year, the first day of the month of Moharram.

In Islam, Friday is the day of the main congregational prayer, and marks a break in the workweek without being a "day of rest" in the formal sense. In contemporary Egypt, the two-day weekend is Friday and Saturday. The regular work and school week is thus Sunday through Thursday, although some also work on Saturday. Christians who work on this schedule attend church in the evenings, and make use of Friday for major gatherings.

The Coptic Orthodox Church is the descendant of the churches associated with the early Christian Patriarchate of Alexandria. It is the main Christian church in Egypt. Its theology is monophysite, holding that in Jesus Christ there is only one nature, both human and divine. The Coptic church is headed by a patriarch and supported by bishops and parish priests. Monasticism is also central to the Coptic church, and the patriarch comes from the ranks of the monks rather than the priests. When a patriarch dies, his successor is chosen by lot (i.e., by God) from a small number of candidates who have survived a vetting process. The monasteries also serve as pilgrimage and retreat centers for Copts. Currently the Virgin Mary is revered, and many churches are dedicated to her.

The two main Christian holidays are the Christmas season and the Easter season. Minor holidays include some that are extensions of these seasons such as 'Id al-Ghattas (Epiphany), the baptism of Christ, Palm Sunday, and some associated with the Virgin Mary (Ascension, in mid-August, is a main one).

In most aspects of life apart from religion, Egyptian Muslims and Christians are indistinguishable. Everyday devotion is common among both, and many religious values are shared at a general level. The attentive observer can sometimes note marks of distinction: "Islamic" dress marks Muslim women; both men and women among Christians may have a cross tattooed on the inside of the right wrist; names are often but not always indicative. For most people, most of the time, the distinction is not relevant. But every so often there are individuals on one side or the other who stress the difference and claim or practice some form of discrimination or injustice. Such speech rarely leads to more violent action. Nonetheless, the boundary is maintained and both groups discourage or prohibit intermarriage and conversion. Muslims and Christians are not residentially segregated; instead, there are clusters of Christians scattered among a Muslim majority. In modern times, the presence of both Muslims and Christians has impeded the drive to define Egypt as a Muslim country and thus at least indirectly has favored secularism.

Rituals and Holy Places. Rituals marking the different stages of life are also an important area of religious practice, and one that is largely shared by Muslims and Christians. Egyptians celebrate a naming ceremony normally one week after a baby's birth; this is a mixture of Islamic (or Coptic) and "traditional" elements, and is basically a family celebration to incorporate the newborn into the family. All boys are circumcised, generally as infants, and girls are usually also "circumcised" before they reach puberty. (Although the form of female genital mutilation varies, surveys suggest that about 97 percent of Egyptian females, both Christians and Muslims, are affected.) Marriage is a major focus of Egyptian culture. For Muslims it is considered a contract the signing of which is later followed by a family celebration; for Christians the sacrament takes place in a church, usually followed the same day by a family celebration.

Death and the Afterlife. After a death, both Muslims and Christians try to bury the body the same day. Condolences are paid immediately, and again after forty days and after a year. The Islamic condolence sessions are often marked by Koran reading. Both Muslims and Christians believe in the soul, distinguishing it from other noncorporeal aspects of the person such as the double, the brother/sister, and the ghost. The "soul" exists before birth and after death, while some of the other aspects disappear with death or only appear at death.

Medicine and Health Care

Health care in Egypt occupies a central place both in people's concerns and in state priorities. There is an extensive network of public hospitals in major towns and cities all over the country. There is a health unit offering basic medical services in practically every village. The standard of the medical service is variable, however, and people often find they have to obtain treatment in private hospitals and clinics. Among more affluent sectors of urban Egypt, people seek out alternative treatments such as homeopathy.

Egyptians tend to combine the modern health system with traditional practices. In villages, the midwife, for example, plays a key role not just during childbirth and the related ceremonial activities, but also in providing general medical advice to women. There are other traditional health practitioners, such as seers and spirit healers. The *zar* ceremony marks a form of spirit possession cult that establishes a relationship between an afflicted person and the spirits afflicting him or her. This

Egyptians at a festival in Cairo. Many public Egyptian holidays mark important events in the recent political history of the country.

relationship must be periodically reaffirmed, with the help of specialists.

Secular Celebrations

The main public holidays are: 25 April, Sinai Liberation Day, which marks the recovery of the Sinai Peninsula in 1982; 1 May, International Labor Day; 23 July, which commemorates the revolution of 1952; and 6 October, Armed Forces Day, which marks the day in 1973 when the Egyptian army crossed the Suez Canal, surprising the Israeli army and scoring a minor military victory that, through later diplomacy, would lead to the return of Sinai to Egypt.

Labor Day in Egypt as elsewhere is used to salute the working class. The others mark important events in the recent political history of the country. All are official affairs, with little popular celebration.

The Arts and Humanities

Literature. Nobel Prize-winning author Naguib Mahfouz (b. 1911) is the best known of the many novelists, poets, and short-story writers whose works have been widely read and translated. Folk tales and folk epics survive but are not robust.

Graphic Arts. Painters are largely self-supporting through the sale of their paintings. There are many art galleries mostly concentrated in Cairo, and the acquisition of paintings has always been a sign of good taste and distinction among members of affluent social groups. Folk painting of house walls is well-known in rural Egypt.

Performance Arts. The Egyptian film industry is one of the oldest in the world. Film production is at once an art, an industry, and a trade. Egyptian films and television dramas are avidly consumed not just in Egypt but all over the Arab world. They range from tacky melodramas to internationally acclaimed, award-winning films of high artistic value. Film production is now almost exclusively in the private sector.

The most famous Egyptian singer was Umm Kalthum (d. 1975), whose songs are still broadcast all over the Arab world. Some more recent singers have also had considerable popularity inside and outside the country. There is also a Cairo Symphony Orchestra, a Cairo Opera Ballet, and other troupes producing classical music and dance.

The State of the Physical and Social Sciences

There are thirteen government universities, some of which have multiple branches, enrolling about one million students. The much smaller American University in Cairo is an old private university, and there are several new ones.

In general, the physical and social sciences are confined to academic departments of the various universities, and to state-sponsored research centers. There is now an increasing tendency to link scientific knowledge to social and economic demands, by emphasizing the "relevance" of such knowledge. Thus, the new Mubarak City for Scientists, which contains one institute for information technology and another for genetics, caters to the demands of industry. The need for research and development is accepted but the realization is more difficult.

The main university subjects took shape at Cairo University in the 1920s. Economics is probably the best developed of the social sciences, and political science and psychology are making progress. Sociology was founded at Cairo in 1925 and is now found in most universities.

The main centers for anthropology are Alexandria and the American University in Cairo. Anthropology is dominated by efforts to come to grips with contemporary patterns of change, often under the heading of development. The main thrust of anthropology in Egypt is not to improve cross-cultural understanding but instead to foster Egyptian development. There are few positions in anthropology, so most trained anthropologists gradually become generalists in development.

Bibliography

Abu Lughod, Lila. *Veiled Sentiments: Honor and Poetry in a Bedouin Society*, 1986

Abu-Zahra, Nadia. *The Pure and Powerful: Studies in Contemporary Muslim Society*, 1997.

Ammar, Hamed. *Growing Up in an Egyptian Village: Silwa, Province of Aswan*, 1954.

Armbrust, Walter. *Mass Culture and Modernism in Egypt*, 1996.

Berger, Morroe. *Islam in Egypt Today: Social and Political Aspects of Popular Religion*, 1970.

Biegman, Nicolaas H. *Egypt: Moulids, Saints, Sufis*, 1990.

Blackman, Winifred S. *The Fellahin of Upper Egypt: Their Religious, Social, and Industrial Life To-day with Special Reference to Survivals from Ancient Times*, 1927 (repr. 1999).

Cole, Donald P., and Soraya Altorki. *Bedouins, Settlers, and Holiday-Makers: Egypt's Changing Northwest Coast*, 1998.

Danielson, Virginia. *The Voice of Egypt: Umm Kulthum, Arabic Song, and Egyptian Society in the Twentieth Century*, 1997.

El-Guindi, Fadwai. *Veil: Modesty, Privacy and Resistance*, 1999.

El-Hamamsy, Laila Shukry. "The Assertion of Egyptian Identity" in George De Vos and Lola Romanucci-Ross, eds. *Ethnic Identity: Cultural Communities and Change*, pp. 276-306. 1975

Fahim, Hussein M. *Egyptian Nubians: Resettlement and Years of Coping*, 1983.

Fakhouri, Hani. *Kafr el-Elow: Continuity and Change in an Egyptian Community* (2nd ed.), 1987.

Fernea, Robert A., et al. *Nubians in Egypt: Peaceful People*, 1973.

Gaffney, Patrick D. *The Prophet's Pulpit: Islamic Preaching in Contemporary Egypt*, 1994.

Gilsenan, Michael. *Saint and Sufi in Modern Egypt: An Essay in the Sociology of Religion*, 1973.

Hobbs, Joseph J. *Mount Sinai*, 1995.

Hoodfar, Homa. *Between Marriage and the Market: Intimate Politics and Survival in Cairo*, 1997.

Hopkins, Nicholas S., and Kirsten Westergaard, eds. *Directions of Change in Rural Egypt*, 1998.

Ibrahim, Barbara, et al. *Transitions to Adulthood: A National Survey of Egyptian Adolescents*, 1999.

Ibrahim, Saad Eddin. *Egypt, Islam, and Democracy*, 1996.

Inhorn, Marcia C. *Quest for Conception: Gender, Infertility, and Egyptian Medical Traditions*, 1994.

Jennings, Anne M. *The Nubians of West Aswan: Village Women in the Midst of Change*, 1995.

Johansen, Julian. *Sufism and Islamic Reform in Egypt: The Battle for Islamic Tradition*, 1996.

Kennedy, John G. *Struggle for Change in a Nubian Community: An Individual in Society and History*, 1977.

MacLeod, Arlene Elowe. *Accommodating Protest: Working Women, the New Veiling, and Change in Cairo*, 1991.

Mitchell, Timothy. *Colonising Egypt*, 1988.

Morsy, Soheir A. *Gender, Sickness, and Healing in Rural Egypt*, 1993.

Nelson, Cynthia. *Doria Shafik: Egyptian Feminist*, 1996.

Reeves, Edward B. *The Hidden Government: Ritual, Clientelism, and Legitimation in Northern Egypt*, 1990.

Reynolds, Dwight F. *Heroic Poets, Poetic Heroes: The Ethnography of Performance*, 1995.

Rodenbeck, Max. *Cairo, The City Victorious*, 1998.

Rugh, Andrea B. *Family in Contemporary Egypt*, 1984.

Saad, Reem. "Shame, Reputation, and Egypt's Lovers: A Controversy Over the Nation's Image." *Visual Anthropology*, 10 (2–4): 401–412, 1998.

Singerman, Diane. *Avenues of Participation: Family, Politics, and Networks in Urban Quarters of Cairo*, 1995.

Starrett, Gregory. *Putting Islam to Work: Education, Politics, and Religious Transformation in Egypt*, 1998.

Sullivan, Denis J. *Private Voluntary Organizations in Egypt: Islamic Development, Private Initiative, and State Control*, 1994.

Tekçe, Belgin, Linda Oldham, and Frederic C. Shorter. *A Place to Live: Families and Child Health in a Cairo Neighborhood*, 1994.

Weyland, Petra. *Inside the Third World Village*, 1993.

Wikan, Unni. *Tomorrow, God Willing: Self-Made Destinies in Cairo*, 1996.

—NICHOLAS S. HOPKINS
AND REEM SAAD

El Salvador

Culture Name

Salvadoran

Alternative Names

Salvadorean, Guanaco, salvadoreño

Orientation

Identification. El Salvador "the Savior," was named by Spanish conquistadors. Guanaco, a type of bird, is a slightly derogative nickname used by other Central Americans and some Salvadorans.

Location and Geography. El Salvador is a country of 8,260 square miles (21,040 square kilometers) in Central America, between Guatemala and Honduras. Mountains separate the country into the southern coastal belt, the central valleys and plateaus, and the northern mountains. These regions have created slight cultural variations because of the different crops grown in each one. Coffee grown in the mountains and cane grown on the coast provide the rural population with paid labor; in the central valleys, corn and beans are grown for private consumption and for sale. Most industry is in the center, where the capital, San Salvador, is located. Other large cities include San Miguel in the east and Santa Ana in the west.

Demography. In 1999 the population was estimated to be 5,839,079, making El Salvador one of the most densely populated countries in the Western Hemisphere. Over a million persons have migrated, starting in the early 1980s during a civil war. Legal and illegal emigration has continued at a high rate since the end of the civil war in 1992.

Linguistic Affiliation. Almost all residents speak Spanish, which was brought in by the conquistadors. Before the Spanish conquest, the area was inhabited by the Pipil Indians. Very few Salvadorans now speak the indigenous language, which virtually disappeared after 1932, when General Maximilio Hernández Martínez suppressed rural resistance by massacring 30,000 mostly Indian rural peasants. Those who survived *la Matanza* ("the massacre") hid their Indian identity by changing their dress and speaking only Spanish. Some remnants of the Pipil language remain in everyday Salvadoran Spanish.

Symbolism. The flag consists of two blue horizontal stripes with a white stripe in the middle. In the center is a coat of arms inscribed "1821," the year of independence. Salvadorans in the United States often have plaques that contain the flag, as a symbol of national pride. Since independence, the blue in the flag has symbolized support for the ruling oligarchy, while the red has symbolized support for communism or resistance. Conservative political parties use blue in their banners; a liberal party, the Farabunda Marti National Liberation Front (FMLN), uses red and centralist parties use blue or green. During the civil war, both sides sang the national hymn.

History and Ethnic Relations

Emergence of the Nation. Before the Spanish conquest, the area that is now El Salvador was made up of two large Indian states and several principalities. Most of the area was inhabited by the Pipil. Spain's first attempt to conquer the area failed as the Pipil forced Spanish troops to retreat. In 1525, the district fell under the control of the Captaincy General of Guatemala, a colony of Spain, which retained authority until independence in 1821. During the colonial period, the Spaniards replaced the communal property of the indigenous population with a system of private property. The *encomienda* system obliged Indians to work for the Spanish in order to pay a large tax. At the top of the colonial hierarchy were the *Peninsulares*, Spaniards born in Spain. Under them were the *criollos*, Spaniards born in the Americas. The *mestizos* were people of mixed Span-

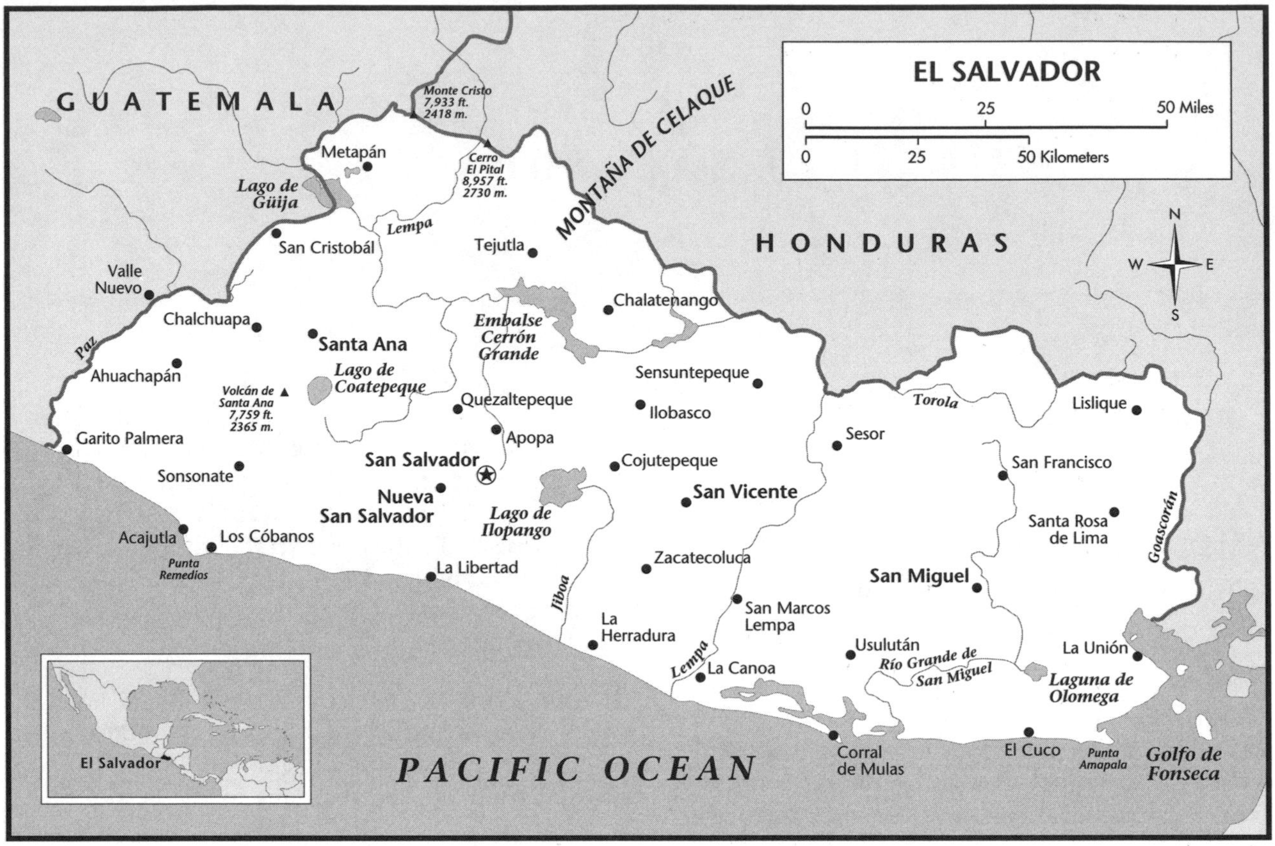

El Salvador

ish and indigenous descent, who had some rights but could not hold private property. The indigenous peoples were exploited and mistreated.

Independence from Spain (1821) was sought by *criollos* who were inspired by the American and French revolutions. They gained support from the Indians and landless peasants by promising to end the abuses committed by landowners. After the revolution, Indians and peasants remained impoverished and largely without land or legal rights.

When the Central American provinces were joined with Mexico in 1822, El Salvador insisted on the autonomy of the Central American countries. Guatemalan troops that were sent to enforce the union were forced out in June 1822. In 1823, José Manuel Arce's army was defeated by the Mexicans. However, in February of that year, a revolution in Mexico ousted the emperor, and a new congress granted independence to the Central American provinces. That year the United Provinces of Central America were formed from five Central American countries. When that federation dissolved in 1838, El Salvador became an independent republic.

The first decades of independence saw uprisings by poor *mestizos* and Indians to protest their impoverishment and marginalization. Before the cultivation of coffee was introduced in the late nineteenth century, indigo was the principal export crop. In 1833, an Indian rebellion of indigo sowers and cutters led by Anastasio Aquino demanded distribution of land to the poor and the just application of the penal laws, the only laws applied to the poor. The rebellion was crushed by the government. Thousands of rural peasants were displaced as new laws incorporated their lands into large "modern" coffee plantations where peasants were forced to work for very low wages. This created a coffee oligarchy made up of fourteen families. The economy is still controlled by a wealthy landowning caste (1 percent of the population still owns 40 percent of the arable land).

The civil war in the 1980s led to a huge population upheaval, with up to 40 percent of the population relocating and close to 20 percent leaving the country. Estimates of deaths in the twelve years of civil war have reached 80,000, including twelve thousand civilians killed in 1981. In 1982, mutilation killings, particularly decapitations, of adults

Motor vehicles, bicycles, and pedestrians crowd a busy street in downtown San Salvador.

and children were used as mechanisms of social terror.

Much of that repression was in response to the political organization of the people in the 1960s and 1970s as workers, peasants, women, students, and shanty town dwellers developed organizations to demand political and economic rights. Many political activists felt that "legal" political organizing would not lead to political change and began organizing the clandestine guerrilla units that formed the nucleus of the FMLN in 1980. By 1979 the FMLN was perceived as a threat by the military dictatorship.

A new spirit of activism emerged within the Catholic Church. Rural peasants and church workers formed Christian "base communities" and agricultural cooperatives in the 1960s and 1970s. Progressive priests and nuns formed Bible study groups in which peasants reflected on local conditions in light of biblical texts. This organizing was considered communist and subversive and became a target of government repression.

A group of young officers staged a military coup and formed a cabinet consisting of civilians from a wide spectrum of political parties. However, the military and the oligarchy frustrated attempts at change. Three more juntas followed, but each was incapable of implementing reform and stopping atrocities.

In 1980, the archbishop of San Salvador, Oscar Romero, who had become a forceful critic of military oppression, was assassinated while saying Mass. This led many people in the base Christian communities and political organizations to turn to armed resistance. Five revolutionary armies joined together to form the FMLN.

In November 1989, the FMLN launched a bloody nationwide offensive, taking parts of the capital. International coverage of the offensive increased the pressure for a negotiated settlement to the conflict. On 31 December 1991, the government and the FMLN signed an agreement under the auspices of the United Nations, and a cease-fire took effect in 1992. The peace accords called for military reforms including a reduction in the size of the military, a new armed forces doctrine stressing democratic values and prohibiting an internal security role, and the banning of paramilitary groups. The National Civilian Police was established to replace the repressive National Police. Judicial, electoral, and social reforms included land reform and government-financed loans for land purchases.

Ideological polarization between the two sides in the conflict has made reconciliation difficult, and the government has failed to prosecute human rights abusers, or address the social injustices. Many Salvadorans, especially rural peasants, do not trust the nation's political leaders.

National Identity. Salvadoran national identity is comprised of a mix of indigenous and Spanish influences expressed in food, language, customs, and religious beliefs.

Ethnic Relations. Indians were at the bottom of the social hierarchy in colonial times and subject to massacre and exploitation well into the twentieth century. Ninety-seven percent of the population in El Salvador is now "mestizo." However, those who have more indigenous features suffer some discrimination and are referred to by the derogatory terms "indios" (Indians) or "negros" (blacks).

Urbanism, Architecture, and the Use of Space

Rural houses are typically made of adobe, with a large front porch (*corredor*) where people spend most of their time when at home. The insides of houses are used mainly for sleeping and storage, and families of seven or eight people may live in one or two small rooms. Urban houses built during the colonial period typically have outdoor space in the middle of the house, making family life more private. Modern urban middle-class and upper-class houses often have a small garden in front instead of in the middle, with the house and garden surrounded by a large wall that often is topped by barbed wire and glass. These houses often cannot be seen from the street. This type of architecture was used in the 1970s for security reasons. Houses for the lower classes are often less protected, with entrances onto the street. Many of the poorest families have houses made of discarded materials such as cardboard and sheet metal.

Food and Economy

Food in Daily Life. Corn is the staple of the diet and is most often made into thick tortillas that are eaten at every meal and also are served as tamales and in a thick corn drink called *atol.* Small red beans are the other staple. A variety of fruits and vegetables are eaten, including mango, papaya, tamarind, oranges, bananas, watermelon, cucumber, *pacayao,* lettuce, tomatoes, and radish. Salvadorans also eat rice, eggs, chicken, pork, beef, fish and seafood, and some game. Coffee is the most common drink, along with highly sugared fruit drinks. *Elotes* (new corn) are eaten in September before the corn hardens. Restaurants are most often cafeterias, *comedores,* where food is ordered from a menu near the kitchen or a buffet table and waitresses bring the food to the table. There are fast food restaurants in the cities which are more expensive, and expensive restaurants where food is ordered from a menu at the table.

Food Customs at Ceremonial Occasions. Tamales are often eaten on special occasions, as is *chumpe,* turkey stewed in a sauce.

Basic Economy. Corn, beans, and rice, are among the principal crops, but El Salvador relies on the importation of these staples.

Land Tenure and Property. The land reform started in the early 1980s transferred land to former combatants who were mostly the rural poor. The purchase of land was financed by a United States-assisted land bank. However, many people find it difficult to sustain their families on small plots of infertile land.

Commercial Activities. Major commercial activities include shoe and textile production.

Major Industries. Major industries include food processing, beverages, petroleum, chemicals, fertilizer, textiles, furniture, and light metals.

Trade. El Salvador is a large exporter of agricultural products, but exports of sugarcane, cotton, and coffee have declined. The nation exports only half the quantity of goods it imports. Traditional exports include coffee, sugarcane, and shrimp. Nontraditional crops include manufactured goods, principally shoes and textiles. Textiles produced in *maquilas* (foreign-owned sweatshops) have replaced coffee as the leading export. However, dollars sent from Salvadorans in the United States to their families provide more income than do any exports.

Division of Labor. Professional jobs, including elementary school teaching, require a university education and are limited mainly to the middle and upper classes. Clerical or technical jobs usually require a high school diploma, which is received by only a small percentage of the population. Semiskilled jobs such as construction and plumbing generally require a period of apprenticeship but not of formal study. Access to education corresponds to the possession of wealth, and poor families are often limited to unskilled positions in industry, agriculture, and small businesses. Others are employed in the informal economy selling candy, fruit, or ta-

A modern sculpture in front of a building in San Salvador. The Salvadoran capital features a mix of modern amenities and extreme poverty.

males on the streets and at bus stops. The majority of working women are employed in the informal sector, along with many children.

Social Stratification

Classes and Castes. About half the population lives below the national poverty line, able to buy food but not clothing and medicine. Over half of these families live in a situation of extreme poverty. Forty-seven percent of the population does not have access to clean water.

The difference between the incomes of the most wealthy and the poorest are extreme and increasing. The poorest 20 percent receive only 2 percent of the national income, whereas the richest 20 percent receive 66 percent. The distinction between the rich and poor is no longer ethnic, as the vast majority of the population is now *mestizo* (about 97 percent).

Symbols of Social Stratification. The rich have more access to American goods and typically dress like Americans. They also have access to education at home and abroad and often speak English, as well as a more grammatical form of Spanish.

Political Life

Government. The constitution provides for a representative government with three independent branches: executive, legislative, and judicial. The president is popularly elected and must receive a majority of the vote. The president is limited to a single five-year term but exercises significant authority in appointing a cabinet with the advice and consent of the assembly. This assembly has one chamber of eighty-four popularly elected deputies who serve three-year terms and may be reelected. The supreme court is the highest court of appeals, with other civil and criminal courts in each of the fourteen departments.

Leadership and Political Officials. Political parties include those of the extreme right, the left, and more central parties. The Partido Alianza Republicana Nacionalista (ARENA), founded in 1981, was associated with the death squads. It continues to have enormous influence. The party has moved from the extreme right to supporting neoliberal structural adjustment policies since the war. More extreme members of ARENA have joined the Partido de Conciliación Nacional (PCN), which was founded in 1961.

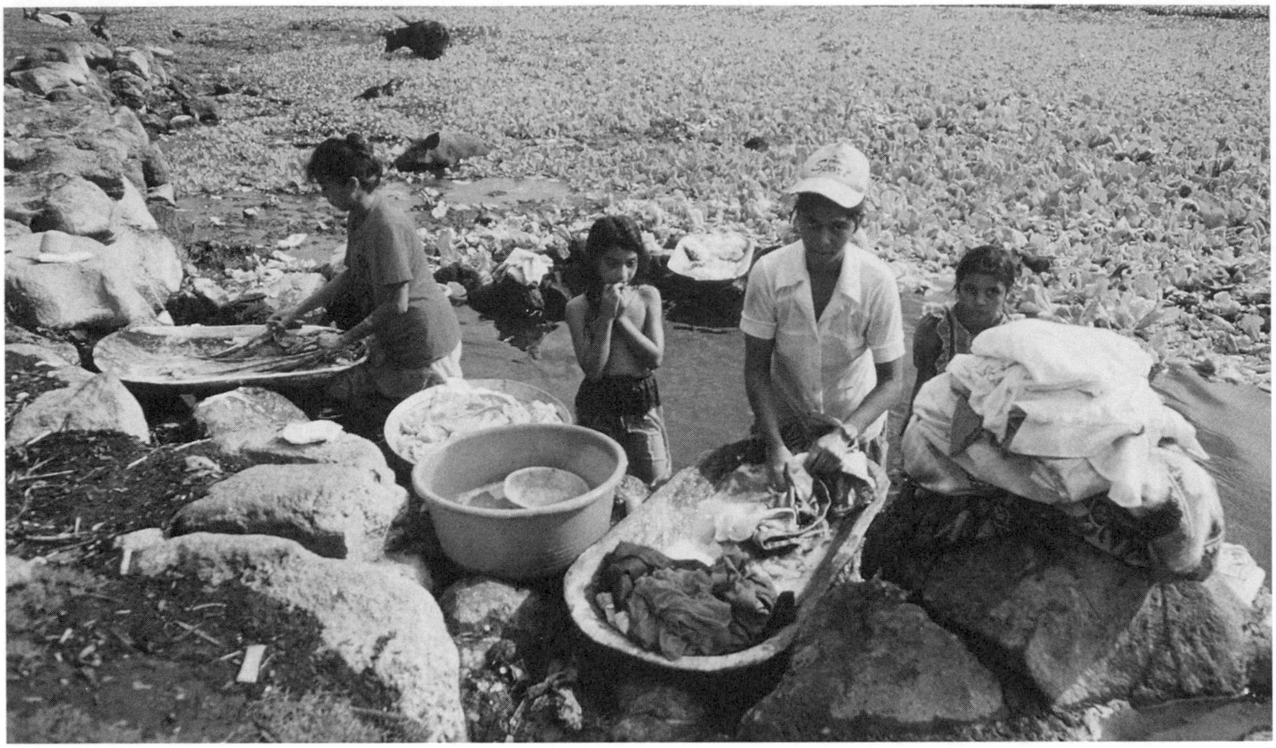

People washing clothes in a lagoon. About half the population of El Salvador lives below the national poverty line.

The FMLN formed a political party after disarming at the end of the war. It has gained political ground since the end of the war, winning a majority of Assembly seats and the mayor's office in San Salvador in 1997. The FMLN is considered a socialist alternative to ARENA, which is seen as protecting the interests of the rich. There has been internal dissent within the FMLN.

The Partido Democrata Cristiano (PDC), which was formed in 1960, failed to address human rights atrocities. Other parties include the Partido Convergencia Democrática, founded in 1993; the Partido Liberal Democrático, founded in 1994; the Partido Popular Laborista, founded in 1997; and the Partido Unión Social Cristiano, founded in 1997.

Social Problems and Control. The number of violent deaths resulting from crime in 1996 was greater than the number of deaths resulting from the conflict during any year of the civil war. In that same year, the murder rates in some parts of the country were among the highest in the Western Hemisphere. Many crime victims do not report crimes to the authorities because of continuing mistrust of the courts and police. The National Civilian Police have poorly trained officers and few resources to investigate crimes. Corrupt courts release criminals, who then seek revenge on those who reported them to the police. Vigilante groups have formed to fight crime by assassinating criminals. Most residents feel that these groups bear a strong resemblance to the former death squads.

Military Activity. The military and paramilitary forces have had an enormous influence on the national culture. From 1932 to 1993, every president but one was an army general. During the civil war the country was highly militarized, with 32,000 soldiers. In spite of the current demilitarization, the culture remains militarized, as evidenced by the high rate of violent crime, armed guards in front of most urban businesses, and the presence of vigilantes.

Social Welfare and Change Programs

Government expenditures on health and education programs declined during the war. The government committed to large expenditures in social welfare programs with the signing of the peace accords to end the civil war. There has been increased spending in health and education, and a number of rural schools have been opened through a special government program. Some health care is provided to students through the Escuela Saludable program. El Salvador has paid for these programs in part through generous foreign aid. The government has also tried to pay for some of these social welfare programs through more efficient collection of the value added tax (VAT).

The transfer of land back to the people at the end of the war and the implementation of agricultural loans also represent massive government and United States-supported social change programs.

Nongovernmental Organizations and Other Associations

Nongovernmental organizations (NGOs) flourished during the war as a result of the civil population's desire for peace, democracy, and development. The NGOs continued to support alternative political, economic, and social projects in the areas which had been most affected by the war and have begun to coordinate their efforts on a national level.

Since the signing of the peace accords, NGOs have grown in importance and experience, particularly in rural zones. They often are connected to the FMLN and have helped distribute land to former combatants, and have represented rural communities politically. They are often involved in rural education, various development projects, agricultural or small business loans, technical assistance, veterinary services, and health services.

Gender Roles and Statuses

Division of Labor by Gender. During the civil war, many women began to take leadership positions outside the traditional domestic sphere, becoming leaders in popular organizations and base Christian communities. While women were often placed in ''supportive roles,'' cooking for the troops and sewing, many became combatants and held key military and political leadership positions in the FMLN.

Although women often work outside the home generating income, they are exclusively responsible for housework and child care.

The Relative Status of Women and Men. Women also began to realize that the revolution could not end the inequalities in society without addressing inequality between men and women. Each of the five branches of the FMLN has its own women's organizations. In those organizations women have fought for women's rights to work outside the home; loans for women's cooperatives and small, women-owned businesses; education; medical care; and economic support for children.

Fathers' abandonment of families increased after the war, and economic support for children is still rare. Families headed by single women often live in extreme poverty, and women are forced to work for low wages. Women's mean salary is 28 percent lower than men's and almost one-third of girls under age sixteen work to support the family. Women are also under-represented in politics.

Violence toward women occurred during the war, and has continued at an alarming rate. Violent crime including murder and rape increased after the signing of the peace accords. Domestic abuse, along with alcohol abuse, is said to be prevalent.

Marriage, Family, and Kinship

Marriage. Among the poor, marriage is the decision of the couple. The most common kind of marriage is informal: a man and a woman set up a household and have children without a civil or church service. These unions are recognized under law but can be dissolved easily. However, men are now required to support children conceived in common law marriage as well as with women with whom they have no formal relationship.

A marriage performed in a church is considered irreversible, and many people wait until they have children to marry. Couples must be 18 years old to marry unless the woman is pregnant or already has children. In both civil and religious marriages, divorce law requires a separation and a cause. The Catholic Church and many Evangelical churches never condone divorce.

Domestic Unit. The domestic unit generally consists of a couple and their children, although other relatives also may live in the household. The man is nominally the head of the household, but women, especially in poorer families, often provide economic support for their children. A large proportion of families are headed by single women.

Kin Groups. The extended family is very important in the national culture. A woman can count on her cousins, uncles, aunts, and grandparents on both sides for support. The Family Code recognizes the importance of the extended family and requires various categories of kin to support their relatives with food, clothing, housing, health care, and education. Either spouse may be required to pay support to the other. Grandparents may be asked to support grandchildren, and vice versa. Parents must support their children, and brothers and sisters may be required to pay support to their siblings.

A road through the village of El Jocotal. Rural housing is typically built of adobe and features a large front porch.

SOCIALIZATION

Infant Care. Infants in poor families are cared for by their mothers, who take them along on their daily tasks. They sleep in a room with their parents, in a crib or hammock of their own or in the parents' bed. People are affectionate with babies and play and talk with them often. They are breast-fed on demand and are not weaned until eighteen months or two years of age. In the upper middle and upper classes, child care often is delegated to a nanny.

Child Rearing and Education. Children are expected to show "respect" to their elders, which involves using respectful greetings and terms of address. They are expected to be obedient and comply with requests from adults immediately. Children may be hit or reprimanded after age six or seven years for not complying with adults' requests, complaining, or answering back. Shaming is another method used to discipline children. Parents loudly complain about a misbehaving child to another adult or child, within earshot of the offending child. Shaming most often occurs in regard to completing assigned tasks, school performance, and propriety in matters such as dress.

Basic education is compulsory until age thirteen, but half the children ages six to sixteen in the poorest families do not attend school. Nine of ten children of the richest families attend school, and a quarter go on to study at a university. Poor families often cannot afford to pay school fees or pay for shoes and school supplies.

Higher Education. Higher education is not emphasized and accounts for a small part of the government budget. Professors and students at the Universidad Centramericana and the National University were killed in the war, and neither university has been given the resources to recover. There has been an explosion of private colleges offering professional and technical degrees, but these schools are not respected and prepare students badly.

ETIQUETTE

Respect is due to older persons from younger person, and to higher-status persons from lower-status individuals. This includes using titles of respect before people's names and using the formal "you" ("*usted*"). Women must show respect to men, should not raise their voices to them, and must serve them food on demand. Greetings are necessary upon entering a store or, in small towns and communities, passing someone on the street. Failure to greet a person is considered offensive.

A Salvadoran man works on his fishing net. Many Salvadorans are employed in low-paying, "informal economy" jobs.

Religion

Religious Beliefs. El Salvador is 75 percent Roman Catholic but has a growing Protestant movement. The Catholic Church returned to its traditional conservative stance after the end of the civil war. Among Protestant denominations, Pentecostal and fundamentalist sects—called evangelical churches—have had the largest growth. There are a number of reasons for the growth of evangelical churches in the last two decades of the twentieth century. First, Catholics were often targets of government repression for their "subversive" involvement in base Christian communities, while evangelicals were safe from government repression. Second, the evangelical emphasis on personal conversion is considered apolitical. Finally, small evangelical churches provide their members with a strong sense of community and family.

Religious Practitioners. While the Catholic Church has allowed greater participation of religious lay workers, the possibilities for leadership in the laity are restricted. There are more possibilities in the evangelical churches for nonspecialists to rise to leadership positions. Such positions are restricted to men.

Death and the Afterlife. Catholics devote nine nights of prayer for deceased persons so that the souls of the dead can be purified and they can rise from purgatory to heaven.

Medicine and Health Care

Most Western-trained doctors who work in clinics and hospitals are located in the metropolitan areas. In the rural zones, most health issues are dealt with by health promoters or midwives who receive some training through the Ministry of Health, a foreign organization, or a local NGO. Salvadorans often treat themselves with modern medicine bought in pharmacies or from ambulatory salesmen. There are traditional remedies for some folk illnesses. The *ojo*, or "evil eye," is said to affect babies with fever. It is cured when the person who gave the eye chews various herbs and spits them into a liquid that is rubbed on the baby's body. Traditional healers are called *curanderos*.

Secular Celebrations

Independence is celebrated on 15 September with parades. It is the only secular holiday, although many religious holidays have become secularized. Many people spend Holy Week, the week preceding Easter, at the beach.

The Arts and Humanities

Literature. Salvadoran literary production in the latter twentieth century has been concerned with a re-examination of the national history. Notable works include the novels and poetry of Manlio Argueta, the poetry of Roque Dalton, and the short stories of José Marie Mendez. The country suffers from a lack of publishing facilities.

Graphic Arts. The village of LaPalma has become famous for a school of art started by Fernando Llort. Images of mountain villages, campesinos, and Christ are painted in bright colors on a variety of wooden objects. The town of Ilobasco is known for its ceramics, while San Sebastián is known for its textile art.

Performance Arts. Most of the music on Salvadoran radio is standard pop fare from the United States, Mexico, and various Latin American countries, but there is a small underground movement of folk music which draws its inspiration from current events in El Salvador.

The State of the Physical and Social Sciences

Academia has suffered much from the war and has not been given the resources to recover. However, there has recently been increased social science research on social problems such as crime, violence, and social and economic inequality. There has also been increased interest in research on the environment. Much of this research is being conducted with funds from foreign agencies.

Bibliography

Aguayo, S., and P. Weiss. *Central Americans in Mexico and the United States*, 1988.

Argueta, Manlio. *Cuzcatlan: Where the South Sea Beats*, 1987.

Berryman, P. *Stubborn Hope: Religion, Politics and Revolution in Central America*, 1994.

Binford, Leigh. *The El Mozote Massacre: Anthropology and Human Rights*, 1996.

Clements, C. *Witness to War: An American Doctor in El Salvador*, 1984.

Craft, Linda Jo. *Novels of Testimony and Resistance from Central America*, 1997.

Dalton, Roque. *Miguel Marmol*, 1982.

A Dream Compels Us: Voices of Salvadoran Women, 1989.

Dickson-Gomez, J. "Lessons of the War: The Psychosocial Effects of the War in El Salvador." Ph.D. dissertation, University of California, Los Angeles, 1999.

Farias, P. "The Socio-Political Dimensions of Trauma in Salvadoran Refugees: Analysis of a Clinical Sample." *Culture, Medicine and Psychiatry* 15:167–192, 1991.

Garaizabal, C., and N. Vazquez. *El Dolor Invisible: Una Experiencia de Grupos de Auto-Apoyo con Mujeres Salvadorenas*, 1994.

Golden, R. *The Hour of the Poor, the Hour of Women: Salvadoran Women Speak*, 1991.

Grande, L. *Our Own Backyard: The United States in Central America*, 1990.

Lindo-Fuentes, Hector. *Weak Foundations: The Economy of El Salvador in the Nineteenth Century 1821–1898*, 1991.

Mahler, Sarah J. *American Dreaming: Immigrant Life on the Margins*, 1995.

Marenn, Lea. *Salvador's Children: A Song for Survival*, 1990.

Martin-Baro, I. "La Violencia Politica y la Guerra como Causas del Trauma Psicosocial en El Salvador." *Revista de Psicologia de El Salvador* 28: 123–141, 1988.

———. "Guerra y Trauma Psicosocial del Niño Salvadoreno." In *Psicologia de la Guerra: Trauma y Terapia*, 1990.

Suarez-Orozco, M. "Speaking of the Unspeakable: Toward Psychosocial Understanding of Responses to Terror." *Ethos* 18:335–383, 1990.

United Nations. *Report of the Commission on the Truth*, 1993.

United States Department of State. *Background Notes: El Salvador*, 1993.

Williams, Philip J. *Militarization and Demilitarization in El Salvador's Transition to Democracy*, 1997.

—Julia Dickson-Gomez

England

Culture Name

English

Alternative Names

British, Britannic

Orientation

Identification. The name of the country and the term "English" derive from the Old English word for one of the three Germanic peoples that invaded the British Isles in the fifth century C.E., the Angles. "Britain" and "British" derive from a Roman term for the inhabitants' language of the British Isles, called "Brythonic" or p-Celtic.

Englishness is highly regionalized. The most important regional divide is between the south and the north. The south, chiefly represented by the regions of the southeast, southwest, East Anglia, and the Midlands, now contains the economically most dynamic sectors of the country, including the City (the chief financial center of the United Kingdom) and the seat of the national government, both in London. The north, the cradle of industrialization and the site of traditional smokestack industries, includes Yorkshire, Lancashire, Northumberland, Cumbria, Durham, Merseyside, and Cheshire. Especially in the last decades of the twentieth century, the north has experienced deindustrialization, severe economic hardship, and cultural balkanization. England is also a culture of many smaller regionalisms, still centered on the old governmental unit of the county and the local villages and towns. Local products, such as ale, and regional rituals and art forms, such as Morris dancing and folk music, many of which date back to the preindustrial era, allow people to shape their attachments to their communities and the nation. Merged with the north–south divide and regionalism are notions of working class, middle class, and upper class as well as rich versus poor.

England's role as a destination for migration also has influenced conceptions of Englishness. Historically, the most prominent immigrant group has been the Irish, who came in two major waves in the modern era: 1847 and 1848 after the potato famine, and during and after World War II. Scots were present in England by the 1700s and settled in England in large numbers during the nineteenth and twentieth centuries, often for economic reasons. Welsh in-migration came to prominence when deindustrialization began in Wales in the 1920s. This in-migration has brought the so-called Celtic fringe into English culture in a host of ways. There has also been the impact of Jewish, Flemish, Dutch, French Huguenot, German, Italian, Polish, Turkish, Cypriot, and Chinese cultures since the twelfth century. The loss of Britain's colonies has brought Afro-Caribbeans, Bangladeshis, Pakistanis, Indians, and migrants from northwestern and eastern Africa in significant numbers. Judgments of whether England's newcomers feel themselves to be "English" vary by group and even by individual.

Location and Geography. England covers 50,357 square miles (130,423 square kilometers) of the main island of the British Isles and lies off the northwestern coast of Europe, separated from the mainland by the English Channel. The Gulf Stream makes the climate mild and rainy. The country is also divided into a highland zone and a lowland zone along a line from the mouth of the River Exe in the southwest to the mouth of the River Tees in the northeast. The highland zone's soil is poor and rocky, mainly suitable for raising livestock, but in the lowlands the land is flatter, the soil is fertile, and there are many navigable rivers. As a result of its favorable topography, the lowland region has always had the majority of the population, supported most agriculture and trade, and had the largest cities including the capital, London. The highland zone did not develop rapidly until the nineteenth century, when its coal and iron deposits allowed it to surge to prominence in the industrial revolution;

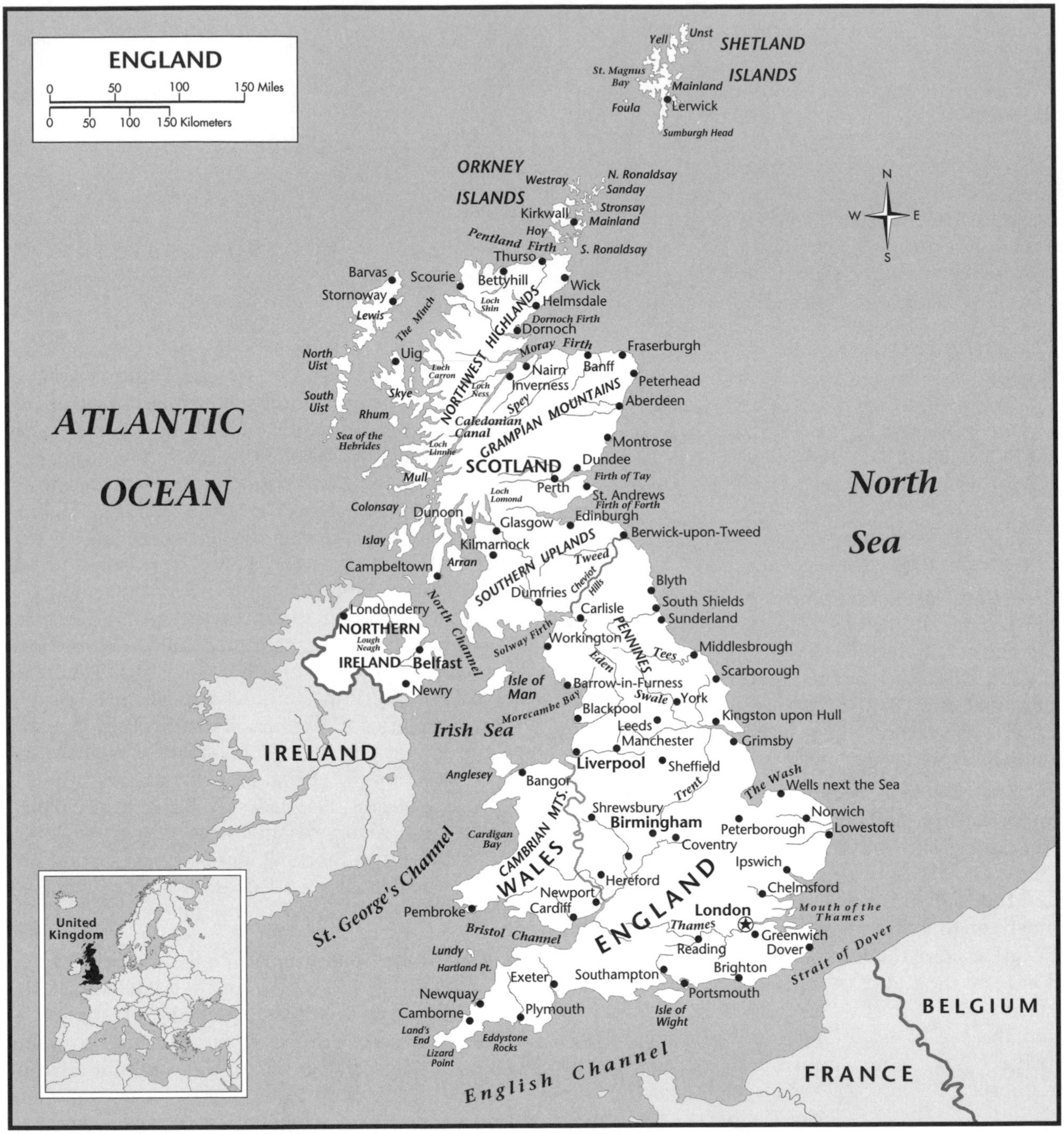

England

its communities struggle in England's postindustrial era.

Demography. The population was 49.5 million in 1998. The estimated nonwhite proportion of the population for that year was 7.3 percent, with the officially designated ethnic groups being black Caribbean, black African, black other, Indian, Pakistani, Bangladeshi, and Chinese.

Celtic in-migrations continues to be a major influence. These migrations are often urban in focus and tend to cluster in particular districts like London and Merseyside. The second important shift in demography from an ethnic standpoint is related to the end of the British Empire. Beginning in the 1950s, peoples from the Indian subcontinent and the Caribbean began to immigrate to England, taking advantage of the 1948 British Nationality Act, which established that all Commonwealth citizens enjoyed British citizenship. Most of these immigrants have settled in London, the West Midlands, Yorkshire and Merseyside. Between 1984 and 1996, the number of nonwhites in England, Scotland, and Wales rose from 2.3 million to 3.39 million (the majority of whom lived in England) for a total increase of 47 percent. In that same period Great Britain grew by just 5.8 percent and England by even less. European, Mediterranean, and East Asian immigrants have been part of the cultural landscape since the Middle Ages, when the Jewish community came to prominence and Flemish clothworkers began arriving. Immigrants to England in particular have been drawn there by the creation of a Common Market in Western Europe and the ending of restrictions on the movement of eastern Europeans.

Linguistic Affiliation. The primary language since the sixteenth century has been some version of English. English, however, is an amalgam of languages brought to the British Isles by invasions that began before written history. The Celts made Gaelic the dominant language until the Romans invaded in 55 and 54 B.C.E., and introduced Latin and Greek, but it was the invasion of England by Germanic tribes in the fifth century (Angles, Saxons, and Jutes) that laid the basis for English. The arrival of Christianity in 597 allowed English to interact with Latin as well as with Greek, Hebrew, and languages as distant as Chinese. Viking invasions a few centuries later brought Scandinavian languages to the British Isles, while the Norman invasion in 1066 introduced French. Gradually, all levels of society adopted English, which had largely supplanted Latin and French in the second half of the fifteenth century.

Modern English comes from the East Midland dialect of Middle English. This divide between the East Midland dialect and all others emerged between the fourteenth and nineteenth centuries when those speaking with a "proper" or "posh" accent separated themselves from those speaking "Cockney" or working-class English. This division is signified by the distinction between "received pronunciation" (r.p.), Standard English, or BBC English and regional or local dialects of English. This linguistic divide has always corresponded with social rank. The elite generally spoke with an r.p. accent (also known as the Queen's or King's English), and other residents spoke a non-standard, locally mediated English. In recent decades the connection between class and accent has begun to loosen.

Except in certain urban communities, bilingualism and multilingualism continue to play a minimal role in England. As of 1980 at least twelve languages other than English had more than 100,000 speakers in Britain, including Punjabi, Urdu, Caribbean patois, Hindi, and Cantonese, which are among England's more influential second languages. In the last decade, the many varieties of spoken English have been thriving. Popular culture, especially music, radio, and television, has brought English creoles and patois; Indian, Pakistani and Bangladeshi English; and Celtic versions of English into the lives of the country's inhabitants. Thus, while Standard English still holds sway, it is no longer an unquestioned standard.

Symbolism. From a political standpoint, the monarchy, Parliament, and the English (or British) constitution are central symbols with both physical and ritual manifestations. Equally powerful are the rituals surrounding Parliament's routine. The monarchy expresses itself physically through the palaces and other residences of the royal family. Ritually, the monarchy permeates national life. From the social functions of the elite, which many people follow in the popular press, to the promotion of public causes, to royal weddings, the monarchy's representatives lend an almost sacral quality to public life.

Images that capture England's past have become a very important element in how people root themselves in a society that is increasingly mobile and in which the past has become a commodity. Idealizations of village and town life from bygone days are common in the speeches of politicians. Other idealizations of the past are equally popular, from the preserved industrial landscapes of the Midlands and the north, to nature walks that refer to the ancient peoples who inhabited the area long before the English arrived, to the appearance of the "English" countryside.

In recent years, popular culture has provided ways for England's immigrants to claim Englishness publicly. Before World War II the majority population insisted that newcomers assimilate and migrants were unable to lay claims to Englishness. More integrated national sports, especially soccer, and sports heroes represent the new ethnic landscape and provide symbols the young and the poor can claim. Similarly, movies, pop music, and plays have given less powerful groups ways of claiming Englishness. Popular festivals such as the Notting Hill Carnival, which is Europe's largest celebration of black identity, are also part of the mix. The New Commonwealth population also has produced widely read literary works.

Participants in the International Worm Charming Festival, a charity event held in Devon, England.

History and Ethnic Relations

Emergence of the Nation. The emergence of the nation took place between 1200 and 1850. The first period when a quasi-national feeling was able to unify the people was the Hundred Years' War with France in the late Middle Ages (1337–1453). Although a dynastic conflict between successive English and French monarchs, this war became a cause in which Anglo-Saxon and Norman culture merged into a recognizably English culture.

In the sixteenth century, nationalism took on another component: anti-Catholicism. Henry VIII created the Church of England by tapping into popular sentiment against the Pope's interference in national affairs. Elizabeth I, his daughter, created a sense of national unity through the conflicts she orchestrated with Catholic Spain. Another manifestation of anti-Catholic sentiment was the Battle of the Boyne in 1689, where William III routed Catholic opposition in Ireland. William subsequently affirmed Catholicism as being contrary to English and Irish law. Beginning with Scotland and Ireland in the thirteenth and fourteenth centuries and continuing with competitions with the Spanish, the Dutch, and the French between 1550 and 1816, the English established a sense of expansionary patriotism. The final step in creating a national sentiment was taken in the seventeenth and eighteenth centuries when the middle classes defined Englishness as a positive morality to which everyone could subscribe.

National Identity. English cultural roots lie in a merging of Anglo-Saxon, Danish, and Norman French culture that has existed as a synthesis since the late Middle Ages. A process of negotiation was at the heart of this cultural creation.

Ethnic Relations. After stripping them of their assets, Edward I expelled the Jewish community in 1290, and Jews did not receive full rights and recognition until the twentieth century. The earliest guest workers, Flemish clothworkers, frequently found their contributions resented by "native" labor. German, French, and Low Countries Protestant refugees in the sixteenth through eighteenth centuries were confronted with ethnic prejudices. The Irish as Celts and Catholics and the Welsh and Scots as Celts also have faced resentment, especially in eras dominated by English nationalism and British imperialism.

In the British Isles and abroad, the English record in colonized areas is no better than that of other European colonizing cultures. Beginning in the 1960s with the Immigration Acts and reaching a low point with the 1981 British Nationality Act, laws have been passed to restrict the rights of foreigners to enter the country and obtain citizenship and benefits. The support of Margaret Thatcher's government for free-market capitalism contributed to the decline of the areas where most ethnic minorities lived, sparking violent protests in the 1980s, such as London's Brixton riots in 1981. Antiracism legislation and the improving economy have lessened public and official attention to the nonwhite population. However, economic migrants and political refugees, chiefly from East Asia, eastern Europe, and Africa, have taken the place of the nonwhite populace as objects of public concern.

Urbanism, Architecture, and the Use of Space

England's urbanism and notions of landscape and countryside are closely tied to the movement of people and economic sectors from major metropolitan areas into new towns, extensions of older towns, smaller towns, villages, and remote rural areas. Cities are thought of as places of decay and degeneration by many people. The central principle in definitions of urban communities is their management and containment; this has been done by designating rings of nondevelopment (green belts) around major cities and urban areas. The emphasis on areas of nondevelopment also has influenced planning within cities and towns, with space being created for private and public gardens, parks, athletic fields, and other so-called greenfield sites. There has also been an emphasis on arranging cities and towns in more livable units, with more thought to the placement of work sites, public amenities, shopping areas, and dwellings and more of a focus on how streets cater to public and private uses.

Villages and small towns that were fairly local or regional have become bedroom communities for large cities such as London or parts of larger regional urban networks. Sometimes they retain their original character, but more often affluent newcomers have changed these localities. Thus, while those in suburban, village, and small-town areas trumpet the rural nature of their lives, they have altered the rural landscape. Outside the towns and villages, two forces dominate the countryside: highly commercialized agriculture and preservation. Agribusiness has played a role in defining the countryside by destroying 95 percent of the nation's wetlands. Countering the trend toward developing the countryside to accommodate more housing are the preservationists, who want to expand parks, preserve a traditional country way of life, and keep urban dwellers out of these areas. Left out of towns, cities, villages, and rolling hills are those with no money and no political voice. Those most excluded from current visions and proposals are the poor and the urban-dwelling ethnic minority groups.

Many different types of Englishness compete in towns, cities, villages, and the countryside. Architecturally, little is left from the Celtic, Anglo-Saxon and Roman periods, although Roman town planning, roads, and walls are still evident and Anglo-Saxon churches and Celtic monuments are still standing. The Middle Ages have left Gothic and Romanesque architecture while the Tudor and Stuart periods of England's history have also left their contributions, notably not just in buildings for the elite and the state but also for the middling sort. The eighteenth century saw Georgian and neo-Gothic architecture, which continued into the nineteenth century when neo-Classical styles arose. The twentieth century has seen the rise of suburban building styles and Modernism and reactions against both in the form of conservation, community architecture, and a tendency to revive old styles such as neo-Classicism.

Government buildings serve a range of symbolic purposes. Monuments more often symbolize particular historical figures or events. The purposes of public spaces also vary. The pews in a typical church promote an orderly separation between congregants while emphasizing togetherness as a congregation. Piccadilly Circus and many museums encourage people to mingle. Tea rooms, coffee shops, public houses, and nightclubs provide separate seating but promote a social atmosphere. People in England prefer to live in detached, suburban dwellings, ideally with a garden. First built in large numbers in the 1920s, many suburban houses were built in twos with a garden in front and rear. Another detached style was the single-story bungalow, which also became popular in the 1920s. Although in the post-war era it became common to build large, boxy modernist apartment blocks, especially for public housing, suburban building continued in additional new towns, some of which used the uniform, modernist styles. Since the 1980s more traditional designs for housing have been popular and both detached and non-detached housing have been constructed to evoke one of England's past eras. In private dwelling spaces, the English tend to fill much of the available space.

Food and Economy

Food in Daily Life. England is known for its bland cuisine. Traditional middle-class notions of diet put

Blossoming croplands in Kent.

meats at the heart of the main meal, which usually was eaten at midday. Along with this main course, there might be a dish such as a meat casserole, and fish also was consumed. Heavy sauces, gravies, soups and stews or puddings (savory and sweet), and pasties and pies also were eaten. Vegetables included potatoes and carrots, turnips and cabbage, and salad vegetables. Fruit was also part of the diet, though in small proportions. Lighter meals included variations of the sandwich. Breakfast foods ranged from hot cereals to tea, toast, and marmalade, to steak, eggs, and kidneys. These foods were not available to most people before World War II. The rural poor, for example, ate a diet based on cheese and bread, with bacon eaten a few times a week, supplemented by fresh milk if available, cabbage, and vegetables if a garden was kept. All the classes drank tea; beer was drunk by the working classes and other alcoholic beverages were drunk by the middle and upper classes.

Since 1950, the English have eaten less red meat, more poultry, and about the same amount of fish. The consumption of fats is down, and that of alternatives such as margarine is up. Fresh fruits are in favor, while vegetables are not, and the focus is on salad vegetables. The main meal is now eaten in the evening and is likely to consist of frozen or ready-made food. In addition to eating out in pubs, inns, and restaurants, people consume fast food. There has been a dramatic increase in the variety of foreign cuisine, ranging from Chinese and Indian to French and Italian.

There are few food-related taboos. People avoid some foods for so-called hygienic reasons, such as onions and leeks, which can cause bad breath. There are also foods that are considered uncivilized. Traditionally, the English have never eaten dogs, horses, other carnivores, or insects. Increasingly, eating meat is looked on as uncivilized. As part of the shift away from meat toward fruit, vegetables, and fish, people have become more distanced from the production of the meat they eat and less willing to eat as wide a variety of meats.

Food Customs at Ceremonial Occasions. Apart from cakes on birthdays, few special foods are eaten at major secular ceremonies, although such ceremonies involve toasting and drinking alcohol. In religious ceremonies, alcohol, usually wine, is common at most celebrations of the Eucharist in Christian churches and also is used at Jewish ceremonies. On Shrove Tuesday, which is both a secular and a religious occasion, many people eat pancakes.

Basic Economy. The economy is developed and highly specialized, and very few inhabitants produce food and other necessities for themselves. In

1998, approximately 13 percent of England's workforce was self-employed, many working in agriculture, fishing, and construction. This group and the few among the economically inactive (21 percent in 1998) who have opted out of the market economy completely are the only people in England who may produce goods for themselves. Given that the majority of both groups are part of the regular economy, the number of people who are completely self-sufficient is small, although at times they are politically and culturally prominent. A rough sense of England's dependence on the world can be gained by looking at trade figures as a proportion of GDP. In 1997 England's exports amounted to about 29 percent of GDP, as did imports.

Land Tenure and Property. The most common form of land tenure is the owner-occupied house, with personal ownership in 1998 at 68 percent and the remainder of the inhabitants renting government-owned rent-controlled or private dwellings. Most dwellings are in urban areas, which occupied about 12 percent of the total land area in 1999. In that same year, 71 percent of England's land was devoted to agriculture: 24 percent was rented and the remaining 47 percent was owned by resident farmers or farming enterprises. Legal rights to property have their origin in the period 1500–1800, when landholders enclosed land and claimed exclusive ownership of it. Their actions extinguished many customary use rights to land and established private claims to rights-of-way. In addition to this division between private and common land, many forms of public and semipublic land have developed. Roads, infrastructure, and official buildings are often public. Also subject to public control are the national parks and nature reserves. Areas of Outstanding Natural Beauty are often in private hands but are under public supervision of the Countryside Agency. Public rights-of-way and common lands are often owned by individuals, but those owners may be obligated to ensure public access. The Department of the Environment, Transport, and the Regions oversees land use, working with local authorities, an arrangement in place since the 1947 Town and Country Planning Act.

Commercial Activities. In addition to manufacturing, the major sectors of the economy are financial services, wholesale and retail trade, communication technology, and education and social services.

Major Industries. The major areas of industrial output are textiles; food, beverages, and tobacco; paper, paper products, wood products; chemicals; metals and fabricated metal items; electrical and optical equipment; and transport equipment and other machinery.

Division of Labor. People with more experience still tend to hold positions with greater responsibility and rewards, but this situation has been changing since the 1970s. Increasingly, older workers are losing jobs because of business strategies to keep workforces small. This trend has hit older working class men particularly hard because the sectors in which they work are rapidly being shifted out of the economy. Ethnic prejudice, ageism, and sexism still prevent many people from advancing. Specialization, educational attainment, and status correspond fairly well, with managerial and professional groups being at the top of society, followed by white-collar workers and then skilled blue-collar workers and semi-skilled and unskilled manual laborers.

SOCIAL STRATIFICATION

Classes and Castes. Class is the primary way in which people approach social stratification. The upper class (the landed gentry, the titled nobility, and members of the royal family) has roughly the same social position it has had since the nineteenth century, when the middle classes began to compete successfully with the landed interests for influence. However, the upper class lost official political influence (and credibility) in the twentieth century. The major change in England's social identity structure has been the shrinking number of workers in manufacturing and the increasing number of people who work in service industries. White-collar and other service workers have replaced blue-collar workers as England's economic backbone. Consequently, the middle class has increased in size and wealth, and home ownership has increased, while union membership has declined dramatically, along with the size of the traditional industrial working class.

Most workers expect unemployment at some point in their careers, especially the unskilled and uneducated. In 1983, only 5 percent of non-manual workers were unemployed. In contrast, skilled manual workers experienced 12 percent and semi-skilled and unskilled manual workers 23 percent unemployment, and manual workers combined accounted for 84 percent of the unemployed.

England is becoming a society of the included and the excluded. There has been a sharp rise in long-term unemployment. The nature of work in a fluid economy does not support long-term employ-

A busy street in Scarborough, York. English architecture is a unique blend of old and new.

ment for low-skilled and moderately skilled workers, and this is reflected in the rise in part-time (24.7 percent of the 1999 workforce), and multiple-job workers. Homelessness has become a fact of English life, with 102,410 families in England accepted as homeless in 1997 alone.

The richest class has increased its share of the national income and national assets. In 1995, the wealthiest 10 percent of the population owned half the assets controlled by households. In 1997 the income of the top 20 percent of households was four times that of the bottom 20 percent. Meanwhile, those earning less than half of the median doubled between 1979 and 1998, reaching 10 percent.

Ethnic minorities have not fared well in the new economic environment. For all minority men, unemployment was 17 percent in the period 1986–1988, for example, compared with 10 percent for whites. Ten years on, in the period 1997–1998, unemployment rates of Pakistanis, Bangladeshis, and blacks were more than three times those for whites. Indians, on the other hand, have faired better, currently occupying a central position in the middle class as entrepreneurs and in the professions, enjoying chances of employment more comparable to whites.

Symbols of Social Stratification. Many of the traditional symbols of social difference have undergone change. Clothing and other consumer goods historically were indicators of class, but are now more ambiguous. Most consumer goods are widely available, and the clothing and fashion industries recycle styles so quickly that rank and clothing do not always correspond. Education, which used to be a clear way to divide people into classes, has also lost some of its defining power. Private primary and secondary schools increased their share of school age children through 1990, and higher education has expanded the number of places available to those who want postsecondary training; by the mid 1990s more than 30 percent of students age eighteen were attending a university. Oxford and Cambridge have been accepting students from an increasingly broad socioeconomic spectrum, and students now have many more universities to choose from. Accent also has become a less reliable class signifier.

Political Life

Government. Unlike Scotland and Wales, England does not have a separate parliament or departments to represent and manage it. Contact with the central government is increasingly achieved through nine Government Offices for the Regions. Day-to-day life in the community is governed by local authorities such as district and parish councils.

Leadership and Political Officials. Political parties and institutions favor those judged to be respectable and, in senior positions, those with political experience. Thus, in the Conservative Party, only members of Parliament (MPs) can elect party leaders. It is still common for politicians and judges to have an elite education and a privileged background. Local politics is a mixed bag, with some local authorities and town and village councils politically polarized and others less so, although the larger the community the more likely it is to be dominated by the Labour Party. In general, those who participate in local politics and local organizations such as arts councils knew someone in government before becoming involved.

England has no national parties that affiliate specifically with the national culture. The main parties are the Labour Party (now often called New Labour), the Conservative Party (Tories), and the Liberal Democrats.

Access to political leaders is achieved most effectively through voluntary sector interest groups. These organizations work with local government authorities, local agencies such as the police, individual MPs, and central government ministries and may acquire an official role.

Social Problems and Social Control. For purposes of policing and criminal justice, England and Wales are treated as one unit. Policing is handled by forty-one locally organized police forces in addition to the Metropolitan Police Service and the City of London police force. Most police officers carry a nightstick, with only designated officers carrying sidearms. Persons suspected of committing a crime may be stopped and searched. More extensive searching is possible with authorization from a senior officer. For most crimes the police require judicial authorization to make arrests, but for "arrestable" offences such as murder, authorization is unnecessary. The maximum period of detention without a charge being leveled is ninety-six hours. The Police Complaints Authority handles cases of police brutality. The national policing bodies are the National Crime Squad and the National Criminal Intelligence Service. The Home Secretary of the United Kingdom has overall responsibility for policing in England as well as for the prison service, the probation service, and the criminal law.

Criminal law is a combination of statute law made by Parliament and common law (case law). Founded in 1985, the Crown Prosecution Service prosecutes criminals arrested by the police. The court system is adversarial, and the accused is defended by a lawyer (a solicitor or barrister) who attempts to disprove the case presented by the Crown Prosecution Service. Cases that go to Crown Court involve a trial by a jury of the accused person's peers with guidance from the presiding judge. In all other cases not on appeal, the defendant is tried in magistrate court by a judge who decides the case with the assistance of a law clerk. The accused or the Crown may appeal a judgment to a higher court, with the highest court being the House of Lords. Except for treason and a few other offenses, the highest penalty is a custodial sentence.

Since the 1980s, ideas about the role of the criminal justice system have been changing, largely as a result of perceived and real increases in violent and property crimes. Local communities with their informal mechanisms for social control are considered an important part of criminal justice. Neighborhood watch schemes have become popular, and victim-offender mediation and reparation, community mediation, and neighborhood mediation have emerged. Police cautioning, in which juvenile offenders and their parents or guardians are informed of the seriousness of their offenses, has become popular. Parole boards administer the punishment of offenders in the community, and the police and other official agencies have formed partnerships with local communities and voluntary organizations. Some people are critical of the trend toward integrating informal social control into the official criminal justice apparatus. They argue that such social control may result in a culture divided into communities suspicious of outsiders. Others have noted that vigilantism, which plays a relatively small role in the culture (exceptions are street gangs, less organized groupings of males termed "the lads," and soccer hooligans), may take root.

Military Activity. Military activity is administered through the armed forces of the United Kingdom, which are directed by the United Kingdom Ministry of Defense.

Social Welfare and Change Programs

Social welfare and change programs are directed toward people who cannot care for themselves (the elderly, children and youth, and the disabled), those in poverty, and those experiencing discrimination. Local government social services authorities provide for children and youth, the elderly, and the disabled, and there are advisory and regulatory bodies such as the National Disability Council and the Mental Health Act Commission. For the elderly, the disabled, and those with learning disabilities, major services include supervised residential and day care, help for those confined to the home, support services for family members caring for those individuals, and counseling. Increasingly, government policy has aimed services for the elderly, the disabled, and persons with learning disabilities at helping those people live at home and in the community. The mentally ill are treated locally, though since there are fewer places for the mentally ill in large hospitals, this has meant farming out patients to smaller hospitals and private and charity-supported facilities. Local authorities have the responsibility for child welfare, and provide aid to families such as advice, guidance, counseling, and day care. They also protect abused children and care for children without parents.

The poor and the unemployed receive support from the Department of Social Security (DSS). The major beneficiaries are the unemployed, families in need, those with short-term or long-term disability, widows, and elderly retirees. Since the early 1980s, more conditions have been placed on the receipt of DSS benefits, with the exception of the elderly and those unable to work. The unemployed,

A row of houses in Shaftesbury, Dorset. Many small villages have made an effort to preserve classic English architecture.

for example, must demonstrate they are looking for work to receive benefits.

Social change programs for ethnic minorities and women are in their infancy. There is a Race Equality Unit in the central government, and the 1976 Race Relations Act set up the Commission for Racial Equality that oversees over one hundred racial equality councils. These changes have not diminished ethnic inequality and tensions, although Britain has a minister for women, a Women's Unit, and an Equal Opportunity Commission (EOC) as well as an umbrella group known as the Women's National Commission.

Nongovernmental Organizations and Other Associations

The Charity Commission for England and Wales registered 188,000 charities in 1998. Across the United Kingdom, charities employed 485,000 people and supervised three million volunteers in 1998. With the move toward privatization in the 1980s, charities became more important, but social and economic dislocation have made it difficult for them to maintain the social safety net. Nongovernmental organizations work with children and youth; marginalized or disadvantaged groups such as the poor, the elderly, the disabled, and those suffering from inequality; environmental conservationists; the science and technology sector; the arts; and the humanities.

Gender Roles and Statuses

Division of Labor by Gender. Gender roles assign homemaking, other domestic activities, and most unpaid labor to women. A man's sense of self is defined chiefly in terms of the paid work he can obtain. The impact of these constructions of gender is now much different than before, but is still felt in English society.

The Relative Status of Women and Men. Although there is no equal rights amendment, in recent decades there has been a more noticeable commitment to equality of opportunity for men and women through bodies such as the Equal Opportunity Commission and laws such as the Abortion Act of 1967 and the 1969 Divorce Act. The rate of women's (especially married women's) participation in the workforce increased in the late twentieth century, as did the nature of that participation. In 1971, only 57 percent of women of working age were economically active, but in 1998 that figure was 72 percent, whereas men's participation declined from 91 percent to 84 percent. Despite their importance in the workforce, women earn only 80 percent of what men do. Women have been confined to lower-status work, are more likely to work part-time, and are under-represented in elite jobs. However, some women have obtained high-status, formerly male-dominated work, and the status of female-dominated work has risen. Women's increasing participation in political life and their progress in religious roles in society—the rise of women MPs in the 1990s and the Church of England's agreement to ordain women priests in 1994—may be an indication of this.

Women have probably made the least progress in the social sphere. They were the victims in 70 percent of cases of domestic violence in 1998, and women still perform most unpaid work, such as running households and raising children. Gender roles among particular subgroups, however, diverge from this picture. Some Muslim and Jewish women are more involved in the domestic sphere, and Afro-Caribbean community women are more likely to be employed and have a higher status than Afro-Caribbean men.

Marriage, Family, and Kinship

Marriage. Among many members of the South Asian and Jewish communities, arranged marriages as a means of cementing family alliances are the norm. Most inhabitants, however, decide independently whom to marry, often choosing to cohabit with the partner before marriage. Social position, social aspirations, and informal social control drive the choice of a marriage partner. Thus, marriages across class lines are not common, especially among unskilled workers and the professional and managerial classes. Marriages across ethnic lines also are not common. As a reason for marriage, economic security is prominent, but so is the desire for sexual and social companionship. In 1997, about half the population over age sixteen was married. While marriage between a man and a woman remains the primary model for long-term relationships, it is not the only one. Same-sex unions and so-called blended families are increasingly common, and experimentation with forms of quasi-polygamy has taken place.

Domestic Unit. The basic domestic unit is a household headed by a married couple—a model that accounted for 59 percent of the households in 1998. Close to 73 percent of inhabitants live in a family headed by a couple (though not necessarily a married couple). It is uncommon for couples to live with the kin of either partner. Current gender roles dictate that men are the primary breadwinners and women are responsible for household management. Who actually controls the household on a daily basis, however, varies by household. Single-parent, usually female-headed households are on the rise, accounting for 9 percent of all households in 1998. The extended family is a visible and important social institution in the South Asian, Asian, Afro-Caribbean, and Jewish communities and still plays a role in the majority population. People living alone represented 28 percent of households in 1998.

Inheritance. Children rarely depend on inherited wealth to become independent and usually inherit movable property rather than real estate. When real estate is involved, it often consists of a home and the attached land, not agricultural land. Most people follow the principle of equal division of inherited wealth among offspring, with some favoritism toward biological offspring in blended families.

Advertisements and a sign for the public underground subway in London's busy Piccadilly Circus.

Kin Groups. People envision themselves as part of a set of interconnected families, the size of which varies with marital status and family traditions. Most people include three to four generations of people in their kin group. Those who are married count the same number of generations of the spouse's family as part of their family. Kin groups do not have prominent status in society formally or informally. Notions of kinship involve a network of individuals who enter into kin relationships. The individual is not subsumed by the kin structure.

Socialization

Infant Care. Good mothering entails stimulating an infant through play and other activities. Many other aspects of infant care are class-specific. For example, middle-class mothers are likely to breast feed babies and wean them early, while working-class mothers tend to use bottle feeding and wean infants later. Middle-class infants are more likely to sleep in a separate room in a crib than are their working-class peers. Working-class infants also are more likely to receive physical chastisement for crying. Working-class fathers are not likely to participate in the upbringing of infant children because of the difficulty of obtaining time off.

Child Rearing and Education. A good child is often termed well adjusted, as opposed to children who are shy, withdrawn, overly aggressive, or hyperactive. Typically, people see children's behavior as the result of interactions with those around them, with the parents being the primary influence. Some children are viewed as having health problems that affect behavior, requiring medical intervention. There are two major areas of emphasis in child-rearing practices and beliefs. First, adults, particularly parents, need to teach children and young adults how to behave by setting limits to what they can and cannot do, teaching them how to solve conflicts and deal with others, and modeling good behavior. Second, adults should stimulate children to learn and be curious and creative to promote the growth of their mental capacities. Children are supposed to be well behaved but capable of interacting with their peers without shyness and should be curious and inquisitive as learners. Models for learning, teaching, and parenting involve intense interaction between teacher and learner and parent and child. Major secular initiation ceremonies for children and young adults revolve around the educational process and clubs. School graduation ceremonies are a primary rite of passage for most children and young adults. Hazing is used to initiate junior members of clubs, schools, and street gangs.

There are three levels of schooling below the university level: preschool, primary school, and secondary school. Depending on the kinds of knowledge tested at the secondary levels, schools emphasize practical knowledge and problem solving as much as the mastery of a body of knowledge.

Higher Education. Government policy since the late 1950s has been aimed at expanding the opportunities for students to benefit from postsecondary education to create a more skilled workforce and increase social mobility. In the 1990s, more than 30 percent of all eighteen-year-olds were attending a university (up from under 5 percent in 1960), although the recent introduction of student fees may cause some to discontinue their education.

Etiquette

Etiquette is changing, but norms for appropriate behavior articulated by the elite and the middle class are still an important normative force. Greetings vary by the class or social position of the person with whom one is dealing. Those with titles of nobility, honorific titles, academic titles, and other professional titles prefer to be addressed by those titles, but like people to avoid calling too much attention to a person's position. Unless invited to do so, one does not call people by their nicknames. Postural norms are akin to those in other Western cultures; people lean forward to show interest and cross their legs when relaxed, and smiles and nods encourage conversation. The English expect less physical expression and physical contact than do many other societies: handshakes should not be too firm, social kissing is minimal, loud talking and backslapping are considered inappropriate, staring is impolite, and not waiting one's turn in line is a serious social blunder.

In conversation the English are known for understatement both in humor and in other forms of expression. On social occasions, small talk on neutral topics is appropriate and modest gifts are given. People reciprocate in paying for food and drink in social exchanges, by ordering drinks by rounds, for example. In public houses (bars), appropriate etiquette includes not gesturing for service. In restaurants it is important to keep one's palms toward the waiter, and tips are in the range of 10 to 15 percent. Standard table manners include holding the fork in the left hand and the knife in the right hand, tipping one's soup bowl away when finishing, and not leaning one's elbows on the table. Deviations from these norms occur in ethnic subcultures and among the working class. These groups usually develop their own version of etiquette, appropriating some rules from the majority standard while rejecting others.

Religion

Religious Beliefs. In 1998, approximately 10 percent of the population claimed to be atheists and 15 percent said they were agnostics, while 20 percent said they believed in God. In 1991, about 25 percent of inhabitants claimed to believe in astrology and good luck charms, and 42 percent believed in fortune-telling and faith healing. The major religious traditions are Christianity, Islam, Hinduism, Sikhism, Judaism, and Buddhism. In recent decades, so-called pagan or cult religions have included Wicca, shamanism, heathenism, druidry, goddess religion, the Unification Church, and Transcendental Meditation.

Religious Practitioners. Christian leaders derive power and authority from their control and dispensation of sacraments. Jewish rabbis and Islamic imams derive their authority from their mastery of a specific set of religious legal texts and the application of those texts to everyday life. Hinduism relies on a wide variety of texts, and traditionally its primary leaders gain authority from their caste position as well as from their adherence to specific ascetic rules and, especially in the case of gurus, their perceived connection to the divine. Sikhism is a monotheistic religion with a single set of texts, and ideally Sikhs associate themselves with a guru who helps believers achieve spirituality. In the most popular form of Buddhism (Mahayana), monks and teachers hold spiritual authority by virtue of their ascetic way of life and mastery of certain texts. In the various forms of Buddhism, monks and teachers hold spiritual authority by virtue of their ascetic way of life, their mastery of certain texts, and their leadership of worship ceremonies. Modern paganism often envisions its priests as deriving their power through a unique connection to the hidden forces in nature. Leaders of other movements rely on charisma or the attractiveness of the skills they teach.

Rituals and Holy Places. Christians celebrate an annual cycle of rituals that vary by denomination. Most celebrate Christmas and Easter and attend services in a church on Sunday. Judaism has particular days of celebration, such as Passover, and weekly services on Saturdays in a synagogue. Islam has special celebrations (the month of Ramadan) and weekly attendance at worship services in a mosque

The House of Parliament and Big Ben are two of London's most famous landmarks.

on Fridays. In Hinduism worship is a daily activity, often taking place at the household shrine but also at the local temple. There are festivals and feasts to honor individual deities (Ram Navami) and particular occasions in the year (e.g. Divali); some are yearly, others weekly and fortnightly. For Sikhs, regular worship at the temple is important, but there are no days that are particularly holy; Sikhs worship on Sunday. For Buddhists, worship is done both at home and at religious centers and occurs on a weekly basis; the birth of the Buddha is an important occasion that is celebrated. Alternative religions vary in where they worship, how often, and on what days.

Death and the Afterlife. In the early 1990s, about 25 percent of the population believed in life after death, although there is a wide range of practices around death. For a majority of the population, ideas about the afterlife are based on typical Victorian notions that are reinforced on television and in film: a place where life is better and those who have lived a good life are rewarded. For most people, funerals have become much cleaner, with the deceased meticulously prepared and cleaned before burial. Cemeteries are kept pristine and immaculate. Others, however, feel that the dead are very much among the living in photographs, videos, and other visual mementos. People used to remember the dead in a yearly cycle of religious days, but with the geographic spread of families, family occasions have become the occasions to recall them. There are organizations that promote awareness of how to die, from living wills to hospice care to palliative measures and euthanasia.

Medicine and Health Care

Since 1946, most people have obtained health care from a physician or other specialist attached to the National Health Service (NHS), a government-controlled and government-funded health care system. Although in the 1980s and early 1990s there were attempts to introduce market-driven principles into the NHS, and the number of privately insured inhabitants has risen; the NHS retains the principles of free services at the point of delivery, and the current Labour government has rescinded many of the measures intended to manage healthcare by market principles.

Most people believe in an approach to medicine that focuses on particular problems and illnesses as opposed to overall wellness. In this type of medicine a patient sees a medical specialist when a health complaint arises. The doctor diagnoses the problem on the basis of the patient's physical symptoms and either prescribes a treatment or sends the patient to a more specialized doctor. In recent years, a very different set of approaches to medicine and health (complementary medicine) has been informed by non-Western traditions such as traditional Chinese medicine and nonstandard approaches such as herbal lore. Rather than trying to cure a specific ailment, practitioners of complementary medicine attempt to restore the well-being of the patient's entire mind and body, often by tapping the body's capacities to heal itself. Examples of complementary medicine are acupuncture, herbal medicine, massage therapy, and healing touch.

Secular Celebrations

New Year's Eve and Day (31 December, 1 January), celebrate the beginning of the new year. April Fool's Day (1 April), is a day on which people play practical jokes on one another. The sovereign's birthday is celebrated in June. Guy Fawkes's Day (5 November) commemorates the foiling of a 1605 Catholic plot to blow up the houses of Parliament and is an occasion for fireworks and revelry. Remembrance Day (11 November) celebrates the contributions of war veterans to defending the freedom of the nation.

The Arts and Humanities

Support for the Arts. In addition to artists' earnings, support for the arts derives from the government, chiefly through the Arts Council and business and private philanthropic sources.

Literature. The elaboration of an expressly English literature began in the medieval period with Geoffrey Chaucer and continued into the Renaissance and then into the Restoration with William Shakespeare, John Milton, and John Dryden. During those periods, drama and poetry were the major literary forms, with popular literature shading into song, cartoons, and storytelling.

The eighteenth century is notable for the emergence of new literary forms such as the novel, the true crime tale, light opera, magazines, and new oral traditions associated with England's port districts. Regionalized music and storytelling from this era still provide the foundation for much currently performed folk music in England.

The nineteenth century is the age of the Romantics and the Victorians. Artists in both movements were social realists, with the Romantics known for recovering older forms and the Victorians known for highly elaborate language. Popular literature offered the penny dreadful and a profusion of magazines that published novels and other literary work serially. New oral traditions sprang up around labor protest movements such as those of the Luddites and Chartists.

In the twentieth century, writers born in England shared the stage with Commonwealth writers such as Derek Walcott, V.S. Naipaul, and Nadine Gordimer and with other non-English writers such as James Joyce, Dylan Thomas, and Alice Walker. The twentieth century also saw the continuance of the phenomenon of Anglicized émigré writers such as T. S. Eliot. Edwardians such as E. M. Forster and moderns such as D. H. Lawrence and Virginia Woolf dominated the period 1900–1950. Edwardians extended Victorian approaches, and moderns worked in older forms such as the novel and helped develop the short story.

Since World War II, the efforts of writers to stretch the bounds of genres expanded. Poetry is now performed in the form of hip-hop music or at poetry slams, while written poetry may be rooted in jazz and has lost prominence. Drama has flourished, as have filmed versions of classic and contemporary works. Novels focus on the everyday and the autobiographical, a reflection in part of women's influence on literature.

Graphic Arts. Most training of graphic artists is provided by universities and art colleges. Art has been incorporated into the school curriculum as part of the nation's educational policy, and all English students receive some training in and exposure to the graphic arts. In 1997 and 1998, 22 percent of the population over age 15 visited a gallery, museum, or other major collection, a figure that has shown little change since the late 1980s. Whether museums are egalitarian in terms of affordability and relevance, however, is debatable. The National Disability Arts Forum and similar organizations are funded by the Arts Council of England and improve access to the arts and training in the arts for the disabled population; the Arts Council promotes cultural diversity as well.

Performance Arts. The Royal Shakespeare Company and musical productions in London's West End are well attended. Musical productions range from orchestras such as the London Philharmonic to jazz, rock, and folk music. Dance forms range from classical ballet to free-form club dancing. Ticket prices limit attendance at elite forms of performance art, although statistics show that in the last decade their audience has not decreased in size.

The State of the Physical and Social Sciences

England supports research and teaching in all areas of science and the social sciences. The government funds most scientific and social scientific research. Larger private corporations and private foundations are also major players. The research sector develops applications for basic primary research in a range of fields. With a long tradition of empirical inquiry,

English scholars have often been active in applied science.

Bibliography

Allan, Graham. *Kinship and Friendship in Modern Britain,* 1996.

Black, Jeremy. *A History of the British Isles,* 1997.

Bruce, Steve. *Religion in Modern Britain,* 1995.

Buchanan, Ann. "The Background." In Ann Buchanan and Barbara L. Hudson, eds., *Parenting, Schooling and Children's Behavior,* 1998.

Burnett, John. *Idle Hands: The Experience of Unemployment, 1790–1990,* 1994.

Cannadine, David. *The Rise and Fall of Class in Britain,* 1999.

Charlesworth, Simon J. *A Phenomenology of Working Class Experience,* 2000.

Christopher, David. *British Culture: An Introduction,* 1999.

The Countryside Agency. *State of the Countryside 2000,* April 2000.

Crawford, Adam. *The Local Governance of Crime: Appeals to Community and Partnerships,* 1997.

Darien-Smith, Eve. *Bridging Divides: The Channel Tunnel and English Legal Identity in the New Europe,* 1999.

Easthope, Anthony. *Englishness and National Culture,* 1999.

Fowler, Jeanane. *Hinduism: Beliefs and Practices,* 1997.

Gillis, John. *A World of Their Own Making: Myth, Ritual and the Quest for Family Values,* 1996.

Goldthorpe, J.E. *Family Life in Western Societies: A Historical Sociology of Family Relationships in Britain and North America,* 1987.

Hakim, Catherine. *Social Change and Innovation in the Labour Market: Evidence from the Census SARs on Occupational Segregation and Labour Mobility, Part-Time Work and Student Jobs, Homework and Self-Employment,* 1998.

Hall, Peter, and Colin Ward. *Sociable Cities: The Legacy of Ebenezer Howard,* 1998.

Harper, Timothy. *Passport United Kingdom: Your Pocket Guide to British Business, Customs & Etiquette,* 1997.

Harvey, Graham, and Charlotte Hardman, eds. *Paganism Today: Wiccans, Druids, the Goddess and Ancient Earth Traditions for the Twenty-First Century,* 1995.

Heyck, Thomas William. *The Peoples of the British Isles: A New History from 1870 to Present,* 1992.

Hirschel, David J., and William Wakefield. *Criminal Justice in England and the United States,* 1995.

Hoggart, Richard. *Townscape with Figures: Farnham: Portrait of an English Town,* 1994.

Kalsi, Sewa Singh. *Simple Guide to Sikhism,* 1999.

Lehmberg, Stanford E. *The Peoples of the British Isles: A New History from Prehistoric Times to 1688,* 1992.

Lewis, Jane. *Women in Britain since 1945: Women, Family, Work and the State in the Post-War Years,* 1992.

Marwick, Arthur. *British Society Since 1945,* 1996.

———. *A History of the Modern British Isles, 1914-1999,* 2000.

McRae, Susan. "Introduction: Family and Household Change in Britain." In Susan McRae, ed., *Changing Britain: Families and Households in the 1990s,* 1999.

Mennell, Stephen. *All Manners of Food: Eating and Taste in England and France from the Middle Ages to the Present,* 1996.

Newman, Gerald. *The Rise of English Nationalism: A Cultural History, 1740–1830,* 1997.

Office for National Statistics. *Britain 2000: The Official Yearbook of the United Kingdom,* 2000.

Rock, Paul. *Helping Victims of Crime: The Home Office and the Rise of Victim Support in England and Wales,* 1990.

Samuel, Raphael. *Theatres of Memory:* Volume I, *Past and Present in Contemporary Culture,* 1994.

Strathern, Marilyn. *After Nature: English Kinship in the Late Twentieth Century,* 1992.

Web Sites

BBC News Online. "That Spiritual Touch," http://news.bbc.co.uk/hi/english/health/newsid_431000/431013.stm, 26 August 1999

Ministry of Agriculture, Fisheries and Food. "England Rural Development Programme, 2000-2006," http://www.maff.gov.uk/erdp/docs/national/programmecontentshome.htm, October 2000

National Statistics. http://www.statistics.gov.uk/statbase/2001

—Douglas Catterall

See Also: United Kingdom

Equatorial Guinea

Culture Name

Equatorial Guinean or Equatoguinean

Alternative Names

In Spanish, the official language, the country is called Guinea Ecuatorial

Orientation

Identification. As a Spanish colony, the area was formerly known as Spanish Guinea. There are two main cultural and ethnic traditions: the Fang, on the mainland, and the Bubi, on the island of Bioko.

Location and Geography. Equatorial Guinea is on the west coast of equatorial Africa, bordered by Cameroon to the north and Gabon to the south and east. The country's total area is 10,830 square miles (28,050 square kilometers; slightly smaller than the state of Maryland). This includes the mainland portion (Río Muni), as well as three coastal islets (Corisco, Elobey Grande, and Elobey Chico) and two islands (Bioko and Annobóon). The larger of these is Bioko, formerly known as Fernando Po. It lies 25 miles (40 kilometers) off the coast of Cameroon, across a bay of the Gulf of Guinea known as the Bight of Biafra, to the northwest of the continental portion of the country. In Río Muni, coastal plains rise to hills, and then to plateaus farther inland. Bioko has three extinct volcanic cones, which contain several crater lakes. Mangrove swamps lie along the coast of the island. Río Muni is mainly tropical rain forest and is home to a variety of animals, including gorillas, chimpanzees, monkeys, leopards, elephants, and crocodiles. However, the wildlife population has suffered greatly as a result of hunting.

Demography. As of 2000, the population is 474,214—80 percent of whom live on the mainland, and of that group, 90 percent are Fang. The original inhabitants of Bioko are of a group called Bubi, descendants of mainland Bantu tribes. Bioko also is home to descendants of former slaves who were freed in the nineteenth century. Many Bubi have recently immigrated to the continent, and along with other, smaller Bantu-speaking tribes, comprise the remaining 10 percent of the population in Río Muni. Minority tribes include the Kombe, Balengue, Bujebas, Ibo, and Ibibo. There is a small group of Europeans (fewer than one thousand), most of them Spanish.

Linguistic Affiliation. Spanish and French are the official languages of Equatorial Guinea, although a very small percentage of the population speaks either of them. Pidgin English is also used as a lingua franca, particularly on Bioko. Most people's daily lives are conducted in tribal languages, either Fang, Bubi, or Ibo, all of which are in the Bantu family of languages.

Symbolism. The coat of arms (which is depicted on the flag) has six yellow six-pointed stars, which stand for the mainland and the five islands that comprise the country. It also includes a picture of a silk-cotton tree.

History and Ethnic Relations

Emergence of the Nation. People of the Pygmy and the Ndowe tribes were the first inhabitants of the area that is today the mainland of Equatorial Guinea. Bantu peoples began to arrive in the twelfth and thirteenth centuries, beginning an ongoing history of tribal wars. The Fang, the most prevalent and warlike of these tribes, predominated. In the seventeenth and eighteenth centuries, the slave trade by the British, French, and Dutch pushed the Fang inland, away from the coast.

In the thirteenth century, the Bubi settled on the island of Bioko. The Portuguese arrived in the fifteenth century and named the island Fernando Po. This was part of other Portuguese holdings in the Gulf of Guinea, including São Tomé and Príncipe. At

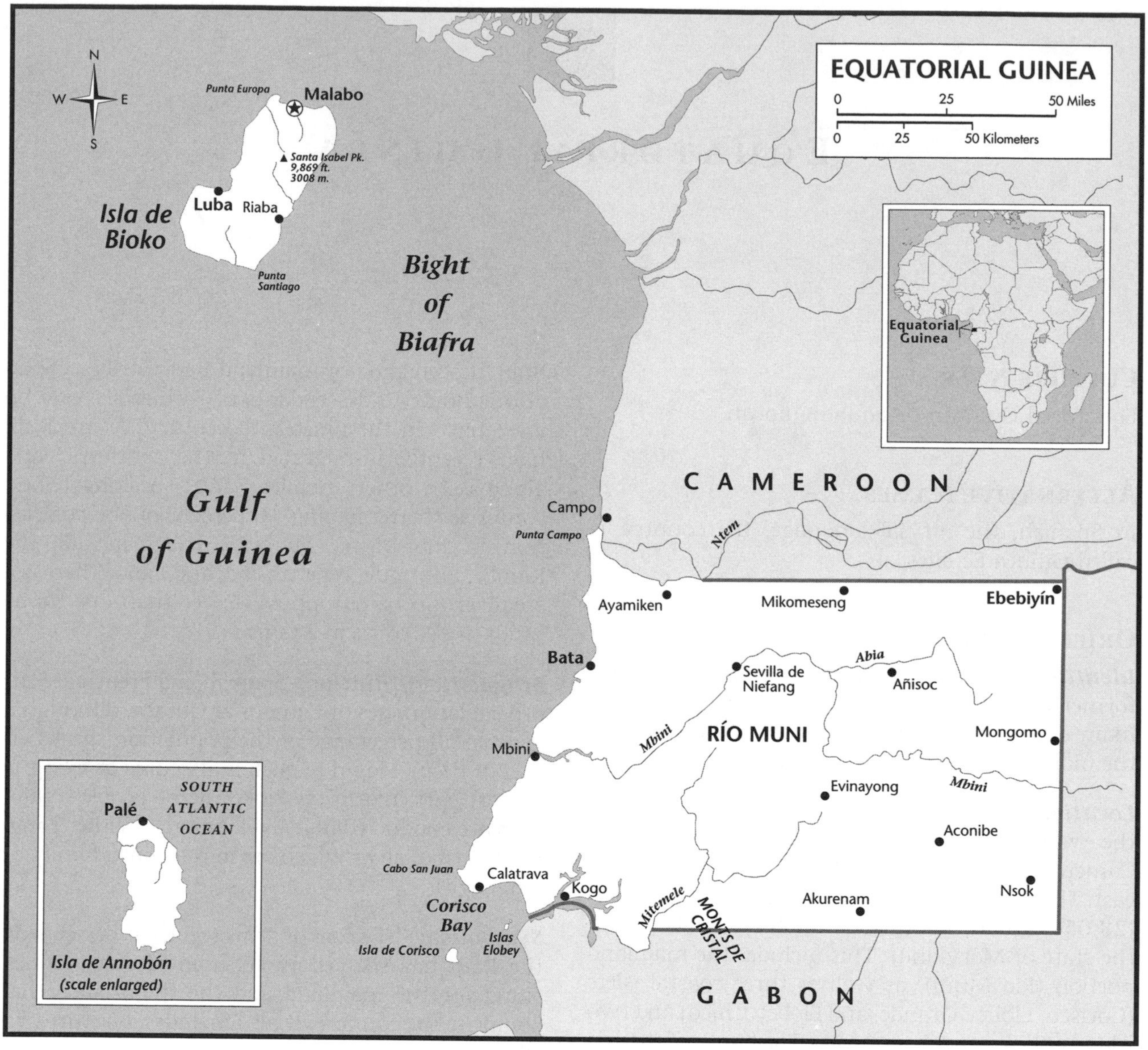

Equatorial Guinea

the end of the 1700s, Spain acquired a large area of Africa from Portugal in a trade; this area included both Río Muni and Bioko.

Bioko was important as a slave trade center, thanks to flourishing cocoa plantations there, and was one of Spain's most profitable territories in Africa. However, the island was administered by the English from 1827 until 1858, at which point the Spanish takeover became official. Spanish rule of the mainland did not begin officially until 1926, despite their long-standing claim to the area. It was only at this time that they began to expand into the interior of Río Muni, territory previously unexplored by Europeans. When the Spanish Civil War ended in 1939, the Spanish began to invest more in the development of Equatorial Guinea. The country experienced increasing prosperity with the aid of the Spanish government and the Catholic Church. Industry grew, and cocoa and timber contributed to a strong economy.

In 1963 Río Muni and Bioko were officially united as Equatorial Guinea, and Spain granted the country partial autonomy. Independence was declared in 1968. However, when Spain pulled out, they left the country in dire straits; violence and economic upheaval ensued, and the fledgling nation declared a state of emergency. The first president, Macias Nguema, ruled as a dictator for eleven years, outlawing all political parties but his own. In 1972 he declared himself ruler for life, presiding over a regime that killed and tortured thousands of its own citizens. Dissidents were sent to work camps or executed, priests were thrown in jail, and schools and churches were shut down. Journalism was declared a crime punishable by death. During this time, Equatorial Guinea had little contact with the rest of the world. By the time of his ouster and subsequent execution in 1979, Macias had managed to kill or force to flee two-thirds of the population.

The coup in 1979 put in place President Teodoro Obiang Nguema. He is part of the same small Fang subclan as Macias. Today the country is still attempting to rebuild and to establish a degree of political and economic stability. However, its record continues to be marred by human rights abuses. Elections have been held, but there are widespread suspicions of vote-rigging. The first presidential election, held in 1993, saw the arrest and imprisonment of an opposition leader. The government later released him under pressure from a number of Western countries.

National Identity. Equatorial Guineans identify first with their tribe or ethnic group, second with the nation. The current country was formed during Spanish rule, linking the main island of Bioko with the mainland territory, despite the fact that the two were culturally distinct. Since the unification of the two, there has been some intermingling and migration, particularly of mainland Fang to Bubi-inhabited Bioko. The Fang tribe itself is not limited to the Río Muni area, but extends also north into Cameroon and south into Gabon.

Ethnic Relations. Legally there is no discrimination against ethnic or racial minorities, but in practice this is not the case. The Bubi have experienced persecution under the postindependence government. Prior to independence, the group formed a majority on Bioko. However, since 1968, many Fang migrated to the island, and a small subclan, the Mongomo, has dominated the government. There is resentment and violence not only between the Bubi and the Fang but also between the Mongomo and other Fang subgroups. Immigrants from Nigeria, Ghana, and francophone Africa also are victims of discrimination and police harassment.

Urbanism, Architecture, and the Use of Space

Thirty-seven percent of the population is urban and 63 percent is rural. On the mainland, the population is dispersed fairly evenly, with the exception of Bata, which is the largest city in the country. Many of its buildings are in the Spanish colonial style and are less than perfectly maintained. Bata is a busy commercial center, with markets, bars, and restaurants. The second-largest town in Río Muni is Ebebiyin in the northeast, near the Cameroon border.

On Bioko, the majority of the population lives in Malabo, which is Equatorial Guinea's capital. The city is fairly clean, and its architecture exhibits Spanish influence. There are shantytowns as well as upper-class neighborhoods, often in close proximity to each other. Luba, with a population of one thousand, is the second-largest town on Bioko.

Food and Economy

Food in Daily Life. The main foods are cassava root, bananas, rice, and yams. People supplement their primarily plant-based diet through hunting and fishing. Palm wine and *malamba* (an alcoholic drink made from sugarcane) are both popular.

Food Customs at Ceremonial Occasions. Chicken and duck are usually served at special occasions.

Basic Economy. The economy has grown significantly in recent years with the discovery and tapping of oil reserves. Other important contributions to the GDP are forestry, fishing, and farming. Most people support themselves through subsistence farming, growing rice, yams, cassava, bananas, and palm oil nuts. Sixty-six percent of the population works in agriculture, 23 percent in services, and 11 percent in industry.

Land Tenure and Property. Most businesses are owned by government officials and their families.

Commercial Activities. The main goods produced for domestic consumption are agricultural. Bananas, cassava, coconuts, and sweet potatoes are all grown and sold locally. Much local commerce is conducted using the barter system. The country also produces timber and national gas for its own use.

Major Industries. Before independence, Equatorial Guinea's main source of income was cocoa production, but it was grown primarily by Spanish colonists, and with their departure, production fell significantly. Forestry cannot keep pace with its preindependence production rates either, as the departure of the Europeans also meant the departure of funds for the industry. The fishing industry was formerly under the control of the Soviets but is currently being developed by Spain, Nigeria, and Morocco.

Trade. Equatorial Guinea's only exports are petroleum, timber, and cocoa. Its main imports are petroleum and manufactured goods and equipment. The primary trading partners are the United States, Spain, France, China, Cameroon, and the United Kingdom.

Division of Labor. There are few specialized or high-status jobs in Equatorial Guinea. While there is a legal working age of eighteen, this is not enforced, and many children are engaged in farm work and street vending. A significant amount of work is performed by prisoners, who are forced to labor both inside and outside the prisons.

Social Stratification

Classes and Castes. The vast majority of the population is poor. The few positions of higher status are generally held by members of the Fang tribe, in particular the Mongomo subclan that controls the government.

Symbols of Social Stratification. In the cities in particular, Western dress is not uncommon. Poorer or rural people (women especially) are more likely to wear the traditional West African attire of brightly colored patterns.

Political Life

Government. Equatorial Guinea declares itself a multiparty democracy, although in practice it is a dictatorship under the leadership of the Democratic Party of Equatorial Guinea (PDGE). The legislature consists of the unicameral House of People's Representatives, a body of eighty elected officials. The president appoints a cabinet. In practice he exercises strong control over all aspects of the government, including the legislative and judiciary branches.

Leadership and Political Officials. The relationship of the people to their government is one of subjugation and fear; the country has no history of democratic processes, as leadership passed from colonial rule to a dictatorship.

Social Problems and Control. The legal system is based on a combination of Spanish law and the tribal system. Violent crime (and even petty theft) is rare compared to rates in other African nations. The government greatly restricts the rights of its citizens. The judicial system does not ensure due process, and prisoners are often tortured. The government has a record of arbitrary arrest, interference with privacy and family, restriction of movement, and lack of freedom of speech, press, and religion, among other abuses.

Military Activity. The military is made up of an army, navy, air force, rapid intervention force, and national police. Males are eligible to serve beginning at age fifteen. The country spends $3 million (U.S.) annually on its military—0.6 percent of its total budget. The armed forces also receive aid and training from Spain.

Social Welfare and Change Programs

The family is responsible for most forms of social welfare, including caring for elderly and sick members.

Nongovernmental Organizations and Other Associations

There are nongovernmental organizations (NGOs), mostly affiliated with the church, such as the Catholic Caritas; however, the government has restricted the functioning of NGOs and does not allow them to act in the area of human rights.

Gender Roles and Statuses

Division of Labor by Gender. Traditional gender roles still hold sway; it is rare to see women employed outside the home in typically male jobs. They are responsible for domestic labor and child care, although rural women also work in agriculture. The lack of women in professional jobs is perpetuated by inequalities in education: The average female receives only one-fifth as much schooling as the average male.

The Relative Status of Women and Men. Although legally granted equal rights, women are in many respects considered second-class citizens. Their status is little higher than that of children, and women are expected to defer to men in general, and to their husbands in particular. Violence against women is common, especially spousal abuse. Women have the right to buy and sell goods, but in actuality women own little property.

Marriage, Family, and Kinship

Marriage. Polygyny is common among the Fang. Traditionally, upon marriage the husband gives a

The Pope visits Bata. Eighty percent of Equatorial Guinea's population is Roman Catholic.

dowry to the family of the bride. Women generally become part of their husband's family upon marriage. Men often beat their wives, and while public beating is illegal, abuse in the home is not, and there is no mechanism for prosecuting domestic violence. According to the custom of most tribes, if the marriage breaks up, the wife is obligated to return the dowry. Additionally, the husband receives custody of all children born in wedlock. (The woman keeps any children born prior to the marriage.)

Domestic Unit. Extended families often live together. When a couple marries, it is traditional for them to move in with the husband's family.

Inheritance. Tribes follow a custom of primogeniture, passing on inheritance to the oldest male child. Although it is legal for women to inherit property, in actuality this rarely happens.

Kin Groups. The Fang are exogamous (they marry outside the clan), whereas the Bubi are endogamous (they marry within the clan). In ancient times, it was even acceptable for a brother and sister to marry, as long as they did not share the same mother.

SOCIALIZATION

Child Rearing and Education. Among the most important lessons children are taught is to respect and obey their elders. Formal education is mandatory between ages six and fourteen. However, only 70 percent of children attend primary school, and even fewer continue on to the secondary level. There are no provisions for children's welfare, and child labor is an ongoing problem, which the government has not addressed. The literacy rate is 79 percent—90 percent for men and 68 percent for women.

Higher Education. The country has two institutions of higher learning, one in Malabo and one in Bata, both run by the Spanish National University of Distant Education. Often, those who can afford it often send their children abroad to Spain or to France to complete their education.

ETIQUETTE

Greetings are an important and often lengthy form of social interaction. They usually involve shaking hands. People stand close when talking, often touching or holding hands. Elders, professionals, and those in positions of authority are treated with particular respect and deference.

Religion

Religious Beliefs. It is necessary for the Ministry of Justice and Religion to approve a religious organization before it is allowed to practice. The government is wary of the Catholic Church, as it has a history of criticizing human rights violations. Nonetheless, Catholic religious study is part of public education, and 80 percent of the population is Roman Catholic. The other 20 percent have held on to their traditional beliefs, and even many who nominally subscribe to Catholicism continue to follow traditional religious practices. There are a few Muslims, mostly Hausa traders in the region. The indigenous beliefs are animist, attributing spiritual energy to natural formations such as rivers, mountains, and trees.

Religious Practitioners. Sorcerers are the leaders of the indigenous religion and occupy an exalted position in the community.

Catholic priests occupy a position not just as religious figures, but often as voices of government opposition as well. Many have been arrested and tortured for speaking out on human rights abuses, social injustice, and corruption.

Rituals and Holy Places. Most rituals involve music and dance. One rite, known as the *abira,* is intended to purge evil from the community. One Bubi ceremony involves placing a pot of water at the entrance to the village, asking good spirits to protect the people and to bless them with more children.

Death and the Afterlife. In the indigenous religion, ancestors are venerated. They are said to live in a place called Borimo, and are thought capable of exerting influence on the living. Bubi villagers often place amulets such as animal bones, feathers, and shells several hundred meters outside the village in remembrance of their dead.

Medicine and Health Care

Health conditions in Equatorial Guinea are not good, and are made worse by lack of adequate sanitation. There is a high infant mortality rate, and the life expectancy is only fifty-three years of age (fifty-one for men and fifty-five for women). Common problems include malnutrition and malaria. The health system concentrates on preventive medicine, but this cannot compensate for the severe lack of supplies and trained personnel.

Secular Celebrations

These are New Year's Day, 1 January; Armed Forces Day, 3 August; Constitution Day, 15 August; Independence Day, 12 October; and Human Rights Day, 10 December.

The Arts and Humanities

Literature. The literary tradition in Equatorial Guinea is oral rather than written. There is a wide range of myths and legends that are passed on from one generation to the next, some meant to preserve the history of the tribes, others to explain natural phenomena. Sorcerers and witches often figure prominently.

Graphic Arts. Equatorial Guinea has a tradition of sculpture and mask-making. Many of the masks depict crocodiles, lizards, and other animals. Fang art is known for its abstract, conceptual qualities.

Performance Arts. Music and dance are central elements of Equatorial Guinean culture, both Fang and Bubi. Many of the songs and dances have religious significance. Drums are a common instrument, as are wooden xylophones; bow harps; zithers; and the *sanza,* a small thumb piano fashioned from bamboo. The accompaniment to a dance usually consists of three or four musicians. The *balélé* dance is usually performed on Christmas and other holidays. The *ibanga,* the Fang national dance, is popular along the coast. Its movements are highly sexual. The men and women who perform it cover their bodies in white powder.

The State of the Social and Physical Sciences

The few facilities for physical sciences in Equatorial Guinea are affiliated with the fledgling petroleum industry and its development.

Bibliography

"The Army Is Mobilized." *Earth Island Journal,* Winter 1999–2000.

"Country Report: Gabon, Equatorial Guinea." *The Economist Intelligence Unit,* 1993.

Fegley, Randall, comp. *Equatorial Guinea,* 1991.

Klitgaard, Robert. *Tropical Gangsters,* 1999.

Liniger-Goumaz, Max. *Historical Dictionary of Equatorial Guinea,* 1988.

———. *Small Is Not Always Beautiful: The Story of Equatorial Guinea,* 1989.

Perrois, Louis, and Marta Sierra Delage. *Art of Equatorial Guinea: The Fang Tribes*, 1990.

Reno, William. "Clandestine Economies, Violence, and States in Africa." *Journal of International Affairs*, Spring 2000.

Rwegera, Damien. "A Slow March Forward." *The UNESCO Courier*, October 1999.

Sundiata, Ibrahim K. *Equatorial Guinea: Colonialism, State Terror, and the Search for Stability*, 1990.

—Eleanor Stanford

ERITREA

CULTURE NAME

Eritrean

ORIENTATION

Identification. The term "eritrea" derives from Sinus Erythraeus, the name Greek tradesmen of the third century B.C.E. gave to the body of water between the Arabian Peninsula and the Africa continent (now known as the Red Sea). Later, during the Roman Empire, the Romans called it Mare Erythraeum, literary meaning "the red sea." When Italy colonized a strip of land along the Red Sea in 1890, they gave it the name Eritrea.

Since the creation of Eritrea was so closely linked to Ethiopia, Eritrea's identity developed in struggles against its ancient and larger neighbor to the south. Many of the nine ethnic groups within Eritrea are also found in Ethiopia, and the dominant Christian Orthodox highland culture of Ethiopia also stretches into the Eritrean highland plateau. Historically, there has been a division in Eritrea between the Christian highlands, which are culturally and linguistically homogenous, and the predominantly Muslim lowlands, which are culturally and linguistically heterogeneous. Eritrea's long war of liberation, however, managed to bridge some of the traditional differences between the highland and lowland populations.

Location and Geography. Located in northeastern Africa, Eritrea has about 620 miles (1,000 kilometers) of coastline along the west coast of the Red Sea. To the north and northwest, the country borders the Sudan, to the south, Ethiopia, and to the southwest, Djibouti. Eritrean territory covers about 48,000 square miles (125,000 square kilometers) and contains a wide variety of rugged landscapes: mountains, desert, highland plateau, lowland plains, and off the coast some 150 coral islands. The topographical variety has affected the social organization and mode of production of the country's nine ethnic groups. In the highland plateau, people live in small villages conducting subsistence plow-agriculture. Many of the lowland groups, however, lead semi-nomadic pastoral or agro pastoral lives. The Eritrean capital, Asmara, is located in the highland plateau, the home region of the biggest ethnic group, the Tigrinya.

Demography. The population in Eritrea is approximately three to three-and-a-half million (1994), divided between nine ethnic groups. The highland Tigrinya group constitutes about half of the population. More than 75 percent of the population lives in rural areas.

Linguistic Affiliation. Although the Eritrean Constitution states that all nine ethnic languages in the country are equal, the government of Eritrea has two administrative languages: Tigrinya and Arabic. Tigrinya is a Semitic language also spoken by the Tigreans of Ethiopia. Arabic was chosen to represent the lowland Muslim groups in the country. Nevertheless, only one ethnic group, the Rashaida, has Arabic as a mother tongue, whereas the other groups use it as a religious language. Many of the groups are bilingual, and because of the legacy of Ethiopian domination over Eritrea, many Eritreans also speak Amharic, the Ethiopian administrative language. Eritrean pupils are today taught in their mother tongue in primary levels (one through five), and English takes over to be the language of instruction from sixth grade (at least in theory). English is taught as a second language from second grade. It appears, however, that Tigrinya is taking over as the dominant language, since the majority of the population are Tigrinya-speakers, the biggest towns are located in the highlands, and most people in government and the state bureaucracy are from the Tigrinya ethnic group.

Symbolism. Since Eritreans fought a thirty-year-long war of liberation (1961–1991) to achieve independence from Ethiopian domination, the national

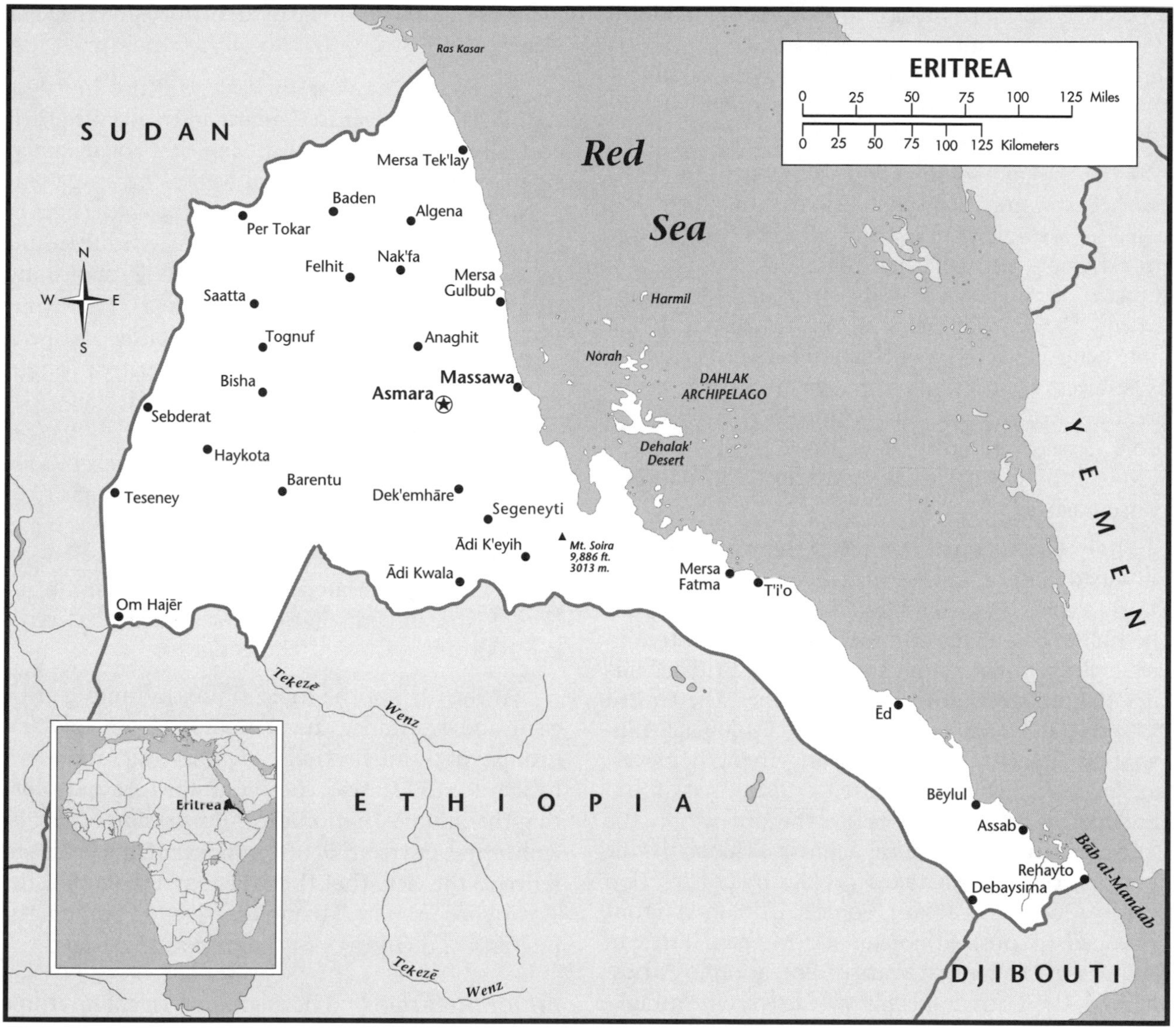

Eritrea

culture endorsed by the government invokes symbols of war and sacrifice. The three main national holidays all commemorate the war of liberation: 24 May, Liberation Day; 20 June, Martyr's Day; and 1 September, a holiday that commemorates the start of the liberation war. The official Eritrean flag, adopted in 1993, is a combination of the flag of the Eritrean People's Liberation Front, the liberation movement that achieved a military victory over the Ethiopian government, and the old flag given to Eritrea by United Nations in 1952.

History and Ethnic Relations

Emergence of the Nation. The Eritrean-Ethiopian region has been exposed to population movements and migrations from northern Africa, across the Red Sea, and from the south. On the border between Eritrea and Ethiopia, one also finds traces of some of Africa's oldest civilizations. The Axumite empire, which emerges into the light of history in the first century C.E., comprised the Akkele-Guzai region of highland Eritrea and the Agame region of Tigray, Ethiopia. The empire expanded and its port city of Adulis, south of present-day Massawa, became an important trading post hosting ships from Egypt, Greece, the Arab world, and other far-off areas. In the early fourth century Enzana, the king of Axum, converted to Christianity. He thus established Christianity as the religion of the court and state, making the Ethiopian/Eritrean Christian Church one of the oldest in the world. The decline of the Axumite empire began around 800, when its area of dominance became too big to administer efficiently.

Moreover, local resistance and uprisings coupled with the domination of overseas trade by the Islamic empire in the Middle East led to the collapse of the kingdom. Ethiopia was subsequently constructed on the legacy of Axum.

The Italian colonization of Eritrea in 1890 marked the first time that Eritrean territory was ruled as a single entity. Under Italian colonial administration, infrastructure was developed, and a modern administrative state structure was established. The development of the Eritrean colonial state helped to create a distinction between Eritreans as subjects of the Italian crown and their ethnic brothers in Ethiopia. The notion that Eritrea was more developed and modern than Tigray and the rest of Ethiopia helped to boost Eritrean national consciousness.

Italy—which had occupied Ethiopia in 1935—saw its dream of an East African empire crushed in World War II. British forces liberated Ethiopia from the Italian colonizers and took control of Eritrea in 1941. Eritrea was administered by the British Military Administration until 1952, when the United Nations (UN) federated Eritrea with Ethiopia. Ethiopia soon violated the federal arrangement, however, and in 1962 Ethiopia annexed Eritrea as its fourteenth province. The year before the annexation, the Eritrean armed resistance against Ethiopian rule commenced. It would take thirty years of liberation war before the Eritrean People's Liberation Front managed to oust Ethiopian forces from Eritrean soil, one of the longest wars of liberation in Africa. In 1993 the Eritrean people voted overwhelmingly in favor of independence in a UN-monitored referendum.

National Identity. Eritrea's long struggle for self-determination and independence has created a feeling of nationhood based on a common destiny. The armed struggle was initiated by the Eritrean Liberation Front (ELF) in 1961, but in 1970 an ELF splinter group formed a new organization that later took the name Eritrean People's Liberation Front (EPLF). During periods of the 1970s, a fierce civil war raged between the ELF and the EPLF. In 1981, the EPLF, with the help of the Tigrean People's Liberation Front in Ethiopia, managed to crush the ELF as a military organization. From then on, the EPLF deliberately used its military struggle and its internal policy of social revolution—which included land reform, gender consciousness, and class equality—to achieve a national cohesion. The EPLF recruited fighters from all the country's ethnic groups. The fighters and the civilian population in the liberated areas were educated in Eritrean history and the EPLF ideology of a strong territorial nationalism.

Following the vote for independence in 1993, the EPLF took power in Asmara and continued their centrally-driven nationalistic policies. For instance, eighteen months of national service became compulsory for all men and women between the ages of eighteen and fifty-five. Moreover, new multiethnic regions (*zoba*) were established in 1997, abolishing the old ethnicity-based regions (*awraja*). The strongest force of Eritrean nationalism after independence derives from the border wars Eritrea fought against Yemen, Djibouti, Sudan, and Ethiopia. The conflict with Ethiopia, which erupted in 1998, escalated into a full-scale war that claimed tens of thousands of casualties. During this war, the majority of the able-bodied population of Eritrea had to serve in the national military forces. A peace treaty with Ethiopia was negotiated by the U.N. and Organization of African Unity (OAU) and signed 12 December 2000.

At the turn of the millennium, mounting criticism and resistance, most notably from lowland groups and intellectuals, against the monopolistic role of EPLF was coming to the fore and splitting the unitary, nationalistic impression of an all-embracing Eritrean identity. Much of the criticism reflected the view that the EPLF was a monopolistic, Tigrinya-dominated front that was subduing the interests and cultures of the minority groups.

Ethnic Relations. The highland Tigrinya ethnic group is the dominant group, numerically, politically, and economically. There is also a minority group of Tigrinya-speaking Muslims called Jeberti in the highlands. The Jeberti, however, are not recognized as a separate ethnic group by the Eritrean government. The lowland groups—the Afar, Beja/Hadarab, Bileyn, Kunama, Nara, Rashaida, Saho, and Tigre—are all, with the exception of the Tigre, relatively small and, taken together, they do not form any homogenous cultural or political blocs. Traditionally, the relationship between the highland and lowland groups has been one of tension and conflict. Raids on livestock and encroachment on land and grazing rights have led to mutual distrust, which is still, to a certain degree, relevant in the relation between the minorities and the state. Many of the groups are also divided between Eritrea and Ethiopia, Sudan, and Djibouti, making cross-border ethnic alliances a possible threat to the national identity.

An Eritrean woman harvesting Teff in Geshinashim. The Eritrean economy is totally dependent on agriculture.

URBANISM, ARCHITECTURE, AND THE USE OF SPACE

The architecture of Eritrean towns reflects the nation's colonial past and the shifting influence of foreign powers. The Italian population in the country called Asmara "Little Rome." The city boasts wide avenues, cafés and pastries, and a host of Italian restaurants. The port of Massawa, on the other hand, is influenced by the Ottoman period, the Egyptian presence, and the long tradition of trade with far-off countries and ports. In the countryside, traditional building customs are still upheld. In the highlands, small stone houses (*hidmo*) with roofs made of branches and rocks dominate. The house is separated into two areas, a kitchen section in the back and a public room in the front that is also used as sleeping quarters. The various lowland groups employ several housing styles, from tentlike structures (*agnet*) among the pastoral nomadic groups, to more permanent straw or stone/mud huts among the sedentary groups.

FOOD AND ECONOMY

Food in Daily Life. Eritrean cuisine is a reflection of the country's history. The *injerra* is commonly eaten in the rural areas. It is a pancake-like bread that is eaten together with a sauce called *tsebhi* or *wat*. The sauce may be of a hot and spicy meat variety, or vegetable based. In the urban centers one finds the strong influence of Italian cuisine, and pasta is served in all restaurants. The lowland groups have a different food tradition than the highlands with the staple food being a porridge (*asida* in Arabic) made of sorghum.

Food Customs at Ceremonial Occasions. Both Islam and the Orthodox Christian tradition require rigorous observance of fasts and food taboos. Several periods of fasting, the longest being Lent among the Orthodox and Ramadan among Muslims, have to be adhered to by all adults. During religious celebrations, however, food and beverages are served in plenty. Usually an ox, sheep, or goat is slaughtered. The meat and the intestines are served together with the injerra. Traditional beer (*siwa*) is brewed in the villages and is always served during ceremonial occasions.

Basic Economy. The Eritrean economy is totally dependent upon agricultural production. Over 75 percent of the population lives in the rural areas and conducts subsistence agricultural production, whereas 20 percent is estimated to be traders and workers. No major goods are produced for export, but some livestock is exported to the Arabian peninsula.

Land Tenure and Property. The granting of equal land right use to all citizens, irrespective of sex, ethnicity, or social class, has been a political priority for the EPLF since the days of the armed struggle. After independence, the Eritrean government passed a new land proclamation abolishing all traditional land tenure arrangements, and granting the ownership of all land to the Eritrean state exclusively. Accordingly, each citizen above the age of eighteen has the right to receive long-term usufruct rights in land in the place he or she resides. The Eritrean government has not yet fully implemented the new land proclamation, and land is still administered under traditional communal tenure forms. Land scarcity is widespread in Eritrea, particularly in the densely populated highland plateau. Thus, any reform touching upon the sensitive issue of access to land necessarily creates controversies.

Commercial Activities. Agricultural production and petty trade make up the bulk of the commercial activity in Eritrea. The informal economy is significant, since petty traders dominate the many marketplaces throughout Eritrea, where secondhand clothing, various equipment, and utensils are sold.

Major Industries. The marginal industrial base in Eritrea provides the domestic market with textiles, shoes, food products, beverages, and building materials. If stable and peaceful development occurs, Eritrea might be able to create a considerable tourism industry based on the Dahlak islands in the Red Sea.

Trade. Eritrea has limited export-oriented industry, with livestock and salt being the main export goods.

Division of Labor. In urban areas, positions are filled on the basis of education and experience. Key positions in civil service and government, however, are usually given to loyal veteran liberation fighters and party members.

A large share of trade and commercial activity is run by individuals from the Jeberti group (Muslim highlanders). They were traditionally denied land rights, and had thus developed trading as a niche activity.

Social Stratification

Classes and Castes. Eritrean society is divided along ethnic, religious, and social lines. Traditionally, there were low caste groups within many of the ethnic groups in the country. The last slave was reportedly emancipated by the EPLF in the late 1970s. The traditional elites were the landowning families. After land reforms both during and after the liberation struggle, however, these elites have ceased to exist. Generally, in the rural areas, the people live in scarcity and poverty and few distinctions between rich and poor are seen. In the urban areas, however, a modern elite is emerging, composed of high-ranking civil servants, businesspeople, and Eritreans returning from the diaspora in the United States and Europe.

Symbols of Social Stratification. In the rural areas, the better-off are able to acquire proper clothing and shoes. The rich may have horses or mules to carry them to the market. A sign of prosperity among the pastoral groups is the display of gold jewelry on women.

Political Life

Government. Eritrea is a unitary state with a parliamentary system. The parliament elects the president, who is head of state and government. The president appoints his or her own cabinet upon the parliament's approval.

No organized opposition to the government party, the People's Front for Democracy and Justice (PFDJ; the re-named EPLF) is allowed in practice. The new constitution, which was ratified in May 1997 but not put fully into effect, guarantees the freedom of organization, but it is too early to say how this will influence the formation of political parties.

Leadership and Political Officials. The president of Eritrea, and the former liberation movement leader, Isaias Afwerki, is the supreme leader of the country. In addition to serving as president, he fills the roles of commander-in-chief of the armed forces and secretary-general of the ruling party, the PFDJ. He is held in high regard among large portions of the population because of his skills as the leader of the liberation movement. Former liberation movement fighters fill almost all positions of trust both within and outside the government.

Social Problems and Control. With the coming to power of the EPLF, strong measures were used to curtail the high rate of criminality in Asmara. At the turn of the millennium, Eritrea probably boasted some of the lowest crime rates on the continent. The people generally pride themselves in being hard working and honest, and elders often clamp down on youths who are disrespectful of social and cultural conventions.

Growing tensions between the lowland minority groups and the Tigrinya—reinforced by the Muslim-Christian divide and Ethiopia's support for Eritrean resistance movements—may threaten the internal stability in the country.

Military Activity. As a result of the 1998–2000 war with Ethiopia, Eritrea was characterized as a militarized society in the early twenty-first century. The majority of the population between the ages of eighteen and fifty-five had been mobilized to the war fronts, and the country's meager funds and resources were being spent on military equipment and defense. Since Eritrea gained independence in 1993, the country has had military border clashes with Yemen, Djibouti, and Sudan, in addition to the war with Ethiopia. This has led to accusations from the neighboring countries that Eritrea exhibits a militaristic foreign policy. There are indications that the Eritrean government uses the military to sustain a high level of nationalism in the country.

Social Welfare and Change Programs

The government of Eritrea is concentrating its development policies on rural agriculture and food self-sufficiency. Few resources are available to social

Women carrying water from a river two hours away from their homes in Adi Baren, Akeleguzay.

welfare programs. Reconstruction of destroyed properties, resettlement of internally displaced people, and demobilization of the army are huge challenges facing the government. Few national or international nongovernmental organizations (NGOs) are allowed to implement social welfare programs on their own initiative.

Nongovernmental Organizations and Other Associations

The Eritrean government prides itself on its policy of self-reliance, rejecting development aid projects that are not the priority of the government. The majority of international NGOs were expelled from the country in 1998, although all were invited back later due to the humanitarian crisis caused by the war with Ethiopia. The government restricts the development of national NGOs, and foreign aid has to be channelled through governmental organizations.

Gender Roles and Statuses

Division of Labor by Gender. Since subsistence agriculture is the main production activity in Eritrea, the division of labor is influenced by custom. Women's input in agricultural production is vital but certain tasks, such as plowing and sowing, are conducted only by men. Animals are generally herded by young boys, while young girls assist in fetching water and firewood for the household.

The Relative Status of Women and Men. Since Eritrean society is still highly influenced by customary principles, the status of women in many communities is inferior to that of men. The war of liberation, where female fighters served side by side with men, was believed to have changed the status of women. The EPLF culture of gender equality, however, did not penetrate deeply into the Eritrean patriarchal culture. Nevertheless, with the government's policies of modernization and gender awareness, changes are slowly occurring in the status of Eritrean women.

Marriage, Family, and Kinship

Marriage. Customary rules of marriage vary among the ethnic groups. Generally, girls marry at an early age, sometimes as young as fourteen. A large share of the marriages in the rural areas are still arranged by the family groups of concern.

Domestic Unit. Generally, people live together in nuclear families, although in some ethnic groups the family structure is extended. The man is the public decision-maker in the family, whereas the woman is responsible for organizing the domestic activities of the household.

Inheritance. Inheritance rules in Eritrea follow the customary norms of the different ethnic groups. Generally, men are favored over women, and sons inherit their parents' household possessions.

Kin Groups. The nuclear family, although forming the smallest kin unit, is always socially embedded in a wider kin unit. The lineage and/or clan hold an organizing function in terms of social duties and obligations and as a level of identity. With the exception of the Kunama who are matrilineal, all ethnic groups in Eritrea are patrilineal, that is, descent is traced through the male line.

SOCIALIZATION

Infant Care. In all ethnic groups, children are raised under the strong influence of parents and close relatives, as well as neighbors and the kin group. While conducting domestic chores or working in the fields, mothers usually carry the infants on their backs.

Child Rearing and Education. From an early age, both boys and girls are expected to take part in the household's activities: boys as herders of the family's livestock, girls as assistants to their mother in domestic affairs. An increasing number of children is joining the formal educational system, although education sometimes conflicts with the children's household obligations. In some of the nomadic and seminomadic communities, children might be unable to regularly attend classes in the formal educational system.

In some ethnic groups, circumcision is used as an initiation ritual into adulthood. The majority of both Eritrean men and women are circumcised. Female circumcision, or female genital mutilation, is carried out both among Christians and Muslims, although the type of circumcision differs from clitoridectomy to infibulation (the removal of the labia and partial closing of the vagina by approximating the labia majora in the midline).

Higher Education. The institutions of higher education in Eritrea are few, and the only university, Asmara University, admits a limited number of students. In the rural areas most people take up farming, which does not presuppose any formal education. The better-off families and those with relatives abroad try to send their children to the United States or Europe for further education and work.

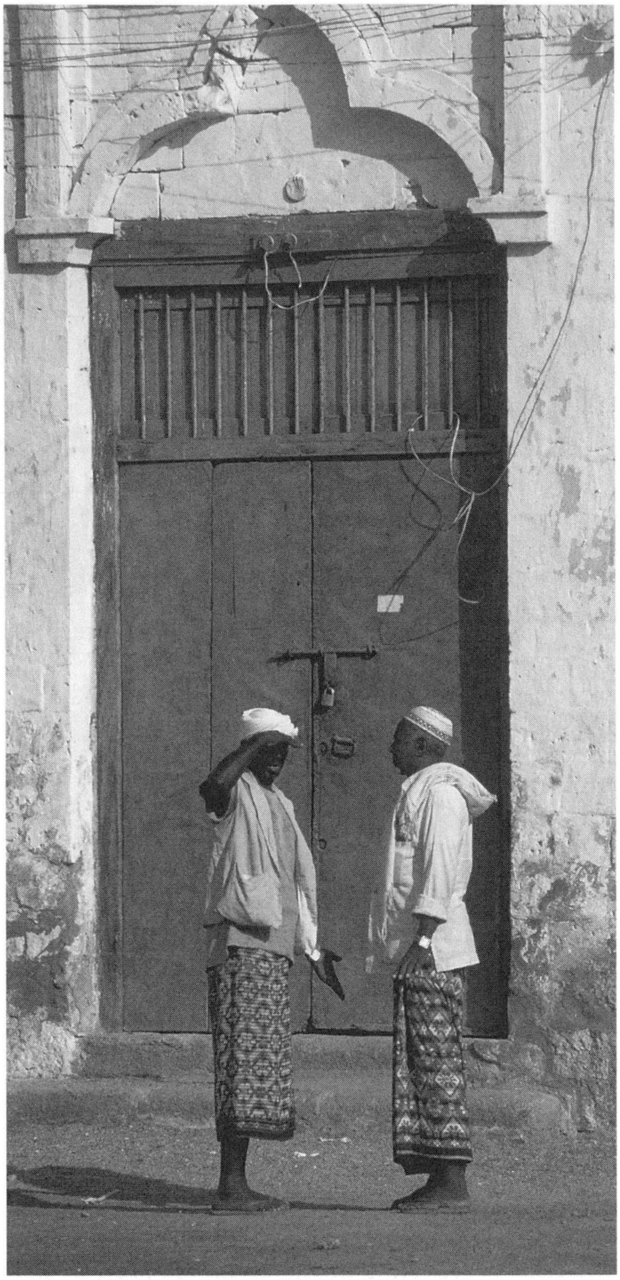

Eritrean men have traditionally been considered the family decision-makers.

ETIQUETTE

Eritreans pride themselves on being hard working and resilient, and they show great social responsibility. Respect for elders and authority is deeply rooted. Compared to the urban population of Asmara, the peasantry keeps a tighter social discipline in relation to open, public affection between two people of the opposite sex. Boys and men, however, are frequently seen holding hands as a sign of friendship.

All traditional foods are eaten using the right hand only and without the use of silverware. The left hand is considered impure.

RELIGION

Religious Beliefs. The population is almost equally divided between Christians and Muslims, with the number of Christians being slightly larger. In addition, there are some followers of traditional beliefs among the Kunama group. The Orthodox Christian tradition in Eritrea stretches back to the fourth century, and Orthodox Christianity forms an integral part of the Tigrinya cultural expression. Catholicism and Lutheranism are also represented. Some syncretism with traditional beliefs is found among both Christians and Muslims. The government has been criticized for discriminating against and persecuting the country's Jehovah's Witnesses.

Religious Practitioners. All Eritreans are either Christians or Muslims (except a few followers of traditional religion among the Kunama), thus the religious practitioners are the formalized clergy and *ulama*, respectively. Since the rural Eritrean community is deeply religious, the clergy and *ulama* have an influential position in the everyday lives of their followers.

Rituals and Holy Places. Since Christianity and Islam are equally recognized by the state, the main religious holidays of both faiths are observed, including both Christian and Muslim celebrations: Both Western and Ge'ez Christmas, the Epiphany, Id Al-Fetir, Good Friday and Ge'ez Easter, Id Al-Adha, and Mewlid El-Nabi.

Death and the Afterlife. The beliefs and practices concerning death, funerals, and the afterlife follow some of the norms of the two religions—Orthodox (Coptic) Christianity and Islam. Funeral practices, however, may vary among the ethnic subgroups who follow Islam.

MEDICINE AND HEALTH CARE

The formal health care system is poorly developed. Poor sanitary conditions in the rural areas and lack of tap water create a high rate of infant mortality. Numerous other health problems, including malaria and HIV/AIDS, lack of food and proper water supplies, and lack of trained personnel, continue to burden Eritrea's development of an efficient health care system. Traditional medical beliefs are widespread in the rural areas.

SECULAR CELEBRATIONS

Upon gaining independence Eritrea changed its calendar from the Julian to the Gregorian. But the reckoning of time according to the Julian calendar exists unofficially and is known as the Ge'ez calendar. The official state holidays are: New Year's Day (1 January); International Women's Day (8 March); May Day (1 May); Liberation Day (24 May); Martyr's Day (20 June); Launching of Armed Struggle (1 September); Ge'ez New Year (11 September; 12 September in leap years); and Meskel (the finding of the true cross) celebrations (27–28 September).

THE ARTS AND HUMANITIES

Because of the protracted war of liberation, the development of arts and humanities has been hindered. Some new artists in postliberation Eritrea are emerging, however, with an artistic focus on the country's struggle for independence.

Support for the Arts. Since the Eritrean society is extremely poor, the government needs to prioritize its funds for development efforts, leaving little for the arts. However, some support is given to cultural shows and exhibits that portray the cultural variety of the Eritrean people. Support is also given to exhibits and shows that display the hardships and sacrifices of the thirty-year war of liberation.

THE STATE OF THE PHYSICAL AND SOCIAL SCIENCES

The Eritrean government gives priority to building academic capacity within scientific fields that relate to the reconstruction of the war-torn country. Priority is also given to research into the environment and agricultural production, in order to secure food self-sufficiency.

BIBLIOGRAPHY

Connell, Dan. *Against All Odds: A Chronicle of the Eritrean Revolution*, 1993.

Erlich, Haggai. *Ras Alula and the Scramble for Africa: A Political Biography: Ethiopia and Eritrea 1875–1897*, 1996.

Gayim, Eyassu. *The Eritrean Question: The Conflict between the Right to Self-Determination and the Interests of States*, 1993.

Gebremedhin, Tesfa G. *Beyond Survival: The Economic Challenges of Agriculture and Development in Post-Independence Eritrea*, 1996.

Gottesman, Les. *To Fight and Learn: The Praxis and Promise of Literacy in Eritrea's Independence War*, 1998.

Iyob, Ruth. *The Eritrean Struggle for Independence: Domination, Resistance, Nationalism, 1941–1993*, 1995.

Nadel, S. F. "Land Tenure on the Eritrean Plateau." *Africa*, 16(1): 1–21; 16(2): 109, 1946.

———. *Races and Tribes of Eritrea*, 1944.

Negash, Tekeste. *Italian Colonialism in Eritrea, 1882-1941: Policies, Praxis and Impact*, 1987.

———. *Eritrea and Ethiopia: The Federal Experience*, 1997.

———, and Tronvoll, Kjetil. *Brothers at War: Making Sense of the Eritrea/Ethiopia War*, 2000.

Pateman, Roy. *Eritrea: Even the Stones Are Burning*, 1990.

Pool, David *Eritrea: Towards Unity in Diversity*, 1997.

Tronvoll, Kjetil. *Mai Weini: A Highland Village in Eritrea*, 1998.

———. "The Process of Nation-Building in Post-War Eritrea: Created from Below or Directed from Above?" *The Journal of Modern African Studies*, 36(3): 461–482, 1998.

———. "Borders of Violence—Boundaries of Identity: Demarcating the Eritrean Nation-State." *Ethnic and Racial Studies*, 22(6): 1037–1060, 1999.

United Nations. *The United Nations and the Independence of Eritrea*, 1996.

—KJETIL TRONVOLL

ESTONIA

CULTURE NAME

Estonian

ALTERNATIVE NAMES

Republic of Estonia; Estonians refer to themselves as *eestlased* and to the country as *Eesti* or *Eesti Vabariik*.

ORIENTATION

Identification. ''Eesti'' can be traced to a first-century mention by the Roman historian Tacitus of a people or place called Aestii or Aestui. The name may derive from a German word referring to the east. Place names have been traced to this period, suggesting a link between language and homeland. The first written evidence of Estonian is in the *Chronican Livoniae* (1180–1227), which includes descriptions of the society and a selection of words and phrases.

Estonians have strong connections to local traditions related primarily to different dialects and reinforced by variations in customs and dress. Islands, including Saaremaa, have their own traditions, and people speak distinctive dialects. Other local cultures with different dialects include the *mulgid* (in southern Viljandimaa), the *vorukad* (from Voru), and the *setud* (from Setumaa, currently divided by the border between Estonia and Russia). Despite local attachments, people feel that they share a common culture. The country has a sizable community of ethnic Russians whose connections to Estonia have begun to develop only recently.

Location and Geography. The country is bordered to the west and north by the Baltic Sea, with Lake Peipsi forming a border with Russia to the east. Most of the country is at or near sea level. The lowest areas, encompassing the islands, western Estonia, and the northern coast and extending along Lake Peipsi, traditionally have been associated with maritime trade and fishing.

A single state is of recent origin. Estonia was divided into two provinces—Estland to the north and Livland (including part of modern Latvia) to the south—during Polish-Swedish rule from the 1560s to 1710 and later under imperial Russia.

Demography. In 1999, the population was about 1.45 million. Estonians account for 65 percent of the population, Russians 28 percent, and Ukrainians 2 percent. Before World War II, the population was about 88 percent Estonian. After the war, the percentage of Estonians steadily declined, reaching a low of 61 percent in 1989, with the Russian population increasing to 30 percent. The percentage of Estonians has increased since that time. Approximately fifty thousand Estonians live in the former Soviet Union, and another fifty thousand to seventy thousand reside in North America, Europe, and Australia.

Linguistic Affiliation. Estonian belongs to the Finno-Ugric linguistic group, related closely to Finnish and more distantly to Hungarian and various languages spoken in Siberia. Speakers of the language probably arrived in the region between 2000 and 3000 B.C.E. Until the nineteenth century, Estonian was spoken by the peasantry, and thus it is central to the national identity. Until the nation regained independence, Estonians were more likely than Russians to speak both Estonian and Russian. This is changing as citizenship and job opportunities push Russians toward learning Estonian. English is gaining popularity as a second or third language.

Symbolism. There is a strong attachment to the mother tongue (*emakeel*) and the fatherland (*isamaa*). The metaphor of the family is common, with a sense of belonging reinforced by a shared understanding of history and roots in rural, peasant values. These values connect Estonians to nature. The cornflower and the barn swallow are common national symbols, and stone and wood have an organic meaning for peasants struggling against nature. The national struggle against foreign occupation is an extension of this historical fight for survival. The most important political symbols are the horizontally striped blue, black, and white flag, symbolizing sky, earth, and virtue and hope, and the coat of arms featuring three lions. The flag represents the nation, and its presence atop the Tall Hermann tower in Tallinn, the capital, represents national and cultural independence.

History and Ethnic Relations

Emergence of the Nation. Estonia was ruled by Poles, Danes, Germans, Swedes, and Russians after the thirteenth century. Before the nineteenth century, the national identity was synonymous with the peasantry. The local nobility and clergy, merchants, and traders were predominantly Baltic Germans; an Estonian could enter the upper classes only by adopting the German language and German customs. Estonians referred to themselves as *maarahvas* (''country folk'') and to a Baltic German as a *saks* (short for ''German''). The first term showed a connection to a place, while *saks* was used to refer to anyone with high status.

The development of a written language was important to cultural awareness. The first Estonian book was printed in 1535, and a Bible was published in 1739. Education in Estonian was a key part of national development. In addition to the peasant tradition of teaching children to read at home, an elementary education system was organized in the 1680s. By 1850, approximately 90 percent of the population was literate.

From 1802 to 1856, the peasantry was emancipated and granted limited property rights. Although these reforms had little effect, they limited the power of Baltic Germans and began to separate ethnic identity from economic status. Under Tsar Nikolai I, Russification policies were introduced to assimilate non-Russian populations into the empire. Under these policies, approximately 17 percent of Estonians were converted to the Russian Orthodox religion. Apart from the actual number of conversions, the policy suggested a cultural basis for challenging the domination of the Baltic Germans, who used religion to justify the socioeconomic status quo.

The middle of the nineteenth century marked the beginning of the national awakening. A small group of intellectuals played a vital role in giving the traditional culture a national meaning. In 1857,

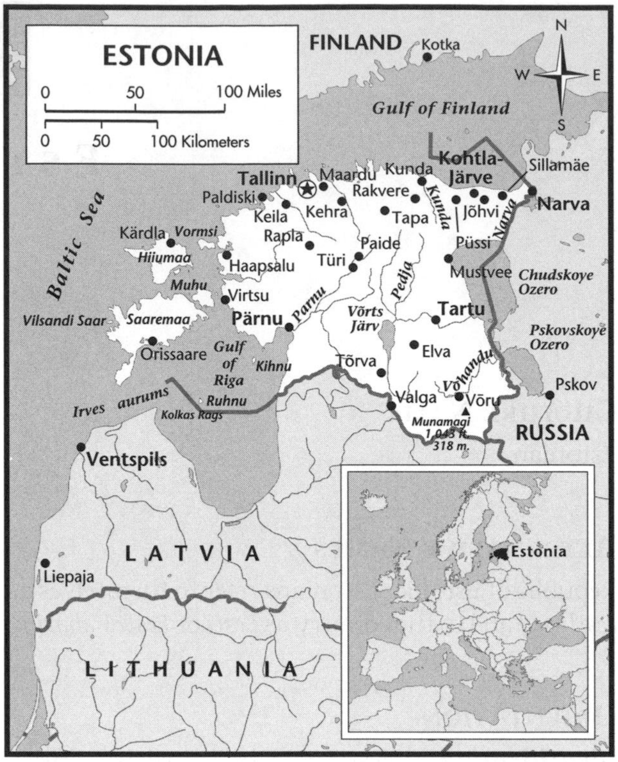

Estonia

a new newspaper, the *Perno Postimees* (*Pärnu Mailman*), published by Johannes Voldemar Jannsen, became the first publication to refer to ''Estonian people'' (*eesti rahvas*) instead of ''country folk'' and catered to a popular readership by publishing articles in colloquial Estonian that dealt with everyday concerns. Other newspapers followed, including *Sakala*, edited by Carl Robert Jakobson. Scholarly interest grew with the founding of the Estonian Alexander School and the Estonian Writer's Society, both headed by Jakob Hurt. Intellectuals also invented traditions. Inspired by the Finnish *Kalevala*, Friedrich Robert Faehlmann outlined and Friedrich Reinhold Kreutzwald completed the Estonian epic *Kalevipoeg*, which was published from 1857 to 1861.

Other aspects of culture were adapted from earlier usages and made ''more Estonian'' as older traditions such as the wearing of folk clothing and singing in the traditional style declined. The first song festival was organized by Jannsen in 1869. Capitalizing on the popularity of church choirs, the festival became the most popular national tradition, although the first one was modest in size and included only two Estonian authors. Poetry, long part of the national song tradition, emerged as a literary form, with Lydia Koidula (Jannsen's daughter) the best loved poet.

In an attempt to undermine the power of the Baltic Germans, Russification was reintroduced by Alexander II and Alexander III. Orders to use Russian in schools had the unintended effect of uniting Estonians against what they saw as an attack on their culture.

By the late 1800s, an Estonian identity had been established and efforts were being made to retrieve the "original culture" by collecting folk poems, sayings, and songs. This process became a national project, pushed originally by Hurt but largely dependent on newspapers. The work later expanded to include folk art and crafts and led to the creation of a national museum in 1908.

Nationalism has continued to evolve. After the Soviet Union occupied the country during World War II, cultural expression was subject to censorship and the use of symbols associated with independence (the flag) was banned.

Estonia was politically independent between 1918 and 1940, and became independent again in 1991. Nationalism survived by adapting forms of expression that could not be controlled by the Soviet authorities. Poetry, music, and film commented on political oppression in ways that only Estonians could understand. The influence of nationalism was reflected in the fact that 250,000 people took part in the 1969 song festival.

National Identity. In both the 1880s and the 1980s, national identity solidified in reaction to Russification policies imposed by the government. The "Letter of Forty," signed by forty well-known artists and intellectuals in 1980, raised concerns about the cultural effects of Russification, setting the stage for the New Awakening in 1987 and 1988.

Ethnic Relations. During the Soviet occupation, policies encouraging the immigration of Russians to Estonia reduced the percentage of ethnic Estonians. The immigrants were seen as occupiers and colonists, and relations between Estonians and Russians are still strained.

Urbanism, Architecture, and the Use of Space

Although built under foreign rule, buildings are important symbols. City walls, towers, churches, and fortresses strongly connect Estonians to the past. Though few unaltered examples remain, the design of an old Estonian farmhouse is considered part of the national culture. The timbered house is long and low, with a relatively low-pitched thatched roof. Farm buildings are often arranged around a central yard area. There are regional variations in fencing, including wood fences (made of sticks or twigs) and low stone walls (mostly in coastal areas). Windmills are part of a remembered past, but only a handful remain for tourist purposes.

Food and Economy

Food in Daily Life. In the fall and winter, soups and stews predominate, with potatoes a staple at most meals. In the spring and summer, fresh tomatoes and cucumbers accompany every meal. Sandwiches are common breakfast fare, and coffee is drunk frequently throughout the day and at social events. In coastal areas, fish is eaten. Many people grow fruits, vegetables, and berries during the summer and can what remains in the fall. Family dinners are infrequent, as both parents usually work. Most families try to share one meal together on the weekend.

Food Customs at Ceremonial Occasions. Christmas dinner includes roast pork or goose, blood sausage, sauerkraut, potatoes, and head cheese, with gingerbread cookies for dessert. Other special occasions such as birthdays, weddings, and funerals do not require special foods, though it is expected that food will be plentiful. Evening social gatherings almost always include meals accompanied by vodka.

Basic Economy. Although the culture emphasizes self-sufficiency, this is no longer possible as Estonia becomes integrated into the global economy. Local production, including agriculture, is augmented by imports, primarily from the European Union. Only 11 percent of the labor force is employed in agriculture and forestry. While these residents may produce enough to be self-sufficient, most citizens are urbanized and purchase food and other necessities.

Land Tenure and Property. The privatization of property once controlled by the Soviet state continues. Not all property can be directly returned to the original owners. Owners are given vouchers for the value of the property that can be exchanged for other property or stock options.

Commercial Activities. In addition to goods for export, the economy is oriented toward food production, clothing, and manufactured goods, especially the production of spare parts for machinery, appliances, and automobiles. A large amount of

Houses in Tallinn, Estonia. Buildings are important symbols to Estonians, who view the structures as an important link to the past.

wealth has been generated by privatization, as commercial interests compete to buy out smaller enterprises that have managed to acquire property.

Major Industries. Light manufacturing and textiles are important for both foreign and domestic markets. Oil shale is mined and used primarily to produce electricity.

Trade. Exports include machinery, parts, and electrical equipment (20 percent of exports in 1998), timber and wood products, textiles, and clothing. The main export markets are Finland, Sweden, and Russia. Imports include machinery and appliances (26 percent), foodstuffs (15 percent), chemical products (10 percent), metals (9 percent), and textiles (8 percent). The primary source of imports is Finland, followed by Russia, Sweden, and Germany.

Division of Labor. In the transition to a market economy, nearly all jobs give priority to younger workers. Education affords status to any employee even if his or her background is in a different field. Privatization has brought back family farms, but they are unlikely to survive the transition to membership in the European Union. Heavy industry and factory jobs have been cut, leaving many Russian workers unemployed.

Social Stratification

Classes and Caste. The top 20 percent of the population earns 40 percent of the total income, while the bottom 20 percent earns only 2 percent. Inequality has increased dramatically since 1991, but the trend has slowed since 1996.

Symbols of Social Stratification. The nouveau riche engage in many forms of conspicuous consumption, including expensive cars, cellular phones, designer clothing, and the display of trophy wives and mistresses.

Political Life

Government. In a parliamentary democracy with a state assembly (*Riigikogu*) of 101 members, the government is headed by a prime minister. The president is the ceremonial head of state and is elected by the assembly.

Leadership and Political Officials. Candidates for political office usually are drawn from a relatively small circle. Officials who leave office frequently work in prominent positions in government or private business. The current political parties are the Pro Patria Union, the Centrist Party,

Harju Street in Tallinn.

the Coalition Party, the Estonian People's Union, the Moderate Party, the Reform Party, and the United People's Party Fraction.

Social Problems and Control. The police operate at the national level. There is a three-tiered legal system: city and county and administrative courts, which hear criminal, civil, and investigative cases; appellate circuit courts; and a supreme court, which hears appeals and constitutional cases. The police and judicial systems are perceived as corrupt and are not trusted. People try to avoid any situation in which the authorities may get involved. Theft and burglary are overwhelmingly the largest crime problems.

Military Activity. Men serve one year in the military. Military service is unpopular and carries little prestige. There is an army, a navy, and a limited air defense system, as well as an internal security force, which is primarily the border patrol. Combined, there are about 4,500 people in the armed services. In addition, the Defense League (*Kaitseliit*) has about 6,000 volunteer members.

Social Welfare and Change Programs

There are limited unemployment benefits, and the elderly receive social security payments. Pensioners consider their benefits inadequate.

Nongovernmental Organizations and Other Associations

There are more than 5,700 civic groups and organizations, along with 3,145 nonprofit organizations. Most have organized only recently and are understaffed and poorly funded.

Gender Roles and Statuses

Division of Labor by Gender. Young women are given jobs in the most visible positions in the service sector, such as retail sales, bank tellers, and secretarial work. Men are almost always preferred for executive positions because they are considered more dependable and less emotional. Although there are some women in politics, they are underrepresented in the government.

The Relative Status of Women and Men. Women are expected to defer to men even when male views are seen as wrong or incorrect. However, women's rights are legally protected by the Constitution, which explicitly forbids gender discrimination.

Marriage, Family, and Kinship

Marriage. There are no formal or informal restrictions on marriage. Marriage to non-Estonians, especially Russians, is not welcomed but is not forbidden. It is estimated that more than half of all marriages end in divorce.

Domestic Unit. The family includes a husband, a wife, and an average of one child. It is not unusual for an elderly parent to live with the family. Both parents are likely to work, but the wife is responsible for household chores. Whether living in the household or separately, grandparents often help with child care.

Inheritance. Private and personal property can be inherited, usually by the children of the deceased.

Socialization

Infant Care. Very small children usually do not leave the home but are taken for walks to get fresh air, which is considered healthy. Crying babies are picked up and calmed by their parents.

Child Rearing and Education. Children are allowed to explore and play on their own. Education is highly valued, and a child is expected to learn how to read, write, and do simple math at home.

Higher Education. A university education is prized and confers a high status.

ETIQUETTE

Estonians are socially introverted and maintain a distance in public and private spaces. People move relatively quickly, seldom make eye contact, and talk in hushed tones in public. Russians are perceived as being loud, boisterous, and not respectful of personal space.

RELIGION

Religious Beliefs. The Evangelical Lutheran Church is the largest denomination, with about 185,000 members. There is a dispute between the Estonian Apostolic Orthodox Church (EAOC) and the Russian Orthodox Church; more ethnic Estonians belong to the EAOC, which has approximately three thousand members. Other churches have small but growing congregations. Most people attend church only at Christmas and do not consider themselves religious, although they believe in an afterlife and have some concept of fate. Astrology, supernatural beliefs, and shamanism (from the country's pre-Christian roots) have gained acceptance.

MEDICINE AND HEALTH CARE

Doctors and modern medicine are beginning to be trusted. For common illnesses, people rely on traditional home remedies.

SECULAR CELEBRATIONS

Traditional weddings are two- or three-day events that include games and generous amounts of food and drink. Birthdays are always celebrated, and christenings and confirmations are celebrated with large parties. The most important holiday remains Christmas. Despite Soviet opposition, Christmas trees were decorated and traditional foods were served. New Year's Eve is considered part of the Christmas holidays. A sauna before midnight cleanses the body and spirit for the upcoming year.

The old folk calender included many days that influenced farming decisions. On Shrove Tuesday, people still go sledding to make flax plants grow taller. On Saint John's Eve (23 June), nearly all Estonians go to the countryside to celebrate midsummer with large bonfires. Saint Martin's Day (10 November) and Saint Catherine's Day (25 November) are celebrated with children dressing up in costumes and going door to door to perform for treats.

A member of an Estonian folk music group performing near Tallinn.

State holidays with official governmental celebrations include Independence Day (24 February), Victory Day (23 June), and Independence Restoration Day (20 August).

THE ARTS AND HUMANITIES

Support for the Arts. Formerly state-subsidized, artists are now self-supporting.

Literature. Nationalism has depended on writing, and Estonians self-identify themselves in fictional works. Early novels mirrored rural hardships in distinctively Estonian settings. In the 1960s, writers began to comment on the lack of cultural and political freedom. Jaan Kross reinvented Estonian cultural heroes in his historical novels.

Graphic Arts. Applied arts, including pottery, ceramics, and textiles, often incorporate national motifs.

Performance Arts. Drama, ballet, and opera have been popular since the nineteenth century. Estonian classical music has gained global recognition through the composers Arvo Pärt, Veljo Tormis, and Eduard Tubin and the conductors Eri Klas and Neeme Järvi.

THE STATE OF THE PHYSICAL AND SOCIAL SCIENCES

Funding comes from international sources, and research frequently is completed in other countries. The study of genetic diseases and gene therapy has been established. Tartu University is known for work in linguistics and semiotics.

BIBLIOGRAPHY

Kaskla, Edgar. "Estonian Nationalism in Comparative Perspective." Ph.D. dissertation, University of California, Irvine, 1992.

Loit, Alexander, ed. *National Movements in the Baltic Countries*, 1985.

Misiunas, Romuald J. and Rein Taagepera. *The Baltic States: Years of Dependence, 1940–1980*, 1983.

Nirk, Endel. *Estonian Literature*, 1987.

Rauch, George von. *The Baltic States: The Years of Independence, 1917–1940*, 1974.

Raun, Toivo U. *Estonia and the Estonians*, 1987.

Taagepera, Rein. *Estonia: Return to Independence*, 1993.

Tedre, Ülo, ed. *Estonian Customs and Traditions*, 1995.

Web Sites

Estonian Institute. "Estonian Information Page by Estonian Institute," http://www.einst.ee

—EDGAR KASKLA

Ethiopia

Culture Name

Ethiopian

Orientation

Identification. The name "Ethiopia" derives from the Greek *ethio*, meaning "burned" and *pia*, meaning "face": the land of burned-faced peoples. Aeschylus described Ethiopia as a "land far off, a nation of black men." Homer depicted Ethiopians as pious and favored by the gods. These conceptions of Ethiopia were geographically vague.

In the late nineteenth century, Emperor Menelik II expanded the country's borders to their present configuration. In March 1896, Italian troops attempted to enter Ethiopia forcibly and were routed by Emperor Menelik and his army. The battle of Adwa was the only victory of an African army over a European army during the partitioning of Africa which preserved the country's independence. Ethiopia is the only African country never to have been colonized, although an Italian occupation occurred from 1936 to 1941.

In addition to the monarchy, whose imperial line can be traced to King Solomon and the Queen of Sheba, the Ethiopian Orthodox Church was a major force in that, in combination with the political system, it fostered nationalism with its geographic center in the highlands. The combination of church and state was an indissoluble alliance that controlled the nation from King 'Ēzānā's adoption of Christianity in 333 until the overthrow of Haile Selassie in 1974. A socialist government (the Derge) known for its brutality governed the nation until 1991. The Ethiopian People's Revolutionary Democratic Front (EPRDF) defeated the Derge, established democratic rule, and currently governs Ethiopia.

The last twenty-five years of the twentieth century have been a time of revolt and political unrest but represent only a small portion of the time during which Ethiopia has been a politically active entity. Unfortunately, however, the country's international standing has declined since the reign of Emperor Selassie, when it was the only African member of the League of Nations and its capital, Addis Ababa, was home to a substantial international community. War, drought, and health problems have left the nation one of the poorest African countries economically, but the people's fierce independence and historical pride account for a people rich in self-determination.

Location and Geography. Ethiopia is the tenth largest country in Africa, covering 439,580 square miles (1,138,512 square kilometers) and is the major constituent of the landmass known as the Horn of Africa. It is bordered on the north and northeast by Eritrea, on the east by Djibouti and Somalia, on the south by Kenya, and on the west and southwest by Sudan.

The central plateau, known as the highlands, is surrounded on three sides by desert with a significantly lower elevation. The plateau is between six thousand and ten thousand feet above sea level, with the highest peak being Ras Deshan, the fourth-tallest mountain in Africa. Addis Ababa is the third-highest capital city in the world.

The Great Rift Valley (known for discoveries of early hominids such as Lucy, whose bones reside in the Ethiopian National Museum) bisects the central plateau. The valley extends southwest through the country and includes the Danakil Depression, a desert containing the lowest dry point on the earth. In the highlands is Lake Tana, the source of the Blue Nile, which supplies the great majority of water to the Nile River Valley in Egypt.

Variation in altitude results in dramatic climatic variation. Some peaks in the Simyen Mountains receive periodic snowfall, while the average temperature of the Danakil is 120 degrees Fahrenheit in the day time. The high central plateau is mild, with a mean average temperature of 62 degrees Fahrenheit.

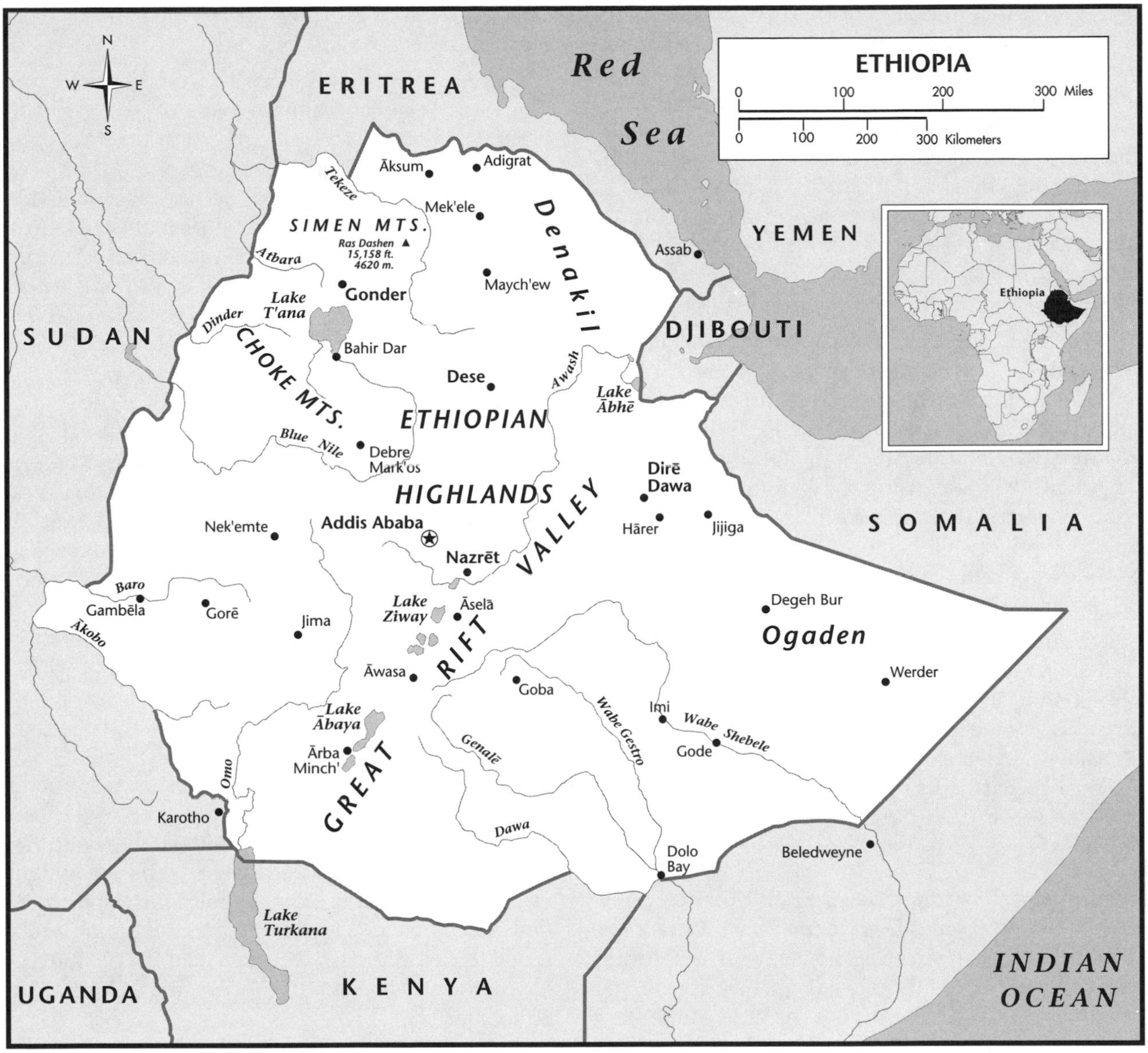

Ethiopia

The bulk of the rain in the highlands falls in the major rainy season from mid-June to mid-September, with an average of forty inches of rain during that season. A minor rainy season occurs from February to April. The northeastern provinces of Tigre and Welo are prone to drought, which tends to occur about once every ten years. The remainder of the year is generally dry.

Demography. In the year 2000, the population was approximately 61 million, with over eighty different ethnic groups. The Oromo, Amhara, and Tigreans account for more than 75 percent of the population, or 35 percent, 30 percent, and 10 percent respectively. Smaller ethnic groups include the Somali, Gurage, Afar, Awi, Welamo, Sidamo, and Beja.

The urban population is estimated to be 11 percent of the total population. The rural lowland population is composed of many nomadic and seminomadic peoples. The nomadic peoples seasonally graze livestock, while the seminomadic peoples are subsistence farmers. The rural highlands economy is based on agriculture and livestock raising.

Linguistic Affiliation. There are eighty-six known indigenous languages in Ethiopia: eighty-two spoken and four extinct. The vast majority of the languages spoken in the country can be classified within three families of the Afro-Asiatic super language family: the Semitic, Cushitic, and Omotic. Semitic-language speakers predominantly live in the highlands in the center and north. Cushitic-language speakers live in the highlands and lowlands of the south-central region as well as in the north-central area. Omotic speakers live predominantly in the south. The Nilo-Saharan super language family accounts for about 2 percent of the population, and these languages are spoken near the Sudanese border.

Amharic has been the dominant and official language for the last 150 years as a result of the political power of the Amhara ethnic group. The spread of Amharic has been strongly linked to Ethiopian nationalism. Today, many Oromo write their language, Oromoic, using the Roman alphabet as a political protest against their history of domination by the Amhara, who account for significantly less of the population.

English is the most widely spoken foreign language and the language in which secondary school and university classes are taught. French is heard occasionally in parts of the country near Djibouti, formerly French Somaliland. Italian can be heard on occasion, particularly among the elderly in the Tigre region. Remnants of the Italian occupation during World War II exist in the capital, such as the use of *ciao* to say ''good-bye.''

Symbolism. The monarchy, known as the Solomonic dynasty, has been a prominent national symbol. The imperial flag consists of horizontal stripes of green, gold, and red with a lion in the foreground holding a staff. On the head of the staff is an Ethiopian Orthodox cross with the imperial flag waving from it. The lion is the Lion of Judah, one of the many imperial titles signifying descent from King Solomon. The cross symbolizes the strength and reliance of the monarchy on the Ethiopian Orthodox Church, the dominant religion for the last sixteen hundred years.

Today, twenty-five years after the last emperor was dethroned, the flag consists of the traditional green, gold, and red horizontal stripes with a five-pointed star and rays emitting from its points in the foreground over a light blue circular background. The star represents the unity and equity of the various ethnic groups, a symbol of a federalist government based on ethnic states.

Sovereignty and freedom are characteristics and thus symbols of Ethiopia both internally and externally. Many African nation-states, such as Ghana, Benin, Senegal, Cameroon, and the Congo adopted Ethiopia's colors for their flags when they gained independence from colonial rule.

Some Africans in the diaspora established a religious and political tradition deemed Ethiopianism. Proponents of this movement, which predates pan-Africanism, appropriated the symbol of Ethiopia to liberate themselves from oppression. Ethiopia was an independent, black nation with an ancient Christian Church that was not a colonial biproduct. Marcus Garvey spoke of viewing God through the spectacles of Ethiopia and often quoted Psalm 68:31, ''Ethiopia shall stretch her hands unto God.'' From Garvey's teachings, the Rastafarian movement emerged in Jamaica in the 1930s. The name ''Rastafari'' is derived from Emperor Haile Selassie, whose precoronation name was Ras Tafari Makonnen. ''Ras'' is both a princely and a military title meaning ''head'' in Amharic. There is a population of Rastafarians living in the town of Shashamane, which was part of a land grant given to the Ethiopian World Federation by Emperor Haile Selassie in return for support during the Italian occupation during World War II.

History and Ethnic Relations

Emergence of the Nation. Ethiopia was home to some of the earliest hominid populations and possibly the region where *Homo erectus* evolved and expanded out of Africa to populate Eurasia 1.8 million years ago. The most notable paleoanthropological find in the country was ''Lucy,'' a female *Australopithicus afarensis* discovered in 1974 and referred to as *Dinqnesh* (''you are marvelous'') by Ethiopians.

The rise of sizable populations with a writing system dates back to at least 800 B.C.E. Proto-Ethiopian script inlaid on stone tablets has been found in the highlands, notably in the town of Yeha. The origin of this civilization is a point of contention. The traditional theory states that immigrants from the Arabian peninsula settled in northern Ethiopia, bringing with them their language, proto-Ethiopian (or Sabean), which has also been discovered on the eastern side of the Red Sea.

This theory of the origin of Ethiopian civilization is being challenged. A new theory states that both sides of the Red Sea were a single cultural unit and that the rise of civilization in the Ethiopian highlands was not a product of diffusion and colonization from southern Arabia but a cultural exchange in which the people of Ethiopia played a vital and active role. During this time period, waterways such as the Red Sea were virtual highways, result-

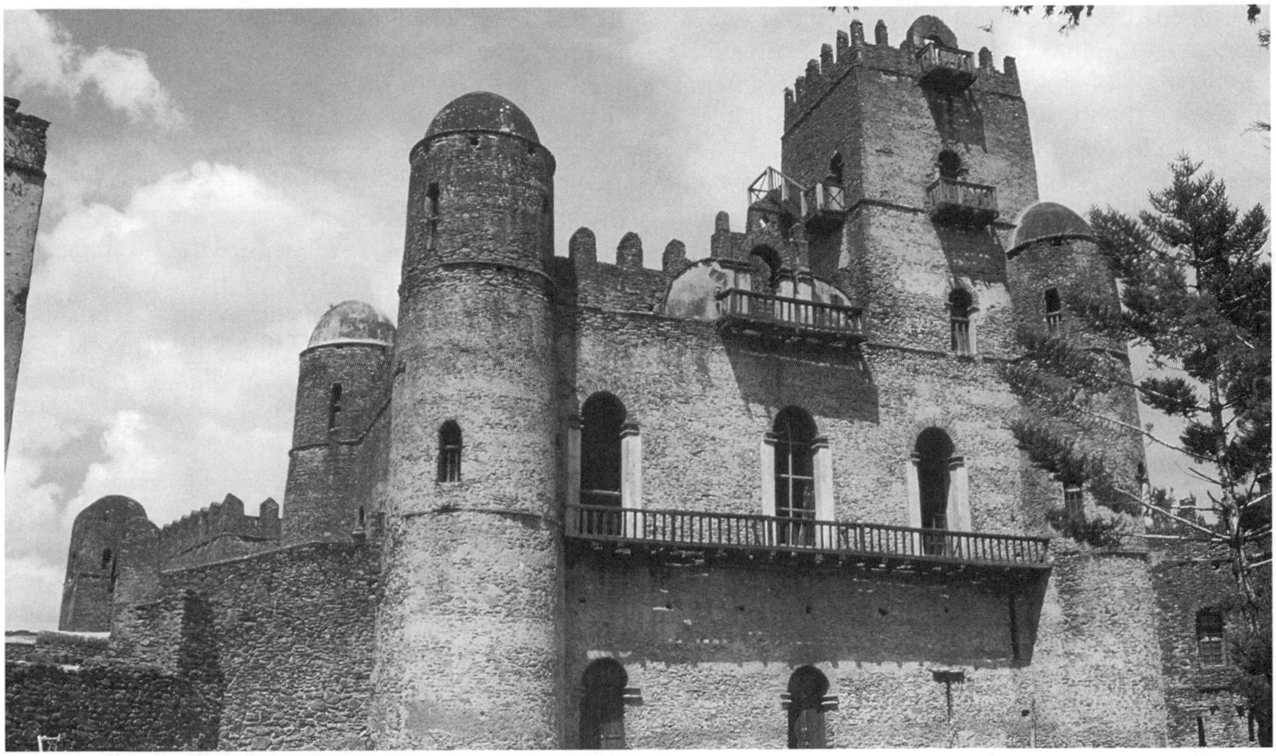

The castle of the Emperor of Fastilida in Gondar.

ing in cultural and economic exchange. The Red Sea connected people on both coasts and produced a single cultural unit that included Ethiopia and Yemen, which over time diverged into different cultures. It is only in Ethiopia that proto-Ethiopian script developed and survives today in Ge'ez, Tigrean, and Amharic.

In the first century C.E., the ancient city of Axum became a political, economic, and cultural center in the region. The Axumites dominated the Red Sea trade by the third century. By the fourth century they were one of only four nations in the world, along with Rome, Persia, and the Kushan Kingdom in northern India, to issue gold coinage.

In 333, Emperor 'Ēzānā and his court adopted Christianity; this was the same year the Roman Emperor Constantine converted. The Axumites and the Romans became economic partners who controlled the Red Sea and Mediterranean Sea trades, respectively.

Axum flourished through the sixth century, when Emperor Caleb conquered much of the Arabian peninsula. However, the Axumite Empire eventually declined as a result of the spread of Islam, resulting in a loss of control over the Red Sea as well as a depletion of natural resources in the region that left the environment unable to support the population. The political center shifted southward to the mountains of Lasta (now Lalibela).

Around 1150, a new dynasty arose in the mountains of Lasta. This dynasty was called the Zagwe and controlled much of northern Ethiopia from 1150 until 1270. The Zagwe claimed descendency from Moses, using genealogy to establish their legitimacy, a characteristic of traditional Ethiopian politics.

The Zagwe were unable to forge national unity, and squabbling over political power led to a decline in the dynasty's authority. A small Christian kingdom in northern Shewa challenged the Zagwe politically and economically in the thirteenth century. The Shewans were led by Yekunno Amlak, who killed the Zagwe king and proclaimed himself emperor. It was Yekunno Amlak who forged national unity and began constructing the nation.

National Identity. Most historians regard Yekunno Amlak as the founder of the Solomonic dynasty. In the process of legitimizing his rule, the emperor reproduced and possibly created the *Kebra Nagast (Glory of the Kings)*, which is regarded as the national epic. The *Glory of the Kings* is a blend of local and oral traditions, Old and New Testament themes, apocryphal text, and Jewish and Muslim commentaries. The epic was compiled by six Tigrean scribes, who claimed to have translated the text from Arabic into Ge'ez. Contained within its central narrative is the account of Solomon and Sheba, an elaborate version of the story found in I Kings of the Bible. In the Ethiopian version, King Solomon and the Queen of Sheba have a child named Menelik (whose name is derived from the Hebrew *ben-melech* meaning "son of the king"), who establishes a duplicate Jewish empire in Ethiopia. In establishing this empire, Menelik I brings the Ark of the Covenant with him, along with the eldest sons of the Israeli nobles. He is crowned the first emperor of Ethiopia, the founder of the Solomonic dynasty.

From this epic, a national identity emerged as God's new chosen people, heir to the Jews. The Solomonic emperors are descended from Solomon, and the Ethiopian people are the descendants of the sons of the Israeli nobles. The descent from Solomon was so essential to the nationalistic tradition and monarchical domination that Haile Selassie incorporated it into the country's first constitution in 1931, exempting the emperor from state law by virtue of his "divine" genealogy.

Both the Orthodox Church and the monarchy fostered nationalism. In the epilogue of the *Glory of the Kings*, Christianity is brought to Ethiopia and adopted as the "rightful" religion. Thus, the empire was genealogically descended from the great Hebrew kings but "righteous" in its acceptance of the word of Jesus Christ.

The Solomonic monarchy had a variable degree of political control over Ethiopia from the time of Yekunno Amlak in 1270 until Haile Selassie's dethroning in 1974. At times the monarchy was centrally strong, but during other periods regional kings held a greater amount of power. Menelik II played a vital role in maintaining a sense of pride in Ethiopia as an independent nation. On 1 March 1896, Menelik II and his army defeated the Italians at Adwa. The independence that emerged from that battle has contributed greatly to the Ethiopian sense of nationalistic pride in self-rule, and many perceive Adwa as a victory for all of Africa and the African diaspora.

Ethnic Relations. Traditionally, the Amhara have been the dominant ethnic group, with the Tigreans as secondary partners. The other ethnic groups have responded differently to that situation. Resistance to Amhara dominance resulted in various separatist movements, particularly in Eritrea and among the Oromo. Eritrea was culturally and politically part of highland Ethiopia since before Axum's achievement of political dominance; Eritreans claim Axumite descendency as much as Ethiopians do. However, in 1889, Emperor Menelik II signed the Treaty of Wichale, leasing Eritrea to the Italians in exchange for weapons. Eritrea was an Italian colony until the end of World War II. In 1947, Italy signed the Treaty of Paris, renouncing all its colonial claims. The United Nations passed a resolution in 1950 establishing Eritrea as a federation under the Ethiopian crown. By 1961, Eritrean rebels had begun fighting for independence in the bush. In November 1962, Haile Selassie abolished the federation and sent his army to quell any resistance, forcefully subordinating Eritrea against the will of its people.

African leaders passed the Cairo Resolution in 1964, which recognized the old colonial borders as the basis for nation-statehood. Under this treaty, Eritrea should have gained independence, but because of Haile Selassie's international political savvy and military strength, Ethiopia retained control. The Eritrean rebels fought the emperor until his deposition in 1974. When the Derge government was armed by the Soviets, the Eritreans still refused to accept external subjugation. The Eritrean People's Liberation Front (EPLF) fought side by side with the EPRDF and ousted the Derge in 1991, at which time Eritrea became an independent nation-state. Political confrontation has continued, and Ethiopia and Eritrea fought from June 1998 to June 2000 over the border between the two countries, with each accusing the other of infringing on its sovereignty.

The "Oromo problem" continues to trouble Ethiopia. Although the Oromo are the largest ethnic group in Ethiopia, never in their history have they maintained political power. During the period of European colonialism in Africa, the Ethiopian highlanders undertook an intra-African colonial enterprise. Many ethnic groups in the present state of Ethiopia, such as the Oromo, were subjected to that colonialization. Conquered ethnic groups were expected to adopt the identity of the dominant Amhara-Tigrean ethnic groups (the national culture). It was illegal to publish, teach, or broadcast in any Oromo dialect until the early 1970s, which marked the end of Haile Selassie's reign. Even today, after an ethnic federalist government has been established, the Oromo lack appropriate political representation.

Urbanism, Architecture, and the Use of Space

Traditional houses are round dwellings with cylindrical walls made of wattle and daub. The roofs are conical and made of thatch, and the center pole has

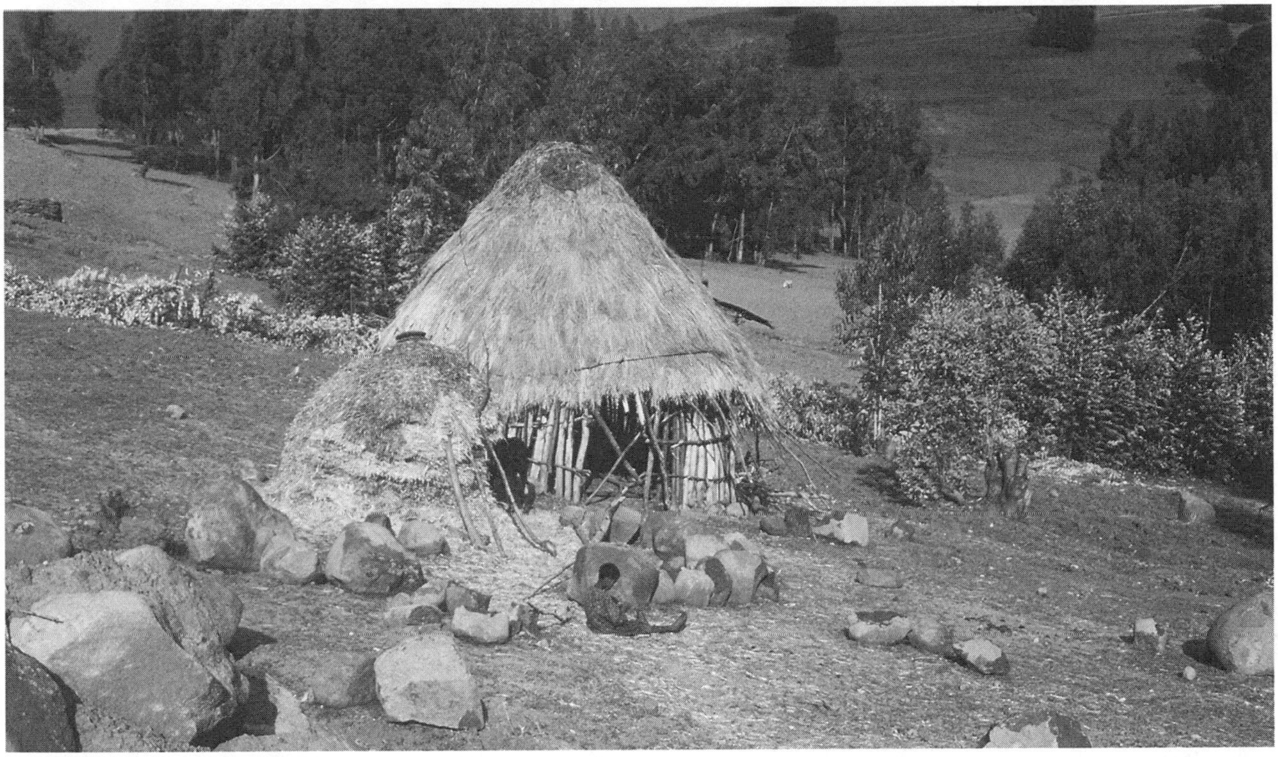

A traditional Ethiopian rural home built in cylindrical fashion with walls made of wattle and daub.

sacred significance in most ethnic groups, including the Oromo, Gurage, Amhara, and Tigreans. Variations on this design occur. In the town of Lalibella the walls of many houses are made of stone and are two-storied, while in parts of Tigre, houses are traditionally rectangular.

In more urban areas, a mixture of tradition and modernity is reflected in the architecture. The thatched roofs often are replaced with tin or steel roofing. The wealthier suburbs of Addis Ababa have multistory residences made of concrete and tile that are very western in form. Addis Ababa, which became the capital in 1887, has a variety of architectural styles. The city was not planned, resulting in a mixture of housing styles. Communities of wattle-and-daub tin-roofed houses often lie next to neighborhoods of one- and two-story gated concrete buildings.

Many churches and monasteries in the northern region are carved out of solid rock, including the twelve rock-hewn monolithic churches of Lalibela. The town is named after the thirteenth-century king who supervised its construction. The construction of the churches is shrouded in mystery, and several are over thirty-five feet high. The most famous, Beta Giorgis, is carved in the shape of a cross. Each church is unique in shape and size. The churches are not solely remnants of the past but are an active eight-hundred-year-old Christian sanctuary.

Food and Economy

Food in Daily Life. *Injera,* a spongy unleavened bread made from teff grain, is the staple of every meal. All food is eaten with the hands, and pieces of *injera* are ripped into bite-sized pieces and used to dip and grab stews (*wat*) made of vegetables such as carrots and cabbage, spinach, potatoes, and lentils. The most common spice is *berberey,* which has a red pepper base.

The food taboos found in the Old Testament are observed by most people as the Ethiopian Orthodox Church prescribes them. The flesh of animals with uncloven hoofs and those that do not chew their cud are avoided as unclean. It is nearly impossible to get pork. Animals used for food must be slaughtered with the head turned toward the east while the throat is cut "In the name of the Father, the Son, and the Holy Ghost" if the slaughterer is Christian or "In the name of Allah the Merciful" if the slaughterer is Muslim.

Food Customs at Ceremonial Occasions. The coffee ceremony is a common ritual. The server starts a fire and roasts green coffee beans while burning frankincense. Once roasted, the coffee beans are ground with a mortar and pestle, and the powder is placed in a traditional black pot called a *jebena*. Water is then added. The *jebena* is removed from the fire, and coffee is served after brewing for the proper length of time. Often, *kolo* (cooked whole-grain barley) is served with the coffee.

Meat, specifically beef, chicken, and lamb, is eaten with *injera* on special occasions. Beef is sometimes eaten raw or slightly cooked in a dish called *kitfo*. Traditionally, this was a staple of the diet, but in the modern era, many of the elite have shunned it in favor of cooked beef.

During Christian fasting periods, no animal products can be eaten and no food or drink can be consumed from midnight until 3 P.M. This is the standard way of fasting during the week, and on Saturday and Sunday no animal products may be consumed, although there is no time restriction on the fast.

Honey wine, called *tej*, is a drink reserved for special occasions. Tej is a mixture of honey and water flavored with *gesho* plant twigs and leaves and is traditionally drunk in tube-shaped flasks. High-quality tej has become a commodity of the upper class, which has the resources to brew and purchase it.

Basic Economy. The economy is based on agriculture, in which 85 percent of the population participates. Ecological problems such as periodic drought, soil degradation, deforestation, and a high population density negatively affect the agricultural industry. Most agricultural producers are subsistence farmers living in the highlands, while the population in the lowland peripheries is nomadic and engages in livestock raising. Gold, marble, limestone, and small amounts of tantalum are mined.

Land Tenure and Property. The monarchy and the Orthodox Church traditionally controlled and owned most of the land. Until the overthrow of the monarchy in 1974, there was a complex land tenure system; for example, there were over 111 different types of tenure in Welo Province. Two major types of traditional land ownership that are no longer in existence were *rist* (a type of communal land ownership that was hereditary) and *gult* (ownership acquired from the monarch or provincial ruler).

The EPRDF instituted a policy of public land use. In rural areas, peasants have land use rights, and every five years there is a reallotment of land among farmers to adapt to the changing social structures of their communities. There are several reasons for the nonexistence of individual land ownership in rural areas. If private ownership were legislated, the government believes that rural class divisions would increase as a result of a large number of peasants selling their land.

Commercial Activities. Agriculture is the major commercial activity. The chief staple crops include a variety of grains, such as teff, wheat, barley, corn, sorghum, and millet; coffee; pulses; and oilseed. Grains are the primary staples of the diet and are thus the most important field crops. Pulses are a principal source of protein in the diet. Oilseed consumption is widespread because the Ethiopian Orthodox Church prohibits the usage of animal fats on many days during the year.

Major Industries. After nationalization of the private sector before the 1974 revolution, an exodus of foreign-owned and foreign-operated industry ensued. The growth rate of the manufacturing sector declined. Over 90 percent of large scale industries are state-run, as opposed to less than 10 percent of agriculture. Under the EPRDF administration, there is both public and private industry. Public industries include the garment, steel, and textile industries, while much of the pharmaceuticals industry is owned by shareholders. Industry accounts for almost 14 percent of the gross domestic product, with textiles, construction, cement, and hydroelectric power constituting the majority of production.

Trade. The most important export crop is coffee, which provides 65 to 75 percent of foreign exchange earnings. Ethiopia has vast agricultural potential because of its large areas of fertile land, a diverse climate, and generally adequate rainfall. Hides and skins are the second largest export, followed by pulses, oilseed, gold, and *chat*, a quasi-legal plant whose leaves possess psychotropic qualities, that is chewed in social groups. The agricultural sector is subject to periodic drought, and poor infrastructure constrains the production and marketing of Ethiopia's products. Only 15 percent of the roads are paved; this is a problem particularly in the highlands, where there are two rainy seasons causing many roads to be unusable for weeks at a time. The two biggest imports are live animals and petroleum. The majority of Ethiopia's exports are sent to Germany, Japan, Italy and the United Kingdom, while imports are primarily brought in from Italy, the United States, Germany, and Saudi Arabia.

A group of women return from Lake Tana with jugs of water. Ethiopian women are traditionally in charge of domestic chores, while men are responsible for activities outside the home.

Division of Labor. Men do the most physically taxing activities outside the house, while women are in charge of the domestic sphere. Young children, especially on farms, get involved in household labor at an early age. Girls usually have a greater amount of work to do than boys.

Ethnicity is another axis of labor stratification. Ethiopia is a multi-ethnic state with a history of ethnic division. Currently, the Tigrean ethnic group controls the government and holds the core positions of power in the federal government. Ethnicity is not the sole basis for employment in the government; political ideology also plays an important role.

Social Stratification

Classes and Castes. There are four major social groups. At the top are high-ranking lineages, followed by low-ranking lineages. Caste groups, which are endogamous, with group membership ascribed by birth and membership associated with concepts of pollution, constitute the third social stratum. Slaves and the descendants of slaves are the lowest social group. This four-tier system is traditional; the contemporary social organization is dynamic, especially in urban areas. In urban society, the division of labor determines social class. Some jobs are esteemed more than others, such as lawyers and federal government employees. Many professions carry negative associations, such as metal workers, leather workers, and potters, who are considered of low status and frequently are isolated from mainstream society.

Symbols of Social Stratification. Symbols of social stratification in rural areas include the amount of grain and cattle a person possesses. While the symbols of wealth in urban areas are different, it is still these symbols which index high social status. Wealth is the chief criterion for social stratification, but the amount of education, the neighborhood in which one lives, and the job one holds are also symbols of high or low status. Automobiles are difficult to obtain, and the ownership of a car is a symbol of wealth and high status.

Political Life

Government. For almost sixteen hundred years, the nation was ruled by a monarchy with close ties to the Orthodox Church. In 1974, Haile Selassie, the last monarch, was overthrown by a communist military regime known as the Derge. In 1991, the Derge was deposed by the EPRDF (internally composed of the Tigrean People's Liberation Front, the Oromo People's Democratic Organization, and the Amhara National Democratic movement), which established a ''democratic'' government.

Ethiopia is currently an ethnic federation composed of eleven states that are largely ethnically based. This type of organization is intended to minimize ethnic strife. The highest official is the prime minister, and the president is a figurehead with no real power. The legislative branch consists of a bicameral legislation in which all people and ethnicities can be represented.

Ethiopia has not achieved political equality. The EPRDF is an extension of the military organization that deposed the former military dictatorship, and the government is controlled by the Tigrean People's Liberation Front. Since the government is ethnically and militarily based, it is plagued by all the problems of the previous regimes.

Leadership and Political Officials. Emperor Haile Selassie ruled from 1930 until 1974. During his lifetime, Selassie built massive infrastructure and created the first constitution (1931). Haile Selassie led Ethiopia to become the only African member of the League of Nations and was the first president of the Organization of African Unity, which is based in Addis Ababa. Micromanaging a nation caught up with the emperor in old age, and he was deposed by the communist Derge regime led by Lieutenant Colonel Mengistu Haile Mariam. Mengistu assumed power as head of state after having his two predecessors killed. Ethiopia then became a totalitarian state financed by the Soviet Union and assisted by Cuba. Between 1977 and 1978, thousands of suspected Derge oppositionists were killed.

In May 1991, the EPRDF forcefully took Addis Ababa, forcing Mengistu into asylum in Zimbabwe. Leader of the EPRDF and current prime minister Meles Zenawi pledged to oversee the formation of a multiparty democracy. The election of a 547-member constituent assembly was held in June 1994, and the adoption of the Federal Democratic Republic of Ethiopia's constitution ensued. Elections for the national parliament and regional legislatures were held in May and June of 1995, although most opposition parties boycotted the elections. A landslide victory was achieved by the EPRDF.

The EPRDF, along with 50 other registered political parties (most of which are small and ethnically based), comprise Ethiopia's political parties. The EPRDF is dominated by the Tigrean People's Liberation Front (TPLF). Because of that, after independence in 1991, other ethnically-based political organizations withdrew from the national government. One example is the Oromo Liberation Front (OLF), which withdrew in June of 1992.

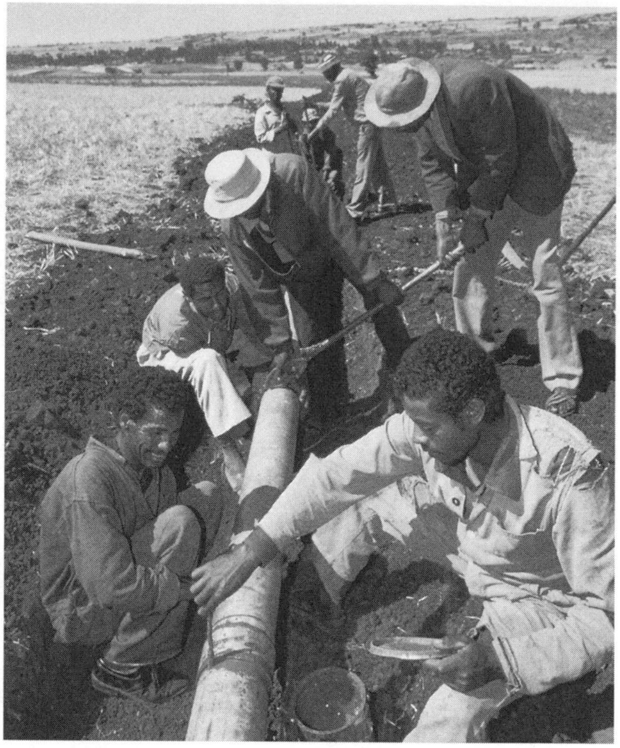

Workers installing a water pipeline for irrigation in Hitosa.

Social Problems and Control. Ethiopia is safer than the neighboring countries, particularly in urban areas. Ethnic issues play a role in political life, but this does not usually result in violence. Christians and Muslims live together peacefully.

Theft occurs infrequently in Addis Ababa and almost never involves weapons. Robbers tend to work in groups, and pickpocketing is the usual form of theft. Homelessness in the capital is a serious social problem, especially among the youth. Many street children resort to theft to feed themselves. Police officers usually apprehend thieves but rarely prosecute and often work with them, splitting the bounty.

Military Activity. The Ethiopian military is called the Ethiopian National Defence Force (ENDF) and is comprised of approximately 100,000 personnel, making it one of the largest military forces in Africa. During the Derge regime, troups numbered around one-quarter of a million. Since the early 1990s, when the Derge was overthrown, the ENDF has been in transition from a rebel force to a professional military organization trained in demining, humanitarian and peacekeeping operations, and military justice.

From June 1998 until the summer of 2000, Ethiopia was involved in the largest war on the African continent with its northern neighbor, Eritrea. The war was essentially a border conflict. Eritrea was occupying the towns of Badme and Zalambasa, which Ethiopia claimed was sovereign territory. The conflict can be traced to Emperor Menelik, who sold Eritrea to the Italians in the late nineteenth century.

Large-scale fighting occurred in 1998 and 1999 with no change in the combatants' positions. During the winter months, fighting was minimal because of the rains, which make it difficult to move armaments. In the summer of 2000, Ethiopia achieved large-scale victories and marched through the contested border area into Eritrean territory. After these victories, both nations signed a peace treaty, which called for United Nations peacekeeping troops to monitor the contested area and professional cartographers to demarcate the border. Ethiopian troops withdrew from undisputed Eritrean territory after the treaty was signed.

Social Welfare and Change Programs

Traditional associations are the major sources of social welfare. There are many different types of social welfare programs in different parts of the country; these programs have religious, political, familial, or other bases for their formation. Two of the most prevalent are the *iddir* and *debo* systems.

An iddir is an association that provides financial assistance and other forms of aid for people in the same neighborhood or occupation and between friends or kin. This institution became prevalent with the formation of urban society. The main objective of an iddir is to assist families financially during times of stress, such as illness, death, and property losses from fire or theft. Recently, iddirs have been involved in community development, including the construction of schools and roads. The head of a family who belongs to an iddir contributes a certain amount of money every month to benefit individuals in times of emergency.

The most widespread social welfare association in rural areas is the debo. If a farmer is having difficulty tending his fields, he may invite his neighbors to help on a specific date. In return, the farmer must provide food and drink for the day and contribute his labor when others in the same debo require help. The debo is not restricted to agriculture but is also prevalent in housing construction.

Nongovernmental Organizations and Other Associations

Nongovernmental organizations (NGOs) are the main sources of aid to alleviate rural poverty. The Swedish International Development Agency was the first NGO in Ethiopia in the 1960s, focusing on rural development. Drought and war have been the two biggest problems in recent years. NGOs played a crucial role in famine relief in Welo and Tigre during the 1973–1974 and 1983–1984 famines through the coordination of the Christian Relief and Development Association. In 1985, the Churches Drought Action Africa/Ethiopia formed a joint relief partnership to distribute emergency food relief to areas controlled by rebel forces.

When the EPRDF took power in 1991, a large number of donor organizations supported and funded rehabilitation and development activities. Environmental protection and food-based programs take precedence today, although development and preventive health care are also activities on which NGO focuses.

Gender Roles and Statuses

Division of Labor by Gender. Traditionally, labor has been divided by gender, with authority given to the senior male in a household. Men are responsible for plowing, harvesting, the trading of goods, the slaughtering of animals, herding, the building of houses, and the cutting of wood. Women are responsible for the domestic sphere and help the men with some activities on the farm. Women are in charge of cooking, brewing beer, cutting hops, buying and selling spices, making butter, collecting and carrying wood, and carrying water.

The gender division in urban areas is less pronounced than it is in the countryside. Many women work outside of the home, and there tends to be a greater awareness of gender inequality. Women in urban areas are still responsible, with or without a career, for the domestic space. Employment at a baseline level is fairly equivalent, but men tend to be promoted much faster and more often.

The Relative Status of Women and Men. Gender inequality is still prevalent. Men often spend their free time socializing outside the home, while women take care of the household. If a man participates in domestic activities such as cooking and child rearing, he may become a social outcast.

The education of boys is stressed more than that of girls, who are supposed to help with household work. Girls are restricted from leaving the home and engaging in social activities with friends much more than boys are.

Marriage, Family, and Kinship

Marriage. Traditional marriage customs vary by ethnic group, although many customs are trans-ethnic. Arranged marriages are the norm, although this practice is becoming much less common, especially in urban areas. The presentation of a dowry from the male's family to the female's family is common. The amount is not fixed and varies with the wealth of the families. The dowry may include livestock, money, or other socially valued items.

The proposal usually involves elders, who travel from the groom's house to the parents of the bride to ask for the marriage. The elders are traditionally the individuals who decide when and where the ceremony takes place. Both the bride's and groom's families prepare food and drink for the ceremony by brewing wine and beer and cooking food. A great deal of food is prepared for the occasion, especially meat dishes.

Christians often wed in Orthodox churches, and a variety of wedding types exist. In the *takelil* type, the bride and groom participate in a special ceremony and agree never to divorce. This type of commitment has become rare in recent years. Wedding garb in the cities is very western: suits and tuxedos for the men and a white wedding gown for the bride.

Domestic Unit. The basic family structure is much larger than the typical Western nuclear unit. The oldest male is usually the head of the household and is in charge of decision making. Men, usually having the primary income, control the family economically and distribute money. Women are in charge of domestic life and have significantly more contact with the children. The father is seen as an authority figure.

Children are socially required to care for their parents, and so there are often three to four generations in a household. With the advent of urban living, however, this pattern is changing, and children often live far from their families and have a much harder time supporting them. Urbanites have a responsibility to send money to their families in rural areas and often try their best to relocate their families to the cities.

Inheritance. Inheritance laws follow a fairly regular pattern. Before an elder passes away he or she orally states his or her wishes for the disposal of possessions. Children and living spouses are typically the inheritors, but if an individual dies without a will, property is allotted by the court system to the closest living relatives and friends. Land, although not officially owned by individuals, is inheritable. Men are more privileged then females and usually receive the most prized properties and equipment, while women tend to inherit items associated with the domestic sphere.

An Ethiopian woman looking at fabric in Fasher.

Kin Groups. Descent is traced through both the mother's and father's families, but the male line is more valued than the female. It is customary for a child to take the father's first name as his or her last name. In rural areas, villages are often composed of kin groups that offer support during difficult times. The kin group in which one participates tends to be in the male line. Elders are respected, especially men, and are regarded as the source of a lineage. In general, an elder or groups of elders are responsible for settling disputes within a kin group or clan.

Socialization

Infant Care. Children are raised by the extended family and community. It is the primary duty of the mother to care for the children as part of her domestic duties. If the mother is not available, the

Colorfully robed deacons at the Timkat Festival in Lalibela.

responsibility falls to the older female children as well as the grandmothers.

In urban society, where both parents often work, babysitters are employed and the father takes a more active role in child care. If a child is born out of wedlock, whoever the women claims is the father is required by law to support the child economically. If parents get divorced, a child five years old or older is asked with whom he or she wants to live.

Child Rearing and Education. During early childhood, children have the greatest exposure to their mothers and female relatives. At around the age of five, especially in urban areas, children start attending school if their families can afford the fees. In rural areas, schools are few and children do farm work. This means a very low percentage of rural youth attend school. The government is trying to alleviate this problem by building accessible schools in rural areas.

The patriarchal structure of society is reflected in the stress on education for boys over girls. Women face discrimination problems as well as physical abuse in school. Also, the belief still exists that females are less competent then males and that education is wasted on them.

Higher Education. Children who do well in elementary school go on to secondary school. It is felt that missionary schools are superior to government schools. Fees are required for missionary schools, although they are reduced considerably for religious adherents.

University is free, but admission is extremely competitive. Every secondary student takes a standardized examination to get into college. The acceptance rate is approximately 20 percent of all the individuals who take the tests. There is a quota for the various departments, and only a certain number of individuals are enrolled in their desired majors. The criterion is the grades of first-year students; those with the highest marks get the first choice. In 1999, enrollment at Addis Ababa University was approximately 21,000 students.

ETIQUETTE

Greeting takes the form of multiple kisses on both cheeks and a plethora of exchanged pleasantries. Any hint of superiority is treated with contempt. Age is a factor in social behavior, and the elderly are treated with the utmost respect. When an elderly person or guest enters a room, it is customary to stand until that person is seated. Dining etiquette is also important. One must always wash the hands before a meal, since all food is eaten with the hands from a communal dish. It is customary for the guest to initiate eating. During a meal, it is proper form to pull *injera* only from the space directly in front of oneself. Depleted portions are replaced quickly. During meals, participation in conversation is considered polite; complete attention to the meal is thought to be impolite.

RELIGION

Religious Beliefs. There has been religious freedom for centuries in Ethiopia. The Ethiopian Orthodox Church is the oldest sub-Saharan African church, and the first mosque in Africa was built in the Tigre province. Christianity and Islam have coexisted peacefully for hundreds of years, and the Christian kings of Ethiopia gave Muhammad refuge during his persecution in southern Arabia, causing the Prophet to declare Ethiopia exempt from Muslim holy wars. It is not uncommon for Christians and Muslims to visit each other's house of worship to seek health or prosperity.

The dominant religion has been Orthodox Christianity since King 'Ēzānā of Axum adopted Christianity in 333. It was the official religion during the reign of the monarchy and is currently the unofficial religion. Because of the spread of Islam in Africa, Ethiopian Orthodox Christianity was severed from the Christian world. This has led to many unique characteristics of the church, which is considered the most Judaic formal Christian church.

The Ethiopian Orthodox Church lays claim to the original Ark of the Covenant, and replicas (called *tabotat*) are housed in a central sanctuary in all churches; it is the *tabot* that consecrates a church. The Ethiopian Orthodox Church is the only established church that has rejected the doctrine of Pauline Christianity, which states that the Old Testament lost its binding force after the coming of Jesus. The Old Testament focus of the Ethiopian Orthodox Church includes dietary laws similar to the kosher tradition, circumcision after the eighth day of birth, and a Saturday sabbath.

Judaism historically was a major religion, although the vast majority of Ethiopian Jews (called Beta Israel) reside in Israel today. The Beta Israel were politically powerful at certain times. Ethiopian Jews often were persecuted during the last few hundred years; that resulted in massive secret airlifts in 1984 and 1991 by the Israeli military.

Islam has been a significant religion in Ethiopia since the eighth century but has been viewed as the religion of the "outside" by many Christians and scholars. Non-Muslims traditionally have interpreted Ethiopian Islam as hostile. This prejudice is a result of the dominance of Christianity.

Polytheistic religions are found in the lowlands, which also have received Protestant missionaries. These Evangelical churches are fast growing, but Orthodox Christianity and Islam claim the adherence of 85 to 90 percent of the population.

Religious Practitioners. The leader of the Ethiopian Orthodox Church is often referred to as the Patriarch or the Pope by Ethiopians. The Patriarch, a Copt himself, was traditionally sent from Egypt to lead the Ethiopian Orthodox Church. This tradition was abandoned in the 1950s when the Patriarch was chosen by Emperor Haile Selassie from within the Ethiopian Church.

The tradition of the Patriarch being sent from Egypt began in the fourth century. The conversion of Emperor 'Ēzānā of Axum to Christianity was facilitated by a Syrian boy named Frumentious, who worked in the emperor's court. After Emperor 'Ēzānā's conversion, Frumentious traveled to Egypt to consult the Coptic authorities about sending a Patriarch to head the Church. They concluded that Frumentious would best serve in that role and he was anointed 'Abba Salama (father of Peace) and became the first Patriarch of the Ethiopian Orthodox Church.

Within the Orthodox Church there are several categories of clergy, including priests, deacons, monks, and lay-priests. It was estimated in the 1960s that between 10 and 20 percent of all adult Amhara and Tigrean men were priests. These figures are much less extraordinary when one considers that at that time there were 17,000 to 18,000 churches in the Amhara and Tigrean regions in the north-central highlands.

Rituals and Holy Places. The majority of celebrations are religious in nature. The major Christian holidays include Christmas on 7 January, Epiphany (celebrating the baptism of Jesus) on 19 January, Good Friday and Easter (in late April), and Meskel (the finding of the true cross) on 17 September. Muslim holidays include Ramadan, Id Al Adha (Arafa) on 15 March, and the birthday of Muhammad on 14 June. During all religious holidays, adherents go to their respective places of worship. Many Christian holidays are also state holidays.

Death and the Afterlife. Death is a part of daily life as famine, AIDS, and malaria take many lives. Three days of mourning for the dead is the norm. The dead are buried the day they die, and special

Taylors' Street in Harrar. Close living conditions, poor sanitation, and lack of medical facilities has lead to an increase of communicable diseases.

food is eaten that is provided by family and friends. Christians bury their dead on the grounds of the church, and Muslims do the same at the mosque. Muslims read from religious texts, while Christians tend to cry for their dead during the mourning period.

Medicine and Health Care

Communicable diseases are the primary illnesses. Acute respiratory infections such as tuberculosis, upper respiratory infections, and malaria are the Ministry of Health's priority health problems. These afflictions accounted for 17 percent of deaths and 24 percent of hospital admissions in 1994 and 1995. Poor sanitation, malnutrition, and a shortage of health facilities are some of the causes of communicable diseases.

AIDS has been a serious health problem in recent years. AIDS awareness and condom usage are increasing, however, especially among the urban and educated populations. In 1988 the AIDS Control and Prevention Office conducted a study in which 17 percent of the sample population tested positive for HIV. A total of 57,000 AIDS cases were reported up to April 1998, almost 60 percent of which were in Addis Ababa. This places the HIV-infected population in 1998 at approximately three million. The urban HIV-positive population is drastically higher than the rural at 21 percent versus under 5 percent, respectively, as of 1998. Eighty-eight percent of all infections result from heterosexual transmission, mainly from prostitution and multiple sex partners.

The federal government has created a National AIDS Control Program (NACP) to prevent the transmission of HIV and reduce the associated morbidity and mortality. The goals are to inform and educate the general population and increase awareness about AIDS. Prevention of transmission through safer sexual practices, condom usage, and appropriate screening for blood transfusion are goals of the NACP.

Government health spending has risen. The absolute level of health expenditure, however, remains far below the average for other sub-Saharan African countries. The health system is primarily curative despite the fact that most health problems are amenable to preventive action.

In 1995-1996, Ethiopia had 1,433 physicians, 174 pharmacists, 3,697 nurses, and one hospital for every 659,175 people. The physician-to-population ratio was 1:38,365. These ratios are very low in comparison to other sub-Saharan developing countries, although the distribution is highly unbalanced in favor of urban centers. For example, 62 percent of the doctors and 46 percent of the nurses were found in Addis Ababa, where 5 percent of the population resides.

SECULAR CELEBRATIONS

The major state holidays are New Year's Day on 11 September, Victory Day of Adwa on 2 March, Ethiopian Patriots Victory Day on 6 April, Labor Day on 1 May, and the Downfall of the Derge, 28 May.

THE ARTS AND HUMANITIES

Literature. The classical language of Ge'ez, which has evolved into Amharic and Tigrean, is one of the four extinct languages but is the only indigenous writing system in Africa that is still in use. Ge'ez is still spoken in Orthodox Church services. The development of Ge'ez literature began with translations of the Old and New Testaments from Greek and Hebrew. Ge'ez was also the first Semitic language to employ a vowel system.

Many apocryphal texts such as the Book of Enoch, the Book of Jubilees, and the Ascension of Isaiah have been preserved in their entirety only in Ge'ez. Even though these texts were not included in the Biblical canon, among Biblical scholars (and Ethiopian Christians) they are regarded as significant to an understanding of the origin and development of Christianity.

Graphic Arts. Religious art, especially Orthodox Christian, has been a significant part of the national culture for hundreds of years. Illuminated Bibles and manuscripts have been dated to the twelfth century, and the eight-hundred-year-old churches in Lalibela contain Christian paintings, manuscripts, and stone relief.

Wood carving and sculpture are very common in the southern lowlands, especially among the Konso. A fine arts school has been established in Addis Ababa that teaches painting, sculpture, etching, and lettering.

Performance Arts. Christian music is believed to have been established by Saint Yared in the sixth century and is sung in Ge'ez, the liturgical language. Both Orthodox and Protestant music is popular and is sung in Amharic, Tigrean, and Oromo. The traditional dance, *eskesta,* consists of rhythmic shoulder movements and usually is accompanied by the *kabaro,* a drum made from wood and animal skin, and the *masinqo,* a single-stringed violin with an A-shaped bridge that is played with a small bow. Foreign influences exist in the form of Afro-pop, reggae, and hip-hop.

THE STATE OF THE PHYSICAL AND SOCIAL SCIENCES

The university system fosters academic research in cultural and physical anthropology, archaeology, history, political science, linguistics, and theology. A large percentage of the leading scholars in these fields went to the University of Addis Ababa. A lack of funding and resources has constrained the development of the university system. The library system is inferior, and computers and Internet access are not available at the university.

BIBLIOGRAPHY

Addis Ababa University. *Addis Ababa University: A Brief Profile 2000,* 2000.

Ahmed, Hussein. "The Historiography of Islam in Ethiopia." *Journal of Islamic Studies* 3 (1): 15–46, 1992.

Akilu, Amsalu. *A Glimpse of Ethiopia,* 1997.

Briggs, Philip. *Guide to Ethiopia,* 1998.

Brooks, Miguel F. *Kebra Nagast [The Glory of Kings],* 1995.

Budge, Sir. E. A. Wallis. *The Queen of Sheba and Her Only Son Menyelek,* 1932.

Cassenelli, Lee. "Qat: Changes in the Production and Consumption of a Quasilegal Commodity in Northeast Africa." In *The Social Life of Things: Commodities in Cultural Perspectives,* Arjun Appadurai, ed., 1999.

Clapham, Christopher. *Haile-Selassie's Government,* 1969.

Connah, Graham. *African Civilizations: Precolonial Cities and States in Tropical Africa: An Archaeological Perspective,* 1987.

Donham, Donald, and Wendy James, eds. *The Southern Marches of Imperial Ethiopia,* 1986.

Haile, Getatchew. "Ethiopic Literature." In *African Zion: The Sacred Art of Ethiopia,* Roderick Grierson, ed., 1993.

Hastings, Adrian. *The Construction of Nationhood: Ethnicity, Religion and Nationalism,* 1995.

Hausman, Gerald. *The Kebra Nagast: The Lost Bible of Rastafarian Wisdom and Faith from Ethiopia and Jamaica,* 1995.

Heldman, Marilyn. "Maryam Seyon: Mary of Zion." In *African Zion: The Sacred Art of Ethiopia,* Roderick Grierson, ed., 1993.

Isaac, Ephraim. "An Obscure Component in Ethiopian Church History." *Le Museon,* 85: 225–258, 1971.

———. "Social Structure of the Ethiopian Church." *Ethiopian Observer,* XIV (4): 240–288, 1971.

——— and Cain Felder. "Reflections on the Origins of Ethiopian Civilization." In *Proceedings of the Eighth International Conference of Ethiopian Studies*, 1988.

Jalata, Asafa. "The Struggle For Knowledge: The Case of Emergent Oromo Studies." *African Studies Review*, 39 (2): 95–123.

Joireman, Sandra Fullerton. "Contracting for Land: Lessons from Litigation in a Communal Tenure Area of Ethiopia." *Canadian Journal of African Studies*, 30 (2): 214–232.

Kalayu, Fitsum. "The Role of NGOs in Poverty Alleviation in Rural Ethiopia: The Case of Actionaid Ethiopia." Master's thesis. School of Developmental Studies, University of Anglia, Norway.

Kaplan, Steven. *The Beta Israel (Falasha) in Ethiopia*, 1992.

Kessler, David. *The Falashas: A Short History of the Ethiopian Jews*, 1982.

Levine, Donald Nathan. *Wax and Gold: Tradition and Innovation in Ethiopian Culture*, 1965.

———. *Greater Ethiopia: The Evolution of a Multiethnic Society*, 1974.

Library of Congress. *Ethiopia: A Country Study*, 1991, http://lcweb2.loc.gov/frd/cs/ettoc.html.

Marcus, Harold. *A History of Ethiopia*,1994.

Mengisteab, Kidane. "New Approaches to State Building in Africa: The Case of Ethiopia's Based Federalism." *African Studies Review*, 40 (3): 11–132.

Mequanent, Getachew. "Community Development and the Role of Community Organizations: A Study in Northern Ethiopia." *Canadian Journal of African Studies*, 32 (3): 494–520, 1998.

Ministry of Health of the Federal Democratic Republic of Ethiopia. *National AIDS Control Program: Regional Multisectoral HIV/AIDS Strategic Plan 2000–2004*, 1999.

———. *Health and Health Related Indicators: 1991*, 2000.

Munro-Hay, Stuart C. "Aksumite Coinage." In *African Zion: The Sacred Art of Ethiopia*, Roderick Grierson, ed., 1993.

Pankhurst, Richard. *A Social History of Ethiopia*, 1990.

Rahmato, Dessalegn. "Land Tenure and Land Policy in Ethiopia after the Derg." In *Papers of the 12th International Conference of Ethiopian Studies*, Harold Marcus, ed., 1994.

Ullendorff, Edward. *The Ethiopians: An Introduction to Country and People*, 1965.

———. *Ethiopia and the Bible*, 1968.

United Nations Development Program. *Health Indicators in Ethiopia, Human Development Report*, 1998.

Web Sites

Central Intelligence Agency. *World Factbook 1999: Ethiopia*, 1999, http://www.odci.gov/cia/publications/factbook/et.html

Ethnologue. *Ethiopia* (Catalogue of Languages), 2000 http://www.sil.org/ethnologue/countries/Ethi.html

United States Department of State. *Background Notes: Federal Democratic Republic of Ethiopia*, 1998, http://www.state.gov/www/background_notes/ethiopia_0398_bgn.html

—Adam Mohr

Falkland Islands

Culture Name

Falklander

Orientation

Identification. The British named the two islands after the naval officer Viscount Falkland.

Location and Geography. The Falklands, located approximately 185 miles (480 kilometers) east of Argentina, consist of two main islands, East Falkland and West Falkland, and over two hundred smaller islets. The combined area is 4,700 square miles (12,170 square kilometers). The terrain is mainly hilly to mountainous grassland. Shrubs abound, but there are no native trees. An impressive diversity of animal life includes elephant seals, sea lions, penguins, and other birds.

Demography. As of the year 2000, there was a population of 2,826 permanent residents, of whom 1,750 lived in the capital, Stanley. The majority are of British descent, although there are a few immigrants from South America, Chile in particular. At any given time, there are about two thousand British military personnel.

Linguistic Affiliation. English is both the official language and the language of daily life.

Symbolism. The coat of arms, which appears on the flag, contains a representation of the sailing ship *Desire,* which was the first to reach the islands, and a white ram symbolizing shepherding, the industry on which the economy was built.

History and Ethnic Relations

Emergence of the Nation. It is thought that Patagonian Indians may have reached the islands by canoe, but when the Europeans encountered the islands in the seventeenth century, they were uninhabited. The British landed in 1690 and claimed the islands. The first settlement was by the French, at Port Louis on East Falkland in 1764. Spain soon after pressured the French to leave, and in 1767, forced the British out of a settlement on West Falkland. Argentina claimed the islands in the late 1820s, and the British reclaimed them in 1833. In the late 1800s, sheep ranching brought some wealth, and the British declared the islands a colony in 1892. Although the Argentinian were forced out in 1833, they did not abandon their claim. In the late 1960s, Britain began to make moves to hand over the colony to Argentina. However, the process was slow, and in 1982, Argentina's government staged an invasion. Britain sent troops to retake the islands. The ensuing war took nearly one thousand lives (three-quarters of them Argentinian), and after seventy-two days, Argentina surrendered and its president resigned. Argentina's government holds to the conviction that it will retake the Falklands, although it declines to use military force to back up its claim.

National Identity. There is no indigenous culture; the population is entirely imported and mainly British. Despite historical ties to Argentina, most inhabitants align themselves with Britain. Since the war in 1972, they have been developing a relationship with Chile.

Urbanism, Architecture, and the Use of Space

There is a low population density, with the majority of people living on farms and ranches in rural settings. Stanley is the only urban center. Its architecture is British in character.

Food and Economy

Food in Daily Life. Food is very similar to British cuisine in terms of ingredients and preparation. A common tradition, called the ''smoko,'' is a midmorning tea or coffee break. Large ''camp

Falkland Islands (Islas Malvinas)

breakfasts'' are popular, especially in rural areas. Seafood is an important part of the diet.

Basic Economy. The currency is the Falkland Island pound. There is no unemployment, but much of the work is seasonal, such as peat cutting and sheep shearing, and many islanders supplement their incomes with small-scale mechanical and agricultural projects.

Commercial Activities. The main goods produced are agricultural. In addition to sheep products (wool, hides, and meat), the islands grow vegetables such as potatoes, cabbages, and cauliflower.

Major Industries. Until recently, sheep shearing and wool processing was the major industry. This business was incorporated in the Falkland Islands Company in 1851, included in the British Royal Charter. The fishing industry has grown rapidly as a result of the government's declaration of the Falkland Islands Interim Conservation and Management Zone (FICZ). Between 1985 and 1987, gross national product tripled.

Trade. The primary products produced for export are wool, hides, and meat. The main imports are food, drink, building materials, and clothing. The major trading partners are the United Kingdom, the Netherlands, and Japan.

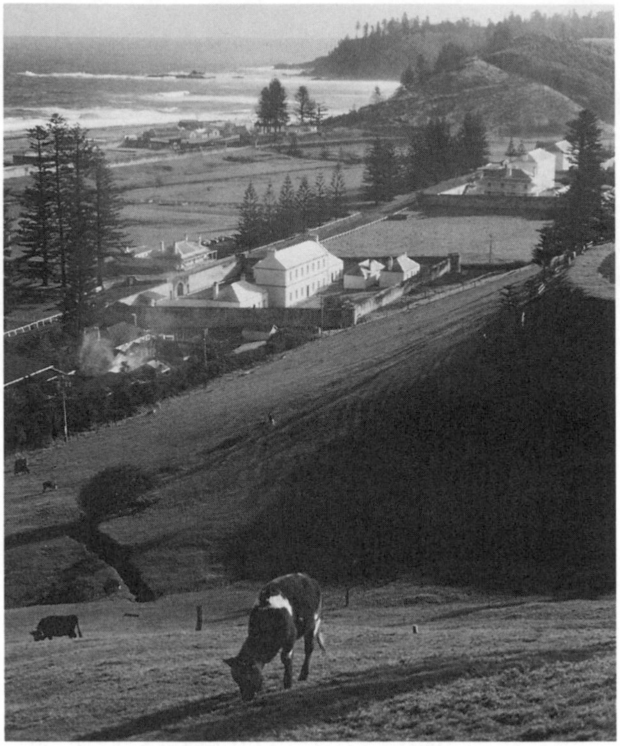

Farms on coastal hills, Kingston, Norfolk Island. Agricultural products, such as wool, meat, and vegetables are the foundation of the country's economy.

Political Life

Government. The Falklands are governed as a colony of the United Kingdom. The highest political official is the governor, who is appointed to represent the British monarchy. Along with an Executive Council of six, the governor is responsible for administration. The Legislative Council is composed of two ex-officio and eight elected members. There is universal suffrage. There is a Supreme Court, the chief justice of which is a nonresident.

Leadership and Political Officials. There are not any political parties; all officials run as independents.

Military Activity. Roughly half the population consists of British personnel; two thousand troops are stationed at the Mount Pleasant airport complex.

Socialization

Child Rearing and Education. Education is free and compulsory from age six through age fifteen. There is a primary school and a secondary school in Stanley, as well as three settlement schools on

Visitors watch a colony of rockhopping penguins. The Falkland's ecosystem includes a wide range of wildlife, including penguins, sea lions, and elephant seals.

farms in rural areas. Students who do not attend these schools are home-schooled with the aid of traveling teachers and radio and telephone lessons.

Higher Education. There are not any institutes of higher learning, but citizens are eligible to receive funding for vocational and higher education classes in Great Britain.

Religion

Religious Beliefs. The vast majority of the population is Anglican.

Medicine and Health Care

The King Edward VII Hospital in Stanley is the only hospital. It was destroyed by a fire in 1984 and rebuilt in 1987. The care provided is free and comprehensive, with the exception of eyeglasses, dentures, and cosmetic dentistry.

Secular Celebrations

Annual sports meetings take place in Stanley on 26 and 27 December; on West Falkland they are held in late February or early March. They include horse racing, bull riding, and sheepdog trials. Also observed are the Queen's Birthday (21 April), Liberation Day (14 June), Falklands Day (14 August), and the Battle of the Falklands Remembrance Day (8 December).

Bibliography

U.S. State Department, Central Intelligence Agency. *Falkland Islands*, 2000.

Web Sites

Destination Falkland Islands, 2000, www.lonelyplanet.com/dest/sam/fal

Falkland Islands Government on the World Wide Web, www.falklands.gov.fk.

—Eleanor Stanford

Faroe Islands

Culture Name

Faroese

Alternative Names

Føroyar; Fóðrøerne

Orientation

Identification. "Faroe" (sometimes "Faeroe") may mean "Sheep Islands." The population is monoethnic, but is culturally distinct within Denmark as a whole. Within Norse Scandinavia, Faroese consider themselves most like Icelanders and least like Swedes.

Location and Geography. The Faroes include seventeen inhabited islands and numerous islets. The area is 540 square miles (1,397 square kilometers). The weather is cool and damp, with frequent winter storms. The landscape is treeless and mountainous, deeply cut with fjords and sounds along whose shores nucleated villages lie surrounded by fields and pastures. The capital has been Tórshavn since Viking times.

Demography. The total population in 1997 was 44,262, up about threefold since 1901(15,230) and about eightfold since 1801 (5,265). Tórshavn, with 14,286 inhabitants, is the only city. Klaksvík has 4,502 inhabitants, and seven other towns have over a thousand. The rest of the population (33.2 percent) lives in smaller places.

Linguistic Affiliation. Faroese is a syntactically conservative west Scandinavian language most closely related to Icelandic and the western dialects of Norwegian, from which it apparently began to diverge significantly after the Reformation while resisting assimilation to Danish. Reduced to writing in 1846 and redeployed for modern use since the late nineteenth century, it is a primary symbol of national identity, spoken and written by all Faroese. Faroese are fluent in Danish and increasingly in English.

Symbolism. Faroese consider themselves "ordinary people" living in "a small country." The primary symbols of national identity are the language, the local past, and the natural environment as these are articulated in oral and written literature, folk and scholarly historiography, and appreciations of the natural setting of social life. Other symbols include the flag (a red cross with a blue border on a white field, internationally recognized in 1940), the ancient tradition of ballad-dancing, the *grindadráp* (pilot whale slaughter), the old-fashioned garb sometimes worn on holidays, and the national bird, the oystercatcher.

History and Ethnic Relations

Emergence of the Nation. Settled by the Norse in the early ninth century, the Faroes became Christian and tributary to Norway in the early eleventh century. They remained subject to the Danish-Norwegian Crown after the Lutheran Reformation (circa 1538). Their point of contact with the Continent passed from Bergen to Copenhagen in the early seventeenth century. In 1709, the Faroe trade (chiefly in exported woolens and imported foodstuffs and timber) became a royal monopoly. The Faroes remained subject to the Danish Crown when Norway passed to Sweden in 1814. In 1816, they were made a Danish county (*amt*) and their ancient parliament, the Løgting, was abolished; it was reconstituted as an advisory assembly in 1852. The monopoly was abolished in 1856, allowing the formation of a native middle class. Traditional open-boat, inshore fishing had already become the mainstay of the export economy, supporting a population that was growing rapidly after centuries of stagnation. The economy grew and diversified as fishing became an increasingly industrialized deep-water pursuit after about 1880. In 1888, a culturally nationalist movement began to gain a wide

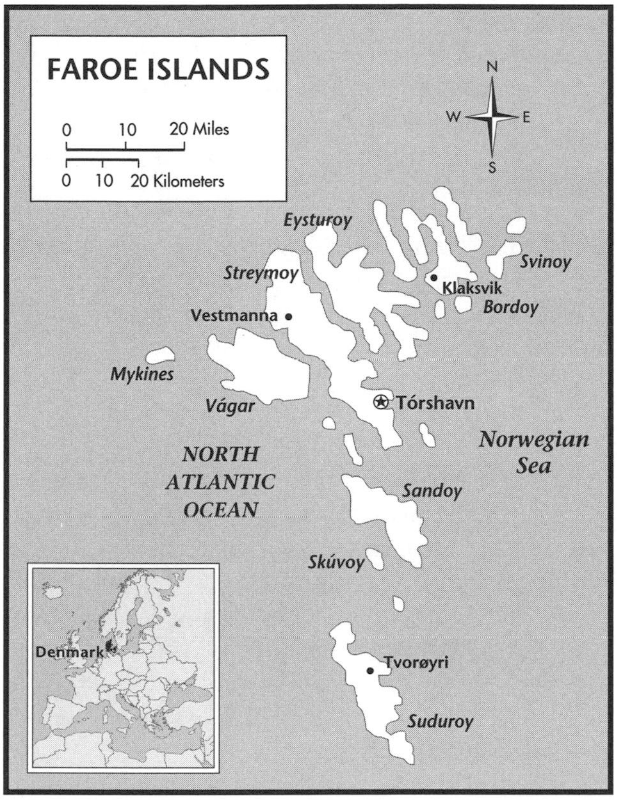

Faroe Islands

following. The movement became politicized around the turn of the century. The nation became internally self-governing in 1948.

National Identity. The principal factors shaping national identity have been the long survival of a distinctive way of life and the vernacular; the continuing integrity of village society as fishing supplanted agriculture; the adoption by an ascendant middle class of Danish National-Romantic ideals, including the notion that formal demonstrations of cultural (chiefly linguistic) distinctiveness should have political consequences; and the relative ease of accommodating socioeconomic change within this ideological framework. Other factors include the example of Iceland; an increasing estrangement between the native and Danish elites in the nineteenth century; and, among both Danes and Faroese, a continuing tradition of parliamentary government, the insignificance of religion, race, or noble blood as markers of cultural distinctiveness, and a mutual interest in maintaining close cultural, economic, and constitutional ties.

Ethnic Relations. The nineteenth-century nationalist movement's ideals were largely realized in 1948, when the Faroes won recognition as a culturally distinct, internally self-governing part of the Danish kingdom. Since then, Faroese citizens have been legally defined as Danish citizens with permanent residence in the Faroe Islands, and the Danish state has recognized the country's cultural and political integrity. Faroese nonetheless experience casual prejudice while in Denmark proper. The Faroes' population is essentially monoethnic, and since immigration from abroad has always been slight, considerable internal migration weakens regional identities, and political parties and cultural (including religious) institutions have been nationally rather than regionally based. Informally, one's Faroese identity is marked primarily by speaking Faroese and by having been born or raised in the country. People recognize differences among themselves on the basis of dialect differences and village origins, but these have no political import.

Urbanism, Architecture, and the Use of Space

There is little explicit architectural symbolism. In formal gatherings, one or more speakers or officials face an audience either directly from a podium or from the open end of a U-shaped table. Members of the audience sit or stand side by side. Ballad-dancers link arms to form a convoluted circle, becoming both audience and leader(s). In a home's more public spaces (the kitchen and parlor), seats often are arranged around a table.

Food and Economy

Food in Daily Life. A standard meal consists of a starch (usually boiled potatoes), a meat (mutton, fish, pilot whale, fowl), and a fat (tallow, blubber, butter, or margarine). Meats are wind-cured or boiled. The main, midday meal ordinarily is eaten in the kitchen, as are breakfast and supper. Snacks are taken at work in midmorning and mid-afternoon, and at any time of day visitors are offered tea or coffee with cakes, cookies, or bread and butter. There is no native tradition of restaurant dining or café going. There are no explicit food taboos, although some things, such as shellfish, are considered unpalatable.

Food Customs at Ceremonial Occasions. There is no major tradition of ceremonial foods. Alcoholic drinks are used for toasts on ceremonial occasions and sometimes are taken in large quantities. However, only men drink as a rule, and teetotaling convictions are widespread.

Basic Economy. The economy depends almost entirely on exports of fish and fish products, which in 1997 accounted for 95.8 percent of exports by value and made up 41.8 percent of the GDP. The Faroes also receive substantial subsidies from the Danish state. The economy is well diversified on this base. Of the wages and salaries paid in 1997, some 20 percent were in primary production (fishing, fish farming, agriculture), 17 percent in the secondary sector (fish processing, construction, shipyards and shipbuilding, trades, etc.), and the remainder in public administration (16 percent), social services (12 percent), commerce (10 percent), etc. Most foodstuffs (except fish, pilot whales, seabirds, and some mutton, eggs, milk, and potatoes) are imported, as well as fuels, building materials, machinery, and clothing. The depletion of fish stocks, a fall in prices, and heavy indebtedness created a social and financial crisis in the early 1990s. In 1992, the Danish government acknowledged Faroese control over undersea resources within Faroese waters. Exploratory drilling for oil is due to begin soon.

Land Tenure and Property. There are two major types of land and two major types of land tenure. Outfield (*hagi*) is uncultivated upland pasturage used for summer grazing. Outfield pasturage rights are associated with rights over patches of infield (*bøur*), on which crops—mostly hay and potatoes—are grown and which is opened for winter pasturage for sheep. Infields and outfields are not internally fenced but are separated by a stone wall. Lands may be held in leasehold (*kongsjørð*, "king's land") or freehold (*óðalsjørð*). King's land is owned by the state. Leaseholds are impartible and inherited by male primogeniture. Freeholdings are divided among their owners' male and female heirs. Houses and house plots are privately owned. Public buildings as well as roadways and harborworks are publicly owned. In general, small fishing boats are owned by individuals, larger vessels by private companies, and ferries by the state.

Commercial Activities. The nation produces a wide array of goods and services, ranging from mutton to hydroelectric power, health care to inter-island ferry service, stern trawlers to rock music and retail groceries.

Major Industries. The most important industries are fishing, fish processing and the construction trades.

Trade. The main exports are fish and fish products. Sales of postage stamps and occasionally ships are also significant. In 1997, the chief export markets (excluding stamps) were Denmark (30.1 percent) and other European Union (EU) countries (52.8 percent). The chief sources of imports were Denmark (30.5 percent), other EU countries (31.6 percent), and Norway (18.6 percent).

Division of Labor. Jobs are increasingly specialized and full-time. They are assigned on the basis of experience and qualifications such as navigation and teaching certificates.

Social Stratification

Class differences are muted by an egalitarian ethos, a progressive tax structure, generous minimum wage provisions, a comprehensive social welfare system, the profitability of manual occupations such as fish processing and construction, and the ambivalent prestige accorded to non-manual work. A previous association between Danishness and a relatively high class status has practically vanished.

Political Life

Government. In 1948, the Faroes became an internally self-governing part of the Danish state. As a Danish electoral district, the Faroes elect two representatives to the Danish parliament. The Danish government controls constitutional matters, foreign affairs, defense, and the currency (the Faroese *króna* is equal to the Danish *krone*). The Danish state is officially represented by an appointed high commissioner called the Rigsombudsmand (Faroese, Ríkisumboðsmaður). The central institution of the Faroe's own government is the Løgting, a popularly elected legislature with twenty-five members from the islands' seven electoral districts and up to seven additional members selected so that its composition closely reflects the overall popular vote. As well as its own chairperson, the Løgting chooses a prime minister called the Løgmaour and a cabinet or executive committee (the Landsstýri) chaired by the prime minister. The high commissioner may participate ex officio in a nonvoting capacity in the Løgting. Partisan coalitions form a working majority in the Løgting. At the local level, there are fifty communes, each consisting of one or more towns or villages. Communes are governed by small, popularly elected councils. It is widely anticipated that the Faroes will become fully independent from Denmark if oil is found in Faroese waters. A new constitution is being prepared.

Two men check the rope of a grip used to collect seabird eggs in Faroe Islands. Outdoor work has traditionally been allotted to men.

Leadership and Political Officials. Six political parties distinguished chiefly by their stands on national and social issues are currently (1998) represented in the Løgting. In the governing coalition are the People's Party (nationalist and conservative), the Republican Party (nationalist and leftist), and the Self-Rule Party (moderately nationalist and centrist). In opposition are the Social Democratic Party (moderately unionist and leftist), the Union Party (unionist and conservative), and the Center Party (centrist). Party affiliation plays only a small role in village-level politics; local leaders are chosen on the basis of individual reputations and expertise and personal and kinship ties. Political figures are not treated with any particular deference or circumspection.

Social Problems and Control. The Faroes' judicial system is thoroughly integrated with Denmark's. The Faroes constitute a Danish judicial district; the chief justice, the head prosecutor, and the police chief are Crown appointees responsible to the Ministry of Justice in Copenhagen; Danish higher courts have appellate jurisdiction; and Faroese are subject, with minor exceptions, to Danish law. Faroese are generally law-abiding, and crimes against persons are rare. Apart from traffic violations, the most frequent crimes are vandalism, burglary, and unlawful entry. Formal punishments include jail sentences, fines, and/or paying restitution. Informal methods of social control are directed against presumption, foolishness, and individualism that goes beyond eccentricity. They include a close, often bemused knowledge of one's fellow villagers, and linguistic expedients such as giving slighting nicknames, telling humorous anecdotes, and composing satirical ballads. Informal controls are shaped and mitigated by the fact that cooperation is highly valued while divisiveness and wanton gossiping are considered scandalous. Thus, slighting nicknames, anecdotes, and topics that might offend someone are avoided in their subjects' hearing.

Military Activity. NATO maintains a small unarmed presence at a radar base. Danish and Faroese vessels provide coast guard services.

Social Welfare and Change Programs

A comprehensive social welfare system whose elements are funded in various proportions by the communal, Faroese, and Danish governments provides old age and disability pensions, health and unemployment insurance, dental, apothecary, midwifery and home-care services, and old-age and nursing facilities. Education, public works, wage and price supports, and transportation and communication services are likewise publicly funded. The Faroese and/or Danish governments own, or oversee or guarantee the operations of most financial institutions.

Nongovernmental Organizations and Other Associations

There are many labor unions and social, athletic, and cultural activity clubs. Alone or in partnership with Denmark, the Faroes are a member of many international cultural and athletic organizations as well as international fisheries regulatory agencies. They participate in the Nordic Council but have not joined the EU despite Denmark's membership.

Gender Roles and Statuses

Division of Labor by Gender. Male and female work roles were traditionally sharply distinguished, with men generally being responsible for outdoor work and women for work within the home and looking after cows. All official positions were held by men. In the late nineteenth century, large numbers of women entered the wage-earning labor force as fish processors, and teaching became a route to upward social mobility for women as well as men. Female suffrage was introduced in 1915. Many women now work outside the home, and frequently hold official positions.

The Relative Status of Women and Men. Women's status was traditionally high and remains so. Legally, men and women are equal.

Marriage, Family, and Kinship

Marriage. Faroese choose their spouses freely. Marriage is always monogamous and usually neolocal. Among the population over 20 years of age, 72 percent are married, widowed, or divorced. Spouses may hold property jointly or individually and how they treat their earnings is a matter of personal preference. Divorce remains uncommon. Divorced and widowed individuals may remarry freely. It has become common for young couples to live together without marrying until the birth of a child.

Domestic Unit. The basic domestic unit is the nuclear family household, sometimes also including an aged parent or a foster child.

Inheritance. As a rule, all property except leaseholds is inherited by a person's children.

Kin Groups. Descent is reckoned bilaterally, with a patrilineal bias. "Family" (colloquially *familja*) means both the members of a household (*hús, húski*) and, more loosely, an individual's closest relatives. An *ætt* is a patrilineage associated with an eponymous homestead, but neolocal marriage attenuates lineage affiliation after a couple of generations except among individuals who still live in the old homestead. There are no corporate kin groups except insofar as the family coincides with the household.

Socialization

Infant Care. Infants generally sleep in cribs in the parents' bedroom. Older children sleep in their own beds, usually in a room with siblings of the same sex and of roughly the same age. Infants and small children play freely in the house where someone can keep an eye on them (often in the kitchen) or occasionally in a playpen. Tucked warmly into a baby carriage, they often are taken for strolls by the mother or an older sister. They are quickly calmed when upset, often dandled or entertained, and distracted from dangerous or unsuitable activities. Men and boys are affectionate with infants and children, but most care is provided by women and girls.

Child Rearing and Education. Children play freely in and around the village, mostly in same-sex, same-age groups, but day care facilities are becoming more common, especially in larger towns. Physical punishment is very rare. Getting along well with others is emphasized at home, among peers, and at school. Formal education usually begins at age 7, in public (communal) primary schools. Children may leave school after the seventh grade, but nearly all continue through the tenth. After leaving their home villages, many go on to pursue general studies or specialized training; some seek further training in navigation, nursing, commerce, teaching, etc. There are no important formal or folk initiation ceremonies. Minor ones include confirmation at about age 13 and school graduation.

Higher Education. The Faroese Academy (Fróðskaparsetur Føroya) in Tórshavn grants higher degrees in a few subjects, but university-level studies in most academic subjects, medicine, and theology are pursued in Denmark or abroad. Learning is respected, and education past secondary schooling is highly valued, in part as a route to high-paying occupations. Especially for men, how-

Tórshavn is the principal harbor and capital of the Faroe Islands. Harbors such as this are the hubs of the islands' vital fishing industry.

ever, occupations requiring practical expertise, public cooperation, and egalitarian relationships provide a more secure reputation.

Etiquette

Social interaction is casual, quiet, and emotionally subdued, with an emphasis on consensus and sociability. The pace of conversation, especially among men, is slow and deliberate. Only one person speaks at a time. Status differentials are muted. Although most public interaction is between men and men, women and women, and age mates, there is no explicit impediment to interaction across genders and ages. People do not publicly greet or otherwise take notice of one another unless they have something to discuss. Casual conversations are initiated and closed with expressions such as "Good day" and "Farewell" without such formalities as handshaking or kissing. People face each other slightly obliquely, and men often stand shoulder to shoulder. Children often stare at strangers; adults do not. Much interaction takes place during casual visits to someone's house. One enters without knocking and removes one's shoes inside the door. The housewife offers something to eat and drink, saying "*Ver so góð[ur]*" or "*Ger so væl*" ("Be so good"). On finishing, one says "*Manga takk*" ("Many thanks"). "*Væl gagnist*" ("May it serve you well"), she replies.

Religion

Religious Beliefs. Since 1990, the Faroes have constituted a bishopric of thirteen parishes within the Evangelical Lutheran Church of Denmark, to which some 75 percent of the population belongs. The Lutheran priesthood is paid by the state and serves sixty-six churches and chapels. Most Faroese are orthodox, moderately observant Lutherans. The Lutheran evangelical movement (Home Mission) has a substantial following, however, and at least 15 percent of the population belongs to evangelical "sects" (*sektir*), the largest of which is the Plymouth Brethren. Belief in a subpantheon of elves, dwarves, and the like is much attenuated.

Religious Practitioners. The only religious practitioners are the twenty-one members of the Lutheran clergy and their assistants (lay readers, deacons, etc.), and the missionaries or local leaders of evangelical congregations.

Rituals and Holy Places. Evangelicals sing hymns and proselytize in the streets. Religious occasions are otherwise limited to church services

Unloading a catch of salt cod in the Faroe Islands. Fish and fish products are the country's chief exports.

on Sundays and holidays (Christmas, Easter, Shrovetide, etc.) and in conjunction with baptisms, weddings, and funerals. There are no shrines or pilgrimage sites.

Death and the Afterlife. Souls are believed to go to heaven after death. Hell is also believed in but receives little emphasis except among evangelicals. A funeral service takes place in church, followed by a procession to the graveyard for burial and a collation at the home of the deceased or of a close relative. The church and graveyard traditionally lie outside the village.

Medicine and Health Care

General practitioners are stationed in each of eleven medical districts. Specialized care is available at two small regional hospitals, at the main hospital in Tórshavn, at two small regional hospitals, and in Denmark. Old and disabled people are cared for in nursing homes or with the help of visiting home-care providers.

Secular Celebrations

The national holiday is Ólavsøka (Saint Olaf's Wake) on 29 July, when the opening of the parliament is celebrated in Tórshavn by a church service, parades, athletic contests, cultural events, and public dances, and informally by strolling about, visiting, and (among men) drinking.

The Arts and Humanities

Support for the Arts. Tórshavn is an artistic and intellectual center with many private and semiprivate organizations devoted to high-cultural activities. Some of these organizations, as well as banks and public buildings, provide exhibit or performance space. Faroe Radio (Útvarp Føroya) and Faroe Television (Sjónvarp Føroya) are state-supported and offer cultural as well as other programming. Most artists are amateurs.

Literature. Vernacular literature has thrived since the late nineteenth century. Faroese publications in 1997 included numerous periodicals and 129 books, including seventy-five original works in Faroese and fifty-four translations.

Graphic Arts. Painting is the most fully developed graphic art, followed by sculpture.

Performance Arts. There are many theatrical and musical groups, primarily in Tórshavn. Similar groups throughout the islands carry on the tradition of ballad-dancing.

The State of the Physical and Social Sciences

Much work in biology, fisheries research, linguistics, history, folklore, and social anthropology is carried out at the Faroese Academy. Other state-supported institutions provide advanced training in nursing, engineering, commerce, and seamanship.

Bibliography

Árbók fyri Føroyar, published annually.

Dansk-F'røsk, Samfund. *Færøerne,* 1958.

Debes, Hans Jacob. *Nú er tann stundin . . . : Tjóðskaparrørsla og sjálvstýrispolitikkur til 1906—við søguligum baksýni,* 1982.

Jackson, Anthony. *The Faroes: The Faraway Islands,* 1991.

Joensen, Jóan Pauli. Føroysk fólkamentan: Bókmentir og gransking." *Fróðskaparrit* 26:114–149, 1978.

———. *Färöisk folkkultur,* 1980.

———. *Fra bonde til fisker: Studier i overgangen fra bondesamfund til fiskersamfund på Færøerne,* 1987.

Lockwood, W. B. *An Introduction to Modern Faroese,* 1964.

Nauerby, Tom. *No Nation Is an Island: Language, Culture, and National Identity in the Faroe Islands*, 1996.

Rasmussen, Sjúrour, et al. *Álit um stýrisskipanarviðurskifti Føroya*, 1994.

Trap, Danmark. Færøerne, 5th ed., 1968.

Vogt, Norbert B., and Uwe Kordeck. *Works in English from and about the Faroe Islands: An Annotated Bibliography*, 1997.

West, John. *Faroe: The Emergence of a Nation*, 1972.

Williamson, Kenneth. *The Atlantic Islands: A Study of the Faeroe Life and Scene*, 1948. second ed., 1970.

Wylie, Jonathan. *The Faroe Islands: Interpretations of History*, 1987.

———. "The Christmas Meeting in Context: The Construction of Faroese Identity and the Structure of Scandinavian Culture." *North Atlantic Studies* 1 (1):5–13, 1989.

———. and David Margolin. *The Ring of Dancers: Images of Faroese Culture*, 1981.

—JONATHAN WYLIE

Fiji

Culture Name

Fijian

Orientation

Identification. The Republic of the Fiji Islands is a multicultural island nation with cultural traditions of Oceanic, European, South Asian, and East Asian origins. Immigrants have accepted several aspects of the indigenous culture, but a national culture has not evolved. Commercial, settler, missionary, and British colonial interests imposed Western ideologies and infrastructures on the native peoples and Asian immigrants that facilitated the operation of a British crown colony.

The indigenous name of the islands is Viti, an Austronesian word meaning "east" or "sunrise." Ethnic Fijians call themselves *Kai Viti* ("the people of Viti") or *i Taukei* ("the owners of the land"). Until the advent of colonial rule in 1873, the population of Viti Levu, the principal island of the Fiji group, was divided into hierarchically organized coastal peoples and more egalitarian highland peoples in the interior.

People from different parts of India, now called Indo-Fijians, came to work as indentured laborers on sugar plantations. After their term of service, many remained in Fiji. Some became merchants and businesspeople, others remained on the land as free peasant cultivators. The early immigrants were joined later by freely-migrating people from India's merchant castes, mostly from Gujarat. European immigrants came primarily from Australia, New Zealand, and Great Britain.

Location and Geography. The republic includes approximately 320 islands, but only about one hundred are inhabited. The land area is 7,055 square miles (18,272 square kilometers); Viti Levu and Vanua Levu account for 87 percent of the landmass. Viti Levu contains the major seaports, airports, roads, schools, and tourist centers, as well as the capital, Suva.

The maritime tropical climate is characterized by high humidity and rainfall along the windward coasts and a drier climate in the interiors and along the leeward coasts, where savanna grassland was the natural vegetation. Much of the original savanna was turned into sugarcane plantations during the colonial period.

Demography. In 1996, the population was 775,077. Fifty-one percent of the population is Fijian, and 44 percent is Indo-Fijian. In the nineteenth century, epidemic diseases decimated the indigenous population, and the arrival of South Asian workers beginning in 1879 caused Fijians to become temporarily a minority in the islands from the late 1930s to the late 1980s. There are small populations of Europeans, Pacific Islanders, Rotumans, Chinese, and persons of mixed European-Fijian ancestry.

Linguistic Affiliation. Fijian, Hindi, and English became the official languages after independence in 1970, and linguistic autonomy was guaranteed by the constitution of 1997. English is the language of interethnic communication, administration, government, trade and commerce, and education. Fijian and Hindi often are spoken at home and are used in religious contexts and on radio and television.

The indigenous languages belong to the Central Oceanic branch of Eastern Austronesian and are divided into eastern and western branches. The Bauan dialect of Fijian was used by Christian missionaries and subsequently became "standard Fijian." The Euro-Fijian community tends to be bilingual, particularly among the educated classes. Fijian Hindi is related to several Hindi-related North Indian languages, and the Chinese community is primarily Cantonese-speaking.

Symbolism. The national flag includes the British Union Jack and Fiji's coat of arms, which still bears

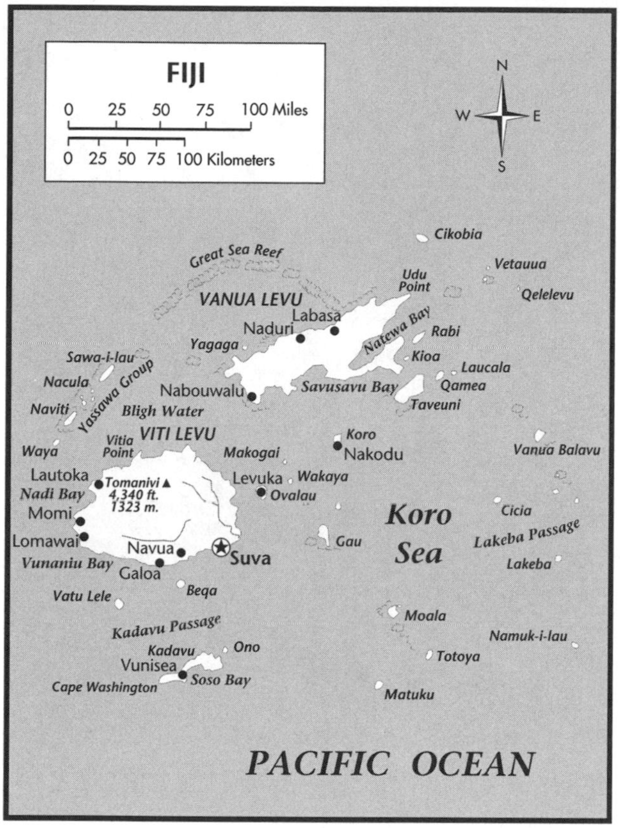

Fiji

British national symbols and, in Fijian, the motto "Fear God and Honor the Monarch." Three of the quadrants of the shield on the coat of arms depict sugarcane, the coconut palm, and bananas, and the fourth quadrant shows a dove of peace. The national anthem is based on a Fijian hymn, but the words are in English. Government offices, police and military uniforms still display the British crown, while the currency (the Fijian dollar) continues to bear a portrait of Queen Elizabeth II.

History and Ethnic Relations

Emergence of the Nation. Indigenous Fijians are descended from the Lapita peoples, a seafaring group from eastern Indonesia or the Philippines who probably arrived in the Fiji Islands during the second millennium B.C.E. and later interbred first with Melanesians from the west and subsequently with Polynesians (also Lapita descendants) from the east. Before European contact, Fijian social organization featured (as it still does) patrilineal clans, subclans, and lineages, and by the nineteenth century there were forty chiefdoms, twelve of which dominated the political scene.

During the nineteenth century there was an influx of European beachcombers, traders, planters, and missionaries. The planters and traders soon attempted to set up a colony on the model of those of Australia and New Zealand. The indigenous chiefs, backed by European settler interests, established several confederated forms of government, the last of which, the United Kingdom of Fiji, represented an attempt at forming a modern independent multiethnic state. Many of the administrative arrangements of the kingdom were subsequently accepted by the British colonial administration. After an initial refusal, in 1874 Great Britain accepted an offer of cession from the self-styled "king of Viti" and other principal Fijian chiefs.

Britain believed that the islands could be economically self-sufficient through the establishment of sugarcane plantations but did not want to end the traditional way of life of the Fijians. In 1879, the first boatload of Indian indentured laborers arrived. In the next forty years, sixty thousand Indians were shipped to the islands, becoming a class of exploited plantation workers who lived in a world of violence, cut off from their cultural roots. Depressed economic conditions in India caused most of those laborers to remain after their contracts expired, finding work in agriculture, livestock raising, and small business enterprises.

National Identity. Common citizenship, multiethnic institutions (some schools, colleges, the police force, civil service, civil aviation authority, etc.), an English-language mass media that caters to a multi-ethnic clientele, national sporting teams that attract intense following, and pride in the beauty and bounty of their oceanic homeland, are some of the factors that help to create a "Fiji Islands" national identity that surmounts the otherwise all-important ethnic affiliations.

Ethnic Relations. The principal ethnic groups—Fijians, Indo-Fijians, and people of mixed Euro-Fijian descent—intermingle with ease at the work place, in shops and markets, and in some educational and recreational settings, but interact much less freely at home. Religion and domestic custom tend to cause greater division than does language. But political aspiration is perhaps the greatest divisive factor, with indigenous Fijians demanding political paramountcy and Indo-Fijians, political equality. Naturalized European and part-European communities tend to mingle more closely with ethnic Fijians than with Indo-Fijians.

Urbanism, Architecture, and the Use of Space

Most of Fiji's eighteen urban centers are on the two largest islands, Viti Levu and Vanua Levu. In the first half of the twentieth century, urban centers were dominated by South Asians and Europeans, while Fijians were considered essentially a rural people. Today, however, 40 percent of ethnic Fijians live in cities and towns. These urban areas are Western rather than Oceanic in appearance, and Suva still retains much of its distinctively British-style colonial architecture, although Asians have influenced the nature of the city and all the ethnic groups trade in the central market. In the colonial period, there was some residential segregation by ethnicity.

Smaller towns usually have a single main street, with shops on both sides, that eventually merges with the countryside; some have a few cross-streets. In most towns the bus station is a center of activity, lying near the market and itself filled with vendors.

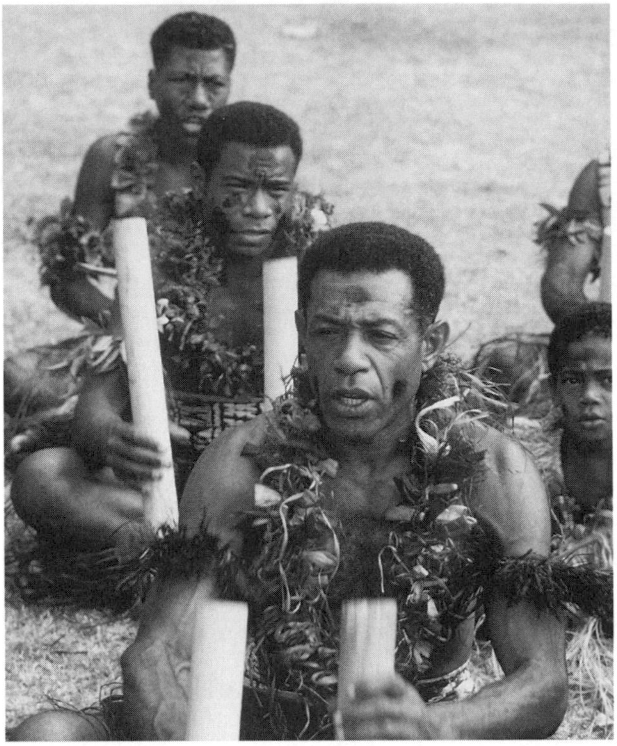

A group of musicians at a Kavo Ceremony. Both sacred and secular music are popular in Fiji.

Food and Economy

Food in Daily Life. Fijians have adopted chili peppers, unleavened bread, rice, vegetables, curries, and tea from the Indian population, while Indians have adapted to eating taro and cassava and drinking kava, a narcotic drink. However, the diets of the two groups remain noticeably different.

A traditional Fijian meal includes a starch, relishes, and a beverage. The starch component, which is referred to as "real food," is usually taro, yams, sweet potatoes, or manioc but may consist of tree crops such as breadfruit, bananas, and nuts. Because of its ease of cultivation, manioc has become the most widely consumed root crop. Relishes include meat, fish and seafood, and leafy vegetables. Canned meat and fish are also very popular. Vegetables often are boiled in coconut milk, another dietary staple. Soup is made of fish or vegetables. Water is the most common beverage, but coconut water and fruit juices also are drunk. Tea and an infusion of lemon leaves are served hot.

People generally eat three meals a day, but there is much variability in meal times and snacking is common. Most food is boiled, but some is broiled, roasted, or fried. Cooked food is served on a tablecloth spread on the floor mat inside the house. The evening meal, which is usually the most formal, requires the presence of all the family members and may not begin without the male head of the household. Men are served first and receive the best foods and the largest portions. Meals are meant to be shared as an expression of social harmony. Traditional food taboos relating to totemic animals and plants generally are ignored.

Indo-Fijian meals also include starch and relishes, and men and women eat separately. The staple tends to be either flatbread made from imported flour or else locally grown rice. Relishes are primarily vegetarian, but some meat and fish is consumed when it is available. Many Indo-Fijians obey religious prohibitions against beef (Hindus) or pork (Muslims). As with Fijians, most cooking is done by women.

Restaurants, tea shops, kava bars, and food stalls are ubiquitous in the towns. In the larger towns, Euro-Fijian, French, Indian, Chinese, Japanese, Korean, and American fast-food restaurants serve a multi-ethnic clientele of local people, resident expatriates, and tourists.

Food Custom at Ceremonial Occasions. In a culture of gift giving, feasting on special occasions is a common practice among ethnic Fijians. The offering of food in substantial quantities (*magiti*) is an essential aspect of traditional community life. Ceremonial foods may be offered cooked or raw and often include entire pigs, oxen, or turtles as well as everyday foods such as canned fish and corned beef. The offering of ceremonial food often is preceded by the presentation of a "lead gift" such as whale's teeth, bark cloth, or kava. Among Indo-Fijians, feasting is associated with marriages and religious festivals. Kava and alcoholic drinks may be drunk on these occasions.

Basic Economy. Most ethnic Fijians who live in villages grow food in gardens where they may use swidden (slash-and-burn) agricultural techniques. The tourist industry draws vacationers primarily from Australia, New Zealand, and North America as well as Japan and Western Europe. Sugar production, begun in 1862, dominates and now engages over half the workforce. A garment industry relies on cheap labor, mostly female. The only commercially valuable mineral is gold, which has declined in importance since 1940, when it generated 40 percent of export earnings. Commercial agriculture consists of the production of copra, rice, cocoa, coffee, sorghum, fruits and vegetables, tobacco, and kava. The livestock and fishing industries have grown in importance.

Land Tenure and Property. The three types of land tenure involve native, state, and freehold land. Native lands (82 percent of the total) are the property of the ethnic Fijian community and consist of all land that was not sold to foreign settlers before colonization. Over 30 percent of native land is classified as "reserved" and can be rented only to ethnic Fijians and "Fijian entities" such as churches and schools. After 1966, Indo-Fijians were given thirty-year leases on their farmlands. The land tenure system dictates not only who can work a plot of land but which crops can be cultivated and what kind of settlement pattern can be established. Fijians who live in villages engage in subsistence farming on descent-group allotments, guided by traditional agricultural practices.

Commercial Activities. Some subsistence farmers earn cash from the sale of copra, cocoa, kava, manioc, pineapples, bananas, and fish. There are many Indo-Fijian and Chinese, but many fewer ethnic Fijian, shopkeepers and small-scale businessmen. The provision of tourist services also provides a living for some members of all the ethnic groups.

Major Industries. Most industrial production involves tourism, sugar, clothing, and gold mining. In 1994, over three hundred thousand tourists and seventeen thousand cruise ship passengers visited the islands. Most hotels are situated on secluded beaches and offshore islands; individual thatched tourist cabins are loosely modeled on village architecture. The largely government-owned Fiji Sugar Corporation has a monopoly on sugar milling and marketing. There is a rum distillery at Lautoka.

Trade. The major export items are sugar, fish, gold, and garments. The main export destinations are Australia, New Zealand, Malaysia, and Singapore. Imports include mutton and goat meat from New Zealand and a wide-range of consumer goods, principally of East Asian origin.

Division of Labor. The majority of indigenous Fijians who live in rural areas are either subsistence farmers and fishermen or small-scale cash croppers, while in town they are largely in service-providing occupations, as unskilled, semi-skilled, or skilled workers. Rural Indo-Fijians are mostly cane farmers on leased land, while Indo-Fijians at the other end of the scale largely dominate the manufacturing, distribution, commercial farming, and service industries. Other non-ethnic Fijians and expatriates also have some input in these sectors, but ethnic Fijians are minimally involved, either as owners or entrepreneurs.

SOCIAL STRATIFICATION

Classes and Castes. Precolonial society was highly stratified, with two major groups: gentry and commoners. Hereditary chiefs were distinguished by refined manners, dignity, honor, and self-confidence. Chiefs had to be addressed in a special "high language." In the nineteenth century, European settlers brought Western ideas of social class, while Indian indentured plantation laborers included people of many castes. The British colonial administration established a social hierarchy generally informed by nineteenth-century Western ideas about race and class. European people had the highest status, but Fijians, especially their chiefs, were ranked above Indo-Fijians who were tainted with the stigma of "coolie" laborers. After independence, Fijian chiefs, allied with foreign and local business interests and some wealthy Indians, dominated the national polity.

Symbols of Social Stratification. Capitalist penetration of the Fijian Islands over more than a hundred years has produced some class stratification, especially in the urban areas. There an elite that has numerous international contacts (both within the Pacific Islands and far beyond) enjoys a material lifestyle which, if not effusively affluent, certainly distinguishes its membership from that of the urban proletariat in terms of housing, the employ-

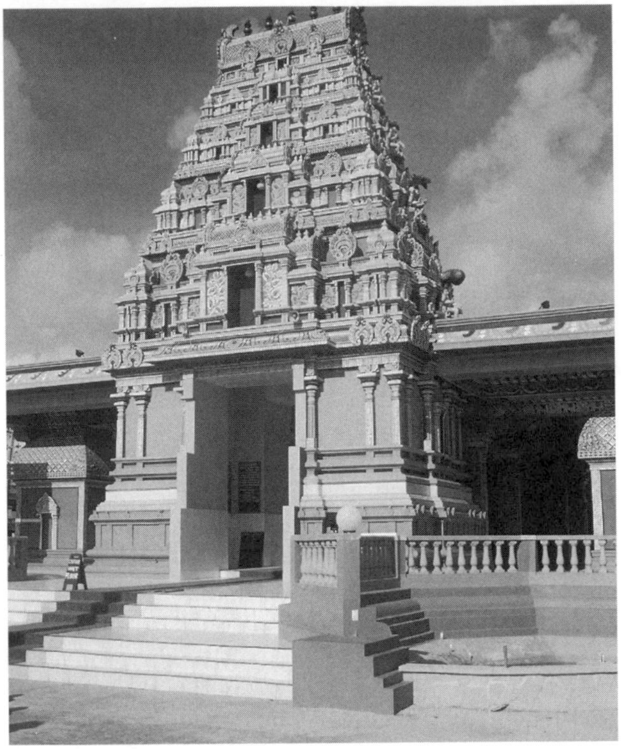

A Hindu temple in Nandi, Viti Levu. Hinduism is Fiji's second largest faith.

ment of domestic servants, household gadgetry, transport facilities, entertainment, and the like.

Political Life

Government. As a British crown colony from 1874 to 1970, Fiji had a dual system of governance: one for the country as a whole, and the other exclusively for the ethnic Fijian population. Although a British governor administered the country and was the ultimate authority, British officials avoided interfering in the affairs of the autonomous Fijian administration. The colony had an executive council dominated by the governor and British administrators and a legislative council that eventually included resident European as well as Fijian legislators. The Indian population received the right to vote in 1929, and Fijians (previously represented by their chiefs) in 1963. The Fijian Affairs Board included an appointed Fijian secretary of Fijian affairs, Fijian members of the legislative council, and legal and financial advisers. The Council of Chiefs was established in 1876 to represent the interests of the chiefly class.

In the 1960s, the British prepared the country for independence by making the government elective rather than appointed. In 1970, Fiji obtained independence as a dominion within the British Commonwealth, and an ethnically-based parliamentary democracy with an independent judiciary was put in place. The House of Representatives had twenty-two seats reserved for Fijians, twenty-two for Indo-Fijians, and eight for all the other ethnic groups. The Senate was appointed by the Council of Chiefs, the prime minister, the leader of the opposition, and the Council of Rotuma.

In 1987, two military coups overthrew Fiji's democratic institutions, supposedly in the interests of the indigenous population. Power was handed over to a civilian government, and the constitution of 1990 provided that the prime minister and president would always be ethnic Fijians. In 1997, the constitution was revised to grant more power to the other ethnic groups, ensure the separation of church and state, guarantee equality before the law for all citizens, and encourage voting across ethnic lines. The appointment of the majority of senators by the Council of Chiefs was meant to safeguard the rights and privileges of the indigenous peoples. In 1999, an Indian-led political party won the first general election under the new constitution and an ethnic Indian became the prime minister. This situation led to an attempted coup in the year 2000.

Leadership and Political Officials. There are ethnically-based political parties as well as those that cross ethnic divides. The Fijian Association, an ethnic Fijian party established in 1956, formed the core of the Alliance Party, a coalition of conservative ethnically-based political organizations. The Federation Party grew out of conflict between Indo-Fijian cane farmers and foreign agricultural interests that culminated in a sugar-cane farmers' strike in 1960. In 1975, more radical Fijians split from the Alliance Party to form the Fijian Nationalist Party, which recommended the repatriation of all Indo-Fijians to India. In 1985, the labor movement founded its own multi-ethnic Fijian Labour Party. In 1987, a multiethnic socialist coalition was overthrown by the military. These parties have continued to vie for election, although in 2000 the constitution of 1997 was abrogated as part of a military takeover after an attempted civilian coup.

Social Problems and Control. Violent crime, alcohol and drug abuse, juvenile delinquency, unwanted pregnancy, and poor health are the major social problems. They have increased in frequency and severity as a result of migration to urban centers, where work is hard to find and traditional social restraints are frequently absent, and due to the inability of the economy to provide an adequate standard of living. Theft and assault are the major crimes.

The high court, a court of appeals, and a supreme court constitute the core of the justice system. The chief justice of the high court and some other judges are appointed by the president. The Republic of Fiji Police Force was established in 1874 as the Fijian Constabulary and now has two thousand members, over half of whom are ethnic Fijians and 3 percent of whom are female. It is responsible for internal security, drug control, and the maintenance of law and order. The police force has been invited to contribute to United Nations peacekeeping activities in Namibia, Iraq, the Solomon Islands, and several other countries. There are prisons in Suva and Naboro.

Military Activity. The Republic of Fiji Military Forces was established to defend the nation's territorial sovereignty. It is staffed almost exclusively by ethnic Fijians, some of whom have received training in Australia, New Zealand, and Great Britain. In the absence of exterior military threats, this force has assumed some policing and civic duties as well as serving abroad under the United Nations. It also fulfills a ceremonial function on state occasions. Since 1987 the army has on three occasions for a limited period of time assumed political control of the nation. A naval squadron was formed in 1975 to protect the country's territorial waters and marine economic zone. After the military coups of 1987, the size of the armed forces was doubled.

Social Welfare and Change Programs

Traditionally, social welfare was the responsibility of religious and private organizations rather than the government, but development plans have consistently stressed the need for primary health care, drinkable water, sanitary facilities, low-cost housing, and electricity for low-income and rural families. Other programs include assistance to poor families, the elderly, and the handicapped; rehabilitation of former prisoners; social welfare training; and legal aid services. The Department of Social Welfare runs a boys' center, a girls' home, and three old-age homes.

Nongovernmental Organizations and Other Associations

Voluntary and religious organizations provide services ranging from kindergartens for poor children to care for the blind, the handicapped, and the cognitively disadvantaged. Christian organizations such as the Salvation Army, YMCA, and Saint Vincent de Paul Society as well as Habitat for Humanity run rehabilitation centers and help construct low-cost housing. Hindu and Muslim religious organizations provide services to their own communities. Secular organizations also help deal with the country's social welfare needs.

Gender Roles and Statuses

Division of Labor by Gender. Men associate primarily with other men, and women's activities are performed mostly with other women. A woman's traditional role is to be a homemaker, a mother, and an obedient wife. Men are the primary breadwinners, although women also contribute to the family economy. Ethnic Fijian women fish, collect shellfish, weed gardens, and gather firewood; men clear land for gardens, hunt, fish, build houses, and mow the grass around the home and village. Among Indo-Fijians, men and women lead largely separate lives. Women help in the cultivation of rice and sugar.

In 1996, the labor force was 76 percent male and 24 percent female, with women working primarily in education and health. Eighty-two percent of legislative and high civil service positions were held by men, along with a similar proportion of executive jobs in the private sector.

The Relative Status of Women and Men. The Fijian and Indo-Fijian societies are strongly patrifocal, and a woman is formally subordinate to her husband in regard to decision making. Unless a woman is of high rank, she has little influence in her village. Although girls do better than boys in schools, fewer women than men receive a higher education. Rising poverty levels have forced many women into the lowest ranks of wage-earning jobs, and there has been an increase in the number of female-headed households and an erosion of traditional family values. Women are often victims of domestic violence and are over-represented among the unemployed and the poor. Fijian women have made greater advances than have Indo-Fijian women, often through the efforts of the National Council of Women, which has a program that encourages greater political involvement among women.

Marriage, Family, and Kinship

Marriage. Among ethnic Fijians, marriages were traditionally arranged, with the groom's father often selecting a bride from a subclan with which his family had a long-term relationship; ties between lineages and families were strengthened in this manner. Today, although individuals choose their spouses freely, marriage is still considered an alliance between groups rather than individuals. When parental approval is refused, a couple may elope. To avoid the shame of an irregular relationship, the husband's parents must quickly offer their apologies and bring gifts to the wife's family, who are obliged to accept them. Marriage is no longer polygynous, but divorce and remarriage are common. Intermarriage is rare with Indo-Fijians, but Fijians often marry Europeans, Pacific islanders, and Chinese. Indo-Fijian marriages traditionally were also parentally arranged. Religiously sanctioned marriages are the norm, but civil registration has been required since 1928.

Domestic Unit. Among ethnic Fijians, *leve ni vale* ("people of the house") include family members who eat together, share their economic resources, and have access to all parts of the house. The domestic unit typically consists of the senior couple, their unmarried children, and a married son with his wife and children and may extend to include an aged widowed parent, a sister of the head of the household, and grandchildren. Older people seldom live alone. Nuclear families are becoming more common in urban areas. The male household head controls the economic activity of the other males, and his wife supervises the other women. Indo-Fijians in rural areas live mostly in scattered homesteads rather than in villages. Their households tend now to comprise a nuclear family rather than the traditional joint-family of the past.

Inheritance. Among Fijians and Indo-Fijians, inheritance is largely patrilineal. Traditionally, a man inherited the symbols, social status, and property rights of his father's subclan, although men sometimes inherit from the mother or wife's family as well. Today property other than native land may be willed to anyone. National law dictates that a surviving widow is entitled to a third of intestate property, with the remaining two-thirds apportioned among the deceased's heirs, including daughters.

Kin Groups. For ethnic Fijians, interpersonal relationships and social behavior are governed by links of kinship. Households affiliate with households with which they share a male ancestor, forming an extended family group with extensive social and economic interactions. These lineages combine to form a patrilineal subclan (*mataqali*), which typically has exclusive claim to part of a village, where its members locate their homes. A village may have several subclans, among which the chiefly subclan dominates, receiving hereditary services from the others. These subclans are exogamous, and the members refer to each other by using kinship terms. Subclans come together to form clans (*yavusa*) that claim a common male ancestor, often from the distant past. Indo-Fijians arrived too recently to have developed extrafamilial kin groups similar to Indian castes. Kin-related activities involve actual or fictive paternal and maternal relatives.

SOCIALIZATION

Infant Care. The Fijian and Indo-Fijian communities pamper infants, providing them with every comfort and convenience and enveloping them in an atmosphere of loving attention. Older people are particularly affectionate toward the very young. As an infant grows, it is disciplined and socialized by both parents but especially the mother, siblings, and other members of the domestic unit.

Child Rearing and Education. Among ethnic Fijians, a child's level of maturity is measured by its capacity to experience shame and fear. Children learn to fear being alone in the dark and to feel safe at home and in the village as opposed to the forest. Mothers warn children that at night the souls of the recent dead can snatch them away, and children are threatened with supernatural misfortune in the form of ogres and devils. Children are given a great deal of freedom but are expected to recognize shame related to bodily functions and to being in the presence of social superiors. Children are socialized between three and six years of age by being taught about their role in the subclan and their familial inheritance.

Indo-Fijians traditionally have permitted their children much less freedom but have now begun to adopt Western ideas about child raising. In traditional homes, the relationship between father and son is formal and reserved, but fathers are more affectionate toward their daughters, who will leave the family after marriage. Mothers are extremely indulgent toward their sons and strict with their daughters, whom they prepare for the role of a daughter-in-law.

Public education is strongly influenced by Western prototypes and is considered the route to economic, social, and political opportunities. Schooling is not compulsory, but every child is guaranteed access to eight years of primary and seven years of secondary education. Primary schools are free, and secondary education is subsidized by the government. Most schools are run by

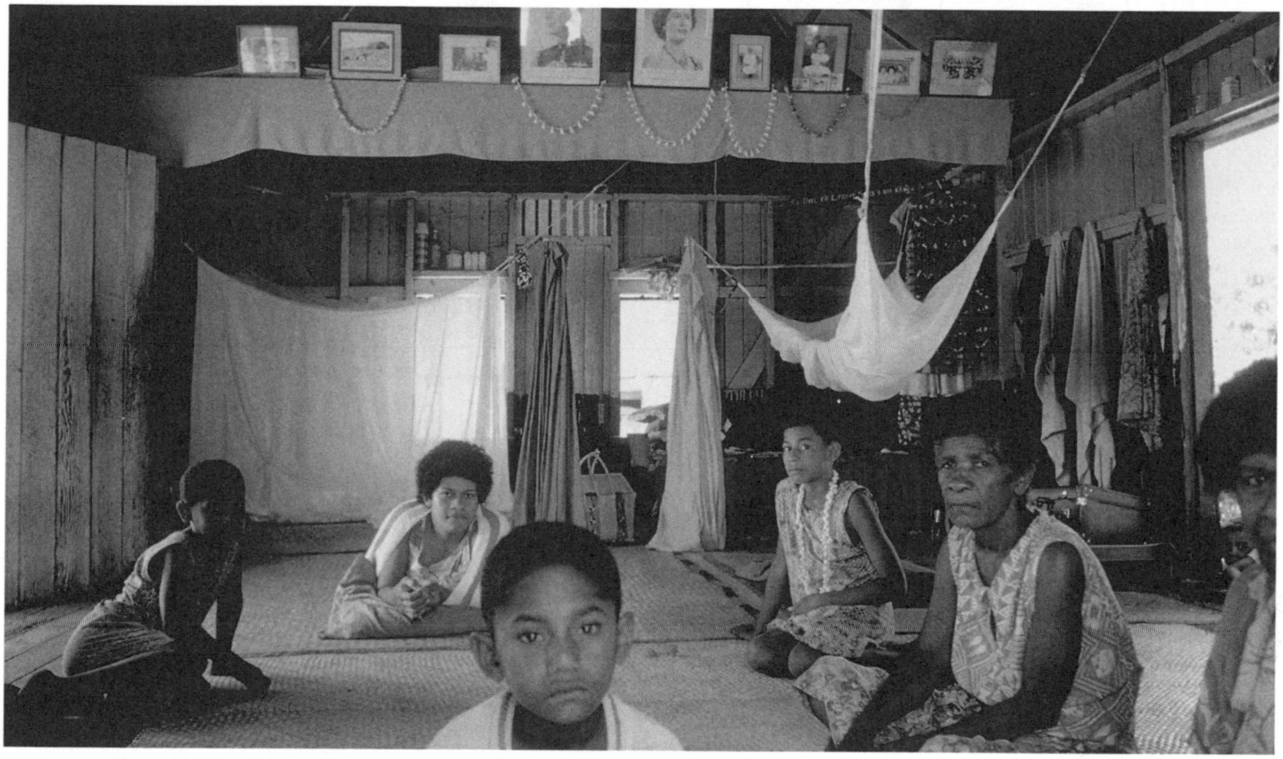

A family inside their house in Shell Village, Fiji. Traditional families might include unmarried children, married sons and their families, an elderly widowed parent, and the sister of the head of the household.

the local community and cater to a specific ethnic group. English becomes the language of education after the fourth year.

Higher Education. The government supports thirty-seven vocational and technical schools, including the Fiji Institute of Technology, the School of Maritime Studies, and the School of Hotel and Catering Services. Agricultural, teacher training, medical, nursing, and theological colleges draw students from other Pacific nations. Fiji makes the largest contribution to the University of the South Pacific (USP), which was founded in 1968; its main campus in Suva has over four thousand students, and there are another four thousand external students. Half the faculty members are from the region, with the remainder coming mostly from Western and South Asian countries.

Etiquette

Ethnic Fijians have informal personal relationships but also follow a tradition of ritual formality in a hierarchical society. In rural areas, people do not pass others without saying a word of greeting; the gentry receive a special form of greeting. In villages, the central area is where the chiefly lineage lives and people must show respect by not wearing scanty dress, hats, sunglasses, garlands, or shoulder bags, and by not speaking or laughing boisterously.

Footwear is removed before one enters a house. Guests are expected to hesitate before entering a house and to seat themselves near the door until invited to proceed further. A complex system of gift giving and receiving has existed for centuries. Sperm whale teeth (*tabua*) are the most precious items of exchange and are given at marriages, funerals and other important ritual occasions. Formal and lengthy speeches accompany the presentation of a whale's tooth. Guests are given kava to drink to promote solidarity between kin, friends, and acquaintances.

Among Indo-Fijians, domestic norms are determined by gender and age, although etiquette is less formal. Sons treat their fathers with great respect, and younger brothers defer to older brothers. Females are socially segregated, but urban living has eroded this practice.

Religion

Religious Beliefs. The population is 53 percent Christian, 38 percent Hindu, and 8 percent Muslim, with small groups of Sikhs and people who profess no religion. The pre-Christian religion of the Fijians was both animistic and polytheistic, and included a cult of chiefly ancestors. There was belief in a life after death. Souls of the departed were thought both to travel to a land of the dead and at the same time to remain close to their graves. Modern Christian Fijians still fear their spirit ancestors.

Christianity was brought to the islands in the 1830s primarily by Methodist missionaries. Other denominations became active after World War II, and fundamentalist and evangelical sects have grown in membership over the last two decades.

Indo-Fijian Hindus follow a variety of religious customs brought by their forebears from India and are divided between the reformed and the orthodox. The religious practices of Hindus, Muslims, and Sikhs inherited from India are characterized by fasts, feasts, and festivals as well as prescribed rituals that cover major life events.

Religious Practitioners. Priests of the traditional Fijian religion were intermediaries between gods and men. Today, Protestant ministers, Catholic priests, and lay preachers are the dominant religious leaders of the Fijians. In the Indo-Fijian community, religious scholars, holy men, and temple priests are the most important religious practitioners.

Rituals and Holy Places. In the pre-Christian Fijian religion, every village had a temple where people made gifts to the gods through a priestly oracle. In the nineteenth century, those temples were torn down and replaced with Christian churches, which became showpieces of village architecture. Indo-Fijian Hinduism relies on stories, songs, and rituals to teach its precepts. Ritualized readings of the Ramayana and worship before divine images at home or in a temple are important aspects of religious life. Annual ceremonies are sponsored by many temples.

Death and the Afterlife. Death evokes strong emotional and elaborate ritual responses in both Fijian and Indo-Fijian communities. But here the similarities end. Ethnic Fijians, almost entirely Christian, have integrated church-focused Christian practices and beliefs with their traditional funerary customs of gift-giving, feasting, kava drinking, and observance of mourning restrictions. Favoring burial over cremation, they also erect elaborate and colorful cloth decorations over their graves. Although Christian ideas of heaven and hell are thoroughly integrated into the Fijians' present-day belief system, old beliefs in the power of ancestral spirits still linger on. Among Indo-Fijians, Hindus may cremate their dead, though this is not the norm, as it is in India; Muslims insist on burial. These two religions offer very different visions of life after death: Hindus assume that the deceased's soul will be reborn and Muslims are confident that the true believer will be rewarded with eternal life in paradise.

Medicine and Health Care

Ethnic Fijians often attribute sickness to supernatural entities in their pre-Christian belief system. Illnesses that are ascribed to natural causes are treated with Western medicine and medical practices, but illnesses that are thought to result from sorcery are treated by traditional healers, including seers, diviners, massage masters, and herbalists. Healing occurs in a ritual context as the forces of good battle those of evil. Muslims and Hindus also turn to religious leaders to request divine intervention in the case of illness.

Government-provided biomedical services are available at several hospitals, health centers, and nursing stations. The Fiji School of Medicine is affiliated with the University of the South Pacific, and there is a Fiji School of Nursing and specialist hospitals in Suva for the treatment of leprosy, psychological disorders, and tuberculosis. Treatment is not free but is heavily subsidized by the government. Government-subsidized contraception is available throughout the islands as part of the family planning program.

Secular Celebrations

National holidays include major Christian, Hindu, and Muslim holy days: Christmas, Easter, the Hindus' Divali, and the prophet Mohammed's birthday. Purely secular festivals include Ratu Sakuna Day, which honors the man whom many regard as the founder of modern Fiji; Constitution Day; and Fiji Day. None of these holidays provokes intense patriotic fervor.

The Arts and Humanities

Support for the Arts. The Fiji Arts Council, the Fiji Museum, and the National Trust are the chief government-backed sponsors of the arts. Most funding for the arts comes from the tourist industry and from galleries and studios, along with aid from foreign governments. The USP's Oceania Center for Arts and Culture, founded in 1997, sponsors workshops and holds exhibitions of paintings and sculpture as well as music and dance performances and poetry readings.

Colorful storefronts in Levuka, Fiji. Urban architecture strongly reflects the influence of Fiji's western colonizers.

Literature. The Fijian tradition of storytelling around the kava bowl has been maintained, as have recitations of the Ramayana in Hindu homes and temples. There is a small community of writers, many of them associated with the USP. Traditional legends and modern social analysis are common themes in Fijian literature, whereas Indo-Fijian literary works tend to concentrate on injustices during the period of indentured servitude.

Graphic Arts. Almost every Fijian girl learns the art of weaving baskets and mats for home and ceremonial use. The production of bark cloth is another traditional female skill; the cloth, which is used as traditional clothing and is still important in Fijian ceremonies, is now also sold to tourists in the form of wall hangings and handbags. War clubs, spears, decorated hooks, kava bowls, and "cannibal forks" are carved by men almost entirely for tourist consumption. Pottery is made by women.

Performance Arts. The traditional dance theater (*meke*) combines singing, chanting, drumming, and stylized movements of the upper body to recreate stories, myths, and legends. Village-based, it is performed on special occasions such as the visit of a chief, a life-cycle event, or a ceremonial gift exchange. The Dance Theater of Fiji now choreographs these performances for modern audiences. Indo-Fijian and Chinese dances have been preserved and are taught in those communities. Ethnic Fijian choral singing is performed both during religious services and for secular entertainment; almost every village church has a choir. Western popular music is played live and on the radio. Among Indo-Fijians too, both secular and sacred music has maintained its popularity.

The State of the Physical and Social Sciences

Social science education and research are centered in the University of the South Pacific's School of Social and Economic Development and the associated South Pacific Social Sciences Association. The Institute of Pacific Studies publishes academic works in sociology, ethnology, religion, culture, and literature. The Institute of Fijian Language and Culture, which was founded in 1987, has been working to produce a Fijian dictionary; it also produces radio and television programs.

Bibliography

Arno, Andrew. *The World of Talk on a Fijian Island: An Ethnography of Law and Communicative Causation,* 1993.

Becker, Anne E. *Body, Self, and Society: The View from Fiji*, 1995.

Belshaw, Cyril S. *Under the Ivi Tree: Society and Economic Growth in Rural Fiji*, 1964.

Biturogoiwasa, Solomoni, with Anthony R. Walker. *My Village, My Life: Life in Nadoria, Fiji*, 2001.

Clunie, Ferguson. *Yalo I Viti: Shades of Viti–A Fiji Museum Catalogue*, 1986.

Derrick, R. A. *The Fiji Islands: A Geographical Handbook*, 1951.

France, Peter. *The Charter of the Land: Custom and Colonization in Fiji*, 1969.

Geddes, W. R. *Deuba: A Study of a Fijian Village*, 1945.

Geraghty, Paul. *The History of the Fijian Languages*, 1983.

Hocart, A. M. *Lau Islands, Fiji*, 1929.

Howard, Michael C. *Fiji: Race and Politics in an Island State*, 1991.

Kaplan, Martha. *Neither Cargo nor Cult: Ritual Politics and the Colonial Imagination in Fiji*, 1995.

Katz, Richard. *The Straight Path: A Story of Healing and Transformation in Fiji*, 1993.

Kelly, John D. *A Politics of Virtue: Hinduism, Sexuality and Countercolonial Discourse in Fiji*, 1991.

Kirch, Patrick Vinton. *The Lapita Peoples: Ancestors of the Oceanic World*, 1997.

Lal, Brij V. *Broken Waves: A History of the Fiji Islands in the Twentieth Century*, 1992.

Mayer, Adrian C. *Peasants of the Pacific: A Study of Fiji Indian Rural Society*, 1961.

Nayacakalou, R. R. *Leadership in Fiji*, 1975.

———. *Tradition and Change in the Fijian Village*, 1978.

Norton, Robert. *Race and Politics in Fiji*, 1977.

Quain, Buell. *Fijian Village*, 1948.

Ravuvu, Asesela. *Vaki I Taukei: The Fijian Way of Life*, 1983.

Routledge, David. *Matanitu: The Struggle for Power in Early Fiji*, 1985.

Sahlins, Marshall D. *Moala: Culture and Nature on a Fijian Island*, 1962.

Thomas, Nicholas. *Planets around the Sun: Dynamics and Contradictions of the Fijian Matanitu*, 1986.

Thompson, Laura. *Fijian Frontier*, 1940.

Toren, Christina. *Making Sense of Hierarchy: Cognition as Social Process in Fiji*, 1990.

———. *Mind, Materiality and History*, 1999.

Ward, R. G. *Koro: Economic Development and Social Change in Fiji*, 1969.

—ANTHONY R. WALKER

FINLAND

CULTURE NAME

Finnish, Finn, Finlander

ALTERNATIVE NAMES

Suomalaiset, Tavastians, or *Hämäläiset* and Karelians or *Karjalaiset*

ORIENTATION

Identification. The terms "Finland" and "Finns" are external obscure derivations from early (first century C.E.) Roman references to people known as Fenni (probably Lapps or Saami) who occupied lands north of the Baltic Sea. In their own language, Finns generally refer to themselves as *Suomalaiset* and their land or country as *Suomi*, which may derive from *suo*, the Finnish expression for a bog or swamp. Finns constitute the majority of the citizens of the Republic of Finland, which has a Swedish-speaking minority as well as Saami (Lapp) and Rom (Gypsy) minorities. While language was a highly divisive issue as late as the 1920s and 1930s, many Finnish speakers now recognize the value of Swedish for communicating with other Nordic countries. A distinction between urban, industrialized, coastal southwestern Finland and the rural interior northeast is an important historical and regional division in terms of culture and identity. However, socialist versus nonsocialist affiliations are more meaningful at the political level. Despite these distinctions, most citizens strongly believe that they share a common culture and heritage.

Location and Geography. Finland is bordered on the east by Russia, on the south by the Gulf of Finland and Estonia, on the west by the Gulf of Bothnia and Sweden, and on the north and northwest by Norway. A quarter of its territory is north of the Arctic Circle. Four physiographic-biotic regions divide the country. An archipelagic belt embraces the southwestern coastal waters and the Åland Islands. A narrow coastal plain of low relief and clay soils, historically the area of densest rural settlement and mixed farming production, extends between the Russian and Swedish borders. A large interior plateau contains dense forests, thousands of lakes and peat bogs, and rocky infertile soils associated with a glacially modified landscape with numerous drumlins and eskers. This district lies north and east of the coastal plain toward the Russian border. Beyond the Arctic Circle, forests give way to barren fells, extensive bogs, rugged mountains, and the large rivers of Lapland. Continental weather systems produce harsh cold winters that last up to seven months in the interior eastern and northern districts, yet long summer days permit farming far to the north. The climate in the south and west is moderated by the waters of the Gulf Stream and north Atlantic drift current.

Demography. In 1997, the population was about 5,147,000 people, of whom 93 percent were ethnically and linguistically Finns. High mortality from wars and famine dampened population growth between the sixteenth and late nineteenth centuries. In the twentieth century, a falling birthrate and emigration led to very low population growth. Dramatic internal migration accompanied an economic transformation between the 1950s and the mid-1970s, when agriculture and the forestry industry were rapidly mechanized. At that time, many young people left the rural east and northeast to work in the urban industrialized south. While 75 percent of the population lived in rural areas just before World War II, by the late 1990s, 62 percent of the people were urban dwellers. About a sixth of the population lives in the Helsinki metropolitan area along the south-central coast in the province of Uusimaa. Helsinki became the capital in 1812 under Russian control, replacing the role Turku had served during Swedish domination. Substantial Finnish populations live in Russia, the United States, Canada, and Sweden, and smaller numbers reside in Australia, South Africa, and Latin America.

Finland

Linguistic Affiliation. Finnish belongs to the family of Finno-Ugric languages in northeastern Europe, Russia, and western Siberia, a group that includes Saami (Lapp) and Hungarian. The most closely related languages are Estonian, Votish, Livonian, Vepsian, and the closely allied Karelian dialects of the Balto-Finnic branch. Although Finnish was established as a written language as early as the sixteenth century, its official status in Finland did not become equivalent to that of Swedish until after the Language Ordinance of 1863. Finnish is a euphonious language with many Germanic and Slavic loan words.

Symbolism. About 1.5 million saunas are significant visual architectural symbols, especially in the rural landscape. Ritualized bathing in the sauna reinforces a web of cultural ideas about sociality, hospitality, cleanliness, health, *sisu* ("gritty perseverance"), and athleticism. The *Kalevala*, an epic poem synthesized by Elias Lönnrot in the early nineteenth century, is a powerful literary evocation of Finnish origins, unity, and destiny as a people. It frequently refers to other aspects of Finnish culture that have become significant symbols of identity, such as the *savusauna* (smoke sauna) and the ancient stringed instrument the *kantele*. Another mid-nineteenth century artistic achievement, the composition *Vårt land* or *Maamme* ("Our Land"), with words by Johan Ludvig Runeberg and music by Fredrik Pacius became the national anthem. Citizens throughout the country fly the national flag, a blue cross on a white background, during the celebration of Midsummer. The national coat of arms, a crowned lion standing on a red field with silver roses, derives from Swedish heraldic crests of the sixteenth century and appears on a variety of postage stamps, banknotes and coins, and official seals.

History and Ethnic Relations

Emergence of the Nation. Human habitation in Finland dates to the early postglacial period in the late eighth millennium B.C.E., long before Finno-Ugric migrations into the area from the east or possibly from eastern Europe. Previous theories held that the ancestors of the Finns migrated into southwestern Finland from Estonia as recently as the first century C.E., during the early Roman Iron Age. Recent research, including paleoecological evidence of agricultural grain pollens dating to the second millennium B.C.E., suggests a much earlier proto-Finnish presence. A combination of archaeological, historical linguistic, and genetic evidence suggests that the spread of the "Comb Ceramic" culture in northern Finland around 4000 B.C.E. may represent the appearance of a proto-Finnic-speaking population in that region that came from an eastern European source area. As the "Battle-Axe or Corded Ware" culture arrived in southwestern Finland around 3000 B.C.E., proto-Finnic began diverging into early Saami-speaking and Finnish-speaking populations. The latter people gradually added farming to their hunting, trapping, and fishing adaptation. By the beginning of the Bronze Age around 1500 B.C.E., these tribes were geographically divided. Those in the southwest were heavily influenced by Scandinavian cultures, while those in the interior and eastern districts had ties with peoples of the Volga region. A series of crusades by the expanding Swedish kingdom between the 1150s and 1293 was the vehicle for spreading the Roman Catholic Church into Finland. By the time of the Lutheran Reformation in the early sixteenth century, the Swedish Crown had strong control of colonial Finland, and a modified estate system forced Finnish peasants to participate in the wars of their Swedish lords. The destruction of Finnish settlements and crops and large population losses resulted from conflicts between the Swedish and Russian empires. By the mid-eighteenth century, there were strong Finnish separatist movements. Russia finally conquered Finland during the Napoleonic wars of 1808–1809, annexing it as an autonomous grand duchy.

National Identity. The nineteenth century was a period of coalescence of feelings of national consciousness in scientific thought, politics, art, and literature, as exemplified by the 1835 compilation of Finnish and Karelian rune songs in the *Kalevala*. This movement served as a counterpoint to a growing Russification of Finnish institutions, and Finland declared itself independent immediately after the Russian Revolution of 1917. The new state was immediately embroiled in a civil war that resulted from growing class tension between property owners (the counterrevolutionary "White" forces) and landless farm, forest, and factory workers (the "Red" forces) who wanted a socialist state. The scars from that conflict had not healed when Finland was united by its battles with the Soviet Union during World War II. Finland surrendered several eastern territories that amounted to 10 percent of its area, and 420,000 Karelian Finns in those areas migrated across the newly formed national boundaries to Finland, requiring a massive resettlement and rural land reform program. Since World War II, the Finnish parliamentary state has actively pursued an official policy of neutrality combined with expanded trade and cultural contacts with the Soviet Union, and then Russia, a political adaptation known as the Paasikivi-Kekkonen Line.

Ethnic Relations. Swedish is the second official language and is spoken by about 6 percent of the population. Living primarily in the southwestern part of the country, Swedish colonists and Swedish-speaking Finns were, for centuries, a ruling elite. Swedish was the language of commerce, the courts, and education, and Finnish was regarded as a peasant language until the nationalist movement of the nineteenth century advanced it as an official written and cultural language of the majority. Political tensions arising from this ethnolinguistic division have largely faded as the Swedish-speaking minority has declined in size and assimilated through marriage with Finnish speakers. By contrast, Finland's 6,500 Saami, or Lapps, have largely avoided assimilation into the cultural mainstream, having been displaced from the southern part of the country by northward-colonizing Finns over the past two thousand years. Separateness is now reinforced as much by the economic marginality and limited educational opportunities in Finnish Lapland as by cultural and linguistic isolation. Gypsies have lived in Finland since the sixteenth century and perhaps have endured the greatest prejudice of any minority. They number between five thousand and six thousand and in recent decades, the government has attempted to improve their economic situation and lessen overt discrimination. Foreigners, while never numerous, have increased to seventy-four thousand and have come mostly from Russia, Estonia, Sweden, and Somalia.

Urbanism, Architecture, and the Use of Space

With the rise of permanent agricultural settlements in the fertile plains of the western and southern regions in the Middle Ages, communal ownership and management created a system in which an entire hamlet, including fifteen to twenty closely spaced farms, assumed joint ownership of fields, forests, and pastures. Land reforms in the eighteenth and nineteenth centuries broke down the communal villages, but the newly created individual farmsteads retained a modified courtyard arrangement with dwelling units, sauna or bathhouse, grain and food storage buildings, livestock barns, and hay sheds enclosing an inner yard. Wooden domestic architecture achieved a high level of craftsmanship and embellishment, with two-story houses marking prosperous farms. However, in the eastern and interior areas, agricultural settlement occurred later and was characterized by a more flexible system of land ownership and farmstead organization. The persistence of "burn-beating" cultivation (*poltta kaskea, kaskiviljelys*), a form of pioneer extensive farming in which patches of conifer forest were cut and burned to create fertilized fields, involved mobile populations and a dispersed pattern of settlement. Remote individual farms or extended dual-family holdings were won from the forest, often along glacial esker ridges or "home hills" (*harju, vaara*). While these historical patterns of settlement affect the current rural landscape, six of ten Finns now live in urban areas. The largest cities are greater Helsinki with about

911,000 people, Tampere with 189,000, Turku with 169,000, and Oulu with 114,000. The majority of residential dwellings of all types have been constructed since World War II, largely consisting of apartment house complexes in large cities. Adapting socially and emotionally to this urban landscape has been problematic for many recent migrants from the countryside. Many city dwellers still view themselves as partly rural, a fact attested to by a weekend and holiday return to cottages in the countryside. Finland remains one of the most sparsely populated countries in Europe, with only 26 people per square mile (16 people per square kilometer). The development of contemporary architectural movements in the twentieth century may be seen as an attempt to adapt the demands of modern housing projects, offices, churches, and public buildings to the forests, lakes, light conditions, and other distinctive features and materials of the landscape. Pioneered by Alvar Aalto and Erik Bryggman, Finnish modern architecture employs a "neoplastic" use of space that emerges directly from the function and surroundings of building structures. Despite the notable innovations of the twentieth century, much of the national architectural identity resides in older buildings that have achieved an iconic status: the medieval castles at Savonlinna and Turku; eighteenth-century vernacular wooden churches; the early nineteenth-century neoclassical center of Helsinki designed by C.L. Engel which now contains the Council of State, the University of Helsinki, and the Helsinki Cathedral; and Helsinki's railway station, designed by Eliel Saarinen and completed in 1914, an imposing granite building that presages the Art Deco skyscrapers built in American cities two decades later.

Food and Economy

Food in Daily Life. Milk is prominent in the diet as a beverage and the basic ingredient in a variety of curdled, soured, and cultured forms; in broths used for soups, stews, and puddings; and in regional specialty dishes such as "cheese bread" (*juustoleipä*). There are notable differences between western and eastern Finland in bread making and the manner of souring milk. A large midday meal in a rural household may include fish baked in a rye loaf (*leipäkukko*), potatoes (*peruna*), barley bread (*rieska*), cheese (*juusto*), pickled beets (*punajuuri*), cloudberries in sauce, milk, and coffee.

Food Customs at Ceremonial Occasions. Coffee is a "national drink" that mediates the distinction between the rural interior and the urban industrial south. In the early nineteenth century, coffee was an expensive imported beverage consumed by the aristocracy, but it has been incorporated into all strata of society. It is the center of the ubiquitous "coffee ceremony," a ritualized display of hospitality, elegance, and self-restraint in which an abundance of delicate pastries is served. Commercially produced sausage (*makkara*), which became increasingly common in the diet after the 1950s, represents a relatively recent shift toward large-scale food-processing industries. Abhorred by nutritionists for its high fat and sodium content and ridiculed and scorned in popular lore and jokes, sausage is nonetheless considered a versatile convenience food. Like coffee, it may appear as a common festival food at occasions such as Midsummer (*juhannus*), along with cheese bread, potato pasties (*perunapiirakka*), yeast coffee bread (*pulla*), beer, and vodka. *Mämmi*, a brown malted porridge, is typically served at Easter. *Sima* (a kind of mead), *talouskalja* (homemade beer), and *viilia* (soured whole milk) also may be served on special occasions.

A Lapp reindeer breeder from Inari. Finland's Lapps have maintained a separate cultural identity.

Basic Economy. Livestock raising was a major element in the peasant economy, along with fishing, hunting, tar production, and peddling. Wood as a commercial product did not become part of the farming economy until liberalized marketing policies, improved sawmilling techniques, and foreign demand converged in the late nineteenth century. The precariousness of crop cultivation, coupled with the emergence of new international markets for butter during the Russian colonial period (1808–1917), intensified the production of dairy cattle. Gradually, cultivated grasses replaced grains and wild hay as a source of cattle pasturage and fodder, and after the turn of the century, farmers began to establish cooperative dairies (*osuusmeijerit*). The general shift toward commercial agriculture coincided with the decline of the burn-beating system. Nonetheless, many farm families in the northern and eastern regions maintained an essentially subsistence orientation until the 1950s. Increased mechanization and specialization in farm production (dairy cattle, hogs, and grains) occurred in the 1960s as the labor force moved into manufacturing and service industries; less than 11 percent of the labor force is now involved in agriculture and forestry. The rural economy is still based on modest family-owned farms where the marketing of timber from privately owned forest tracts is an important means of financing agricultural operations.

Handicraft and artisan traditions were well developed historically, and some have survived the conversion to industrial manufacturing. Men specialized in making furniture, harnesses, wooden vessels or "bushels" (*vakka*), and metalwork. The sheath knife (*puukko*) was a versatile tool, and it continues to symbolize maleness in recreational hunting and fishing. Women specialized in textiles and lace making. The woven woolen wall rug (*ryijy*) has become a particularly popular art form in homes, emblematic of a family's patrimony. By the Middle Ages local markets and fairs were important in the economy, with fairs often held in the vicinity of churches and associated with saints' days or other aspects of the religious calendar.

Land Tenure and Property. Historically, in the west it was customary for a farm to be passed on to the eldest son or the eldest daughter's husband. In the east, the land was divided among all the adult male family members. These regional patterns have largely faded, and intergenerational transfers of land have become highly variable throughout the country. Despite a bias toward patrilineal transmission, farms can be inherited by sons or daughters or the oldest or youngest offspring or can be divided or jointly held by multiple heirs. However, at the beginning of the twentieth century, a landless proletariat constituted half the rural population. Major agrarian reforms included the Crofters' Law of 1918, the *Lex Kallio* of 1922, and the Land Procurement Law of 1945, all of which created holdings for landless rural poor and unfavorably situated tenant farmers. The Land Procurement Law also redistributed land to ex-servicemen and Karelian refugees in the wake of World War II.

Commercial Activities. With two-thirds of total output generated in the service sector, the economy is comparable to those in other advanced industrial nations. Finland joined the European Union (EU) in 1995, primarily to further political integration, but has experienced some economic benefits in the form of lower food prices. The gross domestic product per capita was $18,871 in 1996, close to the mean for EU countries. A recession-spurred unemployment rate exceeding 18 percent in the mid-1990s, has been the largest economic problem, stemming from the Soviet Union's collapse and the deterioration of bilateral Finnish-Soviet trade. The *markka*, or Finnmark, is the basic monetary unit.

Major Industries. In recent years, metal, engineering, and electronics products have accounted for half of the country's exports, with forest products accounting for another third. The revolution in high-technology industries has been dramatic. These industries did not become prominent until the 1990s but now produce a large and growing share of exports. The Nokia Corporation, known in the 1980s primarily for paper and rubber products, has an expanding international market for mobile phones, computers, and related telecommunications products.

Trade. Furs and naval stores constituted a large share of the export trade in the Middle Ages, mainly destined for the cities of the Hanseatic League. German and Swedish merchants were prominent in Finland's early Baltic port cities. After the mid-nineteenth century, foreign trade shifted toward Saint Petersburg and Russian markets with lumber, paper, and agricultural products becoming the chief exports. After World War II, forest products remained crucial to the export economy, but they are now complemented by sophisticated metal, electronics, engineering, and chemical products. In recent years, trade with countries in the European Economic Community has expanded and has been reinforced by Finland's membership in the European Free Trade Association.

Social Stratification

Classes and Castes. Before the nineteenth century, Finnish society was divided into peasants

Light blue vases at the Arabia Factory in Helsinki, which is known for its stoneware, china, and porcelain. Finnish design combines local artistic themes with tools and materials adapted to demanding northern conditions.

(*talonpojat*), city dwellers, clergy, and nobility. Economic change led to the decline of the clergy and nobility and an expansion of the entrepreneurial and working classes. In more recent decades, considerable social mobility and an egalitarian ethos emerged with increasing economic prosperity, a progressive social welfare system, an open educational system, and consensus politics. While Finns may not always recognize clear economic class divisions, they are likely to be conscious of the status attached to educational and honorific titles and political party affiliation. The currently unfolding class system includes farmers, the working class (nonrural manual laborers), the petit bourgeoisie (shop owners, small entrepreneurs), the lower middle class (lower-income service sector), the upper middle class (higher-income white-collar professionals), and the upper class (corporate owners and managers). Symbols of these loosely-drawn social strata, as in many Western democracies, can be rather subtle. Nonetheless, the kinds of work one does, and the level of education, professional training and/or professionalism demanded by one's livelihood, are often strong indicators of the degree of prestige and status one enjoys in Finnish society.

Political Life

Government. The administrative district or commune (*maalaiskunta*) embodies a sense of community and self-identification for its residents. It often coincides with the historical church parish, and is a local unit of self-government that generally collects taxes, regulates economic affairs, and maintains public order. Every four years a communal council is elected to manage local affairs. Much of a council's work is implemented by a communal board composed of members appointed to reflect the council's political party composition.

Leadership and Political Officials. With more than a dozen political parties, *kunta* government sometimes is represented by opposing coalitions of socialist and nonsocialist party interests. The same principle applies at the national level, where the two hundred representatives of the uni-cameral parliament (*Eduskunta*) are often elected by alliances of parties. The Social Democratic Party and the Agrarian Union (Centre) Party formed the basis of all majority governments well into the 1980s. Nonetheless, most parliamentary members follow the positions of their political parties and vote in blocs. The parliament promulgates laws, approves the national budget, monitors the legality of governmental activities, and, in concert with the president, exerts legislative power.

Social Problems and Control. The institution of a village-governing alderman was part of the authoritarian moral environment in the dense rural settlements of the southern and western regions. Village fight groups and fights (*kylätappelut*) were ritualized conflicts, sometimes associated with weddings, which integrated communities via rivalry relationships. In the sparsely settled eastern interior, social life was more individualistic and social control less formal. In contemporary society, independent courts and centrally organized police forces maintain public order. Crime rates generally increased between the 1960s and 1980s paralleling the country's growing wealth and urbanization. The economic recession of the early 1990s was accompanied by a decline in crime, followed by modest increases in recent years. Compared with other Nordic countries, Finland has very low rates for theft and narcotics offenses but an above average rate for assault.

Military Activity. Finland's historical position as a frontier of colonization and military incursions by external empires is part of the collective conscience. Strategic victories against invading Soviet forces during the "Winter War" of 1939–1940 are symbolically integral to the lore and identity of many Finns. By contrast, the "reign of terror" after the civil war of 1917–1918 profoundly polarized the middle classes and working classes, with the working classes remaining alienated and embittered. In foreign relations, Finland initially attempted to establish cooperative ties with other countries that had won their independence from Russia after World War I. However, it soon abandoned that position and began to seek the support of the League of Nations. After the mid-1930s, Nordic cooperation became the predominant orientation in foreign policy.

SOCIAL WELFARE AND CHANGE PROGRAMS

In recent years, expenditures on social insurance (health, pension, accident, and disability programs), social transfers of income (maternity allowances, children's allowances, child support payments, municipal housing allowances), and social welfare (individuals in need) have approached one-fifth of the gross national product. The programs are financed by contributions from the state, municipal governments, employers, and insured individuals. As early as 1895, compensation was instituted for workers injured in accidents. A dramatic increase in medical care needed for disabled war veterans beginning in the 1940s spurred the state to expand public health programs. Finland has been a pioneer in maternity allowances and family welfare, offering one of the most generous systems of payments for mother and child care in the world.

NONGOVERNMENTAL ORGANIZATIONS AND OTHER ASSOCIATIONS

About 10 to 15 percent of the government's aid budget is allocated to nongovernmental organizations (NGOs) involved in development and humanitarian projects. In 1997, as many as one hundred fifty Finnish NGOs maintained four hundred projects in more than seventy countries, mostly in Africa and Asia. The Finnish Evangelical Lutheran Mission, the Finnish Free Foreign Mission, Finnchurchaid, the Finnish Red Cross, and the Trade Union Solidarity Centre account for a large share of NGO activity.

GENDER ROLES AND STATUSES

Division of Labor by Gender. In the rural economy, women are the primary cattle tenders and men are field and forestry workers. Being a good *emäntä* (female head of a farmstead) involves a balance of cow care, child care, food processing, meal preparation, arduous cleaning in cow shed and house, and ritual displays of hospitality for visiting neighbors, friends, and relatives. An *isäntä* (male head of a farmstead) is symbolically and practically associated with the outdoor domain of preparing and maintaining pastures and hay fields, cutting wood, coordinating labor with other farms, and operating and maintaining machinery. However, a decline in the availability of work crews of kin and friends and a concomitant increase in mechanization have contributed to convergence in male and female work roles. A complicating factor is that young women have left the countryside in greater numbers than have men in recent years. Farms have aging personnel and few assisting family members, and some farmers are forced into bachelorhood.

The Relative Status of Women and Men. There is a long tradition of sexual equality in the sense that women's participation in political activity and public life has been encouraged. Finland was the first country to provide equal voting rights to women, instituting female suffrage in elections to the national parliament in 1906. Fully 9.5 percent (nineteen of two hundred members) of the parliament of

Wooden buildings in Porvoo. Few of Finland's residences predate World War II.

1907 consisted of women. Female membership in the parliament currently is about 33 percent. Indeed, Finland's current president, Tarja Halonen, is a woman. The traditional role of rural women as resourceful, powerful workers translates well to urban contexts. The model of a man who works to support a wife who remains at home is not widely embraced. There is an old pattern of sending girls for advanced education while keeping boys in farm work after rudimentary schooling. While women work alongside men in business, forestry, engineering and other fields, women's earnings are only 81 percent of men's, reflecting the greater numbers of women in low-paying service jobs. A lingering area of conservatism and sexual disparity involves men's unchanging attitudes toward their roles and the notion that women, despite their other obligations, are responsible for domestic work and child care.

Marriage, Family, and Kinship

Marriage. Endogamous tendencies characterized marriage in rural society, with mates frequently chosen from the same village, parish, or rural commune. This tendency was most pronounced in the eastern districts among large Karelian joint families and those of the same background and status. Night courting and bundling rituals achieved a high degree of elaboration among the youth in the southwest. Originally, bilocal marriages began with engagement and leave-taking (*läksiäiset*) ceremonies at the bride's home and ended with wedding rites (*häät*) at the groom's home. Under church influence, those customs were replaced by unilocal weddings at the bride's home. In recent years, community and regional endogamy have declined. Marriage rates also have declined as cohabitation has become more common in urban areas, yet that pattern preserves some of the aspects of the "trial marriage" of earlier times, when weddings were performed to finalize a marriage after a woman had conceived a child.

Domestic Unit. Historically, joint families were common in the eastern Karelian area, where a founding couple, their adult male children, and the male children's wives formed multiple-family farm households that were among the largest (twenty to fifty persons) in Scandinavia. Elsewhere, it has been common for only one child to remain on the parents' farmstead, and smaller "stem" and nuclear families have prevailed. Overall, family size has become smaller under the impact of urbanization, dropping from an average of 3.6 persons in 1950 to 2.7 in 1975. Among families with children, the number of offspring declined from an average of 2.27 in 1960 to 1.9 in 1997.

Inheritance. A common historical pattern was for a son to take over a farm and care for his parents in their old age. However, the custom of patrilineal transmission is changing, perhaps as differential migration to cities alters the sex ratios in rural areas. In many cases, relinquishing coheirs (usually siblings who move away) must be compensated for their shares in a farm by the remaining heir; often this is done with timber income from a farm's forest tracts.

Kin Groups. Kinship is basically bilateral, creating overlapping personal kindreds (*sukulaiset*) derived from the father's and mother's relatives.

Socialization

Child Rearing and Education. Gritty perseverance (*sisu*), personal autonomy and independence, and respect for the autonomy of others are central themes in child training and personality formation.

Higher Education. Formal education generally is highly valued. In 1995, 2.2 million people had graduated from a senior secondary school, vocational

Downtown street in Turku, Finland.

school, professional institute, or university. More than 130,000 students currently are enrolled in twenty universities and other institutions of higher education. More than half the students are women. The physical and social sciences are highly developed and well represented at major institutions such as the University of Helsinki, University of Jyvaskyla, University of Oulu, University of Tampere, and the University of Turku.

ETIQUETTE

Finns have a self-conception and reputation for being reserved and sparing with words. Small talk is not valued. Accordingly, words and verbal promises are likely to be taken seriously. To some extent this is a public, formal persona that is belied by the intimacy and voluble conversation shared by good friends and family members. The sauna is a notable context in which people are more open and expressive. The rapid spread of mobile phones, computers, and other communications technology is creating a society that is highly interconnected, regardless of the nature of interpersonal interactions and demeanor. Finland has the highest per capita use of the Internet (nearly 25 percent of the population) and cellular phones (28 percent) in the world. Finns value educational degrees and other qualifications and may expect to be addressed with the appropriate title in professional or work settings. In recent years, there has been some resurgence in traditional conventions of etiquette that require the use of the second person plural as a formal means of address. The second personal singular is appropriate for addressing relatives, friends, and children. Mutual use of first names implies a close personal relationship. The customary greeting involves a firm handshake, direct eye contact, and perhaps a slight nod of the head but rarely embracing or kissing. As a result of women's involvement in politics and public life, relations between men and women are relatively equitable. Condescending attitudes toward women are rarely tolerated. While the social acceptability of intoxication is decreasing among younger people and legal sanctions for drunk driving are severe, Finns have a reputation for weekend binge drinking. This pattern is more prominent among men and, to the extent that it disrupts family life, retards the social progress achieved by women. Although the per capita consumption of alcohol is about average for Europe, Finns have relatively high rates of alcoholism and alcohol-related social and medical problems.

RELIGION

Religious Beliefs. Traditional conceptions of the supernatural had much in common with those of other Balto-Finnic peoples. The creation of the world was associated with the culture hero Väinämöinen, and the cosmos was divided into an underworld of the dead, a middle world of the living, and a sky-heaven supported by a giant pillar. Supernatural beings or deities included a god of the sky (Ilmarinen); a rain-giving god (Ukko), converted to a supreme or universal god under Christian influence; and other spirits of nature such as Tapio, a forest guardian of game. Many old features of Finnish-Karelian religion were preserved within the Russian Orthodox faith, which currently has about fifty-six thousand members in the venue of the Finnish Orthodox Church. However, Lutheranism, which contributed to an erosion of native religion, includes about 88 percent of the population as members of the Evangelical Lutheran Church. Revivalist movements such as Laestadianism have flourished in the context of the Lutheran Church. The distinction between Lutheran and Orthodox traditions ultimately has its roots in early conflicts between the Swedish kingdom and the semi-independent state of Novgorod. The 1323 Peace of Pahkinasaari established a frontier border through Finnish territory. In the ensuing centuries,

Finns to the west of the "Pahkinasaari line" were heavily exposed to Swedish, Scandinavian, and German culture and the Roman Catholic Church (ultimately replaced by Lutheranism), while Finns and Karelians in the Novgorodian realm to the east were influenced by Slavic culture and the Eastern (or Russian) Orthodox Church.

Religious Practitioners. Before Christian and medieval Scandinavian influence, religion involved shamanism, with practitioners mediating between the present world and the upper and nether realms of the universe. Traces of this tradition survive in the divinatory practices of the seer, or *tietäjä*. Evangelical Lutheran clergy, elected by local parish members, are the prominent religious specialists in contemporary society.

Rituals and Holy Places. Bear ceremonialism was part of the ancient hunting traditions. Ritual slaying, feasting, and return of the skull and bones of a bear were fundamental to sending the animal's soul back to its original home and thus facilitating its reincarnation. Ceremonies to promote farming and livestock became associated with holidays and the cult of the saints in the Christian calendar. Lutheran life cycle rites involving baptism, confirmation, marriage, and death remain significant for most people.

Death and the Afterlife. Living and dead formed a close unity in traditional Finnish and Karelian belief, and death was viewed largely as transfer to a new residence. The complex rituals accompanying death were orchestrated by women, who arranged the wake, washed and shrouded the body, and sometimes sang laments to send the deceased, along with food and implements, to the place of the family ancestors. Memorial feasts were held six weeks and one year after death. Those who passed on to the realm of the dead (*Manala* or *Tuonela*) remained a profound moral force among their living descendants. Days set aside for commemorating the dead eventually were adapted to a Christian calendar under Roman Catholic and Russian Orthodox influence.

Medicine and Health Care

As a symbol of cleansing and purity, the sauna was a focus of therapeutic and curing activity as well as ritualized social bathing. It was common to give birth in the saunas before the availability of hospitals in the twentieth century, and cupping and bloodletting were performed there. Generally, the sauna is still seen as a remedy for pain and sickness. Professional medical care and research are highly developed with a network of 265 state financed district health centers providing a wide spectrum of health services. Overall health care expenditures account for a substantial share of Finland's GNP. It is a leading country in research and treatment in the areas of pediatrics, heart disease, and alcoholism.

Secular Celebrations

Kekri, a traditional feast at the end of the harvest season in rural communities, declined in importance as Christmas came to dominate festival life in town and urban settings, yet old *kekri* customs, such as tin casting to foretell the future, still occur in the context of Christmas and New Year celebrations. While Easter retains more of its religious character than do other church holidays, in the 1980s a new Easter custom emerged in which children dress up as witches, carry willow twigs, and travel from house to house seeking treats. Apparently, the Easter witch phenomenon combines ritual elements from older Scandinavian and Eastern Orthodox traditions. Midsummer celebrates the maximum occurrence of light at the summer solstice, a time when towns and cities are deserted for lakeside cottages and farms, where bonfires are lit, food and drink are shared between friends and relatives, and the national flag is flown. Other significant official national holidays include Independence Day (6 December), *Vappu* (May Day), and Mothers' Day (second Sunday of May).

The Arts and Humanities

Support for the Arts. The government maintains a competitive art grants system that allows composers and performing artists to pursue creative work for one to five-year periods.

Literature. Finnish culture is known for its rune song (folk poetry) traditions, which were synthesized in the *Kalevala*, a powerful symbol of national identity. Aleksis Kivi's 1870 novel *Seitsemän Veljestä* (*Seven Brothers*), an unromantic portrayal of the struggle to clear virgin forest, furthered the development of Finnish as a literary language. That novel helped fuel the burgeoning national consciousness and became a source of inspiration in many areas of the arts. Influences from Scandinavian and Russian literature in the late nineteenth century reinforced a trend toward realism and social criticism, as exemplified by Minna Canth's depictions of women and the poor and Juhani Aho's treatment of emotional experience. Despite neoromanticist yearnings, a

A Finnish family in a sauna in Oulu, Finland. Saunas provide a less formal, more open space for reserved Finns to express themselves.

strong realist current infused literature in the early twentieth century. This is seen in Ilmari Kianto's tragicomic portrayal of a tenant farm family's struggles during the prohibition years of the 1920s, *Ryysyrannan Jooseppi* (*Joseph of Ragged Shore*) (1924), and in the Nobel Prize winner F. E. Sillanpää's evocations of rural landscapes that overpower or dwarf human actors. From these roots have arisen versatile recent novelists and prose writers, including Väinö Linna, Antti Tuuri, and Olli Jalonen. The tradition of depicting ordinary people in familiar social settings has continued, although powerlessness, anxiety, and other psychological states have become prominent in contemporary literature.

Graphic Arts. Innovative functionalist movements have distinguished architecture and the design of furniture, ceramics, glass, and textiles. The reputation of Finnish design for combining local artistic themes with tools and materials adapted to demanding northern conditions was established at international fairs and expositions early in the twentieth century. Similar innovations in industrial design since the 1960s are seen in protective equipment, forestry machinery, recreational clothing, sporting goods, and electronics. The arena of contemporary visual arts is complex and evolving. As in architecture and design generally, a concern with the forces, shapes, colors, and textures of the northern landscape and the human relationship to nature have strongly influenced painting, sculpture, and other art forms. This is particularly evident in the representational romantic art that blossomed at the end of the nineteenth century. Akseli Gallen-Kallela's *Great Black Woodpecker* (1893) and his numerous paintings interpreting the *Kalevala* are exemplars. Abstract art movements did not gain a foothold until the 1950s. In recent years, however, graphic artists have experimented with innovative processes of image production and multimedia technologies to create new forms of art that sometimes serve as critiques of society and technology. In addition to a nationwide network of museums that arrange exhibitions, a new Museum of Contemporary Art (KIASMA) has been opened in Helsinki.

Performance Arts. The *Kalevala* had an impact on musical performance. The composer Jean Sibelius drew inspiration from this source in composing his symphony *Kullervo* in the early 1890s, and later his life and work became important symbols of the national identity. Opera gained a significant foothold with the organization of a festival at the fifteenth-century Olavinlinna Castle at Savonlinna between 1912 and 1916. That festival was revived in the 1960s, presaging a revival in opera in the 1970s and 1980s that has continued to the present. Operas drawing from specific historical events or themes, such as *The Last Temptations* and *The Red Line*, have resonated with Finnish audiences. Finland has nearly thirty symphony orchestras and a dozen major festivals offering classical, folk, and contemporary music as well as opera. Theater is another area with a rich history and a vibrant experimental present. There are about sixty institutional theaters, mostly in the cities and larger towns, and outdoor summer theater is often intertwined with community festival life in smaller towns and rural locales where amateur companies predominate. Plays based on the novels of Aleksis Kivi and Väinö Linna, are a popular part of the repertoire in those settings.

Bibliography

Engman, Max, and David Kirby, eds. *Finland: People, Nation, State*, 1989.

Häikiö, Martti. *A Brief History of Modern Finland,*, 1992.

Jarvenpa, Robert. "Agrarian Ecology, Sexual Organization of Labor and Decision Making in Northeastern Finland." In Tim Ingold, ed., *The Social Implications of Agrarian Change in Northern and Eastern Finland*, 1988.

Lander, Patricia Slade. *In the Shadow of the Factory: Social Change in a Finnish Community*, 1976.

Pentikäinen, Juha Y. *Kalevala Mythology*, 1989.

Sarmela, Matti. *Reciprocity Systems of the Rural Society in the Finnish-Karelian Culture Area*, 1969.

Siikala, Anna-Leena. "Finnic Religions." In Mircea Eliade, ed., *The Encyclopedia of Religion*, 1987.

Singleton, Fred. *A Short History of Finland*, 1989.

Solsten, Eric, and Sandra W. Meditz, eds. *Finland: A Country Study*, 1990.

Talve, Ilmar. *Suomen Kansankulttuuri (Finnish Folk Culture)*, 1980.

Vuorela, Toivo. *The Finno-Ugric Peoples*, 1964.

Web Sites

Ministry of Foreign Affairs of Finland. *Virtual Finland*, 1998. http://www.formin.fi.

—Robert Jarvenpa

FRANCE

CULTURE NAME

French

ORIENTATION

Identification. French national identity is based on the historical origins of the nation in Celtic, Gallo-Roman, and Frankish cultures. The name "France" originally was used to refer to several peoples in the lower Rhineland. It gradually was introduced as a more widespread term to denote that territory, formerly known as Gaul, after the Frankish invasion and the retreat of the Romans. The name "Francia" was applied to various territorial units until the Middle Ages, when it came to signify the kingdom of the French sovereign. Regional identities, such as Provencal and Breton have coexisted with political units of state control. The degree to which France is today a homogeneous nation is a highly contested topic. Political and linguistic unification, especially through mass education, has been an ongoing project of nationalism. The immigrant population comes mainly from Portugal and northern Africa, although there has been increasing immigration from eastern Europe. France takes a highly assimilationist approach to its immigrant populations. The social position of *Beurs* (the children of North African immigrants) is an ongoing issue. The population is divided by social class, political party affiliation, generation, ethnicity, and region. Having had a significant rural population well into the twentieth century, the country continues to be marked by a rural-urban split.

Location and Geography. The French often refer to their nation as a hexagon to describe its six-sided shape, and this term is also a symbol for the country. Metropolitan France has an area of over 200,000 square miles (518,000 square kilometers), making it the largest Western European nation. It covers 5 percent of the European continent. Paris is the capital and cultural center, long dominating the rest of the nation. The older provinces, now reconfigured in what are officially called regions, have played an important role in the nation's history. There are currently twenty-two regions. The French Republic includes four overseas departments (*départements d' outre-mer* DOMs): French Guiana, Guadeloupe, Martinique, and Réunion. These DOMs operate primarily as departments within the national system. There are two territorial collectives: Mayotte and Saint Pierre-et-Miquelon. Overseas territories (*territoires d'outre-mer*) include French Polynesia, New Caledonia, Wallis, and Futuna.

France borders Andorra, Belgium, Germany, Italy, Luxembourg, Monaco, Spain, and Switzerland. While tied to the mainland of Europe, the country is open to the Atlantic to the west. It also has coasts on the Mediterranean Sea to the south and the English Channel to the north. France has a large range of terrain and a varied climate and geography. The major mountain ranges are the Alps in the east and the Pyrenees in the southwest. Each forms a natural boundary with other nations. The Massif Central is a large mountainous plateau in the central area, which includes the ancient volcanoes of the Auvergne region. While most of the country is in a temperate zone, the Mediterranean area is considered to have a subtropical climate. The four main rivers are the Seine, the Loire, the Garonne, and the Rhône. The winds that sweep across the territory have regional names and are connected to regional identity, the most famous being *le Mistral* in the Rhône valley.

Demography. In 1999, the population was 58,518,748. France has a low population density compared to other countries in Western Europe. In an attempt to keep the population up, family allowances are given to each family per child, with no income restriction. There is much population mobility from urban to rural areas and from region to

France

region. The population has more than doubled since the mid-nineteenth century, when it was 28.3 million. The post–World War II period saw fertility increases in the French version of the baby boom, but the birthrate began to drop in the early 1970s. Migration has added to the population. At the turn of the twentieth century and after World War I, migration accounted for half the total population growth.

Linguistic Affiliation. The official language is French, which is by far the majority language, having been imposed on the regional populations since the nineteenth century. Regional languages and dialects such as Breton, Catalan, Corsican, Basque, Alsatian, and Flemish are still in use, and some are taught in regional schools. The law of 11 January 1951 permitted the teaching of regional languages in regions in which they were in use. The most recent update of national language policy regarding education came in 1995, permitting the teaching of regional languages at the primary and secondary levels. In all cases, this is voluntary for pupils.

The nation historically has been divided into two linguistic regions: that of the *langue d'oeil* to the north and that of the *langue d'oc* to the south. National identity is closely identified with the French language. The purity of the language is officially protected by the Académie Française established by Cardinal Richelieu in the seventeenth century, whose forty members rule over the inclusion of new words in the language. In 1966, the government instituted a further safeguard by establishing a commission on the French language whose role is to discourage borrowings from English and *franglais* (the combination of the two languages). The Toubon law of 1994 mandates that French be spoken in all official, public spheres of life. The French state also has played a role in the protection of global *francophonie.* Then president François Mitterrand established the Haut Conseil de la Francophonie in 1984, which sponsors summit meetings among French-speaking countries.

Symbolism. Numerous national symbols are associated with the French Revolution, which established the nation as a democratic republic at the end of the eighteenth century. They were further reinforced during the Third Republic at the turn of the twentieth century. Known as the *tricoleur*, the flag is blue, white, and red. White is associated with monarchy, red with the republic, and blue with Charlemagne, Clovis, and other early rulers. *La Marseillaise* became the official national anthem in 1946. It was written in Strasbourg in 1792 but became associated with Marseille when troops from that city entered Paris singing it on 30 July 1792. It was an important rallying song during the First Republic but was not used on official occasions again until the Third Republic. The Gallic rooster (*le coq gaulois*) became associated with the nation during the Renaissance. It was used at first as a royal symbol but during the revolution came to stand for the identity of the nation. Used variously over time and sometimes associated with the figure of Liberty or Marianne, the rooster came to be known as a symbol of the nation during World War I. Today it is often used by sports teams.

Marianne is a symbol of the republic as a motherland and stands for the rallying cry of "liberty, equality, fraternity." Marianne became an official national symbol during the Third Republic, although this female figure developed out of female symbols dating back to the revolutionary period. There are multiple ways of depicting this figure. Statues and images have portrayed Marianne as wearing a helmet and at other times the Phrygian bonnet; during the Third Republic, she began to be seen wearing a crown of ripe wheat. Since the nineteenth century, mayors have commissioned a sculpture of Marianne for their town halls. Now these busts depict popular models, the first of whom was Brigitte Bardot. The most recent model, chosen in 1999 after much discussion and debate, is the actress Laetitia Casta.

History and Ethnic Relations

Emergence of the Nation. The emergence of the modern nation took place over several centuries and resulted from a combination of the cultural influences of Gauls, Romans, and Franks. France was inhabited mainly by the Gauls, a Celtic-language group, when the Roman conquest of the territory began in the first century B.C.E.: The Gallo-Roman period ended when the Frankish peoples began to enter the territory from the Germanic east during the fifth century, led by Clovis.

The term "France" comes from the Franks and has had three historical meanings. It referred to the area around Paris; the Île-de-France region, which was originally a duchy; and the area known as the kingdom of France, ruled by Hugh Capet and his descendants. The Treaty of Verdun in 843 established the kingdom of "Western Francia" when land was divided between the heirs of Charlemagne's son, Louis the Pious. The medieval period was one of political fragmentation even as the state administrative bureaucracy grew. The Church supported the various monarchs, who claimed divine rule. After a long series of wars, France achieved political unity in the sixteenth century under Louis XIV. French became the official language, replacing Latin in official documents, in 1539. The revolution of 1789 established the First Republic and abolished the monarchy. Attempts to form the First and Second Empires by Napoleon and his nephew eventually were overturned by the Third Republic (1870–1940). This period involved a heightened sense of national identity, with a return to the republican values of the revolution. It was also a period of heightened colonial expansion into Africa and Asia. During World War II, with the German occupation and the Vichy regime under Pétain, there was a crisis of national identity and a move toward rejection of the ideals of the revolution. A Fourth Republic was reconstituted after liberation at the end of the war, and this led to the current Fifth Republic, whose first president was Charles de Gaulle, elected in 1958.

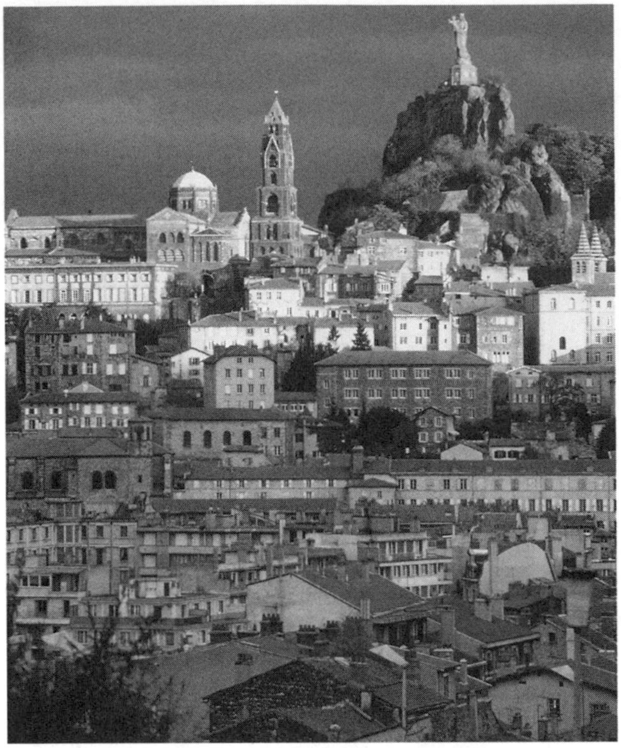

Le Puy lies in the volcanic mountains of south-central France.

France experienced a period of economic prosperity after World War II known as the "thirty glorious years." This was also a time of rural exodus, expanded urbanization, and important sociocultural changes. The events of May 1968 marked a crisis in national identity as workers and students agitated for a more open and equal society.

National Identity. National identity is connected to notions of citizenship, which were established during the revolution. The original criteria included factors such as gender, place of birth, age, and amount of property. Citizenship currently depends on proof of parentage and residence. The national identity is based on several factors, including a concept of shared ancestry coming from the Gallic and Frankish past and territorial roots in the countryside, a shared national language and culture, and the ideals of the revolution. It has also been shaped by religious conflicts between Catholics, Protestants, and Jews and by religious versus secular influences on government, especially in the realm of education. Current national identity is primarily an invention of the Third Republic and has been shaken by various events in recent history. The degree to which a coherent national identity has existed is debatable despite the assimilationist policies of the government. Linguistic unity was achieved less than a century ago, and regional languages and cultural practices persist. The growth of the European Union (EU) and the influx of immigrants eventually will lead to a revised view of what it means to be French.

An important element of national identity is the identity card. Each person on French soil must carry on his or her person a card or document that demonstrates citizenship or another legal status, such as a visa or EU passport. The police have the right to stop anyone at any time to demand to see these documents.

Ethnic Relations. In a multiethnic state, there are two major types of ethnic group identity: that which is associated with territorial groups claiming a separate identity from the dominant French identity and that which is associated with immigrants, such as North Africans. Conflict between the centralized state and regional groups such as the Corsicans, Bretons, and Basques heightened toward the end of the twentieth century, when political autonomy became a major movement. Corsica has won the right to limited administrative autonomy.

About 4.5 million foreigners live in France. These immigrants have come from various nations. The country has offered political asylum to peoples such as Cambodians and Czechs. The largest immigrant groups are the Portuguese, Algerians, Moroccans, Spanish, Italians, and Tunisians. One of the most significant conflicts has been in the area of religious freedom for Islamic groups. The "scarf affair" of 1989, in which three Muslim girls were expelled from high school because they refused to take off their head scarves, drew attention to the conflict between the secular state school system and the religious beliefs of immigrants.

Urbanism, Architecture, and the Use of Space

There has long been a dichotomy between Paris and the rest of the nation or between Paris and the provinces. Paris is by far the major urban center, with Lyon following. Not until the 1960s did the urban population surpass the rural population. Four-fifths of the population now lives in urban areas. More than half the urban population lives in suburbs, however. A movement of population back to rural areas, if not back to farming, has existed since the 1970s. Only 3 percent of the population is employed in agriculture. Regions and cities are linked through an extensive rail system controlled by Societé Nationale des Chemins de Fer de France (SNCF). It is headquartered in Paris, with twenty-three regional areas. High-speed trains (TGV) link

Paris with Lyons, Bordeaux, Calais, Strasbourg, and Montpellier/Marseille-Lyon. Paris is now linked through the English Channel tunnel to the United Kingdom. Several major highways built during the last few decades have improved movement by car.

Architecture ranges from the grand works of the powerful in the cities, such as the Versailles palace and the new National Library in Paris, to the vernacular architecture of rural areas. Buildings dating from the period of state building in the Third Republic are particularly symbolic of nationalism. The architecture of public primary schools built at the turn of the century in small towns and villages symbolizes the presence of the nation-state at the local level. These buildings also house the mayor's office. Churches symbolize the power of the Catholic Church, from Notre Dame in Paris to the village churches whose steeples once dominated the countryside. Vernacular rural architecture varies from region to region, reflecting climate, family forms, and cultural values. Just as each local region had a local dialect, it had its own style of barns and houses.

The use of space in rural areas varies considerably. There is a stark contrast between the south, where there is more open socializing outdoors and in cafés and a stricter gender division of spatial use, and the north, where there is less of an emphasis on these factors. In southern areas, where men tend to associate in cafés or in the town square, married women were traditionally not present in such public spheres but were confined to the household. Across the country, however, there is a strong emphasis on privacy within the walls of the house or *foyer*. Personal space and intimacy are connected, and close friends and relatives have much closeness and physical contact. Acquaintances and intimates are distinguished, and a high degree of formality is used with acquaintances.

Breton girls in costumes for a festival, Arles. Each commune generally holds a festival during the year.

FOOD AND ECONOMY

Food in Daily Life. Food plays a major role in the country's social life. Wine and cheese are sources of national pride and reflect regional differences. Meals are ritualized, and full of social and cultural meaning. There are also political aspects to the meaning of food. For instance, there has recently been much concern about the quality of "engineered" food and a rejection of foods that have been genetically altered. Another recent concern has been *la vache folle* (mad cow disease); the French have rejected the importation of English beef, which has been a major issue in the EU.

The three main meals are *le petit déjeuner* (breakfast), *le déjeuner* (lunch), and *le dîner* (dinner). Although the midday meal had great importance in an agricultural economy and is still the main meal in rural areas, there is a tendency for families to eat the largest meal in the evening. Breakfast is a light meal of bread, cereal, yogurt, and coffee or hot chocolate. Lunch and dinner generally involve several courses, at minimum a first course (*l'entree*) and a main dish (*le plat*), followed by cheese and/or dessert. In restaurants, it is common to have a price that includes all these courses, with a choice of dishes. Children eat a snack after school, *le goûter* or *quatre-heures,* which usually includes cookies, bread and jam or chocolate, and a drink.

Meals involve a succession of courses eaten one at a time. A typical family meal starts with a soup, followed by vegetables and a meat dish and then a salad, cheese, and dessert. Wine is commonly served at meals. Children begin to drink wine during family dinners in their early teens, often drinking wine diluted with water. Most daily food preparation is done by wives and mothers in family settings even if both spouses work full-time. The need to prepare wholesome meals that reflect traditional values is an increasing source of stress for working women who feel pressed for time. Convenience foods are becoming more prevalent, and fast food is a growing trend.

Food Customs at Ceremonial Occasions. Large family gatherings and dinner parties involve more elaborate food preparation and more courses than daily family meals. At such occasions, drink is more important. An *apéritif* is served with small snacks or appetizers before the meal. Different regions have particular *apéritifs*: *pastis* is associated with southern France, and *Suze* (gentian liqueur) with the Auvergne. Wines complement the courses. Champagne often is served to mark ceremonial occasions and is drunk after the meal. This is followed by coffee and a *digestif* (liqueur). It is not uncommon for ceremonial meals to last three or more hours. In Normandy, a tradition that involves having a drink of calvados after each course further lengthens the meal.

Holidays are associated with special foods. Elaborate meals are served on Christmas Eve by Catholic families who attend midnight Mass. These meals involve salmon, oysters, turkey, and *la bûche de noël* cake. In many regions, *crêpes* are eaten on 2 February, the Feast of the Virgin. The ceremonial nature and symbolism of food are evident in rural wedding ceremonies. Often, mixtures of food and drink are presented to the wedding couple in a chamber pot in the early hours of the morning after the wedding. These mixtures can include champagne and chocolate or savory soups with carrots and onion.

In many rural regions, it is still common for families to slaughter a pig each winter and make sausages, patés, hams, roasts, and chops for freezing. These are ceremonial occasions, and each person who helps the family is given a portion of the pig.

Basic Economy. The "thirty glorious years" of expansion of industry after World War II ended with the oil crises of the 1970s. Since then, the country has rebuilt its economy and has one of the four leading economies in Western Europe. Most of the gross national product (GNP) comes from services, with industry generating one fourth of the GNP. France is also a major agricultural nation and is self-sufficient in this sector. Agriculture now accounts for less than 3 percent of the GNP, however. The major agricultural crop is wheat. High unemployment has plagued the country since the 1970s, particularly among youth. The unemployment rate was almost 13 percent in 1997. Inclusion in the EU has had a major impact on the economy, opening some markets and restricting others. In 2002, France will convert from the franc to the euro for all financial transactions. After several decades of nationalization of major industries, France deregulated those sectors in the 1990s, to create a freer market.

Land Tenure and Property. Until the middle of the twentieth century, agriculture was dominated by small holdings and family farms. Two factors have affected rural land holdings since World War II. There has been an acceleration of the rural exodus leading to a strong migration toward cities, along with a consolidation of farm lands that had been scattered through inheritance patterns. This was called *le remembrement* and was more successful in some regions than in others.

Commercial Activities. There are many small businesses and shops on city streets, and street markets thrive in the major cities. In the centers of towns, small shops and specialty boutiques abound. However, there are also large *hypermarchés* or *grandes surfaces* at the outskirts of most cities that sell food, clothing, and furniture. Prices are fixed in stores for the most part, but at markets there is still a lot of bargaining. The commercial services of rural villages have declined during the last twenty years, as a result of depopulation and the attraction of new chain stores. Increasingly, the butchers, bakers, and grocers have closed shop, and people make purchases in small shopping markets or travel to the nearest city to buy less expensive goods.

Major Industries. Industry historically was centered in the northeast and eastern part of the nation, primarily in Paris, Lille, and Lyon. This has changed with the penetration of industry into the hinterlands and the south. The leading industries are steel, machinery, chemicals, automobiles, metallurgy, aeronautics, electronics, mining, and textiles. Tourism is a growing industry in the countryside. Food processing and agribusiness are important to the national economy. The government controls several industrial sectors, including railroads, electricity, aircraft, and telecommunications. A move toward privatizing these industries has been under way since the early 1990s.

Trade. Although the country traditionally took a protectionist stance toward trade and did not play a major role in the world economy, this has changed with the opening of markets through the European Economic Community and the Common Market. Foreign trade grew during the 1950s, under de Gaulle, and by the mid-1960s, France was the fourth largest exporter in the world. Most exports

Men working at a vineyard in France. French wine is a source of national pride and an important part of both simple and elaborate meals.

today go to Europe rather than to former colonies. During the economic crisis of the 1980s, the balance of trade favored imports, but in recent years exports have grown. The major exports are manufactured goods, including cars and luxury items such as clothing, perfume, and jewelry. Wheat and dairy products are also major exports. The country imports raw materials such as oil and agricultural products, as well as machinery, chemicals, and iron and steel products.

Division of Labor. Employment is categorized by the eight PCS (professions and socioprofessional categories): farmers; artisans, small shopkeepers, and small business managers; professionals; middle management; white-collar workers; manual workers; unemployed persons who have never worked; and military personnel. While the nation had a large agricultural population well into the twentieth century, only 3 percent of the people now work in that sector, although 10 percent of the population works in either agriculture or agribusiness. Unemployment (almost 12 percent in 1998) is higher among women and youth. Labor unions are strong. The current thirty-nine-hour workweek will fall to thirty-five hours in 2002.

SOCIAL STRATIFICATION

Classes and Castes. France is a class-stratified society whose middle class did not develop significantly until the 1960s. Historically, society was divided among the nobility, the *bourgeoisie*, the peasants, and the urban proletariat. The French system was the basis for much of Karl Marx's analysis of class struggles during the nineteenth century. The dominant class now is referred to as the bourgeoisie, although this term is difficult to define. Primarily, this class is considered to be the group that controls education and industry. A major source of debate is the issue of social mobility for people of different social origins. Statistics indicate that there is still a strong tendency for children to remain in the occupational class of their parents. For instance, in 1994, almost 50 percent of the children of workers became workers; only 9 percent of them became elite workers. Fifty-six percent of the children of elite workers became elite workers. The school system is blamed for the lack of social mobility.

Symbols of Social Stratification. Social stratification has two main axes: urban versus rural and economic class position. The urban upper class generally has ties to provincial seats of power. The bourgeoisie establish the major tenets of good taste and refinement, of being "civilized." One's taste in music, art, food, and leisure activities generally reveals one's social class origins. Symbols of a higher class position include knowing not only about fine art but about the newest trends in avant-garde art, understanding and being able to purchase fine wines, and dressing with understatement while revealing refined aesthetic sensibilities. Class consciousness is very strong. "Symbolic capital" plays a large role in social class, and not only wealth but family connections and lifestyle determine one's social position and opportunities.

Political Life

Government. France operates under the constitution of the Fifth Republic, which was established in 1958. The government is highly centralized, although the 1982 act of decentralization transferred more power to the regions and communes. Paris is the capital city. The administration of the governmental system is organized through the levels of nation, region, department, arrondissement, canton, and commune. The commune is the smallest administrative level. This system of political administration dates back to the French Revolution. The state controls several state-owned companies in the areas of transportation, energy, and communications. Thirty percent of the workforce is employed by the state. The state bureaucracy is complex and is run by an administrative elite trained at the National School of Administration (ENA).

The executive branch includes the president and the prime minister. The president is elected for a seven-year term by popular vote. The prime minister is appointed by the president and serves as head of the government. In recent years, a form of political "cohabitation" has developed, in which the president and prime minister come from different political parties. The prime minister selects the ministers and secretaries of state, with approval by the president. Legislative power resides in a bicameral parliament composed of the Assemblée Nationale (National Assembly) and the Senat (Senate). The deputies of the Assemblée Nationale are elected by popular vote for five-year terms; senators are elected though an electoral college system for nine-year terms.

The twenty-two metropolitan regions, which recently received a formal role in government, are each composed of several departments. A region is headed by a regional prefect and served by elected regional council members who represent the departments. The regional council elects a president of the council. The department is headed by a prefect, and each canton elects a council member to serve at that level. Communes elect a mayor and a municipal council. There are a little over 36,000 communes, and their populations can range in size from under one thousand to that of a large city. The vast majority of communes are in the countryside.

Leadership and Political Officials. France is politically divided between the right and the left. There are five major political parties. To the far right is the Front National (FN), which has been growing in power since the 1980s under the leadership of Jean-Marie Le Pen. The two major parties on the democratic right are the Rassemblement pour la République (RPR) founded by Jacques Chirac in 1976 and the Union pour la Democratie Française (UDF) founded by Valéry Giscard d'Estaing in 1978. On the left, there is the Parti Socialiste (PS) and the Parti Communiste Française (PCF). In 1981, the PS replaced the earlier SFIO, led by François Mitterrand. The Communist Party was formed in 1920.

Political leaders rise to power by gaining election at the local level, and then accruing more political titles. It is possible for a politician to hold more than one office at different levels simultaneously, and this is a common method for gaining political support. Election to office depends on social networks, as well as on the personal charisma of the politician. The concept of "legitimacy" is crucial; to be viewed as a legitimate candidate is to have local roots and a strong social network. A successful politician must make good use of symbolism and ritual in order to embody various ideals. A high degree of formality is associated with political office, and interactions with elected officials require correct etiquette. One should, for instance, address a mayor as Monsieur or Madame le Mayor.

Social Problems and Control. The police are a noticeable presence, particularly in urban areas and transport centers such as airports and subway stations. Visibly armed, they have the right to stop any person to demand to see documents of identity. The police force is divided between those who work for the minister of the interior and those who work for the minister of defense (*gendarmes*). There is also a National Security Police force (CRS) that is called in during demonstrations and strikes, which occur frequently. An important form of political protest, demonstrations often disrupt urban streets and highways. Labor unions are strong, and striking workers regularly stop social services, such as trash pickup and public transportation, and access to public buildings, such as museums.

People at an outdoor café in France. Cafés are social centers for men in southern France and are also popular among tourists.

Major social problems include AIDS, homelessness, and terrorism. The rate of violent crimes such as homicide is low. Terrorist attacks and bombings occur randomly, if infrequently and were at their height most recently during the Gulf War. The National Security Police justify their strong military presence as a deterrent to terrorism.

Military Activity. The president is the commander in chief of the military, and the minister of defense reports directly to the president. France has an army, navy, and air force. It also contributes to the United Nations military forces and is in the NATO alliance, although its relationship to NATO has been precarious at times. France was involved in several armed conflicts during the twentieth century. After the first and second world wars, it was involved in colonial wars in Algeria and Indochina. The draft is being phased out and will disappear in 2002. Universal compulsory military service for a period of at least sixteen months has been mandatory for all eighteen-year-old males and marked an important rite of passage into adulthood.

Social Welfare and Change Programs

There is an elaborate social welfare program. The social security system was formed in 1946. It is funded not by the state but by employers and workers directly. There are several plans, which vary with one's level of employment and professional status. A minimum level of income is assured for the unemployed and destitute under the RMI (Revenue Minimum d'Insertin), the unemployment assistance payment that is paid for through taxation. Benefits of the social security system include family allowances (paid per child), infant allowances for pregnant women and newborns, single-parent supplements, benefits for sickness and disability, and unemployment insurance.

Nongovernmental Organizations and Other Associations

About half the people belong to a voluntary association, including political parties, and there are 800,000 associations. The 1901 Law of Associations regulates noneconomic activities such as sports clubs, cultural groups, and other clubs. There are clubs for immigrants, the elderly, youth, and leisure activities. Much of civic life is organized through associations.

Gender Roles and Statuses

Division of Labor by Gender. Peasant households traditionally had a strict gender division of labor

Architectural view of Pierrefont Castle, a reminder of the wars that have punctuated French history.

that was incorporated into community life, with the family farm being both a kinship unit and an economic unit. Husband and wife generally worked together, sometimes participating in different tasks related to agricultural labor. The degree to which gender segregation in daily life was upheld varied by region. In general, women carried out domestic tasks of housekeeping, food preparation, and child care; however, they also were involved in farm labor, such as harvesting and tending young animals. With the growth of industrialization, family farms involved much less cooperation between husband and wife in economic activities. A separation of the domestic sphere from the place of work and the growth of wage earning changed the household division of labor. Women worked outside the home as washerwomen, factory workers, and domestics. In bourgeois families in the nineteenth century, husbands controlled wealth and their wives were dependent on them, having limited autonomy in the raising of the children. Today, almost half of all workers are female and the dual-career family is becoming the norm. Women continue to face inequalities in the job market, with lower wages than men for comparable work and more difficult career paths. Women are rare in the highest-paid professions and dominate in clerical work, social work, and primary teaching. There have been proposals for a "maternal wage" that would compensate housewives for their labor.

The Relative Status of Women and Men. The Napoleonic Code of 1803 denied power to women in marriage, and women did not gain the right to vote until 1944. Only in the 1960s did wives gain the right to open bank accounts or work without the husband's permission. The Badinter Law of 1985 established equal rights for women in marriage. The feminist movement has slowly made advances but continues to struggle. The degree to which farm women have lower status than males is a subject of debate. Economic and cultural factors influence the power of women at the level of the family and community.

Marriage, Family, and Kinship

Marriage. Marriage rates and age at marriage are related to socioeconomic class and region. Overall, the marriage rate is declining and the age at marriage is rising. The average age of marriage for men is twenty-nine, and that for women is twenty-seven. Women tend to marry later when they seek higher education. Rural male celibacy has been associated with rural-urban migration since the 1960s. Geographic homogamy is a strong factor in marriage: Over half of all marriages involve partners from the same department. There is also a high level of religious homogamy. The divorce rate has increased in recent years, especially since a 1975 law that made the process easier and faster. One in three marriages ends in divorce. All marriages are sanctioned by a civil ceremony in the town hall. Religious ceremonies must follow the civil ceremony, so that frequently wedding parties make the trip between mayor's office and the church. Payment for the weddings of young people is most often divided equally between the families of the bride and the groom. There has been a rise in cohabitation for unmarried couples. A recent law permitting legal unions that are not marriages for couples has given legal status to cohabitating couples, including homosexual couples. The PACS (*pacte d'association civile et solidaire*) law, passed in 1999, set up an intermediate union between marriage and cohabitation. A *pacte* is easier to dissolve than a marriage.

Domestic Unit. The basic domestic unit is called *le ménage*. This includes all persons living in the same dwelling. These persons are not necessarily related. There has been a rise in single-person households since the 1960s. In 1997, 18 percent of all households were composed of single women, and 12 percent of single men. Most households, however, are composed of couples with (35 percent) or without (28 percent) children. There were three types of domestic units traditionally: the patriarchal family, the stem family, and the nuclear family, which predominates today. In the patriarchal family (a rural model that was prevalent in parts of central France), siblings stayed at home and their spouses joined the household. These large families owned property jointly. In the more hierarchical stem family, which was the most common, there was a pattern of primogeniture. The eldest son would remain in the parental home, but daughters and younger sons were obliged to seek their fortunes elsewhere. That pattern persists in some rural communities, although primogeniture has been illegal since 1804 under the Napoleonic Code. One sibling takes over the farm but "pays off" the parts of the patrimony due to his or her siblings. The nuclear family was most prevalent in southern France and has a more egalitarian basis than the stem family. A young couple would be established in their own household by both sets of parents.

Inheritance. One of the major functions of the domestic unit is the transmission of property to children. Inheritance involves material and symbolic goods. Most property is held in the form of immovable goods such as buildings and land. Social inequalities are perpetuated through unequal access to inheritances among members of different families. Inheritance occurs not just at the death of the parents but at marriage or the setting up of a household for a young person, when loans or gifts are extended by parents. Inheritance also involves "cultural capital," including education, access to various lifestyles, and ways of speaking. Although the Napoleonic Civil Code established uniform regulation of inheritance and authority within the family and equal inheritance among siblings, there are regional variations in the application of the law.

Kin Groups. Kinship is bilateral, with kindreds being recognized as important units of social support. Kinship was historically more important for the peasantry and bourgeoisie than for workers or the petite bourgeoisie, who maintained neighborhood ties that were sometimes stronger than kin ties. Today the family plays a major role in transmitting cultural values, despite the decline in marriage and increasing geographic mobility. Most people continue to live in the region in which they grew up even if they move from a village to a city. Weekend visits to parents and grandparents are common. There is much diversity in the meaning and strength of kin ties across social class and ethnic lines. Ideologies of kinship, in which certain family forms are privileged over others, represent a critique of the kinship patterns of the working classes and immigrants.

SOCIALIZATION

Infant Care. Infant care is done primarily by the mother, although fathers and female relatives participate. In the past, upper-class women sent their children to wet nurses until they were weaned. Children were swaddled with various methods, depending on the region. Baptism is an important familial celebration of the birth of an infant.

Child Rearing and Education. State-sponsored schools for early childhood education begin to take children at the age of three. There are also state-subsidized child care centers for younger children. Although the influence of the family in childhood socialization is very important, there are regional and class-based variations in the methods used. In general, children have been seen as naturally "wild" and in need of learning how to behave in the proper ("civilized") way through guidance from adults. Peer socialization is as important as adult socialization, however, and children generally develop a strong peer culture. There are both public, state-run schools and private (mostly Catholic) schools, which receive some state aid if they follow the state curriculum. Public education was established as mandatory, free, and secular by the Ferry laws of the late nineteenth century. Education is controlled by the Ministry of Education and Research, with the exception of agricultural education, which is under the Ministry of Agriculture. There are three levels of public schooling: the primary school, the college, and the lycee. Schooling is mandatory until age sixteen.

Higher Education. Students receive a higher education after they have completed secondary schooling and successfully taken one of several examinations to earn a *baccalaureat.* Historically, higher education was divided between universities and grandes écoles. Decentralization efforts have been under way to counter the domination of Paris over academic research and teaching. Provincial centers of learning have grown and received increased funding. About 10 percent of all students are foreign. With the growth of the European Union, education initiatives have fostered partnerships between French universities and universities in other European nations.

Etiquette

In French, "*etiquette*" means both "etiquette" and "ceremony." Social class distinctions determine the importance of various forms of correct social behavior. In general when people greet each other, they shake hands or embrace with a kiss on both cheeks (called *faire la bise*). Kissing is only done when two people are close friends or relatives. For the most part, the embrace is done only the first time in a day in which one sees someone and is not repeated again until one says good-bye. There is also formality in verbal greetings, so that one shows respect by adding "Madam," "Monsieur," or "Mademoiselle" to any greeting. There are important public and private distinctions. In public spaces, one generally does not smile at strangers or make eye contact with them (for instance, in the subway or bus) and should keep one's voice low when speaking. Privacy is also maintained in homes, so that doors to bedrooms and bathrooms are kept closed. When shopping in smaller stores, the buyer generally greets the proprietor upon entry, and the proprietor helps the client choose the goods to be purchased. It is less common to have free access in a store, although the growth of large hypermarkets and shopping malls is changing this custom.

Religion

Religious Beliefs. France has been dominated by the influence of the Catholic Church, yet the constitution declares it to be a "secular" country. Secularism does not reject religion but attempts to bar any single religion from gaining political control. The minister of the interior is also the minister of religions, an office established to ensure the representation of various creeds. About 80 percent of the population is Roman Catholic. The second largest religion in terms of adherents is Islam. There are about a million Protestants; 700,000 Jews; and 200,000 Orthodox (Russian and Greek) Christians. There is also a significant Buddhist population. About 15 percent of the population claims the status of a nonbeliever. Religious practice has diminished during the last fifty years, and less than 10 percent of the population attends religious services.

The dominance of Catholicism is historically linked to the conversion of Clovis in 496. In most of the country, communes began as parishes, and most rural villages see the local church building as a symbol of local identity. The church bell rings to mark deaths, wars, and weddings. French history is marked by religious struggles between Catholics and Protestants, especially during the wars of religion in the sixteenth century. Many Protestants fled during the seventeenth century, when their religious rights were rescinded by Louis XIV.

The French Revolution in the eighteenth century was in part a reaction to the power and wealth of the Catholic Church. The 1905 law passed during the Third Republic officially separated church and state. The split between republicans, who supported a secular state, and antirepublicans, who were conservative and Catholic, was strong at the local level in Catholic regions such as Brittany during the turn of the century. Anti-Semitism is symbolized by the Dreyfus Affair, which was sparked at end of the nineteenth century by the false conviction for spying and imprisonment under a death sentence of a Jewish army officer. This divided republican and antirepublican factions across the nation. Anti-Semitism was prevalent during the Vichy regime and has resurfaced with the neofascist Front National.

Folk religion varies by region. Witchcraft beliefs persist in some regions, such as the Vendée. Many Catholic regions combine elements of folk religion and Catholicism in their belief systems.

Religious Practitioners. Because of the strong influence of the Catholic Church, priests are the most important religious practitioners at the local level.

Characteristic stone buildings in the village of Lot. Privacy is strongly valued in French households.

The village priest was historically a major presence in rural areas. The triad of priest, mayor, and schoolmaster was a feature of village life in the nineteenth and early twentieth centuries. Strong anticlerical beliefs, particularly in southern areas, challenged this status. A shortage of priests has reached a crisis point. Reflecting this shortage as well as the decline in religious participation, few village churches hold regular services or have a village priest. People must travel to towns for mass.

France has a variety of religious practices. Immigrants bring new forms of both established and folk religious practices to urban areas. For Muslim immigrants in particular, religious practice is an important way to preserve one's identity in an assimilationist society. In rural areas, folk healers and diviners are consulted. New Age religions are thriving, and herbalists, massage healers, and other practitioners are growing in influence.

Rituals and Holy Places. France was the site of many pilgrimages during the Middle Ages. Most regions have historic churches that are visited regularly on holy days, with processions leading to them. Lourdes is one of the best known pilgrimage sites in the world. Located in the Pyrenees region in the southwest, it is visited by five million people each year. In 1858, the Virgin Mary appeared to a young girl, Bernadette Soubirous, at the grotto in Lourdes. This miracle inspires handicapped and ill people to visit this site and take the waters, which are believed to have healing qualities. Lourdes has a Web site where one can hear the church bells and watch the visitors.

Death and the Afterlife. The Judeo-Christian tradition dominates beliefs about the afterlife, with heaven and hell playing a major role in the cosmology. In traditional rural areas, there was a fatalist approach to death, and in many regions, such as Brittany, a "cult" of death — especially among older women. Funerals are important events, drawing from the entire community. The cemetery in France is a symbolic site of memory, often visited by older female relatives who tend to family plots. Young children often accompany grandmothers for walks through cemeteries.

Medicine and Health Care

The French system of social security manages health care along with family allowances, retirement benefits, and unemployment. The national health system covers medical expenses and hospitalization for French citizens, and is run by a commission composed of representatives of employers and worker organizations. Most of the time, pa-

Only about 3 percent of France's population is employed in agriculture, although people have been moving back to rural areas to live since the 1970s.

tients pay out of pocket for services or medications, and are then reimbursed according to a schedule of rates. Supplemental private health insurance is purchased by many people. There are both public and private hospitals in France, with the latter charging higher fees. The health care system is funded by social security payments taken from wages. Health care is very good in France, since most people have free access to it. Life expectancy is high—80.9 years for women and 72.7 for men.

Death resulting from complications of alcoholism remains a major factor in mortality rates in France, third after heart disease and cancer. The major health issues in France in the past few decades have been AIDS (*SIDA*) and access to birth control. The rate of AIDS in France ranks second after the United States among industrialized countries. The HIV virus was first identified at the Institut Louis Pasteur in Paris, a major scientific research institute.

The sale of birth control and legalization of abortion came much later in France than in other industrialized nations. The role of the Catholic Church in this is important, as is the influence of the women's movement on the changes in policy. Birth control was first permitted to be sold in 1967, and abortion did not become legal until 1975.

Secular Celebrations

France has several civic holidays (*jours feriés*), when schools, museums, and stores close. These public holidays, which include some with a religious origin, are: le Jour de l'An—1 January; May Day or Labor Day—1 May; World War II Victory Day—8 May; Easter (date varies); Ascension Day (after Easter); Pentecost Monday; Bastille Day—14 July; Assumption Day—15 August; All Saints Day or Toussaint—1 November; Armistice Day—11 November; and Christmas—25 December. Along with Bastille Day, Armistice Day is the most patriotic of these holidays, marking the end of World War I. There are speeches and parades in local communities involving local dignitaries and veterans, who place a wreath on the war memorial.

Bastille Day is the most important national holiday, celebrated in every commune with town dances, fireworks, and other festivities. On this day, there is a parade down the Champs-Elysée in Paris, involving the President and other dignitaries. Bastille Day marks the storming of the state prison, known as Bastille, by the citizens of Paris during the French Revolution. Known popularly as the 14th of July (*le quatorze juillet*), Bastille Day celebrates the overthrow of monarchy and the beginnings of the French Republic.

Each commune in France generally holds a town festival during the year. In some regions, these incorporate religious and secular symbolisms. There are dances, parades, sports competitions, and other activities.

The Arts and Humanities

Support for the Arts. There is a great deal of support for the arts in France at the state, regional, and municipal levels. The French Ministry of Culture funds artists as well as restoration projects and museums.

Literature. Oral traditions and folktales predominated in pre-modern France. Up until the mid-twentieth century, rural communities held *veillées*, in which neighbors gathered in someone's home around the hearth to trade stories and tales. French written literature is considered one of the greatest world traditions. The first works of literature in French were the *Chansons de Geste* of the eleventh century, a series of epic poems. During the Renaissance, France's great national literature flourished with works by François Rabelais, Michel Eyquem de Montaigne, and Pierre de Ronsard. Enlightenment writers such as Voltaire, Montesquieu (Charles-Louis de Secondat), and Jean-Jacques Rousseau helped to shape a national consciousness during this time. Nineteenth-century writers took up themes of struggles between social classes, clerical and anticlerical forces, and conservatives and liberals. They also developed a form of realist writing that charted the various regional differences, and urban-rural splits, in France. François-Auguste-René de Chateaubriand, Madame de Staël, George Sand, Victor Hugo, Stendhal (Marie-Henri Beyle), Honoré de Balzac, and Gustave Flaubert were the great novelists of this period. Poets included Charles-Pierre Baudelaire, Alphonse-Marie-Louis de Prat Lamartine, Arthur Rimbaud, Paul Verlaine, and Stéphane Mallarmé. Earlier twentieth century writers include Marcel Proust, Anatole France, Jules Romains, Sidonie-Gabrielle Colette, François Mauriac, Louis-Ferdinand Celine, and André-Georges Malraux. French existentialism during the postwar period is associated with writers Albert Camus and Simone de Beauvoir. The so-called "new novel" came to the fore in the 1950s and its representatives include Nathalie Sarraute and Alain Robbe-Grillet.

France gives several literary prizes each year. These include the Goncourt, the Renaudot, the Medicis, and the Femina.

Graphic Arts. France's most important graphic art forms are painting, sculpture, and architecture. The prehistory of French art is also important, including the famous cave paintings in southwestern France. The nineteenth century period of Romanticism in painting is associated with Eugène Delacroix and Jean-Auguste Ingres. Paintings of peasant life flourished during this century, particularly in the work of Jean Courbet and Jean-François Millet. Impressionism, in which color and light became important, is associated with Claude Monet, (Jean) Pierre Auguste Renoir, Camille Pissaro, Edgar Degas, Édouard Manet, and Morissette. Postimpressionism followed later in the century, with works by Henri Matisse, Paul Cézanne, Georges Seurat, and Pierre Bonnard. Great twentieth century painters include Georges Braque, and Jean Dubuffet. The most famous French sculptor is Auguste Rodin.

Performance Arts. Theater and dance have a strong tradition in France, both in the classical sense and in the realm of folklife. As in most of France's cultural life, Paris dominates the grand traditions of theater. France's great dramatists include Pierre Corneille, Jean Racine, Molière, Victor Hugo, Alexandre Dumas pere and fils, Jean Anouilh, and Jean Genet. The Comédie Française in Paris still presents the classic works of Molière and Racine. Opera is also popular in France, cutting across social class. Street theater, pageants, and regional theatrical productions flourish in the provinces. The city of Toulouse is particularly well-known for its performance arts. French cinema is subsidized more highly by the state than other European movie industries, and the French have access to more nationally-produced films than their neighbors. Many French cities hold movie festivals during the year, the most famous being that in Cannes in early summer.

The State of the Physical and Social Sciences

Most scientific research is supported and sponsored in France through the network of the CNRS (Center for National Research). Scientific research is also funded by the CNES (French National Space Agency) and INSERM (the National Institute for Health and Medical Research). France is among the four world leaders in scientific funding. The CNRS has funded many laboratories in which winners of Nobel prizes and Fields medal for mathematics have worked. CNRS (including the research institutes it funds) and French universities are the major sources of support for scientific research. Very often, professors and researchers at universities also have appointments at CNRS. There is, however, a series of exams that one must pass in order to enter into the CNRS.

French ethnographic research in France is funded by the Mission du Patrimoine Ethnologique, which is part of the Ministry of Culture. The Mission participates in the journal *Ethnologie Francaise* and publishes its own journal, *Terrain.* It also publishes books in association with the Maison des Sciences de l'Homme, an institute for advanced research in Paris. Another major site for the anthropology of France is LAIOS, the Anthropological Laboratory for the Study of Institutions and Social Organizations in Paris.

Bibliography

Abélès, Marc. *Quiet Days in Burgundy: A Study of Local Politics*, 1991.

Agulhon, Maurice. *The French Republic, 1879-1992.* Translated by Antonia Nevill, 1993.

Badone, Ellen. *The Appointed Hour: Death, Worldview and Social Change in Brittany*,1989.

Binet, Alain. *Societé et Culture en France dupuis 1945*, 2000.

Bourdieu, Pierre. *Distinction: A Social Critique of the Judgement of Taste.* Translated by Richard Nice, 1984.

Carroll, Raymonde. *Cultural Misunderstandings: The French-American Experience.* Translated by Carol Volk, 1988.

Corbett, James. *Through French Windows: An Introduction to France in the Nineties.* 1994.

De Planhol, Xavier, and Paul Claval. *An Historical Geography of France.* Translated by Janet Lloyd, 1994.

Levieux, Eleanor, and Michael Levieux. *Insiders' French: Beyond the Dictionary.* 1999.

Mendras, Henri, with Alistair Cole. *Social Change in Modern France: Towards a Cultural Anthropology of the Fifth Republic*, 1992.

Noiriel, Gerard. *The French Melting Pot: Immigration, Citizenship, and National Identity.* Translated by Geoffroy de Laforcade, 1996.

Nora, Pierre. *Realms of Memory.* Vol. I. *Conflicts and Divisions.* Translated by Arthur Goldhammer, 1983.

Pinchemal, Philippe. *France: A Geographical, Social and Economic Survey*, 1987.

Price, Roger. *A Concise History of France*, 1993.

Reed-Danahay, Deborah. *Education and Identity in Rural France: The Politics of Schooling*, 1996.

Rogers, Susan Carol. *Shaping Modern Times in Rural France: The Transformation and Reproduction of an Averyronnais Community*, 1991.

Segalen, Martine. *Historical Anthropology of the Family.* Translated by J. C. Whitehouse and Sarah Matthews, 1986.

Todd, Emmanuel. *The Making of Modern France: Ideology, Politics and Culture*, 1991.

Zeldin, Theodore. *The French*, 1982.

—Deborah Reed-Danahay

French Guiana

Culture Name

French Guianese

Alternative Names

Guyane Francaise

Orientation

Identification. Christopher Columbus sighted the Guiana coast in 1498 during his third trip to the New World. The French first settled the land one hundred years later, calling it Guiana, the French form of an American Indian word that means "land of waters."

Location and Geography. French Guiana is on the northern coast of South America. It is nestled between Suriname to the west and Brazil to the east and south. It covers approximately 34,750 square miles (90,000 square kilometers), about the same size as Indiana. The close proximity of the equator (which lies a few degrees south) contributes to the hot and humid climate, which averages 80 degrees Fahrenheit (27 degrees Celsius) all year.

There are three main regions: the coastal plain in the north, a hilly plateau in the middle, and the Tumac-Humac Mountains in the south. Most of the interior (83 percent of it) is dense tropical rain forest. There are more than twenty rivers that flow into the Atlantic Ocean from French Guiana. The most important of these are the Oyapock, which forms the southeastern border with Brazil, and the Maroni, which forms the border with Suriname.

Demography. The 1998 population in French Guiana was approximately 167,982. Around 40 percent of the population lives in the capital of Cayenne. African and Afro-Europeans make up 66 percent of the total population with Europeans making up another 18 percent and east Asians, Chinese, Amerindians, and Brazilians making up the remainder. In the sparsely populated interior the Oyampi and Palik tribes still follow a traditional pre-columbian way of life. There are also a few tribes descended from African slaves who escaped from plantations to live a lifestyle similar to their native central Africa.

Linguistic Affiliation. The official language is French. All business and most common dialogue is conducted using the mainstream French. The native tribes in the interior, however, use their own language, and the African tribes use Taki-Taki, a pidgin English.

Symbolism. The heavy influence of the French culture is evident throughout the country, and in the capital many of the customs and attitudes of France predominate.

History and Ethnic Relations

Emergence of the Nation. The Arawak Indians are the people first known to inhabit French Guiana. The next major waves of people were the Caribs. These peoples came from the Amazon and traveled to the Antilles (most of the islands of the West Indies). The Caribs displaced many of the Arawak. During the age of discovery and Christopher Columbus's journeys, the Caribs were still traveling through the Caribbean.

The French were the first Europeans to settle in French Guiana. They arrived in the early 1600s, when many of the European powers were colonizing the Americas and looking for the lost city of gold, El Dorado. Between the climate and Indian attacks the first settlement was a failure. In 1634 the French settled again and this time they did not leave. Cayenne was founded as the capital some time later and it has remained the country's largest city.

Plantations were established in parts of the land, forming an economic base. Following a series

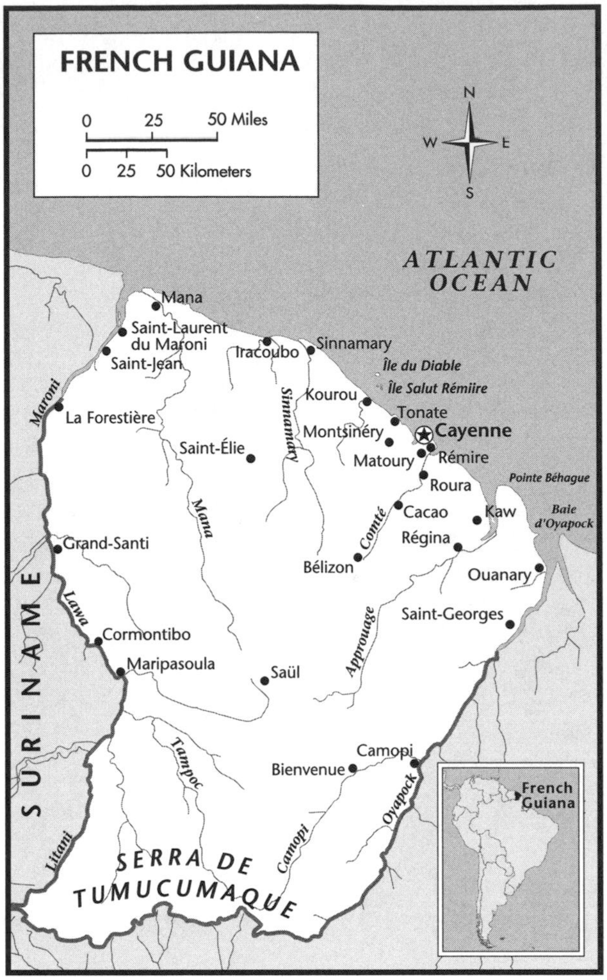

French Guiana

of agricultural failures and culminating with the abolition of slavery in 1848, most of the plantations closed. One of the agricultural settlements located in Kourou became the infamous Devil's Island penal colony. France had sent many political prisoners to French Guiana during the French Revolution; now the most hardened and notorious criminals and dissidents were also sent over the ocean to the penal colony. In nearly one hundred years of operation Devil's Island received more than seventy thousand prisoners. All camps were closed in 1945.

Twenty years later Kourou was once again in the spotlight of France and receiving its people. This time, however, scientists—not prisoners—were arriving, to construct and operate the European Space Agency's rocket-launching center.

In 1946 French Guiana ceased being a colony and became an official overseas department of France. The 1980s saw the rise of a pro-independence party, but ultimately the group lost power because the majority of French Guianese support being a part of France.

National Identity. In the political and cultural sense there is no national identity. The nation for the French Guianese is France. The diversity of ethnic groups and the lack of common history add to the problem of internal national identity. The Amerindians living in the central part of the country seem to identify the least with the French and European way of life.

Ethnic Relations. A complex weave of ethnicity and culture forms French Guiana's population. The Creole population, itself a large mix of ethnicity and culture, comprises the largest ethnic group and has had the greatest influence on the country's culture. Fewer than one hundred of the native settlers, the Arawaks, currently live in the central part of the country. The Caribs have a few small communities along the coast and have mingled with the Creoles. There is also a noticeable settlement of Vietnamese who came over in the early and middle parts of the twentieth century. The cultures interact fairly well and inherently adopt and adapt to local flavors. Considering the small population, the larger culture is forced to recognize all of its peoples.

Urbanism, Architecture, and the Use of Space

With the exception of the Amerindian tribes in the interior, most people live in one of the cities. Cayenne alone has 40 percent of the population. Houses range greatly in size and uniqueness, but the relative prosperity that results from living under the French flag allows the houses to be built of decent quality, and almost all have running water and electricity. They are usually painted light colors such as blue and yellow in keeping with the Caribbean Creole style. Small gardens are often annexed to the houses. The Amerindian residences in the interior are usually simple thatched roof huts, following tradition.

Food and Economy

Food in Daily Life. The diversity of cultures has given the local foods their flavor. Caribbean and Creole style foods are common along with Western foods and such Asian cuisines as Vietnamese and Chinese. Seafood, especially shrimp, is eaten quite often. Rice accompanies most of the dishes.

Basic Economy. The economy is closely tied to France. Shrimp and other seafood production is the

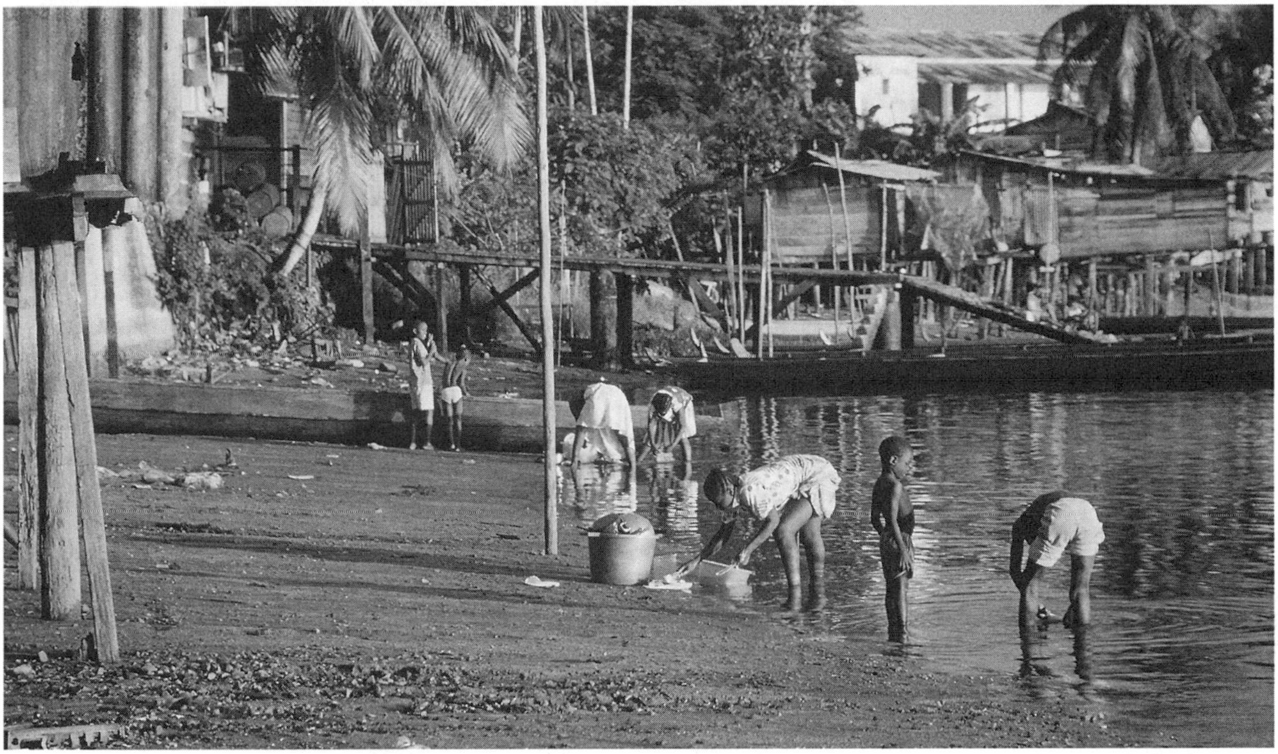

Children washing clothes in a river in Saint Laurent. More than twenty rivers find their way to the Atlantic Ocean from French Guiana.

major economical asset. The space agency has become the second most important asset, with predictions for even more growth. Forestry of the untapped interior holds economic potential. Sugarcane and other cash crops are grown by the agricultural sector.

Commercial Activities. Family members still comprise the farm labor. Locally grown vegetables and fruit are sold in markets along with fish and meats. The demand for livestock is heavy and likewise can be profitable for the sellers. Small craftwork is sold to both tourists and locals. The building materials for these crafts and for carpentry projects are also sold. Among the major buyers of these materials are the many small-scale construction companies. The service sector is also important at the local level.

Major Industries. The major industries are shrimp and fish processing and aerospace. Lumber and construction are secondary industries. The agricultural products are sugar, rice, manioc, cocoa, vegetables, and bananas. Cattle, pigs, and poultry are the main livestock animals.

Trade. The major exports are shrimp, lumber, gold, rice, rum, rosewood essence, and clothing. In 1997 the exports totaled $148 million (U.S.). France bought the bulk of the products, more than 60 percent, with the United States, the European Union, and Japan buying the rest. French Guiana has always bought much more then it sold, resulting in high trade deficits since its inception. In 1997 the country imported $600 million (U.S) of goods, such as processed meats, grains, machinery, fuels, and chemicals. The largest import partner is of course France, with Germany, Belgium, and the United States making up the remainder. A large national debt has accrued because of the constant trade deficit.

Division of Labor. The total labor force in 1997 was 58,800. The bulk of the labor force (60 percent) fell within the service, government, and commerce sectors. Industry accounted for 21 percent and agriculture 18 percent. Unemployment was at nearly a quarter of the total labor force and affected mostly younger workers.

The fishing and forestry sectors rely on local, many times unskilled, labor. The space center in Kourou employs some of the most educated persons in the world. In addition to scientists, the space center employs numerous lower-skilled workers to pave roads, construct buildings, transport goods, and perform service functions ranging from food production to hotel management.

SOCIAL STRATIFICATION

Classes and Castes. The heavy subsidization by the French government has resulted in much more disposable income than if the country would have to rely on its own products alone. This helped create the highest standard of living in South America. The rural parts of the country see the least of the relative prosperity.

Symbols of Social Stratification. The common indicators of wealth in the Western world are also relevant in French Guiana. These include French-fashioned clothes, larger houses, and education.

POLITICAL LIFE

Government. French Guiana is a part of the French Republic and thereby subject to the same regulations and political hierarchy as France. There is a general council that handles local affairs and the relationship with the republic. It is composed of sixteen elected officials from each canton. They elect a president of the department.

Regional councilors are elected by proportional representation of the political parties. This council involves many of the same tasks as the general council but focuses more on long-term economic issues. A prefect, appointed from Paris, technically has the most power in the department but is usually relegated to military and security duties as the local officials are given more say in the running of the country. Two deputies and one senator are sent from French Guiana to Paris to serve in the national parliament. The judicial branch is the same as mainland France with the highest local court based on the Caribbean island of Martinique.

Leadership and Political Officials. The leader credited with exerting the most influence in regard to French Guiana becoming an overseas department is Gaston Monnerville. He was the elected deputy in the years 1932–1946—the last year of his service being the year that departmentalization was enacted. Another important political figure of the time was the mayor of Cayenne, Constant Chlore. He was the founder of the only communist party in French Guiana and became integral to trade union pacts. Since that time French Guiana has had a rotating cast of local politicians in favor of and against French rule. As of 2001, the locally elected prefect was Dominique Vian.

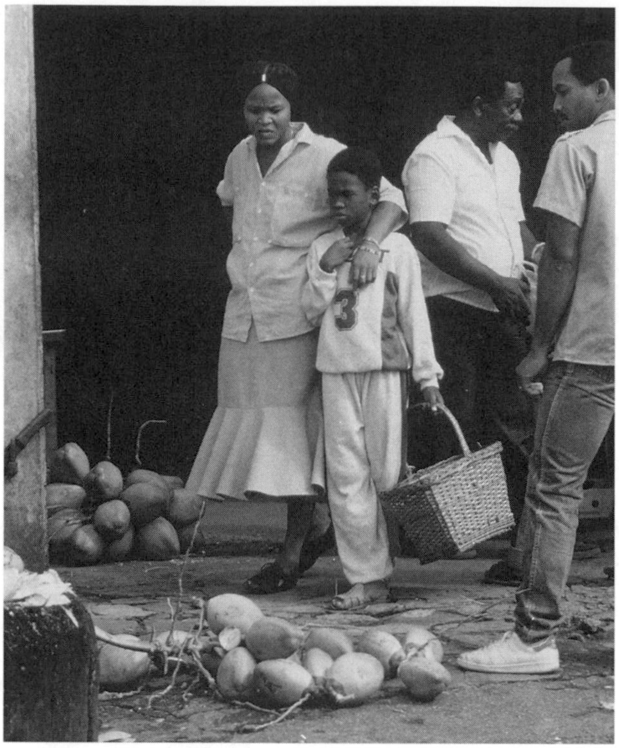

A street scene in Cayenne. French Guianese markets offer a variety of locally grown fruits and vegetables in addition to meat and fish.

Social Problems and Control. French Guiana has had no major human rights abuses in recent times.

Military Activity. The defense of borders is a responsibility of France. This military includes the French Forces and the Gendarmerie. The availability of men fit for service was thirty thousand in 1999.

SOCIAL WELFARE AND CHANGE PROGRAMS

Local officials are in charge of social planning.

NONGOVERNMENTAL ORGANIZATIONS AND OTHER ASSOCIATIONS

European agencies, trade unions, and other associations with France are prevalent in French Guiana.

GENDER ROLES AND STATUSES

Division of Labor by Gender. Women are generally responsible for tending to the children and other household tasks. The men are in charge of providing financial support. This holds especially true in the rural areas, although there is some variation among the different ethnic groups.

Fishing boats are moored on the bank of Laussat Canal, and fishing nets hang out to dry in Cayenne. Shrimp and fish processing are major industries in the country.

The Relative Status of Women and Men. Business and politics are governed by the French system. There is no systematic discrimination against women, but women tend not to be in the upper echelon of either field.

Marriage, Family, and Kinship

Marriage. Most marriage ceremonies take place within the church, as is the custom in most of South America.

Domestic Unit. Families have followed a Western trend of becoming smaller. The average birthrate is 3.31 children per woman. Regardless of size, families maintain their closeness through activities and religion.

Kin Groups. As with families, the members of larger kin groups tend to be close and live within close proximity to one another.

Socialization

Child Rearing and Education. Schooling is compulsory until age sixteen. Primary schools exist all over the country, while secondary schools are located primarily in Cayenne and large towns. The educational system is the same as in France and has contributed to the literacy rate of more than 80 percent.

Higher Education. Professional and university level students get their education overseas, usually in France. Because of the students' European Community status, they are granted all the same privileges as European students.

Etiquette

French values permeate French Guiana. Dress is Western in style in the sense that light colors and short sleeves are worn in warm climates. The people are generally known for their friendliness, although the indigenous peoples in the interior see very few foreigners and therefore may appear to be wary at first.

Religion

Religious Beliefs. The vast majority of French Guianans are Roman Catholic. There are many other religions practiced by the minority groups. These include indigenous Amerindian shamanistic religions, Buddhism, Hinduism, Islam, and African-based religions.

Death and the Afterlife. The Catholic rituals are followed, including a cycle of prayers upon death and a funeral at which friends and family gather.

MEDICINE AND HEALTH CARE

All medical affairs are handled by the State Department of Health. This department works with such organizations as the Pasteur Institute to eradicate diseases. Vaccinations are free and compulsory for tuberculosis, diphtheria, polio, yellow fever, and measles, mumps, and rubella. There are high incidences of malaria (almost six thousand cases in 1995), dengue fever, and various sexually transmitted diseases. A number of AIDS cases have ended in death, accounting for approximately 10 percent of all adult deaths.

There are seven medical doctors per ten thousand people, but these doctors are available only in urban areas. The average life expectancy is 76.4 years.

SECULAR CELEBRATIONS

All major French holidays are celebrated, including Bastille Day, Labor Day, and the Catholic holidays.

THE ARTS AND HUMANITIES

Performance Arts. The various ethnic groups value dance and music. The urban areas listen to modern music; the tribes of African origin produce drumbeat-driven rhythms; and the Amerindians focus more on wind instruments such as flutes.

THE STATE OF THE PHYSICAL AND SOCIAL SCIENCES

French Guiana has perhaps more diversity then any other country in the world in this regard. The interior population has learned little or nothing of the sciences, while on the coast the European Space Agency leads one of the most sophisticated operations in the world. The future seems to hold more of this great divide.

BIBLIOGRAPHY

Burton, Richard, and Fred Reno, ed. *French and West Indian: Martinique, Guadeloupe, and French Guiana Today,* 1995.

Gall, Tim, ed. *Worldmark Encyclopedia of Cultures and Daily Life,* 1998.

Rajewski, Brian, ed. *Countries of the World,* 1998.

U.S. Government, Central Intelligence Agency. *CIA World Factbook,* 2000.

—DAVID MATUSKEY

French Polynesia

Culture Name

French Polynesian

Orientation

Identification. The Territory of French Polynesia consists of five archipelagoes (Society Islands, Marquesas Islands, Tuamotu Islands, Austral Islands, and Gambier Islands) under French administration. While each island group displays a variant of the Polynesian cultural tradition and all are united by over a century of colonial administration, residents maintain cultural identities specific to the home archipelago and home island. These identities are beginning to blend into a general national identity as a result of modern transportation, education, and communication networks.

Location and Geography. French Polynesia includes 121 islands scattered across more than 1,930,500 square miles (five million square kilometers) in the southern Pacific Ocean between Australia and South America. The island groups were formed by undersea volcanoes and include steep volcanic peaks, high islands with fringing coral reefs and large lagoons, and coral atolls surrounding submerged volcanoes. The capital city, Papeete, is on the island of Tahiti, the largest of these islands and the first to experience European conquest.

Demography. The population as of July 2000 is 249,110 on the inhabited islands. Nearly 80 percent of the residents are of Polynesian or mixed Polynesian ethnicity, approximately 12 percent are of European ancestry and 8 percent are of Chinese decent. The population is concentrated in the urban and suburban areas of northern Tahiti, which has nearly 150,000 residents. Only two other islands, Moorea and Raiatea, have populations above ten thousand and many islands have populations below one thousand.

Linguistic Affiliation. A majority of the residents speak both French and Tahitian, the dominant Polynesian language. On the more isolated islands, older residents continue to speak a local Polynesian language; and in the isolated Austral Islands, languages differ from island to island. These languages have become more homogeneous, and Tahitian is beginning to replace local languages. Older Chinese residents speak the Hakka dialect, but younger generations speak French and often Tahitian.

Symbolism. The Territory flies both the French flag and its own flag which shows a red outrigger canoe on a yellow background over a blue sea. The canoe symbolizes the Polynesian seafaring tradition. Other cultural symbols relate to the fertility of the land (the breadfruit), the beauty of the islands (the tiare gardenia blossom and the black pearl), and the indigenous culture (the tiki figure).

History and Ethnic Relations

Emergence of the Nation. The five archipelagoès were joined into a new national entity by the gradual process of French conquest and annexation, beginning with Tahiti in 1843 and ending with the annexation of the Austral group in 1900. French administration and the centralization of authority, jobs, transportation, and services in Papeete contributed to the development of a national identity.

National Identity. French Polynesian identity is more Polynesian than French, but many residents are proud of their relationship to French culture and feel a kinship with French-speaking cultures throughout the world. Residents who favor independence from France advocate a return to a more traditional Polynesian culture.

Ethnic Relations. Tensions between the majority Polynesian ethnic group and the minority European and Chinese communities are due to economic inequalities between those groups and persistent cul-

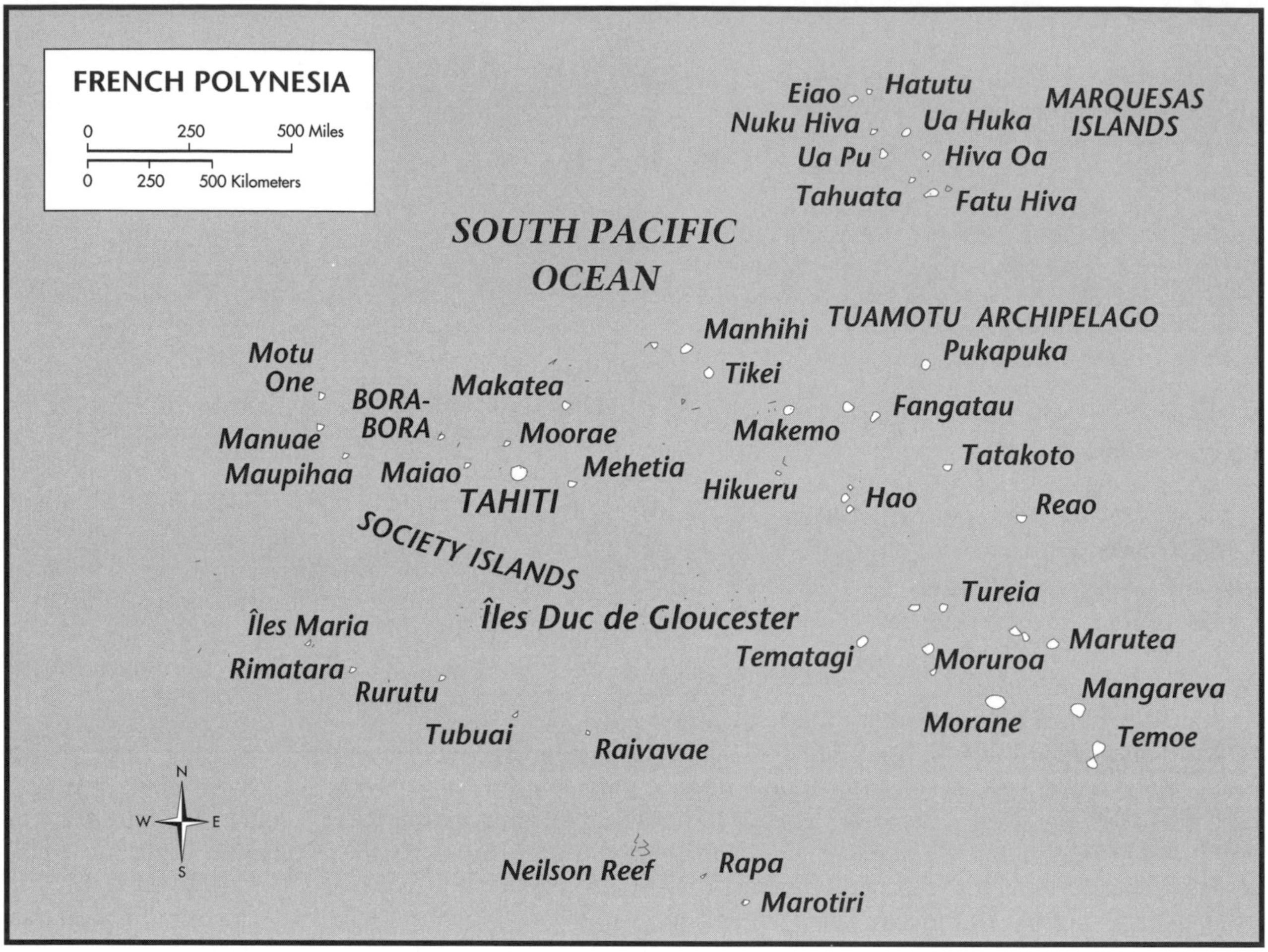

French Polynesia

tural differences. Violence against members of ethnic minorities is rare, and systematic discrimination against the members of any ethnic group is not evident. There has been a great deal of intermarriage between ethnic groups, and European and Chinese families tend to assimilate into the majority culture.

Urbanism, Architecture, and the Use of Space

The only urban center is Papeete and the surrounding communes at the northern end of Tahiti. These are densely developed areas that include a large commercial and government center, military and port facilities, and a wide range of residential housing types. The dominant style of domestic and commercial architecture is International Modern with concrete walls with metal roofs and decorative wood or masonry. Many homes, while built of imported materials, retain traditional spatial organization with a single large sleeping room and an outdoor kitchen. The architecture of public buildings often reflects one of the two regional architectural traditions: Polynesian-style construction from plant materials or colonial construction.

Food and Economy

Food in Daily Life. In rural areas, people provide much of their own food through fishing, animal husbandry, and gardening of indigenous staple foods such as taro, breadfruit, sweet potatoes, and manioc. These local foods are supplemented with imported goods such as rice, canned goods, and fresh bread. In most rural households, only one meal is cooked each day (either lunch or supper) and leftovers are eaten at the other meals. In larger villages and urban areas, Chinese food is available at the local Chinese-owned general store, and in small restaurants. Islands with hotels have restaurants that serve local Polynesian seafood and French-inspired cuisine.

Food Customs at Ceremonial Occasions. On Saturday, Polynesian families prepare an earth oven with traditional foods (fish, pork, taro, breadfruit, sweet potato) to be eaten at large family gatherings on Sunday. Traditional Polynesian food also is served at wedding feasts.

Basic Economy. The economy is heavily dependent on French social programs and military spending. The most important commodity is black pearls, and with the exception of flowers, agricultural exports are insignificant. There is an active internal agricultural trade in which fruits, vegetables, meat, and fish are shipped to market in the urban center from the other islands. Fishing provides some export income, but large-scale commercial fishing is dominated by foreign fleets. Tourism is relatively underdeveloped, but the jobs and income from tourism are significant on islands that have resorts.

Land Tenure and Property. The contemporary system of land ownership and tenure resulted from French efforts to introduce a system of individual land ownership. Land is inherited equally by all the descendants of a landowner and is often held in common by large groups of related people. Co-owners who reside on the family land work out the details of use rights among themselves; these rights are inherited by one's children. Communal land holding is the source of many disputes as heirs petition to divide land into individual holdings or attempt to sell land with competing ownership claims. However, communal ownership has slowed the transfer of land from Polynesian families to recent immigrants. There are few landless Polynesians.

Commercial Activities. A very active import business is dominated by Chinese-Tahitian and French-Tahitian family-owned businesses. Multinational companies are involved in the airline, hotel, construction, and energy sectors, while the importation of building materials, consumer goods, and transport is controlled by local businesses. Locally produced goods include vanilla beans, coconut-oil-based soaps and cosmetics, fruit juice, milk and yogurt, clothing, flowers, and handicrafts.

Major Industries. Within the urban core of Papeete, there are several industrial zones. The port area of Fare includes a number of boat-building and ship-repair businesses, as well as major construction material suppliers. There are only a few factories in French Polynesia: a beer and soft drink bottling enterprise and a few small textile printing studios in Papeete, a fruit juice bottling factory on the neighboring island of Moorea, for example. Other major industrial activities include management of landfills, hydroelectric power, and water purification, all of which are government enterprises. Tourism is also an important industry in the Territory (188,933 tourists in 1998).

A passenger rides on top of the Papeete bus in Tahiti. Papeete is the only urban center in French Polynesia.

Trade. Imports of food and other consumer goods including automobiles, appliances, and building materials are enormous by comparison to exports of locally produced commodities. Trade is also entirely by containers shipped by sea into the large port complex of Papeete. Exports of local goods such as black pearls, coconut products, handicrafts, fresh fruit, and flowers are often transported by air. Most trade occurs within the Pacific basin with major trading partners in Taiwan and Hong Kong, Korea, New Zealand, Australia, Chile, Hawaii, and California. A secondary trade market with the European Union is also important but involves luxury goods such as wine, cheese, automobiles, and clothing.

Division of Labor. In general, Polynesian men dominate in skilled and unskilled physical labor (agriculture, construction, fishing, transportation). The retail and commercial sectors are controlled by Chinese and European-Polynesian families. The government sector is the largest source of jobs, with higher-status jobs typically held by European-Polynesian or Polynesian-Chinese residents with university degrees and lower-status jobs held by Polynesians (clerical work by women, public works jobs by men). Political positions and appointments go almost exclusively to Polynesian men.

Social Stratification

Classes and Castes. The class structure closely mimics that of metropolitan France: small upper class, large middle and lower-middle classes, and a small number of poor people. The upper class includes wealthy Polynesian-European families, Chinese merchant families, and foreign residents. The middle class includes members of all ethnic groups. These families typically own their own homes and have at least one wage earner in the household.

The Polynesian hierarchy of ranked titles and chieftainship has disappeared, but Polynesians continue to keep detailed genealogical records and the descendants of chiefly families are aware of their history. The descendants of the Tahitian monarchy are socially prominent.

Symbols of Social Stratification. Class structure is most evident in the display of imported goods such as automobiles and clothing. There is residential segregation of social classes in the urban areas of Tahiti, with oceanfront and ridgetops dominated by the upper classes, the flat littoral plain by middle-class households, and the interior valleys by lower-class households. On the outer islands, house style and size also mark social stratification, while location is less indicative of class.

Political Life

Government. The country's official status is an overseas territory of France, with internal autonomy since 1984. The territory manages many of its own affairs while remaining a member of the French republic. The French state controls defense and law and order, foreign affairs, nationality and immigration, justice, higher education, and research, communications, and the currency. Residents vote in national elections and elect representatives to the national government in Paris. The country is responsible for territorial administration, exploration and development rights in certain maritime areas, primary and secondary education, taxation, prices, and foreign trade.

The territory's political institutions are the government of French Polynesia, the Assembly of French Polynesia, and the Economic, Social and Cultural Council (CES). The president and the head of the territorial administration are elected by the Polynesian Assembly from among the forty-one territorial council members. The territorial council members, representing the five archipelagoès are elected by direct universal suffrage every five years. The important units of community government are the commune (municipality) and subcommunes (districts). Each island has a mayor and an elected municipal council. France is represented by a high commissioner. The CES is composed of thirty people representing the professions, the trade unions, and other economic, cultural, and social institutions.

Leadership and Political Officials. Public officials control the resources that flow from the government to local communities. Government agencies, social services, employment, and salaries are under the control of municipal, territorial, and state officials. Political patronage is the dominant feature of regional politics, and residents develop personal ties to officials and manipulate those relationships to gain access to political power.

Military Activity. France tested nuclear weapons at Mururoa Atoll in the Tuamotu Archipelago between 1966 and 1996. In August 1999, France maintained a force of 2,300 military personnel and a police force of six hundred.

Social Welfare and Change Programs

In the early 1960s, an accelerated plan for regional development was introduced that involved the creation of a nuclear testing installation in the Tuamotu Islands and the introduction of a colonial welfare state. Funding for regional development and social programs comes primarily from French taxpayers. Aid, subsidies, and loans from France have created many salaried government jobs for islanders. French Polynesians have a fairly high standard of living that is maintained through the money they receive from French entitlement programs, including the elderly pension/retirement system and the family allocation system. Islanders receive free health care and primary education.

Nongovernmental Organizations and Other Associations

Among the most important voluntary organizations and associations are agricultural associations, church-related groups, craft associations, dance groups, and soccer, canoe, and other sports-related teams. There are a few trade unions.

A house on Raivavae, French Polynesia. Traditional homes have a single large sleeping room and an outdoor kitchen.

Gender Roles and Statuses

Division of Labor by Gender. The gendered division of labor resulted from efforts of Christian missionaries and French colonial officials to introduce a Western cultural system. In this system, men were defined as the breadwinners and heads of families and the ideal roles for women were as helpmates and nurturers. Before the introduction of development programs in the 1960s, men were responsible for taro gardens, tree crop plantations, and fishing, and women devoted themselves to motherhood and household maintenance. Women also assisted their husbands in agricultural production and fishing. Men tended to dominate the income-earning opportunities in the processing of copra and vanilla. Rural and urban development schemes after the 1960s expanded men's opportunities in commercial agriculture and introduced wage-earning jobs. Although women in some of the archipelagoès were drawn into wage labor, these opportunities were dominated by men.

The Relative Status of Women and Men. The ability of men to earn money became an essential part of their breadwinning role. After the 1960s, a close association developed between income-earning ability and household decision making. Men's predominance in income-earning activities and greater income were translated into greater control over household decision making. This authority is not supported by an ideology of male superiority. Belief in the interdependence, complementarity, and equality of men's and women's activities and capabilities exists in urban and rural settings.

Marriage, Family, and Kinship

Marriage. Residents recognize several kinds or degrees of marital union. At one end of the continuum is the union of a couple instituted by civil (French) and church ceremonies and celebrated by wedding feasts for relatives, officials, and friends. At the other end are couples that live and eat together without a civil ceremony who are committed to raising a family together and are considered by their neighbors to be married.

Domestic Unit. The most important residential unit is the nuclear family. Many nuclear families include adopted children. Most often couples initially live with the parents of the man or woman and later establish a separate domestic unit.

Inheritance. People recognize bilateral kinship units that control the use of land. Individuals must demonstrate their connections to one of these units in order to claim use rights to plots of family land. Those rights are inherited by one's children.

Kin Groups. All of the mother and fathers' relatives are considered kin. Although not an important corporate or social group in an individual's life, one's bilateral kin group is an important source of mutual aid, and through membership in a kin group, individuals acquire use rights to land.

Socialization

Infant Care. Residents adore children, and most couples look forward to raising a family. Infants and children are raised under the influence of parents as well as grandparents, siblings, and other relatives. Infants are the center of attention in households.

Child Rearing and Education. Children are socialized by a network of kin within and outside the nuclear family household. There is little parental interference in the teaching of skills because people believe in a child's autonomy. The goal is to make children docile so that they will want to act in the "right" way. Children form peer play groups, and much of a child's training takes place in that context.

Higher Education. There is a 98 percent literacy rate. Primary, secondary, and vocational schools were established by the French. Schooling is free and compulsory between ages six and fourteen. Teaching is in French, although a few hours per week of Tahitian are provided in primary and secondary school. Private schools run by churches and subsidized by the government teach the same curriculum as the public schools. Adult education is offered at no charge. French Polynesians can attend college in France or pursue a degree at the French University of the Pacific (UFP), which has a campus in French Polynesia. The geographic fragmentation of the territory complicates the organization of education.

Etiquette

Reciprocity, generosity, and hospitality are central values. When guests are invited for a meal, the hosts are not necessarily expected to eat. Tahitians greet each other by shaking hands and/or exchanging kisses on the cheek. Unless there is a large number of people in the room, it is considered impolite not to shake hands with all of them. It also is considered impolite to keep one's shoes on when entering another person's home.

Roasting a pig at a festival in Atuona, Hiva Oa. Rural Polynesians provide much of their own food and generally cook only one meal each day.

Religion

Religious Beliefs. The conversion of residents to Christianity occurred after the London Missionary School sent evangelical Protestant missionaries to Tahiti in 1797. Catholicism was introduced much later by the French. The Catholic population lives primarily in the Gambier and Marquesas archipelagoès. Protestantism predominates in the Society, Austral, and Tuamotu island groups. Today 49 percent of the population is Protestant, 33 percent is Catholic, 5 percent is Mormon, 5 percent is Sanito, and 4 percent is Seventh-Day Adventist.

Before Western contact, people believed in a pantheon of distant gods and a host of local and family spirits that affected daily life.

Many residents believe in ancestral spirits. These spirits gather around the village and are encountered as the ghosts of formerly living people.

Religious Practitioners. In Protestant areas, the Christian faith, the church, and the pastor are central features of village life. Pastors preside over the religious activities of the community, conduct Sunday school, teach the Bible, conduct weddings and funerals, and provide communion. The village pastor is also a protector of community morality and can affect political decision making. Elders have an important power base in the church, and one of their primary roles is to assist the pastor in enforcing social control. Some contemporary villages have indigenous practitioners (primarily male) who use their knowledge and control of spirits and ghosts to heal people who have a spirit-caused disorder.

Rituals and Holy Places. Many rituals involve the events of the Christian calendar year, such as cemetery visiting on All Saints' Day, or the annual re-enactment of the arrival of the missionaries by boat. There are a number of rituals that involve life-cycle events such as baptisms, weddings, and funerals. For example, traditional weddings include the ceremonial presentation of gifts including traditional speech making and dancing. The annual collection of church tithes by the Protestant churches on May Day also involves ritual oratory and ceremonial visitation of local households.

Ancient Polynesian temple platforms, *marae*, are still considered to be holy places by many Polynesians even though indigenous religious practice has largely ceased. Professional traditional dance companies stage ritual re-enactments of ancient ceremonies on a reconstructed temple platform in the Tahitian district of Paea for tourists and visiting dignitaries.

Death and the Afterlife. Residents traditionally believed that people have both a physical body and a soul. The soul inhabits the body during life, though it can wander during dreaming. Death occurs when the soul leaves the body. Some Christians believe in the existence of two souls. At death, a person's true soul goes to God's world and remains in heaven or hell. A second soul or spirit leaves the body and wanders around the village.

Medicine and Health Care

Health conditions are generally good, with high life expectancy and a low infant mortality rate. In 1998, the major causes of death were cardiovascular problems, cancer, and traumatic injury. Medical care is paid for by the government. There are thirty-four hospitals and 369 doctors in the territory. Some islands lack a resident doctor. Indigenous medicine is widely utilized despite the recent introduction of Western biomedical techniques. Indigenous healing techniques include the use of herbal medicines, herbal baths, massage, and cupping. Indigenous healing has undergone a revitalization, and associations have developed to protect the heritage of local healing and ensure the authenticity of healers and their practice of local medicine.

Secular Celebrations

Public holidays are 1 January (New Year's Day), 5 March (Arrival of the first missionaries), Good Friday, Easter, Easter Monday, 1 May (May Day), 8 May (V-E Day), the last Thursday in May (Ascension), the first Sunday and Monday in June (Pentecost and Pentecost Monday), 29 June (Internal Autonomy Day), 14 July (Bastille Day), 15 August (Assumption), 1 November (All Saints' Day), 11 November (Armistice Day), and 25 December (Christmas). Other popular holidays are Chinese New Year, the Tahiti festival in July, and the Hawaiki Nui Canoe race.

The Arts and Humanities

Support for the Arts. There are a few formal grant programs, but many artists benefit from patronage relationships with government offices and major institutions. Practitioners of traditional handicrafts may register with the government and eventually receive a partial pension. In general, artists are self-supporting.

Literature. Nearly all fiction is written by expatriate European and Americans. Indigenous Polynesian genres such as storytelling, political and religious oratory, and song writing continue to be popular.

Graphic Arts. French Polynesia attracted many European painters and continues to support painters of island landscapes and residents. Indigenous graphic arts such as sculpture in wood, stone, and coral; the creation of hats, mats, and baskets; tattooing; the making of patchwork quilts; and decorative shell work continue to thrive. The practice of decorating bark cloth has largely disappeared, but several artists are attempting to revive this ancient art form.

Performance Arts. Musical performance genres range from highly stylized hymn singing, to humorous storytelling songs, to popular ballads and local rock and pop music. In addition to "classic" local songs, new songs and music are performed and distributed locally. Musical performance is widely practiced, and a favorite activity is to sit with friends and family after supper and sing old classic ballads as a group, accompanied by ukulele, guitar, and spoons. Traditional drumming is widely practiced, often as an accompaniment to dance performances.

Modern ("disco") dance, local variants of ballroom dances, and traditional Polynesian dance are popular. Traditional dance is performed by many amateur and professional troupes.

The State of the Physical and Social Sciences

There are many scientific institutions and programs. At the national level, the Institut de Recherche pour le Developement has the largest scientific library collection. Territorial research organizations operate under government ministries and include the Institut Rechereches Medicales Louis Mallarde, which conducts medical research on tropical diseases, and the Centre Polynesien de Sciences Humains, the sponsoring organization for archaeology, folklore, and ethnographic studies. A number of organizations are devoted to the marine sciences, including territorial government offices and international institutions as well as visiting research ships. The diversity of scientific institutions reflects the territory's relations with France and well-developed local government. Together with the French University of the Pacific, this combination of national, local, and international scientific organizations conducts research activities.

Bibliography

Elliston, Deborah. "En/Gendering Nationalism: Colonialism, Sex and Independence in French Polynesia." Ph.D. dissertation, New York University, 1997.

Finney, Ben. *Polynesian Peasants and Proletarians,* 1973.

Hanson, F. Allan. *Rapan Lifeways: Society and History on a Polynesian Island,* 1970.

Henry, Lisa. *The Reconstruction of Tahitian Healing,* 1999.

Levy, Robert. *Tahitians: Mind and Experience in the Society Islands,* 1973.

Lockwood, Victoria. *Tahitian Transformation: Gender and Capitalist Development in a Rural Society,* 1993.

Oliver, Douglas. *Two Tahitian Villages: A Study in Comparison,* 1981.

—Jeanette Dickerson-Putman and Laura Jones

Gabon

Culture Name

Gabonese

Orientation

Identification. Gabon is a French equatorial country, home to over forty ethnic groups. The largest group is the Fang, forming 40 percent of the population. Other major groups are the Teke, the Eshira, and the Pounou. As in many African countries, the borders of Gabon do not correspond to the borders of the ethnic groups. The Fang, for example, inhabit northern Gabon, Equatorial Guinea, southern Cameroon, and the western part of the Republic of Congo. The cultures of the ethnic groups are akin to other groups in Central Africa, and center around the rain forest and its treasures. Food preferences, farming practices, and quality of life are comparable. The ceremonial traditions vary, however, as do the personalities of the groups. There are ongoing debates about the differences in these groups and their significance.

Location and Geography. Gabon covers 103,347 square miles (267,667 square kilometers). It is slightly smaller than the state of Colorado. Gabon is on the west coast of Africa, centered on the equator. It borders Equatorial Guinea and Cameroon to the north, and the Republic of Congo to the east and south. The capital, Libreville, is on the west coast in the north. It is in Fang territory, though it was not chosen for this reason. Libreville (''free town'') was the landing place for a ship of freed slaves in the 1800s, and later became the capital. Over 80 percent of Gabon is tropical rain forest, with a plateau region in the south. There are nine provinces named after the rivers that separate them.

Demography. There are roughly 1,200,500 Gabonese. There are equal numbers of men and women. The original inhabitants were the Pygmies, but only a few thousand remain. Of the total population, 60 percent live in the cities while 40 percent inhabit the villages. There is also a large population of Africans from other countries who have come to Gabon to find work.

Linguistic Affiliation. The national language is French, which is mandatory in school. It is spoken by the majority of the population under the age of fifty. The use of a common language is extremely helpful in the cities, where Gabonese from all of the different ethnic groups come together to live. Most Gabonese speak at least two languages, as each ethnic group has its own language as well.

Symbolism. The Gabonese flag is made of three horizontal stripes: green, yellow, and blue. Green symbolizes the forest, yellow the equatorial sun, and blue the water from the sky and sea. The forest and its animals are greatly valued as well, and are portrayed on the Gabonese currency.

History and Ethnic Relations

Emergence of the Nation. Tools from the Old Stone Age indicate early life in Gabon, but little is known of its people. The Myene had arrived in Gabon by the thirteenth century and settled as a fishing community along the coast. With the exception of the Fang, Gabon's ethnic groups are Bantu and arrived in Gabon after the Myene. The different ethnic groups were separated from one another by the dense forest and remained intact. Europeans began to arrive at the end of the fifteenth century. The Portuguese, French, Dutch, and English participated in the slave trade that flourished for 350 years. In 1839, the first lasting European settlement was started by the French. Ten years later, Libreville was founded by freed slaves. During this time, the Fang were migrating from Cameroon into Gabon. The French obtained control inland and stymied the Fang migration, thus concentrating them in the north. In 1866, the French appointed a governor with the approval of the Myene leader. At the start of the twentieth century, Gabon became part of

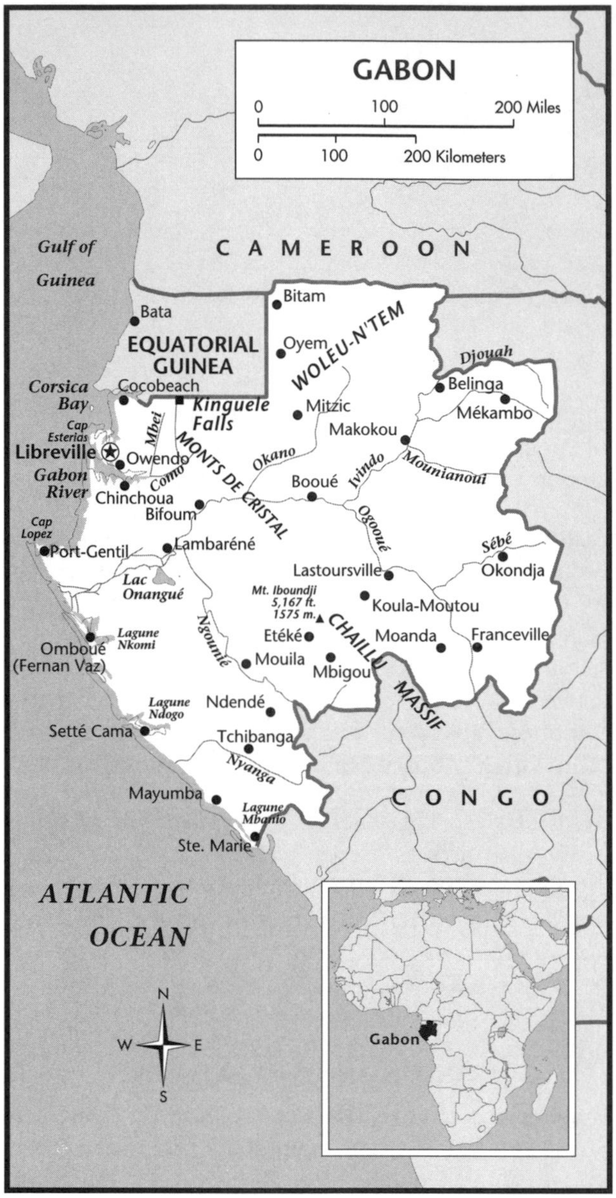

Gabon

French Equatorial Africa, which also included the present-day nations of Cameroon, Chad, the Democratic Republic of Congo, and the Central African Republic. Gabon remained an overseas territory of France until its independence in 1960.

National Identity. The Gabonese are proud of their country's resources and prosperity. They carve their lives from the forest. They fish, hunt, and farm. Each ethnic group has ceremonies for birth, death, initiation, and healing, and for casting out evil spirits, though the specifics of the ceremonies vary widely from group to group. The Gabonese are very spiritual and dynamic.

Ethnic Relations. There are no major conflicts between the groups in Gabon, and intermarriage is common. The ethnic groups are not contained within Gabon. Many groups spill over the borders into the neighboring countries. The borders were chosen by European colonials trying to parcel out territories; little consideration was given to the natural borders formed by the ethnic groups, which were then split by the new lines.

Urbanism, Architecture, and the Use of Space

As a building material, cement is seen as a sign of wealth. The cities are rife with it, and all of the government buildings are constructed in cement. In the capital, it is easy to differentiate between buildings that were styled by Gabonese and those done by outside architects. In the villages, the architecture is different. The structures are impermanent. The most economical houses are made from mud and covered in palm fronds. There are houses built from wood, bark, and brick. The brick houses are often plastered with a thin layer of cement with roofs made from corrugated tin. A wealthy family might build with cinder blocks. In addition to the houses, both men and women have distinctive gathering places. The women each have a *cuisine,* a kitchen hut filled with pots and pans, wood for fire, and bamboo beds set against the walls for sitting and resting. The men have open structures called *corps de guards,* or gatherings of men. The walls are waist high and open to the roof. They are lined in benches with a central fire.

Food and Economy

Food in Daily Life. The staples vary little among the groups in Gabon. The groups share a landscape and climate, and thus are able to produce the same kinds of things. Bananas, papayas, pineapples, guavas, mangoes, bushbutter, avocado, and coconuts are the fruits. Eggplants, bitter eggplants, feed corn, sugarcane, peanuts, plantains, and tomatoes are also found. Cassava is the main starch. It is a tuber with little nutritional value, but fills the stomach. Its young leaves are picked and used as a vegetable. Protein comes from the sea and rivers, as well as from bush meat hunted by the men.

Food Customs at Ceremonial Occasions. Wines are made from palm trees and sugarcane. The palm wine, in conjunction with a hallucinogenic root called eboga, is used during ceremonies for death, healing, and initiation. In small doses, eboga acts as a stimulant, making it useful for all-night ceremonies. In larger quantities, it is hallucinogenic, allowing participants to "see their ancestors." Food and wine are offered to the ancestors during the ceremonies, and both men and women partake in these rituals, which are full of drumming, singing and dancing.

Basic Economy. In the villages, the Gabonese are able to provide themselves virtually everything they need. They buy only soap, salt, and medicine. In the cities, however, most of the goods sold are imported and marketed by foreigners. The Gabonese produce enough bananas, plantains, sugar, and soap to export to nearby cities, but 90 percent of the food is imported. West Africans and Lebanese hold title to many of the shops, and women from Cameroon dominate the open markets.

Land Tenure and Property. Virtually everything is owned by someone. Each village is considered to own three miles (4.8 kilometers) into the forest in every direction. This area is split among the families, and the best locations are given to the elders. Property is passed down paternally or maternally, depending on the ethnic group. The rest of the land belongs to the government.

Major Industries. Gabon has many riches. It is one of the world's largest producers of manganese, and is the world's largest producer of okoume, a softwood used to make plywood. President Omar Bongo has sold the rights to the majority of the forest to French and Asian lumber companies. Oil is another major export, and the petroleum revenues form over half of Gabon's annual budget. Lead and silver have also been discovered, and there are large deposits of untapped iron ore that cannot be reached because of the lack of infrastructure.

Trade. Gabon's currency, the Communaute Financiere Africaine, is automatically converted into French francs, thus giving trading partners confidence in its security. The bulk of the crude oil goes to France, the United States, Brazil, and Argentina. Major export items include manganese, forest products, and oil. Overall, France receives more than one-third of Gabon's exports and contributes half of its imports. Gabon also trades with other European nations, the United States, and Japan.

Division of Labor. In 1998, 60 percent of workers were employed in the industrial sector, 30 percent in services, and 10 percent in agricultural.

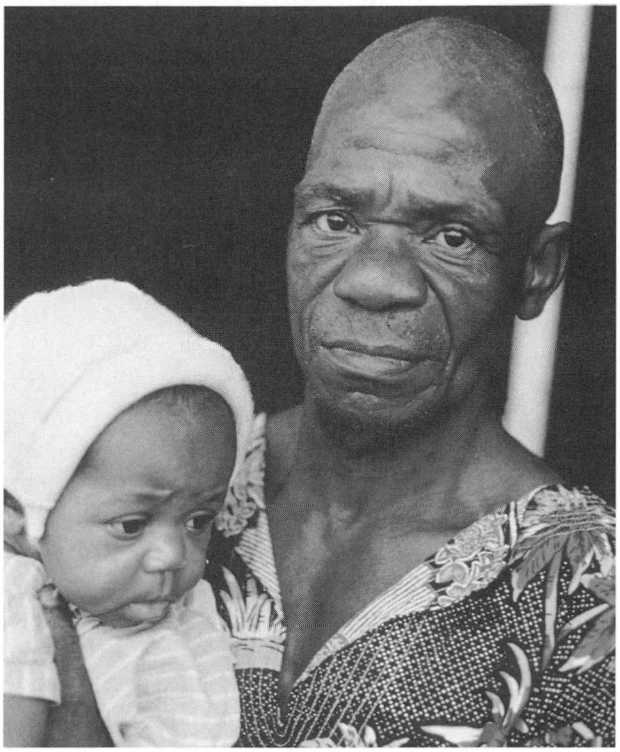

Children born within marriage belong to their fathers; women are expected to have children before marrying so they will still have something should the couple separate.

Social Stratification

Classes and Castes. Though the per capita income is four times that of other sub-Saharan African nations, the majority of this wealth is in the hands of a few. The cities are filled with poverty, which is less noticeable in the villages. The villagers provide for themselves and have less of a need for money. Village families assess relative affluence by how many chickens and goats they have, how many pots are in the kitchen, and how many changes of clothes each person has. Official caste systems are not present.

Symbols of Social Stratification. The more affluent in society wear freshly starched clothes, in both Western and African styles. The Gabonese are accustomed to being shunned and condescended to by government officials, postal workers, and other important figures; once one has reached a higher level oneself, the temptation to respond in kind is enticing. The educated Gabonese speak Parisian French, while the rest of the country speaks a French that has absorbed the rhythm and accent of their local language.

Political Life

Government. Gabon has three branches of government. The executive branch includes the president, his prime minister, and his Council of Ministers, all appointed by him. The legislative branch is made up of the 120-seat National Assembly and the 91-seat Senate, both of which are elected every five years. The judicial branch includes the Supreme Court, the High Court of Justice, an appellate court, and a state security court.

Leadership and Political Officials. When Gabon gained its independence in 1960, Leon M'ba, the former governor to Gabon, slid into the presidency. He survived a coup and remained in power until his death in 1967. Vice President Albert Bernard Bongo took his place. Bongo, who later took the Islamic name El Hadj Omar Bongo, was reelected in 1973 and has been the president ever since. Elections are held every seven years, and Bongo has continued to win by a slender margin. Bongo's party, the Gabon Democratic Party (or PDG) has had competition since other parties were legalized in 1990, but the other two main parties, the Gabonese People's Union and the National Rally of Woodcutters, have been unable to gain control. Before each election, Bongo travels the country giving speeches and handing out money and clothing. He uses the budget to do this, and there is a debate over whether or not the elections are handled fairly.

Social Problems and Control. The formality of crime response is debatable. It hinges on who is victimized as much as who is in charge. Little is done to protect African immigrants, but if a European is hurt the police will try harder. There is a lot of corruption, however, and if money changes hands the criminal could be released and no record kept. For this reason, the law is often more informal. A town will ostracize someone for having stolen something, but no formal charge will be taken. Things will be passed by word of mouth, and the criminal will be cast out. In extreme cases, a village might seek an nganga, or medicine man, to cast a spell on the person.

Military Activity. Gabon's troops stay within its borders. Out of the nation's overall budget, 1.6 percent goes to the military, including an army, navy, air force, the Republican Guard to protect the president and other officials, the National Gendarmerie, and the National Police. The military employs 143,278 people, with concentrations in the cities and along Gabon's southern and eastern borders to repel Congolese immigrants and refugees. There is also a large presence of the French military.

Social Welfare and Change Programs

The PNLS (National Program to Fight Against Aids) has an office in every major city. It sells condoms and educates women on family planning and pregnancy. There is also a Forests and Waters office in every city, working to protect the environment and wildlife from exploitation, though its effectiveness is questioned.

Nongovernmental Organizations and Other Associations

The World Wildlife Fund has ecological and sociological research and wildlife preservation projects in the north and on the coast, and the United Nations supports agricultural advancements in the north by sponsoring extensionists and providing training and mopeds. The United States Children's Fund (UNICEF) is also present, working against child prostitution and infant mortality. A German organization, GTZ, funds the organization of the Gabonese National Forestry School. The Peace Corps is active in Gabon as well, with programs in construction, health, agriculture, fisheries, women in development, and environmental education.

Gender Roles and Statuses

Division of Labor by Gender. The expectations of labor are different for women and men. Women raise their many children, farm, prepare food, and do the household chores. In the villages, the men build a house for the family as well as a cuisine for each wife taken. The men handle cash crops if there are any, and may have jobs fishing or building, or in offices in the cities. The women also work in the cities as secretaries—there are exceptional women who have risen to positions of power in spite of the underlying male dominance in the workplace. The children help with the chores, do laundry and dishes, run errands, and clean house.

The Relative Status of Women and Men. Though debatable, men seem to have higher status than women. They make the financial decisions and control the family, though the women add input and are often outspoken. The men dominate the government, the military, and the schools, while the women do the majority of the manual labor for the family.

Gabon women have traditionally assumed a house-bound role.

Marriage, Family, and Kinship

Marriage. Virtually everyone is married, but few of these marriages are legal. To legalize a marriage it must be done at the mayor's office in a city, and this is rare. Women choose men who will be able to provide for them, while men choose women who will bear children and keep their home. Polygyny is practiced in Gabon, but having more than one woman becomes expensive and has become a sign of wealth as much as it is an indulgence. Divorce is uncommon but not unheard of. Marriages can be business arrangements, at times, though some couples marry for love. It is expected for women to have several children before wedlock. These children will then belong to the mother. In a marriage, however, the children are the father's. If the couple splits up, the husband takes the children. Without premarital offspring, the wife would have nothing.

Domestic Unit. Families stay together. When a couple is wed, they traditionally move to the husband's village. That village will hold his family, including brothers and their families, parents, aunts, uncles, grandparents, children, and nieces and nephews. It is not uncommon for families to share a home with their parents and extended relatives. Everyone is welcome and there is always room for one more.

Kin Groups. Within each ethnic group are tribes. Each tribe lives in the same area and comes from a common ancestor. For this reason, people cannot marry members of their tribe.

Socialization

Infant Care. Babies stay with their mothers. There are no cribs or playpens, and the infants are tied to their mothers' backs with a sheet of cloth when the mothers are busy, and sleep next to the mother on the same bed. Perhaps because they are so physically close all the time, the babies are remarkably calm and quiet.

Child Rearing and Education. Children are raised communally. Mothers care for their children and any neighboring children who may be present. In addition, older siblings take care of the younger ones. The children sleep in the cuisine (kitchen hut) with their mother, but are relatively free within the village during the day. They begin school at age five or six. When there is not money for books and supplies, the children will not go to school until there is. Sometimes a wealthy relative will be called upon to provide these things. Both boys and girls attend school until they are sixteen by law, though this may not always occur for the above reason. The girls may begin to have children at this point, and the boys continue school or begin to work. Approximately 60 percent of Gabonese are literate.

Higher Education. The Omar Bongo University in Libreville offers two to three year programs in many subjects, as well as advanced studies in select fields. The University of Science and Technology in the south is relatively new, and diversifies the options. These schools are dominated by upper-class men. Women have a difficult time excelling in academics, as the subjects and standards are structured for men. Some Gabonese study abroad in other African countries or in France, at both undergraduate and graduate levels.

Etiquette

Gabonese are very communal. Personal space is neither needed nor respected. When people are interested in something, they stare at it. It is not rude to call something what it is, to identify someone by his or her race, or to ask someone for something that is wanted. Foreigners are often offended by this. They may feel personally invaded by having someone stand in their space, insulted at being called white, and put off by people who ask them for their watch and shoes. None of these things are meant in a negative way, however, as they simply reflect the up-front nature of the Gabonese. Conversely, celebrity figures are treated with incredible respect. They are the first to sit, and the first to be fed, and are catered to with detail, regardless of their moral standing in society.

Religion

Religious Beliefs. There are several different belief systems in Gabon. The majority of the Gabonese are Christian. There are three times as many Roman Catholics as Protestants. There are many foreign clergy, though the Protestants have Gabonese pastors in the north. These beliefs are simultaneously held with Bwiti, an ancestral worship. There are also several thousand Muslims, most of whom have immigrated from other African countries.

Rituals and Holy Places. The Bwiti ceremonies, performed to worship the ancestors, are led by ngangas (medicine men). There are special wooden temples for these ceremonies, and participants dress in bright costumes, paint their faces white, remove their shoes, and cover their heads.

Death and the Afterlife. After death, bodies are rubbed and anointed to remove rigor mortis. Because of the tropical climate, the bodies are interred within two days. They are buried in a wooden coffin. The deceased then joins the ancestors who are to be worshiped with the Bwiti ceremonies. They can be asked for advice, and for remedies for disease. There is a *retraite de deuil* ceremony one year after death to end the mourning period.

Medicine and Health Care

Health facilities are inadequate. Hospitals are ill-equipped, and patients buy their own medications from pharmacies before treatment can begin. Malaria, tuberculosis, syphilis, AIDS, and other infectious diseases are widespread and virtually untreated. Many villagers also turn to the ngangas for remedies, as modern health care is expensive and distant.

Secular Celebrations

Gabon's Independence Day, 17 August, is full of parades and speeches. New Year's Day is also celebrated throughout the country.

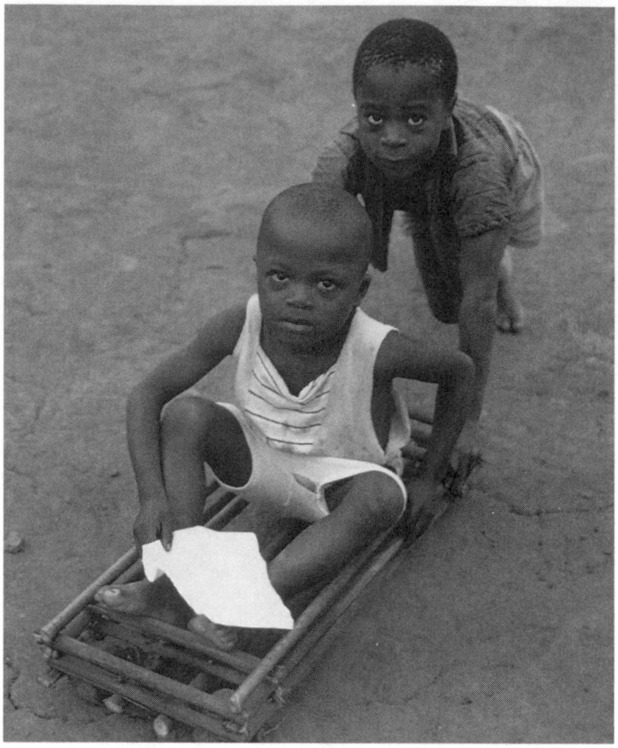

Gabon children enjoy relative freedom in their villages and start school at the age of five or six.

The Arts and the Humanities

Support for the Arts. International Center for Bantu Civilizations was created in Libreville in 1983, and there is a Gabonese Museum featuring Gabon's history and artistic relics. There is also a French Cultural Center in the capital which displays artistic creations and features dance groups and chorales. There is an annual cultural celebration as well, with performances by musicians and dancers from many different groups in celebration of Gabon's diversity.

Literature. Much of Gabon's literature is strongly influenced by France, as many authors received their schooling there. Writers use French, newspapers are in French, and television is broadcast in French. Radio programs use both French and local languages, however, and there is mounting interest in the history of Gabon's peoples.

Graphic Arts. The Fang make masks and basketry, carvings, and sculptures. Fang art is characterized by organized clarity and distinct lines and shapes. Bieri, boxes to hold the remains of ancestors, are carved with protective figures. Masks are worn in ceremonies and for hunting. The faces are painted white with black features. Myene art centers around Myene rituals for death. Female ancestors are represented by white painted masks worn by the male relatives. The Bekota use brass and copper to cover their carvings. They use baskets to hold ancestral remains. Tourism is rare in Gabon, and unlike in other African countries, art is not spurred on by the prospect of capitalism.

The State of the Physical and Social Sciences

The Omar Bongo University in Libreville and the University of Science and Technology in the south are the main facilities in Gabon. Doctoral students and other private individuals and organizations conduct sociological and anthropological studies throughout Gabon, and chemical companies search for new treasures in the rain forest. Resources are dim, however, and when evidence is collected, scholars often travel to other countries to seek superior facilities.

Bibliography

Aicardi de Saint-Paul, Marc. *Gabon: The Development of a Nation,* 1989.

Aniakor, Chike. *Fang,* 1989.

Balandier, Georges, and Jacques Maquet. *The Dictionary of Black African Civilization,* 1974.

Barnes, James Franklin. *Gabon: Beyond the Colonial Legacy,* 1992.

Gardenier, David E. *The Historical Dictionary of Gabon,* 1994.

Giles, Bridget. *Peoples of Central Africa,* 1997.

Murray, Jocelyn. *The Cultural Atlas of Africa,* 1981.

Perrois, Lous. *Ancestral Art of Gabon: From the Collections of the Barbier-Mueller Museum,* 1985

Schweitzer, Albert. *The African Notebook,* 1958.

Weinstein, Brian. *Gabon: Nation-Building on the Ogooue,* 1966.

—Alison Graham

GAMBIA

CULTURE NAME

Gambian

ALTERNATIVE NAMES

The Gambia

ORIENTATION

Identification. Republic of The Gambia is the official name of The Gambia. The country was named after the Gambia River, which flows from East to West for three hundred miles, the entire length of the country. Gambia is a small country with a population of 1.2 million. It straddles the Gambia River on either side.

Location and Geography. Gambia is on the western coast of Africa, surrounded on three sides by Senegal. Situated on a sandy peninsula between the mouth of the Gambia River and the Atlantic Ocean, Banjul, the capital, was founded by the British as Bathurst in 1816 as a base for suppressing the slave trade. The Gambians changed its name to Banjul in 1973, eight years after independence. Gambia is the smallest country in Africa with a total area of 4,363 square miles (11,300 square kilometers), slightly less than twice the size of Delaware. Gambia has the typical West African climate: there is a hot, rainy season (June to November), and a cooler, dry season (November to May). It is a relatively flat land with its lowest point being sea level at the Atlantic Ocean with the maximum elevation being 174 Feet (53 meters) in the surrounding low hills. The Gambia River is the dominant geographical feature of the country, providing both a useful means of transportation and irrigation as well as a rich ground for fishing, boating, and sailing.

Demography. The total population of Gambia, from a July 1999 estimate, is 1,336,320. The main ethnic groups in Gambia are the Mandingo (42 percent of the overall population), Wolof (16 percent), Fulani (18 percent), Jola (10 percent), Serahuli (9 percent), other Africans (4 percent), and non-Africans (1 percent). By age, the population is distributed as follows: (per a 1999 estimate) 0–14 years, 46 percent (male, 305,839; female, 304,905); 15–64 years, 52 percent (male, 341,947; female, 348,163); 65 years and over, 2 percent (male, 18,706; female, 16,760). The population is growing at a rate of 3.35 percent per year. The birthrate is 42.76 births per 1,000 population, and the death rate is 12.57 deaths per 1,000. The infant mortality rate is 75.33 deaths per 1,000 live births. Average life expectancy is 54.39 years; for women it is 58.83 years compared with 52.02 years for men.

Linguistic Affiliation. English is the official language but indigenous languages include Mandinka, Wolof, and Fula.

HISTORY AND ETHNIC RELATIONS

Emergence of the Nation. The first written mention of Gambia is in the work of Hanno the Carthaginian in his writings about his voyage to West Africa in 470 B.C.E. Gambia at various times was part of different West African kingdoms, including the kingdoms of Foni, Kombo, Sine-Saloum, and Fulladou. Its various ethnic groups migrated to Gambia from different areas of West Africa. Trade was vital to Gambia, especially trade with Ghana, Songhai, and the Mali Empire (between the Atlantic Ocean and the River Niger), Kanem-Bornu, and the Hausa States.

By 1500 C.E., trade with Europe was established. In the 1450s, Venetian explorer Alvise Cadamosto, under commission from Portugal, was the first European to reach the Gambia River. The English were not far behind, coming to West Africa to buy gold and spices. The Portuguese successfully barred English trade for one hundred years. At the end of the sixteenth century, however, the English and French managed to establish trade in the area.

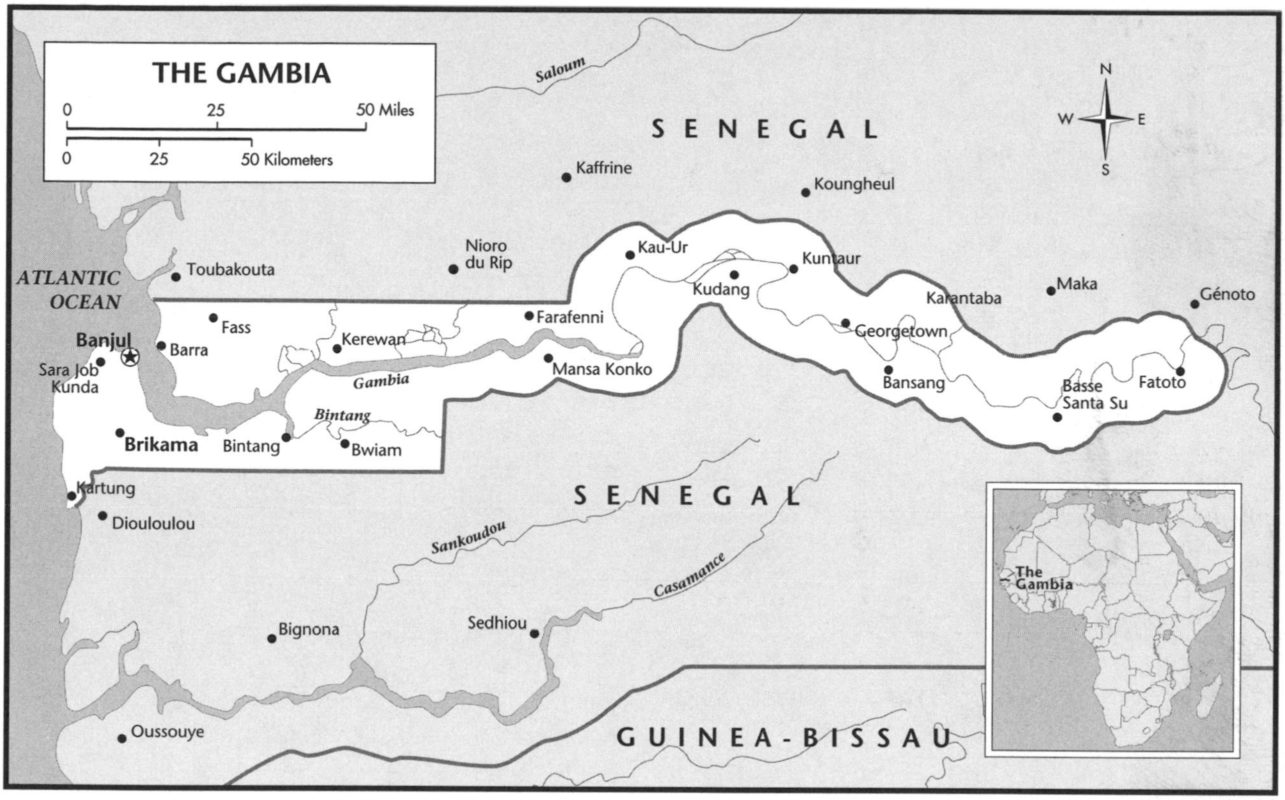

Gambia

After numerous conflicts the British, in the Treaty of Versailles of 1783, gained control of the Gambia River. In 1807, the British abolished slave traffic on the river.

Muslims were involved in the trans-Saharan slave trade, as well as more legitimate trade. Along with trade, merchants brought Islam and Muslim culture to Gambia. More directly, Muslim Berbers from Mauritania were the direct agents of Islam to the Gambia and Senegal. As in other parts of West Africa, rulers in the Gambia became Muslims and used its law, the Shariya, to consolidate their power.

Gambia became part of a larger British colony, the Province of Senegambia, which included present-day Senegal and Gambia. The Senegambia has the distinction of being the first British colony in Africa. The French took Senegal in 1799, and the British agreed to base their trade around Bathurst and Fort James. In 1821, Gambia became a crown colony as part of the colony of Sierra Leone. In 1843, however, the Gambia was separated from Sierra Leone. The Gambia became a British Protectorate in 1888.

The British did not begin to develop Gambia properly until after World War II when administration posts were set up. Internal self-government came in 1963. Independence Day was 18 February 1965 when Gambia became a sovereign republic within the British Commonwealth of Nations. In 1969, Gambia and Senegal formed Senegambia, but in 1982 the confederation was dissolved with the mutual consent of both partners.

National Identity. Although the Gambia is comprised of people of many different ethnic groups, there seems to be relative harmony among them and among people of different religions. Gambia has a generally good human rights record, and there is a great desire among its peoples to have the country taken seriously in the world community.

Ethnic Relations. Gambia is a multiethnic country; major ethnic groups include the Fula, Jola, Mandinka, Serahule, and Wolof. There is no part of The Gambia that is inhabited by one single ethnic group. This close dwelling has led to a sharing of many cultural traits among the groups, which has led to a movement toward a Gambian national culture. There has been a concentrated effort to represent the various minority ethnic groups in government. In addition to indigenous ethnic groups, there has also been an annual migration from Senegal,

Guinea, and Mali. Many people from those countries come to trade in groundnuts (peanuts) and stay to settle.

The Wolof and the Mandinka are the major ethnic groups. The Wolof live mainly in the capital, Banjul. The Mandinka are the largest single ethnic group in the country. These groups represent the former Empire of the Wolof in the Senegambian region and the Mandingo Empires of Mali and Songhai. Creoles form a large element within the local elite. Additionally, there are Mauritanians, Moroccans, and Lebanese in the country. These groups are mainly traders and shopkeepers. English is commonly spoken by members of all ethnic groups since it is the official language of the country. Each ethnic groups speaks its own language as well. Harmony among ethnic groups is the general rule, so much so that Gambia is considered to be a melting pot of West African ethnic groups.

Urbanism, Architecture, and the Use of Space

Banjul is the only real urban center in Gambia. It has a typical former British colonial feel to it. The administrative buildings are built in the center of the city, tending toward Edwardian "majesty." Many of the buildings are done in pastel colors with huge gardens. The colonial bungalow is a typical form of architecture. Squatter settlements resembling poorer versions of rural settlements dot the area. There are large public areas in the British style.

Food and Economy

Food in Daily Life. Not surprisingly, following two hundred years of British colonialism, Western food is available in Gambia. Gambian traditional food includes *benachin* ("Jollof rice," a mixture of spiced meat and rice cooked with tomato puree and vegetables), *base nyebe* (rich stew of chicken or beef with green beans and other vegetables), *chere* (steamed millet flour balls), *domodah* (meat or chicken stewed in groundnut butter and served with rice), *plasas* (meat and smoked fish cooked in palm oil with green vegetables) served with *fu-fu* (mashed cassava), and *chura-gerteh* (a sweet porridge consisting of pounded groundnuts and rice and served with yogurt or sour milk). The most commonly eaten fruits are mangoes, bananas, grapefruit, papayas, and oranges.

Food Customs at Ceremonial Occasions. Food is important at ceremonial occasions such as naming ceremonies, betrothals, marriages, and deaths. At these occasions, meat is served along with Jollof rice and fruit. The more food, the more successful the occasion.

Basic Economy. About 80 percent of the population is comprised of subsistence farmers. A majority of these subsistence farmers are women. Groundnuts make up the majority of export products. Millet is also grown widely in the country. There is very little manufacturing in the country. The Fulani specialize in dairy products and trade them for grain and other products. The fact that there is very little manufacturing in Gambia has resulted in liberal trade policies and the encouragement of tourism. The rapidly growing population of 1.3 million is divided between a rural majority and a growing urban minority. The private sector of the economy is led by tourism, trading, and fisheries. This sector is healthy and is experiencing modest growth. Gambia's high population growth rate has diluted the positive effects of economic expansion. Gambia's per capita gross domestic product is about $360 (U.S.). About 23 percent of the population is in the agricultural sector, 13 percent in the industrial sector, and 64 percent in the service sector.

Land Tenure and Property. All ethnic groups have traditional patterns of inheritance in which priority is given to the male survivors. Islam, however, under the Shari'a law, provides a portion of the estate for widows. Land is traditionally distributed by need, although modern British law is taking root. In the modern sphere, British property law is exerting a greater influence.

Commercial Activities. There is relatively little commercial activity in Gambia. Gambia does rely heavily on trade to obtain industrial goods and, therefore, trades agricultural products, mainly peanuts, to obtain foreign capital. Trade laws are quite liberal.

Major Industries. Gambia has a mining industry that is in its early stages of development in addition to a small oil industry. Electricity is provided by the parastatal utility Gambia Utility Corporation. There have been attempts to develop the fisheries industry and local food processing. Tourism plays a dominant role in the nation's economic development.

Trade. Gambia exported $110.6 million worth of products and imported $164 million in 1994. The bulk of the imported items were comprised of petro-

Workers harvesting rice with threshing machines in Kunuku. About 80 percent of Gambians are subsistence farmers.

leum products, processed food, and manufactured goods.

Division of Labor. Women have entered the modern sphere on a basis of equal pay. Most women, however, are involved in the subsistence farming sector. As in much of West Africa, women do the majority of the day-to-day farming, while men do the heavy clearing.

Social Stratification

Classes and Castes. With the exception of the Fulani, ethnic groups are highly stratified. This stratification is a remnant of the great empires that once ruled the country. In each group, status was essentially inherited from the father. The rulers also inherited their statuses, and administered a feudal domain. The majority of people were peasant farmers who owed various services to their rulers.

Symbols of Social Stratification. Elaborate rituals of rank prevailed in the past. Generally, those of the lower orders abased themselves through prostration in front of those who outranked them. Differences in clothing, food, and the wearing of precious stones also were signs of privilege. Visits to Mecca set some Muslims apart from others.

Political Life

Government. Gambia currently has a multiparty political system. The Constitution of the Second Republic of Gambia provides for elections by universal suffrage for adults eighteen and older. The ballot is a secret one, and elections must be held every five years. The country's National Assembly includes forty-five elected members and four nominated members. The president, popularly elected for a five-year term, is both the chief of state and head of government.

The country's administration is divided into the capital territory (the seat of government), the adjoining Kombo Saint Mary area, and the provinces. Each province has five divisions, each one headed by a commissioner. These divisions are further subdivided into districts locally administered by head chiefs.

The judicial system resembles that of other common law jurisdictions. There is a single system of courts, forming a hierarchy. The subordinate courts consist of Khadis' courts, district tribunals, and magistrate courts. At the higher level are the Supreme Court, the Court of Appeal, and the Privy Council. The latter is the highest court of appeal for the Gambia.

Leadership and Political Officials. In July 1994, junior officers overthrew the government. Lieutenant Yaya Jammeh (later Captain and then Colonel) led the coup. The International community condemned the coup since Gambia had been a model of democracy for over 30 years. It also had been a model of human rights. In spite of promises, there has not yet been a return to political democracy. Rights are denied to opposition politicians, and meetings and a free press are banned. President Jammeh's party, the Alliance for Patriotic Reorientation and Construction (APRC), controls thirty-three of forty-five elected assembly seats and four members appointed by the President. Women are free to participate in government but are poorly represented there. There is only one woman in the assembly. However, the Vice President (who is also Minister of Health) is a woman. Three cabinet members are also women.

Social Problems and Control. The major social problems are poverty, disease, and lack of economic development. A 1994 military coup was an attempt to address these problems by clearing away corruption that stifled democracy. In 1996 and 1997 free elections were held.

Military Activity. Gambia is not at war with any country. Its military is well trained and has returned power to civilian rule. Its military branches include the army (including a marine unit), national police, and national guard. There are currently approximately 150,000 males aged fifteen to forty-nine who are fit for military service. The Gambia spends about $1.2 million on the military, about 2 percent of its budget.

Social Welfare and Change Programs

Like many African states, Gambia has many serious welfare problems. The government is on record as being dedicated to change, and their particular attention is given to children's welfare. The Department of Education and the Department of Health, Social Welfare, and Women's Affairs are heavily funded. However, lack of sufficient resources hinders the full implementation of programs. For example, although free, compulsory primary education is the law of the land, there are insufficient resources to implement the program. In February 1998, the president ended fees for the first six years of schooling. There is even less opportunity for secondary education. Female participation in education is rather low. There are two men for every woman in education, and the ratio is even lower in rural areas.

The government is less concerned with the welfare of children in distress, considering this matter to be a case for parental and family concern. Similarly, although the government requires child support for the children of divorced parents, the requirement is rarely enforced. However, authorities do typically get involved in cases of child abuse that come officially to their attention, although there is little pattern of such abuse. The tourist industry has increased begging and child prostitution. Female genital mutilation (FGM) exists and is widespread. Estimates are that 60 to 90 percent of women in Gambia have been subjected to FGM. Seven of the nine major ethnic groups support FGM. The government considers FGM to be an integral part of the cultural system.

There are no government provisions to aid the disabled. However, there appears to be no discrimination against those people who can perform work. Those who cannot perform work are left to private charity, which often means begging.

Nongovernmental Organizations and Other Associations

Gambia has a number of religious and secular NGOs. There are Muslim brotherhoods, Catholic missions, and international agencies working to care for various problems and to aid development efforts.

Gender Roles and Statuses

Traditionally women are subordinate to men. Polygyny is prevalent and even in groups without traditional patrilineal descent, Islam has strengthened male control of women. In the modern sector, women have equal rights in employment as they have in government. However, relatively few of Gambia's women operate in the modern sector. Most are engaged in subsistence farming. Inheritance in the traditional system also favors women.

Division of Labor by Gender. Women do most of the farming. At one time, women's farm incomes outstripped male incomes in general. Male landholders, however, attempted to use the new ecology movement as a means of erasing women's social and economic gains. Men control tree crops in Gambia, while women control garden farms.

The new ecology movement in anthropology relates to a deeper understanding of the relationship of technology and social organization to the environment. Conscious choices and preferences, as well

Villagers building a water well. Gambia's dry season runs from November to May.

as relationships between different groups, lead to changes in the physical environment.

The Relative Status of Women and Men. In law, there is equality of the sexes. In practice, men tend to exert control over their wives and female children. At the same time, there is a growing women's movement in Gambia.

Marriage, Family, and Kinship

Each ethnic group has its own marriage, residence, and kinship patterns. Additionally, Islam and Christianity have their own regulations. Any particular marriage pattern, kinship system, or residence pattern depends upon a confluence of variables.

Marriage. Marriage in Gambia is regulated by either customary, Shari'a (Muslim), or general law. Customary law is reserved for all non-Muslims and covers inheritance, land tenure, tribal and clan leadership, as well as other relationships. Shari'a law is primarily for Muslims and covers marriage and divorce. General law is based on British law. Rape is illegal in the case of both married and unmarried women and, along with assault, is a crime. The law does not differentiate between married and unmarried women in this regard. Any person who has carnal knowledge of a girl under the age of 16 is guilty of a felony (except in the case of marriage); incest is also illegal. These laws are generally enforced.

Polygyny is the general rule for each of Gambia's ethnic groups. Similarly, each group has arranged marriages. Married women in monogamous or polygynous unions have property and other rights, including the right to divorce their husbands. Their husbands, however, are free to marry other wives without their permission. Shari'a law usually is applied in divorce and inheritance matters for Muslims, who make up approximately 90 percent of the population. Women normally receive a lower proportion of assets distributed through inheritance than do male relatives.

Employment in the formal sector is open to women at the same salary rates as men. No statutory discrimination exists in other kinds of employment. However, women generally are employed in endeavors such as food vending or subsistence farming.

Domestic Unit. There are variations in the domestic units of the various ethnic groups of Gambia. The social structure of the pastoral Fulani is egalitarian, in marked contrast to that of other Muslim groups, such as the Hausa, and to most sedentary Fulani. The influence of Islam on kinship patterns is

Shoppers and cars in downtown Banjul. The capital is Gambia's only urban center.

evident in the general preference for cousin and other intralineage marriages. Most men are polygynous, the typical household unit comprising the family head, his wives, and unmarried children. Other Islamic groups, such as the Soninke, follow the same general pattern. The Wolof are noted for their double descent kinship system. A household unit usually has a nuclear family or a polygynous unit. There may also be other close kin living together.

Kin Groups. The vast majority of Gambia's ethnic groups are patrilineal and patrilocal. This tendency toward male groups is strengthened through Islamic affiliation, as 90 percent of the population is Muslim. Even the Soninke—who practice double descent—have developed a bias toward the patriline.

SOCIALIZATION

Socialization is generally through imitation and proverbs. Older children, especially girls, care for their younger siblings. Generally, male children accompany their fathers, while girls follow their mothers. Segregation by sex is common, and children tend to follow their parents example and occupations. Males tend to be dominant over females. Religion plays its role in supporting the established order. European missionaries have helped bring in Western ideas and modern employment options to the country.

Infant Care. Infant care generally follows West African patterns. Women have general responsibility for child care. Young girls carry their siblings around with them. Any community member can correct any child or commandeer it for reasonable help. Folktales and proverbs illustrate moral ideas.

Child Rearing and Education. Education, in theory, is free and universal for primary school. In practice, that is not always the case. Urban areas tend to have better schools and more reliable attendance.

Literacy in Gambia is defined as those fifteen and older who can read and write. In the total population, the literary rate is 38.6 percent; by gender, it is 52.8 percent for males and 24.9 percent for females.

Higher Education. Relatively few of Gambia's people advance to higher education. In fact, there are no universities in Gambia, but in the late 1990s, university extension programs were offered for the first time.

Etiquette

In general, Gambian ethnic groups prize tranquility of life, and their manners tend to ease the attainment of that goal. Gambians tend to be soft-spoken and gentle in demeanor, seeking to avoid noisy conflicts and striving toward quiet settlement of disputes. Greetings tend to be drawn out while people ask about one another's families.

Religion

Religious Beliefs. The religious distribution is Muslim, 90 percent; Christian, 9 percent; and indigenous believers, 1 percent.

Religious Practitioners. There are a number of traditional religious practitioners as well as Muslim imams, Catholic priests, and Protestant ministers. Each traditional group has its own practitioners.

Rituals and Holy Places. There are no places that are sacred to all peoples; each ethnic group has its own particular local shrines. Muslims go to Mecca on pilgrimage and Catholics increasingly travel to Rome and other Catholic holy places.

Death and the Afterlife. Each group has its own particular beliefs concerning the afterlife and death. Catholics and Muslims tend to combine the particular traditional beliefs of their ethnic group with more universal Catholic or Muslim beliefs.

Medicine and Health Care

Gambia suffers from the usual list of tropical diseases, many of them water borne. Malaria is endemic; blindness afflicts a large percentage of the population. Modern health care is found in urban centers and sporadically in villages.

Secular Celebrations

Independence Day is 18 February. There is a six-month "tourist" festival based on the television series and book *Roots*. It runs from June to January, with variable dates. Christmas, New Year's, and other general holidays are also celebrated.

The Arts and Humanities

Support for the Arts. There is some government support but the Gambia is a poor country and can spare little for the arts.

Literature. Increasingly, there are collections of folk tales, poetry accompanied by the Kora, a lutelike instrument, and novels. No Gambian novelist has reached the stature of other Africans, such as Chinua Achebe or Wole Soyinka, but there are promising young Gambian authors.

Graphic Arts. The masks of Gambia are well known and appreciated.

Performance Arts. The Kora, a lutelike instrument, accompanies much singing and dancing. There are many collections of these performances on audio and videotape.

The State of the Physical and Social Sciences

The Gambian government supports physical and social research for its various development projects. There is a strong tradition of academic freedom in the country.

Bibliography

Davison, Jean, ed. *Agriculture, Women, and Land: The African Experience*, 1988.

Gray, John. *Kora Land Poems*, 1989.

Kelly, Robert, Debra Ewing, Stanton Doyle, and Denise Youngblood, eds. *Country Review: Gambia, 1998/1999*, 2000.

Magel, Emil A., trans. *Folktales from the Gambia: Wolof Fictional Narratives*, 1984.

Marcie-Taylor, C. G. N., ed. *The Anthropology of Disease*, 1993.

Mark, Peter. *The Wild Bull and the Sacred Forest: Form, Meaning, and Change in Senegambian Initiation Masks*, 1992.

McPherson, Malcolm F., and Steven C. Radelet, eds. *Economic Recovery in the Gambia: Insights for Adjustment in Sub-Saharan Africa*, 1996.

Schroeder, Richard A. *Shady Practices: Agroforestry and Gender Politics in the Gambia*, 1999.

Sowa, Shiona, et al. *Trachoma and Allied Infections in a Gambian Village*, 1965.

Wright, Donald R. *Oral Traditions from the Gambia*.

—Frank A. Salamone

Gaza Strip See Palestine, West Bank and Gaza Strip

Georgia

Culture Name

Georgian

Orientation

Identification. The term "Georgian" does not derive from Saint George but from the ancient Persian *Gurg* or *Gorg,* meaning wolf, "supposedly a totemic symbol, or from the Greek *georgios* ("farmer," "cultivator of land").

Self-identification is based mainly on linguistic tradition, and population groups that belong to different ethno-linguistic groups, such as Ossetians, Abkhazians, Armenians, Greeks, and Kurds, are not considered Georgian. There are some exceptions, such as Jews, who speak Georgian as a native language and have surnames with Georgian endings, but historically have had a distinct cultural identity. Georgians are subdivided into smaller regional ethno-cultural entities. All that have specific traditions and customs, folklore, cuisine, and dress and may speak a different language. Ajarans, unlike the Eastern Orthodox majority, are mostly Sunni Muslims. All these groups preserve and share a common identity, literary language, and basic system of values.

Location and Geography. Georgia is on the southern slopes of the Caucasus mountains, forming a natural border with the north Caucasian republics of the Russian Federation. The country, occupying approximately 27,000 square miles (69,900 square kilometers), stretches along the Greater Caucasus ridge, bordered by the Black Sea to the west, the Armenian and Turkish highlands to the South, and Azerbaijan to the east. The topography is varied. The northern region is characterized by high mountains, and the central and southern parts, while mountainous, are much lower and are covered with alpine fields and forests. In the east, the rivers all join the Mtkvari (Kura), forming the Caspian basin, while in the west, the rivers, of which the Rioni and Enguri are the largest, run into the Black Sea.

The climate is temperate and is more mild and humid along the western marine coast. Mountains create temperature zones that vary with elevation. The eastern plains and highlands, which are isolated from the sea, have a continental climate, while year-round snow and glaciers are found in the highest mountains. Climatic zones range from moderately humid Mediterranean, to dry-continental Arab-Caspian, and to cooler mountainous regions. Almost half the land is in agricultural use, with much of the remainder consisting of forests and high mountains. Land use varies with local climatic and soil patterns.

Tbilisi, the capital, was founded by King Vakhtang Gorgasali in the fifth century, and continues to be the most important political and cultural center of the country. Tbilisi is located in the culturally dominant eastern region, Kartli, on the banks of the Mtkvari (Kura), on the ancient cross-roads of one of the great silk roads between Europe and Asia.

Demography. In the 1990s, the population was estimated to be from five to five and a half million, but reliable figures are not available because of extensive uncounted emigration. Just over half the population lives in urban areas, including 1.6 million in Tbilisi. Ethnic Georgians form the great majority of the population in most regions, though there are settlements of Armenians and Azeris in the south and the south-east, respectively; Ossetians in the north-central area; Abkhaz and Armenians in the northwest; Greeks in the southeast; and small numbers of Batsbi, Chechens, Ingushes, and Lezghs in the northeast. Russians and smaller ethnic minorities such as Kurds, Ukrainians, Jews, and Assyrians are concentrated mostly in urban areas. In the 1989 census, ethnic Georgians accounted for seventy percent of the population; Armenians 8 percent; Russians 6 percent, Azeris 6 percent, Ossetians 3 percent, and Abkhazians, under 2 per-

Georgia

cent. This proportion has changed as a result of emigration among ethnic minorities, especially Russians, Jews, Greeks, and Armenians. Most ethnic Georgians were distributed throughout the country, while Abkhazians moved mostly to Russian cities and Ossetians took refuge in Northern Ossetia.

Linguistic Affiliation. The majority language is Georgian, which belongs to the Kartvelian (South Caucasian) language group. However, some subgroups speak other languages in the same linguistic group. The literary language comes from the Kartlian dialect spoken in the historically dominant eastern kingdom of Kartli. Georgian is the only Kartvelian language that is written and taught, and is the literary language used by all Georgians.

The principal minority languages are Abkhazian, Armenian, Azeri, Ossetian, and Russian. Abkhazian is, along with Georgian, the state language in Abkhazia. Most ethnic minorities in urban areas speak Russian rather than Georgian as a second language, but bilingualism and trilingualism are common, and Russian continues to be understood in most of the country. Russian, Armenian, and Azeri are used in schools and as official languages locally.

Symbolism. The competing impact of Asian and western cultures is most prominently expressed in Byzantine and Persian influences. Another overlap is between Christian and pagan, with a much weaker influence from neighboring Muslim patterns. Today, much cultural symbolism reflects a mythologized interpretation of tradition that is influenced by self-perception as belonging to European, Christian contemporary society.

Mythical symbols include the Golden Fleece of the Greek myth of the Argonauts' journey to Colchis and the mythical ancestor of Georgians, Kartlos. Other important mythical figures include Saint George, and Amirani, a noble hero analogous to Prometheus. Mythical symbols of the Abkhazians and Ossetians are both dominated by a mythical cycle dealing with the semidivine people of Narts.

The numbers seven and nine have symbolic meaning, as does the number three, which reflects the Trinity. The snow leopard and lion symbolize noble valor and vigor. The vine symbolizes fertility and the Dionysian spirit, and dominates medieval architectural ornamentation. A very important ornamental symbol is the fire-wheel swastika, a solar symbol traditionally used both as an architectural ornament and in wood carving as well as on the passport and currency. The Cross plays an equally significant role.

The hymn "Thou Art the True Vine" is the most important sacred song. National symbols often refer to language, motherland (national territory), and Confession (Christian Orthodoxy). The ideas of loyalty to kin, honor, and hospitality are held in high esteem. The characteristic metaphor is that of a mother. Other metaphors are linked to the sun, which is interpreted as a source of beauty and light, brotherhood, supreme loyalty, and victory.

State symbolism dates back to the Democratic Republic of Georgia (1918–1921). The most respected national festival (26 May) is linked to the declaration of independence in 1918. The national flag of black and white stripes against a dark crimson background and the state emblem, White George on horseback framed by a septagonal star, repeat the imagery of that period.

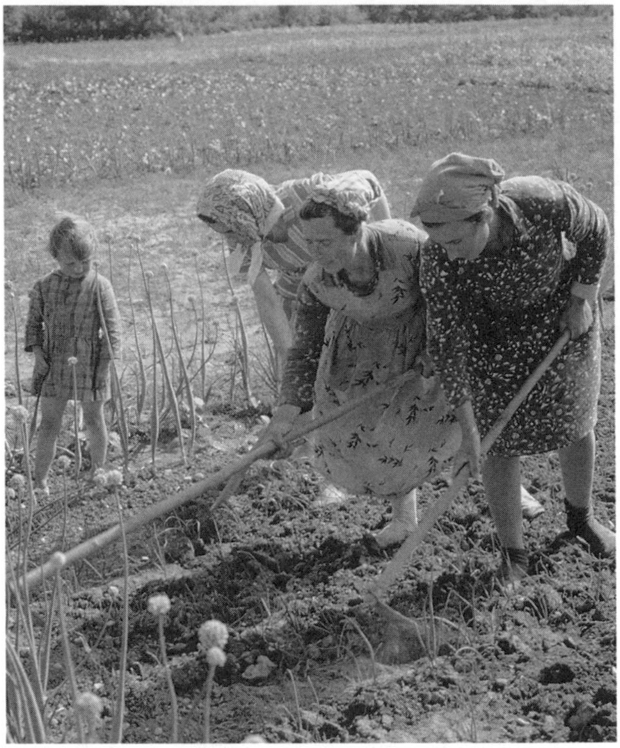

Women hoeing fields near Gori. There is no explicit division of labor by gender in Georgia, except for hard physical labor, such as mining.

History and Ethnic Relations

Emergence of the Nation. Cultural unity was influenced by political unification and fragmentation. In the southern and eastern regions, the state of Kartli (Iberia) united tribes that spoke the Kartvelian language. The first attempt to unite the country occurred under King Parnavaz of Kartli at the beginning of the third century B.C.E. Georgia adopted Christianity in 334, when King Mirian III of Kartli-Iberia, following the instructions of Saint Nino of Cappadocia, declared it the state religion. The alphabet probably was created soon afterward to translate holy texts, replacing Aramaic and Greek scripts and producing both the hieratic script and the contemporary secular alphabet. The first Georgian inscriptions appeared in Jerusalem in the fifth century, followed by the first known literary text, the *Martyrdom of Saint Shushanik.* At about that time, King Vakhtang briefly united eastern and western Georgia. Several centuries later, the new dynasty of the Bagrations took control of the Inner Kartli and the city of Uplistsikhe, and in 978, King Bagrat III Bagration became the first king of both Kartli and Abkhazia. In 1314, Giorgi V the Brilliant reunited Georgia after a long period of decline under the Mongols, but Tamerlain's invasions broke the nation's strength and unity. With the fall of Constantinople in 1453, Georgia became the only Christian stronghold in a region of Muslim kingdoms. In the beginning of the nineteenth century, Georgia was united by the Russian Empire, when the tsars Pavel and Alexander annexed the eastern region, abolishing the kingdom of Kartli-Kakheti.

After the Russian Revolution of 1917, Georgia declared independence in 1918, but the democratic Republic of Georgia, ruled by a social-democratic government, was invaded by the Red Army in 1921, a few days after it was recognized by European states. The Soviet Socialist Republic of Georgia retained formal sovereignty but was a puppet member of the Soviet Empire until its dissolution in 1991, when Zviad Gamsakhurduia proclaimed independence. By the end of that same year, Gamsakhurdia fell victim to a military coup. The military government, unable to cope with international isolation and an economic crisis, invited the former Soviet foreign minister Eduard Shevardnadze to become the chairman of the State Council, keeping real power in its own hands. After two years of civil war and secessionist conflicts in South Ossetia and Abkhazia, Shevardnadze took over the government. A new parliament was elected in 1995, a new constitution was adopted, and Shevardnadze was elected president. The self-proclaimed republics of Abkhazia and South Ossetia continue to be source of conflict, but negotiations on their status is ongoing and virtually no military action has taken place since 1993.

National Identity. The development of the nation is linked to the attempt to unite Georgia by King Parnavaz. However, at that time different parts of the country spoke different languages and had little in common. Western Georgia was inhabited by Colchian, proto-Abkhazian and proto-Svan tribes, with Greek settlements along the Black Sea shore, while in the eastern and southern regions the language was closer to contemporary Georgian, although part of the territory was inhabited by Turkic, Armenian, Alan, and Albanian tribes. Migration of eastern Georgian tribes to the west and the gradual assimilation of other ethnic groups in the east were accompanied by religious unity and unification under the Bagratid dynasty at the end of tenth century. During several centuries of common statehood, the Abkhaz, Armenians, Turks, and Ossetians partly preserved their cultural identities, while Albanians were fully assimilated.

Ethnic Relations. Sub-groups with common cultural identities experienced little conflict, although the medieval feudal system often caused internecine wars and warfare among ethnic kin. Today, despite mass migrations of Svans to southeastern Georgia and Megrel refugees from secessionist Abkhazia to other parts of the country, tensions have calmed. However, among the Abkhaz and Ossetians, tension and radical nationalism after the disintegration of the Soviet Union led to civil wars. There are some tensions with Armenians and between Azeris and Armenians in the rural southeast.

There are significant numbers of predominantly Muslim ethnic Georgians in Iran and Turkey. 100,000 Georgians have preserved their cultural identity in the small Fereydan region near Isfahan. Turkey controls a large territory with a traditionally Georgian population and numerous cultural monuments. These groups of Gürji, as they are called in Turkey, and Laz acknowledge their Georgian origin but have a strong sense of Turkish national identity.

Urbanism, Architecture, and the Use of Space

Settlements tend to be dominated by a church built on a hill nearby if not in the center. However, in the Soviet period, many churches were destroyed or turned into storehouses. Newly built churches are mostly poor replicas of older examples, primitive expressions of a declining tradition. Little is left of the medieval structure of small urban settlements surrounded by a citadel wall.

Urban architecture bears strong traces of Soviet influence. Government buildings and sculptures from the Soviet era are gloomy and pompous. These buildings have flat surfaces and enormous waste spaces in the form of colonnades or halls. In the 1970s and 1980s a new tradition emerged with more light and better use of space but was depersonalized and lacked creativity. Since independence, economic crises have precluded the construction of new government buildings. The older quarters in some cities are elegant and demonstrate an attractive mixture of European and Asian architecture. The majority of smaller towns are overgrown villages that show little effort to organize space or create an urban environment.

Rural architecture is typified by two-story stone buildings with large verandas. In the mountains, villages often are dominated by picturesque towers. Stone houses may surround a family tower or be organized in terraces with small gardens or yards. Traditional dwellings in the southern volcanic highlands were set deep in the ground and had no windows, with polygonal narrowing ceilings with a central opening for light and the exit of smoke. Internal space was organized around the fireplace below the roof opening, and a richly engraved central column played both a functional and a sacral role.

Food and Economy

Food in Daily Life. The greatest culinary divide is between the western and eastern region. In the west, there is a greater emphasis on vegetarian food, predominantly prepared with walnuts. Herbs and spices, especially tarragon, basil, coriander, feuille Grec, and pepper make western Georgian food hot and spicy. Cheese usually is made from cow's milk and is eaten with either corn bread or a corn and flour porridge. *Khachapuri*, a kind of cheese pizza, is common.

In the eastern area, the food is heavier, with more of an accent on mutton and pork. Wheat bread is preferred to corn, and sheep's cheese from

The municipal buildings in Gori. Local governments have small budgets and limited power but may be fairly independent in their policies.

Tusheti is popular. Among people in the mountains, the most popular food is *khinkali,* a cooked meat dumpling that usually is accompanied by beer. The most popular vegetables are tomatoes, potatoes, radishes, pumpkins, eggplant, beans, cucumbers, and cabbage. The most popular sauce, *tkemali,* is made of wild plums; other sauces are based on walnuts with spices, or pomegranate juice. Wine is drunk everywhere, and stronger alcoholic beverages include *araki,* which is made of grapes and other fruit with honey. Fish, especially trout, is eaten universally. A wide variety of locally grown fruit is supplemented by wild and cultured berries, watermelons and other melons. Dried fruit and nuts covered with a mixture of grape juice and wheat or corn flour are eaten in the winter. Jams are prepared from fruit, unripe walnuts, watermelon, eggplant, and green tomatoes.

Food Customs at Ceremonial Occasions. At the New Year's festivity, ground walnuts boiled in honey are served, along with a turkey or chicken in walnut sauce. An Easter meal includes hard-boiled eggs dyed red and other bright colors, roasted piglet and lamb, and special cakes with vanilla and spices. Special dishes are served at a wake: rice with mutton in the east, and meat with sweet rice and raisins in the west. Special wheat porridge with walnuts and honey is served forty days after a person's death.

Basic Economy. Georgians were basically rural people until the beginning of this century, when industrialization caused a mass rural-to-urban migration, especially to the capital. Most families are still linked through kinship relations with the countryside and preserve some traditions of their native localities.

Industrialization and the urban economy have had a limited influence on the national culture. Today, most of the population is urbanized and works in services or industrial production. Industry has been slow in recovering from the economic crisis of the early 1990s. Agriculture has been quicker to recover and accounts for almost 30 percent of the gross domestic product. A significant portion of exports consists of processed or raw agricultural produce such as hazelnuts, tea and wine. However, the country is not self-sufficient in producing grain as a result of the limited arable land.

Land Tenure and Property. After independence, much of land owned by the state was privatized. Over half the cultivated land was privatized by 1994, and that proportion continues to grow. However, in the highlands, where there is little cultivated land, privatization may entail restitution, as families respect traditional ownership. The state continues to control almost all uncultivated land, forests, and pastures; further privatization is expected in these areas.

Commercial Activities. Apart from agricultural goods, mineral water, soft drinks, and beverages, few goods are produced locally for the retail market. Cheaper goods from Turkey, Russia, China, and Bulgaria are sold in the shops. Some locally produced building materials, chemicals, and textiles are sold.

Major Industries. Major industries include metallurgy, metal and chemical works, mining (manganese, arsenic, copper, gold, oil, and raw materials for chemical production such as barite and mineral water), electronic devices, and machinery. A larger role is being played by transportation and especially transhipment because of the development of pipeline routes and transportation projects.

Trade. The principle exports are food, drink, tobacco, metals, and chemicals. The major imports are energy and fuel, mineral products, machinery, and food, drink and tobacco. There is a significant trade deficit. The main trading partners are Russia, Turkey, Azerbaijan, Turkmenistan, Bulgaria, the European Union, and the United States.

Division of Labor. High-paying jobs are available for those with a good command of English and advanced computer skills, while older people remain in poorly paid occupations. However, workers in their forties and fifties continue to occupy leading positions in ownership and management, as result of their advantage in starting capital and business connections from the Soviet era.

Social Stratification

Classes and Castes. The systems of social stratification changed significantly because of the increasing income gap between the impoverished masses and former white-collar workers, and the new rich, who have used financial and social capital to accumulate capital through privatization or trade, or have taken advantage of corruption in the state bureaucracy. Another change is linked to the restructuring of the political and economic system from the Soviet centralized type to a free market, although frequently the same Soviet bureaucrats and Communist officials have become capitalists and advocates of a liberal economy. Much of the new capital is concentrated in Tbilisi, Batumi, and the Black Sea port of Poti and thus is dominated by ethnic Georgians. The Armenian and Jewish economic elite that once played an important role, especially in Tbilisi, has lost its position because of emigration or because they maintain a lower profile.

Symbols of Social Stratification. An advanced position is expressed by a Westernized lifestyle. A Mercedes car symbolizes success, as do an apartment or house in a prestigious district, summering in France, and sending one's children to private European or American schools. Visiting casinos is another sign of upward social mobility.

Political Life

Government. Georgia is a presidential republic. The president is also the head of the executive branch, although the ministers are formally headed by the state minister. The single-chamber (225 members strong) parliament is elected in a mixed majoritarian-proportional system. The last parliamentary elections were won by the president's Citizens' Union of Georgia. The other two parties in the parliament are the Union of Industrialists and the Union of Georgia's Revival. The judicial branch, which was weak in the communist era, is in the process of being reformed. Local governments are partly elected and partly appointed from Tbilisi and have little formal power and small budgets. Depending on personal authority and local conditions, they may be fairly independent in their policies.

Leadership and Political Officials. Political parties, apart from the Union of Georgia's Revival, have little unity and lack well-defined political agendas. They mostly serve as instruments for pursuing a political career. Most parties tend to be social-democratic or moderately nationalistic. Personalities and personal connections play a decisive role in a political career, and the need to balance political issues and personal loyalty makes personnel appointments far from meritocractic. Many politicians are involved in economic activities, and this often creates conflicts of interest.

Social Problems and Control. Since the increase in crime during the civil wars and turmoil of the early 1990s, there has been a significant reduction in law violations and major crimes such as murder and burglary. The most socially dangerous crime is drug trafficking, which has increased the number of young drug addicts. Organized crime is another important concern. Corruption and incompetence in overstaffed law enforcement bodies along with a

The Georgian capital of Tbilisi, which was founded in the fifth century by King Vakhtang Gorgasali.

weak judiciary system have made it difficult to fight crime. The general public is dissatisfied with the existing situation and with the system of law. Sometimes, especially in rural areas with a strong tradition of customary law, the community itself or a victim's relatives will take the law into their own hands and punish the perpetrator of a particularly shocking crime.

Military Activity. There has been little military action since the end of the civil war and the suspension of the conflict in Abkhazia, but the development of the nation's military potential attracts great attention from both the public and the government. Georgia participates in NATO's Partnership for Peace program and aspires to achieve closer cooperation, and even integration, with NATO. There still are four Russian military bases in the country, although their gradual withdrawal is under way.

Social Welfare and Change Programs

The state welfare system is inefficient, and has few resources. Pensions provide only a fifth of the minimum sustenance level, are poorly targeted, and cover too many beneficiaries. Much of the assistance goes to internally displaced persons from Abkhazia. A number of international and intergovernmental organizations are attempting to improve the welfare system.

Nongovernmental Organizations and Other Associations

There are thousands of non-governmental organizations (NGOs), but few of them are active and successful. NGOs participate in defending human rights and freedom of expression as well as environmental protection. However, as virtually all NGOs are funded by western sources, they have to adapt to the preferences and style of foreign funders, which often have only a vague understanding of the real needs of the country.

Gender Roles and Statuses

Division of Labor by Gender. There is no explicit division of labor by gender except in the areas of hard physical labor such as mining. The national culture places women in both the role of breadwinner and housewife. Most urban women work when they have the opportunity, although few have positions in the military and law enforcement. Top-level political and business jobs are less accessible for women, and only a few are in the government. No women can become a priest in the Orthodox church or a mullah among Muslims.

The Relative Status of Women and Men. The national culture strongly values respect for women. Legislation provides for a woman's right to take the children after a divorce. Women receive pregnancy leaves and earlier retirements and are not subject to military conscription. Although men dominate both public and family life, most housework is done by women. With many young educated women getting better paid jobs than their fathers or husbands, traditional stereotypes of gender-defined social roles are changing.

MARRIAGE, FAMILY, AND KINSHIP

Marriage. Marriage is based on the free will of the partners and rarely is prearranged, although that sometimes happens in rural areas, especially in the Muslim population. Mutual attraction is the most common reason for marriage, although for older couples, economic benefits or comfort may be more important. In Muslim areas, unofficial polygamy exists in rare cases. There is a significant incidence of early marriage, but there is a general tendency for later marriage. Married persons who maintain a joint household have equal rights to their possessions.

Domestic Unit. The basic household in cities is the nuclear family, but frequently, grandparents live together with the family and help to bring up the children. In rural and mountainous areas, a few extended families exist, usually including several brothers with their parents and children. In this case the father of the family may control the resources, and assign tasks on the farm, while the mother is responsible for keeping the household. Younger members gradually split off, building a separate house in the neighborhood.

Inheritance. If there is no will after a person's death, the property is divided among all the children, including daughters, or among the closest relatives if there are no children.

Kin Groups. People ascribe great importance to kinship. Relatives up to the third or even fourth generation are considered close, and are expected to share both happy events and grievances. They meet regularly at important social events such as weddings and funerals, and neglecting the social duty to attend is disapproved. The kinship system played an important role in cushioning the effects of economic crisis when the social welfare system was disrupted. Extended kinship relations may create clientelism and protectionism as well as organized crime.

SOCIALIZATION

Infant Care. Customary practices in the care of infants have been abandoned, such as the practice of rearing young infants in a special type of cradle that restricted the movement of a child. Children are the focal point of the family, and much attention is paid to their education and development, especially in the educated classes. Because kindergartens are less available today, retired grandparents often care for the children.

Child Rearing and Education. The early intellectual development of infants is valued, and parents love to show their children's achievements. The values inculcated and the skills taught differ by gender. Boys are taught to be strong and courageous and deal with cars or tools. Girls are supposed to be modest and skilled in housekeeping, sewing, and cooking; play with dolls rather than war toys; and are more often taught to play musical instruments. Although many parents believe in genetically transmitted qualities and talents, education is valued.

Higher Education. Higher education and a university diploma are highly valued even when the quality of education is unsatisfactory. It is almost impossible to have a career without a diploma, although higher education is not always correlated with a higher income.

ETIQUETTE

Both men and women may kiss one another on the cheek in public places. Kissing on the lips and intimate hugging in public are not approved. Shaking hands is common, but women shake hands less often than men do. Either the person with higher social status or the woman is supposed to initiate greeting and define its form. In the countryside, it is common to greet strangers. Men may embrace while walking in the street. In general, the closer the relationship, the smaller the distance at which people stand. Women are not supposed to gaze at a stranger or smoke on the street.

RELIGION

Religious Beliefs. The great majority of the population belongs to the Georgian Orthodox Church, an Eastern (Greek) Orthodox church. Confessional

An apple seller in Tbilisi. A wide variety of fruits are grown in Georgia, although arable land is limited.

identity is a strong cultural factor that defines the prevailing system of social values. The majority of Georgians in Ajara are Sunni Muslims, as are a few inhabitants of the Meskheti region. There are also Shiite Muslims among the Turkic inhabitants in the southeast (Azeris) and Sunni Muslims among the Abkhaz, Ossetians, and Greeks. Several Protestant churches are active, with the Baptists being the most successful. Most ethnic Armenians belong to the Gregorian Christian Church. There are small groups of Yezid Kurds, Russian Molokans and Dukhobors, and Jews; the population of the latter two groups has diminished because of emigration. New emerging cults and sects, such as Jehovah's Witnesses, meet with hostility and aggression from the established churches and the population.

Rituals and Holy Places. The great majority of Orthodox religious ceremonies are carried out by priests in churches. The most important ceremonies, especially those celebrating Easter and Christmas, are carried out by the Patriarch in Svetitskhoveli Cathedral in the ancient town of Mtskheta, or in the Zion Cathedral in Tbilisi. Daily

Most Georgians belong to the Georgian Orthodox Church. Daily services are held, but many seldom attend.

services are held in churches, as well as weddings and baptisms. In some cases priests are invited to other places to bless new initiatives, buildings or organizations. Many people claim to be religious but seldom attend religious ceremonies. In mountainous regions, people who self-identify as Christian continue to follow rituals of pagan origin.

Death and the Afterlife. Many of popular beliefs and rituals regarding death and afterlife stem from a mixture of Christian and pagan concepts, with many superstitions and cultural borrowings. Respecting the deceased is a very important part of social life, and much time is spent attending funerals and wakes and caring for graves. Although people believe in an eternal afterlife, there is no clear understanding of its nature; people observe rules and try to reduce their grief by ritualizing the mourning process.

Secular Celebrations

The most widely observed holiday still is the New Year. Among national holidays, Independence Day is the most respected, and people like to attend even newly invented festivities such as Tbilisoba in October, a holiday invented by the Communist authorities.

The Arts and Humanities

Support for the Arts. Although the state is supposed to support arts through the Ministry of Culture, there are few funds that rarely find the proper application. Some professional unions, once controlled by the government, continue to claim state support despite contributing little to cultural life. Artists whose work depends less on linguistic restrictions, such as painters and craftsmen, look for financial support and markets abroad. Many writers and artists work in politics or business or try to couple them with their art; it is not uncommon for film makers and writers to have a position in the parliament or other agencies of the government.

Literature. Literature is in a dire condition because of the political and economic crisis that started long before independence. There are only a few young talented writers and poets and almost none from the older generation. The literary market is dominated by translations of bestsellers, detective stories, and erotica.

Graphic Arts. Graphic arts are popular, and many young artists are demonstrating high levels of creativity and skill. Many artists sell their work in the West.

Performance Arts. The performance arts are in a crisis because limitations imposed by language hinder the art from finding a wider audience. Several ballet dancers, opera singers, and theater directors have achieved success in other countries. However, in Tbilisi, performance art and dramatic art are alive and rich.

The State of the Physical and Social Sciences

Physical and natural sciences, along with engineering, were highly developed in the Soviet period because of their application to defense. Today there is next to no funding in these areas, as most Western aid goes to the social sciences. This has caused many scientists to emigrate, and the brain drain has helped maintain relations with leading scientific institutions. The social sciences were underdeveloped in the communist era and have not reached international standards in teaching and research.

Bibliography

Allen, W. E. D. *A History of the Georgian People from the Beginning Down to the Roman Conquest in the Nineteenth Century,* 1932, 1971.

Alpago, Novello. *Art and Architecture in Medieval Georgia*, 1980.

Aronson, Howard I. *Georgian: A Reading Grammar*, 1982, 1991.

Ascherson, Neal. *Black Sea: The Birthplace of Civilisation*, 1996.

Avalov (Avalishvili), Zurab. *The Annexation of Georgia to Russia*, 1982.

———. *The Independence of Georgia in International Politics: 1918–1921*, 1940, 1982.

Aves, Jonathan. *Georgia: From Chaos to Stability*, 1996.

Braund, David. *Georgia in Antiquity: A History of Colchis and Transcaucasian Iberia*, 1994, 1996.

Charachidzé, Géorges. *Prométhée ou le Caucase: Essai de Mythologie Contrastive*, 1986.

Chatwin, Mary Ellen. *Socio-Cultural Transformation and Foodways in the Republic of Georgia*, 1996.

Chervonnaya, S. *Conflict in the Caucasus: Georgia, Abkhazia and the Russian Shadow*, 1995.

Crego, Paul. "Religion and Nationalism in Georgia." *Religion in Eastern Europe* 14 (3): 1–9, 1994.

Curtis, Glen E., ed. *Armenia, Azerbaijan and Georgia: Country Studies*, 1995.

Gachechiladze, R. *The New Georgia: Space, Society, Politics*, 1995.

Gamkrelidse Thomas V. *Alphabetic Writing and the Old Georgian Script: A Typology and Provenience of Alphabetic Writing Systems*, 1994.

Georgia: A Travel Reference Map of the Republic of Georgia, 1997.

Grigolia, A. *Custom and Justice in Caucasus: Georgian Highlanders*, 1936, 1939, 1977.

Herzig, Edmund. *The New Caucasus: Armenia, Azerbaijan and Georgia*, 1999.

Kazemzadeh, Firuz. *The Struggle for Transcaucasia (1917–1921)*, 1951, 1981.

Lang, D. M. *The Georgians*, 1966.

MacFarlane, S. Neil. "Democratization, Nationalism and Regional Security in the Southern Caucasus." *Government and Opposition* 32 (3): 399–420, 1997.

Melikidze, V., and G. Tarkhan-Mouravi. *Human Development Report: Georgia 1997*, 1997.

Mepisashvili, Rusudan, and Tsintsadze Vakhtang. *The Arts of Ancient Georgia*, 1979.

Nasmyth, Peter. *Georgia: Mountains and Honour*, 1997.

Rayfield, Donald. *The Literature of Georgia: A History*, 1994.

Rosen, Roger. *The Georgian Republic*, 1995.

Schrade, Brigitta, ed. *The Art of Svanetia: Medieval Treasures from the Caucasus*, 2000.

Suny, R. G. *The Making of the Georgian Nation*, 1989, 1996.

Toumanoff C. *Studies in Christian Caucasian History*, 1963.

Toumanoff, Cyril. "Medieval Georgian Historical Literature (VIII–XV Centuries)." *Traditio* 1: 139–182, 1943.

—George Tarkham-Mouravi

GERMANY

CULTURE NAME

German

ALTERNATIVE NAMES

Germania (Latin), Deutschland (German), l'Allemagne (French)

ORIENTATION

Identification. The name Germany is derived from the Latin word Germania, which, at the time of the Gallic War (58–51 B.C.E.), was used by the Romans to designate various peoples occupying the region east of the Rhine. The German-language name Deutschland is derived from a Germanic root meaning *volk*, or people. A document (written in Latin) from the Frankish court of 786 C.E. uses the term theodisca lingua to refer to the colloquial speech of those who spoke neither Latin nor early forms of Romance languages. From this point forward, the term *deutsch* was employed to mark a difference in speech, which corresponded to political, geographic, and social distinctions as well. Since, however, the Frankish and Saxon kings of the early Middle Ages sought to characterize themselves as emperors of Rome, it does not seem valid to infer an incipient form of national consciousness. By the fifteenth century, the designation *Heiliges Römisches Reich*, or ''Holy Roman Empire,'' was supplemented with the qualifying phrase *der deutschen Nation*, meaning ''of the German Nation.'' Still, it is important to note that, at that point in history, the phrase ''German nation'' referred only to the Estates of the Empire—dukes, counts, archbishops, electoral princes, and imperial cities—that were represented in the Imperial Diet. Nevertheless, this self-designation indicates the desire of the members of the Imperial Estates to distinguish themselves from the curia in Rome, with which they were embroiled in a number of political and financial conflicts.

The area that became known as Deutschland, or Germany, had been nominally under the rule of the German king—who was usually also the Roman emperor—since the tenth century. In fact, however, the various territories, principalities, counties, and cities enjoyed a large degree of autonomy and retained distinctive names and traditions, even after the founding of the nation-state—the *Kaiserreich* or German Empire—in 1871. The names of older territories—such as Bavaria, Brandenburg, and Saxony—are still kept alive in the designations of some of today's federal states. Other older names, such as Swabia and Franconia, refer to ''historical landscapes'' within the modern federal states or straddling their boundaries. Regional identities such as these are of great significance for many Germans, though it is evident that they are often manipulated for political and commercial purposes as well.

The current German state, called the Federal Republic of Germany, was founded in 1949 in the wake of Germany's defeat in World War II. At first, it consisted only of so-called West Germany, that is the areas that were occupied by British, French, and American forces. In 1990, five new states, formed from the territories of East Germany—the former Soviet zone, which in 1949 became the German Democratic Republic (GDR)—were incorporated into the Federal Republic of Germany. Since that time, Germany has consisted of sixteen federal states: Baden-Württemberg, Bavaria, Berlin, Brandenburg, Bremen, Hamburg, Hesse, Lower Saxony, Mecklenburg-West Pomerania, North Rhine-Westphalia, Rhineland-Palatinate, Saarland, Saxony, Saxony-Anhalt, Schleswig-Holstein, and Thuringia.

Location and Geography. Germany is located in north-central Europe. It shares boundaries with nine other countries: Denmark, Poland, the Czech Republic, Austria, Switzerland, France, Luxembourg, Belgium, and the Netherlands. At various

Germany

times in the past, the German Reich claimed bordering regions in France (Alsace-Lorraine) and had territories that now belong to Poland, Russia, and Lithuania (Pomerania, Silesia, and East Prussia). Shortly after the unification of East and West Germany in 1990, the Federal Republic signed a treaty with Poland, in which it renounced all claims to territories east of the boundary formed by the Oder and Neisse rivers—the de facto border since the end of World War II.

The northern part of Germany, which lies on the North Sea and the Baltic Sea, is a coastal plain of low elevation. In the east, this coastal plain extends southward for over 120 miles (200 kilometers), but, in the rest of the country, the central region is dotted with foothills. Thereafter, the elevation increases fairly steadily, culminating in the Black Forest in the southwest and the Bavarian Alps in the south. The Rhine, Weser, and Elbe rivers run toward the north or northwest, emptying into the North Sea. Similarly, the Oder river, which marks the border with Poland, flows northward into the Baltic Sea. The Danube has its source in the Black Forest then runs eastward, draining southern Germany and emptying eventually into the Black Sea. Germany has a temperate seasonal climate with moderate to heavy rainfall.

Demography. In accordance with modern European patterns of demographic development, Germany's population rose from about 25 million in 1815 to over 60 million in 1914, despite heavy emigration. The population continued to rise in the first half of this century, though this trend was hindered by heavy losses in the two world wars. In 1997, the total population of Germany was 82 million. Of this sum, nearly 67 million lived in former West Germany, and just over 15 million lived in former East Germany. In 1939, the year Germany invaded Poland, the population of what was to become West Germany was 43 million and the population of what was to become East Germany was almost 17 million. This means that from 1939 to 1997, both the total population and the population of West Germany have increased, while the population of East Germany has decreased.

Following World War II, the population of both parts of Germany rose dramatically, due to the arrival of German refugees from the Soviet Union and from areas that are now part of Poland and the Czech Republic. In 1950, eight million refugees formed 16 percent of the West German population and over four million refugees formed 22 percent of the East German population. Between 1950 and 1961, however, more than 2.5 million Germans left the German Democratic Republic and went to the Federal Republic of Germany. The building of the Berlin Wall in 1961 effectively put an end to this German-German migration.

From 1945 to 1990, West Germany's population was further augmented by the arrival of nearly four million ethnic Germans, who immigrated from Poland, Romania, and the Soviet Union or its successor states. These so-called *Aussiedler* or return settlers took advantage of a provision in the constitution of the Federal Republic of Germany, which grants citizenship to ethnic Germans living outside of Germany.

Another boost to the population of West Germany has been provided by the so-called *Gastarbeiter* (migrant or immigrant workers), mostly from Turkey, the Balkans, Italy, and Portugal. Between 1961 and 1997, over 23 million foreigners came to the Federal Republic of Germany; seventeen million of these, however, later returned to their home countries. The net gain in population for Germany was still well over 6 million, since those who remained in Germany often established families.

The population of Germany is distributed in small to medium-sized local administrative units, though, on the average, the settlements tend to be larger in West Germany. There are only three cities with a population of over 1 million: Berlin (3.4 million), Hamburg (1.7 million), and Munich (1.2 million). Cologne has just under 1 million inhabitants, while the next largest city, Frankfurt am Main, has a population of 650,000.

Linguistic Affiliation. In the early nineteenth century, language historians identified German as a member of the Germanic subfamily of the Indo-European family of languages. The major German dialect groups are High and Low German, the language varieties of the southern highlands and the northern lowlands. Low German dialects, in many ways similar to Dutch, were spoken around the mouth of the Rhine and on the northern coast but are now less widespread. High German dialects may be divided into Middle and Upper categories, which, again, correspond to geographical regions. The modern standard is descended largely from a synthetic form, which was developed in the emerging bureaucracy of the territorial state of Saxony and which combined properties of East Middle and East Upper High German. Religious reformer Martin Luther (1483–1546) helped popularize this variety by employing it in his very influential German translation of the Bible. The standard language was established in a series of steps, including the emergence of a national literary public in the eighteenth century, the improvement and extension of public education in the course of the nineteenth century, and political unification in the late nineteenth century. In the twentieth century, massive population movements have contributed to further dialect leveling. Nevertheless, some local and regional speech varieties have survived and/or reasserted themselves. Due to the presence of immigrants, a number of other languages are spoken in Germany as well, including Polish, Turkish, Serbo-Croatian, Greek, Italian, Portuguese, Spanish, Mongolian, and Vietnamese.

Symbolism. Any review of national symbols in Germany must take into account the clash of alternative symbols, which correspond either to different phases of a stormy history or to different aspects of a very complex whole. The eagle was depicted in the regalia of the Holy Roman Empire, but since Prussia's victory over Austria in 1866 and the exclusion of Austria from the German Reich in 1871, this symbol has been shared by two separate states, which were united only briefly from 1937 to 1945. Germany is the homeland of the Reformation, yet Martin Luther is a very contentious symbol, since 34 percent of all Germans are Roman Catholic. In the late eighteenth and early nineteenth century, Germany became known as the land of *Dichter und Denker*, that is, poets and philosophers, including such luminaries as Immanuel Kant, Johann Gottfried von Herder, Johann Wolfgang von Goethe, Friedrich von Schiller, and Wilhelm von Humboldt. In the latter nineteenth century this image was supplemented by that of the Prussian officer and the saber-rattling Kaiser. *Der deutsche Michel*—which means, approximately, "Mike the German," named after the archangel Michael, the protector of Germany—was a simpleton with knee breeches and a sleeping cap, who had represented Germany in caricatures even before the nineteenth century. The national and democratic movement of the first half of the nineteenth century spawned a whole series of symbols, including especially the flag with the colors black, red, and gold, which were used for the national flag in the Weimar Republic (1919–1933) and again in the Federal Republic of Germany (as of 1949). The national movement also found expression in a series of monuments scattered over the countryside. The National Socialists were especially concerned with creating new symbols and harnessing old ones for their purposes. In the Federal Republic of Germany, it is illegal to display the *Hakenkreuz* or swastika, which was the central symbol of the Nazi movement and the central motif in the national flag in the Third Reich (1933–1945).

The official symbols of the Federal Republic of Germany are the eagle, on one hand, and the black, red, and gold flag of the democratic movement, on the other. In many ways, however, the capital city itself has served as a symbol of the Federal Republic, be it Bonn, a small, relatively cosy Rhenish city (capital from 1949 to 1990), or Berlin, Germany's largest city and the capital of Brandenburg-Prussia, the German Empire, the Weimar Republic, the Third Reich, and, since 1990, the Federal Republic. From the *Siegessäule* (Victory Column) to the *Reichstag* (parliament), from the Charlottenburg Palace to the former Gestapo Headquarters, from the Memorial Church to the fragmentary remnants of the Berlin Wall, Berlin contains numerous symbols of Germany and German history.

A Bavarian town settlement. Predominantly Catholic, Bavaria is home to many shrines and chapels, as well as the majestic Bavarian Alps.

Given the contentious character of political symbols in Germany, many Germans seem to identify more closely with typical landscapes. Paintings or photographs of Alpine peaks and valleys are found in homes throughout Germany. Often, however, even features of the natural environment become politicized, as was the case with the Rhine during Germany's conflicts with France in the nineteenth century. Alternatively, corporate products and consumer goods also serve as national symbols. This is certainly the case with a series of high-quality German automobiles, such as Porsche, Mercedes-Benz, and BMW.

HISTORY AND ETHNIC RELATIONS

Emergence of the Nation. The emergence of the nation has been understood in very different ways at different times. Humanist scholars of the early sixteenth century initiated a discourse about the German nation by identifying contemporaneous populations as descendants of ancient Germanic peoples, as they were represented in the writings of Roman authors such as Julius Caesar (100–44

B.C.E.) and Cornelius Tacitus (c. 55–c.116 C.E.), author of the famous work *Germania.* From the viewpoint of Ulrich von Hutten (1488–1523), among others, Tacitus provided insight into the origins and character of a virtuous nation that was in many ways equal or superior to Rome. The German humanists found their hero in Armin, or Hermann, who defeated the Romans in the battle of the Teutoburg Forest in 9 C.E.

The interest of German intellectuals in their ancient predecessors, as depicted in the literature of classical antiquity, continued into the eighteenth century, when it inspired the patriotic poetry of Friedrich Gottlieb Klopstock (1724–1803) and of the members of a group of poets called the *Göttinger Hain,* founded in 1772. The twentieth century scholar, Norbert Elias, has shown that the attention that bourgeois Germans of the eighteenth century devoted to the origins and the virtuous character of their nation was motivated in large part by their rejection of powerful aristocrats and courtiers, who modeled themselves on French counterparts.

On the eve of the French Revolution (1789), Germany was divided into nearly three hundred separate political entities of various sizes and with various degrees of sovereignty within the Holy Roman Empire. By 1794, French troops had taken the west bank of the Rhine, which had previously been divided among many different principalities; by 1806, Napoléon Bonaparte (1769–1821) had disbanded the Holy Roman Empire. In the same year, Napoléon's armies defeated Prussia and its allies in the simultaneous battles of Jena and Auerstädt. In its modern form, German nationalism took shape in response to this defeat. In the War of Liberation (1813–1815), in which many patriots participated as volunteers, the allied forces under Prussian leadership were successful in expelling the French from Germany. After the Congress of Vienna (1815), however, those who had hoped for the founding of a German nation-state were disappointed, as the dynastic rulers of the German territories reasserted their political authority.

With the rise of historical scholarship in the first half of the nineteenth century, the earlier emphasis on German antiquity was supplemented by representations of the medieval origins of the German nation. In the age of nationalism, when the nation-state was understood as the end point of a law-like historical development, German historians sought to explain why Germany, in contrast to France and England, was still divided. They believed that they had discovered the answer to this puzzle in the history of the medieval Reich. Shortly after the death of Charlemagne (814), the Carolingian empire split into a western, a middle, and an eastern kingdom. In the teleological view of the nineteenth century historians, the western kingdom became France and the eastern kingdom was destined to become Germany; the middle kingdom was subdivided and remained a bone of contention between the two emerging nations. The tenth century German king, Otto I, led a series of expeditions to Rome and was crowned as emperor by the pope in 962. From this point forward, Germany and the medieval version of the Roman Empire were linked.

German historians of the nineteenth century interpreted the medieval Reich as the beginning of a process that should have led to the founding of a German nation-state. The medieval emperor was viewed as the major proponent of this national development, but modern historians often criticized the actual behavior of the emperors as being inconsistent with national aims. The main villains of medieval history, at least in the eyes of latter-day historians—especially Protestants—were the various popes and those German princes who allied themselves with the popes against the emperor for reasons that were deemed to be "egotistical." This opposition of the pope and the princes was thought to have stifled the proper development of the German nation. The high point in this development was, the nationalist historians believed, the era of the Hohenstaufen emperors (1138–1254). The Hohenstaufen emperor Frederick I was rendered in nineteenth century historiography as a great hero of the German cause. After his reign, however, the empire suffered a series of setbacks and entered into a long period of decline. The early Habsburgs offered some hope to latter-day historians, but their successors were thought to have pursued purely dynastic interests. The low point in the national saga came in the Thirty Years War (1618–1648), when foreign and domestic enemies ravaged Germany.

Among the educated bourgeoisie and the popular classes of nineteenth century Germany, the desire for a renewal of the German Reich was widespread; but there was much disagreement about exactly how this new state should be structured. The main conflict was between those favoring a *grossdeutsch* solution to German unification, that is, a "large Germany" under Austrian leadership, and those favoring a *kleindeutsch* solution, that is, a "small Germany" under Prussian leadership and excluding Austria. The second option was realized after Prussia won a series of wars, defeating Denmark in 1864, Austria in 1866, and France in 1871. In the writings of the Prussian school of national history, Prussia's victory and the founding of the German Reich in 1871 were depicted as the realization of the plans of the medieval emperor, Frederick I. After the founding of the Reich, Germany pursued expansionist policies, both overseas and in the territories on its eastern border. Defeat in World War I led to widespread resentment against the conditions of the Versailles Treaty, which many Germans thought to be unfair, and against the founders of the Weimar Republic, who many Germans viewed as traitors or collaborators. Adolf Hitler, the leader of the National Socialist (Nazi) movement, was able to exploit popular resentment and widespread desires for national greatness. National Socialist propagandists built upon beliefs in the antiquity and continuity of the German nation, augmenting them with racialist theories, which attributed to the Germans a biological superiority over other peoples.

National Identity. Following World War II, German national identity became problematic, since the national movement seemed to have culminated in the Third Reich and found its most extreme expression in the murder of millions of people, including six million Jews. All further reflection on the German nation had to come to grips with this issue in one way or another. There have been many different attempts to explain Nazism and its crimes. Some see Adolf Hitler and his cronies as villains who misled the German people. Others blame Nazism on a flaw in the German national character. Still others see the beginning of Germany's problems in the rejection of the rational and universal principles of the Enlightenment and the adoption of romantic irrationalism. Marxist scholars see Nazism as a form of fascism, which they describe as the form that capitalism takes under certain historical conditions. Finally, some cite the failure of the bourgeois revolution in the nineteenth century and the lingering power of feudal elites as the main cause. Interpretations of this sort fall under the general heading of *Vergangenheitsbewältigung*, or coming to terms with the past. Since the fall of the GDR, West German traditions of coming to terms with the past have been extended to the period of socialist rule in East Germany. Some Germans emphasize the similarities between the two forms of dictatorship, National Socialist and communist, while others, especially many East Germans, view the Third Reich and the GDR as being essentially dissimilar. Lingering differences between the attitudes and practices of West and East Germans are often attributed to the so-called *Mauer in den Köpfen*, or wall in the mind—an allusion to the physical wall that used to divide East and West Germany.

In recent years, German nationalism has been reexamined in accordance with views of the nation as an ''imagined community'' which is based on ''invented traditions.'' Most scholars have concentrated on the organization, the symbolism, and the discourse of the national movement as it developed in the nineteenth century. The most significant contributions to the imagination and the invention of the German nation in this era took place in the context of (1) a set of typical voluntary associations, which supposedly harkened back to old local, regional, or national traditions; (2) the series of monuments erected by state governments, by towns and cities, and by citizens' groups throughout Germany; and (3) the various representations of history, some of which have been alluded to above. In addition, there is a growing body of literature that examines understandings of the nation and the politics of nationhood in the eighteenth century. There is much disagreement on the political implications of the critical history of nationalism in Germany. Some scholars seem to want to exorcize the deviant aspects of modern German nationalism, while retaining those aspects, with which, in their view, German citizens should identify. Others see nationalism as an especially dangerous stage in a developmental process, which Germans, in their journey toward a postnational society, should leave behind.

Ethnic Relations. The framers of the *Grundgesetz* (Basic Law or Constitution) of the Federal Republic of Germany adopted older laws that define citizenship according to the principle of *jus sanguinis*, that is birth to German parents (literally, law of blood). For this reason, many people born outside of Germany are considered to be German, while many people born in Germany are not. Since the 1960s, the country has admitted millions of migrant workers, who have, in fact, played an indispensable role in the economy. Although migrant workers from Turkey, Yugoslavia, Italy, Greece, Spain, and Portugal were called *Gastarbeiter* (literally, guest workers), many stayed in Germany and established families. They form communities, which are to varying degrees assimilated to German lifestyles. Indeed, many of the children and grandchildren of immigrant laborers regard themselves not as Turkish, Greek, or Portuguese, but as German. Nevertheless, they have had great difficulty in gaining German citizenship; and many Germans view them as *Ausländer*, or foreigners. Beginning in the year 2000, new laws granted restricted rights of dual citizenship to children of foreign descent who are born in Germany. This new legislation has been accompanied by intensified discussion about Germany's status as a land of immigration. All major political parties now agree that Germany is and should be a land of immigration, but they differ on many aspects of immigration policy.

Urbanism, Architecture, and the Use of Space

The earliest urban centers in what is now Germany were established by the Romans on or near the Rhine, often on the sites of pre-Roman settlements. Examples include Mainz, Trier, and Cologne. In the Middle Ages, older and newly founded towns became centers for commerce and for the manual trades, which were organized in guilds. Towns developed distinctive forms of social organization and culture, which set them off from the agrarian world of peasants and nobles. Some, called "free imperial cities," enjoyed the protection of the emperor and concomitant political and economic privileges. Others were directly subordinate to territorial lords, but still tried to gain or maintain a degree of autonomy.

By the early modern period, the most important commercial centers were the Hanseatic towns or cities of the northern coastal regions, the Rhenish towns, and the southern German towns, such as Augsburg, Würzburg, Regensburg, and Nuremberg, which were located along trade routes leading to the Mediterranean. There was often a sharp distinction between commercial cities, such as Leipzig, and court cities, such as Dresden. Up until the nineteenth century, however, the urban populations were very modest in size. In 1800, only Berlin and Hamburg had more than 100,000 inhabitants.

In the course of the nineteenth century, Germany experienced the forms of internal migration and urbanization that are typical of the transition from an agrarian to an industrial society. Industrial centers such as Leipzig, Berlin, and the Ruhr Valley grew dramatically in the second half of the century. Essen, in the Ruhr Valley, had 10,000 inhabitants in 1851 and 230,000 in 1905. The inadequate living conditions in the burgeoning cities were a major impetus for the workers' movement, which led to the formation of unions and working-class parties, most notably the Social Democratic and Communist parties.

German cities typically bear witness to all eras in the architectural history of Europe. The sequence of Romanic, Gothic, Renaissance, and Baroque styles is especially evident in churches, many of which have been renovated repeatedly over the centuries. Much of the urban architecture in Germany bears witness to the tastes of the nineteenth century, including the classicism of the first half of the century and the historicism (including neo-Gothic and neo-Renaissance) of the second half of the century. In the period of rapid industrial growth in the late nineteenth and early twentieth centuries, many German cities were largely rebuilt in the styles of the so-called *Gründerzeit*, that is, the founding years of the new German Empire. Most cities dispensed of their medieval walls in the nineteenth century, but they retained their central town square, which is typically flanked by the town hall and sometimes the town church as well. In German cities today, some of the old town halls are still administrative centers, but others have become historical museums. The town square is, however, still used for festivals, weekly farmers' markets, and other special events. Since the late 1970s, inner city areas surrounding the central squares have often been transformed into pedestrian zones, with many shops, cafés, restaurants, and bars.

German cities experienced an unprecedented degree of destruction in the late years of World War II. In the first decades of the postwar era, they were often rebuilt in a modern style that differed sharply from the earlier appearance of the cities. Since the 1970s, cultural preservation has become a higher priority. This emphasis on the preservation of historic aspects of the city corresponds to an increased popular interest in all things historical and to the importance of the international tourist trade. The politics of cultural preservation is characterized by debates over the way in which the past should be represented in urban places. This applies especially to the representation of the Third Reich and World War II. In Berlin, for example, many buildings have been linked to different regimes of the past, including Brandenburg-Prussia, the German Empire, and the Third Reich. The Kaiser Wilhelm Memorial Church, which was largely destroyed in the last war, has been left in ruins. It now serves as a memorial not to Kaiser Wilhelm but to World War II. In Dresden, the federal state of Saxony, the city of Dresden, and various citizens organizations have elected to rebuild the famous Frauenkirche (Church of Our Lady), which was destroyed in the bombing of February 1945. Thus, they have chosen to emphasize the baroque tradition of "Florence on the Elbe," as Dresden was called. At the same time, Dresden—like many other towns and cities of former East Germany—has elected to remove many, though not all, of the monuments of the German Democratic Republic.

People socializing at a festival in Allgau. German beer, a favorite beverage, must be made only of water, hops, and malt.

Food and Economy

Food in Daily Life. Eating habits in Germany vary by social class and milieu, but it is possible to generalize about the behavior of the inclusive middle class, which has emerged in the prosperous postwar era. Most Germans acquire food from both supermarkets and specialty shops, such as bakeries and butcher shops. Bread is the main food at both breakfast and supper. Breakfast usually includes *brötchen*, or rolls of various kinds, while supper—called *Abendbrot*—often consists of bread, sausages or cold cuts, cheese, and, perhaps, a salad or vegetable garnish. The warm meal of the day is still often eaten at noon, though modern work routines seem to encourage assimilation to American patterns. Pork is the most commonly consumed meat, though various sorts of *wurst*, or sausage, are often eaten in lieu of meat. Cabbage, beets, and turnips are indigenous vegetables, which are, however, often supplemented with more exotic fare. Since its introduction in the seventeenth century, the potato has won a firm place in German cuisine. Favorite alcoholic beverages are beer, brandy, and schnapps. German beers, including varieties such as *Pilsner*, *Weizenbier*, and *Alt*, are brewed according to the *deutsche Reinheitsgebot*, i.e., the German law of purity from the sixteenth century, which states that the only admissible ingredients are water, hops, and malt. Large family meals are still common at noontime on Saturdays and Sundays. These are often followed in mid-afternoon by *Kaffee und Kuchen*, the German version of tea time.

Food Customs at Ceremonial Occasions. Special meals usually include meat, fish, or fowl, along with one of a number of starchy foods, which vary by region. Examples of the latter include *klöße* (potato dumplings), *knödel* (a breadlike dumpling), and *spätzle* (a kind of pasta). Alternatively, Germans often celebrate in restaurants, which often feature cuisines of other nations. Greek restaurants tend to be more moderately priced, French restaurants are often more expensive, and the especially popular Italian restaurants span the range of price categories. The most important holiday meal is Christmas dinner. Regional and family traditions vary, but this often consists of goose, duck, or turkey, supplemented by red cabbage and potatoes or potato dumplings.

Basic Economy. Since the late nineteenth century, the German economy has been shaped by industrial production, international trade, and the rise of consumer culture. Consequently, the number of people involved in agricultural production has steadily declined. At the end of the twentieth century, only 2.7 percent of the German workforce was involved in agriculture, forestry, and fishery combined. Nevertheless, 48 percent of the total area of Germany was devoted to agriculture, and agricultural products covered 85 percent of domestic food needs.

Land Tenure and Property. The reform of feudal land tenure was not initiated in Germany until the period of upheaval and change during or following the Napoleonic Wars. In the various German states of those days, land reform was typically part of a broader reform plan that affected many aspects of political, economic, and social life. Programs for land reform, which were begun in the first decades of the nineteenth century, often were not completed until the second half of the century. Subsequently, however, new technologies and new organizational forms allowed agriculture to become an increasingly efficient branch of the modern economy. As the nineteenth century progressed, production rose dramatically. Simultaneously, the workforce shifted away from agriculture and into industry.

Following World War II, agricultural production was subject to further modernization, which resulted in fewer farmers on fewer farms of greater size. Nevertheless, the family farms of West Germany were on the average relatively small, the great majority having less than 100 acres (40 hectares). In East Germany, the postwar reform of agriculture was planned and executed by the state and the ruling socialist party. The most important aspects of this reform were the redistribution of land in 1945, the formation of agricultural collectives between 1952 and 1960, and the regional cooperation among different local collectives in the late 1960s and 1970s. This led to the creation of large, industrialized, cooperative farms. At the end of the Cold War (1989), however, over 10 percent of the East German population was involved in agricultural production, while West German farmers and farm workers made up only 5 percent of the population. After the reunification of Germany in 1990, agriculture in eastern territories was privatized.

The Federal Republic of Germany has liberal property laws which guarantee the right to private property. This right is, however, subject to a number of restrictions, especially with regard to state prerogatives concerning public utilities, public construction projects, mining rights, cultural preservation, antitrust issues, public safety, and issues of national security, to name only a few. Following the German reunification, there were a number of property issues to be resolved, since the GDR had expropriated private property and had not taken appropriate action with regard to private property expropriated during the Third Reich. The farmland taken from landowners between 1945 and 1949 was explicitly excluded from the reunification treaty; otherwise, it was required that expropriated property be restored to private owners. The ruling principle in this process was "restitution over compensation." The restitution of real estate was complicated by multiple claims on single objects. In agriculture, ownership issues were usually clear, since the land exploited by the cooperatives had remained in private hands. Since, however, the cooperatives had worked the land for over thirty years, building roads and buildings irrespective of property boundaries, private owners faced many practical difficulties in gaining access to their land.

Commercial Activities. In Germany, there is a strong tradition of *handwerk*, or manual trades. In the manual trades, training, qualification, and licensing are regulated by special ordinances. Training and qualification occur through vocational schools and internships. These are an integral part of the modern educational system, though some of the vocabulary is reminiscent of guilds, which were abolished in the nineteenth century. For example, the owner or manager of a business enterprise in the manual trades is required to have his or her *Meisterbrief* (master craftsman's certificate). In the mid-1990s, the eleven most important manual trades, in terms of both the number of firms and the total number of employees, were those of barbers and hairdressers, electricians, automobile mechanics, carpenters, housepainters, masons, metalworkers, plumbers, bakers, butchers, and building- and window-cleaners.

Major Industries. Among the industrial countries of Europe, Germany was a late comer, retaining a largely agricultural orientation until the later nineteenth century. Following German unification in 1871, rapid industrial development exploited extensive coal resources in the Ruhr Valley, in the Saarland, in areas surrounding Leipzig, and in Lusatia. Building upon a strong tradition of manual trades, Germany became a leader in steel production and metalworking. Coal reserves also provided the basis for an emerging carbo-chemical industry. When, in the decades following World War II, heavy industry migrated to sites in Asia and Latin America, Germany experienced a dramatic decrease in the number of industrial jobs; this was accompanied by the growth of the service sector (including retail, credit, insurance, the professions, and tourism). At the beginning of the 1970s, over half of the workforce was employed in industry; by 1998, however, this number had dwindled to less than one third. In the early twenty-first century, the most important industries in Germany are automobile manufacturing and the production of automobile parts, the machine industry, the metal products industry, the production of electrical appliances, the chemical industry, the plastics industry, and food processing.

Trade. After the United States, Germany has the second largest export economy in the world. In 1998, export accounted for 25 percent of the gross domestic product and import for nearly 22 percent. Export goods include products from the major industries cited above. Other than coal, Germany lacks fossil fuels, especially oil and natural gas. These products must be imported. Germany's most important trading partners are France, the United States, the United Kingdom, and other European lands. It also trades actively with East Asian countries and has become increasingly involved in eastern Europe.

Division of Labor. The work force in Germany includes laborers, entrepreneurs, employees and clerical workers, managers and administrators, and members of the various professions. Access to particular occupations is determined by a number of factors, including family background, individual ability, and education or training. Laborers in Germany are usually highly skilled, having completed vocational training programs. Beginning in the 1960s, the ranks of the laboring class were augmented by migrant workers from Turkey and other countries bordering on the Mediterranean. Both laborers and employees are represented by well organized and aggressive unions, which, in the postwar era, have often cooperated with entrepreneurial organizations and the state in long range economic planning. Since the 1970s, rising labor costs and the globalization of industrial production have led to high rates of unemployment, especially in areas where heavy industry was dominant, as in Lower Saxony and North Rhine-Westphalia. The problem of unemployment in the Federal Republic of Germany was exacerbated by the entry of the five new federal states of the former GDR in 1990. Once the Iron Curtain fell, East Germany lost its protected markets in Eastern Europe and Central Asia. As a result, its industry collapsed and hundreds of thousands lost their jobs. In 1998, unemployment rates were over 10 percent in former West Germany and 20 percent in former East Germany. The figures for the latter, however, did not take into account those who were involved in make-work and reeducation programs. Since many were pessimistic about the possibility of creating new jobs in eastern Germany, the flow of migrants to western Germany continued to the early twenty-first century.

Social Stratification

Classes and Castes. By the early twentieth century, German society was divided into more or less clear-cut classes. Industrial workers included both the skilled and the unskilled. The former came from the manual trades but became factory laborers when it had proved impossible or undesirable to remain independent. The middle classes included small businessmen and independent members of the trades, white-collar employees, professionals, and civil servants. Finally, the upper or upper middle classes consisted of industrialists, financiers, high government officials, and large landowners, among others. Members of these classes were usually associated with corresponding political organizations and milieus, for example, the workers with unions and socialist or communist organizations, and the middle classes with a range of bourgeois parties, occupational organizations, and patriotic societies. In the German Empire and the Weimar Republic, however, many Catholics of all classes were organized in the *Zentrum*, or Center Party.

The National Socialist (Nazi) Party found supporters among all social classes, especially the middle classes. The Third Reich was, in many ways, an upwardly mobile society, which created new jobs, provided subsidies, and opened career opportunities for party members. The success of many party supporters was gained at the expense of members of the workers' movement and the Jews and other minorities.

In the prosperous West German society of the postwar era, class boundaries seemed to open up and admit more members into a new, more inclusive middle class. Correspondingly, the political distinction between the bourgeois and the socialist parties lessened. In East Germany, the Socialist Unity Party wanted to eliminate the bourgeoisie, which had compromised itself through its support of National Socialism. This was to be achieved by nationalizing larger private enterprises, forcing independent farmers to enter agricultural cooperatives, and favoring the children of workers in education and hiring programs. The GDR described itself as a "workers' and peasants' state," but some social scientists have described it as a leveled middle-class

People collecting pieces of the Berlin Wall in 1989. Built in 1961, the wall was a visible reminder of Germany's defeat in World War II and subsequent division into first four, then two distinct and independent zones.

society, made up of skilled workers, employees, and specialists, who held state-subsidized positions. Since the entry of the five new federal states into the Federal Republic, class relations have been reshuffled in eastern Germany once again, sending many westward in search of work and bringing many eastward to occupy leading positions in government and corporations. Large groups of retired and unemployed persons live side by side with entrepreneurs, managers, employees, civil servants, and others working in the service sector.

Symbols of Social Stratification. Social class in Germany is not only a matter of training, employment, and income but also a style of life, self-understanding, and self-display. The so-called *bildungsbürgertum,* or educated bourgeoisie of the nineteenth and early twentieth centuries, to cite one example, was characterized first and foremost by a particular constellation of artistic and literary taste, habits, and cultural and ethical values. Modern sociologists have tended to focus on the full range of social milieus that make up German society and on the various kinds of consumer behavior that characterize each milieu. Thus, variations in interior design in private residences, eating habits, taste in music and in other entertainment forms, reading materials, personal hygiene and clothing, sexual behavior, and leisure activities can all be viewed as indexes of association with one of a finite set of social milieus. A single example must suffice. Highly educated persons in business, government, or the professions are likely to read the *Frankfurter Allgemeine Zeitung* (a major newspaper, published in Frankfurt), if they are relatively conservative, or the *Süddeutsche Zeitung* or the *Frankfurter Rundschau* (newspapers published in Munich and Frankfurt, respectively), if they are somewhat left of center. Members of both groups will probably also read the politically moderate and rather sophisticated weekly newspaper, *Die Zeit* (Hamburg). Conservatives who are more interested in politics and business than in arts and literature may read *Die Welt* (another Hamburg newspaper), while readers who identify more closely with an alternative leftist milieu are more likely to reach for *die tageszeitung,* or *taz* (a newspaper published in Berlin). In contrast, those with a vocational education, who are small business owners, employees, or workers may read the very popular *Bild* (Hamburg), a daily tabloid newspaper. Finally, those who still feel loyal to the defunct GDR or who hope that socialism will come again often read *Neues Deutschland* (Berlin), which was the official organ of the Socialist Unity Party, that is the East German communist party.

Political Life

Government. Germany is a parliamentary democracy, where public authority is divided among federal, state, and local levels of government. In federal elections held every four years, all citizens who are eighteen years of age or older are entitled to cast votes for candidates and parties, which form the *Bundestag*, or parliament, on the basis of vote distribution. The majority party or coalition then elects the head of the government—the *Kanzler* (chancellor)—who appoints the heads of the various government departments. Similarly, states and local communities elect parliaments or councils and executives to govern in their constitutionally guaranteed spheres. Each state government appoints three to five representatives to serve on the *Bundesrat*, or federal council, an upper house that must approve all legislation affecting the states.

Leadership and Political Officials. Germany's most important political parties are the Christian Democratic Union and its Bavarian sister party, the Christian Social Union; the Social Democratic Party; the Free Democratic or Liberal Party; The Greens; and the Party of Democratic Socialism, the successor to the East German Socialist Unity Party. In 1993, the Greens merged with a party that originated in the East German citizens' movement, called Alliance 90. Since the late 1980s, various right-wing parties have occasionally received enough votes (at least 5 percent of the total) to gain seats in some of the regional parliaments. The growth of right wing parties is a result of political agitation, economic difficulties, and public concern over the increasing rate of immigration. The first free all-German national election since 1932 was held on 2 December 1990 and resulted in the confirmation of the ruling Christian Democratic/Free Democratic coalition, headed by Helmut Kohl, who was first elected in 1982. The Christian Democrats won again in 1994, but in the election of 1998, they were ousted by the Social Democrats, who formed a coalition government with Alliance 90 (the Greens). Like his then counterparts in the United States and Great Britain, Gerhard Schröder, the chancellor elected in 1998, described himself as the champion of the new political "middle."

Social Problems and Control. In the Federal Republic of Germany, police forces are authorized by the Departments of Interior of the sixteen federal states. Their activities are supplemented by the *Bundesgrenzschutz* (Federal Border Police) and the *Bundesamt für Verfassungsschutz* (Federal Office for the Protection of the Constitution). In the early twenty-first century, organized crime and violence by right-wing groups constituted the most serious domestic dangers.

Military Activity. The German armed forces are under the control of the civilian government and are integrated into the North Atlantic Treaty Organization (NATO). German men who are eighteen years of age are required to serve for ten to twelve months in the armed forces—or an equivalent length of time in volunteer civilian service. In 2000, Germans began a public debate about the restructuring of the armed forces.

Social Welfare and Change Programs

Germany's social welfare programs are among the oldest of any modern state. In 1881, the newly founded German Reich passed legislation for health insurance, accident insurance, and for invalid and retirement benefits. The obligation of the state to provide for the social welfare of its citizens was reinforced in the Basic Law of 1949. In the Federal Republic of Germany, the state supplements monthly payments made by citizens to health insurance, nursing care insurance, social security, and unemployment insurance. Beginning in the late twentieth century, questions were raised about the long-term viability of existing social welfare programs.

Nongovernmental Organizations and Other Associations

German society is structured by many different *Verbände*, or associations, which are often organized at federal, regional, and local levels. There are associations for business and industry, for workers and employees (unions), for social welfare, for environmental protection, and for a number of other causes or special interests. Through such associations, members seek to influence policy making or to act directly in order to bring about desired changes in society. Associations that contribute to public welfare typically operate according to the principle of subsidiarity. This means that the state recognizes their contribution and augments their budgets with subsidies.

In local communities in Germany, public life is often shaped to a large degree by *Vereine*, or voluntary associations, in which citizens pursue common

People fill a street in Lindau. Since the late 1970s, many inner-city areas have become pedestrian zones.

interests or seek to achieve public goals on the basis of private initiative. Such organizations often provide the immediate context for group formation, sociability, and the local politics of reputation.

Beginning in the late twentieth century, German society was strongly affected by the so-called new social movements, which were typically concerned with such issues as social justice, the environment, and peaceful coexistence among neighboring states. In the last years of the GDR, several civil rights groups emerged throughout the country and helped usher in the *Wende* (literally, turning or transition) in 1989 and 1990.

Gender Roles and Statuses

Division of Labor by Gender. With the transition from agricultural to industrial society in the late nineteenth and early twentieth century, women, who had been largely restricted to the domestic sphere, began to gain access to a wider range of economic roles. More than a century after this process began, women are represented all walks of life. Nevertheless, they are still more likely to be responsible for childcare and household management; and they are disproportionately represented among teachers, nurses, office workers, retail clerks, hair dressers, and building and window cleaners.

The Relative Status of Women and Men. The Basic Law of the Federal Republic of Germany states that men and women have equal rights under the law. Nevertheless, women did not enjoy juridical equality in marriage and the family until new family legislation was passed in 1977. Previously, family law, which had been influenced by the religious orientation of the Christian Democratic and Christian Social parties, had stated that women could seek outside employment only if this were consistent with their household duties. East German law had granted women equal rights in marriage, in the family, and in the workplace at a much earlier date. Needless to say, in both the Federal Republic and in the former GDR, the ideal of equality of opportunity for men and women was imperfectly realized. Even under conditions of full employment in East Germany, for example, women were under represented in leading positions in government, industry, and agricultural production.

Marriage, Family, and Kinship

Marriage. In Germany, the basic kinship group, as defined by law, is the nuclear family, consisting of opposite sex partners, usually married, and their children; and, in fact, the majority of households are made up of married couples with or without children. Between 1950 and 1997, however, there were fewer and fewer marriages both in total numbers and per capita. In 1950, there were a total of 750,000 marriages, or eleven marriages for every thousand persons; in 1997, by contrast, there were 423,000 marriages, or five marriages for every thousand persons. It is estimated that 35 percent of all marriages ended in divorce in the late twentieth century. In light of these facts, there has been much media speculation on the "crisis of the family," as has been the case in other industrial societies of western Europe and North America as well. Despite the increase in the number of unmarried couples, with or without children, such couples make up only 5 percent of all households. Nevertheless, the rising number of children who are born to unmarried mothers (currently 18 percent, lower than the European Union average), the rising divorce rate, and the growth of alternative forms of partnership have, since 1979, led to a broadening of the concept of family and a liberalization of family law and family policy.

Much more dramatic is the reduction of the birthrate. The annual number of deaths has been greater than the annual number of births since 1972. On the eve of reunification in 1990, there was an annual birthrate of 1,400 children per 1,000 women in West Germany and 1,500 children per 1,000 women in East Germany. In the new federal states of former East Germany, the birthrate had sunken to 1,039 children per 1,000 women by 1997. In both parts of Germany, the reduction of the birthrate is matched by a progressive reduction in the average size of households. In 1998, less than 5 percent of private households had five or more members. Since 1986, the Federal Republic of Germany has provided for the payment of *Kindergeld* (child-raising benefits) to families or single parents with children. As of January 1999, these payments were 250 marks (or approximately half that amount in dollars) per month for the first and second child up until his or her eighteenth birthday—and, in some cases, until the twenty-seventh birthday.

In the new federal states of former East Germany, there are fewer marriages and fewer children; but a disproportionately high number of children are born to unmarried couples. These differences between former East Germany and former West Germany may be attributed, in part, to the economic difficulties in the new federal states. Some of the differences, however, may be understood as lingering effects of the divergence of family law and social policy during the separation of the East and the West. In the GDR, the official policy of full employment for men and women was realized by providing women with benefits and services such as pregnancy leave, nursing leave, day-care centers, and kindergartens. In general, the family law of the GDR served to strengthen the position of women vis-á-vis men in their relationships to their children. With the cutback or elimination of such policies following the entry of the new federal states into the Federal Republic of Germany, there was both a greater hesitancy to have children and a greater tendency to view having children separately from marital status.

Kin Groups. A society the size of Germany lends itself to the statistical analysis of family relations. It is unfortunate, however, that official statistics direct attention so single-mindedly to the nuclear family or variations thereof (unmarried couples, single parents) and cause observers to overlook family ties with grandparents, grown siblings, cousins, and other consanguineal or affinal relatives. Nevertheless, it is clear that ties with more distant relatives are a vital part of kinship in Germany at the onset of the twenty-first century, as is especially evident on holidays, at key points in the lifecycle of individuals, and in large family projects such as moving.

Socialization

Child Rearing and Education. In Germany, infant care and child rearing correspond to typical western European and North American patterns. Childhood is viewed as a developmental stage in which the individual requires attention, instruction, affection, and a special range of consumer products. Child rearing is typically in the hands of the mother and father or the single parent, but here, especially, the importance of the extended family is evident. Variations in child rearing behavior by social class and social milieu are, however, less well studied than other aspects of adult behavior. In light of the critique of the "authoritarian personality" by the German sociologist Theodor Adorno and others, some middle-class parents have tried to practice an anti-authoritarian form of child rearing. Adorno and his colleagues thought that certain child rearing practices, especially strict and arbitrary discipline, encourage stereotypic thinking, submission to authority, and aggression against outsiders or deviants. In the past, they argued, the prevalence of such practices in Germany contributed to the success of National Socialism.

In most federal states, the school system divides pupils between vocational and university preparatory tracks. The vocational track includes nine years of school and further part-time vocational training, together with a paid or unpaid apprenticeship. The university preparatory track requires attendance of the humanistic *Gymnasium*, beginning in the fifth year of school, and successful completion of the *Abitur*, a university entrance examination.

Higher Education. Germany has many universities and technical colleges, almost all of which are self-administered institutions under the authority of the corresponding departments of the individual federal states. University study is still structured according to the humanistic ideals of the nineteenth century, which entrusts students with a great deal of independence. The assignment of grades, for example, is largely independent of class attendance. Grades are given for oral and written examinations, which are administered at the departmental level after the completion of the semester. Students of law and medicine begin with their chosen subject in the first year at the university and pursue relatively specialized courses of study. Admittance to popular

A cowherd leads cows down a rural road at Reit im Winkl, Germany. The cows wear flowered headdresses for an annual celebration.

major subjects is governed by the so-called *Numerus clausus,* which restricts the number of students, usually according to scores on college entrance examinations. German students pay no admission fees and are supported with monthly allowances or loans from the state.

Etiquette

It has often been noted that German society retains a small town ethos, which arose in the early modern period under conditions of political and economic particularism. Indeed, many Germans adhere to standards of *bürgerlichkeit,* or civic morality, which lend a certain neatness and formality to behavior in everyday life. When entering a store, for example, one is not likely to be noticed, unless one announces oneself forcefully by saying, "*guten Tag*" (literally, "good day") or "hello." In former East Germany, it is still common for friends and acquaintances to shake hands when they see each other for the first time each day. West Germans consider it more modern and perhaps more American not to do so. In pronouns of direct address, one uses either the formal *sie* or the informal *du.* Colleagues in the workplace typically address each other as Sie or use a title and the family name, such as, Herr or Frau Doktor Schmidt.

Life in public does not seem to be the highest good for all Germans, as urban centers often appear to be abandoned on Saturday afternoons and Sundays. This is linked to the issue of the operating hours of shops, which has been debated in Germany since the mid-1970s. For different reasons, both the unions and the churches opposed extended operating hours, as do many citizens, who are critical of "consumer societies" or who prefer, on the weekends, to remain with their families or in their private gardens.

Religion

Religious Beliefs. Germany was the homeland of the Protestant Reformation, but, in the politically fragmented Holy Roman Empire of the sixteenth century, many territories remained faithful to Roman Catholicism or reverted back to it, depending of the policy of the ruling house. Today, 34 percent of the population belongs to the Evangelical (Protestant) Church and a further 34 percent belongs to the Catholic Church. Many Germans have no religious affiliation. This is especially true of former East Germany, where, in 1989, the Evangelical Church had

4 million members (out of a total population of 16.5 million) and the Catholic Church had only 921,000 members. Since 1990, the Evangelical Church has lost even more members in the new federal states.

The Evangelical Church is a unified Protestant church, which combines Lutherans, Reformed Protestants, and United Protestants. Reformed Protestants adhere to a form of Calvinism, while United Protestants combine aspects of Lutheranism and Calvinism. Other Protestant denominations make up only a small fraction of the population. Most German Catholics live in the Rhineland or in southern Germany, whereas Protestants dominate in northern and central parts of the country.

In 1933, there were over 500,000 people of Jewish faith or Jewish heritage living within the boundaries of the German Reich. Between 1933 and 1945, German Jews, together with members of the far more numerous Jewish populations of eastern Europe, fell victim to the anti-Semitic and genocidal policies of the National Socialists. In 1997, there are an estimated sixty-seven thousand people of Jewish faith or heritage living in Germany. The largest Jewish congregations are in Frankfurt am Main and Berlin.

In the postwar era, migratory workers or immigrants from North Africa and western Asia established Islamic communities upon arriving in Germany. In 1987, there were an estimated 1.7 million Muslims living in West Germany.

Religious Practitioners. Religious practitioners in Germany include especially the Protestant or Catholic *pfarrer* (minister or priest). In local communities, the minister or priest belongs to the publicly acknowledged group of local notables, which also includes local governmental officials, school officials, and business leaders. Roman Catholic priests are, of course, local representatives of the international church hierarchy, which is centered in Rome. Protestant ministers represent Lutheran, Reformed, or United churches, which are organized at the level of the regional states. These state-level organizations belong, in turn, to the Evangelical Church of Germany.

Rituals and Holy Places. From the smallest village to the largest city, the local church dominates the central area of nearly every German settlement. German churches are often impressive architectural structures, which bear witness to centuries of growth and renovation. In predominantly Catholic areas, such as the Rhineland, Bavaria, and parts of Baden-Württemberg, the areas surrounding the towns and villages are typically strewn with shrines and chapels. The processions to these shrines, which were common until the late nineteenth and early twentieth centuries, have now been largely discontinued.

Despite processes of secularization, which had became intensive by the early nineteenth century, churches retained their importance in public life. Beginning in the 1840s, there was a popular movement to complete the Cologne cathedral, which was begun in the Middle Ages but which remained a construction site for 400 years. With the support of the residents of Cologne, the Catholic Church, and the King of Prussia (who was a Protestant), work on the cathedral was begun in 1842 and completed in 1880. The character of the ceremonies and festivals that accompanied this process indicate that the Cologne Cathedral served not only as a church but also as a national monument. Similarly, the national assembly of 1848, in which elected representatives met to draft a constitution for a united Germany, took place in St. Paul's Church in Frankfurt. (The national and constitutional movement failed when the Prussian king refused the imperial crown, which was offered to him by the representatives of the national assembly.) One of the centers of the popular movement that led to the fall of the GDR in 1989–1990 was the Nikolaikirche (St. Nicolas Church) in Leipzig.

Since the late nineteenth century, churches and other historical buildings in Germany have become the objects of *Denkmalpflege* (cultural preservation), which may be understood as one aspect of a broader culture of historical commemoration. Together with museums, historical monuments constitute a new set of special sites, which may be approached only with a correspondingly respectful attitude.

Graveyards and war memorials occupy a kind of middle ground between holy sites and historical monuments. All settlements in Germany have graveyards, which surviving family members visit on special holidays or on private anniversaries. War memorials from World War I are also ubiquitous. Monuments to World War II often have a very different character. For example, the concentration camp Buchenwald, near Weimar, has, since the early 1950s, served as a commemorative site, which is dedicated to the victims of the National Socialist regime.

Death and the Afterlife. Nearly 70 percent of Germans are members of a Christian church, and many of these share common Christian beliefs in *himmel* (heaven) and *hölle* (hell) as destinations of the soul after death. Many other Germans describe themselves as agnostics or atheists, in which case they view beliefs in an afterlife as either potentially misleading or false. Funerary rites involve either a church service or a civil ceremony, depending on the beliefs of the deceased and his or her survivors.

Medicine and Health Care

Germans were among the leaders in the development of both Western biomedicine and national health insurance. Biomedical health care in Germany is extensive and of high quality. In addition to having advanced medical technology, Germans also have a large number of medical doctors per capita. In 1970, there was one medical doctor for every 615 people, while in 1997, there was one medical doctor for every 290. Forty-one percent of doctors are in private practice, while 48 percent are in hospitals, and 12 percent are in civil service or in similar situations.

In medical research, there is an emphasis on the so-called *zivilisationskrankheiten* (diseases of the "civilized" lands), that is, heart disease and cancer. In 1997, heart disease caused 47 percent of all deaths in former West Germany and 52 percent of deaths in former East Germany. In the same year, cancer was responsible for 25 percent of all deaths in former West Germany and 23 percent of deaths in former East Germany.

Alongside biomedicine, there is a strong German tradition of naturopathic medicine, including especially water cures at spas of various kinds. Water cures have been opposed by some members of the German biomedical establishment but are still subsidized to some extent by statutory health insurance agencies.

Secular Celebrations

German holidays are those of the Roman calendar and the Christian liturgical year. Especially popular are *Sylvester* (New Year's), *Karneval* or *Fastnacht* (Mardi Gras), *Ostern* (Easter), *Himmelfahrt* (Ascension Day), *Pfingsten* (Pentecost), Advent, and *Weihnachten* (Christmas). The new national holiday is 3 October, the *Tag der deutschen Einheit* (Day of German Unity).

The Arts and Humanities

Support for the Arts. The arts in Germany are financed, in large measure, through subsidies from state and local government. Public theaters, for example, gained 26 percent of their revenues from ticket sales in 1969–1970 but only 13.6 percent in 1996–1997. Public subsidies have been threatened in the late twentieth and early twenty-first centuries by budget cuts, which have been accompanied by calls for more sponsorship by private industry. In the new federal states of former East Germany, the once very dense network of theaters and concert halls has been reduced dramatically. In Saxony, for example, the *Kulturraumgesetz* of 1994 (legislation for the creation of arts regions) requires neighboring communities to pool their resources, as, for example, when one community closes its concert hall but retains its theater, while another does just the opposite. Concert- or theatergoers are then required to travel about within the region, in order to take advantage of the full arts program. Still, many major and some minor German cities have excellent theater ensembles, ballets, and opera houses. Berlin and Munich are especially important centers for the performing arts.

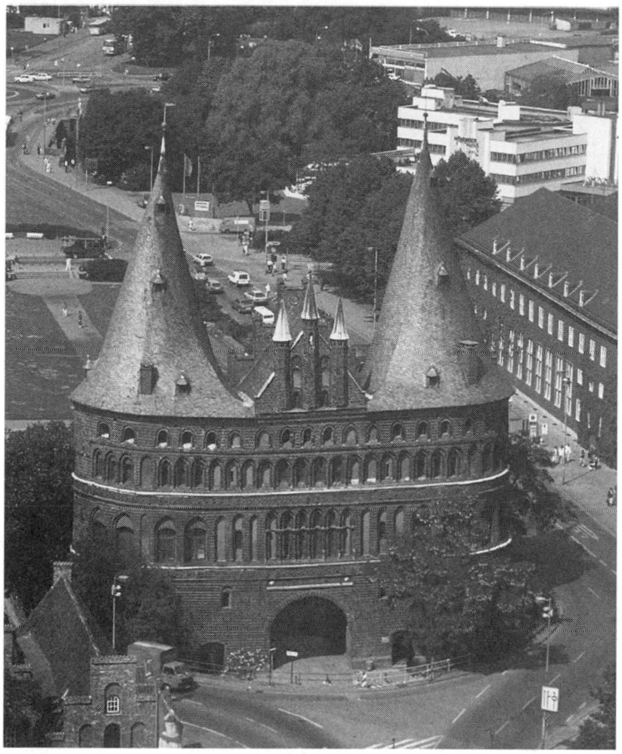

The Holstentor and Holsten gate, built between 1469 and 1478, in Lubeck, Germany.

Literature. Germany was a *Kulturnation*, that is, a nation sharing a common language and literature, before it became a nation-state. As is well known, the printing press was invented by Johannes Gutenberg (c. 1400–1468) in Mainz about a half a century before the onset of the Protestant Reformation.

The Luther Bible, written in the vernacular German of Upper Saxony, spread throughout the German-speaking world and helped to create a national reading public. This reading public emerged among the educated bourgeoisie in the Age of Enlightenment (eighteenth century). Important aspects of this public sphere were newspapers, literary journals, reading societies, and salons. The classical phase in the history of German literature, however, came during the transition from the Enlightenment to Romanticism, the two most important figures being Johann Wolfgang von Goethe (1749–1832) and Friedrich von Schiller (1759–1809). The nineteenth century saw a dramatic expansion of the publishing industry and the literary market and the blossoming of all modern literary genres. Following World War II, there was a split between the literary spheres of East and West Germany. German reunification began with an acrimonious debate over the value of East German literature.

Graphic Arts. German artists have contributed to every era in the history of the graphic arts, especially the Renaissance (Albrecht Dürer), Romanticism (Caspar David Friedrich), and Expressionism (the Brücke and the Blaue Reiter).

Performance Arts. Germans are especially well-known for their contributions in the area of classical music, and the heritage of great German or Austrian composers such as Johann Sebastian Bach, Wolfgang Amadeus Mozart, Ludwig von Beethoven, Johannes Brahms, Richard Wagner, and Gustav Mahler is still cultivated in concert halls throughout the country. Germans developed an innovative film industry in the Weimar Republic, but its greatest talents emigrated to the United States in the 1930s. In East Germany, Babelsberg was the home of DEFA (*Deutsche Film-Aktiengesellschaft*), an accomplished film company. With the help of extensive public subsidies, a distinctive West German cinema emerged in the 1970s. Since then, however, attempts to reinvigorate the German film industry have proven difficult, in light of the popularity of products from Hollywood.

The State of the Physical and Social Sciences

In the course of the nineteenth century, German scientists and scholars cultivated distinct national traditions in the physical sciences, the humanities, and the social sciences, which served, in turn, as important models for other countries. Since the end of the World War II, however, science and scholarship in Germany have become internationalized to such a degree that it is problematic to speak of *deutsche Wissenschaft* (German Science), as was once common. The most important centers for science and scholarship in Germany today are the universities, independent research institutes, such as those sponsored by the Max Planck Society, and private industry.

Bibliography

Adorno, Theodor W., et al. *The Authoritarian Personality*, 1982.

Anderson, Benedict. *Imagined Communities: Reflections on the Origin and Spread of Nationalism*, Rev. Ed., 1991.

Beyme, Klaus von, Werner Durth, Niels Gutschow, Winfried Nerdinger, and Thomas Topfstedt, eds. *Neue Städte aus Ruinen: Deutscher Städtebau der Nachkriegszeit*, 1992.

Blackbourn, David. *The Long Nineteenth Century: A History of Germany, 1780–1918*, 1998.

Blitz, Hans-Martin. *Aus Liebe zum Vaterland: Die Deutsche Nation im 18. Jahrhundert*, 2000.

Borneman, John. *Belonging in the Two Berlins: Kin, State, Nation*, 1992.

Brubaker, Rogers. *Citizenship and Nationhood in France and Germany*, 1992.

Buse, Dieter K., and Jürgen Dörr. *Modern Germany: An Encyclopedia of History, People, and Culture, 1871–1990*, 1998.

Chickering, Roger. *We Men Who Feel Most German: A Cultural Study of the Pan-German League, 1886–1914*, 1984.

Craig, Gordon A. *Germany, 1866–1945*, 1978.

———. *The Germans*, 1991.

Dann, Otto. *Nation und Nationalismus in Deutschland, 1770–1990*, 1993.

Elias, Norbert. *The Germans: Power Struggles and the Development of Habitus in the Nineteenth and Twentieth Centuries.*

———. *The Civilizing Process*, Rev. Ed., 2000.

Forsythe, Diana. "German Identity and the Problem of History." In E. Tonkin, M. McDonald, and M. Chapman, eds., *History and Ethnicity*, 1989.

Francois, Etienne, and Hannes Siegrist, eds. *Nation und Emotion: Deutschland und Frankreich im Vergleich im 19. und 20. Jahrhundert*, 1995.

Hermand, Jost. *Old Dreams of a New Reich: Völkisch Utopias and National Socialism*, 1992.

Hobsbawm, Eric, and Terence Ranger, eds. *The Invention of Tradition*, 1984.

Iggers, Georg G. *The German Conception of History: The National Tradition of Historical Thought from Herder to the Present*, Rev. Ed., 1983.

Koonz, Claudia. *Mothers in the Fatherland*, 1987.

Lowie, Robert H. *Toward Understanding Germany*, 1954.

Maier, Charles. *The Unmasterable Past: History, Holocaust, and German National Identity*, 1988.

Merkel, Ina. *Utopie und Bedürfnis: Die Geschichte der Konsumkultur in der DDR*, 1999.

Mosse, George L. *The Nationalization of the Masses: Political Symbolism and Mass Movements in Germany from the Napoleonic Wars through the Third Reich*, 1975.

Nipperdey, Thomas. *Germany from Napoleon to Bismarck*, 1996.

Peukert, Detlev J. *Inside Nazi Germany: Conformity, Opposition, and Racism in Everyday Life*, 1989.

Schulze, Gerhard. *Die Erlebnisgesellschaft: Kultursoziologie der Gegenwart*, 4th ed., 1993.

Sheehan, James J. *German History, 1770–1866*, 1989.

Siegrist, Hannes. "From Divergence to Convergence: The Divided German Middle Class, 1945–2000." In O. Zunz, ed., *Social Contracts Under Stress*, 2001.

Tacitus, Cornelius. *Agricola; and Germany*, 1999.

Ten Dyke, Elizabeth. "Memory, History and Remembrance Work in Dresden." In D. Berdahl, M. Bunzl, and M. Lampland, eds., *Altering States: Ethnographies of Transition in Eastern Europe and the Former Soviet Union*, 1999.

Tipton, Frank B. *Regional Variations in the Economic Development of Germany During the Nineteenth Century*, 1976.

Walker, Mack. *German Home Towns*, 1971.

—JOHN EIDSON

GHANA

CULTURE NAME

Ghanaian

ALTERNATIVE NAME

Formally known as the Republic of Ghana

ORIENTATION

Identification. Ghana, formerly the British colony of the Gold Coast, assumes a special prominence as the first African country to acquire independence from European rule. Ghanaian politicians marked this important transition by replacing the territory's colonial label with the name of a great indigenous civilization of the past. While somewhat mythical, these evocations of noble origins, in combination with a rich cultural heritage and a militant nationalist movement, have provided this ethnically diverse country with unifying symbols and a sense of common identity and destiny. Over forty years of political and economic setbacks since independence have tempered national pride and optimism. Yet, the Ghanaian people have maintained a society free from serious internal conflict and continue to develop their considerable natural, human, and cultural resources.

Location and Geography. Ghana is located on the west coast of Africa, approximately midway between Senegal and Cameroon. It is bordered by Côte d'Ivoire (Ivory Coast), Burkina Faso, Togo, and the Atlantic Ocean. The land surface of 92,100 square miles (238,540 square kilometers) is dominated by the ancient Precambrian shield, which is rich in mineral resources, such as gold and diamonds. The land rises gradually to the north and does not reach an altitude of more than 3,000 feet (915 meters). The Volta River and its basin forms the major drainage feature; it originates in the north along two widely dispersed branches and flows into the sea in the eastern part of the country near the Togolese border. The Volta has been dammed at Akosombo, in the south, as part of a major hydroelectric project, to form the Lake Volta. Several smaller rivers, including the Pra and the Tano, drain the regions to the west. Highland areas occur as river escarpments, the most extensive of which are the Akwapim-Togo ranges in the east, the Kwahu escarpment in the Ashanti region, and the Gambaga escarpment in the north.

Ghana's subequatorial climate is warm and humid, with distinct alternations between rainy summer and dry winters. The duration and amount of rainfall decreases toward the north, resulting in a broad differentiation between two regions—southern rain forest and northern savanna—which form distinct environmental, economic, and cultural zones. The southern forest is interrupted by a low-rainfall coastal savanna that extends from Accra eastward into Togo.

Demography. The population in 2000 was approximately 20 million and was growing at a rate of 3 percent per year. Approximately two-thirds of the people live in the rural regions and are involved in agriculture. Settlement is concentrated within the "golden triangle," defined by the major southern cities of Accra (the capital), Kumasi, and Sekondi-Takoradi. Additional concentrations occur in the northernmost districts, especially in the northeast. The population is almost exclusively African, as Ghana has no history of intensive European settlement. There is a small Lebanese community, whose members settled in the country as traders. Immigration from other African countries, notably Burkina Faso, Togo, Liberia, and Nigeria, is significant. Some of the better established immigrant groups include many Ghanaian-born members, who are nevertheless classified as "foreign" according to Ghana's citizenship laws.

Linguistic Affiliation. Ghana's national language is English, a heritage of its former colonial status. It is the main language of government and instruc-

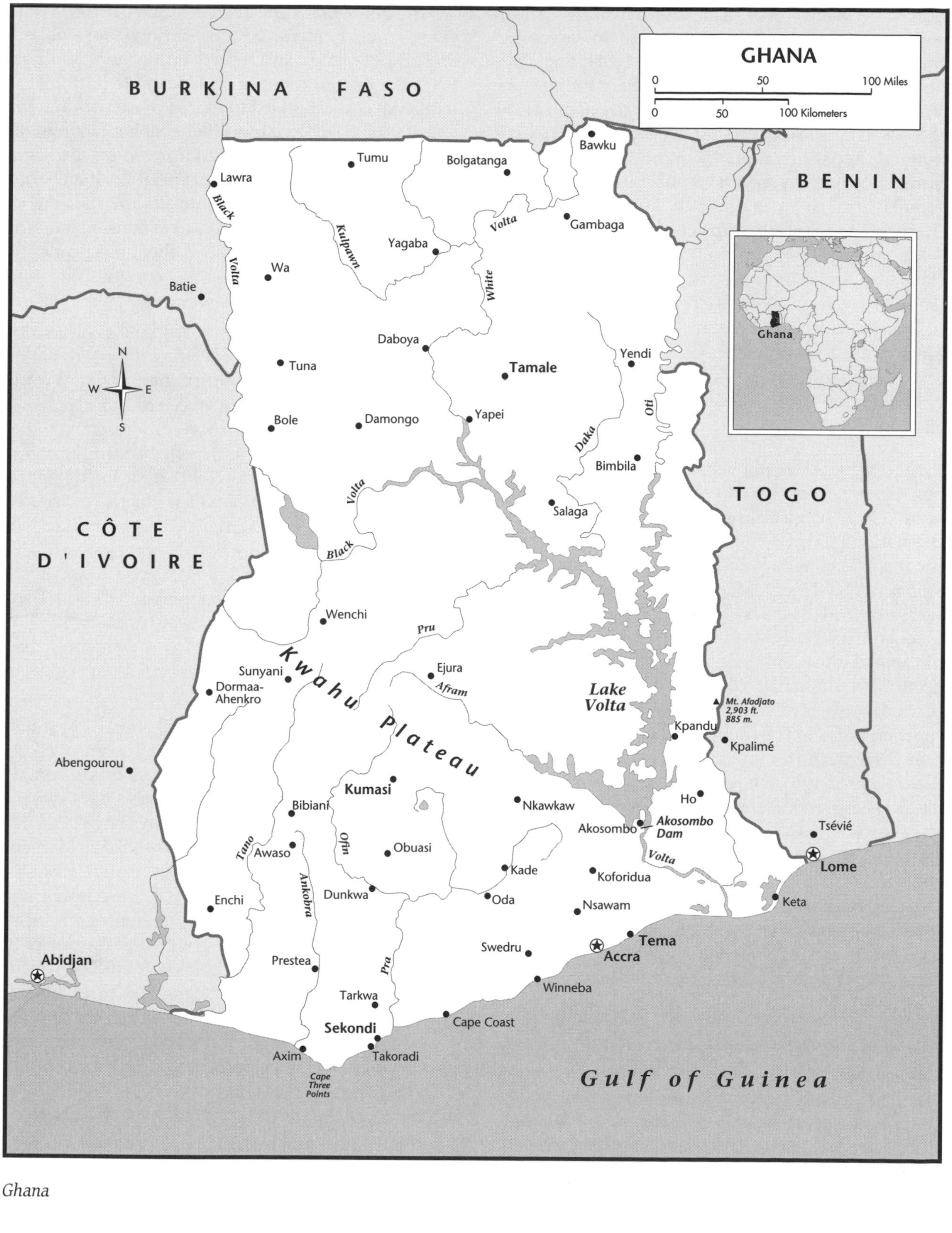

GHANA
0 50 100 Miles
0 50 100 Kilometers
BURKINA FASO
BENIN
TOGO
CÔTE D'IVOIRE
Gulf of Guinea
Ghana
N
W
E
S
Bawku
Tumu
Bolgatanga
Lawra
Gambaga
Black
Volta
Kulpawn
Yagaba
Volta
Wa
White
Batie
Daboya
Yendi
Tuna
Tamale
Yapei
Oti
Bole
Damongo
Daka
Bimbila
Volta
Salaga
Black
Wenchi
Pru
Kwahu Plateau
Sunyani
Dormaa-Ahenkro
Ejura
Afram
Lake Volta
Mt. Afadjato 2,903 ft. 885 m.
Kpandu
Kpalimé
Abengourou
Kumasi
Bibiani
Nkawkaw
Ho
Akosombo
Akosombo Dam
Tsévié
Tano
Awaso
Ofin
Obuasi
Volta
Lome
Kade
Koforidua
Ankobra
Dunkwa
Oda
Keta
Enchi
Nsawam
Tema
Accra
Swedru
Abidjan
Prestea
Pra
Winneba
Tarkwa
Cape Coast
Sekondi
Axim
Takoradi
Cape Three Points

Ghana

tion. Ghanaians speak a distinctive West African version of English as a standard form, involving such usages as chop (eat) and dash (gift). English is invariably a second language. Mother tongues include over sixty indigenous languages. Akan is the most widely spoken and has acquired informal national language status. In addition to the large number of native speakers, many members of other groups learn Akan as a second language and use it fluently for intergroup communication. Ga-Adangme and Ewe are the next major languages. Hausa, a Nigerian language, is spoken as a trade language among peoples from the north. Many Ghanaians are multilingual, speaking one or two indigenous languages beside their native dialects and English. Although Ghana is bounded by francophone nations on all sides, few Ghanaians are proficient in French.

Symbolism. As a relatively new nation, Ghana has not developed an extensive tradition of collective symbols. Its most distinctive emblems originated in the nationalist movement. The most prominent is the black star, which evokes black pride and power and a commitment to pan-African unity, which were central themes for mobilizing resistance against British rule. It is featured on the flag and the national coat of arms, and in the national anthem. It is also the name of Ghana's soccer team and is proudly displayed in Black Star Square, a central meeting point in the capital. Other important symbols derive from Akan traditions that have become incorporated into the national culture. These include the ceremonial sword, the linguist's staff, the chief's stool, and the talking drum. Ghanaian national dress, *kente* cloth, is another source of common identity and pride. It is handwoven into intricate patterns from brilliantly colored silk. Men drape it around their bodies and women wear it as a two-pieced outfit. The main exports—gold and cocoa—also stand as identifying symbols.

HISTORY AND ETHNIC RELATIONS

Emergence of the Nation. Ghana is a colonial creation, pieced together from numerous indigenous societies arbitrarily consolidated, and sometimes divided, according to European interests. There is no written documentation of the region's past prior to European contact. By the time the Portuguese first established themselves on the coast in the fifteenth century, kingdoms had developed among various Akan-speaking and neighboring groups and were expanding their wealth, size, and power. The Portuguese quickly opened a sea route for the gold trade, and the emergence of the "Gold Coast" quickly attracted competition from Holland, England, France, and other European countries. With the development of American plantation systems, slaves were added to the list of exports and the volume of trade expanded. The Ashanti kingdom emerged as the preeminent Akan political force and established its rule over several neighboring groups and into the northern savanna. Some indigenous states on the margins of Ashanti expansion, such as Akim and Akwapem, retained their independence. Coastal peoples were able to resist conquest through alliances with European powers.

In the nineteenth century, England assumed dominance on the coast and developed a protectorate over the local African communities. England came into conflict with Ashanti over coastal expansion and the continuation of the slave trade. At the end of the nineteenth century, it defeated Ashanti and established the colony of the Gold Coast, including the coastal regions, Ashanti, and the Northern Territories beyond. The boundaries of this consolidation, which included many previously separate and independent kingdoms and tribal communities, were negotiated by the European powers to suit their strategic and economic interests. After 1918, England further complicated this arrangement by annexing the trans-Volta region from German Togoland as a spoil of World War I.

The colony was administered under the system of indirect rule, in which the British controlled affairs at the national level but organized local control through indigenous rulers under the supervision of colonial district commissioners. Western investment, infrastructure, and institutional development were concentrated in the urban complexes that emerged within the coastal ports. Educational and employment opportunities were created for Africans, mostly from coastal communities, but only for the purpose of staffing the lower echelons of the public and commercial sectors. The rural masses were disadvantaged by the colonial regime and the exactions of their chiefs but gained some degree of wealth and local development through the growth of a lucrative export trade in cocoa, especially in the forest zone. The north received little attention.

Resistance to British rule and calls for independence were initiated from the onset of colonial rule. Indigenous rulers formed the initial core of opposition, but were soon co-opted. The educated Westernized coastal elite soon took up the cause, and the independence movement remained under their control until the end of World War II. After the war, nationalists formed the United Gold Coast Convention and tried to broaden their base and take advantage of mass unrest that was fed by demobilization, unemployment, and poor commodity prices. They brought in Kwame Nkrumah, a former student activist, to lead this campaign. Nkrumah soon broke ranks with his associates and formed a more radical movement though the Convention People's Party. He gained mass support from all parts of the colony and initiated strikes and public demonstrations that landed him in jail but finally forced the British to grant independence. The Gold Coast achieved home rule in 1951. On 6 March 1957 it became the self-governing country of Ghana, the first sub-Saharan colony to gain independence. In the succeeding decades, Ghana experienced a lot of political instability, with a series of coups and an alternation between civilian and military regimes.

National Identity. In spite of its disparate origins and arbitrary boundaries, Ghana has developed a modest degree of national coherence. British rule in itself provided a number of unifying influences, such as the use of English as a national language and a core of political, economic, and service institutions. Since independence, Ghanaian leaders have strengthened national integration, especially through the expansion of the educational system and the reduction of regional inequalities. They have also introduced new goals and values through the rhetoric of the independence movement, opposition to "neo-colonialist" forces, and advocacy of pan-Africanism. A second set of common traditions stem from indigenous cultures, especially from the diffusion of Akan institutions and symbols to neighboring groups.

Ethnic Relations. Ghana contains great diversity of ethnic groups. The Akan are the most numerous, consisting of over 40 percent of the population. They are followed by the Ewe, Ga, Adangme, Guan, and Kyerepong in the south. The largest northern groups are the Gonja, Dagomba, and Mamprussi, but the region contains many small decentralized communities, such as the Talensi, Konkomba, and Lowiili. In addition, significant numbers of Mossi from Burkina Faso have immigrated as agricultural and municipal workers. Nigerian Hausa are widely present as traders.

Intergroup relations are usually affable and Ghana has avoided major ethnic hostilities and pressure for regional secession. A small Ewe separatist movement is present and some localized ethnic skirmishes have occurred among small communities in the north, mostly over boundary issues. There is, however, a major cultural divide between north and south. The north is poorer and has received less educational and infrastructural investment. Migrants from the region, and from adjoining areas of Burkina Faso, Togo, and Nigeria typically take on menial employment or are involved in trading roles in the south, where they occupy segregated residential wards called *zongos*. Various forms of discrimination are apparent.

Urbanism, Architecture, and the Use of Space

Although Ghana is primarily a rural country, urbanization has a long tradition within indigenous and modern society. In the south the traditional settlement was a nucleated townsite that served as a king's or a chief's administrative base and housed the agricultural population, political elite, and occupational specialists. In precolonial times, populations in these centers ranged from a few hundred to several thousand in a major royal capital, such as Kumasi, which is now Ghana's second largest city. Traditional political nodes also served economic functions concentrated in open-air marketplaces, which still constitute a central feature of traditional and modern towns. Housing consists of a one-story group of connected rooms arranged in a square around a central courtyard, which serves as the primary focus of domestic activity. The chief's or king's palace is an enlarged version of the basic household. Settlement in the north follows a very different pattern of dispersed farmsteads.

The British administration introduced Western urban infrastructures, mainly in the coastal ports, such as Accra, Takoradi, and Cape Coast, a pattern that postcolonial governments have followed. Thus central districts are dominated by European-style buildings, modified for tropical conditions. Neither regime devoted much attention to urban planning or beautification, and city parks or other public spaces are rare. Accra contains two notable monuments: Black Star Square and the Kwame Nkrumah Mausoleum, symbols of Ghana's commitment to independence and African unity.

Much of the vibrancy of urban life is due to the incorporation of indigenous institutions, especially within the commercial sector. Commerce is dominated by open-air markets, such as the huge Markola market in Accra, where thousands of traders offer local and imported goods for sale. Although the very wealthy have adopted Western housing styles, most urban Ghanaians live in traditional dwellings, in which renters from a variety of backgrounds mingle in central courtyards in much

A man builds a small granary from wood and straw for his village in Ghana. The country's economy is primarily agricultural.

the same way that family members do in traditional households. Accordingly, marketplaces and housing compounds provide the predominant settings for public interaction.

FOOD AND ECONOMY

Food in Daily Life. The basic diet consists of a starchy staple eaten with a soup or stew. Forest crops, such as plantain, cassava, cocoyam (taro), and tropical yams, predominate in the south. Corn is significant, especially among the Ga, and rice is also popular. The main dish is *fufu*, pounded plantain or tubers in combination with cassava. Soup ingredients include common vegetables and some animal protein, usually fish, and invariably, hot peppers. Palm nut and peanut soups are special favorites. The main cooking oil is locally produced red palm oil. The northern staple is millet, which is processed into a paste and eaten with a soup as well. Indigenous diets are eaten at all social levels, even by the Westernized elite. Bread is the only major European introduction and is often eaten at breakfast. Restaurants are not common outside of urban business districts, but most local "chop bars" offer a range of indigenous dishes to workers and bachelors. People frequently snack on goods offered for sale by street hawkers.

Food Customs at Ceremonial Occasions. Most households raise chickens and dwarf goats, which are reserved for special occasions, such as christenings, weddings, traditional festivals, and Christmas. Among the Akan, the main indigenous celebration is *odwira*, a harvest rite, in which new yams are presented to the chief and eaten in public and domestic feasts. The Ga celebrate *homowo*, another harvest festival, which is marked by eating *kpekpele*, made from mashed corn and palm oil. Popular drinks include palm wine, made from the fermented sap of the oil palm, and home-brewed millet beer. Bottled European-style beer is widely consumed. Imported schnapps and whiskey have important ceremonial uses as libations for royal and family ancestors.

Basic Economy. Ghana's position in the international economy reflects a heavy dependence on primary product exports, especially cocoa, gold, and timber. International trade accounts for one-third of gross domestic product (GDP), and 70 percent of export income is still derived from the three major commodities. The domestic economy is primarily agricultural with a substantial service and trading sector. Industrial production comprises only 10 percent of national output, and consumers are heavily dependent upon imported manufactures as well as petroleum imports.

Land Tenure and Property. Traditional land use patterns were organized around a slash-and-burn system in which crops were grown for two or three years and then fallowed for much longer periods. This system fostered communal land tenure systems, in which a large group, usually the lineage, held the land in trust for its members and allocated usufruct rights on demand. In the south, reserved lands, known as stool lands, were held by the chief for the wider community. The stool also held residual rights in lineage-owned land, for instance a claim on any gold found. In the north, communal rights were invested in a ritual figure, the *tendana,* who assumed the ultimate responsibility for agriculture rituals and land allocation.

In modern times, land tenure has been widely affected by cocoa farming and other commercial uses, which involve a permanent use of the land and a substantial expansion in demand for new plots. Land sales and long-term leases have developed in some areas, often on stool reserves. Purchased lands are considered private rather than family or communal property and activate a different inheritance pattern, since they can be donated or willed without reference to the standard inheritance rule.

Government regulation of land title has normally deferred to traditional arrangements. Currently, a formally constituted Lands Commission manages government-owned lands and gold and timber reserve leases and theoretically has the right to approve all land transfers. Nevertheless, most transactions are still handled informally according to traditional practice.

Commercial Activities. While strongly export oriented, Ghanaian farmers also produce local foods for home consumption and for a marketing system that has developed around the main urban centers. Rural household activities also include some food processing, including palm oil production. The fishery is quite important. A modern trawler fleet organizes the offshore catch and supplies both the domestic and overseas markets. Small-scale indigenous canoe crews dominate the inshore harvest and supply the local markets. Traditional crafts have also had a long tradition of importance for items such as pottery, handwoven cloth, carved stools, raffia baskets, and gold jewelry. There are also many tailors and cabinetmakers.

Major Industries. Manufactured goods are dominated by foreign imports, but some local industries have developed, including palm oil milling, aluminum smelting, beer and soft drink bottling, and furniture manufacturing. The service sector is dominated by the government on the high end and the small-scale sector, sometimes referred to as the "informal sector," on the low end. Education and health care are the most important public services. Transport is organized by small-scale owner-operators. Construction is handled by the public, private, or small-scale sector depending upon the nature of the project.

Trade. Cocoa is grown by relatively small-scale indigenous farmers in the forest zone and is exclusively a commercial crop. It is locally marketed through private licensed traders and exported through a public marketing board. Gold is produced by international conglomerates with some Ghanaian partnership. Much of the income from this trade is invested outside the country. Timber is also a large-scale formal-sector enterprise, but there is a trend toward developing a furniture export industry among indigenous artisans. Other exports include fish, palm oil, rubber, manganese, aluminum, and fruits and vegetables. Internal trade and marketing is dominated by small-scale operations and provides a major source of employment, especially for women.

Division of Labor. Formal sector jobs, especially within the public service, are strictly allocated on the basis of educational attainment and paper qualifications. Nevertheless, some ethnic divisions are noticeable. Northerners, especially Mossi, and Togolese hold the more menial positions. Hausa are associated with trade. Kwahu are also heavily engaged in trade and also are the main shopkeepers. Ga and Fante form the main fishing communities, even along the lakes and rivers removed from their coastal homelands. Age divisions are of some importance in the rural economy. Extended family heads can expect their junior brothers, sons, and nephews to assume the major burdens of manual labor.

SOCIAL STRATIFICATION

Classes and Castes. Ghana's stratification system follows both precolonial and modern patterns. Most traditional kingdoms were divided into three hereditary classes: royals, commoners, and slaves. The royals maintained exclusive rights to fill the central offices of king and, for Akan groups, queen mother. Incumbents acquired political and economic privileges, based on state control over foreign trade. Unlike European nobilities, however, special status was given only to office-holders and not their extended families, and no special monopoly over land

A busy street in Kumasi. Ghana's urban centers are dominated by European-style buildings, a reminder of its British colonizers.

was present. Moreover, royals regularly married commoners, a consequence of a rule of lineage out-marriage. Freemen held a wide variety of rights, including unhampered control over farm land and control over subordinate political positions. Slavery occurred mainly as domestic bondage, in which a slave could command some rights, including the ability to marry a nonslave and acquire property. Slaves were also used by the state for menial work such as porterage and mining.

Slavery is no longer significant. Traditional royalties are still recognized but have been superseded by Westernized elites. Contemporary stratification is based on education and, to a lesser degree, wealth, both of which have led to significant social mobility since independence. Marked wealth differences have also emerged, but have been moderated by extended family support obligations and the communal rights that most Ghanaians hold in land. Northerners, however, form a noticeable underclass, occupying low status jobs. Bukinabe and Togolese are especially disadvantaged because, as foreigners, they cannot acquire land.

Symbols of Social Stratification. In traditional practice, kings and other hereditary officials marked their status through the use of regalia, such as umbrellas and staves, and the exclusive right to wear expensive clothing, such as kente cloth, and to consume and distribute special imported goods. In modern times, expenditure on Western consumer items has become the dominant status marker. Clothing, both expensive Western and traditional items, is an important symbol of education and wealth. Luxury cars are also significant—a Mercedes-Benz is the most dominant marker of high rank. Status must also be demonstrated in public display, especially in lavish funerals that acclaim both the deceased and their descendants.

Political Life

Government. Although Ghana's national government was originally founded on a British parliamentary model, the current constitution follows an American tricameral system. The country is a multiparty democracy organized under an elected president, a legislature, and an independent judiciary. It is divided into ten administrative regions, exclusively staffed from the central government. Regions are further subdivided into local districts, organized under district assemblies. The majority of assembly members are elected, but some seats are allocated to traditional hereditary rulers. Chiefs also assume the major responsibility for traditional affairs, including stool land transfers, and are significant actors in local political rituals. They are also represented in the National House of Chiefs, which formulates general policies on traditional issues.

Leadership and Political Officials. Indigenous leaders assume hereditary positions but still must cultivate family and popular support, since several candidates within a descent line normally compete for leadership positions. Chiefs can also be deposed. On the national level, Ghana has been under military rule for a good part of its history, and army leadership has been determined by both rank and internal politics. Civilian leaders have drawn support from a variety of fronts. The first president, Nkrumah, developed a dramatic charisma and gave voice to many unrepresented groups in colonial society. K. A. Busia, who followed him after a military interregnum, represented the old guard and also appealed to Ashanti nationalism. Hillal Limann, the third president, identified himself as an Nkrumahist, acquiring power mainly through the application of his professional diplomatic skills. Jerry Rawlings, who led Ghana for 19 years, acquired power initially through the military and was able to capitalize on his position to prevail in civil elections in 1992 and 1996. He stepped down in 2000, and his party was defeated by the opposition, led by John Kufuor.

Ghana has seven political parties. Rawlings National Democratic Party is philosophically leftist and advocates strong central government, nationalism and pan-Africanism. However, during the major portion of its rule it followed a cautious economic approach and initiated a World Bank structural adjustment, liberalization, and privatization program. The current ruling party (as of 2001) is the New Patriotic Party. It has assumed the mantle of the Busia regime and intends to pursue a more conservative political and economic agenda than the previous regime.

Secular politicians are dependent upon the electorate and are easily approachable without elaborate ceremony. Administrators in the public service, however, can be quite aloof. Traditional Akan chiefs and kings are formally invested with quasi-religious status. Their subjects must greet them by prostrating themselves and may talk to them only indirectly through the chief's "linguist."

Social Problems and Control. The Ghanaian legal system is a mixture of British law, applicable to criminal cases, and indigenous custom for civil cases. The formal system is organized under an independent judiciary headed by a supreme court. Its independence, however, has sometimes been compromised by political interference, and, during Rawling's military rule, by the establishment of separate public tribunals for special cases involving political figures. These excesses have since been moderated, although the tribunal system remains in place under the control of the Chief Justice. Civil cases that concern customary matters, such as land, inheritance, and marriage, are usually heard by a traditional chief. Both criminal and civil laws are enforced by a national police force.

People are generally wary of the judicial system, which can involve substantial costs and unpredictable outcomes. They usually attempt to handle infractions and resolve disputes informally through personal appeal and mediation. Strong extended family ties tend to exercise a restraint on deviant behavior, and family meetings are often called to settle problems before they become public. Marital disputes are normally resolved by having the couple meet with the wife's uncle or father, who will take on the role of a marriage counselor and reunite the parties.

Partially because of the effective informal controls, the level of violent crime is low. Theft is the most common infraction. Smuggling is also rampant, but is not often prosecuted since smugglers regularly bribe police or customs agents.

Military Activity. Ghana's military, composed of about eight thousand members, includes an army and a subordinate navy and air force. There is also the People's Militia, responsible for controlling civil disturbances, and a presidential guard. Government support for these services is maintained at approximately 1 percent of GDP. The army leadership has demonstrated a consistent history of coups and formed the national government for approximately half of the time that the country has been independent. Ghana has not been involved in any wars since World War II and has not suffered any civil violence except for a few localized ethnic and sectarian skirmishes. It has participated in peacekeeping operations, though the United Nations, the Organization of African Unity, and the West African Community. The most recent interventions have been in Liberia and Sierra Leone.

Social Welfare and Change Programs

Ghana is a low income country with a per capita GDP of only $400 (U.S.) per year. It has many economic and social problems especially in the areas of employment, housing, health, and sanitation.

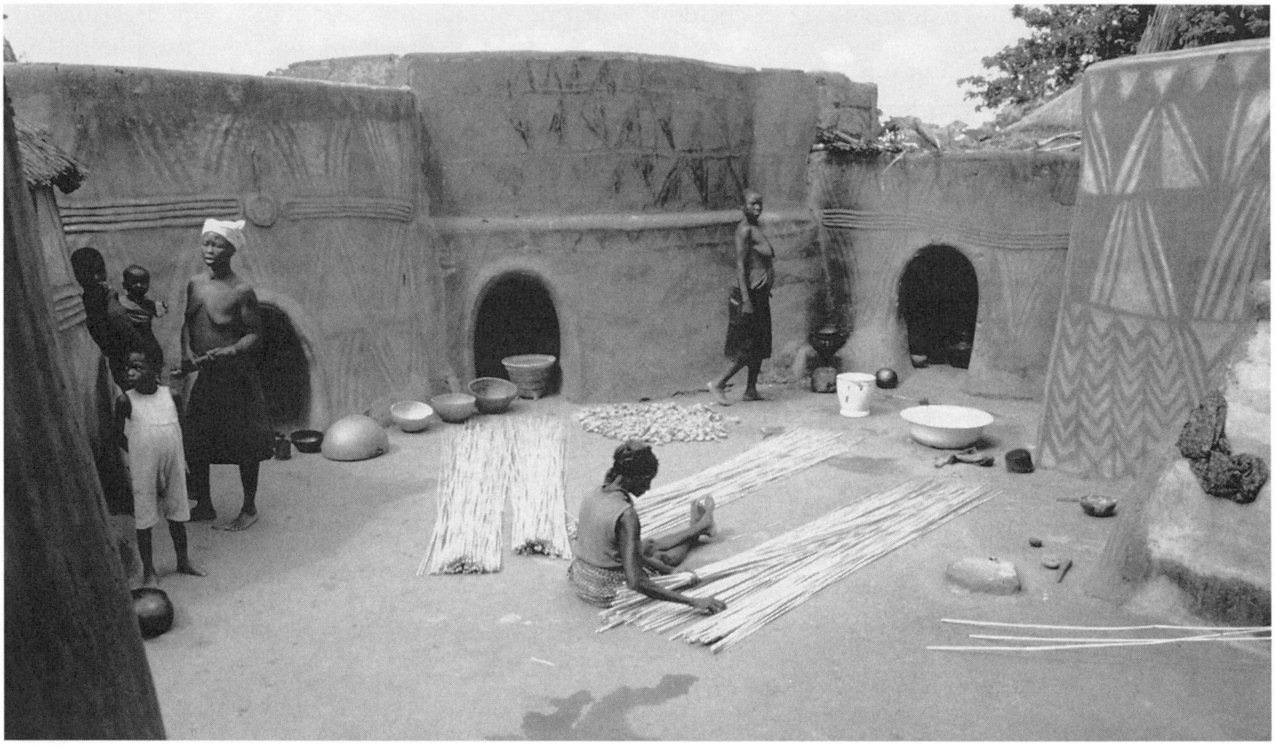

Painted huts enclose a courtyard where a woman weaves mats from millet stalks. Such courtyards serve as the primary focus of domestic activity.

The major thrust of development policy since 1985 has the World Bank–supported Economic Recovery Program, a structural adjustment strategy to liberalize macroeconomic policy. The core initiatives have been expansion and diversification of export production, reduction of government expenditures, especially in the public service, and privatization of state industries. As part of this program, the government instituted a special project to address the attendant social costs of these policies. It involved attempts to increase employment through public works and private-sector expansion, supported by business loans to small-scale entrepreneurs and laid-off public servants. Women were particularly targeted as beneficiaries.

Nongovernmental Organizations and Other Associations

Ghana has an active Nongovernmental Organization (NGO) sector, with over 900 registered organizations that participate in welfare and development projects in health, education, microfinancing, women's status, family planning, child care, and numerous other areas. The longest standing groups have been church-based organizations and the Red Cross. Most are supported by foreign donors. Urban voluntary associations, such as ethnic and occupational unions, also offer important social and economic assistance.

Gender Roles and Statuses

Division of Labor by Gender. Gender division varies across different ethnic groups. Among the Akan, women assume the basic domestic and child-care roles. Both genders assume responsibility for basic agriculture production, although men undertake the more laborious tasks and women the more repetitive ones. Women will work on their husbands' farms but will also farm on their own. Traditional craft production is divided according to gender. Men are weavers, carvers, and metalworkers. Women make pottery and engage in food processing. Petty trade, which is a pervasive economic activity, is almost exclusively a woman's occupation. Women independently control any money that they receive from their own endeavors, even though their husbands normally provide the capital funding. Wives, however, assume the main work and financial responsibility for feeding their husbands and children and for other child-care expenses.

Akan women also assume important social, political, and ritual roles. Within the lineage and extended family, female elders assume authority, predominantly over other women. The oldest women are considered to be the ablest advisers and the repositories of family histories.

Among the Ga and Adangme, women are similarly responsible for domestic chores. They do not do any farmwork, however, and are heavily engaged in petty trade. Ga women are especially prominent traders as they control a major portion of the domestic fish industry and the general wholesale trade for Accra, a Ga homeland. Northern and Ewe women, on the other hand, have fewer commercial opportunities and assume heavier agricultural responsibilities in addition to their housekeeping chores.

The Relative Status of Women and Men. In traditional society, women had considerable economic and political powers which derived in part from their ability to control their own income and property without male oversight. Among the matrilineal Akan they also regularly assumed high statuses within the lineage and the kingdom, even though their authority was often confined to women's affairs. Colonialism and modernization has changed women's position in complex ways. Women have retained and expanded their trading opportunities and can sometimes acquire great wealth through their businesses. Men have received wider educational opportunities, however, and are better represented in government and formal sector employment. A modest women's movement has developed to address gender differences and advance women's causes.

Marriage, Family, and Kinship

Marriage. Tradition dictates that family elders arrange the marriages of their dependents. People are not allow to marry within their lineages, or for the Akan, their wider clan groups. There is a preference, however, for marriage between cross-cousins (children of a brother and sister). The groom's family is expected to pay a bride-price. Polygyny is allowed and attests to the wealth and power of men who can support more than one wife. Chiefs mark their status by marrying dozens of women. Having children is the most important focus of marriage and a husband will normally divorce an infertile wife. Divorce is easily obtained and widespread, as is remarriage. Upon a husband's death, his wife is expected to marry his brother, who also assumes responsibility for any children.

The spread of Western values and a cash economy have modified customary marriage patterns. Christians are expected to have only one wife. Monogamy is further supported by the ability of men to marry earlier than they could in traditional society because of employment and income opportunities in the modern sector. Young men and women have also been granted greater latitude to choose whom they marry. Accordingly, the incidence of both polygyny and cousin marriage is low. There is, however, a preference for marriages within ethnic groups, especially between people from the same town of origin.

Domestic Unit. The basic household group is formed on a complex set of traditional and contemporary forces. Akan custom allows for a variety of forms. The standard seems to have been natalocal, a system in which each spouse remained with his or her family of origin after marriage. Children would remain with their mothers and residential units would consist of generations of brothers, sisters, and sisters' children. Wives, however, would be linked to their husbands economically. Men were supposed to provide support funds and women were supposed to cook for their husbands. Alternative forms were also present including avunculocal residence, in which a man would reside with his mother's brother upon adulthood, and patrilocality, in which children would simply remain with their fathers upon adulthood. In all of these arrangements men would assume the basic role of household head, but women had some power especially if they were elderly and had many younger women under their authority.

The Akan domestic arrangements are based on matrilineal principles. All other Ghanaian ethnic groups are patrilineal and tend toward patrilocal residence. The Ga, however, have developed an interesting pattern of gender separation. Men within a lineage would live in one structure, and their wives and unmarried female relatives would live in a nearby one. In the north, patrilocal forms were complicated by a high incidence of polygynous marriage. A man would assign a separate hut to each of his wives, and, after their sons married, to each of their wives. The man would act has household head but delegate much of the domestic management to his wives, especially senior wives with several daughters-in-law.

Modern forces have influenced changes in domestic forms. Western values, wage employment, and geographical mobility have led to smaller and more flexible households. Nuclear families are now more numerous. Extended family units are still the rule, but they tend to include relatives on an ad hoc basis rather than according to a fixed residence rule.

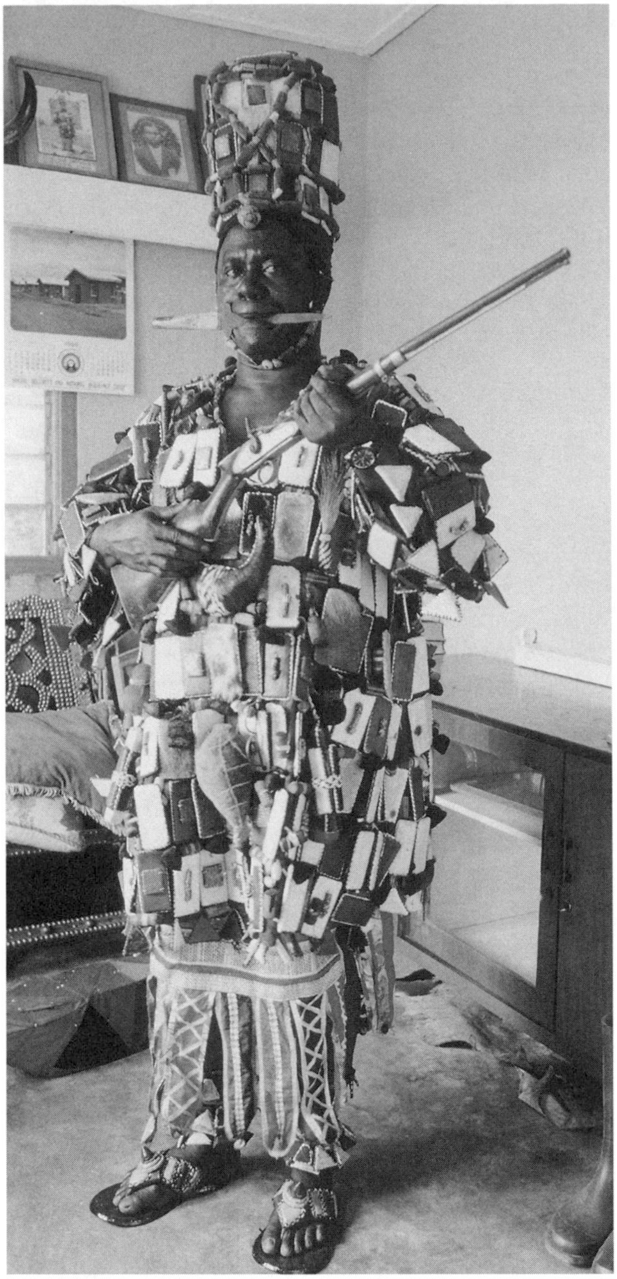

A Fanti chief. Elaborate regalia is a hallmark of traditional kings and officials.

Sibling bonds are strong, and household heads will often include younger brothers and sisters and nieces and nephews from either side of the family within their domestic units. They may also engage resident domestic help, who are often relatives but may come from other families. Important economic bonds continue to unite extended kin who live in separate physical dwellings but still share responsibilities to assist one another and sometimes engage in joint enterprises.

Inheritance. Most Ghanaian inheritance systems share two features: a distinction between family and individual property and a preference for siblings over children as heirs. Among the matrilineal Akan, family property is inherited without subdivision, in the first instance by the oldest surviving brother. When the whole generation of siblings dies out, the estate then goes to the eldest sister's eldest son. Women can also inherit, but there is a preference for men's property to pass on to other men and women's to other women. Private property can be passed on to wives and children of the deceased through an oral or written will. In most cases, it will be divided equally among wives, children, and matrilineal family members. Private property passed on to a child remains private. If it is inherited within the matrilineage, it becomes family property. Among patrilineal groups, sibling inheritance applies as well, but the heir will be expected to support the children of the deceased. If he assumes responsibility for several adult nephews he will invariably share the estate with them.

Kin Groups. Localized, corporate lineage groups are the basic units of settlement, resource ownership, and social control. Among the Akan, towns and villages are comprised of distinct wards in which matrilineal descendants (*abusua*) of the same ancestress reside. Members of this group jointly own a block of farmland in which they hold hereditary tenure rights. They usually also own the rights to fill an office in the settlement's wider administration. The royal lineage holds title to the chief's and queen mother's position. Lineages have an internal authority structure under the male lineage elder (*abusua panyin*), who decides on joint affairs with the assistance of other male and female elders. The lineage is also a ritual unit, holding observances and sacrifices for its important ancestors. Patrilineal groups in Ghana attach similar economic, political, and ritual importance to the lineage system.

Socialization

Infant Care. Young children are treated with affection and indulgence. An infant is constantly with its mother, who carries it on her back wrapped in a shawl throughout the day. At night it sleeps with its parents. Breast-feeding occurs on demand and may continue until the age of two. Toilet training and early discipline are relaxed. Babies receive a good deal of stimulation, especially in social contexts. Siblings, aunts, uncles, and other relatives take a keen interest in the child and often assume caretaking responsibilities, sometimes on an extended basis.

Child Rearing and Education. Older children receive considerably less pampering and occupy the bottom of an age hierarchy. Both boys and girls are expected to be respectful and obedient and, more essentially, to take significant responsibilities for domestic chores, including tending their younger siblings. They are also expected to defer to adults in a variety of situations.

Coming of age is marked within many Ghanaian cultures by puberty ceremonies for girls that must be completed before marriage or childbirth. These are celebrated on an individual rather than a group basis. Boys have no corresponding initiation or puberty rites. Most children attend primary school, but secondary school places are in short supply. The secondary system is based mainly on boarding schools in the British tradition and resulting fees are inhibitive. Most adolescents are engaged in helping on the farm or in the family business in preparation for adult responsibilities. Many enter apprenticeships in small business operations in order to learn a trade. The less fortunate take on menial employment, such as portering, domestic service, or roadside hawking.

Higher Education. Only a tiny percentage of the population has the opportunity to enter a university or similar institution. University students occupy a high status and actively campaign, sometimes through strikes, to maintain their privileges. Graduates can normally expect high-paying jobs, especially in the public sector. Attendance at overseas institutions is considered particularly prestigious.

ETIQUETTE

Ghanaians place great emphasis on politeness, hospitality, and formality. Upon meeting, acquaintances must shake hands and ask about each other's health and families. Visitors to a house must greet and shake hands with each family member. They are then seated and greeted in turn by all present. Hosts must normally provide their guests with something to eat and drink, even if the visit does not occur at a mealtime. If a person is returning from or undertaking a long journey, a libation to the ancestors is usually poured. If someone is eating, he or she must invite an unexpected visitor to join him or her. Normally, an invitation to eat cannot be refused.

Friends of the same age and gender hold hands while walking. Great respect is attached to age and social status. A younger person addresses a senior as father or mother and must show appropriate deference. It is rude to offer or take an object or wave with the left hand. It is also rude to stare or point at people in public. Such English words as "fool(ish)," "silly," or "nonsense," are highly offensive and are used only in extreme anger.

RELIGION

Religious Beliefs. Christianity, Islam, and traditional African religions claim a roughly equal number of adherents. Christians and Muslims, however, often follow some forms of indigenous practice, especially in areas that do not directly conflict with orthodox belief. Moreover, some Christian sects incorporate African elements, such as drumming, dancing, and possession.

Traditional supernatural belief differs according to ethnic group. Akan religion acknowledges many spiritual beings, including the supreme being, the earth goddess, the higher gods (*abosom*), the ancestors, and a host of spirits and fetishes. The ancestors are perhaps the most significant spiritual force. Each lineage reveres its important deceased members both individually and collectively. They are believed to exist in the afterlife and benefit or punish their descendants, who must pray and sacrifice to them and lead virtuous lives. Ancestral beliefs are also built into political rites, as the ancestors of the royal lineage, especially deceased kings and chiefs, serve as major foci for general public observance.

Religious Practitioners. The abosom are served by priests and priestess (*akomfo*), who become possessed by the god's spirit. In this state, they are able to divine the causes of illnesses and misfortunes and to recommend sacrifices and treatments to remedy them. They have also played an important role in Akan history. Okomfo Anokye was a priest who brought down the golden stool, the embodiment of the Ashanti nation, from heaven. Lesser priests and priestesses serve the shrines of fetishes, minor spirits, and focus on cures and magic charms. Family elders also assume religious functions in their capacity as organizers of ancestral rites. Chiefs form the focus of rituals for the royal ancestors and assume sacred importance in their own right as quasi-divine beings.

Other ethnic groups also worship through the intercession of priests and chiefs. Ga observances focus on the *wulomei*, the priests of the ocean, inlets, and lagoons. Their prayers and sacrifices are essential for successful fishing and they serve as advisers to Ga chiefs. In the modern context, the Nai Wulomo, the chief priest, assumes national importance because of his responsibility for traditional ritual in Accra, Ghana's capital. In the north, the *tendana*, priests of the earth shrines, have been the

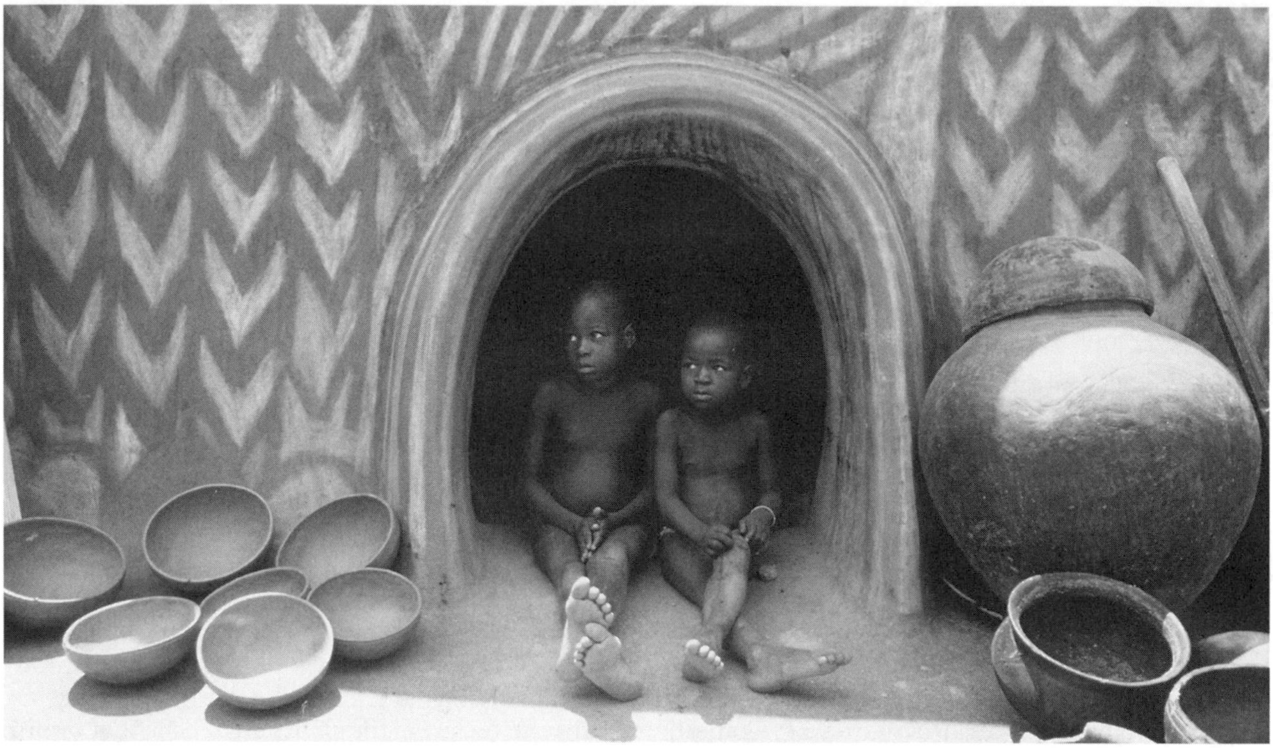

Children taking shelter from the midday heat. Located just north of the equator, Ghana has a warm, humid climate.

key figures of indigenous religion. They are responsible for making sacrifices for offenses against the earth, including murder, for rituals to maintain land productivity, and for allocating unowned land.

Rituals and Holy Places. The most important rituals revolve around the cycle of ancestral and royal observances. The main form is the *adae* ceremony, in which prayers are made to the ancestors through the medium of carved stools that they owned in their lifetimes. These objects are kept in a family stool house and brought out every six weeks, when libations are poured and animals sacrificed. Royal stools are afforded special attention. The *adae* sequence culminates in the annual *odwira* festival, when the first fruits of the harvest are given to the abosom and the royal ancestors in large public ceremonies lasting several days. Royal installations and funerals also assume special ritual importance and are marked by sacrifices, drumming, and dancing.

Death and the Afterlife. Death is one of the most important events in society and is marked by most ethnic groups and religions by elaborate and lengthy funeral observances that involve the whole community. People were traditionally buried beneath the floors of their houses, but this custom is now practiced only by traditional rulers, and most people are interred in cemeteries. After death, the soul joins the ancestors in the afterworld to be revered and fed by descendants within the family. Eventually the soul will be reborn within the same lineage to which it belonged in its past life. People sometimes see a resemblance to a former member in an infant and name it accordingly. They may even apply the relevant kinship term, such as mother or uncle, to the returnee.

Medicine and Health Care

Ghana has a modern medical system funded and administered by the government with some participation by church groups, international agencies, and NGOs. Facilities are scarce and are predominantly located in the cities and large towns. Some dispensaries staffed by nurses or pharmacists have been established in rural areas and have been effective in treating common diseases such as malaria.

Traditional medicine and medical practitioners remain important because of the dearth of public facilities and the tendency for Ghanaians to patronize indigenous and modern systems simultaneously. Customary treatments for disease focus equally on supernatural causes, the psychosociological environment, and medicinal plants. Abosom priests and priestesses deal with illness through prayer, sacrifice, divination, and herbal cures. Keepers of fetish shrines focus more heavily on magical charms and herbs, which are cultivated in a garden adjoining the god's inclosure. More secularly oriented herbalists focus primarily on medicinal plants that they grow, gather from the forest, or purchase in the marketplace. Some members of this profession specialize in a narrow range of conditions, for example, bonesetters, who make casts and medicines for broken limbs.

Some interconnections between the modern and traditional systems have developed. Western trained doctors generally adopt a preference for injections in response to the local belief that medicines for the most serious diseases must be introduced into the blood. They have also been investigating the possible curative efficacy of indigenous herbs, and several projects for developing new drugs from these sources have been initiated.

Secular Celebrations

Aside from the major Christian and Islamic holidays, Ghana celebrates New Year's Day, Independence Day (6 March), Worker's Day (1 May), Republic Day (1 July), and Revolution Day (31 December). New Year's Day follows the usually western pattern of partying. Independence Day is the main national holiday celebrating freedom from colonial rule and is marked by parades and political speeches. The remaining holidays are also highly politicized and provide forums for speeches by the major national leaders. Revolution Day is especially important for the ruling party as it marks the anniversary of Rawlings' coup.

The Arts and the Humanities

Support for the Arts. The arts are primarily self supporting, but there are some avenues of government financing and sponsorship. The publically funded University of Ghana, through the Institute for African Studies, provides a training ground for artists, especially in traditional music and dance, and hosts an annual series of public performances. The government also regularly hosts pan-African arts festivals, such as PANAFEST, and sends Ghanaian artists and performers to similar celebrations in other African countries.

Literature. While there is a small body of written literature in indigenous languages, Ghanaians maintain a rich oral tradition, both through glorification of past chiefs and folktales enjoyed by popular audiences. Kwaku Ananse, the spider, is an especially well-known folk character, and his clever and sometimes self-defeating exploits have been sources of delight across generations. Literature in English is well developed and at least three authors, Ayi Kwei Armah, and Efua Sutherland, and Ama Ata Aiddo, have reached international audiences.

Graphic Arts. Ghana is known for a rich tradition of graphic arts. Wood carving is perhaps the most important. The focus of the craft is on the production of stools that are carved whole from large logs to assume the form of abstract designs or animals. These motifs generally represent proverbial sayings. The stools are not merely mundane items, but become the repositories of the souls of their owners after death and objects of family veneration. Carving is also applied to the production of staves of traditional office, drums, dolls, and game boards. Sculpting in metal is also important and bronze and iron casting techniques are used to produce gold weights and ceremonial swords. Ghanaians do not make or use masks, but there are some funerary effigies in clay. Pottery is otherwise devoted to producing simple domestic items. Textiles are well developed, especially handwoven kente, and stamped *adinkra* cloths.

Most of the traditional crafts involve artists who work according to standardized motifs to produce practical or ceremonial items. Purely aesthetic art is a modern development and there is only a small community of sculptors and painters who follow Western models of artistic production.

Performance Arts. Most performances occur in the context of traditional religious and political rites, which involve intricate drumming and dancing. While these are organized by trained performers, a strong emphasis on audience participation prevails. Modern developments have encouraged the formation of professional troupes, who perform on public occasions, at international festivals, and in theaters and hotel lounges. The University of Ghana houses the Ghana Dance Ensemble, a national institution with an international reputation. More popular modern forms focus on high life music, a samba-like dance style, which is played in most urban nightclubs.

The State of the Physical and Social Sciences

Ghana's economy is not able to support a robust research and development infrastructure. Scientific developments are modest and focus on the most critical practical concerns. The major research establishment is located in Ghana's three universities and in government departments and public corporations. Research in the physical sciences is heavily focused on agriculture, particularly cocoa. The Kwame Nkrumah University of Science and Technology in Kumasi concentrates on civil and industrial engineering and medicine. The Ministry of Health also has an active research agenda, which is complemented by World Health Organization activities. Social sciences focus on economic and development issues. The Institute for Statistical, Social, and Economic Research at the University of Ghana has conducted numerous surveys on rural and urban production and income patterns and on household economies and child welfare. The government statistical service carries out demographic and economic research into such areas as income distribution and poverty. Demographic issues are also investigated through the Population Impact Project at the University of Ghana. Education research and development forms another major concern and is the focus for activities at Ghana's third higher education facility, the University of Cape Coast.

Bibliography

Abu, Katherine. "Separateness of Spouses: Conjugal Resources in an Ashanti Town." In Christine Oppong, ed., *Female and Male in West Africa*, 1983.

Apter, David. *The Gold Coast in Transition*, 1955.

Armstrong, Robert. *Ghana Country Assistance Review: A Review of Development Effectiveness*, 1996.

Asabere, Paul K. "Public Policy and the Emergent African Land Tenure System." *Journal of Black Studies* 24(3): 281–290, 1994.

Berry, LaVerle, ed. *Ghana, a Country Study*, 3rd ed., 1994.

Busia, K. A. *The Position of the Chief in the Modern Political System of the Ashanti: A Study of the Influence of Contemporary Social Change on Ashanti Political Institutions*, 1951.

———. "The Ashanti." In Daryl Forde, ed., *African Worlds*, 1954.

Essien, Victor. "Sources of Law in Ghana." *Journal of Black Studies* 24 (3): 246–263, 1994.

Field, M. J. *Religion and Medicine of the Ga People*, 1937.

———. *Social Organization for the Ga People*, 1940.

Fitch, Robert. *Ghana: End of an Illusion*, 1966.

Fortes, Meyer. *The Dynamics of Clanship among the Talensi*, 1945.

———. "Kinship and Marriage among the Ashanti." In A. R. Radcliffe-Brown and D. Forde, eds., *African Systems of Kinship and Marriage*, 1950.

Goody, Jack. *The Social Organisation of the LoWiili*, 1956.

———. *Changing Social Structure in Ghana*, 1975.

Hill, Polly. *Migrant Cocoa Farmers of Southern Ghana*, 1963.

Jeong, Ho-Won. "Ghana: Lurching toward Economic Rationality." *World Affairs* 159 (2): 643–672, 1996.

———. "Economic Reform and Democratic Transition in Ghana." *World Affairs* 160 (4): 218–231, 1998.

Kaye, Barrington. *Bringing Up Children in Ghana*, 1962.

Lentz, Carola, and Paul Nugent. *Ethnicity in Ghana: The Limits of Invention*, 2000.

Loxley, John. *Ghana: Economic Crisis and the Long Road to Recovery*, 1988.

Manoukian, Madeline. *Tribes of the Northern Territories of the Gold Coast*, 1951.

———. *Akan and Ga-Adangme Peoples*, 1964.

McCall, D. "Trade and the Role of the Wife in a Modern West African Town." In Aidan Southall, ed., *Social Change in Modern Africa*, 1961.

Metcalfe, George. *Great Britain and Ghana: Documents of Ghana History*, 1964.

Nugent, Paul. "Living in the Past: Urban, Rural, and Ethnic Themes in the 1992 and 1996 Elections in Ghana." *Journal of Modern African Studies* 37 (2): 287–319, 1999.

Nukunya, G. A. *Tradition and Change among the Anlo Ewe*, 1969.

Rattray, Robert S. *Ashanti*, 1923.

———. *Ashanti Law and Constitution*, 1929.

Robertson, Claire. *Sharing the Same Bowl? A Socioeconomic History of Women and Class in Accra*, 1984.

Schildkrout, Enid. *People of the Zongo: the Transformation of Ethnic Identities in Ghana*, 1978.

Schwimmer, Brian. "Market Structure and Social Organization in a Ghanaian Marketing System." *American Ethnologist* 6 (4): 682–702, 1979.

———. "The Organization of Migrant-Farmer Communities in Southern Ghana." *Canadian Journal of African Studies* 14 (2): 221–238, 1980.

Vercruijsse, Emile. *The Penetration of Capitalism: A West African Case Study*, 1984.

Wilks, Ivor. *Asante in the Nineteenth Century: The Structure and Evolution of a Political Order*, 1975.

———. *Forests of Gold: Essays on the Akan and the Kingdom of Assante*, 1993.

Web Sites

Aryeetey, Ernest. "A Diagnostic Study of Research and Technology Development in Ghana," 2000. http://www.oneworld.org/thinktank/rtd/ghana1.htm

—Brian Schwimmer

GIBRALTAR

CULTURE NAME

Gibraltarian

ALTERNATIVE NAMES

Yanito (self-name), Llanito, Gibraltareño

ORIENTATION

Identification. The name "Gibraltar" derives from "Tariks Mountain," after Tariq-Ibn-Zayid, the Muslim conqueror who invaded the Iberian peninsula in 711. Although Gibraltar is a multiethnic and a multireligious society, its citizens identify themselves as having a common culture based on common history and territoriality, intermarriage, mutual tolerance, and their status as British colonial subjects.

Location and Geography. Gibraltar is a tiny territory of 4 square miles (6.5 square kilometers) at the southern tip of the Iberian peninsula. The territory consists mainly of rock.

Demography. Among the thirty thousand inhabitants, about twenty-five thousand have the status of British Gibraltarians, two thousand are other British citizens (mainly military), and two thousand are Moroccan workers. There are some Indian and Pakistani workers and about one hundred Russian citizens.

Linguistic Affiliation. The official language is English. Locally, Yanito, an Andalusian-based creole language with many English, Italian, Hebrew, and Maltese words, is spoken. Minority languages include Sindhi and Arabic.

Symbolism. Gibraltarians share a strong sense of unity that is expressed in several cultural symbols: traditional housing arrangements, a common school system, and the Yanito language. A fervent interest in beauty contests is an expression of national identity. Since the early 1990s, much energy has been invested in the creation of national symbolism (the anthem and flag). National Day is celebrated on 10 September to commemorate the pro-British referendum of 1967. The most powerful symbol is the Rock itself, which possesses symbolic meaning in British imperial iconography and is linked to the fortress mentality of Gibraltarians. Like the Rock, the apes of Gibraltar are symbols of British permanence and solidity.

HISTORY AND ETHNIC RELATIONS

Emergence of the Nation. Gibraltar is a colony, not a nation, yet there is a strong nationalist movement that fights for political self-determination as a part of the United Kingdom or a state within the European Union.

National Identity. Nationalist aspirations are the result of two circumstances: the fight for a non-English-based British identity and opposition toward neighboring Spain, whose territorial claim opposes Gibraltarian self-determination. National identity is not based on an ideology of purity but on positively valuing hybridity and multiethnicity.

Ethnic Relations. Gibraltarians include Catholic, Protestant, Jewish, Hindu, and a few Muslim citizens. They were linked to the population of the Spanish hinterland through common customs and intensive intermarriage until 1969, when Spain closed the border for thirteen years. Today this kind of common borderland society is almost nonexistent. While the Sephardic Jews have always been an integrated part of Gibraltar, they tend to segregate themselves. By contrast, the Hindu community politically and culturally has integrated more fully. Moroccan workers are largely excluded from civil society.

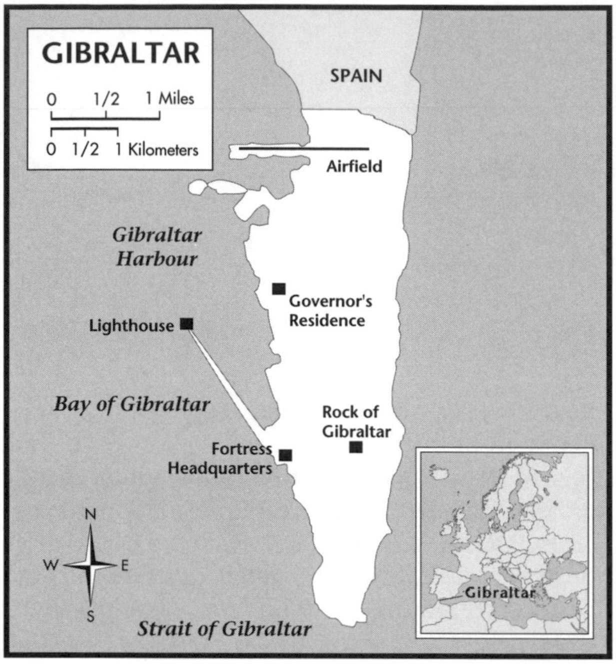

Gibraltar

Urbanism, Architecture, and the Use of Space

Space has always been a problem. Housing is limited by military requirements. Until the military cutback in the 1990s, only 20 percent of the territory was accessible to civilians. Gibraltar's edifices are influenced by British military architecture and by Genoese housing style (also known as ''patios''). Until the 1980s, most Gibraltarians lived densely packed in patios. After the opening of the border in 1982, many wealthier citizens purchased houses in the Spanish hinterland. In the 1990s, enough land was reclaimed from the sea to build extensive housing estates.

Food and Economy

Food in Daily Life. Food is a British-Mediterranean mixture with strong roots in Spanish, Italian, English, and Jewish cuisine. There are no general food taboos within the different religious groups.

Food Customs at Ceremonial Occasions. Calentita, a chickpea pie of Genoese origin, is the national dish.

Basic Economy. Until recently, the local economy depended on the military economy and smuggling (mainly of tobacco). In the 1980s and early 1990s, the economy underwent a heavy transformation and now is based on tourism, the harbor and shipping facilities, and the financial offshore sector. The principal exports are petroleum and manufactured goods. The major trading partners are the United Kingdom, Morocco, Portugal, the Netherlands, Spain, the United States, and Germany. The national currency is the Gibraltar pound.

Land Tenure and Property. Land has been largely in the hands of the British government (92 percent of land and housing in the 1960s). Between 1985 and 1996, 296,663 acres (20.5 percent of the territory) were handed over to the local government. Many Gibraltarians buy property in Spain.

Commercial Activities. Gibraltar is a duty-free harbor. The major goods sold are tobacco, alcohol, perfume, dairy products, and electronics.

Major Industries. Gibraltar is home to the light-manufacturing of tobacco, roasted coffee, ice, mineral waters, candy, beer, and canned fish. Tourism, banking and finance (mostly off-shore), and construction form the larger areas of manufacture, with Gibraltar's main source of industry its support of large UK naval and air bases.

Division of Labor. After the border was closed in 1969, blue-collar jobs were filled by Moroccan migrant workers who replaced the Spanish workforce. Today many Spaniards work on the Rock as shop assistants or cleaning women. Gibraltarians work mainly in the service sector (trade, financial sector, tourism). About 50 percent of young Gibraltarians obtain their education in British universities.

Social Stratification

Classes and Castes. The upper strata consist of a few families of Genoese origin. The upper middle class consists of Catholic, Jewish, and Hindu merchants and lawyers. The working class is made up of families of Spanish, Maltese, and Italian origin. The lower strata consists of Hindu shop assistants of Indian or Pakistani nationality and Moroccan workers. During the time of economical transformation (1980s–1990s), many unemployed and unskilled youth made a living smuggling.

Symbols of Social Stratification. Proper English pronunciation is a symbol of upward social mobility. Suits and ties are symbols of white-collar jobs. Among youngsters, smuggler-type iconography is highly valued.

A donkey grazes outside a farmhouse in Gibraltar. Most of the colony's four square miles of land consists of rock.

Political Life

Government. Gibraltar is a British colony with a local government. The British Crown is represented by a governor. The government is headed by a chief minister and seven ministers who are responsible for most domestic affairs (with the exception of internal security).

Leadership and Political Officials. Politics is strongly influenced by "big men" and a client-based structure based on class but cross-cut by families, personal loyalties, and friendships. The more bourgeois Social Democratic Party forms the government, with socialists and liberals in the opposition. Even though they diverge on domestic affairs and strive for different kinds of links with Britain, all parties strongly reject the Spanish claim to Gibraltar.

Social Problems and Control. The formal mechanisms for dealing with crime are British law, the police system, and the judiciary. Gibraltar can be described as a society of lawyers and trustees. The crime rate is low, and there are strong mechanisms of social control, owing to the small size of the territory and the face-to-face character of its society.

Military Activity. Gibraltar's function as a British military garrison has influenced all aspects of its society. This changed to some extent after the withdrawal of British forces in the 1990s. Today a local regiment of three hundred soldiers is stationed on the Rock.

Social Welfare and Change Programs

Only citizens are entitled to social welfare; this policy excludes Spanish, Moroccan, and Indian workers. To counter the effects of the military cutback, conversion programs partly financed by the European Union have been instituted.

Nongovernmental Organizations and Other Associations

The colony has many social, economical, sports, and leisure associations, such as the Parents Association, the Clergy Fraternal of Gibraltar, the Bankers Association, the Teachers Association, the Hindu Association, the Gibraltar Business Network, the Students Association, the Association of Accountants, the Woman Association, the Spear Fishing Federation, the Gibraltar Sub Aqua Club, the Association of Trust and Company Managers, GA/JPMS,

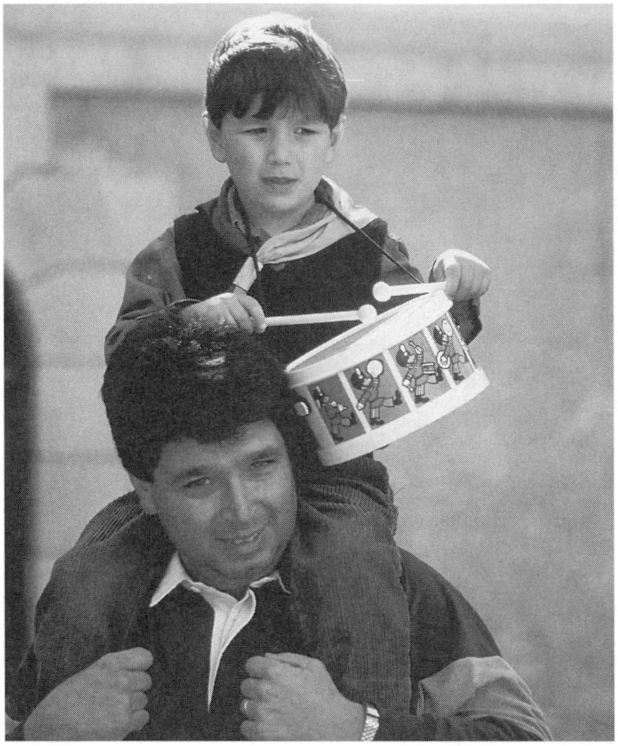

The status of being Gibraltarian is transferred through the male line.

the Hotel Association, the Chamber of Commerce, TGWU/Acts, the Shipping Association, and the Bar Council. Apart from the nationalist movement Self-Determination For Gibraltar Group (SDGG), nongovernmental organizations are politically unimportant.

Gender Roles and Statuses

Division of Labor by Gender. The economy traditionally was gendered, with women keeping the household and men working in dockyards and offices. However, this pattern changed after the closing of the border, when women and Moroccan workers substituted for Spanish workers. Today many women work in the service sector. Women are underrepresented, in political positions, although many women are influential in the informal management of parties. In the field of religion, only Hindu community life is dominated by female specialists.

The Relative Status of Women and Men. Women are still expected to keep out of political life and participate only in social, cultural, and charity affairs. Citizenship is viricentric; the status of being a Gibraltarian can be transferred only through the male line.

Marriage, Family, and Kinship

Marriage. Marriages usually are not arranged. People marry young (around age 20) and often divorce young. Increasingly within the Jewish community and decreasingly within the Hindu community, there is a trend toward arranged marriages. Gays and lesbians tend to cover their identities and marry. Homosexuality was a legal offense until 1992.

Domestic Unit. Until land reclamation began in the 1990s, housing was a major problem. It was common for couples to share an apartment with their in-laws. The household unit was the extended family.

Kin Groups. As Gibraltar is a face-to-face community, frequent contact between members of larger kin groups is unavoidable, though it is not necessarily intense.

Socialization

Higher Education. Higher education is an avenue for upward mobility. An extensive grant system allows about 50 percent of high school graduates to study in British universities.

Religion

Religious Beliefs. The population consists of Catholics (77 percent), Church of England Protestants (7 percent), Muslims (7 percent), other Christians (3 percent), Jews (2.3 percent), and Hindus (2.1 percent).

Religious Practitioners. All the religious groups have seen a struggle for power and control between traditional and orthodox forces. The authority of the Catholic Church, led by a locally-born bishop, is strong. There are four synagogues and one rabbi. Although a Hindu temple was built in 1995, there are no locally based full-time Hindu specialists. The influence of an esoteric guru, Sri Swatchidananda, is especially strong, but there are also followers of the Radha Soami movement.

Rituals and Holy Places. The Rock itself is ascribed spiritual power by Gibraltarians of all religions. The typical Iberian Catholic celebrations (Easter Week, processions, and pilgrimages) are largely absent. Most holy sites for the Jewish community are located in nearby Morocco.

Fishing boats fill the harbor below the Rock of Gibraltar.

Medicine and Health Care

Gibraltar has one civilian hospital. Most health care practitioners have a British degree. Historically, the hospital was organized along religious lines with Catholic, Protestant, and Jewish wards.

Secular Celebrations

The most important celebrations are Commonwealth Day (the second Monday in March), Constitution Day on 30 May (commemorates the constitution of 1969), and, National Day on 9 October (celebrates the pro-British referendum in 1967).

The Arts and Humanities

Support for the Arts. Most artists are self-supporting.

Literature. There are several local poets. As a result of a growing self-identity movement, more Gibraltarians have become interested in local history and biographies.

Graphic Arts. John Mackintosh Hall, the local community center, is the main location for exhibitions of local drawings, paintings, and sculpture.

Performance Arts. There are many dance groups, including Indian and Sevillana groups, as well as modeling and beauty contests. There is a local music scene, as well as some theater groups.

The State of the Physical and Social Sciences

Many Gibraltarians are passionate ornithologists.

Bibliography

Benady, Mesod (''Tito''). ''The Jewish Community of Gibraltar'' In R. D. Barnett and W. M. Schwab, eds., *The Western Sephardim: The Sephardi Heritage*, vol. II, 1989.

Caruana, Charles. *The Rock Under a Cloud*, 1989.

Finlayson, Thomas J. *The Fortress Came First*, 1991.

Haller, Dieter. ''Romancing Patios: Die Aneignung der Stadt im Rahmen der ethnischen und nationalen Neubestimmung in Gibraltar'' In Kokot, Hengartner, and Wildner, eds., *Kulturwissenschaftliche Sichtweisen auf die Stadt*, 1999.

Jackson, Sir William G. F. *The Rock of the Gibraltarians—A History of Gibraltar*, 1987.

Kramer, Johannes. "Bevölkerung und Sprachen in Gibraltar." *Europa Ethnica* 42:88–96, 1985.

Moyer, Melissa Greer. *Analysis of Code Switching in Gibraltar*, 1993.

Stanton, Gareth. "Guests in the Dock—Moroccan Workers on Trial in the Colony of Gibraltar." *Critique of Anthropology* 11 (4):361–379, 1991.

—DIETER HALLER

GREECE

CULTURE NAME

Greek

ALTERNATIVE NAMES

Hellenic, Romeic

ORIENTATION

Identification. Greece, the English name for the Hellenic Republic, derives from an ancient Latin word for that area. "Hellenic" derives from the word ancient Greeks used to refer themselves, while "Romeic" comes from the medieval or Byzantine Greek term. Although Romeic was the most common self-designation early in the nineteenth century, it has declined in favor of Hellenic since that time.

The words "Greek," "Hellenic," and "Romeic" refer not only to the country but also to the majority ethnic group. Greek culture and identity reflect the shared history and common expectations of all members of the nation-state, but they also reflect an ethnic history and culture that predate the nation-state and extend to Greek people outside the country's borders. Since 98 percent of the country's citizens are ethnically Greek, ethnic Greek culture has become almost synonymous with that of the nation-state. However, recent migration patterns may lead to a resurgence of other ethnic groups in the population.

Location and Geography. The Hellenic Republic is in southeastern Europe at the point where the Balkan peninsula juts into the Mediterranean Sea and forms a land-based connection to Anatolia and the Middle East. Initially restricted to the southern mainland and a few islands, Greece grew with the addition of the Dodecanese Islands in 1948. The country is bordered by Albania, the former Yugoslavian Republic of Macedonia, Bulgaria, Turkey, and the Aegean, Ionian, and Cretan seas.

Greece encompasses 50,935 square miles (131,957 square kilometers). The terrain is 80 percent mountainous, with its highest point, at Mount Olympus. Only 25 percent of the land surface is arable, and another 40 percent serves as pasture. There are more than 2,000 islands, 170 of which are inhabited, and a long coastline.

The climate is predominantly Mediterranean. Hot, dry summers alternate with cold, rainy winters.

There are nine recognized regions: Thrace, Macedonia, Epirus, Thessaly, Central Greece, the Peloponnesos, the Ionian Islands, the Aegean Islands, and Crete. Although these regions sometimes operated as separate entities in the past, they have been integrated into the state and their cultural distinctions are diminishing.

Demography. The population rose from slightly over 750,000 in 1836 to 10,264,156 in 1991, reflecting the expansion of national boundaries and the return of ethnic Greeks from the eastern Mediterranean. An even greater increase was prevented by emigration and a declining birth rate.

In the ninteenth and early twentieth centuries, Turks, Bulgarians, and others who were not ethnically Greek left the country in a steady stream that was formalized by the treaties that ended World War I. There has also been a continuing emigration of ethnic Greeks seeking employment and opportunity abroad since the mid-nineteenth century. This emigration was initially aimed at the eastern Mediterranean but was redirected toward the United States, Canada, and Australia by the late nineteenth century. The industrial nations of Western Europe joined the list of destinations in the 1960s.

Birth rates have declined since the early twentieth century. The proportion of elderly people is the highest in Europe at over 20 percent, and the overall rate of natural increase is among the lowest.

Greece

Albanians, Armenians, Bulgarians, Slavic Macedonians, Pomaks (Bulgarian Muslims), Turks, Jews, Roma (Gypsies), Vlachs, Sarakatsanoi, and several other groups have long been part of the country's cultural mosaic, although their numbers have decreased. The 1990s witnessed an unexpected influx of immigrants as refugees and labor migrants entered from Eastern Europe, the Middle East, North Africa, and the Philippines. These newcomers, especially the Albanians, estimated at between one-half million and one million, have placed minority issues at the forefront of public discussion.

Linguistic Affiliation. Greek is the official language and is spoken by nearly all the citizens. It is an Indo-European language that has been used in this area since the second millenium B.C.E., although it has undergone considerable change. A major division exists between the ordinary spoken language known as demotic and a formal version known as *katharevousa*, which was developed in the eighteenth century to revive elements of ancient Greek and develop a national language that did not favor any regional dialect. Katharevousa spread quickly among political leaders and the intelligentsia. Writers initially embraced it, although most turned back to demotic Greek by the twentieth century. Katharevousa was used for most state documents, in many newspapers, and in secondary school instruction until the 1970s but has been displaced by demotic Greek since that time.

Church services are conducted in *koine*, a later form of ancient Greek in which the New Testament is written. There are also regional dialects, of which Pontic Greek may be the most distinctive.

Most minority groups are bilingual; Arvanitika (an Albanian dialect), Ladino (a Jewish dialect), Turkish, Slavic Macedonian, Vlach (a Romanian dialect), Romani (a Gypsy language), Bulgarian, and Pomak are still spoken. Most of the population also is familiar with other European languages, most commonly English and French.

Symbolism. Several widely recognized images and celebrations invoke the identity of the republic. The country is seen as the restoration of an independent Greek civilization, and many symbols establish a strong link between past and present, between larger Greek history and the modern nation-state. National holidays stress the struggle to establish and maintain an independent country in the face of conquest and oppression. The national anthem, "Hymn to Liberty," praises those who fought in the War of Independence. The flag displays a cross symbolizing the Greek Orthodox religion on a field of blue and white stripes that depict the sunlit waves of the seas that surround the nation. Statues of war heroes abound, as do the artistic motifs of antiquity and Orthodox Christianity.

Themes of cultural continuity and endurance, the direct connection to classical antiquity and Orthodox Byzantium, the language, the Mediterranean landscape, democracy, and a history of struggle against domination are central in this imagery. The Aegean area is characterized as a national homeland, and rural villages and ancient ruins are symbolic of long-standing ties to the region. Certain foods, architectural styles, arts, crafts, music, dances, and theatrical performances also evoke the national identity.

History and Ethnic Relations

Emergence of the Nation. A strong sense of a common ethnic identity emerged among Greek speakers of the independent city-states of the Aegean area in the Bronze Age and characterized the city-states of the classical period and their colonies in the Mediterranean and Black Sea regions. It endured over two millennia as these lands were ruled by the Hellenistic, Roman, Byzantine, Frankish, Venetian, and Ottoman empires, and as the area became ethnically heterogeneous.

The last of these empires was run by the Ottoman Turks, who established control over much of Eastern Europe and the Mediterranean after conquering Constantinople in 1453. By the late eighteenth century, the Ottoman Empire was losing ground. A military defeat at Vienna and the growing commercial power of Western Europe led Turkish overlords to institute harsher tactics toward the peasants on their agricultural estates. Increasing discontent in the countryside was matched by difficulty in keeping administrative structures functional. Several regions in which Greeks were numerically dominant developed strong local leadership, while entrepreneurial Greek merchants, sailors, and craftspeople acted as intermediaries between the expanding economies of Western Europe and the declining ones of the empire. Enlightenment ideals of ethnic self-determination were embraced by the merchant diaspora and resonated with the desire of all Greeks to end Ottoman control.

A series of rebellions against the empire led to a full-scale revolution in 1821. The War of Independence aimed at an independent, ethnically based state modeled after the nationalist political philosophies of western Europe. With the aid of armed contingents from Europe and the United States, fighting ended in 1828, when the Turks agreed to cede some lands in which Greeks formed the majority.

The shape and structure of the new country were uncertain and contentious. The desire for a parliamentary form of government was thwarted when the first president was assassinated in 1831. The foreign nations that negotiated the final treaty with the Ottomans then established an absolute monarchy monitored by England, France, and Russia. Otto, the son of Ludwig I of Bavaria, was named the first king. The boundaries of the new state were much smaller than had been hoped. Only the Peloponnesos, central Greece, and some of the Aegean Islands were included.

An 1843 coup resulted in a constitutional monarchy, and another coup in 1862 led to expanded

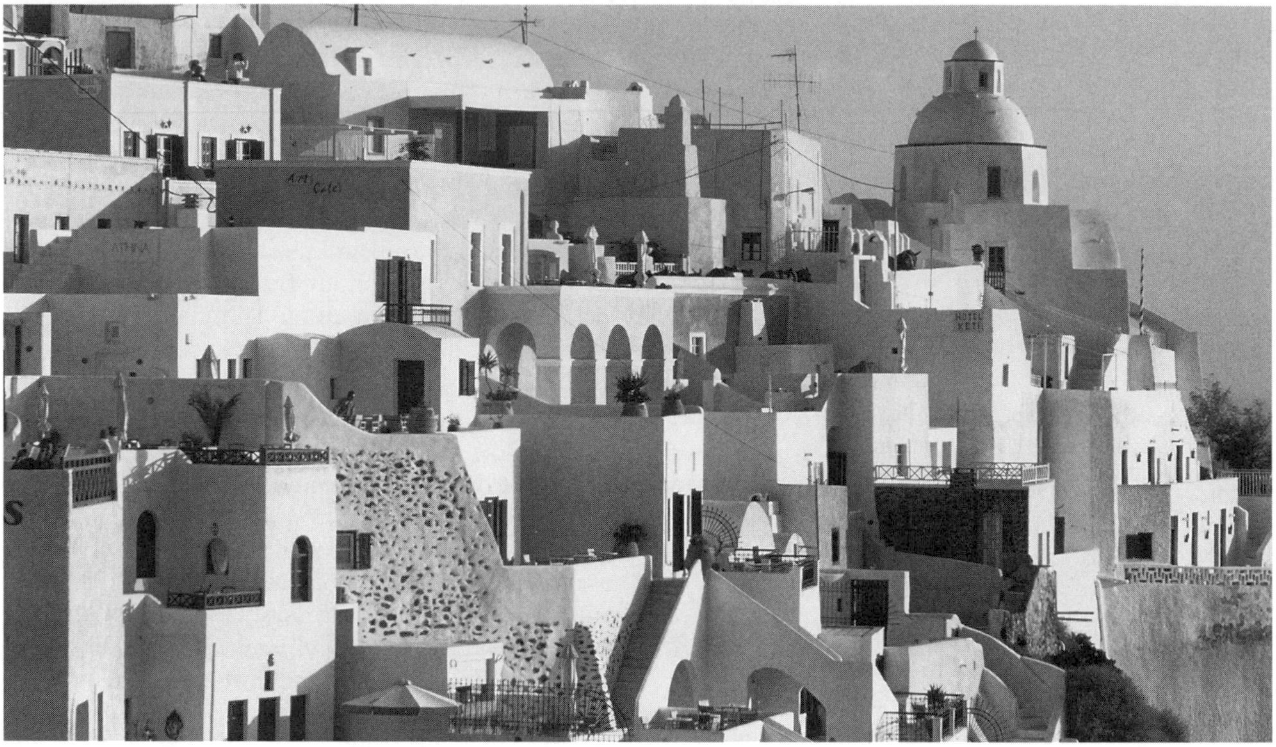

Houses in Santorini, Greece. Much Greek housing has traditionally been small and owner-built, and a high value is placed on home ownership.

powers for the parliament and Otto's removal from the throne. Although Otto was replaced with a Danish-born king, the powers of the monarchy steadily diminished, and the institution was abolished in 1973.

The territorial constriction of the original state was attacked through pursuit of the *Megali Idea:* the belief that the country should eventually encompass all lands in which Greeks were a majority, including Constantinople and western Anatolia. Through a series of wars, treaties, and agreements, most of modern Greece had been transferred by World War I. Greece fought on the side of Allies during the war. In the negotiations that followed, the possibility of allowing the Greek-majority population around Smyrna to vote on union with Greece was discussed. Greek forces were allowed to occupy the area. As Turkish nationalism arose from the ashes of the defeated Ottoman Empire, however, a revived Turkish army routed the Greek troops and destroyed the city. The Anatolian Greeks who survived the conflict fled the area. Although the Dodecanese Islands were granted to Greece after World War II, ideas of a larger state were ended by this event, which is known as the Catastrophe of 1922.

The nation also has been shaped by efforts to limit foreign involvement in its internal affairs. The direct role the original treaty granted to England, France, and Russia faded by the end of the nineteenth century, but the twentieth century was marked by the invasions that accompanied the Balkan Wars and World Wars I and II, including the German occupation of 1941–1944. The Greek Civil War of 1946–1949 saw the forces of the left and right backed by their counterparts in the nations soon to face each other in the Cold War. The outcome of this conflict led to Greece's alignment with the West, its entry into NATO in 1951, massive American aid, and continued foreign involvement in national affairs. Public sentiment against such interference combined with the waning of the Cold War in the 1980s to limit direct foreign intervention.

National Identity. A strong sense of ethnic self-determination initially fueled the construction of the state, erased regional differences, and led to a citizenry largely composed of ethnic Greeks. Nation–state and ethnic group were seen as coterminous. Public consciousness is also characterized by the frustration of unfulfilled hopes, foreign interference, and consignment to marginal status within Europe.

The national identity generally is considered a matter of cultural continuity, with language, religion, democracy, an analytic approach to life, travel, entrepreneurship, cleverness, and personal honor and responsibility as core values that connect contemporary Greeks to the past. An intense relationship to the Mediterranean landscape also plays a role.

The War of Independence, the Catastrophe of 1922, the German occupation, and the civil war figure heavily in national memory. The relationship to the more distant past has, however, been shaped by the important symbolic place reserved for classical Greece in post-Renaissance Europe. While eighteenth-century Greeks called themselves Romeic and looked toward their Byzantine Orthodox heritage, the emphasis Western Europeans placed on classical Greek antiquity led nineteenth-century Greeks to stress European connections over Mediterranean and classical history over medieval. This shift was the source of literary and political debate in the twentieth century, with broader conceptions of Greek identity gradually emerging.

Ethnic Relations. The Balkan peninsula and the Anatolian coast were multiethnic at the start of the nineteenth century. Different groups lived side by side, and there was considerable intermingling and even intermarriage. The pursuit of ethnic nationalism over the last two centuries, however, resulted in increasing ethnic separation. The establishment of ethnically based nation-states led to warfare, territorial disputes, and massive migration. Greece became increasingly monoethnic as members of certain ethnic groups left while Greeks from outside the nation entered. Some sixty thousand of the country's seventy-five thousand Jews were executed or exiled during World War II. Recently, the influx of new immigrants since 1990 is once again creating greater ethnic diversity.

International tension over territorial boundaries and the treatment of minority populations remain high in the region, although the disintegration of Yugoslavia and the former Soviet bloc has unleashed a new dynamic. These tensions often take on an ethnic character. Relations are best with other Orthodox countries and most strained with Turkey, Albania, and the former Yugoslavian republic of Macedonia. The partitioning of Cyprus into Greek and Turkish sides in 1974 remains a bone of contention.

Urbanism, Architecture, and the Use of Space

The population historically has been mobile. Sailors, shepherds, and merchants traveled as a matter of occupation, while peasants frequently moved in response to wars, land tenure policies, and agricultural opportunities. Market towns such as Corinth and Athens have endured for millennia, but smaller settlements appeared and disappeared with regularity. Over the last century, internal migration has overwhelmingly been from mountains to plains, inland to coastal areas, and rural to urban settlements. In this process, hundreds of new villages were founded while others were abandoned, and some towns and cities grew greatly while others declined.

A strongly centralized settlement system revolving around the capital, Athens, has emerged from these moves. The population became predominantly urban after World War II, with only 25 percent living in rural settlements in 1991. The concentration of economic opportunities, international trade, governmental functions, and educational and health facilities in only a few cities has led to the decline of many regional centers and the growth of Athens as a primate city. In 1991, Greater Athens contained 3.1 million people, a third of the population, while the next largest city, Thessaloniki, contained 396,000.

There are distinctive regional architectural styles, such as the pitched roofs of the Arcadian mountains and the flat, rolled ones of the Cyclades. Until recently, much housing was small and owner-built from mud brick, stone, and ceramic tile. Over the last fifty years, the use of industrially produced materials and the construction of more elaborate dwellings has accompanied a dramatic increase in commercial building. International architectural movements have also been influential.

Rural settlements are still characterized by single-family houses, but urban areas contain apartment buildings of five to ten stories. A high value is placed on home ownership, and most urban apartments are owned, not rented. Families tend to buy or remodel homes only after saving the funds needed to do so.

There is a strong public-private distinction in spatial arrangements. Homes are considered private family spaces. Single-family houses often contain walled courtyards that have been replaced in urban apartments with tented balconies. Plazas, open-air markets, shops, churches, schools, coffeehouses, restaurants, and places of entertainment are the major public gathering spots.

An interior view of a home on Crete. Greek homes are private spaces, and hospitality is seen as both a pleasure and a responsibility.

Food and Economy

Food in Daily Life. Grain, grapes, and olives are central to the diet, supplemented with eggs, cheese, yogurt, fish, lamb, goat, chicken, rice, and fruits and vegetables. Certain foods are emblematic of the national identity, including moussaka, baklava, thick coffee, and resinated wine (*retsina*). Coffeehouses have long functioned as daily gathering places for men. Dining out has gained in popularity, with a corresponding increase in the number and variety of restaurants.

Food Customs at Ceremonial Occasions. Guests must always be offered refreshment, and all major ceremonies involve food. At funerals, mourners are given *koliva* (boiled wheat, sugar, and cinnamon), a special cake is baked on New Year's Day, and the midnight Easter service is followed by a feast, generally of lamb.

Basic Economy. Farming, herding, fishing, seafaring, commerce, and crafts were the historical mainstays of the economy. Before the establishment of the modern state, most people were poor, often landless peasants who worked on feudal-like estates controlled by Turkish overlords and Orthodox monasteries. As the Ottoman Empire faced competition from the economies of western Europe, some peasants began producing cash crops such as currants and lumber for sale to England and France, shipbuilders carried produce from the Black Sea to the Atlantic coast, and carpet makers and metal workers sold their wares throughout Eastern and Central Europe.

After the revolution, the nation was deeply in debt to foreign creditors and lacked the capital and infrastructure needed for economic development, nor could it compete with the increasingly industrial economies of western Europe. Families produced most of their own subsistence needs, from food to housing, while engaging in a variety of entrepreneurial activities, producing everything from sponges and currants to tobacco and cotton. The weakness of the economy and the unpredictability of foreign markets led to periods of economic crisis that sparked large-scale emigration by the late nineteenth century.

In the twentieth century, industry was strengthened by the influx of urban refugees after the Catastrophe of 1922 but remained a small sector of the economy. The growth spurred by foreign aid in the 1950s and 1960s was followed by high inflation rates in the 1970s and 1980s. Governmental efforts at economic stabilization and payments from the European Union brought inflation down to 4 percent by the late 1990s. Current economic efforts are focused on industrial development, effective taxation collection, downsizing of the civil service, keeping inflation in check, and resolving the national debt and dependence on European Union payments.

Land Tenure and Property. Through legislation that distributed large agricultural estates to peasant families, most farmland came to be owned by the people who worked it by the early twentieth century. Population growth and partible inheritance practices have produced small individual holdings, often scattered in several plots at a distance from each other. Much grazing land is publicly held, although herders pay fees and establish customary use rights over particular sections.

Commercial Activities. Familial economic strategies were integrated into a market economy and subsistence activities dwindled during the twentieth century. Handmade crafts are generally aimed at the tourist trade, farming is oriented toward sale, and some basic foodstuffs are imported. Family members engage in a variety of cash-producing activities, combining commercial farming with wage labor in canneries, the renting of rooms to tourists with construction work, and sailing in the merchant marine with driving a taxi. A high value is placed on economic flexibility, being one's own boss, and family-run enterprises.

The most common commercial activities are in construction, tourism, transportation, and small-scale shopkeeping. Major cash crops include tobacco, cotton, sugar beets, grains, vegetables, fruits, olives, and grapes. Herders produce meat, milk products, wool, hides, and dung for sale. Fishing contributes little to the GDP. Mining is focused on lignite, bauxite, asbestos, and marble.

Major Industries. Industrial manufacturing contributed 18 percent to the GDP in the 1990s and employed 19 percent of the labor force. The major products are textiles, clothing, shoes, processed food and tobacco, beverages, chemicals, construction materials, transportation equipment, and metals. Small enterprises dominate.

Trade. The international balance of trade has long been negative. The country exports manufactured products (50 percent of exports), agricultural goods (30 percent), and fuels and ores (8 percent), and imports manufactured products (40 percent of imports), food (14 percent), fuels and ores (25 percent), and equipment (21 percent). In the 1990s, trade increasingly focused on European Union countries, with the major partners being Germany, Italy, France, and Britain, followed by the United States.

The negative trade balance is offset by "invisible" sources of foreign currency such as shipping, tourism, remittances from Greeks living abroad, and European Union payments for infrastructure development, job training, and economic initiatives. The merchant fleet is the largest in the world and tourism involves up to eleven million foreign visitors a year.

Division of Labor. The primary sector (farming, herding, and fishing) contributes over 8 percent to the gross domestic product (GDP), the secondary (mining, manufacturing, energy, and construction) sector contributes over 23 percent, and the tertiary sector (trade, finance, transport, health, and education) contributes 68 percent. The primary sector employs 22 percent of workers, the secondary sector 28 percent, and the tertiary sector 50 percent. Immigrants constitute 5 to 10 percent of the labor force.

Social Stratification

Classes and Castes. Despite income differences in the population and a small upper stratum of established families in the larger cities, the class system has been marked by mobility since the establishment of the modern state. Former bases of wealth and power disappeared with the departure of the Ottomans and the dismantling of agricultural estates. A fluid class system fits the strongly egalitarian emphasis of the culture. The degree to which minority groups receive the rights and opportunities of Greeks is a topic of public discussion.

Social status is not coterminous with economic class but results from a combination of wealth, education, occupation, and what is referred to as honor or love of honor (*philotimo*). While sometimes understood only as a source of posturing and argumentation, this concept refers to one's sense of social responsibility, esteem within the community, and attention to proper behavior and public decorum.

Symbols of Social Stratification. The fluidity of class and status means that symbols of social stratification are changeable and diverse, although the trappings of wealth convey a high position, as do urban residence, the use of katharevousa, fluent English and French, and the adoption of Western styles.

A narrow street in the Old Town section of Mykonos, Greece.

Political Life

Government. Greece is a parliamentary republic modeled after the French system. The redrawn constitution of 1975 established a single legislative body with three hundred seats. The president serves as the ceremonial head of state, while the prime minister is the head of government. Suffrage is universal for those over eighteen years of age. A large civil service bureaucracy administers a host of national, provincial, and local agencies. Governmental functioning often is described as hierarchical and centralized. A municipal reorganization in 1998 combined smaller communities into larger ones in an effort to strengthen the power of local government.

Leadership and Political Officials. Greek political history has been marked by frequent moments of uncertainty, and there have been several military coups and dictatorships, the last being the junta that reigned from 1967 to 1974. Since the end of the junta, two major parties have alternated in power: New Democracy, which controlled parliament from 1974 to 1981 and from 1989 to 1993 and the Panhellenic Socialist Movement (PASOK), which controlled it from 1981 to 1989 and from 1993 to the present.

Citizens maintain a wary skepticism toward politicians and authority figures. Support in national elections often was garnered through patronage, extensive networks of ritual kin, and personal ties in the nineteenth century. The rise of the early twentieth-century politician Eleftherios Venizelos initiated a gradual shift toward ideology and policy as the basis of support.

Local-level politics operate differently from politics on the national level. Municipalities elect leaders more on the basis of personal qualities than political affiliation, and candidates for local office often do not run on a party ticket.

Dealing with the large civil service bureaucracy is seen as a matter for creativity, persistence, and even subtle deception. Individuals often are sent from office to office before their affairs are settled. Those who are most successful operate through networks of personal connections.

Social Problems and Control. The legal system is based on modified Roman law, with strong protection for the rights of the accused. There are criminal, civil, and administrative courts, and since 1984, the police force, which previously was divided into urban and rural units, has operated as a single force. There is little violent crime. Tax evasion often is considered the most serious legal concern. Peer pressure, gossip, belief in forces such as the evil eye, and the strong sense of proper behavior and social responsibility engendered by *philotimo* operate as informal mechanisms of social control.

Military Activity. Continuing disputes and past wars are important parts of social memory, but since the Civil War there has been a different climate, especially since the end of the Cold War and the removal of most foreign troops. The country stills spends a high percentage of its budget on defense. The Hellenic Armed Forces are divided into an army, an air force, and a navy. There is a universal draft of all males at age twenty for eighteen to twenty-one months of service, with some deferments and exemptions. There are 160,000 soldiers on active duty and over 400,000 reservists.

Social Welfare and Change Programs

There is a nationalized health care system and a state-directed system of disability and pension payments. There are over 650 different pension programs, with membership depending on type of work. The government also has a system of earthquake and other disaster compensation. Banks have been established to support particular sectors of the economy. Caring for the personal needs of the elderly, infirm, and orphaned is considered a family responsibility.

Nongovernmental Organizations and Other Associations

Voluntary organizations include hobby clubs, scouts, sports organizations, performance ensembles, environmental groups, craft cooperatives, and political pressure groups. Among the most common are urban-based organizations formed by people from the same rural area. These associations enroll as much as one-quarter of the Athenian population and raise funds and exert political pressure on behalf of their areas of origin. Agricultural cooperatives are widespread, enabling family-based farmers to buy and sell in bulk. Trade unions are less well established.

Gender Roles and Statuses

Division of Labor by Gender. Rural men and women traditionally shared agricultural tasks, doing some jointly and dividing others by gender. Land and property have long been owned by both men and women, with husbands and wives contributing fields to the family. As the population became urbanized, this pattern shifted. Among families that operated small shops and workshops, both men and women remained economically active. Among those who sought employment outside the home, women were more likely to work at lower-paid positions and to stop working when they had children. Open access to education and evolving child care arrangements are changing this situation, and women now constitute 45 percent of the paid workforce.

The Relative Status of Women and Men. Gender roles were relatively differentiated and male-dominant until recently. Traditionally, men were associated with public spaces and women with private, with the major exception of the role played by women in attending, cleaning, and maintaining churches. There were nevertheless many arenas in which women asserted power or operated in a female-centered world. Their economic role in the family; ownership of property; position as mother; wife, and daughter; maintenance of the household; religious activities; and artistic expression through dancing, music, and crafts all worked in this direction.

There has been a dramatic decline in gender differentiation in the last few decades. Women received full voting rights in 1956, and the Family Law of 1983 established legal gender equality in family relationships and decision making. A majority (53 percent) of students in universities are women, and the percentage of women in public office has increased. Women are now fully present in public spaces, including restaurants, nightclubs, beaches, stores, and public plazas.

Marriage, Family, and Kinship

Marriage. Families are fundamental units of support and identity, and marriage is considered the normal condition of adulthood. With the exception of monastic orders and the upper echelons of the clergy, nearly all people marry. Arranged marriages in which parents negotiated spouses, dowries, and inheritance for their children were once common but have declined. Marriages are monogamous, and the average age at marriage is the late twenties for women and the mid-thirties for men. The divorce rate is among the lowest in Europe. Until 1982, all marriages occurred in churches, but civil marriages have been legal since that time.

Domestic Unit. Although nuclear family households are the most common, stem, joint, and other forms of extended kin arrangements also exist. Postmarital residence patterns are predominantly neolocal, but rural and urban neighborhoods often contain clusters of matrilineally or patrilineally related households, depending on regional traditions and family dynamics. It is common for elderly parents to join the household of one of their adult children.

Inheritance. Equal partible inheritance is the norm by both law and custom. Sons and daughters receive roughly equivalent shares of their parents' wealth in the form of fields, housing, money, higher education, and household effects. Daughters generally received their portion at marriage, but the Family Law of 1983 made the formal institution of the dowry illegal. However, there continues to be considerable transfer of property from parents to children when the children marry.

Kin Groups. The family-based household unit is the most important kinship group. Bilateral kindreds (loose networks of kin on the mother's and father's sides) provide a larger but less cohesive source of identity and support. Ritual kin in the form of godparents and wedding sponsors retain a special relationship throughout a person's life.

A festival on Skiros, Sporades. Nearly all Greek festivals have a religious component as 98 percent of Greeks are Orthodox Christians.

SOCIALIZATION

Infant Care. Midwives were common until the mid-twentieth century, but most babies are now born in hospitals. Babies are showered with overt displays of affection by male and female relatives. There is special concern over feeding and a belief that children need to be coaxed into eating. The central ceremony of infancy is baptism, which ideally occurs between forty days and a year after birth. This ceremony initiates the baby into the Orthodox community and is the moment at which a baby's name is officially conferred.

Child Rearing and Education. The successful establishment of one's children is a driving goal. Parents willingly sacrifice for children, and there is a continuing emotional bond between parents and children. Both parents are actively involved in child rearing, along with grandparents and other relatives. Adults give children freedom to explore and play, cultivate their abilities to converse and perform, and participate in social occasions. Parents also stress the value of education. The public school system was established in 1833, and 95 percent of the population is literate. Schooling is compulsory and free for the first nine years and optional and free for the next three. Over 90 percent of students attend public schools.

Higher Education. Higher education is strongly valued. There is a state run university, technical, and vocational school system whose capacity is short of demand. Entrance is achieved by nationwide examinations, and many secondary school students attend private afternoon schools to prepare for these tests. In the 1990s, 140,000 students annually vied for 20,000 university seats and 20,000 technical college seats. Many ultimately seek an education abroad.

ETIQUETTE

Much social life takes place within a close circle of family and friends. Group activities revolve around eating, drinking, playing games, listening to music, dancing, and animated debate and conversation. These gatherings often aim at the achievement of *kefi*, a sense of high spirits and relaxation that arises when one is happily transported by the moment and the company. Drinking may contribute to the attainment of kefi, but becoming drunk is considered disgraceful.

A major occasion on which people open their homes to a wide range of visitors is the day honoring the saint for whom a person is named. On those days, it is permissible to call on anyone bearing that saint's name. Guests generally bring sweets or li-

The Parthenon sits above an industrialized Athens, decaying from the exhaust-fouled air.

quor, and the honorees treat their visitors to food and hospitality.

Hospitality is seen as both a pleasure and a responsibility. Hosts are generous, and guests are expected to accept what is offered with only token protests. Hospitality is often extended to foreigners, but the deluge of travelers, ambivalence about the impact of tourism, and the improper or condescending behavior of some tourists complicate the situation.

Religion

Religious Beliefs. Close to 98 percent of the people are Orthodox Christians, just over 1 percent are Muslims, and there are small numbers of Jews, Seventh Day Adventists, Roman Catholics, and members of Protestant denominations. Greeks became involved in Christianity very early. After the Roman Emperor Constantine embraced the new religion, he moved his capital to Constantinople in 330 C.E. The new center grew into the Greek-dominated Eastern Roman or Byzantine Empire. Tension between the Christian patriarchs of Constantinople and Rome ultimately led to the Schism of 1054, which divided the religion into Orthodoxy and Catholicism. The Orthodox church represented and supported the Christian population of Eastern Europe after the Ottoman conquest. In 1833, after the revolution, the Orthodox Church of Greece became the first of several national Orthodox churches in the region, each autonomous while recognizing the spiritual leadership of the patriarch in Constantinople. Today there are sixteen separate Orthodox churches and patriarchates. The Orthodox Church of Greece is officially designated the religion of the nation, its officials exert some influence in state matters, and it receives state funds.

Religious Practitioners. The Orthodox Church of Greece is overseen by the Holy Synod, whose president is the archbishop of Athens. Under this synod are regional bishops as well as monks, nuns, and priests who run specific churches and monastic institutions. Local priests are encouraged to marry, but other members of the clergy may not. Care of local churches is the responsibility of the community of worshipers, and priests are assisted by deacons, chanters, and local women who clean the buildings and bake bread for communion.

Rituals and Holy Places. Orthodoxy includes a series of daily, weekly, and annual rites, including the Sunday liturgy and the Twelve Great Feasts, of which the most important is Easter and the Holy Week that precedes it. Twenty to 25 percent of the population attends weekly services, while many more people are present at annual ones. There are four periods of fasting and saint's days in honor of the three hundred Orthodox saints. There are also rites associated with key events in the life cycle, such as funerals, weddings, and baptisms. Many people integrate religious practice into their daily lives, crossing themselves while passing a church or entering to light a candle, pray, or meditate.

Larger Orthodox churches are often constructed in a cross in-square configuration, and all contain an icon screen separating the sanctuary where communion bread and wine are sanctified from the rest of the building. Icons are pictorial representations of saints in paint or mosaic that serve as symbols of holiness. In many homes, there is a niche where icons and holy oil are displayed. Some churches and monasteries have become national sites of pilgrimage because of their association with miracles and historical events.

Death and the Afterlife. In Orthodox belief, at the time of death, a person's soul begins a journey toward judgment by God, after which the soul is consigned to paradise or hell. Relatives wash and prepare the body for the funeral, which is held in a church within twenty-four hours of death. The body is buried, not cremated, for decomposition is considered part of the process by which a person's sins are forgiven and the soul travels to paradise. The next forty days are a precarious time, at the end of which the soul is judged. Visits are paid to the relatives of the deceased, and additional rituals are held, some with open displays of grief and singing of laments. Three to seven years after burial, the bones of the deceased are exhumed and placed in a family vault or a communal ossuary. The degree to which the body has decomposed and the bones have turned white is seen as evidence of the extent to which the person's sins have been forgiven and the soul has entered a blissful state.

Medicine and Health Care

The state-run National Health Service, a network of hospitals, clinics, and insurance organizations, was established in 1983. The service provides basic health care even in remote areas, but there is an over concentration of hospital facilities, doctors, and nurses in Athens and other major cities. Private health care facilities are used by those who can afford them. The health status of Greek citizens is roughly equivalent to that of Western Europe. Western concepts of biomedicine are well accepted but are supplemented for some individuals by long-standing cultural conceptions concerning the impact that certain foods, the wind, hot and cold temperatures, envy, and anxiety have on health.

Secular Celebrations

Nearly all celebrations have a religious component, and all major rites of the Orthodox church are public holidays. Among celebrations with a predominantly secular orientation are Ochi Day (28 October), commemorating the occasion when Greek leaders refused Mussolini's demand to surrender in 1940; Independence Day (25 March), when Bishop Germanos of Patras raised the flag of revolt against the Ottomans near Kalavryta in 1821; New Year's Day, when people gather, play cards, and cut a special cake that contains a lucky coin; and, Labor Day (1 May), a time for picnics and excursions to the country.

The Arts and Humanities

Support for the Arts. The Ministry of Culture supports all the arts in terms of production, education, publicity, festivals, and national centers, such as the Greek Film Center. There are provincial and municipal theaters, folklore institutes, orchestras, conservatories, dance centers, art workshops, and literary groups.

Literature. Oral poetry and folk songs thrived even under Ottoman domination and developed into more formal, written forms as the nation-state emerged. Poets and novelists have brought contemporary national themes into alignment with the major movements in Western literature. There have been two Greek Nobel laureates: George Seferis and Odysseas Elytis.

Graphic Arts. Long-standing traditions of pottery, metalworking, rugmaking, woodcarving, and textile production have been carried forward by artisan and craft cooperatives. Many sculptors and painters are in the vanguard of contemporary European art, while others continue the tradition of Orthodox icon painting.

Performance Arts. Music and dance are major forms of group and self-expression, and genres vary from Byzantine chants to the music of the urban working class known as *rebetika*. Distinctively Greek styles of music, dance, and instrumentation have not been displaced by the popularity of Western European and American music. Some of the most commonly used instruments are the bouzouki, santouri (hammer dulcimer), lauto (mandolin-type lute), clarinet, violin, guitar, tsambouna (bagpipe), and lyra (a-stringed Cretan instrument), many of which function as symbols of national or regional identity. The popular composers Mikis Theodorakis and Manos Hadjidakis have achieved international fame.

Shadow puppet plays revolving around the wily character known as Karagiozis were very popular in the late Ottoman period. Dozens of theater companies in Athens, Thessaloniki, and other areas, perform contemporary works and ancient dramas in modern Greek. Films are a popular form of entertainment, and several Greek filmmakers and production companies have produced a body of melodramas, comedies, musicals, and art films.

State of the Physical and Social Sciences

The University of Athens was established in 1837, with faculties in theology, law, medicine, and the arts (which included applied sciences and mathematics). The national system has expanded to nearly twenty public universities and technical schools that offer a full range of academic and applied subjects. There are several state-funded research centers, such as the National Centre for Scientific Research, the National Centre for Social Research, and the Center for Programming and Economic Research. The social sciences suffered under some governments in the past but are now flourishing.

Bibliography

Campbell, John. *Honour, Family, and Patronage: A Study of Institutions and Moral Values in a Greek Mountain Community*, 1964.

Clogg, Richard. *A Concise History of Greece*, 1992.

Curtis, Glenn E., ed. *Greece: A Country Study*, 1995.

Danforth, Loring. *The Macedonian Conflict: Ethnic Nationalism in a Transnational World*, 1995.

Dubisch, Jill, ed. *Gender and Power in Rural Greece*, 1986.

Friedl, Ernestine. *Vasilika: A Village in Modern Greece*, 1962.

Gougouris, Stathis. *Dream Nation: Enlightenment, Colonization, and the Institution of Modern Greece*, 1996.

Herzfeld, Michael. *Ours Once More: Folklore, Ideology, and the Making of Modern Greece*, 1982.

Karakasidou, Anastasia. *Fields of Wheat, Hills of Blood: Passages to Nationhood in Greek Macedonia*, 1997.

Leontis, Artemis. *Topographies of Hellenism*, 1995.

Loizos, Peter, and Evthymios Papataxiarchis, eds. *Contested Identities: Gender and Kinship in Modern Greece*, 1991.

Mouzelis, Nicos. *Modern Greece: Facets of Underdevelopment*, 1978.

Panourgia, Neni. *Fragments of Death, Fables of Identity: An Athenian Anthropography*, 1995.

Seremetakis, C. Nadia. *The Last Word: Women, Death, and Divination in Inner Mani*, 1991.

Stewart, Charles. *Demons and the Devil: Moral Imagination in Modern Greek Culture*, 1991.

Sutton, Susan Buck, ed. *Contingent Countryside: Settlement, Economy, and Land Use in the Southern Argolid Since 1700*, 2000.

—Susan Buck Sutton

GREENLAND

CULTURE NAME

Greenlandic

ALTERNATIVE NAMES

Kalaallit Nunaat (used by Inuit Greenlanders)

ORIENTATION

Identification. Greenland was probably originally settled by descendants of the present Inuit culture, who identify the island as Kalaalit Nunaat—meaning "land of the people"—in their native language. It received the name Greenland from Norse explorer Eiríkur Rauðe Þorvaldsson (known today as Erik the Red). He sailed from Iceland to the island in 982 C.E. and spent the next three years farming a plot of land along the southern coastline. He returned to Iceland in 986, intent on encouraging others to settle the rugged island. With this in mind, he referred to the island as Greenland, reasoning that a pleasant name would be more likely to attract settlers. Several colonies subsequently were established in Greenland, but these failed to survive. In 1605 King Christian IV of Denmark claimed Greenland for his kingdom. It remained a colony of Denmark until 1953, when it received county status. This change also gave Greenlanders full Danish citizenship. In 1979, Greenland became a self-governing part of the Danish realm after passage of a popular referendum. But it is still subject to the Danish constitution, and Denmark continues to manage the island's external affairs in areas such as defense. Greenland is currently composed of three administrative divisions: West Greenland (Kitaa in Greenlandic), East Greenland (Tunu), and North Greenland (Avannaa, also known as the Thule District).

Today, about 80 percent of Greenland's population is of Inuit or mixed Inuit/Danish heritage. Most of the remainder are of Danish descent, although a small number trace their heritage back to other regions of Europe. Modern Greenland has undoubtedly been shaped by European values and perspectives, but the island nonetheless features unique Inuit and European cultures that are distinct from one another. These differences in social customs and attitudes do bring tensions, but Greenlanders are united by the commonly held challenges of cold climate and isolation, as well as a genuine affection for the land on which they live.

Location and Geography. Greenland is the largest island in the world. It is located 17 miles northeast of Canada's Ellesmere Island, between the Arctic Ocean and the North Atlantic. The northern tip of Greenland is approximately 460 miles (740 kilometers) from the North Pole, making it the northernmost country on the planet. It is approximately 1,660 miles (2,670 kilometers) long from its northern to southern tips, and is about 650 miles (1,050 kilometers) across at its widest point. The total land area of Greenland is about 804,000 square miles (2,175,600 square kilometers), about three times the size of Texas, but 85 percent of the island's land surface is covered by ice. The country includes about 24,800 miles (40,000 kilometers) of coastline.

Greenland is a forbidding, rugged land that nonetheless possesses a stark beauty. Much of the island's interior lies beneath a vast ice cap that in some places is up to 9,800 feet (3,000 meters) thick. Over the years, the weight of all this ice has reshaped the island's interior into a concave, bowl-like basin that has actually sunk below sea level in several areas. The white surface of this vast ice cap is relieved only by the occasional peaks of mountains (nunataks in Greenlandic) jutting into the sky. Glaciers from this great mass of ice extend through mountain valleys and ravines to reach coastline fjords at many points. At the terminuses of these drainages, thousands of icebergs—many of monstrous size—are formed every year.

The inhospitable interior of the island relegates the entire population of Greenland to its rugged coastlines. Most settlements are on the west and

Greenland

southwest coast, including the capital city of Nuuk. This city, originally founded in 1721, is the island's oldest Danish settlement and by far the largest community in Greenland. It holds about 14,000 of the nation's entire population of 59,000 people.

The climate in Greenland is subarctic, with short, cool summers and bitterly cold winters. Along the fjords of the southwest coast, where most Greenlanders live, temperatures average 50 degrees Fahrenheit (10 degrees Celsius) during the height of summer. But the temperature falls to a mean of 18 degrees Fahrenheit (−8 degrees Celsius) during wintertime. Temperatures are much colder in the northern interior.

Hours of sunlight vary dramatically from season to season in Greenland, three-quarters of which lies north of the Arctic Circle. During the summer, Greenland becomes a land of the "midnight sun," with weeks of 24-hour daylight all along its length and breadth. In fact, northern Greenland receives three months of continual daylight during this time. During the winter, however, Greenland's southern ramparts receive only a meager supply of daylight (several hours each day) and the far north is plunged into darkness for several weeks, bracketed by a month of brief, hazy twilight on either end.

Demography. The total population of Greenland was estimated at 59,300 (31,390 men and 27,910 women) in July 1998. Approximately 26 percent of the total population is 14 years old or younger, while 6 percent are 65 years and over. The remaining 68 percent are between the ages of 15 and 64. Life expectancy for the total population is 69.46 years (65.29 years for men, 73.65 years for women). About 80 percent of Greenland's population is of Inuit or mixed Inuit and Danish-Norwegian heritage. The rest are of European ancestry.

In addition to Nuuk (population 14,000), population centers on Greenland include Holsteinsborg (Sisimiut in Greenlandic), Jakobshavn (Ilulissat), Narsaq (Narssaq), Julianehåb (Qaqortoq), and Ammassalik (Angmagssalik). Greenlandic communities are widely dispersed across the country, and roadways connecting these villages and towns are nonexistent. Transportation within Greenland is via dogsled, snowmobile, coastal ferry, and helicopter.

Linguistic Affiliation. Greenlandic is the official language of the island. It is an Inuit dialect with regional differences (east and west Greenlandic dialects are different in a number of notable respects). "Greenlandic is a polysynthetic language, in which entire ideas are expressed in a single word by addition of prefixes and suffixes to a root subject," note Deanna Swaney and Graeme Cornwallis in *Iceland, Greenland, and the Faroe Islands.* "Hence the impossible-looking mega-syllabic words which intimidate foreigners with their sheer length when written on a page . . . Some outsiders who've lived for years in Greenland still don't have a grasp of the language." In addition, nearly every citizen of Greenland knows the Danish language.

Symbolism. The national flag of Greenland appears as two equal horizontal bands of white and red (with the white on top), broken up by a large circle located slightly to the left of center. The top half of this disk is red, while the bottom half is white. The line dividing the circle in two is aligned with the line that divides the two horizontal bands, creating a single line that extends across the length of the flag.

Greenland is also awash in cultural symbols and slogans that reflect the history and values of traditional Inuit communities. Many of these symbols are closely related to the environment and/or the natural world, which has sustained the Inuit peoples for hundreds of years.

History and Ethnic Relations

Emergence of the Nation. It is believed that Greenland's first inhabitants arrived on the island about 4,500–5,000 years ago (probably from Ellesmere Island). But these early Inuit peoples disappeared from the land about 3,000 years ago for unknown reasons. They were followed by another Stone Age eskimo culture known as the Dorset Culture. This nomadic hunting culture lasted from about 600 B.C.E. to 200 C.E. before disappearing.

In the tenth century, the Thule Culture spread across Greenland. This culture, which developed early kayaks, harpoons, and dogsleds, either absorbed or supplanted existing eskimo cultures. Anthropologists agree that Greenland's modern Inuits are descended from the Thule.

Thule influence spread across the island during the same time that Norse explorers first investigated its coastlines. About 900, a Norwegian named Gunnbjørn Ulfsson became the first European to set foot on Greenland. He was followed more than 80 years later by Eiríkur Rauðe Þorvaldsson (Erik the Red), who organized the first Viking settlements on the island. Around 1000, Leif Eriksson, son of Erik the Red, brought Christianity to Greenland from Norway.

Norse settlements prospered for about 500 years, thanks in large measure to continuing ties with Iceland and Norway. But these settlements eventually dissolved and disappeared. Their disappearance has been attributed to climatic changes and problems with the Thule tribes, but their demise remains largely shrouded in mystery.

Europeans returned to Greenland in 1721, and in 1775 Denmark claimed the island as a colony. In 1953 a new Danish constitution made Greenland a part of Denmark, and financial aid to the island increased dramatically. In 1979, a popular referendum gave Greenland "Home Rule" status as a distinct nation within the Kingdom of Denmark.

National Identity. Greenland features a blend of Inuit and Danish cultures. Many Greenlanders have expressed uneasiness with the increased "Westernization" of Greenland communities in recent years, and many efforts are underway to preserve and sustain traditional Inuit ways, which remain an essential part of the country's national identity. But Greenland's long association with Denmark has benefited the island's inhabitants in many tangible ways, such as in raising standards of living and improving health care and education. Moreover, most Greenlanders of European descent are sensitive to the importance of preserving the historical culture and perspective of the Inuit people.

Urbanism, Architecture, and the Use of Space

Nearly all Greenlandic architecture is extremely utilitarian. Buildings and other structures emphasize functionality over form. Greenlandic homes are typically constructed of stone, sod, or wood. During the summers, some families live in tents made from furs or skins. Communities are typically tightly clustered together, for as Gretel Ehrlich remarked in *National Geographic Adventure*, "for the Eskimo, solitude is a sign of sheer unhappiness. It is thought to be a perversion and absolutely undesirable."

Food and Economy

Food in Daily Life. The typical Greenlandic diet is heavy on consumption of fish, potatoes, vegetables, and canned foods. Seal and polar bear meat is also a staple in many Inuit communities.

Basic Economy. Greenland's economic situation is comparable to that of mainland Europe, in terms of standard of living and unemployment (officially about 10 percent in the mid-1990s, with the public sector accounting for almost two-thirds of all jobs). Its annual gross national product exceeds $1 billion (U.S.), but about one-half of government revenues are received directly from the Danish government. Greenland suffered from recessionary economic conditions in the late 1980s and early 1990s. It has benefited from budget surpluses and low inflation in recent years, but fears that overfishing might trigger crippling fisheries depletion in the near future are growing. In northern and eastern Greenland, the economies of small and isolated Inuit villages are primarily based on subsistence hunting for meat and pelts (of polar bears and seals, most notably) and fishing. In addition, the International Whaling Commission (IWC) has granted Greenland special permission to engage in limited "aboriginal subsistence whaling" in recent years, which has benefited some Inuit communities.

Land Tenure and Property. Community ownership of land and common resources is the rule in Inuit communities, where interdependence is a ne-

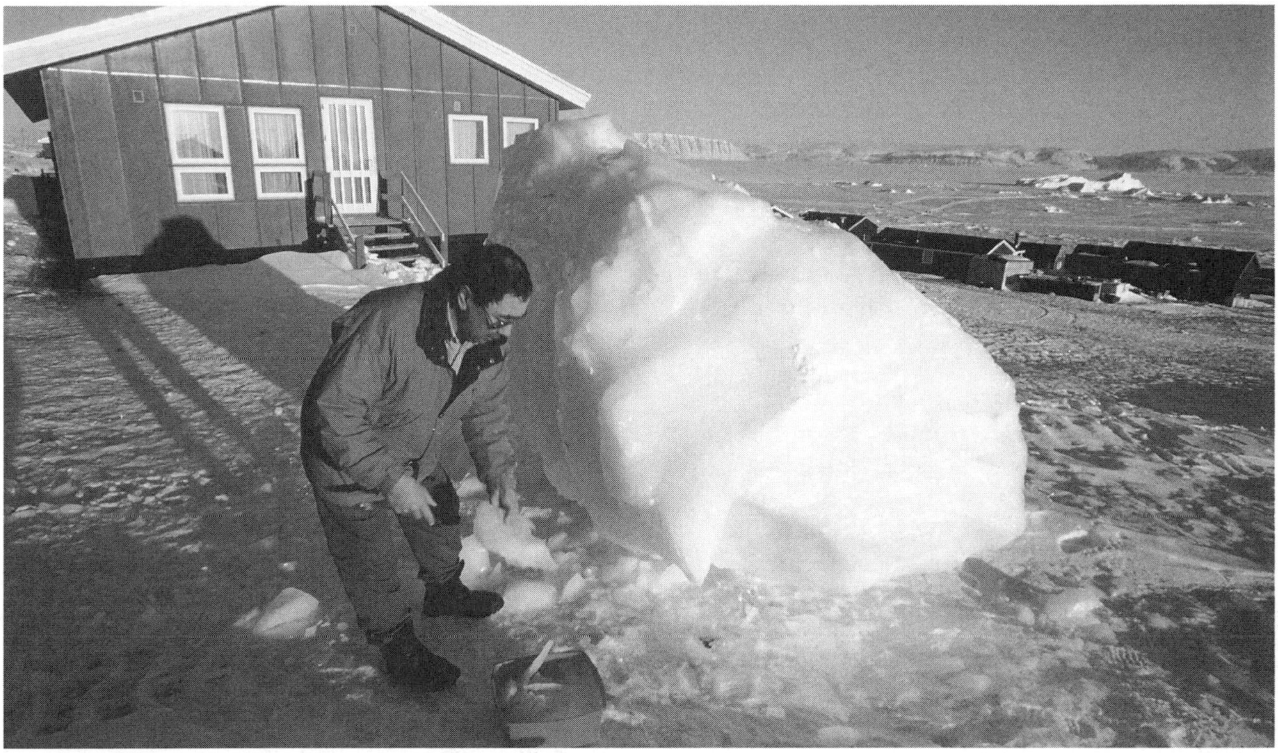

A person collecting ice for drinking water in Qaanaaq, Greenland. In Greenland's subarctic climate, temperatures average only fifty degrees at the height of summer, and only along the southwest coast.

cessity for survival. In fact, Inuit families that exceed "normal" living standards within their community typically distribute excess goods to poorer individuals. In non-subsistence communities such as the capital city of Nuuk, where European influences are more pronounced, private ownership protections are stronger.

Major Industries. Greenland is heavily reliant on fishing and related industries for its economic well-being, and it has gained an international reputation for being a fierce protector of its fishing rights in recurring disputes with Canada and the European Union. Leading fisheries include shrimp, halibut, redfish, salmon, and haddock. Cod was formerly a leader, but its fisheries have been decimated by overfishing. Other important industries include agriculture (sheep, vegetables) and mining. Tourism is emerging as an important economic factor as well, although Greenland's remote location and short summers are hindrances in this regard.

Trade. Most manufactured and consumer goods available in Greenland are imported from Denmark. Fish and fish-related products account for approximately 95 percent of all of Greenland's exports. Leading trading partners are Denmark, Japan, Norway, the United States, and the United Kingdom.

Division of Labor. Many Greenlandic communities continue to maintain a subsistence lifestyle, in which hunting and fishing skills are paramount. The fishing industry is the primary employer of both men and women in Greenland.

Social Stratification

Classes and Castes. Social stratification within Greenlandic communities is not a major factor, since families typically share both common ethnic backgrounds and similar economic circumstances.

Political Life

Government. Greenland has been a self-governing overseas administrative division of Denmark since 1979 (Greenland holds two seats in the Danish parliament). It is divided into 18 separate municipalities. The executive branch of Greenland's government is a seven-member body, known as the *Landsstyre,* that is led by a prime minister. Other members of the Landsstyre administrate departments concerned with a wide variety of areas, including culture, housing, telecommunications, education, transportation, trade, and the environment (responsibilities in the area of foreign relations, defense, and currency remain with the Danish government). Greenland's legislature consists of a 31-member parliament known as the *Landsting.* Members are elected on the basis of proportional representation to serve four-year terms. Their responsibilities include electing Greenland's prime minister (usually the leader of the majority party).

Leadership and Political Officials. Major political parties within Greenland include: Siumut ("Forward"), a moderate socialist party that champions Greenlandic independence within the Kingdom of Denmark; Inuit Ataqatigiit ("Inuit Brotherhood"), which wants complete independence from Denmark; and Atassut ("Solidarity"), which has called for closer ties with Denmark. In recent years, the island has been ruled by a Siumut-Atassut coalition.

Social Problems and Control. Greenland maintains a system of local judicial courts, which hand out judgements based on a Greenlandic—not Danish—criminal code. This code, which reflects traditional Inuit beliefs about punishment, avoids imprisoning most people found guilty of criminal offenses. Instead, sentences usually consist of fines, compulsory counseling, or reform centers in particularly serious cases.

Alcoholism is often cited as a significant social problem in Greenlandic communities. This problem—common in many isolated Arctic communities around the world—is often blamed on cultural stress, seasonal affective disorder (SAD), and genetic intolerance of alcohol within the Inuit community (scientists have noted that Inuit people have lower supplies of important amino acids that break down alcohol). Greenland's government has tried to address this issue by imposing restrictions on hours in which alcohol may be sold, limiting purchases to people 18 years or older, and launching various education programs, but alcohol abuse remains a serious problem in many communities.

Military Activity. The Danish military is responsible for protection of Greenland, which does not maintain its own force.

Social Welfare and Change Programs

Denmark bankrolls an extensive social welfare program that is administered by Greenland's government. Benefits include free health care and other social services.

Gender Roles and Statuses

Division of Labor by Gender. Gender roles in Inuit communities are interchangeable in many respects. Men and women share in many chores associated with their subsistence-oriented lifestyles, although responsibilities related to hunting and fishing still tend to be divided by gender (for instance, men typically do the actual hunting, while women attend to drying the meat, harvesting of the skins, etc.)

The Relative Status of Women and Men. Inuit society has traditionally placed greater value on boys than girls, and these attitudes persist today.

Marriage, Family, and Kinship

Marriage. "Arranged" marriages are not unknown, but most unions are by choice. Most marriages are monogamous, but some men do maintain marriages with more than one wife at a time.

Domestic Unit. Immediate family units are usually modest in size (average two children per family).

Kin Groups. Extended families are very important in Greenlandic communities. These kin groups treat resources as communal property. For example, food obtained from hunting and fishing is generally divided up equally among families of a kin group. But Inuit families also form alliances outside their kin group. These alliances, which stem from historical—and present-day—concerns about survival, are carefully maintained through rituals of respect and gift-giving.

Socialization

Infant Care. Inuit place great importance on the time of year in which children are born. Winter children (axigirn) and summer children (aggirn) are greeted with very different birth rituals, ranging from first foods eaten to selection of garments to clothe them.

Child Rearing and Education. As Greenlandic children grow older, they enjoy great freedom by Western standards. "Greenlanders believe their children are born with complete personalities and are endowed as a birthright with the wisdom, survival instinct, magic and intelligence of their ancestors," explain Swaney and Cornwallis. According to this

Laundry hanging at a farm in Jakobshavn. Most Greenlandic homes are constructed of stone, sod, or wood.

traditional perspective emphasizing ancestral links, punishing children for misbehavior is an insult to their ancestors.

Education is compulsory and free for all Greenlandic children between the ages of 6 and 15. Education standards are identical to those in place in Denmark. Once children complete their primary school education (where courses of instruction include the handling of firearms, an essential skill in many subsistence communities), secondary education is available at boarding schools. Vocational school training is also available. Many of these schools emphasize training youths for careers in the fishing industry, but classes in construction, business, and metalworking are also available. Greenland relies heavily on Danish teachers and administrators to keep their school system operational.

Higher Education. Students who wish to continue their education at the university level usually attend college in Denmark. The lone university on the island is Greenland University (Ilisimatusarfik) in Nuuk.

ETIQUETTE

Greenlanders are friendly of temperament, albeit more restrained in their social interactions than most Westerners. Their strong sense of etiquette is guided by traditional Inuit beliefs and customs.

RELIGION

Religious Beliefs. The majority of the Greenlandic population is associated with the Lutheran Church, which is the national church of Denmark. But traditional Inuit spiritual beliefs remain strong in many of Greenland's remote communities.

Rituals and Holy Places. Members of Greenlandic communities continue to practice a wide range of rituals handed down from their ancestors. These range from giving ritualistic thanks to bears, whales, and other creatures after they have been slain by hunting expeditions to taboos on mixing food and clothing associated with the winter months with those associated with the summer season.

Death and the Afterlife. The Lutheran religion as practiced in Greenland and other nations is based on a belief in the ultimate authority of God. It places great importance on the life of Jesus and the authority of the Bible, and emphasizes the doctrine of salvation through faith.

Communities are typically tightly clustered, and solitude is considered totally undesirable.

Medicine and Health Care

Free health care, subsidized by the Danish government, is available to all Greenlanders. In most of Greenland's small, widely dispersed communities, however, this care is quite limited in scope. The largest hospital in Greenland is Queen Ingrid's Hospital in Nuuk.

Secular Celebrations

Secular holidays celebrated in Greenland include Labour Day (1 May), Danish Constitution Day (5 June), National Day (21 June), and New Year's Eve and Day.

The Arts and Humanities

Support for the Arts. Artists and writers in Greenland enjoy some official support from the Greenlandic and Danish governments, which see the arts as an important element of efforts to increase tourism. The greatest reason for the continued vitality of Greenlandic arts, however, is the Inuit communities' strong artistic tradition.

Literature. Greenland's long tradition of oral storytelling (stories and songs) has always concerned itself primarily with explaining Inuit myths and standards of moral behavior, as well as the relationship between the Inuit people and the creatures (seal, bear, walrus, whale, fox, etc.) on which they relied for survival. This tradition remains a viable one in Greenlandic communities, and its most talented practitioners are respected figures. Written literature is less established in Greenland, but reading and writing are increasingly popular pastimes.

Graphic Arts. Greenland enjoys a distinguished place in the world of native graphic arts. Traditional Inuit clothing features intricate handmade designs, traditional materials, and festive colors. Inuit artists also specialize in the creation of tupilak, small wood or bone carvings of supernatural creatures or arctic animals that have their origins in the island's pre-Christian era.

Performance Arts. As with most other artistic expression in Greenland, performance arts often focus on various aspects of the traditional Inuit hunting and fishing culture. But modern performance art is also present in Greenland in the form of pop music groups, modern dance, etc.

Bibliography

Caulfield, Richard A. *Greenlanders, Whales, and Whaling: Sustainability and Self-Determination in the Arctic*, 1997.

Dahl, Jenns. *Saqqaq: An Inuit Hunting Community in the Modern World*, 2000.

Ehrlich, Gretel. "The Endless Hunt." *National Geographic Adventure*, September/October 2000.

Fitzhugh, William W., and Elisabeth I. Ward, eds. *Vikings: The North Atlantic Saga*, 2000.

Ingstad, Helge. *Land Under the Pole Star: A Voyage to the Norse Settlements of Greenland and the Saga of the People that Vanished*, 1966.

Lassieur, Allison. *Inuit*, 2000.

Mauss, Marcel. *Seasonal Variations of the Eskimo: A Study in Social Morphology*, 1979.

Nuttall, Mark. *Arctic Homeland: Kinship, Community and Development in Northwest Greenland*, 1992.

Seaver, Kirsten. *The Frozen Echo: Greenland and the Exploration of North America, ca AD 1000-1500*, 1996.

Swaney, Deanna, and Graeme Cornwallis. *Iceland, Greenland, and the Faroe Islands*, 1991.

Vaughan, Richard. *Northwest Greenland: A History*, 1991.

—Kevin Hillstrom

Grenada

Culture Name

Grenadian

Orientation

Identification. The Carib Indians violently displaced the Arawak (Taino) tribes around 1000 C.E. and called the island Camerhogne, until they also were driven out. In 1300, Alonso de Hojeda, Amerigo Vespucci, and Juan de la Cosa named the island Mayo while on a mapping mission. Christopher Columbus named the island Concepción when he spotted it in 1498. The name "Granada" was used on maps until the mid-1600s. To the French, the island was known as La Grenade; to the English, Grenada became the permanent title in 1763.

Location and Geography. Grenada is an island of volcanic origin in the Lesser Antilles chain ninety miles north of Venezuela. Grenada measures fourteen miles across and twenty-six miles top to bottom for a total land area of 121 square miles—133 square miles when Carriacou and Petit Martinique are included. Dense rain forest, a jagged coastline, picturesque beaches, and brilliant foliage are enhanced by a mild climate. The wet season lasts from July through September, and the dry season lasts from October through June. Rainfall can be quite heavy but generally does not last long. Grenada's southern position protects it from hurricanes. The capital is Saint George's.

Demography. The population of Grenada was 97,008 in the year 2000, with more than 42 percent of the people under age fifteen and 4 percent over age sixty-five. The youth of the population is reflected in the growing popularity of Western culture and the slow disintegration of the traditional culture. Only a few elderly people in the countryside can speak the French-based Creole (in patois, *Kweyol*) language. However, literary circles are campaigning to expose schoolchildren to the Creole language. Forty-four percent of the population lives outside the urban areas. Saint George's has a population of 4,439.

Linguistic Affiliation. The official language is Standard English—patois is very rarely spoken today. Attempts to revive the French-based patois have not been successful.

Symbolism. The common symbol, which appears on the flag and drives the economy, is nutmeg. As the major export and job provider, nutmeg is an integral part of island life. The flag also displays seven stars in yellow on a red background. Six of the stars are positioned around the flag's border and represent the six parishes named for Saints David, Andrew, Patrick, Mark, John, and Paul. A single star in the center stands for Saint George's Borough, where the capital is located. Nutmeg appears in a field of green to the left of the flag's center. The colors were selected to reflect the natural beauty of the island and the characteristics of its people. Red stands for courage and vitality, yellow represents wisdom and warmth, and green represents agriculture and the island's rich vegetation. These are also the colors of the Rastafarian religion.

History and Ethnic Relations

Emergence of the Nation. The earliest settlers migrated from the Amazonian basin of South America. This Amerindian descent is still evident in the northern countryside where pottery and other Indian crafts are made with traditional methods. Eighty-two percent of the inhabitants are of African origin, descendants of the African slaves who were brought to work the European-owned plantations. Five percent of the people are descended from Asian Indians also brought to the island as indentured servants. The remaining 13 percent of the people are of mixed ancestry, including European and American immigrants.

Long before Columbus sighted the island, the Amazonian Indians had established a tradition of

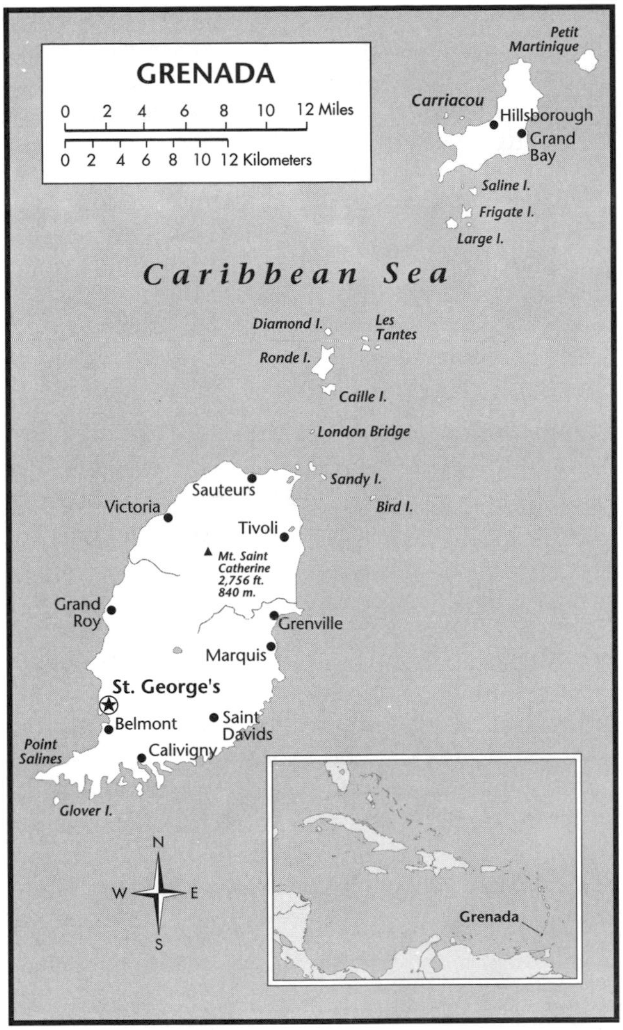

Grenada

territorial dispute. Arawak and Carib Indians originally settled the island around 1100 C.E. After the Caribs defeated the Arawaks, they were conquered by the French in 1651. Rather than submit to conquest, men, women, and children leapt to their death off of a precipice now known as Carib's Leap. The Treaty of Paris of 1763 ceded Grenada to Great Britain. Sixteen years later the French took the island back by force. In 1783, the Treaty of Versailles awarded Grenada again to the British. After another one hundred years, Grenada became a crown colony in 1877. During three hundred years of alternating occupation, the slave population on the sugar plantations grew and gathered strength.

As early as 1700, slaves and a small number of "Free Coloureds" outnumbered white Europeans almost two to one. In the Fedon Rebellion of 1795, Free Coloureds and slaves gathered in an unusual display of disregard for social segregation. In 1974, Grenada gained independence.

National Identity. Grenadians are protective of a local culture that has resulted from a long history of identity crisis. European customs remain an integral part of daily life. Law enforcement officers hold the title of Her Majesty's Royal Police, British spelling is taught in schools, and the Eastern Caribbean dollar displays the queen of England. Many names of streets, rivers, bays, and villages reflect the years of French occupation, along with styles of architecture and food.

Ethnic Relations. Grenada shares a common Caribbean culture base with many other islands in the Lesser Antilles, including music, literature, greetings and salutations, food, and family structure. Not unlike the United States, ethnic groups remain somewhat segregated on Grenada. East Indian families uphold traditions and community ties, as do the African Caribbean island majority. East Indians are viewed by some to own a disproportionately high number of businesses on the island and pay a disproportionately low wage. Stereotypes are changing, however, as the ethnic groups mix and intermarry.

Urbanism, Architecture, and the Use of Space

In the larger and older communities, the legacy of French and British occupation is clearly visible. The architectural styles reflect a strong European influence but have been modified by bright colors and decorative accessories such as hollow eggshells placed on the tips of a cactus branch. Windows are the essential element of residential or commercial buildings. Schools often do not have windows but instead have large open frames that can be battened down during storms. Buildings are designed to take advantage of the Caribbean breeze while providing shelter from the intense sunlight.

Food and Economy

Food in Daily Life. Staples such as bread, rice and peas, fruits, and vegetables figure prominently in the diet. Cocoa tea made from local cocoa and spices is a popular breakfast drink. Lunch is usually a heavier meal that may include salted cod in a "bake," which is fried bread about the size and shape of a hamburger bun. Fish is plentiful and affordable, as is chicken. Beef is scarce. Pork is reserved for special occasions such as Christmas, while goat and lamb are eaten commonly. Dishes are seasoned heavily with local spices. The national dish, "oil down," is a stew-like concoction made in large quantities with local vegetables such as callalou, dasheen, breadfruit, green fig (banana), and plantain. Pig snout, pig tail, salt mackerel, crab, and "back and neck" of chicken are popular additions. The boullion is a mixture of coconut milk, saffron, water, and seasonings.

Food Customs at Ceremonial Occasions. Meals are social occasions, and holidays such as Christmas are spent visiting family, friends, and neighbors, with small "meals" eaten at each stop. Beef, spice cakes, and guava cheese are popular fare. Foods such as ham are expensive and often reserved for just the very important holidays, such as Christmas. Boudin, or blood sausage, is also a holiday favorite, along with a sweet ground cornmeal cake, which is cooked in the wrapped leaves of the banana tree and served tied with a string like a little gastronomic gift. A shot of local rum or creamy rum grog is a traditional accompaniment.

Basic Economy. The currency is the Eastern Caribbean Dollar. Approximately 2.68/2.70 Eastern Caribbean dollars are equivalent to one U.S. dollar. Basic foods are readily available, with the possible exception of grains. Other than nutmeg, virtually all other products are imported. Tourism is growing rapidly.

Land Tenure and Property. Because of the presence of unmonitored squatters in rural areas, the government has been hampered in its actions unless a development prospect is likely. Primitive shacks lack electricity and running water. When these communities grow into villages, programs may be implemented to offer the land for sale at a discounted rate.

Commercial Activities. The economy is driven by nutmeg and tourism. Other spices are produced for local consumption and export, including mace, cinnamon, and cloves.

Major Industries. The major industry is the production of textiles, although they are produced in relatively small amounts by industrial standards. Batik, or hand-designed waxed cloth, is a popular industry for tourism, but not widely worn by the local population.

Trade. The majority (32 percent) of goods are exported to other Caribbean island nations. Another 20 percent of exports goes to the United Kingdom. Virtually everything except perishable food is imported, including, but not limited to, electronics, automobiles, appliances, clothing, and non-perishable foods. Imports come mainly (32 percent) from the United States.

Division of Labor. Service industries account for 29 percent of the labor force, followed by agriculture with 17 percent and construction with 17 percent.

Social Stratification

Classes and Castes. Wealthy areas are inhabited by a disproportionate number of resident foreigners. This situation has led the government to impose stricter regulations on foreign investment and the immigrant population.

Symbols of Social Stratification. Class often is measured by the number of modern conveniences one has. In more rural areas, a concrete "wall" house with modern amenities may stand next to a corrugated shack where a family of six uses an outdoor pipe as its only water source. When the children from these houses leave for school in the morning, it is nearly impossible to distinguish their class origins. School children wear mandatory uniforms that are impeccably maintained even by the poorest households.

Political Life

Government. Grenada is a parliamentary democracy headed by the prime minister who heads the ruling party and the government, which is composed of thirteen appointed senators and fifteen elected members of the House of Representatives. As a member of the British Commonwealth, Grenada has a governor general who is appointed by the British monarch.

Leadership and Political Officials. Adults still have sharp recollection of the revolution of 1979 and the violent circumstances that preceded that upheaval. Protests just before the overthrow of the Eric Gairy government began at the grassroots level and enlisted schoolchildren to march in protests and demonstrate through sit-ins.

Because of the small size of the island, it is common for the majority of constituents to know their local government representatives. Politicians are accessible to the public and are expected to uphold their campaign promises. While the major political figures live in secure and luxurious hous-

Shoppers and vendors at a market in St. George's. Grenada produces a variety of vegetables and spices, and its meats include goat, lamb, fish, chicken, and small quantities of pork and beef.

ing, the majority of politicians cannot be distinguished easily from their neighboring farmers or businessmen.

Social Problems and Control. The rate of violent crime on Grenada is low. Common crimes include petty theft, trespassing, and drug infractions. Prison does not confer great social stigmatism, and exconvicts are readily integrated back into their communities unless the crime was violent or sexual.

Military Activity. The military budget is small. Law enforcement officers often are trained in other countries to gain military expertise.

Social Welfare and Change Programs

Organizations from the United Kingdom, Canada, the United States, and neighboring Caribbean countries assist with child care, education, teacher training, health, and human rights.

Nongovernmental Organizations and Other Associations

Nongovernmental organizations and other associations provide everything from medical supplies to textbooks. Among the more visible groups are the Rotary Club, Save the Children, Crossroads, Peace Corps, Grenada Education (GRENED), Programme for Adolescent Mothers, and the New Life Organisation.

Gender Roles and Statuses

Division of Labor by Gender. Women are beginning to dominate professions such as banking while maintaining a presence in banana fields and at nutmeg processing stations. Financial necessity forces women to support their families. Women are still expected to perform traditional household duties such as cleaning and laundry. Men hold traditional jobs in construction, mechanics, and shipping in which it is unheard of to hire women.

The Relative Status of Women and Men. While women work in politics and professional trades, men are still socially dominant. Typically, after a husband and wife have finished work, the man unwinds at the local rum shop with his friends while the woman attends to household duties.

Marriage, Family, and Kinship

Marriage. Marriage is a strong institution in this predominantly Catholic country. Men are expected

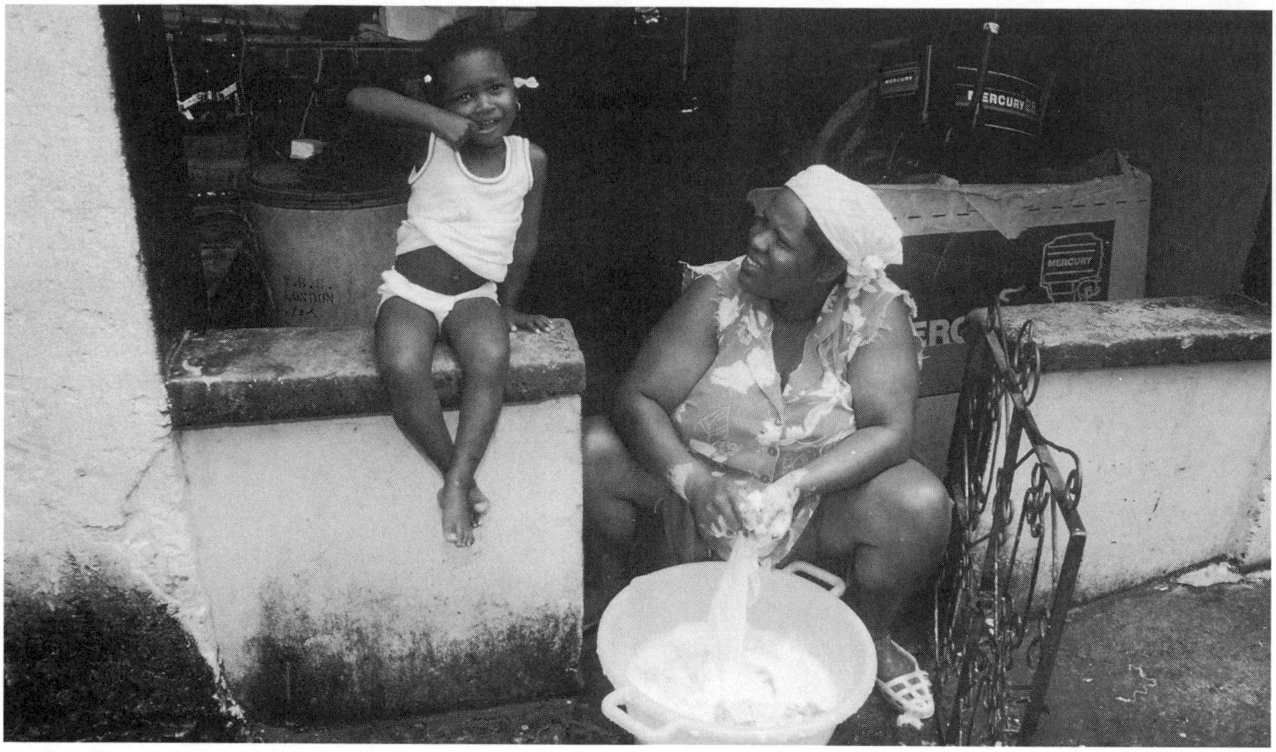

Laundry remains a traditionally female task, although women have also made significant progress in professions such as banking.

to marry and produce children, but having a wife does not preclude having a girlfriend. This practice is beginning to change as women gain greater freedom through education.

Domestic Unit. The family is a powerful unit. Houses of all sizes often contain several generations of at least one family. Children are raised by their parents, grandparents, siblings, and aunts and uncles. If a father figure is present, he most likely is the dominant figure in the household.

Inheritance. Land is the principal unit of inheritance and generally passes along the male line. Since a woman is expected to be cared for by her husband, the man benefits most from an inheritance.

Kin Groups. Communities act as kin groups and are closely knit units. Immediate parents commonly go abroad to earn a better wage, leaving even infant children to be raised by extended family members, and thus, in turn, the community. Members of a community support each other through food exchange and resource pooling.

Socialization

Infant Care. Infants are carried by family members until they can maneuver on their own. Quiet and obedient infants are the ideal. There is not a high level of stimulation, and behavior is often modified by corporal punishment, even at a very young age.

Child Rearing and Education. A good child does not speak out of turn, always does his or her chores, and earns high marks in school. At home and in the classroom, corporal punishment is common. The school system does not support the growing number of youths in its population. Children completing primary school must pass a common entrance exam to move on. Even then, there are never enough available places for student demand. The number of children forced to drop out of school as a result has sparked the growing popularity of "alternative" or trade/skill schools.

Higher Education. Education beyond primary or secondary levels is a luxury that few people can afford. Scholarships or a sponsoring relative abroad is often the only way to reach the college level. An American medical school offers two scholarships a year to local residents.

Etiquette

Salutations are an important part of daily etiquette even among strangers. Public displays of affection are common among schoolchildren, particularly

A house in Sauteurs, Grenada. French and British occupation have strongly influenced Grenadian architecture.

those of the same sex. It is not uncommon to see girls holding hands on the street and boys walking with their arms draped around each other's shoulders. Public transportation may require passengers to sit practically on top of one another. Preferential treatment is almost always granted to women, particularly the aged and those with small children.

Religion

Religious Beliefs. Grenada is predominantly Roman Catholic (53 percent), with Protestants accounting for 33 percent of the population. Among Christians, a substantial number believe to some extent in *obeah*, or white magic. Newspapers occasionally report a spirit who has been raised and is haunting some section of the island.

Religious Practitioners. Priests and clergy, as well as obeah agents, are respected for their higher calling or ability to cast a spell.

Rituals and Holy Places. Churches are formidable institutions where the majority of religious ceremonies take place.

Death and the Afterlife. A funeral is a social occasion to honor the deceased with a banquet of food and drink. The Day of the Dead is celebrated by the family and friends of the departed. Food, drink, and music may be brought to the graveyard and enjoyed amid the glow of candles throughout the night.

Medicine and Health Care

Local remedies are sought with great frequency, and herbs and medicinal plants are widely accepted as having healing powers. The island's bio-medical facilities are substandard.

Secular Celebrations

Holidays and celebrations reflect the influence of religion, particularly Roman Catholicism. The most important holiday is Carnival, which traditionally is celebrated on the weekend culminating on Ash Wednesday. Carnival is now celebrated during the second week of August to generate tourism from neighboring islands. It also coincides with Rainbow City, a celebration in the parish of Saint Andrew's that commemorates Emancipation Day. Other major holidays and celebrations include New Year's Day on 1 January, Independence Day on 7 February, Labour Day on 1 May, the Grenada Jazz Festival in June, Fisherman's Day on 29 June, the Carriacou Regatta in July and August, Emancipation Days in August, Thanksgiving on 25 October, and Boxing Day on 26 December.

The Arts and Humanities

Support for the Arts. The arts are supported largely by tourists, expatriates, and islanders.

Literature. Crick-crack stories often include the spider character Anansi and his friends. These stories are similar to fairy tales and have both oral and written traditions. They often are shared in groups, with the storyteller beginning "Crick," and the audience replying "Crack."

Graphic Arts. Paintings include oil, watercolors, and standard other mediums, but what sets Grenadian art apart is the "canvas" used for various paints. Cloth, bamboo, calabash, cutlass, wood, metal, and many other materials can be used by the Grenadian artist as painting surfaces. Ordinary objects beautifully painted with bright Caribbean colors are a common sight. Local art events usually occur in Saint George's because of its accessibility and population of art patrons.

Performance Arts. Drama, dance, and music are popular, and performances sometimes occur during festivals and at small theaters.

THE STATE OF THE PHYSICAL AND SOCIAL SCIENCES

Higher education, particularly in the sciences, is not adequate. Tuition costs and fees prevent the majority of Grenadians from attending the American medical school. Cuba and the United Kingdom provide scholarship and exchange programs.

BIBLIOGRAPHY

Bendure, Glenda, and Ned Friary. *Lonely Planet—Eastern Caribbean*, 1998.

Brizan, George. *Grenada—Island of Conflict*, 1987.

Ferguson, James. *A Traveller's History of the Caribbean*, 1999.

Froud, J. A. *The English in the West Indies*, 1888.

Gates, Brian. *African Caribbean Religions*, 1980.

Groene, Janet. *Caribbean Guide*, 2000.

Hamlyn, James. *Exploring the Caribbean*, 2000.

Henderson, James. *The Southeastern Caribbean—Windward Islands*, 1994.

Kay, Frances. *This Is Grenada*, 1996.

Knight, F. W., and C. A. Palmer. *The Modern Caribbean*, 1989.

Lunatta, Karl. *The Caribbean: The Lesser Antilles*, 1996.

O'Shaughnessey, Hugh. *Grenada*, 1984.

Parry, J. H., P. M. Sherlock, and Anthony Maingot. *A Short History of the West Indies*, 1987.

Rogozinski, Jan. *A Brief History of the Caribbean*, 1992.

Runge, Jonathan. *Rum and Reggae*, 1995.

Searle, Chris. *Grenada: The Struggle against Destabilization*, 1992.

Walton, Chelle K. *Caribbean Ways: A Cultural Guide*, 1993.

Web Sites

www.grenadaexplorer.com

www.grenada.org

www.travelgrenada.com

—KAREN LYNN PIERZINSKI

GRENADINES SEE SAINT VINCENT AND THE GRENADINES

Guadeloupe

Culture Name

Guadeloupean

Alternative Names

Before its discovery by Christopher Columbus in 1493, the island was called Karukera ("island of beautiful waters") by the Caribs.

Orientation

Identification. Columbus named the island after the Spanish sanctuary Santa Maria de Guadalupe de Estremadura.

Location and Geography. Guadeloupe is an archipelago of eight inhabited islands in the Lesser Antilles, between the tropical Atlantic and the Caribbean Sea. The two principal islands, Basse-Terre and Grande-Terre, are separated by a channel, the Rivière Salée. The capital, Basse-Terre, is on the western wing; the commercial center, Pointe-á-Pitre, is on the eastern wing. The other islands, known as "dependencies," are Marie-Galante, la Désirade, Petite-Terre (uninhabited), and the archipelago Les Saintes, along with Saint Barthélemy and the northern half of Saint Martin to the north. The total area is 660 square miles (1,705 square kilometers). Grande-Terre, essentially limestone, consists of plateaus, plains, and hills (*mornes*). Basse-Terre is volcanic with high mountains and a tropical rain forest. The climate is humid and tropical with a dry season from January to May and a wet season from June to December.

Demography. The total population in 1997 was estimated to be 428,044 with a density of 650 inhabitants per square mile (251 per square kilometer) and a growth rate of 1.5 percent annually. Until recently, population growth was steady because of high levels of fertility and declining mortality as a result of better hygiene and medicine. The youth of the population and high unemployment situation spurred government attempts to control the population through subsidized family-planning programs and a policy of emigration in the period 1961–1981. The majority of the population is of African descent, with a substantial East Indian minority and smaller groups of Syro-Lebanese and white Creoles (*blancs-pays*). In the outlying island dependencies there are distinctive white populations in La Désirade and Saint-Barthélemy and light-skinned inhabitants in Les Saintes.

Linguistic Affiliation. French is the official language of administration and education, but Guadeloupeans speak a French-lexified Creole that dates back to the time of colonization and slavery. In the 1970s and 1980s, Creole became a critical symbol in the nationalist claim for independence from France. Today all social strata recognize the value of Creole in cultural revitalization. Other languages play symbolic roles for ethnic minorities. Syro-Lebanese residents frequently listen to Arabic-language radio stations, and songs and prayers in Tamil have survived in Hindu religious ceremonies.

Symbolism. Creole, drum music, food specialties, and the celebration of carnival operate alongside symbols of the French hegemonic presence such as the tricolor flag and the French national anthem.

History and Ethnic Relations

Emergence of the Nation. In the pre-Columbian period, Arawaks and later Caribs moved to the region from coastal South America. European exploration led to conquest, to colonization, to the eradication of the indigenous population, to the introduction of sugarcane cultivation, and a plantation economy that was dependent on African slave labor. Under French colonial domination since 1635, with brief periods of English occupation, Guadeloupe was shaped by French politics. The first abolition of slavery (1794–1802) and the almost total elimination of the white plantocracy during

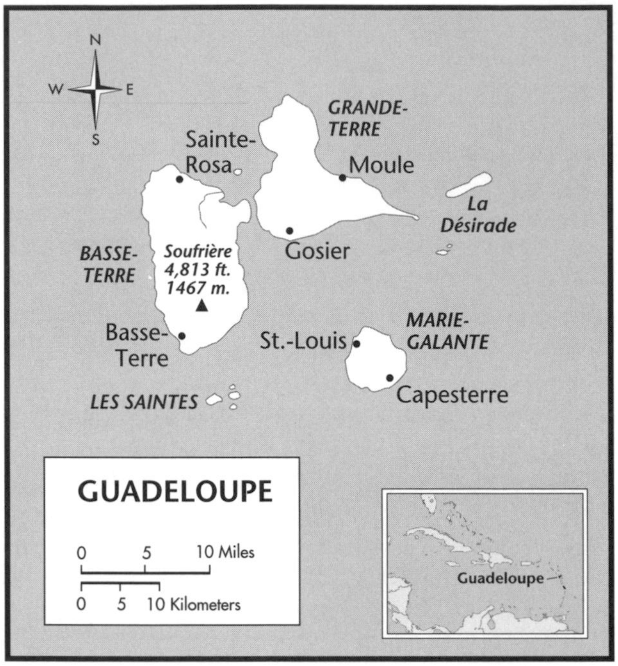

Guadeloupe

the French Revolution had far-reaching social and economic consequences. After the final abolition of slavery in 1848, a crisis of labor and capital led to the introduction of Indian indentured laborers, to the entry of metropolitan capital, and to the centralization of the sugar industry.

During the twentieth century, the local population of color sought to redress political, social, and economic inequalities. With the passage of the Assimilationist Law on 19 March 1946, Guadeloupe became an overseas department of France. This process ushered in wide-scale transplantation of French administrative and political superstructures and educational and social security systems. Integration with France precipitated a decline in both export and subsistence agriculture, a growth in the service sector, a rise in unemployment, massive emigration, and increasing tensions between Guadeloupeans and metropolitan French. In 1974, Guadeloupe was designated a region, ushering in a policy of decentralization.

National Identity. The revolutionary hero Louis Delgrès, who committed suicide in 1802 rather than be subjugated to the restoration of slavery, is credited with starting the formation of a national consciousness. The first independence movements had their origins in Antillean student organizations in France and the decolonization movement after World War II. The Groupe d'Organisation Nationale de la Guadeloupe was formed in the mid-1960s; in the early 1970s the independentist party—the Union pour la Libération de la Guadeloupe—was founded, and in 1981 the Mouvement Populaire pour une Guadeloupe Indépendante was created. Nationalist activity has focused on political demonstrations, trade-union strikes, electoral abstention, and affirmations of cultural difference. The marginal support nationalists enjoyed in the 1980s has eroded with decentralization.

Ethnic Relations. Relations between the black majority and the East Indian minority are basically devoid of tension. Politics and culture remain arenas of debate as a result of increased French integration and the growing presence of the European Union.

Urbanism, Architecture, and the Use of Space

Colonialism created different levels of culture, architecture, and the use of space. A unique architectural style was created in rural areas: the colonial villa with a majestic gallery, verandahs, and jalousied windows for ventilation and the vernacular dwelling (*case créole*) of two or three rooms with a kitchen, yard, and garden. These wooden huts have been supplanted by hurricane-resistant cement houses of one or two stories. The traditional dichotomy between rural and urban landscapes has become less visible as cities and industrial zones expand and suburbs are created. Urban architecture has evolved over time from French military, ecclesiastical, and colonial administrative architecture in the seventeenth to nineteenth centuries to public works in the 1930s, postwar construction such as low-income public housing, and a modern style influenced by local architects who are adapting contemporary construction principles to a tropical environment.

Food and Economy

Food in Daily Life. Food reveals Amerindian, African, East Indian, and French cultural influences. Traditional foods include manioc flour, root crops, breadfruit, avocado, green bananas, peas and beans, okra, curried meats, salted codfish, fish, and tropical fruits. Creole cooking uses hot peppers and spices but has been influenced by French cooking and imported foodstuffs.

Food Customs at Ceremonial Occasions. Special dishes for ceremonial occasions include pork, blood sausage, pigeon peas, rum punches (Christmas), salted codfish, crab *calalou*, rice (Easter and Pentecost), cakes and *chaudeau* (marriages, baptisms, First Communions), and curried goat on banana leaves (Indian ceremonies).

Basic Economy. Agriculture has declined significantly as a percentage of the gross domestic product. Commerce and services now represent 77.9 percent of the total economy. Agricultural productivity is constrained by natural calamities, by the absence of crop diversification, and by rural and agricultural exodus. The primary sector (agriculture and fishing) employs less than 8 percent of the active working population.

Land Tenure and Property. In 1996, 30 percent of the total land area was under cultivation, with sugarcane and bananas the main crops. While the majority of farms registered in 1989 were small, large farms comprise one-quarter of the total cultivated land. Most of the farms registered in 1989 were small. Agricultural land is owned individually or jointly, sharecropped, or rented, and the number of farmers and the amount of land under cultivation have declined consistently. Small farmers produce for the local market, and many people in the countryside maintain small gardens or fruit trees.

Commercial Activities. The weakness of the productive apparatus has caused a serious trade imbalance. In 1997, exports were only 7.4 percent of imports; this has been compensated by the transfer of public funds from France. Imports and exports circulate primarily within the French national territory, with the European union being a secondary partner. Guadeloupe exports principally agricultural products and processed food; most manufactured goods, equipment, and the majority of foodstuffs are imported.

Major Industries. Industrial production remains weak, essentially represented by small enterprises. The manufacturing sector involves primarily food processing and energy. Close to half of industrial production originates in building and public works.

Division of Labor. In 1997, the workforce consisted of 125,900 employed and 52,700 unemployed persons. Jobs are increasingly concentrated in the civil service sector. A major problem is youth unemployment, with persons aged fifteen to twenty-nine accounting for 43 percent of the unemployed.

Social Stratification

Classes and Castes. Social differentiation is based on education, professional orientation, culture, and wealth. Income differentials have been aggravated by inflated civil service salaries that allow greater consumption of imported and luxury goods.

Symbols of Social Stratification. Status markers are linked to consumption patterns and include cars, the type and size of house, leisure activities such as travel abroad and sports, clothing style, and language.

Political Life

Government. Political authority resides in a prefect appointed by the French president, and two subprefects. The Minister for the Overseas Departments and Territories is attached to the French Ministry of the Interior. There are forty-three *cantons* (electoral divisions) from which legislative leaders of the two local assemblies are elected by direct universal suffrage. The Regional Council is the most important local assembly, and the influence of the General Council, or departmental assembly, has declined. Each *commune* has an elected mayor and a municipal council. Two senators and four deputies serve in the French National Assembly.

Leadership and Political Officials. Political parties are distinguished chiefly by their stands on national and social issues. Party orientation follows three main currents: anti-assimilationist/regionalist, autonomist, and independentist. Several parties are formally linked to traditional right-wing parties in France; others are local formations, while the far-left parties are Trotskyist. The anti-assimilationist left is split between a center left committed to autonomy and a far left committed to independence and "socialism." The debate on island status issue is focused on whether to merge the two assemblies into a single local assembly. In December 1999, the presidents of the Regional Councils of Guadeloupe, Martiniques, and French Guiana united in support of autonomy. Personality is important in politics, where patron-client and kin ties play key roles.

Social Problems and Control. Guadeloupe is subject to French law and is part of the French judicial system. There are municipal and national police as well as gendarmeries in each *commune.* In the past, crimes were limited to domestic or local disputes and frequently were handled out of court. Vandalism, burglary, and drug trafficking have become more common as a result of increased economic

Houses and boats along the shore in the fishing village of Bourg, Terre-de-Haut, Iles des Saintes, Guadeloupe. Agriculture and fishing combined employ less than 8 percent of Guadeloupe's workforce.

development and class differentiation. Informal methods of social control include gossip, public defamation, and the use of sorcery.

Military Activity. The French army maintains a presence, and there is a national guard.

Social Welfare and Change Programs

The French government funds a comprehensive social security program that includes a minimum wage, pensions, family allocations, unemployment insurance, workers' compensation, and health insurance.

Nongovernmental Organizations and Other Associations

A variety of organizations operate in the villages, towns, and cities with a focus on sports, culture, carnival, social clubs, and labor unions.

Gender Roles and Statuses

Division of Labor by Gender. In the last few decades, the replacement of agriculture by a state-subsidized economy has been accompanied by a change in women's occupations. While women have entered the workforce in greater numbers, unemployment has disproportionately affected women and youth. With the collapse of the productive sector, most women work in administration, education, health, services, and commercial activities. Women's access to employment lags behind that of men, and women are more likely to be underemployed, to be compensated less, and to hold fewer managerial positions.

The Relative Status of Women and Men. Gender, along with race and class, operates as an important index of status. Although women frequently are heads of households, they have little power outside the home. Continued male domination is manifested by weak political representation of women and their marginalization in the workforce. Feminism and women's reproductive rights have only recently gained a foothold with the formation of women's associations.

Marriage, Family, and Kinship

Domestic Unit. Family organization and the domestic unit are strongly influenced by socioeco-

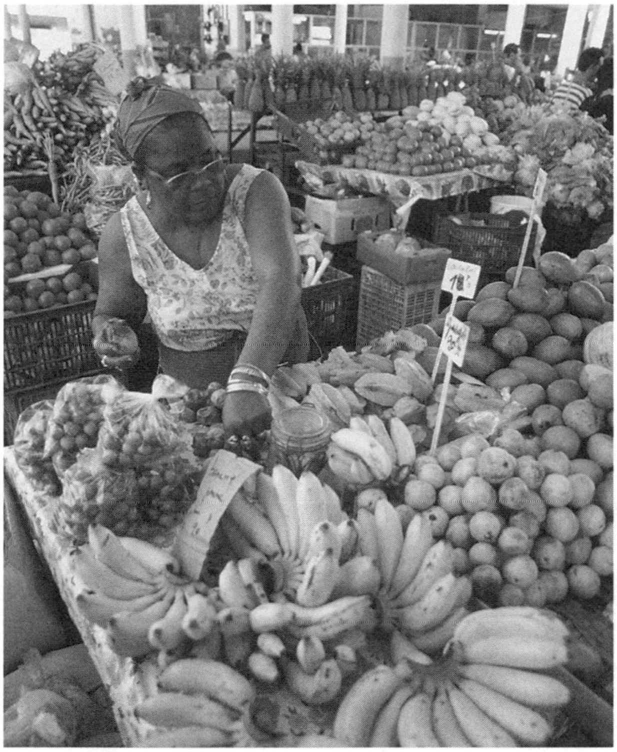

A produce vendor working at a large fruit stand in Basse-Terre. Bananas are a major crop for Guadeloupe.

nomic status. In many domestic units the woman occupies a central position; the man is marginal or completely absent, and the mother-child bond strong. Unions are unstable, and sexual relations are often polygamous, with a high percentage of children born outside legal marriage. Coexisting with the matrifocal model is the Western model of the stable, nuclear family, frequently unified through marriage. While there is greater control over fertility and a decrease in adolescent mothers, other trends are also occurring: a decrease in marriage, an increase in divorce, a pattern of cohabitation occurring later in the life cycle, and a rise of single-parent families.

Inheritance. Inheritance follows French law, which distinguishes between legitimate children with full rights of inheritance, recognized children who are disadvantaged in inheritance if there are legitimate heirs, and "natural" children born of unmarried parents with no rights of inheritance from the father.

Kin Groups. Within the extended family, relations of blood and marriage create a wide circuit of social contacts, including grandparents, godparents (through baptism), cousins, aunts and uncles, half siblings, and neighbors.

Socialization

Infant Care. From the moment of birth an infant is showered with attention and care by family members and extended kin. Frequently an older sibling, a grandmother, or another adult in the family is actively involved in the care of an infant, particularly if the mother works or is a single parent. Baptism occurs within the first few months after birth.

Child Rearing and Education. Child rearing varies with the type of family, the persons in the family, the relationships in the household, the socioeconomic class, and the social milieu. Children participate actively and very early in family life and have responsibilities that vary with age and gender. Being obedient, helpful, polite, and well dressed is valued, and strict discipline frequently is enforced with punishment. School is compulsory from ages two to sixteen. Education is highly valued as a means of social mobility. However, the school system is marked by high failure rates, repeating classes, and students who are below grade level.

Higher Education. The Université des Antilles-Guyane operates a campus in Guadeloupe. Many Antilleans undertake university education in France, which is considered prestigious.

Etiquette

Guadeloupeans are known for hospitality, with an emphasis on food, drink, music, and dancing. Casual conversations often are conducted in Creole. People greet each other by kissing or by shaking hands. The style of life favors multiple social contacts, and interaction is filled with conviviality and humor—with bantering and flirtation between the sexes. Traditional values emphasize "reputation" for men and "respect" for women.

Religion

Religious Beliefs. The Catholic Church is the dominant organized religion, with its own doctrine, rites, social organization, history, and calendar. Since World War II, Protestant sects such as Evangelists, Adventists, and Baptists have competed with the Catholic Church for congregations. Although the cosmology, myths, and theological systems from Africa did not survive, African magico-religious practices and superstitions are prevalent. Many people still believe in the forces of good and evil, spirits and supernatural creatures with powers. Hindu religious rituals are being reactivated

A cruise ship docked at the end of a crowded street in Pointe-a-Pitre, Guadeloupe.

among certain segments of the East Indian population.

Religious Practitioners. In the Catholic Church, metropolitan priests generally outnumber Antillean. Liberation theology is practiced by local priests, but most priests are conservative. Parishioners also frequent the services of *quimboiseurs* (sorcerers) for counsel in affairs of the heart and problems in social relations and in times of sickness. *Marabouts* (sorcerers from Francophone Africa) are active in urban areas.

Rituals and Holy Places. Each village, town, and city has its own church and cemetery where the dead are remembered on All Saints' Day (1 November). There is a Hindu temple in Capesterre Belle-Eau and smaller temples in the countryside.

Death and the Afterlife. Funeral wakes are customary, and the deceased is celebrated with drumming, riddles, storytelling, and rum. Among East Indians, a funeral generally is followed by forty days of fasting.

Medicine and Health Care

Modern Western medical practices coexist with traditional healing methods and the use of medicinal plants. Popular discourse on the body and illness includes notions of "hot" and "cold." While people acknowledge that illness can be attributed to natural causes, there is also a belief in the supernatural causation of illnesses and unhappiness. Whereas in the past, people often used personal and family remedies, visited the local healer if there were no results, and only then resorted to the pharmacy, dispensary, or hospital, today people rely more on Western remedies.

Secular Celebrations

Each town or village observes its own annual *fête patronale.* Islandwide celebrations include French national holidays such as Labor Day (1 May), Bastille Day (14 July), and New Year's Day (1 January) as well as the local celebration of Carnival (linked to the religious calendar) and the anniversary of the Abolition of Slavery (27 May).

The Arts and Humanities

Artists and writers often receive support from the French state. There is a private school of music, and music pervades the culture. Local record labels promote Antillean bands. With the renewed interest in Creole, traditional oral culture is being revived;

there are annual poetry competitions in French and Creole. A regional literature has developed that is receiving recognition overseas.

The State of the Physical and Social Sciences

At the Université des Antilles-Guyane campus in Guadeloupe, natural and biological sciences are taught along with juridical sciences and law. A number of research centers focus on Caribbean studies.

Bibliography

Abenon, Lucien-René. *Petite histoire de la Guadeloupe,* 1992.

"Antilles." *Temps Modernes,* vols. 441-442, April–May 1983.

Bastien, Daniel, and Maurice Lemoine, eds. "Antilles: Espoirs et déchirements de l'âme créole." *Autrement,* vol. 41, October 1989.

Bebel-Gisler, Dany. *La langue créole force jugulée,* 1976.

Benoit, Catherine. *Corps, jardins, memoires: Anthropologie du corps et de l'espace á la Guadelupe,* 2000.

Berthelot, Jack, and Martine Gaumé. *Kaz antiyé jan moun ka rété/Caribbean Popular Dwelling/L'habitat populaire aux Antilles,* 1982.

Burton, Richard D. E., and Fred Reno, eds. *French and West Indian: Martinique, Guadeloupe and French Guiana Today,* 1995.

Centre d'Etudes de Géographie Tropicale du CNRS. *Atlas des Départements Français d'Outre-Mer: III La Guadeloupe,* 1988.

Dictionnaire encyclopédique des Antilles et de la Guyane, edited by Jack Corzani, 6 vols., 1992.

Encyclopédie antillaise, 6 vols., 1971–1973.

INSEE. "Guadeloupe: Une année en demi-teinte." *Antiane Eco,* 41, June 1999.

———. *Tableaux Economiques Régionaux de la Guadeloupe, 1997,* 1998.

Lasserre, Guy. *La Guadeloupe: Etude géographique,* 1961.

Leiris, Michel. *Contacts de civilisations en Martinique et en Guadeloupe,* 1955.

L'Historial Antillais, 6 vols., 1981.

Schnepel, Ellen. *Language, Politics and the Creole Movement in Guadeloupe, French West Indies,* forthcoming.

Singaravélou. *Les Indiens de la Guadeloupe,* 1976.

—Ellen M. Schnepel

Guam

Culture Name

Chamorro

Alternative Names

Guamanian

Orientation

Identification. Guam is the southernmost island in the Mariana Islands chain. The Chamorro people and their language are indigenous throughout the archipelago.

Location and Geography. Guam, the largest island in Micronesia, is fifteen hundred miles southeast of Tokyo and six thousand miles west of San Francisco. It has an area of 212 square miles, (550 square kilometers). A high limestone plateau forms the northern regions. The southern region is of volcanic origin, with a mountainous terrain of red clay hills, waterfalls, rivers, and streams.

Demography. Guam suffered radical depopulation in the late 1600s, when wars against the Spanish and diseases introduced by Spanish settlers resulted in the death of almost 95 percent of the population. Precolonial estimates of the population of the Mariana Islands range from forty thousand to one-hundred thousand. Spanish settlement in 1668, resulted in a population decline to three thousand by 1700. The population in 1990 was nearly 150,000, a six fold increase since 1940, largely as a result of immigration after 1965. In 1990, only 43 percent of the population was of Chamorro ancestry. The largest immigrant population is from the Philippines, followed by American military personnel and other Asian immigrants.

Linguistic Affiliation. The Chamorro language, which is spoken throughout the Mariana Islands, is an Austronesian language.

Symbolism. The most enduring symbol is the latte stone, a megalithic structure used to elevate houses in the precolonial period. First built around C.E. 800, latte stones are large coral blocks composed of two pieces: a trapezoidal stone pillar called a *haligi,* and a hemispherical cap called a *tasa* that rests atop the *haligi.* Because construction of these stones was time and labor consuming, their production ceased after the onset of wars against Spanish colonizers. The latte stone has become a symbol of Chamorro strength, pride, resistance, and survival.

History and Ethnic Relations

Emergence of the Nation. In 1521, Ferdinand Magellan landed on Guam. In 1565, Spain claimed the Mariana Islands, but a colonial settlement was not founded until 1668. After four years of conflict, the leader of the Jesuit mission was killed by Chamorros, leading to thirty years of warfare. Spain maintained a colonial presence until 1898, and contemporary Chamorro culture evidences much Hispanic influence, particularly the preeminence of the Roman Catholic Church.

In 1898, the United States military replaced Spanish rule as a consequence of the Spanish-American War. For the next fifty years, the United States Navy ruled in a nondemocratic, authoritarian fashion. The entire island was designated a naval base, and villagers were expected to conform to naval standards of hygiene and decorum. No political or civil rights were granted to the people until after World War II.

Japanese military forces invaded in 1944. For two and a half years, the Chamorro were forced to provide food and labor to the Japanese military.

The 1944 U.S. military campaign to reoccupy Guam resulted in many ambivalent encounters. Chamorros were elated to see their lives restored to postwar normalcy, but many were disappointed when their lands were seized by the U.S. military. By 1948, the U.S. military and other federal agen-

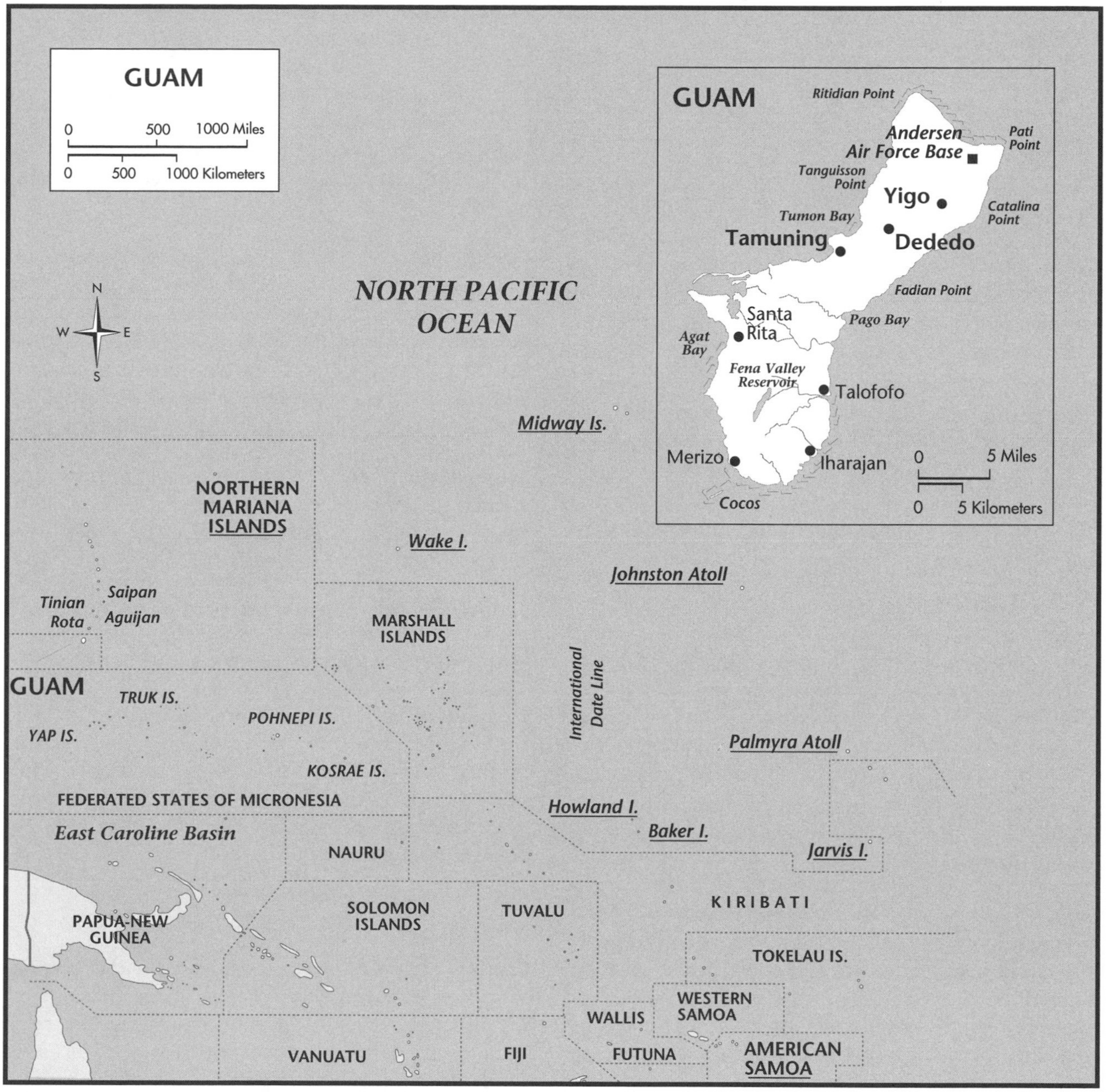

Guam

cies had taken 42 percent of the land, primarily for military bases, but also for restricted recreational areas. The military still controls more than one-third of Guam's land. In over a century of United States rule, the Chamorro have never had an opportunity to decide their political status. Guam remains a colony of the United States, officially classified as an unincorporated territory. A sovereignty movement has sought self-determination for the last two decades.

National Identity. Chamorros have a dual identity as the indigenous people of the Mariana Islands and a part of the United States. The value of *inafa'maolek*, literally translates as "to make good" and connotes a spirit of interdependence and cooperation. This concept bonds people to the idea that residents can live peacefully and productively when they act in the interests of the group rather than the individual.

Ethnic Relations. After the 1970s, ethnic tension between Chamorros and Filipinos became pronounced. Today, there is tension between a growing population of islanders from the Federated States of Micronesia and various indigenous groups. These tensions are exhibited more in the form of racial jokes than in violent acts.

Urbanism, Architecture, and the Use of Space

The latte stone house is the best known form of traditional architecture. Eight to twelve stones are used for each house, lined up in parallel rows of four to six. The stones range from four to sixteen feet high and weigh forty thousand to sixty thousand pounds. The houses built on top of the megaliths were typically long and narrow.

Modern houses are typically concrete structures able to withstand typhoons. Many families live in rural clan compounds where many members of the extended family live in close proximity. The immigrant population dominates the urban areas, living in apartment complexes and condominiums.

Food and Economy

Food in Daily Life. Food is a significant part of the cultural economy, reflecting an affinity with the land. Sharing food is part of a system of reciprocity based on a sense of perpetual interpersonal obligation. Daily foods include traditional staples such as rice, fish, breadfruit, and taro, in addition to growing quantities of imported foods such as canned goods, and fresh and frozen meats and vegetables, readily available for purchase at local grocery stores.

Food Customs at Ceremonial Occasions. Each village celebrates the feast day of its patron saint. These fiestas draw large crowds, with prolific amounts of food prepared for reciprocal exchanges among clan members and friends. Killing a pig or cow and preparing vegetable and seafood dishes are typical aspects of a fiesta.

Basic Economy. By circulating items of food and other material goods, and lending support when labor is needed, Chamorros maintain and strengthen links of kin and friendship. During funerals, family members and friends give food, service, and money for nine days after the death. The family of the deceased acknowledges this support by reciprocating with money, goods, or services when those families are in need.

Guam's modern economy revolves around a growing cash sector and wage labor employment, particularly in the government and tourist industries. Guam's national currency is the U.S. dollar, and U.S. federal government spending and local government expenditures fuel Guam's domestic spending.

Land Tenure and Property. Land traditionally was owned by the clan as a corporate group. During the reoccupation by the U.S. military, almost half the island was taken by the American government. These acts dispossessed many Chamorros, who had few assets other than land. The United States Congress later established private ownership of land.

Commercial Activities. Most residents work for wages and there is subsistence farming of bananas, papaya, guava, mango, breadfruit, and taro. The government funded by local taxes and U.S. federal tax transfers employs the largest proportion of the adult population, while hotels, the service industry, and the military also employ large numbers.

Major Industries. The tourist industry is the largest private sector source of income. Hotels, restaurants, and entertainment provide for millions of tourists, primarily from Japan.

Trade. Imports exceed exports in value by 17 to 1, as almost all of the island's manufactured goods are imported from the United States and Japan.

Division of Labor. Both men and women work in the wage economy. In the nonwage sector, men and women share agricultural responsibilities, while men also engage in fishing and hunting. Women have traditionally managed family resources, including land and food.

Social Stratification

Classes and Castes. Chamorro society emphasizes respect for the elderly. The practice of *manngingi*, ("to smell") entails sniffing the right hand of an elderly person to express one's deep regard. Before colonial rule, Chamorros recognized the power and authority of clan elders. Informal positions of authority were granted to elders who commanded the respect of their clan members. Elders could pool the labor and material resources of their clans in times of need.

The class system has two categories: the *manakhilo* ("high people") and *manakpapa'* ("low people"). The manakhilo includes wealthy families from the capital of Hagåtña who have held positions of power since the colonial era.

Symbols of Social Stratification. Class lines are not strict because most clans have members in both social classes, and the rich and the poor tend to live side by side within family compounds in rural villages. Those outside the clan compound may live in modern housing subdivisions that congregate people along economic lines.

Political Life

Government. In 1950, civil and political rights were granted to the Chamorro people through the passage of an Organic Act for Guam by the United States Congress, which also granted U.S. citizenship to the Chamorro. Guam is an unincorporated territory of the United States. Political life revolves around articulating, explaining, and defining Guam's ambiguous relationship with the United States. The Organic Act established a unicameral legislature, a superior court, and a governor.

Leadership and Political Officials. Leaders are elected and are predominantly of Chamorro ethnicity. These political officials come from the Democratic and Republican parties of Guam. These parties emerged in the 1970s along cultural rather than ideological lines. Party politics express historical clan rivalries more than differences in political ideology.

Social Problems and Control. Uncontrolled population increases have contributed to a diminished level of social welfare in the last decade. Overcrowded schools, hospitals, housing areas, and prisons reflect the social problems of overpopulation. Unresolved land problems, unrestrained immigration, and indigenous rights issues, along with substance abuse and domestic violence, are significant sources of tension.

Military Activity. The U.S. Navy and Air Force occupy one-third of the land and account for approximately 20 percent of the population. An air force base, a naval base, and a naval communications center form the largest concentration of military resources on the island.

Social Welfare and Change Programs

Guam receives welfare assistance from the U.S. government. Additionally, the local government, the Roman Catholic church, and private organizations sponsor programs to assist victims of domestic violence, homelessness, and terminal illness.

Nongovernmental Organizations and Other Associations

The American Red Cross and the American Cancer Society have offices on Guam, and privately funded organizations address social and health problems. Indigenous rights groups have gained international status through the United Nations, including groups such as Chamoru Nation and the Organization of Peoples for Indigenous Rights.

Gender Roles and Statuses

Division of Labor by Gender. Chamorro culture had a balance in gender roles. Power within the clan belonged to both the oldest son and the oldest daughter. Women traditionally held power over the household, while men conducted affairs in the public sphere, including hunting and fishing. The oldest daughter cared for her parents in their older years. Three centuries of colonialism have created much change, particularly in the public sphere. Men dominate political offices, and women are leaders in many social, religious, and cultural organizations.

The Relative Status of Women and Men. After more than three centuries of colonial rule and the dominance of the Roman Catholic church on Guam, the relative status of men and women has changed in favor of higher status for men's roles. Under both Spanish and American rule, men were selected over women to hold positions in any public capacity, whether in the government, business, or church. Women's power in the household has largely been maintained through their control over familial resources, including the paychecks of husbands and children, and the labor resources of all family members. In the past half century, women have successfully found acceptance as elected officials and leaders of numerous government and civic organizations, although men still vastly outnumber women in positions of political leadership.

Marriage, Family, and Kinship

Marriage. The groom's family sponsors the marriage, providing the bride with her wedding dress and other items of value. In addition, they throw a party to demonstrate their ability to provide for their new daughter. Traditionally, upon marriage, the woman was expected to relocate to her husband's clan land, although today this practice often is forgone in favor of whatever housing is available.

Domestic Unit. The extended family or clan, is the core of society. The domestic unit can include grandparents, parents, children, grandchildren, cousins, and other relatives. The practice of *poksai*, a form of adoption, is common. In this system, childless women may raise a niece or nephew and grandparents may exercise parental control over a grandchild.

Inheritance. Sons and daughters generally inherit land and other material possessions equally from both parents, with protections extended to the youngest child and any unmarried children.

Kin Groups. The closest kin group consists of first and second cousins from the mother's and father's lines and may include godparents and their children. The system of clan names allows Chamorros to navigate relationships despite an abundance of duplicate surnames. Clan names reflect kinship along male and female lineages in ways that surnames do not. Persons with different surnames may share a common clan name, revealing a relationship along the lineage. Generally, people place priority in the mother's clan line.

SOCIALIZATION

Infant Care. While biological parents and grandparents are the traditional providers of infant care, the larger extended family provides a network of assistance. People show great affection to infants, frequently smelling and lightly pinching, squeezing, and biting babies. Chamorros believe that feelings of *matgodai* have such spiritually powerful effects that failing to demonstrate affection can make a baby cranky or cause illness.

Child Rearing and Education. Nearly all the major events in a young person's life revolve around celebrations in clan circles. Children are socialized from birth to show respect to their relatives. While the extended family provides a network of assistance for child rearing, some working parents place their children in day care or preschool. There is mandatory schooling from ages five to sixteen.

Higher Education. The University of Guam is the only four-year accredited institution of higher learning in the western Pacific. Most of its students are graduates of Guam's high schools.

ETIQUETTE

Respect for elders and authority figures is a core cultural value. Chamorros demonstrate respect by bending over and sniffing an older person's right hand.

RELIGION

Religious Beliefs. Chamorros believe that their ancestors have lived in the Mariana Islands since the dawn of time. In this world view, the Mariana Islands lie at the center of the universe and all human life began in Guam. While almost all residents are baptized into the Roman Catholic faith or belong to another Christian denomination, animistic beliefs persist, including a respect for ancestral spirits, or *taotaomo'na,* who are believed to occupy certain trees and other areas in the forests. Persons entering the jungle are expected to ask permission from the taotaomo'na and remain quiet and respectful. Those who offend the taotaomo'na may receive bruises or suffer from inexplicable ailments.

Religious Practitioners. In precolonial days, persons referred to as *makahna* mediated between the spiritual and physical worlds. While Spanish Catholic missionaries abolished these practices, many persist. Viewed primarily as herbal healers, *suruhanu* and *suruhana* also function as healers of those with a variety of illnesses.

Rituals and Holy Places. Jungle areas and sites in which latte stones are located are considered sacred. In precolonial years people buried family members beneath latte stones and thus ancestral spirits are assumed to reside there. Ritual behavior in the presence of latte stones or in jungle areas includes maintaining quiet and decorum and showing respect for the environment.

Death and the Afterlife. Many Chamorros continue to observe ancient animistic beliefs. The acceptance of the taotaomo'na "people of before" reveals an enduring belief in the existence of persons' spirits beyond their physical life. Many families tell stories about visits from a deceased relative whose presence has been made known through scent, touch, or appearance. Every year on All Soul's Day, Chamorros remember their ancestors by holding special memorial services and decorating their graves with flowers, candles, photographs, and other mementos.

MEDICINE AND HEALTH CARE

Since World War II, American-trained and licensed doctors and nurses have been the prevalent health care professionals. Chamorro health care specialists continue to practice health care, using a variety of homemade herbal medicines and massage techniques.

SECULAR CELEBRATIONS

American colonialism introduced secular celebrations such as Veterans' Day and Martin Luther King, Jr. Day. The most widely celebrated secular holiday is Liberation Day, commemorated each year on 21 July to observe the retaking of Guam by the U.S. military in 1944. A parade with floats and marching bands is staged to honor military veterans and Chamorros who lived through years of wartime terror.

THE ARTS AND HUMANITIES

Support for the Arts. The Guam Council on the Arts and Humanities, funded by the government of Guam, and the Guam Humanities Council, funded by the U.S. government, sponsor a variety of cultural activities. Public radio and television stations encourage the arts. Public and private art galleries include the Isla Center for the Arts at the University of Guam and the Puntan Dos Amantes Gallery.

Literature. As a culture rooted in oral traditions, Guam has little written literature. A few Chamorro novels have been published. A literary journal published by the university's literature faculty motivates poets and other creative writers.

Graphic Arts. There exists a growing community of local artists, particularly in the fields of painting and woodcarving. A number of locally owned arts shops, such as the Guam Gallery of Art and Jill Benavente's Mangilao store, feature a wide variety of locally produced art pieces.

Performance Arts. The University of Guam's Fine Arts Theater, Southern High School's Performance Center, and the Tiyan Theater are popular venues for locally written and produced plays and musical performances.

THE STATE OF THE PHYSICAL AND SOCIAL SCIENCES

Support for the physical and social sciences comes primarily through the University of Guam's annual College of Arts and Sciences Conference, the annual High School Science Fair, and the university-sponsored journal *Micronesica,* which publishes scientific research.

BIBLIOGRAPHY

Carter, Lee D., William L. Wuerch, and Rosa Roberta Carter, eds. *Guam History: Perspectives, Volume One*, 1997.

Cunningham, Lawrence J. *Ancient Chamorro Society,* 1992.

Hale'-ta: I Ma Gobetna-ña Guam, Governing Guam: Before and After the Wars, 1994.

Hattori, Anne Perez. "Colonial Dis-Ease: U.S. Navy Health Policies and the Chamorros of Guam, 1898–1941." Unpublished dissertation, University of Hawai'ii at Manoa, 1999.

Pacific Island Profiles, 1995.

Rogers, Robert F. *Destiny's Landfall: A History of Guam,* 1995.

Russell, Scott. *Tiempon I Manmofo 'na: Ancient Chamorro Culture and History of the Northern Mariana Islands,* 1998.

Sanchez, Pedro C. *Guahan Guam: The History of Our Island,* 1989.

Souder, Laura Torres. *Daughters of the Island: Contemporary Chamorro Women Organizers on Guam,* 1992.

Wei, Debbie, and Rachel Kamel, eds. *Resistance in Paradise: Rethinking 100 Years of U.S. Involvement in the Caribbean and the Pacific,* 1998.

—ANNE PEREZ HATTORI

GUATEMALA

CULTURE NAME

Guatemalan

ALTERNATIVE NAME

Chapines

ORIENTATION

Identification. The name Guatemala, meaning "land of forests," was derived from one of the Mayan dialects spoken by the indigenous people at the time of the Spanish conquest in 1523. It is used today by outsiders, as well as by most citizens, although for many purposes the descendants of the original inhabitants still prefer to identify themselves by the names of their specific language dialects, which reflect political divisions from the sixteenth century. The pejorative terms *indio* and *natural* have been replaced in polite conversation and publication by *Indígena*. Persons of mixed or non-indigenous race and heritage may be called *Ladino*, a term that today indicates adherence to Western, as opposed to indigenous, culture patterns, and may be applied to acculturated Indians, as well as others. A small group of African–Americans, known as Garifuna, lives on the Atlantic coast, but their culture is more closely related to those found in other Caribbean nations than to the cultures of Guatemala itself.

The national culture also was influenced by the arrival of other Europeans, especially Germans, in the second half of the nineteenth century, as well as by the more recent movement of thousands of Guatemalans to and from the United States. There has been increased immigration from China, Japan, Korea, and the Middle East, although those groups, while increasingly visible, have not contributed to the national culture, nor have many of them adopted it as their own.

Within Central America the citizens of each country are affectionately known by a nickname of which they are proud, but which is sometimes used disparagingly by others, much like the term "Yankee." The term "Chapín" (plural, "Chapines"), the origin of which is unknown, denotes anyone from Guatemala. When traveling outside of Guatemala, all its citizens define themselves as Guatemalans and/or Chapines. While at home, however, there is little sense that they share a common culture. The most important split is between Ladinos and Indians. Garifuna are hardly known away from the Atlantic coast and, like most Indians, identify themselves in terms of their own language and culture.

Location and Geography. Guatemala covers an area of 42,042 square miles (108,889 square kilometers) and is bounded on the west and north by Mexico; on the east by Belize, the Caribbean Sea, Honduras and El Salvador; and on the south by the Pacific Ocean. The three principal regions are the northern lowland plains of the Petén and the adjacent Atlantic littoral; the volcanic highlands of the Sierra Madre, cutting across the country from northwest to southeast; and the Pacific lowlands, a coastal plain stretching along the entire southern boundary. The country has a total of 205 miles (330 kilometers) of coastline. Between the Motagua River and the Honduran border on the southeast there is a dry flat corridor that receives less than forty inches (one hundred centimeters) of rain per year. Although the country lies within the tropics, its climate varies considerably, depending on altitude and rainfall patterns. The northern lowlands and the Atlantic coastal area are very warm and experience rain throughout much of the year. The Pacific lowlands are drier, and because they are at or near sea level, remain warm. The highlands are temperate. The coolest weather there (locally called "winter") occurs during the rainy season from May or June to November, with daily temperatures ranging from 50 to 60 degrees Fahrenheit in the higher altitudes, and from 60 to 70 degrees in Guatemala City, which is about a mile above sea level.

Guatemala

"Summer" denotes the period between February and May, when the temperature during the day in Guatemala City often reaches into the 80s.

The Spanish conquerors preferred the highlands, despite a difficult journey from the Atlantic coast, and that is where they placed their primary settlements. The present capital, Guatemala City, was founded in 1776 after a flood and an earthquake had destroyed two earlier sites. Although the Maya had earlier inhabited the lowlands of the Petén and the lower Motagua River, by the time the first Spaniards arrived, they lived primarily in the Pacific lowlands and western highlands. The highlands are still largely populated by their descendants. The eastern Motagua corridor was settled by Spaniards and is still inhabited primarily by Ladinos. Large plantations of coffee, sugarcane, bananas, and cardamom, all grown primarily for export, cover much of the Pacific lowlands. These are owned by large, usually nonresident, landholders and are worked by local Ladinos and Indians who journey to the coast from highland villages for the harvest.

Demography. The 1994 census showed a total of 9,462,000 people, but estimates for 1999 reached twelve million, with more than 50 percent living in urban areas. The forty-year period of social unrest, violence, and civil war (1956–1996) resulted in massive emigration to Mexico and the United States and has been estimated to have resulted in one million dead, disappeared, and emigrated. Some of the displaced have returned from United Nations refugee camps in Mexico, as have many undocumented emigrants to the United States.

The determination of ethnicity for demographic purposes depends primarily on language, yet some scholars and government officials use other criteria, such as dress patterns and life style. Thus, estimates of the size of the Indian population vary from 35 percent to more than 50 percent—the latter figure probably being more reliable. The numbers of the non-Mayan indigenous peoples such as the Garifuna and the Xinca have been dwindling. Those two groups now probably number less than five thousand as many of their young people become Ladinoized or leave for better opportunities in the United States.

Linguistic Affiliation. Spanish is the official language, but since the end of the civil war in December 1996, twenty-two indigenous languages, mostly dialects of the Mayan linguistic family, have been recognized. The most widely spoken are Ki'che', Kaqchikel, Kekchi, and Mam. A bilingual program for beginning primary students has been in place since the late 1980s, and there are plans to make it available in all Indian communities. Constitutional amendments are being considered to recognize some of those languages for official purposes.

Many Indians, especially women and those in the most remote areas of the western highlands, speak no Spanish, yet many Indian families are abandoning their own language to ensure that their children become fluent in Spanish, which is recognized as a necessity for living in the modern world, and even for travel outside one's village. Since the various indigenous languages are not all mutually intelligible, Spanish is increasingly important as a *lingua franca*. The Academy of Mayan Languages, completely staffed by Maya scholars, hopes its research will promote a return to Proto-Maya, the language from which all the various dialects descended, which is totally unknown today. Ladinos who grow up in an Indian area may learn the local language, but bilingualism among Ladinos is rare.

In the cities, especially the capital, there are private primary and secondary schools where foreign languages are taught and used along with Spanish, especially English, German, and French.

Symbolism. Independence Day (15 September) and 15 August, the day of the national patron saint, María, are the most important national holidays, and together reflect the European origin of the nation-state, as does the national anthem, "Guatemala Felíz" ("Happy Guatemala"). However, many of the motifs used on the flag (the quetzal bird and the ceiba tree); in public monuments and other artwork (the figure of the Indian hero Tecún Umán, the pyramids and stelae of the abandoned and ruined Mayan city of Tikal, the colorful motifs on indigenous textiles, scenes from villages surrounding Lake Atitlán); in literature (the novels of Nobel laureate Miguel Angel Asturias) and in music (the marimba, the dance called son) are associated with the Indian culture, even when some of their elements originated in Europe or in precolonial Mexico. Miss Guatemala, almost always a Ladina, wears Indian dress in her public appearances. Black beans, guacamole, tortillas, chili, and tamales, all of which were eaten before the coming of the Spaniards, are now part of the national culture, and have come to symbolize it for both residents and expatriates, regardless of ethnicity or class.

History and Ethnic Relations

Emergence of the Nation. Guatemala, along with other Central American Spanish colonies, declared its independence on 15 September 1821. Until 1839, it belonged first to Mexico and then to a federation known as the United Provinces of Central America. It was not until 1945 that a constitution guaranteeing civil and political rights for all people, including women and Indians, was adopted. However, Indians continued to be exploited and disparaged until recently, when international opinion forced Ladino elites to modify their attitudes and behavior. This shift was furthered by the selection of Rigoberta Menchú, a young Maya woman, for the Nobel Peace Prize in 1992.

Severe repression and violence during the late 1970s and 1980s was followed by a Mayan revitalization movement that has gained strength since the signing of the Peace Accords in 1996. While Mayan languages, dress, and religious practices have been reintroduced or strengthened, acculturation to the national culture has continued. Today more Indians are becoming educated at all levels, including postgraduate university training. A few have become professionals in medicine, engineering, journalism, law, and social work. Population pressure has forced many others out of agriculture and into cottage industries, factory work, merchandising, teaching, clerical work, and various white-collar positions in the towns and cities. Ironically, after the long period of violence and forced enlistment, many now volunteer for the armed forces.

Ethnic Relations. Some Ladinos see the Indian revitalization movement as a threat to their hegemony and fear that they will eventually suffer violence at Indian hands. There is little concrete evidence to support those fears. Because the national culture is composed of a blend of European and indigenous traits and is largely shared by Maya, Ladinos, and many newer immigrants, it is likely that the future will bring greater consolidation, and that social class, rather than ethnic background, will determine social interactions.

Urbanism, Architecture, and the Use of Space

The Spanish imposed a gridiron pattern on communities of all sizes, which included a central plaza, generally with a public water fountain known as a "pila," around which were situated a Catholic church, government offices, and the homes of high-ranking persons. Colonial homes included a central patio with living, dining, and sleeping rooms lined up off the surrounding corridors. A service patio with a pila and a kitchen with an open fireplace under a large chimney was located behind the general living area. Entrances were directly off the street, and gardens were limited to the interior patios.

Those town and house plans persist, except that homes of the elite now tend to be placed on the periphery of the town or city and have modified internal space arrangements, including second stories. An open internal patio is still popular, but gardens now surround the house, with the whole being enclosed behind high walls. The older, centrally located colonial houses are now occupied by offices or have been turned into rooming houses or hotels.

Indian towns retain these characteristics, but many of the smaller hamlets exhibit little patterning. The houses—mostly made of sun-dried bricks (adobe) and roofed with corrugated aluminum or ceramic tiles—may stretch out along a path or be located on small parcels of arable land. The poorest houses often have only one large room containing a hearth; perhaps a bed, table and chairs or stools; a large ceramic water jug and other ceramic storage jars; a wooden chest for clothes and valuables; and sometimes a cabinet for dishes and utensils. Other implements may be tied or perched on open rafters in baskets. The oldest resident couple occupies the bed, with children and younger adults sleeping on reed mats (*petates*) on the floor; the mats are rolled up when not in use. Running water in the home or yard is a luxury that only some villages enjoy. Electricity is widely available except in the most remote areas. Its primary use is for light, followed by refrigeration and television.

The central plazas of smaller towns and villages are used for a variety of purposes. On market days, they are filled with vendors and their wares; in the heat of the day people will rest on whatever benches may be provided; in early evening young people may congregate and parade, seeking partners of the opposite sex, flirting, and generally having a good time. In Guatemala City, the central plaza has become the preferred site for political demonstrations.

The national palace faces this central plaza; although it once was a residence for the president, today it is used only for official receptions and meetings with dignitaries. More than any other building, it is a symbol of governmental authority and power. The walls of its entryway have murals depicting scenes honoring the Spanish and Mayan heritages. Other government buildings are scattered throughout the central part of Guatemala City; some occupy former residences, others are in a newer complex characterized by modern, massive, high-rising buildings of seven or eight floors. Some of these structures are adorned on the outside with murals depicting both Mayan and European symbols.

Food and Economy

Food in Daily Life. Corn made into tortillas or tamales, black beans, rice, and wheat in the form of bread or pasta are staples eaten by nearly all Guatemalans. Depending on their degree of affluence, people also consume chicken, pork, and beef, and those living near bodies of water also eat fish and shellfish. With improvements in refrigeration and transport, seafood is becoming increasingly popular in Guatemala City. The country has long been known for vegetables and fruits, including avocados, radishes, potatoes, sweet potatoes, squash, carrots, beets, onions, and tomatoes. Lettuce, snow peas, green beans, broccoli, cauliflower, artichokes, and turnips are grown for export and are also available in local markets; they are eaten more by Ladinos than by Indians. Fruits include pineapples,

People walk past fast-food restaurants in Guatemala City, Guatemala. "Fast food" is a fairly recent addition to traditional Guatemalan diets.

papayas, mangoes, a variety of melons, citrus fruits, peaches, pears, plums, guavas, and many others of both native and foreign origin. Fruit is eaten as dessert, or as a snack in-between meals.

Three meals per day are the general rule, with the largest eaten at noon. Until recently, most stores and businesses in the urban areas closed for two to three hours to allow employees time to eat at home and rest before returning to work. Transportation problems due to increased traffic, both on buses and in private vehicles, are bringing rapid change to this custom. In rural areas women take the noon meal to the men in the fields, often accompanied by their children so that the family can eat as a group. Tortillas are eaten by everyone but are especially important for the Indians, who may consume up to a dozen at a time, usually with chili, sometimes with beans and/or stews made with or flavored with meat or dried shrimp.

Breakfast for the well to do may be large, including fruit, cereal, eggs, bread, and coffee; the poor may drink only an *atol*, a thin gruel made with any one of several thickeners—oatmeal, cornstarch, cornmeal, or even ground fresh corn. Others may only have coffee with sweet bread. All drinks are heavily sweetened with refined or brown sugar. The evening meal is always lighter than that at noon.

Although there are no food taboos, many people believe that specific foods are classified as "hot" or "cold" by nature, and there may be temporary prohibitions on eating them, depending upon age, the condition of one's body, the time of day, or other factors.

Food Customs at Ceremonial Occasions. The ceremonial year is largely determined by the Roman Catholic Church, even for those who do not profess that faith. Thus, the Christmas period, including Advent and the Day of the Kings on 6 January, and Easter week are major holidays for everyone. The patron saints of each village, town or city are honored on their respective days. The *cofradia* organization, imposed by the colonial Spanish Catholic Church, is less important now, but where it persists, special foods are prepared. Tamales are the most important ceremonial food. They are eaten on all special occasions, including private parties and celebrations, and on weekends, which are special because Sunday is recognized as being a holy day, as well as a holiday. A special vegetable and meat salad called *fiambre* is eaten on 1 November, the Day of the Dead, when families congregate in the cemeteries to honor, placate, and share food with deceased relatives. Codfish cooked in various forms is eaten at Easter, and Christmas is again a time for gourmet tamales and *ponche*, a rum-based drink containing spices and fruits. Beer and rum, including a fairly raw variety known as *aguardiente* are the most popular alcoholic drinks, although urban elites prefer Scotch whisky.

Basic Economy. Guatemala's most important resource is its fertile land, although only 12 percent of the total landmass is arable. In 1990, 52 percent of the labor force was engaged in agriculture, which contributed 24 percent of the gross domestic product. Although both Ladinos and Indians farm, 68 percent of the agricultural labor force was Indian in 1989. Forty-seven percent of Indian men were self-employed as farmers, artisans, or merchants; the average income for this group was only about a third of that for Ladino men. Agriculture accounts for about one-fourth of the gross domestic product.

The country has traditionally produced many agricultural products for export, including coffee, sugar, cardamom, bananas, and cotton. In recent years flowers and vegetables have become important. However, Guatemala is not self-sufficient in basic grains such as wheat, rice, and even maize, which are imported from the United States. Many small farmers, both Indian and Ladino, have replaced traditional subsistence crops with those grown for export. Although their cash income may be enhanced, they are forced to buy more foods. These include not only the basic staples, but also locally produced "junk" foods such as potato chips and cupcakes as well as condiments such as mayonnaise.

Affluent city dwellers and returning expatriates increasingly buy imported fruits, vegetables, and specialty items, both raw and processed. Those items come from neighboring countries such as Mexico and El Salvador as well as from the United States and Europe, especially Spain, Italy, and France.

Land Tenure and Property. The concept of private property in land, houses, tools, and machinery is well established even though most Indian communities have long held some lands as communal property that is allotted as needed. Unfortunately, many rural people have not registered their property, and many swindles occur, leading to lengthy and expensive lawsuits. As long as owners occupied their land and passed it on to their children or other heirs, there were few problems, but as the population has become more mobile, the number of disputes has escalated. Disputes occur within villages and even within families as individuals move onto lands apparently abandoned while the owners are absent. Sometimes the same piece of land is sold two or more times to different outside persons, often speculators from urban areas who discover the fraud only when they find another person occupying the land. Some land disputes have occurred when agents of the government have illegally confiscated property belonging to Indian communities. In other cases, homeless peasants have taken over unused land on large private plantations and government reserves.

A woman embroidering in Antigua. Handicrafts have been produced and widely traded in Guatemala for centuries.

Commercial Activities. Agricultural products are the goods most commonly produced for sale within the country and for export. Handicrafts have been produced and widely traded since precolonial times and are in great demand by tourists, museums, and collectors, and are increasingly exported through middlemen. The most sought after items include hand woven cotton and woolen textiles and clothing items made from them; baskets; ceramics; carved wooden furniture, containers, utensils and decorative items; beaded and silver jewelry; and hand-blown glassware. These items are made in urban and rural areas by both Ladinos and Indians in small workshops and by individuals in their own homes.

Assembly plants known as *maquilas* produce clothing and other items for export, using imported materials and semiskilled labor. Despite criticisms of this type of enterprise in the United States, many Guatemalans find it a welcome source of employment with relatively high wages.

Major Industries. Guatemala has many light industries, most of which involve the processing of locally grown products such as chicken, beef, pork, coffee, wheat, corn, sugar, cotton, cacao, vegetables and fruits, and spices such as cinnamon and cardamom. Beer and rum are major industries, as is the production of paper goods. A large plastics industry produces a wide variety of products for home and industrial use. Several factories produce cloth from domestic and imported cotton. Some of these products are important import substitutes, and others are exported to other Central American countries and the United States.

Division of Labor. In the Ladino sector, upper-class men and women work in business, academia, and the major professions. Older Ladino and Indian teenagers of both sexes are the primary workers in *maquilas*, a form of employment that increasingly is preferred to working as a domestic. Children as young as four or five years work at household tasks and in the fields in farming families. In the cities, they may sell candies or other small products on the streets or "watch" parked cars. Although by law all children must attend school between ages seven and thirteen, many do not, sometimes because there is no school nearby, because the child's services are needed at home, or because the family is too poor to provide transportation, clothing, and supplies. The situation is improving; in 1996, 88 percent of all children of primary age were enrolled in school, although only 26 percent of those of high school age were enrolled.

Social Stratification

Classes and Castes. Social class based on wealth, education, and family prestige operates as a sorting mechanism among both Indians and Ladinos. Race is also clearly a component, but may be less important than culture and lifestyle, except in the case of the black Garifuna, who are shunned by all other groups. Individual people of Indian background may be accepted in Ladino society if they are well educated and have the resources to live in a Western style. However, Indians as a group are poorer and less educated than are non-Indians. In the 1980s, illiteracy among Indians was 79 percent, compared with 40 percent among Ladinos. In 1989, 60 percent of Indians had no formal education, compared with 26 percent of Ladinos. Indians with thirteen or more years of education earned about one-third less than did Ladinos with a comparable level of education.

Symbols of Social Stratification. Dress varies significantly by class and caste. Professional and white-collar male workers in the cities usually wear suits, dress shirts, and neckties, and women in comparable pursuits dress fashionably, including stockings and high-heeled shoes. Nonemployed upper-class women dress more casually, often in blue jeans and T-shirts or blouses. They frequent beauty salons since personal appearance is considered an important indicator of class.

Poorer Ladinos, whether urban or rural, buy secondhand clothing from the United States that is sold at low prices in the streets and marketplaces. T-shirts and sweatshirts with English slogans are ubiquitous.

Many Mayan women, regardless of wealth, education, or residence, continue to wear their distinctive clothing: a wraparound or gathered, nearly ankle-length skirt woven with tie-dyed threads that produce interesting designs, topped with a cotton or rayon blouse embroidered with flower motifs about the neck, or a more traditional *huipil*. The *huipil* is hand woven on a backstrap loom and consists of two panels sewn together on the sides, leaving openings for the arms and head. It usually is embroidered with traditional designs. Shoes or sandals are almost universal, especially in towns and cities. Earrings, necklaces, and rings are their only jewelry.

Indian men are more likely to dress in a Western style. Today's fashions dictate "cowboy" hats, boots, and shirts for them and for lower-class rural Ladinos. In the more remote highland areas, many men continue to wear the clothing of their ancestors. The revitalization movement has reinforced the use of traditional clothing as a means of asserting one's identity.

Political Life

Government. As of 1993, the president and vice-president and sixteen members of the eighty-member congress are elected by the nation as a whole for non-renewable four-year terms, while the remaining sixty-four members of the unicameral legislature are popularly elected by the constituents of their locales. Despite universal suffrage, only a small percentage of citizens vote.

There are twenty-two departments under governors appointed by the president. Municipalities are autonomous, with locally elected officials, and are funded by the central government budget. In areas with a large Mayan population, there have been two sets of local government leaders, one Ladino and one Mayan, with the former taking precedence. In 1996, however, many official or "Ladino" offices were won by Maya.

Leadership and Political Officials. Political parties range from the extreme right to the left and represent varying interests. Thus, their numbers, size, and electoral success change over time. It generally is believed that most elected officials use their short periods in office to aggrandize their prestige and line their pockets. Most take office amid cheering and accolades but leave under a cloud, and many are forced to leave the country or choose to do so. While in office, they are able to bend the law and do favors for their constituents or for foreigners who wish to invest or do business in the country. Some national business gets accomplished, but only after lengthy delays, debate, and procrastination.

Social Problems and Control. Since the signing of the Peace Accords in December 1996, there has been continued social unrest and a general breakdown in the system of justice. Poverty, land pressure, unemployment, and a pervasive climate of enmity toward all "others" have left even rural communities in a state of disorganization. In many Maya communities, their traditional social organization having been disrupted or destroyed by the years of violence, the people now take the law into their own hands. Tired of petty crime, kidnappings, rapes, and murders and with no adequate governmental relief, they frequently lynch suspected criminals. In the cities, accused criminals frequently are set free for lack of evidence, since the police and judges are poorly trained, underpaid, and often corrupt. Many crimes are thought to have been committed by the army or by underground vigilante groups unhappy with the Peace Accords and efforts to end the impunity granted to those who committed atrocities against dissidents.

Military Activity. In 1997, the army numbered 38,500. In addition, there is a paramilitary national police force of 9,800, a territorial militia of about 300,000, and a small navy and air force.

Social Welfare and Change Programs

Guatemala has governmental and nongovernmental agencies that promote change in agriculture, taxes, banking, manufacturing, environmental protection, health, education, and human and civil rights.

Since 1945 the government has provided social security plans for workers, but only a small percentage of the populace has received these health and retirement benefits. There are free hospitals and clinics throughout the country, although many have inadequate equipment, medicines, and personnel. Free or inexpensive health services are offered as charities through various churches and by private individuals.

Gender Roles and Statuses

Division of Labor by Gender. Among both Maya and Ladinos, women are associated primarily with the domestic world and men work in agriculture, business, and manufacturing. However, well-educated professional women are accepted and often highly respected; many are owners and managers of businesses. More of these women are Ladinas than Mayas. Statistically, women are less educated and lower paid than their male counterparts. Their numbers exceed those of males in nursing, secretarial, and clerical jobs. The teaching force at all levels has attracted women as well as men, but men predominate.

In rural areas, Maya women and men may engage in agriculture, but the crops they grow are different. Men tend to grow basic grains such as corn and beans as well as export crops such as green beans and snow peas. Women grow vegetables and fruits for local consumption and sale, as well as herbs and spices.

Handicrafts also tend to be assigned according to gender. Pottery is most often made by Indian women and Ladino men. Similarly, Indian women are the only ones who weave on backstrap or stick looms, while both Indian and Ladino men weave on foot looms. Indian men knit woolen shoulder bags for their own use and for sale. Men of both ethnicities do woodwork and carpentry, bricklaying, and upholstering. Indian men carve images of saints, masks, slingshots, and decorative items for their own use or for sale. Men and boys fish, while women and girls as well as small boys gather wild foods and firewood. Women and children also tend sheep and goats.

Rural Ladinas do not often engage in agriculture. They concentrate on domestic work and cottage industries, especially those involving sewing, cooking, and processing of foods such as cheese,

A market set up in front of the church in Chichicastenango, Guatemala. Market-based commerce is still a vital part of the Guatemalan economy.

breads, and candies for sale along the highways or in the markets.

The Relative Status of Men and Women. Indian and poor Ladino women (as well as children) are often browbeaten and physically mistreated by men. Their only recourse is to return to their parents' home, but frequently are rejected by the parents for various reasons. A woman from a higher-status family is less likely to suffer in this way, especially if her marriage has been arranged by her parents. While walking, a Maya woman traditionally trails her husband; if he falls drunk by the wayside, she dutifully waits to care for him until he wakes up.

Marriage, Family, and Kinship

Marriage. Marriages are sometimes arranged in Maya communities, although most couples choose each other and often elope. Membership in private clubs and attendance at private schools provides a way for middle-class and upper-class young people to meet prospective mates. Parents may disapprove of a selection, but their children are likely able to persuade them. Marriages are celebrated in a civil ceremony that may be followed by a religious rite. Monogamy is the rule, although many men have a mistress as well as a wife. Among the poorer classes, both Mayan and Ladino, unions are free and ties are brittle; many children do not know, nor are they recognized by their fathers. Formal divorces are more common than many people believe, despite the disapproval of the Catholic Church. Until recently, a divorced woman did not have the right to retain her husband's surname; but she may sue for a share of his property to support herself and her minor children.

Domestic Unit. The nuclear family is the preferred and most common domestic unit. Among both Ladinos and Maya, a young couple may live at first in the home of the man's parents, or if that is inconvenient or overcrowded, with the parents of the woman. Wealthy Ladinos often provide elaborate houses close to their own homes as wedding presents for their sons and daughters.

Inheritance. Inheritance depends on a witnessed written or oral testament of the deceased, and since many people die without indicating their preferences, family disputes after death are very common among both Mayas and Ladinos. Land, houses, and personal belongings may be inherited by either sex, and claims may be contested in the courts and in intrafamily bickering.

A woman carries baskets of textiles along a street in Antigua. Guatemalan textiles are highly regarded for their quality.

SOCIALIZATION

Infant Care. The children of middle-class and upper-class Ladinos are cared for by their mothers, grandmothers, and young women, often from the rural areas, hired as nannies. They tend to be indulged by their caretakers. They may be breastfed for a few months but then are given bottles, which they may continue using until four or five years. To keep children from crying or complaining to their parents, nannies quickly give them whatever they demand.

Maya women in the rural areas depend upon their older children to help care for the younger ones. Babies are breastfed longer, but seldom after two years of age. They are always close to their mothers during this period, sleeping next to them and carried in shawls on their backs wherever they go. They are nursed frequently on demand wherever the mother may be. Little girls of five or six years may be seen carrying tiny babies in the same way in order to help out, but seldom are they out of sight of the mother. This practice may be seen as education for the child as well as caretaking for the infant. Indian children are socialized to take part in all the activities of the family as soon as they are physically and mentally capable.

Child Rearing and Education. Middle-class and upper-class Ladino children, especially in urban areas, are not expected to do any work until they are teenagers or beyond. They may attend a private preschool, sometimes as early as eighteen months, but formal education begins at age seven. Higher education is respected as a means of rising socially and economically. Children are educated to the highest level of which they are capable, depending on the finances of the family.

Higher Education. The national university, San Carlos, has until recently had free tuition, and is still the least expensive. As a result, it is overcrowded, but graduates many students who would not otherwise be able to attain an education. There are six other private universities, several with branches in secondary cities. They grant undergraduate and advanced degrees in the arts, humanities, and sciences, as well as medicine, dentistry, pharmacy, law, engineering, and architecture. Postgraduate work is often pursued abroad by the better and more affluent students, especially in the United States, Spain, Mexico, and some other Latin American countries.

ETIQUETTE

Etiquette varies considerably according to ethnicity. In the past, Indians were expected to defer to Ladinos, and in general they showed them respect and subservience at all times. In turn, they were treated by Ladinos as children or as persons of little worth. Some of those modes of behavior carried over into their own society, especially within the *cofradia* organization, where deliberate rudeness is considered appropriate on the part of the highest-ranking officers. Today there is a more egalitarian attitude on both sides, and in some cases younger Maya may openly show contempt for non-indigenous people. Maya children greet adults by bowing their heads and sometimes folding their hands before them, as in prayer. Adults greet other adults verbally, asking about one's health and that of one's family. They are not physically demonstrative.

Among Ladino urban women, greetings and farewells call for handshakes, arm or shoulder patting, embraces, and even cheek kissing, almost from first acquaintance. Men embrace and cheek kiss women friends of the family, and embrace but do not kiss each other. Children are taught to kiss all adult relatives and close acquaintances of their parents hello and goodbye.

In the smaller towns and until recently in the cities, if eye contact is made with strangers on the street, a verbal "good morning" or "good afternoon" is customary.

Religion

Religious Beliefs. Roman Catholicism, which was introduced by the Spanish and modified by Maya interpretations and syncretism, was almost universal in Guatemala until the early part of the twentieth century, when Protestantism began to make significant headway among both Ladinos and Maya. Today it has been estimated that perhaps 40 percent or more adhere to a Protestant church or sect ranging from established churches with international membership to small local groups celebrating their own set of beliefs under the leadership of lay pastors.

Many Maya combine membership in a Christian fellowship with a continued set of beliefs and practices inherited from their ancient ancestors. Rituals may still be performed to ensure agricultural success, easy childbirth, recovery from illness, and protection from the elements (including eclipses) and to honor and remember the dead. The Garifuna still practice an Afro-Caribbean form of ancestor worship that helps to meld together families broken by migration, plural marriages, and a social environment hostile to people of their race and culture.

Many of the indigenous people believe in spirits of nature, especially of specific caves, mountains, and bodies of water, and their religious leaders regularly perform ceremonies connected with these sites. The Catholic Church has generally been more lenient in allowing or ignoring dual allegiances than have Protestants, who tend to insist on strict adherence to doctrine and an abandonment of all "non-Christian" beliefs and practices, including Catholicism.

Medicine and Health Care

Although excellent modern medical care is available in the capital city for those who can afford it and even for the indigent, millions of people in the rural areas lack adequate health care and health education. The medical training at San Carlos University includes a field stint for advanced students in rural areas, and often these are the only well-trained medical personnel on duty at village-level government-run health clinics.

The less well educated have a variety of folk explanations and cures for disease and mental illnesses, including herbal remedies, dietary adjustments, magical formulas, and prayers to Christian saints, local gods, and deceased relatives.

Most births in the city occur in hospitals, but some are attended at home by midwives, as is more usual in rural areas. These practitioners learn their skills from other midwives and through government-run courses.

For many minor problems, local pharmacists may diagnose, prescribe, and administer remedies, including antibiotics.

The Arts and Humanities

Support for the Arts. The Ministry of Culture provides moral and some economic support for the arts, but most artists are self-supporting. Arts and handicrafts are important to all sectors of the population; artists are respected and patronized, especially in the cities where there are numerous art galleries. Even some of the smaller towns, such as Tecpán, Comalapa and Santiago de Atitlán offer paintings by local artists for sale to both foreign and Guatemalan visitors. There are dozens, perhaps hundreds, of indigenous "primitive" painters, some of whom are known internationally. Their products form an important part of the wares offered to tourists and local collectors. Non-indigenous painters are exhibited primarily in the capital city; these include many foreign artists as well as Guatemalans.

Graphic Arts. Textiles, especially those woven by women on the indigenous backstrap loom, are of such fine quality as to have been the object of scholarly study. The Ixchel Museum of Indian Textiles, located in Guatemala City at the Francisco

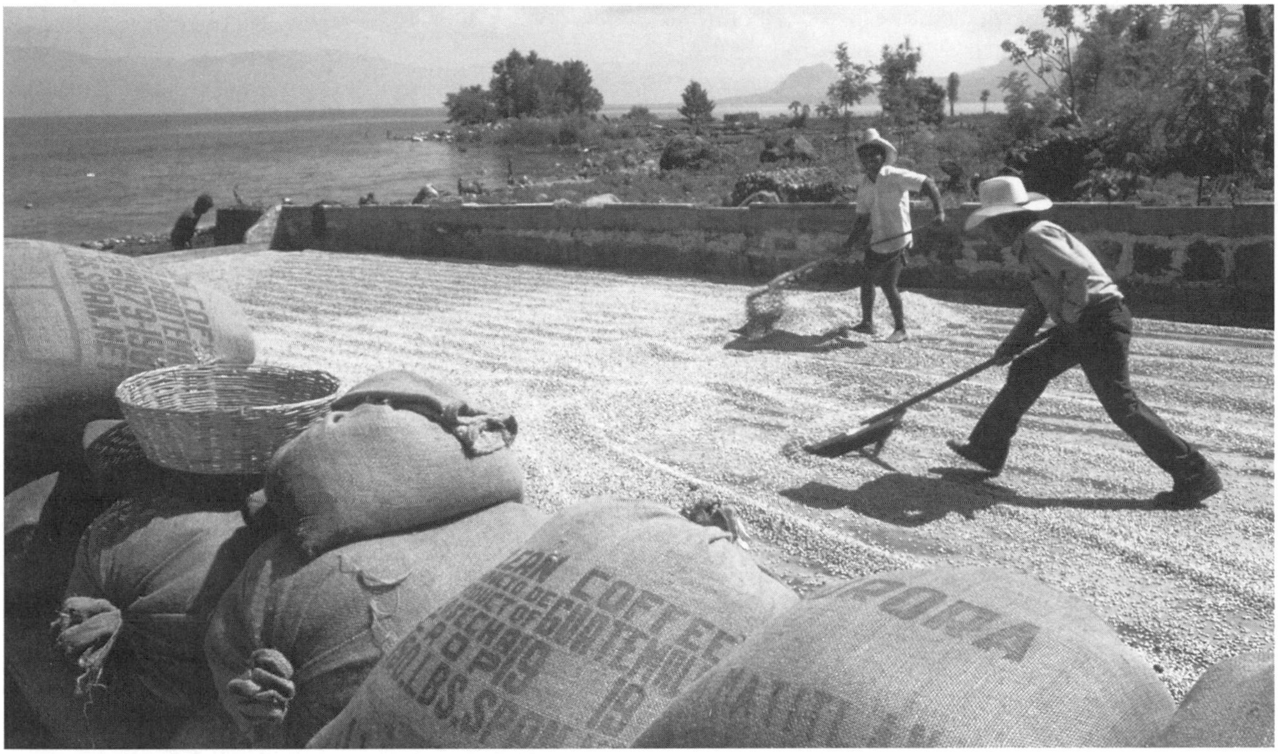

Men spread out coffee beans to dry them in the sun alongside Lake Atitlan. Agriculture is generally considered a male endeavor, although Maya women may grow vegetables and fruits for local sale and consumption.

Marroquín University, archives, preserves, studies, and displays textiles from all parts of the country.

Pottery ranges from utilitarian to ritual wares and often is associated with specific communities, such as Chinautla and Rabinal, where it has been a local craft for centuries. There are several museums, both government and private, where the most exquisite ancient and modern pieces are displayed.

Performance Arts. Music has been important in Guatemala since colonial times, when the Catholic Church used it to teach Christian doctrine. Both the doctrine and the musical styles were adopted at an early date. The work of Maya who composed European-style classical music in the sixteenth and seventeenth centuries has been revived and is performed by several local performance groups, some using replicas of early instruments. William Orbaugh, a Guatemalan of Swiss ancestry, is known internationally for performances of classical and popular guitar music. Garifuna music, especially that of Caribbean origin, is popular in both Guatemala and in the United States, which has a large expatriate Garifuna population. Other popular music derives from Mexico, Argentina, and especially the United States. The marimba is the popular favorite instrument, in both the city and in the countryside.

There is a national symphony as well as a ballet, national chorus, and an opera company, all of which perform at the National Theater, a large imposing structure built on the site of an ancient fort near the city center.

Theater is less developed, although several private semiprofessional and amateur groups perform in both Spanish and English. The city of Antigua Guatemala is a major center for the arts, along with the cities of Guatemala and Quetzaltenango.

The State of the Physical and Social Sciences

Although the country boasts six universities, none is really comprehensive. All of the sciences are taught in one or another of these, and some research is done by professors and advanced students—especially in fields serving health and agricultural interests, such as biology, botany, and agronomy. Various government agencies also conduct research in these fields. However, most of those doing advanced research have higher degrees from foreign universities. The professional schools such as Dentistry, Nutrition, and Medicine keep abreast of modern developments in their fields, and offer continuing short courses to their graduates.

Anthropology and archaeology are considered very important for understanding and preserving the national cultural patrimony, and a good bit of research in these fields is done, both by national and visiting scholars. One of the universities has a linguistics institute where research is done on indigenous languages. Political science, sociology, and international relations are taught at still another, and a master's degree program in development, depending on all of the social sciences, has recently been inaugurated at still a third of the universities. Most of the funding available for such research comes from Europe and the United States, although some local industries provide small grants to assist specific projects.

Bibliography

Adams, Richard N. *Cultural Surveys of Panama, Nicaragua, Guatemala, El Salvador, Honduras*, 1957.

Asturias, Miguel Angel. *Men of Maize*, 1994.

———. *The Mirror of Lida Sal: Tales Based on Mayan Myths and Guatemalan Legends*, 1997.

Asturias de Barrios, Linda, ed. *Cuyuscate: The Traditional Brown Cotton of Guatemala*, 2000.

Aveni, Anthony F. *The Sky in Mayan Literature*, 1995.

Bahl, Roy W., et al. *The Guatemalan Tax Reform*, 1996.

Carlsen, Robert S. *The War for the Heart and Soul of a Highland Maya Town*, 1997.

Carmack, Robert. *Rebels of Highland Guatemala: The Quiche-Mayas of Momostenango*, 1995.

———, ed. *Harvest of Violence*, 1988.

Ehlers, Tracy B. *Silent Looms: Women, Work, and Poverty in a Guatemalan Town*, 1989.

Fischer, Edward F., and R. McKenna Brown, eds. *Maya Cultural Activism in Guatemala*, 1996.

Flannery, Kent, ed. *Maya Subsistence*, 1982.

Garrard, Virginia. *A History of Protestantism in Guatemala*, 1998.

Garzon, Susan, ed. *The Life of Our Language: Kaqchikel Maya Maintenance, Shift and Revitalization*, 1998.

Goldin, C. "Work and Ideology in the Maya Highlands of Guatemala: Economic Beliefs in the Context of Occupational Change." *Economic Development and Cultural Change* 41(1):103–123, 1992.

Goldman, Francisco. *The Long Night of White Chickens*, 1993.

Gonzalez, Nancie L. *Sojourners of the Caribbean: Ethnogenesis and Ethnohistory of the Garifuna*, 1988.

Handy, J. *Gift of the Devil: A History of Guatemala*, 1984.

Hendrickson, Carol. *Weaving Identities: Construction of Dress and Self in a Highland Guatemalan Town*, 1995.

McCreery, David. *Rural Guatemala, 1760–1940*, 1994.

Menchú, Rigoberta, and Ann Wright (ed.). *Crossing Borders*, 1998.

Nash, June, ed. *Crafts in the World Market: The Impact of Global Exchange on Middle American Artisans*, 1993.

Perera, Victor. *Unfinished Conquest: The Guatemalan Tragedy*, 1993. Psacharopoulos, George. "Ethnicity, Education and Earnings in Bolivia and Guatemala," *Comparative Education Review* 37(1):9–20, 1993.

Reina, Ruben E. and Robert M. Hill II. *The Traditional Pottery of Guatemala*, 1978.

Romero, Sergio Francisco and Linda Asturias de Barrios. "The Cofradia in Tecpán During the Second Half of the Twentieth Century." In Linda Asturias de Barrios, ed. *Cuyuscate: The Traditional Brown Cotton of Guatemala*, 2000.

Scheville, Margot Blum, and Christopher H. Lutz (designer). *Maya Textiles of Guatemala*, 1993.

Smith, Carol, ed. *Guatemalan Indians and the State: 1540 to 1988*, 1992.

Steele, Diane. "Guatemala." In *Las poblaciones indígenas y. la pobreza en América Latina: Estudio Empírico*, 1999.

Stephen, D. and P. Wearne. *Central America's Indians*, 1984.

Tedlock, Barbara. *Time and the Highland Maya*, 1990.

Tedlock, Dennis. *Popul Vuh: The Definitive Edition of the Mayan Book of the Dawn of Life and the Glories of the Gods and Kings*, 1985.

Urban, G. and J. Sherzer, eds. *Nation–States and Indians in Latin America*, 1992.

Warren, Kay B. *Indigenous Movements and Their Critics: Pan-Maya Activism in Guatemala*, 1998.

Watanabe, John. *Maya Saints and Souls in a Changing World*, 1992.

Whetten, N. L. *Guatemala, The Land and the People*, 1961.

Woodward, R. L. *Guatemala*, 1992.

World Bank. *World Development Indicators*, 1999.

—Nancie L. González

GUINEA

CULTURE NAME

Guinean

ALTERNATE NAME

Guinea-Conakry

ORIENTATION

Identification. The origin of the word "Guinea" is unclear. The name came into use among European shippers and map makers in the seventeenth century to refer to the coast of West Africa from Guinea to Benin. Some Guineans claim that the word arose from an early episode in the European-African encounter. In Susu, the language spoken by the coastal Susu ethnic group, the word *guinè* means "woman." When a group of Europeans arrived on the coast they met some women washing clothes in an estuary. The women indicated to the men that they were women. The Europeans misunderstood and thought the women were referring to a geographic area; the subsequently used the word "Guinea" to describe coastal West Africa.

The French claimed the coast of present-day Guinea in 1890 and named it French Guinea (*Guinée française*) in 1895. Neighboring colonies also bore the name "Guinea." The British colony of Sierra Leone to the south was sometimes identified as British Guinea, and to the north, Portugal's colony was named Portuguese Guinea.

After Guinea gained independence, the first president, Sekou Touré, named the country the People's Revolutionary Republic of Guinea. The second president, Lansana Conté, changed the official name to the Republic of Guinea. The capital city is Conakry, and the country often is referred to as Guinea-Conakry to distinguish it from other nation-states with the same name.

Location and Geography. Guinea is located on the west coast of Africa, and is bordered by Côte d'Ivoire, Guinea-Bissau, Liberia, Mali, Senegal, and Sierra Leone. Its area is 94,930 square miles (245,857 square kilometers). There are four geographic zones. The coastal maritime region is filled with mangrove swamps and alluvial plains that support palm trees. Lower Guinea receives heavy rains, and Conakry is one of the wettest cities in the world. The coastal belt is home to one of the country's dominant ethnic groups, the Susu, and to many smaller groups, such as the Baga, Landoma, Lele, and Mikiforé. Other important towns include the bauxite mining centers of Fria and Kamsar.

In the interior is the Futa Jallon. This mountainous region has cool temperatures, allowing for the cultivation of potatoes. The Niger, Senegal, and Gambia rivers originate in the Futa Jallon. Many other streams and waterfalls run through this area's rocky escarpments and narrow valleys. The Fulbe ethnic group, also referred to as Peul, is the major population group. Smaller ethnic groups include the Jallonke and the Jahanke. Labé is the largest city, and the town of Timbo was the region's capital in the precolonial era.

To the east of the Futa Jallon is Upper Guinea, a savanna region with plains and river valleys. The Milo and Niger rivers are important for fishing, irrigation, and transportation. Most of the population consists of members of the Maninka ethnic group. Siguiri and Kankan are the major cities, and there are many smaller agricultural settlements in the countryside. Kankan sometimes is referred to as the nation's second capital, although in recent years it has been dwarfed in size by cities in southern Guinea.

The southernmost region is Forest Region. Rainfall is heavy, and the area is dense with rain forests with mahogany, teak, and ebony trees. Agricultural exploitation and the demand for tropical hardwoods have increased the rate of deforestation. Many valuable resources are found, including gold, diamonds, and iron ore. Larger ethnic groups include the Guerzé, Toma, and Kissi. Since the early

Guinea

1990s, the Forest Region has had a substantial rise in population as refugees from wars in Liberia and Sierra Leone have flooded over the border and doubled the size of the towns of Gueckedou, Macenta, and N'Zerekoré.

Demography. The population is approximately 7.5 million, according to 2000 estimates. The Susu ethnic group accounts for 20 percent of the population; the Peul, 34 percent; and the Maninka, 33 percent. Smaller groups, mostly from the Forest Region, such as the Bassari, Coniagui, Guerze, Kissi, Kono, and Toma, make up the remaining 19 percent. There are about five hundred thousand refugees from Sierra Leone and Liberia, although in the year 2000, some started to leave.

Almost half of the population is under the age of fifteen. This generation has known only the rule of the second president, Conté, who came to power in 1984 and is still in office. Fifteen percent of the country was born while the first president, Touré, ruled from 1958 to 1984; only 12 percent of the population witnessed colonial rule.

Many Senegalese merchants, artisans, and tailors live in the country, and they are joined by foreign nationals from other African countries. Some of these are refugees, others come seeking opportunities in Guinea. A substantial number of Europeans and Americans reside in Conakry, most of whom work for embassies and development organizations. Expatriates also live in the mining towns of

Fria and Kamsar (bauxite) and Siguiri (gold). An economically influential Lebanese population conducts commerce in the cities. A tiny group of Korean immigrants operates photo development shops in Conakry.

Linguistic Affiliation. More than thirty languages are spoken, and eight are designated as official national languages: Bassari, Guerzé, Kissi, Koniagui, Maninka, Peul, Susu, and Toma. In the 1960s, President Touré wanted to promote African cultures and languages and abolished the use of French. Schoolchildren started to be taught in local languages. President Conté reversed this policy and resuscitated French as the official language in 1985.

Many people, especially men, speak more than one language. In Conakry, Susu is most commonly spoken on the streets and in the marketplaces, although in certain sectors Peul is more common. Elsewhere, Maninka is the preferred language of commerce. French is used in schools and in high governmental and business circles.

Symbolism. Official national symbols include the flag and the coat of arms. The flag has bands of red, yellow, and green and was first flown during Touré's regime. The coat of arms displays the slogan "Work, Justice, Solidarity." The *nimba*, a wooden headdress that represents fertility among the Bagas in the coastal region, has gained currency as a national symbol. It is found on the Guinean franc and is used as a logo by governmental agencies, businesses, and private organizations. Wood carvers, artisans, and artists reproduce nimbas in various forms and media. Important national sites include the grand mosque in Conakry and the tombs of Alfa Yaya and Samori Touré, two African leaders who confronted the French during the colonial period. The mosque of Dinguiraye in the Futa Jallon is an important monument. Al Hajj Umar Tall, a Muslim state builder in the mid-nineteenth century, constructed the mosque.

History and Ethnic Relations

Emergence of the Nation. Guinea's complex history reflects the diversity of its geographic zones. In the early eighteenth century, Islamic Peul migrants arrived in the Futa Jallon, displacing the ancestors of the Susu, who pushed westward to the coast and encroached on the lands and settlements of coastal peoples, including the Baga and the Landoma. Over the next two centuries, the Susu gained control of the coast by building a series of small states based on clan and town affiliation. The Susu supported themselves by fishing and trading with Europeans. They traded locally produced goods such as beeswax and hides as well as slaves for European cloth, arms, and other manufactured goods. The region participated in but was not a major contributor to the trans-Atlantic slave trade.

In the Futa Jallon, the Peuls constructed a centralized theocratic Muslim state. Two families, the Soriyas and the Alfayas, headed the government of the Futa Jallon. Male members of those families occupied the position of *Almamy*, or leader, for alternating terms of two years. The Futa Jallon was divided into nine *diwals*, or provinces, and people supported themselves through cattle herding, farming, and trade. Slaves lived in small hamlets and did most of the heavy labor.

The savanna of West Africa has been the site of great Maninka kingdoms since the eighth century. The exploits of Sundiata, the builder of the Mali Empire in the thirteenth century, are still recounted by *griots*, or bards, throughout Upper Guinea. Islam also has played an important role in Upper Guinea's history. In the seventeenth century, Muslim migrants came to the banks of the Milo River and formed the small city-state of Baté, with the town of Kankan as its capital. Baté emerged as an enclave of Islam and became a magnet for Muslim traders and scholars. Slaves supported agricultural and commercial activities. Animist Maninka populations tended to have fewer slaves, whom they incorporated into the household. Slaves owned by Maninka Muslims often resided in separate farming villages.

In the Forest Region, political and social affiliations functioned on a small scale because of the density and fragility of the rain forest. Because the ecosystem could not support large population centers, the forest's populations lived in dispersed villages of about one hundred to two hundred people. These villages, often situated on the top of a high hill, could be moved or replaced easily in response to environmental challenges or warfare. The forest stimulated isolated independence. Islam did not make significant inroads in this area.

In the nineteenth century, warfare intensified in several geographic regions. In the 1870s, a Maninka warrior, Samori Turé, created a vast empire through Upper Guinea and present-day Mali. Samori provisioned his armies and administration by trading cattle and slaves for European arms. The French, who were moving eastward to the interior from Senegal, clashed with Samori in the 1880s. They drove him out of Upper Guinea in 1891 and captured him in northern Côte d'Ivoire in 1898. Samori is remembered as a great colonial resistor. In the Futa Jallon, civil war in the 1890s arose over French annexation of Middle Guinea. The French built alliances with disaffected elites and incorporated the area to French Guinea by treaty in 1896. In 1900, the French fixed the borders of the colony.

The French set up a bureaucracy to administer the colony and collected taxes and requisitioned forced labor. The tried to capitalize on the area's natural resources, such as gold, but were largely unsuccessful. The French built schools, courts, and medical clinics. While they brutalized some sectors of the population, colonialism was ameliorated by the lack of French personnel. The French depended on local chiefs and institutions for the day-to-day administration of the colony; as a result, colonial policies were often implemented incompletely.

Sekou Touré led the nation to independence in the 1950s. A postal clerk and union activist, Touré was head of the Democratic Party of Guinea (PDG), which drew support from market women and low-level African bureaucrats. Declaring, "We prefer poverty in freedom to riches in chains," Touré conducted a campaign against the proposed French Union, which would have kept French colonies in a federation.

In September 1958, France's president, granted the nation's independence and ordered a swift withdrawal. All French personnel were deployed back to France, public works in progress were demolished, and the medicines, textbooks, and records used in colonial hospitals, schools, and offices were removed or destroyed. Taking office as the country's first president in 1958, Touré faced immense challenges. Only a handful of doctors, lawyers, engineers, and accountants were left, and the country had only two high schools and no university. Having created an enemy in a powerful Western nation at the height of the Cold War, Guinea was thrust into international isolation.

Touré turned to the Soviet Union and later to the People's Republic of China for help. Those countries provided financial support and expertise and opened their universities to Guinean students. Touré embarked on a socialist program, which he termed African communalism. Advocating unity, egalitarianism, parity between the sexes, and Guinean cultural production, Touré attempted to blend indigenous African institutions with a Marxist agenda. Touré used his presidency to strengthen ties to other African leaders and was hailed internationally as a spokesperson for pan-Africanism. The country's situation varied under those programs of economic centralization, improving with the export of bauxite starting in 1960 but suffering as schemes to collectivize markets and agricultural production foundered in the 1970s. In implementing his programs, Touré tolerated no dissent. He outlawed other political parties and punished his critics severely. Some dissidents lived in exile, and others were interred in detention camps. Economic and political repression prompted many people to flee to neighboring countries.

When he died in 1984, Touré was remembered internationally for his firm stance against colonial rule. But in Guinea, some members of the population celebrated his death. After a brief period of political disarray, Conté, a military general, seized power. After constitutional reform in 1990, Conté instituted civilian rule. Under the auspices of the Party for Unity and Progress, he advocated economic liberalization and privatization, which brought Western donors and aid agencies to the country.

National Identity. At the time of Touré's death, the standard of living was one of the worst in the world, but some people contend that they owe their identity as citizens of a common country to Touré. His legacy is tangible. Buildings, roads, and schools, as well as professionals who speak Chinese, Russian, and Romanian, testify to the assistance he extracted from Eastern bloc nations. Guineans born during Touré's regime who are able to read and write in their own language are proof of Touré's commitment to the use of African languages.

Ethnic Relations. Despite Touré's attempts to minimize ethnic divisions, poverty, a feeble economy, a weak infrastructure, and limited educational and medical resources have exacerbated ethnic tensions. President Conté's has been accused of favoring his own ethnic group, the Susu.

Ethnic and national tensions have coalesced around the issue of refugees. Conté initially welcomed the victims of the Sierra Leonean and Liberian wars in the early and middle 1990s. However, when the country's border towns were attacked in 2000, Conté made a radio address in which he accused the refugee population of harboring rebels and ordered the refugees to leave the country. In the days after that speech, Sierra Leoneans and Liberians were attacked and robbed, and many tried to leave the country.

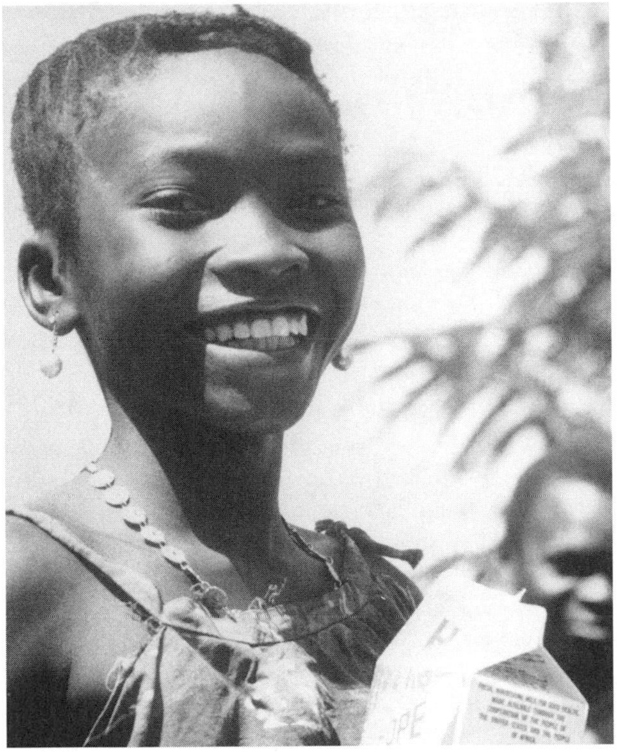

Almost half of all Guineans are younger than fifteen.

Urbanism, Architecture, and the Use of Space

Colonial rule left an imprint on cities and towns, as did the assistance given by the Soviet bloc. The older sections of Conakry are built in a grid pattern interspersed with boulevards and round points. Newer buildings, such as Palace of the People, built by the Chinese, reflect the architecture of the Eastern bloc countries. Conakry radiates fifteen miles outward from the narrow downtown peninsula. Most residential structures there are low buildings with one to four rooms, although some families live in government-owned and privately-owned apartment buildings. Wealthier residents reside in modern, luxurious homes.

Older forms of African and French architecture are better preserved in the interior cities. French-built sections of Kankan, Dalaba, and Siguiri reveal the colonial concern with plotting buildings, houses, and market centers along straight lines. Quarters of towns that were not subject to French intervention reflect the priorities of Africans in arranging their physical space. In Kankan, many people live in small mud huts with thatched roofs, structures that are cool and easy to maintain. Members of the same household often sleep in separate dwellings, but their doors open onto a communal space where cooking and social interaction take place. These family compounds accommodate the large extended families and polygamous marriages that are common among the Maninka ethnic group. This arrangement is repeated in other cities and towns.

Food and Economy

Food in Daily Life. An array of taboos and customs affect food consumption. It is impolite to eat while walking. A visitor who arrives in a compound while a meal is in progress will be invited to join in the meal. Food often is served in large communal bowls and eaten with spoons. In large families, the men will eat from one bowl and the women from another.

The main meal typically is served in the middle of the day and consists of a sauce placed over a staple carbohydrate such as rice or millet. The sauce and staples differ according to region, season, and the wealth of the household. Rice, sorghum, millet, and cassava are common foods. Sauces are made with groundnuts, okra, and tomatoes. They may contain fresh or smoked fish, meat, or poultry. Many people can afford to eat only once a day. Their meals are frequently low in protein, and many children and adults suffer from malnutrition.

Little pork is eaten except in the Forest Region, where there are fewer Muslims and bush pig is favored. Variations in region, ethnicity, and wealth also affect milk and bread consumption. In Middle Guinea, milk is made into a yogurt like sauce that is sweetened and served alone or over sorghum or millet. Wealthier families often eat bread as a morning meal, accompanied by instant coffee or tea with sweetened condensed milk or sugar and powdered milk.

Food Customs at Ceremonial Occasions. Meals often are served at weddings, baptisms, and funerals. Among the wealthier people in large cities, meals on special occasions may include expensive imported goods such as canned peas and costly locally-produced staples such as potatoes. Ramadan is observed, and Tabaski is celebrated with the slaughtering of a sheep, goat, or chicken. Alcohol usually is not served at family celebrations, except for in the Forest Region, where palm wine is frequently consumed.

Basic Economy. Guinea is one of the world's poorest countries. Despite its natural resources and abundant rainfall, Guinea has low life expectancy, a low doctor-patient ratio, and a high rate of infant mortality. The country remains largely rural, and 80 percent of the population is involved in agricultural production. The farming and cattle-herding sectors of the Futa Jallon support 40 percent of the population, while 11 percent of the people are employed in industry and commerce, 5 percent in the service industry, and 4 percent in the civil service. These statistics mask the strategies that people use to support themselves. Many civil servants own livestock or a small store, and some agriculturalists migrate to urban centers to work as day laborers or trade in the dry season.

Land Tenure and Property. A rural–urban divide affects land access and ownership. In rural areas, land is abundant and ownership usually is dictated by local custom. These traditional laws are often highly complex, and in the Futa Jallon, efforts by nongovernmental agencies and the government to streamline property rights have had little success. In urban areas, especially Conakry, demand for land is greater than supply and residents rely on the civic code and legal titles to determine land ownership. Conflict over land rights caused a devastating confrontation in Conakry in 1997, when the government clashed with residents over the building of a road.

Commercial Activities. Most people are not employed in the formal sector, and those who do not engage in agriculture earn a living in an array of occupations. These occupations include auto and motorcycle repair, iron and leather working, marketing, and selling prepared meals.

Major Industries. Guinea has the second largest known deposits of bauxite and produces 25 percent of the bauxite used in the world. The mine in Kamsar was opened in 1960; in the 1990s, bauxite constituted 75 percent of the country's exports. There are also reserves of iron ore, gold, and diamonds. British interests have built a gold mine in Siguiri, but the depressed price of gold has damaged its prospects. Guinean interests have kept careful control over the country's diamond mines, but intermediaries sell to international diamond buyers. Beer, cigarettes, and soft drinks are manufactured in Conakry for local consumption. Tourism is minimal.

Trade. The major export is bauxite. Aluminum, coffee, diamonds, fish, and fruits and vegetables also are exported. Manufactured goods are imported from China, Europe, and the United States. Regional trade networks deal in locally produced agricultural goods, such as potatoes, rice, shea butter, and kola nuts. China supplies bedding, bicycles, buckets, kerosene lamps, motorcycles, and pots, but the abysmal transportation system hinders commerce. The rainy season, aging bridges and roads, and interregional conflicts slow and sometimes stop the movement of goods and people through the country. As a result, the price of goods imported by sea increases dramatically from Lower Guinea to Upper Guinea and the Forest Region. In rural areas, people depend largely on what they can produce or accumulate to support themselves.

Division of Labor. Labor traditionally is divided along lines of class, level of education, gender, and age. Literacy and formal schooling tend to separate manual laborers and petty traders from bureaucrats and professionals, although many successful businesspeople are neither literate nor highly educated. In agricultural settings, boys usually herd livestock, men plow, and women and girls weed and plant gardens for petty trade. The division of labor within a household often is complicated by marital hierarchies and the needs and contributions of elderly parents and grandparents.

Social Stratification

Classes and Castes. While Western education and employment in the formal sector have limited the strength of traditional social orderings, the legacies of caste groupings and domestic slavery continue to shape social relations. In Middle and Upper Guinea, professional artisans such as blacksmiths, leatherworkers, and bards form a social caste. Precolonial social categories are also evident in areas where the descendents of slaves live in the farming villages that were inhabited by their bonded ancestors. In most of the country, marriage between noble women and men of lower status is frowned upon. These traditional rankings have weakened as education, employment, and monetary wealth have created new social hierarchies.

Symbols of Social Stratification. Under the regime of Touré, most people were poor and corruption and embezzlement were forbidden and punished. With the opening of the country under President Conté, the gap between rich people and poor people has increased. A small but significant segment of the population has benefitted from the investment programs that have been started since the mid-1980s. Automobiles and large houses, sometimes equipped with electric generators and swimming pools, symbolize the wealth of the elite sector. Expatriate professionals form a significant part of this sector. The affluence of the wealthy contrasts sharply with the lifestyle of the rest of the people, many of whom do not have access to electricity, running water, and sanitary services.

Outside of Conakry, symbols of success vary according to region and relative means. In small villages, a wealthy household may invest in a concrete house with a corrugated aluminum roof. In this setting, acquiring a bicycle or a motorcycle can demonstrate prosperity while fulfilling practical needs. Sometimes villages or neighborhoods pool their resources to build mosques or schools. In both urban and rural areas, men may use their wealth to take another wife.

POLITICAL LIFE

Government. The constitution, the *Loi Fundamental,* was ratified in 1990. The government is based on the French Napoleonic civil law system and traditional law. The president is democratically elected to five-year terms, and the holder of this office appoints the prime minister and the other ministers. Representatives to the People's National Assembly, the unicameral parliament, are elected by popular vote.

Leadership and Political Officials. Postcolonial Guinea has had only two presidents: Touré (1958–1984) and Conté (1984–present). Under the leadership of Conté, the country went from a one-party state to a multiparty democracy with constitutional reform in 1990. A bill legalized political parties in 1992. Some have questioned whether these reforms have been put into effect, in light of the alleged fraud that marred the presidential elections of 1993 and the parliamentary elections of 1996. Government corruption has increased during Conté's regime, and well-paid contacts are needed to get results from the lethargic and inefficient bureaucracy.

Social Problems and Control. Theft is a problem, and fraud ranges from the banal to the brutal. The regional flood of arms has increased the incidence of armed robbery and other forms of violence. Government officials, particularly soldiers, customs officials, and low-level police officers, sometimes extort money and goods from people. Many Guineans believe that payoffs and embezzlement characterize the country's governance at higher levels. When people have disputes, some seek redress through governmental authorities; others try to settle their differences by resorting to the practices and rules common to their ethnic group or region.

Military Activity. The government is heavily militarized. Conté came to power through the army, and the armed forces continue to be an important source of his support. Soldiering offers a viable, if low-paying, form of employment for many young men, and regional hostilities have reinforced the nation's investment in training and arming its forces. Guinean troops have served in peacekeeping operations in Sierra Leone and with the United Nations.

SOCIAL WELFARE AND CHANGE PROGRAMS

Aid from Western donors has increased significantly during Conté's presidency. Projects initiated by the International Monetary Fund, the World Bank, and the European Union have privatized utilities, such as water and electricity, and improved the infrastructure. Local and international nongovernmental organizations (NGOs) have set up programs that target health, education, and women's and business issues.

The dispersal of donor money and governmental assistance programs varies by region. Historically, Lower and Middle Guinea have received more assistance, and the Forest Region and Upper Guinea have received less. This pattern shifted in the Forest Region in the 1990s as international relief organizations such as the United Nations High Commission of Refugees arrived to contend with the refugee crisis.

NONGOVERNMENTAL ORGANIZATIONS AND OTHER ASSOCIATIONS

While aid organizations and international donor agencies play a large role in the economy, other types of associations thrive. Many ethnic groups practice initiation rights that ritualize the passage to adulthood. Churches and mosques mobilize their members for projects such as the construction of new buildings and schools. A driver's union negotiates the fares charged for long-distance transportation. Veterans clubs testify to the high number of men who served as soldiers in the French army in World War II. Women's trade associations lend money and advocate for demands involving access to and rental of market stalls in major marketing centers.

GENDER ROLES AND STATUSES

Divisions of Labor by Gender. Women are on average less educated and less financially secure than men. A woman often spends part of her life in a polygamous marriage and has only a 22 percent likelihood of being literate. She will live on average

The Wall of Heroes in Conakry. Guinea's often tumultuous history has left a complicated legacy for its citizens.

forty-eight years and have five children, one of whom will die in infancy. In rural areas, women contribute to the household by weeding the fields, planting garden plots, doing the cooking and cleaning, and looking after the children. In urban areas, women constitute a major component of the informal marketing sector.

President Touré recognized the importance of women to cultural, social, and economic production, and instituted programs to promote the education and prosperity of women. Some of Touré's strongest supporters were market women, who, however, successfully led a strike against his marketing reforms in 1972. Touré promoted equal access to education and the enrollment of females in primary, secondary, and professional schools climbed to nearly half in some regions. Touré was the first postindependence leader in Africa to appoint women to key ministerial positions. During the regime of President Conté, these strides have slowed. Women are much less prominent in government, and the rate of female education has declined significantly. Currently, only about 10 percent of students at the university level are women.

The Relative Status of Women and Men. There is a persistent bias in the social hierarchy toward males, and boys are more likely to be educated and as adults are more likely to have a range of economic and employment options. Household heads are almost always men and custom allows them to exercise absolute authority over their wives, sisters, and daughters. These patriarchal structures conceal the power that many women wield on a day-to-day level in family compounds and market stalls, in raising children, earning an income, and allocating household resources.

Marriage, Family, and Kinship

Marriage. Marriage is considered a union of two families, not the choice of two individuals. Family approval and ritual gifts are considered very important in laying a firm marital foundation. The groom typically pays bridewealth to the family of the bride in some combination of cash, cloth, and livestock.

Marriage customs vary widely by region, ethnicity, and social status. In the Futa Jallon, a marriage may be arranged while the wife is still an infant. The couple does not take up residence together until the wife has reached puberty. It is not unusual for a wedding ceremony to take place in the absence of the groom, especially if he lives in a different region than his betrothed. After the ceremony, the bride is sent to her husband. In urban areas, some couples go to the mayor's office to sign official documents, but most couples do not seek civil recognition of their unions. Divorce is not uncommon, and local custom typically prevails over the civil courts.

Domestic Unit. The domestic unit is frequently large and composed of many generations. Polygamy is common and can both complicate and strengthen a household. Custom dictates that the first, or senior, wife mediates conflicts and oversees the division of labor within the household. In rural areas in particular, harmonious polygamous households help ensure sufficient allocations for child care, cooking, marketing, and working in the fields. These large households function less well in urban settings, where space is limited and more challenges exist in dividing scarce material and monetary resources. Tensions, favoritism, and jealousy in either setting can jeopardize a household's viability. Some women, as well as men, reject polygamy. Monogamous unions are most common among Christians and western-educated men and women.

Inheritance. Titles and property typically pass through the male members of a family, from father to son or from brother to brother. Specific patterns and customs of inheritance vary by ethnic group. According to Islamic law, which is sometimes followed, a man inherits the wife or wives of his deceased brother. This rule of inheritance is not always implemented, but this practice can produce results that range from the disastrous to the beneficial for a widow and her children.

Kin Groups. Different types of kin groupings affect social relations. Many people have the same last name and share a common ancestor in the lineage's founder. Family names often inspire jokes and camaraderie; they also can serve as the basis for assumptions about the status and class of their bearers.

Terms such as "cousin" and "sister" frequently are applied to people who are not blood relations. These terms convey respect and affection or indicate certain commonalties. Distance often expands kin relationships: Two acquaintances from the same village in Upper Guinea may refer to each other as "cousin" in the streets of Conakry, and a Guinean studying in France may introduce a neighbor from Conakry as a sister. To distinguish fictive kin from blood ties, people frequently explain their exact relationship to their "real" brothers or sisters. A man may describe his blood brother as having the "same mother, same father" or his half sister as having the "same father, different mother."

Socialization

Infant Care. The mother is typically the primary caretaker of a child, although it is not unusual for a grandmother, aunt, or sister to take charge of the child of one of her relations. Children usually breast-feed until two years of age, a practice that helps them remain healthy while promoting birth spacing. According to custom, a man is not supposed to have intercourse with a woman who is breast-feeding.

At birth, children are given charms to wear around the wrist and waist to protect them from evil spirits. Infants spend most of their waking and sleeping hours with their primary caretaker, usually the mother. A mother typically ties her baby on to her back in a wrapper and carries the child as she goes about her daily tasks.

Child Rearing and Education. Many children, particularly girls, do not have the opportunity to attend school because families cannot afford school fees and uniforms, and because the family needs the child's labor in the fields or the family compound. Girls are more likely than boys to stay home. Children who cannot attend a governmental school may be sent to an Islamic school to learn the Koran. Regardless of whether they are enrolled in school, children tend to work very hard at a young age. Children carry water and firewood, help with food preparation, and go to the market to buy and sell.

Children are brought up by their elders, not just their parents, and are supposed to show respect to their elders at all times. This means that it is culturally acceptable for relatives, friends, and acquaintances to reprimand a child who misbehaves. It is rare for a child to openly confront or contradict an adult.

Higher Education. There are universities in Conakry and Kankan. Students are awarded university scholarships on a competitive basis, but lack of funding severely constrains the universities. Library and computer resources are scarce, and strikes by dissatisfied students and underpaid professors are common. These limitations on higher education mean that students often spend many years completing their university degrees.

Etiquette

Greetings are very important, and it is rude to ask a question or make a request without first inquiring about someone's health and the well-being of his or her family. These questions are formulaic and may be repeated several times. These questions and responses are accompanied by a firm handshake or, among the upper classes, by brief kisses on the cheeks. People still sometimes refer to each other as "comrade," a legacy of Touré's efforts to promote equality and eliminate social hierarchies. It is impolite to use the left hand in any social interaction, whether to shake hands, point, pay, or hand an item to someone.

Rules of etiquette also dictate intergenerational communication. It is not proper for young people to look straight into the eyes of a respected elder; they should instead cast their eyes downward. Under certain circumstances, elders must be approached through an intermediary. A son-in-law is always supposed to approach his mother-in-law with great respect and never treat her with familiarity. It is considered unlucky to compliment the beauty of an infant, and people may instead tell a mother that her child is ugly.

Religion

Religious Beliefs. The vast majority of the population (85 percent) identifies itself as Muslim, while 8 percent of the people are Christians and 7 percent practice traditional religions. Most of the Christians are Roman Catholics. Friday afternoon prayers are widely attended and Muslim holidays are observed. With very rare exceptions, Muslim women do not live in seclusion (*purdah*) or wear the full covering worn by women in other Islamic countries. Most Christians are either from the Forest Region or the Coastal Region, where Catholic missions were more successful. While few people adhere exclusively to animist beliefs, many traditional beliefs are widely practiced and combined with other forms of religious worship. It is not uncommon for a Muslim or a Catholic to wear an amulet or charm.

Medicine and Health Care

There are both traditional and Western practitioners of medicine. Medically-trained doctors and nurses staff government clinics and a few private clinics throughout the country. Every district has a medical dispensary, although many lack supplies and medicine. In recent years, "pay as you go" reforms have placed Western medical care out of the reach of many members of the population. Traditional health practitioners may use a combination of herbal treatments, magic, and counseling to treat patients. Many people are not reluctant to use both traditional and Western methods of care in healing themselves, and some are forced to for financial reasons.

Secular Celebrations

Independence Day is celebrated on 2 October.

The Arts and Humanities

Support for the Arts. Poverty and scarce material resources compel the vast majority of artists and craftspeople to produce goods that serve a practical purpose.

Literature. Traditional literature, particularly among the Maninka, is preserved in a body of oral traditions that are remembered and passed down by bards. Radio broadcasts and recordings of epic tales and local histories told by leading griots have helped transport this literature into the twenty-first century. Authors and academics use the printed word to convey their message, such as Camara Laye, the author of *Dark Child*, a novel about a boy growing up in the colonial era.

Graphic Arts. Woodworkers build and carve furniture such as stools, cabinets, and chairs. Metal workers collect and melt old aluminum cans to make utensils and pots. Villagers weave mats and baskets and dry out and decorate gourds that they use for household tasks. Weavers and dyers sell their cloth to men and women, who take it to tailors to make it into clothing. Most of the graphic arts are thus born of necessity and are evident in daily life.

Performance Arts. A thriving music industry supports a wide range of music. Some artists specialize in traditional music, accompanied by stringed instruments. Others combine the musical forms of their ethnic group or region with influences from Europe or the Middle East. Cassette tapes are cheaper in Guinea than in the rest of West Africa and most of the world, making Guinea a mecca for buyers of recorded music. Festivals and celebrations, whether public or private, usually feature dancing and music. In the 1960s, Touré founded Les Ballet Africains to highlight Guinea's rich cultural tradition. This dance troupe continues to tour nationally and internationally.

The State of the Physical and Social Sciences

The physical and social sciences are not strong as a consequence of a weak and impoverished educational system. The government has developed a program at Conakry's university to train engineers and geologists to work in bauxite, diamond, and gold mines. But many of the Guinea's best students and scholars in all fields seek education and employment outside the country. Those who are able to often move to France, other European countries, the United States, or to the Middle East or Asia.

Bibliography

Amnesty International. *Annual Report, Guinea,* 1973–present.

Barry, Boubacar. *Senegambia and the Atlantic Slave Trade,* 1998.

Barry, Ismaël. *Le Fuuta-Jaloo Face à la Colonisation: Conquête et Mise en Place de l'Administration en Guinée,* 1997.

Derman, William. *Serfs, Peasants, and Socialists: A Former Serf Village in the Republic of Guinea,* 1968.

Dunn, John, ed. *West African States: Failure and Promise,* 1978.

Fairhead, James, and Melissa Leach. *Misreading the African Landscape: Society and Ecology in a Forest-Savanna Mosaic,* 1996.

Kaba, Lansine. *La Guinee Dit "Non" à de Gaulle,* 1989.

Kake, Ibrahima Baba. *Sekou Touré: Le Heros et le Tyran,* 1987.

Lamp, Frederick. *Art of the Baga: A Drama of Cultural Reinvention,* 1996.

Laye, Camara. *The Dark Child,* 1955.

Morgenthau, Ruth Schachter. "French Guinea's RDA Folk Songs." *West African Review,* 1958.

———. "Trade Unionists and Chiefs in Guinea." In *Political Parties in French-Speaking West Africa,* 1967.

Niane, Djibril Tamsir. *Sundiata: An Epic of Old Mali,* 1965.

Person, Yves. *Samori,* 1968–1975.

Rivière, Claude. *Guinea: The Mobilization of a People,* Viriginia Thompson and Richard Adloff, trans, 1973.

Robinson, David. *The Holy War of Umar Tal,* 1985.

Suret-Canale, Jean. *French Colonialism in Tropical Africa (1900–1945),* 1971.

Web Sites

CIA World Factbook http://www.cia.gov/cia/publications/factbook/

Camp Boiro http://guinee.net/camp-boiro/

WebGuinee http://guinee.net/

—Emily Lynn Osborn

Guinea-Bissau

Culture Name

Guinean

Alternative Name

Formally known as The Republic of Guinea-Bissau

Orientation

Identification. "Guinea" was used by European explorers and traders to refer the coast of West Africa. It comes from an Arabic term meaning "the land of the blacks." "Bissau," the name of the capital, may be a corruption of "Bijago," the name of the ethnic group that inhabits the dozens of small islands along the coast. The combined name distinguishes the country from its southern neighbor, Guinea.

Location and Geography. Guinea-Bissau, one of the smallest and poorest West African nation-states, is surrounded by former French colonies. Sharing a border to the north with Senegal and to the south with Guinea, it has a land area of 13,944 square miles (36,125 square kilometers). The terrain is generally flat and nearly at sea level, although there are hills in the southeastern region. Wide tidal estuaries surrounded by mangrove swamps penetrate forty miles into the interior, where coastal rain forest gives way to sparsely wooded savanna.

Demography. In 1998, the population was at 1,206,311. The population is 76 percent rural, but almost 20 percent of the inhabitants live in the capital city. More than half the citizens were born after independence in 1974. Fula and Mandinga, who were traditionally politically centralized and make up the Moslem majority in the interior, account for roughly 30 percent of the population. Balanta, Manjaco, and Papel in the coastal and tidal zone constitute a sizable demographic majority.

Linguistic Affiliation. Government documents are written in Portuguese, students beyond the first few years of elementary school are taught in Portuguese, and government officials speak that language. However, only about 10 percent of the citizens are fluent in Portuguese. The national lingua franca is Criolu, which is derived primarily from Portuguese. Almost all Guineans born after 1974 know Criolu, although most speak it as a second language. Criolu developed in the era of slave trading, when it was used for communication between Portuguese merchant-administrators and the local populations. It became the primary language of Cape Verdeans, who were descendants of West African slaves and resettled in Portuguese coastal enclaves. These people were employed by the government in the lower levels of the colonial bureaucracy and engaged in local commercial activities. Criolu became the de facto national language during the struggle for liberation (1961–1974). Today Criolu is associated with an urban ethnic minority that identifies itself as Cape Verdean. It is also the language of national identity. Patriotic songs and slogans are invariably in Criolu and the national news is broadcast in that language.

Most residents are more comfortable speaking local African languages; close to half the population is monolingual in a local language. Balanta, Manjaco, and Papel speak related but mutually unintelligible languages that are distantly related to languages spoken in Senegal. The language of the Bijagos islanders off the coast is unrelated to that of any neighboring group. The languages spoken by Mandinga and Fula allow them to communicate with their cultural kin in neighboring nations.

Symbolism. The flag, with horizontal stripes of green, red, and yellow and a black star in the center, reflects an explicit concern to define the country in terms of national liberation and as pan-African rather than ethnic. During the revolution, efforts were made to minimize ethnic distinctions, and this

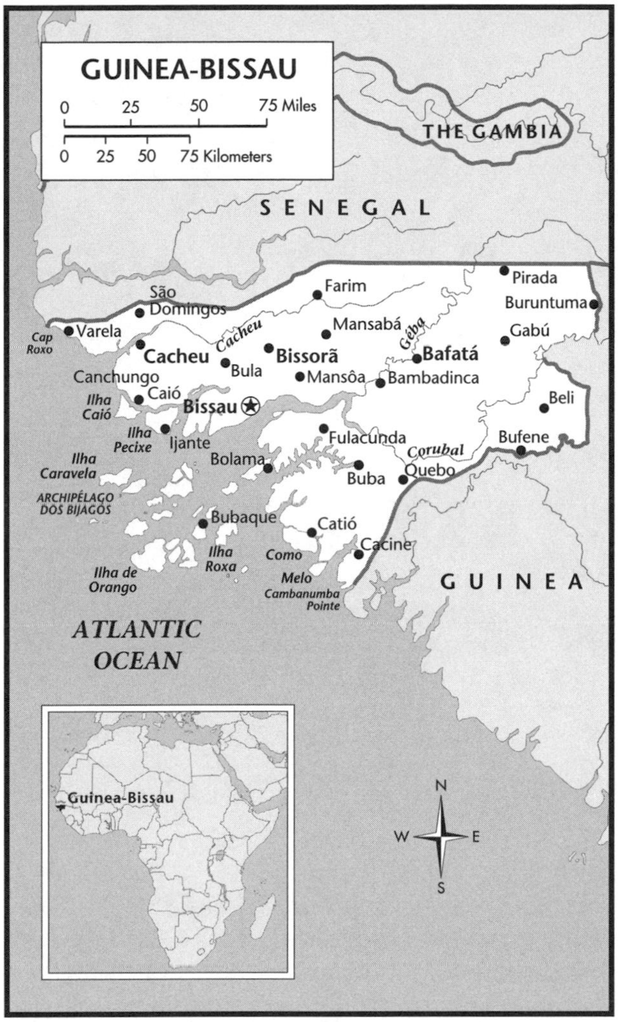

Guinea-Bissau

effort is reflected in the pervasive use of Criolu as the language of political slogans and patriotic celebration. Schools and avenues are named after heroes of the revolution, such as Domingos Ramos, who was killed while leading the first organized guerrilla battalion. Pan-African martyrs to national liberation such as Patrice Lumumba are similarly enshrined.

HISTORY AND ETHNIC RELATIONS

Emergence of the Nation. By the sixteenth century, European traders had established permanent trading posts along the coast and encouraged local peoples to raid their neighbors for slaves. The slave trade created and reinforced ethnic distinctions in the region. Bijagos became notorious slave raiders, and Manjaco and Papel produced food for the coastal trading posts, along with trade goods, such as elaborately patterned textiles.

After the end of the slave trade in the mid-nineteenth century, Bijagos maintained their independence until the 1930s. Manjaco and Papel were among the first people in the region to migrate to Cape Verdean and European *pontas* or concessions, to share-crop peanuts. They were active in the wild rubber trade in the early twentieth century, migrating to Senegal and Gambia. The end of the slave trade led to political collapse and chaos among the more politically centralized Moslem groups in the interior. As Moslem factions fought, they also raided the coast, leading to confrontations with European traders.

The nation began as a colony consisting of the mainland territory and the islands of Cape Verde. Not until the first decades of the twentieth century were the Portuguese able to control the territory. Until then, the Portuguese had ruled only the coastal enclaves and were the virtual hostages of their African hosts, who controlled food and water supplies. In 1913 the Portuguese, under Teixeira Pinto, allied themselves with Fula troops under Abdulai Injai and defeated all the coastal groups. Then the Portuguese exploited divisions among the Moslems to destroy Injai and his followers, becoming the sole power in the region.

During the Salazarist era, the Portuguese built roads, bridges, hospitals, and schools. At the beginning of the 1960s their rule was contested by African nationalists under the leadership of Amilcar Cabral. By 1974, when Portugal recognized the nation's independence, the nationalist forces had developed a political and economic infrastructure providing basic services for the vast majority of local residents.

National Identity. The success of the revolutionary struggle created a strong sense of national identity that was reinforced by linguistic distinctiveness. Because of the upheaval caused by the war for liberation, large numbers of residents migrated to neighboring countries and to Europe.

Efforts to liberalize the economy and democratize the political system have led to corruption and exacerbated the gap in wealth between government officials and the citizens. As a result, the nation-state has come to be perceived as a platform for enriching oneself and one's family and a source of passports and identity papers that allow people to escape from the nation.

Ethnic Relations. In recent national elections, ethnically based parties have not been successful. As the nation becomes increasingly divided economically, ethnicity may become a way to mobilize fac-

Young Bijagos Islands men perform ritual dances to attract wives in this matriarchal society. Most other ethnic groups in Guinea-Bissau are more patriarchal.

tions. Recent coup attempts have divided the military, and animosity toward the wealthy may be increasingly directed at Cape Verdeans. Persons of Cape Verdean descent have been banned from running for the presidency.

Urbanism, Architecture, and the Use of Space

Bissau is a huge city relative to the country's size. Many of the larger buildings were constructed by the Portuguese. The core of the city is a planned colonial capital, with buildings, boulevards, and vistas in the modernist style. The smaller district capitals also feature colonial architecture. There are postcolonial buildings such as the Chinese hospital in Canchungo, but the architecture is largely West African. Rectangular houses with zinc roofs and concrete floors are common in villages and small towns. In villages, much housing is still traditional in form and materials. Dried mud and thatched circular huts in ethnically distinct styles are a common feature.

Food and Economy

Food in Daily Life. Rice is a staple among the coastal peoples. It is also a prestige food, and so the country imports it to feed the urban population. Millet is a staple crop in the interior. Both are supplemented with a variety of locally produced sauces that combine palm oil or peanuts, tomatoes, and onions with fish.

Food Customs at Ceremonial Occasions. Most people participate in elaborate life cycle ceremonies in which family and community celebrates events such as birth, circumcision, marriage, and death. Most of these events, especially funerals, entail the sacrifice of livestock for consumption and ritual offering and the consumption of large quantities of palm wine or rum.

Basic Economy. The economy depends heavily on foreign aid to support the governmental bureaucracy, teachers and health workers, and the oversized military. The economy is basically agricultural; the vast majority of residents live off what they and their neighbors grow. Villagers depend on funds from emigrant workers. Urban government workers at all but the highest levels depend on their village kin for food. The West African franc (C.F.A.) is the currency used.

Land Tenure and Property. Traditional land tenure practices and systems of property ownership

Thatched houses in a Buboque Island village in the Bijagos Islands. Although cities display colonial architecture, villages feature these more traditional dwellings.

were not altered significantly by the colonial government or the independent state. A range of customary practices tend to protect the livelihoods of rural families and promote economic cooperation at the village level. There are no landless poor, but with economic liberalization and attempts to generate an export income, so-called empty lands have been granted to members of the government. Known as *pontas*, these concessions are enlarged extensions of earlier colonial practices. Ponta owners provide materials to local farmers who grow cash crops in exchange for a share of the profits or for wages.

Commercial Activities. There is a thriving rural market in livestock and foodstuffs. Most significantly Fula, Mandinga, and Balanta breed cattle and other livestock for consumption among the coastal groups who pay with funds repatriated by emigrant kin living in Senegal and Europe. There is some local business activity in Bissau but firms are small and relatively unimportant economically.

Trade. Guinea-Bissau produces and exports cashews, peanuts, fish and shellfish, and palm nuts. Export partners include Spain, Portugal, and Sweden. The country imports food, primarily rice, petroleum products, transport equipment, and consumer goods from Portugal, Russia, Senegal, and France.

Division of Labor. In urban centers, women work alongside men in the government. Urban men who are not employed by the government drive taxis, work in local factories, and are employed as laborers, sailors, and dock workers. Urban women do domestic work and trade in the markets. In the villages, children herd livestock, and young people work collectively to weed or prepare fields. Women do most domestic tasks. In some regions, women perform agricultural tasks that once were done by their husbands.

Social Stratification

Classes and Castes. In the colonial era, there were castes in Mandinga and Fula society, along with specific occupational groups. Among Manjaco and Papel, distinctions were made between aristocratic groups and commoners. Aristocrats among coastal and Moslem peoples continue to enjoy the privileges of rank.

Symbols of Social Stratification. Markers of wealth include business suits, cars, and cell phones. In the villages, funerals in wealthy families involve large slaughters of cattle; the dead are wrapped in greater quantities of cloth, and the guests are more numerous and better fed.

Political Life

Government. Until 1994, the country was a one-party republic with widespread participation and support. Today opposition parties have gained a considerable following and the current president ran against the revolutionary party.

The president selects a cabinet of ministers. Basic laws are enacted by the hundred delegates to the National Assembly, who are elected by universal sufferage.

Since the early 1990s, the government has increasingly privatized basic services and industries but continues to be the largest employer of workers outside the agricultural sector.

Leadership and Political Officials. Until the elections of 1999, almost all political leaders and officials came from the ranks of those who fought in the revolution. Midlevel and regional leaders often came from local aristocratic families.

Social Problems and Control. Social problems include smuggling, corruption, and emigration of the educated. With joblessness high in the capital city, there has been a rise in crime and prostitution.

Military Activity. The military forces that fought in the revolution emerged with prestige, organizational skill, and political authority. The armed forces were also large in proportion to the population. With the end of the Cold War and with economic and political liberalization, the army has become an economic burden and a threat to political stability. Several coups have been attempted since independence. The coup attempt of 1998 paralyzed the nation for six months and sent a flood of refugees to Senegal and Europe, because of protracted fighting in Bissau.

Marriage, Family, and Kinship

Marriage. Rural Mandinga and Fula and the peoples of the coastal ethnic groups continue to practice arranged marriage in which a brideprice or groom service is given. However, young people can make matches on their own. Interethnic marriage rates are low but increasing. Men marry later than do women. Polygamy is accepted. Widows often remarry the husband's brother, thereby remaining in the same domestic household group.

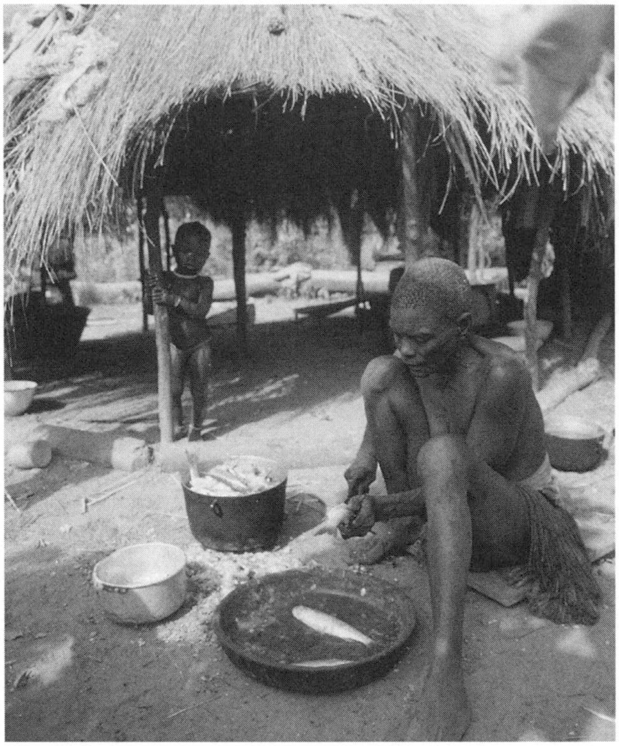

Women prepare fish of Buboque Island. Fish and shellfish are important in both Guinean diet and exports.

Domestic Unit. In the villages, the domestic unit is a large kinship group with common rights to agricultural property and obligations to work for one another.

Inheritance. Land passes from fathers to sons or from older brothers to younger brothers. Among the Manjaco and Papel, rice fields owned by domestic groups are inherited by a sister's sons, who act as caretaker-managers, dividing use rights to portions of the fields.

Kin Groups. All the ethnic groups are organized in fairly large kin groups known as clans or lineages. Most kin groups tend to be patrilineal and patrilocal, although there are also large categories of matrilineal kin who share rights to land and to local religious and political offices.

Socialization

Infant Care. High infant mortality rates result from a lack of modern health services.

Child Rearing and Education. Education at the primary school level is almost universal.

A peanut harvester in Bissau. These nuts, along with cashews and palm nuts, are among Guinea-Bissau's chief exports.

Higher Education. In the colonial era, only a handful of residents, primarily of Cape Verdean ancestry, went to Portugal for a higher education. Guineans in Senegal received degrees from French colonial institutions. During the revolution, many young people were sent to East Germany, the Soviet Union, Cuba, and China to be educated at the university and postgraduate level. After the revolution, the government was able to increase the literacy rate and the numbers of students who earned a high school diploma. Some of these students study in technical schools, but it is still necessary to go abroad for training in a university. Many students with such educations remain abroad.

Religion

Religious Beliefs. Despite centuries of Catholic and Protestant missionary activity, few people claim to be Christian. The overwhelming majority (over 60 percent) of residents practice indigenous religions.

Rituals and Holy Places. The coastal groups believe that ancestor spirits exercise power over their living descendants, and those spirits are recognized in household shrines at which periodic offerings are made. In every village, there are dozens of shrines to tutelary or guardian spirits. These spirits are recognized at public ceremonies in which food and alcohol offerings are made and animals are sacrificed. Such spirits are thought to protect the community against misfortune. Individuals visit the shrines to request personal favors. Certain shrines have gained a transethnic reputation for reliability and power. Guineans abroad continue to return to those shrines and send money to pay for sacrifices and ceremonies.

Over 30 percent of Guineans are Moslem and recognize their allegiance to Islam through practices such as circumcision and fasting and various forms of Islamic mysticism.

Death and the Afterlife. The most elaborate and expensive life cycle rituals are associated with death, burial, and the enshrinement of ancestors.

Medicine and Health Care

Malaria and tuberculosis are rampant. Infant mortality rates are high and life expectancy is generally low because Western medicine is available only intermittently. Most residents seek out local healers, go to diviners, and make offerings at shrines. The government has made efforts to provide primary nursing care in the villages, but the country continues to rely on foreign doctors. There is a hospital in

Teenagers from Bijagos Islands playing the drums. Almost all children receive primary education in Guinea-Bissau.

the district capital of Canchungo that is run by Chinese medical personnel but also employs European doctors. Cubans once provided advance care in the hospital in Bissau.

Secular Celebrations

Independence Day, celebrated on 24 September, is the major national holiday. Carnival in Bissau, once a festival associated with Catholic Criolu culture, has become a multiethnic celebration.

The Arts and Humanities

Support for the Arts. National television programming and radio programming provide some support for the arts.

Literature. Amilcar Cabral wrote extensively on the goals and theories of national liberation. His speeches are widely read today. Guineans of Cape Verdean ancestry such as Fausto Duarte, Terencio Anahory, and Joao Alves da Neves have begun to write fiction in Criolu. The Manjaco poet Antonio Baticam Ferreira has been published in Europe.

Graphic Arts. Art tends to be religious and traditional, and is made and used by villagers. There is not much of a market for tourist art, but Bijagos islanders produce carvings for the tourist markets.

The State of the Physical and Social Sciences

Until the civil war of 1998, there was a research program in Bissau called the Instituto Nacional de Estudos e Pesquisas (INEP). During the war, the INEP building was damaged and its archives and library were vandalized.

Bibliography

Bigman, Laura. *History and Hunger in West Africa: Food Production and Entitlement in Guinea-Bissau and Cape Verde,* 1993.

Bowman, Joye. *Ominious Transition: Commerce and Colonial Expansion in the Senegambia and Guinea, 1857–1919,* 1997.

Brooks, George E. *Luso-African Commerce and Settlement in the Gambia and Guinea-Bissau Region,* 1980.

Cann, John P. *Counterinsurgency in Africa: The Portuguese Way of War, 1961–1974,* 1997.

Forrest, Joshua. *Guinea-Bissau: Power, Conflict, and Renewal in a West African Nation,* 1992.

Galli, Rosemary, and Jocelyn Jones. *Guinea-Bissau: Politics, Economics, and Society,* 1987.

Lobban, Richard Andrew, Jr., and Peter Karibe Mendy. *Historical Dictionary of the Republic of Guinea-Bissau*, 3rd ed., 1999.

Lopes, Carlos. *Guinea-Bissau: From Liberation Struggle to Independent Statehood*, 1987.

Rodney, Walter. *A History of the Upper Guinea Coast, 1545–1800*, 1970.

Rudebeck, Lars. *Guinea-Bissau: A Study in Political Mobilization*, 1974.

—ERIC GABLE

Guyana

Culture Name

Guyanese

Orientation

Identification. Guyana is an Amerindian word meaning "the land of many waters." Attempts to forge a common identity have foundered, and it is more accurate to speak of African, Indian, and Amerindian Guyanese cultures. There were small European, Portuguese "colored," and Chinese communities before large-scale migration to Canada and the United States in the late 1960s. British Guiana was referred to as "the land of six peoples."

Location and Geography. Guyana is on the northeastern shoulder of South America, bounded on the north by the Atlantic Ocean, on the east by Suriname, on the northwest by Venezuela, and on the south and southwest by Brazil. The capital city is Georgetown. In an area of 83,000 square miles (212,000 square kilometers), there are three regions: the narrow coastal belt of rich alluvium; the densely forested, hilly sand and clay belt; and the Rupununi grasslands between the rain forests and the frontier with Brazil. Over 90 percent of the population lives on the coastal belt, which is below sea level. The Dutch, using African slaves in the eighteenth century, made this area habitable. Every square mile of cultivated land has forty-nine miles of drainage canals and ditches and sixteen miles of high-level waterways.

Demography. The population was 758,619 in 1980. It had declined to 723,800 in 1991, and an estimated 720,700 in 1996. In 1991, the population consisted of 49 percent Indians; 35 percent Africans; 7 percent mixed race peoples; and 6.8 percent Amerindians. Indians are of the following religions: Hindu, 65 percent; Muslim, 20 percent; and Christian, 15 percent. Massive migration has led to the virtual disappearance of Chinese, mixed, Europeans, and Portuguese.

Linguistic Affiliation. The official language is English. No African languages survived slavery, nor have those of the indentured laborers (Indians, Madeiran Portuguese, and Chinese). Guyanese speak creole dialects of English with varying ethnic lexical imprints. However, all dialects are mutually intelligible.

Symbolism. There are few national symbols or metaphors. The national hero, Cuffy, the leader of the Berbice Slave Rebellion in 1763, is primarily an African Guyanese hero whose statue in Georgetown evokes Indian antipathy. Indians tend to identify with an India of the imagination and the Hindu and Muslim religions. Africans often look to an imagined Africa. The utopian vision of Guyana—El Dorado—created by Sir Walter Raleigh in the 1590s, claims the imagination of most Guyanese today.

History and Ethnic Relations

National Identity. The colonial rulers promoted images of Britishness to inculcate loyalty to the empire, but although various ethnic groups absorbed aspects of that culture, they retained their identities. The Portuguese attempted to selectively Anglicize their Madeiran Catholic culture to stress their European-ness. Most Africans adapted British culture to an essentially African core. Indians, coming after the Africans (between 1838 and 1917), sustained a stronger sense of their national identity. This process of "creolization" affected all groups but did not forge a national culture.

Ethnic Relations. After adopting British cultural idioms, the African and mixed middle class deprecated the "backward coolie" culture of Indians. The Indians, steeped in ancient notions of caste, brought rigid ideals of color and physical features to their judgment of African people, although most Indian immigrants were themselves dark. Africans and Indians thus constructed distinct

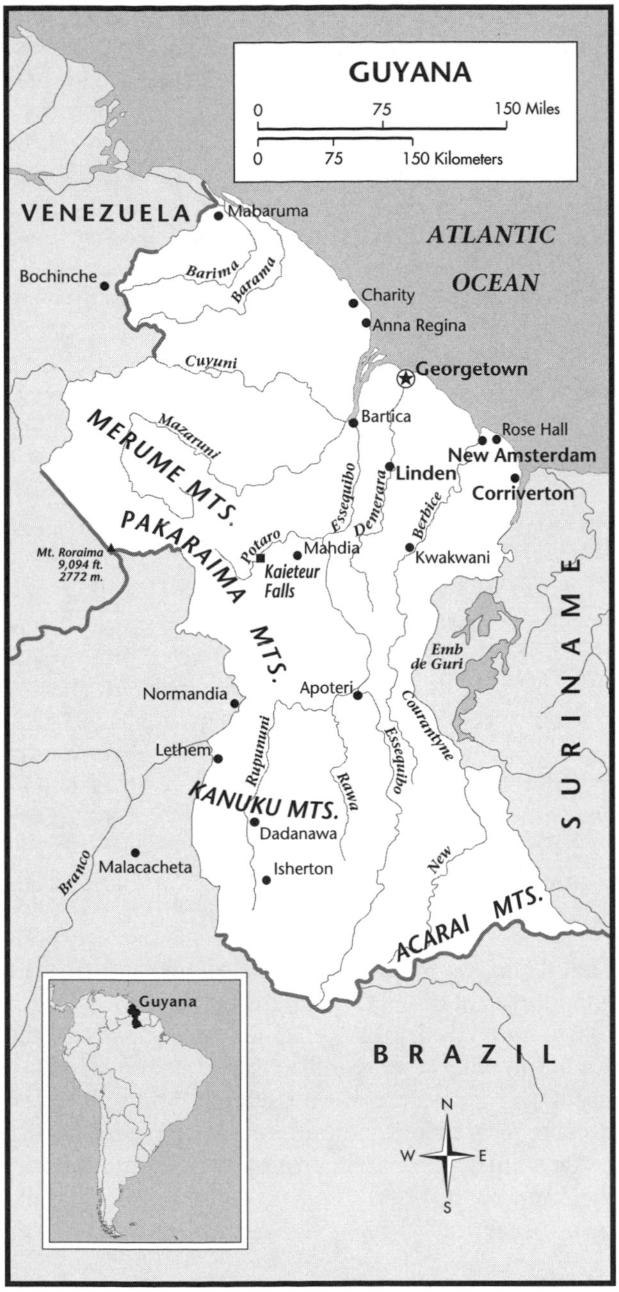

Guyana

identities. A brief political compromise in the early 1950s could not moderate their mutual incomprehension. In the early 1960s, both groups violently contested the space being vacated by the British; this has left a legacy of racial hatred. Ethnic relations since independence in 1966 have been undermined by the notion that politics consists of the allocation of the spoils of power to the ruling ethnic section. Alternating ruling African and Indian elites publicly criticize the role of culture and ethnicity in political mobilization while exploiting it.

Urbanism, Architecture, and the Use of Space

The two main commercial centers are Georgetown and New Amsterdam. The colonial architecture found in parts of Georgetown is still impressive wooden buildings with jalousies and high ceilings to facilitate ventilation, some featuring large, wooden verandas. In rural areas, there are many wooden buildings made up of many eclectic styles, but all are built on stilts to protect them from floods. Wooden buildings are fading into the past, however, as concrete buildings are becoming more common.

Food and Economy

Food in Daily Life. Basic foods reflect ethnic preferences, but there has been considerable cross-fertilization. The creole foods created by Africans have been adopted by all the other groups. Dishes made from "ground provisions" now constitute a national menu: crab or fish soups with plantains, eddoes, cassava, dasheen, and coconut milk; "cook-up rice" with black-eyed peas, pigs tail, green plantain, and cassareep; and Indian curries and roti.

Food Customs at Ceremonial Occasions. At African festivals and life cycle rites, creole foods are served. Vegetarian curries are provided at Hindu weddings; the day after a wedding, curried meat is served.

Basic Economy. Most food is produced locally, including rice, fruits and vegetables, sugar, cooking oils, fish and seafood, meat, and rum. Colonial tastes survive in the form of sardines, corned beef and mutton, chocolate, and whiskey. Imports largely consist of fuels and lubricants, cars, agricultural machinery, clothing and footwear, and consumer durables.

Commercial Activities. In a primarily agricultural country, the main exports are sugar and rum. Rice is grown primarily on small farms, and coconuts also are an important crop. The major industrial products are bauxite, gold, and lumber. Fishing is established, as is livestock rearing. Tourism, mainly to the wild interior, is in its infancy.

Major Industries. Industry is still in its infancy in Guyana. The one exception to this are the companies that process bauxite and the facilities in rural areas set up to dredge for gold.

Trade. Guyana trades primarily with the European Union (mainly the United Kingdom), Canada, the United States, and the Caribbean community. Most of the country's main export, sugar, is sold to the European Union. The bulk of rice production goes to the Caribbean, and bauxite is exported to Canada and the United States.

Division of Labor. Eighty percent of workers in the sugar industry and 90 percent of rice farmers are Indian, as are many growers of fruits and vegetables and forestry and fishing workers. Africans tend to go into the professions, work in public service, and seek employment as skilled workers in urban centers and the interior.

Social Stratification

Classes and Castes. There are class differences within each ethnic group. One can identify an Indian middle class based primarily in commerce and an African middle class in the professions and the upper echelons of public service. Middle class consciousness across ethnic lines is weak, and includes very few Amerindians. Between 1988 and 1996, gross domestic product increased by forty percent, with remarkable growth in sectors where Indians are disproportionately represented. The public sector, where Africans dominate, experienced no growth in that period.

Symbols of Social Stratification. Markers that locate people as middle class regardless of ethnicity include place of residence, the employment of security guards, the type of car driven, the type of English spoken, the frequency of travel overseas, where and what the men drink, where the women shop, clubs, and access to private tutors for children.

Political Life

Government. The 1992 and 1997 general elections were won by the predominantly Indian People's Progressive Party (PPP). The elections of 1968, 1973, 1980, and 1985 and the referendum of 1978 were widely seen to be rigged in favor of the predominantly African People's National Congress (PNC), which ruled from 1964 to 1992. The electoral system has been one of proportional representation since 1964. Fifty-three seats in the national Parliament are allocated proportionally. Another tier of government serves the ten regions; the President, who is the leader of the victorious party, heads the government but does not sit in Parliament.

Leadership and Political Officials. Elections are a demonstration of ethnic strength rather than a reflection of popular will. Cheddi Jagan and L. F. S. Burnham were the cofounders of the PPP, a loose coalition of the two main ethnic groups. The first PPP government, elected in April 1953, was thrown out by the British for fear of communism. Party rivalries since that time have involved different versions of Marxism, and the various parties have failed to deal with racial antagonism.

Military Activity. Before the 1990s, the army was crucial to the projection of political power, and was a source of employment for African youths. In 1992, the Guyana Defence Force was 97 percent African and 3 percent Amerindian, with Indians accounting for less than one percent.

Gender Roles and Statuses

Division of Labor by Gender. The economic and political spheres are dominated by men, but a few women are senior officials in the government. Although there has been one female president, there is a paucity of women in the cabinet, the legislature, and the leadership of political parties. Women play a significant role as farmers, market vendors, teachers, nurses, civil servants, and clerks, as well as doing housework. In recent years girls have outperformed boys in regional examinations, and more women than men attend university.

The Relative Status of Women and Men. The abandonment of children by fathers and a culture of male-centered drinking frequently leave women with the sole responsibility for their children. In urban areas, where the extended family is often nonexistent, many African women are the family breadwinners. The state provides virtually no social welfare assistance.

Marriage, Family, and Kinship

Marriage. Among Hindus and Muslims, arranged, comparatively early marriages are common. Middle-class Indians have greater freedom in choosing a spouse, especially if the woman is a professional. Marriage usually occurs later, and the family is smaller. Indian families are patriarchal and often function as corporate economic units. Formal marriage is less common among the African working class, and the middle classes marry later.

Domestic Unit. There is a high incidence of multigenerational women-centered households in working-class families. Younger men may belong to and contribute to the household, and older men may join later. Men usually marry late and often engage

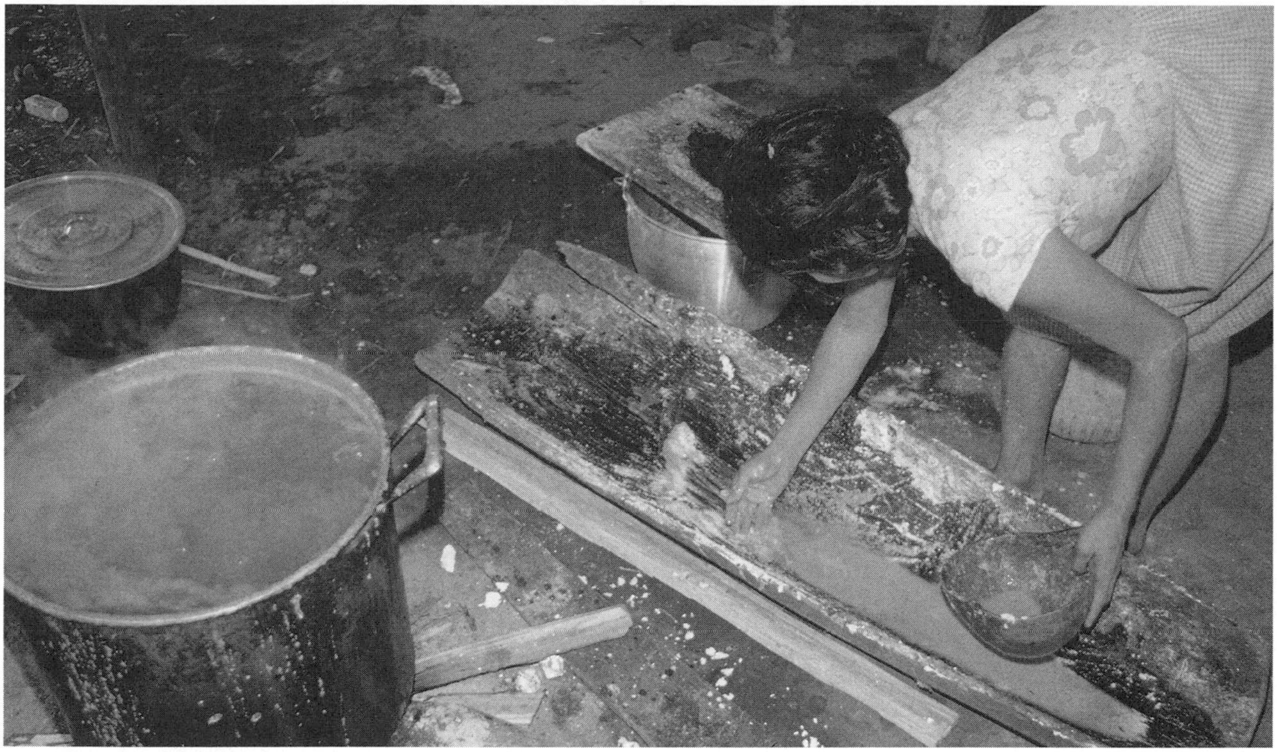

A woman prepares cachiri, an alcoholic drink, in a workshop.

in serial monogamy before forming a stable relationship.

Socialization

Infant Care. Among all the ethnic groups, the extended family plays a role in the socialization of children. In an outdoor society, children are allowed to roam. In rural communities, discipline is a communal responsibility. Children and younger adults address elders not by their names but as "auntie" or "uncle." Children usually are carried by parents, siblings, and relatives.

Child Rearing and Education. Teaching children "correct" behavior is a priority. Corporal punishment is considered indispensable, and attendance at church, temple, or mosque is used to inculcate moral values. Life cycle rites and rituals are central to the shaping of a child.

Higher Education. Mixed people and Africans were pioneers in education. Until the 1930s, Indians tended to resist educating girls, but the example of other groups and the emergence of an Indian middle class have led to a changed attitude. Until decolonization in the late 1960s, secondary schools were excellent. The University of Guyana, founded in 1963, has produced many distinguished scholars and professionals, but it has also suffered from the mass exodus of Guyanese academics.

Religion

Religious beliefs. African, Amerindian, and Indian traditional cultures have sustained folk practices that have penetrated Christianity, Hinduism, and Islam. Obeah has its roots in African folk religion but influences Indians as well, and Indian spirit possession has affected rural African religious sensibility.

Religious Practitioners. Christian ministers, Hindu priests (Brahmins), and Muslim imams command considerable deference. However, folk religious leaders such as obeah men and women, charismatic leaders in Afro-Christian sects, and similar leaders in folk Hinduism compete with the established religious leaders.

Death and the Afterlife. Death requires the public articulation of grief; the "wake" or vigil, facilitates communal support for the bereaved, who reciprocate by providing a feast for the community. Hindus believe in reincarnation, and Africans believe that the spirit of the dead must be placated and assisted.

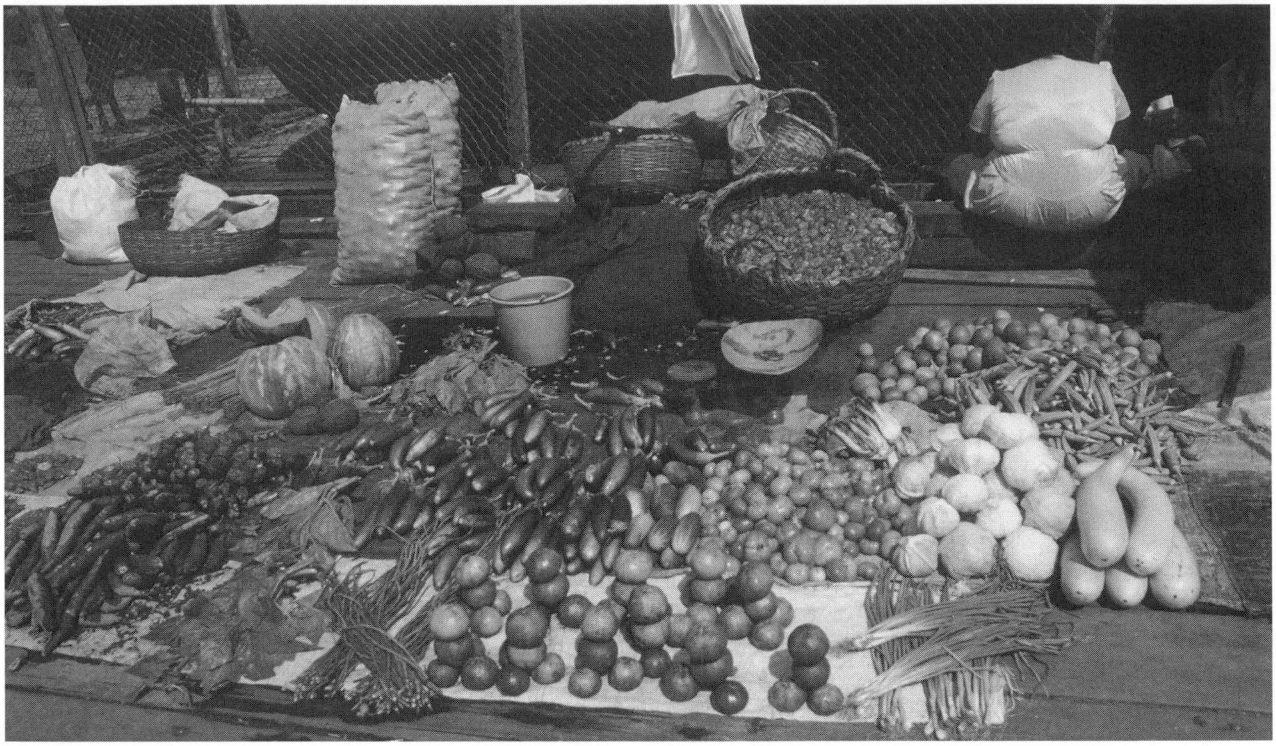

Produce displayed for sale at a market in Parika Quayside. Agriculture is Guyana's principal commercial activity.

Secular Celebrations

Most festivals are based on Christian, Hindu, and Islamic beliefs, so there are few truly secular holidays or events. However, "Mashramani" is celebrated to mark the country's Republic Day on 23 February, and the anniversary of the Berbice Slave Rebellion of 1763 is also noted.

The Arts and Humanities

Support for the Arts. It is extremely difficult for artists to survive as public funding is very limited. Many artists have migrated.

Literature. Africans celebrate their history of resistance and achievement through Anancy tales, proverbs, songs, and stories. This tradition has shaped Guyanese literary sensibility. The first major Guyanese novelist was Edgar Mittelholzer (1909–1965), who lived and worked in England most of his life. His first novel, *Corentyne Thunder*, was published in 1941 and was followed by 22 additional novels. Another noted Guyanese author, Wilson Harris (1923–), also did most of his writing in England. His works were greatly influenced by Amerindian myths and the haunting solitude of the rain forests and its majestic rivers. The country's best-known poet is Martin Carter (1927–1996), whose work was influenced by the political turmoil of the 1940s and early 1950s.

Graphic Arts. The country's most accomplished painter, Aubrey Williams, was steeped in Amerindian motifs and images of the hinterland. The work of the sculptor Philip Moore is informed by West African artistic forms and motifs. In pottery, woodcraft, and basketry, Amerindians produce for the domestic and foreign markets. There is a national collection of paintings but no national gallery.

Performance Arts. There is a rich heritage of folk music, dance, and drama in each of the main ethnic groups but no art form to project a national identity. The impact of the national School of Dance has been limited; music and dance are still essentially ethnic. The Theatre Guild in Georgetown has sustained a dramatic tradition, as has the professional Theatre Company, but drama appeals mainly to the elite.

Bibliography

Adamson, Alan H. *Sugar without Slaves: The Political Economy of British Guiana, 1838–1904*, 1972.

Benjamin, Joel, Lakshmi Kallicharan, Ian McDonald, and Lloyd Searwar, eds. *They Came in Ships: An Anthology of Indo-Guyanese Prose and Poetry*, 1998.

Brown, Stewart ed. *The Art of Martin Carter*, 2000.

Carter, Martin. *Selected Poems*, 1997.

Jagan, Cheddi. *The West on Trial: My Fight for Guyana's Freedom*, 1966.

McGowan, Winston F., James G. Rose, and David A. Granger, eds. *Themes in African Guyanese History*, 1998.

Menezes, Mary Noel. *The Portuguese of Guyana: A Study in Culture and Conflict*, 1994.

Moore, Brian. *Cultural Power, Resistance and Pluralism: Colonial Guyana, 1838–1900*, 1995.

Rodney, Walter. *A History of the Guyanese Working People, 1881–1905*, 1981.

Seecharan, Clem. *"Tiger in the Stars": The Anatomy of Indian Achievement in British Guiana, 1919–1929*, 1997.

———. "The Shaping of the Indo-Caribbean People: Guyana and Trinidad to the 1940s." *Journal of Caribbean Studies* 14 (1–2): 61–92, 1999–2000.

Smith, Raymond T. *The Negro Family in British Guiana: Family Structure and Social Status in the Villages*, 1956.

———. *British Guiana*, 1962.

Spinner, Thomas J., *A Political and Social History of Guyana, 1945–1983*, 1983.

St. Pierre, Maurice. *Anatomy of Resistance: Anti-Colonialism in Guyana, 1823–1966*, 1999.

Sue-a-Quan, Trev. *Cane Reapers: Chinese Indentured Immigrants in Guyana*, 1999.

—CLEM SEECHARAN

HAITI

CULTURE NAME

Haitian

ORIENTATION

Identification. Haiti, a name that means "mountainous country," is derived from the language of the Taino Indians who inhabited the island before European colonization. After independence in 1804, the name was adopted by the military generals, many of them former slaves, who expelled the French and took possession of the colony then known as Saint Domingue. In 2000, 95 percent of the population was of African descent, and the remaining 5 percent mulatto and white. Some wealthy citizens think of themselves as French, but most residents identify themselves as Haitian and there is a strong sense of nationalism.

Location and Geography. Haiti covers 10,714 square miles (27,750 square kilometers). It is located in the subtropics on the western third of Hispaniola, the second largest island in the Caribbean, which it shares with the Spanish-speaking Dominican Republic. The neighboring islands include Cuba, Jamaica, and Puerto Rico. Three-quarters of the terrain is mountainous; the highest peak is the Morne de Selle. The climate is mild, varying with altitude. The mountains are calcareous rather than volcanic and give way to widely varying microclimatic and soil conditions. A tectonic fault line runs through the country, causing occasional and sometimes devastating earthquakes. The island is also located within the Caribbean hurricane belt.

Demography. The population has grown steadily from 431,140 at independence in 1804 to the estimate of 6.9 million to 7.2 million in 2000. Haiti is one of the most densely populated countries in the world. Until the 1970s, over 80 percent of the population resided in rural areas, and today, over 60 percent continue to live in provincial villages, hamlets, and homesteads scattered across the rural landscape. The capital city is Port-au-Prince, which is five times larger than the next biggest city, Cape Haitian.

Over one million native-born Haitians live overseas; an additional fifty thousand leave the country every year, predominantly for the United States but also to Canada and France. Approximately 80 percent of permanent migrants come from the educated middle and upper classes, but very large numbers of lower-class Haitians temporarily migrate to the Dominican Republic and Nassau Bahamas to work at low-income jobs in the informal economy. An unknown number of lower-income migrants remain abroad.

Linguistic Affiliation. For most of the nation's history the official language has been French. However, the language spoken by the vast majority of the people is *kreyol,* whose pronunciation and vocabulary are derived largely from French but whose syntax is similar to that of other creoles. With the adoption of a new constitution in 1987, *kreyol* was given official status as the primary official language. French was relegated to the status of a secondary official language but continues to prevail among the elite and in government, functioning as marker of social class and a barrier to the less educated and the poor. An estimated 5–10 percent of the population speaks fluent French, but in recent decades massive emigration to the United States and the availability of cable television from the United States have helped English replace French as the second language in many sectors of the population.

Symbolism. Residents attach tremendous importance to the expulsion of the French in 1804, an event that made Haiti the first independently black-ruled nation in the world, and only the second country in the Western Hemisphere to achieve independence from imperial Europe. The most noted national symbols are the flag, Henri Christophe's citadel and the statue of the "unknown maroon" (*Maroon inconnu*), a bare-chested revolutionary

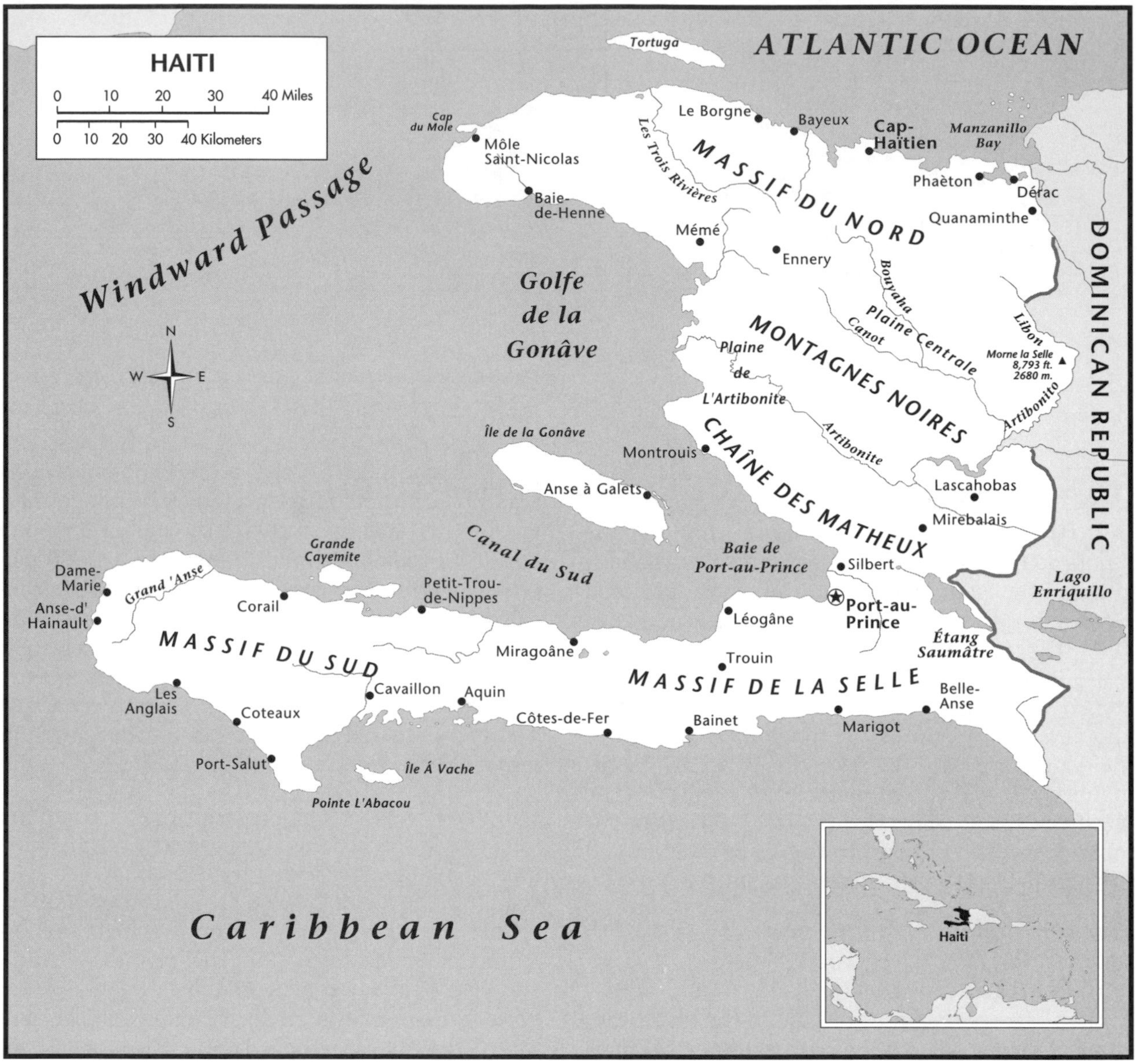

Haiti

trumpeting a conch shell in a call to arms. The presidential palace is also an important national symbol.

History and Ethnic Relations

Emergence of a Nation. Hispaniola was discovered by Christopher Columbus in 1492 and was the first island in the New World settled by the Spanish. By 1550, the indigenous culture of the Taino Indians had vanished from the island, and Hispaniola became a neglected backwater of the Spanish Empire. In the mid-1600s, the western third of the island was populated by fortune seekers, castaways, and wayward colonists, predominantly French, who became pirates and buccaneers, hunting wild cattle and pigs unleashed by the earliest European visitors and selling the smoked meat to passing ships. In the mid-1600s, the French used the buccaneers as mercenaries (freebooters) in an unofficial war against the Spanish. In the Treaty of Ryswick of 1697, France forced Spain to cede the western third of Hispaniola. This area became the French colony of Saint Domingue. By 1788, the colony had become the "jewel of the Antilles," the richest colony in the world.

In 1789, revolution in France sparked dissension in the colony, which had a population of half a million slaves (half of all the slaves in the Caribbean); twenty-eight thousand mulattoes and free blacks, many of whom were wealthy landowners; and thirty-six thousand white planters, artisans, slave drivers, and small landholders. In 1791, thirty-five thousand slaves rose in an insurrection, razed a thousand plantations, and took to the hills. Thirteen years of war and pestilence followed. Spanish, English, and French troops were soon battling one another for control of the colony. The imperial powers militarized the slaves, training them in the arts of "modern" warfare. *Grands blancs* (rich white colonists), *petits blancs* (small farmers and working-class whites), *mulatres* (mulattoes), and *noirs* (free blacks) fought, plotted, and intrigued. Each local interest group exploited its position at every opportunity to achieve its political and economic objectives. From the mayhem emerged some of the greatest black military men in history, including Toussaint Louverture. In 1804, the last European troops were soundly defeated and driven from the island by a coalition of former slaves and mulattoes. In January 1804 the rebel generals declared independence, inaugurating Haiti as the first sovereign "black" country in the modern world and the second colony in the Western Hemisphere to gain independence from imperial Europe.

Since gaining independence, Haiti has had fleeting moments of glory. An early eighteenth century kingdom ruled by Henri Christophe prospered and thrived in the north, and from 1822 to 1844 Haiti ruled the entire island. The late nineteenth century was a period of intense internecine warfare in which ragtag armies backed by urban politicians and conspiring Western businessmen repeatedly sacked Port-au-Prince. By 1915, the year in which U.S. marines began a nineteen year occupation of the country, Haiti was among the poorest nations in the Western Hemisphere.

National Identity. During the century of relative isolation that followed independence, the peasantry developed distinct traditions in cuisine, music, dance, dress, ritual, and religion. Some elements of African cultures survive, such as specific prayers, a few words, and dozens of spirit entities, but Haitian culture is distinct from African and other New World cultures.

Ethnic Relations. The only ethnic subdivision is that of the *syrians*, the early twentieth-century Levantine emigrants who have been absorbed into the commercial elite but often self-identify by their ancestral origins. Haitians refer to all outsiders, even dark-skinned outsiders of African ancestry, as *blan* ("white").

In the neighboring Dominican Republic, despite the presence of over a million Haitian farm workers, servants, and urban laborers, there exists intense prejudice against Haitians. In 1937, the Dominican dictator Rafael Trujillo ordered the massacre of an estimated fifteen to thirty-five thousand Haitians living in the Dominican Republic.

Urbanism, Architecture, and the Use of Space

The most famous architectural accomplishments are King Henri Christophe's postindependence San Souci palace, which was almost entirely destroyed by an earthquake in the early 1840s, and his mountaintop fortress, the Citadelle Laferrière, which survives largely intact.

The contemporary rural landscape is dominated by houses that vary in style from one region to another. Most are single-story, two-room shacks, usually with a front porch. In the dry, treeless areas, houses are constructed of rock or wattle and daub with mud or lime exteriors. In other regions, walls are made from the easily hewn native palm; in still other areas, particularly in the south, houses are made of Hispaniola pine and local hardwoods. When the owner can afford it, the outside of a house is painted in an array of pastel colors, mystic symbols are often painted on the walls, and the awnings are fringed with colorful hand-carved trimming.

In cities, early twentieth century bourgeoisie, foreign entrepreneurs, and the Catholic clergy blended French and southern United States Victorian architectural styles and took the rural gingerbread house to its artistic height, building fantastic multicolored brick and timber mansions with tall double doors, steep roofs, turrets, cornices, extensive balconies, and intricately carved trim. These exquisite structures are fast disappearing as a result of neglect and fires. Today one increasingly finds modern block and cement houses in both provincial villages and urban areas. Craftsmen have given these new houses traditional gingerbread qualities by using embedded pebbles, cut stones, preformed cement relief, rows of shaped balusters, concrete turrets, elaborately contoured cement roofing, large balconies, and artistically welded wrought iron trimming and window bars reminiscent of the carved fringe that adorned classic gingerbread houses.

Haitians in Gonaïves celebrate the deposition of President Jean-Claude Duvalier in February, 1986.

Food and Economy

Food in Daily Life. Nutritional deficits are caused not by inadequate knowledge but by poverty. Most residents have a sophisticated understanding of dietary needs, and there is a widely known system of indigenous food categories that closely approximates modern, scientifically informed nutritional categorization. Rural Haitians are not subsistence farmers. Peasant women typically sell much of the family harvest in regional open-air market places and use the money to buy household foods.

Rice and beans are considered the national dish and are the most commonly eaten meal in urban areas. Traditional rural staples are sweet potatoes, manioc, yams, corn, rice, pigeon peas, cowpeas, bread, and coffee. More recently, a wheat-soy blend from the United States has been incorporated into the diet.

Important treats include sugarcane, mangoes, sweetbread, peanut and sesame seed clusters made from melted brown sugar, and candies made from bittermanioc flour. People make a crude but highly nutritious sugar paste called *rapadou*.

Haitians generally eat two meals a day: a small breakfast of coffee and bread, juice, or an egg and a large afternoon meal dominated by a carbohydrate source such as manioc, sweet potatoes, or rice. The afternoon meal always includes beans or a bean sauce, and there is usually a small amount of poultry, fish, goat, or, less commonly, beef or mutton, typically prepared as a sauce with a tomato paste base. Fruits are prized as between-meal snacks. Non-elite people do not necessarily have community or family meals, and individuals eat wherever they are comfortable. A snack customarily is eaten at night before one goes to sleep.

Food Customs at Ceremonial Occasions. Festive occasions such as baptismal parties, first communions, and marriages include the mandatory Haitian colas, cake, a spiced concoction of domestic rum (*kleren*), and a thick spiked drink made with condensed milk called *kremass*. The middle class and the elite mark the same festivities with Western sodas, Haitian rum (Babouncourt), the national beer (Prestige), and imported beers. Pumpkin soup (*bouyon*) is eaten on New Year's day.

Basic Economy. Haiti is the poorest country in the Western Hemisphere and one of the poorest in the world. It is a nation of small farmers, commonly referred to as peasants, who work small private landholdings and depend primarily on their own labor and that of family members. There are no contemporary plantations and few concentrations of land. Although only 30 percent of the land is considered suitable for agriculture, more than 40 percent is worked. Erosion is severe. Real income for the average family has not increased in over twenty years and has declined precipitously in rural areas. In most rural areas, the average family of six earns less than $500 per year.

Since the 1960s, the country has become heavily dependent on food imports—primarily rice, flour, and beans—from abroad, particularly from the United States. Other major imports from the United States are used material goods such as clothes, bicycles, and motor vehicles. The Haitian has become primarily domestic, and production is almost entirely for domestic consumption. A vigorous internal marketing system dominates the economy and includes trade not only in agricultural produce and livestock but also in homemade crafts.

Land Tenure and Property. Land is relatively evenly distributed. Most holdings are small (approximately three acres), and there are very few landless households. Most property is privately held, though there is a category of land known as State Land that, if agriculturally productive, is rented under a long-term lease to individuals or families and is for all practical purposes private. Unoccupied land frequently is taken over by squatters. There is a vigorous land market, as rural households buy and sell land. Sellers of land generally need cash to finance either a life crisis event (healing or burial ritual) or a migratory venture. Land is typically bought, sold, and inherited without official documentation (no government has ever carried out a cadastral survey). Although there are few land titles, there are informal tenure rules that give farmers relative security in their holdings. Until recently, most conflicts over land were between members of the same kin group. With the departure of the Duvalier dynasty and the emergence of political chaos, some conflicts over land have led to bloodshed between members of different communities and social classes.

Commercial Activities. There is a thriving internal market that is characterized at most levels by itinerant female traders who specialize in domestic items such as produce, tobacco, dried fish, used clothing, and livestock.

Major Industries. There are small gold and copper reserves. For a short time the Reynolds Metals Company operated a bauxite mine, but it was closed in 1983 because of conflict with the government. Offshore assembly industries owned principally by U.S. entrepreneurs employed over sixty thousand people in the mid-1980s but declined in the later 1980s and early 1990s as a result of political unrest. There is one cement factory—most of the cement used in the country is imported—and a single flour mill.

Trade. In the 1800s, the country exported wood, sugarcane, cotton and coffee, but by the 1960s, even the production of coffee, long the major export, had been all but strangled through excessive taxation, lack of investment in new trees, and bad roads. Recently, coffee has yielded to mangoes as the primary export. Other exports include cocoa and essential oils for the cosmetics and pharmaceutical industries. Haiti has become a major transshipment point for illegal drug trafficking.

Imports come predominantly from the United States and include used clothing, mattresses, automobiles, rice, flour, and beans. Cement is imported from Cuba and South America.

Division of Labor. There is a large degree of informal specialization in both rural and urban areas. At the highest level are craftsmen known as bosses, including carpenters, masons, electricians, welders, mechanics, and tree sawyers. Specialists make most craft items, and there are others who castrate animals and climb coconut trees. Within each trade there are subdivisions of specialists.

Social Stratification

Class and Castes. There has always been a wide economic gulf between the masses and a small, wealthy elite and more recently, a growing middle class. Social status is well marked at all levels of society by the degree of French words and phrases used in speech, Western dress patterns, and the straightening of hair.

Symbols of Social Stratification. The wealthiest people tend to be lighter-skinned or white. Some scholars see this apparent color dichotomy as evidence of racist social division, but it also can be explained by historical circumstances and the immigration and intermarrying of the light-skinned elite with white merchants from Lebanon, Syria, Germany, the Netherlands, Russia, other Caribbean countries, and, to a far lesser extent, the United States. Many presidents have been dark-skinned, and dark-skinned individuals have prevailed in the military.

Both music and painting are popular forms of artistic expression in Haiti.

Political Life

Government. Haiti is a republic with a bicameral legislature. It is divided into departments that are subdivided into arrondissments, communes, commune sectionals, and habitations. There have been numerous constitutions. The legal system is based on the Napoleonic Code, which excluded hereditary privileges and aimed to provide equal rights to the population, regardless of religion or status.

Leadership and Political Officials. Political life was dominated between 1957 and 1971 by the initially popular, but subsequently brutal, dictator François "Papa Doc" Duvalier, who was succeeded by his son Jean-Claude ("Baby Doc"). The Duvalier reign ended after popular uprising throughout the country. In 1991, five years and eight interim governments later, a popular leader, Jean Bertrand Aristide, won the presidency with an overwhelming majority of the popular vote. Aristide was deposed seven months later in a military coup. The United Nations then imposed an embargo on all international trade with Haiti. In 1994, threatened with the invasion by United States forces, the military junta relinquished control to an international peacekeeping force. The Aristide government was reestablished, and since 1995 an ally of Aristide, Rene Preval, has ruled a government rendered largely ineffective by political gridlock.

Social Problems and Control. Since independence, vigilante justice has been a conspicuous informal mechanism of the justice system. Mobs have frequently killed criminals and abusive authorities. With the breakdown in state authority that has occurred over the last fourteen years of political chaos, both crime and vigilantism have increased. The security of life and property, particularly in urban areas, has become the most challenging issue facing the people and the government.

Military Activity. The military was disbanded by United Nations forces in 1994 and replaced by the *Polis Nasyonal d'Ayiti* (PNH).

Social Welfare and Change Programs

The infrastructure is in a very poor condition. International efforts to change this situation have been under way since 1915, but the country may be more underdeveloped today than it was one hundred years ago. International food aid, predominantly from the United States, supplies over ten percent of the country's needs.

Nongovernmental Organizations and Other Associations

Per capita, there are more foreign nongovernmental organizations and religious missions (predominantly U.S.-based) in Haiti than in any other country in the world.

Gender Roles and Statuses

Division of Labor by Gender. In both rural and urban areas, men monopolize the job market. Only men work as jewelers, construction workers, general laborers, mechanics, and chauffeurs. Most doctors, teachers, and politicians are men, although women have made inroads into the elite professions, particularly medicine. Virtually all pastors are male, as are most school directors. Men also prevail, although not entirely, in the professions of spiritual healer and herbal practitioner. In the domestic sphere, men are primarily responsible for the care of livestock and gardens.

Women are responsible for domestic activities such as cooking, housecleaning and washing clothes by hand. Rural women and children are responsible for securing water and firewood, women help with planting and harvesting. The few wage-

Haitians expect to haggle when making a purchase.

earning opportunities open to women are in health care, in which nursing is exclusively a female occupation, and, to a far lesser extent, teaching. In marketing, women dominate most sectors, particularly in goods such as tobacco, garden produce, and fish. The most economically active women are skillful entrepreneurs on whom other market women heavily depend. Usually specialists in a particular commodity, these *marchann* travel between rural and urban areas, buying in bulk at one market and redistributing the goods, often on credit, to lower-level female retailers in other markets.

The Relative Status of Women and Men. Rural women are commonly thought by outsiders to be severely repressed. Urban middle-class and elite women have a status equivalent to that of women in developed countries, but among the impoverished urban majority, the scarcity of jobs and the low pay for female domestic services have led to widespread promiscuity and the abuse of women. However, rural women play a prominent economic role in the household and family. In most areas, men plant gardens, but women are thought of as the owners of harvests and, because they are marketers, typically control the husband's earnings.

Marriage, Family, and Kinship

Marriage. Marriage is expected among the elite and the middle classes, but less than forty percent of the non-elite population marries (an increase compared with the past resulting from recent Protestant conversions). However, with or without legal marriage, a union typically is considered complete and gets the respect of the community when a man has built a house for the woman and after the first child has been born. When marriage does occur, it is usually later in a couple's relationship, long after a household has been established and the children have begun to reach adulthood. Couples usually live on property belonging to the man's parents. Living on or near the wife's family's property is common in fishing communities and areas where male migration is very high.

Although it is not legal, at any given time about 10 percent of men have more than a single wife, and these relationships are acknowledged as legitimate by the community. The women live with their children in separate homesteads that are provided for by the man.

Extra residential mating relationships that do not involve the establishment of independent households are common among wealthy rural and urban men and less fortunate women. Incest restrictions extend to first cousins. There is no brideprice or dowry, although women generally are expected to bring certain domestic items into the union and men must provide a house and garden plots.

Domestic Unit. Households typically are made up of nuclear family members and adopted children or young relatives. Elderly widows and widowers may live with their children and grandchildren. The husband is thought of as the owner of the house and must plant gardens and tend livestock. However, the house typically is associated with the woman, and a sexually faithful woman cannot be expelled from a household and is thought of as the manager of the property and the decision maker regarding use of funds from the sale of garden produce and household animals.

Inheritance. Men and women inherit equally from both parents. Upon the death of a landowner, land is divided in equal portions among the surviving children. In practice, land often is ceded to specific children in the form of a sales transaction before a parent dies.

Kin Groups. Kinship is based on bilateral affiliation: One is equally a member of one's father's and mother's kin groups. Kinship organization differs from that of the industrial world with regard to ancestors and godparentage. Ancestors are given ritual attention by the large subset of people who serve the *lwa*. They are believed to have the power to influence the lives of the living, and there are certain ritual obligations that must be satisfied to appease them. Godparentage is ubiquitous and derives from Catholic tradition. The parents invite a friend or acquaintance to sponsor a child's baptism. This sponsorship creates a relationship not only between the child and the godparents but also between the child's parents and the godparents. These individuals have ritual obligations toward one another and address each other with the gender-specific terms *konpè* (if the person addressed is male) and *komè*, or *makomè* (if the person addressed is female), meaning "my coparent."

SOCIALIZATION

Infant Care. In some areas infants are given purgatives immediately after birth, and in some regions the breast is withheld from newborns for the first twelve to forty-eight hours, a practice that has been linked to instruction from misinformed Western-trained nurses. Liquid supplements usually are introduced within the first two weeks of life, and food supplements often are begun thirty days after birth and sometimes earlier. Infants are fully weaned at eighteen months.

Child Rearing and Education. Very young children are indulged, but by the age of seven or eight most rural children engage in serious work. Children are important in retrieving household water and firewood and helping to cook and clean around the house. Children look after livestock, help their parents in the garden, and run errands. Parents and guardians are often harsh disciplinarians, and working-age children may be whipped severely. Children are expected to be respectful to adults and obedient to family members, even to siblings only a few years older than themselves. They are not allowed to talk back or stare at adults when being scolded. They are expected to say thank you and please. If a child is given a piece of fruit or bread, he or she must immediately begin breaking the food and distributing it to other children. The offspring of elite families are notoriously spoiled and are reared from an early age to lord it over their less fortunate compatriots.

Tremendous importance and prestige are attached to education. Most rural parents try to send their children at least to primary school, and a child who excels and whose parents can afford the costs is quickly exempted from the work demands levied on other children.

Fosterage (*restavek*) is a system in which children are given to other individuals or families for the purpose of performing domestic services. There is an expectation that the child will be sent to school and that the fostering will benefit the child. The most important ritual events in the life of a child are baptism and the first communion, which is more common among the middle class and the elite. Both events are marked by a celebration including Haitian colas, a cake or sweetened bread rolls, sweetened rum beverages, and, if the family can afford it, a hot meal that includes meat.

Higher Education. Traditionally, there has been a very small, educated urban-based elite, but in the last thirty years a large and rapidly increasing number of educated citizens have come from relatively humble rural origins, although seldom from the poorest social strata. These people attend medical and engineering schools, and may study at overseas universities.

There is a private university and a small state university in Port-au-Prince, including a medical school. Both have enrollments of only a few thousand students. Many offspring of middle-class and

The carnival that preceeds Lent is the most popular Haitian festival.

elite families attend universities in the United States, Mexico City, Montreal, the Dominican Republic, and, to a much lesser extent, France and Germany.

ETIQUETTE

When entering a yard Haitians shout out *onè* (''honor''), and the host is expected to reply *respè* (''respect''). Visitors to a household never leave empty-handed or without drinking coffee, or at least not without an apology. Failure to announce a departure, is considered rude.

People feel very strongly about greetings, whose importance is particularly strong in rural areas, where people who meet along a path or in a village often say hello several times before engaging in further conversation or continuing on their way. Men shake hands on meeting and departing, men and women kiss on the cheek when greeting, women kiss each other on the cheek, and rural women kiss female friends on the lips as a display of friendship.

Young women do not smoke or drink alcohol of any kind except on festive occasions. Men typically smoke and drink at cockfights, funerals, and festivities but are not excessive in the consumption of alcohol. As women age and become involved in itinerant marketing, they often begin to drink *kleren* (rum) and use snuff and/or smoke tobacco in a pipe or cigar. Men are more prone to smoke tobacco, particularly cigarettes, than to use snuff.

Men and especially women are expected to sit in modest postures. Even people who are intimate with one another consider it extremely rude to pass gas in the presence of others. Haitians say excuse me (*eskize-m*) when entering another person's space. Brushing the teeth is a universal practice. People also go to great lengths to bathe before boarding public buses, and it is considered proper to bathe before making a journey, even if this is to be made in the hot sun.

Women and especially men commonly hold hands in public as a display of friendship; this is commonly mistaken by outsiders as homosexuality. Women and men seldom show public affection toward the opposite sex but are affectionate in private.

People haggle over anything that has to do with money, even if money is not a problem and the price has already been decided or is known. A mercurial demeanor is considered normal, and arguments are common, animated, and loud. People of higher class or means are expected to treat those beneath them with a degree of impatience and contempt. In interacting with individuals of lower status or even equal social rank, people tend to be candid in referring to appearance, shortcomings, or handicaps. Violence is rare but once started often escalates quickly to bloodshed and serious injury.

RELIGION

Religious Beliefs. The official state religion is Catholicism, but over the last four decades Protestant missionary activity has reduced the proportion of people who identify themselves as Catholic from over 90 percent in 1960 to less than 70 percent in 2000.

Haiti is famous for its popular religion, known to its practitioners as "serving the *lwa*" but referred to by the literature and the outside world as voodoo (*vodoun*). This religious complex is a syncretic mixture of African and Catholic beliefs, rituals, and religious specialists, and its practitioners (*sèvitè*) continue to be members of a Catholic parish. Long stereotyped by the outside world as "black magic," *vodoun* is actually a religion whose specialists derive most of their income from healing the sick rather than from attacking targeted victims.

Many people have rejected voodoo, becoming instead *katolik fran* ("unmixed Catholics" who do not combine Catholicism with service to the *lwa*) or *levanjil*, (Protestants). The common claim that all Haitians secretly practice voodoo is inaccurate. Catholics and Protestants generally believe in the existence of *lwa*, but consider them demons to be avoided rather than family spirits to be served. The percentage of those who explicitly serve the family *lwa* is unknown but probably high.

Religious Practitioners. Aside from the priests of the Catholic Church and thousands of Protestant ministers, many of them trained and supported by evangelical missions from the United States, informal religious specialists proliferate. Most notable are the voodoo specialists known by various names in different regions (*houngan, bokò, gangan*) and referred to as *manbo* in the case of female specialists. (Females are viewed as having the same spiritual powers as males, though in practice there are more *houngan* than *manbo*.) There are also bush priests (*pè savann*) who read specific Catholic prayers at funerals and other ceremonial occasions, and *hounsi*, initiated females who serve as ceremonial assistants to the *houngan* or *manbo*.

Rituals and Holy Places. People make pilgrimages to a series of holy sites. Those sites became popular in association with manifestations of particular saints and are marked by unusual geographic features such as the waterfall at Saut d'Eau, the most famous of sacred sites. Waterfalls and certain species of large trees are especially sacred because they are believed to be the homes of spirits and the conduits through which spirits enter the world of living humans.

Death and the Afterlife. Beliefs concerning the afterlife depend on the religion of the individual. Strict Catholics and Protestants believe in the existence of reward or punishment after death. Practitioners of voodoo assume that the souls of all the deceased go to an abode "beneath the waters," that is often associated with *lafrik gine* ("L'Afrique Guinée," or Africa). Concepts of reward and punishment in the afterlife are alien to *vodoun*.

The moment of death is marked by ritual wailing among family members, friends, and neighbors. Funerals are important social events and involve several days of social interaction, including feasting and the consumption of rum. Family members come from far away to sleep at the house, and friends and neighbors congregate in the yard. Men play dominoes while the women cook. Usually within the week but sometimes several years later, funerals are followed by the *priè*, nine nights of socializing and ritual. Burial monuments and other mortuary rituals are often costly and elaborate. People are increasingly reluctant to be buried underground, preferring to be interred above ground in a *kav*, an elaborate multi chambered tomb that may cost more than the house in which the individual lived while alive. Expenditures on mortuary ritual have been increasing and have been interpreted as a leveling mechanism that redistributes resources in the rural economy.

MEDICINE AND HEALTH CARE

Malaria, typhoid, tuberculosis, intestinal parasites, and sexually transmitted diseases take a toll on the population. Estimates of HIV among those ages twenty-two to forty-four years are as high as 11 percent, and estimates among prostitutes in the capital are as high as 80 percent. There is less than one doctor per eight-thousand people. Medical facilities are poorly funded and understaffed, and most health care workers are incompetent. Life expectancy in 1999 was under fifty-one years.

In the absence of modern medical care, an elaborate system of indigenous healers has evolved, in-

Women are typically responsible for household maintenance and marketing garden produce.

cluding herbal specialists know as leaf doctors (*medsin fey*), granny midwives (*fam saj*), masseuses (*manyè*), injection specialists (*charlatan*), and spiritual healers. People have tremendous faith in informal healing procedures and commonly believe that HIV can be cured. With the spread of Pentecostal evangelicalism, Christian faith healing has spread rapidly.

Secular Celebrations

Associated with the beginning of the religious season of Lent, Carnival is the most popular and active festival, featuring secular music, parades, dancing in the streets, and abundant consumption of alcohol. Carnival is preceded by several days of rara bands, traditional ensembles featuring large groups of specially dressed people who dance to the music of *vaccines* (bamboo trumpets) and drums under the leadership of a director who blows a whistle and wields a whip. Other festivals include Independence Day (1 January), Bois Cayman Day (14 August, celebrating a legendary ceremony at which slaves plotted the revolution in 1791), Flag Day (18 May), and the assassination of Dessalines, the first ruler of independent Haiti (17 October).

The Arts and Humanities

Support for the Arts. The bankrupt government provides occasional token support for the arts, typically for dance troupes.

Literature. Haitian literature is written primarily in French. The elite has produced several writers of international renown, including Jean Price-Mars, Jacques Roumain, and Jacques-Stephen Alexis.

Graphic Arts. Haitians have a predilection for decoration and bright colors. Wood boats called *kantè*, second hand U.S. school buses called *kamion*, and small enclosed pickup trucks called *taptap* are decorated with brightly colored mosaics and given personal names such as *kris kapab* (Christ Capable) and *gras a dieu* (Thank God). Haitian painting became popular in the 1940s when a school of "primitive" artists encouraged by the Episcopal Church began in Port-au-Prince. Since that time a steady flow of talented painters has emerged from the lower middle class. However, elite university-schooled painters and gallery owners have profited the most from international recognition. There is also a thriving industry of low-quality paintings, tapestries, and wood, stone, and metal handicrafts that supplies much of the artwork sold to tourists on other Caribbean islands.

Performance Arts. There is a rich tradition of music and dance, but few performances are publicly funded.

BIBLIOGRAPHY

Cayemittes, Michel, Antonio Rival, Bernard Barrere, Gerald Lerebours, and Michaele Amedee Gedeon. *Enquete Mortalite, Morbidite et Utilisation des Services*, 1994–95.

CIA. *CIA World Fact Book*, 2000.

Courlander, Harold. *The Hoe and the Drum: Life and Lore of the Haitian People*, 1960.

Crouse, Nellis M. *The French Struggle for the West Indies 1665–1713*, 1966.

DeWind, Josh, and David H. Kinley III. *Aiding Migration: The Impact of International Development Assistance in Haiti*, 1988.

Farmer, Paul. *The Uses of Haiti*, 1994.

———. "Aids and Accusation: Haiti and the Geography of Blame." Ph.D. dissertation. Harvard University, 1990.

Fass, Simon. *Political Economy in Haiti: The Drama of Survival*, 1988.

Geggus, David Patrick. *Slavery, War, and Revolution: The British Occupation of Saint Domingue 1793–1798*, 1982.

Heinl, Robert Debs, and Nancy Gordon Heinl. *Written in Blood: The Story of the Haitian People*, 1978.

Herskovits, Melville J. *Life in a Haitian Valley*, 1937.

James, C. L. R. *The Black Jacobins*, 1963.

Leyburn, James G. *The Haitian People*, 1941, 1966.

Lowenthal, Ira. "Marriage is 20, Children are 21: The Cultural Construction of Conjugality in Rural Haiti." Ph.D. dissertation. Johns Hopkins University, Baltimore, 1987.

Lundahl, Mats. *The Haitian Economy: Man, Land, and Markets*, 1983.

Metraux, Alfred. *Voodoo in Haiti*, translated by Hugo Charteris, 1959,1972.

Metraux, Rhoda. "Kith and Kin: A Study of Creole Social Structure in Marbial, Haiti." Ph.D. dissertation: Columbia University, New York, 1951.

Moral, Paul. *Le Paysan Haitien*, 1961.

Moreau, St. Mery. *Description de la Partie Francaise de Saint-Domingue*, 1797, 1958.

Murray, Gerald F. "The Evolution of Haitian Peasant Land Tenure: Agrarian Adaptation to Population Growth." Ph.D. dissertation. Columbia University, 1977.

Nicholls, David. *From Dessalines to Duvalier*, 1974.

Rotberg, Robert I., with Christopher A. Clague. *Haiti: The Politics of Squalor*, 1971.

Rouse, Irving. *The Tainos: Rise and Decline of the People Who Greeted Columbus*, 1992.

Schwartz, Timothy T. "Children Are the Wealth of the Poor": High Fertility and the Rural Economy of Jean Rabel, Haiti." Ph.D. dissertation. University of Florida, Gainesville, 2000.

Simpson, George Eaton. "Sexual and Family Institutions in Northern Haiti." *American Anthropologist*, 44: 655–674, 1942.

Smucker, Glenn Richard. "Peasants and Development Politics: A Study in Class and Culture." Ph.D. dissertation. New School for Social Research, 1983.

—TIMOTHY T. SCHWARTZ

HERZEGOVINA SEE BOSNIA AND HERZEGOVINA

Honduras

Culture Name

Honduran

Alternative Names

Hondureño catracho (the national nickname; can be amusing, insulting, or friendly, depending on the context. "Catracho" comes from the name of Florencio Xatruch, the general who led the Honduran expeditionary force against William Walker in Nicaragua in 1856.)

Orientation

Identification. The name of the country means "depths." It was so named by Christopher Columbus on his fourth voyage because of the deep waters at the mouth of the Tinto o Negro River off the Mosquito Coast. Regional traditions exist in the south (Choluteca and Valle) and the north coast as well as among the minority ethnic groups. All these people self-identify as Hondurans, however. Spanish-speaking people in the center of the country are the most numerous and are culturally dominant. They do not use a special name to refer to themselves or their region.

Location and Geography. The nation has an area of 43,266 miles (112,492 square kilometers). Honduras is in the middle of Central America. The physical environment is tropical, with a long dry season (six months or more) in the south and the interior and a shorter dry season in the north. The center of the country originally was covered with pine and broadleaf forests of oak and other trees, but much of the pine forest has been logged and much of the oak forest has been cut for farming. The north coast was once primarily rain forest, but much of it has been cleared for commercial banana plantations. The northeast is called the Mosquitia. It includes the "Mosquito Coast," which is actually a long series of white sand beaches and freshwater lagoons. Inland from the coast, the Mosquitia has one of the last great stands of tropical rain forest left in North America, plus pine woods and grasslands.

Different ethnic groups live in specific environments. The Anglo-African-Caribbean "Bay Islanders" live on the Bay Islands off the north coast. The Garífuna people live along the Caribbean Coast of Central America, from Belize to Nicaragua. The Miskito and Tawahka people live in the rain forests of the eastern lowlands, and in similar lands in neighboring areas of Nicaragua. The Pech and Jicaque people live in some of the more remote areas in the central highlands. The Chortí and Lenca peoples live in the rugged western highlands. Hispanic-Hondurans live in the north, south, and center of the country.

The capital city, Tegucigalpa, was chosen because it is near the geographic center of the country. It completely fills a small, deep valley in the headwaters of the Choluteca River, in the central highlands.

Demography. Honduras had a population of 5,990,000 in 1998. In 1791, the population was only 93,501. The pre-Hispanic population was probably much higher, but conquest, slavery, and disease killed many people. The population did not reach one million until 1940.

The major ethnic group include the Chortí, a native people with a population of about five thousand in the department of Copán. There may still be a few people who can speak the Chortí language, which belongs to the Mayan family. The Lenca are a native people in the departments of La Paz, Intibucá, and Lempira, as well as some other areas. The Lenca language is extinct, and culturally the Lenca are similar in many ways to the other Spanish-speaking people in the country. The Lenca population is about one hundred thousand. The Jicaque are a native people who live in the department of Yoro and the community of Montaña de la Flor (municipality of Orica) in the department of

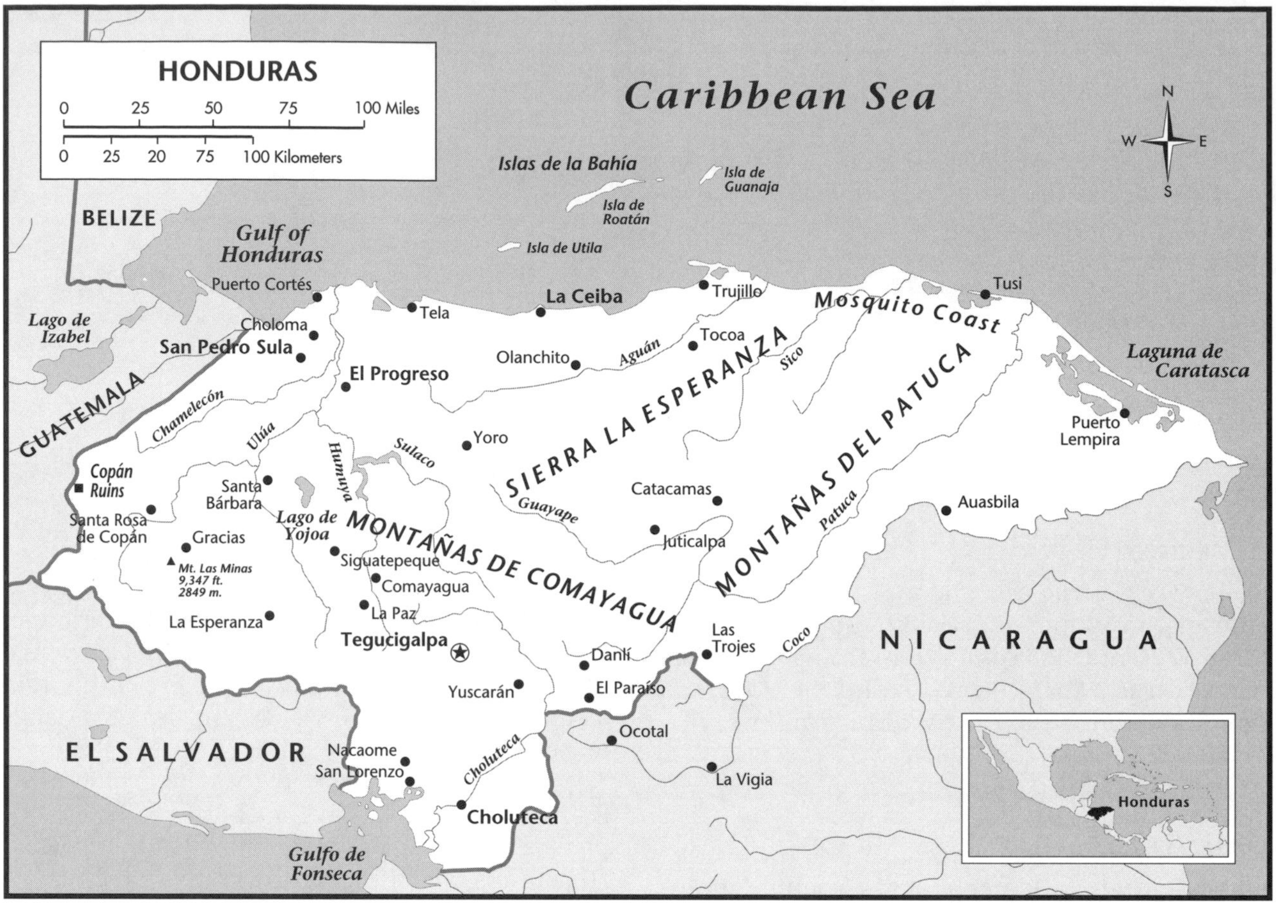

Honduras

Francisco Morazán. Only those in Montaña de la Flor still speak the Tol (Jicaque) language, which is in the Hokan family. The Jicaque group in Yoro is much larger and has been almost completely assimilated into the national culture. There are about nineteen thousand Jicaque in Yoro and about two hundred in Montaña de la Flor. The Pech are a native people in the departments of Olancho and Colón, with a few living in Gracias a Dios in the Mosquitia. They speak a Macro-Chibchan language and have a population of under three thousand. The Tawahka are a native people in the department of Gracias a Dios in the Mosquitia. Tawahka is a Macro-Chibchan language that is very closely related to Sumo, which is spoken in Nicaragua. Most Tawahkas also speak Misquito and Spanish. The Tawahka population is about seven hundred. The Misquitos are a native people with some African and British ancestry who reside in the department of Gracias a Dios in the Mosquitia. Misquito is a Macro-Chibchan language, although most Misquitos speak fluent Spanish. The Misquito population is about thirty-four thousand. The Garífuna are a people of African descent with some native American ancestry. They originated on the Caribbean island of Saint Vincent during colonial times from escaped slaves who settled among a group of Arawak-speaking Carib Indians and adopted their native American language. In 1797, the Garífuna were forcibly exiled by the British to Roatán in the Bay Islands. The Spanish colonial authorities welcomed the Garífuna, and most of them moved to the mainland. The Garífuna population is about one hundred thousand. The Bay Islanders are an English-speaking people who are long settled in the Caribbean. Some are of African descent, and some of British descent. The Bay Islanders population is about twenty-two thousand.

Linguistic Affiliation. Spanish is the dominant national language. Although originally imposed by the *conquistadores*, it has been widely spoken in Honduras for over two hundred years. Almost all residents speak Spanish, although some also speak English or one of the Native American languages discussed in the previous paragraph. Honduran Spanish has a distinct accent. Hondurans use some words that are not heard in other Spanish-speaking countries, and this gives their speech a distinctive character.

Symbolism. In spite of the 1969 war with El Salvador and tense relations with Nicaragua, the Honduran people feel that they are part of a larger Central American community. There is still a sense of loss over the breakup of Central America as a nation. The flag has five stars, one for each Central American country (Guatemala, El Salvador, Honduras, Nicaragua, and Costa Rica). Factory goods are not labeled "made in Honduras," but "Central American product, made in Honduras." Independence Day (15 September) is shared with the other Central American countries, and is a fairly muted national holiday. Some people complain that there is little point celebrating independence from Spain, since Honduras has become virtually a colony of the United States. By 1992, Columbus Day had become a day of bereavement, as Hondurans began to realize the depth of cultural loss that came with the Spanish conquest. May Day is celebrated with parades and speeches. In the 1990s, the national government found this symbol of labor unity threatening and called out the army to stand with rifles before the marching workers.

History and Ethnic Relations

Emergence of the Nation. Francisco Morazán led the fight for independence from Spain (achieved in 1821) and resistance to the breakup of Central America (1830). In 1855, North American soldiers of fortune (filibusterers) led by William Walker tried to convert Central America into a United States colony. They held Nicaragua until they were expelled in 1857 by Nicaraguan regular troops and volunteer fighters. In 1860 Walker invaded Honduras, at Trujillo, where he ended up before an army firing squad. United States banana companies dominated Honduran politics after 1911. Fruit companies were able to choose presidents and as late as the 1970s were powerful enough to refuse to pay higher taxes imposed on banana exports by the military government. A 1920 letter by a U.S. fruit company executive describing how easily Honduran politicians could be bribed and dominated is still a source of national embarrassment.

National Identity. Because of the relationship of Honduras with the United States, the national culture often is defined in opposition to that of the United States. Hondurans feel an affinity with other Latin Americans and Central Americans, although this is mixed with fear and resentment of some neighboring countries, especially El Salvador and Nicaragua.

The Spanish conquest was a violent episode of genocide and slavery. It produced a people with blended European, native American, and African ancestry. Many Latin American countries have a similar large ethnic group called *mestizos* or *criollos*, but what is unusual about Honduras is that the Spanish-speaking people of mixed ancestry, who make up about 88 percent of the population, proudly call themselves *indios* (Indians). Hondurans call indigenous peoples *indígenas*, not indios.

Ethnic Relations. Music, novels, and television shows circulate widely among Spanish-speaking countries and contribute to a sense of Latin culture that transcends national boundaries. Ethnic relations are sometimes strained. For centuries, most indigenous peoples lost their land, and the nation did not value their languages and cultures. The Indian and Garífuna people have organized to insist on their civil and territorial rights.

The Bay Islanders (including those of British decent and those of African descent) have ties with the United States. Because the Islanders speak English, they are able to work as sailors on international merchant ships, and despite their isolation from the national culture, they earn a higher income than other residents.

Arab-Hondurans are descended from Christian Arabs who fled Muslim persecution in the early twentieth century after the breakup of the Ottoman Empire. Many have successful businesses. Some Hispanic-Hondurans envy the economic status of Arab-Hondurans, who are usually called *turcos*, a name they dislike since they are not of Turkish descent. (Many of the original Arab immigrants carried passports of the Ottoman Empire, whose core was Turkey.)

Urbanism, Architecture, and the Use of Space

In the cities, houses are made of store-bought materials (bricks, cement, etc.), and some of the homes of wealthy people are large and impressive. In the countryside, each ethnic group has a distinct architectural style. Most of the homes of poor rural people are made of local materials, with floors of packed earth, walls of adobe or wattle and daub, and roofs of clay tiles or thatch.

The kitchen is usually a special room outside the house, with a wood fire built on the floor or on a

Rural homes vary in style but are usually made of local materials.

raised platform. Porches are very common, often with one or more hammocks. The porch often runs around the house and sometimes connects the house to the kitchen. When visiting a rural home, one is received on the breezy porch rather than inside the house. The porch is used like the front parlor. The house is often plastered with mud, and people paint designs on it with natural earths of different colors.

A central plaza forms the heart of most towns. Important government buildings face it, as does a Catholic chapel or cathedral. Successful businesses are situated on or near the plaza. People are attracted to their city centers, and some municipal governments have started converting inner-city streets to pedestrian walkways to accommodate the crowds. Plazas are formal parks. People sit on benches under the trees and sometimes chat with friends or strangers. Villages have an informal central place located near a soccer field and a few stores and a school. In the afternoon, some people tie their horses to the front porch of the store, have a soft drink, and watch children play ball.

Food and Economy

Food in Daily Life. Beans and corn tortillas are the mainstays of the diet. The beans are usually fried, and the tortillas are small, thick, and usually handmade; ideally, they are eaten warm. A farm worker's lunch may be little more than a large stack of tortillas, a few spoonfuls of beans, and some salt. The ideal meal includes fried plantains, white cheese, rice, fried meat, a kind of thickened semisweet cream called *mantequilla*, a scrambled egg, a cabbage and tomato salad or a slice of avocado, and a cup of sweet coffee or a bottled soft drink. These meals are served in restaurants and homes for breakfast, lunch, and dinner year-round. Plantains and manioc are important foods in much of the country, especially the north and the Mosquitia. Diners often have a porch or a door open to the street. Dogs, cats, and chickens wander between the tables, and some people toss them bones and other scraps. There are Chinese restaurants owned by recent immigrants. In the early 1990s, North American fast-food restaurants became popular.

Food Customs at Ceremonial Occasions. Special and holiday foods are an improved version of the typical meal but feature more meat and perhaps more of an emphasis on cream and fried plantains. Christmas food includes *torrejas*, a white bread soaked in hot syrup, and *nacatamales*, which are like the Mexican tamales, but are larger and moister with a more gelatinous dough and are wrapped in banana leaves.

Basic Economy. Fifty-four percent of economically active people work in agriculture. Most are smallholder farmers who call themselves *campesinos*. Because the internal food market is irregular, *campesinos* try to grow their own maize (corn), beans, and plantains. Once they have achieved that goal, they raise a cash crop. Depending on whether they live in a valley, the mountains, or along the coast and on whether they live near a good road, a *campesino* household may raise a cash crop of coffee, cattle, cabbage, tomatoes, citrus fruit, maize, beans, or other vegetables. Long-term donations of wheat from the United States have kept food prices low but have provided a disincentive for grain farmers. Some large-scale commercial farmers produce melons, beef, coffee, and shrimp for export.

Land Tenure and Property. Land may be private, communal, cooperative, or national. Private land includes buildings and most of the agricultural and grazing land and some forested land. Communal land usually consists of the forest or rough pasture traditionally used by a rural community. Forest trees are owned by the government even if an individual owns the land. Many smallholders and rural communities do not have clear title to or ownership papers for their land even though their families have worked it for generations.

Cooperatives were formed in the mid-1970s to manage land taken from large landowners under agrarian reform policies. Much of this land is of good quality, and cooperatives can be several hundred acres in size. Most of the members or their parents once worked on large estates that were expropriated, usually by the workers and occasionally with some violence, and often suffered some repression while doing so. These farms are still owned cooperatively, although in almost all cases the farmers found it too difficult to work them collectively, and each household has been assigned land to work on its own within the cooperative's holdings. By 1990, 62,899 beneficiaries of agrarian reform (about 5 percent of the nation, or 10 percent of the rural people) held 906,480 acres of land (364,048 hectares, or over 4 percent of the nation's farmland). In the 1970s and 1980s, wealthy people, especially in the south, were able to hire lawyers to file the paperwork for this land and take it from the traditional owners. The new owners produced export agricultural products, and the former owners were forced to become rural laborers and urban migrants or to colonize the tropical forests in eastern Honduras.

As late as the 1980s there was still national land owned but not managed by the state. Anyone who cleared and fenced the land could lay claim to it. Some colonists carved out farms of fifty acres or more, especially in the eastern forests. By the late 1980s, environmentalists and indigenous people's advocates became alarmed that colonization from the south and the interior would eliminate much of the rain forest and threaten the Tawahka and Miskito peoples. Much of the remaining national land has been designated as national parks, wilderness areas, and reserves for the native peoples.

Commercial Activities. In the 1990s, Koreans, Americans, and other foreign investors opened huge clothing factories in special industrial parks near the large cities. These *maquilas* employ thousands of people, especially young women. The clothing they produce is exported.

Major Industries. Honduras now produces many factory foods (oils, margarine, soft-drinks, beer), soap, paper, and other items of everyday use.

Trade. Exports include coffee, beef, bananas, melons, shrimp, pineapple, palm oil, timber, and clothing. Half the trade is with the United States, and the rest is with other Central American countries, Europe, Japan, and the rest of Latin America. Cotton is now hardly grown, having been replaced by melon and shrimp farms in southern Honduras. Petroleum, machinery, tools, and more complicated manufactured goods are imported.

Division of Labor. Men do much of the work on small farms. Tortilla making is done by women and takes hours every day, especially if the maize has to be boiled, ground (usually in a metal, hand-cranked grinder), slapped out, and toasted by hand, and if the family is large and eats little else. *Campesino* children begin playing in the fields with their parents, and between the ages of about six and twelve, this play evolves into work. Children specialize in scaring birds from cornfields with slingshots, fetching water, and carrying a hot lunch from home to their fathers and brothers in the field. Some villagers have specialties in addition to farming, including shopkeeping, buying agricultural products, and shoeing horses. In the cities, job specialization is much like that of other countries, with the exception that many people learn industrial trades (mechanics, baking, shoe repair, etc.) on the job.

Social Stratification

Classes and Castes. Large landholdings and, to a lesser extent, successful businesses generate income for most of the very wealthy. Some of these people,

In cities such as Tegucigalpa, extended families may share the same house until the younger couple can afford their own home.

especially in the city of Danlí, consider themselves a kind of aristocracy, with their own social clubs and old adobe mansions downtown. These people import new cars and take foreign vacations.

Educated, professional people and the owners of mid size businesses make up a group with a lifestyle similar to that of the United States middle class. However, some professionals earn only a few hundred dollars a month. They may work several jobs and tend to have old cars and small houses that are often decorated with much care.

Urban workers are often migrants from the countryside or the children of migrants. They tend to live in homes they have built for themselves, gradually improving them over the years. Their earnings may be around $100 a month. They tend to travel by bus.

Campesinos may earn only a few hundred dollars a year, but their lifestyle may be more comfortable than their earnings suggest. They often own land, have horses to ride, and may have a comfortable, if rudimentary home of wood or adobe, often with a large, shady porch. If a household has a few acres of land and if the adults are healthy, these people usually have enough to feed their families.

Symbols of Social Stratification. As in many countries, wealthier men sometimes wear large gold chains around their necks. Urban professionals and workers dress somewhat like their counterparts in northern countries. Rural people buy used clothing and repair each garment many times. These men often wear rubber boots, and the women wear beach sandals. In the late 1980s and early 1990s, many men carried pistols, usually poked barrel-first into the tops of their trousers. By 2000 this custom had become somewhat less common. Many *campesinos*, commercial farmers, and agricultural merchants carried guns at that time.

There is a subtle difference in accent among the different classes. The highest-status people pronounce words more or less as in standard Spanish, and working-class pronunciation uses a few systematic and noticeable modifications.

Political Life

Government. The most important political offices are the national president, members of congress (*diputados*) and city mayors. In addition to the executive branch (a president and a cabinet of ministers) and a unicameral congress, there is a supreme court.

Leadership and Political Officials. Honduras still has the two political parties that emerged in the nineteenth century: the Liberales and the Nacionalistas. The Liberales originally were linked to the business sector, and the Nacionalistas with the wealthy rural landowners, but this difference is fading. Both parties are pro–United States, and probusiness. There is little ideological difference between them. Each is associated with a color (red for Liberals and blue for Nationalists), and the Nationalists have a nickname (*los cachurecos* which comes from the word *cacho*, or "horn," and refers to the cow horn trumpet originally used to call people to meetings). People tend to belong to the same party as their parents. Working on political campaigns is an important way of advancing in a party. The party that wins the national elections fires civil servants from the outgoing party and replaces them with its own members. This tends to lower the effectiveness of the government bureaucracy because people are rewarded not for fulfilling their formal job descriptions but for being loyal party members and for campaigning actively (driving around displaying the party flag, painting signs, and distributing leaflets).

Political officials are treated with respect and greeted with a firm handshake, and people try not to take up too much of their time. Members of congress have criminal immunity and can literally get away with murder.

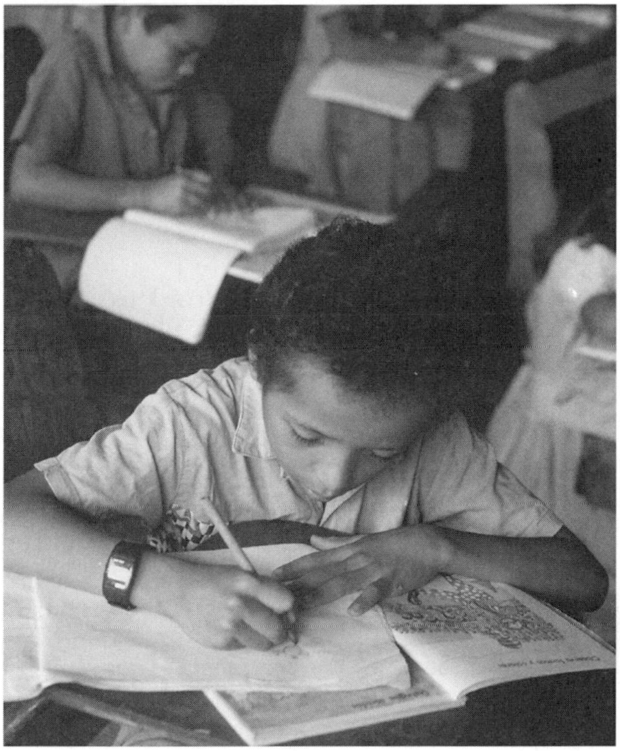

Rural children help with farm chores in addition to their school work.

Social Problems and Control. Until the 1990s, civilians were policed by a branch of the army, but this force has been replaced by a civil police force. Most crime tends to be economically motivated. In cities, people do not leave their homes unattended for fear of having the house broken into and robbed of everything, including light bulbs and toilet paper. Many families always leave at least one person home. Revenge killings and blood feuds are common in some parts of the country, especially in the department of Olancho. Police are conspicuous in the cities. Small towns have small police stations. Police officers do not walk a beat in the small towns but wait for people to come to the station and report problems. In villages there is a local person called the *regidor*, appointed by the government, who reports murders and major crimes to the police or mayor of a nearby town. Hondurans discuss their court system with great disdain. People who cannot afford lawyers may be held in the penitentiary for over ten years without a trial. People who can afford good lawyers spend little time in jail regardless of the crimes they have committed.

Until after the 1980s, crimes committed by members of the armed forces were dismissed out of hand. Even corporals could murder citizens and never be charged in court. In 1991, some military men, including colonels, raped and murdered a university student. Her school and family, the press, and the United States embassy exerted pressure until two men were sent to prison. This event was the start of a movement to modernize and improve the court system.

Military Activity. The Cold War was difficult for Honduras. In the past thirty years, the military has gone through three phases. The military government of the 1970s was populist and promoted land reform and tried to control the banana companies. The governments in the 1980s were nominally civilian, but were dominated by the military. The civilian governments in the 1990s gradually began to win control of the country from the military.

In the 1980s, the United States saw Honduras as a strategic ally in Central America and military aid exceeded two hundred million dollars a year. The army expanded rapidly, and army roadblocks became a part of daily life. Soldiers searched cars and buses on the highways. Some military bases were covers for Nicaraguan contras. In the mid-1990s, the military was concerned about budget cuts. By 2000, the military presence was much more subtle and less threatening.

For several reasons, the Honduran military was less brutal than that of neighboring countries. Soldiers and officers tended to come from the common people and had some sympathies with them. Officers were willing to take United States military aid, but were less keen to slaughter their own people or start a war with Nicaragua.

Social Welfare and Change Programs

The most important social change in the last few years has been the influence of Evangelical Protestant missionaries, who have converted many Hondurans to Pentecostal religions. There are also urban social change agencies, and many that work in the villages. Their fields of activity include soil conservation, gardening, and natural pest control. One of the most important reformers was an agronomist educator-entrepreneur named Elías Sánchez, who had a training farm near Tegucigalpa. Sánchez trained tens of thousands of farmers and extension agents in soil conservation and organic fertilization. Until his death in 2000, he and the people he inspired transformed Honduran agriculture. Farmers stopped using slash-and-burn agriculture in favor of intensive, more ecologically sound techniques.

Nongovernmental Organizations and Other Associations

United States military aid was accompanied by economic aid. Much of this money was disbursed to nongovernmental organizations (NGOs), and during the 1980s there were over two hundred of these groups. About a hundred worked in agricultural programs. CARE, Catholic Relief Services, World Neighbors, and Habitat for Humanity were some of the many international organizations that opened offices in Honduras. By the early 1990s, Honduran biologists and some foreign scientists and activists were able to attract attention to the vast forests, which were often the homes of native peoples and were under threat from logging, colonial invasion and cattle ranching. The Miskito people's NGO, Mopawi, was one of several native people's organizations that attracted funding, forged ties with foreign activists, and were able to reverse destructive development projects. Most native peoples now have at least one NGO that promotes their civil rights. In the large cities there are some organizations that work in specific areas such as street children and family planning. Rural people receive much more attention from NGOs than do the urban poor.

Gender Roles and Statuses

Division of Labor by Gender. Men are more prominent than women in public life, but women have served as judges, big city mayors, trial lawyers, members of congress, cabinet members, and heads of the national police force. Women have been especially active in religious life. To counter the inroads made by Evangelical missionaries, the Catholic Church encourages lay members to receive ecclesiastical training and visit isolated communities, to perform religious services. These people are called *celebradores de la palabra* ("celebrators of the word"). They hold mass without communion. Many of them are women. Women also manage stores and NGOs and teach at universities. Male-only roles include buying and trucking agricultural products, construction, bus and taxi drivers, and most of the military.

The Relative Status of Women and Men. Honduran people occasionally say that theirs is a *machista* (macho, sexist) country. This is mostly a stereotype, but some men shout catcalls at women on the street, especially when the men are in groups. There are also cases of sexual harassment of office staff. However, most men are fond of their families, tolerant of their behavior, and sensitive to women, who often have jobs outside the home or run small stores. Adolescents and young adults are not subject to elaborate supervision during courtship.

Marriage, Family, and Kinship

Marriage. Marriage is based on the Western ideal of falling in love. There are few formal rules prohibiting marriage with people of different social backgrounds, although people tend to marry neighbors or people they meet at school or work. Almost everyone eventually marries or lives with someone and has children. Founding a household is a financial struggle for most couples, and so women's earnings are appreciated. Divorce and remarriage are fairly common and are slightly stigmatized. Monogamy is the formal rule, although a middle-aged man who can afford to may set up a separate house with a younger woman. If they find out about the younger women, most wives find the idea disgusting and threatening to the marriage.

Domestic Unit. The ideal household of a couple and their children is not always possible. When young couples cannot afford housing, they may live with their parents until they have several children of their own. As in other Latin American coun-

Horses and mules provide transportation for some small landholders.

tries, when a couple marries, their new family assumes both of their names. For example, if a woman named María García marries a man named Carlos Martínez, they and their children become the Martínez-García family. In many households, men and women make major decisions together regarding household expenses, children's education, etc. In the cities, many households with only a moderate income include a live-in domestic servant who does the housekeeping.

Inheritance. Inheritance practice varies widely, but in general when a person dies the widow or widower inherits half the property (called the *parte conyugal*, or "the spouse's part") and the children get the other half, unless a will was made to the contrary. The spouse's part provides economic security for widows and helps preserve farms more or less intact. Sometimes there is a preference for the oldest son to inherit a larger share. There is also a tendency for sons to inherit land and daughters to inherit livestock, furniture, and money.

Kin Groups. In the cities, families tend to spend Sunday afternoon having an elaborate meal with the wife's parents. The ideal is for married children to live near their parents, at least in the same city, if not in the same neighborhood or on a contiguous lot. This is not always possible, but people make an effort to keep in touch with the extended family.

SOCIALIZATION

Child Rearing and Education. Urban professionals and elites are indulgent toward children, rarely punishing them and allowing them to interrupt conversations. In stores, middle-class shoppers buy things their children plead for. Obedience is not stressed. Bourgeois children grow up with self-esteem and are encouraged to feel happy about their accomplishments.

The urban poor and especially the *campesinos* encourage children to play in small groups, preferably near where adults are working. Parents are not over protective. Children play in the fields where their parents work, imitating their work, and after age of six or seven they start helping with the farm work. *Campesinos* expect children to be obedient and parents slap or hit disobedient children. Adults expect three- to four-year-old children to keep up with the family while walking to or from work or shopping, and a child who is told to hurry up and does not may be spanked. *Campesino* children grow up to be disciplined, long-suffering, and hard working.

Higher Education. Higher education, especially a degree from the United States or Europe, is valued, but such an education is beyond the reach of most people. There are branches of the National University in the major cities, and thousands of people attend school at night, after work. There are also private universities and a national agricultural school and a private one (Zamorano).

ETIQUETTE

A firm handshake is the basic greeting, and people shake hands again when they part. If they chat a bit longer after the last handshake, they shake hands again just as they leave. Among educated people, when two women greet or when a man greets a woman, they clasp their right hands and press their cheeks together or give a light kiss on the cheek. *Campesinos* shake hands. Their handshakes tend to be soft. Country women greeting a person they are fond of may touch the right hand to the other person's left elbow, left shoulder, or right shoulder (almost giving a hug), depending on how happy they are to see a person. Men sometimes hug each other (firm, quick, and with back slapping), especially if they have not seen each other for a while and are fond of each other. This is more common in the cities. *Campesinos* are a little more inhibited with body language, but city people like to stand close to the people they talk to and touch them occasionally while making a point in a conversation. People may look strangers in the eye and smile at them. People are expected to greet other office workers as they pass in the hall even if they have already greeted them earlier that day. On country roads people say good-bye to people they pass even if they do not know each other. In crowded airports and other places where people have to wait in a long, slow line, some people push, shove, cut in front of others, go around the line, and attract attention to themselves to get served first.

RELIGION

Religious Beliefs. Almost all Hondurans believe in God and Jesus Christ, though sometimes in a vague way. In a traditionally Catholic country, many people have joined Evangelical Protestant churches. People usually keep their religious beliefs to themselves but Catholics may wear a crucifix or religious medal around their necks. Many people have a sense of divine destiny. Accidental death is attributed to the will of God rather than to a seat belt that was not buckled or another physical cause. The upper classes are still predominantly Catholic, while many of the urban poor are now Evangelical. Newspapers carry stories of witchcraft, writing about people who were ill until a healer sucked a toad or a sliver of glass from their bodies.

Religious Practitioners. The Catholic Church is the national religion, as stated in the Constitution. However, the liberal reforms of the 1820s led to the confiscation of Church property, the closing of the seminary, and a great decline in the number and morale of the Catholic clergy. By the 1960s mass was only heard regularly in the larger towns. At that time, foreign clergy, including French Canadians, began revitalizing the Honduran Church. Many priests supported *campesino* movements in the 1970s, and some were killed for it by the military. In the 1980s the bishops were strong enough to play a key role in resisting pressure from the United States for Honduras to go to war with Nicaragua. Various Protestant churches have been active in Honduras since the early twentieth century, especially since the 1970s, and have gained many converts. The Evangelical clergy is an informal lay clergy for the most part and small Pentecostal chapels are common in villages and in poorer neighborhoods in the cities.

Rituals and Holy Places. Most Catholics go to church only on special occasions, such as Christmas and funerals. Evangelicals may go to a small chapel, often a wood shack or a room in a house, for prayer meetings and Bible readings every night. These can be important havens from the pressures of being impoverished in a big city.

There is a minor ritual called *cruzando la milpa* ("crossing the cornfield") practiced in the Department of El Paraíso in which a magico-religious specialist, especially one who is a twin, eliminates a potentially devastating corn pest such as an inchworm or caterpillar. The specialist recites the Lord's Prayer while sprinkling holy water and walking from one corner to the other of the cornfield in a cross pattern. This person makes little crosses of corn leaves or caterpillars and buries them in four spots in the field.

Death and the Afterlife. Beliefs about the afterlife are similar to the general Western tradition. An additional element is the concept of the *hejillo*, (standard Spanish: *hijillo*) a kind of mystic contagion that comes from a dead human body, whether death was caused by age, disease, or violence. People who must touch the body wash carefully as soon as possible to purify themselves.

Commercial agriculture is an important part of the Honduran economy.

Medicine and Health Care

Sickness or an accident is a nightmare for people in the countryside and the urban poor. It may take hours to get a patient to a hospital by traveling over long dirt roads that often lack public transportation. Doctors may be unable to do much for a patient if the patient's family cannot afford to buy medicine. If the patient is an adult, the household may have to struggle to make a living until he or she recovers. Some traditional medical practitioners use herbal medicines and set broken bones.

Secular Celebrations

Independence Day falls on 15 September and features marches and patriotic speeches. Labor Day, celebrated on 1 May, includes marches by workers. During Holy Week (the week before Easter), everyone who can goes to the beach or a river for picnics and parties. On the Day of the Cross (*Día de la Cruz*) in May in the countryside, people decorate small wooden crosses with flowers and colored paper and place the crosses in front of their homes in anticipation of the start of the rainy season. Christmas and the New Year are celebrated with gift giving, festive meals, dancing, and fireworks.

The Arts and Humanities

Support for the Arts. Some art is publicly supported through the Ministry of Culture, as well as through sales of tickets, CDs, etc. Some artists also have day jobs.

Literature. There is a modest tradition of serious literary fiction. The novel *Prisión Verde* (*Green Prison*) by Ramón Amaya is perhaps the best known work of fiction. It describes the sufferings of workers on an early twentieth century banana plantation.

Graphic Arts. There is a Honduran school of impressionist painting whose favorite themes include village street scenes. This style was first developed by Antonio Velázquez of the historic mining village of San Antonio de Oriente, department of Francisco Morazán, in the 1950s. Velázquez was the barber at the nearby agricultural college at Zamorano. He was self-taught, and Hondurans refer to his style as "primitivist." Newspaper cartoons are popular and important for social critique. The cartoonist Dario Banegas has a talent for hilarious drawings that express serious commentary.

Performance Arts. There are various theater groups in San Pedro Sula and Tegucigalpa, of which the most important is the National Theater of Honduras (TNH), formed in Tegucigalpa in 1965. Its directors have been faculty members of various public schools and universities. Other groups include University Theater of Honduras (TUH) and the Honduran Community of Theater Actors (COMHTE), formed in 1982. These groups have produced various good plays. Honduras also has a National School of Fine Arts, a National Symphonic Orchestra, and various music schools. There are a handful of serious musicians, painters, and sculptors in Honduras, but the most well-known group of artists may be the rock band Banda Blanca, whose hit single "Sopa de Caracol" (Conch Soup) was based on Garífuna words and rhythms. It topped Latin music charts in the early 1990s. There are still some performances of folk music at fiestas and other events, especially in the country. The accordion, guitar, and other string instruments are popular.

THE STATE OF THE PHYSICAL AND SOCIAL SCIENCES

Perhaps the most highly developed social science is the archaeological study of the ancient Maya at the site of Copán and elsewhere in western Honduras. Much of this work is done by foreigners, but many Hondurans also conduct research. Among the applied sciences, the best known institution is the Pan-American School of Agriculture (Zamorano), near Tegucigalpa, where scientists and students conduct agricultural research. Zamorano attracts an international student body and faculty and offers the best practical education in commercial agriculture in Latin America. The Honduran Agricultural Research Foundation (FHIA) on the north coast, was once a research center for the banana industry. It is now supported by the Honduran and United States governments and other donors and conducts research on tropical crops.

BIBLIOGRAPHY

Aguilar Paz, Jesús. *Tradiciones y Leyendas de Honduras*, 1972.

Becerra, Longino. *Evolución Histórica de Honduras*, 1999.

Beneditt, Leonardo, Ismael Zepeda, José Antonio Montoya et al. *Enciclopedia Multimedia Honduras Nuestro País*, 1999.

Bentley, Jeffery W. *Diccionario Campesino Hondureño*, in press, probable date of publication 2001.

Chapman, Anne. *Masters of Animals: Oral Traditions of the Tolupan Indians, Honduras*, 1978.

———. *Los Hijos del Copal y la Candela*, 1992.

Coelho, Ruy Galvão de Andrade. *Los Negros Caribes de Honduras*, 1995.

Durham, W. H. *Scarcity and Survival in Central America: The Ecological Origins of the Soccer War*, 1979.

Fash, William L. & Ricardo Agurcia Fasquelle. *Visión del Pasado Maya*, 1996.

Gamero, Manuel. "Iberoamérica y el Mundo Actual." In A. Serrano, O. Joya, M. Martínez, and M. Gamero (eds.), *Honduras Ante el V Centenario del Descubrimiento de América*, 1991.

Joya, Olga. "Identidad Cultural y Nacionalidad en Honduras." In A. Serrano, O. Joya, M. Martínez, and M. Gamero (eds.), *Honduras Ante el V Centenario del Descubrimiento de América*, 1991.

Martínez Perdomo, Adalid. *La Fuerza de la Sangre Chortí*, 1997.

Murray, Douglas L. *Cultivating Crisis: The Human Cost of Pesticides in Latin America*, 1994.

Pineda Portillo, Noé. *Geografía de Honduras*, 1997.

Pineda Portillo, Noé, Fredis Mateo Aguilar Herrera, Reina Luisa Portillo, José Rolando Díaz, and Julio Antonio Pineda. *Diccionario Geográfico de América Central*, 1999.

Salinas, Iris Milady. *Arquitectura de los Grupos Étnicos de Honduras*, 1991.

Salomón, Leticia. *Poder Civil y Fuerzas Armadas en Honduras*, 1997.

Stonich, Susan C. *I Am Destroying the Land: The Political Ecology of Poverty and Environmental Destruction in Honduras*, 1993.

Tucker, Catherine M. "Private Versus Common Property Forests: Forest Conditions and Tenure in a Honduran Community." *Human Ecology*, 27 (2): 201–230, 1999.

—JEFFREY W. BENTLEY

Hong Kong

Culture Name

Hong Kong

Alternative Names

Heung Gong (Cantonese), *Xianggang* (Mandarin)

Orientation

Identification. Hong Kong means "fragrant harbor." Once administered by the United Kingdom, it has been known since 1997 as the Hong Kong Special Administrative Region (SAR) of the People's Republic of China (PRC). Many residents do not identify with either Britain or China. The generation born and raised in Hong Kong from 1949 to 1979 (when China was isolated) has a much more local identity than do their parents.

Location and Geography. The total area is 425 square miles (1,097 square kilometers). Hong Kong Island is only ten square miles. Only 15 percent of the area is built up, while 67 percent consists of grassland, scrub, and woods. Forty percent of the territory is designated as recreational parks, largely hills and mountains.

Demography. The population was 6,805,600 in 1998. At the end of World War II, the population was only about 600,000; it swelled with refugees when the Communist Party won the civil war in China in 1949. Both fertility and infant mortality are low, and life expectancy is the seventh highest in the world. Hong Kong is one of the world's most crowded cities. The proportion of the population born in Hong Kong is about 60 percent, but among those under age 15, the proportion is about 88 percent.

Linguistic Affiliation. Cantonese is spoken in 89 percent of households. Other languages include Fukienese (2 percent), Hakka (1 percent), Mandarin or Putonghua (1 percent), Chiu Chau (1 percent), Shanghainese (less than 1 percent), and Sze Yap. English is spoken as the primary language at home by 3 percent of the population. Thirty-eight percent of the population claims the ability to speak English, and 25 percent claims to speak Mandarin (or Putonghua), the national language of China. In the colonial period, English was used in business and the courts. Chinese was added as a second official language in 1974 in response to anti-colonial riots. This Chinese was Cantonese, not Mandarin (or Putonghua) which is the official in the mainland, Taiwan, and Singapore. The Cantonese spoken in Hong Kong is similar to that used in Guangzhou (Canton), but the accent and some vocabulary are slightly different.

Hong Kong uses the traditional complex Chinese characters, while mainland China and Singapore have adopted simplified characters. Since the 1970s, popular magazines and newspapers have taken to writing using many new characters to represent the Cantonese spoken locally.

Symbolism. Hong Kong prides itself on being "the gateway to China" and the place "where East meets West." In tourist brochures, a junk is used to capture the idea of a traditional port, although by 1990 there was only one junk left. The Star Ferry, which until 1972 was the only way to cross the harbor, is also a common symbol of the city. The skyline of the harbor, with skyscrapers and Victoria Peak, is a famous view.

Many symbols are in flux. Holidays related to Britain and local events have been replaced with Chinese holidays such as 1 July, celebrating the restoration of Hong Kong to Chinese rule in 1997, and 1 October, commemorating the founding of the PRC in 1949. A newly created "Buddha's Birthday" in May has replaced Queen's Birthday in June. The Hong Kong flag is now considered a regional flag that must fly lower than the PRC national flag. It is pinkish red with a stylized bauhinia flower in white in the center.

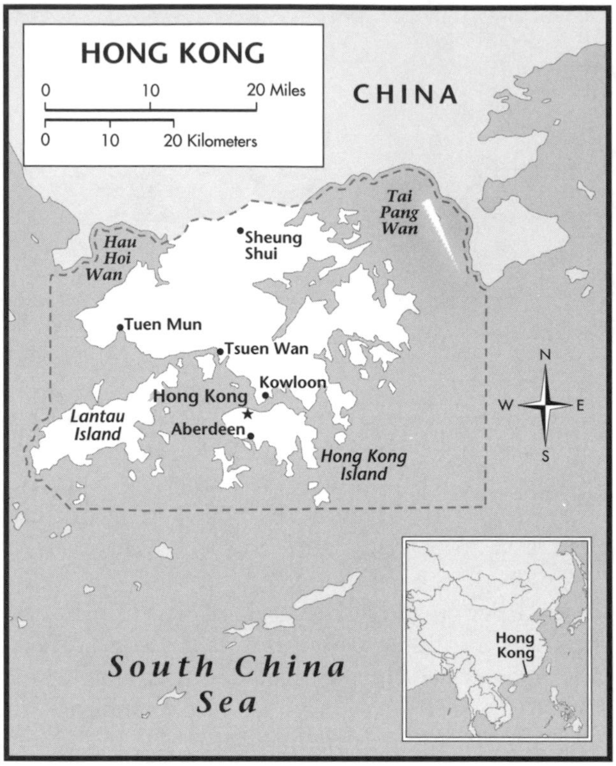

Hong Kong

History and Ethnic Relations

Emergence of the Nation. Hong Kong was claimed by Great Britain in three steps: Hong Kong island was handed over to Britain by China "in perpetuity" in 1842 after the Opium War, the peninsula of Kowloon was ceded in 1860, and the New Territories were leased to the United Kingdom for ninety-nine years in 1898. The PRC never accepted these "Unequal Treaties," which it viewed as products of imperialism. The end of the lease to the New Territories led to the return of the entire territory to China. Under the Sino-British Joint Declaration signed in 1984, Hong Kong is to be ruled "with a high degree of autonomy" until 2047. The guiding principle is "one country, two systems," meaning that the territory can keep its distinctive lifestyle and economic system for fifty years, by which time Hong Kong and China are expected to be more alike.

The population is descended primarily from long-term urban residents, the aboriginal Chinese population of the New Territories, and the refugees who fled China. These refugees were a source of cheap and willing labor.

The key to Hong Kong's emergence was its status as a free port at the edge of China, but the emergence of a national identity dates to the early 1970s, when a generation of young people born and raised in Hong Kong came of age. Before the victory of the Chinese Communists in 1949, Hong Kong had no border with China; it was a British-administered city with a constant flow of people in and out. From 1949 to the late 1970s, there was little movement across the border. After twenty years of division from mainland China, people identified with the locality rather than the nation. Popular songs began to focus on the territory as home. Hong Kong was also different from the rest of China in its use of English. Once Chinese immigrants began coming in the 1980s, local residents felt superior to and more sophisticated than their mainland brethren.

Since the handover in July 1997, there have been few changes. None of the place names with colonial connotations have been changed, though the word "royal" has been dropped from names. Textbooks have stopped referring to China as a foreign country, and the flag of the "Republic of China" (Taiwan) can no longer be flown in public.

National Identity. Hong Kong sees itself as a modern city and is proud of its state-of-the-art airport and subway system. It has its own style of life, currency (the Hong Kong dollar), and economic and legal systems. Hong Kong is still governed by common law, and judges wear robes and wigs as they do in Britain. Other continuing legacies of British rule include the rule of law, open government, civil and press freedoms, and high professional standards.

Ethnic Relations. Ethnicity and nationality (citizenship) do not overlap. In 1996, 90 percent of the population had some form of Hong Kong Chinese nationality: 59 percent had British nationality overseas, and 31 percent had Chinese nationality with the right to live in Hong Kong. In 1997, Hong Kong began issuing its own passports.

The population is predominantly Cantonese Chinese from the counties of the Pearl River Delta and Guangzhou. A small minority are of Shanghainese, Hokkien (southern Fujian), and Boat People ("Tanka") descent. The younger generation tends to ignore these origins.

Only a small percentage of people claim long descent in the territory, and most live in New Territories villages. The British allowed these villages to follow traditional law. Inheritance of land was exclusively through the male line. Forty-five percent of residents have close relatives living permanently abroad, and about two-thirds have relatives in mainland China.

Unskilled jobs such as rickshaw driver hold low status.

"New immigrants" are defined as persons who have arrived since the 1980s. Those who adapt quickly can pass as locals; the term "new immigrant" is used to refer to those whose accent, low educational level, lack of skills, and manners are considered typical of mainland China. The term thus combines place of origin with class and education. Many immigrants who arrived in the 1970s and 1980s became brokers and entrepreneurs who invested and worked in factories that moved to China in the 1990s.

Eurasians were a recognized ethnic category until the mid-twentieth century, but have largely disappeared as an ethnic group. Eurasians are considered Chinese if they speak Cantonese or Westerners if they have received a Western education.

Hong Kong is cosmopolitan and multicultural and had a foreign population of 485,760 in 1998, including large groups from the Philippines, Indonesia, the United States, Canada, Thailand, the United Kingdom, India, Australia, Japan, and Nepal. Most persons from the Philippines are female "domestic helpers" who have special visas that prevent them from becoming residents. Professionals who live in the territory for seven years can become permanent residents. Many British, American, and Canadian citizens are ethnic Hong Kong Chinese who have returned to work after receiving citizenship.

Urbanism, Architecture, and the Use of Space

The Peak, the area at the top reaches of Victoria Peak, has expensive estates; the higher up the mountain the estate, the higher one's relative rank in business and government. Before World War II, Chinese had to live lower down the hill, mostly in the crowded areas at sea level. After the war, the inflow of refugees from China forced many families to share quarters and live in squatter huts. In 1953, the government began to build public housing, in part because of the realization that the refugees would not go back to the mainland and to allow developers to build on squatter-occupied land. Land reclamation along Kowloon and the north of the island has added significantly to urban space.

Homes are tiny, and bunk beds for families living in single rooms are common. Sidewalks and shopping areas are dense with people. Bumping into others is not uncommon and normally is not acknowledged.

The New Territories include new towns with hundreds of thousands of residents living in high-rise apartment blocks, but there still are villages in which nearly all the residents are descendants of a single male ancestor.

Hong Kong has not preserved much colonial architecture. Colonial history is reflected in road names, a few English place names, and structures such as the Legislative Council Building and Government House. The Anglican Saint John's Cathedral, with its neo-gothic style, is also a reminder of the past. Most older buildings have been replaced with modern structures, although a few colonial-era monuments remain. Notable modern buildings include the Hong Kong and Shanghai Bank building, the Bank of China building, and the Hong Kong Exhibition Centre.

Food and Economy

Food in Daily Life. There is a wide variety of ethnic foods, including Italian, Japanese, French, and American. Most people, however, eat Cantonese-style Chinese food. Soups are especially important in most meals. A typical Cantonese food is *dim sum,* also known as *yam chah,* which is small snacks cooked in bamboo steamers. This meal is served seven days a week, and family members and friends often meet over tea on the weekend. Residents prefer to buy seafood live and meat freshly butchered. Hong Kong has one of the highest per capita consumption rates of fast food in the world, and students buy snacks such as potato chips, fried rice crackers, and prawn crackers from school snack shops.

Food Customs at Ceremonial Occasions. Eating out banquet-style is a common form of entertainment, especially for businesspeople. Banquets differ from everyday meals in that most dishes are meat or fish, and starch is only served at the end of the meal. Alcohol normally accompanies a banquet; beer and brandy are popular drinks, and grape wine has grown rapidly in popularity.

Some holidays and ceremonial occasions are associated with certain kinds of food. Lunar New Year's Eve features chicken, roast pork, and fruit; at the Dragon Boat Festival, people eat rice dumplings wrapped in lotus leaves; and the Mid-Autumn Festival is associated with moon cakes, pomelo, and persimmons. Meals when the family reunites, including New Year's Eve, often include rice flour balls in sweet soup. Birthday banquets for older people include a bowl of long noodles symbolizing long life, and eggs dyed red traditionally are given out at the celebration of a baby's first month.

Basic Economy. Nearly all food comes from mainland China and overseas, as less than 1 percent of the population engages in farming or fishing. The economy has grown rapidly; the real growth of the median household income from 1986 to 1996 was 51 percent.

In 1996, 11 percent of workers are in manufacturing, 67 percent in service industries, 11 percent in transport and communications, 9 percent in construction, and less than one percent in agriculture.

The economy is nearly completely open to the world economy. Most products have no tariffs; only automobiles, petroleum, and alcohol have high import tariffs. Taxes are low. There are no value-added or sales taxes, and less than half of the working population earns enough to pay income tax, which has a minimum rate of 15 percent.

Land Tenure and Property. The government earns enormous revenues from land auctions because it is the owner as well as the principal leaseholder of all land. Once acquired from the government at auctions, land leases can be transferred through private deals, subject to a stamp duty. In 1998, 34 percent of the population lived in public rental housing and 12 percent lived in government-subsidized sale flats.

Commercial Activities. Hong Kong has always been primarily a trade and shipping center, but a sizable amount of light industry has developed. Textile and clothing, toys, and electronics were among the first products manufactured for export in the territory. In the early 1980s, factories began to move across the border into mainland China, and Hong Kong has been transformed into a service center.

Major Industries. Most industry produces for export, such as textiles and clothing, electronic products, watches and clocks, jewelry, gold and silverware, printed matter, plastic products, metals, toys and dolls, and electrical appliances. Hong Kong also is one of the world's leading financial centers.

Much of the economy, though free and competitive externally, is dominated internally by a few large companies. A handful of real estate development companies build the vast majority of new housing and office space, two companies control nearly all the supermarkets, and exclusive importers-distributors of products such as automobiles and compact discs dominate the market.

Trade. Hong Kong, with no natural resources other than a deepwater port, was the world's eighth largest trading economy in 1997. Its port is one of the world's busiest for container throughput, and the airport was the world's busiest in terms of international cargo. The leading trading partners in 1998 were mainland China, the United States, Japan, Taiwan, and Singapore. Textiles and clothing are the major exports but most are made in China and pass through the territory for quality control, packaging, and distribution. Major imports include electronics and consumer goods, raw materials, semimanufactured goods, and machinery. Many are exported for processing in mainland Chinese factories.

SOCIAL STRATIFICATION

Classes and Castes. The gap between rich and poor is extremely large in a territory with a capitalist economy and minimal government interference. Economic inequality is increasing, although from 1986 to 1996 all groups had real growth in income. The only caste-like group is the Boat People. This occupational group of fisherfolk was traditionally marginalized and ritually humiliated. Most have now moved onto land and melted in with the rest of the population. A disproportionate number of the members of the political and economic elite are of Shanghainese descent.

Skyscrapers along Aberdeen Harbour accommodate the high population density.

Symbols of Social Stratification. Membership in elite clubs is a mark of status. Designer fashions and gold and diamond jewelry are popular among all classes, but only the very wealthy can afford the latest styles. Ownership of an automobile is another sign of wealth. Habits such as not standing in line, spitting, and wearing ''mainlander'' clothes mark a person as a new immigrant and low on the social scale. Chinese who speak only Mandarin or speak Cantonese with a Guangzhou accent are also déclassé. Tanned or dark skin is also viewed negatively, suggesting a working-class origin.

Political Life

Government. In an executive-led government, the chief executive has replaced the British governor of the colonial period. The chief executive is selected by an electoral assembly picked by China, and is assisted by an executive council whose members tend to be leading industrialists. A Legislative Council (Legco) approves executive decisions, although its members can introduce bills and investigate the administration. Only a third of the members are elected by districts; the others are representatives of

The majority of unmarried women in Hong Kong are part of the labor force.

occupational groups or are appointed. The Legco represents the people but has little power.

Hong Kong has a free and very competitive press. The press and public demonstrations have been important in pressuring the government, as has call-in talk radio.

Hong Kong residents are said to be politically apathetic. The executive-led government and strong bureaucracy left little room for public participation. However, voting rates have risen dramatically, and the slogan ''Hong Kong people ruling Hong Kong'' has been effective and popular.

Social Problems and Control. The crime rate is very low, and there is little vandalism. The most common violent crime is common assault; nonviolent crimes include shoplifting and burglary. Corruption is relatively rare, partly as a result of the Independent Commission Against Corruption established in 1974. Hong Kong has been unable to stamp out the smuggling of narcotics, intellectual piracy of software, and organized crime. Overall, residents have confidence in the police and court system. Maintenance of the common law system and the independence of the judiciary is guaranteed by the Basic Law.

Military Activity. The police force is staffed by local Chinese and some remaining British officers. A small military force from mainland China is stationed in Hong Kong, but Chinese soldiers are not allowed to be in uniform on the street.

Social Welfare and Change Programs

Spending on social welfare has been rising rapidly, including Comprehensive Social Security Assistance for families that cannot meet their basic needs in food, clothes, and rent. There is a Social Security Allowance for the severely disabled, services for the elderly, and community services. The government passes funds to private organizations that provide services and monitors their effectiveness. Government subsidies are used for the elderly, rehabilitation of the disabled, family and child welfare services, youth services, community services, and services for offenders.

Nongovernmental Organizations and Other Associations

Nongovernmental organizations are important because the government prides itself on nonintervention. Among the charitable associations are Po Leung Kuk (a Chinese benevolent association that ran an orphanage and provided paupers' funerals and now runs schools and hospitals), the Tung Wah Group of Hospitals, the Community Chest, and the Hong Kong Jockey Club Charities Trust. There are associations of missionary origin such as the YMCA, YWCA, and Caritas and chapters of international organizations such as the Red Cross, Boys' and Girls' Clubs, and Amnesty International. There are also provincial associations for people from various regions of China and surname associations.

Gender Roles and Statuses

Division of Labor by Gender. In 1999, 60 percent of men and 40 percent of women were in the labor force. The labor force participation rate in 1996 for married and unmarried men was 86 and 73 percent respectively; for women, it was 46 and 68 percent. The average salary of women was 87 percent that of men.

The Relative Status of Women and Men. Traditional Chinese and British societies were patriarchal, and men continue to have more power and authority than do women. In 1996, the Equal Employment Opportunity Commission was established; among its first acts was ending the practice of specifically asking for men or "pretty girls" in job advertisements. Although women do housework in addition to outside employment, the availability of domestic live-in help allows many women to pursue a career.

Marriage, Family, and Kinship

Marriage. Polygamy was allowed until 1971. In 1996, 34 percent of men and 29 percent of women age 15 and over had never married. Marriage depends on becoming economically established, finding housing, and reserving auspicious days. Couples line up in advance at the marriage registry office to reserve wedding dates that are believed to be lucky. A common surname is no longer a hindrance to a marriage. Couples may marry legally first in order to get government housing and hold the customary banquet later when they are socially married. The rate of remarriage of divorced men and women is rising rapidly.

Domestic Unit. The average household size has been declining. The single unextended nuclear family is the dominant household type, accounting for 64 percent of households in 1996. Traditionally the children of divorced parents stayed with the father. The father is formally the head of the household, but more equal conjugal relations are common among younger couples.

Inheritance. All children can inherit property, but an estate typically is divided equally among sons in accordance with the traditional Chinese practice, especially if the family owns a business; a half share for each daughter is also common. In 1994 in the New Territories, lineage leaders complained about urban and colonialist meddling when the government decided to let women inherit land when the deceased had no sons and died intestate. Since the lineages are patrilineal, leaders claimed this would disperse assets and ruin the unity of the lineage.

Socialization

Infant Care. Pregnancy leave for women is commonly ten to twelve weeks in large companies. Breast-feeding is rare. Chinese tend to indulge infants' and preschool children's demands and do not attempt to control their impulsive behavior. After age five or six, however, rigorous discipline and self-control are expected.

Child Rearing and Education. Parents value obedience, proper behavior, and the acceptance of social obligations rather than independence, spontaneity, and creativity. A "good" child is one who obeys, is quiet, and compliant. School-age children are expected to control their impulses, especially aggression. There are not many formal preschool programs for children. Grandmothers are important help in caregiving.

Education is highly valued. Preschool children are taught Chinese characters, and most schools expect children to know up to two hundred characters before they begin their formal education. Most children attend school only half a day since many schools have two sessions. All children have several hours of homework every day. There is great pressure to enter good schools, and school is very competitive, with frequent testing. Education theories such as learning through play are not widely accepted; parents believe in rote memorization and drilling. Many of the best schools are officially English-language schools, but many teachers conduct classes in Cantonese. Sports are not emphasized, in part because of the lack of space in many schools and housing areas.

Higher Education. A university education is highly valued in Hong Kong, with 34 percent of university-age students receiving a tertiary education. Eighteen percent attend school in Hong Kong, while the rest attend schools overseas. There are seven publicly-funded universities in Hong Kong, including the University of Hong Kong, Chinese University, Hong Kong University of Science and Technology, City University of Hong Kong, Polytechnic University, Hong Kong Baptist University, and Lingnan University.

Etiquette

Higher Education. Acquaintances greet each other with a nod or may shake hands if they stop to talk. Good-byes require a handshake only in business settings. Hierarchy is important in social settings; senior or higher ranking persons are introduced or served first. In family gatherings, older people are greeted first. Younger people are expected to greet older people by title and name. The idea of "ladies first" is sometimes used, though it is recognized as a Western notion. It is easier to break the ice by being introduced by a mutual acquaintance. It is common to use the title and family name until one is invited to use a first name. Many Chinese residents use English names for business. In business situations, it is common to exchange bilingual business cards. The cards are given and received with two hands;

Crew members prepare to race in the Dragon Boat Festival while drummers beat their drums. The Dragon Boat Festival is held annually in June in Hong Kong.

this is the proper way to accept any object, even a gift and cup of tea.

Hong Kong Chinese stand close together. They tend to be uncomfortable with body contact, though women often walk hand in hand. When standing in line or visiting museums, foreigners may mistake the smaller personal space as pushiness. Gift giving is important at visits to a home and at a first business meeting. Gifts are given wrapped and are not opened in front of the giver.

RELIGION

Religious Beliefs. Most Chinese residents practice Chinese folk religion which is an amalgam of Taoism, Buddhism, and ancestor worship. Many individuals say they have no religion, but nearly all people have religious ceremonies at funerals. There are 540,000 Christians, and Christianity is growing among the young and university-educated. There are eighty thousand Muslims, twelve thousand Hindus, one thousand Sikhs, and one thousand Jews. There are many beliefs regarding luck and fortune. Certain numbers are considered lucky, while others are unlucky. Many people visit temples for fortune-telling, to consult gods about specific problems, and to ask for protection and good luck.

Religious Practitioners. Taoist priests officiate at village festivals, but along with Buddhist monks and nuns, their most prominent activity is conducting funeral ceremonies. Christian ministers and priests have a more prominent role for Christians because they lead congregations. Fengshui masters help businessmen in the layout of offices.

Rituals and Holy Places. Major holy places include the Wong Tai Sin Temple, the Che Kong Temple in Shatin, and the Tin Hau Temple in Joss House Bay. These temples are popular destinations for worshipers at the lunar new year. Most villages have small temples that hold annual festivals on a god's birthday, and some in the New Territories have lineage halls at which annual worship and division of pork for lineage members are held. The Po Lin Buddhist Monastery on Lantau Island is a popular site for weekend visits.

Death and the Afterlife. Funerals are conducted in traditional Chinese or Christian forms, with Buddhist monks or nuns or Taoist priest officiating at Chinese ceremonies and a priest or minister han-

Visitors to a terraced cemetery in Hong Kong place flowers on the graves of their relatives during the Qing Mong festival, which promotes ancestral worship.

dling Christian funerals. Because of the lack of space, Hong Kong residents have had to accept cremation instead of burial, with ashes stored in columbaria. Traditionally, Chinese people have believed in a continuing relationship with ancestors and in the reincarnation of the soul, but many now express doubt or skepticism, although they continue to follow traditional rituals.

Medicine and Health Care

There is a modern medical system with government-funded hospitals that provide inexpensive care; these hospitals offer what is called "Western medicine." People turn to Chinese (herbal) medicine, acupuncture, moxibustion (in which users place cones of burning leaves on the skin; it is used to cure rheumatism and other ailments), and other alternative treatment for illnesses and chronic problems that are not cured by modern medicine.

Secular Celebrations

Among the major holidays are New Year's Day on 1 January, the Chinese New Year in January and/or February, Ching Ming (a grave-sweeping holiday) on 5 April, Labor Day on 1 May, Buddha's birthday in mid-May, Tuen Ng (the Dragon Boat Festival) in May and/or June, SAR Establishment Day on 1 July, the Mid-Autumn Festival in September, Chinese National Day on 1 October, and Chung Yeung (another grave-sweeping holiday) in October.

The Arts and Humanities

Support for the Arts. The arts have not developed as quickly as the economy, and Hong Kong is often considered a cultural desert. Financial support for the arts comes almost entirely from the government.

Literature. A few local authors write about Hong Kong identity and culture. In literature, the territory is considered a small part of Greater China. Hong Kong is famous for comic books (often with martial themes and set in a vague imperial past) that are read throughout the Chinese-speaking world.

Graphic Arts. Graphic arts are modern and range widely in style. Institutions that collect graphic arts include the Hong Kong Museum of Art (prints) and the Hong Kong Heritage Museum, Contemporary

Art and Design Gallery, which has prints and a poster collection. Other exhibition venues include the government-run Visual Arts Centre and the Hong Kong Arts Centre, which holds international and local exhibitions of paintings, photography, design, and crafts.

Performance Arts. Cantopop concerts are the most popular type of performance. The Hong Kong Philharmonic Orchestra, Hong Kong Repertory Theatre, Hong Kong Chinese Orchestra, and Hong Kong Dance Company are all government-subsidized, and are far less popular. There are also a Hong Kong Dance Company, City Contemporary Dance Company, and Hong Kong Repertory Company. In recent years, the number of small theater troupes has risen, as their alternative productions explore and reflect on Hong Kong identities. They usually are founded by local Chinese residents who are often graduates of the Academy of Performing Arts. The annual Hong Kong Arts Festival brings in dozens of performers every year in January and February. Hong Kong is also famous for its movies, which are popular among Chinese speakers worldwide.

The State of the Physical and Social Sciences

A major expansion of university funding in the 1990s has increased the number of tertiary students and has led to an increase in internationally recognized research at Hong Kong's universities. The three main universities University of Hong Kong, Chinese University, and the Hong Kong University of Science and Technology feature world-class facilities and faculties in many disciplines.

Bibliography

Castells, Manuel, Lee Goh, and R. Yin-Wang Kwok *The Shek Kip Mei Syndrome: Economic Development and Public Housing in Hong Kong and Singapore,* 1990.

Chan, Selina Ching. "Politicizing Tradition: The Identity of Indigenous Inhabitants in Hong Kong." *Ethnology* 37(1):39–54, 1998.

Cheung, Sidney C.H., and Siumi Maria Tam. *Culture and Society of Hong Kong: A Bibliography,* 1999.

Constable, Nicole. *Maid to Order in Hong Kong: Stories of Filipina Workers in Hong Kong,* 1997.

Evans, Grant, and Maria Siu-Mi, Tam, eds. *Hong Kong: The Anthropology of a Chinese Metropolis,* 1997.

Hong Kong Anthropologist, annual.

Hong Kong Census and Statistics Department. *1996 Population by Census,* 1997.

Journal of the Hong Kong Branch of the Royal Asiatic Society, annual.

Lang, Graeme, and Lars Ragvald. *The Rise of a Refugee God: Hong Kong's Wong Tai Sin,* 1993.

Lau, C. K. *Hong Kong's Colonial Legacy: A Hong Kong Chinese's View of the British Heritage,* 1997.

Lau, Siu-kai, and Kuan Hsin-chi. *The Ethos of the Hong Kong Chinese,* 1988.

Leung, Benjamin K. P. *Perspectives on Hong Kong Society,* 1996.

——— and Teresa Y. C. Wong, eds. *25 Years of Social and Economic Development in Hong Kong,* 1994.

Mathews, Gordon. "Heunggongyahn: On the Past, Present, and Future of Hong Kong Identity." *Bulletin of Concerned Asian Scholars* 29 (3):3–13, 1997.

The Other Hong Kong Report, annual.

Salaff, Janet W. *Working Daughters of Hong Kong: Filial Piety or Power in the Family?* 1995.

Siu, Helen F. "Remade in Hong Kong: Weaving into the Chinese Cultural Tapestry." In Tao Tao Liu and David Faure, eds., *Unity and Diversity: Local Cultures and Identities in China,* 1996.

Ward, Barbara E. *Through Other Eyes: An Anthropologist's View of Hong Kong,* 1989.

Watson, James L. *Emigration and the Chinese Lineage: The Mans in Hong Kong and London,* 1975.

—Joseph Bosco

HUNGARY

CULTURE NAME

Hungarian

ALTERNATIVE NAMES

Magyar

ORIENTATION

Identification. Hungarian derives from Onogur, a Bulgarian-Turkish tribe's self-name. Between the sixth and eight centuries C.E., both the Hungarian tribes and the Onogurs lived just northeast of the Black Sea.

Location and Geography. Hungary is a landlocked country in central Europe. Covering an area of 35,934 square miles (93,030 square kilometers), the country is in the Carpathian Basin, surrounded by the Carpathian Mountains, the Alps, and the Dinaric Alps. The Danube River divides Hungary and bisects the capital, Budapest. Hungary lies within the temperate zone and has four distinct seasons.

Demography. Hungary has lost population since the early 1980s. The population was 10,065,000 in 1999, 48,000 less than it had been a year earlier. As in several European countries, the population of the elderly is on the rise and that of children on the decrease.

The officially recognized minorities are Armenians, Bulgarians, Croats, Germans, Greeks, Poles, Romanians, Roma (Gypsy), Ruthenians, Serbs, Slovaks, Slovenes, and Ukrainians. The largest minority is the Roma, who make up about 5 percent of the population, numbering approximately 500,000. The second largest minority are the Germans, who number an estimated 170,000. There are 80,000 to 110,000 Slovaks as well as about 35,000 Croatians, 15,000 to 25,000 Romanians, 80,000 to 100,000 Jews, and 5,000 Serbs.

Linguistic Affiliation. Hungarian belongs to the Ugor branch of the Finno-Ugric language family. Before World War II, German was the most important and frequently used second language. During the socialist period, Russian was mandatory in schools and universities. English has become the most valued second language, particularly for younger people with entrepreneurial ambitions and in academia, the sciences, and various businesses and services.

Symbolism. The Hungarian language constitutes one of the most significant national symbols. History also has a central meaning in national awareness and identity. Related to history is the national coat of arms, which depicts the House of Árpád's coat of arms. Árpád led the Hungarian conquest in 896 C.E. and his offspring founded the state and ruled until the male line died out in the early fourteenth century. On this family crest is the crown that national tradition connects with the person of King István (997–1038) (Saint Stephen), the country's first Christian king.

This crown, usually called Sacred Crown or Holy Crown, has always been endowed with a mystical and transcendent meaning. Historically, the crown validated and legitimated the ruler. Even though the kingdom of Hungary ceased to exist in 1918, the crown continues to hold deeply meaningful national significance.

The red, white, and green flag also is a powerful national symbol. The national anthem, written in 1823, is symbol of the eastern origins and history of the Hungarians in the form of a prayer that begs God to help the nation.

The gigantic painting entitled "The Arrival of the Hungarians" is another national symbol. Feszty originally painted it for the millennial celebration (1896).

The most significant manifestation of national unity is the sense of linguistic and cultural connection that includes the national language, literature,

Hungary

music, folk culture, folk literature, folk traditions, and history.

A deep, permeating consciousness is another integral element of national identity. It can be summarized as ''we are all alone'' and is based on historical reasons and the ''otherness'' of the language and the origins of Hungarians. While the consciousness of ''we are all alone'' was dormant during the socialist period (1948–1989), it still remained a recognizable and crucial part of the national identity.

History and Ethnic Relations

Emergence of the Nation. There is evidence that the Hungarian nation was a unit in the Middle Ages. In Latin chronicles dating back to the tenth century, there are colorful origin myths of the Hungarians ''conquering'' and occupying the Carpathian Basin and their conversion to Christianity under King Stephen. Many Hungarians consider their nation ''the final fortress of Western Christianity and civilized Europe.''

National Identity. In the Middle Ages, groups and nationalities that were not ethnically Hungarian lived in the nation. After the late Middle Ages, a dual national consciousness is demonstrable. On the one hand, there was a nation–state that ethnic Hungarians and non-Hungarians could share. On the other hand, there was a narrower sense of belonging to the Hungarian linguistic, cultural, and ethnic community.

In 1526, a young Hungarian king fell in a battle with the Ottoman Turks. On the basis of a marriage contract, the Habsburgs claimed the Hungarian throne. After conquering the Ottomans in 1686 and 1712, the Habsburgs ruled all of Hungary. The population accepted their right to rule but kept and observed their own laws, legislative powers, parliament, and administrative division. From time to

Houses in the village Holloko in northern Hungary in 1980. At the end of the twentieth century more than half of Hungarians grew food for their own use and for supplemental income.

time there were anti-Habsburg revolts, conspiracies, and political unrest.

In 1848, a revolution led by Lajos Kossuth demanded democratic reforms and more independence from Austria. However, Austria defeated the revolution. This was the first time that the general population, including the peasantry, experienced a sense of national unity. While some of the nationalities shared that experience, most turned against the Hungarians.

The Austrian tyranny that followed the revolution of 1848 ended with the 1867 Austrian-Hungarian Compromise. With this accord, the Austro-Hungarian monarchy was established. The Austro-Hungarian monarchy ended after World War I. The Trianon Treaty of 1920 ended the territorial integrity of Hungary. Nearly 70 percent of its historical territory and 58 percent of its former population were ceded to neighboring countries. One-third of ethnic Hungarians came under foreign rule. With the assent of the Western powers, Hungary came under Soviet occupation after World War II. Under the leadership of Moscow and the Moscow-led Hungarian Communist Party, the "building of socialism" began. In 1956, the nation rose up against the Communist rule and occupation by the Soviet Union. The revolt was defeated and approximately two hundred thousand Hungarians, mostly young people, skilled workers, white-collar workers, professionals, and intellectuals, escaped to the West.

By 1968 Hungary had become the "happiest barrack in the lager" as a result of the economic reforms of the New Economic Mechanism and with some social and political liberalization. In 1989, Hungary was the first Socialist Bloc country to open the "Iron Curtain," providing a transit route for thousands people emigrating from East Germany to West Germany, precipitating the fall of the Berlin Wall and the reunification of Germany.

The "softer" regime under János Kádár was successful in weakening traditional national consciousness, along with previously closely knit community networks and religious worldviews and values. After forty years of socialism, the general tendency among many in the population is to be individualistic, survival-oriented, and likely to work out strategies of compromise.

Ethnic Relations. After the 1989 change of regime, the Hungarian government assumed responsibility for the ethnic and linguistic maintenance of ethnic Hungarians living outside the nation's borders. The government tries to establish and maintain fair and friendly relations with the governments of neighboring countries. There are frequent complaints, however, that the Hungarian minorities' ethnic and cultural maintenance is made difficult by the host countries.

Hungary continues to strive for friendly relations with the surrounding countries. Ethnic and national minorities are encouraged to set up their own self-governing councils, and their cultural and educational institutions receive state support.

Among the minorities, the Roma are in an extremely difficult situation. Their high birth rate, disadvantageous economic position and social status, and the subjection to prejudice have worsened their economic circumstances and social integration.

Urbanism, Architecture, and the Use of Space

Until the middle of the nineteenth century, Hungary was a primarily rural agrarian society. Often Hungarian villages had large populations. The church was always in the center of the village. Many settlements were "two-church villages," indicating that two groups settled there at different periods.

On the Great Hungarian Plain instead of villages, there was a loose network of huge agrotowns that were located far from one another, each with a population from 20,000 to 100,000. Until recently, most Hungarians engaged in agriculture. The large agrotowns were administered as villages, with most of their inhabitants living like peasants. In the early eighteenth century, individual, isolated homesteads sprang up. Only seasonally occupied at first, they eventually became permanent residences of mostly extended families. However, even though about 50 percent of the people in the agrotowns lived and worked outside towns on these homesteads, they still considered themselves townspeople.

As a result of industrialization after the establishment of the Austro-Hungarian monarchy in 1867, a number of industrial-commercial-merchant cities sprang up. Between 1867 and the beginning of World War I, Budapest grew into a huge metropolis with a population of over a million.

In the center of cities there are city halls and other public buildings as well as churches, shopping districts, and remnants of traditional marketplaces. Some churchyards still have small cemeteries.

Until recently, it was customary to have a *tiszta szoba* (clean room) in peasant houses that was used mainly for special visits and particular rituals and occasions such as births, christenings, weddings, and funerals. There were also "sacred corners" that were decorated with pictures of various saints and pictures and statues brought back from Catholic pilgrimages. In Protestant households, the walls of those rooms depicted religious reformers and the heroes of the 1848 revolution.

Food and Economy

Food in Daily Life. *Magyar kenyér* (Hungarian bread) remains very important in the rural and urban cuisine. For the last one hundred fifty years, wheat has been one of the most important crops both for domestic use and exportation. Pig breeding became the most important type of animal breeding in the 1870s, and since then the meat and byproducts of pigs have predominated in the national diet.

Food Customs at Ceremonial Occasions. The cuisine at most village weddings includes chicken soup with special *csiga* noodles that were traditionally believed to have fertility-inducing properties, *gulyás*, stuffed cabbage, sweetened millet, sweetened rice and other rice dishes, and butter-cream tortes and other baked goods.

According to the national self-image, Hungarians are wine drinkers, but beer drinking is more common. Since the early 1990s there has been an attempt to familiarize the population with regional wines.

Basic Economy. Before World War II, Hungary was an agricultural country. During the socialist regime, forced industrialization took place. However, more than half the population does some agricultural work for household use and supplemental income.

Major Industries. Tourism continues to be a great Hungarian success. The production of barley, corn, potatoes, wheat, sugar beets, and sunflower seeds, along with grapes and wine making, is important. Mines are no longer subsidized by the government, and many mines have closed.

Trade. Imports include metal ores and crude petroleum, while exports include agricultural products, consumer goods, leather shoes, machinery, transport equipment, chemicals, textiles, wines, iron, and steel.

Between 1948 and 1989, more than half of foreign trade was with the Soviet Union and other socialist countries. Since the early 1990s, foreign

The towns of Buda and Pest (shown in 1995), on opposite sides of the Danube River, joined to become Budapest in 1873.

trading partners have been Germany, Italy, Austria, the United States, and some of the formerly socialist countries.

Social Stratification

Classes and Castes. Early in the socialist period, the nationalization of industries, commerce, and most services, along with the forced collectivization of agrarian landholding, brought about the end of private property. Communist Party leaders, secretaries, and members lived better and had access to more goods than did the rest of the population. Privatization of industry, commerce, and some services took place after 1990 as Western capital flowed into Hungary. As a result of a complex and controversial system of property compensation, most arable land and real properties were reprivatized after more than four decades. The income gap then widened between the rich and the poor. It increased in 1998 as 38 percent of the population earned below the minimum annual wage. In contrast, the rich seem to have increased their wealth at a rapid rate.

Upward social mobility still depends on the channeling of students into educational institutes. A disproportionate number of students in high schools, colleges, and universities come from intellectual, upper management, or otherwise "elite" families.

Symbols of Social Stratification. Western-style clothes, especially American jeans, are worn by the bulk of the younger population in both urban and rural areas. New clothes are very expensive and brand names such as Levi-Strauss can be bought only by a small segment of the population. Shiny polyester or nylon leisure suits worn with expensive, name-brand sports shoes are signs of new and successful entrepreneurs. Many of the new rich drive expensive foreign cars. The number of cell phones and their frequent and public uses are striking. There are numerous luxurious new or elaborately remodeled villas in Budapest that are owned by the new economic elite. Foreign travel has become a flaunted symbol of wealth and status.

Political Life

Government. All levels of government were under the control of the Communist Party between 1948 and 1989. The change of regime in 1989 brought in a multiparty government and a parliamentary democracy with elected representatives. At the end of the twentieth century, there were 182 officially registered political parties.

A woman paints a flower design which will be used to make a traditional Hungarian dress in Kalocsa, Hungary.

Leadership and Political Officials. There is a president, who is the head of the state and may be elected for two five-year terms. The prime minister is the leader of the party with the most seats. The parliament is called the National Assembly, with 386 deputies who are elected for four-year terms. The Constitutional Court was established in 1990. There is a Judicial Supreme Court that is essentially a final court of appeal.

Social Problems and Control. Alcoholism is a widespread and significant problem. In addition, drug abuse has increased since the end of the socialist regime. After the outbreak of the war in the former Yugoslavia in 1991, Hungary became a favorite place for international organized crime organizations that engage in drug, weapons, and people smuggling; prostitution rings; and money laundering. The crime rate is rapidly increasing. The population worries about the lack of public safety and generally blames crimes on the Roma as well as refugees and other foreigners. Psychological problems, particularly depression, increased significantly between 1988 and 1996, and, although the number of suicides has been declining, Hungary continues to have the highest rate of suicide in the world.

Military Activity. Modernization of the army began in the early transition period (1990–1994) and has continued since the country has become part of the North Atlantic Treaty Organization (NATO). There is an ongoing process of integrating the Hungarian armed forces with NATO organizations and the filling of alliance posts. The army is being converted to a mixed structure that is composed of volunteers and conscripts. All males between ages 18 and 55 are required to serve in the armed forces, but conscription is selective. For example, students in universities serve for a very short time or not at all and conscientious objectors are given civilian jobs. There are 80,000 people serving in the army, air force, border guards, and the small fleet guarding the Danube River.

Gender Roles and Statuses

Division of Labor by Gender. Men are expected to work, earn, and provide for their families, while women are expected to take care of the children and the domestic chores. These ideal roles are rarely achieved today. In the last couple of generations, the rate of divorce and remarriage has increased dramatically. Since the change of regime (in 1989), cohabitation of unmarried couples and the number of children born outside of marriage have grown. These patterns are more common among those with less formal education, money, and social prestige.

Most Hungarian men do not help with the housework, and few women object to this arrangement. Only among a small percentage of young, mostly urban couples and an even smaller segment of middle-aged intellectuals and professionals is there evidence of a changing pattern in the gendered division of labor in the domestic sphere.

The Relative Status of Women and Men. The images of the mother and motherland are expressed in the national literature and culture. Since the early nineteenth century, the centrality of the mother-son relationship has been idealized in literature and the public consciousness. The mother is often hailed as the core of the national identity, the guardian and cultivator of a "real" culture that is untouched by foreign influences.

Marriage, Family, and Kinship

Marriage. Marriages are no longer arranged. Young people usually marry for love or to have children. The perpetual shortage of apartments is a problem for married couples. Young married couples frequently move into the small apartment of either set of parents. While traditionally a young married couple lived near the parents of the groom, today, if a couple cannot set up an independent new household, they move in with the set of parents who will welcome them and has the most room. Most households consist of a married or unmarried couple and their children.

Even when a couple lives in a separate household, great value is placed on having the help of a grandmother or grandfather.

Kin Groups. Kin groups are often large in villages and smaller in urban centers. Godparenthood is still much valued. Extended families living in the same household are very rare.

Socialization

Infant Care. Traditionally, newborns were swaddled; today they are wrapped in warm blankets when they are very young, but swaddling is no longer practiced. Infants and toddlers are usually put into a separate space to sleep and play. Parents try to calm an active baby rather than stimulate it. There seems to be a growing child centeredness that is manifested in focusing on children and often giving them more material goods and privileges than the family can afford. Good children are obedient, mindful, diligent, respectful, industrious, quiet, and good students. In rural areas, more emphasis is placed on respect and industrious behavior. The actual behavior of children rarely approximates these expectations.

Child Rearing and Education. Formal education is compulsory between six and sixteen years of age. The rate of literacy is 98 percent. Traditionally, most people considered a high school diploma as the final formal educational goal.

Higher Education. Since the 1980s more value has been placed on college or university education. This is illustrated by a slightly increased enrollment in colleges and universities and in an expansion of educational opportunities in institutes of higher learning.

Etiquette

Hospitality entails an extraordinary effort to feed and care for guests. Guests are always encouraged to step into one's home first.

On the streets, it is customary for men to walk on the left side of women, ostensibly because in the past gentlemen kept their swords on the left side and women had to be on the opposite side of the sword. A Hungarian man enters first into a pub, restaurant, coffeehouse, or other public establishment.

Friends, family members, and close acquaintances who have not seen one another for a while greet and part from one another with pecks on both the left and right cheeks. Touching the hands, arms, and shoulders of partners in conversation is common. It is customary for a woman to offer her hand first both to men of all ages and to younger women and children.

Differentiated formal terms of address are seldom used among younger people. Informal styles of greeting and terms of address are used from the moment of initial meeting. Considerably less time is spent visiting and socializing in coffeehouses and on the streets than in the past.

Bodily contact is rather intimate on public transportation and in malls and shopping centers. In isolated rural settlements, villagers still stare at strangers.

Religion

Religious Beliefs. According to surveys in the early 1990s, 72 percent of Hungarians are Roman Catholic, 21 percent are Calvinist Reformed, 4 percent are Lutherans, nearly 1 percent are Jewish, and

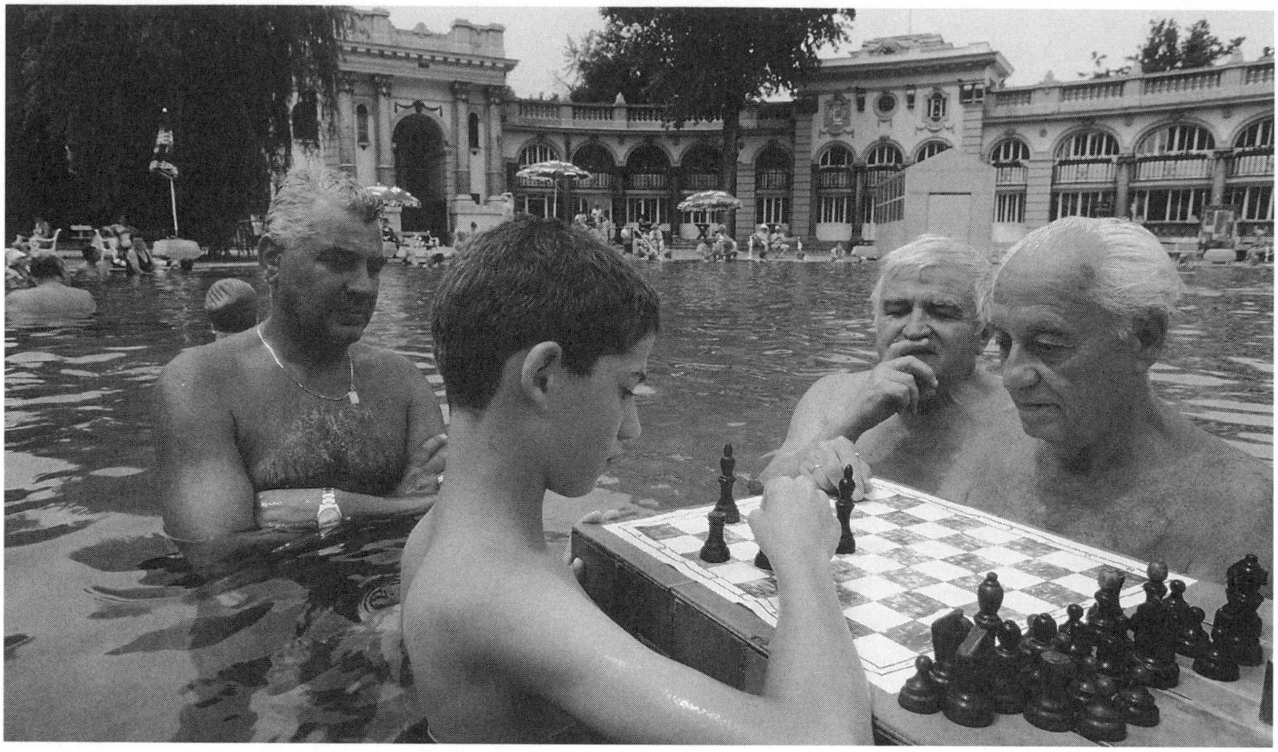

Hungarians frequent the Szechenyi Thermal Baths in Budapest and other spas to promote good health.

about 2 percent are "nondenominational" or "other."

After Russia, Hungary has the largest Jewish population in its region. About 80 percent of Hungarian Jews live in the capital city. About half the Jewish population is over the age of 65.

There was an official campaign against all religions during the socialist regime. Those who openly practiced a religion were discriminated against and often punished. The state closed most parochial schools and dissolved or disbanded religious orders and institutions. After 1989 and during the periods of privatization, many schools and other formerly parochial buildings were returned to the churches. As compensation for the confiscated properties, the state financially supports parochial schools and other religious institutions.

Among large segments of the population, religious indifference and often explicitly antireligious attitudes prevail. This is an outcome of the lax, individualist, atomizing policies of the last decade of socialism. Alongside the major denominations, there are an increasing number of small sects, religious movements, and Eastern religious practices, along with a growing number of followers of proselytizing Western missionaries.

Many Hungarians do not formally belong to or regularly practice any religion, but baptisms, weddings, and funerals tie them informally to churches.

Rituals and Holy Places. Among the sacred places of the Hungarian Roman Catholic Church are the city of Esztergom, where Saint Stephen was born; Pannonhalma, where the first Benedictine Order was founded in 996 C.E.; the city of Eger; and a number of provincial rural settlements and places of annual pilgrimage. Calvinists in eastern Hungary consider Debrecen the "Calvinist Rome." The religious centers for Lutherans are Budapest and Sopron. Budapest has the largest synagogue in Europe.

Death and the Afterlife. In addition to traditional in-ground burial, cremation with special places to put funerary urns has been practiced since before World War II. Because of a lack of cemetery space in the cities and the great expense of traditional funerals, cremation is widely practiced.

Medicine and Health Care

Western medicine is practiced, although many individuals have turned to alternative medicine such as acupuncture and herbal and homeopathic remedies. In addition to Western medical treatment, frequenting medicinal spas, getting professional deep tissue and other types of massage, and drinking mineral water continue to be very popular.

Secular Celebrations

Major national holidays include 20 August, commemorating the death of King Stephen. This day is also an ecclesiastical feast day. During the socialist regime (1948–1989), 20 August was renamed the Day of the Constitution and the Day of New Bread. Another major national holiday is 15 March, which commemorates the bloodless democratic civil revolution that broke out in 1848. Since the change of regime in 1989, 23 October has been a day of remembrance of the revolution of 1956, when Hungarians rose against the Soviet occupation. Though not an official holiday, the Day of the Martyrs of Arad (6 October) is a significant time of remembrance.

In addition, there are numerous local memorial celebrations, art festivals, and folk festivals. Among the many festivals and fairs are the southern Folklore Festival along the Danube, the northern region's annual Palóc Festival, and the annual Bridge Fair. In the annual Budapest Spring Festival, there are art exhibits and musical and theatrical events.

The Arts and Humanities

Support for the Arts. Support for the arts during the socialist period was provided primarily by the State. Since 1989, there has been much less governmental support and more private, individual, and corporate sponsors for artists.

The State of the Physical and Social Sciences

The physical and social sciences are taught on sophisticated and advanced levels in universities, research facilities, and other institutes. State funding continues to be a key resource, but it has decreased in the last decade. There has been a "brain drain" as younger and middle-aged scientists leave temporarily or permanently for better wages and opportunities and more advanced laboratories and instruments in Western Europe, the United States, Canada, and Australia.

Bibliography

Bárány, George. *Stephen Széchenyi and the Awakening of Hungarian Nationalism*. 1968.

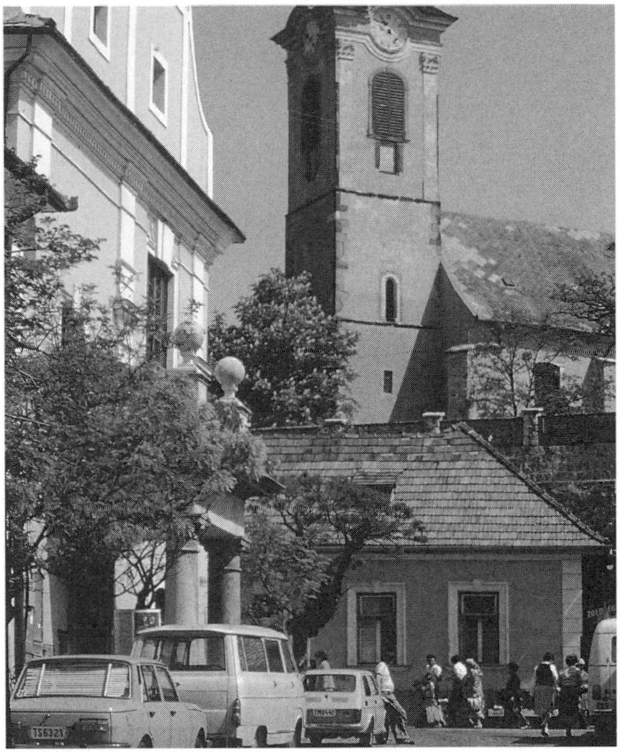

Remnants of past centuries such as this clock tower still dominate many towns.

———. "Hungary: From Aristocratic to Proletarian Nationalism." In Peter Sugar and Ivo Lederer, eds., *Nationalism in Eastern Europe*, 1969.

Bibó, István. *Democracy, Revolution, Self-Determination. Selected Writings*, 1991.

Csalog, Zsolt. "'We Offer Our Love': Gypsies in Hungary." *New Hungarian Quarterly* 33, (127):70–80, 1992.

Csepeli, György. *Structures and Contents of Hungarian National Identity: Results of Political Socialization and Cultivation*,, 1989.

———. *National Identity in Contemporary Hungary*, 1997.

Crowe, David. "The Gypsies of Hungary." In David Crowe and J. Kolsti, eds., *The Gypsies of Eastern Europe*, 1990.

Deák, István. "Uncovering Eastern Europe's Dark History." *Orbis*, Winter 1990.

———. *Beyond Nationalism: A Social and Political History of the Habsburg Officer Corps*,, 1992.

Erõs, Ferenc. "The Construction of Jewish Identity in Hungary in the 1980s." In Ferenc Erõs, David Schers, and David Zisenwine, eds., Yitzak Kashti, *A Quest for Identity: Post War Jewish Biographies. Studies in Jewish Culture, Identity and Community, School of Education*, 1996.

Fél, Edit, and Hofer Tamás. *Proper Peasants: Tradtional Life in a Hungarian Village*, 1969.

Fenyõ, Marió D. *Hitler, Horthy and Hungary*, 1972.

Gerõ, András. *Modern Hungarian Society*, 1995.

Gombár, Csaba, Elemér Hankiss, László Lengyel, and György Várnai, eds. *The Appeal of Sovereignty: Hungary, Austria, and Russia*, 1998.

Hanák, Peter, ed. *The Corvina History of Hungary: From Earliest Times Until the Present Day*, 1991.

Hofer, Tamás, and Edit Fél. *Hungarian Folk Art*, 1979.

Huseby-Darvas, Éva. "The Search for Hungarian National Identity." In Lola Romanucci-Ross and George DeVos, eds., 1995.

———. "'Feminism, the Murderer of Mothers': Neo-Nationalist Reconstruction of Gender in Hungary." In Brackette F. Williams, ed., *Women out of Place: The Gender of Agency and the Race of Nationality*, 1996.

János, Andrew. *The Politics of Backwardness in Hungary*, 1982.

Jászi, Oszkár. *The Dissolution of the Habsburg Monarchy*, 2nd ed., 1958.

Kereszty, András, ed. *The Reliable Book of Facts Hungary '98*, 1999.

Kis, János, *Politics in Hungary: For a Democratic Alternative*, 1989.

Kisbán, Eszter "Parasztételbôl nemzeti jelkép: A Gulyás esete 1800 körül [From Peasant Food to National Symbol: The Case of the Gulyás]." *Janus IV.*

Kolosi, Tamás, István G. Tóth, and György Vukovich, eds., *Social Report 1998*, 1999.

Kontra, Miklós. "Hungary." In *Sprachkontakte in Mitteleuropa Kontaktlinguistik*, Hans Goeble, Peter H. Nelde, Zdenek Stary, and Wolfgang Wolk, eds., 1997.

Kuti, Éva. *Hivjuk talán non-profitnak [Perhaps We Ought to Call It Non-Profit]*, 1998.

Lázár, István. *An Illustrated History of Hungary*, 1995.

Lukács, John. *Budapest 1900: A Historical Portrait of a City and Its Culture*, 1988.

Makkai, Ádám, ed. *In Quest of the Miracle Stag*, 1996.

McCagg, William O. *Jewish Nobles and Geniuses in Modern Hungary*, 1973.

Macartney, Aylmer C. *National States and National Minorities*, 1934.

Örkény, Antal, and Mária Székelyi. "Justice and Legitimacy: Post-Transformation Trends in Eastern Europe." In Kolosi, Tóth, Vukovics, eds., 1999.

Szathmáry, Lajos. "How Festive Foods of the Old World Became Commonplace in the New, or the American Perception of Hungarian Gulyás." *Oxford Symposium on Foods and Eating Habits Proceedings* 2(1):137–143, 1983.

—Éva V. Huseby-Darvas

ICELAND

CULTURE NAME

Icelandic

ORIENTATION

Identification. Scandinavian sailors discovered Iceland in the mid-ninth century, and the first settler recognized in the literary-historical tradition, Ingólfur Arnason, arrived in 874. The book of settlements (*Landnámabók*), which contains information on four hundred settlers, was compiled in the twelfth century. The story set down there and repeated to this day is that a Norse Viking named Flóki sailed to Iceland, but spent so much energy hunting and fishing that he did not lay up hay for his livestock, which died in the winter, and had to return. He then gave the island its unpromising name.

Among the settlers and the slaves the Scandinavians brought were people of Irish as well as Norse descent; Icelanders still debate the relative weight of the Norse and Irish contributions to their culture and biology. Some date a distinctive sense of "Icelandicness" to the writing of the *First Grammatical Treatise* in the twelfth century. The first document was a recording of laws in 1117. Many copies and versions of legal books were produced. Compilations of law were called *Grágas* ("gray goose" or "wild goose").

In 930, a General Assembly was established, and in 1000, Iceland became Christian by a decision of the General Assembly. In 1262–1264, Iceland was incorporated into Norway; in 1380, when Norway came under Danish rule, Iceland went along; and on 17 June 1944, Iceland became an independent republic, though it had gained sovereignty in 1918 and had been largely autonomous since 1904.

The sense of Iceland as a separate state with a separate identity dates from the nineteenth-century nationalist movement. According to the ideology of that movement, all Icelanders share a common heritage and identity, though some argue that economic stratification has resulted in divergent identities and language usage.

Location and Geography. Iceland is an island in the north Atlantic Ocean between Greenland and Norway just south of the Arctic Circle. It covers 63,860 square miles (103,000 square kilometers), of which about 620 are cultivated, 12,400 are used for grazing, 7,500 are covered by glaciers, 1,900 are covered by lakes, and 41,500 are covered by lava, sands, and other wastelands. The Gulf Stream moderates the climate. The capital is Reykjavík.

Demography. In 1993, the population was 264,922. In 1703, when the first census was done, the population was 50,358. In 1992, there were 63,540 families that averaged three members. In 1993, the population of the capital area was 154,268.

Linguistic Affiliation. Icelandic is a Germanic language related to Norwegian. Medieval Icelandic, the language of the historical-literary tradition, sometimes is called Old Norse. Icelandic has been said to be virtually unaltered since medieval times, although many Icelanders disagree. There are no family names. Everyone has one or two names and is referred to as the son or daughter of his or her father. Thus, everyone has a patronymic, or father's name. Directories are organized alphabetically by first name. There is some debate about the uniformity of the language. Purists of the nationalist-oriented independence tradition insist that there is no variation in Icelandic, but linguistic studies suggest variation by class. While all the people speak Icelandic, most also speak Danish and English.

Symbolism. The international airport is named Leif Erikson Airport after the first voyager to North America, and a statue of Erikson stands in front of the National Cathedral. A heroic statue of the first

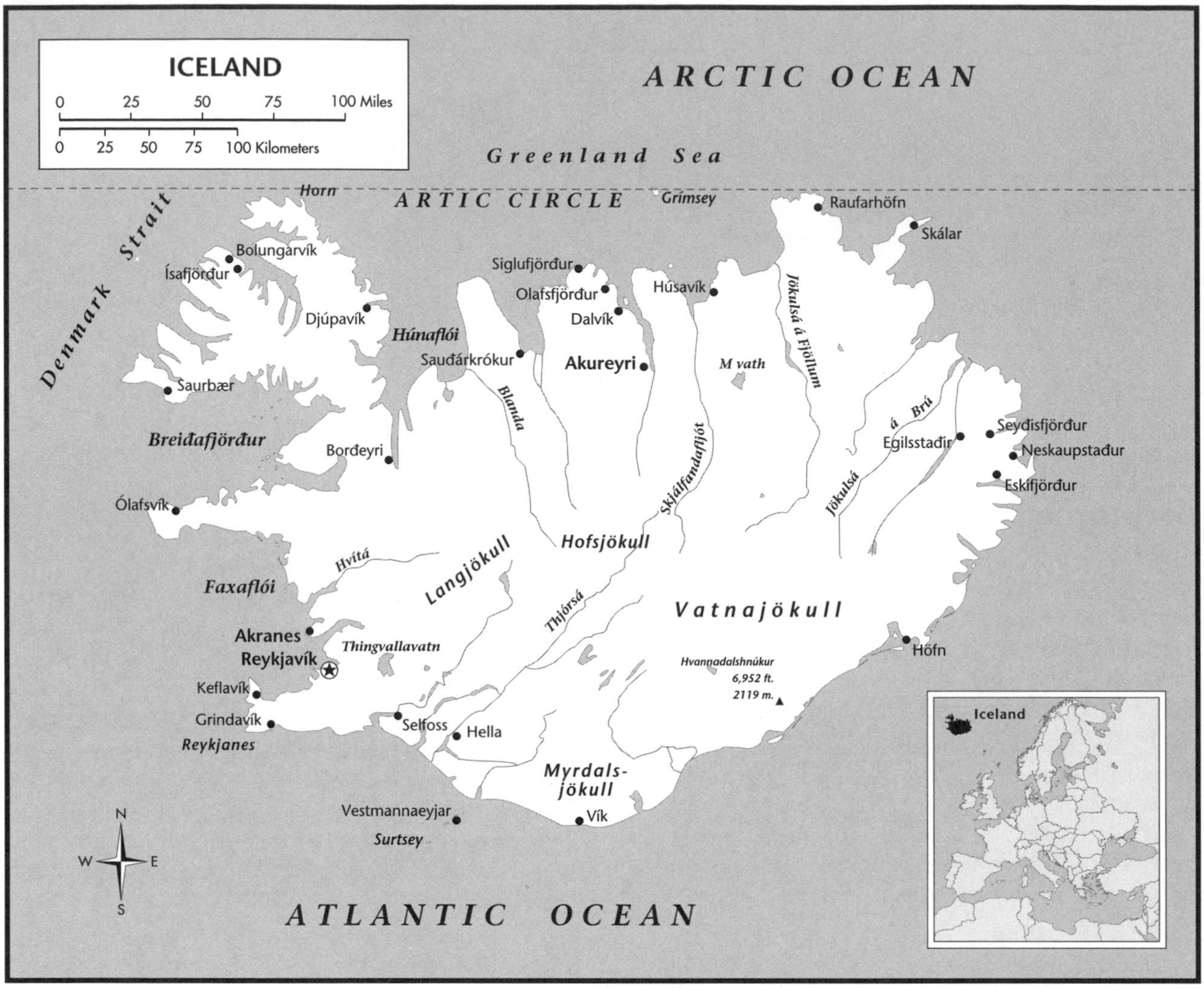

Iceland

settler is in the downtown area of the capital. The nationalist-oriented ideology stresses identification with medieval culture and times while downplaying slavery and later exploitative relations of the aristocracy and commoners. This romantic view of the saga tradition informs nationalist symbolism and nationalist-influenced folklore. There is a whole genre of romantic landscape poetry depicting the beauty of the island. Some of it goes back to the saga tradition, quoting Gunnar, a hero of Njal's saga, who refused to depart after being outlawed because as he looked over his shoulder when his horse stumbled, the fields were so beautiful that he could not bear to leave. More recently, rhetoric about whaling has achieved symbolic proportions as some have viewed attempts to curtail the national tradition of whale hunting as an infringement on their independence. Independence Day on 17 June is celebrated in Reykjavík. Neighborhood bands march into the downtown area playing songs, and many people drink alcoholic beverages. The major symbols of Icelandicness are the language and geography, centered on the beauty of the landscape. Many people know the names of the farms of their ancestors and can name fjords and hills, and the map in the civic center in Reykjavík has no place names because it is assumed that people know them. The folkloristic tradition contains many stories of trolls, among them the ones that come from the wastelands to eat children at Christmas and their twelve sons who play pranks on people. Various features of landscape are associated with stories recorded in the official folklore.

History and Ethnic Relations

Emergence of the Nation. Between 1602 and 1787, Denmark imposed a trade monopoly that re-

Swimmers bathe in the Blue Lagoon thermal baths in Iceland.

stricted imports and kept fishing under its control. A farming elite developed a system of self-contained farms and opposed the development of fishing, which would threaten the supply of cheap labor if relied on. After independence, fishing finally developed. The trade monopoly organized Iceland as a tributary state for mercantile purposes and created a class of farmers with entrenched interests and power to defend them against the fisheries. The trade monopoly created the autonomous Icelandic farm as the primary social, economic, and political unit. When the tributary system became a hindrance to organizing for capitalism, the elite engineered backwardness to serve its interests. This backwardness was not a local dynamic and was not culturally determined but served a large international Danish system. When Denmark's absolute monarchy was replaced by a nation-state, this provided a context for Icelandic independence. Although farmers tried to perpetuate their hold over the economy, industrial fishing became the backbone of the national economy. The "independence struggle" started in the mid-nineteenth century. Nationalist ideology presents the movement as an autonomous great awakening. In the service of the independence movement, the elite developed distinctive images of what it meant to be Icelandic, aided by historians and legalists, folklorists, and linguists. These images described an ideal lifestyle of an elite. Danes thought Icelandic culture embodied the most noble elements in the Norse experience and looked to Iceland for inspiration. Thus, Icelandic leaders could argue that the nation's future should match the glories of its past. Icelandic students in Denmark began to import ideas of nationalism and romanticism. The Icelandic elite followed the Danes in identifying with a romantic image of a glorious Icelandic past. As the Danes began to modernize and develop, they set the conditions for Icelandic independence. Finally it was conditions beyond Danish control—when Denmark was occupied by Germany in World War II, followed by the occupation of Iceland by British and then American troops—that pushed Iceland into independence. Given independence and population growth, along with new sources of outside capital, the government focused on the development of industrial fishing and the infrastructure to support it.

National Identity. The working class identified with national political movements and parties and thus helped ratify the elite's vision of Iceland. The ideology developed by members of the farming elite was one of the individual, the holiness and purity of the countryside, and the moral primacy of the farm and farmers. The most significant individuals were the farmers. This ideology was perpetuated in academic writings, schools, and law. Foreign scholars and anthropologists, along with local folklorists, created a bureaucratic folklorism that considered the intellectual superior to the rural people and the rural people as the most superior of all exotics. Such constructs could not be perpetuated as most people abandoned the countryside in favor of fishing villages and wage work or salaried positions in Reykjavík. Icelanders generalized and democratized the concept of the elite and combined it with competitive consumerism. This led to a new cultural context that weakened the ideology of the farmer elite. The main ideological task of the independence movement was to develop a paradigm that would prove that the nationalistic power struggle would change the lives of ordinary people. The past and the countryside were emphasized as pure, while working people in the cities were considered trash. The folklore movement displaced discussions of competition for power to earlier times and reduced diversity to uniformity in service of the state. As the population grew and the economy turned more toward fishing in the coastal towns and villages, farmers lost their economic place. The main goal of the nationalist ideology that the elite promulgated was to conserve the old order. The glory of the sagas was held up as a model, and certain celebrations were revived to emphasize the connection. However, today most Icelanders live in the area of the capital, and their culture is international.

Urbanism, Architecture, and the Use of Space

In 1991, there were 4,754 farms. More than half the people (154,268) live in the Reykjavík area. The next largest town is Akurery, with a population of 14,799. Keflavík, where the NATO base and the international airport are, has a population of 7,581. The Westman Islands are home to 4,883 people. The realities of daily life for most people are urban and industrial or bureaucratic. Until recently, social life was centered on households and there was little public life in restaurants, cafés, or bars. There is a thriving consumer economy. People are guaranteed the right to work, health care, housing, retirement, and education. Thus, there is no particular need to save. People therefore purchase homes, country houses, cars, and consumer goods to stock them. Private consumption in 1993 reached $10,600 per capita.

Food and Economy

Food in Daily Life. The writer Halldor Laxness once observed that "life is salt fish." During some of the events inspired by the romantic folkloric revival, people consume brennivín, an alcoholic beverage called "black death," along with fermented shark meat and smoked lamb, which is served at festive occasions. Icelanders are famous for the amount of coffee they drink and the amount of sugar they consume.

Food Customs at Ceremonial Occasions. For homecomings and family gatherings, there is usually a sumptuous spread of cakes and pastries, including crullers and thin pancakes rolled around whipped cream.

Basic Economy. The major occupations in 1991 were agriculture, fishing, and fish processing. The main industries were building, commerce, transportation and communications, finance and insurance, and the public sector. Fish and fish products are the major export item. While dairy products and meat are locally produced, grain products are imported. Some vegetables are produced in greenhouses, and some potatoes are locally produced. Other food is imported, along with many consumer goods. In 1993, consumer goods accounted for 37.2 percent of imports, intermediate goods 28 percent, fuels 8 percent, and investment goods 25.8 percent.

Social Stratification

Classes and Castes. There is a lack of extreme stratification in a country that values egalitarian relationships. Working-class people are likely to indicate their class status by language use, incorporating into their speech what purists call "language diseases."

Political Life

Government. Iceland has a multiparty parliamentary system, and there is a written constitution. Presidents are elected for four-year terms by direct popular vote but serve a parliamentary function and do not head a separate executive branch. The parliament is called *Althingi* after the medieval general assembly. It has sixty three members elected by popular vote for four-year terms. Each party puts forward a list of candidates, and people vote for parties, not candidates. The seats in the parliament are then distributed to parties according to the placement of people in their lists. Thus, elections

Flowers adorn a public square. Icelanders take extreme care in the upkeep of public areas.

have more to do with policies and positions on issues than with personalities.

Leadership and Political Officials. After elections, the president asks one party, usually the one with the largest number of votes, to form a government of cabinet officers. There has never been a majority in the parliament, and so the governments are coalitions. The real political competition starts after elections, when those elected to the parliament jockey for positions in the new government. If the first party cannot form a coalition, the president will ask another one until a coalition government is formed. Cabinet ministers can sit in the parliament but may not vote unless they have been elected as members. This cabinet stays in power until another government is formed or until there are new elections. The president and the *Althingi* share legislative power because the president must approve all the legislation the parliament passes. In practice, this is largely a ritual act, and even a delay in signing legislation is cause for public comment. Constitutionally, the president holds executive power, but the cabinet ministers, who are responsible to the *Althingi*, exercise the power of their various offices. The parliament controls national finances, taxation, and financial allocations and appoints members to committees and executive bodies. There is an autonomous judicial branch. The voting age is 18, and about 87.4 percent of the people vote. The major parties include the Independence Party, Progressive Party, People's Alliance, Social Democrats, Women's Party, and Citizens/ Liberal Party. Each party controls a newspaper to spread and propagate its views. The mode of interaction with political officials is informal.

Social Problems and Control. There are few social problems, and crime is minimal. There is some domestic abuse and alcoholism. The unemployment rate is very low. Police routinely stop drivers to check for drunkenness, and violators have to serve jail time, often after waiting for a space in the jail to become available. There are no military forces.

Social Welfare and Change Programs

Since independence, there has been a high standard of living. From 1901 to 1960, real national income rose tenfold, with an annual average growth rate over 4 percent. This was the period in which the national economy was transformed from a rural economy based on independent farms to a capitalist fishing economy with attendant urbanization.

Gender Roles and Statuses

The Relative Status of Women and Men. There is more gender equality than there is in many other countries. The open nature of the political system allows interested women to organize as a political party to pursue their interests in the parliament. There are women clergy. Fishing is largely in the hands of men, while women are more prominent in fish processing.

Marriage, Family, and Kinship

Marriage. There is a relative lack of formal marriage, and out-of-wedlock births (13 to 36 percent) have never been stigmatized. Women frequently have a child before they marry. Many people are related to numerous half siblings from their parents' other children by other mates.

Domestic Unit. The domestic unit is the household, and larger kin groups come together for annual reunions. Friendship and other connections are very important, and many people who are referred to by kin terms are not genealogically related.

Socialization

Infant Care. Infants are isolated in carriages and cribs, not continuously held. Public health nurses check on newborns to be sure they are on the growth curves and check for signs of neglect, abuse, or disease. Since both men and women usually work, it is common for children to be kept in day care centers from an early age.

Child Rearing and Education. Children are centers of attention, and classes are given on child rearing and parenting. Thus, even teenagers are familiar with approved methods of child rearing. Education is respected and considered a basic right. University education is available to all who want it and can afford minimal registration fees. Education is compulsory between ages 7 and 16 but may be continued in middle schools or high schools, many of which are boarding schools.

Higher Education. A theological seminary was founded in 1847, followed by a medical school in 1876 and a law school in 1908; these three schools were merged in 1911 to form the University of Iceland. A faculty of philosophy was added to deal with matters of ideology (philology, history, and literature). Later, faculties of engineering and social sciences were added.

Etiquette

Social interaction is egalitarian. Public comportment is quiet and reserved.

Religion

Religious Beliefs. The state church is the Evangelical Lutheran Church, of which 92.2 percent of the population are nominal if not practicing members. Other Lutherans constitute 3.1 percent of the population, Catholics 0.9 percent, and others 3.8 percent. There is a Catholic church and churches of other groups in Reykjavík. There are many Lutheran churches, and their clergy substitute for social service agencies. Other religions include Seventh-Day Adventists, Pentecostals, Jehovah's Witnesses, Bahai, and followers of the Asa Faith Society, which looks to the gods represented in the saga tradition. Less than 2 percent of the population in 1993 was not affiliated with a religious denomination. Confir-

Icelandic fishermen provide the key ingredient for one of the country's main exports, fish and fish products.

mation is an important ritual for adolescents, but many who are confirmed are not active.

Medicine and Health Care

Universal medical care is provided as a right. There is a modern medical system.

Secular Celebrations

Most holidays are associated with the Christian religious calendar. Others include the first day of summer on a Thursday from 19 to 25 April, Labor Day on 1 May, National Day on 17 June, and Commerce Day on the first Monday of August. These holidays are observed by having a day off from work and possibly traveling to the family summer house for a brief vacation.

The Arts and Humanities

Support for the Arts. There is an art museum in Reykjavík, and several artists have achieved the status of "state artists" with government-funded studios, which become public museums after their deaths. There is a theater community in Reykjavík. Literature has a long history.

The State of the Physical and Social Sciences

The University of Iceland is the center for scientific research. There is much work on geothermal energy sources. The National Science Foundation funds research, and Iceland belongs to international federations for the support of physical and social science research. There is a faculty of engineering and a faculty of social science at the university.

Bibliography

Durrenberger, E. Paul. *The Dynamics of Medieval Iceland: Political Economy and Literature*. University of Iowa Press, 1992.

———. *Icelandic Essays: Explorations in the Anthropology of a Modern Nation*, 1995.

——— and Gísli Pálsson. *The Anthropology of Iceland*, 1989.

Pálsson, Gísli. *Coastal Economies, Cultural Accounts: Human Ecology and Icelandic Discourse*, 1990.

———. *The Textual Life of Savants: Ethnography, Iceland, and the Linguistic Turn*, 1995.

——— and E. Paul Durrenberger. *Images of Contemporary Iceland: Everyday Lives and Global Contexts*, 1996.

—E. Paul Durrenberger

India

Culture Name

Indian, Hindu, Bharati

Orientation

Identification. India constitutes the largest part of the subcontinental land mass of South Asia, an area it shares with six other countries, including Nepal, Pakistan, and Bangladesh. It has highly variable landforms, that range from torrid plains, tropical islands, and a parched desert to the highest mountain range in the world.

Location and Geography. India, on the southern subcontinent of Asia, is bounded on the northwest by Pakistan; on the north by China and Tibet, Nepal and Bhutan; on the northeast by Bangladesh and Burma (Myanmar); and on the southwest and southeast by the Indian Ocean, with the island republics of Sri Lanka and the Maldives to the south. Excluding small parts of the country that are currently occupied by Chinese or Pakistani military forces, the area of the Republic of India is 1,222,237 square miles (3,165,596 square kilometers).

Demography. The 1991 census enumerated 846,302,688 residents, including 407,072,230 women, and 217 million people defined as urban dwellers. However, with a population growth rate estimated at 17 per one thousand in 1998, by May 2000 the national figure reached one billion. Life expectancy in the 1991 census was sixty years, and in 1997 it was estimated that almost 5 percent of the population was age 65 or older. The population is still primarily rural, with 73 percent of the population in 1997 living outside the cities and towns. In 1991, the largest urban centers were Bombay or Mumbai (12,596,243), Calcutta or Kolkata (11,021,915), Delhi (8,419,084), Madras or Chennai (5,421,985), Hyderabad (4,253,759), and Bangalore (4,130,288).

Linguistic Affiliations. There are four major language families, each with numerous languages. Indo-Aryan, a branch of Indo-European, covers the northern half of the country, and the Dravidian family covers the southern third. In the middle regions a number of tribal languages of the Munda or Austroasiatic family are spoken. In the northeastern hills, numerous Tibeto-Burman languages are spoken.

Symbolism. The national flag, which was adopted in 1947, is a tricolor of deep saffron, white, and green, in horizontal bands (with green at the bottom). In the center of the white band is a blue wheel, the *chakra*, which also appears on the lion column-capital of the Emperor Asoka at Sarnath. This carving, which is over 2,200 years old, is also a national emblem that is preserved in the Sarnath Museum. The sandstone carving features four lions back to back, separated by wheels (*chakra*, the wheel of law), standing over a bell-shaped lotus. The whole carving once was surmounted by the wheel of law. The national anthem is a song composed by Rabindranath Tagore in 1911 entitled *Jana-gana mana*. The nearly useless Saka-era calendar also may be considered a national symbol, adopted in 1957 and still often used officially alongside the Gregorian calendar.

History and Ethnic Relations

Emergence of the Nation. India has a history going back thousands of years and a prehistory going back hundreds of thousands of years. There was a long phase of Paleolithic hunting and gathering cultures parallel in time and characteristics with the Paleolithic peoples of Europe and East Asia. This was followed, eight thousand to ten thousand years ago, by the development of settled agricultural communities in some areas.

In 2700 B.C.E., the first genuinely urban civilization in the Indus Valley and western India

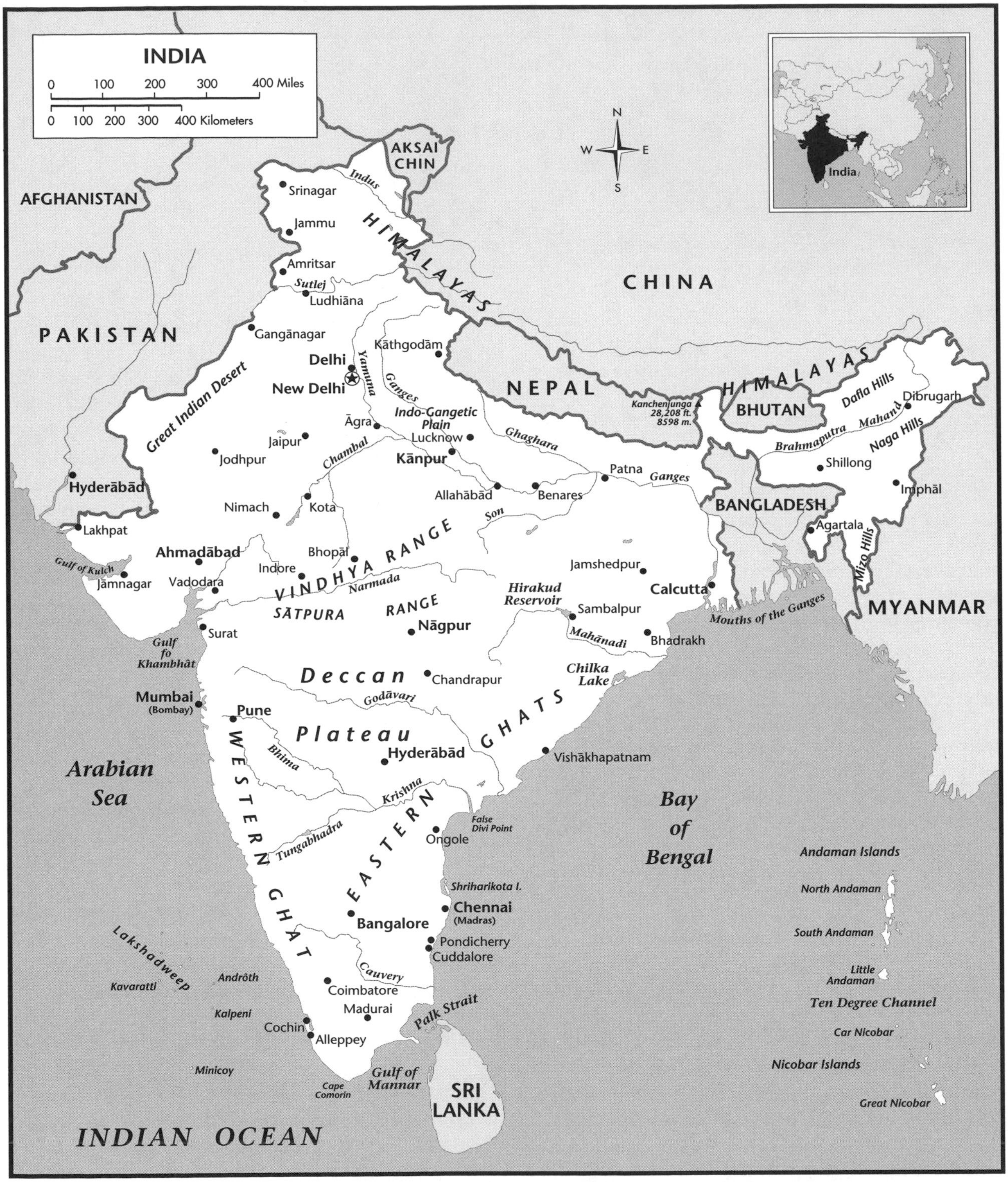

India

emerged. After its disappearance around 1500 B.C.E., there was a bewildering variety of princely states and kingdoms, small and large, throughout the subcontinent, creating a long history of war and conquest that was punctuated by foreign invasions and the birth of some of the world's largest religions: Buddhism, Jainism, Hinduism, and Sikhism.

Despite the extent of the Empire of Asoka (272–232 B.C.E.) and the Mughal Empire (1526–1707), it was left to the last foreign invaders, the British, to establish a unified empire that covered most of the subcontinent during its final century.

India was ruled by the British government after 1858 through a viceroy and a council, although several hundred "princely states" continued to maintain a measure of independence. The Indian National Congress, founded in 1885, slowly moved from a position of advisor and critic for the British administration toward demanding the transference of power to native Indian politicians. In 1930, the Indian National Congress, led by Jawaharlal Nehru and Mahatma Gandhi, adopted a policy of civil disobedience with a view to achieving full national independence. It was to be a long struggle, but independence was achieved in 1947, with the condition that predominantly Muslim areas in the north would form a separate country of Pakistan. Mohammed Ali Jinnah was to be Pakastani's first prime minister, while Nehru became the prime minister of the Republic of India. The departure of the colonial authorities, including the British armed forces, was peaceful, but the splitting off of Pakistan caused a massive population movement and bloodshed on both sides as a result of "communal passions." A quarter century later, the eastern wing of Pakistan split from that country to become the independent country of Bangladesh.

National Identity. National identity is not a major political issue; regional identity and the mother tongue seem to be more important. There are still millions of illiterate people who seem hardly aware that they are Indians but can be vociferous in their support of chauvinistic regional politicians. Thus, India has been plagued with secessionist struggles since independence, the most prominent of which have been a Dravidistan movement in the south, an armed struggle among Kashmiri Muslims for a union of their state with Pakistan, a Khalistan movement among Panjabi Sikhs, and a guerilla movement seeking independence for all the Naga tribes in the northeast.

Ethnic Relations. India is home to several thousand ethnic groups, tribes, castes, and religions. The castes and subcastes in each region relate to each other through a permanent hierarchical structure, with each caste having its own name, traditional occupation, rank, and distinctive subculture. Tribes usually do not have a caste hierarchy but often have their own internal hierarchical organization. The pastoral and foraging tribes are relatively egalitarian in their internal organization.

India is no stranger to ethnic conflict, especially religious wars. Nevertheless, in most parts of the country there has long been a local intercaste and intertribal economy that commonly is based on barter or the exchange of goods and services; since this system has satisfied economic necessities at least partially, ethnic conflict commonly has been dampened or kept under control because of the mutual benefits these economic arrangements provide.

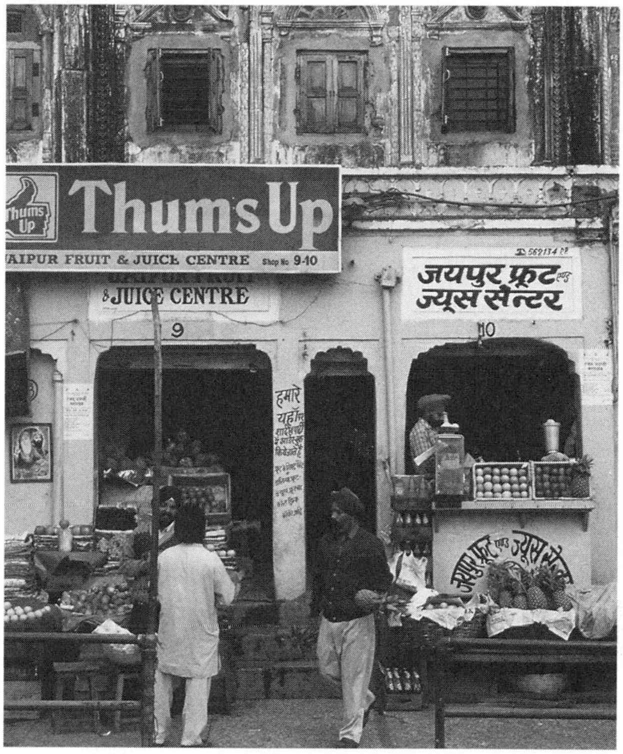

Indian shop workers in the main bazaar in Jaipur, Rajasthan.

Urbanism, Architecture, and the Use of Space

In the Indus civilization of 2700 to 1500 B.C.E., India developed one of the earliest urban societies in the world, along with an extensive trading economy to support it.

The walled citadels in some early cities developed into elaborate palisades, walls, and moats to protect the multitude of Iron Age and medieval cities throughout much of the country. The towns and cities are of eight historic types: (1) ancient pilgrimage centers, such as Madurai; (2) local market towns, roughly one every 20 miles; (3) medieval fortified towns, such as Gwalior; (4) ancient and medieval seaports, such as Bharuch (Broach); (5) military cantonments first set up by the British, such as Pune; (6) modern administrative centers such as New Delhi; (7) new industrial centers, such as Jamshedpur; and (8) great modern metropoles such as Bombay (Mumbai) and Calcutta (Kolkata).

Architecture developed distinct regional styles that remain apparent. These styles reflect the relative influence of the medieval Tamil kingdoms, Persian and Turkic invaders in the north, Portuguese and British Christianity, and all the distinctive features of the religious monuments of Jainism, Buddhism, Islam, and medieval Hinduism.

The landscape is dotted with over half a million villages, and each region has distinctive forms of domestic architecture and village layout. Holy places of the various religions are commonly within villages and towns, but the numerous pilgrimage sites are not necessarily located there.

Food and Economy

Food in Daily Life. About half the people eat rice as their staple, while the remainder subsist on wheat, barley, maize, and millet. There are thus major geographic differences in diet. Just as fundamental is the division between those who eat meat and those who are vegetarian. Muslims, Jews, Sikhs, and Christians all eat meat, with the important proviso that the first three groups do not consume pork. Lower-caste Hindus eat any meat except beef, whereas members of the higher castes and all Jains are normally vegetarian, with most even avoiding eggs.

Food Customs at Ceremonial Occasions. Every caste, tribe, town, village, and religion has a panoply of traditional ceremonies that are observed with enthusiasm and wide participation. Most of these ceremonies have a religious basis, and the majority are linked with the deities of Hinduism.

Basic Economy. With a large proportion of the population being located in rural areas (73 percent), farming is the largest source of employment; for hundreds of millions of people, this means subsistence farming on tiny plots of land, whether owned or rented. In most parts of the country, some farmers produce cash crops for sale in urban markets, and in some areas, plantation crops such as tea, coffee, cardamom, and rubber are of great economic importance because they bring in foreign money.

In 1996, the gross domestic product (GDP) per capita was $380, and the GDP growth rate was almost 6 percent from 1990 to 1996. In that period, the average annual inflation was 9 percent. In 1994, national debt was 27 percent of GDP. Over the past half century the economy has been expanding slowly but at a steady rate on the basis of a wide range of industries, including mining operations.

Major cities such as Bombay are considered residential creations of British administrators.

The United States has been the principal export market in recent years, receiving 17 percent of exports in 1995 and 1996. Clothing, tea, and computer software are three major categories of exports to the United States.

Land Tenure and Property. In an economy based on agriculture, the ownership of land is the key to survival and power. In most parts of the country, the majority of the acreage is owned by a politically dominant caste that is likely to be a middle-ranking one, not a Brahmin one. However, the various regions still have different traditions of land tenure and associated systems of land taxation.

India has only recently seen the last of the rural serfs who for centuries supplied much of the basic farm labor in some parts of the country. There are still numberless landless wage laborers, tenant farmers, and landlords who rent out their extensive lands, and rich peasants who work their own holdings.

Commercial Activities. India has had many traders, transport agents, importers, and exporters since the days of the Indus civilization four thousand years ago. Market places have existed since that time, and coinage has been in circulation among urban people for 2500 years.

In modern times, an expanding investment scene, combined with continuing inflation, has formed the background to an extensive import and export trade. The major industries continue to be tourism, clothing, tea, coffee, cotton, and the production of raw materials; in the last few years, there has been a surge in the importance of the computer software industry. Russia, the United States, Germany, and Great Britain are among the major importers of Indian products.

Major Industries. The modern infrastructure was created by the British administration in the nineteenth and early twentieth centuries. The country still relies on a vast network of railroad track, some of it electrified. Railroads are a government monopoly. Roadways, many of them unsurfaced, total about 1.25 million miles. The first air service, for postal delivery, grew into Air India which, along with Indian Airlines, the internal system, was nationalized in 1953. In the 1980s a number of private airlines developed within the country, while international connections are provided by a multitude of foreign companies as well as Air India.

International Trade. The major trading partners are Russia, the United States, the United Kingdom, and Germany. Political animosities have long ensured that trade with neighboring South Asian countries remains minimal, although there is now considerable transborder trade with Nepal, Sri Lanka, Bangladesh, and Bhutan.

Division of Labor. The division of work is based on gender. Age also separates out the very old and the very young as people unable to perform the heaviest tasks. Those jobs are done by millions of adult men and women who have nothing to offer but their muscles. Beyond these fundamental divisions, India is unique in having the caste system as the ancient and most basic principle of organization of the society. Each of many hundreds of castes traditionally had one occupation that was its specialty and usually its local monopoly. Only farming and the renouncer's life were open to all.

Social Stratification

Classes and Castes. The caste system is more elaborate than that in any of the other Hindu or Buddhist countries. Society is so fragmented into castes that there can be twenty or thirty distinct castes within a village.

This society has a hierarchy of endogamous, birth-ascribed groups, each of which traditionally is characterized by one distinctive occupation and had its own level of social status. Because an individual cannot change his or her caste affiliation, every family belongs in its entirety and forever to only one named caste, and so each caste has developed a distinctive subculture that is handed down from generation to generation.

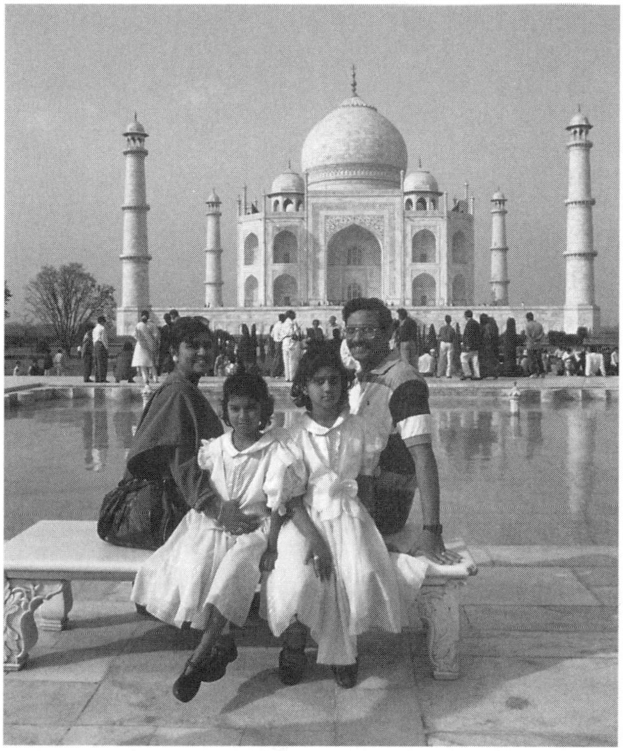

A family at the Taj Mahal, one of the most famous buildings in the world.

Hindu religious theory justifies the division of society into castes, with the unavoidable differences in status and the differential access to power each one has. Hindus usually believe that a soul can have multiple reincarnations and that after the death of the body a soul will be reassigned to another newborn human body or even to an animal one. This reassignment could be to one of a higher caste if the person did good deeds in the previous life or to a lower-status body if the person did bad deeds.

The highest category of castes are those people called *Brahmins* in the Hindu system; they were traditionally priests and intellectuals. Below them in rank were castes called *Ksatriya*, including especially warriors and rulers. Third in rank were the *Vaisyas*, castes concerned with trading and land ownership. The fourth-ranking category were the *Sudras*, primarily farmers. Below these four categories and hardly recognized in the ancient and traditional model, were many castes treated as "untouchable" and traditionally called *Pancama*. Outside the system altogether were several hundred tribes, with highly varied cultural and subsistence patterns. The whole system was marked not just by extreme differences in status and power but by relative degrees of spiritual purity or pollution.

A curious feature of the caste system is that despite its origins in the Hindu theory of fate and reincarnation, caste organization is found among Indian Muslims, Jews, and Christians in modern times. In the Buddhist lands of Korea, Japan, and Tibet, there are rudimentary caste systems, their existence signaled especially by the presence of untouchable social categories.

The major cities in modern times—Bombay (Mumbai), Madras (Chennai), Calcutta (Kolkata), New Delhi, and Bangalore—were essentially residential creations of the British administrators. Architecturally, professionally, and in other ways, they are therefore the most Westernized cities in India today. In these cities and their suburbs, there is now a developed class system overlying and in many respects displacing the more traditional caste system. As a consequence, there are many modern cases of intercaste marriage in all the cities, although this practice remains almost unthinkable to the great majority of Indians.

Symbols of Stratification. There are many symbols of class differentiation because each caste tends to have its own persisting subculture. People's location in this stratification system thus can be gauged accurately according to the way they dress, their personal names, the way they speak a local dialect, the deities they worship, who they are willing to eat with publicly, the location of their housing, and especially their occupations. The combination of all these subcultural features can be a sure sign of where individuals and their families are situated in the caste hierarchy.

Political Life

Government. The national system of government is a liberal democratic federal republic, making India the largest democracy in the world. The country is divided for administrative purposes into twenty-eight linguistically-based states, plus a further seven small "Union Territories" administered directly by the central government in New Delhi, the national capital.

Leadership and Political Officials. The central parliament in New Delhi consists of the House of the People (*Lok Sabha*) and the Council of States (*Rajya Sabha*).

The states all have legislative assemblies (*Vidhan sabha*) and legislative councils (*Vidhan parishad*). Members of parliament and the state legislatures are selected in democratic elections. An exception to this procedure is that the Lok Sabha has two seats reserved for Anglo-Indian members, and of the 4,072 seats in all the state legislative assemblies, 557 have been reserved for candidates from the Scheduled Castes and a further 527 for candidates from the Scheduled Tribes. These provisions have ensured that the main minority populations have legislative representation and an interest in pursuing the electoral process. The Lok Sabha recently had sitting members from twenty one different parties. State legislatures also host a multiplicity of political parties.

The head of state is the president, and there is also a vice-president, neither elected by general franchise but instead by an electoral college. The president is aided by a council of ministers, and appoints the prime minister of each government. This prime minister is the leader of the dominant party or of a coalition of prominent parties and has been elected as a member of parliament. The president has the power to dissolve a government and order new elections or to dismiss a problematic state government and declare "president's rule."

Social Problems and Control. Indians have lived under the rule of law since ancient times. Hindu law was codified over two thousand years ago in the books called *Dharmasastras*. There is now one legal hierarchy throughout the land, with the Supreme Court at its head. Legal procedure is based on the Indian Penal Code (IPC) which was drafted in the mid-nineteenth century, and the Code of Criminal Procedure of 1973. The constitution promulgated in 1950 went further than any other South Asian country has gone in curtailing the influence of traditional legal systems that in practice applied only to the followers of a particular religion, whether Hindu, Buddhist, Muslim, Christian, Jewish, or Parsi.

The huge legal profession helps push cases slowly through the complex apparatus of magistrates' and higher-level courts, sometimes creating the impression that litigation is a national sport. While fines and imprisonment are the most common punishments, the Supreme Court has upheld the legality of the death penalty.

Military Activity. Five wars with Pakistan and one with China since independence have provided training for several generations of soldiers. India thus has a strong program of national defense, with four national services: the army, navy, air force, and coast guard (since 1978). In 1996, these branches

An Indian shopkeeper with his wares. Small shops still make up a big part of the Indian economy.

had 1,145,000 personnel. In 1998, the nation exploded a nuclear bomb as a test.

Social Welfare and Change Programs

Traditionally the family was responsible for the care of the poor, incapacitated, elderly, and very young. For rural populations this is still largely true. In recent decades, underfunded state governments, often with international help, have tried to create more jobs for the poor as a direct way of helping them. Beyond this, welfare organizations have helped, but they are largely private and often religious foundations with relatively little financing. The population in need of social welfare support is too vast for the facilities that are available, and these people are disproportionately concentrated in the cities.

Nongovernmental Organizations and Other Associations

There are numerous nongovernmental organizations of social, political, religious, educational, or sporting natures. Every village, town, and caste and most temples have at least one associate formal organization and sometimes dozens. Beyond some attempts at registration, for example, of cooperative societies and charitable endowments, the government does not attempt to control organizations.

Gender Roles and Statuses

Division of Labor by Gender. Gender provides the basis for a fundamental division of the work force, with perhaps only the lowest day-labor jobs and the most modern professions being regularly staffed by people of both genders.

The Relative Status of Women and Men. "Patriarchal" is the word most commonly used to describe the traditional Indian family and the gender relationships within it. This is true in all family systems except the defunct matrilineal system of the Nayar castes in Kerala. Within all branches of Hinduism, priests can only be male, though they may be boys. In Islam, the leaders of a prayer group are males. In Zoroastrianism and Roman Catholicism, only men can function as priests.

It is said that a woman must first obey her father, then her husband, and then her son; this seems to be the normal pattern as she goes through life. The opinion of the male head of household is especially important in the arrangement of marriages, because in most religious communities these are effectively marriages between two families. At such times, romantic preferences get little consideration. Since it is the male head who typically controls the family's finances, it is he who pays or receives a dowry at the time of a child's marriage. Although older women may be very influential behind the scenes, they wield little legal authority in property and marriage matters.

Marriage, Family, and Kinship

Marriage. Although the different regions and religions have considerable variety in marital arrangements, the arranged marriage is a traditional feature of virtually every community; today, except among the urban middle classes, it still is widely practiced. Marriages that are not arranged by the couple's parents, often termed "love marriages," are looked down on as impulsive acts of passion. The more usual style of marriage unites a couple who have barely met beforehand. It is through the institution of arranged marriage and its correlate, caste endogamy, that parents exercise control not only over their adult children but also over the social structure and the caste system.

Generally, the country has two main types of marriage: a north Indian one in which the man must not marry a closely related cousin and a south Indian one in which a cross-cousin, whether the mother's brother's daughter or the father's sister's daughter, is the ideal spouse. Many south Indian castes also permit uncle-niece marriage. Maharashtra state has intermediate forms.

Domestic Unit. The residential unit is normally the household, but this unit varies widely in its structure, from housing a large extended family of three or four generations to a household made up of a lone widow. In large buildings with many rooms, it is common to find a number of discrete households, especially in cities; each of these households may be distinguished by its use of a common cooking hearth and perhaps by depending on a common source of funds. In crowded urban conditions, each room may constitute a separate household, as may each small grass hut in a roadside encampment.

Inheritance. The written will is largely unknown except in modern urban areas. The tradition has always been that sons inherit property and status from their fathers and that daughters can hope to receive a dowry at the time of their marriage. However, there is much local and caste variation in precisely who inherits. In some groups, the oldest son inherits everything and then makes an accommodation for his younger brother and provides his sisters' dowries. In other groups, the brothers may inherit equal shares, except that the youngest brother inherits the house. Other patterns occur, but in general, although modern law states that daughters should inherit equally with their brothers, this almost never happens except in Islamic families.

Kin Groups. The largest kin-based group is the caste, of which there are several thousand. A caste is an endogamous unit with its own traditional occupation and rank. It is made up of a number of clans, which are also kin-based but are exogamous and often intermarrying units. The clan in turn is made up of smaller and more localized groups called lineages, which are also exogamous. A caste may include hundreds of lineages of varying size and status, depending on how many generations of depth they claim. Major lineages commonly are composed of minor lineages, but the smallest are so localized that they are made up of a number of neighboring and closely related extended or nuclear families. Thus, a caste is endogamous, but all the kin-based units below it are exogamous and follow rigid rules about which clans or lineages are allowed to intermarry.

Socialization

Infant Care. Infant care is almost completely the responsibility of mothers, older siblings, and grandmothers. When the mother works in the fields or a factory, a grandmother commonly is the chief provider of daytime care for an infant. After about the age of two, older sisters spend much of their time in this activity.

Child Rearing and Education. In 1995, the government spent over 2 percent of its resources on education. Although the government's goal of eradicating illiteracy among people age fifteen to thirty five by the year 2000 has not been achieved, there has been a steady decrease in illiterary since the late nineteenth century. Among people above age six in 1991, 52 percent were literate, a 9 percent increase from 1981. Kerala state has the highest rates of literacy. However, nationally there remains a great sexual disparity: While 64 percent of men were literate in 1991, only 39 percent of women were. The central government is more interested in military power than in literacy, and millions of rural parents, especially Muslims, feel that the schooling of girls is a waste of time and money. Only the establishment of sixteen as the minimum legal age for marriage has made it possible for many girls to get their parents' reluctant permission to attend school.

While in earlier times missionary-run schools were important, especially in rural areas, in the last century local and state schools have educated the vast majority of students. Over the last half century universal school attendance for eight years, equal opportunities for female students, relevant vocational training, and improvement in the quality of classes and textbooks have been national goals, with an emphasis on free and compulsory education for everybody from ages six to fourteen. However, there has been a recent growth of privately run schools, many associated with religious organizations, which tend to do a better job but commonly charge fees.

Higher Education. There were 166 universities in 1996, including thirteen central universities which are the oldest, best known, and best funded. The rest are run by state governments or religious foundations. Funding, hiring professors, and setting educational standards in all universities are centralized through the University Grants Commission, which was established in 1956. About a hundred colleges throughout the country have an autonomous status, but others are branches of major universities within their states. In 1996 there were 6.4 million university students enrolled throughout the country, of whom 5.7 million were undergraduates and 2.2 million were women. There are 418 institutions that grant degrees in engineering and technology and1,029 that award diplomas.

Adult education programs combat illiteracy, lack of knowledge about family planning, and inadequate understanding of new farming techniques. Such programs tend to be more accessible in urban areas. A major hurdle has been the language of university instruction. The central universities generally teach in English and produce graduates with internationally acceptable credentials, but most of the smaller universities teach in the local (state) language so that their students' skills are not easily transferable even to other parts of the country. The opportunities for graduate study overseas are much reduced for this category of students, and even the acquisition of up-to-date textbooks can be a problem.

Etiquette

Indians are usually very hospitable even when poor and go to considerable lengths to make a visitor feel comfortable. Women normally adopt a deferential attitude toward men, especially to their husbands and fathers-in-law. All the people tend to show deference to religious figures and government officials.

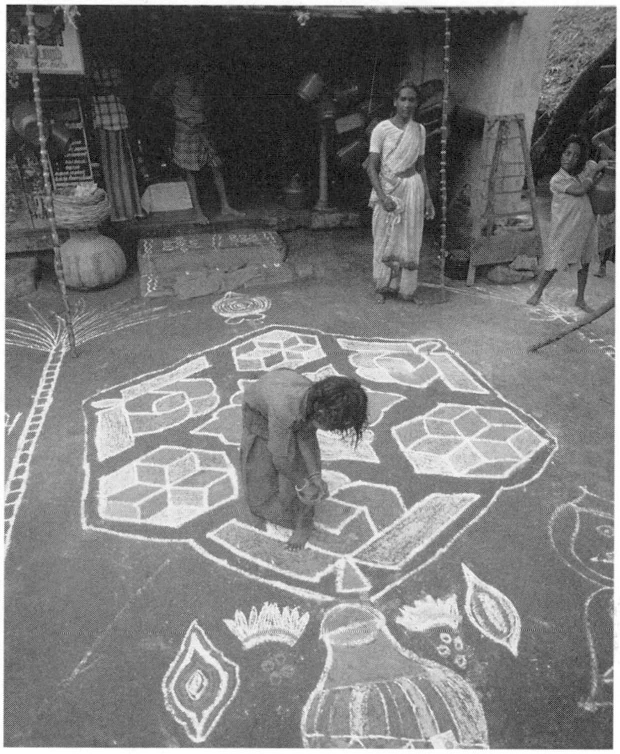

A woman decorates the streets with vibrantly colored rice powder paintings during a festival in Madurai, India.

Religion

Religious Beliefs. In the 1991 census, 82 percent of the population was enumerated as Hindu. However, 12 percent of Indians are Muslim, a fact that makes this one of the largest Islamic nations in the world. The next largest religious category is Christians, who make up only over 2 percent of the population and are closely followed in number by Sikhs. The only other groups of numerical significance are the Buddhists (less than 1 percent) and the Jains (less than half a percent).

Rituals and Holy Places. The thousands of rituals and millions of shrines, temples, and other holy places of many faiths defy categorization here. For Hindus, large pilgrimage temples are the holiest centers, whereas for Muslims the tombs of saints (*pir*) are the most important. For Buddhists, many of them overseas visitors, the sites associated with the Buddha are crucial.

Death and the Afterlife. While Muslims, Jews, and Christians pray that their individual souls will go to a paradise after death, Hindu ideas about the afterlife are very different. Muslims, Jews, and Christians bury their dead in cemeteries, as do most Zoroastrians today. However, Zoroastrians are

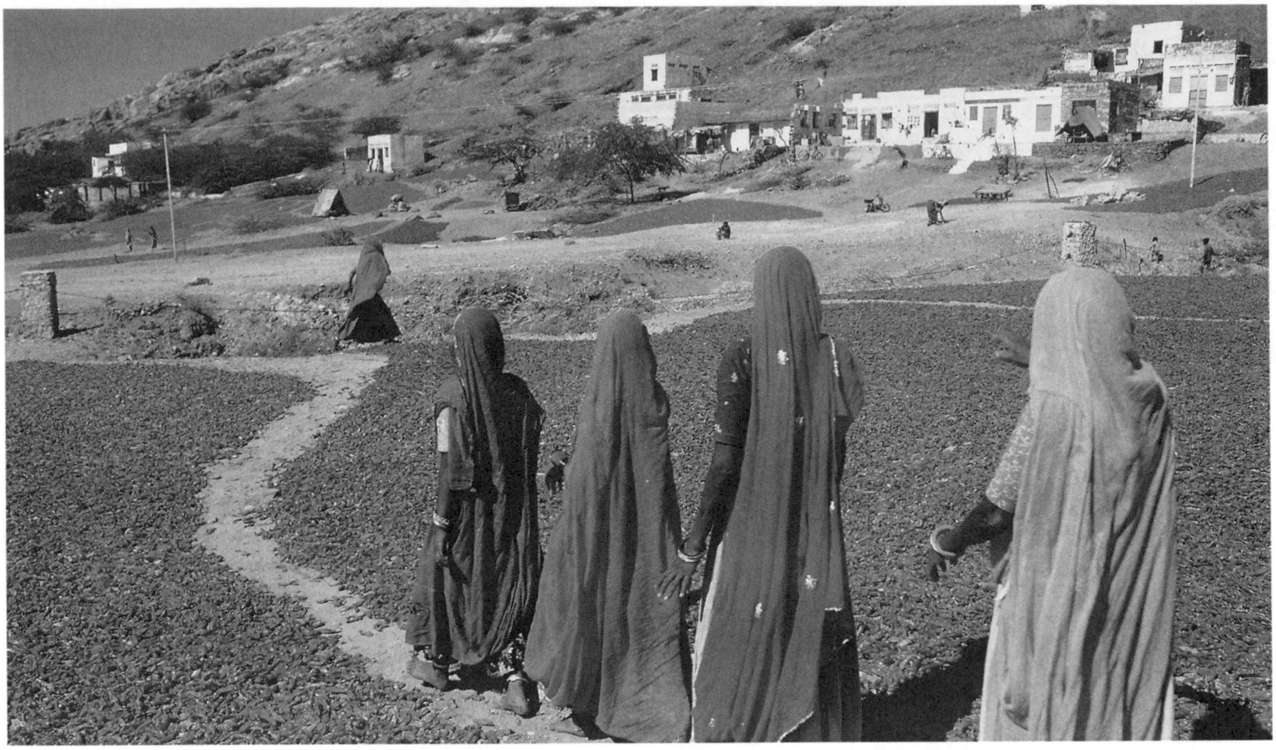

Women walk on a trail through drying chilies in the Bundi District of Rajasthan.

noted for their Towers of Silence in Bombay and a few other cities: stone structures where corpses are exposed to the air and particularly to the vultures that congregate there.

Most Hindu communities have a fundamental belief in reincarnation. The basic idea is that one's soul can be reincarnated for an unknown number of rebirths and that what the soul is to be reincarnated into depends on the balance of one's sins and good deeds in past lives. This belief provides the justification for the inequities of the caste system: One is born into a particular caste, whether high or low, as a result of the accumulated virtues or sins of one's soul in a previous life. One can never hope to move out of one's caste in this life but may do so in the next reincarnation. Particularly evil individuals may be reincarnated as animals.

Hindus normally cremate the dead on a pile of logs, but the very poor may resort to burial. Extremely saintly figures may be buried in a sitting position, as are members of the Lingayat sect.

Medicine and Health Care

India has a tradition of medical healing, teaching, and research that goes back more than two thousand years to the two basic medical treatises written by Charaka and Sushruta. Today the country has four major medical systems as well as dozens of localized and tribal ones that depend on herbal treatments. The oldest of the four systems is still widely followed under the name of *Ayurveda*, meaning "science of long life". It is highly developed, with its own hospitals, clinics, pharmaceutical factories, and medical textbooks. It depends primarily on non invasive herbal treatments. The diagnosis and treatment emphasize a holistic approach. *Sidda* is a distinct tradition that developed in south India and follows principles of physiology close to those of Ayurveda. Diagnosis depends on a careful reading of the pulse. Treatment is mostly herbal and psychological. A third medical tradition is called *Unani.* This system came to India with Muslim travelers and was developed under the patronage of the Mughals. It emphasizes holistic diagnosis and treatment, but the theory of human physiology is distinct. All three of these systems attribute disease to an imbalance between underlying constituents. The fourth and most widely favored system is biomedicine, or scientific medicine. It has been used in the cities for three centuries and is practiced in the best hospitals and training colleges. India has about 140 medical colleges.

Public health is a major concern of every state government because of the continuing incidence of epidemic diseases, high rates of infant mortality, and the need for family planning (usually sterilization) to control the growth of the population.

Secular Celebrations

Public holidays in most states include 1 January (Gregorian New Year), 26 January (Republic Day, when the constitution was adopted), 1 May (International Labor Day), 30 June, and 15 August (Independence Day), 2 October (Gandhi's birthday), 25 December (Christmas), and 31 December (New Year's Eve). Parsi New Year and Telugu New Year, both locally celebrated, fall at different times.

The Arts and Humanities

Support for the Arts. Historically, the arts flourished under the support of two main categories of patron: the larger Hindu temples and the princely rulers of states both small and large. Over the last two centuries, the patronage of British residents and art collectors has become important. In independent India, a national art institute, the Lalit Kala Akademi, promotes the visual arts through lectures, prizes, exhibitions, and publications.

The government supports the Sahitya Akademi, which was set up in 1954 to promote excellence in literature; the National School of Drama (1959); and the Sangeet Natak Akademi (1953), which promotes dance.

Literature. India has some of the earliest literature in the world, beginning with Sanskrit, which may be the oldest literature in any Indo-European language. The *Rig Veda* is the oldest of the four *Vedas*, long religious texts composed in an early form of Sanskrit some time late in the second century B.C.E. It was followed by three other *Vedas*, all liturgical in character, and then by the principal *Upanishads* during the eighth through fifth centuries B.C.E.

The first significant secular document in Sanskrit was a sophisticated grammar that fixed the structure of the language, probably in the fourth century B.C.E. Then, during the reign of Chandragupta Maurya, the text of the great epic *Mahabharata*, the world's longest poem, was established around 300 B.C.E., although it continued to be developed until about 100 C.E. About 200 B.C.E. there emerged the second great Sanskrit epic, the *Ramayana*, which probably took on its final form four centuries later. Both epics incorporated material from extant folklore.

By roughly the third century B.C.E., the *Tripitaka* or *Three Baskets*, the Buddhist canon in the Pali language (closely related to Sanskrit), was fixed. It was soon to become the most influential body of literature in the eastern half of Asia and has remained so to the present day, especially in Chinese and Japanese translations.

In that era the image of the social structure of India was codified by two books. During the late fourth century Kautilya, who is said to have been the prime minister Chanakya, wrote the *Arthasastra*, a *Treatise on the Good*, which was rediscovered in 1909. Shortly thereafter came the compilation of Manu's *Laws (Manusmrti)*. This treatise on religious law and social obligation described in detail a society, possibly a utopian one, in which there were four caste blocks, the *varna*, each of which had its own occupation, status, and religious duties. This book continued to exercise an immeasurable influence on Indian society for the next two thousand years and the *varna model* is still a popular image of Hindu caste society.

Around 150 C.E., there began in south India the Tamil Sangam, an academy of poets and philosophers that lasted for decades. While its history is shrouded, it set the stage for an outpouring of medieval poetry in Tamil, a Dravidian language. Some of this work was devotional, but much was secular in its appeal, including the first known work of Indian women writers. The most famous example of this poetry was the *Purananuru*, an anthology of four hundred poems praising Tamil rulers. Equally important, the *Kural* was a collection of moral maxims compiled by Tiruvalluvar in perhaps the third and fourth centuries. It has been likened to a Tamil Koran. At about the same time, there was a flowering of Sanskrit drama in the northerly parts of India. In the fourth or fifth century lived the greatest Sanskrit poet, Kalidasa. The best known plays that have survived from this era are *Shakuntala* and *The Little Clay Cart*, the former written by Kalidasa and the latter a comedy also perhaps written by him.

During the Middle Ages, science and philosophy flourished in Sanskrit texts. Perhaps the best known, if the least scientific, work was the *Kama Sutra* or a treatise on love by Vatsyayana, who wrote it in a legal style of Sanskrit in about the third century. The Middle Ages witnessed an outpouring of religious and philosophical literature not just in Sanskrit, which was still the prime liturgical and scholarly language, but also in a number of regional languages. Logic, metaphysics, devotional poetry, and commentary developed over the centuries.

In the period 850–1330 there appeared an important new philosophical literature in Karnataka, beginning with the *Kavirajamarga*. This was Jain

A farmer leans under the burden of a harvest as it is carried to the top of a building in Zanskar Valley, Ladakh.

literature written in the medieval Kannada language. At the end of the twelfth century *Lilavati* was written by Nemichandra, the first novel in that language. It was followed by other allegorical novels, as well as Kesiraja's grammar of medieval Kannada.

Around 1020, another Dravidian literature, in Telugu, made its debut with the grammarian Nannaya Bhatta and the poet Nannichoda. At about that time the Malayalam language became differentiated from Tamil. A century later the oldest known manuscript was written in Bengali. In the twelfth and thirteenth centuries Mukundaraj became the first man to write poetry in Marathi.

Early in the fifteenth century two poets brought Bengali literature into prominence: Chandidas and Vidyapati, with the latter writing in Sanskrit as well as Bengali. Contemporary with them were two Telugu poets, Srinatha and Potana, as well as the best-loved Hindi poet, Kabir (1440–1518). Kabir wrote in a medieval regional language closely related to Sanskrit. Although Kabir was a low-caste Hindu, he drew inspiration from Sufism and criticized the caste system, ritualism, and idolatry. He was followed in 1540 by the first important Muslim poet of India, Mohamed of Jais who wrote the allegorical poem *Padmavat* in Hindi. Contemporary with Kabir was one of the greatest of woman poets, the Rajput Mirabai, who wrote in both Hindi and Gujarati. A century before her, Manichand had written an important historical novel in Gujarati.

In 1574 the Hindi version of the *Ramayana*, by Tulsidas, appeared it was to be a forerunner of numerous versions of the *Ramayana* in regional languages.

At that time there was a strong Persian cultural influence in some parts of the country. One ruler of the Muslim province of Golconda (later Hyderabad) was Mohammed Quli Qutub Shah, a poet who wrote in both Persian and Urdu, which was a new form of Hindi containing many Persian words and written in an Arabic script.

In 1604, the *Adi Granth*, the canonical text of the Sikh religion, was established in Punjabi. Thirty years later there appeared, also in northwestern India, a book in Urdu prose, the *Sab Ras* of Vajhi. In more southern parts of the subcontinent the middle of the seventeenth century also saw the writing of the Kannada poem *Rajasekhara*, by Sadakshara Deva, the works of the Gujarati storyteller Premanand (1636–1734), and the influential Marathi poems of Tukaram (1607–1649).

With the arrival of the printing press in south India, Tamil literature underwent a renaissance. Arunachala Kavirayar wrote *The Tragedy of Rama* in

India has the largest film industry in the world.

1728, and the Italian Jesuit Beschi wrote the Tamil poem *Tembavani* in 1724 under the pen name Viramamunivar (it was not published until 1853). Also of interest was the eighteenth century "Indian Pepys" Anandaranga Pillai, a Tamil living in the French colony of Pondicheåry. His lengthy diary has been published in Tamil, French, and English. Another outstanding Tamil poet and bard was Tyagaraja.

In the eighteenth century, there was a further flowering of Urdu poetry by Vali, Hatim, Sauda, Inch'a, and Nazir. By the time of Nazir, the British hegemony in India was well established, and along with it went the spread of regional printing presses, the opening of the first modern universities, and the increasing influence of European literary forms, especially in the English language. This influence is evident even in writers who published in their native languages. Bengal in particular experienced a great literary and intellectual renaissance in both English and Bengali, including the novels of Bankim Chandra Chatterji and India's first Nobel Prize Winner, the poet and dramatist Rabindranath Tagore. A parallel literary renaissance occurred in Hindi at the beginning of the twentieth century, with the first novels by Premchand. Tamil also began to produce novels with an English influence.

The twentieth century saw a continuation of this modernization, fueled by the ease of publication and the increasing size of the reading public. An unexpected development during that century was the emergence of numerous world-class and prize-winning novelists writing in English, and often not residing in India. Pre-eminent today are the London-based Salman Rushdie, from Bombay, and the Delhi-based Arundati Roy, from Kerala.

Graphic Arts. India has a multiplicity of visual arts extending back over four thousand years. Early painting has not survived, but urban architecture and some small sculptures have. Most of the thousands of stamp seals that have been found are masterpieces of glyphic art, showing the large animals of northwestern India in miniature relief.

The main visual arts arose in the context of religious worship. Sanskrit handbooks still survive stipulating the rules for the production of Hindu religious statues, temples, and paintings. Distinctive regional styles of temple architecture are a feature of the landscape and a clear marker of the presence of Islam, Sikhism, Jainism, Christianity, and Hinduism in each part of the country. Within the Hindu temples there is a great variety of images of the deities, some skilfully carved in stone, some cast in bronze or silver, and some modeled in terra-cotta or wood.

Painting was an ancient accomplishment, although the climate has not been conducive to preservation. One can still see second and third-century wall paintings and monumental Buddhist sculptures in caves in Ajanta (Madhya Pradesh).

Despite Islamic prohibitions on the representation of the human face, painting and drawing flourished under the Moghul emperors. Realistic portraits, historical scenes, and botanical and zoological subjects were evoked with a sensitive line and a subtle pallet of colors during that period.

Painting in oils dates back two centuries, to the time when the first European portrait painters began to work in India. Today there are many professional graphic artists, some inspired by old Indian traditions and some by modern abstract expressionism. Art schools, public exhibitions, and coffee-table books are the means of reaching their public today, while religious patronage has practically evaporated.

Performance Arts. India has the largest film industry in the world. In 1996, 683 feature films were certified by the Board of Censors. Although television came to even rural India more than twenty years ago, the cinema remains the major popular visual art form. In 1996, India had 12,623 cinemas, with an attendance of ninety to one hundred million weekly. Radios are widespread, primarily as a source of light music, but not as a major source of information.

The State of the Physical and Social Sciences

India has long had government-sponsored national research organizations for the sciences, including the Archaeological Survey of India (1861), the Botanical Survey of India (1890), the Census of India (1867), the Ethnological Survey of India (1901, later the Anthropological Survey of India, 1946), the Geological Survey of India (1851), the Indian Forestry Service (1865), the Indian Medical Service (1786), the Indian Council of Medical Research (1912), the Indian Meteorological Department (1875), the Linguistic Survey of India, and the Zoological Survey of India. The antecedent of all these institutions was the Survey of India (1832), which did the first scientific mapmaking of the subcontinent. There has been an annual Indian Science Congress, a national conference, which began as the Indian Association for the Cultivation of Science in 1876.

With independence, an overarching bureaucratic organization came into being, the Council of Scientific and Industrial Research, as well as an Atomic Energy Commission and the Tata Institute of Fundamental Research. To avoid centralization of these organizations in and around Delhi and Bombay, regional institutes of technology were set up in a number of large cities. The government also supports four national academies: the Indian National Science Academy in New Delhi, the Indian Academy of Sciences in Bangalore, the National Academy of Science in Allahabad, and the Indian Science Congress Association in Calcutta. Other centrally supported research councils include the Indian Council of Agricultural Research, the Indian Council of Historical Research, the Indian Council of Philosophical Research, the Indian Council of Social Sciences Research, and the National Council of Educational Research and Training.

Bibliography

Achaya, K. T. *Indian Food: A Historical Companion*, 1994.

Basham, A. L. *The Wonder That Was India*. Rev. ed., 1963.

———. *Cultural History of India*, 1975.

Berreman, Gerald D. *Caste and Other Inequities: Essays on Inequality*, 1979.

Bishop, Donald H., ed. *Indian Thought: An Introduction*, 1975.

Bonnefoy, Yves, and Wendy Doniger, eds. *Mythologies*, 1991.

Bose, Sugata, and Ayesha Jalal. *Modern South Asia: History, Culture, Political Economy*, 1998.

Burrow, Thomas, and Murray B. Emeneau. *A Dravidian Etymological Dictionary*, 2nd ed., 1984.

Council of Scientific and Industrial Research. *The Wealth of India: A Dictionary of Indian Raw Materials and Industrial Products*, 1948–1990.

Dumont, Louis. *Homo Hierarchicus: An Essay on the Caste System*, 1970.

Embree, Ainslie T., and Stephen Hay, eds. *Sources of Indian Tradition. 2nd ed.* 1970.

Farmer, B. H. *An Introduction to South Asia, 2nd ed.*, 1993.

Garrett, John. *A Classical Dictionary of India Illustrative of the Mythology, Philosophy, Literature, Antiquities, Arts, Manners, Customs, etc. of the Hindus*, 1973.

Gole, Susan. *Indian Maps and Plans from Earliest Times to the Advent of European Surveys*, 1989.

Government of India. *India 2000: A Reference Annual*, 2000.

Hawkins, R. E. *Encyclopedia of Indian Natural History*, 1986.

Hockings, Paul ed., *Encyclopedia of World Cultures. Vol. 3: South Asia*, 1992.

Hutton, John H. *Caste in India: Its Nature, Function, and Origins*, 1963.

Johnson, Gordon, et al. eds. *The New Cambridge History of India*, 1987.

Keay, John. *India Discovered: The Achievement of the British Raj*, 1981.

Kramrisch, Stella. *The Hindu Temple*, 1980.

Kulke, Hermann, and Dietmar Rothermund. *A History of India*, 1986.

Kumar, Dharma, Tapan Raychaudhuri, et al., eds. *The Cambridge Economic History of India*, 1982.

Majumdar, R. C., H. C. Raychaudhuri, and Kalikinkar Datta. *An Advanced History of India*, 1961.

——— et al., eds. *The History and Culture of the Indian People, 2nd ed.* 1970–1988.

Maloney, Clarence. *Peoples of South Asia*, 1980.

Mandelbaum, David G. *Society in India*, 1970.

Masica, Colin P. *Defining a Linguistic Area: South Asia*, 1976.

Mehra, Parshotam. *A Dictionary of Modern Indian History 1707–1947*, 1987.

Mitchell, George, and Philip Davies. *The Penguin Guide to the Monuments of India*, 1989.

Mode, Heinz, and Subodh Chandra. *Indian Folk Art*, 1985.

Muthiah, S., ed. *A Social and Economic Atlas of India*, 1986.

Queneau, Raymond, ed. *Histoire des Littératures: I. Littératures Anciennes, Orientales et Orales*, 1956.

Radhakrishnan, Sarvepalli, and Charles A. Moore, eds. *A Source Book in Indian Philosophy*, 1957.

Rapson, E.J., et al. eds. *The Cambridge History of India*, 1922–1947.

Robinson, Francis, ed. *The Cambridge Encyclopedia of India, Pakistan, Bangladesh, Sri Lanka, Nepal, Bhutan and the Maldives*, 1989.

Rowland, Benjamin. *The Art and Architecture of India, Buddhist /Hindu / Jain*, 3rd ed., 1967.

Schwartzberg, Joseph E., ed. *A Historical Atlas of South Asia*, 1969.

Sebeok, Thomas A., et al. eds. *Current Trends in Linguistics: Vol. 5. Linguistics in South Asia*, 1969.

Shapiro, Michael C., and Harold F. Schiffman. *Language and Society in South Asia*, 1981.

Sindh, R. D. *India: A Regional Geography*, 1971.

Sivaramamurti, Calambur. *The Art of India*, 1977.

Smith, Vincent A. *The Oxford History of India*, 1958.

Srinivas, M. N., M. S. A. Rao, and A. M. Shah, eds. *A Survey of Research in Sociology and Social Anthropology*, 1972–1974.

Stutley, Margaret, and James Stutley. *Harper's Dictionary of Hinduism: Its Mythology, Folklore, Philosophy, Literature, and History*, 1977.

Thapar, Romila, and Percival Spear. *A History of India*, 1965–1966.

Turner, Jane, ed. "Indian Subcontinent." In Jane Turner, ed., *The Dictionary of Art*, 1996.

Tyler, Stephen A. *India: An Anthropological Perspective*, 1973.

Watt, George. *The Commercial Products of India, Being an Abridgement of "The Dictionary of the Economic Products of India,"* 1966.

Williams, L. F. Rushbrook, ed. *A Handbook for Travellers in India, Pakistan, Nepal, Bangladesh & Sri Lanka (Ceylon), 22nd ed.*, 1975.

Yule, Henry, and A. C. Burnell. *Hobson-Jobson: A Glossary of Colloquial Anglo-Indian Words and Phrases, and of Kindred Terms, Etymological, Historical, Geographical, and Discursive*, rev. ed., 1968.

—PAUL HOCKINGS

INDONESIA

CULTURE NAME

Indonesian

ORIENTATION

Identification. The Republic of Indonesia, the world's fourth most populous nation, has 203 million people living on nearly one thousand permanently settled islands. Some two-to-three hundred ethnic groups with their own languages and dialects range in population from the Javanese (about 70 million) and Sundanese (about 30 million) on Java, to peoples numbering in the thousands on remote islands. The nature of Indonesian national culture is somewhat analogous to that of India—multicultural, rooted in older societies and interethnic relations, and developed in twentieth century nationalist struggles against a European imperialism that nonetheless forged that nation and many of its institutions. The national culture is most easily observed in cities but aspects of it now reach into the countryside as well. Indonesia's borders are those of the Netherlands East Indies, which was fully formed at the beginning of the twentieth century, though Dutch imperialism began early in the seventeenth century. Indonesian culture has historical roots, institutions, customs, values, and beliefs that many of its people share, but it is also a work in progress that is undergoing particular stresses at the beginning of the twenty-first century.

The name Indonesia, meaning Indian Islands, was coined by an Englishman, J. R. Logan, in Malaya in 1850. Derived from the Greek, *Indos* (India) and *nesos* (island), it has parallels in Melanesia, "black islands"; Micronesia, "small islands"; and Polynesia, "many islands." A German geographer, Adolf Bastian, used it in the title of his book, *Indonesien*, in 1884, and in 1928 nationalists adopted it as the name of their hoped-for nation.

Most islands are multiethnic, with large and small groups forming geographical enclaves. Towns within such enclaves include the dominant ethnic group and some members of immigrant groups. Large cities may consist of many ethnic groups; some cities have a dominant majority. Regions, such as West Sumatra or South Sulawesi, have developed over centuries through the interaction of geography (such as rivers, ports, plains, and mountains), historical interaction of peoples, and political-administrative policies. Some, such as North Sumatra, South Sulawesi, and East Java are ethnically mixed to varying degrees; others such as West Sumatra, Bali, and Aceh are more homogeneous. Some regions, such as South Sumatra, South Kalimantan, and South Sulawesi, share a long-term Malayo-Muslim coastal influence that gives them similar cultural features, from arts and dress to political and class stratification to religion. Upland or upriver peoples in these regions have different social, cultural, and religious orientations, but may feel themselves or be perforce a part of that region. Many such regions have become government provinces, as are the latter three above. Others, such as Bali, have not.

Location and Geography. Indonesia, the world's largest archipelago nation, is located astride the equator in the humid tropics and extends some 2,300 miles (3,700 kilometers) east-west, about the same as the contiguous United States. It is surrounded by oceans, seas, and straits except where it shares an island border with East Malaysia and Brunei on Borneo (Kalimantan); with Papua New Guinea on New Guinea; and with Timor Loro Sae on Timor. West Malaysia lies across the Straits of Malaka, the Philippines lies to the northeast, and Australia lies to the south.

The archipelago's location has played a profound role in economic, political, cultural, and religious developments there. For more than two thousand years, trading ships sailed between the great civilizations of India and China via the waters and islands of the Indies. The islands also supplied

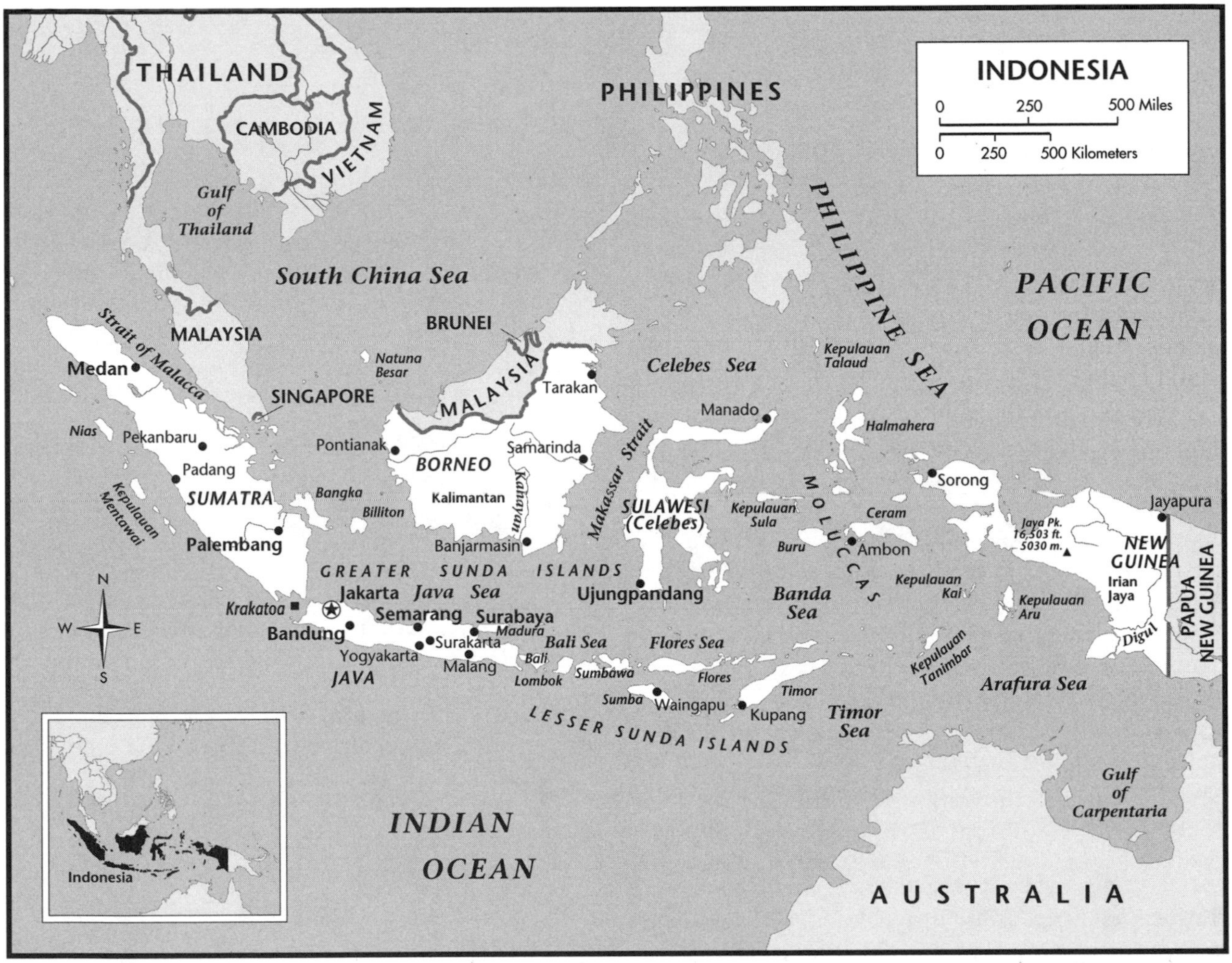

Indonesia

spices and forest products to that trade. The alternating east and west monsoon winds made the Indies a layover point for traders and others from diverse nations who brought their languages, ideas about political order, and their arts and religions. Small and then large kingdoms grew as a result of, and as part of, that great trade. Steamships altered some trade patterns, but the region's strategic location between East and South Asia and the Middle East remains.

Indonesia consists of all or part of some of the world's largest islands—Sumatra, Java, most of Kalimantan (Borneo), Sulawesi (Celebes), Halmahera, and the west half of New Guinea (Papua)—and numerous smaller islands, of which Bali (just east of Java) is best known. These islands plus some others have mountain peaks of 9,000 feet (2,700 meters) or more, and there are some four hundred volcanos, of which one hundred are active. Between 1973 and 1990, for example, there were twenty-nine recorded eruptions, some with tragic consequences. Volcanic lava and ash contributed to the rich soils of upland Sumatra and all of Java and Bali, which have nurtured rice cultivation for several thousand years.

The inner islands of Java, Madura, and Bali make up the geographical and population center of the archipelago. Java, one of the world's most densely settled places (with 2,108 people per square mile [814 per square kilometer] in 1990), occupies 78 percent of the nation's land area but accounts for about 60 percent of Indonesia's population. (About the size of New York state, Java's population is equivalent to 40 percent of that of the United States.) The outer islands, which form an arc west, north, and east of the inner ones, have about 90 percent of the land area of the country but only about 42 percent of the population. The cultures of the inner islands are more homogeneous, with only four major cultural groups: the Sundanese (in West

Java), the Javanese (in Central and East Java), the Madurese (on Madura and in East Java), and the Balinese (on Bali). The outer islands have hundreds of ethnolinguistic groups.

Forests of the inner islands, once plentiful, are now largely gone. Kalimantan, West Papua, and Sumatra still have rich jungles, though these are threatened by population expansion and exploitation by loggers for domestic timber use and export. Land beneath the jungles is not fertile. Some eastern islands, such as Sulawesi and the Lesser Sundas (the island chain east of Bali), also have lost forests.

Two types of agriculture are predominant in Indonesia: permanent irrigated rice farming (*sawah*) and rotating swidden or slash-and-burn (*ladang*) farming of rice, corn, and other crops. The former dominates Java, Bali, and the highlands all along the western coast of Sumatra; the latter is found in other parts of Sumatra and other outer islands, but not exclusively so. Fixed rain-fed fields of rice are prominent in Sulawesi and some other places. Many areas are rich in vegetables, tropical fruit, sago, and other cultivated or forest crops, and commercial plantations of coffee, tea, tobacco, coconuts, and sugar are found in both inner and outer islands. Plantation-grown products such as rubber, palm oil, and sisal are prominent in Sumatra, while coffee, sugar, and tea are prominent in Java. Spices such as cloves, nutmeg, and pepper are grown mainly in the outer islands, especially to the east. Maluku (formerly the Moluccas) gained its appellation the "Spice Islands" from the importance of trade in these items. Gold, tin, and nickel are mined in Sumatra, Bangka, Kalimantan, Sulawesi, and Papua for domestic and international markets, and oil and liquified natural gas (especially from Sumatra) are important exports. Numerous rivers flowing from mountainous or jungle interiors to coastal plains and ports have carried farm and forest products for centuries and have been channels for cultural communication.

Demography. Indonesia's population increased from 119,208,000 in 1971 to 147,500,000 in 1980, to 179,300,000 in 1990, and to 203,456,000 in 2000. In the meantime the fertility rate declined from 4.6 per thousand women to 3.3; the crude death rate fell at a rate of 2.3 percent per year; and infant mortality declined from 90.3 per thousand live births to 58. The fertility rate was projected to fall to 2.1 percent within another decade, but the total population was predicted to reach 253,700,000 by 2020. As of the middle of the twentieth century, Indonesia's population was largely rural, but at the beginning of the twenty-first century, about 20 percent live in towns and cities and three of five people farm.

Cities in both inner and outer islands have grown rapidly, and there are now twenty-six cities with populations over 200,000. As in many developing countries, Indonesia's population is still a young one. The above patterns are national, but there are ethnic and regional variations. Population has grown at different rates in different areas owing to such factors as economic conditions and standard of living, nutrition, availability and effectiveness of public health and family planning programs, and cultural values and practices.

Migration also plays a part in population fluctuations. Increased permanent or seasonal migration to cities accompanied economic development during the 1980s and 1990s, but there is also significant migration between rural areas as people leave places such as South Sulawesi for more productive work or farm opportunities in Central Sumatra or East Kalimantan.

Linguistic Affiliation. Nearly all of Indonesia's three hundred to four hundred languages are subgroups of the Austronesian family that extends from Malaysia through the Philippines, north to several hill peoples of Vietnam and Taiwan, and to Polynesia, including Hawaiian and Maori (of New Zealand) peoples. Indonesia's languages are not mutually intelligible, though some subgroups are more similar than others (as Europe's Romance languages are closer to each other than to Germanic ones, though both are of the Indo-European family). Some language subgroups have sub-subgroups, also not mutually intelligible, and many have local dialects. Two languages—one in north Halmahera, one in West Timor—are non-Austronesian and, like Basque in Europe, are not related to other known languages. Also, the very numerous languages of Papua are non-Austronesian.

Most people's first language is a local one. In 1923, however, the Malay language (now known as Bahasa Malaysia in Malaysia where it is the official language) was adopted as the national language at a congress of Indonesian nationalists, though only a small minority living in Sumatra along the Straits of Malaka spoke it as their native language. Nevertheless, it made sense for two reasons.

First, Malay had long been a commercial and governmental lingua franca that bound diverse peoples. Ethnically diverse traders and local peoples used Malay in ports and hinterlands in its grammatically simplified form known as "market Malay." Colonial

A row of tongkona houses in the Toraja village of Palawa. The buffalo horns tied to the pole supporting the massive gable of these houses are a sign of wealth and reputation.

governments in British Malaya and the Netherlands Indies used high Malay in official documents and negotiations and Christian missionaries first translated the Bible into that language.

Second, nationalists from various parts of the archipelago saw the value of a national language not associated with the largest group, the Javanese. Bahasa Indonesia is now the language of government, schools, courts, print and electronic media, literary arts and movies, and interethnic communication. It is increasingly important for young people, and has a youth slang. In homes, a native language of the family is often spoken, with Indonesian used outside the home in multiethnic areas. (In more monolingual areas of Java, Javanese also serves outside the home.) Native languages are not used for instruction beyond the third grade in some rural areas. Native language literatures are no longer found as they were in colonial times. Many people lament the weakening of native languages, which are rich links to indigenous cultures, and fear their loss to modernization, but little is done to maintain them. The old and small generation of well-educated Indonesians who spoke Dutch is passing away. Dutch is not known by most young and middle-aged people, including students and teachers of history who cannot read much of the documentary history of the archipelago. English is the official second language taught in schools and universities with varying degrees of success.

Symbolism. The national motto, *Bhinneka Tunggal Ika*, is an old Javanese expression usually translated as ''unity in diversity.'' The nation's official ideology, first formulated by President Sukarno in 1945, is the Pancasila, or Five Principles: belief in one supreme God; just and civilized humanitarianism; Indonesian unity; popular sovereignty governed by wise policies arrived at through deliberation and representation; and social justice for all Indonesian people. Indonesia was defined from the beginning as the inheritor of the Netherlands East Indies. Though West Papua remained under the Dutch until 1962, Indonesia conducted a successful international campaign to secure it. Indonesia's occupation of the former Portuguese East Timor in 1975, never recognized by the United Nations, conflicted with this founding notion of the nation. After two decades of bitter struggle there, Indonesia withdrew.

Since 1950 the national anthem and other songs have been sung by children throughout the country to begin the school day; by civil servants at flag-raising ceremonies; over the radio to begin and close broadcasting; in cinemas and on television;

and at national day celebrations. Radio and television, government owned and controlled for much of the second half of the twentieth century, produced nationalizing programs as diverse as Indonesian language lessons, regional and ethnic dances and songs, and plays on national themes. Officially recognized "national heroes" from diverse regions are honored in school texts, and biographies and with statues for their struggles against the Dutch; some regions monumentalize local heros of their own.

History and Ethnic Relations

Emergence of the Nation. Though the Republic of Indonesia is only fifty years old, Indonesian societies have a long history during which local and wider cultures were formed.

About 200 C.E., small states that were deeply influenced by Indian civilization began to develop in Southeast Asia, primarily at estuaries of major rivers. The next five hundred to one thousand years saw great states arise with magnificent architecture. Hinduism and Buddhism, writing systems, notions of divine kingship, and legal systems from India were adapted to local scenes. Sanskrit terms entered many of the languages of Indonesia. Hinduism influenced cultures throughout Southeast Asia, but only one people are Hindu, the Balinese.

Indianized states declined about 1400 C.E. with the arrival of Muslim traders and teachers from India, Yemen, and Persia, and then Europeans from Portugal, Spain, Holland, and Britain. All came to join the great trade with India and China. Over the next two centuries local princedoms traded, allied, and fought with Europeans, and the Dutch East India Company became a small state engaging in local battles and alliances to secure trade. The Dutch East India Company was powerful until 1799 when the company went bankrupt. In the nineteenth century the Dutch formed the Netherlands Indies government, which developed alliances with rulers in the archipelago. Only at the beginning of the twentieth century did the Netherlands Indies government extend its authority by military means to all of present Indonesia.

Sporadic nineteenth century revolts against Dutch practices occurred mainly in Java, but it was in the early twentieth century that Indonesian intellectual and religious leaders began to seek national independence. In 1942 the Japanese occupied the Indies, defeating the colonial army and imprisoning the Dutch under harsh conditions.

On 17 August 1945, following Japan's defeat in World War II, Indonesian nationalists led by Sukarno and Mohammad Hatta declared Indonesian independence. The Dutch did not accept and for five years fought the new republic, mainly in Java. Indonesian independence was established in 1950.

National Identity. Indonesia's size and ethnic diversity has made national identity problematic and debated. Identity is defined at many levels: by Indonesian citizenship; by recognition of the flag, national anthem, and certain other songs; by recognition of national holidays; and by education about Indonesia's history and the Five Principles on which the nation is based. Much of this is instilled through the schools and the media, both of which have been closely regulated by the government during most of the years of independence. The nation's history has been focused upon resistance to colonialism and communism by national heroes and leaders who are enshrined in street names. Glories of past civilizations are recognized, though archaeological remains are mainly of Javanese principalities.

Ethnic Relations. Ethnic relations in the archipelago have long been a concern. Indonesian leaders recognized the possibility of ethnic and regional separatism from the beginning of the republic. War was waged by the central government against separatism in Aceh, other parts of Sumatra, and Sulawesi in the 1950s and early 1960s, and the nation was held together by military force.

The relationships between native Indonesians and overseas Chinese have been greatly influenced by Dutch and Indonesian government policies. The Chinese number about four to six million, or 3 percent of the population, but are said to control as much as 60 percent of the nation's wealth. The Chinese traded and resided in the islands for centuries, but in the nineteenth century the Dutch brought in many more of them to work on plantations or in mines. The Dutch also established a social, economic, and legal stratification system that separated Europeans, foreign Asiatics and Indo-Europeans, and Native Indonesians, partly to protect native Indonesians so that their land could not be lost to outsiders. The Chinese had little incentive to assimilate to local societies, which in turn had no interest in accepting them.

Even naturalized Chinese citizens faced restrictive regulations, despite cozy business relationships between Chinese leaders and Indonesian officers and bureaucrats. Periodic violence directed toward Chinese persons and property also occurred. In the colonial social system, mixed marriages between

Chinese men and indigenous women produced half-castes (*peranakan*), who had their own organizations, dress, and art forms, and even newspapers. The same was true for people of mixed Indonesian-European descent (called Indos, for short).

Ethnolinguistic groups reside mainly in defined areas where most people share much of the same culture and language, especially in rural areas. Exceptions are found along borders between groups, in places where other groups have moved in voluntarily or as part of transmigration programs, and in cities. Such areas are few in Java, for example, but more common in parts of Sumatra.

Religious and ethnic differences may be related. Indonesia has the largest Muslim population of any country in the world, and many ethnic groups are exclusively Muslim. Dutch policy allowed proselytization by Protestants and Catholics among separate groups who followed traditional religions; thus today many ethnic groups are exclusively Protestant or Roman Catholic. They are heavily represented among upriver or upland peoples in North Sumatra, Kalimantan, Sulawesi, Maluku, and the eastern Lesser Sundas, though many Christians are also found in Java and among the Chinese. Tensions arise when groups of one religion migrate to a place with a different established religion. Political and economic power becomes linked to both ethnicity and religion as groups favor their own kinsmen and ethnic mates for jobs and other benefits.

Urbanism, Architecture, and the Use of Space

Javanese princes long used monuments and architecture to magnify their glory, provide a physical focus for their earthly kingdoms, and link themselves to the supernatural. In the seventeenth through nineteenth centuries the Dutch reinforced the position of indigenous princes through whom they ruled by building them stately palaces. Palace architecture over time combined Hindu, Muslim, indigenous, and European elements and symbols in varying degrees depending upon the local situation, which can still be seen in palaces at Yogyakarta and Surakarta in Java or in Medan, North Sumatra.

Dutch colonial architecture combined Roman imperial elements with adaptations to tropical weather and indigenous architecture. The Dutch fort and early buildings of Jakarta have been restored. Under President Sukarno a series of statues were built around Jakarta, mainly glorifying the people; later, the National Monument, the Liberation of West Irian (Papua) Monument, and the great Istiqlal Mosque were erected to express the link to a Hindu past, the culmination of Indonesia's independence, and the place of Islam in the nation. Statues to national heroes are found in regional cities.

Residential architecture for different urban socioeconomic groups was built on models developed by the colonial government and used throughout the Indies. It combined Dutch elements (high-pitched tile roofs) with porches, open kitchens, and servants quarters suited to the climate and social system. Wood predominated in early urban architecture, but stone became dominant by the twentieth century. Older residential areas in Jakarta, such as Menteng near Hotel Indonesia, reflect urban architecture that developed in the 1920s and 1930s. After 1950, new residential areas continued to develop to the south of the city, many with elaborate homes and shopping centers.

The majority of people in many cities live in small stone and wood or bamboo homes in crowded urban villages or compounds with poor access to clean water and adequate waste disposal. Houses are often tightly squeezed together, particularly in Java's large cities. Cities that have less pressure from rural migrants, such as Padang in West Sumatra and Manado in North Sulawesi, have been able to better manage their growth.

Traditional houses, which are built in a single style according to customary canons of particular ethnic groups, have been markers of ethnicity. Such houses exist in varying degrees of purity in rural areas, and some aspects of them are used in such urban architecture as government buildings, banks, markets and homes.

Traditional houses in many rural villages are declining in numbers. The Dutch and Indonesian governments encouraged people to build "modern" houses, rectangular structures with windows. In some rural areas, however, such as West Sumatra, restored or new traditional houses are built by successful urban migrants to display their success. In other rural areas people display status by building modern houses of stone and tile, with precious glass windows. In the cities, old colonial homes are renovated by prosperous owners who put newer contemporary-style fronts on the houses. The roman columns favored in Dutch public buildings are now popular for private homes.

Food and Economy

Food in Daily Life. Indonesian cuisine reflects regional, ethnic, Chinese, Middle Eastern, Indian, and Western influences, and daily food quality, quan-

Women carry towering baskets of fruit on their heads for a temple festival in Bali.

tity, and diversity vary greatly by socioeconomic class, season, and ecological conditions. Rice is a staple element in most regional cooking and the center of general Indonesian cuisine. (Government employees receive monthly rice rations in addition to salaries.) Side dishes of meat, fish, eggs, and vegetables and a variety of condiments and sauces using chili peppers and other spices accompany rice. The cuisine of Java and Bali has the greatest variety, while that of the Batak has much less, even in affluent homes, and is marked by more rice and fewer side dishes. And rice is not the staple everywhere: in Maluku and parts of Sulawesi it is sago, and in West Timor it is maize (corn), with rice consumed only for ceremonial occasions. Among the Rotinese, palm sugar is fundamental to the diet.

Indonesia is an island nation, but fish plays a relatively small part in the diets of the many people who live in the mountainous interiors, though improved transportation makes more salted fish available to them. Refrigeration is still rare, daily markets predominate, and the availability of food may depend primarily upon local produce. Indonesia is rich in tropical fruit, but many areas have few fruit trees and little capacity for timely transportation of fruit. Cities provide the greatest variety of food and types of markets, including modern supermarkets; rural areas much less so. In cities, prosperous people have access to great variety while the poor have very limited diets, with rice predominant and meat uncommon. Some poor rural regions experience what people call "ordinary hunger" each year before the corn and rice harvest.

Food Customs at Ceremonial Occasions. The most striking ceremonial occasion is the Muslim month of fasting, Ramadan. Even less-observant Muslims fast seriously from sunup to sundown despite the tropical heat. Each night during Ramadan, fine celebratory meals are held. The month ends with Idul Fitri, a national holiday when family, friends, neighbors, and work associates visit each other's homes to share food treats (including visits by non-Muslims to Muslim homes).

In traditional ritual, special food is served to the spirits or the deceased and eaten by the participants. The ubiquitous Javanese ritual, *selamatan,* is marked by a meal between the celebrants and is held at all sorts of events, from life-cycle rituals to the blessing of new things entering a village. Life-cycle events, particularly marriages and funerals, are the main occasions for ceremonies in both rural and urban areas, and each has religious and secular aspects. Elaborate food service and symbolism are features of such events, but the content varies greatly in different ethnic groups. Among the Meto of

Timor, for example, such events must have meat and rice (*sisi-maka'*), with men cooking the former and women the latter. Elaborate funerals involve drinking a mixture of pork fat and blood that is not part of the daily diet and that may be unappetizing to many participants who nonetheless follow tradition. At such events, Muslim guests are fed at separate kitchens and tables.

In most parts of Indonesia the ability to serve an elaborate meal to many guests is a mark of hospitality, capability, resources, and status of family or clan whether for a highland Toraja buffalo sacrifice at a funeral or for a Javanese marriage reception in a five-star hotel in Jakarta. Among some peoples, such as the Batak and Toraja, portions of animals slaughtered for such events are important gifts for those who attend, and the part of the animal that is selected symbolically marks the status of the recipient.

Basic Economy. About 60 percent of the population are farmers who produce subsistence and market-oriented crops such as rice, vegetables, fruit, tea, coffee, sugar, and spices. Large plantations are devoted to oil palm, rubber, sugar, and sisel for domestic use and export, though in some areas rubber trees are owned and tapped by farmers. Common farm animals are cattle, water buffalo, horses, chickens, and, in non-Muslim areas, pigs. Both freshwater and ocean fishing are important to village and national economies. Timber and processed wood, especially in Kalimantan and Sumatra, are important for both domestic consumption and export, while oil, natural gas, tin, copper, aluminum, and gold are exploited mainly for export. In colonial times, Indonesia was characterized as having a "dual economy." One part was oriented to agriculture and small crafts for domestic consumption and was largely conducted by native Indonesians; the other part was export-oriented plantation agriculture and mining (and the service industries supporting them), and was dominated by the Dutch and other Europeans and by the Chinese. Though Indonesians are now important in both aspects of the economy and the Dutch/European role is no longer so direct, many features of that dual economy remain, and along with it are continuing ethnic and social dissatisfactions that arise from it.

One important aspect of change during Suharto's "New Order" regime (1968–1998) was the rapid urbanization and industrial production on Java, where the production of goods for domestic use and export expanded greatly. The previous imbalance in production between Java and the Outer Islands is changing, and the island now plays an economic role in the nation more in proportion to its population. Though economic development between 1968 and 1997 aided most people, the disparity between rich and poor and between urban and rural areas widened, again particularly on Java. The severe economic downturn in the nation and the region after 1997, and the political instability with the fall of Suharto, drastically reduced foreign investment in Indonesia, and the lower and middle classes, particularly in the cities, suffered most from this recession.

Land Tenure and Property. The colonial government recognized traditional rights of indigenous peoples to land and property and established semicodified "customary law" to this end. In many areas of Indonesia longstanding rights to land are held by groups such as clans, communities, or kin groups. Individuals and families use but do not own land. Boundaries of communally held land may be fluid, and conflicts over usage are usually settled by village authorities, though some disputes may reach government officials or courts. In cities and some rural areas of Java, European law of ownership was established. Since Indonesian independence various sorts of "land reform" have been called for and have met political resistance. During Suharto's regime, powerful economic and political groups and individuals obtained land by quasi-legal means and through some force in the name of "development," but serving their monied interest in land for timber, agro-business, and animal husbandry; business locations, hotels, and resorts; and residential and factory expansion. Such land was often obtained with minimal compensation to previous owners or occupants who had little legal recourse. The same was done by government and public corporations for large-scale projects such as dams and reservoirs, industrial parks, and highways. Particularly vulnerable were remote peoples (and animals) in forested areas where timber export concessions were granted to powerful individuals.

Commercial Activities. For centuries, commerce has been conducted between the many islands and beyond the present national borders by traders for various local and foreign ethnic groups. Some indigenous peoples such as the Minangkabau, Bugis, and Makassarese are well-known traders, as are the Chinese. Bugis sailing ships, which are built entirely by hand and range in size from 30 to 150 tons (27 to 136 metric tons), still carry goods to many parts of the nation. Trade between lowlands and highlands and coasts and inland areas is handled by these and other small traders in complex market systems

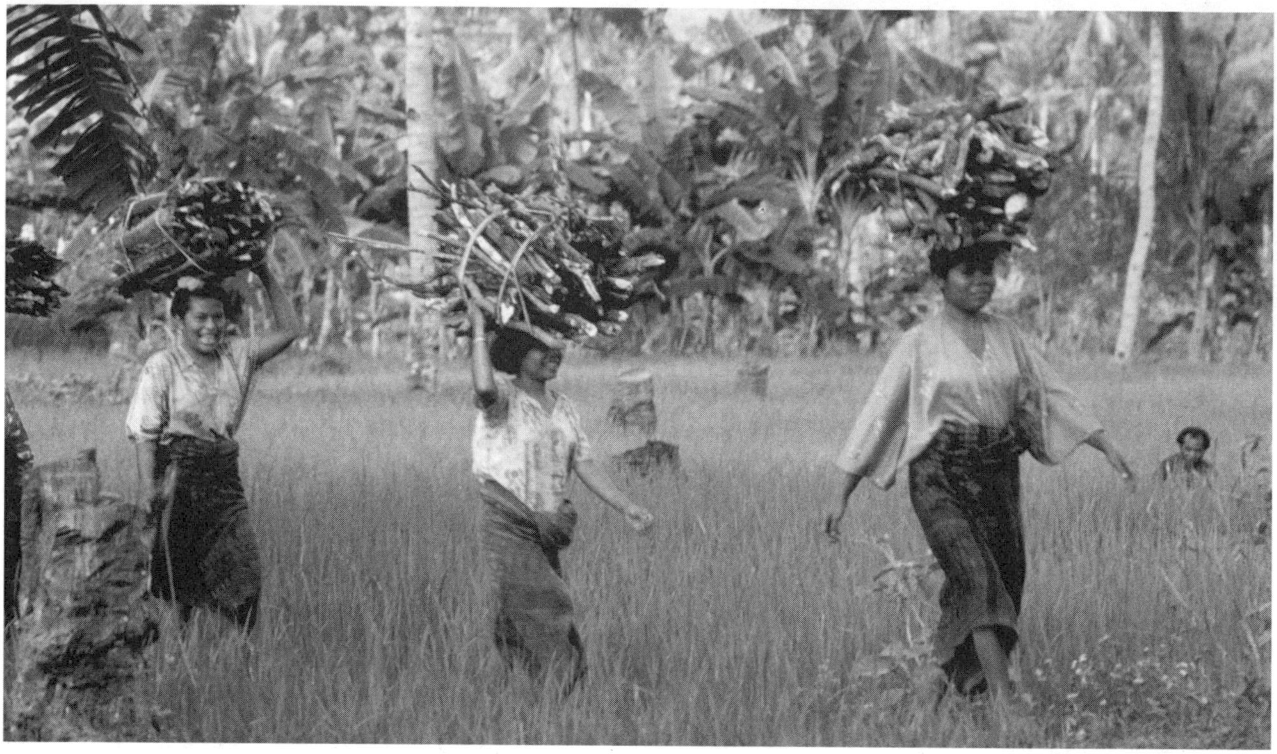

Women carrying firewood in Flores. In Indonesia, men and women share many aspects of village agriculture.

involving hundreds of thousands of men and women traders and various forms of transport, from human shoulders, horses, carts, and bicycles, to minivans, trucks, buses, and boats. Islam spread along such market networks, and Muslim traders are prominent in small-scale trade everywhere.

In the nineteenth and twentieth centuries the Dutch used the Chinese to link rural farms and plantations of native Indonesians to small-town markets and these to larger towns and cities where the Chinese and Dutch controlled large commercial establishments, banks, and transportation. Thus Chinese Indonesians became a major force in the economy, controlling today an estimated 60 percent of the nation's wealth though constituting only about 4 percent of its population. Since independence, this has led to suppression of Chinese ethnicity, language, education, and ceremonies by the government and to second-class citizenship for those who choose to become Indonesian nationals. Periodic outbreaks of violence against the Chinese have occurred, particularly in Java. Muslim small traders, who felt alienated in colonial times and welcomed a change with independence, have been frustrated as New Order Indonesian business, governmental, and military elites forged alliances with the Chinese in the name of "development" and to their financial benefit.

Major Industries. Indonesia's major industries involve agro-business, resource extraction and export, construction, and tourism, but a small to medium-sized industrial sector has developed since the 1970s, especially in Java. It serves domestic demand for goods (from household glassware and toothbrushes to automobiles), and produces a wide range of licensed items for multinational companies. Agro-business and resource extraction, which still supply Indonesia with much of its foreign exchange and domestic operating funds, are primarily in the outer islands, especially Sumatra (plantations, oil, gas, and mines), Kalimantan (timber), and West Papua (mining). The industrial sector has grown in Java, particularly around Jakarta and Surabaya and some smaller cities on the north coast.

Social Stratification

Classes and Castes. Aristocratic states and hierarchically-ordered chiefdoms were features of many Indonesian societies for the past millennium. Societies without such political systems existed, though most had the principle of hierarchy. Hindu states that later turned to Islam had aristocracies at the top and peasants and slaves at the bottom of society. Princes in their capitals concentrated secular and spiritual power and conducted rites for their principalities, and they warred for subjects, booty and land, and control of the sea trade. The Dutch East India Company became a warring state with its own forts, military, and navy, and it allied with and fought indigenous states. The Netherlands Indies government succeeded the company, and the Dutch ruled some areas directly and other areas indirectly via native princes. In some areas they augmented the power of indigenous princes and widened the gap between aristocrats and peasants. In Java, the Dutch augmented the pomp of princes while limiting their authority responsibility; and in other areas, such as East Sumatra, the Dutch created principalities and princely lines for their own economic and political benefit.

In general, princes ruled over areas of their own ethnic group, though some areas were multiethnic in character, particularly larger ones in Java or the port principalities in Sumatra and Kalimantan. In the latter, Malay princes ruled over areas consisting of a variety of ethnic groups. Stratified kingdoms and chiefdoms were entrenched in much of Java, the Western Lesser Sundas and parts of the Eastern Lesser Sundas, South Sulawesi, parts of Maluku, parts of Kalimantan, and the east and southeast coast of Sumatra.

Members of ruling classes gained wealth and the children of native rulers were educated in schools that brought them in contact with their peers from other parts of the archipelago.

Not all Indonesian societies were as socially stratified as that of Java. Minangkabau society was influenced by royal political patterns, but evolved into a more egalitarian political system in its West Sumatran homeland. The Batak of North Sumatra developed an egalitarian political order and ethos combining fierce clan loyalty with individuality. Upland or upriver peoples in Sulawesi and Kalimantan also developed more egalitarian social orders, though they could be linked to the outside world through tribute to coastal princes.

Symbols of Social Stratification. The aristocratic cultures of Java and the Malay-influenced coastal principalities were marked by ceremonial isolation of the princes and aristocrats, tribute by peasants and lesser lords, deference to authority by peasants, sumptuary rules marking off classes, the maintenance by aristocrats of supernaturally powerful regalia, and high court artistic and literary cultures. The Dutch in turn surrounded themselves with some of the same aura and social rules in their interaction with native peoples, especially during the late colonial period when European women came to the Indies and Dutch families were founded. In Java in particular, classes were separated by the use of different language levels, titles, and marriage rules. Aristocratic court culture became a paragon of refined social behavior in contrast to the rough or crude behavior of the peasants or non-Javanese. Indirection in communication and self-control in public behavior became hallmarks of the refined person, notions that spread widely in society. The courts were also exemplary centers for the arts—music, dance, theater, puppetry, poetry, and crafts such as batik cloth and silverworking. The major courts became Muslim by the seventeenth century, but some older Hindu philosophical and artistic practices continued to exist there or were blended with Muslim teachings.

In the late nineteenth and early twentieth centuries a more complex society developed in Java and some other parts of the Indies, which created a greater demand for trained people in government and commerce than the aristocratic classes could provide, and education was somewhat more widely provided. A class of urbanized government officials and professionals developed that often imitated styles of the earlier aristocracy. Within two decades after independence, all principalities except the sultanates of Yogyakarta and Surakarta were eliminated throughout the republic. Nevertheless, behaviors and thought patterns instilled through generations of indigenous princely rule—deference to authority, paternalism, unaccountability of leaders, supernaturalistic power, ostentatious displays of wealth, rule by individuals and by force rather than by law—continue to exert their influence in Indonesian society.

Political Life

Government. During 2000, Indonesia was in deep governmental crisis and various institutions were being redesigned. The 1945 constitution of the republic, however, mandates six organs of the state: the People's Consultative Assembly (*Majelis Permusyawaratan Rakyat*, or MPR), the presidency, the People's Representative Council (*Dewan Perwakilan Rakyat*, or DPR), the Supreme Advisory Council (*Dewan Pertimbangan Agung*), the State Audit Board (*Badan Pemeriksa Keuangan*), and the Supreme Court (*Mahkamah Agung*).

The president is elected by the MPR, which consists of one thousand members from various walks of life—farmers to businesspeople, students to soldiers—who meet once every five years to elect the president and endorse his or her coming five-year plan. The vice president is selected by the president.

The DPR meets at least once a year and has five hundred members: four hundred are elected from the provinces, one hundred are selected by the military. The DPR legislates, but its statutes must be approved by the president. The Supreme Court can hear cases from some three hundred subordinate courts in the provinces but cannot impeach or rule on the constitutionality of acts by other branches of government.

In 1997, the nation had twenty-seven provinces plus three special territories (Aceh, Yogyakarta, and Jakarta) with different forms of autonomy and their own governors. East Timor ceased to be a province in 1998, and several others are seeking provincial status. Governors of provinces are appointed by the Interior Ministry and responsible to it. Below the twenty-seven provinces are 243 districts (*kabupaten*) subdivided into 3,841 subdistricts (*kecamatan*), whose leaders are appointed by the government. There are also fifty-five municipalities, sixteen administrative municipalities, and thirty-five administrative cities with administrations separate from the provinces of which they are a part. At the base of government are some sixty-five thousand urban and rural villages called either *kelurahan* or *desa*. (Leaders of the former are appointed by the subdistrict head; the latter are elected by the people.) Many officials appointed at all levels during the New Order were military (or former military) men. Provincial, district, and subdistrict governments oversee a variety of services; the functional offices of the government bureaucracy (such as agriculture, forestry, or public works), however, extend to the district level as well and answer directly to their ministries in Jakarta, which complicates local policy making.

Leadership and Political Officials. During the New Order, the Golkar political party exerted full control over ministerial appointments and was powerfully influential in the civil service whose members were its loyalists. Funds were channeled locally to aid Golkar candidates, and they dominated the national and regional representative bodies in most parts of the country. The Muslim United Development Party and the Indonesian Democratic Party lacked such funds and influence and their leaders were weak and often divided. Ordinary people owed little to, and received little from, these parties. After the fall of President Suharto and the opening of the political system to many parties, many people became involved in politics; politics, however, mainly involves the leaders of the major parties jockeying for alliances and influence within the representative bodies at the national and provincial levels, as well as within the president's cabinet.

Fish drying. Both freshwater and ocean fishing are important to village economies.

The civil and military services, dominant institutions since the republic's founding, are built upon colonial institutions and practices. The New Order regime increased central government authority by appointing heads of subdistricts and even villages. Government service brings a salary, security, and a pension (however modest it may be) and is highly prized. The employees at a certain level in major institutions as diverse as government ministries, public corporations, schools and universities, museums, hospitals, and cooperatives are civil servants, and such positions in the civil service are prized. Membership carried great prestige in the past, but that prestige diminished somewhat during the New Order. Economic expansion made private sector positions—especially for trained professionals—more available, more interesting, and much more lucrative. Neither the number of civil service positions nor salaries have grown comparably.

The interaction of ordinary people with government officials involves deference (and often payments) upward and paternalism downward. Officials, most of whom are poorly paid, control access to things as lucrative as a large construction contract or as modest as a permit to reside in a neighborhood, all of which can cost the suppliant special fees. International surveys have rated Indonesia among the most corrupt nations in the world. Much of it involves sharing the wealth between private persons and officials, and Indonesians note that bribes have become institutionalized. Both the police and the judiciary are weak and subject to the same pressures. The unbridled manipulation of contracts and monopolies by Suharto family members was a major precipitant of unrest among students and others that brought about the president's fall.

Social Problems and Control. At the end of the colonial period, the secular legal system was divided between native (mainly for areas governed indirectly through princes) and government (for areas governed directly through administrators). The several constitutions of the republic between 1945 and 1950 validated colonial law that did not conflict with the constitution, and established three levels of courts: state courts, high courts (for appeal), and the supreme court. Customary law is still recognized, but native princes who were once responsible for its management no longer exist and its position in state courts is uncertain.

Indonesians inherited from the Dutch the notion of "a state based upon law" (*rechtsstaat* in Dutch, *negara hukum* in Indonesian), but implementation has been problematic and ideology triumphed over law in the first decade of independence. Pressure for economic development and personal gain during the New Order led to a court system blatantly subverted by money and influence. Many people became disenchanted with the legal system, though some lawyers led the fight against corruption and for human rights, including the rights of those affected by various development projects. A national human rights commission was formed to investigate violations in East Timor and elsewhere, but has so far had relatively little impact.

One sees the same disaffection from the police, which were a branch of the military until the end of the New Order. Great emphasis was placed upon public order during the New Order, and military and police organs were used to maintain a climate of caution and fear among not just lawbreakers but also among ordinary citizens, journalists, dissidents, labor advocates, and others who were viewed as subversive. Extrajudicial killings of alleged criminals and others were sponsored by the military in some urban and rural areas, and killings of rights activists, particularly in Atjeh, continue. The media, now free after severe New Order controls, is able to report daily on such events. In 1999–2000, vigilante attacks against even suspected lawbreakers were becoming common in cities and some rural areas, as was an increase in violent crime. Compounding the climate of national disorder were violence among refugees in West Timor, sectarian killing between Muslims and Christians in Sulawesi and Maluku, and separatist violence in Atjeh and Papua; in all of which, elements of the police and military are seen to be participating, even fomenting, rather than controlling.

In villages many problems are never reported to the police but are still settled by local custom and mutual agreement mediated by recognized leaders. Customary settlement is frequently the only means used, but it also may be used as a first resort before appeal to courts or as a last resort by dissatisfied litigants from state courts. In multiethnic areas, disputes between members of different ethnic groups may be settled by leaders of either or both groups, by a court, or by feud. In many regions with settled populations, a customary settlement is honored over a court one, and many rural areas are peaceful havens. Local custom is often based upon restorative justice, and jailing miscreants may be considered unjust since it removes them from oversight and control of their kinsmen and neighbors and from working to compensate aggrieved or victimized persons. Where there is great population mobility, especially in cities, this form of social control is far less viable and, since the legal system is ineffective, vigilantism becomes more common.

Military Activity. The Armed Forces of the Republic of Indonesia (*Angkatan Bersenjata Republik Indonesia*, or ABRI) consist of the army (about 214,000 personnel), navy (about 40,000), air force (nearly 20,000), and, until recently, state police (almost 171,000). In addition, almost three million civilians were trained in civil defense groups, student units, and other security units. The premier force, the army, was founded and commanded by members of the Royal Netherlands Indies Army and/or the Japanese-sponsored Motherland Defenders. Many soldiers at first came from the latter, but many volunteers were added after the Japanese left. Some local militias were led by people with little military experience, but their success in the war of independence made them at least local heroes. The army underwent vicissitudes after independence as former colonial officers led in transforming guerilla-bands and provincial forces into a centralized modern army, with national command structure, education, and training.

From its beginning the armed forces recognized a dual function as a defense and security force and as a social and political one, with a territorial structure (distinct from combat commands) that paralleled the civilian government from province level to district, subdistrict, and even village. General Suharto came to power as the leader of an anticommunist and nationalist army, and he made the military the major force behind the New Order. Its security and social and political functions have included monitoring social and political developments at national and local levels; providing personnel for important government departments and state enterprises; censoring the media and monitoring dissidents; placing personnel in villages to learn about local concerns and to help in development; and filling assigned blocs in representative bodies. The military owns or controls hundreds of businesses and state enterprises that provide about three-quarters of its budget, hence the difficulty for a civilian president who wishes to exert control over it. Also, powerful military and civilian officials provide protection and patronage for Chinese businesspeople in exchange for shares in profits and political funding.

Social Welfare and Change Programs

The responsibility for most formal public health and social welfare programs rests primarily with government and only secondarily with private and religious organizations. From 1970 to 1990, considerable investment was made in roads and in health stations in rural and urban areas, but basic infrastructure is still lacking in many areas. Sewage and waste disposal are still poor in many urban areas, and pollution affects canals and rivers, especially in newly industrializing areas such as West Java. Welfare programs to benefit the poor are minimal compared to the need, and rural economic development activities are modest compared to those in cities. The largest and most successful effort, the national family planning program, used both government and private institutions to considerably reduce the rate of population increase in Java and other areas. Transmigration, the organized movement of people from rural Java to less populated outer island areas in Sumatra, Kalimantan, Sulawesi, and West Papua, was begun by the Dutch early in the twentieth century and is continued vigorously by the Indonesian government. It has led to the agricultural development of many outer island areas but has little eased population pressure in Java, and it has led to ecological problems and to ethnic and social conflicts between transmigrants and local people.

Nongovernmental Organizations and Other Organizations

Despite government dominance in many areas of social action, nongovernmental organizations (NGOs) have a rich history, though they often have had limited funds, have operated under government restraint, and have been limited in much of their activity to urban areas. They have served in fields such as religion, family planning, education, rural health and mutual aid, legal aid, workers' rights, philanthropy, regional or ethnic interests, literature and the arts, and ecology and conservation Muslim and Christian organizations have been active in community education and health care since the early twentieth century. Foreign religious, philanthropic, and national and international organizations have supported welfare efforts by government and NGOs, though most NGOs are homegrown. The authoritarian nature of the New Order led to tensions between the government and NGOs in areas such as legal aid, workers' rights, and conservation, and the government sought to co-opt some such organizations. Also, foreign support for NGOs led to tensions between the various governments, even cancellations of aid, when that support was viewed as politically motivated. With the collapse of the New Order regime and pressures for reform since 1998, NGOs are more active in serving various constituencies, though economic upset during the same period has strained their resources.

Gender Roles and Statuses

Division of Labor by Gender. Women and men share in many aspects of village agriculture, though plowing is more often done by men and harvest groups composed only of women are commonly seen. Getting the job done is primary. Gardens and orchards may be tended by either sex, though men are more common in orchards. Men predominate in hunting and fishing, which may take them away for long durations. If men seek long-term work outside the village, women may tend to all aspects of farming and gardening. Women are found in the urban workforce in stores, small industries, and markets, as well as in upscale businesses, but nearly always in fewer numbers than men. Many elementary schoolteachers are women, but teachers in secondary schools and colleges and universities are more frequently men, even though the numbers of male and female students may be similar. Men predominate at all levels of government, central and regional, though women are found in a variety of positions and there has been a woman cabinet min-

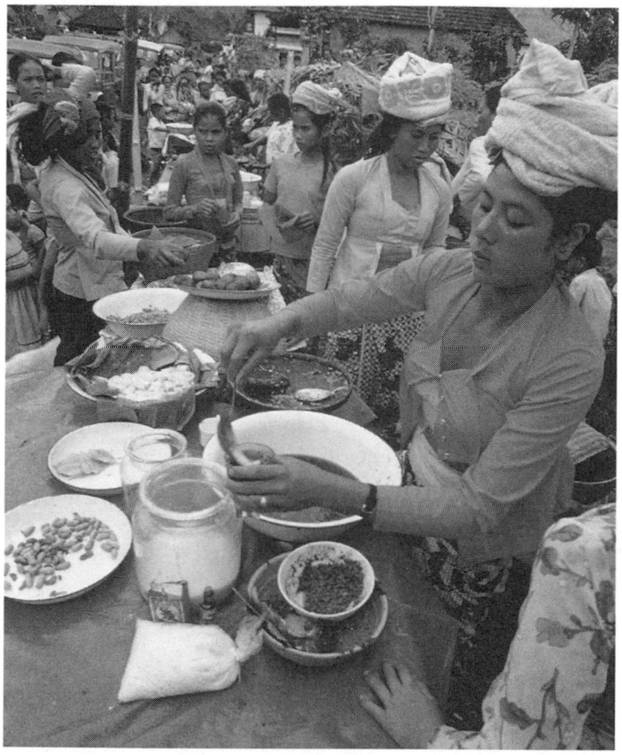

A woman serves food at a market stand. Urban Indonesian women often find work in markets.

ister. The vice president, Megawati Sukarnoputri, a woman, was a candidate for president, though her reputation derives mainly from her father, Sukarno, the first president. She was opposed by many Muslim leaders because of her gender, but she had the largest popular following in the national legislative election of 1999.

The Relative Status of Women and Men. Though Indonesia is a Muslim nation, the status of women is generally considered to be high by outside observers, though their position and rights vary considerably in different ethnic groups, even Muslim ones. Nearly everywhere, Indonesian gender ideology emphasizes men as community leaders, decision makers, and mediators with the outside world, while women are the backbone of the home and family values.

Marriage, Family, and Kinship

Marriage. People in Indonesia gain the status of full adults through marriage and parenthood. In Indonesia, one does not ask, "Is he (or she) married?," but "Is he (or she) married yet?," to which the correct response is, "Yes" or "Not yet." Even homosexuals are under great family pressure to marry. Certain societies in Sumatra and eastern Indonesia practice affinal alliance, in which marriages are arranged between persons in particular patrilineal clans or lineages who are related as near or distant cross-cousins. In these societies the relationship between wife-giving and wife-taking clans or lineages is vitally important to the structure of society and involves lifelong obligations for the exchange of goods and services between kin. The Batak are a prominent Sumatran example of such a people. Clan membership and marriage alliances between clans are important for the Batak whether they live in their mountain homeland or have migrated to distant cities. Their marriages perpetuate relationships between lineages or clans, though individual wishes and love between young people may be considered by their families and kinsmen, as may education, occupation, and wealth among urbanites.

In societies without lineal descent groups, love is more prominent in leading people to marry, but again education, occupation, or wealth in the city, or the capacity to work hard, be a good provider, and have access to resources in the village, are also considered. Among the Javanese or Bugis, for example, the higher the social status of a family, the more likely parents and other relatives will arrange a marriage (or veto potential relationships). In most Indonesian societies, marriage is viewed as one important means of advancing individual or family social status (or losing it).

Divorce and remarriage practices are diverse. Among Muslims they are governed by Muslim law and may be settled in Muslim courts, or as with non-Muslims, they may be settled in the government's civil court. The initiation of divorce and its settlements favors males among Muslims and also in many traditional societies. Divorce and remarriage may be handled by local elders or officials according to customary law, and terms for such settlements may vary considerably by ethnic group. In general, societies with strong descent groups, such as the Batak, eschew divorce and it is very rare. Such societies may also practice the levirate (widows marrying brothers or cousins of their deceased spouse). In societies without descent groups, such as the Javanese, divorce is much more common and can be initiated by either spouse. Remarriage is also easy. Javanese who are not members of the upper class are reported to have a high divorce rate, while divorce among upper-class and wealthy Javanese is rarer.

Polygamy is recognized among Muslims, some immigrant Chinese, and some traditional societies, but not by Christians. Such marriages are probably few in number. Marriages between members of different ethnic groups are also uncommon, though they may be increasing in urban areas and among the better educated.

Domestic Unit. The nuclear family of husband, wife, and children is the most widespread domestic unit, though elders and unmarried siblings may be added to it in various societies and at various times. This domestic unit is as common among remote peoples as among urbanites, and is also unrelated to the presence or absence of clans in a society. An exception is the traditional, rural matrilineal Minangkabau, for whom the domestic unit still comprises coresident females around a grandmother (or mothers) with married and unmarried daughters and sons in a large traditional house. Husbands come only as visitors to their wife's hearth and bedchamber in the house. Some societies, such as the Karo of Sumatra or some Dayak of Kalimantan, live in large (or long) houses with multiple hearths and bedchambers that belong to related or even unrelated nuclear family units.

Inheritance. Inheritance patterns are diverse even within single societies. Muslim inheritance favors males over females as do the customs of many traditional societies (an exception being matrilineal ones where rights over land, for example, are passed down between females). Inheritance disputes, similar to divorces, may be handled in Muslim courts, civil courts, or customary village ways. Custom generally favors males, but actual practice often gives females inheritances. In many societies, there is a distinction between property that is inherited or acquired; the former is passed on in clan or family lines, the latter goes to the children or the spouse of the deceased. Such a division may also be recognized at divorce. In many areas land is communal property of a kin or local group, while household goods, personal items, or productive equipment are familial or individual inheritable property. In some places economic trees, such as rubber, may be personally owned, while rice land is communally held. With changing economic conditions, newer ideas about property, and increasing demand for money, the rules and practices regarding inheritance are changing, which can produce conflicts that a poorly organized legal system and weakened customary leaders cannot easily manage.

Kin Groups. Many of Indonesia's ethnic groups have strong kinship groupings based upon patrilineal, matrilineal, or bilateral descent. Such peoples are primarily in Sumatra, Kalimantan, Maluku, Sulawesi, and the Eastern Lesser Sundas. Patrilineal descent is most common, though matriliny is found in a few societies, such as the Minangkabau of West Sumatra and southern Tetun of West Timor. Some societies in Kalimantan and Sulawesi, as well as the Javanese, have bilateral kinship systems.

Kinship is a primordial loyalty throughout Indonesia. Fulfilling obligations to kin can be onerous, but provides vital support in various aspects of life. Government or other organizations do not provide social security, unemployment insurance, old age care, or legal aid. Family, extended kinship, and clan do provide such help, as do patron-client relationships and alliances between peers. Correlated with these important roles of family and kin are practices of familial and ethnic patrimonialism, nepotism, patronage, and paternalism in private sectors and government service.

SOCIALIZATION

Child Rearing and Education. In the government education system, generally, quantity has prevailed over quality. Facilities remain poorly equipped and salaries remain so low that many teachers must take additional jobs to support their families.

Higher Education. The colonial government greatly limited education in Dutch and the vernaculars, and people were primarily trained for civil service and industrial and health professions. At the time of independence in 1950, the republic had few schools or university faculties. Mass education became a major government priority for the next five decades. Today many Indonesians have earned advanced degrees abroad and most have returned to serve their country. In this effort the government has received considerable support from the World Bank, United Nation agencies, foreign governments, and private foundations. Increasingly, better-educated people serve at all levels in national and regional governments, and the private sector has benefitted greatly from these educational efforts. Private Muslim and Christian elementary and secondary schools, universities and institutes, which are found in major cities and the countryside, combine secular subjects and religious education.

Higher education has suffered from a lecture-based system, poor laboratories, a shortage of adequate textbooks in Indonesian, and a poor level of English-language proficiency, which keeps many students from using such foreign textbooks as are available. Research in universities is limited and mainly serves government projects or private enterprise and allows researchers to supplement their salaries.

From the late 1970s through the l990s, private schools and universities increased in number and quality and served diverse students (including Chinese Indonesians who were not accepted at government universities). Many of these institutions' courses are taught in afternoons and evenings by faculty members from government universities who are well paid for their efforts.

The colonial government limited education to an amount needed to fill positions in the civil service and society of the time. Indonesian mass education, with a different philosophy, has had the effect of producing more graduates than there are jobs available, even in strong economic times. Unrest has occurred among masses of job applicants who seek to remain in cities but do not find positions commensurate with their view of themselves as graduates.

Students have been political activists from the 1920s to the present. The New Order regime made great efforts to expand educational opportunities while also influencing the curriculum, controlling student activities, and appointing pliant faculty members to administrative positions. New campuses of the University of Indonesia near Jakarta, and Hasanuddin University near Makassar, for example, were built far from their previous locations at the center of these cities, to curb mobilization and marching.

ETIQUETTE

When riding a Jakarta bus, struggling in post-office crowds, or getting into a football match, one may think that Indonesians have only a push-and-shove etiquette. And in a pedicab or the market, bargaining always delays action. Children may repeatedly shout "Belanda, Belanda" (white Westerner) at a European, or youths shout, "Hey, Mister." In some places a young woman walking or biking alone is subject to harassment by young males. But public behavior contrasts sharply with private etiquette. In an Indonesian home, one joins in quiet speech and enjoys humorous banter and frequent laughs. People sit properly with feet on the floor and uncrossed legs while guests, men, and elders are given the best seating and deference. Strong emotions and rapid or abrupt movements of face, arms, or body are avoided before guests. Drinks and snacks must be served, but not immediately, and when served, guests must wait to be invited to drink. Patience is rewarded, displays of greed are avoided, and one may be offered a sumptuous meal by a host who asks pardon for its inadequacy.

Whether serving tea to guests, passing money after bargaining in the marketplace, or paying a clerk for stamps at the post office, only the right hand is used to give or receive, following Muslim custom. (The left hand is reserved for toilet functions.) Guests are served with a slight bow, and elders are passed by juniors with a bow. Handshakes are appropriate between men, but with a soft touch (and between Muslims with the hand then lightly touching the heart). Until one has a truly intimate relationship with another, negative feelings such as jealousy, envy, sadness, and anger should be hidden from that person. Confrontations should be met with smiles and quiet demeanor, and direct eye contact should be avoided, especially with social superiors. Punctuality is not prized—Indonesians speak of "rubber time"—and can be considered impolite. Good guidebooks warn, however, that Indonesians may expect Westerners to be on time! In public, opposite sexes are rarely seen holding hands (except perhaps in a Jakarta mall), while male or female friends of the same sex do hold hands.

Neatness in grooming is prized, whether on a crowded hot bus or at a festival. Civil servants wear neat uniforms to work, as do schoolchildren and teachers.

The Javanese emphasize the distinction between refined (*halus*) and crude (*kasar*) behavior, and young children who have not yet learned refined behavior in speech, demeanor, attitude, and general behavior are considered "not yet Javanese." This distinction may be extended to other peoples whose culturally correct behavior is not deemed appropriate by the Javanese. The Batak, for example, may be considered crude because they generally value directness in speech and demeanor and can be argumentative in interpersonal relationships. And a Batak man's wife is deemed to be a wife to his male siblings (though not in a sexual way), which a Javanese wife might not accept. Bugis do not respect persons who smile and withdraw in the face of challenges, as the Javanese tend to do; they respect those who defend their honor even violently, especially the honor of their women. Thus conflict between the Javanese and others over issues of etiquette and behavior is possible. A Javanese wife of a Batak man may not react kindly to his visiting brother expecting to be served and to have his laundry done without thanks; a young Javanese may smile and greet politely a young Bugis girl, which can draw the ire (and perhaps knife) of her brother or cousin; a Batak civil servant may dress down his Javanese subordinate publicly (in which case both the Batak and the Javanese lose face in the eyes of the Javanese). Batak who migrate to cities in Java organize evening lessons to instruct newcomers in proper behavior with the majority Javanese and Sundanese with whom they will live and work. Potential for interethnic conflict has increased over the past decades as more people from Java are transmigrated to outer islands, and more people from the outer islands move to Java.

Religion

Religious Beliefs. Indonesia has the largest Muslim population of any nation, and in 1990 the population was reported to be 87 percent Muslim. There is a well-educated and influential Christian minority (about 9.6 percent of the population in 1990), with about twice as many Protestants as Catholics. The Balinese still follow a form of Hinduism. Mystical cults are well established among the Javanese elite and middle class, and members of many ethnic groups still follow traditional belief systems. Officially the government recognizes religion (*agama*) to include Islam, Christianity, Hinduism, and Buddhism, while other belief systems are called just that, beliefs (*kepercayaan*). Those who hold beliefs are subject to conversion; followers of religion are not. Belief in ancestral spirits, spirits of diverse sorts of places, and powerful relics are found among both peasants and educated people and among many followers of the world religions; witchcraft and sorcery also have their believers and practitioners. The colonial regime had an uneasy relationship with Islam, as has the Indonesian government. The first of the Five Principles extols God (*Tuhan*), but not Allah by name. Dissidents have wanted to make Indonesia a Muslim state, but they have not prevailed.

The Javanese are predominantly Muslim, though many are Catholic or Protestant, and many Chinese in Java and elsewhere are Christian, mainly Protestant. The Javanese are noted for a less strict adherence to Islam and a greater orientation to Javanese religion, a mixture of Islam and previous Hindu and animist beliefs. The Sundanese of West Java, by contrast, are ardently Muslim. Other noted Muslim peoples are the Acehnese of North Sumatra, the first Indonesians to become Muslim; the Minangkabau, despite their matriliny; the Banjarese of South Kalimantan; the Bugis and Makassarese of South Sulawesi; the Sumbawans of the Lesser Sunda Islands; and the people of Ternate and Tidor in Maluku.

The Dutch sought to avoid European-style conflict between Protestants and Catholics by assigning particular regions for conversion by each of them. Thus today the Batak of Sumatra, the Dayak of Kalimantan, the Toraja and Menadonese of Sulawesi, and the Ambonese of Maluku are Protestant; the peoples of Flores and the Tetun of West Timor are Catholic.

Religious Practitioners. Islam in Indonesia is of the Sunni variety, with little hierarchical leadership. Two major Muslim organizations, *Nahdatul Ulama* (NU) and *Muhammadiyah*, both founded in Java, have played an important role in education, the nationalist struggle, and politics after independence. The New Order regime allowed only one major Muslim political group, which had little power; but after the fall of President Suharto, many parties (Muslim and others) emerged, and these two organizations continued to play an important role in the elections. The leader of NU, Abdurrahman Wahid (whose grandfather founded it), campaigned successfully and became the country's president; an opponent, Amien Rais, head of Muhammadiyah, became speaker of the DPR. During this time of transition, forces of tolerance are being challenged by those who have wanted Indonesia to be a Muslim state. The outcome of that conflict is uncertain.

Muslim-Christian relations have been tense since colonial times. The Dutch government did not proselytize, but it allowed Christian missions to convert freely among non-Muslims. When Christians and Muslims were segregated on different islands or in different regions, relations were amicable. Since the 1970s, however, great movements of people—especially Muslims from Java, Sulawesi, and parts of Maluku into previously Christian areas in Kalimantan, Sulawesi, Maluku, and West Papua—has led to changes in religious demography and imbalances in economic, ethnic, and political power. The end of the New Order regime has led to an uncapping of tensions and great violence in places such as Ambon (capital of the Maluku province), other Maluku islands, and Sulawesi. A loss of authority by commanders over Muslim and Christian troops in the outer islands is playing a part. Christians generally have kept to themselves and avoided national politics. They lack mass organizations or leaders comparable to Muslim ones, but disproportionate numbers of Christians have held important civil, military, intellectual, and business positions (a result of the Christian emphasis upon modern education); Christian secondary schools and universities are prominent and have educated children of the elite (including non-Christians); and

Village living is often dictated by established custom and mutual agreement by recognized leaders.

two major national newspapers, *Kompas* and *Suara Pembaruan*, were of Catholic and Protestant origin, respectively. Some Muslims are displeased by these facts, and Christians were historically tainted in their eyes through association with the Dutch and foreign missionaries and the fact that Chinese Indonesians are prominent Christians.

During the New Order, those not having a religion were suspected of being Communist, so there was a rush to conversion in many areas, including Java, which gained many new Christians. Followers of traditional ethnic beliefs were under pressure as well. In places such as interior Kalimantan and Sulawesi, some people and groups converted to one of the world religions, but others sought government recognition for a reorganized traditional religion through both regional and national politicking. Among the Ngaju Dayak, for instance, the traditional belief system, Kaharingan, gained official acceptance in the Hindu-Buddhist category, though it is neither. People who follow traditional beliefs and practices are often looked down upon as primitive, irrational, and backward by urban civil and military leaders who are Muslim or Christian—but these groups formed new sorts of organizations, modeled on urban secular ones, to bolster support. Such moves represent both religious and ethnic resistance to pressure from the outside, from neighboring Muslim or Christian groups, and from exploitative government and military officers or outside developers of timber and mining industries. On Java, mystical groups, such as Subud, also lobbied for official recognition and protections. Their position was stronger than that of remote peoples because they had followers in high places, including the president.

Rituals and Holy Places. Muslims and Christians follow the major holidays of their faiths, and in Makassar, for example, the same decorative lights are left up for celebrating both Idul Fitri and Christmas. National calendars list Muslim and Christian holidays as well as Hindu-Buddhist ones. In many places, people of one religion may acknowledge the holidays of another religion with visits or gifts. Mosques and churches have the same features found elsewhere in the world, but the temples of Bali are very special. While centers for spiritual communication with Hindu deities, they also control the flow of water to Bali's complex irrigation system through their ritual calendar.

Major Muslim annual rituals are Ramadan (the month of fasting), Idul Fitri (the end of fasting), and the hajj (pilgrimage). Indonesia annually provides the greatest number of pilgrims to Mecca. Smaller pilgrimages in Indonesia may also be made to

Workers harvest rice on a terraced paddy on the island of Bali.

graves of saints, those believed to have brought Islam to Indonesia, Sunan Kalijaga being the most famous.

Rituals of traditional belief systems mark life-cycle events or involve propitiation for particular occasions and are led by shamans, spirit mediums, or prayer masters (male or female). Even in Muslim and Christian areas, some people may conduct rituals at birth or death that are of a traditional nature, honor and feed spirits of places or graves of ancestors, or use practitioners for sorcery or countermagic. The debate over what is or is not allowable custom by followers of religion is frequent in Indonesia. Among the Sa'dan Toraja of Sulawesi, elaborate sacrifice of buffalos at funerals has become part of the international tourist circuit, and the conversion of local custom to tourist attractions can be seen in other parts of Indonesia, such as on Bali or Samosir Island in North Sumatra.

Death and the Afterlife. It is widely believed that the deceased may influence the living in various ways, and funerals serve to ensure the proper passage of the spirit to the afterworld, though cemeteries are still considered potentially dangerous dwellings for ghosts. In Java the dead may be honored by modest family ceremonies held on Thursday evening. Among Muslims, burial must occur within twenty-four hours and be attended by Muslim officiants; Christian burial is also led by a local church leader. The two have separate cemeteries. In Java and other areas there may be secondary rites to assure the well-being of the soul and to protect the living. Funerals, like marriages, call for a rallying of kin, neighbors, and friends, and among many ethnic groups social status may be expressed through the elaborateness or simplicity of funerals. In clan-based societies, funerals are occasions for the exchange of gifts between wife-giving and wife-taking groups. In such societies representatives of the wife-giving group are usually responsible for conducting the funeral and for leading the coffin to the grave.

Funeral customs vary. Burial is most common, except for Hindu Bali where cremation is the norm. The Sa'dan Toraja are noted for making large wooden effigies of the deceased, which are placed in niches in sheer stone cliffs to guard the tombs. In the past, the Batak made stone sarcophagi for the prominent dead. This practice stopped with Christianization, but in recent decades, prosperous urban Batak have built large stone sarcophagi in their home villages to honor the dead and reestablish a connection otherwise severed by migration.

Medicine and Health Care

Modern public health care was begun by the Dutch to safeguard plantation workers. It expanded to hospitals and midwifery centers in towns and some rural health facilities. During the New Order public health and family planning became a priority for rural areas and about seven thousand community health centers and 20,500 sub-health centers were built by 1995. In Jakarta medical faculties exist in a number of provincial universities. Training is often hampered by poor facilities, and medical research is limited as teaching physicians also maintain private practices to serve urban needs and supplement meager salaries. Physicians and government health facilities are heavily concentrated in large cities, and private hospitals are also located there, some founded by Christian missions or Muslim foundations. Many village areas in Java, and especially those in the outer islands, have little primary care beyond inoculations, maternal and baby visits, and family planning, though these have had important impacts on health conditions.

Traditional medicine is alive throughout the archipelago. Javanese curers called *dukun* deal with a variety of illnesses of physical, emotional, and spiritual origin through combinations of herbal and magical means. In north Sumatra, some ethnic curers specialize; for example, Karo bonesetters have many clinics. Herbal medicines and tonics called *jamu* are both home blended and mass produced. Commercial brands of tonics and other medicines are sold throughout the archipelago, and tonic sellers' vehicles can be seen in remote places.

Various forms of spiritual healing are done by shamans, mediums, and other curers in urban and rural areas. Many people believe that ritual or social missteps may lead to misfortune, which includes illness. Traditional healers diagnose the source and deal with the problems, some using black arts. Bugis transvestite healers serve aristocratic and commoner households in dealing with misfortune, often becoming possessed in order to communicate with the source of misfortune. In Bali, doctors trained in modern medicine may also practice spirit-oriented healing. Accusations of sorcery and attacks on alleged sorcerers are not uncommon in many areas and are most liable to arise in times of social, economic, and political unrest.

Secular Celebrations

The most important national celebration is Independence Day, 17 August, which is marked by parades and displays in Jakarta and provincial and district capitals. Provincial celebrations may have local cultural or historical flavor. Youth are often prominent. Kartini Day, 21 April, honors Indonesia's first female emancipationist; schools and women's organizations hold activities that day. The military also has its celebrations. New Year's is celebrated 1 January when businesses close and local fairs with fireworks are held in some places. Western-style dances are held in hotels in cities. Public celebration by the Chinese of their New Year was not allowed for decades, but this rule was lifted in 1999 and dragons again danced in the streets. Previously it was celebrated only in homes, though businesses did close and for two days the bustle of Jakarta traffic was stilled. Local celebrations recognize foundings of cities, historical events and personages, or heroes (some national, others regional), while others mark special events, such as bull racing on Madura and palace processions in Yogyakarta or Surakarta. On Bali a lunar calendar New Year's day is celebrated with fasting, prayer, silence, and inactivity. All people (including tourists) must remain indoors and without lights on so that harmful spirits will think Bali is empty and will leave.

The Arts and Humanities

Support for the Arts. In the past in Java and Bali, royal courts or rich persons were major patrons of the arts. They continue their support, but other institutions joined them. The Dutch founded the Batavia Society for the Arts and Sciences in 1778, which established the National Museum that continues to display artifacts of the national culture. The Dutch-founded National Archive seeks to preserve the literary heritage, despite poor funding and the hazards of tropical weather and insects. Over the past several decades, regional cultural museums were built using national and provincial government funding and some foreign aid. Preservation of art and craft traditions and objects, such as house architecture, batik and tie-dye weaving, wood carving, silver and gold working, statuary, puppets, and basketry, are under threat from the international arts and crafts market, local demands for cash, and changing indigenous values.

A college for art teachers, founded in 1947, was incorporated in 1951 into the Technological Institute of Bandung; an Academy of Fine Arts was established in Yogyakarta in 1950; and the Jakarta Institute of Art Education was begun in 1968. Academies have since been founded elsewhere; the arts are part of various universities and teacher training institutes; and private schools for music and dance have been founded. Private galleries for painters and batik designers are legion in Yogyakarta and Jakarta. Academies and institutes maintain traditional arts as well as develop newer forms of theater, music, and dance.

Literature. Indonesia's literary legacy includes centuries-old palm, bamboo, and other fiber manuscripts from several literate peoples, such as the Malay, Javanese, Balinese, Buginese, Rejang, and Batak. The fourteenth century *Nagarakrtagama* is a lengthy poem praising King Hayam Wuruk and describing the life and social structure of his kingdom, Majapahit. The *I La Galigo* of the Bugis, which traces the adventures of their culture hero, Sawerigading, is one of the world's longest epic poems.

In colonial times some literature was published in regional languages, the most being in Javanese, but this was stopped after Indonesian independence. The earliest official publishing house for Indonesian literature is Balai Pustaka, founded in Batavia in 1917. National culture was expressed and, in some ways formed, through spoken Malay-Indonesian (understood by many people) and newspapers, pamphlets, poetry, novels, and short stories for those who could read. By the time of independence, literary production was not great, but it has grown considerably since the 1950s. The literary tradition is now rich, but one should note that reading for pleasure or enlightenment is not yet part of the culture of average urban Indonesians and plays little if any part in the life of village people. Indonesia has made literacy and widespread elementary education a major effort of the nation, but in many rural parts of the country functional literacy is limited. For students to own many books is not common; universities are still oriented toward lecture notes rather than student reading; and libraries are poorly stocked.

In the conflict between left-and right-wing politics of the 1950s and early 1960s, organizations of authors were drawn into the fray. In the anticommunist purges of the late 1960s, some writers who had participated in left-wing organizations were imprisoned. The most famous is Pramoedya Ananta Toer, a nationalist who had also been imprisoned by the Dutch from 1947 to 1949. He composed books as stories told to fellow prisoners in exile on the island of Buru from 1965 to 1979. He was released from Buru and settled in Jakarta, but remained under city arrest. Four of his novels, the *Buru Quartet*, published between 1980 and 1988 in Indonesian, are rich documentaries of life in turn-of-the-century colonial Java. They were banned in Indonesia during the New Order. Pram (as he is commonly known, rhyming with Tom) received a PEN Freedom-to-Write Award in 1988 and a Magsaysay Award in 1995. In English translation, the *Buru Quartet* received critical acclaim, and after the end of the New Order in 1999, Pram made a tour of the United States. He is the only Indonesian novelist to have received such acclaim overseas.

Graphic Arts. Stone sculptures of the elaborate Hindu variety in Java or the ornate sarcophagi of Sumatra are archaeological remains of value, but only in Bali is elaborate stone carving still done (apart from that which may decorate some upscale Jakarta homes or public buildings). Wood carving is more common. The cottage carving industry of Bali finds a wide domestic and international market for its statues of people, deities, and animals, many of which are finely artistic, some hackneyed. Perhaps the most common carving is in the urban furniture industry, mainly in Java, where ornately carved sofas and chairs are very popular. Traditional puppet or animal carvings of the mountain Batak of Sumatra or the upriver Dayak of Kalimantan are now mainly for tourists, though they once showed rich artistry (now largely seen in museums). The Toraja homes are still elaborately carved, and small examples of these carvings are sold to tourists. Toraja carve decorations on large bamboo tubes used for carrying palm wine or rice, and people in eastern Indonesia decorate small bamboo tubes that carry lime used in betel chewing. Among contemporary urban artists, painting on canvas or making batik is much more common than making sculpture.

Indonesian textiles are becoming more widely known overseas. Batik is the Javanese word for "dot" or "stipple"; ikat, a Malay-Indonesian word for "to tie," is a type of cloth that is tie-dyed before weaving. Batik textiles were made in royal courts and cottages, but also became a major commercial industry in Java and Bali, an industry that has experienced economic vicissitudes over the decades. Batik cloth varies enormously in artistry, elaboration, quality, and cost. Formal occasions require that Javanese, Sundanese and Balinese women wear whole cloths wrapped ornately to form a skirt. Men nowadays do so only at their marriage (or if they are in royal courts or are performers in gamelan, dance, or theater). Long-sleeved batik shirts are now accepted formal social wear for men of all ethnic backgrounds, though formal wear for men also includes civil service uniforms, shirts and ties, or Western suits.

Performance Arts. Performance arts are diverse and include: Javanese and Balinese gong-chime orchestras (gamelan) and shadow plays (*wayang*), Sundanese bamboo orchestras (*angklung*), Muslim orchestral music at family events or Muslim holiday celebrations, trance dances (*reog*) from east Java, the dramatic barong dance or the monkey dances for tourists on Bali, Batak puppet dances, horse puppet dances of south Sumatra, Rotinese singers with *lontar* leaf mandolins, and the dances for ritual and life-cycle events performed by Indonesia's many outer island ethnic groups. All such arts use indigenously produced costumes and musical instruments, of which the Balinese barong costumes and the metalworking of the gamelan orchestra are the most complex. Best known in Indonesia is the Javanese and Balinese shadow puppet theater based on the *Ramayana* epic, with its brilliant puppeteers (*dalang*) who may manipulate over a hundred puppets in all-night oral performances accompanied by a gamelan orchestra. Bali is best known for the diversity of its performance arts. Despite the fact that Bali draws visitors from around the world, and its troupes perform overseas, most Balinese performers are villagers for whom art complements farming.

Contemporary (and partly Western-influenced) theater, dance, and music are most lively in Jakarta and Yogyakarta, but less common elsewhere. Jakarta's Taman Ismail Marzuki, a national center for the arts, has four theaters, a dance studio, an exhibition hall, small studios, and residences for administrators. Contemporary theater (and sometimes traditional theater as well) has a history of political activism, carrying messages about political figures and events that might not circulate in public. During the New Order, poets and playwrights had works banned, among them W. S. Rendra whose plays were not allowed in Jakarta. There is a long Javanese tradition of the poet as a "voice on the wind," a critic of authority.

THE STATE OF THE PHYSICAL AND SOCIAL SCIENCES

The development of science and technology has formed part of Indonesia's five-year plans and is directed toward both basic science and applied technology, with emphasis on the latter. Health, agriculture and animal husbandry, defense, physical sciences, and applied technology have had priority. The Indonesian Institute of Sciences has its headquarters and main library in Jakarta. Its task is to oversee and encourage research in diverse fields, to coordinate between institutions, and to advise on national science and technology policy. It also approves research by foreign scholars. Indonesia's major scientific research training centers are the Technological Institute, in Bandung, and the Agricultural Institute, in Bogor, founded in the colonial period, which draw top secondary school graduates.

Among social sciences, economics has received the greatest attention since the 1950s when the Ford Foundation launched a major program to train economists abroad. These so-called technocrats rose to great importance during the early decades of the New Order and molded economic policy throughout the country's growth period, from the 1970s through the 1990s. Social sciences are included in the national mandate largely as they contribute to supporting development activities. Fields such as political science and sociology received far less attention during the New Order, owing to their potential for, and actual involvement in, social and political criticism.

BIBLIOGRAPHY

Abdullah, Taufik, and Sharon Siddique, eds. *Islam and Society in Southeast Asia*, 1987.

Abeyasekere, Susan. *Jakarta: A History*, 1987.

Alisyahbana, S. Takdir. *Indonesia: Social and Cultural Revolution*, 1966.

Anderson, Benedict R. O'G. *Language and Power: Exploring Political Cultures in Indonesia*, 1990.

Bellwood, Peter, James J. Fox, and Darrell Tryon, eds. *The Austronesians: Historical and Comparative Perspectives*, 1995.

Boomgaard, Peter. *Children of the Colonial State: Population Growth and Economic Development in Java, 1795–1880*, 1989.

Brenner, Suzanne April. *The Domestication of Desire: Women, Wealth, and Modernity in Java*, 1998.

Bresnan, John. *Managing Indonesia: The Modern Political Economy*, 1993.

Buchori, Mochtar. *Sketches of Indonesian Society: A Look from Within*, 1994.

Covarrubias, Miguel. *Island of Bali*, 1937.

Cribb, Robert. *Historical Dictionary of Indonesia*, 1992.

Cunningham, Clark E. "Celebrating a Toba Batak National Hero: An Indonesian Rite of Identity." In Susan D. Russell and Clark E. Cunningham, eds., *Changing Lives, Changing Rites*, 1989.

———. "Indonesians." In David Levinson and Melvin Ember, eds., *American Immigrant Cultures*, 1997.

Dalton, Bill. *Indonesia Handbook*, 6th ed., 1995.

Emmerson, Donald K., ed. *Indonesia beyond Suharto: Polity, Economy, Society, Transition*, 1999.

Fontein, Jan. *The Sculpture of Indonesia*, 1990.

Fox, James J. *Harvest of the Palm: Ecological Change in Eastern Indonesia*, 1977.

Furnivall, J. S. *Colonial Policy and Practice: A Comparative Study of Burma and Netherlands India*, 1948.

Geertz, Clifford. *The Religion of Java*, 1976.

———. *Agricultural Involution: The Process of Ecological Change in Indonesia*, 1970.

———. *Negara: The Theatre State in Nineteenth-Century Bali*, 1980.

Geertz, Hildred. *The Javanese Family: A study of kinship and socialization*, 1961.

———. "Indonesian Cultures and Communities." In Ruth T. McVey, ed., *Indonesian*,1963.

Geertz, Hildred, and Clifford Geertz. *Kinship in Bali*, 1975.

Gillow, John. *Traditional Indonesian Textiles*, 1992.

Grant, Bruce. *Indonesia*, 3rd ed., 1996.

Hefner, Robert W., and Patricia Horvatich, eds. *Islam in an Era of Nation-States*, 1997.

Hoskins, Janet. "The Headhunter as Hero Local: Traditions and Their Reinterpretation in National History." *American Ethnologist* 14 (4): 605–622, 1987.

Josselin de Jong, P. D. de, ed. *Unity in Diversity Indonesia as a Field of Anthropological Study*, 1984.

Kahin, George Mc T. *Nationalism and Revolution in Indonesia*, 1952.

Kartodirdjo, Sartono. *Modern Indonesia Tradition and Transformation*, 1984.

Kayam, Umar. *The Soul of Indonesia: A cultural journey*, 1985.

Keeler, Ward. *Javanese Shadow Puppets*, 1992.

Kipp, Rita Smith, and Susan Rodgers, eds. *Indonesian Religions in Transition*, 1987.

Koentjaraningrat. *Introduction to the Peoples and Cultures of Indonesia and Malaysia*, 1975.

———. *Javanese Culture*, 1985.

———. ed. *Villages in Indonesia*, 1967.

Kwik, Greta. "Indos." In David Levinson and Melvin Ember, eds., *American Immigrant Cultures*, 1997.

Lev, Daniel, S. and Ruth McVey, eds. *Making Indonesia Essays on Modern Indonesia in Honor of George McT. Kahin*, 1996.

Levinson, David, and Melvin Ember, eds. *American Immigrant Cultures: Builders of a Nation*, 1997.

Liddle, R. William. *Leadership and Culture in Indonesian Politics*, 1996.

Loveard, Keith. *Suharto: Indonesia's Last Sultan*, 1999.

Lubis, Mochtar. *The Indonesian Dilemma*, 1983.

McVey, Ruth T., ed. *Indonesia*, 1963.

Miksic, John. *Borobudur: Golden Tales of the Buddhas*, 1990.

Mulder, Niels. *Individual and Society in Java*, 1989.

———. *Inside Indonesian Society: An Interpretation of Cultural Change in Java*, 1994.

Peacock, James L. *The Muhammadijah Movement in Indonesian Islam*, 1978.

Pemberton, John. *On the Subject of "Java,"* 1994.

Ricklefs, M. C. *A History of Modern Indonesia since c. 1300*, 2nd ed.,1993.

Russell, Susan D., and Clark E. Cunningham, eds. *Changing Lives, Changing Rites: Ritual and Social Dynamics in Philippine and Indonesian Uplands*, 1989.

Schwarz, Adam. *A Nation in Waiting: Indonesia in the 1990s*, 1994.

Siegel, James T. *Solo in the New Order: Language and Hierarchy in an Indonesian City*, 1986.

Sumarsam. *Gamelan: Cultural Interaction and Musical Development in Central Java*, 1995.

Suryadinata, Leo, ed. *Ethnic Chinese as Southeast Asians*, 1997.

Taylor, Paul Michael, ed. *Fragile Traditions: Indonesian Art in Jeopardy*, 1994.

——— and Lorraine V. Aragon. *Beyond the Java Sea: Art of Indonesia's Outer Islands*, 1991.

Toer, Pramoedya Ananta. *The Buru Quartet: This Earth of Mankind*, 1982; *Child of All Nations*, 1982; *Footsteps*, 1990; *House of Glass*, 1992.

Walean, Sam A., ed. *Indonesia Year Book, 1996–1997*, 1998.

Waterson, Roxana. *The Living House: An Anthropology of Architecture in South-East Asia*, 1990.

Watson, C. W. *Of Self and Nation: Autobiography and the Representation of Modern Indonesia*, 2000.

Wiener, Margaret J. *Visible and Invisible Realms: Power, Magic, and Colonial Conquest in Bali*, 1995.

Williams, Walter L. *Javanese Lives: Women and Men in a Modern Indonesian Society*, 1991.

Wolters, O. W. *History, Culture, and Region in Southeast Asian Perspectives*, 1982, rev. ed., 1999.

Woodward, Mark R. *Islam in Java: Normative Piety and Mysticism in the Sultanate of Yogyakarta*, 1989.

—CLARK E. CUNNINGHAM

IRAN

CULTURE NAME

Iranian, Persian

ALTERNATIVE NAMES

The term "Persian" is used as an adjective—especially pertaining to the arts—and to designate the principal language spoken in Iran. The term is often used to designate the larger cultural sphere of Iranian civilization. This includes populations living in Iraq, the Persian Gulf region, the Caucasus region, Central Asia, Afghanistan, Pakistan, and northern India. The formal name of the Iranian state is *Jomhuri-ye Islami-ye Iran*, the Islamic Republic of Iran.

ORIENTATION

Identification. The terms "Iran" as the designation for the civilization, and "Iranian" as the name for the inhabitants occupying the large plateau located between the Caspian Sea and the Persian Gulf have been in continual use for more than twenty-five hundred years. They are related to the term "Aryan" and it is supposed that the plateau was occupied in prehistoric times by Indo-European peoples from Central Asia. Through many invasions and changes of empire, this essential designation has remained a strong identifying marker for all populations living in this region and the many neighboring territories that fell under its influence due to conquest and expansion.

Ancient Greek geographers designated the territory as "Persia" after the territory of Fars where the ancient Achamenian Empire had its seat. Today as a result of migration and conquest, people of Indo-European, Turkic, Arab, and Caucasian origin have some claim to Iranian cultural identity. Many of these peoples reside within the territory of modern Iran. Outside of Iran, those identifying with the larger civilization often prefer the appellation "Persian" to indicate their affinity with the culture rather than with the modern political state. This is also true of some members of modern Iranian émigré populations in the United States, Europe, and elsewhere who do not wish to be identified with the current Islamic Republic of Iran, established in 1979.

Location and Geography. Iran is located in southwestern Asia, largely on a high plateau situated between the Caspian Sea to the north and the Persian Gulf and the Gulf of Oman to the south. Its area is 636,300 square miles (1,648,000 square kilometers). Its neighbors are, on the north, Azerbaijan, Armenia, and Turkmenistan; on the east, Pakistan and Afghanistan; and on the west Turkey and Iraq. Iran's total boundary is 4,770 miles (7,680 kilometers). Approximately 30 percent of this boundary is seacoast. The capital is Tehran (Teheran).

Iran's central plateau is actually a tectonic plate. It forms a basin surrounded by several tall, heavily eroded mountain ranges, principally the Elburz Mountains in the north and the Zagros range in the west and south. The geology is highly unstable, creating frequent earthquakes. Several important volcanoes, including Mount Damāvand, the nation's highest peak at approximately 19,000 feet, (5,800 meters) also ring the country.

The arid interior plateau contains two remarkable deserts: the Dasht-e-Kavir (Kavīr Desert) and the Dasht-e-Lut (Lūt Desert). These two deserts dominate the eastern part of the country, and form part of an arid landscape extending into Central Asia and Pakistan.

Iran's climate is one of extremes, ranging from subtropical to subpolar, due to the extreme variations in altitude and rainfall throughout the nation. Temperatures range from as high as 130 degrees Fahrenheit (55 degrees Celsius) in the southwest and along the Persian Gulf coast to −40 degrees Fahrenheit (−40 degrees Celsius). Rainfall varies from less than two inches (five centimeters) annually in Baluchistan, near the Pakistani border, to

Iran

more than eighty inches (two hundred centimeters) in the subtropical Caspian region where temperatures rarely fall below freezing.

Demography. Iran's population has not been accurately measured since the Islamic Revolution of 1979. Recent population estimates range from sixty-one to sixty-five million. The population is balanced (51 percent male, 49 percent female), extremely young, and urban. More than three-quarters of Iran's habitants are under thirty years of age, and an equal percentage live in urban areas. This marks a radical shift from the mid-twentieth century when only 25 percent lived in cities.

Iran is a multiethnic, multicultural society as a result of millennia of migration and conquest. It is perhaps easiest to speak of the various ethnic groups in the country in terms of their first language. Approximately half of the population speaks Persian and affiliated dialects as their primary language. The rest of the population speaks languages drawn from Indo-European, Ural-Altaic (Turkic), or Semitic language families.

The principal non-Persian Indo-European speakers include Kurds, Lurs, Baluchis, and Armenians, making up approximately 15 percent of the population. Turkic speakers constitute approximately 20 to 25 percent of the population. The largest group of Turkic speakers lives in the northwest provinces of East and West Azerbaijan. Other Turkic groups include the Qashqa'i tribe in the south and southwest part of the central plateau, and the Turkmen in the northeast. Semitic speakers, constituting approximately 10 percent of the population, include a large Arabic-speaking population in the extreme southwest province of Khuzestan, and along the Persian Gulf Coast, and a small community of Assyrians in the northwest, who speak Syriac. The remains of a miniscule community of Dravidian speakers lives in the extreme eastern province of Sistan along the border with Afghanistan.

It is important to note that, with some minor exceptions, all ethnic groups living in Iran, whatever their background or primary language, identify strongly with the major features of Iranian culture and civilization. This also applies to many non-Iranians living in Afghanistan, Central Asia, northern India, and parts of Iraq and the Persian Gulf region.

Linguistic Affiliation. In English, "Persian" is the name for the primary language spoken in Iran. It is incorrect, but increasingly common in English-speaking countries to use the native term, "Farsi," to identify the language. This is somewhat akin to using "Deutsch" to describe the principal language of Germany.

Modern Persian, a part of the Indo-Iranian branch of the Indo-European languages, is a language of great antiquity. It is also a language of extraordinary grace and flexibility. Over many centuries, it absorbed Arabic vocabulary and many Turkish elements, swelling its vocabulary to well over 100,000 commonly used words. At the same time, over the many centuries when Arabic was dominant, Persian lost much of its grammatical complexity. The resulting language is mellifluous, easy to learn, and ideally suited for the unsurpassed poetry and literature Iranians have produced over the ages. The language is remarkably stable; Iranians can read twelfth century literature with relative ease.

The majority of Iranian residents whose first language is not Persian are bilingual in Persian and their primary language. Persons whose first language is Persian are usually monolingual.

Symbolism. Iranian culture is rich in cultural symbolism, much of which derives from prehistoric times. Iran is the only nation in the Middle East that uses the solar calendar. It is also the only nation on earth marking the advent of the New Year at the spring equinox.

The Islamic and the pre-Islamic world have both provided national symbols for Iran, and these have come in conflict in recent years. Mohammad Reza Pahlavi, the shah who was deposed in 1979, tried to make the twenty-five-hundred-year-old monarchy itself a central symbol of Iranian life. He designed a series of lavish public celebrations to cement this image in the public imagination. The ancient emblem for the nation was a lion holding a scimitar against a rising sun. This emblem was a symbol not only of Iran, but also of the ancient monarchy, and was prominently displayed on the national tricolor flag of red, white, and green. The Persian lion is now extinct, and since the 1979 Revolution, so is this emblem. It has been replaced by a nonfigurative symbol that can be construed as a calligraphic representation of the basic Islamic creed, "There is no god but God." The tricolor background has been maintained.

Much symbolism in daily life derives not just from Islam, but from the "Twelver" branch of Shi'a Islam that has been the official state religion since the seventeenth century. It is essential to note the central symbolic importance of Imam Hassain, the grandson of the prophet Muhammad, who was martyred in Karbala in present-day Iraq during the Islamic month of Muharram in the seventh century. His martyrdom is a "master symbol" in Iranian life, serving as an inexhaustible source of imagery and rhetoric.

History and Ethnic Relations

Emergence of the Nation. The Iranian nation is one of the oldest continuous civilizations in the world. Upper Paleolithic and Mesolithic populations occupied caves in the Zagros and Elburz mountains. The earliest civilizations in the region descended from the Zagros foothills, where they developed agriculture and animal husbandry, and established the first urban cultures in the Tigris-Euphrates basin in present day Iraq. The earliest urban peoples in what is today Iranian territory were the Elamites in the extreme southwest region of Khuzestan. The arrival of the Aryan peoples—Medes and Persians—on the Iranian plateau in the first millennium B.C.E. marked the beginning of the Iranian civilization, rising to the heights of the great Achaemenid Empire consolidated by Cyrus the Great in 550 B.C.E. Under the rulers Darius the Great and Xerxes, the Achaemenid rulers extended their empire from northern India to Egypt.

Down to the present, one pattern has repeated again and again in Iranian civilization: the conquerors of Iranian territory are eventually them-

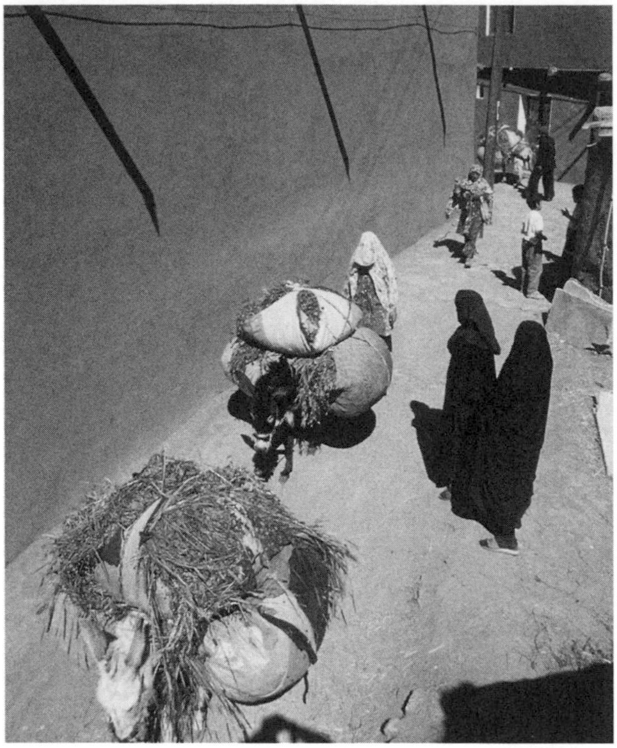

Donkeys carry grass loads past typical mud-brick buildings in a small Iranian village.

selves conquered by Iranian culture. In a word, they become Persianized.

The first of these conquerors was Alexander the Great, who swept through the region and conquered the Achaemenid Empire in 330 B.C.E. Alexander died shortly thereafter leaving his generals and their descendants to establish their own subempires. The process of subdivision and conquest culminated in the establishment of the entirely Persian Sassanid Empire at the beginning of the third century C.E. The Sassanians consolidated all territories east to China and India, and engaged successfully with the Byzantine Empire.

The second great conquerors were the Arab Muslims, arising from Saudi Arabia in 640 C.E. They gradually melded with the Iranian peoples, and in 750, a revolution emanating from Iranian territory assured the Persianization of the Islamic world through the establishment of the great Abbassid Empire at Baghdad. The next conquerors were successive waves of Turkish peoples starting in the eleventh century. They established courts in the northeastern region of Khorassan, founding several great cities. They became patrons of Persian literature, art, and architecture.

Successive Mongol invasions of the thirteenth century resulted in a period of relative instability culminating in a strong reaction in the early sixteenth century on the part of a resurgent religious movement—the Safavids. The Safavid rulers started as a religious movement of adherents of Twelver Shi'ism. They established this form of Shi'ism as the Iranian state religion. Their empire, which ranged from the Caucasus to northern India, raised Iranian civilization to its greatest height. The Safavid capital, Isfahan, was by all accounts one of the most civilized places on earth, far in advance of most of Europe.

Subsequent conquests by the Afghans and the Qājār Turks had the same result. The conquerors came and became Persianized. During the Qājār period from 1899 to 1925, Iran came into contact with European civilization in a serious way for the first time. The industrial revolution in the West seriously damaged Iran's economy, and the lack of a modern army with the latest in weaponry and military transport resulted in serious losses of territory and influence to Great Britain and Russia. Iranian rulers responded by selling "concessions" for agricultural and economic institutions to their European rivals to raise the funds needed for modernization. Much of the money went directly into the pockets of the Qājār rulers, cementing a public image of collaboration between the throne and foreign interests that characterized much of twentieth century Iranian political life. A series of public protests against the throne took place at regular intervals from the 1890s to the 1970s. These protests regularly involved religious leaders, and continued throughout the reign of the Pahlavi dynasty (1925–1979). These protests culminated in the Islamic Revolution of 1978–1979, hereafter referred to as "the Revolution."

National Identity. The establishment of the theocratic Islamic Republic of Iran under Ayatollah Ruhollah Khomeini marked a return to religious domination of Iranian culture. Khomeini's symbols were all appropriately appealing to Iranian sensibilities as he called on the people to become martyrs to Islam like Hasan, and restore the religious rule of Hasan's father, Ali, the last leader of both Sunni and Shi'a Muslims. Now, more than twenty years after the Revolution and following Khomeini's death, Iran is once again undergoing change. Its youthful population is demanding liberalization of the strict religious rule of its leaders, and a return to the historic balance of religion and secularism that has characterized the nation for most of its history.

Ethnic Relations. Iran has been somewhat blessed by an absence of specific ethnic conflict. This is noteworthy, given the large number of ethnic groups living within its borders, both today and in the past. It is safe to conclude that the general Iranian population neither persecutes ethnic minorities, nor openly discriminates against them.

Some groups living within Iranian borders do assert autonomy occasionally, however. Chief among these are the Kurds, living on Iran's western border. Fiercely independent, they have pressed the Iranian central government to grant economic concessions and autonomous decision-making powers. However, outside of the urban areas in their region, the Kurds already have formidable control over their regions. Iranian central government officials tread very lightly in these areas. The Kurds in Iran, along with their brethren in Iraq and Turkey, have long desired an independent state. The immediate prospects for this are dim.

The nomadic tribal groups in the southern and western regions of the Iranian central plateau have likewise caused problems for the Iranian central government. Because they are in movement with their sheep and goats for more than half of the year, they have historically been difficult to control. They are also generally self-sufficient, and a small minority are even quite well-off. Attempts to settle these tribes in the past have met with violent action. At present they entertain an uneasy peace with Iranian central authorities.

The Arab population of the southwestern trans-Zagros Gulf province of Khuzestan has entertained political aspirations of breaking away from Iran. These aspirations have been encouraged by Iraq and other Arab states. In times of conflict between Iran and Iraq, Iraqi leaders have supported this separatist movement as a way of antagonizing Iranian officials.

The severest social persecution in Iran has been directed at religious minorities. Periods of relative tolerance have alternated with periods of discrimination for centuries. Under the current Islamic republic, these minorities have had a difficult time. Although theoretically protected as "People of the Book" according to Islamic law, Jews, Christians, and Zoroastrians have faced accusations of spying for Western nations or for Israel. Islamic officials also take a dim view of their tolerance of alcohol consumption, and the relative freedom accorded to women. The one group that has been universally persecuted since its nineteenth century founding is the Baha'i community, because its religion is viewed as heretical by Shi'a Muslims.

Urbanism, Architecture, and the Use of Space

Until recently Iran was primarily a rural culture. Even today with rampant urbanization, Iranians value nature and make every attempt to spend time in the open air. Because Iran is largely a desert, however, the ideal open space is a culturally constructed space—a garden. At the same time Iranians will try to bring the outdoors inside whenever possible. The wonderfully intricate carpets that every family strives to own are miniature gardens replete with flower and animal designs. Fresh fruit and flowers are a part of every entertainment, and nature and gardens are central themes in literature and poetry.

This underscores a fascinating central motif in Iranian architecture—the juxtaposition of "inside" and "outside." These two concepts are more than architectural themes. They are deeply central to Iranian life, pervading spiritual life and social conduct. The inside, or *andaruni*, is the most private, intimate area of any architectural space. It is the place where family members are most relaxed and able to behave in the most unguarded manner. The outside, or *biruni*, is by contrast a public space where social niceties must be observed. Every family creates both kinds of spaces, even if living in a single room. Until the nineteenth century, Iranians did not use chairs. They normally sat cross-legged on the floor, preferably on a carpet with bolsters or pillows. In the twentieth century, furniture became the hallmark of the *biruni*, and now every family of any standing has a room stuffed with uncomfortable furniture for receiving important visitors. When the guests leave, family members give a sigh of relief and go to the *andaruni* where they can relax on the plush carpet.

An Iranian home is one where any room, with the exception of those used for cooking and bodily functions, can be used for any social purpose—eating, sleeping, entertainment, business, or whatever else one can conceive. One spreads a dinner cloth, and it is a dining room. After dinner, the cloth is removed, cotton mattresses are spread, and the room becomes a bedchamber. Contrast this to an American home where each room has specific functions, or is designated the specific territory of a given family member. As a result, Iranian families can live and entertain many guests in much less space than in the West. This is a social necessity, since the members of one's extended family, and even their friends and acquaintances, have an ironclad claim on virtually unlimited hospitality.

One must be prepared to entertain many overnight guests at a moment's notice.

In addition to intimacy, the notion of the *andaruni* pertains to modesty for women. This is a consideration in all public arrangement of space, especially since the advent of the Islamic Republic. Some zealots will not allow men to sit on a spot that is still warm from a woman's presence. By contrast, public space occupied by persons of the same sex can be very close and intimate with no hint of eroticism or immodesty.

The historical Iranian city is constructed around the commercial center—the bazaar. Architect Nader Ardalan has likened the city to the human body. The bazaar is the spine of the city. Emanating from it are all the institutions needed by the urban population. At the top of the bazaar sits the "head" of this body—the great congregational mosque where all citizens gather on Friday for common prayers and perhaps a sermon. The bazaar is divided into sections inhabited by the various trade guilds. Thus all the carpenters are in one section, the goldsmiths in another, and the shoemakers in yet another.

The bazaar is punctuated with the "outside brought inside" in the form of pools and running water, and even perhaps a religious school with a small garden. The urban space surrounding the bazaar is likewise punctuated by the "inside brought outside" in the form of enclosed public gardens for private discourse in public. Houses in residential neighborhoods are built with abutting walls, each home having its bit of the outside in the form of an open courtyard with a pool, and a tree and a few flowers or a kitchen garden.

In the twentieth century, however, the needs of modern motor transportation and increased urban population density have destroyed much of the texture of the traditional city. Wide avenues have been cut through the traditional quarters in almost every city, disrupting the integrity of the old neighborhoods. Faceless apartment buildings have sprung up depriving residents of their gardens, save for a pot or two of flowers on a small balcony.

Public architecture has always been the essence of *biruni* in Iran. Grandiose in style, it almost demands formal social behavior. This has been true since Achaemenid times, as a visit to the ruins of their capital, Persepolis, will attest. The grandiose public mosques, shrines, and squares of Isfahan, Mashhad, Shīrāz, and Qom are overwhelming in their beauty and architectural excellence. Unfortunately, the great public buildings of Tehran built in the twentieth century have the bad fortune to have been built to emulate the most stark Western architectural styles.

Food and Economy

Food in Daily Life. As one might expect from Iran's geographic situation, its food strikes a medium between Greek and Indian preparations. It is more varied than Greek food, and less spicy and subtler than Indian food with a greater use of fresh ingredients.

Iranians have a healthy diet centered on fresh fruits, greens and vegetables. Meat (usually lamb, goat, or chicken) is used as a condiment rather than as the centerpiece of a meal. Rice and fresh unleavened or semileavened whole-grain bread are staple starches. The primary beverage is black tea. The principal dietary taboo is the Islamic prohibition against pork.

Breakfast is a light meal consisting of fresh unleavened bread, tea, and perhaps butter, white (feta-style) cheese, and jam. Eggs may also be eaten fried or boiled. Meat is not common at breakfast.

The main meal of the day is eaten at around one o'clock in the afternoon. In a middle-class household it usually starts with a plate of fresh greens—scallions, radishes, fresh basil, mint, coriander, and others in season. This is served with unleavened bread and white cheese. The main dish is steamed aromatic rice (*chelow*) served with one or more stews made of meat and a fresh vegetable or fruit. This stew, called *khoresht* resembles a mild curry. It centers on a central ingredient such as eggplant, okra, spinach, quince, celery, or a myriad of other possibilities. One particularly renowned *khoresht*, *fesenjun*, consists of lamb, chicken, duck, or pheasant cooked in a sauce of onions, ground walnuts, and pomegranate molasses. In addition to its preparation as chelow, rice may also be prepared as a pilaf (*polow*) by mixing in fresh herbs, vegetables, fruit, or meat after it is boiled, but before it is steamed.

The Iranian national dish, called *chelow kabab*, consists of filet of lamb marinated in lemon juice or yogurt, onions, and saffron, pounded with a knife on a flat skewer until fork tender and grilled over a hot fire. This is served with grilled onions and tomatoes on a bed of *chelow* to which has been added a lump of butter and a raw egg yolk. The butter and egg are mixed with the hot rice (which cooks the egg), and ground sumac berries are sprinkled on top. A common drink with a meal is *dough*, a yogurt and salted water preparation that is similar to Turkish ayran, Lebanese lebni, and Indian lassi.

An Iranian woman sits on the ground while she makes knitted crafts in the Maseleh village located 1,050 meters above sea level in the Alborz Mountains.

Sweets are more likely to be consumed with tea in the afternoon than as dessert. Every region of the country has special confections prized as travel souvenirs, and served casually to guests. Among the most famous are *gaz*, a natural nougat made with rose water, and *sohan*, a saffron, butter, and pistachio praline. After a meal Iranians prefer fresh fruit and tea. In fact, fruit is served before the meal, after the meal—indeed, at any time.

The evening meal is likely to be a light meal consisting of leftover food from the noon meal, or a little bread, cheese, fruit, and tea. Urban dwellers may eat a light meal at a café or restaurant in the evening.

Outside of large cities, restaurants are not very common in Iran. On the other hand, teahouses are ubiquitous, and widely frequented at all times of day. One can always get some kind of meal there.

Alcoholic beverages are officially forbidden in Iran today under the Islamic republic, but their consumption is still widely practiced. Armenian, Jewish, and Zoroastrian communities still produce wine, and local moonshine is found everywhere in rural areas. The principal alcoholic beverage is "vodka" distilled from grain, grapes, or more commonly, raisins. It is consumed almost exclusively by men in the evening or at celebrations such as weddings.

Food Customs at Ceremonial Occasions. Ritual foods fall into two categories—foods that are eaten in celebration, and foods that are prepared and consumed as a charitable religious act.

A few foods are traditional for the New Year's celebration. Fish is widely consumed as the first meal of the New Year, along with a *polow* made with greens. One food appears on the ritual New Year's table, but is rarely eaten. This is a kind of sweet pudding made of ground sprouted wheat called *samanou.*

During the Islamic month of fasting, Ramadan, no food or drink is consumed from sunrise to sunset. Families rise before dawn to prepare heavy breakfasts that look like the noon meal. The process is repeated at sundown. Special crispy fried sweets made from a yogurt batter and soaked in syrup are frequently served. Two forms are popular: *zulbia,* which looks a bit like a multi stranded pretzel, and *bamieh,* which looks a bit like the okra pods it is named after.

Food is frequently prepared for distribution to the community as a charitable religious act. When a sheep is slaughtered for a special occasion it is common to give meat to all of one's neighbors. To give thanks for fulfillment of a desire, a community meal is frequently prepared. Likewise, during the mourning ceremonies for Hossein during the months of Muharram and Safar, communal meals are paid for by charitable individuals. The most common food served on these occasions is a *polow* made with yellow peas and meat.

Basic Economy. Historically Iran has been an agricultural nation with fairly rich resources both for vegetable crops and animal husbandry. In the twentieth century, Iran's economy changed in a radical fashion due to the discovery of oil. By the time of the Revolution the nation received more than 80 percent of its income from oil and oil-related industry. While in 1955 more than 75 percent of the population lived in rural areas, distribution has reversed. Now more than 75 percent of Iranians live in urban areas, deriving their incomes either from manufacturing or from the service sector (currently the largest sector of the economy).

The goals of the Islamic Republic include a drive for self-sufficiency in food and manufacture. At present, however, only about 10 percent of the nation's agricultural land is under cultivation, and subsistence farming is all but dead. Iran remains a net importer of food and manufactured goods, a condition that will not change soon. Inflation is a continual problem. Were it not for oil income, the nation would be in difficult straits.

Land Tenure and Property. Absentee landlords in Iran held traditional agricultural land for many hundreds of years. They employed a sharecropping arrangement with their tenant farmers based on a principle of five shares: land, water, seed, animal labor, and human labor. The farmer rarely supplied more than human and animal labor, and thus received two-fifths of the produce. Additionally landlords hired some agricultural laborers to work land for them for direct wages.

Sharecropping farmers received the land they farmed in the land reform movements of the 1960s and 1970s, but the wage farmers received nothing, and largely abandoned agricultural pursuits.

Nomadic tribes claim grazing rights along their route of migration, with the rights parceled out by family affiliation. Government officials have contested and opposed these rights at various times on environmental grounds (overgrazing), but they have not been able marshal effective enforcement. Tribal members also maintain agricultural land both at their summer and winter pasture headquarters.

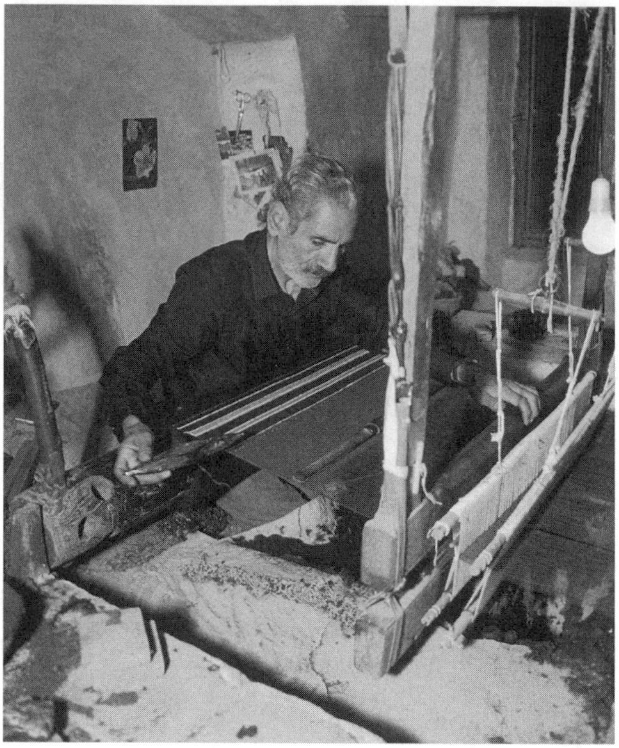

A carpet maker works on a loom at his shop in Na'in.

Religious bequest (*waqf*) land plays a large role in Iranian life. Large landowners on their death have willed whole villages as well as other kinds of property to the religious bequest trust. Nearly the entire city of Mashhad is waqf land. Individuals in that city can buy houses and office buildings, but not the land on which they stand. Part of the strategic plan of the Pahlavi rulers was to break the economic power of the clergy who controlled this vast property by nationalizing it, and placing its administration under a government ministry. This was one of the government actions most vehemently opposed by the clergy before the Revolution. Nevertheless, the waqf is still administered by a government ministry.

Major Industries. Iran today has a steel plant, automobile and bus assembly plants, a good infrastructure of roads, a decent telecommunication system, and good broadcast facilities for radio and television. These have all been extended under the Islamic Republic, as has rural electrification. Mining and exploitation of Iran's extensive mineral wealth other than oil is largely moribund. Moves to privatize industry have been slow; 80 percent of all economic activity is under direct government control.

Trade. Aside from oil products, the nation's exports include carpets, caviar, cotton, fruits, textiles, minerals, motor vehicles, and nuts. A small amount of fresh produce and meat is exported to the states of the Persian Gulf.

Social Stratification

Classes and Castes. Iranian society presents a puzzle for most standard social science analysis of social structure. On the one hand there is an outward appearance of extensive social stratification. When one peers beneath the surface, however, this impression breaks down almost immediately.

In Iran one can never judge a book by its cover. A traditional gentleman in ragged clothes, unshaven, and without any outward trapping of luxury may in fact be very rich, and as powerful as the mightiest government official; or he may be a revered spiritual leader. On the other hand a well-dressed gentleman in an Italian suit driving a fine European car may be mired in debt and openly derided behind his back.

Social mobility is also eminently possible in Iran. Clever youths from poor backgrounds may educate themselves, attach themselves to persons of power and authority, and rise quickly in status and wealth. Family connections help here, and hypergamy (marriage into a higher class) for both men and women is very important.

High status is precarious in Iran. There is a symbiotic relationship between superior and inferior. Duty is incumbent on the inferior, but the noblesse oblige incumbent on the superior as a condition of maintaining status is often greater, as the last shah, Mohammad Reza Pahlavi, discovered in the Revolution.

Nevertheless there are genuinely revered figures in public life. Public respect is largely accorded by diffuse and generalized acclimation, this being a form of status recognition that Iranians trust. The public has a tendency to dismiss awards, promotions, and public accolades as the result of political or social intriguing. The clerical hierarchy in Shi'a Islam is a good model for genuine advancement in social hierarchy because clerics advance through the informal acknowledgment of their peers.

Political Life

Government. Iran has made the transition in the last twenty years from a nominal constitutional monarchy to a democratic theocracy. As the United States has checks and balances in its governmental system, so does Iran. There is a strong president elected for a four-year term, and a unicameral legislature (*majles*) of 270 members, elected directly by the people, with some slots reserved for recognized minorities. The position of speaker is politically important, since there is no prime minister. Suffrage is universal, and the voting age is sixteen. The president selects a Council of Ministers, an Expediency Council, and serves as the head of the Council of National Security.

Over and above these elected bodies there is a supreme jurisprudent selected by an independent Assembly of Experts—a council of religious judges. The office of chief jursiprudent (*faqih*) was created for Ayatollah Ruhollah Khomeini at the time of the Revolution. It was designed to implement a controversial philosophy unique to Khomeini's teachings—a "guardianship" to be implemented until the day of return of the twelfth Shi'a Imam, Muhammad al-Mahdi, who is in occultation (being hidden from view). Alongside the chief jurisprudent is a twelve-member Council of Guardians, six selected by the chief jurisprudent, and six by the Supreme Judicial Council ratified by the majles. The Council of Guardians rules on the Islamic suitability of both elected officials and the laws they pass. They can disqualify candidates for election both before and after they are elected. Another council mediates between the Council of Guardians and the legislature.

The judiciary consists of a Supreme Judge and a Supreme Judicial Council. All members must be Shi'a Muslim jurisprudents. Islamic Shari'a law is the foundation for the court's decisions. Freedom of the press and assembly are constitutionally guaranteed so long as such activities do not contradict Islamic law.

The units of governmental division are the province (*ostan*), "county" (*sharestan*), and township (*dehestan*). Each governmental unit has a head appointed by the Ministry of the Interior.

Military Activity. Although there is a standing army, navy, and air force, the Revolutionary Guards (*Pasdaran-e Engelab*), organized shortly after the Revolution, dominate military activities, often coming into conflict with the standard military forces. The Revolutionary Guards either accompany or lead all military activities, both internal and international. A national police force oversees urban areas, and a gendarmerie attends to rural peacekeeping.

Social Welfare and Change Programs

The Islamic Republic of Iran is replete with charitable organizations. It is incumbent upon all Muslims to devote a proportion of their excess income to the support of religious and charitable works. This contribution is voluntary, but the government collects this tithe and uses the income to support hospitals, orphanages, and religious schools. The government is also committed to rural development projects. A movement called the "sacred development struggle" (*jihad-e sazandegi*) was launched early in the Islamic Republic and was successful in bringing important development projects—electrification, drinking water and roads—to remote rural areas. There are many small private charitable organizations organized to help the poor, fatherless families, children, and other unfortunate citizens. The Iranian Red Crescent Society (the local version of the Red Cross) is active and important in the instance of national disaster. Iran is a net exporter of charity to neighboring countries. It has assisted with disaster relief in Central Asia, the Caucasus, Lebanon, and the Persian Gulf region.

Nongovernmental Organizations and Other Associations

There are very few international nongovernmental organizations (NGOs) operating independent development or health programs in Iran at present, except in conjunction with Iranian governmental organizations. The current regime views independent NGOs with deep suspicion, and in its aim for self-sufficiency views the work of many international charities as unnecessary. The United Nations (UN) is the one important exception. Iran has supported the UN since its inception, and a number of UN programs in health, development, population, and the preservation of cultural antiquities are active. The nation's Mostazafin ("downtrodden people") Foundation and the Imam Khomeini Foundation have operated in the international sphere.

Gender Roles and Statuses

The Relative Status of Women and Men. The question of gender roles is one of the most complex issues in contemporary Iranian society. Women have always had a strong role in Iranian life, but rarely a public role. Their prominent participation in political movements has been especially noteworthy. Brave and often ruthlessly pragmatic, women are more than willing to take to the streets for a good public cause. Moreover, although the world focuses increasingly on the question of female dress as an indicator of progress for women in Iran (and indeed, in the Islamic world altogether), this is a superficial view. In the years since the Revolution, women have made astonishing progress in nearly every area of life.

Both the Pahlavi regime and the leaders of the Islamic Republic have gone out of their way to emphasize their willingness to have women operate as full participants in government and public affairs. Women have served in the legislature and as government ministers since the 1950s. The average marriage age for women has increased to twenty-one years. Iran's birthrate has fallen steadily since before the Revolution, now standing at an estimated 2.45 percent. Education for women is obligatory and universal, and education for girls has increased steadily. The literacy rate for women is close to that of men, and for women under 25 it is over 90 percent, even in rural areas.

Female employment is the one area where women have suffered a decline since the Revolution. Even under the current Islamic regime, virtually all professions are theoretically open to women—with an important caveat. The difficulty for the leaders of the Islamic republic in allowing women complete equality in employment and public activity revolves around religious questions of female modesty that run head-to-head with the exigencies of public life. Islam requires that both women and men adopt modest dress that does not inflame carnal desire. For men this means eschewing tight pants, shorts, short-sleeved shirts, and open collars. Iranians view women's hair as erotic, and so covering both the hair and the female form are the basic requirements of modesty. For many centuries women in Iran have done this by wearing the chador, a semicircular piece of dark cloth that is wrapped expertly around the body and head, and gathered at the chin. This garment is both wonderfully convenient, since it affords a degree of privacy, and lets one wear virtually anything underneath; and restricting, since it must be held shut with one hand. Makeup of any kind is not allowed. In private, women dress as they please, and often exhibit fashionable, even daring, clothing for their female friends and spouses.

Any public activity that would require women to depart from this modest dress in mixed company is expressly forbidden. Professions requiring physical exertion outdoors are excluded, as are most public entertainment roles. Interestingly, film and television are open to women provided they observe modest dress standards. This has created an odd separate-but-equal philosophy in Iranian life. Some

Vehicles travel on a street near the Eman Reza Shrine in Mashhad.

activities, such as sports events, have been set up for exclusively female participants and female spectators.

Westernized Iranian women have long viewed obligatory modest dress in whatever forms as oppressive, and have worked to have standards relaxed. These standards certainly have been oppressive when forced on the female population in an obsessive manner. Revolutionary Guards have mutilated some women for showing too much hair or for wearing lipstick. But the majority of women in Iran have always adopted modest dress voluntarily, and will undoubtedly continue to do so in the future no matter what political decisions are made on this matter.

The emotional roles of Iranian men and women are different from those in the United States and many other Western countries. In particular, it is considered manly for men to be emotionally sensitive, artistically engaged, and aesthetically acute. Women, by contrast, can be emotionally distant and detached without seeming unfeminine. Open weeping is not shameful for either sex. Both sexes can be excessively tender and doting toward their same-sex friends with no intention of eroticism. Kissing and hand-holding between members of the same sex is common.

By contrast, physical contact between members of the opposite sex is assiduously avoided except between relatives. Western men offering to shake a traditional Iranian woman's hand may see her struggling between a desire to be polite, and a desire not to breech standards of decency. The solution for many a woman is to cover her hand with part of her chador and shake hands that way. Under no circumstances should a proper man or woman willingly find themselves alone in a closed room with a member of the opposite sex (except for his or her spouse).

Marriage, Family, and Kinship

Marriage. In Iran women control marriages for their children, and much intrigue in domestic life revolves around marital matters. A mother is typically on the lookout for good marriage prospects at all times. Even if a mother is diffident about marriage brokering, she is obliged to "clear the path" for a marriage proposal. She does this by letting her counterpart in the other family know that a proposal is forthcoming, or would be welcome. She then must confer with her husband, who makes the formal proposal in a social meeting between the two families. This kind of background work is essential, because once the children are married, the two families virtually merge, and have extensive rights and obligations vis-á-vis each other that are close to a sacred duty. It is therefore extremely important that the families be certain that they are compatible before the marriage takes place.

Marriage within the family is a common strategy, and a young man of marriageable age has an absolute right of first refusal for his father's brother's daughter—his patrilateral parallel cousin. The advantages for the families in this kind of marriage are great. They already know each other and are tied into the same social networks. Moreover, such a marriage serves to consolidate wealth from the grandparents' generation for the family. Matrilateral cross-cousin marriages are also common, and exceed parallel-cousin marriages in urban areas, due perhaps to the wife's stronger influence in family affairs in cities.

Although inbreeding would seem to be a potential problem, the historical preference for marriage within the family continues, waning somewhat in urban settings where other considerations such as profession and education play a role in the choice of a spouse. In 1968, 25 percent of urban marriages, 31 percent of rural marriages, and 51 percent of tribal marriages were reported as endogamous. These percentages appear to have increased somewhat following the Revolution.

In Iran today a love match with someone outside of the family is clearly not at all impossible, but even in such cases, except in the most westernized families, the family visitation and negotiation must be observed. Traditional marriages involve a formal contract drawn up by a cleric. In the contract a series of payments are specified. The bride brings a dowry to the marriage usually consisting of household goods and her own clothing. A specified amount is written into the contract as payment for the woman in the event of divorce. The wife after marriage belongs to her husband's household and may have difficulty visiting her relatives if her husband does not approve. Nevertheless, she retains her own name, and may hold property in her own right, separate from her husband.

The wedding celebration is held after the signing of the contract. It is really a prelude to the consummation of the marriage, which takes place typically at the end of the evening, or, in rural areas, at the end of several days' celebration. In many areas of Iran it is still important that the bride be virginal, and the bedsheets are carefully inspected to ensure this. A wise mother gives her daughter a vial of chicken blood "just in case." The new couple may live with their relatives for a time until they can set up their own household. This is more common in rural than in urban areas.

Iran is an Islamic nation, and polygyny is allowed. It is not widely practiced, however, because Iranian officials in this century have followed the Islamic prescription that a man taking two wives must treat them with absolute equality. Women in polygynous marriages hold their husbands to this and will seek legal relief if they feel they are disadvantaged. Statistics are difficult to ascertain, but one recent study claims that only 1 percent of all marriages are polygynous.

Divorce is less common in Iran than in the West. Families prefer to stay together even under difficult circumstances, since it is extremely difficult to disentangle the close network of interrelationships between the two extended families of the marriage pair. One recent study claims that the divorce rate is 10 percent in Iran. For Iranians moving to the United States the rate is 66 percent, suggesting that cultural forces tend to keep couples from separating.

Children of a marriage belong to the father. After a divorce, men assume custody of boys over three years and girls over seven. Women have been known to renounce their divorce payment in exchange for custody of their children. There is no impediment to remarriage with another partner for either men or women.

Domestic Unit. In traditional Iranian rural society the "dinner cloth" often defines the minimal family. Many branches of an extended family may live in rooms in the same compound. However, they may not all eat together on a daily basis. Sons and their wives and children are often working for their parents in anticipation of a birthright in the form of land or animals. When they receive this, they will leave and form their own separate household. In the meantime they live in their parents' compound, but have separate eating and sleeping arrangements. Even after they leave their parents' home, members of extended families have widespread rights to hospitality in the homes of even their most distant relations. Indeed, family members generally carry out most of their socializing with each other.

Inheritance. Inheritance generally follows rules prescribed by Islamic law. Male children inherit full shares of their father's estate, wives and daughters half-shares. An individual may make a religious bequest of specific goods or property that are then administered by the ministry of waqfs.

Kin Groups. The patriarch is the oldest male of the family. He demands respect from other family members and often has a strong role in the future of young relatives. In particular it is common for members of an extended family to spread themselves out in terms of professions and influence. Some will go into government, others into the military, perhaps others join the clergy, and some may even become anti-government oppositionists. Families will attempt to marry their children into powerful families as much for their own sake as for the son or daughter. The general aim for the family is to extend its influence into as many spheres as possible. As younger members mature, older members of the family are expected to help them with jobs, introductions, and financial support. This is not considered corrupt or nepotistic, but is seen rather as one of the benefits of family membership.

Socialization

Infant Care. The role of the mother is extremely important in Iran. Mothers are expected to breastfeed their babies for fear the babies will become "remorseless."

Child Rearing and Education. Mothers and children are expected to be mutually supportive. A mother will protect her children's reputation under all circumstances. Small children are indulged, and not just by their parents. They are magnets for attention from everyone in the society. Some parents worry about their children becoming vain and spoiled, but have a difficult time denying their wishes.

Older children often raise younger children, especially in rural settings. It is very common to see an older child with full responsibility for care of a toddler. Children are usually more than up to this task, and develop strong bonds with their siblings. There is some rivalry between children in a family, but the rule of primogeniture is strong, and older children have the right to discipline younger children.

The father is the disciplinarian of the family. Whereas most fathers dote on their small children, they can become fierce and stern as children approach puberty. It is the father's responsibility to protect the honor of the family, and this means keeping close watch on the women and their activities. A girl is literally a treasure for the family. If she remains chaste, virginal, modest, and has other attributes such as beauty and education she has an excellent chance of making a marriage that will benefit everyone. If she falls short of this ideal, she can ruin not only her own life, but also the reputation of her family.

Boys are far more indulged than girls. Their father teaches them very early, however, that the protection of family honor also resides with them. It is not unusual to see a small boy upbraiding his own mother for some act that shows a lack of modesty. This is the beginning of a life long enculturation that emphasizes self-denial, collectivism, and interdependence with regard to the family.

Families place a very strong emphasis on education for both boys and girls. For girls this is a more modern attitude, but it was always true for boys. The education system relies a great deal on rote memorization, patterned as it is on the French education system. Children are also strongly encouraged in the arts. They write poetry and learn music, painting, and calligraphy, often pursuing these skills privately.

Higher Education. All Iranians would like their children to pursue higher education, and competition for university entrance is fierce. The most desired professions for children are medicine and engineering. These fields attract the best and the brightest, and graduates receive an academic social title for both professions (*doktor* and *mohandess*). The social rewards are so great for success in these professions that families will push their children into them even if their interests lie elsewhere. Many young people receive an engineering or medical degree and then pursue a completely different career.

Etiquette

The social lubricant of Iranian life is a system known as *ta'arof*, literally "meeting together." This is a ritualized system of linguistic and behavioral interactional strategies allowing individuals to interrelate in a harmonious fashion. The system marks the differences between *andaruni* and *biruni* situations, and also marks differences in relative social status. In general, higher status persons are older and have important jobs, or command respect because of their learning, artistic accomplishments, or erudition.

Linguistically, ta'arof involves a series of lexical substitutions for pronouns and verbs whereby persons of lower status address persons of higher status with elevated forms. By contrast, they refer to themselves with humble forms. Both partners in an interaction may simultaneously use other-raising and self-lowering forms toward each other. Ritual

An Iranian family eating a meal in Shiraj. Even after they leave home, members of extended families have hospitality rights in the homes of their most distant relatives.

greetings and leave-takings such as *ghorban-e shoma* (literally, "your sacrifice") underscore this sensibility.

In social situations, this linguistic gesture is replicated in behavioral routines. It is good form to offer a portion of what one is about to eat to anyone nearby, even if they show no interest. One sees this behavior even in very small children. It is polite to refuse such an offer, but the one making the offer will be sensitive to the slightest hint of interest and will continue to press the offer if it is indicated.

Guests bring honor to a household, and are eagerly sought. When invited as a guest a small present is appreciated, but often received with a show of embarrassment. It will usually not be unwrapped in front of the giver. It is always expected that a person returning from a trip will bring presents for family and friends.

An honored guest is always placed at the head of a room or a table. The highest status person also goes first when food is served. It is proper form to refuse these honors, and press them on another.

One must be very careful about praising any possession of another. The owner will likely offer it immediately as a present. Greater danger still lies in praising a child. Such praise bespeaks envy, which is the essence of the "evil eye." The parent will be alarmed, fearing for the child's life. The correct formula for praising anything is *ma sha' Allah*, literally, "What God wills."

Iranians can be quite physically intimate with same-sex friends, even in public. Physical contact is expected and is not erotic. In restaurants and on buses and other public conveyances people are seated much closer than in the West. On the other hand, even the slightest physical contact with non-family members of the opposite sex, unless they are very young children, is taboo.

A downward gaze in Iran is a sign of respect. Foreigners addressing Iranians often think them disinterested or rude when they answer a question without looking at the questioner. This is a cross-cultural mistake. For men, downcast eyes are a defense measure, since staring at a woman is usually taken as a sign of interest, and can cause difficulties. On the other hand, staring directly into the eyes of a friend is a sign of affection and intimacy.

In Iran the lower status person issues the first greeting. In the reverse logic of ta'arof this means that a person who wants to be polite will make a point of this, using the universal Islamic *salaam* or the extended *salaam aleikum*. The universal phrase for leave-taking is *khoda hafez*—"God protect."

RELIGION

Religion Beliefs. The state religion in Iran is *Ithna-ashara* or Twelver Shi'ism, established by the Safavid Dynasty in the seventeenth century. This branch of Islam has many distinctive practices and beliefs that differ from the Sunni Islam practiced in most of the Muslim world. Shi'a Muslims revere the descendants of Fatimah, daughter of the prophet Muhammad, and her husband, Ali, Muhammad's cousin. There are twelve Imams recognized by this branch of Shi'ism. All were martyred except the twelfth, Muhammad al-Mahdi, who disappeared, but will return at the end of time with Jesus to judge mankind. A common symbol seen throughout Iran is an open hand. This is a complex symbol with a number of interpretations, but one is that the five fingers represent the "five bodies" central to Shi'ism—Muhammad, Fatimah, Ali, and the two sons of Fatimah and Ali, Husayn and Hassain.

It is Hassain, however, who is the true central figure in Iranian symbolic life. Hassain was martyred in a struggle for power between rival sects, later concretized as Shi'a and Sunni. This martyrdom is ritually observed throughout the year on every possible occasion. Pious individuals endow recitation of the story by professional panegyrists on a regular basis. The Islamic months of Muharram and Safar are months of ritual mourning for Hassain, with processions, self-flagellation, and ten-day dramatic depictions of the events of the martyrdom.

Just as Hassain is a central figure, everyone associated with him and his descendants who lived in Iran are equally revered—in particular Imam Reza, the eighth leader of Shi'a Muslims. Whereas all other Shi'a Imams are buried in modern Iraqi territory, Imam Reza is buried in the northeastern Iranian city, Mashhad. His astonishingly lavish shrine is one of the major pilgrimage destinations for Shi'a Muslims.

Although the vast majority of Iranians are Twelver Shi'a Muslims, important religious minorities have always played an important role in Iranian life. Zoroastrians date back to the Achaemenid Empire more than two thousand years ago. Iranian Jews claim to be the oldest continuous Jewish community in the world, dating back to the removal to Babylon. Armenians, an ancient Christian people, were imported by Iranian rulers for their artisanry, and Assyrian Christians, who follow a non-Trinitarian doctrine, have been continually resident in Iran since the third century. Sunni Muslims are represented by Arab and Baluchi populations in the south and Turkish populations in the north and west. One religious group is homegrown. The Baha'i movement, a semi-mystical nineteenth-century departure from Shi'ia Islam, won converts not only from Islam, but also from Judaism, Zoroastrianism, and Christianity. Considered a heresy by many Shi'a Muslims, Baha'i has spread from Iran to virtually every nation on earth.

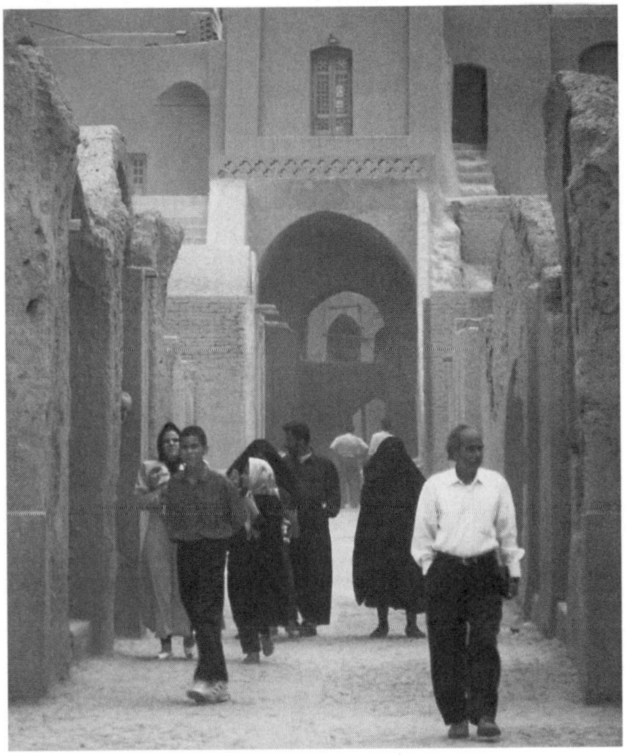

Local Iranian families tour the mud city of Bam to learn of its history.

Religious Practitioners. There is no formal certification for Islamic clergy. Technically, all sincere Muslims can establish themselves as religious practitioners. Women cannot preach to men, but female clerics ministering to women are not uncommon. In the normal course of training a young man attends a religious school. He takes classes from revered scholars who give him a certificate when he has completed a course of study to their satisfaction. After some time he may receive a call to take up residence in a community needing a cleric.

In time, he may acquire a reputation as a *mujtahed* or "jurisprudent," capable of interpreting Islamic law. Since there is no fixed theological doctrine in Shi'ism beyond the Koran and the Hadith (traditions of the prophet Muhammad), believers are free to follow the religious leader of their choice, and his interpretation of Islamic law. In time, as a mujtahed gains respect and followers, he may rise to become an ayatollah (literally, Reflection of God''). Ayatollah Ruhollah Khomeini, who in the 1970s had the largest number of followers of all religious leaders, led the Iranian Revolution.

Mysticism plays an important role in Iranian religion. Religious orders of Sufi mystics have been active in Iran for many centuries. Sufis focus on an inward meditative path for the pursuit of religious truth that may include group chanting and dance. Because they believe religion to be a personal spiritual journey, they eschew the outward trappings of social and economic life, and are highly revered.

Rituals and Holy Places. Shrines of Islamic saints are extremely important in Iranian religious practice. Most of these burial places, which receive regular visits from believers, are purported graves of the descendants of the prophet Muhammad through the Shi'a Imams. A pilgrimage to a local shrine is a common religious and social occasion. Longer pilgrimages to Karbala, Mashhad, or Mecca are greatly respected.

Most holidays in Iran are religious holidays revolving around the birth or death of the various Shi'a Imams. There are thirty of these days, all calculated according to the lunar calendar, which is always at variance with the Iranian solar calendar. This can complicate people's lives. It is necessary to have a Muslim cleric in the community just to calculate the dates. Most of these holidays involve mourning, at which time the story of Hassain's martyrdom at Karbala is recited. The exception is the birthday of the Twelfth Imam, which is a happy celebration.

MEDICINE AND HEALTH CARE

Health care in Iran is generally very good. Life expectancy is relatively high (70 years) and the nation does not have any severe endemic infectious diseases. The principal cause of death is heart and circulatory disease. Many physicians emigrated at the time of the Islamic Revolution, but a sufficient number, supplemented by doctors from South Asia, continue to serve the population.

Health care programs in recent years have been highly successful. Malaria has been virtually eliminated, cholera and other waterborne diseases are generally under control, and family planing programs have resulted in dramatic decreases in fertility rates. The infant mortality rate remains somewhat elevated (twenty-nine per thousand) but it has declined significantly over the past twenty years. AIDS figures are suppressed.

Opium addiction has been a continual medical concern in Iran. The Pahlavi regime attempted to phase out its use by licensing the sale of state-produced raw opium only to certified addicts born after a specified date. It was thought that all the addicts would eventually die, and the problem would be solved. Of course, the availability of opium on the free market simply guaranteed that it would be resold to younger people at a profit, and the problem continued. The use of opium persists as a casual drug for all classes of society, with a small proportion of continued addicts.

A folk belief prevalent in Iran revolves around dietary practice. This philosophy tries to maintain balance between the four humors of the body—blood, phlegm, yellow bile, and black bile—through judicious combinations of foods. Although more sophisticated Iranians use the full range of four humors in their dietary calculations, most adhere to a two-category system: hot and cold. For example, visitors quickly learn that their friends will not allow the simultaneous consumption of watermelon and yogurt (both cold foods), for fear that this combination will cause immediate death.

SECULAR CELEBRATIONS

Most holidays in Iran are religious in nature. The few secular holidays relate to pre-Islamic practices, or modern political events.

The Iranian New Year's Celebration (*Now Ruz*) is the nation's principal secular holiday. The Now Ruz celebration is replete with pre-Islamic symbolism, beginning with the practice of jumping over bonfires on the Wednesday before the equinox. An array of symbols emphasizing agricultural renewal is displayed throughout the long period of celebration, which lasts for thirteen days. Accompanying the festivities is the celebratory presence of a black-faced clown, *Hajji Firouz*. In some parts of the country a ''king'' of the New Year is selected and catered to during the holiday. On the thirteenth day he is ritually sacrificed.

In some parts of Iran the winter solstice is celebrated in a special manner. Watermelons are saved from the summer and hung in a protected place. On the longest night of the year, family and friends stay up all night, tell stories, and eat the watermelons.

The nation also celebrates Islamic Republic Day on 1 April to mark the 1979 Revolution.

The Arts and Humanities

Support for the Arts. The role of the arts in Iran is highly complex. On the one hand, Iranians have one of the richest and most elaborate artistic traditions in the world. On the other hand, Islamic leaders disapprove of many forms of artistic expression. Under the Pahlavi regime, especially under the patronage of the empress, Farah Diba, the arts were heavily supported and promoted. Under the Islamic republic this support has continued, but with many fits, starts, and caveats. Moral censorship has invaded virtually every form of artistic expression, but the inventive Iranians somehow manage to produce marvelous art despite these restrictions.

Two Islamic prohibitions affect arts in the most direct way: a prohibition against music, and one against the depiction of humans and animals in art. The prophet Muhammad disapproved of music because it acted to transport listeners to another mental sphere, distracting them from attention to the world created by God. The depiction of humans and animals is disapproved on two grounds: first, because it could be construed as idolatry; and second, because it could be seen as an attempt to create an alternate universe to that created by God. Additionally, the early Muslims considered poetry to be suspect, since it was thought to be inspired by jinn. For these reasons the Koran, certainly one of the most poetic works ever created, is explicitly not poetry. Chanting of the Koran is likewise not music. Over the centuries Iranians have taken these prohibitions somewhat lightly.

Literature. Iranian poets have penned some of the most wonderful, moving poetry in the history of humankind. The great poets Firdawsī, Hāfez, Sa'adī, and Jalāl ad-D n ar-R m and a host of others are an intimate part of the life of every Iranian. Modern poets writing in non-metric styles are equally revered, and the nation has developed a distinguished coterie of novelists, essayists, and exponents of belles lettres, both male and female.

Graphic Arts. Persian miniature paintings illustrating Iranian epics and classic stories are among the world's great art treasures. These miniatures depicted both humans and animals. Another tradition, more religiously approved, is the artistic development of calligraphy. This is a highly developed Iranian art, as it is throughout the Middle East. Iran has its own styles of Arabic calligraphy, however, and has developed many modern artists who fashion common words into figurative art of great beauty. Iran's modern painters often use classic themes from miniatures combined with calligraphy for a uniquely Persian effect. Geometric design is also approved, and is seen in architectural detail and carpet design.

No discussion of Persian art would be complete without mention of carpet making. Carpets are Iran's most important export item after oil, and their creation is an art of the highest order. Carpets are hand-knotted. The finest take years to complete and have hundreds of knots per square inch. The designs are drawn from a traditional stock of motifs, but are continually elaborated upon by weavers. Each region of Iran has its own traditional designs. Carpets are not only beautiful works of art, they are investments. Older carpets are worth more than new carpets. Every Iranian family will try to own one, with the secure knowledge that if they take care in their purchase it will always increase in value.

Also of significance are the centuries-old traditions of silverwork, wood-block printing, enamel ware, inlay work, and filigree jewelry manufacture. These arts were revived during the Pahlavi era in government-sponsored workshops and training programs. This support has continued after the Revolution, and owning excellent examples of these artistic products has become a hallmark of good taste in Iranian homes.

Performance Arts. Persian classical music is one of the most elaborate and inspiring artistic forms ever created. The musical system consists of twelve modal units called *dastgah.* These are divided into small melodic units called *gusheh*, most of which are associated with classic Persian poetic texts. A full performance of classical music consists of alternating arhythmic and rhythmic sections from a single dastgah. The instrumentalist and the vocal artist improvise within the modal structure, creating a unique performance. Traditional instruments include the *tar*,: a lute like instrument with a body shaped something like a figure eight; the *setar*, a smaller lute with three strings and a small, round body; the *nei*, a vertical flute; the *kemanche*, a small vertical fiddle with a long neck and a small body; the *qanun*, a larger, broader vertical fiddle; the *santur*, a hammer dulcimer; the *dombak*, a double-headed drum; and the *daf*, a large tambourine. Popular music forms are largely based on the more melodic structures of classical music, and are highly disapproved by the religious authorities. Many popular Iranian musicians now live abroad, where

Pipelines and storage tanks at a gas liquification plant in Bandar Mah Shar.

they record and export their music back to Iran. Women are not allowed to perform music in public under the current government.

Iran has two unique traditional dramatic forms. The first, *ta'zieh*, is an elaborate pageant depicting the death of Imam Hassain. In its full form, it lasts ten days during the month of Muharram, and involves hundreds of performers and animals. The other dramatic form is less elevated, but equally unique. It is a comic improvisatory form known commonly as *ru-howzi* theater, because it was typically performed on a platform placed over the pool (*howz*) in a courtyard. Ru-howzi theater is performed by itinerant troupes at weddings and other celebrations, and is greatly appreciated. It has undergone a revival since the Revolution. Modern Western drama entered Iran at the end of the nineteenth century and attracted a number of fine playwrights whose works are regularly performed in live theater and on television.

Iranian film has captured the interest of the entire world in recent years, winning major international prizes. The Iranian film industry is decades old, but in the 1970s it began to develop as a serious art form under the sponsorship of National Iranian Radio and Television. Young film makers remained in Iran after the Revolution to create masterpieces of film art, despite censorship restrictions. This is somewhat confounding for the religious officials of the Islamic republic, since the most conservative officials condemned film attendance as immoral before the Revolution. Now they realize that Iranian film makers give Iran a progressive, positive image, and they grudgingly lend their support to the industry.

The State of the Physical and Social Sciences

Iran has had a long and proud national tradition in mathematics and the sciences. Iranians view this as an emanation of their cultural heritage. During the period from the ninth to the twelfth centuries the greatest scientists in Baghdad, often thought of as Arabs, were in fact Iranian scholars. Avicenna (Ibn Sīnā) is perhaps the most famous of these. The high regard for medicine and engineering has produced the strongest education and research programs in the country. More than half of all university students are enrolled in these fields.

There are forty-four universities (fifteen in Tehran) currently active in Iran along with a number of other institutes of higher learning and technical training. Approximately 450,000 students are enrolled, men outnumbering women two to one. The University of Tehran, Tehran Polytechnic University, the University of Isfahan, the University of Shīrāz, and the University of Tabrīz are premier educational institutions operating at a high international standard.

One of the more interesting developments following the Revolution was the establishment of the Islamic Open University. This was largely due to student discontent with the restrictive admission policies of the existing universities. Set up throughout the country, it is truly a university without walls, enrolling nearly 400,000 students. Although admission examinations are required, it is not necessary for applicants to submit standard high school diplomas for admission.

A third innovation in higher education has been the establishment of a correspondence institution, the Remote University. This is open to everyone, but in practicality it serves primarily government officials, teachers, and civil servants who wish to further their education.

The nation has enough applied scientists to carry out the functions of infrastructure maintenance and health care. Nevertheless, research institutes have suffered severe declines since the Revolution. Many of the country's best scientists and researchers emigrated to Europe and the United States. A few have returned, but the combination of the massive brain drain and the relatively young population of the nation indicate that it will be some time before much rebuilding can take place.

The government has realized that this is a problem and has increased appropriations to research institutes in recent years. The National Research Council formulates national research policy. The Industrial and Scientific Research Organization of the Culture and Higher Education Ministry carries out research for the government. Other institutes, such as the Institute for Theoretical Physics and Mathematics and the Institute for Oceanographic Research, are given little support.

Social science research is somewhat underdeveloped in Iran. Where it exists it has been developed on French models. The University of Tehran has strong faculties in sociology, psychology, and linguistics, and an active Institute for Social Studies and Research. The University of Shīrāz also has instruction and research in anthropology and sociology.

Bibliography

Abrahamian, Ervand. *Iran Between Two Revolutions*, 1982.

Afshar, Haleh. *Islam and Feminisms: An Iranian Case-Study*, 1998.

——— ed. *Iran: A Revolution in Turmoil*, 1985.

Akhavi, Shahrough. *Religion and Politics in Contemporary Iran: Clergy-State Relations in the Pahlavi Period*, 1980.

Amān Allāhī Bahārvand, Sikander. *Tribes of Iran*, 1988.

Amjad, Mohammed. *Iran: From Royal Dictatorship to Theocracy*, 1989.

Ardalan, Nader, and Laleh Bakhtiar. *The Sense of Unity: The Sufi Tradition in Persian Architecture*, 1973.

Arjomand, Said Amir. *The Shadow of God and the Hidden Imam: Religion, Political Order, and Societal Change in Shi'ite Iran from the Beginning to 1890*, 1984.

Azimi, Fakhreddin. *Iran: The Crisis of Democracy*, 1989.

Baghban, Hafiz. "The Context and Concept of Humour in Magadi Theatre." Ph.D. dissertation, Indiana University, 1977.

Bakhash, Shaul. *The Reign of the Ayatollahs: Iran and the Islamic Revolution*, rev. ed., 1990.

Batmanglij, Najmieh. *The New Food of Life: A Book of Ancient Persian and Modern Iranian Cooking and Ceremonies*, 1992.

Bayat, Mangol. *Mysticism and Dissent: Socioreligious Thought in Qajar Iran*, 1982.

Beck, Lois. *The Qashqa'i of Iran*, 1986.

Beeman, William O. "A Full Arena: The Development and Meaning of Popular Performance Traditions in Iran." in Michael Bonine, and Nikki R. Keddie, eds., *Modern Iran: The Dialectics of Continuity and Change*, 1981.

———. *Culture, Performance, and Communication in Iran*, 1982.

———. "Religion and Development in Iran from the Qajar Era to the Islamic Revolution of 1978–1979." In James Finn, ed., *Religion and Global Economics*, 1983.

———. *Language, Status and Power in Iran*, 1986.

———. "Theatre in the Middle East." in Martin Banham, ed., *Cambridge Guide to World Theatre*, 1995.

———. "The Iranian Revolution of 1978–1979." in *The Encyclopedia of the Modern Islamic World*, 1996.

Bill, James A. *The Eagle and the Lion: The Tragedy of American-Iranian Relations*, 1988.

Bonine, Michael, ed. *Population, Poverty, and Politics in Middle East Cities*, 1997.

Bosworth, C.E., and Carole Hillenbrand, eds. *Qajar Iran: Political, Social, and Cultural Change, 1800–1925*, 1983.

Brosius, Maria. *Women in Ancient Persia, 559–331 BC*, 1996.

Chelkowski, P. J., ed. *Ta'ziyeh: Indigenous Avant-Garde Theater of Iran*, 1979.

Chubin, Shahram, and Charles Tripp. *Iran and Iraq at War*, 1988.

Cook, J. M. *The Persian Empire*, 1983.

Cordesman, Anthony H. *Iran's Military Forces in Transition: Conventional Threats and Weapons of Mass Destruction*, 1999.

Farhat, Hormoz. *The Traditional Art Music of Iran*, 1973.

———. *The Dastgāh Concept in Persian Music*, 1990.

Fathi, Asghar, ed. *Women and the Family in Iran*, 1985.

Ferrier, R.W., ed. *The Arts of Persia*, 1989.

Fesharaki, Fereidun. *Development of the Iranian Oil Industry: International and Domestic Aspects*, 1976.

Fischer, Michael M. J. *Iran: From Religious Dispute to Revolution*, 1980.

Fischer, Michael M. J., and Mehdi Abedi. *Debating Muslims: Cultural Dialogues in Postmodernity and Tradition*, 1990.

Friedl, Erika. *Women of Deh Koh: Lives in an Iranian Village*, 1989.

———. *Children of Deh Koh: Young Life in an Iranian Village*, 1997.

Frye, Richard N. *The Golden Age of Persia: The Arabs in the East*, 1975.

———. *The History of Ancient Iran*, 1984.

Gaffary, Farrokh. "Evolution of Rituals and Theater in Iran." *Iranian Studies* 17 (4): 361–90.

Ghods, M. Reza. *Iran in the Twentieth Century: A Political History*, 1989.

Graham, Robert. *Iran: The Illusion of Power*, rev. ed., 1980.

Haeri, Shahla. *Law of Desire: Temporary Marriage in Shi'i Iran*, 1989.

Hojat, Mohammadreza, Reza Shapurian, Habib Nayerahmadi, Mitra Farzaneh, Danesh Foroughi, Mohin Parsi, and Maryam Azizi. "Premarital Sexual, Child Rearing, and Family Attitudes of Iranian Men and Women in the United States and in Iran." *Journal of Psychology Interdisciplinary and Applied*, 133 (1) [January]: 19–52, 1999.

Hole, Frank, ed. *The Archaeology of Western Iran: Settlement and Society from Prehistory to the Islamic Conquest*, 1987.

Hooglund, Eric J. *Land and Revolution in Iran, 1960–1980*, 1982.

Horne, Lee. *Village Spaces: Settlement and Society in Northeastern Iran*, 1994.

Jaffery, Yunus, ed. *History of Persian Literature*, 1981.

Kamshad, Hassan. *Modern Persian Prose Literature*, 1996.

Karsh, Efraim, ed. *The Iran-Iraq War: Impact and Implications*, 1989.

Keddie, Nikki R. *Roots of Revolution: An Interpretive History of Modern Iran*, 1981.

———, ed. *Religion and Politics in Iran: Shi'ism from Quietism to Revolution*, 1983.

Keddie, Nikki R., and Eric Hooglund, eds. *The Iranian Revolution and the Islamic Republic*. 1986.

Khadduri, Majid. *The Gulf War: The Origins and Implications of the Iraq-Iran Conflict*, 1988.

Lamberg-Karlovsky, C. C. *Excavations at Tepe Yahya, Iran, 1967–1975: The Early Periods*, 1986.

Lambton, Ann K. S. *Qajar Persia: Eleven Studies*, 1987.

Lenczowski, George, ed. *Iran Under the Pahlavis*, 1978.

Lewis, Franklin, and Farzin Yazdanfar. *In A Voice of Their Own: A Collection of Stories by Iranian Women Written since the Revolution of 1979*, 1996.

Looney, Robert E. *Economic Origins of the Iranian Revolution*, 1982.

Maull, Hanns W., and Otto Pick, eds. *The Gulf War: Regional and International Dimensions*, 1989.

Metz, Helen Chapin, ed. *Iran: A Country Study*, 4th ed., 1989.

Milani, Farzaneh. *Veils and Words: The Emerging Voices of Iranian Women Writers*. 1992.

Milani, Mohsen M. *The Making of Iran's Islamic Revolution: From Monarchy to Islamic Republic*, 1988.

Miller, Lloyd. *Music and Song in Persia: the Art of Āvāz*, 1999.

Mir-Hosseini, Ziba. *Islam and Gender: The Religious Debate in Contemporary Iran*, 1999.

Moghadam, Valentine M. *Revolution En-Gendered: Women and Politics in Iran and Afghanistan*, 1990.

Momen, Moojan. *An Introduction to Shi'i Islam*, 1985.

Morgan, David. *The Mongols*, 1986.

Mottahedeh, Roy P. *Loyalty and Leadership in an Early Islamic Society*, 1980.

———. *The Mantle of the Prophet: Religion and Politics in Iran*, 1985.

Najmabadi, Afsaneh. *Land Reform and Social Change in Iran*, 1987.

Nashat, Guity, ed. *Women and Revolution in Iran*, 1983.

Nassehi-Behnam, V. "Change and the Iranian Family." *Current Anthropology*, 26: 557–562, 1985.

Negahban, Ezat O. *Excavations at Haft Tepe, Iran*, 1991.

Nettl, Bruno. *Daramad of Chahargah: A Study in the Performance Practice of Persian Music*, 1972.

———. *The Radif of Persian Music: Studies of Structure and Cultural Context*, 1987.

O'Ballance Edgar. *The Gulf War*, 1988.

Parsa, Misagh. *Social Origins of the Iranian Revolution*, 1989.

Salzman, Philip Carl. *Black Tents of Baluchistan*, 2000.

Sanasarian, E. "The Politics of Gender and Development in the Islamic Republic of Iran." *Journal of Developing Societies*, 13: 56–68, 1992.

Savory, Roger. *Iran under the Safavids*, 1980.

Sciolino, Elaine. *Persian Mirrors: The Elusive Face of Iran*, 2000.

Shay, Anthony. *Choreophobia: Solo Improvised Dance in the Iranian World*, 1999.

Tabari, Azar, and Nahid Yeganeh. *In the Shadow of Islam: The Women's Movement in Iran*, 1982.

Tabataba'i, 'Allamah Sayyid Muhammad Husayn. *Shi'ite Islam*, 2nd ed., 1977.

Talattof, Kamran. *The Politics of Writing in Iran: A History of Modern Persian Literature*, 1999.

Tapper, Richard. *The Conflict of Tribe and State in Iran and Afghanistan*, 1983.

Wilbur, Donald N. *Iran, Past and Present: From Monarchy to Islamic Republic*, 9th ed., 1981.

Wright, Robin. *Sacred Rage: The Crusade of Modern Islam*, rev. ed., 1986.

———. *In the Name of God: The Khomeini Decade*, 1989.

Wulff, Hans E. *The Traditional Crafts of Persia: Their Development, Technology, and Influence on Eastern and Western Civilizations*, 1966.

Yarshater, Ehsan, ed. *Encyclopædia Iranica*, 1985–.

Zabih, Sepehr. *Iran since the Revolution*, 1982.

Zonis, Ella. *Classical Persian Music: An Introduction*, 1973.

—William O. Beeman

IRAQ

CULTURE NAME

Iraqi

ORIENTATION

Identification. Modern Iraq covers almost the same area as ancient Mesopotamia, which centered on the land between the Tigres and the Euphrates Rivers. Mesopotamia, also referred to as the Fertile Crescent, was an important center of early civilization and saw the rise and fall of many cultures and settlements. In the medieval era, Iraq was the name of an Arab province that made up the southern half of the modern-day country. In today's Republic of Iraq, where Islam is the state religion and claims the beliefs of 95 percent of the population, the majority of Iraqis identify with Arab culture. The second-largest cultural group is the Kurds, who are in the highlands and mountain valleys of the north in a politically autonomous settlement. The Kurds occupy the provinces of As Sulaymaniyah, Dahuk and Irbil, the area of which is commonly referred to as Kurdistan.

Location and Geography. Iraq, in the Middle East, is 168,754 square miles (437,073 square kilometers), which is comparable to twice the size of Idaho. Iraq is bordered by Iran, Jordan, Kuwait, Saudi Arabia, Syria, Turkey, and the Persian Gulf. Baghdad was the name of a village that the Arabs chose to develop as their capital and is in the central plains. The northern border areas near Iran and Turkey are mountainous and experience cold, harsh winters, while the west is mostly desert. The differences in climate have influenced the economies of the various areas and ethnic groups, especially since a large part of the economy used to be agriculturally based.

Demography. The estimated Iraqi population for 2000 is 22,675,617 people. Arabs comprise about three-fourths of the population, and Kurds compose about one-fifth. The remaining people are divided into several ethnic groups, including Assyrian, Turkoman, Chaldean, Armenian, Yazidi, and Jewish.

Linguistic Affiliation. Almost all Iraqis speak and understand their official language, Arabic. Arabic, a Semitic language, was introduced by the Arab conquerors and has three different forms: classical, modern standard, and spoken. Classical Arabic, best known by scholars, is the written language of the Qur'an. Modern standard Arabic, which has virtually the same structure in all Arabic-speaking countries, is taught in schools for reading and writing. The spoken language is Iraqi Arabic, and is extremely similar to that which is spoken in Syria, Lebanon, and parts of Jordan. Those who go to school learn Modern Standard Arabic, and many that do not attend school are likely to at least understand it. The major differences between modern standard and Iraqi Arabic are changes in verb form, and an overall simplicity in grammar of the spoken Arabic.

Kurdish is the official language in Kurdistan, and serves to distinguish Kurds from other Iraqis. It is not of Semitic origin nor an Arab or Persian dialect, but a distinct language from the Indo-European family. Other minority languages include Aramaic, Turkic, Armenian, and Persian.

Symbolism. In the 1970s a cultural campaign was launched to influence a national consciousness based on Iraq's history, including the pre-Islam era and the former glory of Mesopotamia and Babylon. The goal was to focus on a new cultural life for modern Iraq and to emphasize Iraq's uniqueness, especially in the Arab world. Archaeological museums were built in several cities, which held exhibitions and educational programs especially for children, so that they were made aware of the historical importance of their culture and nation. In order to promote this center of attention on history, several ancient sites from the city of Babylon were reconstructed, such as the Ziggurat of Aqarquf, the ruins of Babylon, the temple of Ishtar, the southern

Iraq

fortress of Nebuchadnezzar, and the Greek amphitheater.

The Iraqi flag is also an important national symbol, and is composed of three colored, horizontal sections, starting with red on the top, white, and black. On the white band there are three green five-pointed stars. During the Persian Gulf War in 1991, the phrase *Allahu Akbar* (God is great) was added to the flag. The flag resembles other Arab countries' flags and demonstrates Iraqi faith in Allah and Arab unity.

History and Ethnic Relations

Emergence of the Nation. Starting from prehistory, the area of Mesopotamia has been under the

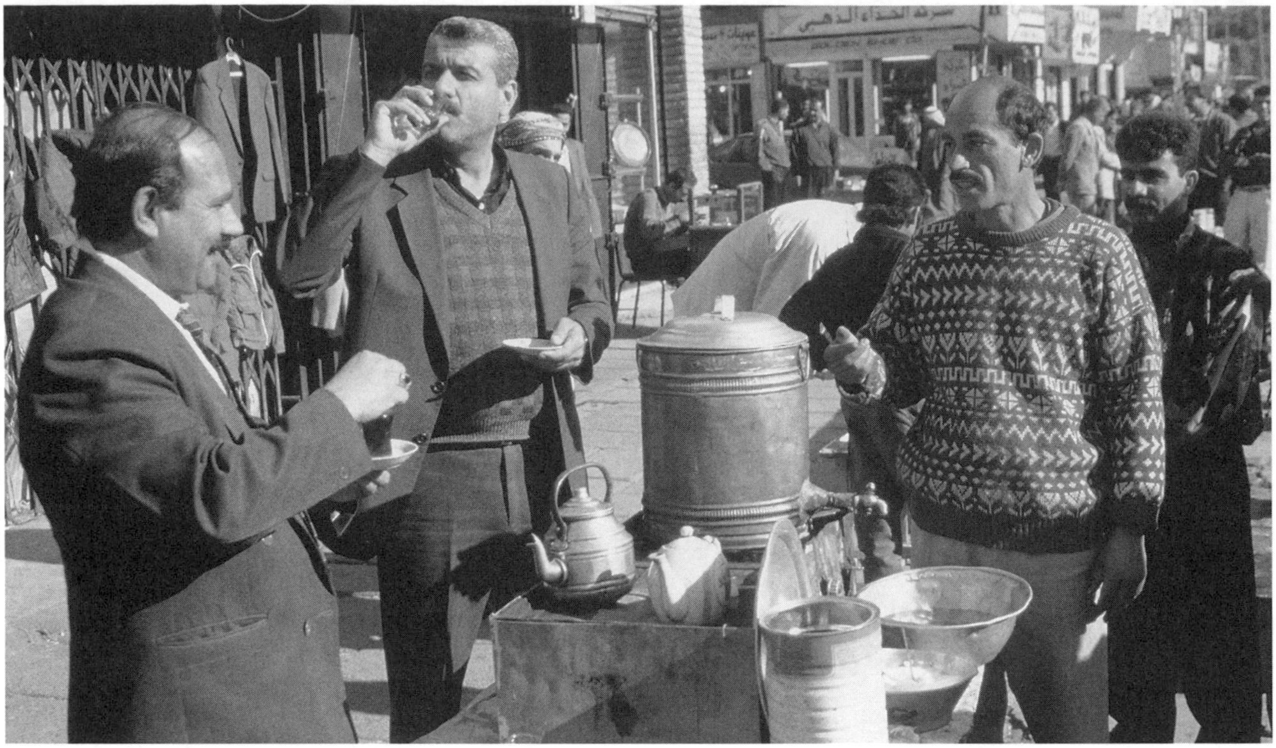

Iraqi men socialize at a tea stall in Baghdad.

control of several civilizations. In about 4000 B.C.E. the land belonged to the Sumerians, who built advanced irrigation systems, developed cereal agriculture, invented the earliest form of writing, a math system on which time in the modern world is based, the wheel, and the first plow. Literature was produced, including the first known recorded story, the Epic of Gilgamesh. Unlike their Egyptian counterparts who believed that all land belonged to the pharaoh, Sumerians believed in private property, still an important notion in Iraq today.

When the Sumerian civilization collapsed in about 1700 B.C.E., King Hammurabi took over the area and renamed it Babylonia. Hammurabi, a great leader known for creating the first recorded legal code in history, united the Assyrians and Babylonians in harmony. Following several changes in power, Nebuchadnezzar II came to rule from 604 to 562 B.C.E., and restored Babylonia to its former glory. Babylon, which is about thirty miles (forty-eight kilometers) south of modern-day Baghdad, became the most famous city in the world, and boasted, among other things, the Hanging Gardens of Babylon.

In 323 B.C.E. Babylonia became part of the Persian Empire, until Arab Muslims overtook it in 634 C.E. At the time of the invasion, the people of Mesopotamia were mostly Christian, and paid non-Muslim taxes to the invaders. As the Persians were eventually defeated, the people of Mesopotamia began to convert to Islam and intermarry with Arabs. In 762 C.E. the capital city of Baghdad was founded, and it became an important commercial, cultural, and educational center. It linked Asia to Mediterranean countries via trade; welcomed visitors, scholars, and commercial traders from all over the world; and produced incredible philosophical and scientific works by both Arab and Persian thinkers.

The 1200s witnessed yet another invasion, and control went to the Mongols, who ruled until the 1400s. The Ottoman Turks took control in the sixteenth century, in a reign that lasted until the end of World War I. When the Ottoman Empire was defeated in that war, the League of Nations assigned Britain to set up the administration in Mesopotamia. The British defined the territory of Iraq, and in doing so paid little attention to natural boundaries and ethnic divisions. They set up the institutional framework for government and politics, which included installation of a monarchy and influence in writing the constitution. On 14 July 1958 the monarchy was overthrown, and Iraq was declared a republic. The following ten years were followed by much political instability. Then, on 17 July 1968, another coup d'état occurred, which brought to power the Baath Party, today's government leader.

National Identity. Arab rule during the medieval period had the greatest cultural impact on modern Iraq. The dominating culture within Iraq is Arab, and most Arabs are Muslim. Iraqi Muslims are split into two groups, the Sunnis and the Shias (Shiites). The Sunnis, a majority in Islam, are a minority in Iraq, and the Shias, a minority in the Arab world, are the majority in Iraq. Between the Shia and Sunni Muslims, loyalty to Iraq has come to be a common factor. Though they have differing views, both Sunnis and Shias hold high leadership positions in the government (including the Sunni Saddam Hussein), as do some Christians.

The Arab culture, as influenced by the conquerors in the seventh century, withstood many changes of power throughout the centuries, and managed to remain influential. In the nineteenth century, while the Ottoman Empire was focusing on the "Turkification" of its people, rebels in Mesopotamia were building their Arab nationalist movement. They were granted an opportunity to act during World War I, when the British agreed to recognize Arab independence in Mesopotamia if they helped fight against the Turks. Though Iraq was subject to British mandate rule following the defeat of the Ottoman Empire, Arab nationalism stood strong. For the next few decades, even after independence from Britain, the government's attitude wavered between being pro-British and Arab nationalist. Today Iraq stands firm in its belief in pro-Arab nationalism.

Ethnic Relations. The largest minority in Iraq, the Kurds, continually battle with the majority Arabs, and the sparring between these two cultural groups has contributed to a survivalist mentality for the Kurds. The Turkomans, who populate the northern mountainous areas, also have had strained relations with the Kurds due to their historical role as buffers between Arab and Kurdish areas. Other cultural groups who are sometimes subject to the will of the Arab majority are the Yazidis, who are of Kurdish descent, but differ from the Kurds because of their unique religion. There are the Assyrians, who are direct descendents of the ancient Mesopotamian people and speak Aramaic. They are mainly Christian, and though they compose a significant minority in Iraq, the government does not officially recognize them as an ethnic group. Regarding relations with other countries, Iraq's Shias have been the traditional enemies of Persians for centuries; this contributed to Iraq fighting Iran in a costly war from 1980 to 1988 over a land dispute. The Iraqi Kurdish population is surrounded by fellow Kurds in the countries of Iran, Turkey, Syria, and Azerbaijan.

URBANISM, ARCHITECTURE, AND THE USE OF SPACE

Iraq's economy was once based on agriculture, which stipulated a large rural population. However, due to oil production, an economic boom hit Iraq in the 1970s, and with the change of economic basis, much of population migrated toward urban centers. Modern apartment and office buildings sprang up in Baghdad, and programs and services such as education and health care developed with the shift from rural areas to urban population centers. In addition to modernization, the influx of monetary resources allowed Iraq to do things for its cultural identity and preservation, especially in architecture. High priority was placed on restoring and building according to historic style, and the structures targeted included archaeological sites, mosques, and government buildings. Some of the traditional aspects of the architecture include rooms surrounding an open center or courtyard, and use of multiple colors, tiles, and arches.

FOOD AND ECONOMY

Food in Daily Life. Prior to the United Nations economic sanctions, the traditional diet included rice with soup or sauce, accompanied by lamb and vegetables. Today, because food is tightly rationed, most people eat rice or another grain sometimes with sauce. Both vegetables and meat are hard to come by. In rural areas it is customary for families to eat together out of a common bowl, while in urban areas individuals eat with plates and utensils.

Food Customs at Ceremonial Occasions. It is traditional to sacrifice a lamb or a goat to celebrate holidays. However, today few Iraqis have the means to do this, and celebrations are now minimal.

Basic Economy. Iraq's economy is currently in a difficult position. Following the 1991 Persian Gulf War, the United Nations imposed Security Council Resolution 687, which requires Iraq to disclose the full extent of its programs to develop chemical and nuclear weapons and missiles, and to eliminate its weapons of mass destruction. Until Iraq complies with these requirements, the United Nations attests that there will be an economic embargo and trade sanctions against Iraq. At first the resolution meant that Iraq could not assume trade relations with any foreign country. In 1996 the United Nations modi-

The Dora Oil Refinery in Baghdad. The most important industries in Iraq produce crude oil, petroleum products, and natural gas.

fied the sanctions and implemented the oil-for-food program, which allows Iraq to pump and sell a limited amount of oil for humanitarian purposes, with no direct exchange of cash, but rather with all transactions taking place through an offshore escrow account. Two-thirds of the proceeds are to be spent on food and medicine for the Iraqi people; the remaining third is to be directed to victims of Iraq's occupation of Kuwait.

Prior to the sanctions, Iraq imported about 70 percent of its food. However, food shortages have forced people to grow their own, but given the severity of the economic situation of the country, it is difficult for Iraqis to find the means to do this. Items that are imported through the oil-for-food program are distributed to people in a food basket on the first of each month. The rations are estimated to last twenty to twenty-three days and include flour, tea, sugar, rice, beans, milk, cooking oil, soap, and salt.

Land Tenure and Property. Private property was an important notion first introduced by the Sumerians during their control of Mesopotamia, and emerged again in the late nineteenth century. The reintroduction of private property had a major impact on Iraq's social system, as it went from a feudal society where sheikhs provided both spiritual and tribal leadership for the inhabitants, to one separated between landowners and sharecroppers. At present many people have sold or are selling their land to the government to purchase essentials such as food and medicine. Though private property does exist, fewer and fewer people can now claim it.

Commercial Activities. Oil, mining, manufacturing, construction, and agriculture are the major types of goods and services produced for sale.

Major Industries. Crude oil, refined petroleum products, and natural gas are products produced by the most important industry in Iraq. Other products and services include light manufacturing, food processing, textiles, and mining of nonmetallic minerals.

Trade. Iraq may only legally trade with other countries through the oil-for-food program, wherein they are allowed to sell oil to buy basic food supplies. However, diplomatic reports have indicated that Iraq has been illegally exporting some of its medical supplies and food, purchased through the oil-for-food program, to Lebanon, Syria, and Jordan. Prior to the sanctions, Iraq's main exports were crude oil, refined petroleum products, natural gas, chemical fertilizers, and dates. Its major trade partners were Russia, France, Brazil, Spain, and Japan.

Division of Labor. It is common for jobs to be assigned through knowing people in the government. Those who enter the military may have more opportunity locating work, as they are trained for jobs that are specifically needed in the country.

Social Stratification

Classes and Castes. Arabs, Kurds, and other ethnic groups each have their own social stratospheres, and no one ethnicity dominates another in a caste system. In terms of social class there is great disparity between rich and poor. Those who compose the high class in society of Iraq are essentially chosen by the government, since there is no opportunity to start a business or make a name for oneself without the endorsement of the government. The once-dominant middle class of the 1970s has deteriorated in the face of the economic crisis. These people, who are very well educated, now perform unskilled labor, if they have jobs at all, and have joined the ranking of the majority lower or poor class.

Political Life

Government. Iraq is a republic divided into eighteen provinces, which are subdivided into districts. There is a National Assembly elected every four years, and they meet twice annually and work with the Revolutionary Command Council (RCC) to make legislative decisions. The RCC holds ultimate authority over legislative decisions, and the chairman of the RCC is also president of the country. The president exercises all executive decision-making powers, and he as well as the vice presidents are elected by a two-thirds majority vote of the RCC. There is universal suffrage at age eighteen, and the popular vote elects 220 of the 250 seats in the National Assembly. The president chooses the remaining 30 seats, which belong to the three provinces of Kurdistan; he also appoints judges.

Leadership and Political Officials. On 16 July 1979 Saddam Hussein became president of Iraq, and has been reelected since. He is also the prime minister, as well as chairman of the RCC. The Baath Party, which stands for Arab Socialist Resurrection, is the controlling party of the government and the most powerful political party. Its authority is the Regional Command, and the secretary general of the Regional Command is Saddam Hussein.

Political activities are carried out through the Progressive National Front (PNF), which is an official organization of political parties. PNF participants include the Iraqi Communist Party, Kurdish political parties, and other independent groups. Politics that try to be exercised outside the framework of the PNF are banned.

Though granted the right to vote for some positions, many Iraqis feel that elections are fixed. They also fear that they might vote for the "wrong" candidate and that they may be punished for doing so. It is a crime for any Iraqi to speak out against the government, and those who disagree with it place themselves and their families at great risk of being persecuted, as many citizens will turn in fellow Iraqis they feel are not loyal to the government or Saddam Hussein.

Social Problems and Control. The head of the formal judicial system is the Court of Cassation, which is the highest court in the country. There are other levels of courts, and all judges are government-appointed. Personal disputes are handled by religious community courts, which are based on Islamic law. Normally punishment is swift for crimes, with no long court trials and with severe sentences.

The crime rate has been traditionally low, but following the United Nations embargo, there has been an increase in crime, especially theft. In addition to crimes by the general public, many crimes by corrupt police and military forces have been reported, the most common being bribery and blackmail. Conditions in prisons are said to be extremely harsh. Prisoners are housed with more than twenty people in a cell meant for two, with no sanitation system, and no food is given unless brought by relatives. Other punishment practices include torture, often in front of family members, and execution.

Military Activity. Current statistics about Iraq's military are not available, though it is believed to be one of the strongest in the world. In 1994 a report indicated that Iraq spent $2.6 billion (U.S.) on its military. Iraq has not officially stated that military service is compulsory, but another statistic from 1994 stated that most of the 382,000 service people were required to be in the military. The average length of service was eighteen to twenty-four months, and there were another 650,000 in the reserves. Regarding compensation, wages for those who fought in the Iran-Iraq War were generous. Journalists reported that families who lost a son in the fighting would receive compensation in such

A residential district in Baghdad. After the economic boom of the 1970s, high priority was placed on restoring and building according to historic style.

forms as an automobile, a generous pension for life, real estate, and loans with easy terms for repayment. It is estimated that current compensation to the military has changed, but no specific information is available.

Social Welfare and Change Programs

Before the Persian Gulf War, welfare benefits such as Social Security, pensions for retirees and disabled people, and money for maternity and sick leaves were available. Currently the only known welfare programs are food distribution and medical aid food. Some nongovernmental organizations (NGOs) have been involved, but unless the Iraqi government can direct NGO operations, they are not permitted to function.

Nongovernmental Organizations and Other Associations

The most important NGOs are those that are responsible for food rationing and distribution, medical aid, and rebuilding of water and sewage treatment facilities. Many of the NGOs, such as the World Food Program, are associated with the United Nations. Currently Iraqi leaders have been turning down humanitarian efforts and have refused offers of relief from private medical groups. They recently expelled representatives of the Middle East Council of Churches, and denied entry of a Russian envoy from the United Nations who was to investigate the cases of missing persons since 1990. The only NGOs Iraq allows are foreign antisanctions protesters, who bring in small amounts of aid but who are welcome principally because of the propaganda they provide.

The presence of NGOs is different between the south and the three provinces of Kurdistan in the north. The Kurds welcomed NGOs in 1991, immediately following the Persian Gulf War, while they were not allowed in the South until 1996. Kurdistan hosts more than thirty NGOs, while in 1999 there were eleven in the south, with even fewer in 2000. Local Kurdish officials work with the United Nations to manage food, health, and economic programs, while the resources and control of the NGOs are restricted in the south. Due to the attitude toward NGOs as well as other contributing factors such as arable land, population, and availability of natural resources, the north is more productive agriculturally and economically and has a more advanced health system infrastructure. The south, under Iraqi control and closed to outside help, has

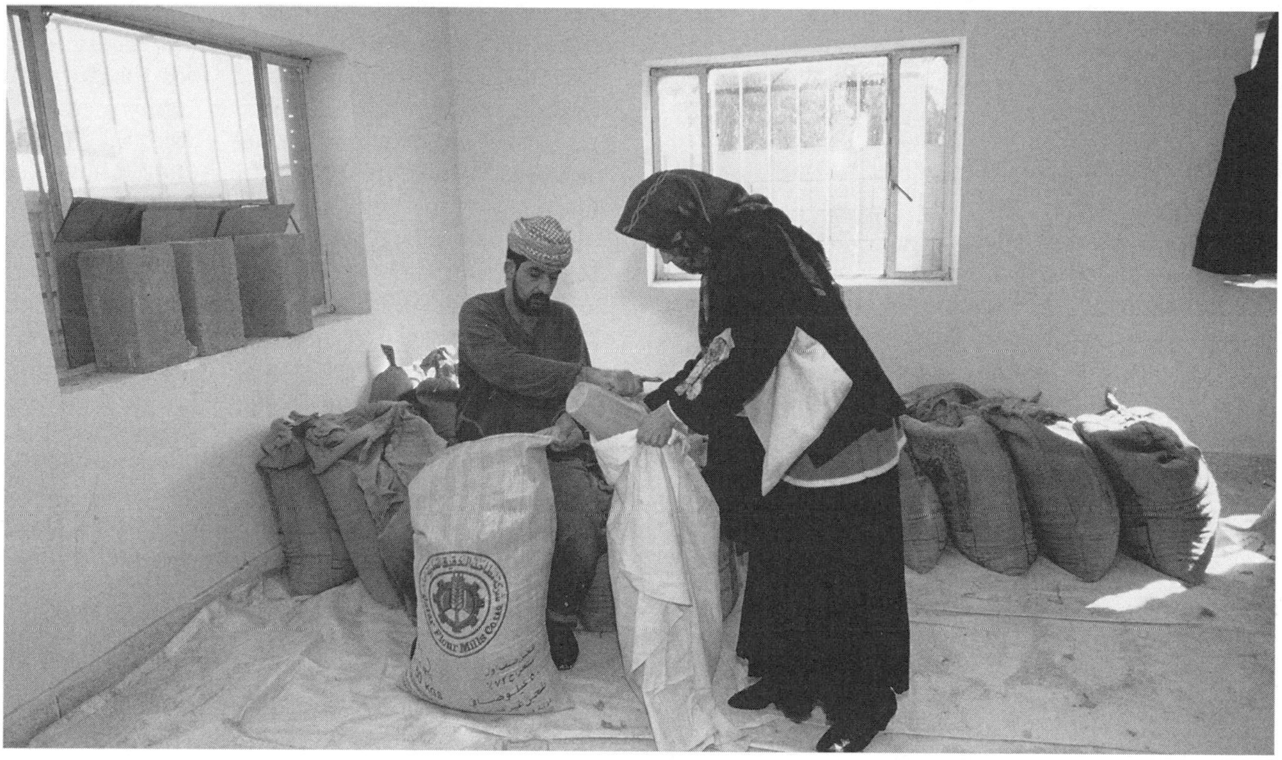

An Iraqi woman collects her monthly food rations from the Red Cross in Baghdad.

suffered with more food, health, and economic problems.

GENDER ROLES AND STATUSES

Division of Labor by Gender. During the Iran-Iraq War, with so many men fighting in the military, women were required to study in fields and to work in positions normally filled by men. Many women joined the labor force as teachers, physicians, dentists, factory workers, and civil servants, with the majority performing unskilled labor. Women professionals, such as doctors, are normally pediatricians or obstetricians, so that they work with only women or children. Those drafted into the workforce during the Iran-Iraq War were also made to comply with about a one-third deduction from their salary to go toward the war effort.

The Relative Status of Women and Men. The General Federation for Iraqi Women (GFIW) is a government organization for women with eighteen branches, one in each province. Its stated goal is to officially organize women, promote literacy and higher education, and encourage women in the labor force. The federation supported big legislative steps, such as a 1977 law that said a woman may be appointed an officer in the military if she has a university degree in medicine, dentistry, or pharmacy. However, it has had little impact on issues that affect women as individuals, such as polygamy, divorce, and inheritance.

Many believe that the GFIW is not really functioning in the interests of women, but rather in the interests of the Baathist regime. Instead of trying to improve the situation of women in Iraq, the government seems to use the federation as a means to exercise control over them. In an address to the federation, Saddam said that an educated and liberated mother is one who will give back to the country conscious and committed fighters for Iraq. An underlying goal of the GFIW, whether it is stated or not, is to encourage women to "liberate" themselves through commitment to the Iraqi revolution.

In politics Iraq was the first Arab country ever to elect a woman to a parliamentary position. Though an incredible advancement for women in the Arab world, many believe that rather than exercising real authority, she was put in power to falsely demonstrate the controlling regime as a progressive one. Today there are women in politics, though the legitimacy of their authority is often questioned. In Islam, the state religion, women do not hold any leadership roles. Many cannot go to the mosque to pray, and if they do, they are segregated from the men. It is largely due to Islamic influence that women do not enjoy the same social rights and privileges as men, and if gender reform is to take place, it will have to be within the context of Islamic law.

Marriage, Family, and Kinship

Marriage. In the past, arranged marriages were common. However, this practice is becoming more rare, and a law was passed that gave authority to a state-appointed judge to overrule the wishes of the father in the event of an early marriage. The Muslim majority traditionally views marriage as a contract between two families, as the family's needs are considered most important. In urban settings, women and men have more options in choosing their spouses, though the proposed spouse still must have parental approval. Partners often come from the same kin group, and though marriage between different ethnic groups is accepted, it is not too common. The ruling Baath regime considers marriage to be a national duty that should be guided and encouraged. Starting in 1982, women were forbidden to marry non-Iraqi men. If they were already married, they were prohibited from transferring money or property to their spouses.

Following the Iran-Iraq War, the loss of men's lives was so severe that the government embarked on a campaign to increase the population. Government grants were given to men to marry war widows, and polygamy, once rare, became more common. Divorce is accepted, but usually is left solely as a decision of the husband. If the husband wishes to be divorced, it is normally without question or problem, while it is close to impossible for a woman to initiate a divorce proceeding. In the event of divorce, custody is supposed to be granted based on what is best for the child's welfare.

Domestic Unit. Couples can live in either of two ways: with the husband's extended family, or as a nuclear family. At present, with economic hardships, families tend to live with extended households. The extended family unit consists of the older couple, sons, their wives and families, and unmarried daughters. Other dependent relatives also may make up part of this group, and the oldest male heads the group. He manages property and makes the final decisions regarding such things as the type of education the children receive, their occupations, and whom they will marry. In this living arrangement household and child-rearing tasks are shared among all female members of the larger families. If the couple can afford to live in a nuclear household, women, even though they work outside the home, retain all domestic and child-care responsibilities. The challenge of the woman's role in this situation is that there is no change in cooking methods or materials, and they are isolated from the help and emotional support of other female family members. Families often grow large, because the Iraqi government has stated that every family should have five children, as four children or fewer is considered a threat to national security. Considering the extreme hardships families now face in light of economic hardship and harsh living conditions, the goal of many is now to simply feed their families and preserve a semblance of some sort of home life.

Inheritance. Based on the Islamic rule, a man inherits twice as much as a woman. The justification for this is that women are to be protected by their male relatives, so men need to be granted more means to provide. Normally, property and belongings are passed down through the family, split two-to-one between sons and daughters.

Kin Groups. Large kin groups are the fundamental social units, and are of higher importance than ethnic, social class, and sectarian lines. Familial loyalty is considered an essential quality, and the family is mutually protective of each other. The kin group usually is organized through descent and marriage and involves three generations, many of whom live together. They often cooperate in areas such as agriculture and land ownership. If some family members live in nuclear families, they keep up practices such as depending on one another and asking the elders for advice. Individual status within the group is determined by the family's position and the individual's position within that group.

Socialization

Infant Care. Children are the mother's responsibility, and in extended domestic units other female members also take care of the children. Children normally imitate older siblings, and obedience and loyalty to elders are of vital importance. Boys and girls have different upbringings, as a boy's birth into the family is usually celebrated, while a girl's typically is not. The boy is thought to be more valuable to a family, given his potential to work, while the girl is considered more of a dependent. At puberty girls are separated from boys and have much less freedom than boys.

Child Rearing and Education. The family holds an important role in teaching values, and they consider it their duty and feel responsible for other family members' behaviors. A good child is loyal, obedient, and does not question authority. The

In March 1991, two million Kurds fled Iraq, settling at camps on the border to wait for humanitarian aid.

most important value impressed upon young girls and boys is premarital chastity. In addition, girls are taught ideas of weakness, naïveté, resignation, and passivity, while boys go with men at an early age to learn the worth of authority and dominance.

In urban settings, more authority is found in schools rather than with the family. Schools teach about religion and values that stem from it. One present problem, however, is that differing values are taught in schools than are taught in families. State schools tend to emphasize national sovereignty, Arab unity, economic security, and socialism, while families usually focus on such values as love, people, generosity, and religion. Many families also fear that their children acquire violent views and habits such as spying while in school.

Higher Education. Prior to the Persian Gulf War higher education was greatly prized, and the state used to pay for all of it, even literacy classes for adults. In the 1980s the literacy rate was about 80 percent, and there were several plans to build new universities and expand existing ones. During the Iran-Iraq War the government refused to recruit or draft university students, claiming that they would ensure the future of Iraq. However, the situation has gravely changed since the Persian Gulf War. No current literacy statistic is available, but in 1995 the rate was estimated to be 42 percent, a sharp drop from the previous decade. Also, there is no indication that the universities were ever expanded. Fewer women than men receive the highest levels of education.

Etiquette

In general, both adults and children keep to themselves and are not loud and boisterous, especially in public. Men commonly hold hands or kiss when greeting each other, but this is not the case for men and women. Respect is given to the elderly and women, especially those with children, as men give up their seats to them on buses and trains.

Religion

Religious Beliefs. Islam is the officially recognized religion of Iraq and is practiced by 95 percent of the population. Islam itself does not distinguish between church and state, so any distinctions between religious and secular law are the result of more recent developments. There are two forms of Muslims in Iraq, the majority Shias (Shiites) and the minority Sunnis. The Shias believe that the original twelve im-

The ziggurat of Nanna, built around 2100 B.C.E. in the ancient city of Ur by Shulgi.

ams (Islamic leaders) were both spiritual and temporal leaders and that the caliph, or successor of Muhammad and leader of Islam, is selected through lineage and descent. The Sunnis believe that the imams were strictly temporal leaders and that the caliph should be elected. The Sunni sect is considered the orthodox branch of Islam. A small percentage of the population is Christian, divided into four churches: Chaldean, Nestorian, Jacobite (Syrian) Orthodox, and Syrian Catholic. The Yazidis, a cultural group living in the northern mountains, believe in a religion that combines paganism, Zoroastrianism, Christianity, and Islam. They are concentrated in the Sinjar Mountains in the north and are herders and cultivators. In the past they have been victims of persecution due to their religious beliefs and practices, often being called heretical.

Religious Practitioners. There are five pillars of Islam: praise of Allah as the only God, with Muhammad as his prophet; prayer five times per day; almsgiving; fasting; and pilgrimage to Mecca. *Muezzins* invoke a call to prayer, reminding everyone it is either time to pray or to call them to the mosque, and imams lead the prayers. Imams are not required to go through formal training, but usually are men of importance in their communities and are appointed by the government. During Ramadan, men gather in homes or the marketplace to participate in readings of the Qur'an led by *mumins* (men trained at a religious school in An Najaf) or by *mullahs* (men apprenticed with older specialists). Christians are organized under a bishop who resides in Baghdad, and gather for Mass on Sundays.

Rituals and Holy Places. Muslims gather at the mosque every Friday for afternoon prayer. Ramadan falls in the ninth month of the Muslim calendar, which is on a lunar cycle and thus falls during different times of the year. The month entails a period of fasting from all food, drink, and activities such as smoking and sexual intercourse during daylight hours. At night the fast is broken, and on the first day of the tenth month there is a celebration, Id al Fitr, to acknowledge the end of the fast. During Id al Adha, on the tenth day of the twelfth month, there is a sacrificial festival. Both this and the one following Ramadan last for three or four days, and people dress up, visit each other, exchange gifts, and also visit cemeteries.

Death and the Afterlife. Funerals are very simple and somber events. People are buried on the day following their death, and are wrapped in a white cloth and placed in a plain box, if available. Whether the person is rich or poor, funerals are generally the same for everyone.

Medicine and Health Care

Health care is socialized, with a few private hospitals. The current situation of hospitals is dire, as they are tremendously understaffed, under-equipped, and overbooked. There has been a dramatic rise in disease since 1990, due to chemicals used in the fighting of the Persian Gulf War, and from malnutrition and bacterial disease exacerbated by conditions resulting from the economic embargo. In the 1980s Iraq was extremely advanced in health care, but lack of resources and education has compromised medical advancement, and in fact has caused it to regress. Doctors who could once cure many diseases through medicine or surgery are no longer able to do so due for lack of resources. Because Iraq was so advanced in medical expertise in the past, there was little reliance on traditional medicine. The current situation is disheartening for older physicians, because they are not able to do medical procedures that they have the capability to perform, and young physicians are no longer educated in the available techniques that older physicians know. The health care situation is rapidly deteriorating, and once-controlled diseases such as malnutrition, diarrhea, typhoid fever, measles, chicken pox, and cholera are reappearing in great numbers; in addition, there is a large increase in diseases such as leukemia and other cancers.

Secular Celebrations

The Anniversary of the Revolution is 17 July and the most important secular holiday. It was on this day in 1968 that the Baath Party took control of the Republic of Iraq. Other holidays celebrate Islamic feasts and include the day following the month-long fast of Ramadan (Id al Fitr), the sacrificial festival of Id al Adha, the birth of Muhammad, and a pilgrim's return from Mecca.

The Arts and Humanities

Support for the Arts. The government supports artists, provided they are chosen by the state and do works requested by the state. For example, all writers, when commissioned by the state, must include praise to Saddam Hussein in their work. In general, artistic forms of thought and expression have been banned. Private ownership of typewriters and photocopiers is prohibited, so that no independent writings may be published or distributed. In addition, publishing houses, distribution networks, newspapers, art galleries, theaters, and film companies are subject to state censorship and must register all writing equipment with authorities. The end result is that artists are unable to express themselves freely.

Graphic Arts. Islamic art is very important, as are ceramics, carpets, and Islamic-style fashion design. In 1970 the Iraqi Fashion House opened, and design concentrated on the preservation of traditional attire and historical style. At present historical art, which is colorful and fine, has been reduced to art produced for function, such as sculptures of political figures and propaganda for the government.

Performance Arts. Music festivals have been important, such as the Babylon International Music and Arts Festival (last held in 1987 and 1995). International orchestras and performance troupes were invited to perform in the restored sites of Babylon, and people from all over the world attended. At present due to the harsh and severe living conditions, there are no resources to allocate to performance arts.

Bibliography

Al-Khalil, Samir. *Republic of Fear: The Politics of Modern Iraq*, 1991.

Al-Khayyat, Sana. *Honor and Shame: Women in Modern Iraq*, 1990.

Baram, Amatzia. *Culture, History, and Ideology in the Formation of Ba'thist Iraq, 1968–89*, 1991.

Calabrese, John, ed. *The Future of Iraq*, 1997.

CARDRI (Committee Against Repression and for Democratic Rights in Iraq). *Saddam's Iraq: Revolution or Reaction?*, 1986.

Chalian, Gerard, ed. *A People Without a Country: The Kurds and Kurdistan*, 1993.

Crossette, Barbara. "Iraq Won't Let Outside Experts Assess Sanctions' Impact." *New York Times*, 12 September 2000.

Fernea, Elizabeth and Robert. *The Arab World: Personal Encounters*, 1985.

Fisher, W. B. *The Middle East and North Africa 1995*, 1994.

Hazelton, Fran, ed. *Iraq Since the Gulf War: Prospects for Democracy*, 1994.

Hopwood, Derek; Ishow, Habib; and Kozinowski, Thomas, eds. *Iraq: Power and Society*, 1993.

Lewis, Bernard. *The Middle East: A Brief History of the Last 2000 Years*, 1995.

Lukitz, Liora. *Iraq: The Search for National Identity*, 1995.

Marr, Phebe. *The Modern History of Iraq*, 1985.

Miller, Judith and Laurie Mylroie. *Saddam Hussein and the Crisis in the Gulf*, 1990.

Roberts, Paul William. *The Demonic Comedy: Some Detours in the Baghdad of Saddam Hussein*, 1998.

Simons, G.L. *Iraq: From Sumer to Saddam*, 1994.

Taylor, Marisa. "The Great Iraqi Exodus: Arrival of Chaldeans at Border Part of 'Enormous' Migration." *San Diego Union Tribune*, 30 September 2000.

Web Sites

Hickey, Brian; Danielle LeClair; Brian Sims; and Jack Zylman. "Iraq Trip Report." Congressional Staffers Report, 16 March 2000, www.nonviolence.org/vitw/pages/94.htm

Metz, Helen Chapin, ed. "Iraq: A Country Study." Federal Research Division, Library of Congress, May 1988. www.loc.gov (search "Iraq")

Saleh. "Iraq History and Culture from Noah to the Present." www.achilles.net/~sal/iraq_history.html

U.S. State Department. *CIA World Factbook 2000: Iraq.* www.odci.gov/cia/publications/factbook/geos/iz.html

—ELIZABETH C. PIETANZA

IRELAND

CULTURE NAME

Irish

ALTERNATIVE NAMES

Na hÉireanneach; Na Gaeil

ORIENTATION

Identification. The Republic of Ireland (Poblacht na hÉireann in Irish, although commonly referred to as Éire, or Ireland) occupies five-sixths of the island of Ireland, the second largest island of the British Isles. Irish is the common term of reference for the country's citizens, its national culture, and its national language. While Irish national culture is relatively homogeneous when compared to multinational and multicultural states elsewhere, Irish people recognize both some minor and some significant cultural distinctions that are internal to the country and to the island. In 1922 Ireland, which until then had been part of the United Kingdom of Great Britain and Ireland, was politically divided into the Irish Free State (later the Republic of Ireland) and Northern Ireland, which continued as part of the renamed United Kingdom of Great Britain and Northern Ireland. Northern Ireland occupies the remaining sixth of the island. Almost eighty years of separation have resulted in diverging patterns of national cultural development between these two neighbors, as seen in language and dialect, religion, government and politics, sport, music, and business culture. Nevertheless, the largest minority population in Northern Ireland (approximately 42 percent of the total population of 1.66 million) consider themselves to be nationally and ethnically Irish, and they point to the similarities between their national culture and that of the Republic as one reason why they, and Northern Ireland, should be reunited with the Republic, in what would then constitute an all-island nation-state. The majority population in Northern Ireland, who consider themselves to be nationally British, and who identify with the political communities of Unionism and Loyalism, do not seek unification with Ireland, but rather wish to maintain their traditional ties to Britain.

Within the Republic, cultural distinctions are recognized between urban and rural areas (especially between the capital city Dublin and the rest of the country), and between regional cultures, which are most often discussed in terms of the West, the South, the Midlands, and the North, and which correspond roughly to the traditional Irish provinces of Connacht, Munster, Leinster, and Ulster, respectively. While the overwhelming majority of Irish people consider themselves to be ethnically Irish, some Irish nationals see themselves as Irish of British descent, a group sometimes referred to as the "Anglo-Irish" or "West Britons." Another important cultural minority are Irish "Travellers," who have historically been an itinerant ethnic group known for their roles in the informal economy as artisans, traders, and entertainers. There are also small religious minorities (such as Irish Jews), and ethnic minorities (such as Chinese, Indians, and Pakistanis), who have retained many aspects of cultural identification with their original national cultures.

Location and Geography. Ireland is in the far west of Europe, in the North Atlantic Ocean, west of the island of Great Britain. The island is 302 miles (486 kilometers) long, north to south, and 174 miles (280 kilometers) at its widest point. The area of the island is 32,599 square miles (84,431 square kilometers), of which the Republic covers 27, 136 square miles (70,280 square kilometers). The Republic has 223 miles (360 kilometers) of land border, all with the United Kingdom, and 898 miles (1,448 kilometers) of coastline. It is separated from its neighboring island of Great Britain to the east by the Irish Sea, the North Channel, and Saint George's Channel. The climate is temperate maritime, modified by the North Atlantic Current. Ireland has mild

Ireland

winters and cool summers. Because of the high precipitation, the climate is consistently humid. The Republic is marked by a low-lying fertile central plain surrounded by hills and uncultivated small mountains around the outer rim of the island. Its high point is 3,414 feet (1,041 meters). The largest river is the Shannon, which rises in the northern hills and flows south and west into the Atlantic. The capital city, Dublin (Baile Átha Cliath in Irish), at the mouth of the River Liffey in central eastern Ireland, on the original site of a Viking settlement, is currently home to almost 40 percent of the Irish population; it served as the capital of Ireland before and during Ireland's integration within the United Kingdom. As a result, Dublin has long been noted as the center of the oldest Anglophone and British-oriented area of Ireland; the region around the city has been known as the "English Pale" since medieval times.

Demography. The population of the Republic of Ireland was 3,626,087 in 1996, an increase of 100,368 since the 1991 census. The Irish population has increased slowly since the drop in population that occurred in the 1920s. This rise in population is expected to continue as the birthrate has steadily increased while the death rate has steadily decreased. Life expectancy for males and females born in 1991 was 72.3 and 77.9, respectively (these figures for 1926 were 57.4 and 57.9, respectively). The national population in 1996 was relatively young: 1,016,000 people were in the 25–44 age group, and 1,492,000 people were younger than 25. The greater Dublin area had 953,000 people in 1996, while Cork, the nation's second largest city, was home to 180,000. Although Ireland is known worldwide for its rural scenery and lifestyle, in 1996 1,611,000 of its people lived in its 21 most populated cities and towns, and 59 percent of the population lived in urban areas of one thousand people or more. The population density in 1996 was 135 per square mile (52 per square kilometer).

Linguistic Affiliation. Irish (Gaelic) and English are the two official languages of Ireland. Irish is a Celtic (Indo-European) language, part of the Goidelic branch of insular Celtic (as are Scottish Gaelic and Manx). Irish evolved from the language brought to the island in the Celtic migrations between the sixth and the second century B.C.E. Despite hundreds of years of Norse and Anglo-Norman migration, by the sixteenth century Irish was the vernacular for almost all of the population of Ireland. The subsequent Tudor and Stuart conquests and plantations (1534–1610), the Cromwellian settlement (1654), the Williamite war (1689–1691), and the enactment of the Penal Laws (1695) began the long process of the subversion of the language. Nevertheless, in 1835 there were four million Irish speakers in Ireland, a number that was severely reduced in the Great Famine of the late 1840s. By 1891 there were only 680,000 Irish speakers, but the key role that the Irish language played in the development of Irish nationalism in the nineteenth century, as well as its symbolic importance in the new Irish state of the twentieth century, have not been enough to reverse the process of vernacular language shift from Irish to English. In the 1991 census, in those few areas where

Irish remains the vernacular, and which are officially defined as the *Gaeltacht*, there were only 56,469 Irish-speakers. Most primary and secondary school students in Ireland study Irish, however, and it remains an important means of communication in governmental, educational, literary, sports, and cultural circles beyond the Gaeltacht. (In the 1991 census, almost 1.1 million Irish people claimed to be Irish-speaking, but this number does not distinguish levels of fluency and usage.)

Irish is one of the preeminent symbols of the Irish state and nation, but by the start of the twentieth century English had supplanted Irish as the vernacular language, and all but a very few ethnic Irish are fluent in English. Hiberno-English (the English language spoken in Ireland) has been a strong influence in the evolution of British and Irish literature, poetry, theater, and education since the end of the nineteenth century. The language has also been an important symbol to the Irish national minority in Northern Ireland, where despite many social and political impediments its use has been slowly increasing since the return of armed conflict there in 1969.

Symbolism. The flag of Ireland has three equal vertical bands of green (hoist side), white, and orange. This tricolor is also the symbol of the Irish nation in other countries, most notably in Northern Ireland among the Irish national minority. Other flags that are meaningful to the Irish include the golden harp on a green background and the Dublin workers' flag of "The Plough and the Stars." The harp is the principal symbol on the national coat of arms, and the badge of the Irish state is the shamrock. Many symbols of Irish national identity derive in part from their association with religion and church. The shamrock clover is associated with Ireland's patron Saint Patrick, and with the Holy Trinity of Christian belief. A Saint Brigid's cross is often found over the entrance to homes, as are representations of saints and other holy people, as well as portraits of the greatly admired, such as Pope John XXIII and John F. Kennedy.

Green is the color associated worldwide with Irishness, but within Ireland, and especially in Northern Ireland, it is more closely associated with being both Irish and Roman Catholic, whereas orange is the color associated with Protestantism, and more especially with Northern Irish people who support Loyalism to the British crown and continued union with Great Britain. The colors of red, white, and blue, those of the British Union Jack, are often used to mark the territory of Loyalist communities in Northern Ireland, just as orange, white, and green mark Irish Nationalist territory there. Sports, especially the national ones organized by the Gaelic Athletic Association such as hurling, camogie, and Gaelic football, also serve as central symbols of the nation.

History and Ethnic Relations

Emergence of the Nation. The nation that evolved in Ireland was formed over two millennia, the result of diverse forces both internal and external to the island. While there were a number of groups of people living on the island in prehistory, the Celtic migrations of the first millennium B.C.E. brought the language and many aspects of Gaelic society that have figured so prominently in more recent nationalist revivals. Christianity was introduced in the fifth century C.E., and from its beginning Irish Christianity has been associated with monasticism. Irish monks did much to preserve European Christian heritage before and during the Middle Ages, and they ranged throughout the continent in their efforts to establish their holy orders and serve their God and church.

From the early ninth century Norsemen raided Ireland's monasteries and settlements, and by the next century they had established their own coastal communities and trading centers. The traditional Irish political system, based on five provinces (Meath, Connacht, Munster, Leinster, and Ulster), assimilated many Norse people, as well as many of the Norman invaders from England after 1169. Over the next four centuries, although the Anglo-Normans succeeded in controlling most of the island, thereby establishing feudalism and their structures of parliament, law, and administration, they also adopted the Irish language and customs, and intermarriage between Norman and Irish elites had become common. By the end of the fifteenth century, the Gaelicization of the Normans had resulted in only the Pale, around Dublin, being controlled by English lords.

In the sixteenth century, the Tudors sought to reestablish English control over much of the island. The efforts of Henry VIII to disestablish the Catholic Church in Ireland began the long association between Irish Catholicism and Irish nationalism. His daughter, Elizabeth I, accomplished the English conquest of the island. In the early seventeenth century the English government began a policy of colonization by importing English and Scottish immigrants, a policy that often necessitated the forcible removal of the native Irish. Today's nationalist conflict in Northern Ireland has its historical roots in this pe-

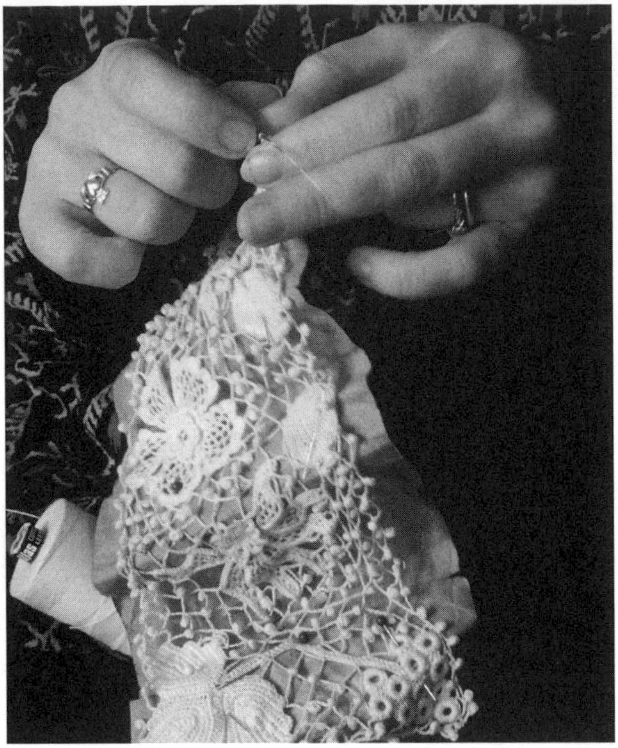

A woman makes clones knots between the main motifs in a piece of hand-crochet.

riod, when New English Protestants and Scottish Presbyterians moved into Ulster. William of Orange's victory over the Stuarts at the end of the seventeenth century led to the period of the Protestant Ascendancy, in which the civil and human rights of the native Irish, the vast majority of whom were Catholics, were repressed. By the end of the eighteenth century the cultural roots of the nation were strong, having grown through a mixture of Irish, Norse, Norman, and English language and customs, and were a product of English conquest, the forced introduction of colonists with different national backgrounds and religions, and the development of an Irish identity that was all but inseparable from Catholicism.

National Identity. The long history of modern Irish revolutions began in 1798, when Catholic and Presbyterian leaders, influenced by the American and French Revolutions and desirous of the introduction of some measure of Irish national self-government, joined together to use force to attempt to break the link between Ireland and England. This, and subsequent rebellions in 1803, 1848, and 1867, failed. Ireland was made part of the United Kingdom in the Act of Union of 1801, which lasted until the end of World War I (1914–1918), when the Irish War of Independence led to a compromise agreement between the Irish belligerents, the British government, and Northern Irish Protestants who wanted Ulster to remain part of the United Kingdom. This compromise established the Irish Free State, which was composed of twenty-six of Ireland's thirty-two counties. The remainder became Northern Ireland, the only part of Ireland to stay in the United Kingdom, and wherein the majority population were Protestant and Unionist.

The cultural nationalism that succeeded in gaining Ireland's independence had its origin in the Catholic emancipation movement of the early nineteenth century, but it was galvanized by Anglo-Irish and other leaders who sought to use the revitalization of Irish language, sport, literature, drama, and poetry to demonstrate the cultural and historical bases of the Irish nation. This Gaelic Revival stimulated great popular support for both the idea of the Irish nation, and for diverse groups who sought various ways of expressing this modern nationalism. The intellectual life of Ireland began to have a great impact throughout the British Isles and beyond, most notably among the Irish Diaspora who had been forced to flee the disease, starvation, and death of the Great Famine of 1846–1849, when a blight destroyed the potato crop, upon which the Irish peasantry depended for food. Estimates vary, but this famine period resulted in approximately one million dead and two million emigrants.

By the end of the nineteenth century many Irish at home and abroad were committed to the peaceful attainment of "Home Rule" with a separate Irish parliament within the United Kingdom while many others were committed to the violent severing of Irish and British ties. Secret societies, forerunners of the Irish Republican Army (IRA), joined with public groups, such as trade union organizations, to plan another rebellion, which took place on Easter Monday, 24 April 1916. The ruthlessness that the British government displayed in putting down this insurrection led to the wide-scale disenchantment of the Irish people with Britain. The Irish War of Independence (1919–1921), followed by the Irish Civil War (1921–1923), ended with the creation of an independent state.

Ethnic Relations. Many countries in the world have sizable Irish ethnic minorities, including the United States, Canada, the United Kingdom, Australia, and Argentina. While many of these people descend from emigrants of the mid- to late nineteenth century, many others are descendants of more recent Irish emigrants, while still others were born in Ireland. These ethnic communities identify in varying degrees with Irish culture, and they are distinguished by their religion, dance, music, dress, food, and secular and religious celebrations (the most famous of which is the Saint Patrick Day's parades that are held in Irish communities around the world on 17 March).

While Irish immigrants often suffered from religious, ethnic, and racial bigotry in the nineteenth century, their communities today are characterized by both the resilience of their ethnic identities and the degree to which they have assimilated to host national cultures. Ties to the "old country" remain strong. Many people of Irish descent worldwide have been active in seeking a solution to the national conflict in Northern Ireland, known as the "Troubles."

Ethnic relations in the Republic of Ireland are relatively peaceful, given the homogeneity of national culture, but Irish Travellers have often been the victims of prejudice. In Northern Ireland the level of ethnic conflict, which is inextricably linked to the province's bifurcation of religion, nationalism, and ethnic identity, is high, and has been since the outbreak of political violence in 1969. Since 1994 there has been a shaky and intermittent cease-fire among the paramilitary groups in Northern Ireland. The 1998 Good Friday agreement is the most recent accord.

Urbanism, Architecture, and the Use of Space

The public architecture of Ireland reflects the country's past role in the British Empire, as most Irish cities and towns were either designed or remodeled as Ireland evolved with Britain. Since independence, much of the architectural iconography and symbolism, in terms of statues, monuments, museums, and landscaping, has reflected the sacrifices of those who fought for Irish freedom. Residential and business architecture is similar to that found elsewhere in the British Isles and Northern Europe.

The Irish put great emphasis on nuclear families establishing residences independent of the residences of the families from which the husband and wife hail, with the intention of owning these residences; Ireland has a very high percentage of owner-occupiers. As a result, the suburbanization of Dublin is resulting in a number of social, economic, transportation, architectural, and legal problems that Ireland must solve in the near future.

The informality of Irish culture, which is one thing that Irish people believe sets them apart from British people, facilitates an open and fluid approach between people in public and private spaces. Personal space is small and negotiable; while it is not common for Irish people to touch each other when walking or talking, there is no prohibition on public displays of emotion, affection, or attachment. Humor, literacy, and verbal acuity are valued; sarcasm and humor are the preferred sanctions if a person transgresses the few rules that govern public social interaction.

Food and Economy

Food in Daily Life. The Irish diet is similar to that of other Northern European nations. There is an emphasis on the consumption of meat, cereals, bread, and potatoes at most meals. Vegetables such as cabbage, turnips, carrots, and broccoli are also popular as accompaniments to the meat and potatoes. Traditional Irish daily eating habits, influenced by a farming ethos, involved four meals: breakfast, dinner (the midday meal and the main one of the day), tea (in early evening, and distinct from "high tea" which is normally served at 4:00 P.M. and is associated with British customs), and supper (a light repast before retiring). Roasts and stews, of lamb, beef, chicken, ham, pork, and turkey, are the centerpieces of traditional meals. Fish, especially salmon, and seafood, especially prawns, are also popular meals. Until recently, most shops closed at the dinner hour (between 1:00 and 2:00 P.M.) to allow staff to return home for their meal. These patterns, however, are changing, because of the growing importance of new lifestyles, professions, and patterns of work, as well as the increased consumption of frozen, ethnic, take-out, and processed foods. Nevertheless, some foods (such as wheaten breads, sausages, and bacon rashers) and some drinks (such as the national beer, Guinness, and Irish whiskey) maintain their important gustatory and symbolic roles in Irish meals and socializing. Regional dishes, consisting of variants on stews, potato casseroles, and breads, also exist. The public house is an essential meeting place for all Irish communities, but these establishments traditionally seldom served dinner. In the past pubs had two separate sections, that of the bar, reserved for males, and the lounge, open to men and women. This distinction is eroding, as are expectations of gender preference in the consumption of alcohol.

Food Customs at Ceremonial Occasions. There are few ceremonial food customs. Large family gatherings often sit down to a main meal of roast chicken and ham, and turkey is becoming the preferred dish for Christmas (followed by Christmas cake or plum pudding). Drinking behavior in pubs

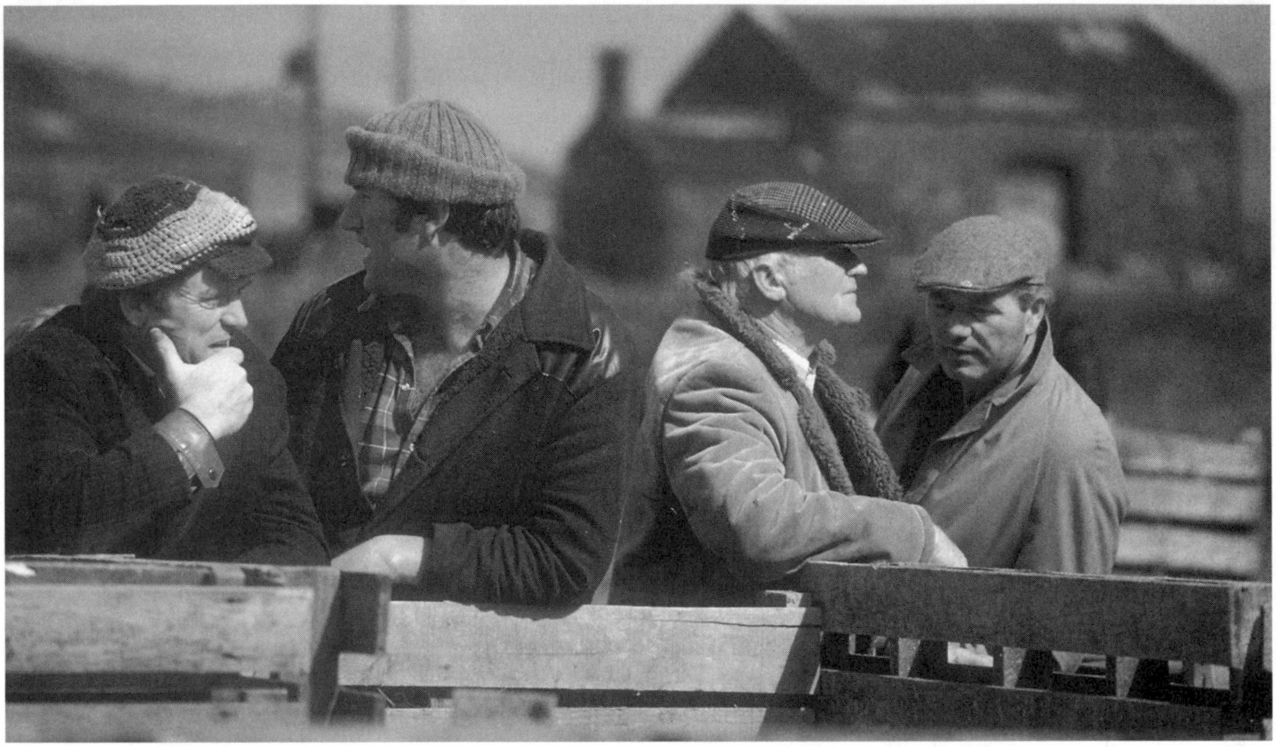

The informality of Irish culture facilitates an open and fluid approach between people in public places.

is ordered informally, in what is perceived by some to be a ritualistic manner of buying drinks in rounds.

Basic Economy. Agriculture is no longer the principal economic activity. Industry accounts for 38 percent of gross domestic product (GDP) and 80 percent of exports, and employs 27 percent of the workforce. During the 1990s Ireland enjoyed annual trade surpluses, falling inflation, and increases in construction, consumer spending, and business and consumer investment. Unemployment was down (from 12 percent in 1995 to around 7 percent in 1999) and emigration declined. As of 1998, the labor force consisted of 1.54 million people; as of 1996, 62 percent of the labor force was in services, 27 percent in manufacturing and construction, and 10 percent in agriculture, forestry, and fishing. In 1999 Ireland had the fastest growing economy in the European Union. In the five years to 1999 GDP per capita rose by 60 percent, to approximately $22,000 (U.S.).

Despite its industrialization, Ireland still is an agricultural country, which is important to its self-image and its image for tourists. As of 1993, only 13 percent of its land was arable, while 68 percent was devoted to permanent pastures. While all Irish food producers consume a modest amount of their product, agriculture and fishing are modern, mechanized, and commercial enterprises, with the vast bulk of production going to the national and international markets. Although the image of the smallholding subsistence farmer persists in art, literary, and academic circles, Irish farming and farmers are as advanced in technology and technique as most of their European neighbors. Poverty persists, however, among farmers with small holdings, on poor land, particularly in many parts of the west and south. These farmers, who to survive must rely more on subsistence crops and mixed farming than do their more commercial neighbors, involve all family members in a variety of economic strategies. These activities include off-farm wage labor and the acquisition of state pensions and unemployment benefits ("the dole").

Land Tenure and Property. Ireland was one of the first countries in Europe in which peasants could purchase their landholdings. Today all but a very few farms are family-owned, although some mountain pasture and bog lands are held in common. Cooperatives are principally production and marketing enterprises. An annually changing proportion of pasture and arable land is leased out each year, usually for an eleven-month period, in a traditional system known as conacre.

Major Industries. The main industries are food products, brewing, textiles, clothing, and pharmaceuticals, and Ireland is fast becoming known for its roles in the development and design of information technologies and financial support services. In agriculture the main products are meat and dairy, potatoes, sugar beets, barley, wheat, and turnips. The fishing industry concentrates on cod, haddock, herring, mackerel, and shellfish (crab and lobster). Tourism increases its share of the economy annually; in 1998 total tourism and travel earnings were $3.1 billion (U.S.).

Trade. Ireland had a consistent trade surplus at the end of the 1990s. In 1997 this surplus amounted to $13 billion (U.S). Ireland's main trading partners are the United Kingdom, the rest of the European Union, and the United States.

Division of Labor. In farming, daily and seasonal tasks are divided according to age and gender. Most public activities that deal with farm production are handled by adult males, although some agricultural production associated with the domestic household, such as eggs and honey, are marketed by adult females. Neighbors often help each other with their labor or equipment when seasonal production demands, and this network of local support is sustained through ties of marriage, religion and church, education, political party, and sports. While in the past most blue-collar and wage-labor jobs were held by males, women have increasingly entered the workforce over the last generation, especially in tourism, sales, and information and financial services. Wages and salaries are consistently lower for women, and employment in the tourism industry is often seasonal or temporary. There are very few legal age or gender restrictions to entering professions, but here too men dominate in numbers if not also in influence and control. Irish economic policy has encouraged foreign-owned businesses, as one way to inject capital into underdeveloped parts of the country. The United States and the United Kingdom top the list of foreign investors in Ireland.

Social Stratification

Classes and Castes. The Irish often perceive that their culture is set off from their neighbors by its egalitarianism, reciprocity, and informality, wherein strangers do not wait for introductions to converse, the first name is quickly adopted in business and professional discourse, and the sharing of food, tools, and other valuables is commonplace. These leveling mechanisms alleviate many pressures engendered by class relations, and often belie rather strong divisions of status, prestige, class, and national identity. While the rigid class structure for which the English are renowned is largely absent, social and economic class distinctions exist, and are often reproduced through educational and religious institutions, and the professions. The old British and Anglo-Irish aristocracy are small in number and relatively powerless. They have been replaced at the apex of Irish society by the wealthy, many of whom have made their fortunes in business and professions, and by celebrities from the arts and sports worlds. Social classes are discussed in terms of working class, middle class, and gentry, with certain occupations, such as farmers, often categorized according to their wealth, such as large and small farmers, grouped according to the size of their landholding and capital. The social boundaries between these groups are often indistinct and permeable, but their basic dimensions are clearly discernible to locals through dress, language, conspicuous consumption, leisure activities, social networks, and occupation and profession. Relative wealth and social class also influence life choices, perhaps the most important being that of primary and secondary school, and university, which in turn affects one's class mobility. Some minority groups, such as Travellers, are often portrayed in popular culture as being outside or beneath the accepted social class system, making escape from the underclass as difficult for them as for the long-term unemployed of the inner cities.

Symbols of Social Stratification. Use of language, especially dialect, is a clear indicator of class and other social standing. Dress codes have relaxed over the last generation, but the conspicuous consumption of important symbols of wealth and success, such as designer clothing, good food, travel, and expensive cars and houses, provides important strategies for class mobility and social advancement.

Political Life

Government. The Republic of Ireland is a parliamentary democracy. The National Parliament (*Oireachtas*) consists of the president (directly elected by the people), and two houses: *Dáil Éireann* (House of Representatives) and *Seanad Éireann* (Senate). Their powers and functions derive from the constitution (enacted 1 July 1937). Representatives to Dáil Éireann, who are called *Teachta Dála*, or TDs, are elected through proportional representation with a single transferable vote. While legislative

People walk past a colorful storefront in Dublin.

power is vested in the Oireachtas, all laws are subject to the obligations of European Community membership, which Ireland joined in 1973. The executive power of the state is vested in the government, composed of the *Taoiseach* (prime minister) and the cabinet. While a number of political parties are represented in the Oireachtas, governments since the 1930s have been led by either the Fianna Fáil or the Fine Gael party, both of which are center-right parties. County Councils are the principal form of local government, but they have few powers in what is one of the most centralized states in Europe.

Leadership and Political Officials. Irish political culture is marked by its postcolonialism, conservatism, localism, and familism, all of which were influenced by the Irish Catholic Church, British institutions and politics, and Gaelic culture. Irish political leaders must rely on their local political support—which depends more on their roles in local society, and their real or imagined roles in networks of patrons and clients—than it does on their roles as legislators or political administrators. As a result there is no set career path to political prominence, but over the years sports heroes, family members of past politicians, publicans, and military people have had great success in being elected to the Oireachtas. Pervasive in Irish politics is admiration and political support for politicians who can provide pork barrel government services and supplies to his constituents (very few Irish women reach the higher levels of politics, industry, and academia). While there has always been a vocal left in Irish politics, especially in the cities, since the 1920s these parties have seldom been strong, with the occasional success of the Labour Party being the most notable exception. Most Irish political parties do not provide clear and distinct policy differences, and few espouse the political ideologies that characterize other European nations. The major political division is that between Fianna Fáil and Fine Gael, the two largest parties, whose support still derives from the descendants of the two opposing sides in the Civil War, which was fought over whether to accept the compromise treaty that divided the island into the Irish Free State and Northern Ireland. As a result, the electorate does not vote for candidates because of their policy initiatives, but because of a candidate's personal skill in achieving material gain for constituents, and because the voter's family has traditionally supported the candidate's party. This voting pattern depends on local knowledge of the politician, and the informality of local culture, which encourages people to believe that they have direct access to their politicians. Most national and local politicians have regular open office hours where constituents can discuss their problems and concerns without having to make an appointment.

Social Problems and Control. The legal system is based on common law, modified by subsequent legislation and the constitution of 1937. Judicial review of legislation is made by the Supreme Court, which is appointed by the president of Ireland on the advice of the government. Ireland has a long history of political violence, which is still an important aspect of life in Northern Ireland, where paramilitary groups such as the IRA have enjoyed some support from people in the Republic. Under emergency powers acts, certain legal rights and protections can be suspended by the state in the pursuit of terrorists. Crimes of nonpolitical violence are rare, though some, such as spousal and child abuse, may go unreported. Most major crimes, and the crimes most important in popular culture, are those of burglary, theft, larceny, and corruption. Crime rates are higher in urban areas, which in some views results from the poverty endemic to some inner cities. There is a general respect for the law and its agents, but other social controls also exist to sustain moral order. Such institutions as the Catholic Church and the state education system are partly responsible for the overall adherence to rules and respect for authority, but there is an anarchic quality to Irish culture that sets it off from its neighboring British cultures. Interpersonal forms of informal social control include a heightened sense of humor and sarcasm, supported by the general Irish values of reciprocity, irony, and skepticism regarding social hierarchies.

Military Activity. The Irish Defence Forces have army, naval service and air corps branches. The total membership of the permanent forces is approximately 11,800, with 15,000 serving in the reserves. While the military is principally trained to defend Ireland, Irish soldiers have served in most United Nations peacekeeping missions, in part because of Ireland's policy of neutrality. The Defence Forces play an important security role on the border with Northern Ireland. The Irish National Police, *An Garda Siochána*, is an unarmed force of approximately 10,500 members.

Social Welfare and Change Programs

The national social welfare system mixes social insurance and social assistance programs to provide financial support to the ill, the aged, and the unemployed, benefitting roughly 1.3 million people. State spending on social welfare comprises 25 percent of government expenditures, and about 6 percent of GDP. Other relief agencies, many of which are connected to the churches, also provide valuable financial assistance and social relief programs for the amelioration of the conditions of poverty and inequity.

Nongvernmental Organizations and Other Associations

Civil society is well-developed, and nongovernmental organizations serve all classes, professions, regions, occupations, ethnic groups, and charitable causes. Some are very powerful, such as the Irish Farmers Association, while others, such as the international charitable support organization, *Trócaire*, a Catholic agency for world development, command widespread financial and moral support. Ireland is one of the highest per capita contributors to private international aid in the world. Since the creation of the Irish state a number of development agencies and utilities have been organized in partly state-owned bodies, such as the Industrial Development Agency, but these are slowly being privatized.

Gender Roles and Statuses

While gender equality in the workplace is guaranteed by law, remarkable inequities exist between the genders in such areas as pay, access to professional achievement, and parity of esteem in the workplace. Certain jobs and professions are still considered by large segments of the population to be gender linked. Some critics charge that gender biases continue to be established and reinforced in the nation's major institutions of government, education, and religion. Feminism is a growing movement in rural and urban areas, but it still faces many obstacles among traditionalists.

Marriage, Family, and Kinship

Marriage. Marriages are seldom arranged in modern Ireland. Monogamous marriages are the norm, as supported and sanctioned by the state and the Christian churches. Divorce has been legal since 1995. Most spouses are selected through the expected means of individual trial and error that have become the norm in Western European society. The demands of farm society and economy still place great pressure on rural men and women to marry, especially in some relatively poor rural districts where there is a high migration rate among

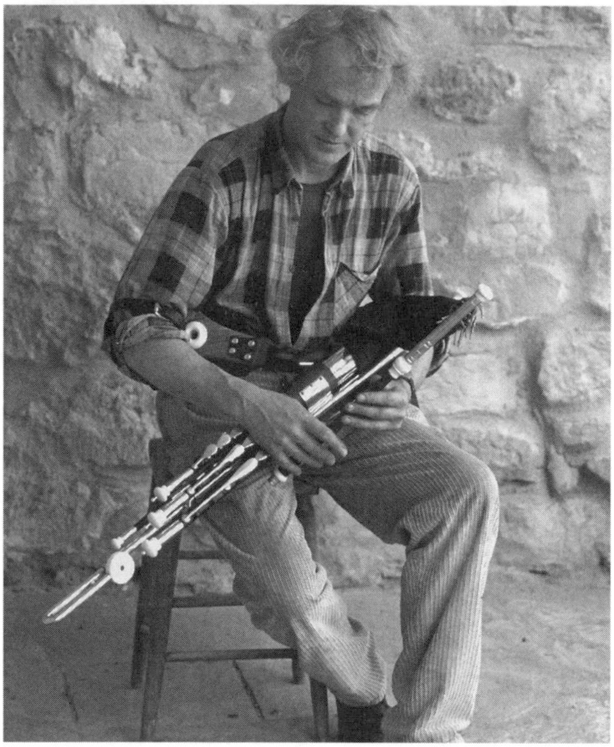

Eugene Lamb, an uillean pipe maker in Kinvara, County Galway, holds one of his wares.

women, who go to the cities or emigrate in search of employment and social standing commensurate with their education and social expectations. Marriage festivals for farm men and women, the most famous of which takes place in the early autumn in Lisdoonvarna, has served as one way to bring people together for possible marriage matches, but the increased criticism of such practices in Irish society may endanger their future. The estimated marriage rate per thousand people in 1998 was 4.5. While the average ages of partners at marriage continues to be older than other Western societies, the ages have dropped over the last generation.

Domestic Unit. The nuclear family household is the principal domestic unit, as well as the basic unit of production, consumption, and inheritance in Irish society.

Inheritance. Past rural practices of leaving the patrimony to one son, thereby forcing his siblings into wage labor, the church, the army, or emigration, have been modified by changes in Irish law, gender roles, and the size and structure of families. All children have legal rights to inheritance, although a preference still lingers for farmers' sons to inherit the land, and for a farm to be passed on without division. Similar patterns exist in urban areas, where gender and class are important determinants of the inheritance of property and capital.

Kin Groups. The main kin group is the nuclear family, but extended families and kindreds continue to play important roles in Irish life. Descent is from both parents' families. Children in general adopt their father's surnames. Christian (first) names are often selected to honor an ancestor (most commonly, a grandparent), and in the Catholic tradition most first names are those of saints. Many families continue to use the Irish form of their names (some "Christian" names are in fact pre-Christian and untranslatable into English). Children in the national primary school system are taught to know and use the Irish language equivalent of their names, and it is legal to use your name in either of the two official languages.

Socialization

Child Rearing and Education. Socialization takes place in the domestic unit, in schools, at church, through the electronic and print media, and in voluntary youth organizations. Particular emphasis is placed on education and literacy; 98 percent of the population aged fifteen and over can read and write. The majority of four-year-olds attend nursery school, and all five-year-olds are in primary school. More than three thousand primary schools serve 500,000 children. Most primary schools are linked to the Catholic Church, and receive capital funding from the state, which also pays most teachers' salaries. Post-primary education involves 370,000 students, in secondary, vocational, community, and comprehensive schools.

Higher Education. Third-level education includes universities, technological colleges, and education colleges. All are self-governing, but are principally funded by the state. About 50 percent of youth attend some form of third-level education, half of whom pursue degrees. Ireland is world famous for its universities, which are the University of Dublin (Trinity College), the National University of Ireland, the University of Limerick, and Dublin City University.

Etiquette

General rules of social etiquette apply across ethnic, class, and religious barriers. Loud, boisterous, and boastful behavior are discouraged. Unacquainted people look directly at each other in public spaces, and often say "hello" in greeting. Outside of formal introductions greetings are often vocal and are not accompanied by a handshake or kiss. Individuals maintain a public personal space around themselves; public touching is rare. Generosity and reciprocity are key values in social exchange, especially in the ritualized forms of group drinking in pubs.

Religion

Religious Beliefs. The Irish Constitution guarantees freedom of conscience and the free profession and practice of religion. There is no official state religion, but critics point to the special consideration given to the Catholic Church and its agents since the inception of the state. In the 1991 census 92 percent of the population were Roman Catholic, 2.4 percent belonged to the Church of Ireland (Anglican), 0.4 percent were Presbyterians, and 0.1 percent were Methodists. The Jewish community comprised .04 percent of the total, while approximately 3 percent belonged to other religious groups. No information on religion was returned for 2.4 percent of the population. Christian revivalism is changing many of the ways in which the people relate to each other and to their formal church institutions. Folk cultural beliefs also survive, as evidenced in the many holy and healing places, such as the holy wells that dot the landscape.

Religious Practitioners. The Catholic Church has four ecclesiastical provinces, which encompass the whole island, thus crossing the boundary with Northern Ireland. The Archbishop of Armagh in Northern Ireland is the Primate of All Ireland. The diocesan structure, in which thirteen hundred parishes are served by four thousand priests, dates to the twelfth century and does not coincide with political boundaries. There are approximately twenty thousand people serving in various Catholic religious orders, out of a combined Ireland and Northern Ireland Catholic population of 3.9 million. The Church of Ireland, which has twelve dioceses, is an autonomous church within the worldwide Anglican Communion. Its Primate of All Ireland is the Archbishop of Armagh, and its total membership is 380,000, 75 percent of whom are in Northern Ireland. There are 312,000 Presbyterians on the island (95 percent of whom are in Northern Ireland), grouped into 562 congregations and twenty-one presbyteries.

Rituals and Holy Places. In this predominantly Catholic country there are a number of Church-recognized shrines and holy places, most notably that of Knock, in County Mayo, the site of a reported apparition of the Blessed Mother. Traditional holy places, such as holy wells, attract local people at all times of the year, although many are associated with particular days, saints, rituals, and feasts. Internal pilgrimages to such places as Knock and Croagh Patrick (a mountain in County Mayo associated with Saint Patrick) are important aspects of Catholic belief, which often reflect the integration of formal and traditional religious practices. The holy days of the official Irish Catholic Church calendar are observed as national holidays.

Death and the Afterlife. Funerary customs are inextricably linked to various Catholic Church religious rituals. While wakes continue to be held in homes, the practice of utilizing funeral directors and parlors is gaining in popularity.

Medicine and Health Care

Medical services are provided free of charge by the state to approximately a third of the population. All others pay minimal charges at public health facilities. There are roughly 128 doctors for every 100,000 people. Various forms of folk and alternative medicines exist throughout the island; most rural communities have locally known healers or healing places. Religious sites, such as the pilgrimage destination of Knock, and rituals are also known for their healing powers.

Secular Celebrations

The national holidays are linked to national and religious history, such as Saint Patrick's Day, Christmas, and Easter, or are seasonal bank and public holidays which occur on Mondays, allowing for long weekends.

The Arts and Humanities

Literature. The literary renaissance of the late nineteenth century integrated the hundreds-year-old traditions of writing in Irish with those of English, in what has come to be known as Anglo-Irish literature. Some of the greatest writers in English over the last century were Irish: W. B. Yeats, George Bernard Shaw, James Joyce, Samuel Beckett, Frank O'Connor, Seán O'Faoláin, Seán O'Casey, Flann O'Brien, and Seamus Heaney. They and many others have constituted an unsurpassable record of a national experience that has universal appeal.

Graphic Arts. High, popular, and folk arts are highly valued aspects of local life throughout Ire-

Walls separate individual fields on Inisheer, one of Ireland's Aran Islands.

land. Graphic and visual arts are strongly supported by the government through its Arts Council and the 1997-formed Department of Arts, Heritage, Gaeltacht, and the Islands. All major international art movements have their Irish representatives, who are often equally inspired by native or traditional motifs. Among the most important artists of the century are Jack B. Yeats and Paul Henry.

Performance Arts. Performers and artists are especially valued members of the Irish nation, which is renowned internationally for the quality of its music, acting, singing, dancing, composing, and writing. U2 and Van Morrison in rock, Daniel O'Donnell in country, James Galway in classical, and the Chieftains in Irish traditional music are but a sampling of the artists who have been important influences on the development of international music. Irish traditional music and dance have also spawned the global phenomenon of Riverdance. Irish cinema celebrated its centenary in 1996. Ireland has been the site and the inspiration for the production of feature films since 1910. Major directors (such as Neill Jordan and Jim Sheridan) and actors (such as Liam Neeson and Stephen Rhea) are part of a national interest in the representation of contemporary Ireland, as symbolized in the state-sponsored Film Institute of Ireland.

The State of the Physical and Social Sciences

The government is the principal source of financial support for academic research in the physical and social sciences, which are broadly and strongly represented in the nation's universities and in government-sponsored bodies, such as the Economic and Social Research Institute in Dublin. Institutions of higher learning draw relatively high numbers of international students at both undergraduate and postgraduate levels, and Irish researchers are to be found in all areas of academic and applied research throughout the world.

Bibliography

Clancy, Patrick, Sheelagh Drudy, Kathleen Lynch, and Liam O'Dowd, eds. *Irish Society: Sociological Perspectives*, 1995.

Curtin, Chris, Hastings Donnan, and Thomas M. Wilson, eds. *Irish Urban Cultures*, 1993.

Taylor, Lawrence J. *Occasions of Faith: An Anthropology of Irish Catholics*, 1995.

Wilson, Thomas M. "Themes in the Anthropology of Ireland." In Susan Parman, ed., *Europe in the Anthropological Imagination*, 1998.

Web Sites

CAIN Project. *Background Information on Northern Ireland Society—Population and Vital Statistics*. Electronic document. Available from: http://cain.ulst.ac.uk/ni/popul.htm

Government of Ireland, Central Statistics Office, *Principal Statistics*. Electronic document. Available from http://www.cso.ie/principalstats

Government of Ireland, Department of Foreign Affairs. *Facts about Ireland*. Electronic document. Available from http://www.irlgov.ie/facts

—THOMAS M. WILSON

ISRAEL

CULTURE NAME

Israeli

ORIENTATION

Identification. According to the Bible, Israel is the name given by God to Jacob. The modern country of Israel includes two distinct nationalities, the Palestinian and the Jewish. Each nationality is inextricable from its religious identity. The Palestinians are Arabs whose traditions are founded in Muslim culture; the Jews define their culture in large part around their religion as well. Each group identifies as part of a larger, international religious and cultural community, and each has a history in the region that goes back to ancient times.

Location and Geography. Israel is in the Middle East on the Mediterranean Sea, bordering Egypt, the Gaza Strip, Jordan, Lebanon, Syria, and the West Bank. Its total area is 8,019 square miles (20,770 square kilometers), slightly smaller than New Jersey. The Negev Desert covers the south of the country. Mountains rise in the central region from the low coastal plain along the Mediterranean. The Jordan River stretches 200 miles (322 kilometers) from Syria in the north, emptying into the Dead Sea. The Dead Sea (technically a lake) is, at 1,312 feet (400 meters) below sea level, the lowest inland sea on earth.

Demography. Israel's population in 2000 was 5,842,454. This includes an estimated 171,000 Israeli settlers in the West Bank, 20,000 in the Israeli-occupied Golan Heights, 6,500 in the Gaza Strip, and 172,000 in East Jerusalem. The population is roughly 80 percent Jewish; of the total population, 32.1 percent were born in Europe or America; 20.8 percent in Israel; 14.6 percent in Africa; and 12.6 percent in Asia. Most of the 20 percent who are not Jewish are Arab.

Linguistic Affiliation. Hebrew is the nation's official language. The modern Hebrew language was designed by Eliezer Ben-Yehuda, a Lithuanian Jew who moved to Palestine in the 1880s. Previously, biblical Hebrew had been the language of prayer, whereas the vernacular of most Jews was Yiddish (Ladino for Spanish and Portuguese Jews). David Ben-Gurion's vision of a national language, which would allow Jews from different parts of the world to communicate with each other, was an important element of the Zionist movement. Arabic is the official language of the Arab minority. English is studied in school and is the most commonly spoken foreign language. Immigrants from various countries also bring their languages with them, and Spanish, Italian, African dialects, and especially Russian are often heard.

Symbolism. The flag consists of a blue six-pointed star on a white background, with a horizontal blue stripe above and one below. The star, called a Magen David, or Shield of David, is a symbol of the Jewish faith.

The Israeli national anthem, *Hatikva*, is over one hundred years old. Its melody is of unknown origin, although some believe it comes from an Eastern European fold song. Its lyrics are explicitly Zionist, extolling the return of the Jews to their holy land. The song was banned from the airwaves during the British mandate, and it continues to be somewhat controversial today; there has been some debate as to whether its Zionist message is still valid.

HISTORY AND ETHNIC RELATIONS

Emergence of the Nation. There is archaeological evidence of settlements in Israel dating from nine thousand to eleven thousand years ago. It is thought that the first people of the kingdom of Israel migrated from Mesopotamia. Much of the history of ancient Israel is laid out in the Bible. The Israelites were slaves in Egypt from about 1750 to

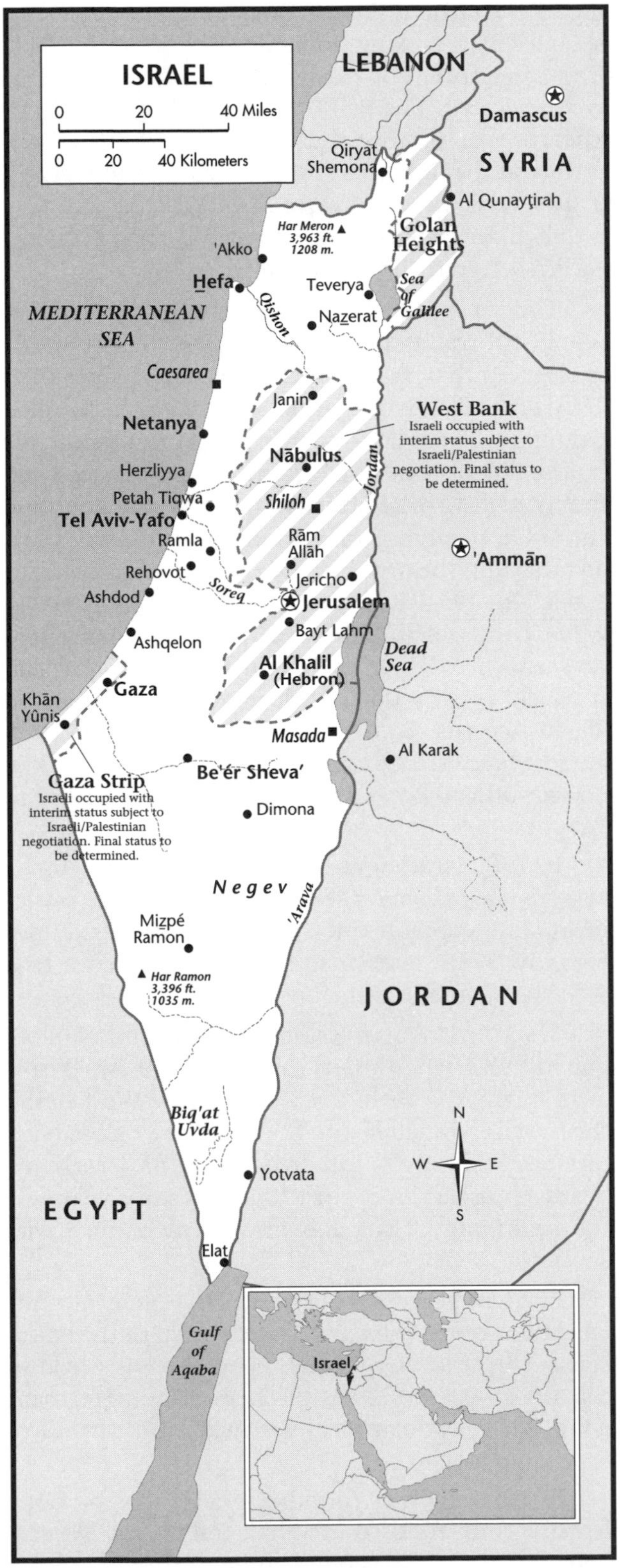

Israel

1280 B.C.E., when Moses led the Jewish people in Exodus. They wandered in the desert for forty years. Moses died, and Joshua took the helm and led the people into the land of Canaan, or the Promised Land. The epoch that followed was known as the period of the judges, when Israel was ruled by judges and priests. Saul became the first king of Israel in 1020 B.C.E. He was succeeded by his rival, David, in 1004. Under David's rule, Jerusalem became the capital. Solomon ascended to the throne in 965 B.C.E., and ruled for nearly forty years, during which time the First Temple was built. In 925 the kingdom split into two parts, Israel and Judah. In 721 Israel was conquered by Assyria, and in 586 it was taken over by Babylonia. The city of Jerusalem was destroyed, and the Jews were exiled to Babylon.

In 538 Babylon was conquered by the king of Persia, who allowed the Jews to return to their homeland, where they rebuilt the Temple and began what became known as the Second Jewish State. In 322 B.C.E., Alexander the Great defeated the Persians and took control of Israel. Between 322 and 160 B.C., the land of Israel changed hands several times under various Greek and Syrian rulers. In 160 Judas Maccabee led a rebellion that allowed the Jews to reclaim Jerusalem, a victory that Jews still celebrate in the festival of Hanukkah. Judah became an independent state in 141 B.C.E.

Herod conquered Judah in 37 B.C.E. In 19 B.C.E., under his rule, the Temple was again rebuilt. The First Revolt against Rome occurred in 66 C.E.; however, Jerusalem fell to the Romans in 70 C.E. The Temple was destroyed, and the majority of the Jews were dispersed throughout the world.

Byzantines ruled the area from 313 to 635, although toward the end of this period, from 614 to 629, the Jews ruled Jerusalem under Persian jurisdiction. The years 622 to 632 saw the founding of Islam by Muhammad. In 638 Arab Muslims conquered Jerusalem, where their rule lasted until the Turkish conquest in 1078. The First Crusaders took the city in 1099. In 1187 Saladin, the Kurdish ruler of Egypt, conquered Jerusalem. In 1516 the land of Israel, known at this time as Palestine, was taken over by the Ottoman Turks, who ruled for four hundred years. In 1799 Napoleon unsuccessfully attempted to take the territory, but did not succeed.

The first modern Jewish settlement in Palestine was established in 1870, and was followed at the end of the nineteenth century by others, as Jews fled pogroms in Russia and Poland. In 1897 the First Zionist Conference was held in Basel, Switzerland, and under the initiative of the Hungarian Jew Theodor Herzl, the Zionist movement began its mission to create a Jewish homeland in the territory from which the Jews had been expelled nearly two thousand years earlier.

The Balfour Declaration, issued by Britain in 1917, expressed support for the establishment of a Jewish state in Palestine. The British used a 1920 mandate from the League of Nations as license to rule the area for the ensuing decades, during which time they kept control by feeding the animosity between Palestinian Arabs and Jewish settlers. The British also restricted Jewish immigration to the region, even by Jews who were experiencing persecution at the hands of the Russians, and later the Nazis. The Arabs attempted unsuccessfully to revolt against the British from 1936 to 1938; tensions between Arabs and Jews also escalated, and there were several anti-Jewish riots.

From the time Hitler came to power in 1933 until the beginning of World War II in 1939, a large number of German Jews managed to immigrate to Palestine despite British restrictions, fleeing the increasingly oppressive regime. Between 1939 and 1945 more than six million Jews were killed in the Holocaust, a horror that gave new impetus to the movement to form a Jewish state and that caused European nations to recognize the legitimacy of such a claim.

In Palestine, a truce with the British lasted through World War II, but when the war ended, violence again increased, both between Jews and Arabs and against the British. In 1947 the United Nations voted to partition Palestine into two states, one Jewish and one Arab. The Palestinians rejected this plan.

On 14 May 1948, when Israel proclaimed its independence, the declaration was met by an invasion on behalf of the Palestinians by the armies of Egypt, Jordan, Syria, Lebanon, and Iraq. The war that followed lasted until the Arab defeat in January 1949. A mass immigration of Jews from Europe and Arab countries took place over the first few years after the state's founding, and the economy grew. While some Palestinians chose to take up Israeli citizenship, many others immigrated to the primarily Arab West Bank and Gaza Strip, or sought refuge in other Arab nations.

When Egypt took control of the Suez Canal from France and Britain in 1956, Israel, fearing the increase in power of their unfriendly neighbor, staged an attack in Egypt's Sinai Desert. Several days later, Britain and France joined the offensive. The United Nations sent peacekeepers, who stayed in the region until 1967. When they pulled out, Egypt sent its military back into the Sinai, obstructing the southern Israeli port of Eilat. Israel responded by attacking on 5 June. Syria, Jordan, and Iraq came to Egypt's defense, but all four nations were defeated. The Six-Day War, as it came to be known, won Israel not just the Sinai but the Gaza Strip and the Golan Heights as well. It also resulted in a Jewish occupation of the West Bank and a reunited Jerusalem. (The city had been partitioned earlier between the Jews and the Arabs.)

The Arab League vowed that the situation would not rest and proceeded to put Israel in a state of siege. Arab terrorists highjacked Israeli airplanes. They also killed Israeli athletes at the 1972 Munich Olympics. The following year, on Yom Kippur, the holiest day of the Jewish calendar, Egypt and Syria mounted a surprise attack on Israel at the Suez and the Golan Heights. Israel managed to defeat the two armies, but the resulting situation was far from stable. In 1977 Egyptian president Anwar Sadat went to Jerusalem to talk with Israeli prime minister Menachem Begin, and in the following year U.S. president Jimmy Carter helped to broker the Camp David Accords. Sadat and Begin shared the 1978 Nobel Peace Prize for their efforts at reconciliation, and an official peace treaty was signed in 1979 in Paris.

In 1982 Israel agreed to give up the Sinai, but it also invaded Lebanon, to leave its northern settlements less vulnerable to Palestinian attacks. However, by 1985, Israel had limited its presence to a security strip along the border.

The Palestinian uprising called the Intifadah began in 1987. Palestinians threw rocks at Israeli soldiers occupying the Gaza Strip and the West Bank; the Israelis retaliated, and the violence escalated, ultimately resulting in hundreds of deaths. Israel proposed a peace initiative in 1989. This same year saw the beginning of a mass immigration by Soviet Jews.

The first peace talks between Israel and Palestinian Arabs, represented by Yasser Arafat of the Palestinian Liberation Organization (PLO), were held in Madrid in October 1991. The resulting agreement gave the Palestinians responsibility for the Gaza Strip and Jericho.

In 1993 another round of peace talks, between Israeli prime minister Yitzhak Rabin and Arafat, resulted in further compromise, including Israel handing over most of the Gaza Strip and parts of the West Bank to the Palestinian National Authority (PNA). By moving in this direction, the agreements presumed eventual statehood for the Palestinians. Other deals included resolving the issue of Israeli settlements in the West Bank and Gaza, as well as

A Sephardic family celebrates the Jewish festival of Passover by sharing a picnic in West Jerusalem.

the status of Jerusalem. Arafat was to confiscate illegal arms from Palestinians, and both sides were to protect and preserve access to holy sites. These agreements, known as the Oslo Accords (after the city where the first secret rounds of talks were held), were seen as momentous steps in the peace process, and concluded at Camp David with a historic handshake between Arafat and Rabin.

Israel went on to sign a peace agreement with Jordan in 1994, and to begin talks with Syria as well. However, despite progress at the upper echelons, violence continued. In 1995 Israeli prime minister Rabin was assassinated at a peace rally in Tel Aviv. The killer was an ultraconservative Jew who was angered by what he saw as Rabin's overly conciliatory stance toward the Palestinians.

In October 1998 a conference at the Wye River in Maryland resulted in an agreement by the PLO to get rid of its terrorist groups, to confiscate illegal weapons, and to imprison their own terrorists, in exchange for more land on the West Bank. The meetings also resulted in the creation of a U.S.-Palestinian-Israeli committee, to convene several times a month to prevent terrorism and assess the state of affairs. These meetings had some degree of success, and the incremental progress appeared promising. In September 2000, violence again broke out. The fragile peace established by the Oslo Accords crumbled. By the end of November more than 280 people had been killed, most of them Palestinian, with no end to the conflict in sight.

National Identity. National identity for Israelis is to a large extent bound up with their identity as Jews. For the more devout, national identity takes on a spiritual element, in which the observance of religious ritual becomes an expression of national pride. However, there are also a large number of secular Jews in Israel, for whom Judaism is more a cultural and ethnic identity than a spiritual practice. Many Palestinians living in Israel do not identify as Israelis at all, but rather with the displaced Palestinian nation (and with the rest of the Arab world as well). Much of their national identity is also based on both religious and cultural elements of the Muslim faith.

Ethnic Relations. Relations between Jews and Arabs are extremely antagonistic. Each side sees the other as the aggressor. Palestinians resent the fact that the Jews took over their homeland, and that they have exercised their far superior military technology to maintain it, whereas the Jews feel that they are making a claim to land that is rightfully theirs, and from which they have been exiled for thousands of years. Palestinians have often resorted to terrorist action, which further aggravates the situation. Atrocities have been committed on both sides of the divide, and there is little sign of reconciliation in the near future.

Relations within the Jewish community itself also have been problematic. Many of the Orthodox and ultra-Orthodox oppose any compromise with the Palestinians and want the state to follow a more strictly religious line. They do not consider more Reform or Conservative Jews Jewish, because these more liberal branches do not strictly follow all the religious laws.

Urbanism, Architecture, and the Use of Space

Ninety percent of Israel's population is urban. Jerusalem is the capital and largest city, with a population of 602,100. It is in the center of the country, straddling the border between Israel and the West Bank. The city has been continuously settled for more than three thousand years and is home to many sites of historical and religious significance for Jews, Christians, and Muslims. These include the Dome of the Rock, the Wailing Wall, the Church of the Holy Sepulchre, and the Tomb of the Virgin Mary, among others. The Old City is divided into quarters: Jewish, Christian, Muslim, and Armenian. Outside the walls of this oldest district, the city sprawls in neighborhoods containing residential zones, parks, museums, and government buildings.

Tel Aviv is a more modern city, and the commercial and industrial capital of the country. It is in fact a combination of two cities, Tel Aviv and Jaffa. Jaffa's history dates back to biblical times, whereas Tel Aviv was founded in 1909 by European Jewish immigrants. The third-largest city in the country is Haifa, in the north. It is the country's main port and also is an industrial center.

Israel's architecture is diverse, spanning many centuries and styles. There is a good deal of Islamic architecture, most of which dates from 1250 to 1517. Today most Israelis live in modern high-rise apartments, which are overseen by committees elected by the inhabitants of the building. Some Jewish settlers in Palestinian territory, and many Palestinians themselves, live in shacks, unfinished houses, or other modest dwellings.

Food and Economy

Food in Daily Life. *Falafel,* ground chickpeas mixed with onions and spices formed into balls and fried, are served in pita bread as a sandwich. Other popular dishes include *tabuleh* (a salad of bulgar wheat and chopped vegetables), *hummus* (chickpea paste), grilled meats, and eggplant. Cumin, mint, garlic, onion, and black pepper are used for flavoring. *Baklava* is a popular dessert of Arabic origin and consists of flaky dough layered with honey and nuts. Coffee is often prepared in the Turkish style, extremely strong and thick and served in small cups.

Jews are bound by a set of dietary laws called *kashrut*, which, among other restrictions, forbid the consumption of pork and shellfish, as well as the consumption of both meat and milk products at the same meal. Not all Israelis observe these rules, but many restaurants do.

Food Customs at Ceremonial Occasions. Food plays an important role in nearly all Jewish celebrations. The Sabbath, observed on Saturday, is ushered in on Friday evening with a family meal including an egg bread called *challah.* At the Jewish New Year the challah is baked in a circle, symbolizing the cyclical nature of life. Apples and honey also are eaten, symbolizing the wish for a sweet new year. *Hamentaschen* are traditionally served at Purim, the celebration of Queen Esther's triumph over the evil Haman, who was trying to annihilate the Jewish people. These are cookies filled with *lekvar* (prune preserves) and baked in the shape of a triangle. Some believe hamentaschen symbolizes the tricornered hat of Haman; others think it is his pockets, and still others think it represents his ears, which were clipped as a sign of shame. During Passover, Jews abstain from eating all leavened foods (bread, pasta, etc.). Instead they eat *matzoh*, a flat, crackerlike bread. This is in memory of the Exodus from Israel, when the Jews could not wait for their bread to rise, and so carried it on their backs to bake in the sun. Passover also is observed with a ritual meal called a seder. Four glasses of wine, representing God's four promises to Israel ("I will bring you out of Egypt;" "I will deliver you;" "I will redeem you;" and "I will take you to be my people"), are drunk throughout the evening. Other symbolic foods at the occasion include boiled eggs (symbolizing new life) and *charosis* (a mixture of apples and walnuts, representing the mortar the Jews used as slaves). On Shavuot in the late spring, dairy-based treats are served. Because cooking is forbidden on the Sabbath, a traditional Saturday meal is *cholent*, a thick stew that is left in the oven to simmer overnight.

Basic Economy. Israel's economy was originally based on a socialist model, in which the Histadrut

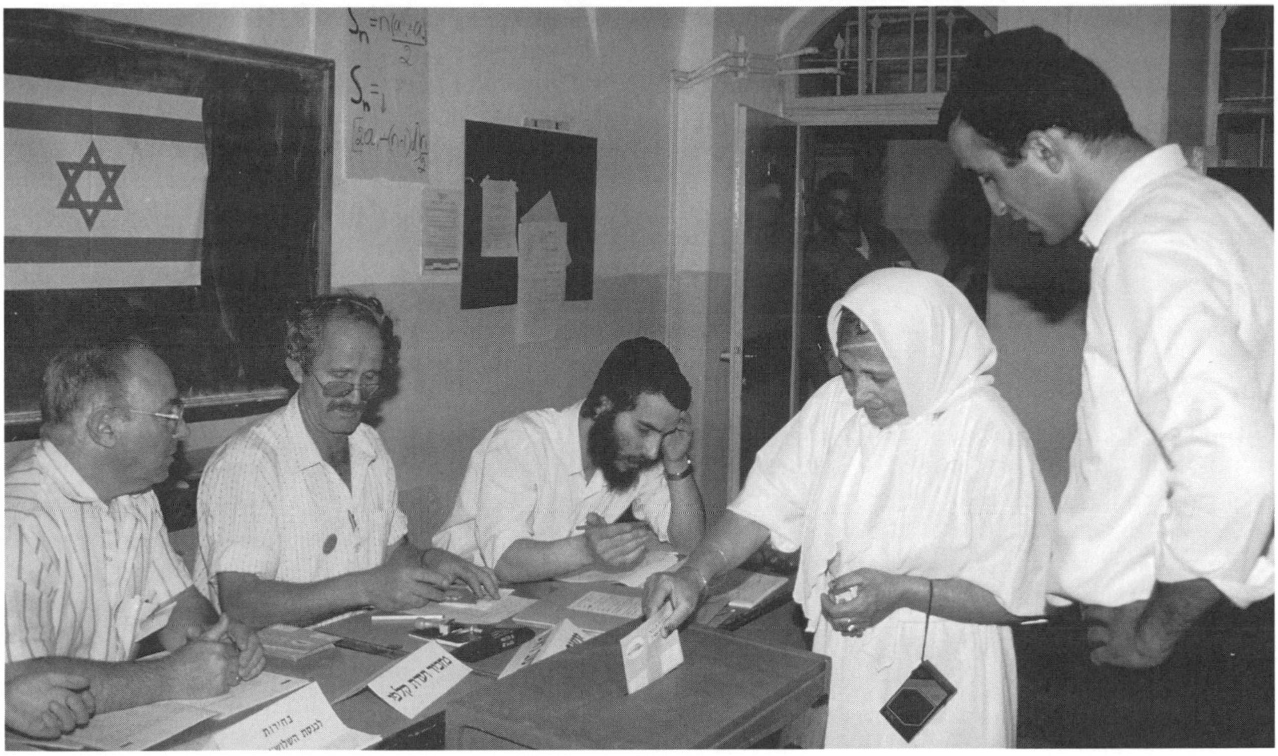

People voting in an election. Israel is a parlimentary democracy, divided into six administrative districts.

trade union was the most powerful organization, controlling most of agriculture, industry, and health care. However, in the past few decades, Histadrut's power has been diluted as the country has adopted more capitalist policies. The economy today is based largely on advanced technology. Its high-tech firms play an important role in the global economy, and foreign investment in these firms is abundant. Despite its limited natural resources, the country has become nearly self-sufficient in food production (with the exception of grains). Still, agriculture accounts for only 2 percent of the GDP and employs roughly 2 percent of the labor force. Services account for 81 percent and industry for 17 percent. The Israeli economy grew significantly during the 1990s, thanks to an influx of skilled immigrants and growth in the technology sector. While 2000 was the most financially successful year in Israel's history, gains in prosperity, and particularly foreign investments, feel somewhat tenuous after the recent outbreaks of violence.

Land Tenure and Property. Some land is privately owned and some is public property. Israel also has a system of *kibbutzim* (singular: *kibbutz*), cooperative farms in which property is collectively owned. Residents share chores, and instead of a salary receive housing, medical care, education, and other necessities. There are also *moshav*, farming communities in which each family owns its own house and is responsible for its own land, but in which other functions, such as selling their products, are done collectively.

Commercial Activities. Israel produces a variety of agricultural goods, including meat and dairy products, vegetables, citrus, and other fruits. Computer industries and technology account for a large amount of the nation's commercial activity. Tourism is another important sector. Israel draws roughly two million tourists each year, with its historical and religious sites as well as resorts and health spas near the Dead Sea.

Major Industries. Israel has a variety of industries, including food processing, textiles, diamond cutting and polishing, metal products, military equipment, high-technology electronics, and tourism.

Trade. The main exports are machinery and equipment, software, cut diamonds, textiles, and agricultural products. These go primarily to the United States, the United Kingdom, Hong Kong, the Benelux countries, and Japan. Israel imports raw materials, military equipment, rough diamonds, fuel, and consumer goods from the United States, the

Benelux countries, Germany, and the United Kingdom.

Division of Labor. Palestinian Israelis generally do not have access to as good an education as Israeli Jews and therefore are more likely to occupy less skilled and poorly paid positions. Immigrants as well, even highly educated ones, often are forced to take jobs of a low status, and many are unemployed.

SOCIAL STRATIFICATION

Classes and Castes. Israel is not highly stratified economically; most people have a similarly comfortable standard of living. However, the majority of the poor are Palestinian. Recent immigrants from Africa and Eastern Europe also tend to be at a disadvantage economically.

Symbols of Social Stratification. Among Israeli Jews, clothing is often an indication of religious or political affiliation. Men wear *yarmulkes*, or skullcaps, for prayer; more observant men wear them at all times. Conservative Jewish men can be distinguished by their black hats, whereas liberal Jews wear white crocheted caps. In the strictest Orthodox communities, men dress all in black and wear *peyes*, long sidelocks. Women keep their heads covered; traditionally, after marriage, they shave their heads and wear wigs. Secular or less conservative Jews, who comprise the majority of the population, wear Western-style clothes. Many Arabs wear traditional Muslim dress, which for men is a turban or other headdress and long robes, and for women is a long robe that covers the head and the entire body.

POLITICAL LIFE

Government. Israel is a parliamentary democracy, divided into six administrative districts. There is no formal constitution; instead, there is the Declaration of Establishment, from 1948, the Basic Laws of the parliament (*Knesset*), and the Israel citizenship law. The head of government is the prime minister, elected by popular vote for a four-year term. The 120 members of the Knesset also are elected for four years. The Knesset selects the president, who serves as chief of state.

Leadership and Political Officials. There about twelve political parties represented in the Knesset, ranging from the far right wing to the far left, and many in between. The most powerful of the conservative parties is the fairly centrist *Likud*. The Labor Party is the liberal party with the most clout, and the one Palestinian Israelis tend to support. The Palestinian Liberation Organization, headed by Yassar Arafat, is the main political representation of Palestinians seeking the formation of a separate state. There also are several militant and terrorist organizations with this same objective, including *Hamas* and *Hezbollah*.

Social Problems and Control. The legal system is a combination of English common law and British mandate regulations. For personal matters, Jews, Muslims, and Christians are subject to separate jurisdictions.

The role of the police force is sometimes virtually interchangeable with that the army—for example, in the case of the border guards in the West Bank. The Palestinian National Authority has its own police and security forces, which have a record of human rights abuses. Palestinian civilians have a reputation for violence against Israeli soldiers and law-enforcement officers, who in turn have a reputation for responding brutally.

Military Activity. The military consists of the Israel Defense Forces (ground, naval, and air troops), the Pioneer Fighting Youth, the Frontier Guard, and Chen (composed of women). All citizens, men and women, are required to serve in the armed forces. For unmarried women, two years of active duty are required (not in combat); for men, a minimum of four years. Military expenditures total $8.7 billion annually, 9.4 percent of the GDP.

SOCIAL WELFARE AND CHANGE PROGRAMS

Social welfare programs include pensions for the elderly, maternity insurance, workers' compensation, and allowances for large families. The government also provides assistance for recent immigrants, although these programs have been criticized for helping well-off immigrants at the expense of poorer native-born Israelis.

NONGOVERNMENTAL ORGANIZATIONS AND OTHER ASSOCIATIONS

A number of nongovernmental Jewish organizations make considerable economic contributions to Israel, such as the international World Zionist Organization, which supports the immigration of Jews to Israel from around the world. Synagogues in the United States and Europe also send aid and sponsor tree-planting drives. Israel also has a system of "national institutions," which are not part of the government but function alongside it in the

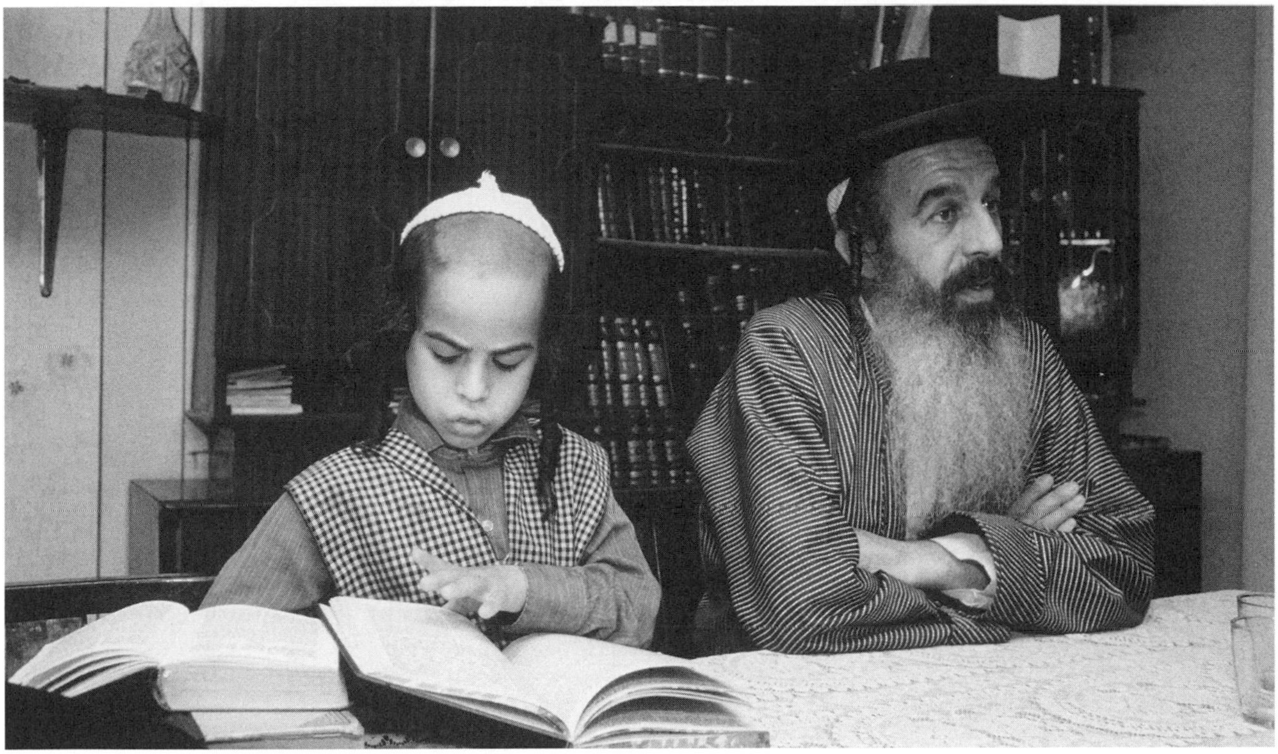

A Torah scribe works with his son. Judaism is the official Israeli religion, and the Torah is the most sacred text.

realms of social welfare services, education, and culture.

Gender Roles and Statuses

Division of Labor by Gender. Women are well represented in many fields, both traditional (teaching, nursing, child care), and nontraditional (law, politics, the military). Israel even elected a female prime minister, Golda Meir, who served from 1969 to 1974. Some strides toward equality have been reversed; while it used to be a hallmark of kibbutzim that labor was divided without respect to gender, today women are more likely to be found in the kitchen and in child care facilities. Women, like men, are required to serve in the armed forces, and during the war for independence fought in the front lines alongside men. Today women are not permitted combat. Instead they are mostly confined to adminstration and education, and usually do not achieve high-ranking positions.

The Relative Status of Women and Men. In the Orthodox tradition, women and men live very separate lives. Women are considered inferior, and are excluded from many traditional activities. However, most of Israeli society is more progressive, and women are generally accorded equal status to men, both legally and socially. (The main exception to this is the divorce law.)

Marriage, Family, and Kinship

Marriage. Traditionally, in both Arab and Jewish societies, marriages were often arranged, but that is uncommon nowadays. However, there are powerful social taboos against intermarriage, and it is illegal for a Jew to marry a non-Jew in Israel. Those wishing to do so must go abroad for the ceremony. Even within the Jewish community, it is unusual for a very observant Jew to marry someone secular. Divorce is legal, but Orthodox Jewish law applies. According to this statute, men have the power to prevent their ex-wives from remarrying. If the woman enters into another relationship, the courts refuse to recognize it, and any children from such a union are considered illegitimate and themselves cannot marry in the State of Israel.

Domestic Unit. The most common family unit consists of a nuclear family. In more traditional families, grandparents are sometimes included in this. In the original kibbutz system, the living arrangements were different. Husband and wife lived in separate quarters from their children, who were housed with the other young people. Some kibbutzim still operate in this way, but it is now more common for children to live with their parents, although their days are still spent separately.

Socialization

Infant Care. Babies are generally adored and showered with affection. The extended family plays an important role in helping to raise the baby, but the mother generally takes primary responsibility. Jewish boys are circumcised eight days after birth in a religious ceremony called a *bris.*

Child Rearing and Education. In most of Israeli society, children are raised in the setting of a nuclear family. However, collective child care is common, especially for mothers who work outside the home. In kibbutzim, they stay separately from their parents, and usually see them only at night or on weekends. Children are generally indulged and are not strictly disciplined.

In the Arab tradition, boys and girls are raised separately. They have different responsibilities at home, where girls are expected to help much more with domestic chores. The schools are also usually gender-segregated.

Education is mandatory from the ages five through fifteen. The state runs both religious and nonreligious schools; 70 percent of children attend the nonreligious ones. There is a separate education system for Arab children, where the language of instruction is Arabic. The quality of education in these schools is often lower due to a relative unavailability of teachers and poor resources, and they have at times been subject to closings due to violence and political instability. Arab schools receive some funding from the government, as well as from religious institutions. There are three types of high schools: academic, vocational, and agricultural.

Higher Education. Israel has seven universities. Entrance standards are high, and students must pass a national exam before being admitted. The oldest and most prestigious of these is Hebrew University in Jerusalem, which also has one of the strongest medical schools in the Middle East. Ben-Gurion University, in Beersheba, specializes in natural conservation, and Technion in Haifa focuses on science and engineering. The Weizmann Institute in Rehovot supports postgraduate study. There also are vocational, agricultural, and teacher training institutes. *Yeshivot* are religious academies (generally not open to women) that train future rabbis and Jewish scholars.

Etiquette

Israelis are very informal in social interactions. Their standards would, in many other countries, be considered rude. For example, store clerks do not act at all solicitous or even acknowledge a customer's presence until the customer approaches. "Please" and "thank you" are not uttered lightly. Despite this apparent brusqueness, touching and eye contact are common in social interactions.

Religious etiquette dictates that women dress conservatively when visiting holy sites (shorts are not acceptable for either gender) and that men cover their heads with a yarmulke.

Arabs are physically affectionate people, but in Arab society, men and women are often separated socially and there is less physical contact between men and women in public. It is customary to remove one's shoes before entering an Arab household.

Religion

Religious Beliefs. Judaism is the official religion. Eighty percent of the population are Jewish, 15 percent are Muslim, and 4 percent are Christian or Druze. Jews believe in the Hebrew Bible, or Tenakh, which corresponds to the Christian Old Testament. The most sacred text is the Torah, or the five books of Moses. The Bible is seen as both historical record and religious law. Different communities follow the Holy Book with varying degrees of literalness. The strictest are the ultra-Orthodox, who believe that the Scriptures were physically handed down from God. There are also Conservative, Reform, and Reconstructionist congregations, who interpret the law more leniently, and who allow women more of a role in the religion. There also are different sects of Judaism, such as the Hasidim and the Lubbavicher.

There are five pillars of faith that Muslims follow. They are: a declaration of faith in Allah; praying five times a day; giving alms to the poor; fasting from sunrise to sundown during the holy month of Ramadan; and making a pilgrimage at some point in one's life to the holy city of Mecca.

Religious Practitioners. Rabbis are the religious leaders of the Jewish community. They are ordained in Jewish law, and often are scholars in addition to delivering sermons and offering spiritual guidance. The Chief Rabbinate is a body of rabbis who make the religious laws to which Israeli Jews are subject.

An overview of Haifa and the bay area, in 1989.

The main religious figures in the Muslim community are muezzins, who are scholars of the Koran and sound the call to prayer from mosques.

Rituals and Holy Places. Jews worship in synagogues. In the most traditional, men sit in the front and women in the back, separated by a partition, or in a balcony. There are a number of places in Israel, in Jerusalem in particular, that have religious significance to Jews, Muslims, and Christians. The Dome of the Rock is an ancient Muslim shrine. Christians often make pilgrimages to the Church of the Holy Sepulcher, also in Jerusalem. The Wailing Wall, the remains of the Temple destroyed by the Romans in 70 C.E., is a sacred spot for Jews. There is a separate section of the wall for men and women. People often write their prayers on pieces of paper and slip them in cracks between the stones. The Jewish New Year, called Rosh Hashana, falls in September or October. Jews attend synagogue for two days and listen to readings from the Torah. The ten days following Rosh Hashana are known as the Days of Awe, a period of reflection and penitence. This culminates in Yom Kippur, the Day of Atonement, and the holiest day of the year. Jews fast from sundown to sundown and attend synagogue, where they repent for their sins and ask God to be inscribed in the Book of Life for another year. Sukkot, the harvest festival, is later in the fall. Hanukkah, which falls in December, is an eight-day holiday celebrating the victory of the Maccabees over the Greeks in C.E. 165. Purim, in the spring, celebrates Queen Esther's outsmarting Haman, who wished to kill the Jewish people. Passover, which falls later in the spring, remembers Jewish liberation from slavery in Egypt.

The bar mitzvah (for boys) or bat mitzvah (for girls) is an important coming-of-age ceremony in Judaism. Children study for years to prepare for the event that occurs when they turn thirteen. They are called to read from the Torah before the congregation; the service is followed by a party with food and dancing.

Death and the Afterlife. Judaism focuses more on the here and now, rather than the concept of an afterlife. A death is followed by a mourning period of seven days, a process called sitting *shiva*, during which friends and relatives pay visits to the family of the deceased and bring food. Mourners dress in black, sit on low stools, and recite prayers. Another traditional practice is for mourners to tear their clothes; today they generally rip only the lapel of their shirts. When visiting a Jewish cemetery, it is customary to place a stone on the gravestone in memory of the deceased.

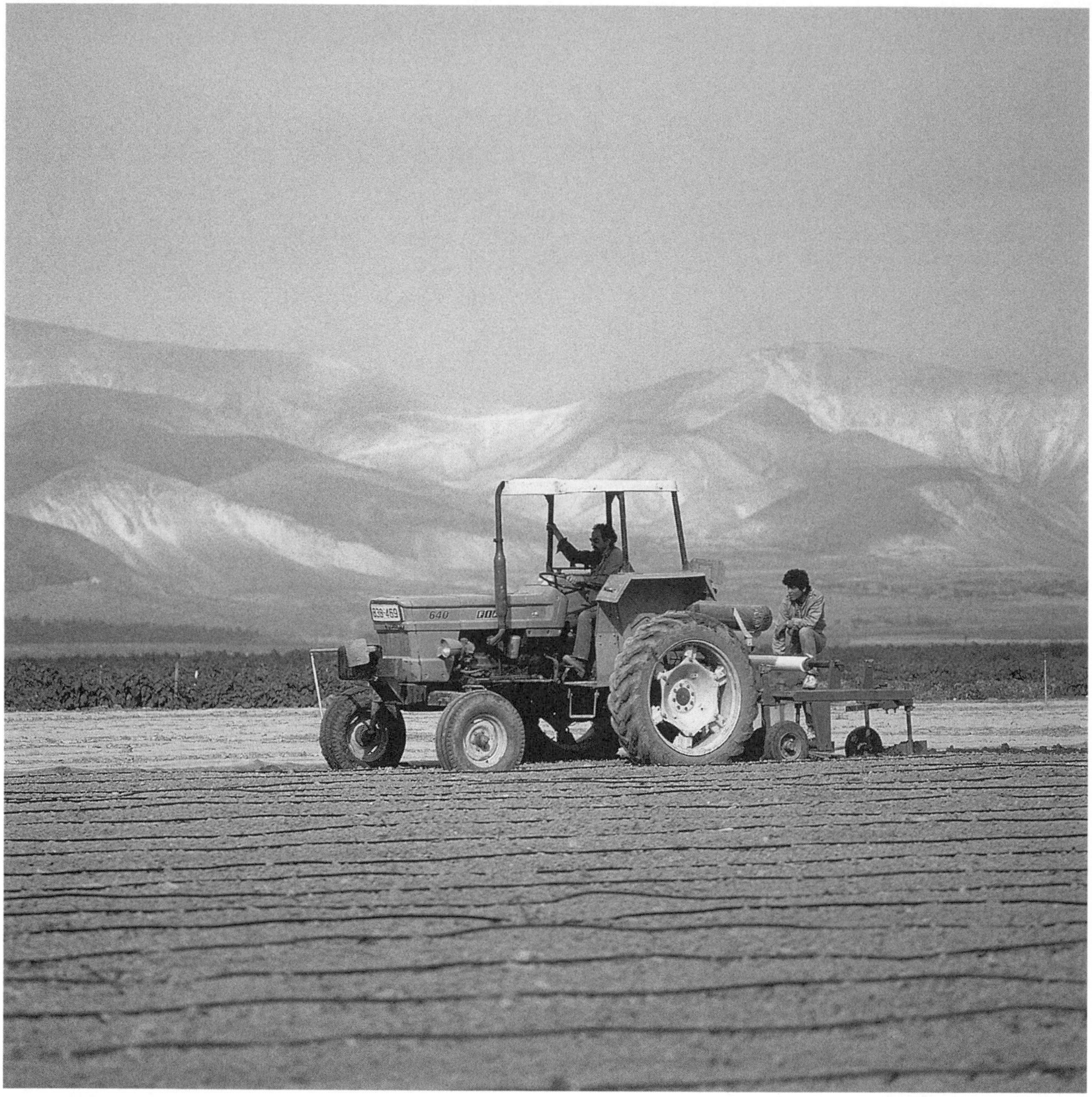

Making the desert bloom in the arid Jordan Valley, kibbutz members prepare the ground for planting winter crops.

Medicine and Health Care

Israel has a well-developed health care system. It has one of the highest ratios of doctors to general population in the world. Since independence, sanitation has improved, and the rate of infectious diseases has decreased. Histadrut, the labor federation, runs Kupat Cholim, or Sick Fund, which provides health care to members through regional hospitals and local clinics. The Ministry of Health provides for those who do not receive care from a sick fund. In general, Jews receive better health care than Arabs. The life expectancy is longer for Jews, and the infant mortality rate is significantly lower.

Secular Celebrations

Noted here are the more secular Israeli holidays, but virtually all celebrations and commemorative occasions have some religious significance. The dates of these holidays vary from year to year, because the Jewish calendar does not correspond to the Gregorian: Holocaust Memorial Day, April/May; Memorial Day, April/May; Independence Day,

April/May; Jerusalem Day, May/June; National Day (Palestinian), November.

The Arts and Humanities

Support for the Arts. The government founded the magazine *Ariel* to promote literary endeavors. The publication now has a web page as well. There is a national drama company, Habima, as well as dance troupes, a national orchestra, and museums and galleries, including the Museum of Contemporary Art in Tel Aviv and the Israel Museum in Jerusalem.

Literature. Israel has a varied literary scene. Many of its writers have come to the country from abroad, including Zbigniew Herbert from Poland, Vasko Popa from Yugoslavia, and Robert Friend from the United States. The Israeli writer Shmuel Yosef Agnon, a German who immigrated to Israel in 1913, won the Nobel Prize for literature in 1966. The poet Arnon Levy, who was born in Jerusalem, has also gained international recognition, as has Yehuda Amichai, whose verses have been translated into a variety of languages. Amos Oz is perhaps the best-known Israeli writer internationally. Both his novels and his nonfiction have been translated into a number of languages.

Graphic Arts. Contemporary painting and sculpture are alive and well in Israel. The Israeli style is highly influenced by European art, but much of it deals explicitly with Jewish themes and issues. Israeli artists who have gained international acclaim include the painters Ya'akov Agam, Menashe Kadishman, Avigdor Arikha, and the sculptors Dany Karavan and Ygael Tumarkin.

Ritual Jewish art includes beautifully crafted menorahs (candelabra), wine cups, candlesticks, *tallilot* (prayer shawls), and other ceremonial objects.

Performance Arts. Israel has a well-known philharmonic orchestra. The country has produced such classical music stars as violinist Yitzhak Perlman and pianist and conductor Daniel Barenboim. The Leonard Bernstein International Music Competition in Jerusalem gives annual awards in classical music. Pop music and rock and roll also have a large following, particularly in Tel Aviv, where local stars such as Ofra Haza, Ilanit, and Shalom Hanoch perform to enthusiastic audiences. *Klezmer*, a form of Jewish music that originated in Eastern Europe during the seventeenth century, is a raucous blend of drums, violins, clarinets, keyboards, and tambourines that is common at wedding celebrations.

The Israel Ballet Company is world-famous. There are several modern dance troupes as well, most notably Inbal, Batsheeva, and Bat Dor. Israeli choreographer Ohad Nahrin is well known in the dance world. Israel also has a lively tradition of folk dances, which are performed by professional troupes and at occasions such as weddings. The *hora*, a circle dance, is one of the most commonly performed.

Theater also is popular in Israel. Jewish theater is traditionally highly melodramatic, although many contemporary productions adopt many Western theatrical conventions and social issues. There are companies that stage productions in Russian and English as well as in Hebrew and Arabic. The film industry, also thriving, is best known for its documentaries, including Yaakov Gross's *Pioneers of Zion*, produced in 1995, and *Toward Jerusalem*, Ruth Beckermann's 1992 production.

The State of the Physical and Social Sciences

The country's scientific and technological progress has been aided in recent years by an influx of well-educated immigrants from the former Soviet Union. Israeli scientists have made contributions in electronics, nuclear and solar power, and computer hardware and software, as well as in weapons-related technology. Cutting-edge firms have developed wireless and cellular telephone technology, as well as new applications for the Internet.

Bibliography

Cohen, Asher, and Susser, Bernard. *Israel and the Politics of Jewish Identity: The Secular-Religious Impasse*, 2000.

Doran, Gideon, and Harris, Michael. *Public Policy and Electoral Reform: The Case of Israel*, 2000.

Gross, David C. *Israel: An Illustrated Dictionary*, 2000.

Hamad, Jamil. "No Patience for a Peace Deal." *Time*, 13 November 2000.

———. "Arafat May Now Want to Calm the Situation." *Time*, 15 November 2000.

Heller, Joseph. *The Birth of Israel 1945–49: Ben-Gurion and His Critics*, 2000.

Herzog, Hanna. *Gendering Politics: Women in Israel*, 1999.

Karsh, Efraim. *Israel: The First Hundred Years*, 2000.

Leshem, Elazar, and Shuval, Judith T., eds. *Immigration to Israel: Sociological Perspectives*, 1998.

MacFarquhar, Neil. "Arafat Asks U.N. Council to Send Force to Protect Palestinians." *New York Times*, 11 November 2000.

Matza, Michael. "Seven Years After Oslo Pacts, Mideast Peace Is Elusive." *Philadelphia Inquirer*, 24 November 2000.

Morris, Nomi. "Jewish Group Helps Arabs Harvest Olives." *Philadelphia Inquirer*, 27 November 2000.

Orme, William A. "Fighting in Mideast Blocks Wave of Christian Tourism." *New York Times*, 11 November 2000.

Pappé, Ilan, ed. *The Israel/Palestine Question*, 1999.

Rees, Matt. "At the Speed of Hate." *Time*, 13 November 2000.

———. "Into the War Zones." *Time*, 30 November 2000.

Reich, Bernard, and Goldberg, David H. *Political Dictionary of Israel*, 2000.

Rejwan, Nissim. *Israel in Search of Identity: Reading the Formative Years*, 1999.

Said, Edward. *The End of the Peace Process: Oslo and After*, 2000.

Shafir, Gershon, and Peled, Yuav. *New Israel: Peacemaking and Liberalization*, 2000.

Wanna, Butros. "Israel Attacks South Lebanon." *Philadelphia Inquirer*, 27 November 2000.

Zielenziger, Michael. "Clashes in Israel Sound Across the High-Tech World." *Philadephia Inquirer*, 23 November 2000.

—ELEANOR STANFORD

Italy

Culture Name

Italian

Alternative Names

Republic of Italy, Italia, Repubblica Italiana

Orientation

Identification. The Romans used the name *Italia* to refer to the Italian peninsula. Additionally, Italy has been invaded and settled by many different peoples. Etruscans in Tuscany preceded the Romans and Umbria, while Greeks settled the south. Jews entered the country during the period of the Roman republic, and Germanic tribes came after the fall of Rome. Mediterranean peoples (Greeks, North Africans, and Phoenicians) entered the south. The Byzantine Empire ruled the southern part of the peninsula for five hundred years, into the ninth century. Sicily had many invaders, including Saracens, Normans, and Aragonese. In 1720, Austrians ruled Sicily and at about the same time controlled northern Italy. There is a continuing ethnic mixing.

Location and Geography. Italy is in south central Europe. It consists of a peninsula shaped like a high–heeled boot and several islands, encompassing 116,300 square miles (301,200 square kilometers). The most important of the islands are Sicily in the south and Sardinia in the northwest. The Mediterranean Sea is to the south, and the Alps to the north. A chain of mountains, the Apennines, juts down the center of the peninsula. The fertile Po valley is in the north. It accounts for 21 percent of the total area; 40 percent of Italy's area, in contrast, is hilly and 39 percent is mountainous. The climate is generally a temperate Mediterranean one with variations caused by the mountainous and hilly areas.

Italy's hilly terrain has led to the creation of numerous independent states. Moreover, agriculture in most of the country has been of a subsistence type and has led to deforestation. Since World War II, many Italians have turned away from rural occupations to engage in the industrial economy.

Rome was a natural choice for the national capital in 1871 when the modern state was united after the annexation of the Papal States. Rome recalls Italy's former grandeur and unity under Roman rule and its position as the center of the Catholic Church.

Demography. Italy's population was approximately 57 million in 1998. The population growth rate is .08 percent with a death rate of 10.18 per 1,000 and a birthrate of 9.13 per 1,000. Life expectancy at birth is 78.38 years. Population growth declined quickly after World War II with the industrialization of the country.

The majority of the people are ethnically Italian, but there are other ethnic groups in the population, including French–Italians and Slovene–Italians in the north and Albanian–Italian and Greek–Italians in the south. This ethnic presence is reflected in the languages spoken: German is predominant in the Trentino–Alto Adige region, French is spoken in the Valle d'Aosta region, and Slovene is spoken in the Trieste–Gorizia area.

Linguistic Affiliation. The official language is Italian. Various "dialects" are spoken, but Italian is taught in school and used in government. Sicilian is a language with Greek, Arabic, Latin, Italian, Norman French, and other influences and generally is not understood by Italian speakers. There are pockets of German, Slovene, French, and other speakers.

Symbolism. Italian patriotism is largely a matter of convenience. Old loyalties to hometown have persisted and the nation is still mainly a "geographic expression" (i.e., there is more identity with one's home region than to the country as a

Italy

whole) to many Italians. The national anthem, *Fratelli d'Ialia*, generally is seen as something to be played at sporting events with teams from other countries. The red, green, and white flag has meaning for most citizens but does not stir a great deal of fervor. The strongest ties are to one's family. Therefore, politicians make appeals for loyalty to the nation based on loyalty to the family, stressing ties to the *patria* ("fatherland").

History and Ethnic Relations

Emergence of the Nation. It was not until the middle of the nineteenth century that Italy as we know it today came to be. Until that time, various city-states occupied the peninsula, each operating as a separate kingdom or republic.

Forces for Italian unification began to come together with the rise of Victor Emmanuel to the throne of Sardinia in 1859. That year, after the French helped defeat the Austrians, who had come to rule regions through the Habsburg Empire, Victor Emmanuel's prime minister, Count de Cavour of Sardinia, persuaded the rest of Italy except the Papal States to join a united Italy under the leadership of Victor Emmanuel in 1859. In 1870 Cavour managed to be on the right side when Prussia defeated France and Napoleon III, the Pope's protector, in the Franco-Prussian War. On 17 March 1861, Victor Emmanuel of Sardinia was crowned as king of Italy. Rome became the capital of the new nation.

Italy's history is long and great. The Etruscans were the first major power in the Italian peninsula and Italy was first united politically under the Romans in 90 B.C.E. After the collapse of the Roman Empire in the fifth century C.E., Italy became merely a "geographic expression" for many centuries. Chaos followed the fall of the Roman Empire. Charlemagne restored order and centralized government to northern and central Italy in the eight and ninth centuries. Charlemagne brought Frankish culture to Italy, and under the Franks, the Church of Rome gained much political influence. The popes were given a great deal of autonomy and were left with control over the legal and administrative system of Rome, including defense.

The Carolingian line became increasingly weak and civil wars broke out, weakening law and order. Arabs invaded the mainland from their strongholds in Sicily and North Africa. In the south, the Lombards claimed sovereignty, where they established a separate government, until they were replaced by the Normans in the eleventh century.

City governments, however, had profited from Carolignian rule and remained vibrant centers of culture. Local families strengthened their hold on the rural areas and replaced Carolingian rulers. Italy had become difficult to rule from a central location. It had become a collection of city–states.

Through the ensuing years, numerous rulers from beyond the Alps, with or without the consent of the papacy, failed to impose their authority. Throughout the fourteen and fifteenth centuries of *campanilismo* (local patriotism), only a minority of people would have heard the word "Italia." Loyalties were predominantly provincial. However, there were elements that made a strong contrast to the world beyond the Alps: a common legal culture, high levels of lay education and urban literacy, a close relationship between town and country, and a nobility who frequently engaged in trade.

Three features in particular from this period solidified the notion of a unified culture. The first was the maturing of the economic development that had originated in the earlier centuries. Northern and central Italian trade, manufacture, and financial capitalism, together with increasing urbanization, were to continue with extraordinary vigor and to have remarkable influence throughout much of the Mediterranean world and Europe as a whole—a development that served as the necessary preliminary for the expansion of Europe beyond its ancient bounds at the end of the fifteenth century. Second came the extension of de facto independent city–states, which, whether as republics or as powers ruled by one person or family, created a powerful impression upon contemporaries and posterity. Finally, and allied to both these movements, it was from this society that was born the civilization of the "Italian Renaissance" that in the fifteenth and sixteenth centuries was to be exported to the rest of Europe.

Italian rivalries of status, class, family, and hometown prevented unity throughout its history. The period from the fifteenth through the mid-eighteenth centuries was no exception. Nations grew and their ambitions, as well as those of the Italian city–states, continued to plague Italy. France and Spain in particular intervened in Italian affairs. Moreover, the chaos caused by these invasions led the Italian states to seek to further their own particular goals.

Italy became part of the Spanish Habsburg inheritance in 1527 when the Spanish king Charles I (Holy Roman Emperor Charles V) sent his troops in to take over Rome. Spain established complete control over all the Italian states except Venice.

Italy was ready for the new ideas of the French Enlightenment after the economic depression, plagues, wars, famines, and invasions of the seventeenth century. Italian intellectuals resented the supranational character of the papacy, the immunities of clerics from the state's legal and fiscal apparatus, the church's intolerance and intransigence in theological and institutional matters, and its wealth and property, and demanded reforms. Some changes in administration, taxation, and the economy were made by Habsburg rulers Maria Theresa and Joseph, but these reforms did not go far enough. The French Revolution and Napoleon's army demonstrated that a united Italy was possible and that arms might be the only way to achieve it.

Under the leadership of Victor Emmanuel, Count de Cavour, and Giuseppe Garibaldi, the various city-states moved toward unity. The writings of Allessandro Manzoni in the common tongue aided the forging of an Italian identity. His *I Promessi*

A man in elaborate costume at an outside café celebrates during the Venice Carnival in Piazza San Marco, Venice.

Sposi provided a romantic image of Italy struggling against outside forces. Giuseppe Mazzini's Young Italy organization and his fiery writings during and after the revolutions of 1848 did much to stir Italian nationalism and hatred of outside rule.

National Identity. The issue of regionalism has plagued Italy to the present day. Originally, the issue was one of the more developed north against the poor south. Italian regions had their own separate histories over a fourteen–hundred–year period. Many different "dialects" were spoken, and customs varied from area to area. In the period since the Risorgimento, the Italian unification movement, there has been a great deal of unity achieved. There is still a difference between the north, the central region, and the south. However, literacy has made a common language the norm. Television, radio, and newspapers have aided education by fostering a sense of national culture.

Ethnic Relations. Many countries and peoples have occupied Italy over the centuries. Italians resented each of these conquerors. However, they intermarried with them and accepted a number of their customs. Many customs, for example, in Sicily are Spanish in origin.

Italians have assimilated a number of people within their culture. Albanians, French, Austrians, Greeks, Arabs, and now Africans have generally found a welcome in peaceful social interaction. This mixture is reflected in the wide variety of physical characteristics of the people—skin and hair colorings, size, and even temperaments. Italians easily incorporate new foods and customs into the national mix. In all, there are about one million resident foreigners.

Urbanism, Architecture, and the Use of Space

The northern area is highly industrialized and urbanized. Milan, Turin, and Genoa form the "industrial triangle." After World War II, there was a great migration to urban areas and into industrial occupations.

In spite of the previous agricultural and rural nature of Italy's *Mezzogiorno* (south), architecture there as well as in more industrialized areas of Italy has followed urban models. The architecture throughout Italy has strong Roman influences. In Sicily, Greek and Arabic ones join these influences. Throughout, a strong humanistic tone prevails but it is a humanism touched with deep religious feeling. There is a "family" feeling about the divine that often baffles non–Italians.

Italians tend to cluster in groups, and their architecture encourages this clustering. The piazzas of each town or village are famous for the parading of people through them at night with friends and relatives. Public space is meant to be used by the people, and their enjoyment is taken for granted.

FOOD AND ECONOMY

Food in Daily Life. Food is a means for establishing and maintaining ties among family and friends. No one who enters an Italian home should fail to receive an offering of food and drink. Typically, breakfast consists of a hard roll, butter, strong coffee, and fruit or juice. Traditionally, a large lunch made up the noon meal. Pasta was generally part of the meal in all regions, along with soup, bread, and perhaps meat or fish. Dinner consisted of leftovers. In more recent times, the family may use the later meal as a family meal. The custom of the siesta is changing, and a heavy lunch may no longer be practical.

There are regional differences in what is eaten and how food is prepared. In general, more veal is found in the north, where meals tend to be lighter. Southern cooking has the reputation of being heavier and more substantial than northern cooking.

Food Customs at Ceremonial Occasions. There are special foods for various occasions. There is a special Saint Joseph's bread, Easter bread with hard–boiled eggs, Saint Lucy's "eyes" for her feast day, and the Feast of the Seven Fishes for New Year's Eve. Wine is served with meals routinely.

Basic Economy. Only about 4 percent of the gross national product comes from agriculture. Wheat, vegetables, fruit, olives, and grapes are grown in sufficient quantities to feed the population. Meat and dairy products, however, are imported.

Lombardy is, perhaps, the richest area of Italy. It is the location of the fertile Po river valley as well as Milan, the chief commercial, industrial, and financial center. It is also the major industrial area of Italy. Textiles, clothing, iron and steel, machinery, motor vehicles, chemicals, furniture, and wine are its major products. It stands in marked contrast to the southern area of the country that has only recently begun to emerge from its agricultural economy.

Italy began its major shift from agriculture to a major industrial economy after World War II. At the beginning of the twenty-first century, it is the fifth-largest economy in the world. Italy has only recently abandoned its interventionist economic policies that created periods of recession. Under pressure from the European Union it has begun to face its federal deficit, crime, and corruption. The state has begun a major retreat from participating in economic activities. Unemployment, however, has remained around 12 percent and economic growth has risen barely above the 1 percent level as the new millennium began.

Land Tenure and Property. Italy's economy is basically one of private enterprise. The government, however, owns a large share of major commercial and financial institutions. For example, the government has major shares in the petroleum, transportation, and telecommunication systems. In the 1990s Italy began to more away from government ownership of business.

Commercial Activities. Most of Italy's commercial centers are in the developed northern region. Milan is the most important economic center of Italy. It is located in the midst of rich farmland and great industrial development. It has extensive road and rail connections, aiding its industrial power. Milan is predominant in the production of automobiles, airplanes, motorcycles, major electric appliances, railroad materials, and other metalworking. It is also important for its textiles and fashion industry. Chemical production, medicinal products, dyes, soaps, and acids are also important. Additionally, Milan is noted for its graphic arts and publishing, food, wood, paper, and rubber products. It has kept pace with the world of electronics and cybernetic products.

Genoa remains Italy's major shipbuilding center. However, it also produces petroleum, textiles, iron and steel, locomotives, paper, sugar, cement, chemicals, fertilizers, and electrical, railway, and marine equipment. It is also a center for finance and commerce. Genoa is Italy's major port for both passengers and freight.

Florence, located about 145 miles (230 kilometers) northwest of Rome, is renowned for its magnificent past. Tourists flock to Florence to see its unparalleled art treasures. Turin, in contrast, is noted for automobile manufacturing and its modern pace of life. It is located just east of the Alps. In addition to Fiats and Lancias, Turin manufactures airplanes, ball-bearings, rubber, paper, leatherwork, metallurgical, chemical, and plastic products, and chocolates and wines.

Major Industries. Italy is important in textile production, clothing and fashion, chemicals, cars, iron

Boats float in a canal lined by houses in Venice.

and steel, food production, wine, shipbuilding, and other industrial activities.

Trade. Italy exports metals, textiles and clothing, production machinery, motor vehicles, transportation equipment, and chemicals. In 1996, Italy exported almost 2 billion gallons of wine. It exports about $250 billion in material and imports about $190 billion. Imports include industrial machinery, chemicals, petroleum, metals, food and agricultural products, and transportation equipment.

Division of Labor. There is a great hierarchy of prestige according to one's occupation. Those in professional jobs have greater prestige than those in manual labor. The importance of tailoring one's lifestyle to the appropriate job is significant. Thus, anyone who works with a pencil and paper, or today a computer, is above others who get their hands dirty.

Social Stratification

Classes and Castes. There is a vast difference in wealth between the north and the south. There are also the usual social classes that are found in industrial society. Italy has a high unemployment rate, and differences between rich and poor are noticeable. New immigrants stand out since they come from poorer countries. The government has had a vast social welfare network that has been cut in recent years to fit the requirements of the European Union. These budget cuts have fallen on the poorer strata of society.

Symbols of Social Stratification. Speech is a social boundary marker in Italy. The more education and "breeding" a person has, the closer that person's speech comes to the national language and differs from a dialect. Style of dress, choice of food and recreation, and other boundary markers also prevail. Clothes from Armani, Versace, and other fashion designers are beyond the reach of the poor. There is a difference also in what food one eats, certain food being more prestigious, such as veal or steak, than others. Although pasta and bread are still staples for all classes, it is what else and in what quantity meat is available that marks social classes.

Leisure and the manner in which it is spent are also class boundary markers. The more leisure and the great the amount of travel mark off groups from each other. The more private the beaches, the longer the siesta, the more opulent the family villa, the greater the prestige. Soccer is for everyone, but more expensive entertainment is restricted by cost.

Political Life

Government. Italy is a republic with twenty regions under the central government. In 1861, the Italian states were unified under a monarch. The republic was formed on 2 June 1946 and on 1 January 1948, the republic's constitution was proclaimed. There are three branches of government: executive, judicial, and legislative. The legal system is a combination of civil and ecclesiastical law. The system treats appeals as new trials. There is a Constitutional Court that has the power of judicial review. A chief of state (the president) and a head of government (the prime minister) head the executive branch. There have been numerous changes of government since the end of World War II. There are two houses in the parliament: the Senate and the Chamber of Deputies. Both houses have elected and appointed members chosen through a complicated system of proportional representation and appointed. Voters must be 25 years old to vote for senators but only 18 in all other elections.

Leadership and Political Officials. Italy has been plagued with too many political parties and, in some sense, every Italian is his or her own political party. Recent reforms have not ended the problem. New parties have grown from combinations or alliances of a number of parties. The major parties are Olive Tree, Freedom Pole, Northern League, Communism Refoundation, Italian Social Movement, Pannella–Sgarbi's List, Italian Socialist, Autonomous List, and Southern Tyrol's List. The Olive Tree is the party of the democrat left. The Freedom Pole is the party of the right to center. Other parties occupy various positions on the political spectrum. There are certain rules of respect toward those in power. Presents are usually given, and support is promised in return. People approach those in power through intermediaries.

Social Problems and Control. Italians resent intrusions into private and family life. They have had centuries of practice in evading what they consider unjust laws. The major crime problem comes from the Mafia. Special courts and task forces have made some headway against the Mafia. Scandals linking politicians and judges to the Mafia have led to greater action in seeking its extermination. Street crime, such as robbery, is prevalent in the larger cities, and murder is a serious problem, with about one thousand five hundred per year, and an additional two thousand attempted murders per annum. The national police are found throughout the country. The judicial system operates on an inquisitorial system. There is no presumption of innocence, and judges routinely question defendants. The Catholic Church, family, and friends serve as strong informal social controls.

Military Activity. The country's president is the commander of the armed forces. He also chairs the Supreme Council of Defense. Male military service is compulsory. Italy is a member of the North Atlantic Treaty Organization (NATO). The first significant deployment of troops outside Italy took place in 1997, when troops were sent to Albania to help control the chaos that resulted with the collapse of the economy. As a member of NATO, the country allowed its air bases to be used in attack on Yugoslavia.

Italian architecture—especially the use of public space—encourages socializing.

Social Welfare and Change Programs

Until the 1990s Italy had a cradle-to-grave social welfare system. Italy began to cut its involvement in these programs in response to pressure from its European partners to cut its budget deficits. These changes affected unemployment insurance, retirement pensions, child support, and other major programs. However, Italy's system is still impressive when compared with that of the United States.

Nongovernmental Organizations and Other Associations

The Catholic Church is deeply involved in various charitable activities in Italy. In addition to the Church's activities on behalf of the homeless, poor, orphans, prisoners, and others, there are a number of other NGOs operating in Italy. The Italian Red Cross and Caritas, for example, are involved in various projects to resettle refugees in Italy. The Association for Minority People works on behalf of minorities worldwide, including in Italy. COSPE is another agency that works with minorities and refugees, teaching languages to minority ethnic groups in Italy, and with programs in Africa, Asia, Latin America, and Eastern Europe.

Gender Roles and Statuses

Division of Labor by Gender. Traditionally, men went out to work and women took care of the home. After World War II, that arrangement changed rapidly. While old notions of gender segregation and male dominance prevail in some rural areas, Italian women have been famous for their independence and many anthropological and historical works point out that their assumed past subordination was often overstated. Currently, women participate in every aspect of political, economic, and social life. Women are equal under the law and attend universities and work in the labor force in numbers commensurate with their share of the population.

A sign of female independence is Italy's negative population growth. It is true, however, that women continue to perform many of the same domestic tasks they did in the past while assuming new responsibilities.

The Relative Status of Women and Men. In Italian culture, men were given preferential status and treatment. Women were assigned the position of the "soul" of the family, while men were the "head." Men were to support and defend the family while women raised the children and kept themselves chaste so as not to disgrace the family. How much of the ideal was ever found in the real world is problematic. Women in general always had more power than they were traditionally supposed to have. Currently, Italian women are often considered the most liberated in Europe.

Marriage, Family, and Kinship

Marriage. In the past, marriages were arranged and women brought a dowry to the marriage. However, there were ways to help one's parents arrange marriage with the right person. The poorer classes, in fact, had more freedom to do so than did the wealthier ones. Dowries could be waived and often were. Currently, marriage is as free as anywhere else in the world. Except for those who enter the clergy, almost all Italians marry. But there is a custom in many families for a child to remain unmarried to care for aged parents. Divorce was forbidden until recently.

Domestic Unit. The family is the basic household unit. It may vary in size through having other relatives live with the nuclear family or through taking in boarders. Often two or more nuclear families may live together. It is common for newly married couples to live for a time with the bride's parents. Traditionally the husband was the ruler of the family, in theory, while the wife took care of the day-to-day operations. The reality may have been quite different. Tasks have traditionally been assigned according to age and sex. There is evidence that there is some change in this system as more and more often both parents work outside the home.

Inheritance. By law, all members of the family inherit equally. Special personal items may be given to loved ones before death to assure their being received by the designated heir.

Kin Groups. Italians are famous for their family lives. They are often tied to one another by relationships on both sides of the family. They can and do expand or contract their extended kin groups by emphasizing or de-emphasizing various kinship ties. Usually, children of the same mother feel a necessity to cooperate against the outside world. Other ties may be egocentric. Generally, a male feels closest for many reasons to his mother's sisters and their kin. These kin traditionally protected him from the father's side, traditionally the side of "justice" as opposed to "mercy" and unmitigated love.

Socialization

Infant Care. There is a fear that others will be jealous of a healthy and bright baby. Care is taken not to be foolish and boast too much about one's child. There are many charms and practices to ward off dangers, such as the evil eye. Children are coddled and held to keep them happy and content. They eat at will, are allowed to sleep with their parents, and are taken on family outings. Although times are changing it is still common to have families go to nightclubs and restaurants together. Parents are glad to see signs of activity in children and tease youngsters almost mercilessly to teach them to stand up for themselves. Older children routinely care for younger ones.

Child Rearing and Education. Children are indulged when young. As they grow older, they are expected to obey their parents and contribute to the

Tiled rooftops on brick buildings and homes in Siena. Architecture throughout Italy shows strong Roman influences.

work of the household. They are trained to be loyal to the family and defend it against others. The Catholic Church is still important in Italian lives through providing a structure for rites of passage. A good child is one who obeys, does not disgrace the family, and loves his or her parents. Children are seen to resemble other family members, often dead ones. Although inheritance of personality traits is given a great deal of credence, there is still an intense effort made to shape the child's personality. Directions are given, surveillance is constant, and physical punishment is common.

Higher Education. Current Italian society emphasizes formal education, including higher education. However, Italy currently ranks last in expenditure per pupil in higher education in the European Union. There are a number of notable universities, many with long lineages: the universities of Bologna and Salerno, among others, go back to medieval times.

Etiquette

Italians generally are effusive in their public behavior. There is a great deal of public embracing and kissing upon greeting people. It is also polite to sit close to people and to interact by lightly touching people on the arms. Italian gazes are intense. It is felt that someone who cannot look you in the eyes is trying to hide something. Elders expect and get respect. They enter a room first. Men stand for women and youngsters for adults. Children tend to be used to run errands and help any adult, certainly any adult in the family. Gazing intently at strangers is common, and Italians expect to be looked at in public. Traditionally, younger women deferred to men in public and did not contradict them. Older women, however, joined in the general give and take of conversation without fear. Italians have little respect for lines and generally push their way to the front. There is great care given to preserving one's bella figura, dignity. Violating another's sense of self–importance is a dangerous activity.

Religion

Religious Beliefs. Ninety percent of the population is Roman Catholic. The other 2 percent is mainly comprised of Jews, along with some Muslims and Orthodox and Eastern Rite Catholics. The general supernatural beliefs are those of the Catholic Church as mixed with some older beliefs stretching back to antiquity. In Sicily, for example, Arabic and Greek influences have mixed with popular Spanish beliefs and been incorporated into Catholicism.

A woman purchases produce at the Campo de Fiori Market in Rome.

Thus, there are beliefs in the evil eye, charms, spells, messages through dreams, and various other types of omens. Witches have powers and there are anti–witches. Many of these beliefs, of course, have yielded to the rationalism of the modern age. Others, however, exist below the surface.

Religious Practitioners. Rome, or more precisely Vatican City, is the center of the Roman Catholic religion. Thus, the Pope, cardinals, bishops, monsignors, priests, members of various male and female religious orders, and others are omnipresent. The seven sacraments form a framework for religious life. Churches are plentiful and also attract the tourist dollar. There are more folk–like practitioners who carry on ''magic'' or ''superstitious'' practices—various healers who may have the gift of hands, witches, purveyors of charms and spells, and many others.

Rituals and Holy Places. Italy is filled with over 2000 years' worth of holy places. Rome and the Vatican City alone have thousands of shrines, relics, and churches. There are relics of Saint Peter and other popes. Various relics of many saints, places holy to Saint Francis of Assisi, shrines, places where the Virgin Mary is reputed to have appeared, and sites of numerous miracles are found across the country. Similarly, religious ceremonies are frequent. There are the usual holy days of the Roman Catholic Church—Christmas, Easter, Pentecost, the Immaculate Conception and others. In addition, there are local saints and appearances by the Pope. The sanctification of new saints, various blessings, personal, family, and regional feast days and daily and weekly masses add to the mix. There are also various novenas, rosary rituals, sodalities, men's and women's clubs, and other religious or quasi–religious activities.

Death and the Afterlife. Italians generally believe in a life after death in which the good are rewarded and the evil punished. There is a belief in a place where sins are purged, purgatory. Heaven and hell are realities for most Italians. The deceased are to be remembered and are often spoken to quietly. Funerals today take place in funeral parlors. Respect for the dead is expected. Failure to attend a wake for a family member or friend is cause for a breach of relationship unless there is a patently valid reason.

MEDICINE AND HEALTH CARE

Italy was a pioneer in modern health care with its medieval centers for medical study. Although modern Italy has a number of modern doctors and health specialists, it has had a history of healers and potion–makers. There was a prevalent belief, for example, in people having "healing hands." These people, it was felt, could heal soreness and broken bones by touch and manipulation. Others could cause disease through incantations or spells. Various faith healers practiced their arts.

Secular Celebrations

Most secular celebrations also are tied to religious holidays, like Christmas or New Year's (the Circumcision of Jesus). These celebrations tend to be family affairs. The Anniversary of the Republic is celebrated on 2 June. There is a show of patriotism through air shows and fireworks. Generally, it, too, is a day off and a family holiday. Independence Day is March 17 and provides another opportunity for family activity.

The Arts and Humanities

Support for the Arts. Italian art has a long history. Part of that history is the support it has received from public and private benefactors. That tradition continues into the present day with numerous benefactors who support the arts and humanities. These include the Agnelli Foundation, La FIMA (Foundazione Italiana per la Musica Antica), and numerous others.

Literature. Italian literature has its roots in Roman and Greek literature. Until about the thirteenth century Italian literature was written in Latin. There were various poems, legends, saint's lives, chronicles and similar literature. French and Provencal was also used. This literature concerned Charlemagne and King Arthur.

In the thirteenth century Sicilians composed the earliest poetry written in Italian at the court of Frederick II. Frederick and his son Manfred administered the Holy Roman Empire from Sicily. This poetry was a courtly poetry, following the Provencal models closely. When the Hohenstaufen dynasty fell in 1254, the capital of Italian poetry moved north. There were poets before Dante, especially Guittone d'Arezzo and Guido Guinizelli, the founder of the *dolce stil nuovo*—sweet new style. Dante's *La Vita Nuova* (1292) is in this style, and it influenced Petrach and other Renaissance writers. At about the same time as the dolce stil nuovo appeared, Saint Francis of Assisi began another type of poetry, a devotional style filled with love for all of God's creatures. Dante's greatest work was *La Divine Comida.*

Petrarch was the next great literary figure in Italy. He worked to restore classical Latin as the language of scholarship and literature. Petrarch believed that Italy was the heir of Rome, and he worked to foster Italian nationalism and unity. In spite of his classical scholarship, his work in Italian is Petrarch's greatest contribution to literature. His sonnets to Laura bring a fiery passion to Italian literature. Boccaccio's *Decameron* (1353) drew on both Dante and Petrarch as influences and in turn influenced numerous writers. It not only uses the vernacular but also uses true–to–life stories.

The fifteenth century was the period of the High Renaissance and included "universal men" such as Michelangelo, Leon Battista Alberti, and Leonardo da Vinci, among others. These men generally profited from patrons of the arts such as Lorenzo de'Medici and the Popes, such as Alexander VI. The first major Italian drama was *Orfeo* (c. 1480) written by Angelo Poliziano. There were still works done in the medieval geste style, which were based on the medieval romances.

In the sixteenth century, Italian rose to great heights with the writing of Pietro Bembo, Nicolo Machiavelli, and Ariosto. Machiavelli is best known for *The Prince* (1640), the first realistic work of political science and a call for Italian unity. Ariosto's poem, *Orlando furioso* (1516) is an epic dealing with Charlemagne, an old theme but with a new sophistication. There were numerous fine works written during century. The early exuberance was stifled, however, by the mood of the Counter–Reformation. Nonetheless, Torquato Tasso's masterpiece, *Geusalemme liberata* (1575), managed to break through the fog of repression. However, it received such petty criticism that Tasso wrote a poor new version of the poem.

The seventeenth and eighteenth century saw a decline in the standard of living in Italy. Trade had shifted to the Atlantic and Italy was under the political domination of Spain, France, and Austria. It was also the period of the baroque. The one great work of the period is Giambattista Marino's *Adone* (1623). The majority of other work in the century is depressingly gloomy, as befits the general tenor of Italian life of the period.

The next century saw a movement toward simplicity, the Arcadia movement. It was a period of naivete in style and simplicity in narrative. Greek models were used. The period was also influenced by the French Enlightenment.

The nineteenth century was the century of the Risorgimento. Giacomo Leopardi wrote magnificent lyric poems. Leopardi shows great feeling in his works as well as a deep nationalism. Alessandro Manzoni's *I promessi sposi* (1825–1827) is a great work of nationalistic fiction. Manzoni called for a

A mountain shepherd with goats in Lenola, circa 1985. After World War II, Italy began moving from an agricultural economy to an industrial economy.

return to the pure Tuscan dialect. However, nationalism also inspired a realist movement that extolled the beauty of regional dialects and life. The Sicilian Giovanni Verga was a leader of the movement and its greatest novelist.

The eaarly twentieth century has witnessed a number of different styles. Gabriele D'Annunzio, who began writing in the previous century, had great influence in the twentieth century. Benedetto Croce and others carried on the work of modern though in Italy. Luigi Pirandello, a 1934 Nobel Prize winner, was an innovator in style and thought. Fascism threatened to destroy Italian literature, and many of its great writers went abroad. Ignazio Silone, for example, produced *Fonatamara* and *Bread and Wine* overseas.

After World War II Italian literature blossomed again. All the major movements found in the West had their counterparts in Italy. A simple listing of major figures is sufficient to suggest the importance of modern Italian literature. In poetry, there are Giuseppe Ungaretti, Eugenio Montale, and Sal-

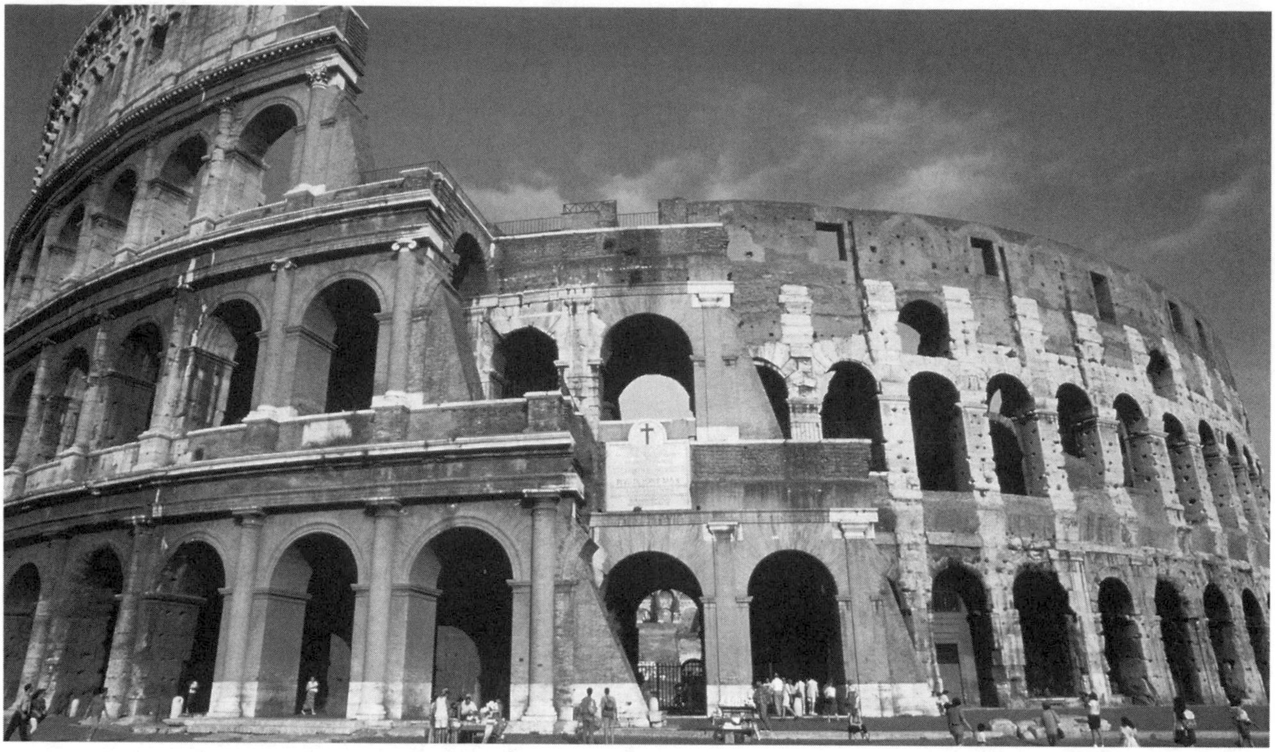

The Coliseum in Rome, a popular tourist spot.

vatore Quasimodo. In fiction, there are Carlo Levi, Elio Vittorini, Vasco Pratolini, Mario Doldati, Cesare Pavese, Vitaliano Brancati, Giuseppe Tomasi di Lampedusa, Alberto Moravia, Giorgio Bassani, Dino Buzzati, Elsa Morante, Natalia Levi Ginzburg, Primo Levi, and Umberto Ecco.

Graphic Arts. The history of Italian graphic arts is at least as long as that of literature. Italian artists such as Michelangelo, Leonardo, Fra Angelico, Raphael, and numerous others are known throughout the world. There is not one type of art in which Italy is not famous.

Italy has a cultural heritage that is felt everywhere in the country. Remains of Greek and Etruscan material culture are found throughout the south and middle of the peninsula. Roman antiquities are found everywhere. Pompeii and Herculaneum are famous for their well–preserved archeological remains. The city of Rome is itself a living museum. Throughout the country there are churches, palaces, and museums that preserve the past. There are, for example, over 35 million art pieces in its museums. Moreover, Italy has 700 cultural institutes, over 300 theaters, and about 6,000 libraries, which hold over 100 million books.

Italy's museums are world famous and contain, perhaps, the most important collections of artifacts from ancient civilizations. Taranto's museum, for example, offers material enabling scholars to probe deeply into the history of Magna Gracie. The archaeological collections in the Roman National Museum in Rome and in the National Archaeological Museum in Naples are probably among the world's best. Similarly, the Etruscan collection in the National Archaeological Museum of Umbria in Perugia, the classical sculptures in the Capitalize Museum (Museo Capitolino) in Rome, and the Egyptian collection in the Egyptian Museum in Turin are, perhaps, the best such collections in the world.

The classical age is not the only age represented in Italy's museums. The Italian Renaissance is well represented in a number of museums: the Uffizi Gallery (Galleria degli Uffizi), Bargello Museum (Museo Nazionale del Bargello), and Pitti Palace Gallery (Galleria di Palazzo Pitti, or Galleria Palatina) are all located in Florence.

The Uffizi contains masterpieces by Michelangelo, Leonardo da Vinci, Botticelli, Piero della Francesca, Giovanni Bellini, and Titian. The Bargello has specialized in Florentine sculpture, with works by Michelangelo, Benvenuto Cellini, Donatello, and the Della Robbia family. The Pitti Palace has a fine collection of paintings by Raphael, as well as about five hundred important works of the sixteenth and seventeenth centuries, which were collected by the Medici and Lorraine families.

Performance Arts. Italian music has been one of the major glories of European art. It includes the Gregorian chant, the troubadour song, the madrigal, and the work of Giovanni Palestrina and Claudio Giovanni Monteverdi. Later composers include Antonio Vivaldi, Alessandro and Domenico Scarlatti, Gioacchino Rossini, Gaetano Donizetti, Giuseppe Verdi, Giacomo Puccini, and Vincenzo Bellini. The most famous of Italy's opera houses is La Scala in Milan. There are other famous venues for opera, including San Carlo in Naples, La Fenice Theatre in Venice, and the Roman arena in Verona. Additionally, there are fifteen publically-owned theaters and numerous privately-run ones in Italy. These theaters promote Italian and European plays as well as ballets.

The State of the Physical and Social Sciences

All forms of the physical and social sciences are practiced in Italy. There is no area in which Italian scholars are not prominent. Government and private funding is extensive. Schools of engineering, social work and other applied work are prominent.

Bibliography

Belmonte, Thomas. *The Broken Fountain*, 1989.

Blok, Anton. *The Mafia of a Sicilian Village, 1860–1960: A Study of Violent Peasant Entrepreneurs*, 1988.

Buck, Joan Juliet. "Italian Spirit—A Generosity of Style." *Vogue* 171: 293–319, 1981.

Cole, Jeffrey. *The New Racism in Europe: A Sicilian Example*, 1998.

Cornelisen, Ann. *Women of the Shadows: A Study of the Wives & Mothers of Southern Italy*, 1991.

Galt, Anthony H. *Town & Country in Locorotondo*, 1992.

Gentile, Emilio. "The Struggle for Modernity: Echoes of the Dreyfus Affair in Italian Political Culture, 1898–1912." *Journal of Contemporary History* 33(4): 497–511, 1998.

Gibson, Mary S. "Visions and Revisions: Women in Italian Culture." *Journal of Women's History* 8(2): 169–180, 1996.

Hauser, Ernest. *Italy: A Cultural Guide*, 1981.

Holmes, Douglas R. *Cultural Disenchantments Worker Peasantries in Northeast Italy*, 1989.

Kertzer, David I. *The Family in Italy from Antiquity to the Present*, 1993.

"The Lessons of History: Italy's Lack of Nationalism." *The Economist* 327(7817) pp. 14–16.

Magliocco, Sabina. *The Two Madonnas: The Politics of Festival in a Sardinian Community*, 1993.

Silverman, Sydel. *The Three Bells of Civilization: The Life of an Italian Hill Town*, 1975.

"The Triumph of La Dolce Vita?" *New Scientist* 144 (1957-58): 73–74, 1971.

Thompson, Doug. *State Control in Fascist Italy. Culture and Conformity, 1925–1943*, 1994.

—Frank A. Salamone

JAMAICA

CULTURE NAME

Jamaican

ORIENTATION

Identification. In 1494, Columbus named the island Santiago. The Spanish wrote the name used by the native Taino, "Yamaye," as "Xaymaca." The Taino word is purported to mean "many springs." The abbreviated name, "Ja" and the Rastafarian term "Jamdung" (Jamdown) are used by some residents, along with "Yaahd" (Yard), used mainly by Jamaicans abroad, in reference to the deterritorialization of the national culture.

Location and Geography. Jamaica, one of the Greater Antilles, is situated south of Cuba. Divided into fourteen parishes, it is 4,244 square miles (10,990 square kilometers) in area. In 1872, Kingston, with a quarter of the population, became the capital.

Demography. The population in 1998 was 2.75 million. Fifty-three percent of the population resides in urban areas. The population is 90 percent black, 1 percent East Indian, and 7 percent mixed, with a few whites and Chinese. The black demographic category includes the descendants of African slaves, postslavery indentured laborers, and people of mixed ancestry. The East Indians and Chinese arrived as indentured laborers.

Linguistic Affiliation. The official language is English, reflecting the British colonial heritage, but even in official contexts a number of creole dialects that reflect class, place, and social context are spoken.

Symbolism. The national motto, which was adopted after independence from Great Britain in 1962, is "Out of many, one people." In the national flag, the two black triangles represent historical struggles and hardship, green triangles represent agricultural wealth and hope, and yellow cross-stripes represent sunshine and mineral resources.

HISTORY AND ETHNIC RELATIONS

Emergence of the Nation. Jamaica was a Spanish colony from 1494 to 1655 and a British colony from 1655 to 1962. The colonial period was marked by conflict between white absentee owners and local managers and merchants and African slave laborers. After independence, there was conflict between plantation and industrial economic interests and those of small, peasant cultivators and landless laborers. In the 1920s, rural, landless unemployed persons moved into the Kingston-Saint Andrew area in search of work. The new urban poor, in contrast to the white and brown-skinned political, merchant, and professional upper classes threw in sharp relief the status of the island as a plural society. In 1944, with the granting of a new constitution, Jamaicans gained universal suffrage. The struggle for sovereignty culminated with the gaining of independence on 6 August 1962.

National Identity. Class, color, and ethnicity are factors in the national identity. Jamaican Creole, or Jamaica Talk, is a multiethnic, multiclass indigenous creation and serves as a symbol of defiance of European cultural authority. Identity also is defined by a religious tradition in which there is minimal separation between the sacred and the secular, manipulable spiritual forces (as in *obeah*), and ritual dance and drumming; an equalitarian spirit; an emphasis on self-reliance; and a drive to succeed economically that has perpetuated Eurocentric cultural ideals.

Ethnic Relations. The indigenous Taino natives of the region, also referred to as Arawaks, have left evidence of material and ideational cultural influence. Jews came as indentured servants to help establish the sugar industry and gradually became part of the merchant class. East Indians and Chinese were recruited between the 1850s and the 1880s to fill the labor gap left by ex-slaves and to keep plantation wages low. As soon as the Chinese finished their indentured contracts, they established small businesses. East Indians have been moving gradually from agricultural labor into mercantile and professional activities.

The major ethnic division is that between whites and blacks. The achievement of black majority rule has led to an emphasis on class relations, shades of skin color, and cultural prejudices, rather than on racial divisions. Jamaica has never experienced entrenched ethnic conflict between blacks and Indians or Chinese.

Urbanism, Architecture, and the Use of Space

Settlement patterns were initiated by plantation activities. Lowland plantations, complemented by urban trade and administrative centers, ports, and domestic markets, were the hub of activity. As the plantations declined and as the population grew, urban centers grew faster than did job opportunities, leading to an expanding slum population and the growth of urban trading and other forms of "informal" economic activities.

Architecture reflects a synthesis of African, Spanish, and baroque British influences. Traces of pre-Columbian can be seen in the use of palm fronds thatch and mud walls (daub). Styles, materials, size, and furnishings differ more by class than by ethnicity. Since much of Caribbean life takes place outdoors, this has influenced the design and size of buildings, particularly among the rural poor. The Spanish style is reflected in the use of balconies, wrought iron, plaster and brick facades, arched windows and doors, and high ceilings. British influence, with wooden jalousies, wide porches, and patterned railings and fretwork, dominated urban architecture in the colonial period. Plantation houses were built with stone and wood, and town houses typically were built with wood, often on a stone or cement foundation. The kitchen, washroom, and "servant" quarters were located separately or at the back of the main building. The traditional black peasant dwelling is a two-room rectangular structure with a pitched thatched roof and walls of braided twigs covered with whitewashed mud or crude wooden planks. These dwellings are starting to disappear, as they are being replaced by more modern dwellings with cinder block walls and a corrugated metal roof.

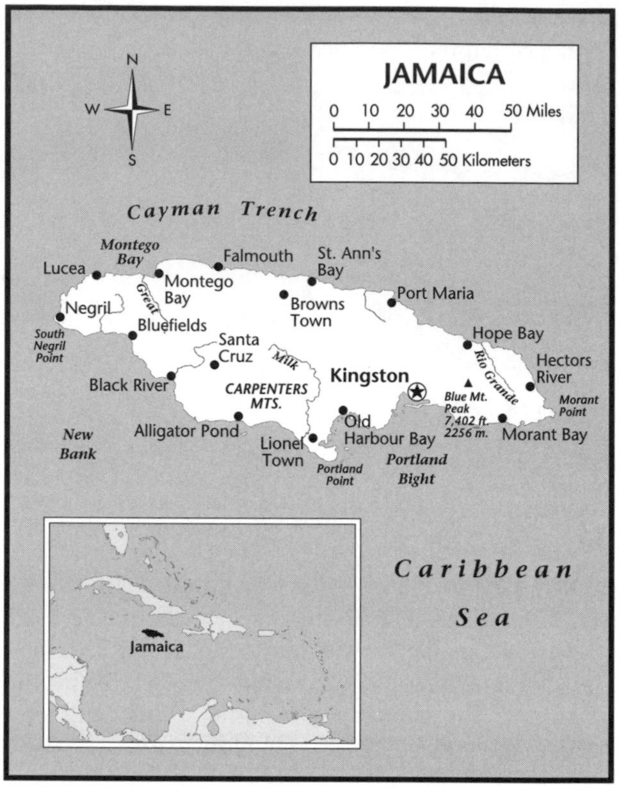

Jamaica

Food and Economy

Food in Daily Life. A "country" morning meal, called "drinking tea," includes boiled bananas or roasted breadfruit, sauteed callaloo with "saal fish" (salted cod), and "bush" (herbal) or "chaklit" (chocolate) tea. Afro-Jamaicans eat a midafternoon lunch as the main meal of the day. This is followed by a light meal of bread, fried plantains, or fried dumplings and a hot drink early in the evening. A more rigid work schedule has forced changes, and now the main meal is taken in the evening. This meal may consist of stewed or roasted beef, boiled yam or plantains, rice and peas, or rice with escoviched or fried fish.

Food Customs at Ceremonial Occasions. Rice is a ubiquitous ceremonial food. Along with "ground provisions" such as sweet potato, yam, and green plantains, it is used in African and East Indian ceremonies. It also is served with curried goat meat as the main food at parties, dances, weddings, and funerals. Sacrificially slaughtered animals and birds are eaten in a ritual context. Several African-religious sects use goats for sacrifice, and in Kumina, an Afro-religious practice, goat blood is mixed with rum and drunk.

Basic Economy. Since the 1960s, the economy, which previously had been based on large-scale agricultural exportation, has seen considerable diversification. Mining, manufacturing, and services are now major economic sectors.

Land Tenure and Property. Land tenure can be classified into legal, extralegal, and cultural-institutional. The legal forms consist of freehold tenure, leasehold and quitrent, and grants. The main extralegal means of tenure is squatting. The cultural-institutional form of tenure is traditionally known as "family land," in which family members share use rights in the land.

Commercial Activities. The economy is based primarily on manufacturing and services. In the service economy, tourism is the largest contributor of foreign exchange. The peasantry plays a significant role in the national economy by producing root crops and fruits and vegetables.

Trade. The main international trading partners are the United States, the United Kingdom, Canada, and the Caribbean Economic Community. The major imports are consumer goods, construction hardware, electrical and telecommunication equipment, food, fuel, machinery, and transportation equipment. The major exports are bauxite and alumina, apparel, sugar, bananas, coffee, citrus and citrus products, rum, cocoa, and labor.

Division of Labor. In the plantation economy, African slaves performed manual labor while whites owned the means of production and performed managerial tasks. As mulattos gained education and privileges, they began to occupy middle-level positions. This pattern is undergoing significant change, with increased socioeconomic integration, the reduction of the white population by emigration, and the opening of educational opportunities. Blacks now work in all types of jobs, including the highest political and professional positions; the Chinese work largely in retail and wholesale trades; and Indians are moving rapidly into professional and commercial activities. Women traditionally are associated with domestic, secretarial, clerical, teaching, and small-scale trading activities.

Social Stratification

Classes and Castes. The bulk of national wealth is owned by a small number of light-skinned or white families, with a significant portion controlled by individuals of Chinese and Middle Eastern heritage. Blacks are confined largely to small and medium-size retail enterprises. While race has played a defining role in social stratification, it has not assumed a caste-like form, and individuals are judged on a continuum of color and physical features.

Symbols of Social Stratification. Black skin is still associated with being "uncivilized," "ignorant," "lazy," and "untrustworthy." Lifestyle, language, cuisine, clothing, and residential patterns that reflect closeness to European culture have been ranked toward the top of the social hierarchy, and symbols depicting African-derived culture have been ranked at the bottom. African symbols are starting to move up in the ranks, however.

Political Life

Government. Jamaica, a member of the British Commonwealth, has a bicameral parliamentary legislative system. The executive branch consists of the British monarch, the governor general, the prime minister and deputy prime minister, and the cabinet. The legislative branch consists of the Senate and the sixty-member elected House of Representatives. The judicial branch consists of the supreme court and several layers of lower courts.

Leadership and Political Officials. The two major parties are the People's National Party (PNP) and the Jamaica Labor Party (JLP). Organized pressure groups include trade unions, the Rastafarians, and civic organizations.

Social Problems and Control. The failure of the socialist experiment in the 1970s and the emphasis on exports have created a burgeoning mass of urban poor (scufflers) who earn a meager living in the informal, largely small-scale trading sector and engage in extralegal means of survival. Also, globalization has led to the growth of the international drug trade. The most serious problem is violent crime, with a high murder rate. Governmental mechanisms for dealing with crime-related social problems fall under the Ministry of National Security and are administered through the Criminal Justice System.

Military Activity. The military consists of the Jamaica Defense Force (which includes the Ground Forces, the Coast Guard, and the Air Wing) and the Jamaica Constabulary Force. Both branches include males and females. The military is deployed mainly for national defense and security purposes but occasionally aids in international crises.

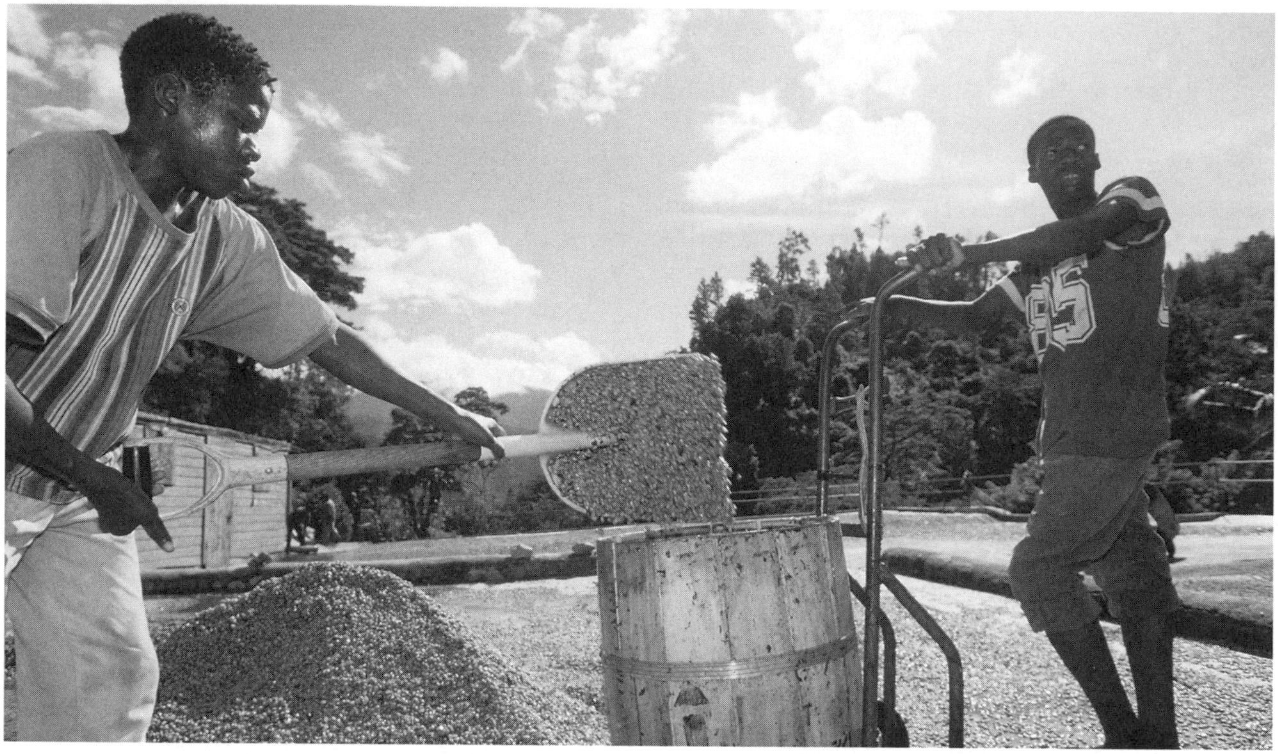

Two men shoveling coffee beans into a barrel. Agriculture is now only one of many fields open to black Jamaicans, once enslaved to work the plantations.

Social Welfare and Change Programs

The social development system combines local governmental programs and policies, international governmental support, and local and international nongovernmental organization (NGO) participation. It is administered largely by the Ministry of Youth and Community Development. The social security and welfare system includes the National Insurance Scheme (NIS) and public assistance programs. NIS benefits include employment benefits; old age benefits; widow and widower, orphan, and special child benefits; and funeral grants.

Nongovernmental Organizations and Other Associations

Over 150 NGOs are active in areas such as environmental protection, the export-import trade, socioeconomic development, and education.

Gender Roles and Statuses

Division of Labor by Gender. Men are predominant in leadership positions in government, the professions, business, higher education, and European-derived religions and engage in physical labor in agriculture. Women work primarily in paid and unpaid in household labor, formal and informal retail trades, basic and primary education, clerical and administrative jobs, and social welfare.

The Relative Status of Women and Men. Traditionally, woman's place is in the home and women receive less remuneration than men. The appropriate place for men is outside the home, in agriculture, business, government, or recreation. This attitude is changing.

Marriage, Family, and Kinship

Marriage. There are two types of marriage patterns: the legally recognized and socially preferred Western-style monogamous union and the so-called consensual union. The selection of a spouse is made by individual choice, but in more traditional communities, the approval of parents and close relatives is sought. Among the Indians and Chinese, monogamous unions predominate. Traditionally, among African Jamaicans there has been a link between socioeconomic status and type of marriage, with the consensual union associated with the rural and urban poor and the legal union associated with economically stable, landholding peasants, and the middle and upper classes. A consensual union often occurs among young people, with

The Kingston business district. Jamaica's economy now includes mining, manufacturing, and services in addition to agriculture.

a legal union taking place when economic stability is achieved.

Domestic Unit. The domestic unit typically consists of a grandmother, a mother, and the mother's offspring from the current and previous unions. The father may be a permanent part of the unit, may visit for varying periods, or may be absent. Often the unit includes children of kin who are part of other households.

Inheritance. Inheritance generally passes bilaterally from parents to children and grandchildren. Among the poor, land that is inherited helps to maintain strong family and locality relationships.

Kin Groups. The concept of family applies to blood and nonblood kin who maintain an active, functional relationship with respect to material and social support. It is not limited to the household. Family relations are of great importance, and children of the poor often are shifted from household to household for support. Kin relations are traced bilaterally for four or five generations.

Socialization

Infant Care. The use of midwives is still popular, and breast-feeding is done in all the ethnic groups. A baby is named and registered within a few days of its birth, and soon afterward it is "christened." Infants typically sleep with the mother and are carried in her arms. A crying baby is rocked in the mothers arms and hummed to. As a baby ages, the parents and grandparents try to accommodate their expectations to the child's unique qualities; the baby is allowed to "grow into itself."

Child Rearing and Education. Firm discipline underlies child care until a child leaves home and/or becomes a parent. The mother is central, but all members of the household and other close kin have some responsibility in rearing a child. It is believed that the behavior of the pregnant mother influences what the child will become. Children are said to "take after" a parent or to be influenced by "the devil" or the spirits of ancestors. Children are given progressively demanding responsibilities from the age of five or six. For poor parents in all ethnic groups, the single most important route out of poverty is the education of their children. In more traditional settings, the child is "pushed" by the entire family and even the community. The national stereotype is that Indians and Chinese pay greater attention to their offspring, who perform better than blacks.

Higher Education. Higher education is considered essential to national success, and the parliament has established the National Council on Education to oversee higher education policy and implementation. Expenditures on education have continued to rise. There are two universities the University of the West Indies, and the University of Technology.

Etiquette

Politeness and courtesy are highly valued as aspects of being ''raised good.'' They are expressed through greetings, especially from the young to their elders. A child never ''backtalks'' to parents or elders. Men are expected to open doors for women and help with or perform heavy tasks. Women are expected to ''serve'' men in domestic contexts and, in more traditional settings, to give the adult males and guests the best part of a meal.

Religion

Religious Beliefs. The Anglican church is regarded as the church of the elite, but the middle class in all ethnic groups is distributed over several non-African-derived religions. All the established denominations have been creolized; African-Caribbean religious practices such as Puk-kumina, revivalism, Kumina, Myalism, and Rastafarianism have especially significant African influences.

Religious Practitioners. Among less modernized African Jamaicans, there is no separation between the secular and the sacred. Afro-Jamaican leaders are typically charismatic men and women who are said to have special ''gifts'' or to be ''called.''

Rituals and Holy Places. Rituals include ''preaching'' meetings as well as special healing rituals and ceremonies such as ''thanksgiving,'' ancestral veneration, and memorial ceremonies. These ceremonies may include drumming, singing, dancing, and spirit possession. All places where organized rituals take place are regarded as holy, including churches, ''balm yards,'' silk cotton trees, burial grounds, baptismal sites at rivers, and crossroads.

Death and the Afterlife. Death is regarded as a natural transformation, and except in the case of the very old, its cause is believed to be the violation of a cultural norm, evil spirits, or envy. After a death, kin and community gather at the home of the deceased to lend support and assist in funeral preparations, which involve washing and tying the body. People gather at the home of the deceased each night until the burial in a ritual called ''setup.'' Funerals are one of the most important African-Jamaican rituals. A large harmonious funeral is considered a sign of good living.

A Rastafarian man.

Medicine and Health Care

Jamaicans use a mix of traditional and biomedical healing practices. The degree of use of traditional means, including spiritual healing, is inversely related to class status. Among the African Jamaicans, illness is believed to be caused by spiritual forces or violation of cultural taboos. Consequently, most illnesses are treated holistically. When traditional means fail, modern medicine is tried.

Secular Celebrations

Independence Day is celebrated on the first Monday in August. Other noteworthy holidays are Christmas, Boxing Day, New Year's Day, and National Heroes Day, which is celebrated the third Monday in October. Chinese New Year is celebrated.

The Arts and Humanities

Support for the Arts. The arts and humanities have a long tradition of development and public support, but state support has been institutionalized only since independence. Most artists are self-supporting.

Literature. Indians, Chinese, Jews, and Europeans brought aspects of their written tradition, yet current literary works are overwhelmingly African Jamaican. The oral tradition draws on several West African-derived sources, including the griot tradition; the trickster story form; the use of proverbs, aphorisms, riddles, and humor in the form of the "big lie"; and origin stories. The 1940s saw the birth of a movement toward the creation of a "yard" (Creole) literature.

Graphic Arts. The tradition of graphic arts began with indigenous Taino sculpting and pottery and has continued with the evolution of the African tradition. Jamaica has a long tradition of pottery, including items used in everyday domestic life, which are referred to as *yabbah*. There is a West African tradition of basket and straw mat weaving, seashell art, bead making, embroidery, sewing, and wood carving.

Performance Arts. Most folk performances are rooted in festivals, religious and healing rituals, and other African-derived cultural expressions. Traditional performances take the form of impromptu plays and involve social commentary based on the African Caribbean oratorical tradition ("speechifying" or "sweet talking"). Music is the most highly developed of the performing arts. There is a long tradition of classical music interest, but the country is best known for its internationally popular musical form, reggae. Jamaica also has a strong tradition of folk and religious music. Drama is the least developed performing art, but it has been experiencing a new surge of energy.

The State of the Physical and Social Sciences

There are physical and social science programs at the University of West Indies (UWI) and the Institute of Jamaica and its ancillary research bodies such as the African Caribbean Institute of Jamaica. The UWI has a medical school and a law school, and there is a University of Technology. Most social science research is done with support from the Institute of Social and Economic Research.

Bibliography

Alleyne, Mervyn. *The Roots of Jamaican Culture*, 1989.

Carnegie, Charles V., ed. *Afro-Caribbean Villages in Historical Perspective*, 1987.

Cassidy, Frederic. *Jamaica Talk: Three Hundred Years of the English Language in Jamaica*, 1971.

Chevannes, Barry. *Rastafari: Roots and Ideology*, 1994.

Curtin, Philip D. *Two Jamaicas: The Role of Ideas in a Tropical Colony, 1830–1865*, 1955.

Dance, Daryl C. *Folklore from Contemporary Jamaicans*, 1985.

Kerr, Madeline. *Personality and Conflict in Jamaica*, 1963.

Mintz, Sidney W. *Caribbean Transformations*, 1974.

Nettleford, Rex. *Caribbean Cultural Identity: The Case of Jamaica*, 1979.

Olwig, Karen Fog. "Caribbean Family Land: A Modern Commons." *Plantation Society in the Americas*, 4 (2 and 3): 135–158, 1997.

Rouse, Irving. *The Tainos: Rise and Decline of the People Who Greeted Columbus*, 1992.

Senior, Olive. *A–Z of Jamaica Heritage*, 1985.

Sherlock, Philip, and Hazel Bennett. *The Story of the Jamaican People*, 1998.

Smith, Michael G. *The Plural Society in the British West Indies*, 1974.

—Trevor W. Purcell

Japan

Culture Name

Japanese

Orientation

Identification. The Japanese names, *Nihon* and *Nippon,* are alternative readings of written characters that mean "origin of the sun" ("Land of the Rising Sun").

European names for the country probably originated with Marco Polo, who most likely adopted a name for Japan used in a Chinese dialect.

The name "Yamato" is used by archaeologists and historians to distinguish Japanese artistic genres from their Chinese counterparts. When used as a contemporary term, Yamato has strong associations with the imperial system, and thus with conservative nationalist ideologies.

Contemporary Japan is considered a highly homogeneous society, but regional variation in social and cultural patterns has always been significant. Pride of place and identification with local cultural patterns remain strong. Japanese people often attribute personality traits to people from particular regions, and regional identity often is expressed through local culinary specialties and dialects.

Location and Geography. The Japanese archipelago consists of four major islands and over six-thousand minor ones, covering approximately 234,890 square miles (378,000 square kilometers), and has enormous climatic variation. The four major islands are Hokkaidō, Honshū, Shikoku, and Kyūshū. The southern island group of Okinawa (the Ryūkyū Islands) is geographically, historically, and culturally distinct.

Japan faces the Pacific Ocean along the entire eastern and southern coastline. To the north and west are the Sea of Okhotsk, the Sea of Japan, and the East China Sea. The Korean peninsula is the closest point on the Asian mainland. Japanese life has always been oriented toward the ocean. The currents that converge offshore create fertile and varied fishing grounds.

The climate is shaped by Asian-Pacific monsoon cycles, which bring heavy rains from the Pacific during the summer and fall, followed by icy winds from North Asia during the winter that dump snow in the mountains.

There are approximately 1,500 volcanoes, and because the islands lie on major fault lines, earthquakes are common occurrences. Only about 15 percent of the land is level enough for agriculture, and so the population density in coastal plains and valleys is extremely high. Because of the steep mountains, there are almost no navigable inland waterways.

Demography. The population in 1999 was 127,000,000. The country is heavily urbanized, and urban areas have extremely high population densities. According to the 1995 census, 81 million people (65 percent) live in urban areas; that constitutes only 3 percent of the land area.

During the last 150 years of industrialization and economic development, the population has grown from around thirty million to its present size. This increase occurred as a result of a rapid demographic transition characterized by an enormous movement of people from rural to urban areas, dramatic decreases in infant mortality, increases in longevity, widespread reliance on birth control, and transformations of family composition from large, multigenerational extended households to small nuclear families.

Life expectancy is the highest in the world, and the birthrate has been declining dramatically. Because of these trends, the population is projected to peak early in the twenty-first century and then shrink.

Linguistic Affiliation. The official and predominant language is Japanese (Nihongo). After the

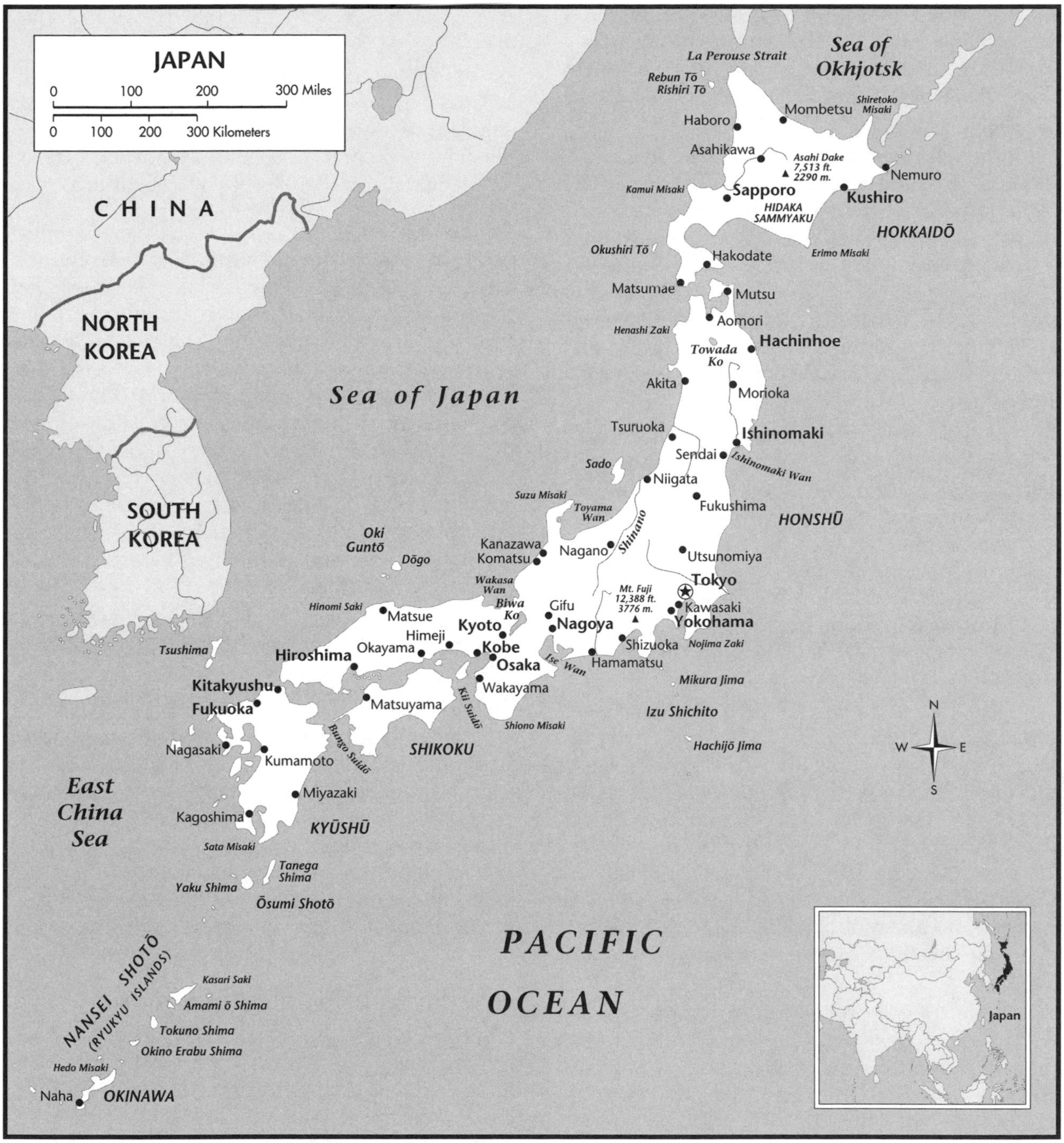

Japan

Meiji Restoration in 1868, the government attempted to create a strong centralized state. Linguistic unification was a step toward shaping the national identity. Through the national educational system and the military, a dominant national dialect replaced local and regional dialects. The resulting dialect, *hyōjungo* (''the standard language''), was based on the linguistic patterns of Tōkyō's samurai (''warrior'') classes and has become the norm in the educational system, the mass media, government, and business.

Japanese is linguistically related to Korean, and both languages are thought to be members of the Ural-Altaic family. Despite similarity in syntax, vocabulary, and grammar, the contemporary languages are mutually unintelligible. Japanese also has close connections to various Oceanic (Malayo-Polynesian) languages, suggesting that in prehistoric times the archipelago may have been settled by populations from Oceania as well as from the Asian mainland.

Although Chinese and Japanese are fundamentally unrelated and differ in phonology, syntax, and grammar, Chinese has had enormous impact on the Japanese language and civilization. The Chinese system of writing was introduced along with Buddhism in the sixth century, and Chinese orthography was used to transform Japanese into a written language. Until the nineteenth century, stylized versions of written Chinese remained a hallmark of elite culture.

The introduction of Chinese characters 1,500 years ago established semantic and orthographic systems that make Japanese one of the most complicated languages in the world. The contemporary language relies on an enormous number of words and terms that are Sino-Japanese in origin as well as words derived from indigenous Japanese terminology. Most written characters can be read in contemporary Japanese with both a Sino-Japanese pronunciation and a Japanese reading.

In addition to the adaptation of Chinese characters to preexisting Japanese vocabulary, two phonetic systems of writing were developed after the ninth century. Those orthographies made it possible to write Chinese phonetically and to write spoken Japanese terms that had no equivalent Chinese characters. Literacy therefore became attainable for people not educated in the Chinese classics, and many masterpieces of classical Japanese literature, including the *Tale of Genji*, were written in those scripts.

The writing system *rōmaji* (''Roman characters'') is used to transcribe Japanese into the Roman alphabet. *Rōmaji* is widely used on signs, in advertising, and in the mass media. An alternative system, adopted but not mandated by the government, is much less commonly used.

Although spoken and written forms of Japanese are largely standardized throughout the nation, there are several linguistically distinctive ethnic and regional dialects. The most distant dialects are those spoken in the Okinawan islands. Okinawan dialects are considered by many linguists to be distinct from Japanese. After the Kingdom of Ryūkyū was annexed in 1879, the national government tried to replace the use of the Ryūkyū language with standard Japanese, but the isolation of the islands, their lack of development before World War II, and the American occupation until 1970, enabled Okinawans to maintain the use of their dialects.

Other linguistic minorities include the Korean-Japanese and the Ainu. Most Korean-Japanese are bilingual or, especially among the younger generations, monolingual speakers of Japanese. There are only a handful of native speakers of Ainu.

Symbolism. National identity and unity are formally symbolized by a number of conventional icons and motifs, including the cherry blossom, the red and white national flag portraying the rising sun, and the chrysanthemum. These symbols have contested meanings because they are associated with the imperial family and World War II. The chrysanthemum, for example, serves as the crest of the imperial family, and cherry blossoms were invoked in wartime propaganda to represent the glory of kamikaze suicide pilots. Progressive political groups resist flying the national flag and singing the national anthem (Kimigayo) because of their wartime associations.

Stereotypical images that are deployed in foreign representations of Japan, such as Mount Fuji, geisha, and samurai, are not regarded by Japanese people as symbols of contemporary identity.

Contemporary Japanese culture emphasizes symbolic expressions of local or regional identity. For example, local identity and pride are commonly expressed through ''famous local products.'' Almost every village, town, and city is famous for something, often a locally distinctive folk craft, a local culinary specialty, or a traditional song or performing art.

History and Ethnic Relations

Emergence of the Nation. The peoples of the Jōmon period (8000 B.C.E.–300 B.C.E.) were Neolithic hunting-and-gathering bands. During the Yayoi period (ca. 300 B.C.E.– ca. 300 C.E.) extensive cultural contact with and migration from the Asian mainland occurred, and a society arose that was based on irrigated rice cultivation. The basic genetic stock of the population and the fundamental patterns of the language were established during that period.

Japan came to the attention of China in the fourth century. During the Yamato period (300 C.E.–552 C.E.), small chieftainships coalesced into a rudimentary state-level society. The mythologies of the indigenous Japanese religion, Shintō, date from that period; they intertwine accounts of the divine origins of the islands with chronicles of struggles among gods whose descendants eventually came to be regarded as the imperial family, which claims an unbroken line of descent since this period.

In 552, emissaries from the Korean kingdom of Paekche established contact with the Yamato rulers. They introduced Buddhism and thus brought Japan into systematic contact with Chinese civilization. Almost every aspect of Japanese life—agricultural technology, written language, philosophy, architecture, poetry, medicine, and law—was transformed. The Yamato state adopted the conventions of the Chinese imperial court and tried to model society along the lines of Chinese civilization.

In the late eighth century, a new capital was established at what is now Kyōto, and during the Heian period (794–1185) Japanese classical civilization blossomed. Kyōto became the aristocratic center of a refined culture that was influenced by contact with China but developed independent and sophisticated aesthetic, literary, and artistic styles. *The Tale of Genji*, the world's first novel, epitomizes the culture of the Heian period.

By the end of the Heian period, economic, social, and military power had shifted to provincial landholders and warriors. From the beginning of the Kamakura period (1185–1333) the imperial court appointed a Shōgun: a supreme military commander who acted in the name of the imperial court but was in fact the supreme political authority. Several successive hereditary dynasties occupied this position until 1868. Central control was in the hands of the Shōgun's court, while regional lords governed individual provincial domains and commanded the personal loyalty of warrior retainers (samurai). The Kamakura period and the following periods were characterized by a warrior culture, including the development of Japanese forms of austere Zen Buddhism, martial arts, and the philosophic code of warrior life now called *Bushidō.*

The medieval period ended in a century of civil war lasting from the late fifteenth to the late sixteenth century. Contacts with the West began in the mid-sixteenth century with the arrival of the Portuguese Jesuit missionary Francis Xavier. The introduction of Western weaponry hastened the consolidation of power among a few increasingly dominant warlords who unified the country and ended the civil war.

In 1603 Tokugawa Ieyasu decisively defeated most of the remaining opponents, and established a dynasty that lasted until 1868. For over 260 years, Japan experienced political stability, peace, and rising prosperity. Ieyasu established his capital in Edo (renamed Tōkyō in 1868), which commanded the Kantō region and was distant from the imperial court in Kyōto. The Tokugawa regime ruled through a complicated network of alliances with approximately 250 regional lords, some closely allied to the Tokugawa and others in opposition but permanently subdued. Each fief retained its own castle town, and as a political strategy, some fiefs maintained a high degree of economic, social, and cultural autonomy.

During the Tokugawa period, culture and society became codified and somewhat uniform across the country. Patterns established during this period shaped, propelled, and constrained the country's modernization after 1868. By the 1630s, the Tokugawa regime had ruthlessly suppressed Christian communities and broken off most ties with European nations. It disarmed the peasantry and imposed rigid household registration requirements to keep the population spatially and socially immobile. Traffic along the great highways was scrutinized at heavily guarded checkpoints. Trade was controlled through feudal guilds, and detailed sumptuary regulations governed the lives of all social classes.

These social policies reflected the ideology of neo-Confucianism, which valued social stability and the social morality of ascribed status. Tokugawa social structure was organized around principles of hierarchy, centralized authority, and collective responsibility. Individuals were expected to subordinate themselves to the specific obligations of their ascribed social roles, and virtue consisted of perfecting one's ability to fit the requirements of one's role. In the upper reaches of society, the kinship system upheld neo-Confucian ideals of the family as a microcosm of the social order. Neo-Confucianism also established a rigid system of ranked social classes: warriors, peasants, artisans, and merchants. Status reflected ideals of social utility, not wealth. Beyond those four hereditary official classes, Tokugawa society included a tiny stratum of imperial nobility, a large clerical establishment, and a population of outcastes.

Throughout this period, regional castle towns and the major urban centers under the direct control of the Tokugawa authorities became increasingly integrated into a national economic, social, and cultural network. Urban economic power increased over the agrarian sectors. This undermined Tokugawa political power, which depended on the control of agricultural land and taxes.

In the cities, bourgeois culture flourished: *kabuki* drama, *bunraku* puppet theater, *sumō* wrestling, *ukiyo-e* woodblock prints, and geisha enter-

Irrigated fields in front of a housing development near Kyōto. Only about 15 percent of Japan is level enough for agriculture.

tainers were all creations of the urban culture. Japanese cities equaled or surpassed their European counterparts in infrastructure and public amenities, but Japanese urbanites lacked a political voice commensurate with their economic and cultural capital.

Tokugawa social patterns and institutions laid the foundations for modernization. The urban merchant classes stimulated the development of sophisticated national economic institutions and the beginning of industrial production. Literacy and computational ability were widespread among samurai, merchants, and the upper levels of the peasantry. The samurai became a hereditary class of bureaucrats whose qualifications for leadership depended on education. Society was characterized by discipline and regulation.

The Tokugawa dynasty surrendered its authority to the imperial court in 1868 after a long struggle. The political crisis included major internal economic problems and the unexpected confrontation with the Western powers precipitated by the arrival of Commodore Matthew Perry and a squadron of American warships in 1853. Opponents of the Tokugawa demanded that it take a firm stand against foreign intrusions and then overthrew the regime. The result was a largely peaceful coup known as the Meiji Restoration, which marked the beginning of the nation's modernization.

The Meiji regime reconnected imperial rule with civil political authority and military power. Under the nominal leadership of Emperor Meiji, the imperial government was run by the young samurai who had defeated the Tokugawa dynasty. They were fiercely nationalistic and attempted to bring Japanese society into parity with European and North American powers. Society was thoroughly transformed as the leaders created a strong centralized state centered on the imperial line, built a modern military, avoided European colonization, began imperialist expansion into other parts of East Asia, and launched industrialization and economic development.

Although they had come to power under the slogan "Revere the Emperor; Expel the Barbarians," the Meiji leaders built a strong state and society along the lines of an industrial European country. Meiji leaders balanced Western powers again each other to avoid domination by any single patron. The government sent delegations to study legal institutions, commerce and industry, science and technology, military affairs, architecture, arts, and medicine in Europe and North America. Foreign experts were hired, and young Japanese were sent to study at Western universities. The new slogan was "Eastern values; Western science."

Meiji leaders also emphasized the imperial family as the foundation of the state and strengthened institutions and ideologies, including Shintō religious beliefs, that supported the imperial family. From the late nineteenth century until 1945, an official cult (State Shintō) dominated the national ideology. The Meiji grafted the trappings of contemporary Western monarchies onto the sacred imperial institution, creating a court nobility that resembled European aristocracies. Samurai ranks were abolished in 1872. The centrality of the state was strengthened by a new national educational system, and a growing military.

Treaties signed by the Tokugawa regime had created zones where Western citizens lived independently of Japanese laws. These "treaty ports" were important sources of Western influence, and many schools, hospitals, and other institutions created by foreign missionaries became prominent. The system of extraterritoriality, however, was considered degrading, and the government tried to transform social life and culture in ways that would command the respect of the Western powers.

Japan rapidly built a Western-style navy and army and attempted to expand its influence in East Asia. It annexed the Ryūkyū islands, took control of Formosa (Taiwan) after its success in the Sino-Japanese War, and was granted equal status with the Western powers in dealings with China. Extraterritoriality ended in 1899, and victory in the Russo-Japanese War (1904–1905)—resulted in the possession of several islands north of Hokkaidō and Russia's extensive interests in Manchuria. In 1910, Japan annexed Korea. By the 1920s, Japan considered itself a world military power.

This military might was made possible by industrialization after the 1870s. The state built industries such as shipyards, iron smelters, and spinning mills and sold them to well-connected entrepreneurs. Domestic companies became consumers of Western technology and applied it to the production of goods that could be sold cheaply on the world market. Industrial zones grew enormously, and there was steady migration from the countryside to the newly industrializing centers. Industrialization was accompanied by the development of a national railway system and modern communications.

In addition to state-sponsored innovations such as uniform national education and the creation of a single national dialect, popular interest in Western life increased throughout the Meiji period, starting at elite levels and eventually extending to almost all social groups, especially in the largest cities. Not all social changes were modeled on the West, however. The goal of the state was to promote nationalist ideolōgies centered on imperial institutions and the Shinto religion and to preserve a strong consciousness of national identity. Many aspects of tradition and history were codified. From Shintō to sumō, from the celebration of political loyalty and social conformity to the organization of kinship patterns, almost all aspects of life were suffused with consciousness of the national identity.

Nation building and industrialization were complete by the early twentieth century. During the Taishō period (1912–1926), the political and intellectual climate became more liberal, shaped by the large new middle classes that formed in major urban areas. Mass media and popular culture developed in parallel to the Jazz Age in the West. Political democracy was encouraged; and leftist groups agitated for political freedom and workers' rights.

With the beginning of the Shōwa period in 1926 (when Hirohito, the Emperor Shōwa, succeeded to the throne), society shifted increasingly toward the right. The military assumed a larger role in politics, and conservative forces made international "respect," military expansion, and the sanctity of imperial institutions the cornerstones of public life. Throughout the 1930s, military and colonial adventures in Manchuria and elsewhere in China led to open war, and society became increasingly militarized. The war in China grew more intense, and international condemnation of Japanese atrocities poisoned relations with the Western nations. Japan joined with Italy and Germany in the Axis because its military planners saw the United States and its interests in Asia as inimical.

Diplomatic relations with the Western powers grew worse, and on 7 December 1941, Japanese forces attacked Pearl Harbor. Japan almost simultaneously attacked all the major territories claimed by Western colonial powers, including American possessions such as Hawaii and the Philippines. The stated goal was to create a "Greater East Asian Co-Prosperity Sphere" in which Western imperialism would be banished.

In the first year and a half of the Pacific War, Japanese forces were on the offensive, but by 1944, Allied forces were recapturing the Western Pacific. Allied naval victories destroyed Japan's fleets and shipping, and bombing raids began in 1944. They destroyed most of the domestic infrastructure and took an enormous toll on civilians. Anticipating that an invasion of Japan would be a bloodbath, American military planners proceeded with the development of the atomic bomb. American military

A Japanese bride and groom hold their champagne glasses during a traditional Shintō wedding ceremony. Japanese weddings are elaborately staged and usually held in banquet halls or hotels.

scientists developed the atomic bomb in secrecy, and it was dropped on Hiroshima and Nagasaki after the Allies called for Japan's unconditional surrender. On 15 August 1945, the Emperor announced that his government had capitulated.

From 1945 until 1952, Japan was occupied by Allied troops under the command of U.S. General Douglas MacArthur. The early postwar years were a time of massive rebuilding. Millions of people were homeless, and millions more were repatriated from the former colonies. The economy was shattered, and mass starvation was a threat. Disillusionment with the cultural and social frameworks of prewar and wartime life was widespread.

The Occupation launched social and cultural reforms, including a democratic constitution and political system, universal adult suffrage, the emperor's renunciation of divinity and separation of religion from state control, agricultural land reform, the dismantling of major economic and industrial combines, the expansion of education, language reform, and expanded civil liberties.

By the mid-1950s, the initial reconstruction of society and economy had largely been accomplished, and the government had built a conservative consensus that the national priorities were economic growth and social stability, which would be achieved through the close cooperation of business and a government directed by bureaucratic elites. After the late 1950s, this "developmental state" created the social, economic, and political contexts in which ordinary people could experience middle-class urban lifestyles.

The characteristics of postwar urban middle-class life included small nuclear families in which mothers focused on their children's education and from which fathers were largely absent because of their occupational obligations. The typical white-collar urban family was secure in the knowledge that lifetime employment was the norm.

In the 1960s and 1970s, success in the domestic economy began to be felt around the world as consumer products from Japan began to dominate overseas markets. Economic growth was politically unassailable, but the costs in terms of pollution, declines in the agricultural sector, and massive urban growth without adequate infrastructure were enormous. Grassroots movements developed to combat problems spawned by the developmental ethos; those movements were limited in their effectiveness.

Throughout the 1970s and 1980s, Japan experienced unprecedented prosperity. Riding massive trade surpluses and producing top-quality products, the economy was regarded as a model for other industrial and postindustrial societies. That economic strength allowed investment in overseas assets. The affluence of ordinary consumers manifested itself in a growing market for luxury items, conspicuous consumption, and very short product cycles. Although work schedules permitted little leisure time, travel became a desired commodity. High levels of disposable income, however, masked the astronomical cost of real estate and the growing division in urban society between the wealthy and the poor.

Political leaders have rarely acknowledged Japan's role as a conqueror of neighboring countries, and the nation has not expressed explicit regret. National self-identity after the war focused instead on the pursuit of peace, and many Japanese stress their own country's losses. Because of the intensity of pacifism in contemporary society, opposition to the military runs very strong, and the article in the constitution that prohibits military involvement is of great symbolic importance.

The Shōwa Emperor died in 1989, succeeded by his son, who became the Emperor Heisei. His coronation and the elaborate Shintō rites that accompanied it were reminders of prewar rituals that evoked unwelcome memories of nationalism. The Heisei period (1989 to the present) began with great hopes that it would usher in the "Japanese century," but the era of prosperity sputtered to a halt. The Heisei period has thus far been a time of unremitting economic stagnation. Simultaneously, the political system has been shaken by the breakup of the long-ruling Liberal Democratic Party in 1993 and by widespread corruption scandals. At the beginning of the twenty-first century, there is a general sense that the postwar model of a stable, prosperous, and well-governed society has run its course.

National Identity. Throughout the Meiji period, the national government attempted to create institutions that would unify the Japanese people as citizens of a new nation-state and erase local identities and regional loyalties. The establishment of a national educational system and a national conscript army, the growth of an efficient transportation system, and the development of mass media significantly hastened the homogenization of regional differences, as did industrialization, urban development, and economic and social change. Today, variations in most aspects of daily life are more likely to reflect urban, suburban, and rural differences than regionalism.

Alternating currents of isolation from and embrace of foreign cultures form a central strand in contemporary conceptions of the national identity. Ideas about Japanese culture frequently weigh the relative contributions of indigenous inspiration and adaptations of foreign practices in forming the national culture.

Ethnic Relations. Several distinct minority populations together total less than 5 percent of the population. The minority populations whose identities have regional dimensions include Korean-Japanese, who are spread across the country but are most prominent in Ōsaka and other parts of the Kansai region; Okinawans, mainly in Okinawa but also with a sizable community in and around Ōsaka: Ainu, most of whom live in Hokkaidō; and the so-called outcaste population, who are found primarily in the Kansai region. There is a small population of Chinese-Japanese, mainly from Taiwan.

The rivalry between the Kantō region (Tōkyō and the surrounding prefectures) and the Kansai region (centered on Ōsaka and Kyōto) is the most prominent expression of regionalism. The two regions are economic and political as well as social and cultural competitors. Tōkyō is the national capital and the center of political, economic, and cultural life; Ōsaka is also a major economic center, and Kyōto was the imperial capital for a thousand years. In describing the opposition between the two regions, people point to different personalities, orientations toward tradition, openness to social change, and ways of expressing emotions. The two regions have markedly different dialects, and linguistic differences are sometimes taken as evidence of cultural sophistication, level of education, politeness, personality, and other social traits.

Urbanism, Architecture, and the Use of Space

Japan today is a highly urbanized society. Cities have a long history, beginning with the first imperial capitals, such as Nara and Kyōto. Those cities were patterned after the Chinese T'ang dynasty capital of Ch'ang-an and reflected the architectural principles of the Chinese imperial court, with walls and gates enclosing a checkerboard grid of streets organized around the institutions of imperial power and centered on an imperial compound.

During the civil wars of the fifteenth and sixteenth centuries, the characteristic urban place was the castle town, a fortified city that served as headquarters for the provincial warlord. Castle towns

Rows of apartment houses in Osaka. Approximately 65 percent of Japan's population lives in cities.

remained the key regional administrative and economic centers throughout the Tokugawa period. They were spatially segregated along class lines, and their spatial layout and social organization put priority on the defensive needs and domestic convenience of the lord and his retinue.

After the Meiji restoration, many castle towns declined as migration to new centers of industrial and economic opportunity led to a reconfiguration of the urban network. In several "treaty ports," enclaves of Western and Asian traders formed thriving cosmopolitan communities. Industrialization centered on established cities such as Tōkyō and Ōsaka but also on towns and cities that flourished around mining, shipbuilding, and textiles. The corridor along the Pacific seaboard between Tōkyō and Ōsaka gradually emerged as the central axis of the industrial complex.

Almost all the cities were heavily damaged by bombing during World War II. They were rebuilt quickly after the war, and a massive urban migration occurred throughout the 1950s and 1960s as a result of large-scale industrialization and economic development. By the 1960s, urban sprawl had created enormous megalopolises. Roughly a quarter of the population lives in the greater Tōkyō region, and less than 10 percent of the people live in rural areas. During the 1950s and 1960s, the concentration of heavy industrial facilities in densely populated areas caused environmental pollution on an unprecedented scale. Quality of life issues, including population density, environmental pollution, and the quality of the housing stock, continue to be problems.

The earliest forms of architecture are reflected in the austere simplicity of some Shintō shrines. This style is thought to reflect prehistoric influences from Oceania and Austronesia. Its features include floors raised off the ground and steeply pitched roofs with deep overhanging eaves.

In the sixth century, Chinese architectural styles were adopted, particularly for Buddhist temples and imperial structures. The construction style of such buildings proved to be resistant to earthquakes.

During the aristocratic Heian period, a distinctively Japanese architectural style began to develop. Its features include the use of thick straw mats on floors, the use of sliding and folding screens to partition larger spaces, and the use of verandas and covered walkways to link rooms. Many elements of this architectural style were adapted to more ordinary living circumstances, and by the Tokugawa period, samurai and wealthy merchant homes included many of these elements.

Since World War II, housing has been built along Western lines. Many homes still have traditional elements, but the majority of living space is equipped with generically modern furnishings. Contemporary apartments and condominiums are even less likely than single-family dwellings to have Japanese-style rooms.

Contemporary cultural attitudes toward and uses of space rely on clear distinctions between public and private spaces defined along the dimensions of sight, sound, touch, and smell. In crowded public spaces, bodies are pressed together without comment, while in many private settings it would be unthinkable to touch a stranger.

Within private settings that are used and occupied by a group of people on an ongoing basis, clear spatial patterns reflect the internal hierarchies of social position within the group and between the group and others.

FOOD AND ECONOMY

Food in Daily Life. An extremely varied diet makes use of culinary elements from around the world, including the cuisines of Korea, China, South and Southeast Asia, Europe, and North America. However, notions of "traditional" Japanese cuisine are an important element of cultural identity.

The defining characteristics include ingredients, styles of preparation, and aesthetics. White rice is a staple component of virtually every meal; other typical ingredients include soy products and seafood that is served grilled or raw. Vegetables and seafood are often prepared as pickles. The cuisine does not rely on intense flavorings. Meals ideally contrast flavors and textures among different dishes and include many small dishes rather than a main course. The visual presentation of a meal is important.

During the premodern period, meat was proscribed under the tenets of Buddhism. Vegetarian cuisine prepared in Zen monasteries relied heavily on soy products, including miso soup and tofu.

Since the late nineteenth century, tastes have been influenced by foreign cuisines, many of which have been adapted and absorbed into the national diet. Since World War II, consumption of dairy products, beef, bread, and other Western foods has increased dramatically.

Eating habits have been reshaped by changes in domestic life. Families eat fewer meals together, and sophisticated kitchen appliances have transformed domestic cooking. Food manufactures have created vast numbers of prepared dishes.

Basic Economy. The cornerstone of the economy is high-quality, high-technology manufacturing, with a focus on exports.

Commercial Activities. The wholesale, retail, and service sectors have grown dramatically as domestic standards of living have risen. Despite economic problems in the 1990s, Japan continues to be a major financial market. Primary sectors such as agriculture, fishing, and forestry have declined enormously since World War II. In 1999, less than 5 percent of the labor force was employed in agriculture, compared to 21 percent in manufacturing, 23 percent in the wholesale and retail sectors, and 26 percent in service industries.

Major Industries. *Keiretsu*—groups of companies that are closely linked through overlapping stock ownership, preferential supply relationships, coordination of economic activities, and extensive subcontracting relationships—play a central role in the economy. The flagships of such groups are heavy industrial firms, banks, and general trading companies, and the largest keiretsu control dozens of firms in sectors that range from mining to mass media.

Since World War II, business and government have maintained extremely close ties. Government agencies set both broad economic policies and measures targeted at specific sectors, and business generally cooperates with government planning. The business establishment has been a major backer of the Liberal Democratic Party, and its successors.

SOCIAL STRATIFICATION

Classes and Castes. Japanese society has been portrayed as being essentially classless or as having a class structure in which very tiny elite groups and underclasses bracket an enormous number of middle-class people. However, there are significant social differences among rural and urban residents, including family composition, educational attainment, and labor force participation. Within the urban population, social differentiation exists between the white-collar, salaried "new middle class," blue-collar industrial workers, and the self-employed petty entrepreneurial classes of shopkeepers and artisans.

The neo-Confucian class system was abolished in the 1870s, but remnants of it continue to influence cultural attitudes toward social position, including the entitlement of elite groups to lead society and ideas about conformity to social expectations. Other legacies of premodern stratification include the continued existence of "outcaste" populations. This "untouchable" status results

A farmhouse in Hokkaido. Only a small portion of Japan's work force is employed in agriculture.

from stigmas associated with Shinto and Buddhist beliefs about purity and pollution. The status is hereditary, but the people so stigmatized are indistinguishable from other residents in terms of language, ethnic background, or physical appearance.

Other marginalized urban social categories include a large floating population of day laborers and migrant laborers, who have been joined by an increasing number of illegal and quasi-legal immigrants from China, Southeast Asia, Latin America, and the Middle East.

Symbols of Social Stratification. One of the most important determinants of social stratification is educational attainment. Japanese people refer to a "credential" society, and educational credentials have often been regarded as the most important criteria for employment and marriage, particularly among the urban middle classes.

Political Life

Government. Japan has been a constitutional monarchy since the Meiji constitution of 1890. In 1947, a new constitution was drafted by advisers to the Allied occupation forces and adopted by the parliament. This constitution guarantees equality of the sexes, extends suffrage to all adult citizens, underscores the emperor's postwar renunciation of claims to divine status, and assigns the emperor a symbolic role as head of state.

Japan's parliament, known as the Diet, consists of the House of Councilors and the House of Representatives. Upper House members are elected from national and local constituencies; Lower House member are elected from local constituencies. The political power of the Lower House is much greater than that of the Upper House; prime ministers are elected from the Lower House, and most cabinet positions are also filled from the membership of that chamber.

At the local level, each prefecture has an elected governor and an elected assembly. Prefectures have limited authority over taxation and legal codes and act primarily as agents of the national government. Cities, towns, and villages have elected chief executives and assemblies. Municipalities also have limited autonomous powers and are primarily providers of daily services. Education, police, and fire protection are organized around municipal units but are controlled or standardized at the national level.

Administratively, the country is divided into forty-seven prefectures that vary in terms of their political structures. There are forty-three ordinary prefectures, three metropolitan prefectures with special administrative powers, and one administrative region for the northernmost island. Lower levels of local government and administration include counties and municipalities that are classified by population size: cities, towns, and villages.

Leadership and Political Officials. Throughout most of the postwar period, the Liberal Democratic Party (LDP), a conservative party with close ties to business and the national bureaucracy, dominated national politics. The LDP was in effect a coalition among leaders of semiautonomous factions, and its hallmark was intricate compromises and backroom deals. In 1993, the LDP split apart, and many of its factions have become independent political parties.

At the national level, government ministries wield enormous power. Since the late nineteenth century, the elite levels of the national bureaucracy have been accorded enormous respect. In many areas, ministries set policy and politicians ratify the opinions of the bureaucrats. The prestige and respect accorded to government ministries have plunged since the 1980s in response to the economic downturn and widely publicized incidents of corruption and incompetence.

Military Activity. The constitution of 1947 renounced the use of military force and forbids the state from maintaining armed forces. However, Japan maintains a "self-defense force" with substantial personnel and weaponry, supported by a growing budget.

Social Welfare and Change Programs

There is a long-standing ethos of support for education, public safety, and public health, which have been government priorities since the nineteenth century. However, many aspects of social welfare continue to be the responsibility of families, communities, and other social groups. Traditionally, villages were organized around mutual assistance, and cultural norms still encourage social groups to take care of the needs of their individual members. Care for the elderly was traditionally a family responsibility, but it has become an enormous public issue because of Japan's rapidly aging population and the decline in multi-generational households.

Nongovernmental Organizations and Other Associations

Japanese religious traditions have not emphasized charity or philanthropy. Since the nineteenth century, however, Japanese Christians have been leaders in social reform movements, and many educational, medical, and other institutions have been sponsored by Christian groups. The growth of social movements has been limited because of deferential attitudes toward the state's role in public affairs. Throughout the twentieth century, the government harnessed or supervised the activities of many nominally independent social groups and organizations. During the 1960s and 1970s, citizen movements that confronted the government became common, particularly in response to environmental issues. Since the early 1990s, there has been a dramatic increase in the numbers and range of activities of nonprofit organizations, stimulated in part by skepticism over the efficiency of government, the failure of government agencies to respond to major public issues and emergencies, and the desire to create institutions that will give more autonomy to citizens in shaping social policy.

Gender Roles and Statuses

Division of Labor by Gender. Because of Shintō beliefs about ritual purity and pollution, women were excluded from many aspects of ritual life. Women were not permitted to enter certain sacred spaces, and in some communities were forbidden to board fishing vessels or enter mines or tunnels. Most of these prohibitions have vanished, but in some ritual contexts they continue. For example, women are still excluded from sumō wrestling rings.

Neo-Confucianism defined all social roles in terms of hierarchical relationships; including the domination of husband over wife and of father over children. In the late nineteenth century, when new legal codes institutionalized family norms, the control of husband over wife was codified. In virtually all legal, political, and social contexts outside the home, women were subordinate to the male household head.

The Relative Status of Women and Men. Authority and autonomy for women traditionally were confined to domestic matters. A male household head represented the family to the outside world and controlled its public affairs; within the home, his wife might exercise great control in managing the day-to-day life of the family. Changes in family structure since the end of World War II have eroded the patriarchal domination of households.

The constitution of 1947 made equality of the sexes an established principle, and the legal framework of the traditional family structure has been dismantled. However, the practical impact of legal changes on women's status has been gradual. De-

Downtown Hiroshima and the memorial of the atomic bomb. The bombing of Hiroshima and Nagasaki brought Japan to unconditional surrender in World War II.

spite new employment laws, equality in education, and employment, career advancement remains an ideal, and "glass ceilings," gender gaps in salaries, and different educational and employment tracks remain common.

Women's social participation also reflects various gendered divides. The Japanese language includes sharply divergent styles of speech for men and women. Women often are expected to use a more polite and formal style of speech that implies deference and observance of the established hierarchy.

Marriage, Family, and Kinship

Marriage. Marriage is generally based on mutual attraction between individuals; this is known as a "love marriage" in contrast to the traditional "arranged marriage" in which a go-between negotiated a match in a process that might give parental opinions more weight than those of the prospective bride and groom. Some vestiges of arranged marriage continue and many couples rely on matchmakers to find mates. Background checks on a prospective spouse and his or her family are routine.

Weddings are almost always held in hotels or wedding halls, with a lavish banquet for several dozen guests. The ceremonies blend elements from Shintō marriage rituals and stylized adaptations of Christian weddings. Weddings are elaborately staged, and the bride and groom typically go through several changes of costume.

Domestic Unit. Most families, especially in urban areas, are nuclear, consisting of the parents and their children. Slightly extended families, such as an elderly parent living with a married couple and their children, are not uncommon, but in general extended kin groups no longer play a major role in people's daily lives.

Inheritance. The primary imperative of the family as a social institution was to survive across the generations. The household head's role ideally was to be steward for a family's intergenerational fortunes, honoring the memories of ancestors who had established the family's position and ensuring that family assets, traditions, and social standing would be passed on intact to an unbroken line of future heirs.

In traditional agrarian life, land was almost never divided, because to do so might imperil the next generation's ability to survive. So in most cases, inheritance was by a single child, usually the eldest son. In the case of an extremely prosperous family, they might be able to establish other children in newly independent family lines, which would remain forever subservient to the original line.

Various kinds of fictive kinship modeled on patterns of adoption and relationships between family banches have been used to sustain other kinds of social relationships. Patron-client relationships sometimes are referred to as parent-child ties, and may involve elaborate formal rituals of bonding. Traditional artistic life is structured around master-apprentice relationships that involve adoption and the establishment of lineages.

Kin Groups. The kinship system before World War II was based on upper-class family patterns established during the late Tokugawa period. In the late nineteenth century, the Meiji government put in place legal norms and standards that defined an ideal family structure. It established clear rules about membership, inheritance patterns, and the authority of the household head over assets and

Women in costume at the Needle Festival in Tokyo.

marriages. This legal structure was radically altered after World War II, by reducing patriarchal authority, increasing the legal rights of women, and requiring that estates be shared among children and widows.

Patterns of traditional kinship still shape the social conventions of family life. The traditional family system was organized around a multigenerational household with a single central authority: the male household head. Inheritance of a family's estate and succession to a family's occupation, social position, and obligations devolved to a single child. In most regions, this involved inheritance and succession by the oldest son. All other children were expected to leave the natal household and become members of another family system through marriage or adoption. In terms of social participation, the household was considered as a single unit rather than the sum of its members.

SOCIALIZATION

Infant Care. Infants and young children are doted on, and child rearing is a considered a very important responsibility for women in their twenties and thirties. Many women give birth to their first child after little more than a year of marriage, and married couples without children are uncommon.

Child Rearing and Education. Child rearing involves a high degree of physical and emotional interaction between mother and child; fathers are less involved. Traditionally, sons were favored over daughters, and the oldest son was raised quite differently from the other sons. Particularly close bonds between oldest sons and their mothers were not uncommon. In modern urban nuclear families, close psychological ties between mothers and children are extremely common.

Childhood socialization is guided by the widespread belief that a child is a passive and malleable being; innate talent or ability is less important than is its being properly shaped, particularly by maternal influences. These attitudes carry over into the early years of education. Differentiation of students by academic ability does not take place until the end of elementary school, and the emphasis in primary education is on social integration, self-discipline, and the fundamental skills of reading, writing, and arithmetic.

Responsibility for curriculum standards and textbook approval lies with the Ministry of Education, which must approve public and private educational institutions. There are two levels of preschool: nursery school from about three years of age and kindergarten from about five years of age. Compulsory education begins at about age six with elementary school, which lasts for six years, followed by three years of middle school. Mandatory education ends with middle school, but most students go on to high school.

Entrance examinations are generally are required for admission to all levels of private schools and for public schools beyond elementary school. At better schools, these exams can be extremely competitive. In preparation for college entrance examinations, sometimes for high school, and occasionally even at lower levels, a student may leave school to devote an entire year to studying at an examination academy.

The examination system is a source of anxiety for children and their families (pushy mothers are dubbed "education mamas"). Bullying among students is a common problem. A related problem is the reintegration of students who have studied overseas.

Higher Education. Half of high school graduates receive an advanced education. There are 165 public and 460 private universities and four-year colleges and almost 600 two-year colleges. A college degree is a prerequisite for most middle-class occupations, and many companies formally restrict their recruiting to graduates of specific universities. This creates enormous pressure to enter top-ranked schools. High schools are evaluated in terms of their success in placing their graduates prestigious universities. For many students, college is seen as an opportunity to take a break from years of preparation for examinations, and college life often is regarded as a relaxing interlude before one starts a career.

Etiquette

Etiquette can be a full-time occupation, especially in the context of traditional artistic pursuits, such as the tea ceremony, where its principles are incorporated as elements of performance. Even in more prosaic circumstances, many points of etiquette are elaborately codified, including an extensive vocabulary and grammar for polite conversation; specific principles for the selection, presentation, and reciprocation of gifts; and standards for bowing and exchanging name cards. Many people find the intricacies of etiquette daunting, and books that offer advice on these situations are steady sellers. Etiquette hinges on principles of proportional reciprocity in social hierarchies based on determinations of relative status between superior and subordinate. These relative statuses may reflect an individual's age, gender, or social role or may reflect relationships among different social institutions.

Religion

Religious Beliefs. Shintō is the contemporary term for a system of gods and beliefs about the relationship between people, the natural environment, and the state. Shintō teaches that Japan is uniquely the land of the gods. The religion has no formal dogma or scripture. During much of Japanese history, Shintō and Buddhism have coexisted and influenced each other. Shintō is closely linked to the imperial family and a nationalist ideology.

Buddhism was introduced into Japan from Korea and China during the sixth century A.D. It consists of two major branches, known as Teravada and Mahayana Buddhism. Teravada Buddhism, in general, is the branch practiced in South Asia, Central Asia, and Southeast Asia, and Mahayana is the branch that influenced Chinese, Korean, and Japanese civilizations. In essence, Teravada (a Sanskrit term meaning "the lesser or smaller vessel") teaches that salvation is available only to an elect few, those who strive to achieve enlightenment and practice good works that will enhance one's ability to transcend the snares of mortal existence. The Teravada tradition emphasizes monastic communities.

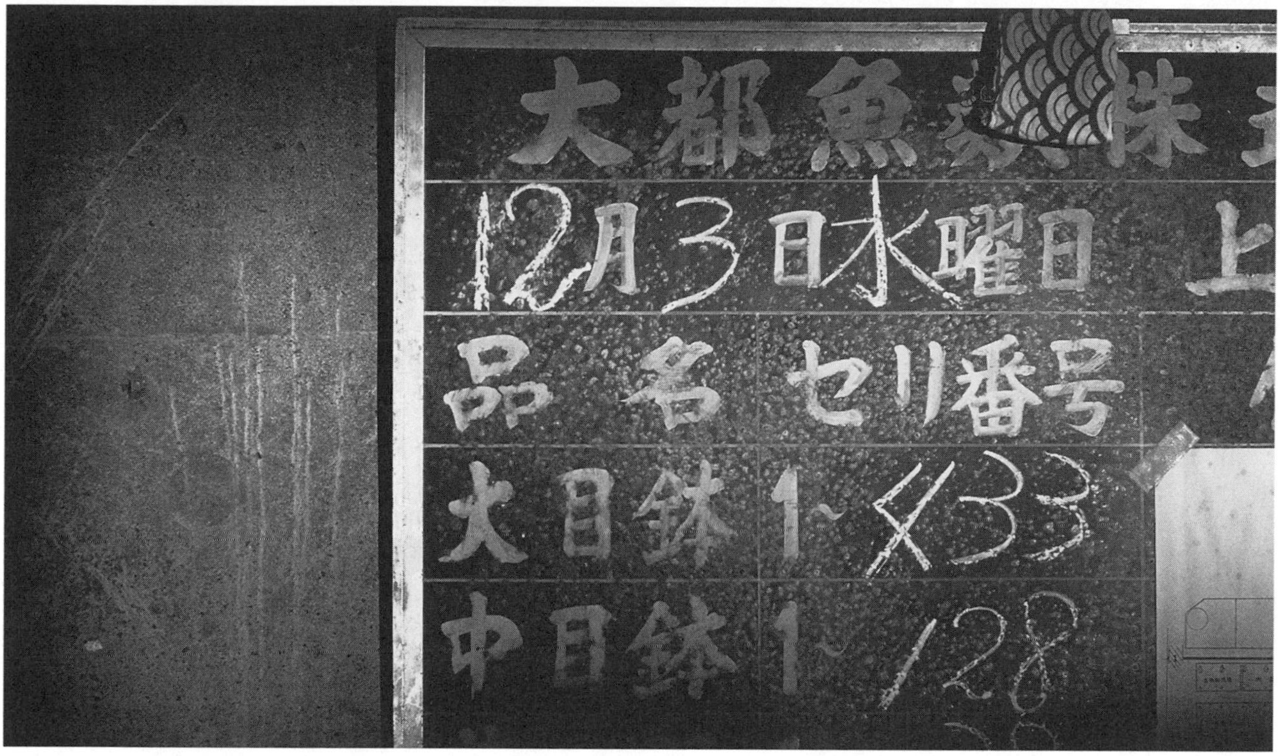

The light of dawn falls on a sign at the Tsukiji Fish Market during a tuna auction. Japanese did not become a written language until the sixth century, when Chinese orthography was introduced.

Mahayana (a Sanskrit term meaning "the greater (larger) vessel") teaches that the grace and mercy of the Buddha and the bodhisattvas (saints) lead them to intercede on behalf of the masses of humanities, and that through proper devotion anyone can hope for salvation while, during their lives on earth, remaining a part of the mundane world.

The sects of Buddhism popular in Japan have emphasized the accessibility of salvation and enlightenment of ordinary people. These include: esoteric Buddhism (e.g., the Shingon and Tendai sects) that teach mystical practices as a means of apprehending the sacred; the so–called " Pure Land Sects" that teach that prayer and devotion to Buddhist saints offer a means for salvation, through divine intercession; and Zen, which teaches that enlightenment can be obtained through meditation in which one attains an intuitive spiritual revelation or catharsis through intensive, introspective contemplation, negating the intellect (and the attachments, desires, and obsessions that human thought embodies) precisely through the effort to think through insoluble puzzles of life. The one major branch of Japanese Buddhism that does not have close connections to Chinese Buddhist traditions are the various sects of the Nichiren tradition which developed an intensely nationalistic ideology and a militant orientation to proselytizing that is uncharacteristic of other Japanese Buddhist sects.

Confucianism, Taoism, and shamanism have also influenced Japanese religion. Confucianism established ideal relations between ruler and subject, husband and wife, father and child, older brother and younger brother, and friend and friend. Although the cultural legacies of neo-Confucianism are still evident in social patterns of hierarchy and deference, neo-Confucianism did not survive beyond the nineteenth century in Japan. Taoism is a Chinese philosophical tradition that emphasizes the spiritual and mystical connection between human beings and nature. Shamanism involves mystical and ecstatic contact through mediums between the supernatural and the human world.

Since the sixteenth century, religious life has been influenced by Christianity. Frances Xavier visited the country in 1549 to initiate Catholic missionizing. By the early seventeenth century, there were an estimated three hundred thousand Catholics. The Tokugawa regime expelled the Catholic clergy in 1614 and tried to eliminate the Catholic community. However, communities of "hidden Christians" maintained their faith in isolation and secrecy. In 1870, the ban on Christianity was lifted. Although, only about 1 per cent of Japanese today consider themselves Christian, a number of intellectuals and political figures in the late nineteenth and twentieth centuries adopted Christianity. Liberal American Protestantism influenced progressive reformers and established many private universities; Catholic universities and hospitals are equally prominent.

After World War II, many new religious sects were founded and existing sects expanded enormously. Today there are hundreds of religious sects, a dozen of which are prominent. The Sōka Gakkai, an offshoot of Buddhism, has several million adherents and in the 1960s formed a conservative national political party. Buddhist and Shintō beliefs are central for most "New Religions," but many sects also incorporate eclectic elements from religions around the world.

Rituals and Holy Places. O-Shōgatsu, the New Year's holiday is the major holiday season of the year and is a time for ritual reaffirmations of social obligations. O-Bon in mid-August marks the season when the spirits of the deceased return to their homes, and many people go to their hometowns to clean graves and celebrate memories of the departed. Infants often are taken to Shintō shrines thirty days after their birth, and the holiday Shichigosan in November is an occasion for children to be honored at shrines. Shintō includes beliefs about unlucky ages, and many shrines offer purification rituals to ward off ill fortune for people passing through those dangerous years. Community celebrations generally echo Shintō observances of the agricultural cycle. Local festivals vary, but most center on the celebration of the tutelary deity of a specific village, town, or neighborhood. Today local festivals are often expressions of community sentiment rather than religious events.

Medicine and Health Care

Medical practice includes sophisticated biomedical research facilities and advanced training of physicians. An extensive system of national health insurance provides access to high quality health care for almost all people through a combination of public hospitals and physicians in private practice.

East Asian medical traditions, including herbal therapy, acupuncture, and moxibustion, are widely practiced and incorporated into popular and professional medical conceptions of health and illness. Traditional East Asian medicine is based on holistic principles that view the human organism in terms of its integration with the social and physical environment. The goal of these treatments is to restore or enhance flows of *ki* (energy or spirit) within the body and between the human body and its environment. Foods, weather conditions, types of activity, human relations, and organs of the body are regarded as possessing varying qualities of *in* and *yō*, and if these qualities are out of balance, the flow of energy within the body is impaired. A healthy body must maintain a dynamic balance, and the goal of therapy is to preserve or restore that balance by introducing countervailing elements. Treatment ideally addresses all the aspects of a person's condition from diet and sleep to exercise, personal habits, and work.

Although traditional East Asian medicine is still widely practiced, since the late nineteenth century, the dominant form of medicine has been Western-oriented biomedicine.

Secular Celebrations

In the premodern calendar, a sequence of holidays occurred on numerologically auspicious days (such as 1 January, 3 March, 5 April); these remain popular holidays.

Other important traditional holiday seasons include O-ch gen and O-seib, in late June and late December, respectively, when one is expected to repay social obligations and exchange gifts with colleagues.

The following national holidays are observed: 1 January, New Year's Day; 15 January, Adult's Day; 11 February, National Foundation Day; 21 March, spring equinox; 29 April, Green Day; 3 May, Constitution Day; 5 May, Children's Day; 20 July, Ocean Day; 15 September, Respect for the Aged Day; 21 September, the autumnal equinox; 10 October, Sports Day; 3 November, Culture Day; 23 November, Labor Thanksgiving Day; 23 December, Emperor's Birthday.

The week between 29 April and 5 May is known as Golden Week because of the three successive national holidays. Many businesses close for the entire week, and vacation travel peaks during this period.

Several Western holidays, including Christmas and Valentine's Day, have become very popular secular holidays. Valentine's Day in particular has been adapted to conform to the Japanese gift-giving etiquette of reciprocity.

The Arts and Humanities

Support for the Arts. Support for and appreciation of artistic activities is widespread in terms of popular participation and governmental encouragement.

From the high school level onward, there are public and private schools that emphasize training in the arts, and there are many arts colleges and academies in which students can prepare for careers as professional artists.

The Ministry of Education is responsible for most official support and patronage of the arts, including arts education in the schools and museums, libraries, and other institutions. The ministry generally takes a conservative stance that favors traditional arts and crafts and "high culture."

One interesting aspect of Japanese arts policy is the designation of "national treasures" by the Ministry. National treasures include great works of art—paintings, sculptures, or architectural masterpieces—but also include art forms and artists. Many folk crafts, for example, have been designated as "intangible cultural properties," and sometimes specific individual artists—a noted potter, or a weaver, or a sculptor—will be designated as a "living national treasure."

Many traditional artistic forms and aesthetic genre are regarded as distinctively Japanese: *ukiyo-e* woodblock prints, dramatic forms such as *Nō* and *Kabuki*, landscape gardening, architectural styles, poetic genre such as *haiku* (the 17-syllable verse form), Zen philosophy, flower arranging (*ikebana*), tea ceremony, and *taiko* drum music are simply a few examples.

Literature. The very flow of Japanese history is defined in artistic terms, for example in the iconic role of *The Tale of Genji*, often regarded as the world's first novel, as exemplar of the Heian period (eighth to twelfth centuries) and the sophisticated crystallization of Japanese art and civilization.

Popular culture includes *manga* (comic books) and *anime* (animation), both of which are extremely popular and have gained an international audience. New electronic media have diminished the popularity of books, magazines, and newspapers, but the publishing industry is still enormous and rates of readership remain high.

Performance Arts. Many of the traditional arts and crafts which attract the participation of hundreds of thousands of aficionados—such tea ceremony, traditional dance, flower arranging, and the like—are organized around a distinctive institutional pattern, known in Japanese as *iemoto*. Literally, the iemoto is the master or highest ranking teacher-practitioner of a particular art form and as such he or she heads a particular "school" of that art form. The position of iemoto, which is often hereditary, stands at the official head of hierchies of teachers and pupils in a hierarchical structure based on ranks of proficiency and teaching credentials certified by the iemoto organization. In this system, a pupil studies an art form with an accredited teacher and as he or she achieves greater proficiency, attains ranks that may eventually enable the student to take on lower-ranking pupils on his or her own. Even high-ranking teachers are still considered pupils of still higher ranking teachers, up to the iemoto at the apex, and some portion of each pupil's fees goes to support the teacher's teacher. Iemoto of the leading schools of flower arranging and tea ceremony routinely appear on lists of Japan's wealthiest individuals.

A large and diverse popular music industry is closely tied to television programs; popular stars ("idols") are constantly in the public view on broadcasts several times a day as singers, comedians, hosts, and advertising spokespeople and as subjects of articles in the tabloid press.

The State of the Physical and Social Sciences

Scientific and technological research is a priority of both government and industry, and since the early twentieth century the Japanese have conducted sophisticated research. In some technological fields, particularly in commercial applications of technology, Japan has been a world leader. Scientific research is carried out through universities, government research institutes, and research and development (R&D) laboratories of private industry. High levels of investment in R&D were long regarded as a critical component of industrial success.

In the social sciences, economics and econometrics are the most widespread and highly developed fields. Psychology, political science, sociology, geography, and cultural anthropology are important academic fields, as is social history. The government has an elaborate statistical system that produces detailed data with a high level of reliability. Public opinion polling is carried out by government agencies, the mass media, trade organizations, and academic researchers.

Bibliography

Allinson, Gary D. *Japan's Postwar History*, 1997.

Allison, Anne. *Nightwork*, 1994.

———. *Permitted and Prohibited Desires*, 2000.

Befu, Harumi. (ed.). *Cultural Nationalism in East Asia*, 1993.

Ben-Ari, Eyal, et al. eds. *Unwrapping Japan*, 1990.

Benedict, Ruth. *The Chrysanthemum and the Sword*, 1946.

Bestor, Theodore C. *Neighborhood Tōkyō*, 1989.

———. *Tōkyō's Marketplace*, 2001.

———, Patricia G. Steinhoff, and Victoria Lyon Bestor, eds. *Doing Fieldwork in Japan*, 2001.

Brinton, Mary C. *Women and the Economic Miracle*, 1993.

Curtis, Gerald L. *The Japanese Way of Politics*, 1988.

Dore, Ronald. *Shinohata*, 1978.

———. *Taking Japan Seriously*, 1987.

Embree, John F. *Suye Mura*, 1939.

Fields, George. *From Bonsai to Levi's*, 1983.

Fowler, Edward. *San'ya Blues*, 1997.

Garon, Sheldon. *Molding Japanese Minds*, 1997.

Gluck, Carol, and Stephan Graubard, eds. *Shōwa: The Japan of Hirohito*, 1993.

Gordon, Andrew, ed. *Postwar Japan as History*, 1993.

Hamabata, Matthews. *Crested Kimono*, 1990.

Hanley, Susan B. *Everyday Life in Premodern Japan*, 1997.

Hardacre, Helen. *Marketing the Menacing Fetus in Japan*, 1997.

Hendry, Joy. *Wrapping Culture*, 1993.

———. *Understanding Japanese Society*, 2nd ed., 1995.

Imamura, Anne E., ed. *Re-Imagining Japanese Women*, 1996.

Ivy, Marilyn. *Discourses of the Vanishing*, 1995.

Jinnai, Hidenobu. *Tōkyō A Spatial Anthropology*, 1995.

Kelly, William W. *Deference and Defiance in Nineteenth Century Japan*, 1985.

Kondo, Dorinne. *Crafting Selves*, 1990.

———. *About Face*, 1997.

Krauss, Ellis S. *Broadcasting Politics in Japan*, 2000.

——— eds. *Conflict in Japan*, 1984.

LaFleur, William R. *Liquid Life: Abortion and Buddhism in Japan*, 1992.

LeBlanc, Robin M. *Bicycle Citizens*, 1999.

Lebra, Takie S. *Japanese Women*, 1984.

———. *Above the Clouds*, 1993.

Lock, Margaret M. *East Asian Medicine in Urban Japan*, 1980.

———. *Encounters with Aging*, 1993.

Martinez, D. P. ed. *The Worlds of Japanese Popular Culture*, 1998.

McConnell, David L. *Importing Diversity*, 2000.

McCreery, John. *Japanese Consumer Behavior*, 2000.

McVeigh, Brian. *Wearing Ideology: State, Schooling, and Self-Production in Japan*, 2001.

Moeran, Brian. *Lost Innocence: Folk Craft Potters of Onta, Japan*, 1985.

———. *A Japanese Advertising Agency*, 1996.

Nakane, Chie. *Japanese Society*, 1970.

Nakano, Makiko. *Makiko's Diary: A Merchant Wife in 1910 Kyōto*, translated by Kazuko Smith. 1995.

Nelson, John K. *A Year in the Life of a Shintō Shrine*, 1996.

Noguchi, Paul. *Delayed Departures, Overdue Arrivals*, 1990.

Ohnuki-Tierney, Emiko. *Rice as Self*, 1995.

Okimoto, Daniel, and Thomas P. Rohlen eds. *Inside the Japanese System*, 1988.

Plath, David W. *Long Engagements*, 1983.

Reader, Ian. *A Poisonous Cocktail? Aum Shinrikyō's Path to Violence*, 1996.

———, and George J. Tanabe, Jr. *Practically Religious*, 1998.

Roberson, James. *Japanese Working Class Lives*, 1998.

Roberts, Glenda. *Staying on the Line*, 1994.

Robertson, Jennifer. *Takarazuka*, 1998.

Rohlen, Thomas P. *For Harmony and Strength*, 1974.

———. *Japan's High Schools*, 1983.

Ryang, Sonia. *North Koreans in Japan*, 1997.

Singleton, John., ed. *Learning in Likely Places*, 1998.

Skov, Lise, and Brian Moeran, eds. *Women, Media, and Consumption in Japan*, 1995.

Smith, Robert J. *Japanese Society*, 1983.

Stevens, Carolyn S. *On the Margins of Japanese Society*, 1997.

Tobin, Joseph J., ed. *Re-Made in Japan*, 1992.

Treat, John W., ed. *Contemporary Japan and Popular Culture*, 1996.

Turner, Christena. *Japanese Workers in Protest*, 1995.

Varley, H. Paul. *Japanese Culture*, 3rd ed. 1984.

Vlastos, Stephen, ed. *Mirror of Modernity: Invented Traditions of Modern Japan*, 1998.

Weiner, Michael, ed. *Japan's Minorities*, 1997.

White, Merry I. *The Japanese Educational Challenge*, 1987.

———. *The Material Child*, 1994.

Web Site

Japan in Figures and *Japan Statistical Yearbook.* http://www.stat.go.jp/English/1.htm

—THEODORE C. BESTOR

Jordan

Culture Name

Jordanian

Orientation

Identification. The Emirate of Transjordan was the name given to this small state when it was recognized in 1921, after the collapse of the Ottoman Empire and the promulgation of the Balfour Declaration. It was not until 1946 that Transjordan became a completely sovereign state. In 1950, Transjordan merged with part of Palestine to form the Hashemite Kingdom of Jordan. Amman is the capital and the largest city.

Location and Geography. Jordan has an area of about 35,475 square miles (91,900 square kilometers). It lies in the center of the Middle East, sharing its northern border with Syria, eastern border with Iraq, it's southern and eastern borders with Saudi Arabia, and western border with the Jordan River, the Dead Sea, and Israel. Its only seaport is the port of Aqaba. Jordan has barren deserts, fertile valleys, and colorful rock and sand mountains. It contains the lowest point on earth, the Dead Sea, and the Great Rift Valley, which was created twenty million years ago when tectonic plates shifted, stretching from Lake Tiberius south through Jordan and into eastern Africa.

Demography. In 1946, the population was about 400,000; in 1997, it reached 4.6 million, a figure twice that of 1981. After the 1967 war with Israel and Iraq's 1990 invasion of Kuwait, there were sudden and massive influxes of Palestinian Arab refugees, who now make up more than two-thirds of the population. In 1996, 1,359,000 Palestinian refugees living in Jordan were registered with United Nations; 250,000 Palestinians continue to live in ten refugee camps. Nomadic people, predominantly Bedouin, account for more than 10 percent of the total population. The population is young, with a birthrate that is double the world average; 43 percent of the people are under age fifteen. By the year 2012, the population is expected to double.

Linguistic Affiliation. Arabic is the official language. English is taught to all students and is widely spoken.

Symbolism. The flag has black, white, and green horizontal stripes with a red triangle on the hoist side bearing a white seven-pointed star. The flag of the Palestinian people is identical but does not have the white star.

History and Ethnic Relations

Emergence of the Nation. The Nabateans built the capital of their ancient Arab kingdom, Petra, in what is now Jordan between 400 B.C.E. and 160 C.E. From Mount Nebo in western Jordan, many people believe that Moses saw the Promised Land. When the Ottoman Empire collapsed after four hundred years of rule, Britain divided up the Fertile Crescent, and modern Jordan was born.

National Identity. Jordan is the only Arab country where Palestinians can become citizens. The differentiation between Jordanians, Bedouins, and Palestinians is clear in this society. Jordanians are defined as residents who have lived east of the Jordan River since before 1948. Palestinians are defined as residents whose birthright extends back to areas west of the Jordan River. People of Bedouin descent are considered to be of the purest Arab stock.

Ethnic Relations. In deserts with little vegetation and water, Bedouin families have lived in the traditional way for thousands of years. They roam freely and pay little attention to borders. Bedouins form the core of the army, occupying key positions, even though their political influence is diminishing. Palestinians are typically referred to as educated, hard-working people, and their influence in Jordan has resulted in a greater emphasis on education and

Jordan

the development of a richer, global economy. Jordanians who no longer espouse the Bedu nomad lifestyle are gradually accepting the standards of the modern Arab world.

Urbanism, Architecture, and the Use of Space

Most people live in one- or two-room apartments or houses. Affluent urban families live in larger apartments or individual homes. Buildings and homes are made of concrete, and some are made of mud and stone, with a design that allows more floors to be added, to create apartments for married sons. Privacy is very important, and many homes and other buildings open into private courtyards with concrete walls. Nomadic farmers live in tents made from the hides and fur of their animals. Amman's appearance reflects a Western influence, with modern hotels and commercial buildings. Streets are identified and numbered in an inefficient manner, and maps are hard to read and often useless.

Food and Economy

Food in Daily Life. An ancient legend tells of an Arabian shepherd who six thousand years ago put his supply of milk in a pouch made from a sheep's stomach before making a journey across the desert. The rennet in the lining of the pouch, combined with the heat of the sun, caused the milk to form curds, and cheese was discovered. Bedouin farmers keep herds of goats and sheep whose milk is used to produce cheese and yogurt. A popular cheese is called *halloumi* (similar to feta), made from goat or sheep milk and often served in a sandwich of pita-style bread or cubed in salads. Rice, legumes, olives, yogurt, flat breads, vegetables (cauliflower, eggplant, potatoes, okra, tomatoes, and cucumbers), lamb or chicken, and fruits (apricots, apples, bananas, melons, and oranges) form the basis for most meals. Main dishes of rice with spices are eaten almost daily. The main meal typically is served during the middle of the afternoon. A covering is placed on the floor, with a large tray of rice and meat placed in the center surrounded by small dishes of yogurt and salad. Torn pieces of bread are folded in half and used to scoop the food. The left hand is never used to feed oneself.

Food Customs at Ceremonial Occasions. When people visit family and friends, tea, Turkish-style or Arabic-style coffee, or fruit juice is served. Often this meal includes sweets, especially on holidays. The national main dish is *Mansaf*, which consists of lamb cooked in dried yogurt and served with seasoned rice on flat bread. *Mansaf* is always served on holidays and special family occasions such as visits to relatives or friends, engagements, and weddings.

Basic Economy. The economy is based on free enterprise. The service sector, consisting of government, tourism, transportation, communication, and financial services contributes the most to the economy, employing 70 percent of the workforce. Amman has developed into a regional business center.

Land Tenure and Property. Land ownership is the goal of many, but few can afford the cost. Except for the very wealthy, most people live in rented housing.

Commercial Activities. Because most of the country is desert, less than 4 percent of the land is cultivated. Natural resources are scarce, and no oil has been found. The country's archaeological sites draw more than two million visitors a year.

Major Industries. Potash, phosphate, and gypsum mining and the manufacturer of cement, fertilizers, and refined petroleum products are the largest industries.

Trade. Jordan is among the world's top three potash exporters. Since the Gulf War, the number of immigrants has increased greatly, leading to a severe trade deficit and a labor market that has not produced enough jobs.

Division of Labor. Jordan's economy is heavily impacted by its location in the Middle East, the arid landscape, its relationship with its neighbors, and its dependence on foreign aid. Its largest sectors are finance, which employs 22 percent of its labor force; transportation, which employs 16 percent; and the industrial sector, which employs 17 percent. Tourism offers the greatest prospect for development.

Social Stratification

Jordan's political and social systems are a mix of new and old, traditional and non-traditional, Bedouin and Palestinian.

Classes and Castes. All social and political systems of Jordan are centered around extended patriarchal family units based on ancestry and wealth. Family units are often led by sheikhs whose rule depends on the size of their families, their wealth, and the will of their personalities. After the death of a sheikh, the eldest son ascends to the position of head of the family.

Symbols of Social Stratification. The emerging modern Arab culture values a college education, Mercedes cars, and a home in an urban area as symbols of success. However, in traditional Arab culture, camel breeders are still considered to be highest on the social scale. Traditional clans consider anyone outside their clan to be inferior, so the tradition of only marrying a person from within their families continues.

Political Life

Government. Since 1951, Jordan has been a constitutional hereditary monarchy with a parliamentary form of government. It is politically stable, with freedom of religion, the press, and private property guaranteed. There is an ongoing program of democratization. In 1989 parliamentary elections were instituted, and since that time, martial law has been lifted and political parties have been legalized. Elections were held in 1993 and 1997.

Leadership and Political Officials. In 1999, King Hussein, the longest-serving head of state in the world, died. Hussein's oldest son, Prince Abdullah,

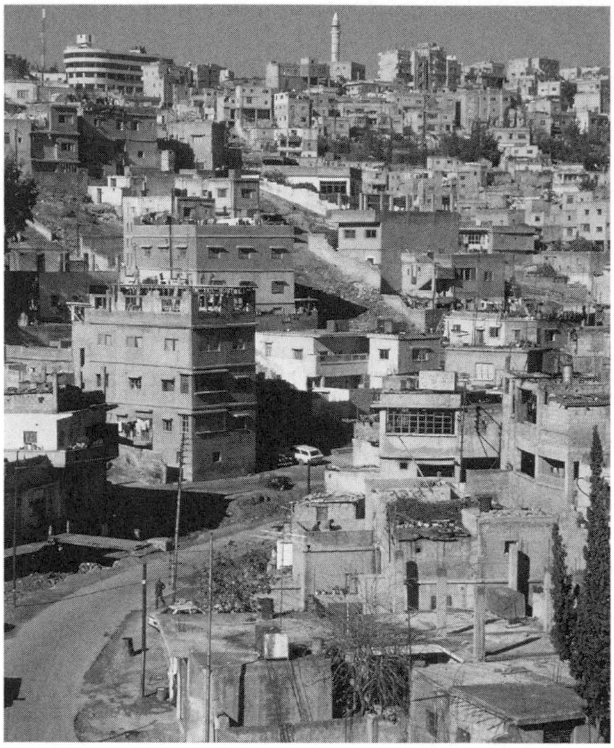

Buildings in Amman, a city that reflects western influence.

succeeded him. King Abdullah Ibn al-Hussein has indicated that he intends to follow his father's policies. He wields wide power over the government and appoints the prime minister.

Jordan's present legislative branch consists of an eighty-member elected Lower House and a forty-member Upper House. After a bill is approved by the Lower House and Senate, it is given to the King, who either grants consent by Royal Decree or returns the bill unapproved. Jordan's Constitution guarantees an independent judicial branch, dividing the courts into three categories: civil, religious, and special courts. The Jordanian civil legal system has its foundations in the Code Napoléon, a French legal code.

Social Problems and Control. Many of the country's laws are based on the Koran and the Hadith, a collection of Mohammed's sayings. These laws are enforced in religious courts called Sharia courts, which have jurisdiction over personal matters. Chastity is demanded of all single women. If a woman's chastity is compromised, a male relative may feel obligated to murder her to save the family's honor. When these cases go to court, often the charges are dropped or the murderer receives a short sentence.

Jordan has a low crime rate by international standards, with few petty crimes such as robbery reported.

Military Activity. Jordan maintains an army, an air force, and a small navy. The total strength of the armed forces in 1998 was 104,000 active members and 35,000 reserves. There is a paramilitary force that includes twenty thousand civil militia members and ten thousand public security officers. Jordan is a leader of peace efforts in the Middle East and is at peace with its neighbors.

Social Welfare and Change Programs

There is not a comprehensive welfare scheme, but the government administers medical and health services.

Nongovernmental Organizations and Other Associations

Nongovernmental organizations are involved with the environment, women, children, and economic issues. The royal family is supportive of many charitable foundations. Thirty miles north of Amman, Jerash hosts an annual summer Festival of Culture and Arts administered by the Noor Al-Hussein Foundation. The Jordanian Hashemite Fund for Human Development has social development centers throughout the country that help women and children.

Gender Roles and Statuses

Division of Labor by Gender. Most women have their lives controlled by their closest male relatives. Despite the limitations placed on them, they have made advances in education in a country where the practice of educating women only began three or four decades ago. Balancing customs and traditions at home with obedience to their husbands and the demands of a career remains a difficult challenge. When women work, they receive extensive benefits and sometimes equal pay. The 1997 census placed the proportion of women in the workforce at 14 percent, up from 8 percent in 1979. The unofficial unemployment rate for women is 65 percent.

The Relative Status of Women and Men. Sons are prized, and this status continues throughout adulthood. Most Muslim women cover their heads with scarves. A small minority cover their heads and faces with a veil. Segregation of the sexes occurs all public situations, and there is limited interaction be-

Workmen lay a water pipeline in the Jordan Valley. Most of Jordan is desert.

tween men and women. It is common for women to eat apart from men in restaurants. Unless they are married or related, men and women do not sit together on public transportation.

Marriage, Family, and Kinship

Marriage. Getting married and having children are top priorities. Most marriages are arranged by the father of the bride. Often cousins marry each other, and the couple may barely know each other until the engagement is announced. The wedding has two celebrations: an engagement party and a wedding party. After the engagement party, the process of dating and getting to know each other begins. After the engaged woman and man have signed the papers at the engagement party, they are legally married. If they choose not to proceed, even though they have not lived together, they must divorce. Brides must be virgins on the wedding night. After marriage, every aspect of a woman's life is dictated by her husband. She cannot obtain a passport or travel outside the country without his written approval. At any time, a husband may take another wife. Polygamy with up to four wives is legal. Divorce is legal. When there is a divorce, custody of the children automatically goes to the father, and for this reason, women choose to remain in a marriage even when there are other wives. Divorced women are viewed as outcasts.

Domestic Unit. The typical family is extended, with family size decreasing since 1979 to about six members per family. The scarcity of natural resources, especially the chronic shortage of water, makes population control vital. To slow the rapid growth rate, birth spacing programs have increased awareness of the benefits of family planning, and many wives now use contraceptives.

Inheritance. Inheritance is guided by Islamic law. A woman receives half the amount that a man receives.

Kin Groups. Kinship relationships are patriarchal. Extended family ties govern social relationships and tribal organization.

Socialization

Infant Care. Women are primary caregivers for infants and small children. After the first son is born, the father and mother take the name of the son. If the son's name is Mohammed, the father becomes Abu Mohammed, meaning "father of Mohammed," and the mother becomes Om Mohammed, or "mother of Mohammed."

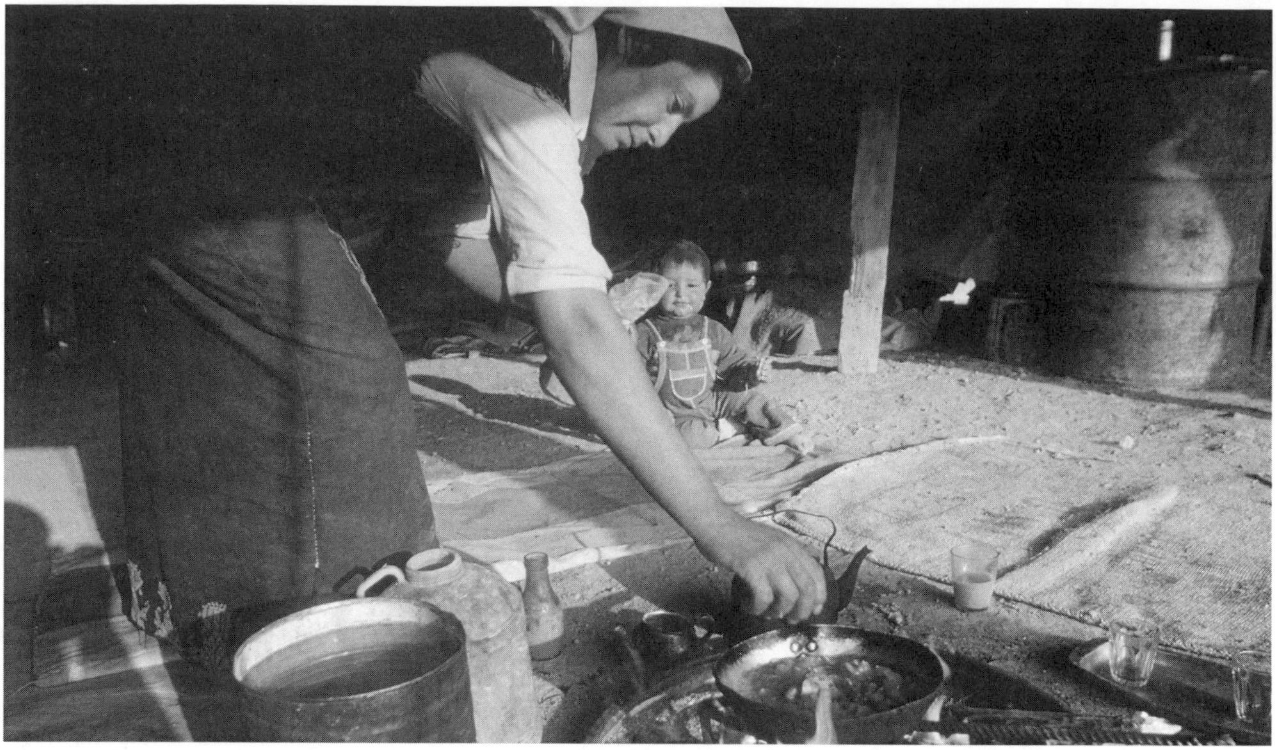

Bedouin woman preparing a meal. Free-wandering Bedouins have lived in the traditional way for thousands of years.

Child Rearing and Education. Children love to belly-dance with people watching and clapping their hands and women making a vocal expression by moving their tongues rapidly back and forth between their lips. Primary education is free and compulsory, starting at the age of six years until a child is sixteen years old. The United Nations Relief and Works Agency for Palestine Refugees provides schooling for Palestinian refugees. Outside the classroom, children participate in few activities away from the family.

Higher Education. All students are required to take an extensive examination called *Tawjehieh* before graduating from secondary school and as a prerequisite for entering universities and colleges. The top male and female students attend state universities and numerous private colleges. The literacy rate is over 86 percent.

ETIQUETTE

Greetings and farewells are lengthy and sincere. Even answering a telephone involves saying "how are you?" in several different ways. Visitors and/or friends frequently are invited into homes for dinner, where they are showered with kindness and food. Women dress modestly and often are offended by exposed flesh. Most Muslims do not drink alcohol. Shoes are always removed before entering a mosque, and this custom extends to homes as well. *Shib-shibs* (flip-flop sandals) are always put on before entering a bathroom, the feet and are never put on a coffee table, footstool, or desk. It is forbidden and disrespectful to expose the bottoms of the feet. Same-sex friends hold hands, hug, and kiss in public, but there is limited touching between men and women. A man does not shake hands with a woman unless she offers her hand first.

RELIGION

Religious Beliefs. The state religion is Muslim, as indicated in the constitution. Ninety percent of the population adheres to the Sunni branch. About 6 percent of the people are Christian.

Religious Practitioners. Imams, leaders of prayer in a Muslim mosque, hold an important role in this Muslim country. In most smaller and rural communities they are the political leaders as well.

Rituals and Holy Places. Jordan has a rich religious history. For Jews and Christians, it is part of the Holy Land, sacred for its connection to the Jewish patriarchs Abraham and Moses, as well as Christian biblical figures such as John the Baptist. Jordan is equally important in the history of Islam, as many tombs of Prophet Mohammed's companions are located in Jordan. Jordan is where the non-Arab world first contacted Islam more than fifteen hundred years ago.

One of the five essential Pillars practiced by Muslims is the recitation of prayers five times a day. Calls to prayers are announced publicly by mosques and can be heard throughout the nation. The devout unroll a small prayer rug and face Mecca to pray. Ramadan, the ninth month of the Islamic calendar, is a time of fasting from sunrise until sunset. Most public restaurants do not open for business until just before sunset. Throughout Ramadan and the celebration commemorating its end, of families mark the occasion with large feasts and special sweets. Another Pillar of Islam is the Hajj, the holy pilgrimage made at least once during a lifetime to Mecca. Many pilgrims travel through Jordan on the way to Mecca in Saudi Arabia.

Medicine and Health Care

Excellent medical care is available, especially in Amman. For the typical family, finding the money to pay for medical insurance and preventive care is difficult. Life expectancy is sixty-seven years for mens and seventy years for women. Most children are fully immunized.

Secular Celebrations

Jordanians follow the Islamic calendar. National holidays include Arbor Day (15 January), Arab League Day (22 March), and Independence Day (25 May). Religious holidays include Id al-Fitr (the end of Ramadan), Id al-Adha (the Feast of the Sacrifice), the Islamic New Year, the birthday of Mohammed, and Leilat al-Meiraj (the Ascension of Mohammed).

The Arts and Humanities

Support for the Arts. In 2000, King Abdullah ordered that government workers be given Fridays and Saturdays off, hoping they would find time to develop new interests and travel to sites such as Petra. The government promotes cultural festivals, encourages the revival of handicrafts, and takes steps to preserve the country's archaeological and historical heritage.

Literature. The country's most famous poet is Mustafa Wahbi al-Tal, who is among the major Arab poets of the twentieth century. Al-Tal was a political and social activist who devoted twenty years of his life to regaining the rights of gypsies and became a member of the gypsy community.

Graphic Arts. Folk art survives in tapestries, leather crafts, pottery, and ceramics. Wool and goat hair rugs with colorful tribal designs are manufactured.

Performance Arts. Popular culture takes the form of songs, ballads, and storytelling. Villagers have special songs for births, weddings, funerals, planting, plowing, and harvesting.

The State of the Physical and Social Sciences

Since the 1960s, a number of higher learning institutions have opened in Jordan, foremost among them the University of Jordan (1962) in Amman, Yarmouk University (1976) in Irbid, and Jordanian University Science and Technology (1996) in Irbnil. These centers are recognized for their Islam, Arabic language, and Middle East peace and conflict studies.

Bibliography

Chebaro, Lina, Halawani, Bassam, and Nada Mosbah. *Arabic Cooking Step by Step,* 1997.

Dallas, Roland. *King Hussein: A Life on the Edge,* 1998.

De Blij, H. J., and Peter O. Muller. *Geography: Regions and Concepts,* 6th ed., 1991.

Discovery Channel. *Jordan Insight Guide,* 1999.

Fernea, Elizabeth Warnock. *In Search of Islamic Feminism: One Woman's Global Journey,* 1998.

Friedman, Thomas L. *From Beirut to Jerusalem,* 1995.

Goodwin, Jan. *Price of Honor: Muslim Women Lift the Veil of Silence on the Islamic World,* 1994.

Hussein, King of Jordan. *Uneasy Lies the Head: The Autobiography of His Majesty King Hussein I of the Hashemite Kingdom of Jordan,* 1962.

———. *My War With Israel,* 1969.

Sedlaczek, Brigitte. *Petra: Art and Legend,* 1997.

Shumsky, Adaia and Abraham. *A Bridge across the Jordan: The Friendship between a Jewish Carpenter and the King of Jordan,* 1997.

Viorst, Milton. *Sandcastles: The Arabs in Search of the Modern World,* 1994.

Web Sites

The Hashemite Kingdom of Jordan (official government site). http://www.kinghussein.gov.jo

The Jordan Star. http://star.arabia/com

Palestinian National Authority. http://www.pna.net

—Darlene Schmidt

KAZAKHSTAN

CULTURE NAME

Kazakh, Kazakhstani, Republic of Kazakhstan (note the spelling of Kazakhstan can be found with or without an *h*; currently it is officially spelled with an *h*)

ALTERNATIVE NAMES

Kazak, Central Asian or Post-Soviet People

ORIENTATION

Identification. The Kazakh steppeland, north of the Tien Shan Mountains, south of Russian Siberia, west of the Caspian Sea, and east of China, has been inhabited since the Stone Age. It is a land rich in natural resources, with recent oil discoveries putting it among the world leaders in potential oil reserves. The newly independent Republic of Kazakhstan ranks ninth in the world in geographic size (roughly the size of Western Europe) and is the largest country in the world without an ocean port.

The Kazakhs, a Turkic people ethnically tied to the Uighur (We-goor) people of western China and similar in appearance to Mongolians, emerged in 1991 from over sixty years of life behind the Iron Curtain. Kazakhstan, which officially became a full Soviet socialist republic in 1936, was an important but often neglected place during Soviet times. It was to Kazakhstan that Joseph Stalin exiled thousands of prisoners to some of his most brutal gulags. It was also to Kazakhstan that he repatriated millions of people of all different ethnicities, in an effort to "collectivize" the Soviet Union. Kazakhstan was also the site of the Soviet nuclear test programs and Nikita Khrushchev's ill-conceived "Virgin Lands" program. These seventy years seem to have had a profound and long-lasting effect on these formerly nomadic people.

The process of shedding the Soviet Union and starting anew as the democratic Republic of Kazakhstan is made difficult by the fact that a large percentage of Kazakhstan is not Kazakh. Russians still make up 34.7 percent of the population, and other non-Kazakhs such as Ukrainians, Koreans, Turks, Chechnians, and Tatars, make up another 17 percent. Many of the non-Kazakh people of Kazakhstan have met attempts by the Kazakh government to make Kazakh the central, dominant culture of Kazakhstan with great disdain and quiet, nonviolent resistance. The picture is further complicated by the fact that many Kazakhs and non-Kazakhs are struggling (out of work and living below the poverty level). Democracy and independence have been hard sells to a people who grew accustomed to the comforts and security of Soviet life.

Location and Geography. Kazakhstan, approximately 1 million square miles (2,717,300 square kilometers) in size, is in Central Asia, along the historic Silk Road that connected Europe with China more than two thousand years ago. Five nations border current-day Kazakhstan: China to the east; Russia to the north; the Caspian Sea to the west; and Turkmenistan, Uzbekistan, and Kyrgyzstan to the south. A pair of beautiful mountain ranges, the Altay and the Tien Shan, with peaks nearly as high as 22,966 feet (7,000 meters), runs along Kazakhstan's southeastern border. The area north and west of this is the vast Kazakh steppe. Life on the steppe is harsh, with extreme temperatures and intense winds. The lands leading up to the Caspian Sea in the west are below sea level and rich in oil. The historic Aral Sea is on Kazakhstan's southern border with Uzbekistan. In recent years the sea has severely decreased in size and even split into two smaller seas due to environmental mismanagement. The climate of Kazakhstan is extremely variable. The very south experiences hot summers, with temperatures routinely over 100 degrees Fahrenheit (38 degrees Celsius). The very north, which is technically southern Siberia, has extreme winters, with lows of well below 0 degrees Fahrenheit (−18 degrees Celsius), with strong winds, making the temperature feel like −50 to −60 degrees Fahrenheit

Kazakhstan

(−46 to −51 degrees Celsius). There are beautiful parts of Kazakhstan, with lakes and mountains that would rival many tourist destinations in the world. There are also parts of Kazakhstan that are flat and barren, making it seem at times like a forsaken place.

The capital of Kazakhstan was moved in 1996 to Astana, in the north-central part of the country far from any of Kazakhstan's borders. The former capital, Almaty, is still the largest city and most important financial and cultural center. It is located at the base of the Tien Shan Mountains in the far southeast near both China and Kyrgyzstan.

The move of the capital was very controversial among many in Kazakhstan. There are three main theories as to why the move was made. The first theory contends that the move was for geopolitical, strategic reasons. Since Almaty is near the borders with China and Kyrgyzstan (which is a friend but too close to the Islamic insurgent movements of Tajikistan and Afghanistan), this theory maintains that the new, central location provides the government with a capital city well separated from its neighbors. A second theory asserts that the capital was moved because Kazakh president Nursultan Nazarbayev wanted to create a beautiful new capital with new roads, buildings, and an airport. The final theory holds that the Kazakh government wanted to repatriate the north with Kazakhs. Moving the capital to the north would move jobs (mostly held by Kazakhs) and people there, changing the demographics and lessening the likelihood of the area revolting or of Russia trying to reclaim it.

Demography. The population of Kazakhstan was estimated to be 16,824,825 in July 1999. A census taken just after the fall of the Soviet Union in 1991 indicated a population of more than 17 million. The decreasing nature of Kazakhstan's population (−.09 percent in 1999) is due, in part, to low birthrates and mass emigration by non-Kazakhs, mainly Russians and Germans (Kazakhstan's net migration rate was −7.73 migrants per 1,000 people in 1999). Given the emigration, Kazakhstan's ethnic make up is ever-changing. For 1999 the best estimates were Kazakhs 46 percent, Russians 34.7 percent, Ukrainians 4.9 percent, Germans 3.1 percent, Uzbeks 2.3 percent, Tartar 1.9 percent, and others 7.1 percent. Many observers predict that continued emigration by non-Kazakhs and encouraged higher birthrates of Kazakhs by the government will lead to Kazakhs increasing their numbers relative to other ethnicities in Kazakhstan.

Linguistic Affiliation. Language is one of the most contentious issues in Kazakhstan. While many countries have used a common language to unite disparate ethnic communities, Kazakhstan has not been able to do so. Kazakh, the official state language of Kazakhstan, is a Turkic language spoken by only 40 percent of the people. Russian, which is spoken by virtually everyone, is the official language and is the interethnic means of communications among Russians, Kazakhs, Koreans, and others.

The move to nationalize Kazakhstan through the use of Kazakh has presented two main problems. During Soviet times, when Russian was the only real language of importance, Kazakh failed to keep up with the changing vocabulary of the twentieth century. In addition, Russian is still very important in the region. Knowledge of Russian allows Kazakhstan to communicate with the fourteen other former Soviet republics as well as with many people in their own country.

Symbolism. Kazakhs are historically a nomadic people, and thus many of their cultural symbols reflect nomadic life. The horse is probably the most central part of Kazakh culture. Kazakhs love horses, riding them for transportation in the villages, using them for farming, racing them for fun, and eating them for celebrations. Many Kazakhs own horses and keep pictures of them in their houses or offices. Also a product of their formally nomadic lives is the *yurt,* a Central Asian dwelling resembling a tepee, which was transportable and utilitarian on the harsh Central Asian steppe. These small white homes are still found in some parts of Kazakhstan, but for the most part they are used in celebrations and for murals and tourist crafts.

Also central to Kazakh symbolism are Muslim symbols. Kazakhs are Muslim by history, and even after seventy years of Soviet atheism, they incorporate Islamic symbols in their everyday life. The traditionally Muslim star and crescent can be widely seen, as can small Muslim caps and some traditionally Muslim robes and headscarves in the villages.

Kazakhs are also very proud of their mountains, rare animals such as snow leopards, eagles, and falcons (a large eagle appears on the Kazakh flag under a rising sun), and their national instrument, the dombra, a two-stringed instrument with a thin neck and potbelly base, resembling a guitar.

The symbols of Soviet Kazakhstan still exist and are important to some people. At its peak there was hardly a town that did not have a statue of Lenin; a street named after the revolution; or a large hammer, sickle, and Soviet red star on many of its houses and public buildings. Much like the attempt to assert the Kazakh language, the increased use of Kazakh symbols on money, in schools, on television, and in national holidays has been tempered by those who do not wish to part with the Soviet symbols of the past.

History and Ethnic Relations

Emergence of the Nation. Humans have inhabited the Central Asian steppe since the Stone Age. Dramatic seasonal variations coupled with movements, conflicts, and alliances of Turkic and Mongol tribes caused the people of Central Asia often to be on the move.

In the eighth century a confederation of Turkish tribes, the Qarluqs, established the first state in Kazakhstan in what is now eastern Kazakhstan. Islam was introduced to the area in the eighth and ninth centuries, when Arabs conquered what is now southern Kazakhstan. The Oghuz Turks controlled western Kazakhstan until the eleventh century.

The eleventh through the eighteenth centuries saw periodic control over Kazakhstan by Arabs, Turks, and Mongols. The people of Kazakhstan consider themselves great warriors and still honor many of the war heroes of this time period.

What might be called the modern-day history of Kazakhstan started in the eighteenth century, when the three main hordes (groups) of Kazakh nomads (who had begun to distinguish themselves linguistically and culturally from the Uzbeks, Kyrgyz, and Turkmen) started seeking Russian protection from Oryat raiders from the Xhinjian area of western China.

In 1854 the Russian garrison town of Verny (modern-day Almaty) was founded. It was not long before Russian incursions into Central Asia became much more frequent. By the end of the nineteenth century the Russians had a firm foothold in the area and were starting to exert their influence on the nomadic Kazakhs, setting the stage for the twentieth century transformation of the region by the Soviets.

The Soviet Union's interaction with Kazakhstan started just after the 1917 October Revolution, with Lenin granting the peoples of Central Asia the right to self-determination. This did not last long, and during the 1920s Moscow and the Red Army put down Muslim revolts throughout Central Asia after the Russian civil war. Centuries of nomadic tribal wars among Turks, Mongols, and Arabs were being replaced by a new kind of domination: the military might of the Red Army and the propagandistic Soviet machine of Stalin's Kremlin.

In 1924 Kazakhstan was given union republic status, and in 1936 full Soviet socialist republic status—a status that did not change until Kazakhstan was the last Soviet republic to break from Moscow and declare independence, on 16 December 1991.

The years between 1924 and 1991 were truly transformative for the people and land of Kazakhstan. Factories were built, schools reorganized, borders closed, and life changed in almost every facet. Soviet years were a time of immigration into Kazakhstan. Stalin's collectivization campaign after World War II brought people from the Caucasus, southern Russia, and the Baltic to Kazakhstan. Khrushchev's "Virgin Land" campaign in 1954 made much of Kazakhstan into farmland, run by huge collective farms, largely made up of the Russian and Ukrainian settlers brought in to run them.

Soviet wars were also very difficult for this region. World War II and the war in Afghanistan in the late 1970s killed many young Kazakh men and women. Kazakhstan was integral to the Soviet Union for its oil and minerals, fertile farmlands, tough warriorlike heritage, and its vast, wide-open lands suitable for nuclear testing.

In 1986 the Soviet Union and the world got a glimpse of how intact Kazakh nationalism remained. Riots broke out on 16 December in reaction to the Russian Gennady Kolbin being named head of the Kazakh Communist Party machine. Kazakhstan had been changed by the Soviet Union; its people looked and acted differently and its language had partially been neglected, but the Kazakh people were still proud of their history and their heritage.

In 1991, then Kazakh Communist Party leader Nursultan Nazarbayev declared independence for Kazakhstan. He had stayed faithful to Moscow the longest and supported Mikhail Gorbachev's efforts to keep the Union intact. The years since 1991 have seen many changes in Kazakhstan and its people. Democracy is attempting to take root in a land that hasn't known democracy at any time in its three thousand-year history. Nomadism, tribal warfare, Mongol dynasties, foreign domination, and Soviet communism have been all the Kazakh land has known.

National Identity. Several factors that are unique to Kazakhstan, its land, and its history, unite its people. Kazakhstanis are proud of the nation's abundant natural resources, agricultural potential, and natural beauty. They are also united in their shared history as a neglected republic during the Soviet years. While they toiled under Soviet rule, producing much of the agricultural and industrial product for the Soviet Union, the rest of the Union looked upon Kazakhstan as a barren place.

A very structured and uniform educational system exists in Kazakhstan. All ethnicities, whether urban or rural, study a similar curriculum. Thus, students throughout the country share the same education.

Ethnic Relations. According to many people of Kazakhstan, during the Soviet years they wanted for very little. Everyone had jobs, everyone had a house or an apartment, and food was abundant. The Kazakhs were part of a powerful union that challenged the United States and the other powers of the world. They lived in a socialist system that based its success on the hard work of its people. But to say that everything was equal and that there were no underlying tensions, especially between Russians and Kazakhs, would be untrue. Since the very days of Russian influence in Central Asia, many Kazakhs have met their presence with contempt and skepticism. This was furthered during the Soviet years when Russian language, Russian culture, and the power in Moscow took very prominent places in Kazakhstan. While tensions between the two groups were often subtle and barely visible, they erupted violently during the 16 December, 1986 riots over Russian control of the Kazakh Communist Party. The day of 16 December is a very important and proud one in recent Kazakh history, as evidence of their nationalism and unity as a people (in 1991, when independence was declared, 16 December was symbolically chosen as Independence Day).

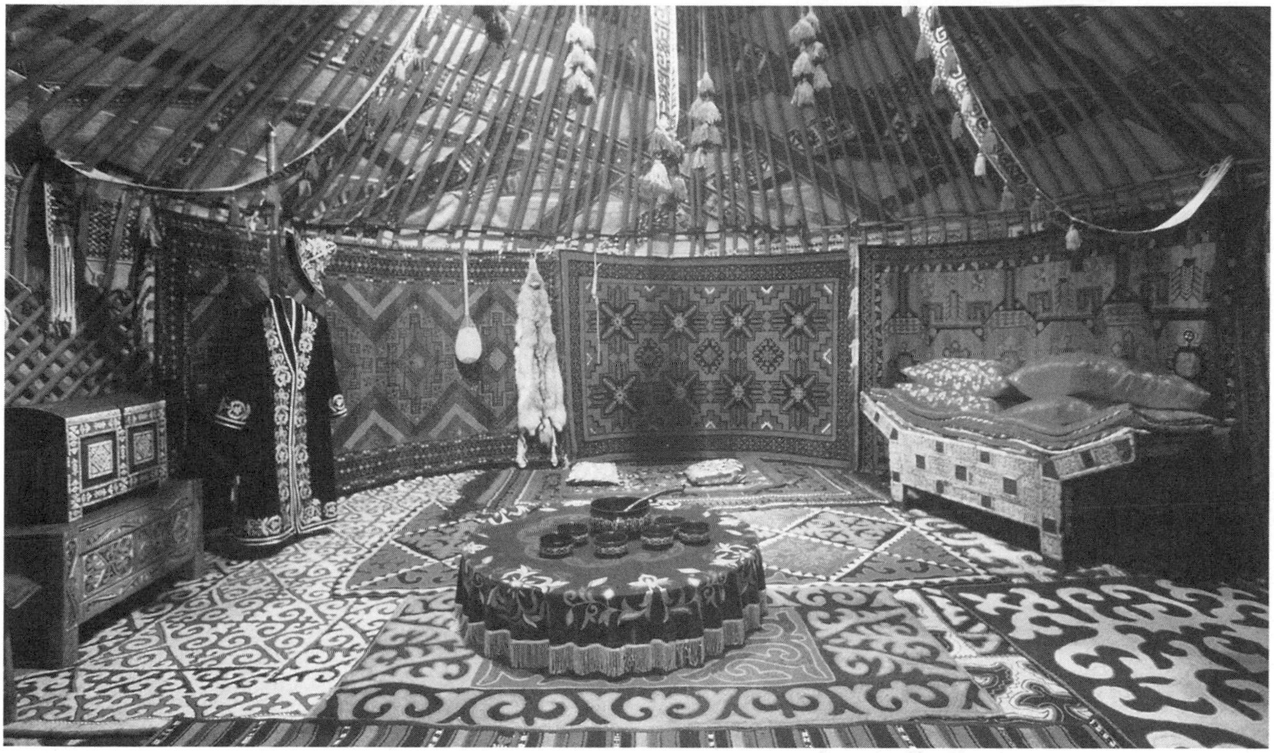

Interior of a yurt, a mobile dwelling used by nomadic Kazakhs.

The latent tensions of 150 years of Russian influence in Kazakhstan, coupled with the increasingly more visible disapproval by Kazakhs of Russian domination, set the stage for the difficult first years of post-Soviet life. Kazakh nationalism has been unpopular with many non-Kazakhs, especially the Russians, and thousands have left as a result. Streets and schools have been renamed, statues of Lenin taken down, the national anthem and flag changed, old Soviet holidays forgotten, and new Kazakh holidays promoted. Ethnic tensions have been further strained by an economy and a political system that has produced extreme haves and have-nots. The guarantee of work, an apartment, free health care, and higher education that kept tensions low for seventy years have been replaced by unemployment, decaying health care, and expensive higher education.

Urbanism, Architecture, and the Use of Space

The yurt is the main architectural remnant from the Kazakh nomadic years. The yurt is a round, transportable dwelling not unlike the Native American tepee (the yurt being shorter and flatter than the tepee). The yurt was very useful to the nomadic Kazakhs, who needed a sturdy dwelling to protect them from the elements of the harsh plains, and its inhabitants would sit and sleep in them on thick mats on the floor. Very few Kazakhs live in yurts today, but sitting on the floor is still very common in many Kazakh homes, many preferring it to sitting in chairs or at a regular table. Yurts are widely used in national celebrations and in Kazakh arts and poetry as reminders of the Kazakhs' nomadic past.

Russian settlers in Kazakhstan also had an effect on Kazakhstani architecture. Small A-frame houses, Russian orthodox churches, and many new wooden buildings went up as Russians settled the area in the eighteenth and nineteenth centuries. Very few of these building have survived the times besides some churches, which have been restored and protected.

The twentieth century and the Soviet Union brought many architectural changes to Kazakhstan. Hard work and unity were two central themes of the socialist years in Kazakhstan, and the architecture from this period is a large reflection of that. Most of the buildings built during this period were big and utilitarian. Hospitals, schools, post offices, banks, and government buildings went up from Moscow to Almaty in basically the same shape, size, and color. The materials used were usually just as rough, with concrete and brick being the most common.

Large Soviet apartment blocks went up in all of the cities across Kazakhstan. Arranged in small microdistricts, these buildings were usually five or six stories high and had three to four apartments of one, two, or three bedrooms each per floor.

The villages and collective farms of Kazakhstan were of a different kind of Soviet architecture. Small two- to three-room, one-story houses, usually painted white and light blue (the light blue is thought to keep away evil spirits), adorn the countryside in Kazakhstan. The government built all houses, and there was no individualizing, excessive decorating, or architectural innovation. Very few, if any, houses were allowed to be more than one story high. A big house or an elaborate apartment was thought to be gaudy and very bourgeois.

While work and utilitarianism had definite effects on Kazakhstan's architecture, so did the belief in unity and the rights of the people. Public space was very important to the Soviets; in fact, nothing was privately owned, including one's home. Large collective farms were formed, transforming small villages into working communities, all with the same goal. Large squares and parks were built in almost every town and city. Everything belonged to the people, through the Communist apparatus in Moscow.

Times have certainly changed, as has the architecture in these post-Soviet days of independence. The old buildings, and the people who designed and built them, still exist. Some parts of Kazakhstan are in good repair and upkeep, while other parts look like an old amusement park that hasn't been used in years. In some cases cranes and forklifts stand in the exact places they were in when independence was declared and government money ran out. Rusted and covered in weeds and grass, much of the Soviet architecture and the people occupying it are in desperate need of help. This picture is further complicated and contrasted by the introduction of new buildings and new wealth by some people in Kazakhstan.

Oil money, foreign investments, and a new management style have created a whole new style in Kazakhstan. Almaty and Astana both have five-star high-rise hotels. The big cities have casinos, Turkish fast food restaurants, and American steak houses; modern bowling alleys and movie theaters are opening up amid old and decaying Soviet buildings. Private homes are also changing; sometimes next to or between old Soviet-style one-story austere houses, new two- and three-story houses with two-car garages and large, fenced-in yards are being built.

FOOD AND ECONOMY

Food in Kazakh culture is a very big part of their heritage, a way of respecting guests and of celebrating. When sitting down to eat with a Kazakh family one can be sure of two things: There will be more than enough food to eat, and there will be meat, possibly of different types.

Food in Daily Life. In daily life Kazakhs eat some of their own national dishes, but have borrowed some from the Russians, Ukrainians, Uzbeks, and Turks that they live among. Daily meals for Kazakhs usually are very hearty, always including bread and usually another starch such as noodles or potatoes and then a meat. One common dish is pilaf, which is often associated with the Uzbeks. It is a rice dish usually made with carrots, mutton, and a lot of oil. Soups, including Russian borscht, also are very common. Soups in Kazakhstan can be made of almost anything. Borscht is usually red (beet-based) or brown (meat-based), with cabbage, meat, sometimes potatoes, and usually a large dollop of sour cream. Pelimnin, a Russian dish that is made by filling small dough pockets with meat and onions, is very popular with all nationalities in Kazakhstan and is served quite often as a daily meal.

A more traditional Central Asian dish, although not conclusively Kazakh, is *manti,* a large dough pocket filled with meat, onions, and sometimes pumpkin.

Bread (commonly loaves or a flat, round bread called *leipioskka*) and seasonal fruits and vegetables are served with almost every meal. Kazakhstan is known for its apples, and the Soviets are known for their love of potatoes (for both eating and making vodka).

Shashlik, marinated meat roasted over a small flame and served on a stick, is of great popularity in this region. The style of meat, which locals claim originated in the Caucasus is not often eaten on a daily basis at home but is eaten quite often at roadside cafés and corner shashlik stands. High quality shashlik in large quantities is served at home on special occasions or if an animal is slaughtered.

With their daily meals, Kazakhs drink fruit juices, milk, soft drinks, beer, water, and tea. Tea is an integral part of life in Kazakhstan. Many people sit down and drink tea at least six or seven times a day. Every guest is always offered tea, if not forced to stay and drink some. Tea is almost always consumed hot, as people in Kazakhstan think that drinking cold beverages will make one sick. Soft drinks, beer, and other drinks are drunk cold but never too cold, for fear of sickness.

Two children peruse movies advertisements in Alma Ata.

Tea drinking habits vary between Russians and Kazakhs. Russians drink their tea in teacups filled to the brim with hot tea. Kazakhs drink their tea in small wide-mouthed saucers called *kasirs* that they never fill more than halfway (usually only a quarter full). The intent is that the tea should never get cold, and the passing of the empty cup by a guest or a family member to the woman pouring tea serves as a way to keep them interacting, a way of showing respect. Kazakhs take tea drinking very seriously, and the ritualistic brewing, drinking, passing, and refilling of teacups take on a real rhythm and beauty when observed.

Kazakhs are both very traditional and superstitious and thus have a multitude of food and drink taboos. As Muslims, Kazakhs do not eat pork. This is a general rule, followed much more closely in the villages than in the more secular cities. Kazakhs also have great respect for bread. It should never be wasted or thrown away and should always be placed on the table right side up. Kazakhs will often forbid you to leave their house unless you have eaten at least some of their bread, even if it is just a small crumb.

A national habit is eating with one's hands. This is naturally more common in the villages, where traditions are more evident, but it is not uncommon to see Kazakhs in cities eat with their hands. In fact, the Kazakh national dish *beshbarmak* means "five fingers" in Kazakh.

Food Customs at Ceremonial Occasions. Kazakhs have always held guests in high regard. Certain traditional Kazakh foods are usually served only on special occasions such as parties, holidays, weddings, and funerals. The most notable of these is *beshbarmak*, most traditionally made of horse meat. It is essentially boiled meat on the bone served over noodles and covered in a meat broth called *souppa*. The host, usually a man, takes the various pieces of meat and gives them out in an order of respect usually based on seniority or distance traveled. Each different piece of the horse (or goat, sheep or cow, never chicken or pig) symbolizes a different attribute such as wisdom, youth, or strength. *Beshbarmak* is always served in large quantities and usually piping hot.

When beshbarmak is made of sheep, the head of the sheep also will be boiled, fully intact, and served to the most honored guest. That guest then takes a bit of meat for himself or herself and distributes other parts of the head to other people at the table.

Another national food that is present at all celebrations is *bausak*, a deep-fried bread with nothing in the middle and usually in the shape of a triangle or a circle. The bread is eaten with the meal, not as dessert, and is usually strewn all over the traditional Kazakh table, which is called *destrakan* (the word refers more to a table full of traditional food than to an actual table). Bausak is strewn all over the table so that no part of the table is showing. Kazakhs like to have every inch of service area covered with food, sometimes with more food than will fit on the table, as a way of showing respect and prosperity.

A fermented horse's milk called *kumis* in Kazakh is also occasionally drunk at ceremonial occasions. This traditional milk dates back to the nomadic days, and many people in Central Asia think that the intoxicating beverage is therapeutic.

Vodka is consumed at all ceremonies. It is usually consumed in large quantities, and can be homemade or bought from a store (although usually only Russians make it at home). Toasts almost always precede a drink of vodka, and are given not only at special events but also at small, informal gatherings. Vodka permeates Kazakh and non-Kazakh culture and is central to all important meals and functions.

Basic Economy. Because of the richness of its land and resourcefulness of its people, the Kazakh basic economy is not very dependent on foreign trade and imports. The degree to which this is true varies greatly between the cities and towns, and the villages of the countryside. Almost every rural Kazakh has a garden, sheep and chickens, and some have horses. There are many meals in rural Kazakhstan where everything people eat and drink is homemade and from the person's garden or livestock. People in this region have been taught to be very resourceful and careful with what little they have. Most men can fix their own cars, houses, and farm equipment; women can cultivate, cook, sew, or mend almost everything they use in daily life. In fact, many rural dwellers make a living of growing foods or handmaking goods for sale in the local markets or in the cities.

For other goods, Kazakhs rely on a local market, where they buy clothes, electronics or other goods, mostly from Russia, Turkey, China, and South Korea. Urban Kazakhs rely much on grocery stores and now even big shopping malls in some cities for their goods and services.

Land Tenure and Property. Most people in Kazakhstan now own a house or an apartment for which they paid very little. Houses and property built and subsidized by the former Soviet government were very cheap and available to all during the Soviet years. With the collapse of the USSR most people retained the property that they had during Soviet years. New houses have been built and new property developed, and these are bought and sold in much the same way property is in any Western country. Most apartments are bought outright, but slowly the concept of developing an area and renting out the apartments and stores is becoming more popular. The area may face a real crisis as the houses and apartments that remain from the Soviet era need to be torn down or rebuilt, as people do not have much money for property or building supplies.

Commercial Activities. Seventy years of living in a land without imports or major foreign trade made the people of Kazakhstan rely heavily on their Soviet neighbors and on producing for themselves. In local markets, all types of goods and services are for sale, from produce to clothes, cars, and livestock. Kazakh carpets and handicrafts are probably some of the most famous exports from Kazakhstan. In addition, mineral and oil exports bring in much-needed revenue.

Major Industries. The major industries of Kazakhstan are oil, coal, ore, lead, zinc, gold, silver, metals, construction materials, and small motors. Kazakhstan produces 40 percent of the world's chrome ore, second only to South Africa. Besides the major fossil fuels and important minerals extraction, which is being supported by both foreign investment and the Kazakh government, much of the major industrial production in Kazakhstan has slowed or stopped. An industrial growth rate of −2.1 percent in 1998 was very frustrating to a country and people with such a rich land but with such a poor infrastructure and rate of capital investment.

Trade. Kazakhstan trades oil, ferrous and nonferrous metals, chemicals, grains, wool, meat, and coal on the international market mostly with Russia, the United Kingdom, Ukraine, Uzbekistan, the Netherlands, China, Italy, and Germany. For the years between 1990-1997, 28 percent of working males were active in agriculture; 37 percent in industry; and 35 percent in services. During that same time period, 15 percent of working women were engaged in agriculture; 25 percent in industry; and 60 percent in services.

Division of Labor. Liberal arts colleges have only existed in Kazakhstan since independence in 1991. Until that time all institutes of higher education trained workers for a specific skill and to fill a specific role in the economy. This is still very much the case with high school seniors deciding among careers such as banking, engineering, computer science, or teaching.

A system of education, qualifications, work experience, and job performance is for the most part in place once a graduate enters the workforce. In recent years there have been widespread complaints of nepotism and other unfair hiring and promotion practices, often involving positions of importance. This has lead to cynicism and pessimism regarding fairness in the job market.

In villages, women are responsible for the domestic chores.

Social Stratification

Class and Castes. Some would argue that there is no bigger problem in Kazakhstan than rising social stratification at all levels. Kazakh capitalism has been a free-for-all, with a few people grabbing almost all of the power regardless of who suffers.

The terms "New Kazakh" or "New Russian" have been used to describe the *nouveau riche* in Kazakhstan, who often flaunt their wealth. This is in contrast to the vast number of unemployed or underpaid. A culture of haves and have-nots is dangerous for a country composed of many different ethnic groups used to having basic needs met regardless of who they were or where they came from. Poverty and accusations of unfair treatment have raised the stakes in tensions between Kazakhs and non-Kazakhs, whose interactions until recently have been peaceful.

Symbols of Social Stratification. The symbols of stratification in Kazakhstan are much like they are in many developing countries. The rich drive expensive cars, dress in fashionable clothes, and throw lavish parties. The poor drive old Soviet cars or take a bus, wear cheap clothes imported from China or Turkey, and save for months just to afford a birthday party or a wedding.

Political Life

Government. American legal and constitutional experts helped the Kazakhstani government write their constitution and form their government in 1995. The system is a strong presidential one, with the president having the power to dissolve the parliament if his prime minister is rejected twice or if there is a vote of no confidence. The president also is the only person who can suggest constitutional amendments and make political appointments. There are some forms of checks and balances provided by a bicameral legislature called the Kenges. The Majlis, or lower house, has sixty-seven deputies and the upper house, the Senate, has forty-seven senators. The powers of the legislature are severely limited; most glaringly, they don't even have the power to initiate legislation. The legal system is based on the civil law system. There is a Supreme Court of forty-four members and a Constitutional Court of seven members. While much of the control is centered in Astana with the president, legislature, and courts, there are fourteen provinces or states, called *oblasts* in Russian, with governors and certain rights.

Leadership and Political Officials. The president, Nursultan Nazarbayev, was the top Communist leader of the Kazakh Soviet Socialist Republic when the Soviet Union disbanded in 1991. After independence, Nazarbayev was easily elected president in November 1991. In March 1995 he dissolved parliament, saying that the 1994 parliamentary elections were invalid. A March 1995 referendum extended the president's term until 2000, solidifying Nazarbayev's control and raising serious doubts among Kazakhstani people and international observers as to the state of Kazakhstani democracy.

Multiparty, representative democracy has tried to take hold in Kazakhstan but has been met by opposition from Nazarbayev's government. The main opposition parties are the Communist Party, Agrarian Party, Civic Party, Republican People's Party, and the Orleu, or progress movement. A number of smaller parties have formed and disbanded over the years. The opposition parties have accused Nazarbayev and his Republican Party of limiting any real power of the opposition by putting obstacles and loopholes in their way, if not actually rigging the elections.

The most notable example of suppression of political opposition has been the case of Akezhan Kazhageldin, who was Nazarbayev's prime minister from 1994 to 1997. In 1999 Kazhageldin was banned from running in the 1999 presidential elections. He and his wife were charged with tax evasion (the conviction of a crime under the Kazakhstani constitution prevents a potential candidate from running for office) and arrested in September 1999 at the Moscow airport after arriving from London. Sharp criticism by the Organization for Security and Cooperation in Europe (OSCE) over how the arrest was set up and carried out allowed Kazhageldin to return to London. The end result was that he was still not registered for the October election, and Nazarbayev won easily, with more than 80 percent of the vote. The OSCE and the United States criticized the election as unfair and poorly administered.

Social Problems and Control. In urban areas, robberies and theft are common. Murder, suicide, and other violent crimes are on the rise. The system for dealing with crime in Kazakhstan is based, in theory, on a rule of law and enforced by the police and the courts. Local and state police and local and national courts are set up much as they are in the United States and much of the rest of the Western world. The problem is the lack of checks and controls on this system. There are so many police and so many different units (remnants of the Soviet apparatus still exist, such as intelligence gatherers, visa and registration officers, and corruption and anitgovernmental affairs divisions, as well regular police and border controls) that it is often that jurisdiction is unclear. The strong sense of community, with neighbors looking out for each other, acts as a deterrent against crime. Civic education and responsible citizenry is emphasized in schools, and the schools work closely with local communities in this area.

The drug trade from Afghanistan and long, hard-to-patrol borders have given rise to organized crime, putting a strain on Kazakhstan's police and border patrol.

White-collar crime, such as embezzlement, tax fraud, and abuse of power and privilege are almost daily events, which seem to be tacitly accepted.

Military Activity. The military of the Soviet Union was very strong and well-trained. The armies of the post-Soviet republics are much weaker and less supported by the government. The available Kazakhstani military manpower of males between ages fifteen and forty-nine was estimated at 4.5 million in 1999, with about 3.5 million of those available being fit for service. All males over age eighteen must serve in the military for two years. Exemptions are made for those in school and the disabled. The 1998 fiscal year expenditures on the military were $232.4 million (U.S.)—1 percent of the GDP of Kazakhstan.

Kazakhstan is in a semiprecarious location. It has a friendly, although weakened, neighbor to the north in Russia. Recent complaints by Russians in Kazakhstan have begun to resonate in Moscow, putting some strain on relations that are for the most part friendly. Kazakhstan has a historical fear of China and thus watches its border with that country closely, but the most unstable areas for Kazakhstan involve its neighbors to the south. Movements in Afghanistan have spread to the failed state of Tajikistan, forming a center of Islamic fundamentalism not far to Kazakhstan's south. Kyrgyzstan and Uzbekistan have already dealt with attacks from rebel groups in Tajikistan, and Kazakhstan has significantly increased its military presence on its borders with Kyrgyzstan and Uzbekistan. The region does not seem to be one that will readily go to war, while memories of the war in Afghanistan in the late 1970s are fresh in most people's minds.

Social Welfare and Change Programs

There is a government-sponsored program of pension and disability benefits. There is also support for single mothers with multiple children. The problem is that there is very little money for these programs. Pension levels have not kept up with inflation, and pensions are rarely paid on time, with those elderly, disabled, or unemployed often going months without payment.

Nongovernmental Organizations and Other Associations

Kazakhstan and the rest of the former Soviet Union have seen a massive infusion of nongovernmental organizations (NGOs) and international aid programs. The passage of the Freedom Support Act by the United States' Congress has provided millions of dollars for direct U.S. governmental involvement in Kazakhstan and much-needed money for NGOs to operate there. The Peace Corps, United Nations Volunteers, and many other aid and educational organizations have been working hard in Kazakhstan. The groups are well received by the people and, for the most part, allowed to do their work by the Kazakhstani government.

Gender Roles and Statuses

Division of Labor by Gender. There is a large distinction between work and the home in Kazakhstani society. Women occupy very important roles in the Kazakhstani workforce. Women are, for example, school principals, bank presidents, teachers, accountants, police officers, secretaries, and government workers and make up almost half of the workforce. This may be a carryover from Soviet times when women were very important parts of a system that depended on every citizen to work and contribute.

Women are often the best students in a school and more qualified than men for many of the jobs in Kazakhstan. However, often women have not been promoted to the top positions in national government and the private sector. With alcoholism on the rise, especially among men, and educational performance among men often lower than average, women may play an even more significant role in the future Kazakhstani economy.

The Relative Status of Women and Men. Kazakh culture is traditionally a patriarchal one, with much respect being given to men, especially elderly men. Symbols in the culture often represent power and warriorlike behavior, often associated with men. This can be seen in many Kazakh households. In villages and small towns women always prepare the food, pour the tea, and clean the dishes. Men will often lounge on large pillows or stand outside and smoke while women prepare food or clean up after a meal. Men do work around the house, but it is usually with the horses, garden, or car. There are many marriage and courtship customs that further assert the male as dominant in Kazakh society.

Marriage, Family, and Kinship

Marriage. Marriage in Kazakhstan is similar to that in the United States and Europe. The reasons and even the process of marriage in Kazakhstan are also very similar. While years ago it was common for women to marry very young, times have changed; education has become much more important for both genders, and marriages for people in their mid-twenties are becoming more common. Marriages are not arranged by the parents but are usually formed through dating and courtship. Interracial marriage is rare but tolerated.

Three aspects of traditional Kazakh culture still occasionally affect marriage today in Kazakhstan. Marriage is forbidden to any couple related over the past seven generations. In addition, the male should be older than the female. Finally, the nomadic tradition of stealing a bride is still practiced, although rarely, by some Kazakhs.

Families of the bride and groom are usually heavily involved in the process of the wedding and subsequent marriage. The families meet before the wedding, and exchange gifts and dowries. Kazakh weddings are three-day events.

Divorce is not uncommon, especially in the urban centers. It is viewed in Kazakhstan as it is in other parts of the world—it is never ideal but some marriages were not meant to last. There are no formal rules for who gets what when a marriage ends, but women usually keep the children.

Domestic Unit. Households vary greatly in Kazakhstan. Some couples have only one or two children, while other families have eight or nine. Kazakhs tend to have more children than Russians. Men exercise most of the symbolic authority in both Kazakh and non-Kazakh households. But there are many very strong women and powerful matriarchs who wield all practical control.

Domestic units in Kazakhstan are very rarely just a mother, father, and their children. The practice of grandparents and extended family living

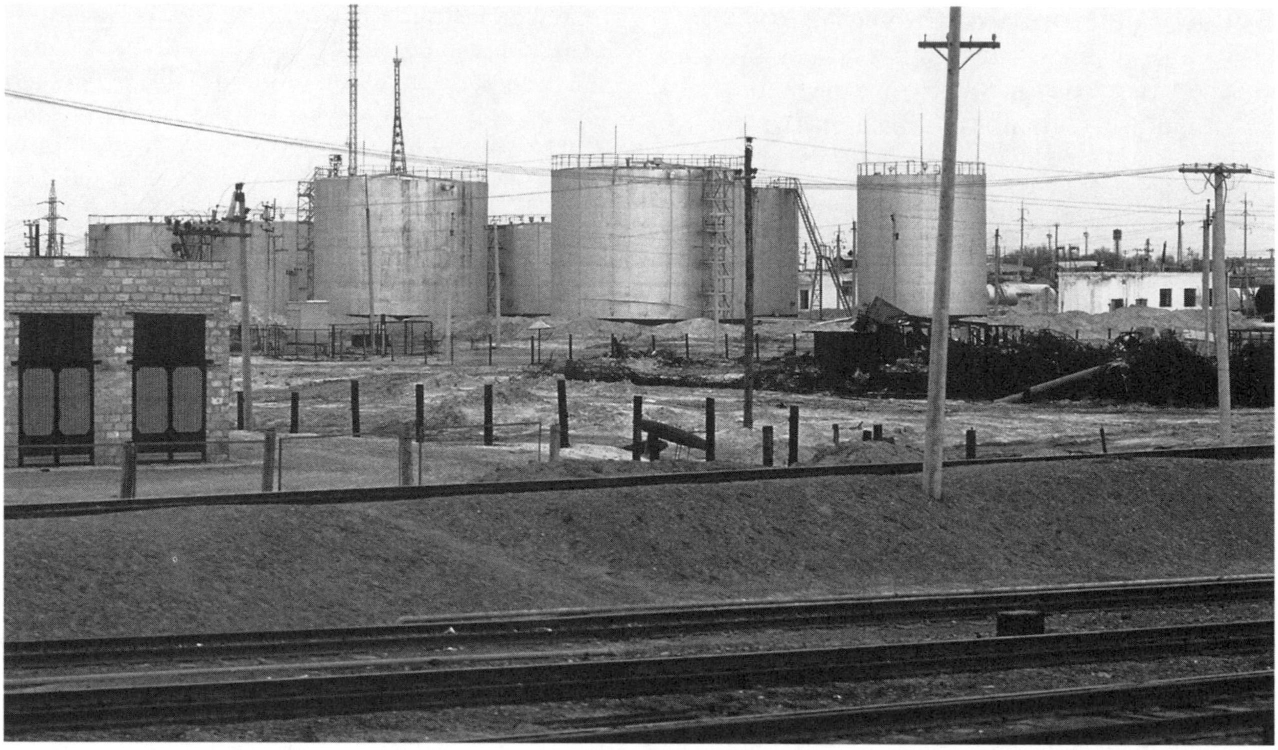

Oil refineries next to train tracks near Kul'Sary, Kazakhstan. Oil is one of the major industries in Kazakhstan.

within one household is very common. Kazakhs especially make very little distinctions among cousins, second cousins, aunts, uncles, and grandparents. Kazakhs also still largely adhere to an old custom of care for the elderly. The youngest son in Kazakh families is expected to stay at home until his parents die. He may take a wife and have a family of his own, but he is expected to care for his parents into their old age.

Kin Groups. Kin groups are central to the life of almost every Kazakh life. Who you are, who your family is, and where you are from are very important. Dating back hundreds of years to the times when the Kazakhs were divided into three distinct hordes or large tribes, it has been important to know about your kin groups. Extended families are large support networks, and relatives from far away can be expected to help financially in times of crisis.

Socialization

Infant Care. Childbirth in Kazakhstan occurs in a hospital under the care of a doctor whenever possible. Every district in the country has a hospital, and medical care is free; patients only pay for drugs and specialized tests and care. Mothers usually stay in the hospital with their infants for a few days after birth. Some Kazakhs practice a custom of not letting anyone besides close family members see a newborn for the first forty days of life; then the family holds a small party and presents the baby to extended family and friends. Babies are well cared for and cherished by all cultures in Kazakhstan. Independence and access to markets have brought improved access to infant care products.

Child Rearing and Education. Generally children go to kindergarten at ages four or five in Kazakhstan. First grade and formal schooling start at age six, when many Kazakhs have large parties celebrating the event.

Children in Kazakhstan are assigned to classes of about twenty-five students in the first grade; the class remains together through the eleventh grade. The class has the same teacher from the first through the fourth grade and then a different teacher from the fifth through the eleventh grade. These teachers become like second mothers or fathers to the students in that class, with discipline being an important factor. Homework is extensive and grades difficult, and students are very grade-conscious.

Kazakhstani schools stress the basics: literature, math, geography, history, grammar, and foreign languages. Workdays are held where students clean the school and the town. Classes on citizenship and army training are required. After school, arts and dance performances are very popular.

Higher Education. Many high school students—often as high as 75 percent—go on to attend some form of schooling after graduation. Liberal arts schools, many run by foreigners, are opening in the bigger cities. Technical schools and state universities are widespread and very popular. A tendency still exists to pigeonhole students by making them choose a profession before they enter school—a Soviet remnant that preached that every citizen had a specific role in society and the sooner he or she realized it and learned the trade the better. Unfortunately this practice is less flexible in the ever-changing Kazakhstani economy, leaving many young people underqualified for many of the emerging jobs.

ETIQUETTE

Etiquette and cultural norms related to acceptable and unacceptable behavior vary between urban and rural Kazakhs. As a rule, rural Kazakhs tend to follow the cultural norms more strictly.

Kazakh men always shake hands with someone they know when they see each other for the first time in a day. Usually the younger man initiates this, and shows respect by extending both hands and shaking the older man's hand.

Both Kazakhs and non-Kazakhs remove their shoes when inside a house. Guests always remove their shoes at the door and often put on a pair of slippers provided by the host or hostess. Central Asian streets often can be very dusty or muddy, so wearing shoes indoors is a serious social offense.

Greetings are also very structured in Kazakhstan. In Kazakh culture, elder women and men are greeted with certain phrases showing respect. A Russian system of patronymics is still widely used.

Kazakhs can be superstitious, and whistling inside a house is unacceptable in almost all Kazakh homes. It is believed that whistling inside will make the owner of the house poor.

In general smoking by women is not accepted, especially in rural areas, and women who are seen walking and smoking at the same time are considered prostitutes.

Kazakhs, and many other people from the former Soviet Union, often don't smile at people in public except to those they know. Kazakhs rarely form lines when boarding crowded buses.

Many people in Kazakhstan treat foreigners with a visible degree of skepticism. With the work of the Peace Corps and many other international groups and companies, the image of a foreigner as a spy is starting to fade. Nevertheless Kazakhstani people will often stare at foreigners as they walk by.

Public affection between friends is very common. Women and girls often hold hands as they walk; boys wrestle and often hook arms or walk with their arms around each other. Kissing cheeks and embracing is perfectly acceptable between good friends.

RELIGION

Religious Beliefs. Religion in Kazakhstan is in a time of change. Arabs brought Islam to the region in the ninth century, and more than a thousand years later, Russian Orthodoxy was introduced by Russian settlers from the north. For all intents and purposes no religion was practiced for the seventy years of Soviet influence over the region; religious participation was banned, and many churches and mosques were destroyed—religious traditions were lost in the name of Soviet atheism. At the beginning of the twenty-first century, 47 percent of the people profess to be Muslim (mainly Sunni branch) and 44 percent Russian Orthodox. However, few people practice religion in any formal way, but Kazakhs have incorporated religion into some parts of their everyday life; for example, they cover their faces in a short prayer when they pass graveyards where someone they know is buried, and they often say prayers after meals. Sayings such as "God willing" and "this is from God" are very common in everyday speech.

There are virtually no visible tensions between Muslims and Christians in Kazakhstan. Religion was such a nonfactor for so many years, and continues to occupy so little of everyday life, that it is simply not an issue of importance between Russians and Kazakhs.

Religious Practitioners. Most town mosques are cared for and staffed by a mullah, who conducts religious services at the mosque as well as funerals, weddings, and blessings. Russian Orthodox churches are in many parts of Kazakhstan, especially in the north and in large cities. Orthodox priests perform services and baptize children much as in the West.

Death and the Afterlife. Both Kazakhs and non-Kazakhs believe that the deceased go to a heaven after they die. Funerals and burials reflect this, as

A farm on the steppe grasslands near Kul'Sary, Kazakhstan. Many rural Kazakhs acquire the food they eat from their own land.

great care is taken in preparing bodies and coffins for burial. Funerals in this part of the world are very intense, with wailing being a sign of respect and love for the dead.

Funerals are usually held in the home of the deceased with people coming from afar to pay their respects. Russians and Kazakhs are usually buried in separate sections of the graveyard. If the means are available, a Kazakh can be buried in a mausoleum.

Medicine and Health Care

There are some hospitals in Kazakhstan where it is possible to get good health care, but many more are in poor repair, without heat or electricity, lacking basic drugs and medical supplies, and staffed by underqualified and severely underpaid doctors and nurses.

Doctors are still trained under the Soviet system of specialties, with very few general practitioners. Doctors also rely heavily on symptomatic diagnosis, as they do not have access to the latest machines and testing devices; often simple blood tests cannot be done. Nevertheless, doctors are trusted and respected.

People also rely heavily on home remedies such as hot teas, honey, vodka and *Banya* (a very hot version of a sauna used mainly for cleaning purposes, but also for sweating out diseases and impurities).

Secular Celebrations

Some of the principal secular celebrations are 8 March, Women's Day, a very important day in Kazakhstan and celebrated by all. Women are honored on this day and showered with flowers and entertained with skits and jokes by their male co-workers and family members. Narooz, Kazakh New Year—a holiday mainly celebrated by Kazakhs on 22 March, but also observed by Kyrgyz, Uzbeks, Turkmen, Iranians. It occurs on summer solstice. Kazakhs cook traditional foods, have horse races, and set up many yurts.

Victory Day on 9 May commemorates the Soviet victory over Nazi Germany. Day of the Republic, 25 October, was the day independence was declared. This day is a day of Kazakh nationalism, with many speeches, songs, and performances in Kazakh. Independence Day is celebrated on 16 December—this date was chosen to remember the riots in Almaty on 16 December 1986. The riots were the first display of Kazakh nationalism and solidarity. Independence day is celebrated much like the Day of the Republic.

The Arts and Humanities

Support for the Arts. Under the Soviet Union, funding and support of the arts were available for those who enrolled in specialized schools for artists, dancers, and musicians. However today, government money for arts, besides what is provided through public schools and municipals houses of culture, has virtually dried up. Many artisans are supported through NGOs such as Aid to Artisans and the Talent Support Fund.

Literature. Students study both Kazakh and Russian literature. Great Russian and Kazakh writers such as Tolstoy, Pushkin, and Abai are well known in Kazakhstan. A high societal value is put on those who have read the famous works and can quote and discuss them.

Performance Arts. Despite funding cutbacks, plays, dance performances, art museums, and the upkeep of historical museums are very important to the people of Kazakhstan. There are beautiful theaters in the larger cities, and almost every town has a house of culture where plays, art classes, concerts, and dance performances can take place. Many cultures in Kazakhstan have a strong tradition of instrument playing, traditional dancing, and theatrical performances.

The State of the Physical and Social Sciences

The Soviet Union had, and its now independent republics have, some very well respected science universities in the world. Higher education is very specialized in Kazakhstan, with many universities or programs focusing on specialized fields of physics, technology, engineering, math, philosophy, and politics. Many famous academics have come from this part of the world, and education in these fields has remained important, although funding for them has slowed with the economic downturn in the region.

Bibliography

Abazov, Rafis. *The Formation of Post-Soviet International Politics in Kazakhstan, Kyrgyzstan, and Uzbekistan,* 1999.

Abraham, Kurt S. "A World of Oil—Kazakhstan, an Oasis in FSU Bureaucratic Quagmire; International Deals." *World Oil,* 220 (11): 29, 1999.

Agadjanian, Victor. "Post-Soviet Demographic Paradoxes: Ethnic Differences in Marriage and Fertility in Kazakhstan." *Sociological Forum,* 14 (3): 425, 1999.

Akiner, Shirin. *Central Asia: A Survey of the Region and the Five Republics,* 1999.

Arenov, M. M., and Kalmykov, S. K. "The Present Language Situation in Kazakhstan." *Russian Social Science Review: A Journal of Translations,* 38 (3): 56, 1997.

Asia and Pacific Review: World of Information, 6 September 2000.

Auty, R. M. *The IMF Model and Resource-Abundant Transition Economies: Kazakhstan and Uzbekistan,* 1999.

Bhavna, Dave. "Politics of Language Revival: National Identity and State Building in Kazakhstan." Ph.D. Dissertation, Syracuse University, 1996.

Benko, Mihaly. *Nomadic life in Central Asia,* 1998.

Berler, Rouza. *Cattle car to Kazakhstan: a Woman Doctor's Triumph of Courage in World War II,* 1999.

Burkitbayev, S. "Rail transport in Kazakhstan." *Rail International,* 31 (3): 18, 2000.

Campbell, Craig E. *Kazakhstan: United States Engagement for Eurasian Security,* 1999.

Eizten, Hilda. "Scenarios of Statehood: Media and Public Holidays in Kazakhstan." Ph.D. dissertation, Columbia University, 1999.

Grant, Steven. *Charms of Market, Private Sector Continue to Elude Three Central Asian Republics,* 2000.

———. *Order Trumps Liberty for Many in Three Central Asian Nations: Ethnic Differences Brewing?,* 2000.

Hoffman, Lutz. *Kazakhstan 1993–2000: Independent Advisors and the IMF,* 2000.

Landau, Jacob M. *Politics of Language in the ex-Soviet Muslim States: Azerbaijan, Uzbekistan, Kazakhstan, Kyrgyzstan, Turkmenistan, Tajikistan,* 2000.

Luong, Pauline Jones and Weinthal, Erika. "The NGO Paradox: Democratic Goals and Non-democratic Outcomes in Kazakhstan." *Europe-Asia Studies,* (7): 1267–1294, 1999.

Mitrofanskaya, Yuliya, and Bideldinov, Daulet. "Modernizing Environmental Protection in Kazakhstan." *Georgetown International Environmental Law Review,* 12 (1): 177, 1999.

Pirseyedi, Bobi. *The Small Arms Problems in Central Asia: Features and Implications,* 2000.

Pohl, Michaela. "The Virgin Lands between Memory and Forgetting: People and the Transformation of the Soviet Union, 1954–1960. Ph.D. dissertation, Indiana University, 1999.

Privratsky, Bruce G. "Turkistan: Kazakh Religion and Collective Memory." Ph.D. dissertation, University of Tennessee, Knoxville. 1998.

Sabol, Steven. "'Awake Kazak!': Russian Colonization of Central Asia and the Genesis of Kazakh National Consciousness, 1868–1920." Ph.D. dissertation, Georgia State University, 1998.

Schatz, Edward. "The Politics of Multiple Identities: Lineage and Ethnicity in Kazakhstan." *Europe-Asia studies*, 52 (3): 489–506, 2000.

Smith, Dianne L. *Opening Pandora's Box: Ethnicity and Central Asian Militaries*, 1998.

Sullivan, Barry Lynn. "Kazakhstan: An Analysis of Nation-Building Policies." M.A. dissertation, University of Texas, El Paso, 1999.

Svanberg, Ingvar. *Contemporary Kazakhs: Cultural and Social Perspectives*, 1999.

Timoschenko, Valery, and Krolikova, Tatiana. "Oil Pipeline Imperils the Black Sea." *Earth Island* 12 (3): 23, 1997.

Vartkin, Dmitri. *Kazakhstan: Development Trends and Security Implications*, 1995.

Werner, Cynthia Ann. *A Profile of Rural Life in Kazakhstan, 1994–1998: Comments and Suggestions for Further Research*, 1999.

—ERIC M. JOHNSON

KENYA

CULTURE NAME

Kenyan

ALTERNATIVE NAMES

Jamhuri ya Kenya

ORIENTATION

Identification. The country takes its name from Mount Kenya, located in the central highlands.

Location and Geography. Kenya is located in East Africa and borders Somalia to the northeast, Ethiopia to the north, Sudan to the northwest, Uganda to the west, Tanzania to the south, and the Indian Ocean to the east. The country straddles the equator, covering a total of 224,961 square miles (582,600 square kilometers; roughly twice the size of the state of Nevada). Kenya has wide white-sand beaches on the coast. Inland plains cover three-quarters of the country; they are mostly bush, covered in underbrush. In the west are the highlands where the altitude rises from three thousand to ten thousand feet. Nairobi, Kenya's largest city and capital, is located in the central highlands. The highest point, at 17,058 feet (5,200 meters), is Mount Kenya. Kenya shares Lake Victoria, the largest lake in Africa and the main source of the Nile River, with Tanzania and Uganda. Another significant feature of Kenyan geography is the Great Rift Valley, the wide, steep canyon that cuts through the highlands. Kenya is also home to some of the world's most spectacular wildlife, including elephants, lions, giraffes, zebras, antelope, wildebeests, and many rare and beautiful species of birds. Unfortunately, the animal population is threatened by both hunting and an expanding human population; wildlife numbers fell drastically through the twentieth century. The government has introduced strict legislation regulating hunting, and has established a system of national parks to protect the wildlife.

Demography. According to an estimate in July 2000, Kenya's population is 30,339,770. The population has been significantly reduced by the AIDS epidemic, as have the age and sex distributions of the population. Despite this scourge, however, the birth rate is still significantly higher than the death rate and the population continues to grow.

There are more than forty ethnic groups in the country. The largest of these is the Kikuyu, representing 22 percent of the population. Fourteen percent is Luhya, 13 percent is Luo, 12 percent is Kalenjin, 11 percent Kamba, 6 percent Kisii, and 6 percent Meru. Others, including the Somalis and the Turkana in the north and the Kalenjin in the Great Rift Valley, comprise approximately 15 percent of the population. These ethnic categories are further broken down into subgroups. One percent of the population is non-African, mostly of Indian and European descent.

Linguistic Affiliation. The official languages are English and Kiswahili (or Swahili). Swahili, which comes from the Arabic word meaning "coast," is a mix of Arabic and the African language Bantu. It first developed in the tenth century with the arrival of Arab traders; it was a *lingua franca* that allowed different tribes to communicate with each other and with the Arabs. The major language groups native to the region include Bantu in the west and along the coast, Nilotic near Lake Victoria, and Cushitic in the north.

English is the language generally used in government and business. It is also used in most of the schools, although there has been movement towards using Kiswahili as the teaching language. English is not spoken solely by the elite, but only people with a certain level of education speak it.

Symbolism. The Kenyan flag has three horizontal stripes—red, black, and green—separated by thin

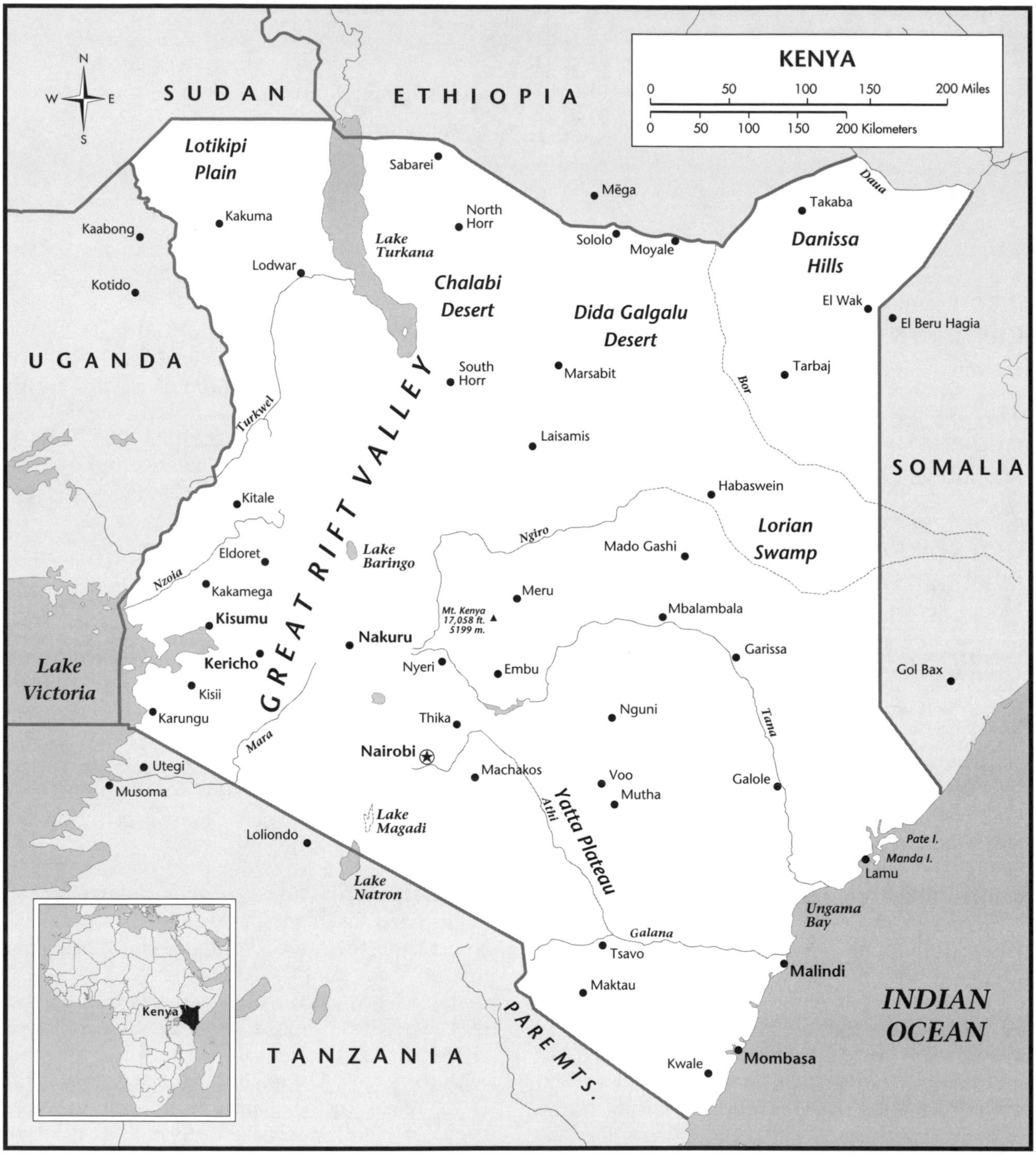

Kenya

white bands. The black symbolizes the people of Kenya, the red stands for the blood shed in the fight for independence, and the green symbolizes agriculture. In the center of the flag is a red shield with black and white markings and two crossed spears, which stands for vigilance in the defense of freedom.

History and Ethnic Relations

Emergence of the Nation. The Great Rift Valley is thought to be one of the places where human beings originated, and archeologists working in the valley have found remains of what they speculate are some of the earliest human ancestors. The first known inhabitants of present-day Kenya were

Cushitic-speaking tribes that migrated to the northwest region from Ethiopa around 2000 B.C.E. Eastern Cushites began to arrive about one thousand years later, and occupied much of the country's current area. During the period from 500 B.C.E. to 500 C.E., other tribes arrived from various parts of Africa. Tribal disagreements often led to war during this time.

In the 900s, Arab merchants arrived and established trading centers along the coast of East Africa. Over the ensuing eight centuries, they succeeded in converting many Kenyans to Islam. Some Arabs settled in the area and intermarried with local groups.

Portuguese explorer Vasco da Gama landed at Mombasa in 1498, after discovering a sailing route around the Cape of Good Hope. The Portuguese colonized much of the region, but the Arabs managed to evict them in 1729. In the mid-1800s, European explorers stumbled upon Mount Kilimanjaro and Mount Kenya, and began to take an interest in the natural resources of East Africa. Christian missionaries came as well, drawn by the large numbers of prospective converts.

Britain gradually increased its domain in the region, and in 1884–1885, Kenya was named a British protectorate by the Congress of Berlin, which divided the African continent among various European powers. The British constructed the Uganda Railway, which connected the ports on Kenya's coast to landlocked Uganda. The increasing economic opportunities brought thousands of British settlers who displaced many Africans, often forcing them to live on reservations. The Africans resisted—the Kikuyu in particular put up a strong fight—but they were defeated by the superior military power of the British.

During the early twentieth century, the British colonizers forced the Africans to work their farms in virtual slavery, and kept the upper hand by making it illegal for the Kenyans to grow their own food. In the early 1920s, a Kikuyu named Harry Thuku began to encourage rebellion among his tribe and founded the East Africa Association. He was arrested by the British in 1922, provoking a popular protest. The British reacted violently, killing twenty-five people in what came to be called the Nairobi Massacre.

Desire for self-rule continued to build and in 1944 the Kenya African Union, a nationalist party, was founded. In 1946, the Kikuyu leader Jomo Kenyatta returned after sixteen years in England and began agitating for Kenyan independence. Back on his home soil, he was elected president of the Kenya African Union. His rallying cry was *uhuru*, Swahili for freedom. While Kenyatta advocated peaceful rebellion, other Kikuyu formed secret societies that pledged to win independence for Kenya using whatever means necessary, including violence. In the early 1950s, members of these groups (called Mau Mau) murdered 32 white civilians, as well as 167 police officers and 1,819 Kikuyu who disagreed with their absolutist stance or who supported the colonial government. In retaliation for

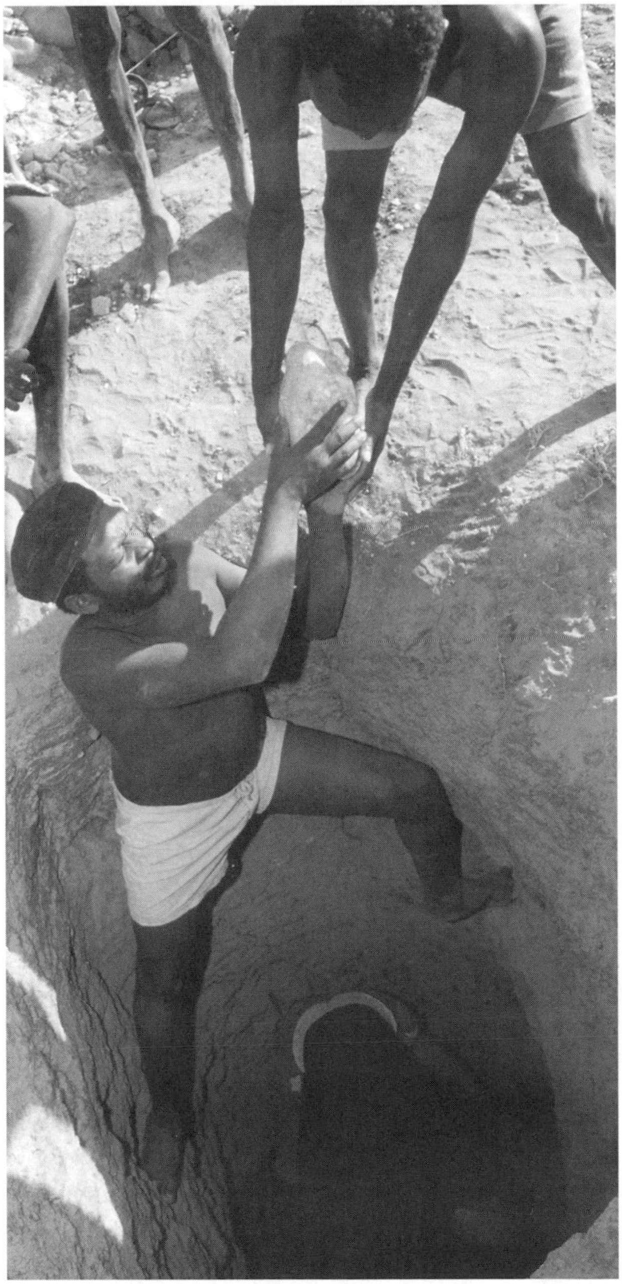

Turkana men working at a gold mine in northern Kenya pass blocks of gold-bearing ore to the surface of a shaft. The mines often lie sixty or so feet below the ground.

these murders, the British killed a total of 11,503 Mau Mau and their sympathizers. British policy also included displacing entire tribes and interning them in barbed-wire camps.

Despite Kenyatta's public denouncement of the Mau Mau, the British tried him as a Mau Mau leader and imprisoned him for nine years. While Kenyatta was in jail, two other leaders stepped in to fill his place. Tom Mboya, of the Luo tribe, was the more moderate of the two, and had the support of Western nations. Oginga Oginga, also a Luo, was more radical, and received support from the Soviet bloc. One common goal of the two was to give blacks the right to vote. In a 1957 election, blacks won their first representation in the colonial government and eight blacks were elected to seats in the legislature. By 1961, they constituted a majority of the body.

In 1960 at the Lancaster House Conference in London the English approved Kenyan independence, setting the date for December 1963. Kenyatta, released from prison in 1961, became prime minister of a newly independent Kenya on 12 December 1963 and was elected to the office of president the following year. Although he was a Kikuyu, one of Kenyatta's primary goals was to overcome tribalism. He appointed members of different ethnic groups to his government, including Mboya and Oginga. His slogan became *harambee,* meaning "Let's all pull together." In 1966, however, Oginga abrogated his position as vice-president to start his own political party. Kenyatta, fearing cultural divisiveness, arrested Oginga and outlawed all political parties except his own. On 5 July 1969, Tom Mboya was assassinated, and tensions between the Luo and the Kikuyu increased. In elections later that year, Kenyatta won reelection and political stability returned. Overall, the fifteen years of Kenyatta's presidency were a time of economic and political stability. When Kenyatta died on 22 August 1978, the entire nation mourned his death. The vice-president, Daniel Toroitich arap Moi (a Kalenjin of the Tugen subgroup) took over. His presidency was confirmed in a general election ninety days later.

Moi initially promised to improve on Kenyatta's government by ending corruption and releasing political prisoners. While he made some progress on these goals, Moi gradually restricted people's liberty, outlawing all political parties except his own. In 1982, a military coup attempted to overthrow Moi. The coup was unsuccessful, and the president responded by temporarily closing the University of Nairobi, shutting down churches that dissented from his view, and giving himself the power to appoint and fire judges. Moi did away with secret ballots, and several times changed election dates spontaneously to keep people from voting. Moi's opposition has faced even more blatant obstacles: Legislator Charles Rubia, who protested the policy of waiting in line to vote, was arrested and later lost his seat in a rigged election; Robert Ouko, Moi's Minister of Foreign Affairs, threatened to expose government corruption, and was later found with a bullet in his head, his body severely burned. Pro-democracy demonstrations in the early 1990s were put down by paramilitary troops, and leaders of the opposition were thrown in jail. Western nations responded by demanding that Kenya hold multi-party elections if they wanted to continue to receive foreign aid, and in December 1992 Moi won reelection, despite widespread complaints of bribery and ballot tampering. During this time, the economy floundered: inflation skyrocketed, the Kenyan currency was devalued by 50 percent, and unemployment rose.

In 1995, the various opposition groups united in an attempt to wrest the presidency from Moi and formed a political party called Safina. Opposition efforts have been unsuccessful so far, however. In July 1997, demonstrators demanding constitutional reforms were teargassed, shot, and beaten, resulting in eleven deaths.

Despite Moi's unpopularity and his advanced age (he was born in 1924), he maintains his grip on the presidency. Kenya continues to suffer from tribalism and corruption, as well as high population growth, unemployment, political instability, and the AIDS epidemic.

National Identity. Kenyans tend to identify primarily with their tribe or ethnic group, and only secondarily with the nation as a whole. The Kikuyu, who were better represented in the independence movement than other groups, and who continue to dominate the government, are more likely to identify themselves as Kenyans.

Ethnic Relations. The Kikuyu are the largest tribe in the highlands, and tend to dominate the nation's politics. Over the centuries, they consolidated their power by trading portions of their harvests to the hunter-gatherers for land, as well as through intermarriage. This gradual rise to domination was peaceful and involved a mingling of different ethnic groups. While the Kikuyu have enjoyed the most power in the post–independence government, they were also the hardest–hit by brutal British policies during the colonial period. The Kikuyu traditionally had an antagonistic relationship with the Maasai, and the two groups often raided each other's villages and cattle herds. At the same time, there was a good deal of intermarriage and cultural borrowing between the two groups. Relations among various other ethnic groups are also fraught with tension, and this has been a major obstacle in creating a united Kenya. These conflicts are partly a legacy of colonial rule: the British exaggerated ethnic tensions and played one group against another to reinforce their own power. Under British rule, different ethnic groups were confined to specific geographic areas. Ethnic tensions continue to this day, and have been the cause of violence. In the early 1990s tribal clashes killed thousands of people and left tens of thousands homeless. Conflicts flared again in the late 1990s between the Pokots and the Marakwets, the Turkanas and the Samburus, and the Maasai and the Kisii.

Kenya has a fairly large Indian population, mostly those who came to East Africa in the early twentieth century to work on the railroad. Many Indians later became merchants and storeowners. During colonial times, they occupied a racial netherland: they were treated poorly by the British (although not as poorly as blacks), and resented by the Africans. Even after independence, this resentment continued and half of the Indian population left the country.

Urbanism, Architecture, and the Use of Space

About 70 percent of the population is rural, although this percentage has been decreasing as more Kenyans migrate to the cities in search of work. Most of those who live in urban areas live in either Nairobi or Mombasa. Nairobi was founded at the beginning of the twentieth century as a stop on the East African Railway and its population is growing rapidly. Nairobi is a modern city with a diverse, international population and a busy, fast-paced lifestyle. The city is in close proximity to Nairobi National Park, a forty-four square mile preserve inhabited by wild animals such as giraffes and leopards. Around the perimeter of the city, shantytowns of makeshift houses have sprung up as the population has increased, and the shortage of adequate housing is a major problem in urban areas.

Mombasa is the second-largest city; located on the southern coast, it is the country's main port. Its history dates back to the first Arab settlers, and Mombasa is still home to a large Muslim population. Fort Jesus, located in the old part of the city, dates to the Portuguese settlement of the area in 1593, and today houses a museum. Kisumu, on Lake Victoria, is the third-largest city and is also an important port. Two smaller cities of importance are Nakuru in the Eastern Rift Valley and Eldoret in western Kenya.

In the cities, most people live in modern apartment buildings. In the countryside, typical housing styles vary from tribe to tribe. *Zaramo* houses are made of grass and rectangular in shape; *rundi* houses are beehive-like constructions of reed and bark; *chagga* houses are made from sticks; and *nyamwezi* are round huts with thatched roofs. Some rural people have adapted their houses to modern building materials, using bricks or cement blocks and corrugated iron or tin for roofs.

Food and Economy

Food in Daily Life. Corn (or maize) is the staple food of Kenyans. It is ground into flour and prepared as a porridge called *posho*, which is sometimes mixed with mashed beans, potatoes, and vegetables, to make a dish called *irio*. Another popular meal is a beef stew called *ugali*. This is eaten from a big pot, and each diner takes a piece of *ugali*, which he or she uses as a spoon to pick up beans and other vegetables. Boiled greens, called *mboga*, are a common side dish. Banana porridge, called *matoke*, is another common dish. Meat is expensive, and is rarely eaten. Herders depend on milk as their primary food, and fish is popular on the coast and around Lake Victoria. Mombasa is known for its Indian foods brought by the numerous immigrants from the subcontinent, including curries, samosas, and *chapatti*, a fried bread. Snacks include corn on the cob, *mandazi* (fried dough), potato chips, and peanuts.

Tea mixed with milk and sugar is a common drink. Palm wine is another popular libation, especially in Mombasa. Beer is ubiquitous, most of it produced locally by the Kenyan Breweries. One special type of brew, made with honey, is called *uki*.

Food Customs at Ceremonial Occasions. For special occasions, it is customary to kill and roast a goat. Other meats, including sheep and cow, are also served at celebrations. The special dish is called *nyama choma*, which translates as "burnt meat."

Basic Economy. Kenya's economy has suffered from inefficiency and government corruption. The tourist industry has also been harmed by political violence in the late 1990s. Seventy-five to 80 percent of the workforce is in agriculture. Most of these

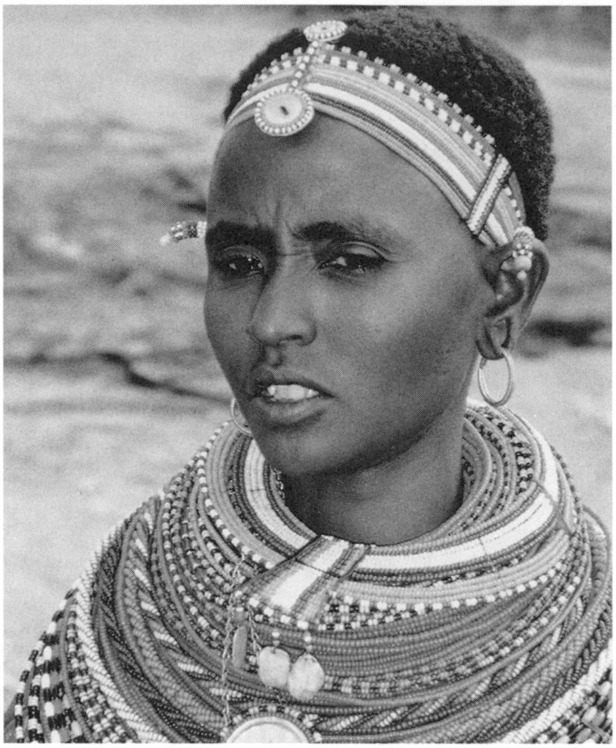

A young Samburu woman wearing traditional ornamentation.

workers are subsistence farmers, whose main crops are corn, millet, sweet potatoes, and such fruits as bananas, oranges, and mangoes. The main cash crops are tea and coffee, which are grown on large plantations. The international market for these products tends to fluctuate widely from year to year, contributing to Kenya's economic instability.

Many Kenyans work in what is called the *jua kali* sector, doing day labor in such fields as mechanics, small crafts, and construction. Others are employed in industry, services, and government, but the country has an extremely high unemployment rate, estimated at 50 percent.

Land Tenure and Property. During colonial rule, Kenyan farmers who worked the British plantations were forced to cultivate the least productive lands for their own subsistence. After independence, many of the large colonial land holdings were divided among Kenyans into small farms known as *shambas.* The government continues to control a large part of the economy, although in the late 1990s it began selling off many state farms to private owners and corporations.

Commercial Activities. The main goods produced for sale are agricultural products such as corn, sweet potatoes, bananas, and citrus fruit. These are sold in small local markets, as well as in larger markets in the cities, alongside other commercial goods and handicrafts. Bargaining is an expected, and at times lengthy, process in financial interactions.

Major Industries. The main industries are the small-scale production of consumer goods, such as plastic, furniture, and textiles; food processing; oil refining; and cement. Tourism is also important to Kenya's economy, due mainly to game reserves and resorts along the coast, but the industry has been hurt by recent political instability.

Trade. The primary imports are machinery and transportation equipment, petroleum products, iron, and steel. These come from the United Kingdom, the United Arab Emirates, the United States, Japan, and Germany. Kenya exports tea, coffee, horticultural products, and petroleum products to Uganda, the United Kingdom, Tanzania, Egypt, and Germany.

Division of Labor. Kikuyu are the best represented ethnic group in jobs of the highest status, followed by the Luo. Members of these two groups hold most of the highest positions in government, business, and education. Many Luo are fishermen and boatbuilders; those who have moved to the cities often take up work as mechanics and craftsmen, and dominate Kenyan trade unions. A number of Maasai and Samburu have taken jobs as park rangers and safari guides. Along the coast, most merchants and storekeepers are of Indian or Arab descent. In farming communities, work is divided among people of all different ages; children begin helping at a very young age, and the elderly continue to work as long as they are physically able.

Social Stratification

Classes and Castes. There is a great deal of poverty in Kenya. Most of the wealthiest people are Kikuyu, followed by the Luo. Kenyans of higher economic and social class tend to have assimilated more Western culture than those of the lower classes.

Symbols of Social Stratification. Among herders such as the Masai, wealth is measured in the number of cattle one owns. Having many children is also a sign of wealth. In urban areas, most people dress in Western-style clothing. While western clothing does not necessarily indicate high status, expensive brand-name clothing does. Many women wear a colorful *kanga,* a large piece of cloth that can be wrapped around the body as a skirt or shawl and head scarves are also common. Some ethnic groups, such as the Kikuyu and the Luo, have adopted Western culture more readily than others, who prefer to retain their distinctive styles of dress and ornamentation. Women of the northern nomadic tribes, for example, wear *gorfa*, a sheepskin or goatskin dyed red or black and wrapped around the body, held in place with a leather cord and a rope belt.

Among some ethnic groups, such as the Rendille, a woman's hairstyle indicates her marital status and whether or not she has children. A man's stage of life is revealed by specific headdresses or jewelry. The Pokot and Maasai wear rows of beaded necklaces, as do the Turkana women, who wear so many strands that it elongates their necks. The above practices are indicators of marital and social standings within Kenyan society.

Political Life

Government. Kenya is divided into seven provinces and one area. The president is both chief of state and head of the government. He is chosen from among the members of the National Assembly, and is elected by popular vote for a five-year term. The president appoints both a vice-president and a cabinet. The legislature is the unicameral National Assembly, or Bunge. It consists of 222 members, twelve appointed by the president and the rest elected by popular vote.

Leadership and Political Officials. According to Kenya's constitution, multiple parties are allowed, but in fact it is President Moi's Kenya African National Union (KANU) that controls the government. The main opposition groups (which have little clout) are the Forum for the Restoration of Democracy-Kenya (FORD–Kenya), the National Development Party, the Social Democratic Party, and the Democratic Party.

Social Problems and Control. Crime (mostly petty crime) and drug use are rampant in the cities. Kenya has a common law system similar to that of Britain. There are also systems of tribal law and Islamic law, used to settle personal disputes within an ethnic group or between two Muslims. Citizens are not granted free legal aid except in capital cases, and as a result many poor Kenyans are jailed simply for lack of a legal defense. Kenya has a spotty record in the area of human rights, and does not allow independent monitoring of its prison system.

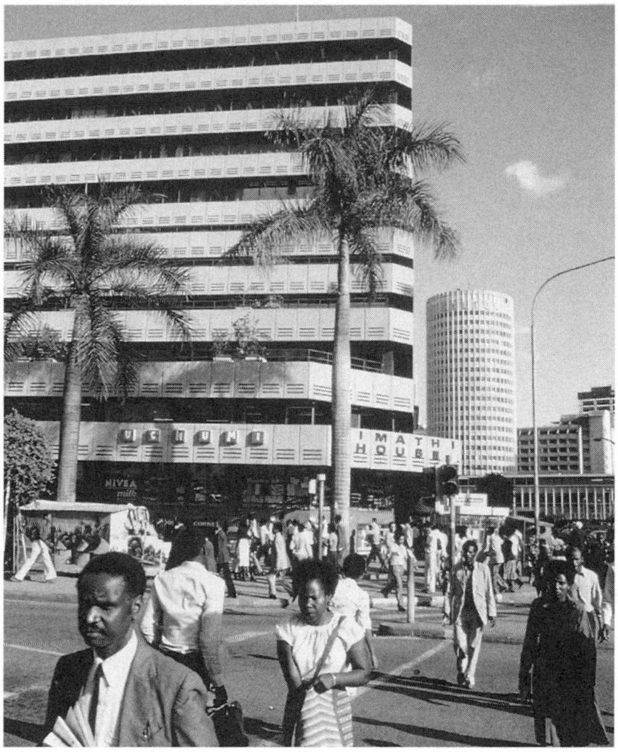

Nairobi, Kenya, is a thriving urban center.

Military Activity. Kenya's military includes an army, navy, air force, and the paramilitary General Service Unit of the Police, which has been used to put down civilian rebellions and protests. The country's military expenditures total 2 percent of the gross domestic product (GDP). Serving in the military is voluntary.

Social Welfare and Change Programs

Most social welfare is provided by the family rather than the government. There are government-run hospitals and health clinics, as well as adult literacy programs.

Nongovernmental Organizations and Other Associations

There are a number of international organizations that work in Kenya to provide humanitarian aid and to help with the state of the economy and health care. These include the World Health Organization, the United Nations Educational, Scientific, and Cultural Organization (UNESCO), the United States Agency for International Development (USAID), and others. There are also a number of human rights organizations, including the Kenya Antirape Organization, the Legal Advice Center, and the Catholic Justice and Peace Commission. Kenya is a member of the United Nations, the Commonwealth of Nations, and the Organization of African Unity.

Gender Roles and Statuses

Division of Labor by Gender. Among herders, men are responsible for the care of the animals. In agricultural communities, both men and women work in the fields but it is estimated that women do up to 80 percent of the work in rural areas: in addition to work in the fields, they take care of the children, cook, keep a vegetable garden, and fetch water and are also responsible for taking food to market to sell. It is common for men to leave their rural communities and move to the city in search of paying jobs. While this sometimes brings more income to the family, it also increases the women's workload. In urban areas women are more likely to take jobs outside the home; in fact, 40 percent of the urban work force is female. For the most part, women are still confined to lower-paying and lower status jobs such as food service or secretarial work, but the city of Kisumu has elected a woman mayor, and there are several women in Parliament.

The Relative Status of Men and Women. For the most part, women are treated as second-class citizens in Kenya. Despite the disproportionate amount of work that women do, men usually control the money and property in a family. Wife beating is common, and women have little legal recourse. Another women's issue is clitoridectomy, or female genital mutilation, which leaves many women in continual pain and vulnerable to infection. As women gain access to education, their status in society is increasing. Women's groups such as the National Women's Council of Kenya have been instrumental in pushing for just laws and in teaching women skills that allow them to earn a living.

Marriage, Family, and Kinship

Marriage. Polygamy is traditional, and in the past it was not uncommon for men to have five or six wives. The practice is becoming less typical today as it has been opposed by Christian missionaries, and is increasingly impractical as few men can afford to support multiple partners. When a man chooses a potential wife, he negotiates a bride price of money or cattle with the woman's father. The price is generally higher for a first wife than for subsequent ones. The wedding ceremony and feast are celebrated in the husband's home.

Domestic Unit. In the traditional living arrangement, a man builds a separate hut for each of his wives, where she will live with her children, and a hut for himself. In a family with one wife, the parents often live together with girls and younger boys, while the older boys have smaller houses close by. It is common for several generations to live together under the same roof. According to tradition, it is the responsibility of the youngest son to care for his aging parents. Among the Maasai, houses are divided into four sections: one section for the women, one section for the children, one section for the husband, and one section for cooking and eating.

Inheritance. According to the tradition, inheritance passes from father to son. This is still the case today, and there are legal as well as cultural obstacles to women inheriting property.

Kin Groups. Extended families are considered a single unit; children are often equally close to cousins and siblings, and aunts and uncles are thought of as fathers and mothers. These large family groups often live together in small settlements. Among the Maasai, for example, ten or twelve huts are built in a circle surrounded by a thornbush fence. This is known as a *kraal.*

Socialization

Infant Care. Mothers usually tie their babies to their backs with a cloth sling. Girls begin caring for younger siblings at a very early age, and it is not uncommon to see a five- or six-year-old girl caring for a baby.

Child Rearing and Education. Child rearing is communal: responsibility for the children is shared among aunts, uncles, grandparents, and other members of the community. Boys and girls have fairly separate upbringings. Each is taught the duties and obligations specific to their sex: girls learn early how to carry water, cook, and care for children, while boys are schooled in the ways of herding or working in the fields. Children are also grouped into "age sets" with peers born in the same year. Members of a given age set form a special bond, and undergo initiation rituals as a group.

Primary school, which children attend from the age of seven to the age of fourteen, is free. Secondary school for students ages fourteen to eighteen is prohibitively expensive for most of the population. Only half of all children complete the first seven years of schooling, and only one-seventh of these

Farms in the Great Rift Valley of Kenya. In the 1990s, the government began selling state farms to private enterprises.

continue on to high school. After each of the two levels, there is a series of national exams which students must pass in order to continue in their studies.

Kenya's education system has been plagued with widespread accusations of cheating, and there is a shortage of qualified teachers to educate the burgeoning population of school-age children. In addition to government-run schools, churches and civic groups have established self-help or *harambee* schools, with the help of volunteers from the United States and Europe. These schools now outnumber government-run secondary schools.

Higher Education. There are eight universities in Kenya. The largest of these is the University of Nairobi, the Kenyatta University College is also located in the capital. In addition to universities, Kenya has several technical institutes which train students in agriculture, teaching, and other professions. Those who can afford it often send their children abroad for post-secondary education.

ETIQUETTE

Kenyans are generally friendly and hospitable. Greetings are an important social interaction, and often include inquiries about health and family members. Visitors to a home are usually offered food or tea, and it is considered impolite to decline. Elderly people are treated with a great deal of respect and deference.

RELIGION

Religious Beliefs. The population is 38 percent Protestant and 28 percent Roman Catholic. Twenty-six percent are animist, 7 percent are Muslim, and 1 percent follow other religions. Many people incorporate traditional beliefs into their practice of Christianity, causing some tension between Kenyans and Christian churches, particularly on the issue of polygamy. Religious practices of different ethnic groups vary, but one common element is the belief in a spirit world inhabited by the souls of ancestors. The Kikuyu and several other groups worship the god Ngai, who is said to live on top of Mount Kenya.

Religious Practitioners. In traditional religions, diviners are believed to have the power to communicate with the spirit world, and they use their powers to cure people of diseases or evil spirits. Diviners are also called upon to help bring rain during times of drought. Sorcerers and witches are also believed to have supernatural powers, but unlike the diviners they use these powers to cause harm. It is the job of the diviners to counter their evil workings.

Rituals and Holy Places. Among the Masai, the beginning of the rainy season is observed with a celebration which lasts for several days and includes singing, dancing, eating, and praying for the health of their animals. For the ritual dances, the performers die their hair red, paint black stripes on their bodies, and don ostrich-feather headdresses. The Kikuyu mark the start of the planting season with their own festivities. Their ceremonial dances are often performed by warriors wearing leopard or zebra skin robes and carrying spears and shields. The dancers dye their bodies blue, and paint them in white patterns.

Initiation ceremonies are important rites of passage, and they vary from tribe to tribe. Boys and girls undergo separate rituals, after which they are considered of marriageable age. Kikuyu boys, for example, are initiated at the age of eighteen. Their ears are pierced, their heads shaved, and their faces marked with white earth. Pokot girls are initiated at twelve years old, in a ceremony that involves singing, dancing, and decorating their bodies with ocher, red clay, and animal fat.

Weddings are important occasions throughout the country, and are celebrated with up to eight days of music, dance, and special foods.

Death and the Afterlife. At death, Kenyans believe that one enters the spirit world, which has great influence in the world of the living. Many Kenyans believe in reincarnation, and children are thought to be the embodiment of the souls of a family's ancestors.

Medicine and Health Care

The health care system in Kenya is understaffed and poorly supplied. The government runs clinics throughout the country that focus primarily on preventive medicine. These clinics have had some success in reducing the rate of sleeping sickness and malaria through the use of vaccines, but the country is still plagued with high rates of gastroenteritis, dysentery, diarrhea, sexually transmitted diseases, and trachoma. Access to modern health care is rare, particularly in rural areas, and many people still depend on traditional cures including herbal medicines and healing rituals.

Kenya has one of the world's highest birth rates, and birth control programs have been largely ineffective. The life expectancy, while higher than in some other African nations, is still only fifty-four years. AIDS has been devastating to the country, and at least five hundred Kenyans die of the disease each day. President Moi has declared the AIDS epidemic a national disaster, but has nonetheless refused to encourage condom use.

Secular Celebrations

New Year's Day is celebrated on 1 January, and Labor Day, 1 May. Other holidays include Madaraka Day anniversary of self-rule, 1 June; Moi Day commemorating the president's installation in office, on 10 October; Independence Day also called Jamhuri Day, on 12 December; Kenyatta Day, celebrating Jomo Kenyatta as the national hero, on 20 October. Also called Harambee Day, this festival includes a large parade in the capital and celebrations throughout the country.

The Arts and Humanities

Support for the Arts. The National Gallery in Nairobi has a special gallery and studio space set aside for emerging artists. The University of Nairobi also supports a national traveling theater company.

Literature. Kenya has a strong oral tradition. Many folktales concern animals or the intervention of the spirits in everyday life; others are war stories detailing soldiers' bravery. The stories are passed from generation to generation, often in the form of songs. Contemporary Kenyan literature draws extensively from this oral heritage, as well as from Western literary tradition. Ngugi wa Thiong'o, a Kikuyu, is Kenya's most prominent writer. His first novels, including *Weep Not, Child* (1964) and *Petals of Blood* (1977) were written in English. Though they were strong messages of social protest, it was not until he began to write exclusively in Swahili and Kikuyu that Ngugi became the victim of censorship. He was jailed for one year, and later exiled to England. Other contemporary Kenyan writers, such as Sam Kahiga, Meja Mwangi and Marjorie Oludhe Macgoye, are less explicitly political in their work.

Graphic Arts. Kenya is known for its sculpture and wood-carving, which often has religious significance. Figures of ancestors are believed to appease the inhabitants of the spirit world, as are the elaborately carved amulets that Kenyans wear around their necks. In addition to wood, sculptors also work in ivory and gold. Contemporary sculptors often blend traditional styles with more modern ones.

Only half of Kenyan children complete the first seven years of schooling.

Artists also create the colorful masks and headdresses that are worn during traditional dances, often fashioned to represent birds or other animals. Jewelry is another Kenyan art form, and includes elaborate silver and gold bracelets and various forms of colorful beadwork.

In some tribes, including the Kikuyu and the Luhya, women make pottery and elaborately decorated baskets.

Performance Arts. Dancing is an important part of Kenyan culture. Men and women usually dance separately. Men perform line dances, some of which involve competing to see who can jump the highest. Dance is often an element of religious ceremonies, such as marriage, child naming, and initiation. Costume is an important element of many traditional dances, as are props: dancers often don masks and carry shields, swords, and other objects.

The music of Kenya is polyrhythmic, incorporating several different beats simultaneously. The primary instruments are drums but lutes, woodwinds, and thumb pianos are also used. Singing often follows a call-and-response pattern, and singers chant rhythms that diverge from those played on the instruments. Kikuyu music is relatively simple; the main instrument is the *gicandi*, a rattle made from a gourd. Other groups, such as the Luhya, have more complex music and dance traditions, incorporating a variety of instruments.

In the cities, *benga*, a fusion of Western and Kenyan music, is popular. *Benga* was originated by the Luo in the 1950s, and incorporates two traditional instruments, the *nyatiti*, a small stringed instrument, and the *orutu*, a one-string fiddle, as well as the electric guitar. *Taarab* music, which is popular along the coast, shows both Arabic and Indian influence. It is sung by women, with drums, acoustic guitar, a small organ, and sometimes a string section accompanying the singers.

The State of the Physical and Social Sciences

Kenya has few facilities for the study of physical sciences. The National Museum in Nairobi has collections of historical and cultural artifacts and the museum at Fort Jesus in Mombasa is dedicated to archeology and history.

Much of what scientific activity there is in Kenya revolves around conservation. There are a number of National Parks where the animals are protected, and scientists come from around the world to study the nation's rich and diverse wildlife.

Bibliography

Aieko, Monica. *Kenya: Water to Unburden Women*, 1999.

Clough, Marshall S. *Mau Mau Memoirs: History, Memory, and Politics*, 1998.

Kyle, Keith. *Politics of the Independent Kenya*, 1999.

Maxon, Robert M. and Thomas P. Ofacansky. *Historical Dictionary of Kenya*, 2000.

McGeary, Johanna, et al. "Terror in Africa." *Time South Pacific*, 17 August 1999.

"Moi, Lord of the Empty Dance." *The Economist*, 15 May 1999.

Morton, Andrew. *Moi: The Making of an African Statesman*, 1998.

"No Pastures New." *The Economist*, 18 January 1997.

Oded, Arye. *Islam and Politics in Kenya*, 2000.

Ogot, B. A. and W. R. Oghieng', eds. *Decolonization and Independence in Kenya 1940–93*, 1995.

Oucho, John O. *Urban Migrants and Rural Development in Kenya*, 1996.

Patel, Preeti. "The Kenyan Election." *Contemporary Review*, 1 April 1998.

Robinson, Simon. "Free as the Wind Blows." *Time*, 28 February 2000.

———. "A Rough Kind of Justice." *Time South Pacific*, 10 May 1999.

Russell, Rosalind. "Kenya Calls AIDS National Disaster, Bars Condom News Alerts." *Reuters NewMedia*, 30 November 1999.

Sayer, Geoff. *Kenya: Promised Land?*, 1998.

"Serial Killer at Large." *The Economist*, 7 February 1998.

Simmons, Ann M. "'Inherited' Kenya Widows Fear Spread of AIDS." *Los Angeles Times*, 13 March 1998.

Srujana, K. *Status of Women in Kenya: A Sociological Study*, 1996.

Turner, Raymond M., et al. *Kenya's Changing Landscape*, 1998.

Vine, Jeremy. "View from Nairobi." *New Statesman*, 2 January 1999.

Watson, Mary Ann, ed. *Modern Kenya: Social Issues and Perspectives*, 2000.

Women and Land Rights in Kenya, 1998.

—Eleanor Stanford

KIRIBATI

CULTURE NAME

I-Kiribati or kaini Kiribati. "Kiribati" is a transliteration of "Gilberts," the British colonial name for part of the Gilbert and Ellice Islands Colony.

ALTERNATIVE NAMES

The Kiribati name for the Gilbert Islands is Tungaru, and the archipelago's inhabitants sometimes refer to themselves as *I-Tungaru*. Island of origin is an important aspect of identification that predates colonialism, and *I-Kiribati* differentiate themselves by birthplace.

ORIENTATION

Identification. Kiribati is located at the interface of the Micronesian and Polynesian cultural areas and is generally considered Micronesian. The overwhelming majority of the population is I-Kiribati, with very small minorities (less than 2 percent) of Tuvaluans and *I-Matang* (Westerners).

Location and Geography. The country consists of 33 islands in three primary groups—the western Tungaru chain (sixteen islands), the Phoenix Islands (eight islands), and the Line Islands (eight of the ten islands in the chain)—plus Banaba (Ocean Island) at the western edge of the nation. Ocean-rich and land-poor, these equatorial islands are scattered over millions of square kilometers of the central Pacific Ocean, with a total land area of about 284 square miles (736 square kilometers). Kiritimati (Christmas Island) in the northern Line Islands accounts for about 48 percent of this land area. Banaba is a raised limestone island, but the other islands are all coral atolls, and most have lagoons. These atolls rise less than thirteen feet (four meters) above sea level, raising concerns over rising sea levels as a result of global warming. The thin alkaline soils are extremely infertile, and there is no fresh surface water. Mean daily temperatures vary only slightly, averaging approximately 83 degrees Fahrenheit (28 degrees Celsius). The north of the Tungaru chain is wetter, more verdant, and less prone to drought than the south.

Demography. Banaba and the sixteen most westerly islands have been inhabited for over three thousand years by ancestors of the contemporary I-Kiribati. The Phoenix Islands and Line Islands were not permanently inhabited before the twentieth century. Twenty of the islands are permanently settled. The majority of the population (92 percent) lives in the Tungaru chain, with over one-third living on urban South Tarawa.

The population reached 84,000 in 1998, and is growing at a rate of 1.4–1.8 percent per year. Population has been growing rapidly since the early 1900s, and overpopulation is a serious concern of the government. While family-planning methods were introduced in 1968 and are delivered free, fertility remains moderately high and large families are culturally valued. Despite government efforts to maintain and improve life on the outer islands, there has been substantial migration to the capital on South Tarawa. There are several thousand I-Kiribati in other countries, most serving as temporary workers. There is a small migrant community of I-Kiribati in Vanuatu. Most Banabans were resettled on Rabi Island in Fiji, and became Fijian citizens in 1970. However, they retain ownership of land on Banaba and rights of residence and representation in Kiribati.

Linguistic Affiliation. The I-Kiribati language, sometimes referred to as Gilbertese, is a Micronesian language in the Austronesian family and is spoken in a relatively uniform manner throughout the islands. While the language shows considerable borrowing from Polynesia, it is distinct from the language of neighboring Tuvalu and the Marshall Islands. English is the official language and is taught in primary and secondary schools. Many adults on the outer islands speak little English.

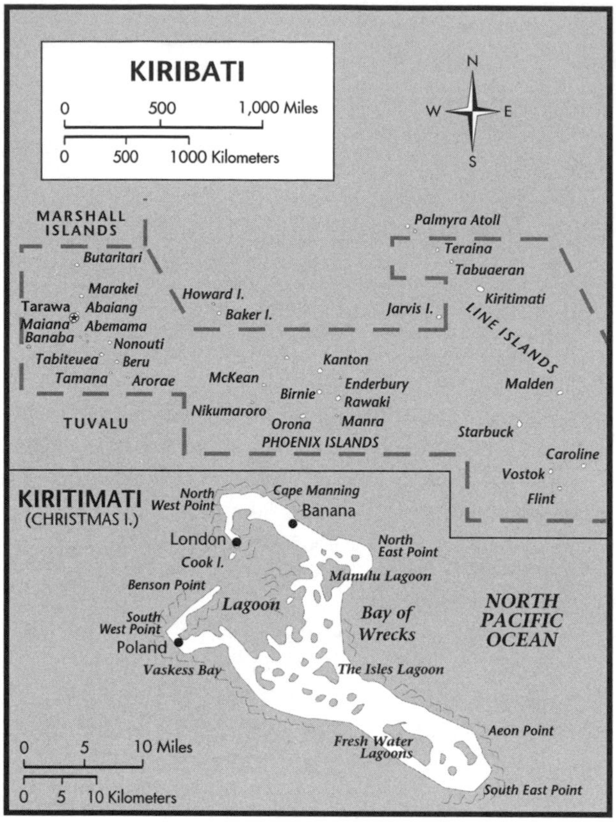

Kiribati

Symbolism. Symbols of nationalism are linked centrally to independence. The primary symbol of the republic is the flag, which depicts a frigate bird over an ocean sunrise. Seventeen rays of sunlight represent the sixteen Tungaru islands and Banaba, and three waves represent the Tungaru, Phoenix, and Line island groups. On the flag is the motto *te mauri te raoi ao te tabomoa* (''Good Health, Peace, and Honor''). The national anthem is *Teirake kaini Kiribati* (*Stand Up, I-Kiribati*).

History and Ethnic Relations

Emergence of the Nation. In 1892, the Gilbert Islands became a protectorate of Great Britain and were joined with the Ellice Islands protectorate in 1916 to form the Gilbert and Ellice Islands Colony. In that year, Banaba, Fanning Island (Tabuaeran), Washington Island (Teraina), and the Union Islands (Tokelau) became part of the colony, as did Kiritimati in 1919 and most of the Phoenix Islands in 1937.

Despite a centralized colonial government, a schism developed over time between the culturally and linguistically different Gilbert and Ellice Islanders concerning jobs and other political issues. This ultimately resulted in the separation of the Ellice Islands to become Tuvalu in 1978. In contrast to Kiribati, Tuvalu opted for membership in the British Commonwealth. In July 1979, the Gilberts, Banaba, and the Phoenix and Line Islands became the independent Republic of Kiribati.

Several islands in northern and central Kiribati were occupied by the Japanese in World War II, and the Battle of Tarawa in November 1943 was one of the bloodiest of that war. However, there was little ongoing impact from the Japanese occupation.

National Identity. Precolonially, the people of the Tungaru islands formed small, shifting political units, and there was no unified economic or political system or cultural identity. A single national identity emerged only after World War II as a result of colonial policies intended to move the area toward political independence.

Differences between the northern, central, and southern islands of Tungaru, especially in terms of social and political organization, traditions, and group characteristics, are clearly identified by I-Kiribati and underlie national politics. Traditionally, the north had a more complex social organization with a kingship and chiefly classes compared with the more egalitarian social structure of the south. Currently the north and central islands are seen as more progressive than the south, which is more politically and socially conservative.

Ethnic Relations. I-Kiribati can be considered culturally and ethnically homogeneous, with a shared genetic history, cultural traditions, values, historical experience, and language. I-Kiribati distinguish themselves from neighboring island groups and see the greatest conceptual divide between themselves and I-Matang (''Westerners''). The culture and language of Banaba are basically I-Kiribati. The primary issue in Banaban independence movements has been the distribution of phosphate revenues, not cultural differences.

Urbanism, Architecture, and the Use of Space

Rural houses usually are built of traditional materials and are open-sided rectangular structures with thatched roofs and raised floors. In towns, more houses are built with imported materials such as concrete block and corrugated iron. The most symbolically important structure is the rectangular, open-sided *maneaba* (meeting house), which may be owned by a family, church community, or village. The *maneaba* functions as a central place for formal

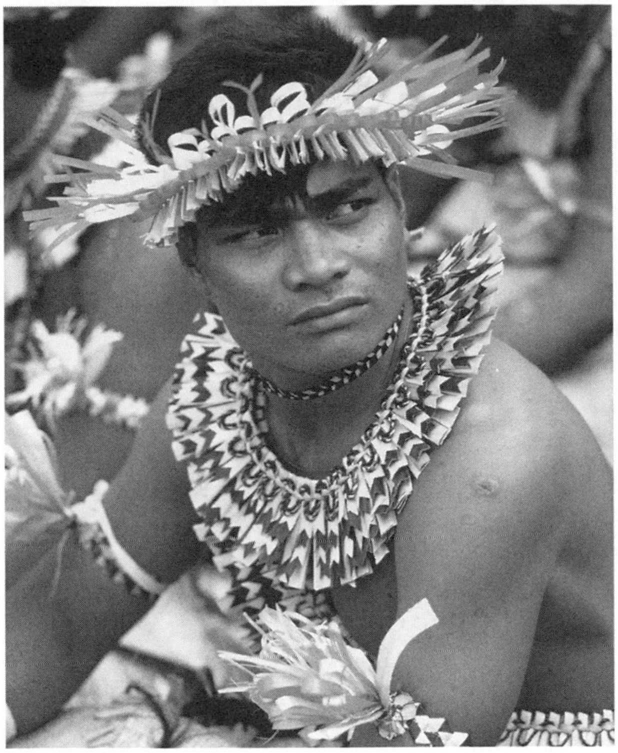

A man wearing traditional dress for a ceremony in Kiribati.

and informal group activities. *Maneaba* built with modern materials follow the traditional prescriptions of style, aspect, and orientation. The floor is composed of unmarked but known sitting places termed *boti* arranged around the perimeter, with one belonging to each family represented in the *maneaba*; this is the place from which a representative (usually the oldest male) of each family participates in community discussions and decision making. Churches are architecturally European and often are the largest structures in a village.

Food and Economy

Food in Daily Life. Fish and marine resources are a primary food source, as the ecological nature of atolls mean that only the most hardy plants can grow there. Local crops include coconut, giant swamp taro, breadfruit, pandanus, and a native fig. Coconut is central to the diet and is especially valued for the sweet, vitamin-rich toddy (sap) cut from the flower spathe. Toddy is used as a children's drink or as a base for syrup. It can also be soured into vinegar and fermented into an alcoholic drink. Drunkenness is a widespread problem that is dealt with on some islands by the prohibition of alcohol. Imported goods, especially rice, but also flour, canned butter, and canned fish and meat, are becoming increasingly important in the daily diet.

Food Customs at Ceremonial Occasions. The display and eating of prestige foods is central to all celebrations and banquets. Although imported goods are increasingly available, local foods are more important in feasting, such as crayfish, giant clam, pig, chicken, and giant swamp taro. The most symbolically valued crop is giant swamp taro, which is grown in pits dug into the water lens under each atoll.

Basic Economy. Around 80 percent of the population engages in subsistence agriculture and fishing. The cash economy is limited largely to South Tarawa, where the private sector of the economy is very small and there are few manufacturing enterprises. Independence in 1979 coincided with the end of phosphate mining on Banaba, which in 1978 had accounted for 88 percent of the nation's export earnings. The cash economy has now shifted to dependence on remittances from I-Kiribati employed in phosphate mining on Nauru or working as seamen on foreign-owned merchant ships, as well as foreign aid. Accounting for some 60 percent of the gross domestic product in 1995, aid is received mainly from Japan, Australia, New Zealand, South Korea, and the European Union. The government has determined that there is potential for the development of tourism. However, economic development is constrained by a shortage of skilled workers, weak infrastructure, and geographic remoteness.

Land Tenure and Property. Access to and ownership of land underlie and cement social relations. A vital unit in I-Kiribati society, the *utu* includes all those people who are linked as kin and share common ownership of land plots. Everyone on an island belongs to several utu; people may inherit the land rights for each utu from either parent. The *kainga*, or family estate, sits at the heart of each utu, and those who live on the particular kainga of one of their utu have the greatest say in utu affairs and the largest share of produce from the land in that utu. The colonial government attempted to reorganize the land tenure system to encourage the codification of individual land holdings, in part to reduce land disputes. As a result, land transfers are now registered.

Commercial Activities. Marine resources have emerged as the most important natural resource for Kiribati, particularly the licensing of foreign fishing vessels to fish in the two hundred nautical miles of the exclusive economic zone in the waters surrounding the islands. Efforts to develop a competitive local fishing company have been less successful but large stocks of tuna fish remain in Kiribati waters. Copra, fish, and farmed seaweed are major exports.

Trade. The primary imports are food, manufactured goods, vehicles, fuel, and machinery. Most consumer goods are imported from Australia, and the Australian dollar is the unit of currency.

Social Stratification

Classes and Castes. Generally, postcolonial Kiribati can be considered a relatively classless society. A new social class of young leaders is emerging, however, threatening the village-based traditional authority of elders. There are also growing income disparities, and access to higher education is emerging as a key differentiating factor.

Political Life

Government. The *boti,* or clan, system, which according to oral tradition was imported from Samoa around 1400 C.E., remained the central focus of social and political life in Tungaru until around 1870. By the time of the establishment of the British protectorate in 1892, the traditional boti system had largely been eradicated, replaced judicially and administratively by a central government station on each island. Another major change came when the colonial administration completely reorganized the land tenure system before the 1930s, taking households that had been dispersed as hamlets in the bush and lining them up in villages along a central thoroughfare. At that time, control over village and family activities started to move to the heads of families. In 1963, the British colonial government abolished the kingship (*uea*) system that was part of the traditional political structure of the northern islands. The council of elders (*unimane*) that historically included all the male senior family heads is now responsible for overseeing village and island affairs. Local government consists of statutory island councils with elected members and limited administrative and financial powers and government-appointed administrators.

The government consists of a *Maneaba ni Maungatabu,* or parliament, which is unicameral. The *Beretitenti,* or president, is elected by popular vote every four years and is both head of government and chief of state. There is no tradition of formal political parties, although there are loosely structured political parties. There is universal suffrage at age 18.

Leadership and Political Officials. The council of elders in each community continues to be an effective local political force. The village household is the most important unit, and within it the most important person is the oldest male.

Social Problems and Control. The judicial branch of the government includes a court of appeals and a high court, as well as a magistrate's court on each inhabited island. The jurisdiction of the magistrates' courts is unlimited in land matters but limited in criminal and civil cases. There are small police forces on all the islands. Emerging substantial problems include embezzlement (often connected with the practice of *bubuti,* or requests by kin that cannot be refused), robbery, sexual coercion, and child and domestic abuse, often linked to alcohol use.

Military Activity. There is no standing army. Kiribati has shown some assertiveness in its foreign relations, for example, in the 1986 fishing rights treaty that was negotiated with the Soviet Union despite strong opposition from the United States.

Nongovernmental Organizations and Other Associations

Nongovernmental organizations (NGO) include the Catholic and Protestant women's organizations and the Scouting Association and Guiding Association. An NGO of traditional healers was recently formed. Australian, British, Japanese, and American volunteer organizations are active in Kiribati.

Gender Roles and Statuses

Division of Labor by Gender. Labor is divided by gender, with men fishing and collecting toddy and doing heavy construction tasks, while women handle child care and cook and keep house; both genders cultivate crops. While women may fish and often collect shellfish in the lagoon, only men may collect toddy. There is a clear status ranking in each household, which is usually headed by the oldest male unless he is too elderly to be active. The control of domestic activities lies with a senior married woman.

The Relative Status of Women and Men. While Kiribati society is currently egalitarian, democratic, and respectful of human rights, in the traditional culture women occupy a subordinate role. Job opportunities for women are limited, and there is no

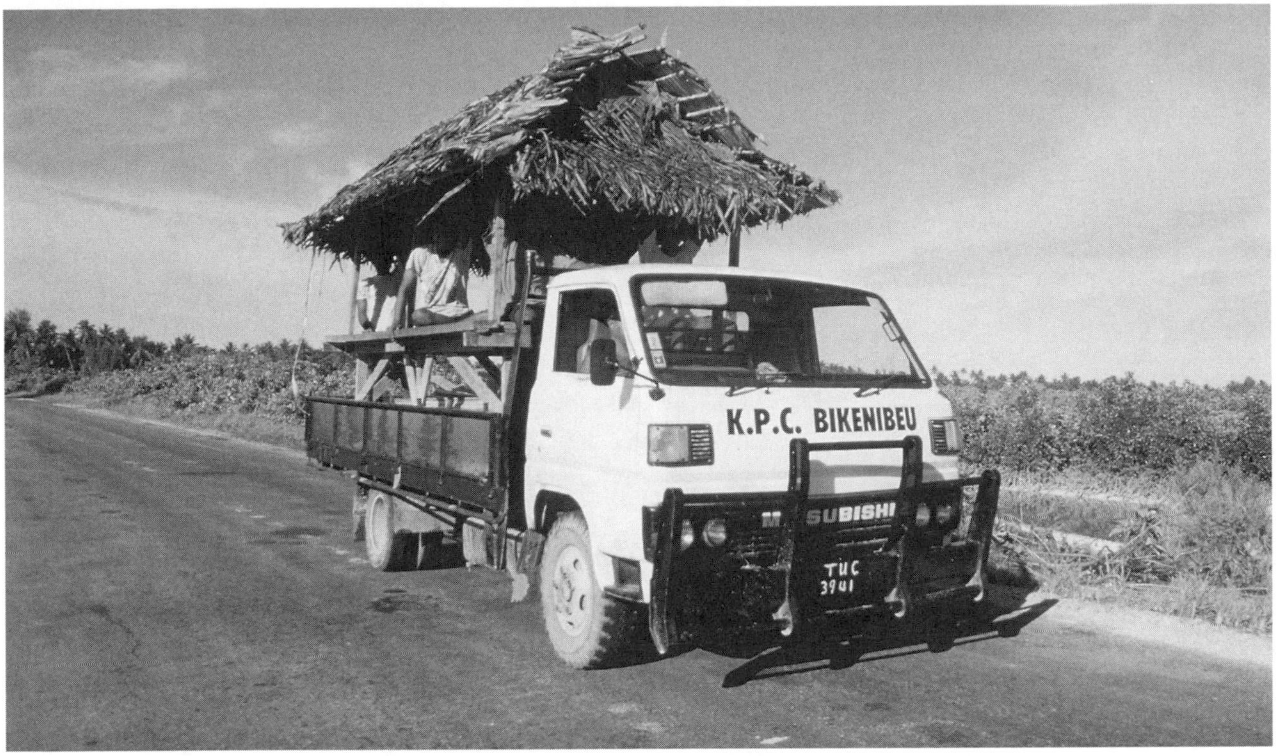

A new home in transit on the back of a truck in Tarawa. Rural houses are built with traditional materials while imported materials are used for homes in towns.

law against gender discrimination. Few women have served in key governmental or political positions. Women have started to play a more prominent role through women's associations and they now occasionally speak in the *maneaba*.

Marriage, Family, and Kinship

Marriage. Although historically polygamy was practiced, the marriage system is now monogamous. Arranged marriages remain common, especially in rural areas. "Love matches" and elopements have become more common and are tolerated by most families. Virginity tests of the bride remain valued despite criticism by churches. Marriage is almost universal, and divorce is unpopular and uncommon.

Domestic Unit. The household is commonly based on a single nuclear family and may include aging parents and adoptive kin. Patrilocal residence remains common in rural areas, with married women moving to live on the husband's *kainga*.

Kin Groups. The main kinship units are *mwenga* ("household"), utu ("related family"), and kainga. Membership in *mwenga* is determined by residence, in utu by kin relations, and in kainga by common property holding and descent from a common ancestor. Inheritance of property and kinship are traced through both the mother's and the father's families. Adoption is widely practiced, especially between close kin.

Socialization

Infant Care. In this pro-natal society, infants are showered with attention and care by both parents and by the extended family. In the first few months after a birth, the mother stays in the house with the baby, and breast-feeding on demand is standard until at least six months of age. Kiribati has one of the highest infant death rates in the world as a result of diarrheal disease and respiratory infection.

Child Rearing and Education. After infancy, care by siblings, especially sisters, is very common, even by siblings as young as eight years. Children are indulged until they are about four years old, after which they become subject to strict parental and kin authority reinforced by corporal punishment. Crying and emotional outbreaks are not tolerated, and a good child is obedient, helpful, and respectful. By age eight or nine, children are expected to start helping around the house.

Beach houses in Tarawa, Kiribati, consist of thatched roofs and native wood.

Schooling is compulsory for children from age six. Approximately 20 percent of primary students go on to receive secondary education. Education is highly valued by parents as a means of increasing their children's wage-earning abilities.

Higher Education. Higher education is expanding and increasingly valued. Kiribati participates with eleven other Pacific Island countries in funding the University of the South Pacific with its main campus in Suva, Fiji. Technical education is available in South Tarawa at the Teacher's Training College, Tarawa Technical Institute, and the Marine Training Centre.

Etiquette

The most important aspect of etiquette for locals and guests involves behavior in the *maneaba*, where there are appropriate places and ways to sit and interact. In all aspects of life, humility and humbleness are admired. Direct eye contact is uncommon, and it is inappropriate to look directly at one of higher status or cut between the gaze of talking individuals. Touching of heads is considered extremely intimate, and the top of the head is a taboo area. Modest dress is important for women, and cleanliness of the body and clothing is valued.

Religion

Religious Beliefs. According to I-Kiribati mythology, the giant spider Nareau was the creator, followed by spirits (*anti*), half spirits, half humans, and finally humans. The *anti* were the most important figures in I-Kiribati worship before Christian missionaries arrived, and they remain respected in everyday life.

Conversion activity began in 1852 with the arrival of Protestant missionaries. There was a rivalry between the Catholic and Protestant missions, resulting in deep-seated animosities that remain as an undercurrent in national and island politics. Just over half of all I-Kiribati are Catholic, almost half are Protestant, and the remainder are Seventh-Day Adventist, Baha'i, and members of the Church of God and the Church of Latter-Day Saints.

Medicine and Health Care

Life expectancy is low, and the most common causes of adult death are infectious diseases, including tuberculosis. Liver cancer is a common cause of male death, exacerbated by widespread infection with hepatitis B and heavy alcohol use. There have been several cases of AIDS. Traffic-related accidents are increasing.

While a new central hospital was completed in Tarawa in 1992 and the Ministry of Health and Family Planning provides free medical care in most villages, medical supplies and services are not always available. A pluralistic system of traditional herbal and massage treatments is maintained alongside biomedical services, and many women give birth at home. Healing traditions are passed on as special knowledge within families.

Secular Celebrations

The most important holiday is the annual celebration of independence on 12 July, which includes sports competitions, parades, and feasts. Other national holidays include New Year's Day, Easter, Christmas, and Youth Day (4 August).

Bibliography

Brewis, Alexandra. *Lives on the Line: Women and Ecology on a Pacific Atoll*, 1996.

Grimble, Arthur Francis and H. E. Maude, eds. *Tungaru Traditions: Writings on the Atoll Culture of the Gilbert Islands*, 1989.

Macdonald, Barrie. *Cinderellas of the Empire: Toward a History of Kiribati and Tuvalu*, 1982.

Mason, Leonard, ed. *Kiribati: A Changing Atoll Culture*, 1984.

Talu et al. *Kiribati: Aspects of History*, 1979.

Van Trease, Howard, ed. *Atoll Politics: The Republic of Kiribati*, 1993.

—Alexandra Brewis
and Sandra Crismon

North Korea

Culture Name

North Korean

Alternative Name

The Democratic People's Republic of Korea

Orientation

Identification. The Democratic People's Republic of Korea, usually known as North Korea, is a state that occupies the northern half of the Korean peninsula. North Korea is a new state, founded in 1948 as a result of the postcolonial settlement handed down by the United States and the Soviet Union (USSR). The United States and the USSR replaced the Japanese in 1945 and divided the peninsula into the American south and the Soviet north. For much of its short history, North Korea was regarded as a Soviet satellite state. With the fall of the Soviet Union in 1991, however, North Korea's unique socialism has stood out in the post-Cold War world.

Little is known about North Korea in the United States, or in the world for that matter; except for the rare but striking news story about its international terrorism, the nuclear arms threat, and the devastating famine of recent years, nothing substantial is known about North Korea. This is due to the nation's strict closed-country policy: not many outsiders have visited there and not many North Koreans have traveled to the outside world.

Widely regarded as one of the few Stalinist regimes persisting into the post-Cold War era, North Korea—along with its culture, history, and society, and the daily lives of its residents—is hidden behind iron curtains. So little is known about North Korea that the country is often demonized in the Western media. This is in a stark contrast to South Korea, from which millions have emigrated to the United States, forming a substantial Korean American population. South Korea and North Korea share a half-century history of confrontation and antagonism, often involving bloodshed, as manifested in the Korean War of 1950-1953. Nevertheless, South and North Korea stem from one nation.

Location and Geography. North Korea shares borders with China and Russia to the north and the military demarcation line with South Korea in the south. The total area measures 46,540 square miles (120,540 square kilometers), with land boundaries of 1,037 miles (1,673 kilometers), and a coastline of 1,547 miles (2,495 kilometers). It is divided into 14 percent arable land, 2 percent permanent cropland, and 61 percent forest- and woodland. The country's terrain is mostly covered with hills and mountains. The highest point is Mount Paektu, which rises to 9,003 feet (2,744 meters).

North Korea's capital is P'yongyang. At the founding of North Korea in 1948, it was the only city located in the northern half of the peninsula that had a notable historical heritage going back to the premodern era. Kaesong, which once was an ancient capital of the Koryo kingdom (935–1392), located in the middle of the peninsula, became incorporated into North Korean territory only after the 1953 truce agreement that ended the Korean War. Kaesong, P'yongyang, and Namp'o, a new industrial city, are special cities with independent juridical authorities. The rest of the country is divided into nine provinces.

Demography. As of July 1998, North Korea's population was 21,234,387, with a sex ratio from birth to the age 15 of 1.05 males per female; 15–64 years, 0.96 males per female; and 65 years and over, 0.44 males per female. The infant mortality rate stood at 87.83 deaths per thousand live births. The life expectancy was 48.88 years for males and 53.88 years for females. The total fertility rate measured 1.6 children born per woman, although the population growth rate was −0.03 percent, likely because of the high infant mortality rate. The population is more or less homogeneously Korean, with a small Chinese community in the north and a few hundred

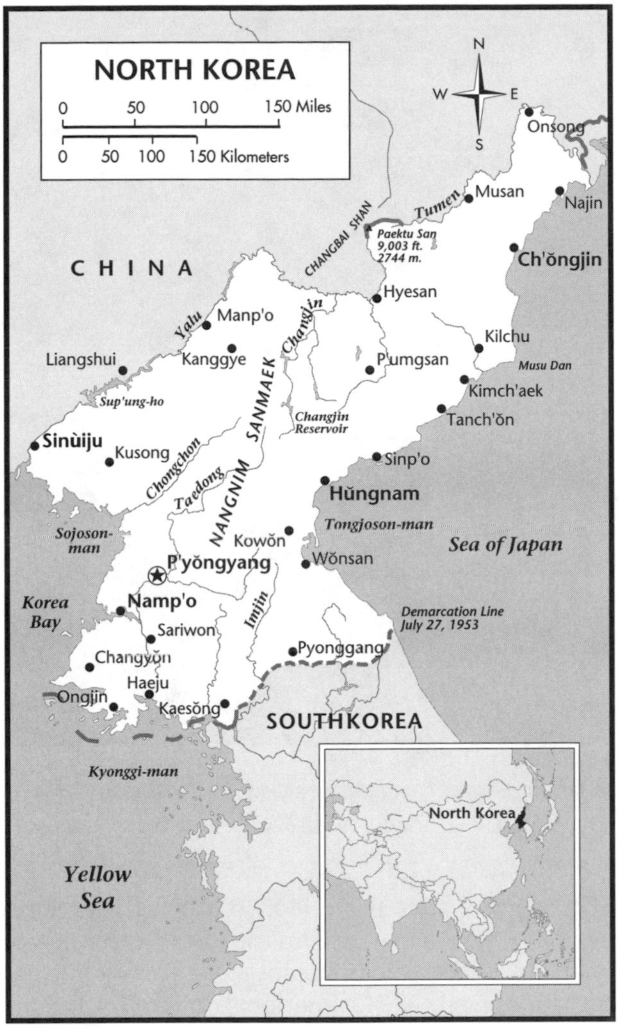

North Korea

Japanese who are mainly wives of the Korean and repatriated with their husbands after the war.

Linguistic Affiliation. Technically, North Korea uses the same Korean language as the one spoken in South Korea. The cultural and sociopolitical division of more than half a century, however, pushed the languages in the peninsula far apart, if not in syntax, at least in semantics. When North Korea faced the task of building a new national culture, it faced a serious problem of illiteracy. For example, over 90 percent of women in northern Korea in 1945 were illiterate; they in turn made up 65 percent of the total illiterate population. In order to overcome illiteracy, North Korea adopted the all-Korean script, eliminating the use of Chinese characters.

Traditionally, the Korean language operated on a dual system: in premodern Korea, oral language was indigenous Korean, but the script was classical Chinese. The syntax of the Chinese and Korean languages are distinct and for those who did not have access to formal education, the world of writing was remote and unknowable. In 1444, under the initiative of King Sejong of Yi dynasty Korea, court scholars invented a Korean script named *hunminjongum* ("the correct sound to be taught the commoners"). The original set consisted of seventeen consonants and eleven vowels. The script represented the phonetic sounds of Korean; using the script, therefore, one could write the language that people actually spoke. The advantage of using this script instead of the classical Chinese was obvious: the former corresponded to the oral utterance of Korean, helping those in lower strata and women express themselves in writing; the latter, consisting of thousands of ideographs which expressed meaning, was monopolized by the highly–ranked in the social strata. For example, the bureaucrats' qualification examinations and court documentation were all in classical Chinese, while popular stories were written in Korean script.

With more reforms over many centuries, the Korean of the late nineteenth century had developed more vowels and consonants. North Korea inherited this modern form of Korean vernacular script consisting of nineteen consonants and twenty-one vowels. The abolition of the use of Chinese characters from all public printing and writing helped achieved nationwide literacy at a remarkable speed. By 1979, the United States government estimated that North Korea had a 90 percent literacy rate. At the end of the twentieth century, it was estimated that 99 percent of North Korea's population could read and write Korean sufficiently.

Symbolism. The national symbols, such as the national emblem and flag, were all created in 1948 or thereafter. The North Korean flag consists of three colors: red, blue, and white. The top and bottom edges of the flag are thin blue stripes, paralleled by thinner white stripes, leaving the large middle field red. Toward the left, there is a white disk with a red five-pointed star. There is a national anthem, the *Aegukka* ("the song of patriotism"), but due to the worship of the longtime national leader, songs that praise Kim Il Sung have more or less replaced the anthem. With the rise of Kim Il Sung's son, Kim Jong Il, to public office, two songs, each praising Kim Il Sung and Kim Jong Il, began to be sung in public meetings.

North Koreans are strongly loyal to Kim Il Sung's family, and often refer to North Korea as "one big revolutionary family" with Kim Il Sung as household head. With Kim Il Sung's death in July 1994, his son Kim Jong Il is widely seen as the successor, although he has not yet assumed the presidency. On public occasions, every individual in North Korea wears a Kim Il Sung badge on the upper left side of the chest as a proof of loyalty; this practice continues even after Kim Il Sung's death. The type of badge one wears reflects one's status. It is almost impossible to see a North Korean not wearing a Kim Il Sung badge. The badge has become an important national symbol.

History and Ethnic Relations

Emergence of the Nation. Korea's unified history dates at least from the kingdom of Silla (c.670–935), which unified the peninsula in the seventh century C.E. The Buddhist-influenced kingdom of Koryo (935–1392) followed. (The English name "Korea" comes from "Koryo.") The Yi dynasty (1392–1910) adopted Neo-Confucianism as the state ideology and established a vassal-tributary relationship with China. For centuries, China never directly interfered with the internal affairs of the dynasty. It was Japan that came to rule the Koreans directly, when that country subordinated the Yi royal family in the colonial annexation of 1910.

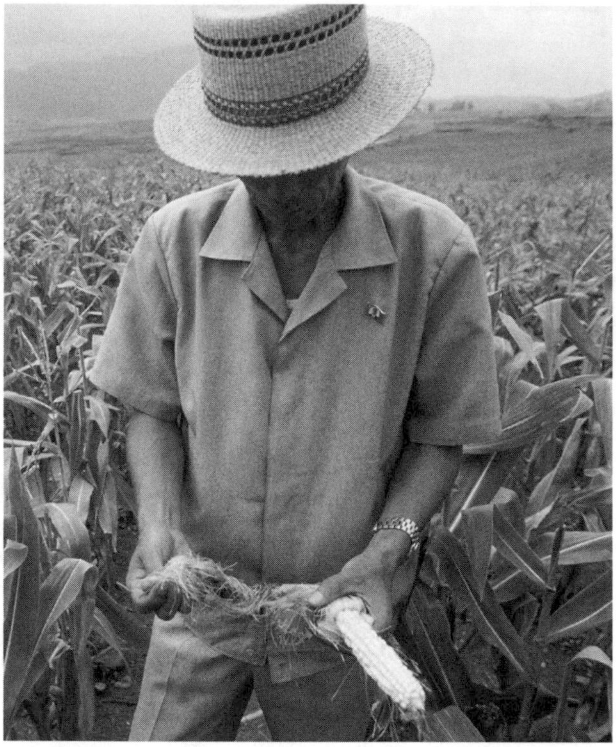

A farmer assesses crop damage caused by flooding in North Korea. Severe food shortages have occurred in recent years.

The end of Japanese rule following World War II (1939–1945) marked the beginning of a peculiar era for Korean history that continues today. In 1945, upon the surrender of the Japanese armed forces, Korea was partitioned into northern and southern halves along the 38th parallel, governed respectively by the Soviet Union and the United States. The Soviets endorsed a group of former guerrilla fighters as national leaders. This included a thirty-two-year-old legendary anti-Japanese guerrilla fighter, Kim Il Sung. Kim Il Sung's advantage over other patriots was that he was never apprehended by the Japanese colonial authorities; the consistency of his track record authenticated his quality as a national leader.

The North Korean state was founded on September 9, 1948, three years after the nation was divided into north and south, and approximately three weeks after the South Korean state was established with the sponsorship of the United Nations and the United States. But the preparation for North Korean state-building had already begun in 1945. With Soviet support, the northern leaders had carried out socioeconomic reforms including free distribution of land to the farmers, a gender equality law, and public ownership of key industries.

National Identity. A national identity as such was not born automatically with the emergence of the North Korean state. The northern leaders held the official view that the establishment of the North Korean state was an interim measure, with the ultimate goal being the unification of the entire peninsula in a single Korean national state. Kim Il Sung was not considered the national leader from the outset, either. He and his faction of the ruling Workers' Party of Korea (originally named the Communist Party of Korea) systematically eliminated rival factions and individuals over several decades. Kim Il Sung's ascendancy to absolute leadership started during the Korean War with the elimination of Pak Hon-yong, who headed the South Korean Workers' Party. After the war, Kim took leadership in close connection to North Korea in its sociopolitical form from traditional Korean culture, enabling it to start anew. North Korean national identity is indissolubly connected with loyalty to Kim and North Korean-style socialism.

Despite the heavy Soviet influence, Northern Korea was driven by patriotic and nationalist zeal and anti-Japanese sentiment, rather than by an ideological commitment to socialism and communism.

In contrast to the south, where Korea's high society had been traditionally located, the north had no notable political and cultural center except for P'yongyang, which was an obvious choice for the capital. With this lack of centralized political power and cultural tradition, North Korea was able to start largely from scratch. This proved useful for constructing a brand-new North Korean cultural identity, stemming from the Soviet cultural current but distinctly North Korean at the same time.

Urbanism, Architecture, and the Use of Space

Except for a total of perhaps ten cities, vast areas of North Korea are rural—or even untouched. These are areas that are not just underdeveloped, but undeveloped. For example, in 1985 a mining town in the northeastern part of North Korea had houses with no running water, no electric or fuel heating system, no lavatories or bath, no washbasin, no kitchen, and almost no furnishings. The residents used communal facilities and lived in tiny two-room houses heated by coal. Houses were equipped with electricity for lights, but its use was strictly controlled.

Located throughout North Korea—in towns such as the above, in the remotest of the villages, and in the capital P'yongyang, are the ubiquitous slogans praising Kim Il Sung's leadership and mobilizing the citizens to the revolutionary struggle and the socialist cause. The capital's landscape is also marked by austere buildings, vast streets with almost no cars, children and pedestrians in orderly lines, no trace of trash—almost clinically beautiful, but somewhat lifeless. Behind the formal facades, though, the back streets are very different. There are muddy streets and alleyways, chaotic residential quarters, and the normal confusion and noise of everyday life.

P'yongyang is marked by a planned cityscape, clustered around Kim Il Sung-related monuments such as the 20-foot-high gold statue of Kim that looks down on the city. The capital is located on the Taedong, an extremely beautiful river with small islands and a riverbank covered with swinging willows and nicely kept flowerbeds. Everything in the center of the capital is carefully designed and built, including the People's Study Hall, Children's Palace, Mansudae Art Hall, P'yongyang Grand Theatre, the Parisien style arch, and recently built international hotels and restaurants. During the 1960s and 1970s, the peak of P'yongyang's reconstruction after the Korean War, the basic austere style and layout of the city was established. Some buildings, such as the Korean Revolutionary Museum and Kim Il Sung University, bear the features of European modernist architecture. These are mixed with the more tradition-inspired architecture of the 1980s, including the People's Study Hall and the city gate.

A majority of P'yongyang's residents live in apartments. Individual houses with their own electricity and heating systems are reserved for high-ranking party members and army officers. In the late 1990s, individual dwellings became popular among postwar repatriates from Japan, who, through financial support from their families remaining in Japan, are able to purchase houses. The majority of North Korean citizens do not own a car.

Apart from the capital and a very few cities that are comparable to it, the national landscape is divided into semi-urban, undeveloped, and agricultural areas. As visitors are not allowed, not much is known about the agricultural areas.

North Korean nature reserves can be extremely beautiful. National resorts such as Mount Myohyang and Mount Kumgang are magical in their charm and grandiose beauty. Here too one finds the revolutionary slogans, such as "Long Live the Great Leader Kim Il Sung!" One can see these slogans not only on panels that can be removed if necessary, but also carved on the rocky walls of mountains, filled with permanent red paint.

North Korea has constructed a revolutionary pilgrimage route, marking important locations connected to Kim Il Sung's anti-Japanese resistance. These include the Mount Paektu and the forest surrounding it, Hyesan city in the central north and its vicinity, and other areas mainly concentrated on the Chinese border. Another pilgrimage site is Kim Il Sung's birthplace in Man'gyongdae, near P'yongyang, where the cottage where he grew up is preserved.

Food and Economy

Food in Daily Life. White rice and meat soup was once a symbol of good food in the North Korean rhetoric. It is not certain whether the population still eats white (steamed) rice due to the severe food shortage that became clear only in recent years. The visitors from overseas are normally given abundant food to eat, including meat, vegetables, dairy products, and fruits. However, ordinary citizens do not eat such a variety of food. Also, the North Korean diet does not include spicy food using chili and garlic, traditional in the Korean diet: There is no *kimchee* as found elsewhere. Another point to stress is that they do not seem to have candies or sweets for children: sugar is in short supply and regarded

A group of North Korean girls walk to school. Education in North Korea is geared toward furthering the influence of state socialism.

as a highly luxurious ingredient. Only when one visits the ranking officers' stores where one can use foreign currency is there a poor variety of sugary sweets. Basic food is rationed, while one can buy canned meat or a small amount of vegetables either from a store or farmers' market.

Food Customs at Ceremonial Occasions. All the food is state regulated, and this precludes obtaining any special food. For state-sponsored banquets, food is supplied abundantly, accompanied with nearly endless supply of wines and liqueurs. However, for ordinary people's ceremonies, such as the sixtieth birthday that is traditionally celebrated as a commemoration of longevity, it would not be the case.

Basic Economy. The Korean War (1950–1953) and the almost total destruction of the northern infrastructure by the allied bombing that flattened P'yongyang and napalmed the civilians paved the way for North Korea to emerge as a new, fresh, and truly heroic nation of Koreans. This was, according to North Korean officials, in contrast to South Korea, which was labeled a U.S. puppet regime. The destruction of economy was thorough, while the war casualties reached a phenomenal number and millions fled to the south as refugees. With Soviet and Chinese aid, reconstruction began immediately after the war. In the process of reconstructing the economy, the North Korean government collectivized agriculture, reinforced state and public ownership of heavy and light industries, and nationally unified education and the arts and sciences. By 1960, North Korea had a typical Soviet-style socialist economy and the party's hegemony had been consolidated.

In this process, a new form of leader-subject relations emerged, referred to in Korean as *hyonjichido*—on-the-spot teaching or guiding. Film footage and photographs from the post-Korean War economic reconstruction period show numerous scenes of Kim Il Sung visiting steel mills and factories. In the 1950s and 1960s, Kim visited the workplaces nationwide, encouraging people to participate more vigorously in production. Kim's presence carried weight and the people were impressed that the country's top man had visited their hometown; the visits boosted morale and enhanced national pride. As a result, the North Korean economy recovered at a remarkable speed.

Following the three-year post-Korean War reconstruction, the North Korean government launched a five-year economic plan in 1956. Two years later, the socialist reform of production was declared complete and agriculture and industry became publicly owned and managed. Some key industries were placed under state ownership. In 1961, another economic plan was initiated; in November 1970, the party's Fifth Congress declared North Korea to be a socialist industrial state. These were the high times for the North Korean economy, and in April 1974, North Korea abolished all taxes. Until about 1976, North Korea's per capita gross national product (GNP) was higher than the equivalent figure in South Korea.

In December 1972, the North Korean Supreme People's Congress established the North Korean socialist constitution. The same session elected Kim Il Sung president of North Korea for the first time; he was reelected in 1977 and 1982, and remained president until his death in 1994.

The famine of the late 1990s, caused by floods and other natural calamities, revealed the shortcomings of the North Korean economy. The world had known for some time that North Korea's economy lagged far behind South Korea's, but the news of the famine was alarming to the West. Following massive floods in 1995 and 1996, a dry summer accompanied by typhoon damage in 1997 devastated North Korean agriculture. In 1997, the per capita daily grain ration fell from 24.5 ounces (700 grams) to 3.5 ounces (100 grams). The ration distribution also became intermittent. Because of the increasing deaths by starvation and undernourishment, funerals were allowed only in small scale and in the evening, and were attended only by the immediate family. As poverty increased and the lack of food intensified, there were reports that crimes related to the situation were on the increase—from petty theft to organized gang robbery, often involving murder. North Korea began relying heavily on foreign aid from South Korea, Japan, the United States, and other Western nations. Since the beginning of 1999, North Korean publication has placed more emphasis on economy than on military affairs. It was scheduled to receive 100,000 tons of rice from Japan as of March 1999 as a result of the newly activated contact between the North Korean and Japanese governments. This and other aids from foreign governments is contributing to North Korea's slow recovery from a serious food shortage.

Land Tenure and Property. All land is state-owned or owned collectively, in the case of agricultural farms. Individuals do own movable goods such as furniture. All the houses are de jure state-provided; although it is said to be possible to buy off good housing, that would be through a personal connection rather than buying the property itself. Material goods are scarce in North Korea and generally people do not have opportunities to be exposed to expensive commodities. This works to suppress any desire to own something.

Commercial Activities. There are stores and even department stores in the big cities if one wishes to buy anything. However, basic goods are provided by the state either through ration or as a "gift" from the government (e.g. children's school textbooks or uniforms). In this sense, commercial activities among the ordinary citizens are minimal. In recent years, collaboration between Korean merchants in Japan took off with restaurant and hotel operation, but such ventures ran into serious difficulty since North Korea's food shortage became clear. There is an ongoing project of building a free trade zone in the northeastern region of North Korea, with collaboration of South Korean and Chinese capitals. This again is a tardy project and contrary to initial hopes, little success is expected.

Major Industries. North Korea's major industries are geared toward its domestic resources, and so include iron and steel production, mining, machinery, and other heavy industries. Its light industry also revolves around the domestic supply and lacks variety in products.

Trade. In the past, North Korea confined its trade counterparts to socialist states third world countries, particularly Africa. However, since the end of the Cold War, it has been trying to establish more stable relationships with Japan and the United States, while its former trade partners are shifting the emphasis from friendship-based trade to a more business-minded attitude. One of its major imports is weapons imported from Russia and China.

Division of Labor. Heavy industry is assigned to men, light industry to women. Jobs are assigned by the state in accordance to its judgment of family rank, ability, and qualifications. It is highly unlikely for the family of high-ranking party officers to work as a manual laborer or miner, for example. It is not acceptable for one to freely change occupation: Everything must be decided by higher authorities.

SOCIAL STRATIFICATION

Classes and Castes. Although the government officially claims that North Korea is a classless society that has done away with the remnants of feu-

People attend the funeral and cremation of a Buddhist monk. North Korea. Though there are Buddhist monks and nuns in the country, North Koreans do not have much religious freedom.

dalism and capitalism, it is clearly a class society starkly divided between the politically powerful and politically powerless, with an unequal distribution of monetary and nonmonetary privileges. The highest ranking people in North Korea are Kim Il Sung's family and relatives, followed by his old comrades and their families, who used to be referred to as revolutionary fighters, denoting their participation in the anti-Japanese armed resistance. The next stratum is made up of the families of Korean War veterans and anti-South Korea sabotage officers. The children of this class typically are educated in schools for the bereaved children of the revolutionaries and face better career opportunities. Women generally lag behind men in high-status positions in society, but a daughter of an established revolutionary can rank very high in both the party and the government.

The vast majority of North Koreans are ordinary citizens who are divided and subdivided into ranks according to their family history and revolutionary or unrevolutionary origin. Status is regularly reviewed, and if any member of the family commits an antirevolutionary crime, other members of the family are also demoted in status.

Political Life

Government. North Korea's government is made of a presidency, a central government that is divided into various departments, and local governments. The equivalent to the United States Congress, for example, is the people's congress. The Supreme People's Congress passes the laws, which are carried through by local people's committees that are organized in a top-down fashion following the administrative units such as province, county, city, and agricultural collectives and co-ops. Offices for the People's Congress and committees are based on the election that takes place every five years.

There is normally only one candidate per office and the turn-out rate for voting marks near 100 percent every time, according to the official media report.

Leadership and Political Officials. The ruling Worker's Party of Korea has the largest decision-making power. The party is not just a political organization, but a moral and ethical icon for the people. The party is also divided top-down from the central committee to the local party offices. Since Kim Il Sung's death, it is Kim Jong Il, his son, who holds the supreme authority inside the party. Kim

Jong Il is also the supreme commander of the army. He is so deemed in not only North Korea but by the South Korean government. When in June 2000 the South Korean president Kim Dae Jung visited North Korea to meet with the northern leader for the first time in the fifty years of Korea's division, Kim Jong Il appeared in person to greet Kim Dae Jung and the meetings between the two leaders took place in a highly cordial and mutually respectful atmosphere. It has been decided that Kim Jong Il will pay the return visit to the south, which will confirm his authority in the eyes of the South Korean citizens. The north-south meetings put forth some measures for reuniting the families that were separated during the Korean War and cultural collaboration between the two Koreas, ultimately aiming at reunification. The North Korean leadership enhanced its legitimacy through this recent move.

Social Problems and Control. The participation in political organizations occupies an important place in the everyday lives of North Koreans. By definition, every citizen in North Korea belongs to at least one political organization and this replaces a system of social control: the Korean Democratic Women's Union, the Korean Congress of Trade Unions, the Korean Socialist Labor Youth League, the Korean Farmers' Union, the Korean Press Association, the Korean Association of Writers and Artists, or the Korean Young Pioneers.

Technically, all those who live on North Korean soil are North Korean citizens except for those who already have foreign citizenship, such as diplomats and visitors. North Koreans have citizens' certificates identifying their class origin and current address. No one in North Korea is allowed to change their residence at will: they have to apply to move to another province or town and have a legitimate reason, such as marriage. Not even weekend journeys or holidays are left to individual discretion; one has to apply for such a trip through the appropriate authorities. Family holidays must be approved by the authorities, and normally families have to wait for their vacation quota. Sometimes individuals who distinguish themselves in devotion to the party and the state are rewarded with a family vacation.

Contrary to the traditional registration system of Korea, which was based on family registration, North Korean registration is based on individual identification. Each individual is subject to regular investigation by the authorities for the purpose of classification and reclassification according to class origin. For example, a person who commits a crime might be reclassified in terms of "soundness" of origin.

Military Activity. Although it has been said that in North Korea, the military has the ultimate say in decision making, it is hard to determine the degree of exercise of power by the military. North Korea's military leader, Kim Jong Il, is also the supreme commander of the Korean People's Army. In 1998, it became known that North Korea's military launched a missile across the Japanese archipelago into the Pacific. The incident is still being debated, but it is evident that North Korea's expenditure on military affairs is severely constraining its economy. The conscription is not mandatory, but many gifted young men and women join the army in order to obtain a ticket to the higher education through the army's recommendation after several years' service. The duration of the service is not clearly defined. Some stay five to six years, others less; women tend to stay shorter than men do. To go to the army even for a couple of years is an honor in North Korea, since it is a demonstration of one's readiness to devote one's life to the motherland.

Nongovernmental Organizations and Other Associations

All citizens in North Korea join one or more of the following political organizations in the course of their lives: the Korean Democratic Women's Union, the Korean Congress of Trade Unions, the Korean Socialist Labor Youth League, the Korean Farmers' Union, the Korean Press Association, the Korean Association of Writers and Artists, the Korean Young Pioneers, and so on. In addition, there are three political parties: the Workers' Party of Korea, the Korean Democratic Party, and the Ch'ondo Religious Friends Party. The latter two, however, have disappeared from North Korea's public politics since the 1980s. The local headquarters and branches of these organizations form the basis of political life of individuals. Rather than home or family, the political organizations one belongs to are, in principle, the primary basis for social identification and the most important vehicle for socialization for North Koreans. Also, if one comes from an ordinary background, to do well in these organizations would create better opportunities.

Gender Roles and Statuses

Division of Labor by Gender. In North Korea it is widely accepted that men run the heavy industry and women work in light industry. Beyond this, the division is highly diverse. For example, agriculture is not necessarily regarded specifically as a man's or

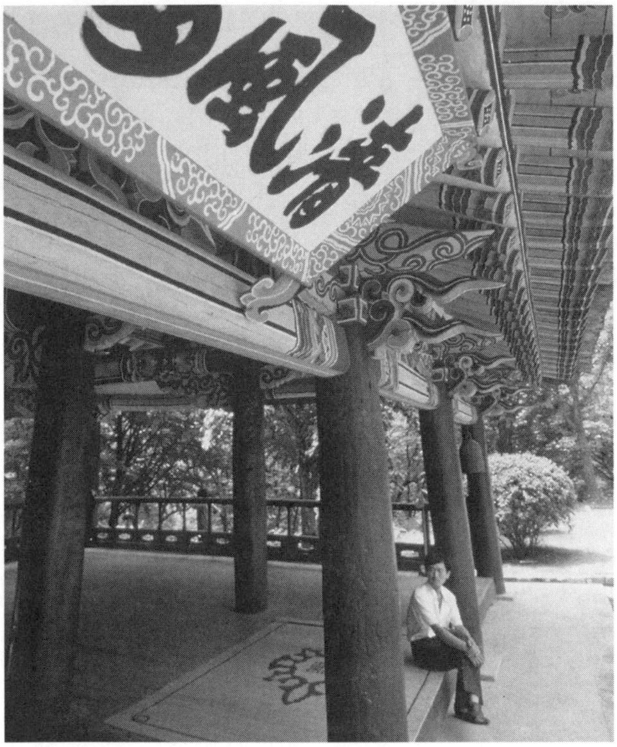

Gables of a Zen Buddhist monastery.

woman's job. When it comes to the domestic division of labor, although the state and the party try to minimize the work by introducing canned food and electrical appliances, it remains that women do most of the housework and child rearing even while working as many hours as men outside of the home. This effectively doubles women's burdens in society.

The Relative Status of Women and Men. Women's status is not equal to that of men. Men have a far better chance in advancing in politics, while women, particularly after marriage, are seen as "done" with a political career. This is different for women from the high-ranking families, whose background and connections would outmaneuver handicaps that ordinary woman would have to bear. In North Korea, women are supposed to have certain mannerisms that are regarded as feminine. They are not supposed to wear trousers unless they are factory workers or agricultural laborers.

In professional settings, however, women are often as assertive as their male counterparts. The only occupation where behavior is sometimes flirtatious or subservient is as a waitress, but for women it is an honor to hold this position as they are selected for their beauty, good family background, and educational qualifications.

Marriage, Family, and Kinship

Marriage. Individual registration has had a significant effect on the North Korean marriage system. In Korean tradition, marriage between a man and a woman who share the same family origin is not allowed. Since all Koreans were required to keep family records since the time of the Yi dynasty, everyone can trace their family origin. If two people share the same ancestral name, they were regarded as brother and sister, and hence subject to the incest taboo. Since North Korea abolished the family registry, marriages between individuals from the same ancestral clan—as long as they are not direct relatives—are lawful.

A primary consideration in marriage is the compatibility of class origins. If a man comes from the family of a high-ranking party member, and a woman from a family that does not have a comparable sociopolitical status, a marriage between the two would not be approved of by the society. If a man comes from a family that was originally repatriated from Japan in the postwar period and a woman comes from a family that is "native" North Korean, a marriage between the two is considered difficult since, generally speaking, repatriates are regarded with suspicion and distrust due to their ongoing connection with families in Japan. Hence, classes tend to marry within themselves just as in capitalist societies.

Upon marriage, a couple is given a house or, if they live in an urban area, an apartment. Ordinary couples, however, often have to wait until their application for a residence is approved by the authorities. The case of a couple from high-ranking families will be different: they will receive preferential treatment when seeking housing. Normally, newlyweds conduct a small ceremony, inviting close friends, neighbors, and family members, take a photo if they can afford it, and register their marriage. There is no feast or party and no honeymoon. Even wedding dresses are made from state-rationed fabrics, and therefore brides of a certain period all look more or less alike.

Domestic Unit. The domestic unit is a nuclear family with some degree of stem family practice, i.e. the family of one of the children (most likely a son) living with aged parents. Houses are small throughout the country and this restricts having large families as a norm. Adoption takes place through orphanages.

Socialization

Child Rearing and Education. The process of economic recovery following the Korean War was also the process by which the population was successfully turned into members of the newly emerging nation. Compulsory education and the general literacy program played a decisive role in forming individuals into new subjects of state socialism, subjects capable of reproducing the state-coined, politically correct vocabulary and revolutionary rhetoric. Starting on 1 November 1958, all education up to middle school became compulsory and free of charge. By 1975, North Korea had extended this to eleven years of free compulsory education, including one year in a collective preschool. In addition, factories and collective farms have nursery schools where children are introduced to socialization and taken care of collectively away from home, since mothers are usually full-time workers.

In North Korea's linguistic practice, Kim Il Sung's words are frequently quoted as a gospel-like reference point. People learn the vocabulary by reading publications of the state and the party. Since the print industry and the entire publishing establishment are strictly state-owned and state-controlled, and no private importation of foreign-printed materials or audiovisual resources is permitted, words that do not conform with the interest of the party and the state are not introduced into the society in the first place, resulting in efficient censorship.

The vocabulary that the state favors includes words relating to such concepts as revolution, socialism, communism, class struggle, patriotism, anti-imperialism, anticapitalism, the national reunification, and dedication and loyalty to the leader. By way of contrast, the vocabulary that the state finds difficult or inappropriate, such as that referring to sexual or love relations, does not appear in print. Even so-called romantic novels depict lovers who are more like comrades on a journey to fulfill the duties they owe to the leader and the state.

Limiting the vocabulary in this way has made everyone, including the relatively uneducated, into competent practitioners of the state-engineered linguistic norm. On the societal level, this had an effect of homogenizing the linguistic practice of the general public. A visitor to North Korea would be struck by how similar people sound. In other words, rather than broadening the vision of citizens, literacy and education in North Korea confine the citizenry into a cocoon of the North Korean-style socialism and the state ideology.

Higher Education. Higher education is regarded as an honor and a privilege, and as such, it is not open to the general public at will. Men and women who have served in the military would be recommended to subsequent higher education. There are also "gifted" entries to the universities and colleges, where the candidate's intellectual merit is appreciated. Normally, however, it depends on one's family background in determining whether or not one obtains the opportunity of learning at a college for years at the state's expense. (Hence, for ordinary men and women, the military is a secure detour.) Sometimes, candidates are recommended from factories and agricultural collectives, with the endorsement of the due authorities.

Religion

Religious Beliefs. What most characterizes North Korean socialism is its leadership, built on the basis of the cult of personality of Kim Il Sung. Through the state-engineered education system, Kim and his family are introduced as role models for men and women, young and old. By the time they are in kindergarten, children can recite stories from Kim's childhood. Moral ideological education in North Korea is allegorically organized, with Kim Il Sung and his pedigree as protagonists.

Kim Il Sung's name is ubiquitous in North Korea. For example, if one is asked how one is, the model answer would be "thanks to the Great Leader Kim Il Sung, I am well," and the North Korean economy is remarkably strong "thanks to the wise guidance of Marshal Kim Il Sung." The ideology that represents the leader cult is called the *Juche* idea. *Juche* literally means "subject" and is often translated as self-reliance. In North Korea, slogans such as "Let us model the whole society on the *Juche* idea!" are heard daily. North Korea's official history claims that Kim Il Sung first established the *Juche* ideology in 1927 when he founded the Anti-imperialism Youth League in Jilin in northeastern China. The *Juche* idea is quite unlike Marxist historical materialism. Rather, it is a sort of idealism, placing emphasis on human belief; in this sense, it resembles a religion rather than a political ideology. Under the ideology of *Juche,* North Korea achieved many remarkable goals, including the economic recovery from the ashes of the Korean War. In the name of loyal dedication to Kim Il Sung, national unity was accomplished and national pride instilled North Korean citizens.

Religion is theoretically permitted in North Korea, and a visitor may meet a Buddhist monk or

A soldier guards the DMZ (Demilitarized Zone) between North and South Korea.

nun. But North Koreans hardly have freedom of religion. The monks and nuns that tourists meet may not have any public followers; indeed, they themselves may be loyal followers of the leader. Traditionally, northern Korea had strong centers of Christianity, and Christianity played an important role in organizing anti-Japanese resistance during the colonial period. Similarly, the Ch'ondo religion that emerged in the nineteenth century as an indigenous Korean religion was strengthened in the process of anti-Japanese resistance. In fact, many Ch'ondo leaders were included in the initial state-building of North Korea. Decades of Kim Il Sung worship transformed the religious plurality, though; with the leader's ascendancy, non-*Juche* ideas came to be regarded as heterodox and dangerous, or as bourgeois and capitalist.

Korean culture has an age-old Confucian tradition, although this heritage does not exist in today's North Korea as it did in the past. Rather, its form and direction changed due to the intervention of leader-focused socialism. Kim Il Sung often is depicted in a paternalistic manner, personified as a benevolent father (and at times, father-mother, asexually or bisexually) who looks after the whole population as children and disciples. Kim Il Sung created the notion of a family state with himself as the head of the nation. Indeed, a popular North Korean children's song includes this refrain: "Our Father is Marshal Kim Il Sung/ Our home is the bosom of the party/ We are one big family/ We have nothing to envy in the whole wide world."

Secular Celebrations

National celebrations include the Foundation of the People's Army (8 February), Kim Jong Il's birthday (16 February), Kim Il Sung's birthday (15 April), May Day (1 May), Young Pioneers Day (6 June), National Foundation Day (9 September), and the Workers' Party Day (10 October). Some of these celebrations are carried out with a Soviet-style military parade, while others are commemorated with art festivals and official congregations in local and central government units.

The Arts and Humanities

Support for the Arts. The production of arts and literature in North Korea is controlled entirely by the state. Their ideological line, form of presentation, dissemination to the public, and availability are all under the administration of state authorities. This does not mean that North Koreans suffer from a poverty of art. On the contrary, there is quite a rich variety of art genres and distinct fashions that come and go over time. Film is more fully developed than literature, perhaps because of Kim Jong Il's involvement in the medium.

Literature. Literature is produced by state-salaried official writers whose novels and poems tend to be pedantic, predictable, and outright boring. For example, a long-selling popular novel *Ode to Youth* (first published in 1987 and continuously reprinted until 1994) is a story of a technician in a steel mill, whose relationship with his girlfriend is interwoven with other human relations among his colleagues. The story in the end reconfirms that in North Korea all relations, including romantic ones, exist to encourage loyalty to the leader. This has been the pattern in literature since the 1960s. Typically, human relationships are depicted in simplistic ways, with romantically-involved couples never hesitating to help each other become heroes for the revolution. There is no complex web of psychology, diversity of personality, or unexpected events that are quite often part of the ordinary lives of individuals. North Korean literature is full of barren, lifeless language, which is to be expected given the limited vocabulary the North Korean state makes available to the public.

Graphic Arts. North Korea has distinct graphic arts related to a mixture of Korean traditional drawing and the techniques of western watercolor. Large mural art is commonly seen inside the public buildings in North Korea, and the theme is usually leader worship—typically Kim Il Sung in the middle, larger than other people surrounding him. People of al ages, occupation, and dress circle him with adoration and admiration in their eyes. The commission of such art is done by the state, and in this sense, there is no private artist. Also commonly seen are large sculptures depicting history patriotically, such as Korean War heroes and anti-Japanese guerrilla fighters; there are usually portrayed in the Soviet style. No individual artist is endorsed in this type of public art display. One cannot miss in North Korea ubiquitous statues and sculptures, paintings and even embroidery art that portray in beautified form Kim Il Sung and his family. These are displayed in public spaces; in terms of art to purchase privately, there are paintings and other products that use traditional Korean (or East Asian) ink paint or oil paint. These are most readily found in the international hotel shops and are not readily available for ordinary citizens to purchase.

Performance Arts. Under the direct intervention of Kim Jong Il, a new form of films has emerged in North Korea, especially since the 1980s. Sin Sang-ok and Ch'oi Un-hui—married former South Korean citizens, a director husband and an actress wife—played an important role in introducing this new version of North Korean film. The Sin-Ch'oi team, which enjoyed the endorsement of Kim Jong Il, produced many realist films. Their work is based on Korean literature of the 1930s, which was very strongly influenced by Russian realism as well as the Japanese proletarian literary movement. Classics such as *The Blanket* by Ch'oi So-hae were made into films that represented family life and the misery of poverty in an unprecedented vivid style. Also popular was the long-running series *Heroes without Name,* which depicted romantic relations among North Korean spies who worked undercover in South Korea after the Korean War.

Films in North Korea are inexpensive entertainment for the general public, while other more specialized genres such as circuses or song and dance ensembles are reserved for foreign guests and national festivals. Only selected individuals—either by their revolutionary heritage or by being recognized as meritorious contributors to the revolution—are invited to enjoy such entertainment.

BIBLIOGRAPHY

Buzo, Adrian. *The Guerrilla Dynasty: Politics and Leadership in North Korea,* 1999.

Cumings, Bruce. *Korea's Place in the Sun: A Modern History,* 1997.

———. *The Origins of the Korean War, Volume 1,* 1981.

———. *The Origins of the Korean War, Volume 2,* 1990.

Henriksen, Thomas, and Jongryn Mo. *North Korea after Kim Il Sung,* 1997.

Hunter, Helen-Louise. *Kim Il-Song's North Korea,* 1999.

Kim, C. I. Eugene, and B. C. Koh, eds. *Journey to North Korea: Personal Perceptions,* 1983.

Kim, Yun, and Eui Hang Shin, eds. *Toward a Unified Korea: Social, Economic, Political, and Cultural Impacts of the Reunification of North and South Korea,* 1995.

Park, Han S., ed. *North Korea: Ideology, Politics, Economy,* 1996.

Suh, Dae-Sook. *Kim Il Sung: The North Korean Leader,* 1995.

Suh, Dae-Sook, ed. *North Korea after Kim Il Sung,* 1998.

—Sonia Ryang

South Korea

Culture Name

South Korean

Alternative Names

Republic of Korea; Corean, Han'guk, Taehan, Taehanmin'guk

Orientation

Identification. Koryo (918–1392) and Choson (1392–1910) were the last two Korean dynasties. Korean immigrants and their descendants in Russia, China, and Japan use the names of those dynasties as a reference for their ethnicity. Despite the continued use of Choson as a self-name in North Korea, the Japanese convention of referring to the Korean nation by that name (pronounced Chosen in Japanese) can be offensive to South Koreans because of its evocation of Japanese colonization of the nation (1910–1945).

Koreans share a common culture, but a sense of regionalism exists between northerners and southerners and between southeasterners and southwesterners in terms of customs and perceived personality characteristics. Some suggest that this regionalism dates back to Three Kingdoms of Koguryo (37 B.C.E.–668 C.E.), Silla (57 B.C.E.–935 C.E.), and Paekche (18 B.C.E.–660 C.E.). In South Korea politicized regionalism has emerged between the southeastern (Kyongsang Province) and southwestern regions (Cholla Province) since the late 1960s as a result of an uneven pattern of development that benefits people in the southeast.

Location and Geography. South Korea occupies the southern half of the Korean peninsula, which protrudes about 620 miles (1,000 kilometers) southward from the Eurasian landmass between Soviet Siberia in the northeast and Chinese Manchuria to the north. About three thousand islands belong to Korea, among which the Province of Cheju Island is the largest. The total area of the peninsula, including the islands, is about 85,000 square miles (222,000 square kilometers), of which about 45 percent or about 38,000 square miles (99,000 square kilometers) constitutes the territory of South Korea.

Geopolitically, the peninsula is surrounded on three sides by the sea and by Russia, China, and Japan. Korea has suffered from the attempts of these neighboring countries to dominate it, particularly in the twentieth century. Each of them considers Korea to be of major importance to its own security, and since 1945 the United States has had a major security interest in the nation. The peninsula was divided at the 38th Parallel in an agreement between the United States and the Soviet Union at the end of the World War II. Subsequently, the Military Demarcation Line established by the Armistice Agreement of 1953 to bring a cease-fire to the Korean War (1950–1953) replaced the boundary. A 2.5-mile (four-kilometer) wide strip of land that runs along the cease-fire line for about 150 miles (241 kilometers) is fixed at the Demilitarized Zone (DMZ) as the no man's land between North Korea and South Korea.

Korea is mountainous, and only about 20 percent of the land in the south is flat enough for farming. Seoul, the capital, is in the northwestern part of the country on the Han River, which flows toward the Yellow Sea. Seoul was first established as the walled capital of the Choson Dynasty in 1394. Before Japan colonized Korea in 1910, Seoul was the first city in east Asia to have electricity, trolley cars, a water system, telephones, and telegraphs. Seoul has grown into a metropolis of more than ten million residents. The palaces, shrines, and other vestiges of the Choson Dynasty are still prominent features of the city north of the Han River, serving as major tourist attractions. In the last few decades, the area south of the Han River has built trendy commercial centers and high-rise con-

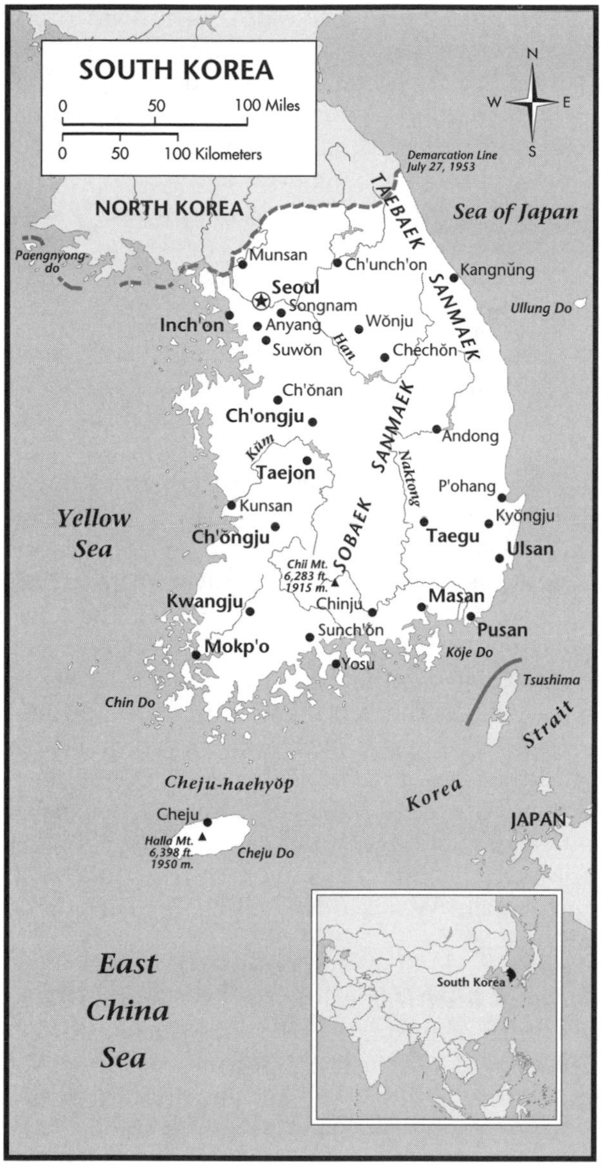

South Korea

dominium complexes for the middle and upper-middle classes.

Demography. In 1997, the population was 45.9 million, with 1,200 persons per square mile (463 persons per square kilometer). Since the mid-1980s, when Korea stabilized at a low level of fertility, remarkably high sex ratios at birth have resulted from son-selective reproductive behaviors such as prenatal sex screening and sex-selective abortion. Another notable demographic trend is the increasing ratio of the elderly: the 1997 census revealed that 6.3 percent of the total population was 65 years of age or older.

Linguistic Affiliation. About seventy million people speak Korean. Most live on the peninsula, but more than five million live across the globe. Korean is considered part of the Tungusic branch of the Altaic group of the Ural-Altaic language family. It also has a close relationship to Japanese in general structure, grammar, and vocabulary. The form of Korean spoken around Seoul is regarded as standard. Major dialects differ mainly in accent and intonation. Except for old Cheju dialect, all are mutually intelligible.

Koreans value their native tongue and their alphabet, *han'gul*, which was invented in the mid-fifteenth century. Until then, Korea's aristocratic society used Chinese characters, while the government and people used the writing system known as *idu* (a transcription system of Korean words invented in the eighth century by Silla scholars using Chinese characters). The Chinese writing system requires a basic knowledge of several thousand characters. Commoners who did not have the time or means to master Chinese could not read or write. Moreover, it is difficult to express spoken Korean in Chinese characters.

Considering the frustrating situation of mass illiteracy and troubled by the incongruity between spoken Korean and Chinese ideographs, King Sejong (1397–1450), the fourth ruler (1418–1450) of the Choson Dynasty, commissioned a group of scholars to devise a phonetic writing system that would represent the sounds of spoken Korean and could be learned by all the people. The result was Hunmin Chong'um ("the Correct Sounds to Teach the People"), or *han'gul*, as it is called today. The system was created in 1443 and promulgated in 1446. South Koreans observe *Han'gul* Day on 9 October with a ceremony at King Sejong's tomb.

Han'gul is easy to learn since each letter corresponds to a phoneme, and Korea now has one of the highest literacy rates in the world. UNESCO established the King Sejong Literacy Prize in 1988 and offers it annually to an individual or group that contributes to the eradication of illiteracy worldwide.

Symbolism. The national flag, *T'aegukki*, is a unique symbol. The flag of *T'aeguk* ("Supreme Ultimate"), symbolizes the basic ideas of east Asian cosmology shared by the peoples in the Chinese culture area. In the center of a white background is a circle divided horizontally in two by an S-shaped line. The upper portion in red represents the *yang*, and the lower portion in blue symbolizes the *um* (*yin* in Chinese), depicting the *yinyang* principle of a universe in perfect balance and harmony. The central symbolism in the *T'aeguk* form is that while there is a constant movement of opposites in the universe (day and night, good and evil, masculinity and femininity), there is also balance. The four trigrams at the corners of the flag also express the ideas of opposites and balance. The three unbroken lines in the upper left corner represent heaven while the three broken lines placed diagonally in the lower right corner represent the earth. The trigram in the upper right corner represents water, while the one placed diagonally at the lower left corner represents fire.

In contrast to the cosmological symbolism in the flag, the national anthem, *Aegukka*, conjures a sense of the national identity of the Taehan people by making territorial references to the East Sea (Sea of Japan), Paektusan ("White Head Mountain," on the northern border with China), and the beautiful land of *mugunghwa* (the rose of Sharon, the national flower). The phrase *samch'ol-li kangsan* ("three-thousand-li land of range and river"), which is included in the national anthem, refers to the national territory.

The phrase *han p'it-chul* ("one bloodline") often is used by Koreans at home and abroad to symbolize their shared identity as the members of a homogeneous nation. Blood and territory thus are the most frequently invoked metaphors associated with the nation.

National days of celebration include Liberation Day (*Kwangbokchol*) on 15 August and National Foundation Day (*Kaech'onjol*) on 3 October. *Kwangbokchol* (the Day of Recovering the Light) celebrates the nation's liberation from Japanese colonial rule in 1945. *Kaech'onjol* (Heaven Opening Day) commemorates the founding of the first Korean kingdom, KoChoson, by the legendary priest-king Tan'gun Wanggom.

History and Ethnic Relations

Emergence of the Nation. The Korean peninsula has been inhabited for more than half a million years, and a Neolithic culture emerged around 6,000 B.C.E. The legendary beginning date of the Korean people is said to be 2333 B.C.E., when Tan'gun established the kingdom of Choson ("Morning Freshness," often translated as the "Land of Morning Calm") around today's P'yongyang. To distinguish it from the later Choson Dynasty, it is now referred to as Ko ("Old") Choson.

In the legend, Tan'gun was born of a divine father, Hwan-ung, a son of the heavenly king, and a woman who had been transformed from a bear. The bear and a tiger had pleaded with Hwan-ung to transform them into human beings. Only the bear achieved the transformation by following Hwan-ung's instructions, which included a hundred-day seclusion to avoid sunlight and the ingestion of a bunch of mugwort (*ssuk*) and twenty pieces of garlic. This bear turned woman then married Hwan-ung, and their offspring was Tan'gun. A recent interpretation of the bear woman is that she came from a bear totem tribe.

The Old Choson period is divided into the Tan'gun, Kija, and Wiman periods. Shortly after the fall of Wiman Choson in 108 B.C.E. and the establishment of Chinese military control in the north, the Three Kingdoms (Silla, Koguryo, and Paekche) period began. In 668, Silla unified the Three Kingdoms. Silla's decline in the late ninth century brought about the rise of Later Paekche and Later Koguryo. Wang Kon, who established the Koryo Dynasty, eventually reunified the nation. A series of Mongol invasions that began in 1231 devastated the country in the thirteenth and fourteenth centuries. General Yi Song-gye overthrew Koryo and established the Choson Dynasty in 1392. Despite invasions by Japan and Manchu (Qing) in the sixteenth and seventeenth centuries, respectively, Choson continued for more than five centuries until 1910, when Japan colonized the nation for three and a half decades.

National Identity. Before the 1945 national division of the peninsula and the subsequent establishment of the two political regimes of North and South Korea in 1948, Koreans identified themselves as the people of Choson. Tan'gun as the founding ancestor has had a symbolic meaning for Koreans throughout the nation's history. A temple erected in Tan'gun's honor in 1429 stood in P'yongyang until its destruction during the Korean War. In 1993, North Korea announced the discovery of Tan'gun's tomb and a few remains of his skeleton at a site close to P'yongyang. Some Korean calendars still print the Year of Tan'gun (*Tan'gi*) along with the Gregorian calendar year, which the South Korean government officially adopted in 1962.

Ethnic Relations. Korea is one of the few countries in which ethnicity and nationality coincide. The only immigrant ethnic minority group is a Chinese community of about 20,000 that is concentrated mainly in Seoul and has existed since the late nineteenth century. Since the Korean War, the continued presence of the United States Forces–Korea has resulted in the immigration of over one hundred thousand Korean women to the United States as

A house in Oh Ju Kon village, Kangnung, South Korea, reflects a more modern approach to South Korean rural housing.

soldiers' wives. Since the early 1990s, an increasing number of foreign workers from Asian countries (including Korean Chinese) and Russia have entered South Korea in pursuit of the "Korean Dreams."

Urbanism, Architecture, and the Use of Space

Traditionally, dwellings with thatched roofs and houses with clay-tile roofs symbolized rural—urban as well as lower-class—upper-class distinctions. The traditional houses of *yangban* (gentry) families were divided by walls into women's quarters (*anch'ae*), men's quarters (*sarangch'ae*), and servants' quarters (*haengnangch'ae*), reflecting the Confucian rules of gender segregation and status discrimination between the yangban and their servants in the social hierarchy of the Choson Dynasty. Western architecture was introduced in the nineteenth century. The Gothic-style Myongdong Cathedral (1898) is a prominent example of the earliest Western architecture in Seoul.

As part of government-sponsored rural development projects since the late 1960s, thatched-roof houses in rural areas have mostly been replaced by concrete structures with a variety of brightly colored slate roofs. The tile-roofed traditional urban residential houses have also become almost extinct, partly because of the ravages of the Korean War and the rush toward modernization and development. Now a wide range of architectural styles coexists. For example, the Toksu Palace of the Choson Dynasty built in the traditional style, the Romanesque Seoul City Hall built during Japanese rule, and modem high-rise luxury hotels can all be seen from City Hall Plaza in downtown Seoul.

According to the 1995 national census, about 88 percent of the population lives in urban areas. Lack of land for construction and changes in people's lifestyle have combined to make condominium apartments the dominant housing type in urban areas. Close to half the urban population consists of condominium dwellers, but the bedrooms in most condos still feature the *ondol* floor system. Traditional ondol floors were heated by channeling warm air and smoke through a system of under-the-floor flues from an exterior fireplace. Those floors typically were made of large pieces of flat stone tightly covered with several square-yard-size pieces of lacquered paper in light golden brown to present an aesthetically pleasing surface and prevent gas and smoke from entering the room.

Customarily, the "lower end" of the room (*araemmok*), which is the closest to the source of heat, was reserved for honored guests and the senior members of the household, while people of lower social status occupied the "upper end" (*ummok*), farthest from the source of heat and near the door. This customary practice reflected the social hierarchy. This distinction does not exist in the modern apartments because the heating system is centrally controlled.

Food and Economy

Food in Daily Life. The rapid changes in lifestyles that have accompanied economic development since the 1960s have changed the traditional pattern of eating rice at each meal. Some urbanites may eat toast, eggs, and milk for breakfast, using a fork and knife. Nonetheless, for many people a bowl of steamed white rice, a soybean-paste vegetable soup, and a dish of *kimch'I* may still constitute the basic everyday meal, to which steamed or seasoned vegetables, fish, meats, and other foods may be added as side dishes (*panch'an*). Many people eat at a low table while sitting on the ondol floor, using a spoon and chopsticks.

Kimch'I is the national dish. It is a pungent, often hot, mixture of fermented and/or pickled vegetables. Almost any vegetable can be fermented to make kimch'I, but Chinese cabbage and daikon radishes are the most commonly used. As part of the national diet for centuries, it has many variations depending on the region, season, occasion, and personal taste of the cook. Kimch'I has long been the test of a housewife's culinary skills and a family tradition. A South Korean consumes an average of forty pounds (eighteen kilograms) of kimch'I a year. Many companies produce kimch'I for both domestic consumption and export.

Meat dishes such as *pulgogi* (barbecued meat) and *kalbi* (short ribs) are popular among both Koreans and foreigners. They are traditionally charcoal-roasted after the meat has been marinated in soy sauce, sesame oil, sugar, minced garlic, and other spices. The foods available at restaurants range from sophisticated Western cuisine, to various ethnic specialty foods, to both indigenous and foreign fast foods. There are no food taboos, although Buddhist monks may practice vegetarianism and observe other food taboos.

Food Customs at Ceremonial Occasions. A variety of *ttok* (rice cake), other traditional confectionery, and fresh fruits are served to celebrate birthdays, marriages, and the *hwan'gap* (the sixtieth birthday). The offerings at *ch'arye*, memorial services for one's ancestors performed on special holidays, include rice wine, steamed white rice, soup, barbecued meats, and fresh fruits. After ritual offerings of the wine and food to the ancestral spirits, the family members consume the food and wine. Their ingestion symbolizes the receiving of blessings from the ancestral spirits.

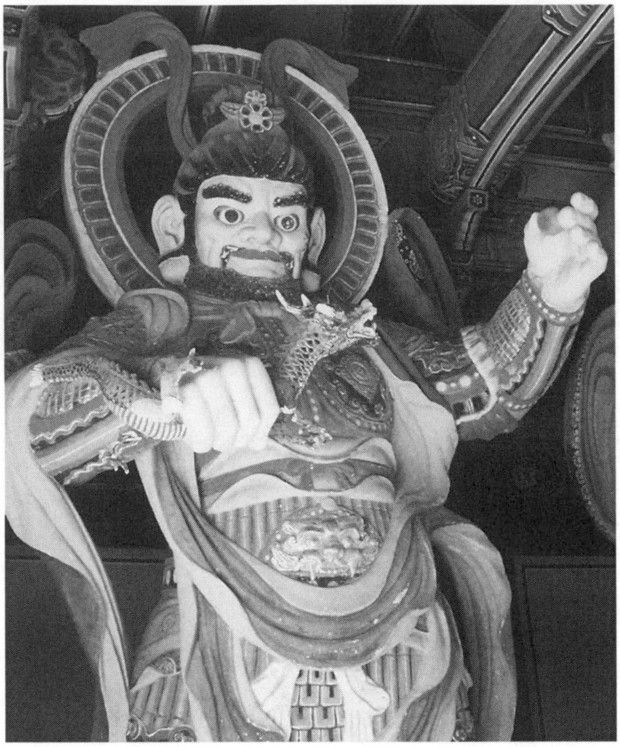

Kwang-mok-chong-wang, the guardian of the West at Pulguk-sa Temple in Kyongju, South Korea.

Basic Economy. South Korea transformed its traditional agrarian subsistence economy to a primarily industrialized one in little more than a generation. In 1962, when the First Five-Year Economic Development Plan was launched, per capita gross national product was $87 (U.S.), in contrast with $10,543 (U.S.) in 1996. However, rapid increases in short-term debt precipitated by overinvestments by *chaebols* (family-owned and -managed conglomerates) and insufficient foreign exchange reserves caused the financial crisis of 1997, which necessitated emergency financial aid from the International Monetary Fund (IMF) in December 1997. After a year of rising unemployment, negative economic growth, and reforms of the financial sector in 1998, the economy began to recover. For gross domestic product (GDP) of $406.7 billion (U.S.), the country ranked thirteenth and for per capita GDP it ranked thirtieth among the world's nations in 1999.

The working-age population (15 years or above) numbered 34.7 million, and 62.2 percent

(21.6 million) of those people were in the labor force in 1997. More than two thirds of them were employed in the service sector in 1997.

South Korea still produces most of its domestically consumed rice. Traditional cash crops such as ginseng, tobacco, tea, and silkworms remain important. The livestock industry raises beef and dairy cattle, hogs, and chickens. Meat production has increased, largely in response increased consumption and government support. South Korea imports beef and milk, exports pork to Japan, and maintains self-sufficiency in chickens and most vegetable products.

Land Tenure and Property. Traditionally, land, especially farmland, was the main form of wealth, and tenants had customary rights that allowed them to farm the same plots year after year. The land survey and tax structure under colonial rule changed the nature and extent of land tenure, forcing many owner-farmers to sell their land to the Japanese. Some people argue that the violation of tenants' customary rights predates the Japanese incursion. The majority of the agricultural population became impoverished, landless tenants by the end of the colonial rule.

After the liberation, redistributions of land were effected in 1948, when former Japanese-owned agricultural lands were sold to the incumbent tenants, and in 1950–1952, when the government under the Land Reform Act (promulgated in 1949) acquired tenanted land owned by absentee landlords and the balance of properties larger than 7.4 acres held by owner-farmers. That property was sold to tenant farmers and those with no land. The imposition of a maximum of three *chongbo* (7.4 acres) on legal land holdings meant that large-scale landlords were eliminated, and the average farm size became less than 2.5 acres. The land reform was a political and social success, destroying the colonial landlord class. However, it contributed to a fragmentation of the land into small holdings, making cultivation inefficient and not conducive to mechanization. Since the 1960s, systematic efforts have been made to increase, rearrange and consolidate farmland by reclaiming mountain slopes and seashores as arable land to expand farm mechanization and increase the utility of farmland. In 1975, the Arable Land Preservation Law was modified to limit the use of arable land for purposes other than farms.

In a country where natural resources are scarce, the efficient use of the land is essential. Government land development projects started in the 1960s with the 1963 Law on Integrated National Land Development, the 1964 Export Industrial Estates Assistance Law, and the 1967 National Parks Law. Those laws were followed by the 1972 Law on the Management of National Land and the 1973 Law on the Promotion of Industrial Estates. In addition to the development of large-scale industrial estates at Ulsan, P'ohang, and elsewhere, a superhighway linking Seoul and Pusan and large-scale water resources development projects such as the Soyang Dam were constructed. A basic land price pattern was officially determined to allow an equitable distribution of the profits from land development. Despite a variety of regulations, however, speculation in real estate has been a major device for accumulating wealth rapidly and irregularly.

Major Industries. The share of primary industry in the economic structure decreased steadily from 26.6 percent in 1970 to 5.7 percent in 1997. Farmwork increasingly is done by women and old men as young people leave for urban jobs. As a result of structural reforms in the economy, Korea has built a strong industrial foundation, especially in the areas of electronics, automobiles, shipbuilding, and petrochemicals. The shipbuilding industry is second only to Japan's and has a 32 percent share of the world market. In the semiconductor industry, Korea ranks third in the world market. Three Korean companies supply more than 40 percent of the global demand for computer memory chips. The Korean automobile and petrochemicals industries rank fifth in the world in terms of production.

Trade. The economy is export-oriented and at the same time heavily dependent on overseas raw materials. In 1999 exports were $143.7 billion (U.S.) and imports were $119.8 billion (U.S.). Korea ranked twelfth for exports and fourteenth for imports among the countries in the world. The major trading partners are the United States and Japan. Since the 1980s, main export items have included computers, semiconductors, automobiles, steel, shipbuilding, electronic goods, machinery, textiles, and fishery products. Overseas construction is a critical source of foreign currency and invisible export earnings. Major import items are steel, chemicals, timber and pulp, cereals, petroleum and petroleum products, and electronics and electrical equipment. The current account balance for the first half of 2000 marked a surplus of $4.4 billion (U.S.).

Division of Labor. Leading *chaebol* companies such as Hyundai, Samsung, and the LG Group recruit white-collar workers from among college graduates through the *kongch'ae* system (an open competitive

A farmer hauls rice on his back in Pong Hwang, Naju, South Korea. Rice is a staple of the South Korean diet.

written examination and interviews). Smaller companies often rely on social connections to hire employees. For executive and upper-level management jobs, companies may scout the desired personnel by using a variety of means, including professional headhunting services. Employment in the civil service, which is based on a grade system, reflects a strong tradition of seniority. Positions are assigned strictly according to grade, and remuneration is based on grade and length of service. Recruitment from outside is allowed only at certain grade levels through the civil service examination system, with age limitations that favor the young. Vacant positions, except at the lowest grade level, are filled mostly by promotions based on seniority. The tradition of seniority, however, is being challenged as part of the wide-ranging restructuring taking place in the public sector as well as in the financial and corporate sectors as a result of the 1997 economic crisis.

SOCIAL STRATIFICATION

Classes and Castes. The traditional gentry (*yangban*) status was formally abolished by the Kabo Reforms of 1894, but the legacy of the class system is seen in social psychological and behavioral patterns. In 1994, 60 percent of South Koreans regarded themselves as belonging to the middle class. The subjective perception of one's class position was closely correlated with one's level of educational attainment. Eighty-three percent of those with a college education perceived themselves as belonging to the middle class, compared with 41 percent of those with a primary school education. In general, industrialization and urbanization have contributed to a leveling of the nonkin hierarchy in social life, but the income gap between the working classes and the industrialist class as a new power elite has grown. Family background, education, occupation, and the general acceptance of a meritocracy are major social factors that contribute to the unequal distribution of wealth by class.

Symbols of Social Stratification. Major symbols of social status include the size of one's condominium or house, the location of one's residence, chauffeur-driven large automobiles, style and quality of dress, membership in a golf club, and the use of honorifics in speech. According to the government classification, residential space between eighteen and 25.7 *p'yong* (one p'yong equals 3.95 square yards) is regarded as medium-sized housing. People in the middle and upper-middle classes tend to live in apartment units of over thirty p'yong. The precise number of p'yong of one's condominium often is interpreted as a barometer of one's wealth. Academic degrees such as a doctorate and professional occupations such as medicine also symbolize higher social status.

POLITICAL LIFE

Government. Koreans lived under a dynastic system until 1910. After liberation from Japanese colonization in 1945, the southern half of the peninsula was occupied by the United States and the northern half by the Soviet military until 1948, when two Koreas emerged. Since then, South Korea has traveled a rocky road in its political development from autocratic governments to a more democratic state, amending its constitution nine times in the wake of tumultuous political events such as the Korean War, the April Revolution of 1960, the 1961 and 1979 military coups, the 1980 Kwangju uprising, and the 1987 democracy movement. The government has maintained a presidential system except in 1960–1961, when a parliamentary system was in place. Government power is shared by three branches: the executive, legislative, and judicial. The Constitutional Court and the National Election Commission also perform governing functions.

The executive branch under the president as the head of state consists of the prime minister, the State Council, seventeen executive ministries, seventeen independent agencies, the Board of Inspection and Audit, and the National Intelligence Service. The president is elected by popular vote for a single five-year term. The prime minister is appointed by the president with the approval of the National Assembly. The legislature consists of a single-house National Assembly whose 273 members serve four-year terms. Some degree of local autonomy was restored for the first time since 1961 by the implementation of local assembly elections in 1991 and popular elections of the heads of provincial and municipal governments in 1995. The judiciary has three tiers of courts: the Supreme Court, the high courts or appellate courts, and the district courts.

Leadership and Political Officials. Political parties have been organized primarily around a leader instead of a platform. The hometown and school ties of the founding leader of a party have often influenced voting patterns, contributing to emotional regionalism among voters as well as politicians. The political parties represented in the Fifteenth National Assembly (1996–2000) are the National Congress for New Politics (NCNP), the United Liberal Democrats (ULD), and the New Korea Party. The NCNP (founded by Kim Dae-jung) and the ULD (founded by Kim Jong-pil) as opposition parties formed a coalition for the 1997 presidential election to help D. J. Kim win the election. The so-called DJP alliance, named for the coalition of Kim Dae-jung and Prime Minister Kim Jong-pil, promised to change the executive branch into a cabinet system with the prime minister as the head of state. The constitutional amendment for a parliamentary government thus has become a major political issue in the Kim Dae-jung administration.

Social Problems and Control. According to the National Statistical Office, the number of reported major penal code offenses was 864 per 100,000 in 1997, and the most common crime was theft. Since the 1980s, sexual violence against women has drawn public concern, and legislation to deal with it was enacted in the 1990s.

Public prosecutors and the police are authorized to conduct investigations of criminal acts, but theoretically, police authority to investigate criminal acts is subject to the direction and. review of prosecutors. The National Police Agency is under the authority of the Ministry of Government Administration and Home Affairs, while the Supreme Public Prosecutor's Office, the penal administration, and other legal affairs are supervised by the Ministry of Justice. The supreme prosecutor general is appointed by the president. Historically, the executive branch exercised great influence on judicial decisions. There is no jury system. Cases that involve offenses punishable by the death penalty, life imprisonment, or imprisonment for more than one year are tried by three judges of a district or branch court; other cases are heard by a single judge.

Military Activity. The North Korean invasion in June 1950 led to the fratricidal Korean War that ended in 1953, killing a million South Korean civilians. Since then, the armed forces have grown to be the largest and most influential government organization. According to the 1998 Defense White Paper, the nation has 690,000 troops. The 1997 defense expenditure accounted for about 15 percent of the national government budget. Weapons and equipment modernization and the operational costs of the three armed services and the armed forces reserves are the main items in the defense budget. Based on the 1953 Korean-American Mutual Defense Treaty, the two countries hold the joint exercise Team Spirit every spring to promote military cooperation and readiness. The Korean peninsula is the world's most densely armed zone with over 1.8 million combat-ready troops confronting each other across the DMZ.

The traditional Korean Confucian New Year's Day celebration in Seoul, South Korea, includes prayer and special food.

SOCIAL WELFARE AND CHANGE PROGRAMS

Much progress has been made in the area of social welfare since the 1970s, especially in the health care system. The National Health Insurance Program, which started in 1977 with coverage of less than 10 percent of the population, covered the entire population by 1989. The government also enacted the National Health Program Law and the Mental Health Law in 1995 to promote health education, antismoking campaigns, and the improvement of the civil rights of the mentally ill. The budget of the Ministry of Health and Welfare has been growing rapidly.

NONGOVERNMENTAL ORGANIZATIONS AND OTHER ASSOCIATIONS

Until the late 1980s, civil organizations generally developed in opposition to the government and contributed to democratization. In the past decade, nongovernmental organizations (NGOs) have increased in numbers and services. The Citizens' Coalition for Economic Justice, the Korean Federation for the Environment Movement, the Korean Women's Associations United, and the Korean Council for Women Drafted for Military Sexual Slavery by Japan (known as *Chongdaehyop*) are well-known NGOs. Since its formation in 1990, Chongdaehyop has achieved remarkable success in bringing to the attention of the world community the ''comfort women'' who served Japanese troops before and during World War II. Its activities have improved the living conditions of the surviving victims and strengthened feminist human rights movement. Many Christian church supported NGOs send missionaries and provide on-site aid in Africa and other regions.

GENDER ROLES AND STATUSES

Division of Labor by Gender. Gender and age have been the two fundamental influences in patterns of social organization. Housework is most commonly regarded as women's work even when a woman works outside the home. Industrialization and democratization have given women more opportunities to play diverse roles in public life, but the basic structure of a gender division of labor is observable in public life. As of April 1998, 47.7 percent of all adult females worked outside the home. Women's average earnings were 63.4 percent of those of men in the same jobs. In June 1999, there was one woman among seventeen cabinet members and no woman vice minister. Women occupied 2.3 percent of the provincial and local assembly seats in 1999. Women as professional leaders in religious life are limited in numbers in both Christian churches and Buddhist temples. The exception to this pattern is seen in shamanism, in which women dominate as priestesses.

The Relative Status of Women and Men. The constitution stipulates equality of all citizens before the law, but the norms and values that guide gender relations in daily life continue to be influenced by an ideology of male superiority. The interplay between these gender role ideologies complicates the patterns and processes of social change in the area of gender role performance and the relative status of women and men.

One of the consequences of these dual gender role ideologies is the behavioral pattern that compartmentalize the social arena into public versus private spheres and formal versus informal situations within each sphere of social action. The patriarchal gender role ideology tends to guide people's behavior at group levels in public informal situations as well as private formal situations. Democratic egalitarianism is more readily practiced at the societal level in public, informal situations, and at the individual level in private, informal situations. Thus, a woman can and did run for the presidency, but women are expected to behave in a submissive manner in public, informal gatherings such as dinner parties among professional colleagues. In private, informal situations such as family affairs, however, urban middle-class husbands tend to leave the decision making to their wives. Nonetheless, male authority as the household head (*hoju*) is socially expected and the law favors husbands and sons over wives and daughters.

The main sources of social change in gender status have been the women's movement and the role of the state in legislating to protect women's rights and improve their status. In response to feminist activism, some men organized the first National Men's Association in 1999. Complaining of reverse sexism, they asserted that laws enacted to prevent domestic violence and sexual harassment unfairly favor women and vowed to campaign to abolish the exclusively male duties of military service so that both sexes may shoulder the duties of national defense.

Marriage, Family, and Kinship

Marriage. Family background and educational level are important considerations in matchmaking. Marriage between people with a common surname and origin place (*tongsong tongbon*) was prohibited by law until 1997. Many urbanites find their spouse at schools or workplaces and have a love marriage. Others may find partners through arranged meetings made by parents, relatives, friends, and professional matchmakers.

In urban centers, the arranged meeting often takes place in a hotel coffee shop where the man, the woman, and their parents may meet for the first time. After exchanging greetings and some conversation, the parents leave so that the couple can talk and decide whether they would like to see each other again. Most individuals have freedom in choosing a marital partner.

Marriage has been regarded as a rite of passage that confers a social status of adulthood on an individual. Marriage also is thought of as a union of not just a man and a woman but of their families and a means to ensure the continuity of the husband's family line. Ninety percent of women marry in their twenties, although the average age of first-time brides has increased from 20.4 years in 1950 to 25.9 years in 1997. Traditionally, divorce was rare, but it tripled from 1980 to 1994.

Remarriages constituted 10.9 percent of all marriages in 1997. Traditionally, remarriages of widows were not allowed and remarriages of divorced women were difficult. However, changes are occurring in the remarriage pattern, especially for divorced women. The ratio of a divorced woman marrying a bachelor used to be lower than that of a divorced man marrying a never-married woman. Since 1995, however, this situation has reversed in favor of women, with a 1997 ratio of 2.9 to 2.6 percent. Divorced women with independent economic means, especially successful professionals, no longer face the traditional gender bias against their remarriage and can marry bachelors who are younger and less occupationally advanced. This phenomenon clearly reveals the importance of the economic aspect of marriage.

Domestic Unit. Two-generation households constituted 73.7 percent of the 11.1 million households in 1995, one-generation and three-generation households constituted 14.7 percent and 11.4 percent, respectively. Traditionally, three-generation stem families were patrilineally composed. That custom continues, but some couples now live with the parents of the wife. In an extended family, the housekeeping tasks usually are performed by the daughter-in-law unless she works outside the home.

Inheritance. Traditionally, the oldest son received a larger proportion of an inheritance than did younger sons because of his duty to coreside with aging

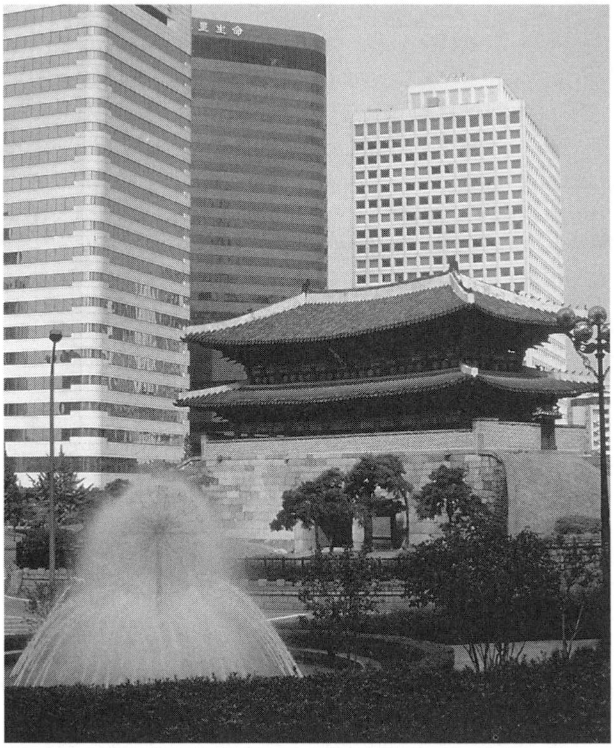

South Gate in downtown Seoul, South Korea, provides greenspace in the urban center.

parents and observe ancestor ceremonies. After the 1989 revision of the Family Law, family inheritance must be divided equally among the sons and daughters. The children may inherit real estate, money from savings accounts, furniture, and other family heirlooms.

Kin Groups. Outside the family, the patrilineal kin group (*tongjok*) is organized into *tangnae* and *munjung*. Consisting of all the descendants of a fourth-generation common patrilineal ancestor, the members of a tangnae participate in death-day and holiday commemoration rites of the kin group. Munjung as a national-level organization is composed of all the patrilineal descendants of the founding ancestor and owns and manages corporate estates for conducting the annual rites to honor ancestors of the fifth generation and above at their grave sites. The main purpose of these lineage organizations and ancestor rites is to assert gentry (*yangban*) status and reaffirm agnatic ties. Since food offerings and ritual equipment are costly, only a small number of kin groups have formal lineage organizations. The Kimhae Kim, the largest lineage, is said to have more than 3.7 million members. "Kim" as the most common Korean surname is composed of about one hundred fifty groups of that name with different places of origin, accounting for approximately one-fifth of the population. The Hahoe Yu of the Hahoe Iltong village in Kyongsang Province are the best known example of kin groups living in the same village.

SOCIALIZATION

Infant Care. Because of rapid changes in lifestyles in the last few decades, the care of infants varies widely, depending, among other things, on the class positions of a family. Generally, during the first two years children receive great deal of affection, indulgence, and nurturing from their parents. Infants seldom are separated from their mothers. They used to be carried on the mother's back but today may ride in baby carriages. Many parents sleep with their infants in the same room. Infant care practices encourage emotional dependence of the children on their parents.

Child Rearing and Education. Obedience, cooperation, respect for the elders, and filial piety are the major values inculcated in a child's early years. Most children receive traditional gender role socialization from early childhood. Parents go to great lengths to provide the best education for their children, especially their sons, since parents traditionally have depended on their children in old age. Children, particularly sons, maintain a strong sense of dependence on their parents throughout adolescence and until after marriage. The differential treatment sons and daughters receive from their parents is considered a fundamental source of the gender structure in Korean society, where women are likely to be more self-reliant and individualistic than men.

Higher Education. The traditional high regard for education as a means to improve one's socioeconomic status continues in contemporary Korea. The annual college entrance examinations are extremely competitive. Many unsuccessful applicants repeat the examinations in order to enter elite universities. From only nineteen institutions of higher education in 1945, the number has increased to nine hundred fifty. Over 26 percent of men and about 13 percent of women age twenty-five and over received higher education as of 1995.

ETIQUETTE

Koreans are very status conscious, and their speech behavior reflects the hierarchical relationship between social actors. Except among former classmates and other very close friends, adults do not use first names to address each other. Position titles such as "professor," "manager," "director," and "president" are used in combination with the honorific suffix *nim* to address a social superior.

Koreans are generally courteous to the extent of being ceremonious when they interact with social superiors but can be very outgoing and friendly among friends and acquaintances of equal social status. Their behavior with strangers in urban public situations may be characterized by indifference and self-centeredness. Koreans appear to be rude to strangers since they generally do not say a word when they accidentally push or jostle other people on the streets, and in the stores, train stations, and airports. Traditional Confucian teaching emphasized propriety in the five sets of human relationships, which included the relations between sovereign and subject, father and son, husband and wife, senior and junior, and friend and friend. Confucianism still serves as the standard of moral and social conduct for many people.

Religion

Religious Beliefs. As a result of constitutional guarantees of freedom of religion, there is a wide range of religious beliefs, from shamanism, Confucianism, and Buddhism to Christianity, Islam, and other religions. Indigenous folk beliefs and shamanism have co-evolved, sharing a fundamental belief in the existence of a myriad of gods (such as the mountain gods, the house gods, and the fire god) and spirits of the dead, all of which may influence people's fortunes. Korean Buddhism has both doctrinal and meditative traditions. Buddhists believe that human suffering is caused mainly by desire. Thus, some Buddhists try to obtain enlightenment by cultivating an attitude of detachment, while others seek to fulfill their desires by offering prayers of requests to Kwanum, the Bodhisattva of Compassion. Confucianism is a political and social philosophy that emphasizes the virtues of *in*, usually translated as "human-heartedness," and *hyo* or filial piety, which is expressed through ceremony such as ancestor rites. The Confucian concept of heaven is an impersonal yet willful force in nature and society, and is beyond human control.

Early Korean Catholics who embraced Catholicism as part of Western Learning (*Sohak*), suffered persecution during the Choson Dynasty for renouncing their ancestral rites as "pagan" rites. Christianity, including both Catholicism and Protestantism, has become a major religion. Lay Christians seek material and spiritual richness through fervent prayers, while some theologians have advocated new theologies focusing on the plight of the underprivileged *minjung* (the "masses") and/or women. Ch'ondogyo (the Teaching of the Heavenly Way), which began as Tonghak (Eastern Learning), founded by Ch'oe Che U in 1860, is a syncretistic religion that grew on the grassroots level. "Humanity and heaven are one and the same" is its basic tenet, which emphasizes human dignity and gender equality.

Religious Practitioners. Shamans derive their power from their ability to serve as a medium between the spirit world and their clients during *kut* (shaman rituals). The Buddhist and Christian clergy derive their power from their knowledge of scripture. Another source of power for the clergy of major religions is the wealth their churches have accumulated from the contributions of followers. The activities of the Christian clergy include not only sermons but also routine personal visits to the homes of their congregants. Buddhist monks may perform personalized prayer services in return for monetary donations.

Rituals and Holy Places. A shaman keeps a shrine where her guardian deity and the instruments for ritual services are kept. *Kut*, which include songs, dances, and incantations, are performed at various places to secure good fortune, cure illnesses, or guide the spirit of a deceased person to heaven. Numerous Koreans perform Confucian-style ceremonies to commemorate their ancestors on death dates and special holidays at home and/or grave sites. The National Confucian Academy in Seoul holds semimonthly and semiannual ceremonies to honor Confucius, his disciples, and other Confucian sages. Christian churches are ubiquitous in urban and rural areas. Some offer services not only on Sundays but also at predawn hours on weekdays. Leading Christian churches have huge new buildings that can accommodate several thousand worshipers. Buddhist temples used to be located away from urban centers near the mountains, but more temples are now being erected in urban areas.

Death and the Afterlife. Many Koreans believe in ancestral spirits and observe Confucian rituals concerning funerals, mourning practices, and memorial services. Folk beliefs about the afterlife are somewhat influenced by Buddhism but are characterized by diversity. Mourning periods vary, depending on the social status of the deceased, from one day to two years. Selecting good grave sites according to geomantic principles is regarded as important for both the ancestral spirit and the descen-

Shoppers indulge in the markets and stores of the Namdaemun shopping district in downtown Seoul, South Korea.

dants' fortune. At domestic rites performed on the eve of the death day and on major holidays, the ancestral image is that of living, dependent, and inactive parents to whom food and wine are offered.

Medicine and Health Care

The health care system includes both Western and traditional medicine. As a result of increasing public demand for traditional medicine, the Oriental Medicine Bureau was established in the Ministry of Health and Welfare in 1966. There were 62,609 Western doctors and 9,289 traditional doctors in 1997. Traditional doctors practice acupuncture and prescribe herbal medicine for the prevention and treatment of illness. Some people turn to a shaman for elaborate kut performance to cure illnesses attributed to evil spirits.

Secular Celebrations

The two most important national holidays are New Year's Day and Ch'usok (which falls on the eighth full moon by the lunar calendar). Koreans observe both solar and lunar New Year's holidays of which many people wear *hanbok* (traditional dress), offer *sebae* (New Year's greetings with a "big bow") to their parents, eat *ttok-kuk* (rice-cake soup), play traditional games, and observe ancestor rites. On Ch'usok, the harvest festival celebrations include eating special foods such as *songp'yon* (half-moon-shaped rice cakes) and making family visits to ancestral graves to tidy the tomb area and offer fruits and other foods, including steamed rice cooked with newly harvested grain.

The Arts and Humanities

Literature. Korean classical literature was written in Chinese, and the late Koryo and early Choson *sijo* poems dealt mainly with the theme of loyalty. The *kasa* form of Choson poetry expressed individual sentiments and moral admonitions. After the creation of the Korean alphabet, many works of fiction were written in *Han'gul* and royal ladies wrote novels depicting their personal situations and private thoughts. Modern literature started in the mid-nineteenth century as a result of the new Western-style education and the Korean language and literature movement. The themes of twentieth-century literature reflect the national experiences colonization, postliberation division of the homeland, the Korean War, urbanization, and industrialization. Translations of literary works began to appear in foreign countries in the 1980s. The novelists whose works have been most widely translated are Hwang Sun-won and Kim Tong-ri.

Graphic Arts. Traditional brush paintings include realistic landscapes; genre paintings of flowers, birds, and the daily lives of ordinary people; and calligraphic presentations of Chinese phrases extolling Confucian virtues such as filial piety and loyalty decorated with designs and pictures. Traditional sculptures in bronze, stone, and rock were inspired by Buddhism. The Sakyamuni Buddha in the rotunda of the Sokkuram Grotto is regarded as a national masterpiece.

Performance Arts. Korean music and dance evolved over three thousand years from the religious ceremonies of shamanism and Buddhism and often were linked to the agricultural cycle. Traditional music has two genres: *Chong'ak* (''correct music''), a genre of chamber music with a leisurely tempo and a meditative character, and *minsok'ak* (folk music), characterized by spontaneity and emotionality. *P'ansori* as a category of folk vocal music is a unique combination of singing and storytelling by a single vocalist with the accompaniment of a *changgo* (traditional drum). The *Tale of Ch'unhyang*, a love story and one of the five extant traditional p'ansori compositions, requires more than eight hours to perform. Among folk instrumental music, *samul nori* has been the most popular form since the 1970s. The primarily percussive music is played on gongs made of bronze and leather and double-headed hourglass and barrel drums. Koreans also enjoy classical and popular Western music. South Korea has thirty-one symphony orchestras and has produced internationally renowned violinists such as Kyung-hwa Chung and Sarah Chang.

There are two categories of traditional dance: court dances and folk dances performed by farmers, shamans, and villagers. Kut and *nong-ak* (farmers' festival music), which combine music and dance with ritual and entertainment, continue to be popular. Mask dances performed by villagers combined dance with satiric drama, making fun of erring officials and monks for entertainment and ethical edification. The Traditional Dance Institute of the Korean National University of Arts was established in 1998 to educate future generations in the traditional dance heritage.

The State of the Physical and Social Sciences

The Korean Advanced Institute of Science and Technology was established by the government in 1971 as a model for research-oriented universities producing scientists and engineers. The Pohang University of Science and Technology was founded with similar aims by the Pohang Steel Corporation in 1986. The Korean Science and Engineering Foundation and the Korea Research Foundation are the major funding agencies for university research in basic science. The Academy of Korean Studies was founded in 1978 to encourage in-depth social science and humanities studies of the heritage of the Korean nation. Since 1980, it has offered graduate courses in Korean studies.

Bibliography

Abelmann, Nancy. *Echoes of the Past, Epics of Dissent: A South Korean Social Movement*, 1996.

An, Myung-soo. ''The Scientific Significance of Traditional Korean Food.'' *Koreana* 7 (3): 12–13, 1993.

Brandt, Vincent S. R. *A Korean Village: Between Farm and Sea*, 1971.

Buswell, Robert E., Jr. *The Zen Monastic Experience: Buddhist Practice in Contemporary Korea*, 1992.

Cho, Soon. *The Dynamics of Korean Economic Development*, 1994.

Choi, Gil-sung. ''Annual Ceremonies and Rituals.'' In Shin-yong Chun, ed., *Customs and Manners in Korea*, 1982.

Clark, Donald N. *Christianity in Modern Korea*, 1986.

Cumings, Bruce. *Korea's Place in the Sun: A Modern History*, 1997.

Hahm, Pyong-Choon. *The Korean Political Tradition and Law: Essays in Korean Law and Legal History*, 1967.

Harvey, Youngsook Kim. *Six Korean Women: The Socialization of Shamans*, 1979.

Janelli, Roger L., and Dawnhee Yim Janelli. *Ancestor Worship and Korean Society*, 1982.

———. *Making Capitalism: The Social and Cultural Construction of a South Korean Conglomerate*, 1993.

Kang, K. Connie. *Home Was the Land of Morning Calm: A Saga of a Korean-American Family*, 1995.

Kendall, Laurel. *Shamans, Housewives, and Other Restless Spirits: Women in Korean Ritual Life*, 1985.

———. *Getting Married in Korea: Of Gender, Morality, and Modernity*, 1996.

Kim, Choong Soon. *Faithful Endurance: An Ethnography of Korean Family Dispersal*, 1988.

———. *The Culture of Korean Industry: An Ethnography of Poongsan Corporation*, 1992.

Kim, Won-yong. *Art and Archaeology of Ancient Korea*, 1986.

Kim, Yung-chung, ed. and trans. *Women of Korea: A History from Ancient Times to 1945*, 1979.

Koo, Hagen, ed. *State and Society in Contemporary Korea*, 1993.

Koo, John. "The Term of Address 'You' in South Korea Today." *Korea Journal* 32: (1), 1992.

Korean Overseas Culture and Information Service. *A Handbook of Korea*, 1998.

Lee, Chong-sik. *The Politics of Korean Nationalisms*, 1965.

Lee, Kwang-kyu. *Kinship System in Korea*, 1975.

Lie, John. *Han Unbound: The Political Economy of South Korea*, 1998.

Nahm, Andrew C. *Introduction to Korean History and Culture*, 1993.

Rutt, Richard. *The Bamboo Grove: An Introduction to Shijo*, 1971.

Saccone, Richard. *Koreans to Remember: Fifty Famous People Who Helped Shape Korea*, 1993.

"Sejong the Great." *Koreana: Korean Art & Culture* 11: (3), Autumn 1997.

Shima, Mutsuhiko, and Roger L. Janelli, eds. *The Anthropology of Korea: East Asian Perspectives*, 1998.

Soh, Chunghee Sarah. *Women in Korean Politics*, 1993.

———. "Compartmentalized Gender Schema: A Model of Changing Male-Female Relations in Korean Society." *Korea Journal* 33 (4): 34–48, 1993.

———. "The Status of the Elderly in Korean Society." In S. Formanek and S. Linhart, eds., *Aging: Asian Experiences Past and Present*, 1997.

Song, Byung-Nak. *The Rise of the Korean Economy*, 2nd ed., 1997.

Vos, Ken. *Korean Painting: A Selection of Eighteenth to Early Twentieth Century Painting from the Collection of Cho Won-kyong*, 1992.

Whitfield, Roderick, ed. *Treasures from Korea: Art through 5,000 Years*, 1984.

Yang, Sung Chul. *The North and South Korean Political Systems: A Comparative Analysis*, 1994.

Yang, Sunny. *Hanbok: The Art of Korean Clothing*, 1997.

—CHUNGHEE SARAH SOH

KUWAIT

CULTURE NAME

Kuwaiti

ALTERNATIVE NAMES

State of Kuwait, Dawlat al Kuwayt

ORIENTATION

Identification. Modern day Kuwaitis are the descendants of several nomadic tribes and clans who ultimately settled on the coast of the Arabian Gulf during the eighteenth century to avoid the persistent drought of the desert. When they arrived at the coast, the clans built forts to protect themselves from other nomadic tribes who still traversed the desert. The name Kuwait is derived from *kut*, an Arabic word for "fort."

Location and Geography. Kuwait is a small country located in the Middle East on the Persian Gulf, between Iraq and Saudi Arabia. It is a desert country with intensely hot summers and short, cool winters. The terrain varies minimally, between flat and slightly undulating desert plains.

Demography. The population of Kuwait in 2000 was estimated at 1,973,572, including 1,159,913 non-Kuwaiti citizens. A variety of ethnic groups reside in this country, and only around 40 percent of the population is Kuwaiti. People from surrounding Middle Eastern nations, such as Egypt, Palestine, Jordan, Lebanon, Oman, Saudi Arabia, and Yemen, constitute 35 percent of the population. This make up is often in flux, depending on the dynamics and relationships between surrounding countries. After the Gulf War the entire population of Palestinians was expelled from Kuwait, because they were believed to sympathize with Iraq. In addition to these Arabian and African populations, approximately 9 percent of the population is Indian, 4 percent of the population is Iranian, and the remaining 7 percent is consists of other foreign nationals. Approximately 29 percent of the population is 14 years or under, 68 percent is between the ages of 15 and 64, and 2 percent of the population is over 65 years of age. Around 60 percent of the population is male, while 40 percent of the population is female.

Linguistic Affiliation. Arabic is the official language, and English is widely spoken.

HISTORY AND ETHNIC RELATIONS

Emergence of the Nation. For centuries Kuwait was merely a transitory home for Arabic nomads. Located between Mesopotamia and the Indus river valley, this arid terrain was a trade link between these two civilizations. In the early 16th century Portuguese invaded the Arabian Gulf and built a fort where Kuwait City now stands. The Portuguese used the area as a base from which to make further excursions north, but their residence in the Arabian Desert was short-lived. Thus, up until the 18th century, Kuwait was a territory of shifting communities.

It was in 1710 that the Sabahs, a nomadic community of people of Arabian descent, settled in what is now Kuwait city. In the mid 18th century, members of the Utab clan, from what is now Saudi Arabia, began to settle in Kuwait. Within a span of fifty years, the town burgeoned into an important trading post, with boat building and the excavation and cultivation of pearls being the two main industries.

National Identity. Kuwaitis are increasingly a minority in their own country. The fear that has arisen from this loss of dominance, compounded by the country's precarious relationship with neighboring nations such as Iraq, has led to extremist policies and practices regarding the assertion of nationality and the rights of Kuwaiti nationals.

Ethnic Relations. Ethnic Kuwaitis struggle to maintain their cultural dominance in an increasingly complex society. Dominant Kuwaiti culture is homogeneous, and adheres to traditional values de-

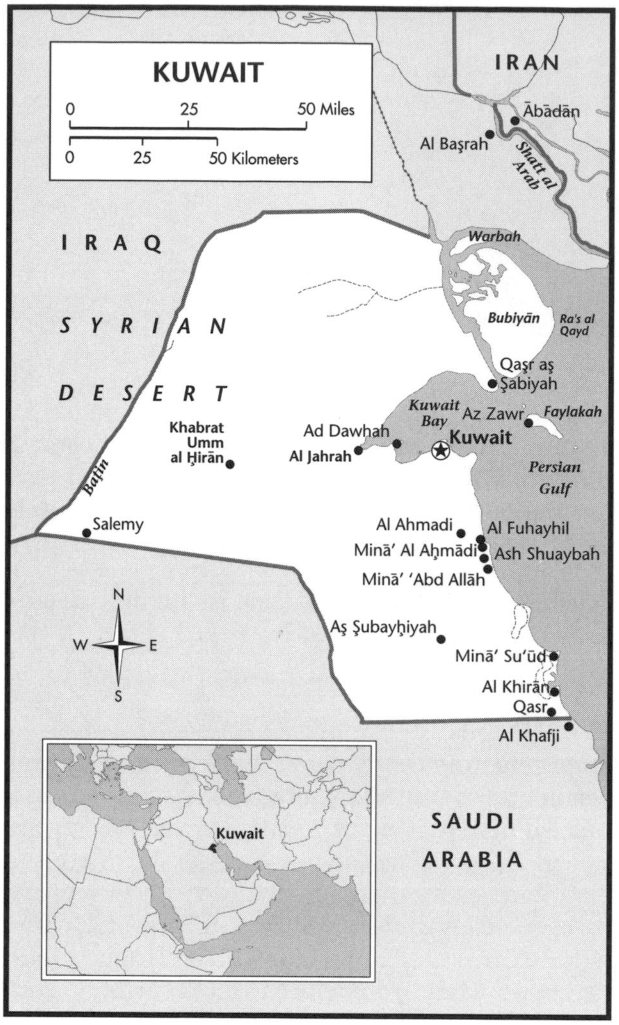

Kuwait

veloped in the desert plains in accordance with the teachings of Islam. There is tension, however, between these cultural norms and the other ethnic groups who reside in Kuwait. Most Kuwaiti workers have government jobs, an opportunity generally denied to foreign nationals. Also, there are restrictions against foreigners owning property and businesses. These social and economic gaps between nationals and other ethnic groups increases the friction between Kuwaitis and non-Kuwaitis residing in the country.

Urbanism, Architecture, and the Use of Space

Over the span of just two hundred years, Kuwait shifted from a nomadic population to an urban population. The development of the urban environment has largely been influenced by Islam, and Kuwaiti homes reflect the tenets of Islam as clearly as they reflect the influence of desert life and culture. Most homes are rectangular in shape and are organized around an inner courtyard. This courtyard allows for an enclosed yet open environment, and at the same time protects from the wind and direct sunlight in the arid desert climate. Generally homes are clustered together to unite and serve the needs of an extended family. As family size increases, more rooms are built on to accommodate the new members.

The manner in which space is used in Kuwait reflects the traditional relationship between men and women. In nomadic times, tents would be separated by screens or a cloth, so that men could entertain unrelated men, as is their custom, without having the guests come into contact with female kin. With the advent of urban living, homes were built with what is known as a ''double circulation system'' so that men and women could avoid contact with one another, and most importantly so that women were not in contact with strange men.

Food and Economy

Food in Daily Life. After centuries of living as nomads, surviving off of subsistence farming and animal husbandry, the relatively recent increase in the income of many Kuwaitis has lead to a rapid rise in the relative obesity of the general population. Still operating under the precept that plump children are healthy, Kuwaitis eat a very rich diet, and do not engage in physical exercise like they did in the past. The shift from a nomadic to sedentary lifestyle happened quickly with industrialization and urbanization coinciding with the advent of the oil industry in the past century, and habits of nutrition have not completely changed to accommodate the present environment.

An average Kuwaiti person eats three meals each day. Breakfast often includes some meat, such as fried liver or kidneys, and a dairy product such as cheese or yogurt. For lunch and dinner, several meat dishes may be served. In the desert, vegetables and grains were largely unavailable. Subsequently, meat was a staple of the desert nomad's diet. As in the past, meat remains a central part of the Kuwaiti diet.

Food Customs at Ceremonial Occasions. For Kuwaitis, it is very important to be generous in providing food for guests. For ceremonial occasions such as weddings, people will roast an entire sheep and serve it on a bed of saffron rice.

As Kuwait is predominately an Islamic country, alcohol is illegal within its borders. Islam influences many customs regarding food, the most prominent of which is the fasting month of Ramadan. During Ramadan, practitioners of Islam fast between sunrise and sunset. Also at this time, the consumption of food, drink, and tobacco in public is forbidden.

Basic Economy. With only 5 percent of the land suitable for farming, Kuwait is dependent on international trade for the provision of most basic necessities, including food, clothing, and construction materials. However, that dependency is tempered by the fact that Kuwait is one of the largest oil producing countries in the world, an energy source upon which virtually every developed nation is dependent. Kuwait's relationship with trading partners is thus defined by the countries respective interdependence.

Land Tenure and Property. Many people live in urban areas because of the necessity of sharing scarce resources in the desert. This factor also influences the price of available property: prices are high and the general population has limited ability to actually own property.

Major Industries. The economy of Kuwait is dependent on the oil industry. During the war with Iraq many oil refining facilities were destroyed, but this industry remains of enormous importance to Kuwait. To protect oil interests, and to protect against larger countries taking advantage of Kuwait, the country was one of the founding members of the Organization of Petroleum Exporting Countries (OPEC).

Trade. Kuwait was built on the trade between Mesopotamia and the Indus river valley. Throughout its history Kuwait has depended on trade, and today exports total $13.5 billion each year in oil, refined products, and fertilizers. Japan, India, the United States, South Korea, and Singapore are the major recipients of their exports. Kuwait imports $8.1 billion a year in food, construction materials, vehicles and parts, and clothing from the United States, Japan, the United Kingdom, Germany, and Italy.

Division of Labor. The labor force includes 1.3 million people. The government and social services employ 50 percent of the labor force, businesses employ 40 percent, and the remaining 10 percent are employed in agriculture. This labor force is divided along ethnic lines, with Kuwaitis holding most of the government jobs and owning most of the of businesses in the private sector. Non-Kuwaitis generally labor in various businesses and in the oil industry.

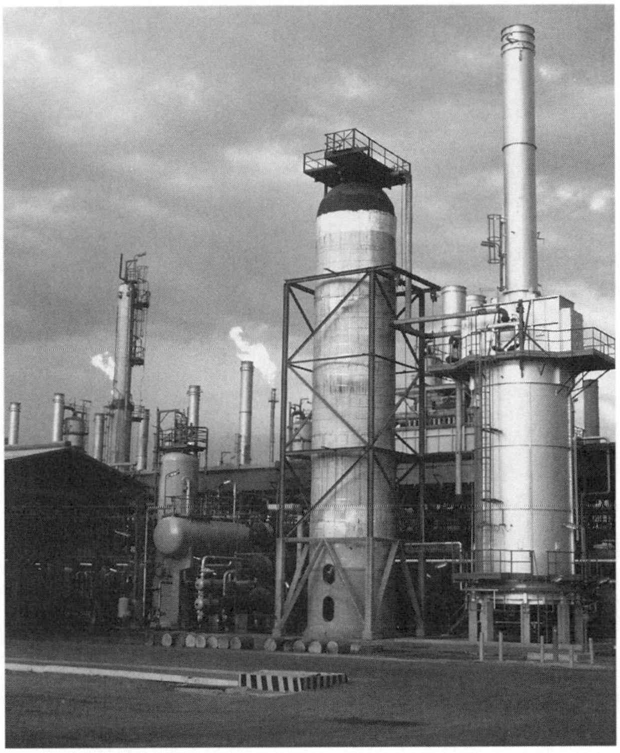

The towers and pipes of a Kuwait oil refinery contribute to the nation's most important industry.

Social Stratification

Classes and Castes. There are five levels of social stratification in Kuwaiti society, and these divisions are based on wealth. At the apex of the social hierarchy is the ruling family. Below that are old Kuwaiti merchant families. In the middle of the strata are former Bedouins, Arabian Desert nomads, who settled in Kuwait with the advent of the oil industry. Next come Arabs from neighboring countries, and at the bottom of this hierarchy are foreigners.

Within classes there are strong kinship bonds, which help maintain the social structure. Social stratification is perpetuated by the state, as in the legal ability to own property by cultural factors, such as marriage patterns, and by social rights, such as the provision or lack of state funded education, healthcare, and housing. Within this hierarchy there are enormous gaps between the vastly rich, the middle class, and the extraordinarily poor migrants.

Political Life

Government. Kuwaiti government is nominally a constitutional monarchy, headed by the Amir. The constitution was approved and implemented on 11 November 1962. Upon the development of this con-

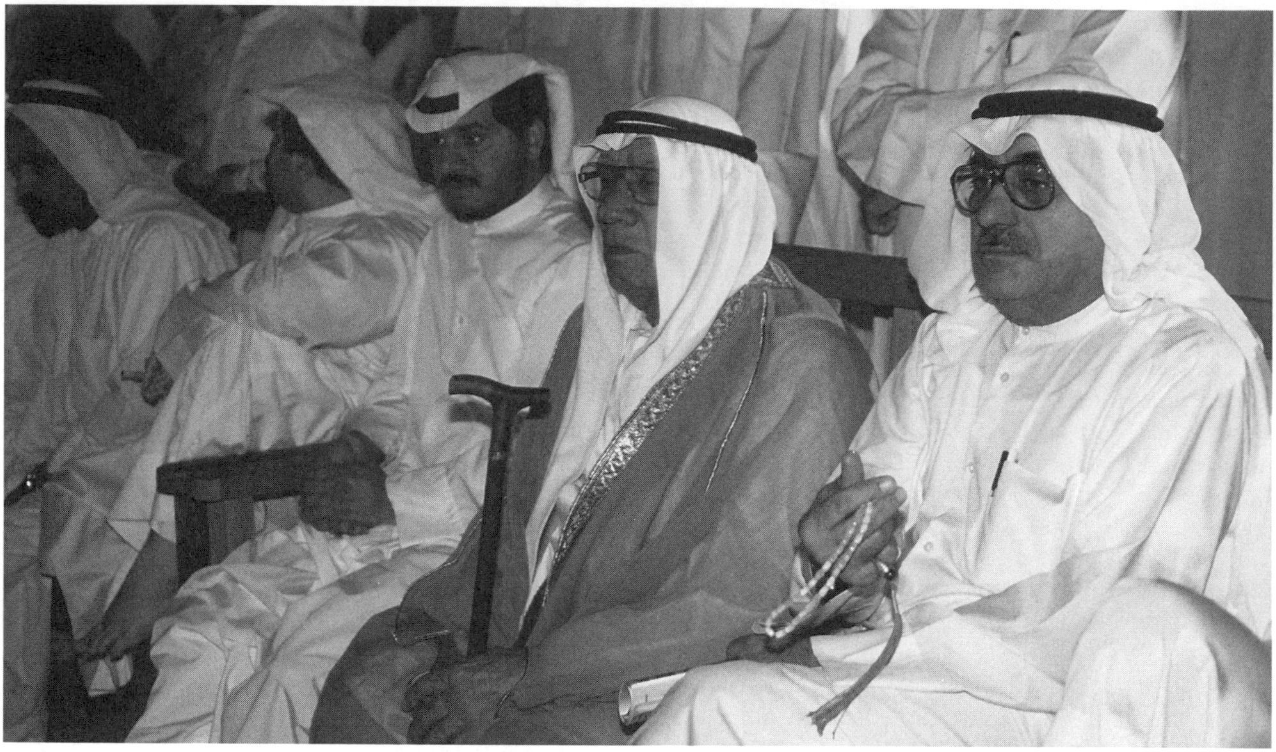

Kuwaiti men in traditional robes attend a meeting in Kuwait.

stitutional monarchy, Kuwait developed a National Assembly. This form of democracy was short-lived, however. In August 1976, Sheikh Sabah dissolved the assembly under the premise that legislation was being manipulated to increase private gain for officials. As a political system built on a hierarchy of clans, nepotism is rampant in the Kuwaiti government. Therefore, it is in the Amir's power to dissolve the parliament, and within two months it must be re-elected, or the previous parliament will be instituted again.

Leadership and Political Officials. There are not any national political parties or leaders, yet several political groups act as de facto parties; these include the Bedouins, merchants, nationalists, Sunni and Shi'a activists, and secular leftists. These de facto parties are divided along the lines of class and religion.

Social Problems and Control. Social problems stem predominantly from the various systemic hierarchies. Within these structures, groups and individuals are constantly struggling to either improve or maintain their position. As of late, the position of women within these structures has been a subject of great debate. Similarly, the degree to which Islam should influence political structures is also a source of debate and contention. Presently, political and social controls are influenced by a combination of Islam and tradition, but this is being questioned in the increasingly multicultural environment of Kuwait.

Military Activity. Kuwait has an army, navy, and air force. The national police force, national guard, and coast guard are also part of the military. During 1999-2000, $2.5 billion (U.S.) was spent on the military.

Social Welfare and Change Programs

Social service programs have long been an important agenda item for Kuwait's government, with education and health being two of the country's major expenditures. In the past there have been many programs providing housing and subsidizing services such as water, electricity, and gasoline. Recently, however, these programs have been cut back and are being re-evaluated, as they have lead to an extreme amount of reliance on the state for basic services.

Nongovernmental Organizations and Other Associations

In the past the Kuwait Fund for Arabic Economic Development was one of the largest and most influ-

Kuwaiti women demonstrate for suffrage. These women reflect the emerging prominence of women in Kuwaiti political and social life.

ential nongovernmental organizations in the country. Founded in 1961, the organization made massive loans and provided technical expertise to assist Arab and other developing nations develop their economies. In the aftermath of the war with Iraq, Kuwait has been the recipient of assistance from neighboring countries.

Gender Roles and Statuses

Division of Labor by Gender. Both Kuwaiti custom and law enforce a division of labor by gender. Unlike other Arabic countries, women are involved various aspects of the labor force, but the percentage of women involved in labor outside of the home is small. Those women who are gainfully employed often work in the social services, in clerical positions, and as teachers. Few women are owners or managers of small businesses.

The Relative Status of Women and Men. The tension between traditional Kuwaiti Islamic values and Western values is evidenced in the roles and status afforded to men and women within Kuwaiti society. Many women still go veiled and wear the traditional black, but many girls in the younger generation follow the dictates of western fashion. Female students are a majority at Kuwait University, and women are prominent in the country's commercial life and in the civil service. Women are openly agitating for the relaxation of social restrictions on females, more women's rights, and an increase in job opportunities.

Marriage, Family, and Kinship

Marriage. Most marriages in Kuwait are arranged, in accordance with tradition. Intermarriage occurs within clans, but not between social classes. Women, regardless of their age, need their father's permission to marry. Also, a woman cannot marry a non-Muslim, although a man is afforded this privilege. In addition, a woman can only marry one spouse, while a man has the legal right to four wives.

Domestic Unit. Family forms the basis of Kuwaiti society. Extended families live together, both out of necessity caused by limited housing space, and so that all family members can be involved in the socialization of future generations and maintain familial and cultural traditions.

Inheritance. In accordance with Islam, both men and women have equal property rights.

Socialization

Child Rearing and Education. All schooling for Kuwaitis is free, and between the ages of six and fourteen, attendance is compulsory. While the government stresses the importance of education regardless of gender, most schools are segregated on the basis of gender after kindergarten. The definition of literacy used by the government is that one must be over the age of fifteen and capable of reading and writing. With this in mind, 79 percent of the population is literate, with 82 percent of men and 75 percent of women meeting these criteria.

Higher Education. There is only one university in the country, but because of the great value placed on education, the government awards scholarships for many Kuwaitis to pursue higher education. There are also several post-secondary technical institutes where one may pursue knowledge of electronics, air-conditioning, and diesel and petrol engines, all necessary to the major industries of Kuwait.

Etiquette

Kuwaitis, like other Arab populations, have different personal boundaries than Westerners. In general, they sit, talk, and stand closer to one another. It is common for members of the same sex to touch one another during their interactions as an expression of their friendship, and men often shake hands upon greeting and departure. Socially, physical contact between men and women is not acceptable. To Kuwaitis, honor, reputation, and respect are primary concerns.

Religion

Religious Beliefs. The main religion in Kuwait is Islam: approximately 85 percent of the population is Muslim. There are two main sub-sects of Islam in Kuwait, 45 percent of the population is Sunni Muslim, while 40 percent of the population is Shi'a Muslim. The remaining 15 percent of the population practices Christianity, Hinduism, Parsi, and other religions.

Rituals and Holy Places. For practitioners, the most essential tenet of Islam is the purification of the soul through prayers, known as *salat,* five times each day. The purpose of this activity is to strengthen one's commitment to god. Cleanliness and proper hygiene are prerequisites for the ritual prayers—in Islam good physical health and good spiritual health are intertwined.

Medicine and Health Care

In Islam the importance of good health cannot be overemphasized. With this in mind every Kuwaiti citizen is provided both care in sickness and preventative medicine.

Secular Celebrations

Both New Years Day on 1 January and Kuwaiti National Day on 25 February are celebrated.

The Arts and Humanities

Graphic Arts. In Kuwait, as in many Islamic countries, the art of calligraphy is one of the most longstanding and thriving forms of expression. Arabic calligraphy is considered to be the ultimate expression of god's words. Because in traditional Islam sculptural and figurative forms of art were perceived as idolatry, calligraphy was considered an acceptable, alternative form of art and expression.

Bibliography

Al-Rabie, Ahmad. "The Absence of Plans for the Future." *Asharq Al-Aswat,* 1997.

Crystal, Jill. *Kuwait: The Transformation of an Oil State,* 1992.

Devine, E. and N. L. Braganti, eds. *The Travelers Guide to Middle Eastern and North African Customs and Manners,* 1991.

Hasan, Alia F. "Architecture 101: Some Basics," *Arabic and Islamic Architecture,* July 26, 2000.

———. "The Art of Calligraphy." *Arabic and Islamic Architecture,* November 7, 1999.

Ismael, Jacqueline. *Kuwait: Social Change in Historical Perspective,* 1982.

Milmo, Sean, ed. *The Gulf Handbook 1978,* 1977.

Osborne, Christine. *The Gulf States and Oman,* 1977.

Web Sites

Amnesty International 1999 Human Rights Reports. Available at www.amnesty.org

"Arab Net-Kuwait." Available at http://arab.net/kuwait

CIA Fact Book. Available at http://www.odci.gov/cia/publications/factbook/geos/ku.htm

"Islamic Architecture." Available at http://www.islamicart.com/main/architecture/intro.htm

"Kuwait On-Line." Available at http://kuwaitonline.com/aboutkw/aboutkw.htm

U.S. Department of State 1999 Report: Kuwait, Available at http://www.usis.usemb.se/human/index

—Heather Loew

KYRGYZSTAN

CULTURE NAME

Kyrgyz

ALTERNATIVE NAMES

Kirgiz, Kirghiz, Kara-Kyrgyz, Kirghizstan

ORIENTATION

Identification. The name *qirqiz* or *kyrgyz* dates back to the eighth century. The Kyrgyz people originated in the Siberian region of the Yenisey Valley and traveled to the area of modern-day Kyrgyzstan in response to pressure from the Mongols. The Kyrgyz people believe that their name means *kirk-kyz,* (forty girls), and that they are descended from forty tribes. Today the majority of Kyrgyz people live in the Kyrgyz Republic, also known as Kyrgyzstan, but there are large populations living in China, Afghanistan, Tajikistan, and Uzbekistan. Kyrgyzstan was formerly the Kirghiz Soviet Socialist Republic, or Kirghizia.

Location and Geography. Kyrgyzstan has an area of 76,500 square miles (198,500 square kilometers). Its neighbors are China to the southeast, Kazakstan to the north, Tajikistan to the southwest, and Uzbekistan to the northwest. In addition, Tajikistan and Uzbekistan control two enclaves each within Kyrgyzstan's borders in the southern part of the country. Ninety-four percent of the land is mountainous, and only 20 percent of the land is arable. The valleys are densely populated along the few paved roads.

The capital, Bishkek, is in the north, near the Kazak border, where it was known as Frunze during the Soviet era. The country is divided into north and south by mountain ranges. Northern culture has been influenced by Russians, while southern culture has absorbed Uzbek traditions. The Naryn region in central Kyrgyzstan is relatively isolated, and it is here that the Kyrgyz culture is most "pure."

Demography. In 1998 the population of Kyrgyzstan was estimated at more than 4.5 million. Approximately 52.4 percent of the inhabitants are ethnically Kyrgyz. Ethnic Russians (22.5 percent) and Uzbeks (12.6 percent) make up the largest minorities. Many smaller groups, including Ukrainians, Germans, Dungans, Kazaks, Tajiks, Uighours, Koreans, and Chinese, make up the remainder. Many Kyrgyzstan-born Germans and Russians emigrated after the fall of the Soviet Union, but due to government efforts, Russian emigration has slowed. The Kyrgyz have a high birth rate, and have become the ethnic majority since independence.

Linguistic Affiliation. Kyrgyz is a Turkic language, most closely related to Kazak. Kyrgyz is mutually intelligible with both Kazak and Uzbek. Northern pronunciation varies from southern and has more Russian loanwords. Many Uzbek loanwords are used in the south.

Kyrgyz was originally written in Arabic script, but Soviet policy changed its alphabet first to Latin and then to a modified Cyrillic. After independence the Kyrgyz government discussed returning to the Latin alphabet, but this transition has not taken place. In 2000 Russian was adopted as an official national language. It is still commonly used as the language of business, and many ethnic Russians cannot speak Kyrgyz. All children study Kyrgyz, Russian, and English in school.

Symbolism. Public art abounds in the form of statues, murals, roadside plaques, and building decorations. One of the most popular themes is Manas, the legendary father and hero of the Kyrgyz people. His deeds are commemorated in the national epic *Manas,* which is chanted by *manaschis.* Manas is the symbol of Kyrgyz bravery and is often shown astride a rearing horse, with sword in hand, fighting the enemies of the Kyrgyz people.

Kyrgyzstan

While they call Manas their "father," the Kyrgyz do not see themselves as a warlike people. Instead, they are a family of artists. This identity is embodied in the yurt, or *boz-ui*, the traditional Kyrgyz dwelling. The boz-ui is an important cultural symbol, as both the center of the Kyrgyz family and the showplace of Kyrgyz art. The Kyrgyz flag reflects this. On a field of red a yellow sun is centered with forty rays coming from it. In the center of the sun is a *tunduk*, the top of the boz-ui. It was under this that the family gathered.

Inside the boz-ui are hung all the forms of Kyrgyz craftsmanship, including rugs called *shirdaks*. They are made of brightly colored appliquéd wool felt, with stylized nature motifs that have been passed down for generations. These motifs are also often used for borders and decorations on public art.

Other important symbols are taken from the Kyrgyz landscape. The unofficial national anthem is "*Ala-Too*," which names the various features of Kyrgyzstan's landscape. The mountains are described as a body wearing snow and sky, and Lake Issyk-Kul is the eye. Issyk-Kul, in the northeastern part of the country, is called the "Pearl of Kyrgyzstan," and its beauty is a source of great pride. Both the mountains and the lake are on the Kyrgyz seal behind a large golden eagle, flanked by *shirdak* designs, cotton, and wheat.

History and Ethnic Relations

Emergence of the Nation. The Kyrgyz people were originally settled in Siberia. Pressure from the Mongols forced their group to splinter into nomadic tribes and move to the region now known as Kyrgyzstan. Here they were subdued by the Kokandian Khanate, but there were many rebellions. The Kyrgyz allied with Russia as it expanded to the south. Russia then conquered the Kokands and ruled the Kyrgyz as a part of Russian Turkestan. The Kyrgyz rebelled in 1916 against the Russian peasant influx and the loss of grazing land. After the Communists took control, groups such as the Basmachi movement continued to fight for independence. Stalin's collective farms caused protests in the form of killing herds and fleeing to China.

National Identity. Until the advent of Communist control, the Kyrgyz were still a nomadic people made up of individual tribes. The idea of a Kyrgyz nation was fostered under Soviet rule. Kyrgyz traditions, national dress, and art were defined as distinct from their neighbors. Today people will name the Kyrgyz national hat (*kalpak*), instrument (*komuz*), sport (*uulak*), house (boz-ui), drink (*kumyss*), and foods. Stalin then intentionally drew borders inconsistent with the traditional locations of ethnic populations, leaving large numbers of ethnic Uzbeks and Turkmen within Kirghizia's borders. This was supposed to maintain a level of interethnic tension in the area, so that these closely related groups would not rise up against him.

Kyrgyzstan, like many of its neighbors, voted against independence when the Soviet Union collapsed. With no history as an independent nation, they have struggled with the loss of centralized government control. The people of Kyrgyzstan are, however, meeting these challenges, and Kyrgyzstan is held up as the most democratic and market-oriented country in Central Asia.

Ethnic Relations. Kyrgyzstan is an ethnically diverse country, which leads to tensions between and among different groups. Unlike in neighboring Uzbekistan, the Russian people are not vilified or considered morally corrupt. However, Russians claim there is discrimination by Kyrgyz people. In addition, smaller groups, such as the Uighours and the Dungans, complain of widespread discrimination.

The strongest ethnic tensions are felt between the Uzbeks and the Kyrgyz, particularly in the southern region of Osh. In 1990 riots and fighting broke out between these groups over competition for housing and job segregation. It is estimated that two hundred to a thousand people were killed in the fighting. Intergovernmental tension is also high, fueling ethnic conflicts.

Urbanism, Architecture, and the Use of Space

The Kyrgyz people did not have an established architecture of their own before they came under Russian rule. Governmental and urban architecture is in the Soviet style. Cities were designed with many parks and plazas filled with benches that focused on monuments to Soviet achievements. Much of the housing in urban centers consists of large apartment blocks, where families live in two- or three-room apartments. Bazaars come in all sizes, and are divided so that products of the same type are sold side by side.

Most houses are of one story, with open-ended peaked roofs that provide storage space. Outer decorations vary by ethnicity. Families live in fenced-in compounds that may contain the main house, an outdoor kitchen, barns for animals, sheds for storage, gardens, and fruit trees. The traditional dwelling was the portable boz-ui, made of wool felt on a collapsible wooden frame, which people still live in when they take their animals to the summer pastures.

Skaters in Ala-Too Square, Bishkek.

Furniture is a Western adaptation, and its use varies between the north and the south. In the north most families will have a kitchen table with chairs. They also may have a low table for meals, with either stools or sitting mats called *tushuks.* They sleep on beds or convertible couches, and usually there is a couch in the room where the television is kept. Many families also have an outdoor cooking area and eating place for summer use. Sleeping, cooking, and formal areas are kept separate.

In the south there is minimal furniture. A table, sofa, and chairs are kept in a formal room, along with a cabinet full of the family's glassware and books. Large social gatherings usually take place in a special room with two alcoves built into a wall. Decorative chests are placed in the alcoves, and the family's embroidered sleeping mats and pillows are displayed on top.

Southern families may have a low table, or they may spread a *dastarkon* (tablecloth) directly on the floor and surround it with tushuks to sit on. The dastarkon is treated as a table and is never stepped on. People sleep on the floor on layers of tushuks, which are neatly folded and placed in a corner of the room during the day. In summer, platforms are set out in the garden for eating and sleeping on, often with railings to lean against. Families may sleep in the kitchen in the winter if there is a woodstove.

Throughout the country, floors and walls are lined with carpets and fabric hangings. Furniture usually is placed along the walls, leaving most of a room empty.

FOOD AND ECONOMY

Food in Daily Life. Common dishes include: *lagman* (hand-rolled noodles in a broth of meat and vegetables), *manti* (dumplings filled with either onion and meat, or pumpkin), *plov* (rice fried with carrots and topped with meat), *pelmeni,* (a Russian dish of small meat-filled dumplings in broth), *ashlam-foo* (cold noodles topped with vegetables in spicy broth and pieces of congealed corn starch), *samsa* (meat or pumpkin-filled pastries), and fried meat and potatoes. Most meat is mutton, although beef, chicken, turkey, and goat are also eaten. Kyrgyz people don't eat pork, but Russians do. Fish is either canned or dried. Lagman and manti are the everyday foods of the north, while plov is the staple of the south.

Most people eat four or five times a day, but only one large meal. The rest are small, mostly consisting of tea, bread, snacks, and condiments. These include *vareynya* (jam), *kaimak,* (similar to clotted cream), *sara-mai* (a form of butter), and various salads.

Kyrgyz cafes, *chaikanas,* and *ashkanas* usually will have six or seven dishes, as well as two or three side dishes, on the menu. Many places also will serve *shashlik,* which is marinated mutton grilled on a skewer. It is common for only a few of the menu items to be available on any given day. Drink options are limited to tea, soda, and mineral water. Patrons are expected to order as a group and all eat the same entree. *Ristoran* (restaurants) usually have more varied European and Russian dishes.

Food Customs at Ceremonial Occasions. During holidays and personal celebrations, a sheep is killed and cooked. In the north, the main course is *besh-barmak,* which is accompanied by elaborate preparations. The sheep is slaughtered by slitting its throat, and the blood is drained onto the ground. Then the carcass is skinned and butchered, and the organ meats are prepared. The intestines are cleaned and braided. The first course is *shorpo,* a soup created from boiling the meat and organs, usually with vegetables and pieces of chopped fat. The roasted sheep's head is then served and distributed among the honored guests. The fat, liver, other organs, and the majority of the meat are divided equally and served to the guests, with the expectation that they will take this home. Guests receive a cut of meat that corresponds to their status. The remaining meat goes into the besh-barmak. It is shredded into small pieces and mixed with noodles and a little broth, which is served in a communal bowl and eaten with the hands.

In the south, the main course is most often *plov.* The sheep is killed and prepared in the same manner as in the north. Shorpo also is served, and the meat, fat, and organ meats are shared and taken home in the same way; however, it is rare for the head to be eaten. Plov is served in large platters shared by two or three people, and often is eaten with the hands.

For a funeral and sometimes a marriage, a horse will be killed instead of a sheep. The intestines are then used to make sausage.

In the summer a traditional drink called *kumyss* is available. This is made of fermented mare's milk, and is drunk at celebrations when it is in season. Multiple shots of vodka are mandatory at all celebrations.

Basic Economy. After the dissolution of the Soviet Union, Kyrgyzstan went into a deep recession. The economy seemed to be improving in 1997, with low inflation and high growth percentages predicted for 1998, but the troubled Russian economy caused renewed economic difficulties.

Kyrgyzstan is considered self-sufficient in both food and energy. Despite this, electricity is either unpredictable or rationed in the winter. About 35 percent of the people are involved in agriculture, and nearly every village family has a garden where they grow food to support their needs. Most people have a small amount of livestock, such as sheep, cows, and chickens. Excess produce and dairy products are commonly sold to neighbors or at the bazaar.

Unemployment is high, but many people make money by selling goods at the bazaar or by using their private cars as taxis. Kyrgyzstan is dependent on other countries, such as Turkey and China, for consumer goods and chemical products. Since independence, most manufacturing plants and factories have closed or are working at reduced capacities.

Average salaries are higher in the north. State employees may not be paid for months at a time. Pensioners receive minimal monthly payments as well as flour and cooking oil. In 1998, a total of 23 percent of households could not meet their basic food needs.

Land Tenure and Property. Early attempts at privatization led to rioting in Osh in 1990, so this process was put on hold. Farmland cannot be owned by individuals, but it is possible to hold land rights for up to ninety-nine years.

Commercial Activities. Kyrgyzstan is a country with few natural resources. The economy is based on agriculture, mining, and animal products. Most exports are in the form of raw materials. Kyrgyzstan has deposits of gold, coal, bismuth, mercury, antimony, tungsten, and copper. The most important export is hydroelectric power.

Major Industries. Craftsmanship accounts for nearly half of Kyrgyzstan's yearly production. Artisans make saddles, carpets such as *shirdaks* and *alakiis*, embroidered hangings called *tushkiis*, and are skilled at goldsmithing. Other industries include metallurgy as well as those for mechanical and electrical materials, motors and electronic components, and some textiles. The processing of animal products such as in tanning, shoe manufacturing, wool production, and animal slaughter also are important.

The Kumtor gold mine has been rated as the seventh biggest in terms of world importance. Agriculturally, wheat, potatoes, sugar beets, and tobacco are the most important crops. Cotton and silkworms for silk production also are grown.

Trade. Kyrgyzstan trades with one hundred other countries. Within the CIS, its largest-volume trading partners are Russia, Kazakstan, and Uzbekistan; outside the CIS, they are Germany, China, Turkey, the United States, and Korea. In 1998, Kyrgyzstan's exports came to $513.7 million (U.S.), and its imports equaled $841.5 million (U.S.). Kyrgyzastan's major exports are precious metals, power resources, tobacco, and cotton, while major imports include fuel and energy, commodity goods, equipment, and machinery.

Division of Labor. The law states that those under eighteen cannot work, but children often help their parents in the fields and by selling goods. At harvest time, village schools often close so that the children can work.

Jobs are scarce, and people take whatever is available. Russians tend to work in cities, where service sector jobs are available. Uzbeks typically work in the bazaar, selling goods. Many Kyrgyz grow crops and tend livestock. These divisions of labor are often a result of where people choose to live.

Social Stratification

Classes and Castes. Because of the economic hardships endured since independence, Kyrgyzstan has a very small upper class and a large lower class. While ethnic Kyrgyz may be in either class, it is more rare to find other ethnic groups in the upper class, which consists mainly of politicians and community leaders.

Symbols of Social Stratification. Speaking Russian and dressing in a Western manner, having a two-story house, a Mercedes, or a BMW are all signs of wealth. Poor knowledge of Russian is considered a sign of lower-class status.

Political Life

Government. The Kyrgyz government is basically democratic, with three governmental branches: the president and his advisers; the Parliament, which has two houses; and the courts. Parliament is made up of the Legislative Assembly and the Assembly of People's Representatives. In February 1996 a referendum was passed that expanded the president's powers with respect to Parliament, but Parliament has shown its ability to function separately from the president.

Leadership and Political Officials. As of 1996, there were fifteen political parties active within Kyrgyzstan. The parties with the most support are the "Bei Becharalar" Party with thirty-two thousand members, the Communist Party with twenty-five thousand members, the Party of Protection of Industrial, Agricultural Employees and Low Revenue Families with fifteen thousand members, and the Democratic Party "Erkin Kyrgyzstan" with nearly thirteen thousand members. Other parties include the Social Democratic Party, the Democratic Party of Women, the Democratic Party of Economic Unity, and the Agrarian Labor Party.

Political power is closely linked to wealth, both locally and on a national scale. Corruption and buying votes, as well as ballot box stuffing, are common during elections. Kyrgyzstan was the first Central Asian country to hold a presidential election after independence.

Social Problems and Control. The Ministry of Internal Affairs (MIA) is primarily responsible for the prevention and investigation of crime. Because of Kyrgyzstan's economic difficulties, funding for these activities has dropped since independence. Organized crime and drug trafficking are considered the most high-profile crimes, and this is where

Roadside yurt restaurants in rural Kyrgyzstan.

Kyrgyzstan's crime prevention resources are being utilized.

The national police force, or *militzia*, is underpaid and understaffed, so bribes and invented fines are common. Corruption and nepotism are widespread. Many people feel that the rich can do what they want and that the poor are helpless. The media have much more freedom than in other parts of Central Asia.

Military Activity. Kyrgyzstan has a small national guard and navy but no air force. Kyrgyzstan has signed accords with both Uzbekistan and Kazakstan for joint air defense. Military activity has been limited to dealing with an Islamic fundamentalist group in the southern region of Batken; the group began fighting in August 1999.

Social Welfare and Change Programs

The first program to offer social assistance was the National Program to Overcome Poverty. Its goal is to eliminate extreme poverty by developing entrepreneurship, particularly among women. Nongovernmental organizations (NGOs) are central to the implementation of the program.

Under this program, the Kyrgyz government has set up employment promotion companies. Their programs include infrastructure development, social assistance, public education, vocational training for youth and women, and assistance for rural migrants in urban areas.

There are also numerous international organizations working with and supplying funding for projects in Kyrgyzstan.

Nongovernmental Organizations and Other Associations

In 1995 there were three hundred NGOs in Kyrgyzstan. Fifty of them covered gender issues, and eighteen specifically targeted women. NGOs often are seen as vehicles for obtaining foreign aid and grants, and there have been problems with corruption. However, many small NGOs play important roles within their communities. Counterpart Consortium provides important training and assistance to developing NGOs.

Gender Roles and Statuses

Division of Labor by Gender. Historically, women had a fair amount of equality with men in the Kyrgyz culture. Soviet policies maintained this equality, providing women with jobs outside the home and a role in politics. Today women still work

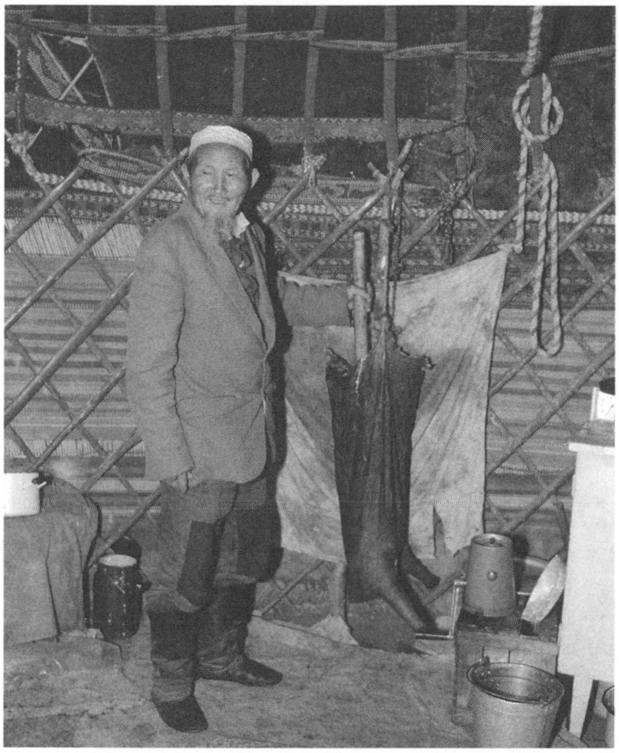

A Kyrgyz man in a yurt.

outside of the home, primarily in education and agriculture. However, women hold few managerial or political positions. In addition to these jobs, women are responsible for all work inside the home. Men are dominant in business and politics.

The Relative Status of Women and Men. While Kyrgyz women are not sequestered, like those in many other Muslim societies, they tend to have less status than men. Age is the most important determinant for status, however, and an older woman will be given respect by younger men.

Within the household women are often the seat of power, making everyday decisions about running the household. It is common for them to hold positions of power in schools as well. In politics and business, however, men have greater power.

Marriage, Family and Kinship

Marriage. Arranged marriages were once common, but are no longer. While couples may choose each other, they often know each other for no more than a few months before they are married. People are expected to marry in their early twenties, after they have finished secondary school, and to have children quickly.

The bride must have a dowry, consisting of clothing, sleeping mats, pillows, and often a handknotted rug. The groom is expected to pay a bride price in the form of cash and several animals. Some of the cash may go toward furnishing the bride's dowry, and often the animals are eaten at the wedding feast.

A typical wedding lasts three days. The first day consists of the bride and groom going to the city with friends and classmates to have the marriage license signed. The bride wears a Western-style wedding dress, and the couple's car is decorated with wedding rings or a doll in bridal clothes.

On the second day the bride and groom celebrate separately with their friends and family. There is food and dancing through the night.

On the third day the bride and her family travel to the groom's family's house. The bride is expected to cry, because she is leaving her family. At the groom's house there are more celebrations and games. Gifts are exchanged between the couple's parents. At the end of the night, a bed is made from the bride's dowry. Two female relatives of the groom are chosen to make sure that the marriage is consummated and that the bride was a virgin.

If the groom is the youngest son he lives with his parents and takes care of them in their old age. The new bride is known as a *kelin*, and it is her responsibility to take over the household duties from her mother-in-law. If the groom is not the youngest, the couple will live with his family only until they can provide the couple with a house.

An alternate marriage tradition is that of wife-stealing. A man may kidnap any unmarried woman and make her his wife. Usually the girl spends one night alone with her future husband. The next day she is taken to meet her mother-in-law, who ties a scarf around the girl's head to indicate that she is now married. She may run away, and it is legal to sue the man who steals her, but it is shameful to do so and unlikely that another man would marry her. Often a lesser bride price is still paid after a girl is stolen, but a dowry is not provided. Girls may be stolen when they are fifteen or sixteen years old.

Polygamy is not practiced, but it is common for people to have lovers when they are married. It is more acceptable for men to do so, and they may refer to their mistresses as their second wives. More than one in five couples get divorced.

Domestic Unit. Because of the tradition of the youngest son taking care of his parents, it is common for a family to consist of grandparents, parents, and children. Individuals live with their parents until they marry. Most families have three or more children, with larger families common in rural villages. Members of the extended family also may visit and live with the immediate family for months at a time.

Inheritance. The youngest son lives with his parents until their deaths, at which time he inherits the house and the livestock. He may decide to share this livestock with his brothers, and is expected to do so if they are in need. Daughters do not inherit from their parents because they become members of their husbands' families.

Kin Groups. Tribal ties were important just after independence, but now regional ties are more important. Favoritism for those from the same tribe or region is common.

There are three main tribal branches: the *ong, sol* and the *ichkilik.* Within these branches there are many smaller tribes.

Tribes become important during marriage. Two people from the same tribe may not marry, unless they do not share a common ancestor for seven generations.

SOCIALIZATION

Infant Care. Infants are primarily cared for by their mothers or other female family members. For the first forty days of an infant's life, he or she cannot be taken outside the home or be seen by anyone but the immediate family. Infants are strapped into their cradles much of the time and quieted when they make noise. When a mother visits another woman the mother usually will take her infant along. A child is rarely taken from his or her mother without the child's consent, and sometimes bribes are used to make the child reach out to another family member.

Child Rearing and Education. Children are expected to be quiet. They are not brought to parties or official functions, and so are prevented from disturbing guests. Girls begin to take on household duties when they are six or seven years old. By the time she is sixteen, the eldest daughter may be responsible for running the household. Boys are considered rowdy and active and often have fewer household chores.

Education is mandatory for both boys and girls. Public schools are found in all towns and villages, and they offer schooling from first to eleventh grade.

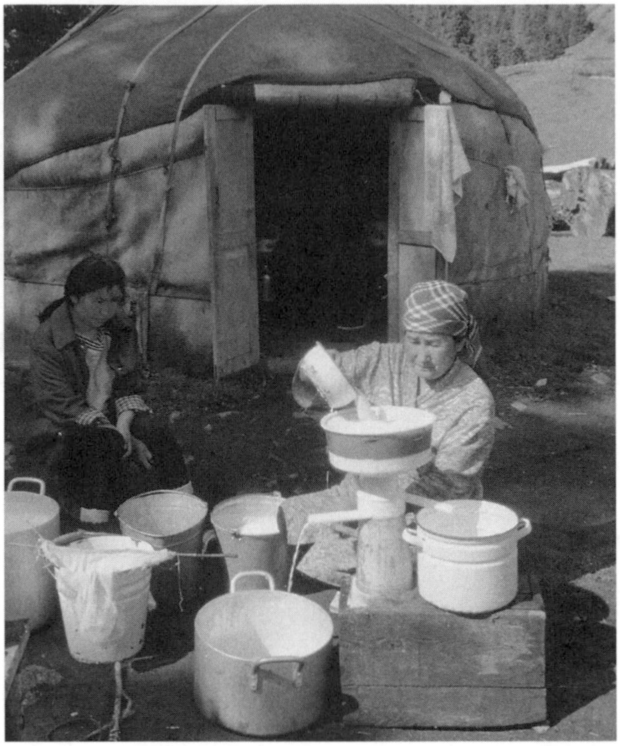

Woman making sour cream in Kjety Oguz, Kyrgyzstan.

Higher Education. Primary and secondary education are free and nearly universal within Kyrgyzstan. Higher education is highly prized but expensive, and there is little financial aid.

ETIQUETTE

The most important element of etiquette is respect. Respect is given to elders and authority figures. Verbal respect is given by using the polite pronoun and endings, and by using the titles *eje* (older sister) and *baikay* or *aga* (older brother). People always use these polite forms, even with close friends and relatives.

Respect also is shown physically. Men and women alike will give up their seats to elders on public transportation. A person's position at a table also shows his or her status. Men and women usually sit on opposite sides of a table, with the eldest and most respected at the head of the table, farthest from the door.

Strangers do not usually acknowledge each other while passing on the street. Any close contact, however, such as sitting near each other on public transportation or making a transaction at the bazaar, will open the way to introductions. It is common to invite new acquaintances into the home.

Friends greet each other differently in the north and the south. In the south, men and women both greet friends of the same gender by shaking hands, often with the left hand over the heart. The opposite gender usually is ignored. Greetings are a series of questions with no pause and spoken over the other person's greetings. Older women and female relatives often will kiss on the cheek while shaking hands. The Arabic greeting *assalom aleikum* is frequently used between men.

In the north, greetings are shorter, and only men shake hands with each other. Assalom aleikum is used only by a younger man to an elder, as a form of deep respect. Good-byes in both the north and the south are brief.

There is less personal space than in the United States, and strangers brush against each other in public without apologizing. People tend to sit shoulder-to-shoulder, and physical affection is common between members of the same sex. People usually don't form lines. Pushing to the front of a group for service is normal and inoffensive.

In the more conservative south, men and women often occupy separate rooms at large celebrations. Boys and girls do not commonly befriend each other.

Bread is considered sacred by the Kyrgyz and must never be placed on the ground or left upside down. It is never thrown away, and leftovers are fed to animals.

At the end of a meal, a quick prayer may be said. This is from the Qur'an, but it honors the ancestors. The hands are held out, palms up, and then everyone at the table cover their face in unison while saying *omen.*

RELIGION

Religious Beliefs. The Kyrgyz consider themselves Sunni Muslim but do not have strong ties to Islam. They celebrate the Islamic holidays but do not follow Islamic practices daily. Many areas were not converted to Islam until the eighteenth century, and even then it was by the mystical Sufi branch, who integrated local shamanistic practices with their religion. Ethnic Russians and Ukrainians tend to be Orthodox Christians.

Religious Practitioners. In the past, the Kyrgyz people relied on shamans as healers. Some theorize that the *manaschis* were originally shamanistic and that the *Manas* epic is derived from calling on ancestor spirits for help. There are still professional shamans, called *bakshe,* and usually there are elders who know and practice shamanistic rituals for families and friends. The Islamic *mullah* is called for marriages, circumcisions, and burials.

Rituals and Holy Places. Both graves and natural springs are holy places to the Kyrgyz people. Cemeteries stand out on hilltops, and graves are marked with elaborate buildings made of mud, brick, or wrought iron. Visitors say prayers and mark the graves of holy people or martyrs with small pieces of cloth tied to the surrounding bushes. Natural springs that come from mountainsides are honored in the same fashion.

Death and the Afterlife. Burials are done in Islamic fashion, but funerals are not. Contrary to Islamic law, the body will remain on display for two or three days so that all close family members have time to arrive and say good-bye. When someone dies, a boz-ui must be erected. This is the traditional home of the nomadic Kyrgyz, a round, domed tent made of wool felt on a collapsible wooden frame. A man is laid out inside on the left, while a woman is laid on the right.

Only women are allowed inside the boz-ui to lament, while men mourn through the tent wall, from the outside. The wife and daughters of the deceased sit by the body to sing mourning songs and greet each person who comes to view the body. A wife wears black, while daughters wear deep blue. As each visitor pays respects, the mullah recites from the Qur'an.

The burial usually takes place at noon. The body is washed and wrapped in a shroud, then cloth, and then sometimes a felt rug. The body is displayed outside the boz-ui and a final prayer, the *janaza,* is said. Only men go to the cemetery for[fj] the burial, but the women visit the grave early the next day.

Every Thursday for the next forty days the family must kill a sheep in remembrance. At this time, those who could not attend the funeral may come to pay their respects. At the end of the forty-day period there is a large memorial feast called *kirku,* where a horse or a cow is killed.

On the first anniversary another memorial feast is given, called *ash* or *jildik,* which takes place over two days. The first day is for grieving, and the second is for games and horse races.

The Kyrgyz believe that the spirits of the dead can help their descendants. Ancestors are "offered" food in prayers, and people pour water on graves when they visit so the dead will not be thirsty. It is forbidden to step on a grave, and cemeteries are placed on hilltops because high places are sacred.

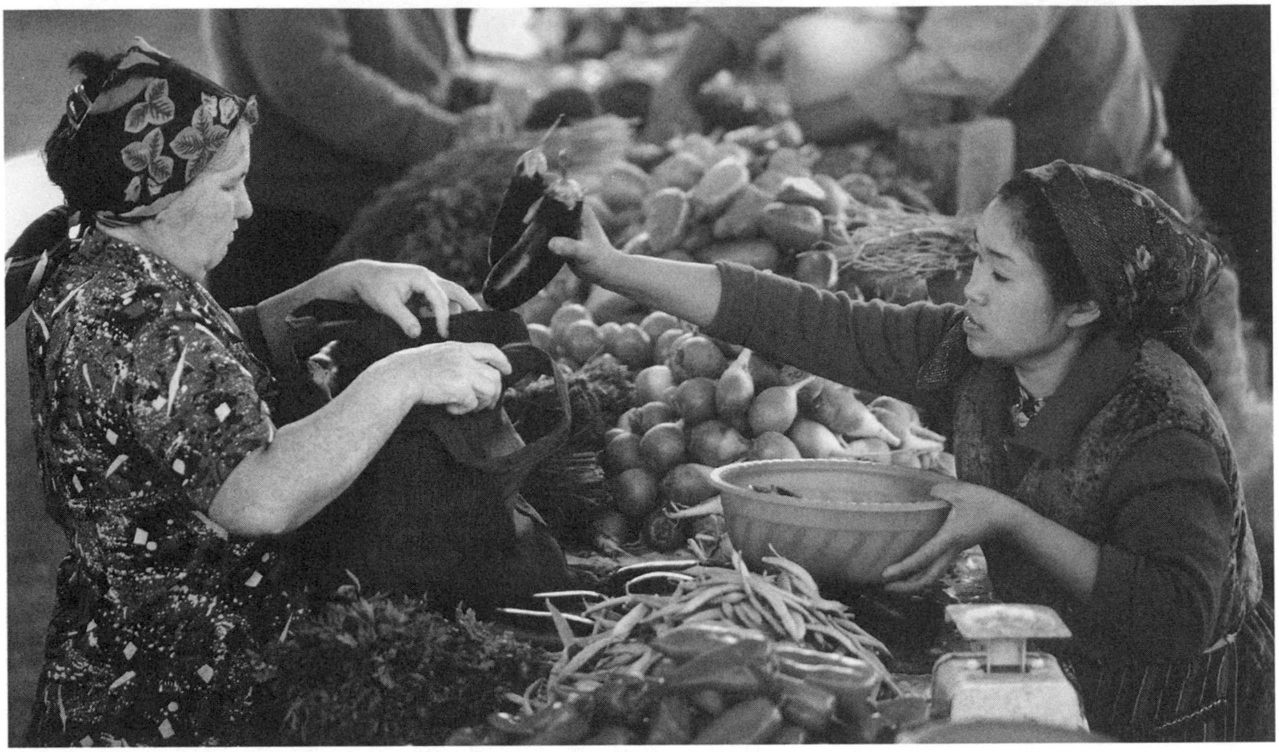

A produce vendor places eggplants in a customer's bag at the Osh Market. Bishkek, Kyrgyzstan.

Medicine and Health Care

Many people still go to the hospital for most illnesses, as they did before independence, but health care is limited by lack of funds. Food and medicine are not provided by the hospital, so friends and family must bring these in daily.

Traditional beliefs blame cold for most forms of illness: Sitting on cold stones or the ground can result in grave illnesses or hurt a woman's reproductive organs; drinking cold beverages will result in a sore throat or a cold; being exposed to cold drafts is considered the cause of most minor illnesses. People treat illnesses by wrapping a blanket or a shawl around the affected body part to keep it warm. Some home remedies that derive from shamanistic beliefs are still practiced as well. Certain grasses are burned because the smoke is believed to purify the air and to prevent sickness. The air above and the waters of Lake Issyk-Kul are attributed healing properties, and swimming in the lake is a popular cure for tuberculosis.

Secular Celebrations

Secular holidays include International Women's Day (8 March), May Day (1 May), Constitution Day (5 May), Victory Day (9 May), Last Bell (mid-June), Independence Day (31 August), First Bell (1 September), and New Year's Eve (31 December). Most holidays are celebrated with parties at work and at home that involve eating, drinking, dancing, and singing.

New Year's Eve is more elaborate, and many of the traditions come from Russian practices. There are costume parties, as well as performances at schools. At these performances, Det Moroze (called Ayaz-Ata in Kyrgyz) and his granddaughter give presents to good children. Det Morose wears a robe trimmed in fur and rides in a horse-drawn sleigh. Naughty children are chased by the witch Baba Yaga. People decorate *yulkes*, or fir trees, with garlands, ornaments, and lights, and set off fireworks at midnight. Kyrgyz people follow the Chinese zodiac, where each year is assigned an animal, and people whose sign is the same animal as the incoming year must wear something red and then give it away for good luck.

The Arts and Humanities

Support for the Arts. Support for the arts mostly comes from selling pieces or paid performances. There is little to no funding available from the government.

Literature. Kyrgyz was not written until the twentieth century. The Kyrgyz oral tradition included several epics about mythical warriors, including Manas, Jayin-Bayis, Kurmanbek, and Er Tabildi. The epic *Manas* is most widely known, and is still widely performed by *manaschis*. It is not a memorized piece; the best manaschis take the outline of the story and improvise verses, which have a distinct rhythmic beat and are accompanied by expressive hand gestures. Thirteen versions and four million verses have been recorded.

During the twentieth century, novel-writing in the historical and romance genres developed. The best-known Kyrgyz novelist is Chingiz Aitmatov, who is known for his critical novels about life in Soviet Central Asia.

Graphic Arts. Traditional crafts are taught in school, and the graphic arts are well developed. In most cases artisans create objects to be sold either as souvenirs to tourists or as heirlooms for people's homes. Some are displayed in the National Gallery or in museums abroad. Most of these are done in wool or silk, including the wool carpets called *shirdaks* and *alakiis*, embroidered wall hangings called *tush-kiis*, and small animal or human figures. Wood, horn, leather, and clay are also used. There are a number of painters as well, whose works are sold mostly to foreigners. These often have traditional Kyrgyz themes but often use modern and postmodern styles of painting. Galleries and art exhibits are almost exclusively in the capital city.

Performance Arts. Kyrgyz folk singing and music lessons are frequently offered in schools. There are several Kyrgyz children's performance groups, which feature traditional songs and dance as well as performances using Kyrgyz instruments. The best-known instruments are the komuz (a three-stringed lute), *oz-komuz* (mouth harp), the *chopo choor* (clay wind instrument), and the *kuiak* (a four-stringed instrument played with a bow). There also are adult folk, classical, and operatic musicians and groups who perform in the capital regularly. Popular television shows feature Kyrgyz pop and folk singers and musicians. There is a small but active film industry.

The State of the Physical and Social Sciences. Scientists teach at the university level, but funding for research is limited. Most scientists have moved to other professions for financial reasons.

Bibliography

Abazov, Rafis. *The Formation of Post-Soviet International Politics in Kazakstan, Kyrgyzstan and Uzbekistan*, 1999.

Anderson, John R. *Kyrgyzstan: Central Asia's Island of Democracy*, 1999.

Asian Development Bank. *Technical Assistance to the Kyrgyz Republic for Support to the National Strategy for Poverty Reduction*, 2000.

Bauer, Armin. *A Generation at Risk: Children in the Central Asian Republics of Kazakstan and Kyrgyzstan*, 1998.

———. *Women and Gender Relations: The Kyrgyz Republic in Transition*, 1997.

Bloch, Peter C. *Land and Agrarian Reform in the Kyrgyz Republic*, 1996.

Caspisani, Giampolo R. *The Handbook of Central Asia*, 2000.

Commission on Security and Cooperation in Europe. *Political Reform and Human Rights in Uzbekistan, Kyrgyzstan, and Kazakstan*, 1998.

Country Economic Review: The Kyrgyz Republic, 1999.

Decentralization: Conditions for Success, 2000.

Department of Economic and Social Affairs. *Decentralization: Conditions for Success*, 2000.

Economist Intelligence Unit. *Country Profile: Kyrgyz Republic, Tajikistan*, 1998.

Giovarelli, Renee. *Land Reform and Farm Reorganization in the Kyrgyz Republic*, 1998.

Imart, Guy G. *From 'Roots' to 'Great Expectations': Kirghizia and Kazakstan between the Devil and the Deep-Green Sea*, 1990.

Kotlov, Eugeny. *Generous Manas*, 1995.

Kyrgyzstan: 1998 Post Report, 1998.

Kyrgyzstan: Social Protection in a Reforming Economy, 1993.

Kyrgyzstan: Then and Now, 1993.

Kyrgyzstan: The Transition to a Market Economy, 1993.

Peace Corps, World Wise Schools. *Destination, Kyrgyzstan*, 1997.

Pirseyedi, Bobi. *The Small Arms Problem in Central Asia: Features and Implications*, 2000.

Ruffin, M. Holt, and Waugh, Daniel. *Civil Society in Central Asia*, 1999.

Slobin, Mark. *Kirgiz Instrumental Music*, 1969.

Smith, Diane L. *Breaking Away from the Bear*, 1998.

—Tiffany Tuttle